For Laura Morris

Build your film on white, on silence, and on stillness.
—Robert Bresson

. . . the frenzy on the wall . . .
—Jean-Paul Sartre

"Have You Seen...?"

A Personal Introduction to 1,000 Films including masterpieces, oddities, guilty pleasures and classics (with just a few disasters)

DAVID THOMSON

PENGUIN BOOKS

PENGUIN BOOKS

Published by the Penguin Group
Penguin Books Ltd, 80 Strand, London WC2R 0RL, England
Penguin Group (USA), Inc., 375 Hudson Street, New York, New York 10014, USA
Penguin Group (Canada), 90 Eglinton Avenue East, Suite 700, Toronto, Ontario, Canada M4P 2Y3
(a division of Pearson Penguin Canada Inc.)
Penguin Ireland, 25 St Stephen's Green, Dublin 2, Ireland (a division of Penguin Books Ltd)
Penguin Group (Australia), 250 Camberwell Road, Camberwell, Victoria 3124, Australia
(a division of Pearson Australia Group Pty Ltd)
Penguin Books India Pvt Ltd, 11 Community Centre, Panchsheel Park, New Delhi – 110 017, India
Penguin Group (NZ), 67 Apollo Drive, Rosedale, North Shore 0632, New Zealand
(a division of Pearson New Zealand Ltd)
Penguin Books (South Africa) (Pty) Ltd, 24 Sturdee Avenue, Rosebank,
Johannesburg 2196, South Africa

Penguin Books Ltd, Registered Offices: 80 Strand, London WC2R 0RL, England

www.penguin.com

First published in the United States of America by Alfred A. Knopf,
a division of Random House, Inc., New York, 2008
First published in Great Britain by Allen Lane 2008
Published in Penguin Books 2010

005

Printed and bound in Great Britain by Clays Ltd, Elcograf S.p.A.

A CIP catalogue record for this book is available from the British Library

978-0-141-02075-4

www.greenpenguin.co.uk

MIX
Paper from
responsible sources
FSC™ C018179

Penguin Books is committed to a sustainable
future for our business, our readers and our planet.
This book is made from Forest Stewardship
Council™ certified paper.

Acknowledgments

I was first approached to try this book by Nigel Wilcockson of Penguin in London. It was a prolonged process. After *The Biographical Dictionary of Film*, I did not believe it was a sane idea to write another very long book on the same subject. But Nigel was not to be told no and saw little evidence that I was sane. He talked to me. He sent me superb books on the churches of England as inspiration. He never stopped until he had persuaded me to say yes. Then he left Penguin, and for all I know he is now leading other authors astray for other houses. The one thing Nigel omitted to say in his campaign—that I would enjoy doing the book—came through with such surprise that I knew I must always thank him first. His role at Penguin, as my editor, was then filled by Simon Winder, who proved to be a dedicated friend, a patient and invaluable editor, and a tower of strength, even though I declined illustrations and a rating system.

In America, the book was taken up by Knopf, who had published me often before: thus, I fell into the hands of a proven team—Bob Gottlieb as editor, Katherine Hourigan as managing editor, Kevin Bourke as production editing maestro, Kathy Zuckerman as publicity director, and Carol Carson, who designed the jacket. These people are some of the best friends I have had, in or out of publishing. If I mark Bob Gottlieb down as captain of the team, it is only fair. Bob is a book man, and a very good writer (though he only found that out, I think, after he had stopped commissioning and editing so many books). There's a lot that we don't agree on, but there is no one with whom sporting disagreements can be so thoroughly enjoyed and explored. I have been lucky enough to be there in need at a time in his life when his passion moved toward film. He is a great editor—and all he does is read you, think about it, argue, and guide you into being a little better.

Beyond the publishing assistance, I rely on a group of friends and family with whom I see or discuss films. Again, we do not agree all the time. But we have seen that as the point. I have benefited from remarks, recommendations, and insights, and helpless cries of pain and ecstasy from so many people. But these are the ones I can remember now: Mark Feeney; Tom Luddy; Edith Kramer; Pierre Rissient; Jean-Pierre Gorin; Scott Foundas; Richard and Mary Corliss; Andrew Sarris and Molly Haskell; Richard Schickel; Richard Roud; Richard Jameson and Kathleen Murphy; Patrick McGilligan; Greil Marcus; Peter Bogdanovich; Mark Cousins; Ty Burr; Michael Ondaatje; Anthony Lane, Quentin Curtis, Gilbert Adair, and Jonathan Romney (all in their time fellow film critics at the *Independent on Sunday* in London); Antonia Quirke; Jim Toback; Paul Schrader; David Packard; Steven Bach; Jeffrey Selznick; Holly Goldberg Sloan and Garry Rosen. Many of these people are all the more remarkable for being interested in many things beside film. And that leads me to the vital company in any filmgoer's life—the other people in the dark—Anne, Lucy, and five children (Kate, Mathew, Rachel, Nicholas, and Zachary), most of whom know the problem of keeping me awake at some films. It is the just reward for insomnia that I sleep most easily at the movies. Why not? I always suspected they were dreams.

Introduction

I wanted a "bumper" book for your laps, a volume where you could keep turning the pages and coming upon juxtapositions of the fanciful and the fabulous (Abbott and Costello go to Zabriskie Point?) or some chance alphabetical poetry that might make your scalp tingle—like *Bad Day at Black Rock* leading into *Badlands*. I wanted old favorites to be neighbors with films you've never heard of. I wanted you to entertain the unlikely possibility that "everything" is here. Of course, it is not—everything remains out in our scattered "there."

Choosing their top ten is a game most film critics are accustomed to—and one that allows depressives to ask, "Are there really ten worth keeping?" (This is a healthy doubt, more useful than the routine thumbs up on two or three fresh masterpieces every week.) Writing about a select hundred is a regular form of bookmaking—the exercise of taste makes a moderate-sized book and a harmless pantheon. But going for a thousand is a gesture toward history—it seems to require that the selector weighs the old against the new. It's like wondering whether Beowulf can talk to Lolita.

How is it that a thousand seems to omit so many more than a whimsical ten? How can ten hundred escape being an outline of the history of the medium and of our jumping tastes? If you're picking ten, you may not consider the silent era in Sweden. But if you're doing a thousand, then those Stillers and Sjöströms deserve reappraisal. And they may be among the best early films we have.

Equally, it's touching to find in Irene Mayer Selznick's private letters that, in 1927, the cool, inside crowd in Hollywood reckoned *Sunrise* was the best film they'd ever seen—and surely the harbinger of great creative changes. (The newly founded Academy actually created two types of Best Picture—the Hollywood prize, for *Wings*, and an arty one for *Sunrise*.) So it's a surprise that in Brussels in 1958, a gang of historians put Murnau's *The Last Laugh* way ahead of his *Sunrise*. I can recall a time when "film writing" took that estimate for granted. Yet now *The Last Laugh* feels like an academic exercise—while *Sunrise* is different and dangerous every time you see it.

This book is not simply my one thousand preferred films offered with whatever mixture of authority I can muster or generosity you will allow. I like or love many of these movies and I hope you will feel that in the reading and come closer to sharing my pleasure. The first purpose or wish behind the question in my title is not to establish you as an expert in film studies but to give you a good time—or a better time than you have been having.

More than that this is a book created to meet the question frequently asked of anyone with a reputation for knowing about films. It's "What should I see?" So "Have you seen . . . ?" is a response to that uncertainty.

I knew early on in thinking about this book that I could not face it as David Thomson's "best" films. My favorites are here—but there is a monotony in writing or reading about just the splendid. As my editor, Bob Gottlieb, observed on reading an early draft, "We're snowed under with 'greats' and I'm still on B!" Enthusiasm is too easy and it can lead to lazy writing and formulaic thinking. Very often in a book like this you can signal your critical stance to a reader with just one bad-tempered dismissal as easily as and more rapidly than a hundred raves will permit. (So *The Sound of Music* is in here, along with *Doctor Zhivago, The Ten Commandments, The Last Laugh,* and others. You'll find them.) A little severity in such writing can be as welcome as the song of the blackbird at the end of a hot day.

So this is a thousand fiction films, going back to 1895 and ranging across the world—the landmarks are here, the problem films, a few guilty pleasures, a few forlorn sacred cows, some surprises, a thousand for you to see. They are arranged alphabetically—but in the back of the book you will find a chronology, too.

The pantheon of film culture is an untidy place: it is every year's top ten or the survey of critics and filmmakers that *Sight & Sound* attempts every ten years—with *Citizen Kane* rated the best film on every survey since 1962 (yet nowhere on the first such list in 1952). It is what "everyone" thinks and knows and takes for granted. God bless "everyone," but watch how slippery he is. For example, I write for *The Guardian* in London. I have read that paper most of my life; I love it and its readers. But not so long ago, in 2007, it took it into its head to poll readers on the best foreign language films ever made. *Cinema Paradiso* won (and it had won a previous poll in 1993). And that's not the fault of the film in question or of those who made it—and it has little to do with whether *Cinema Paradiso* is sublime or pleasant. Or not. But *Cinema Paradiso* surpassed *M, L'Atalante, Les Enfants du Paradis, Belle de Jour, L'Eclisse, La Ronde, Ugetsu Monogatari, The Travelling Players, Pierrot le Fou, Tokyo Story, La Règle du Jeu,* and *Pather Panchali* because, clearly, more people in the *Guardian*'s electorate had seen *Cinema Paradiso* than the others. If you haven't read much else, then Ian Fleming's *Goldfinger* may be the best book you've ever read.

And as we have to learn sooner or later, it is no counter to democracy and general education to deplore the public's not voting for people not on the ticket. History is, first of all, what happens; and historians know the terrible fallacy of wishing that something else (wiser, more honorable, or funnier) had happened. So the *Guardian* results in 2007 and 1993 were inescapable history, even if most film writers on the paper kept their fingers crossed and their remarks guarded.

To compile a book like this, you immerse yourself in the history of the best—but in film studies the best has sharply different meanings. One is all about numbers: it deals with which films did best at the box office. And from *Birth of a Nation* to *Titanic,* those landmark films claim that their ripeness was our taste. Their sensation testifies to our innocence—or worse. The other measure is all about opinion—and generally speaking it is in the area of opinion that any chance for art in film remains. So I was intrigued to discover a poll in Brussels in 1958 at one of those exhibitions that now and then occur. On that occasion 117 historians and critics were asked to vote on the twelve best films ever made. The results were as follows: *Battleship Potemkin* (Sergei Eisenstein), 100 votes; *The Gold Rush* (Charlie Chaplin) and *Bicycle Thieves* (Vittorio De Sica), 85; *La Passion de Jeanne d'Arc* (Carl Dreyer), 78; *La Grande Illusion* (Jean Renoir), 72; *Greed* (Erich von Stroheim), 71; *Intolerance* (D. W. Griffith), 61; *Mother* (V. I. Pudovkin), 54; *Citizen Kane* (Orson Welles), 50; *Earth* (Alexander Dovzhenko), 47; *The Last Laugh* (F. W. Murnau), 45; *The Cabinet of Dr. Caligari* (Robert Weine), 43.

First of all, don't doubt that this was an honest vote by an informed electorate. In which case you have to allow that in 1958, nine out of thirteen films chosen were silent. But did 1958 really believe that the great work in film had been done thirty years earlier? There's another remarkable conclusion to that list by today's standards. It seems unaware of so many things from the fifties that now impress us: for instance, *The Searchers* (John Ford); *The River* or *The Golden Coach* (Jean Renoir); *Diary of a Country Priest* and *A Man Escaped* (Robert

Bresson); *Madame de . . .* or *Lola Montès* (by Max Ophüls); *Ugetsu* and *Sansho the Bailiff* (by Kenji Mizoguchi); *Seven Samurai* and *Living* (by Akira Kurosawa); *In a Lonely Place* (by Nicholas Ray); *Les Enfants Terribles* (Jean-Pierre Melville); *Europa '51* (Roberto Rossellini); *Sunset Blvd.* (Billy Wilder); *The Third Man* (Carol Reed); *Singin' in the Rain* (Gene Kelly and Stanley Donen). Further, the poll was just too early for *Wild Strawberries, Touch of Evil, Vertigo,* and the thing called the New Wave (though *Touch of Evil* played in another part of the Brussels fiesta—and won a prize).

Some observers in 1958 pointed out how much the Brussels poll lagged behind history. But in those days it was an orthodoxy that Chaplin, Griffith, and Eisenstein were the rocks on which film was built. And notice how few conventional or mainstream films made the list. The only Hollywood films (*Intolerance, Greed,* and *Kane*) were notable for having been made against the grain of box-office and popular expectation—and they were all flops. For the rest, so many pictures had come from countries or production systems that could be said to favor individual (or subsidized) expression. That fact predicted the omission of so many "mainstream" things that now seem personal and important—the work of Lubitsch, Hawks, and Keaton, film noir, the musical, screwball comedy.

But 1958 was more of a cusp than anyone appreciated. A year later—at Cannes—we would begin to see the films of a young French generation who had been critics (Godard, Truffaut, Rivette, Rohmer, and Chabrol). These writers had been steadily building an auteur theory for Hollywood and proclaiming the virtues of many of the directors just mentioned. But in the late fifties, the pantheon of film criticism was still closed to this point of view. *Sight & Sound* (the most reputable film magazine in English) was horrified and amused by the outrageous things being said in *Cahiers du Cinema.* And film magazines, festivals, and archives held sway in film culture. There was as yet nothing like film academia (we had the Academy instead). There were few books on film. There was hardly any film history. And the ways of seeing films were restricted. There was nothing like video. It was very difficult to see old films, except at the archives, the museums, and the film societies. The Brussels poll was the voice of those film societies and voters who had been young in the twenties or thirties. That *Citizen Kane* never figured in the *Sight & Sound* poll for 1952 was because, a failure on release, Welles's film had gone out of circulation. It was hard to see.

In retaliation against the Brussels poll, the *Cahiers du Cinema* writers declared their own top twelve in December 1958. They voted first on the best twelve directors, and then the best film by those directors. The result is *Cahiers*-like in its show-off long-shots, but it's a more interesting list than Brussels managed: *Sunrise; La Règle du Jeu; Journey to Italy* (Rossellini); *Birth of a Nation; Confidential Report* (Welles); *Ordet* (Dreyer); *Ugetsu Monogatari; L'Atalante; The Wedding March* (Stroheim); *Under Capricorn* (Hitchcock); *Monsieur Verdoux* (Chaplin).

This matter of youth is important, and not the least thing about 1958 in my mind was my being seventeen and available to discover the movies for myself. Young people had always made the movies and gone to see them, but in the forties, say, that was less palpable—perhaps because there was never an age when the cinema was so much everyone's sport. But by the late fifties, and not just in Paris, a group of young firebrands stood ready to redefine the movies. You could find them all over the world just as young people seemed determined to make movies—as opposed to writing novels or poetry. These people became the first great wave of film students in a climate that saw film ushered into the academy and become a part of general knowledge—not just as film-buff trivia, but as a general, educated awareness of Renoir, Hitchcock, and Welles, say, as styles and attitudes.

That audience found its reward: not just the New Wave films from France but the next generation in Italy (Antonioni, Fellini, Bertolucci), in Germany (Fassbinder, Herzog, Wenders), to say nothing of Scandinavian film, Indian, Japanese, Latin American, and even American. For it's clear now, I think, that just as Hollywood was in decline by its own standards in the late fifties and sixties, so at the end of the sixties film students were pushing to make their first pictures. Francis Coppola and Martin Scorsese, George Lucas and Steven Spielberg, led that generation and helped deliver a "silver age" of Hollywood in the early seventies—from about the time of *Bonnie and Clyde* to *Taxi Driver.*

One way of tracing that shift is to look at the films voted in the top ten in the *Sight & Sound* polls of 1952, 1962, and 1972. Like it or not, this is the movies changing from current sensation to a subject for study and reflection. It's the dark now giving way to the library.

1952	1962	1972
1. Bicycle Thieves	1. Citizen Kane	1. Citizen Kane
2. City Lights	2. L'Avventura	2. La Règle du Jeu
2. The Gold Rush	3. La Règle du Jeu	3. Battleship Potemkin
4. Battleship Potemkin	4. Greed	4. 8½
5. Louisiana Story	4. Ugetsu Monogatari	5. L'Avventura
5. Intolerance	6. Battleship Potemkin	5. Persona
7. Greed	7. Bicycle Thieves	7. La Passion de Jeanne d'Arc
7. Le Jour Se Lève	7. Ivan the Terrible	8. The General
7. La Passion de Jeanne d'Arc	9. La Terra Trema	8. Magnificent Ambersons
10. Brief Encounter	10. L'Atalante	10. Ugetsu Monogatari
10. La Règle du Jeu		10. Wild Strawberries

What's most striking about these lists is not the disappearance of Chaplin, Clair, De Sica, and Carné, the persistence of Dreyer's *Joan of Arc,* and the arrival of Bergman, Antonioni, and Mizoguchi but the supremacy of foreign language or art-house films. Welles has two films in the top ten by 1972 (and why not?), yet both are anti-Hollywood productions. It's worth adding that in the runners up in 1972, you could find such relatively recent pictures as *Hiroshima Mon Amour, Pierrot le Fou, Vertigo, Mouchette, The Searchers,* and *2001.* Notice that every film, listed and runner-up, is pretty solemn in outlook—apart from *The General.* Our talking comedies of undying appeal—*Trouble in Paradise, My Man Godfrey, Bringing Up Baby, His Girl Friday, The Lady Eve, The Shop Around the Corner, The Philadelphia Story, Midnight, Twentieth Century, To Be or Not to Be* (now *there* is a ten best built for fun)—are not mentioned or remembered. Yet one principle of the book you are holding is that Hollywood has a record of being most entertaining (and most serious) when making comedies. This is a truth that the Academy (the one that gives the statuettes) has had as much trouble with as *Sight & Sound* polls.

When I was asked to do this book (as something like a companion to *A Biographical Dictionary of Film,* first published in 1975), I wondered whether I would be idiot enough to take on another half-a-million-word project. Writing the *Dictionary* had put me in the position of having to reckon which films—as of then—were keepers. And in some ways, I had caught larger moods: the *Dictionary* argues that Hawks is very important, and Buñuel and Renoir and Mizoguchi and Ophüls—and it asks, really, what is all the fuss over Chaplin, Griffith, Eisenstein, René Clair (really a faded glory), and so on. It's not regarded as dotty now to say that Cary Grant is the most intriguing actor in the history of movies—yet in 1975 that was still fanciful.

So if you think you were right you don't allow much room for your mind to change—especially as you grow older and shall we say firmer. This is a book that has had to accommodate that ugly process, and it would not have surprised me if I had included just about every film by my favorite directors. I am an auteurist still. But as I began to sketch out lists (and asked advice from others), a number of things struck me—not least that Chaplin and Eisenstein may be in need of some recovery. Those wheels of fashion keep turning. I still think Keaton is funnier, and sadder, but historically Chaplin towers over so much.

I wondered how different figures and nations would fare, and I started the immense process of reviewing old films. As I worked on the *Dictionary*, my chief aid was going to the movies—essentially the National Film Theatre in London. There were films on television, of course, but video had not yet begun and it remained very difficult to see certain films. But in doing this book, living in San Francisco, I have access not just to my library of tapes and the libraries of friends but to the resources of Le Video (on 9th Street), one of many outstanding stores in the U.S. There are so many fewer films that are hard to see.

This means that I go to the movies less often—I see fewer films in real dark, in great prints, on enormous screens. I watch the videos on television, and try to adjust to the diminution. There is no going back, and it may be that film studies is about to enter a time of theater withdrawal. But *The Testament of Dr. Mabuse*, say, is one thing on video and another being projected on a big screen. I lament the loss, but I know that everything in the business and in the treatment of movies is shifting toward small-screen study. Otherwise sensible people write Ph.D. theses on particular movies without ever seeing them on a large screen. And if their writing is a little dry, or a little short of what I recall as magical effects, well, the Ph.D. is a professional achievement. Is it possible that the movies are going to end up as museum pieces—like the way we now study old newspapers? We should remember that the "meaning" of newspaper content had to do not just with the "news" preserved but with the dailiness of the paper, its feel in the hands, its smell, and its illusion of opening up the grubby world.

Movies are always of their time—they never again mean as much as on the day they open. So it's important to *Citizen Kane* that it was an anxious look at American success at a moment when most Americans guessed an almighty effort was coming for the sake of survival. That effort required positive thinking (the only critic of America who got away with that in those years was Preston Sturges). Similarly, one reason why *Gone With the Wind* succeeded in 1939 was that it was a step toward preparing Americans for a new conflict. In *Meet Me in St. Louis* (1944), a white lie is told to people far from home—this enchanted Smith family will not leave for New York. They will stay at home, "right here in St. Louis."

The spirit that makes film wants them to succeed *now*—this weekend above all—and not in that whimsical place, posterity. No one thinks much of fifty years from now, or whether the films will still be seen long after their makers are dead. Yet literary and artistic cultures ask how Dickens, Joyce, George Eliot, and Faulkner are wearing in changing times. It is a marvel to see that things written four hundred years ago are still read or attended to. Will films stand up that long, or are they more perishable? Maybe in the best of our young generation it can be seen and felt that *Citizen Kane* is as good or as worthy or as much fun as *The Great Gatsby*, a Frank Lloyd Wright house, an Edward Hopper window, or Louis Armstrong doing "Potato Head Blues."

But when I say movies are of their time, I have to agree that they share in our time, too. I have a game with film experts, of asking them not just their official pantheon but the pictures they love the most—like your favorite teddy bear. Chances are, those beloveds were seen between ten and fifteen (years of age). So don't rule out the possibility that the movies are most fit for kids. Sometimes we stretch our youth unreasonably far—and I think there is an interesting book in how far film people (battling being grown up) are especially prey to that sentimentality. My time was 1945 to 1960, I suppose, and it was American film mixed with French—and then the two together in that new ice cream flavor, Nouvelle Vague. If you were to make a graph of when the films in this book were made, there is a great hump that stands for the thirties, the forties, the fifties. I can try to moderate it, but I do not apologize for it. It may just be that I was lucky when I was young.

As I said, I re-encountered many films I had not seen for decades. The results were mixed, as you might expect. But when a film reminded me of what it had meant once, that only encouraged me to believe that there might be a tradition in which films are made and seen, where the past naturally enriches the present. Yet is that so? Films are not what they were. Far fewer of us go to see them. Young people coming to this book are being asked to bear with "restrictions" that they resist in the marketplace—silence, black and white, a lot of smart talk, a sense of morality, et cetera. Very few pictures contribute to the overall wonder at films, a thing that existed from around 1920 to the 1950s, a mood that no one born in that time can forget. Yet many films today are merciless and mercenary, and increasingly they are not even photographed. Story, character, and the innate beauty of the medium are being sacrificed. What does that leave, apart from desperate novelty? Well, *The Lives of Others; Eastern Promises; No Country for Old Men; You, the Living . . . You, the Living*? What on earth is that? I can hear you asking. One of the best films of this century, so far. That's all.

Of course, the latest films do not fare as well in this book as pictures from the thirties and the forties. Too many new films are gestures trying to grab the interest of kids set on war games and PlayStations. We are so ready for shallow amusement that it may be harder to enjoy profound entertainment (like those comedies I listed earlier). This book may come off as helplessly nostalgic—a tribute to an age that is not coming back. But if Preston Sturges does well at video stores—and he does—what would happen to someone like that today if he offered *The Lady Eve*?

Film is now more or less a hundred-year history. A lot of the estimates of quality made along the way seem ludicrous. For instance, I fill quite a bit of space in this book talking about Academy Awards. In part that is because I have found that readers are interested in such things. But in larger part I do so because so many of the Oscar decisions make us so wary of passing judgments. The Best Picture award in its time has gone to *Mrs. Miniver, Gentleman's Agreement, The Greatest Show on Earth, Around the World in 80 Days, Ordinary People, Terms of Endearment, Driving Miss Daisy, Patton, Dances with Wolves, Braveheart,* and *Crash.* I have to say that the Academy's opinion seems to me as often wrong as right—and that tells us a lot about how a business system tries to pledge itself to a scheme of quality that it does not quite understand.

The Academy has a modern face, represented by its excellent archive and research library. It is considering a grand movie museum in Los Angeles. But the Academy still insists on awarding prizes for a type of film that is hardly made anymore. And that is misleading and unhelpful in the intelligent regard for movies in America. In a history of excellence, the Academy shows itself in desperate need of reform. Its annual "march past" is as misleading and as vulgar as the display of weaponry that once attended every birthday of the Soviet Union.

None of those winners is in this book. Which doesn't mean that Oscar splendor is always cut off from real glory. Oscar is supposed to have helped American pictures; I think, more often, he has led them astray. So don't trust anyone's opinion or what is called history's verdict. *The Birth of a Nation* funded the picture business and it gathered together so many innovations in visual storytelling—still, it is shameful. *The Night of the Hunter* was a crushing failure when it opened. And today it is treasured as an American masterpiece. For those changes to occur, one thing is necessary: *you* must look and see and think and decide. I hope there will be films in this book you have never heard of. Be ready to be shocked by what I have left out, but try to see what I have offered.

The last time *Sight & Sound* polled 145 critics on the ten best, in 2002, this was the result: *Citizen Kane,* top again, but only five votes clear of *Vertigo* (46–41), and then *La Règle du Jeu* (second three times and third once over the decades), the first two parts of *The Godfather* (now regarded as one film—a natural but sweeping artistic assertion, denying the business reality), Ozu's *Tokyo Story* (a welcome newcomer in top tens), *2001, Battleship Potemkin, Sunrise, 8½,* and *Singin' in the Rain.* That looks pretty good for Hollywood, with six entries, even if *2001* was made in London or Stanley Kubrick's head, while *Sunrise* was set in a visitor's dream of America. Why not? One day we shall see that all movies live in the same place—on a screen, or in dreamscape.

And 2012? Well, I doubt that *Vertigo* will have passed *Kane*—though *The Godfather* might. (I think the urge is growing in what is supposed to be a modern, technological medium to overthrow a film that will be seventy years old.) I'll guess that *La Règle du Jeu* and *Sunrise* will still be in the top ten. I think Dreyer's *La Passion de Jeanne d'Arc* will be back. But I look forward to at least one white-hot sensation made between now and then, and as unimaginable now as *Kane* was in 1936. That's the year Orson did his voodoo *Macbeth* up in Harlem. When he was twenty-one. We are famous for our brilliant kids now (or is it just our childlike cool?), but it's a long time since anyone met a twenty-five-year-old like Welles.

“Have You Seen…?”

Abbott and Costello Meet Frankenstein (1948)

Begin as you mean to go on: Practice complete candor. So it was that at one stage in this book's history I had *Abe Lincoln in Illinois* as my opening page, trapped by alphabetical order. Now, that is not the worst film you could ever see: It's Robert Sherwood's prizewinning play about the young Lincoln, as directed by John Cromwell, with Raymond Massey working hard as Lincoln and Ruth Gordon clearly disturbed as his wife, Mary.

But then a good friend, Michael Barker (of Sony Classics), was looking at my alphabetical list, and he had the wit and the delicacy to know that *Abe Lincoln in Illinois* could not be first. That film on the first page of the book—no matter how earnest my support for it in five hundred words or so—could not fail to depress the ordinary heart. "You need something wilder, something far greater or far sillier," said Barker. He was right, of course (and he did not even suggest a Sony Classics picture!). When I offered *Abbott and Costello Meet Frankenstein,* his face lit up with the showman's true excitement. I thank him.

You can argue that this glorious venture of a film was a kind of going-out-of-business sale at what was then Universal Studios. As television closed in, the staples of old movie entertainment were often jammed together into B pictures. At Universal, the original home of so many haunted creatures, Frankenstein was meeting the Wolf Man. What next? Let the monsters of one genre have at those from another: Let Dracula confront Lou Costello, and see which of them cracked up first.

The boys are in the railroad shipping business, you see, when they get two very large crates that turn out to hold Drac and Frankenstein's monster. By now, alas, the creatures are lovable old frauds serving up comic situations for the boys. In turn, that means this is a movie about Lou's jitters and his total romantic self-absorption. The plot gives him two sophisticated women (Lénore Aubert and Jane Randolph) who would like to get their hands on his love handles, and Lou can hardly tell one sort of touch from another. The other extras are Bela Lugosi himself, looking very dapper as the count; Glenn Strange as the monster; and Lon Chaney, Jr.—that saddest of all actors—as the Wolf Man.

Charles T. Barton directed (and he was a veteran with the boys), three people were credited with the script, but still Bud Abbott manages to be the most forbidding figure in sight. Deep down, we know that Bud has abused Lou—it is the secret in their films never quite arrived at. So alphabetical order is rescued—with this reminder: Just as the book ends with *Zabriskie Point,* so it is at the heart of picture romance that Bud and Lou could just as easily have invaded that solemn desert land, or how about *Abbott and Costello Meet Persona*?

Ace in the Hole (1951)

In the biography of Billy Wilder, *Ace in the Hole* may be the most important picture. His partnership with Charles Brackett dated from *Bluebeard's Eighth Wife* (1938), which they wrote together for Ernst Lubitsch. It included *Midnight, Ninotchka,* and *Hold Back the Dawn* as writing projects, not to mention *The Lost Weekend, A Foreign Affair,* and *Sunset Blvd.*, for which they had been joint writers as Brackett produced and Wilder directed. And then Wilder wanted out of the arrangement. It was clearly his initiative, and Brackett was bewildered by it to the end of his days. Did Wilder want more credit and more of the money? He got both, so it's worth asking.

Wilder would direct and produce a story started by Walter Newman and Lesser Samuels. Set in the American Southwest, it features a fallen newspaperman, Chuck Tatum (Kirk Douglas), who gets wind of a human-interest story. Leo Minosa (Richard Benedict) is trapped in a cave where he was hunting for Indian relics. Tatum will milk the story into a national sensation to regain his position.

Some charges of cruelty and cynicism had been leveled at Wilder already. Phyllis is hateful in *Double Indemnity.* Walter is not the insurance man we hope for. The nurse and the barman are harsh figures in *The Lost Weekend.* And we don't have to spell out the cruelty in *Sunset Blvd.* But *Ace in the Hole* goes much further in its portrayal of a kind of gloating malice. Kirk Douglas holds nothing back. In one scene he slaps Jan Sterling (Minosa's wife), and she snarls, "Don't do that again, I might get to like it." It was even Wilder's plan to redo the studio logo: The arc of stars would rise above, not the famous mountain, but a rattlesnake in the desert sand. The studio killed the idea, but the snake's poison runs all through this deeply misanthropic film.

It was shot in New Mexico, in Albuquerque and Gallup, where a huge set was constructed for the cave. Charles Lang was the photographer—John Seitz had been dropped, and Wilder never went back to him. Hal Pereira and Earl Hedrick were the art directors. Hugo Friedhofer did the music. It is a film made under complete control; there seems to be no doubt about the justice in loathing everyone in sight. People are idiots or they are vicious. It is a mercy when Tatum is killed, though the method is hideous—scissors in the stomach—and the scene exploits Kirk Douglas's masochistic streak to the full.

What is remarkable is that Wilder is uttering these curses from the pulpit of great success. Is it a boast at being free from Brackett, or a kind of self-loathing for the way he got free? No one interested in Wilder should miss the film, but the public hated it and the Academy turned a cold shoulder (Brackett was president of the Academy!). Wilder took shelter in easier films, softer and stranger (*The Spirit of St. Louis*), and he did not really come back until the end of the fifties, when he was a comedy director—nothing he would have been accused of in 1951.

Act of Violence (1948)

A great film noir out of Metro-Goldwyn-Mayer doesn't sound quite right, a picture in which the "villainy" of Robert Ryan is left uncorrected is unexpected, and a film that begins to destroy your faith in humanism doesn't feel like Fred Zinnemann's preferred territory. Yet *Act of Violence* is all these things. Neglected for years, it is as unforgettable as the dragging sound of Ryan's limp.

The film came from a story by Collier Young and a script by Robert Richards. We find a young married couple in a small Californian town outside Los Angeles—they are Van Heflin and Janet Leigh. They have a brief idyll. He is a respected citizen, based on war heroism. The sun shines. The world smiles. But then a limping menace appears—Robert Ryan, a gaunt man with little left in life but malice—and he is looking for Heflin. As it turns out, Ryan has a cause, for during the war Heflin behaved like a coward in a prisoner-of-war camp. Men were killed because of his betrayal. Ryan was wounded—and now he is implacable. Not even the pretty wholesomeness of Leigh and her family can prevent fate from taking its toll.

The action shifts to L.A. at night, and Zinnemann was justifiably proud of the location work there, with atmospheric noir imagery from cinematographer Robert Surtees. Another character appears in the city—a hooker, played by Mary Astor—and she is in a way the heart of the film, the one person who knows that bad character and bad luck usually prevail. As a rule, Fred Zinnemann's films are about the community surviving as heroes stand by principle: The Army endures in *From Here to Eternity* even if Montgomery Clift dies, the town and law are intact in *High Noon* despite the civil betrayal. But in *Act of Violence,* there is a rare, bleak absence of hope, of lives that cannot avoid being destroyed by consequences. It is an unusual picture of the slow stain of war.

So it's fascinating to see the crack-up in the Heflin character and the gradual way in which Ryan is reclaimed for battered ordinariness. To that extent, it's a welcome change for Ryan, who was so often encouraged or allowed to be just a very nasty, if not psychotic, guy. But here he is something else: a helpless menace, yet not really possessed by uncommon powers or malice. Equally, Heflin—so often more interesting than his roles—gets a chance to explore panic and a wish to cover up his own past.

So here we have an eighty-two-minute picture, not quite an A movie, not quite a B, but a tough, tight script done economically and effectively, doing its damaging bit to present a real Americana, crowded with weak people and desperate compromises. Later in life, alas, Zinnemann did grander films with big themes and issues and a kind of official tidiness or optimism. Most of those films are nowhere near as absorbing or challenging as this small picture. By 1973's *The Day of the Jackal,* Zinnemann was doing set-piece best sellers about empty figures. This is a story of real wrecks.

Adam's Rib (1949)

It is the case that George Cukor did many successful adaptations, so it's nice to be able to point out a few works that were movie originals: *Pat and Mike, A Double Life,* and *Adam's Rib.* However, all three of those screenplays were by Garson Kanin and Ruth Gordon, who brazenly wrote their movies as if they had had a couple of years onstage first. Another way of putting it is to say that this team believed in situation, crisis, comedy, and humanity—but situation above all. Thus Adam and Amanda (Spencer Tracy and Katharine Hepburn) are lawyers who are married, and who come to take opposite sides in a domestic-violence case involving Tom Ewell and Judy Holliday.

At first, Tracy and Hepburn are regarded as the sophisticated couple, with Ewell and Holliday the rednecks driven to violence. But as time passes, it is the fun of the enterprise to show that you pick sides at your own risk. So here we are in 1949, amid the dire Cold War, the threat of A and H bombs, et cetera, and Kanin and Gordon have a gem that foreshadows feminism, women in the workplace, and that crackling battle of the sexes for which Hepburn and Tracy were so suited. It was only about fifteen years ahead of Betty Friedanism!

You can hear Kanin and Gordon saying, "Well, you just film it, George"—as if nothing could be easier. And it is very hard to find a hint of strain anywhere, not even when Hope Emerson lifts Spencer Tracy up in court. When Cukor comes to the scene where Holliday (in jail) needs to tell her story to Hepburn, he reads the script and agrees it's a little piece of theater. Except that he then gives it an uninterrupted nine-minute take, which is something only movies can do. Some said Judy had "stolen" the scene, but Cukor was entirely correct in his counterassertion that the scene belonged to her. That was the only way to play it. If anyone would have banned cutaway reaction shots from Hepburn, it would have been Kate herself.

It's fair to admit that in most of these sexual duels, the woman caves in first—to get a happy ending and to avoid real subversion. But along the way enormous fun is made of male arrogance, and Tracy has the great good sense to feel the pain and let the prospect of real tragedy sink in. One reason why Cukor's comedies are so good is that he seldom set out if he didn't believe in the human or dramatic substance. As with *The Philadelphia Story,* this could end very badly if Amanda goes another inch too far. As it is, self-pity is not entirely avoided.

There's also a song from Cole Porter, "Farewell, Amanda," with David Wayne caustic as the songwriter. As for Judy Holliday, it is a stunning debut in which we have to pick out her huge cunning from her lovely show as a dummy. Jean Hagen is also a lot of fun.

Adaptation (2002)

Screenwriters in America want it every way they can get it. They want the health scheme and the pension, yet they also regret having surrendered their copyright so long ago. Equally, they enjoy the reputation of being the ordinary, decent, regular guys in the picture business as well as the shunned geniuses. But sometimes you get a feeling that they wouldn't mind the health plan *and* copyright, attention and worship *and* the reputation for being filled with lovable common sense. Enough, they say, of the jokes about the actress who was so dumb she screwed the writer! (You take your actresses where you can find them.) To put it yet another way, they'd like their name on a smash-hit franchise and on Charlie Kaufman's droll *Adaptation*.

Adaptation was a late admission to this book—to be honest, it was the last, after a weekend spent with old friends, screenwriters both. They pitched me *Adaptation* just as if it were something they were offering to write, but then they sat me down with the videotape to watch it again. To tell you the truth, I fell asleep just as I had the first time I saw the film, but I remember thinking as I dropped off that *Adaptation* was very nice and unexpected and very clever and . . .

No, it is not as startling or transforming as *Being John Malkovich*, the earlier film written by Kaufman and directed by Spike Jonze. But I could see what my friends meant about the marvel of Kaufman—apparently a very shy fellow—mustering the authority and audacity to write a Sterne-like inquiry into the dilemma of a blocked screenwriter, in which the film itself is compelled to digress because of the writer's anxiety. Thus, one Nicolas Cage—very untidy and sweaty—is attempting to write an adaptation of Susan Orlean's book *The Orchid Thief*, but needs the cheery advice of his much more confident twin brother, a sweat-free Nicolas Cage. Incidentally, Charlie Kaufman plays with the idea that he, too, has a screenwriting partner, just like Cage's Kaufman does—Donald Kaufman, who in real life seems to be serenely nonexistent.

We see the blocked screenwriter with Tilda Swinton (a very sharp performance as the executive who has commissioned him), with author Orlean (Meryl Streep), and even with the central character from her book, a piratical orchid hunter, John Laroche (Chris Cooper). The result is clever, amusing, and good-natured to all parties. It is a very odd film to come out of America, and it is a halfway witty elaboration on the ghostly identity of the writer in film. At the same time, its intricacy, its achieved comic and dramatic impact, and its intelligence are fairly slight when compared with *Celine and Julie Go Boating*, a film that effectively summarizes the whole place of movie fiction in our culture. Whether Jonze and Kaufman represent a new wavelet or an authentic fresh hope remains to be seen. I am happy with what they—and a few others—have done, though again, I think they are trailing along behind a man like Paul Thomas Anderson (and not that far ahead of the Buster Keaton of *Sherlock Jr.*). But it is good for screenwriters to have and pursue enthusiasms, and to seem as daft and lovely as actresses.

The Adventures of Robin Hood (1938)

It may turn out one day that Robin of Locksley was a fraud, a drunk, or someone waiting to be put in a Sam Peckinpah film in which the forest of Sherwood is gradually being cleared by the Weyerhaeuser Company. Meanwhile, if you happen to live in a kingdom where your King Richard (Ian Hunter) has gone off on some reckless foreign adventure called a Crusade, it's more than likely that the wretched, envious, lifelong supporting player, Prince John (Claude Rains), is going to do all he can to spoil camp life for the boys in Lincoln green.

No, this isn't history, and don't look for any kind of peasants' revolt in this gloss on Olde England. As soon as Richard comes back, our outlaws are bending the knee and tugging the forelock. This Robin Hood is as much of a monarchist as the David O. Selznick who wept when that other "David," Edward VIII, abdicated.

Enough. In Hollywood, history is just a matter of his story. And I'm not sure if this kind of thing was ever done better. First, equip yourself with a man-child, because the average five-year-old is going to want to watch this splashy revel in stained-glass colors again and again. And since you're going to be watching with him, you want a movie in which freshness comes back like the dew every morning. Once or twice, plug your ears and simply gaze upon the dye-rich Technicolor—not just the greens but the violet and mauve of Maid Marian's gown (she is Olivia de Havilland), the reds like spilled strawberry jam on a white cloth. Then close your eyes to get the most out of Errol Flynn's charming twang, the hiss of arrows, the *click-clack* of dueling swords, and the flawless enthusiasm of the music by Erich Wolfgang Korngold. Korngold was a child prodigy who wrote operas, and maybe we do him a severe injustice by not knowing that music. On the other hand, his score (it won an Oscar) is not just the perfect accompaniment to this adventure; it is its bloodstream. When people bleed in this film, they bleed music. When they laugh, they sing.

You have Alan Hale as Little John, Eugene Pallette as Friar Tuck, Una O'Connor as Marian's maid. Then there is Basil Rathbone as Sir Guy of Guisborne, a fencing match for Flynn's Robin—the faster they fence, the quicker our hearts beat. This is one of the great duels in film history, and honestly, what is sword fighting but pure fun? And Errol Flynn? Yes, he was a joke, but no one laughed or enjoyed it more than he did. And he moved as if hearing the lovely mingle of his own chuckle and Korngold's flourish.

Michael Curtiz directed—and it looks as if the film is directing itself. There are only seven or eight Curtiz films like that, and they're all different. So maybe it's time we thanked Curtiz and saw that he was not merely lightly likeable but a genius who copied the blithe lack of self-regard in Errol Flynn. Sometimes knowing everyone wants you is enough.

Advise and Consent (1962)

Here is the calm antidote to the rising hysteria in Frank Capra's Washington films. For whereas his idealism was a brittle front for reaction, self-pity, and a refusal to play ball with politics, so this Otto Preminger film is a cool, ironic portrait of an argumentative chamber set on compromise, bargaining, and a final adherence to the virtues of the Code. Democracy is hard work, not righteousness. It is always middling, muddled, and sociable—and very seldom extreme, fierce, filibustering, or based on the incredibly naïve beauty of James Stewart in 1939. Preminger's ideal senator is homely, sarcastic, seasoned, weary, and ready to deal—witness Seab Cooley (Charles Laughton in his last performance).

Preminger bought the film rights to Allen Drury's 1959 novel early on, and asked Wendell Mayes to make a script of it. Mayes found the novel very conservative in tone, and he and Preminger wanted to make a picture that was not partisan except in its appreciation of the American process and its checks and balances. Two politicians are caught by life. Robert Leffingwell (Henry Fonda), in the running for Secretary of State, lies to the Senate about his past as a Communist. It is the lie, not the history, that ruins him. Brigham Anderson (Don Murray) has a homosexual past, and again it is the reluctance to be true to the rules and the clubbiness of the Senate that brings him down.

Above all, in Preminger's chamber, men who sit on opposite sides of the aisle are joined by space and camera movements. They believe in their commitment to the process, no matter the fierce separation of personal opinions. And nothing works better in the film than its spatial integration at the time of crisis, and the way in which "opponents" become players on the same side, or in the same game. It is not so much a forum for brilliance as a place where association and agreement can be made shining examples. And, of course, Preminger the historian of controversy put his finger on issues that meant a lot in 1962—a Red past or a gay subtext.

The picture is beautifully photographed by Sam Leavitt in black-and-white Panavision (a choice that means the film is not seen much today). But the frame lends itself to space, and the monochrome deromanticizes the political figures (or the actors playing them). Above all, Preminger feels for Lew Ayres as the vice president taken too much for granted, and as the man uneasy at being promoted when the president (Franchot Tone) dies.

But those two, and even Laughton, accommodate themselves to what is truly a group portrait. The man who makes this Senate work is actually the majority leader, Senator Munson (Walter Pidgeon), far more urbane than Lyndon Johnson but a nod to that Texan for his major impact on Senate affairs. His chief assistant is played very well by Paul Ford—and with supporting players like Peter Lawford, Gene Tierney, Burgess Meredith, and George Grizzard (as the only villain in sight), the starrier names (Fonda et cetera) are tamed by the casting.

The African Queen (1951)

The C. S. Forester novel had been published in 1935, and there had been movie interest from the outset. Charles Laughton and Elsa Lanchester had thought of doing it together, and then Warners bought the property for Bette Davis. But in 1950, Sam Spiegel and John Huston were able to buy the rights together and float the movie as a Horizon-Romulus production (Romulus being a British company able to send sterling to British East Africa, where the film would be based).

Huston asked his chum James Agee to write a script, and Agee is credited, but it seems that most of his work was unusable and had to be supplanted by the joint efforts of Huston and Peter Viertel. Forester had always been in doubt over his ending (the English and American versions of the novel had different finales), but Huston settled for a happy ending in which Rose and Charlie succeed in their mission to dispose of a German gunboat. A good deal of the filming would be on the Congo River, and it was a heroic, adventurous venture—there is a book by Katharine Hepburn, and there is Viertel's less than flattering portrait of Huston in the novel *White Hunter, Black Heart*.

Spiegel and Huston were rascals who never trusted each other, but the picture was delivered—thanks to the photography by Jack Cardiff (a Technicolor triumph) and the art direction of Wilfred Shingleton, but also to the long-suffering attitude of all those on location. Humphrey Bogart was uncertain about taking on Charlie Allnutt, and purists have always had some amusement over his cockney accent—but Huston knew there was a weasel in Bogart, if not a rat, and he happily coaxed the creature out into the light. As for Katharine Hepburn, apart from falling half in love with Huston on the venture, she decided at first to do the relationship as a battle. So Huston had to take her aside and caution her: Be a lady, don't allow Charlie to be your equal, be like Eleanor Roosevelt.

Would we recognize that from the picture? Probably not. Rose and Charlie are opportunities for eccentric acting; they are an odd couple more than real people. And the problems over their nature are more or less disguised by a great deal of physical action, from manhandling the boat in leech-infested waters to combat with the Germans. For most of the time, it is a two-man show and so odd that plausibility hardly comes into consideration. Let's just say they got away with it.

Even with two big stars and shooting on location in Africa, the film cost barely $1 million, and it took in more than $4 million. Bogart won an Oscar (defeating Marlon Brando in *Streetcar,* Montgomery Clift in *A Place in the Sun,* and Fredric March in *Death of a Salesman*). Hepburn and Huston were also nominated, but the picture did not get a nod, probably out of a healthy dislike of Spiegel—something Huston and Bogart learned to their rue as their returns on the laborious project were first delayed and then squeezed. Huston and Spiegel never worked together again, though this had been their third picture.

L'Âge d'Or (1930)

Here is the first great film that begins with an essay on scorpions—from which the scene shifts to an absurd desert island, a pile of burning rocks being adopted in the name of Christendom . . . the saving bishops become skeletons. The History comes back with a second Empire. The foundation stone for a church is laid, with ceremony and dignitaries. Then a cry is heard. Not far away a man and a woman are lying on the ground, "lasciviously rolling in the mud." Though the action will switch to what is called Imperial Rome and a world of social gatherings, concerts, and jewel-wearing not unlike that of Ernst Lubitsch, these muddied fuckers are the trouble in paradise—or are they the paradise nearly buried in trouble?

L'Âge d'Or is 63 minutes long. I suppose it is a feature film, and I do think that playing it in the same room as Lubitsch's *Trouble in Paradise* would be an interesting experiment—I like the idea of that film's Herbert Marshall, his walk so proper despite his wooden leg, rolling up his trouser leg (with a smile to the middle class) and unscrewing the rifle he uses for a false limb.

This is again a collaboration between Luis Buñuel and Salvador Dali, though I think that Buñuel was by now the leading force—and years later, under the godly Franco, Dali was moved to denounce the film's anti-Catholicism. I like *L'Âge d'Or,* and I am fascinated by the way in which its imagery of gamekeepers and orchestral conductors brings not just René Magritte to mind, but many things in *La Règle du Jeu*—don't forget that the man in *L'Âge d'Or* is played by Gaston Modot, the actor who did such a fine job as the frustrated gamekeeper Schumacher in Renoir's final film of the thirties.

It would be easy to claim mere coincidence, but certain gestures of the gamekeeper figure are so resonant and the role of the conductor is the inner music in *La Règle du Jeu.* The Renoir film is closer to orgy or abandon than you might think. Just as I would claim that Alfred Hitchcock used his memories of *Portrait of Jennie* in *Vertigo,* so I suspect that Renoir had been stirred by *L'Âge d'Or.* And I am, too—apart from which I am a dedicated believer in Buñuel. But, truth to tell, if I had seen this in 1930, I think I would have still found the island opening fussy, just as I feel only literary shock in the final allusions to the Marquis de Sade.

Whereas the shock in *Un Chien Andalou* is always in the imagery and the editing, in the sublime transitions, and in the way serene inconsequence keeps blooming with ugly, awkward, hard-on meanings. *L'Âge d'Or* may be a surreal classic, funded by the Vicomte de Noailles, with Jacques Brunius as assistant director and a cast that includes Max Ernst, Pierre Prévert, and Lya Lys as the woman. But I continue to find *Un Chien Andalou* more magical and expressive, and a greater clue to the traps and springboards in Surrealist film.

Aguirre, Wrath of God (1972)

Long before its ending, you feel the momentum of this hypnotic film—like a great falls on the river that cannot be avoided—carrying us over the edge. But for what? Is the title, and the last tableau, ironic, mordant, a warning? Or is it exultant?

First things first: It is 1560, and we are with a party of conquistadors in Peru. The leader is named Pizarro (we think we know there was such a man), and he sends a party of forty down the river on a raft. They are looking—so they say, so they think—for El Dorado. Ursua (Ruy Guerra) heads the forty, with his wife, Inez (Helena Rojo). Ursua looks Spanish. But his lieutenant, Aguirre, looks and sounds like Klaus Kinski. There is a priest, Gaspar de Carvajal (Del Negro) and a nobleman, Guzman (Peter Berling). Aguirre has a fifteen-year-old daughter, Flores (Cecilia Rivera).

Things do not go well. There are Indian attacks. Ursua is killed. Inez disappears. Illness and poison arrows pick them off one by one. But the raft is left, with the crooked figure of Aguirre in command, despite the swarming mass of small monkeys, announcing himself as the Wrath of God, with plans to found a dynasty. It is a superb image, and it seems to me mean-spirited to say that it is simply the ultimate disaster. In the blazing eyes of Aguirre, it is a triumph that he has organized—it is madness run riot. The monkeys are his audience. And it is very hard to detect a demurring spirit in Werner Herzog's film. Whatever the intent of the other conquistadors, their sensible desire for gold and silver, slaves and power, you feel that everything has worked out as Aguirre wished. For the last image is megalomania in excelsis. And from Herzog's point of view, no matter that he came back from the jungles with a very viable movie, and his own greatest art-house hit, you do feel that some exultant nihilism was ready for only the film to survive. Herzog, Kinski, and everyone else might still be going up the river.

I put it that way because I have never been able to feel that Herzog was much interested in sixteenth-century colonialism, its pluses and minuses. Nor is this film even—like *Apocalypse Now,* say—a study in how differing manias struggle to command an expedition. Aguirre's madness is far too sweeping and ultimate, and I think Herzog found it magnificent, just as he found Klaus Kinski very dangerous as an actor or a companion, but irresistible.

Aguirre, Wrath of God is not an adventure film. It's not a parable about power. Rather, it is a game played on the threat of making a film as daft and giddy as this. In Aguirre, we see so many of Herzog's future beasts, including the grizzly bears, the ones that man should not talk to. But in this era, the 1970s, Herzog was locked in a wrestling match with Kinski in which each one, I think, played with the idea of killing the other. The spectacle (it was filmed by Thomas Mauch) is stunning, but it's like watching two mad boys in a dare contest. You wonder if you shouldn't shoot them both.

Air Force (1943)

Major General Henry (Hap) Arnold, chief of the Army Air Forces, and Howard Hawks had been friends for years. At the moment of Pearl Harbor, Arnold spoke to Jack Warner and called for a movie that would stand up for the air force. Warner, proud of his own rank of "Colonel," put Hawks on the project with Dudley Nichols to do a script. But it was Arnold who suggested the story of one B-17 bomber flying from Hamilton Field in California as news of Pearl Harbor comes in. This was ideally suited to Hawks's delight in the small, self-contained unit—this could be *Only Angels Have Wings* in uniform, flying for the flag. Hal Wallis was put in charge of it all as producer. Warner wanted the picture ready for the first anniversary of Pearl.

But as Hawks researched Florida airfields, Nichols got himself into writing a heartfelt masterpiece. By June 1942, he delivered a 207-page script. A key problem was to get the right B-17 mock-up for scenes supposedly done in the air. To film in the air was to incur many extra problems and flaws in the image—witness the documentary footage done that way. Clearly, the aim of *Air Force* was to make audiences believe in the real guys, but Hawks was always determined to do it as a feature. It was just that, as a flier, he wanted the air stuff to look as good as *Only Angels Have Wings,* with its uncanny circular tracking shot for the mountain landing.

The Nichols script was never cut down before shooting. Rather, Wallis trusted Hawks to economize, on the basis of the director's habit of rewriting. With James Wong Howe as cameraman, and working miracles when lights failed, they shot in Florida and then came back to Los Angeles for the mock-up footage. And Hawks was rewriting (though he liked the Nichols script) and incurring Wallis's wrath because of it. Wallis was a controlling force, and Hawks was one of the few directors at that time who could make a film up as he went along.

This led to a major row, during which Hawks said he was "ill" and Vincent Sherman was brought in to take over. But Sherman could do nothing with the loyal cast, who played every scene Sherman shot at Hawks's underplayed level—plus a few degrees further under. So Hawks came back, and when he felt that the pilot Quincannon's death scene Nichols had written was too sentimental, he enlisted William Faulkner to rewrite it; the result may be the best bit of writing Faulkner ever did for the screen.

So it got done and cut down to 124 minutes, with a Franz Waxman score. It opened in February 1943, taking over from *Casablanca*—and, truly, it has the same panache, granted its lack of romance and the stress on doing a job. It is hokey, it is fond, it is lyrical—and war is seldom those things. But *Air Force* was a film for its moment, with John Ridgely (as Quincannon), John Garfield, Gig Young, Arthur Kennedy, Charles Drake, Harry Carey, and George Tobias.

Alexander Nevsky (1938)

One day, we may have a great comedy over the making of *Alexander Nevsky—Some Like It Cold, Some Like It Hot, Some Don't Ask.* Here's how it goes. Sergei Eisenstein, the great Russian filmmaking genius, is in poor standing with his Soviet masters. Early in the thirties, he went off to Hollywood and then to Mexico (see *Que Viva Mexico*) and was in disgrace at home. Once restored to Mother Russia, he started *Bezhin Meadow,* but the project was stopped. Desperately, Sergei needed a film. The authorities offered one last chance, and they gave him a list of subjects.

With Russia's delicate political situation in 1937, the friends of Sergei assessed the list most carefully. They opted for the story of Alexander Nevsky's defeat of the Germans in the thirteenth century. Why? asked Sergei. Because no one knows anything about him, said the friends, but it's pro-Russia and anti-Germany. A done deal.

It is clearly a battle film, the good Russians in dark tunics and pointed helmets, the Germans in white with upside-down coal buckets for helmets. I know, it is a masterpiece, but it is a very silly masterpiece, even with the Prokofiev music bubbling along beside it. Eduard Tisse did the photography—and it still looks like a lovely summer's day. They filmed in summer, with filtered lenses, and melted glass for the ice. It is a prolonged battle, and Nevsky wins—thanks in part to this actor, Nikolai Cherkasov, who played Nevsky: seven feet tall, a bit like Gary Cooper, really good-looking.

So the friends of Sergei watched over the editing, and they told their man, please, no fancy montage stuff—just the battle. And Sergei did as he was told, so it's one of his dullest pictures, unless you love axes coming down on helmets. There is a sneak preview at the Kremlin, and the word is that Stalin loved it. But when the print comes back, one reel is missing: lost, or did Stalin not like it? No one dares ask. They recompose the film to hide the missing reel. It opens in November 1938 and is acclaimed.

Less than a year later, the great and merciful nonaggression pact is signed between Russia and Germany. Sergei gets ready to cringe. The film is withdrawn. All mention of it is dropped. But then, a couple of years later, with Germany invading the Soviet Union, the film is back, and it's a masterpiece again!

And more or less, in the history books, that's where it stands now. But it's the movie of someone who has had good reason to become nervous. Indeed, the story is that Eisenstein encouraged a codirector, Dmitri Vasiliev, to do a good deal of the shooting, perhaps on the principle of "That was Vasiliev!" Why not? Compared with a film like *Strike,* say, the eye has gone dead and little is left but the bloodthirsty urge. Still, there are good scenes of Teutonic knights hurling naked children into the flames. To be candid, it is spectacular propaganda rubbish, and an unnerving if sidelong portrait of the lengths to which even great talent will go to survive.

Alice Adams (1935)

When Bette Davis won her first Oscar, in 1936, for *Dangerous,* one of the people she beat was Katharine Hepburn as Alice Adams. And it leaves you wondering, because Hepburn's performance as the unlikeable but yearning Alice is still so good as to take your breath away. The only possible resemblance is to some of the work done by Meryl Streep while still young—and it may help to explain Hepburn's failure to win public affection in the 1930s that she and Streep are so good, so clever, that we sometimes watch the cleverness more than the story.

Alice Adams is Midwest America, from a Booth Tarkington novel. Alice wants it all, and she gets little except embarrassment. Indeed, it isn't going too far to say that she could be Fanny (Agnes Moorehead) from *The Magnificent Ambersons,* perhaps twenty years younger.

This is an RKO film, produced by Pandro Berman and adapted for the screen by Jane Murfin and then scripted by Dorothy Yost and Mortimer Offner. But I think it's more to the point that this was a pact between Hepburn and her director, the very able George Stevens. The story lingers that they were lovers. No hard evidence survives, but Stevens was exactly the man's man she liked—and they clearly saw eye to eye on the richness of Alice as a role, the awkward version of the dazzling American heroine, the girl who can't help seeming gauche or fake in the upper set to which she aspires.

The film is kinder than the Tarkington novel—it has a more conventional romantic ending in which we suppose Alice is going to get her man (Fred MacMurray). The novel is far more set on the kind of solitude that affects Fanny, and therefore more certain of the loneliness that could settle over single women. Hepburn was not good casting, therefore, in anything except intelligence. And there are scenes here—set pieces of misery—in which we wince for Alice while wanting to see the shit hit her. This is rare in American cinema and accounts for the rather hurried coziness of the ending.

Robert De Grasse did the photography, Van Nest Polglase and Perry Ferguson did the art direction, and Max Steiner did the music. Stevens directs it beautifully, but without ever reaching the despair that Orson Welles got at in *Ambersons.* The cast includes Fred Stone, Evelyn Venable, Frank Albertson, Ann Shoemaker, Charley Grapewin, Grady Sutton, Hedda Hopper, Jonathan Hale, and Hattie McDaniel.

Alice Adams got a Best Picture nomination, as well as the nod to Hepburn, but it's clear historically that this great success led her down a dangerous path. Alice seemed chilly, a snob and a poseur. Not a happy mixture. And what is so impressive about Hepburn is the way she resolved to be likeable, and how to get there. Of course, this was tantamount to admitting that in American movies there was no other way in the 1930s. And she wanted to be an American success, as well as a famously independent self. Nobody had as much cake, ate as much, and stayed so slim.

Alien (1979)

There are those who say that James Cameron's *Aliens* (1986), the second film in the series, was the fullest exploitation of the original's many potent ideas. And the case can even be argued that David Fincher's *Alien 3* is a very interesting picture, though it proudly begins to dismantle the suspense dynamic of the series and is ready to sacrifice Sigourney Weaver's sturdy Ripley in the process. No one has much good to say about *Alien Resurrection,* though I have argued elsewhere that even that tone-dead picture had several fascinating ideas in play. But *Alien,* the original, is a favorite all round. Nostalgists shudder again to recall how high they jumped when that first stickleback poked its way out of John Hurt's tubercular chest. And no one has ever denied the allure of Weaver in her underwear, prepared for a last battle with the great monster.

I think a large part of the appeal is the way in which the *Nostromo*—a very beaten-up, underrepaired piece of the space fleet, with a crew that is equally tattered at its edges—should have the ill luck to encounter such a supreme, streamlined, Eigeresque monster. Remember, though, that that meeting is clearly signaled as something ordained, something desired by the creature. And from the very outset, it was not just that the monster was uncommonly visceral and psychically alarming (it was); it also had ideas, personality, and even a macabre wit. It hides as cunningly as an uncle who is skilled at hide-and-seek, and its timing is without rival. As *Aliens* will discover, this is a species made for a battle royal, only really vulnerable at that nexus of the film's other plot, the surrogate motherhood that makes Ripley so appealing.

But the first film is so slow, so stealthy, so gradual in finding its battle. There is time to smell out this lugubrious, neurotic crew—just think of being cooped up with Harry Dean Stanton, Veronica Cartwright, a zombie Ian Holm, Yaphet Kotto, and poor John Hurt. Yes, Weaver and Tom Skerritt are more regular and wholesome, and there was even a thought once of some sex between them. But Ridley Scott and his writers eschewed it, and rightly so—romance is too fanciful in outer space. Ripley's real mate is the rapist monster, and it all feels better if she has not been touched before.

So take the time to study Howard Hanson's mournful music, the fabulous striations of vulcanized rubber on the dead planet. The meanings in *Alien* are myriad, and it's telling that the film came along just ahead of an unexpected and irrational invasion of the human immune system. For finally the alien here is not simply a monster, the great shadow of the id stepping into life, but DNA flipped over so that it says *And?* in the most menacing way. It is about things that are alien to us, and one regrets that the series could never quite see its way through to that, instead of settling for one genre display after another. But *Alien* is not just a monster movie, or science fiction, or horror even. It is a study of the loneliness of the human species, dismaying and moving because of unknowns it is on the point of disclosing.

Aliens (1986)

Generally speaking, the industrial strategy known as franchising—of doing sequels until the end of time—was a disaster in the 1980s and 1990s. But every now and then, something quite wonderful came of the plodding method. If you put *Alien* and *Aliens* side by side (and it may be one of the last great double bills in American film), you get not just the thumping and very satisfactory sequence of prolonged combat after great unnerving threat. You also get the emergence of the secret love story in these *Alien* pictures, the way in which no matter what happens in her movie career, Sigourney Weaver is never going to meet a more faithful lover than the creature. Indeed, its only rivals were the gorillas in the mist.

Ripley comes back from the first film like Sleeping Beauty in her spacecraft. She looks lovely still, but the journey has taken fifty-seven years. She is brought back to Earth's drab reality, but she has nightmares. And then she hears that the planet the *Nostromo* went to—it is called LV-426 now—has a small community of miners on it, a few families. And now, as Ripley comes home and wakes after fifty-seven years, the regular signal from LV-426 cuts out. Is there a clearer way the Alien has of calling to Ripley?

The second film is said to be written by director James Cameron after a story by Cameron, David Giler, and Walter Hill. Hill and Giler were set on doing a combat film this time, but Cameron was in such control that they weren't asked for too much. So a patrol goes back to LV-426 and discovers a little girl, Newt (Carrie Henn), the only human left alive on a planet writhing with monsters and pods ready to make more. As such, Cameron made a terrific action film (there is a director's cut of 153 minutes, compared with the release print of 136). Of course, the patrol is no match for the creatures; but Ripley becomes Newt's surrogate mother, and the "marines" all go down in a blaze of glory. The film has a lot of Cameron's actors in this capacity—Michael Biehn, Bill Paxton, William Hope, Al Matthews, Jenette Goldstein—as well as brilliant imagery of intestinal corridors, flamethrowers, and the sudden lunge of the monster's jaws.

But it has extras: a very nasty Paul Reiser as a kind of scientist in charge, who wants to keep the alien alive; and Lance Henricksen, who is very touching as Bishop, the replicant who is ripped to shreds in his valiant effort to help Ripley. There is not enough time for much else, but Cameron served the franchise well: He delivered a blazing adventure film that made a ton of money and so stressed Ripley's courage and resourcefulness that Weaver would get an Oscar nomination for it. So the sequel speaks to the insinuating muscle of the inner story, the subtext, that the bond between Ripley and the alien, and the strange play upon motherhood, is still there, pale and plaintive. When Ripley turns the flamethrower on pods of baby aliens-to-be, the ripe smell of necessary abortion fills the air, but motherhood is a far cry that lurks in Ripley's gaze. She has a dream from the start of this film that she is pregnant by the monster.

So it proved, but alas *Alien 3* and then *Alien Resurrection* proved dismal failures (though the third film is filled with intriguing ideas and beautiful, devastated imagery).

All About Eve (1950)

Whereas *Sunset Blvd.* was a first step toward autopsy for the film industry, *All About Eve,* made the same year, is by contrast a celebration of theater—of theatricality, acting, and great lines that may bring the house down. Of course, by the standard of 1950, caught between *A Streetcar Named Desire* and *Death of a Salesman,* this is old-fashioned theater. It is the well-made play par excellence, it is about people who will talk until they drop, and it has no ulterior motive beyond saying that the theater is a fiercely competitive place, and quite wonderful. The meanings for *Sunset Blvd.* are vastly more alarming. They even suggest that you might not want to be a great actress. *All About Eve* can see no other goal in sight as bright or commanding.

So it's not really surprising that *All About Eve* got fourteen Academy Award nominations and six Oscars (the Sarah Siddons award, of course, it keeps for itself in perpetuity)—though, as the years go by, doesn't every prolonged Oscars show cry out for the sardonic commentary of Addison DeWitt and the realization that this winner we see before us is a bitch on wheels? *Eve* won for Best Picture. Joseph L. Mankiewicz won for directing and screenplay (for the second year in a row). George Sanders won for supporting actor. Bette Davis and Anne Baxter were both losers in the Best Actress category. So were Gloria Swanson in *Sunset Blvd.* and Eleanor Parker in *Caged.* The Oscar went to Judy Holliday in *Born Yesterday.* But it's all acting.

Over the years, the objection has been raised that Mankiewicz was not a very interesting director in the sense of moving the camera, composition and cutting. It's a fair claim, and there are films where this lack of facility gets in the way (even *The Barefoot Contessa,* I fear, seems pretty heavy-handed nowadays). But Mankiewicz could answer that when he had his script right and his cast in line, no one really noticed how static or plain the film was.

But that comes nowhere near conveying the pleasure of *All About Eve.* After all, it is as cinematic as, say, crosscutting to have George Sanders's sarcastic comments daubed like a mustache on Anne Baxter's Mona Lisa gaze. It is as visual as Marlene Dietrich praying in the gloom in *Shanghai Express* to see Bette Davis's smug Pekingese face emerging from a thick collar of fur. And remember that this was not meant to be Davis. Claudette Colbert was the original casting, and she lost the role of Margo because of an injury. How would Colbert have been? Funny? Of course. Sophisticated? Surely. But was Colbert as vulnerable to hurt and envy as Davis? I'm not so sure of that—and Colbert was helplessly prettier, whereas in 1950 anyone could see that Bette Davis was turning into a gargoyle.

This is very much the theater before Kazan and the Actors Studio, but there was a theater then—and may be again. *All About Eve* is modest, self-contained, and brilliant. Could it be more? I doubt it, not with Mankiewicz putting it together, not with his eternally comic perspective on actors. But on the whole, I'd sooner poke fun at playacting than take it too seriously. I like the idea of Miss Caswell coming from the Copacabana School of Dramatic Art, and I love the happy look on Marilyn Monroe's face as much as I cherish the sour demeanor of Thelma Ritter.

It was also, I think, a talky, snob film. It cost $1.4 million, and even after all the awards, its domestic rentals were only $2.9 million. *Samson and Delilah* did $11 million—as George Sanders might have purred, "And I was in both."

All Quiet on the Western Front (1930)

Erich Maria Remarque's novel was published in 1929, and it became an international sensation. As never before in the history of combat, the daily texture of military life (and death) was spelled out—perhaps because the condition of the First World War was so static. The same dreadfully plowed land was the site of friendly trenches, then enemy lines, and back again. If the soldier survived, he found a grim archaeology in the mud. Moreover, the casualty figures in that war had ripped apart the social fabric of Europe. It may be that the poetry of the war was more trenchant and shocking, but *All Quiet on the Western Front* had the broad brush of a best-selling novel. It was the duty of the film industry to live up to that challenge. And it was fitting that Carl Laemmle, Jr., at Universal, born in Chicago but the son of a German, should be resolved to produce a film from the novel—and to maintain the thrust of Remarque's narrative by following a group of German soldiers as they move from school to death.

It was always intended to be a big production, with an eventual budget of $1.2 million. Lewis Milestone was hired as director (he had been on a wartime film unit), and it was hoped that he would clarify the contributions of a great many writers. Maxwell Anderson did the major adaptation of the novel, but several other people, including George Abbott, had a hand in the writing. Milestone's most remarkable contribution is not exactly what the film is about, but anyone who knows the film remembers it. In the great frontal assaults, Milestone used very exciting tracking shots, moving with the advancing soldiers. (All his life he loved that shot—he also used it in *Pork Chop Hill*, about the Korean War.) But, truth to tell, the shot is arousing. It associates the movement of the attack with the energy of the camera. It makes us feel that the attack will be successful, whereas the opposite is the grim message of that war—and to get the opposite effect, just look at Stanley Kubrick's doomed tracking shots in *Paths of Glory*. In other words, the reality—of rows of men cut down—is still rather avoided in this celebrated antiwar film.

What remains is the progress of the soldiers (a group that includes Louis Wolheim, Lew Ayres, Slim Summerville, and many others). They are German, yet they are universal, too, and although their talk is very stilted, the description of their tragedy remains powerful—you have to realize that such scenes had never really been played before. Moreover, Ayres, only twenty-two, had a freshness that made the loss of him nearly unbearable.

The camera work was done by Arthur Edeson and Karl Freund, and Edeson was credited with developing sound cameras light enough for Milestone's traveling shots. Everyone saw the film. It made a huge profit and won Best Picture and Best Director for 1930. But it's a tough experience these days, in great part because the audience has to face its own defiant appetite for "war scenes" no matter the logic of pacifism. The single temptation of war on film is to make it look easy. Sooner or later, most war films become recruiting material.

All That Jazz (1979)

This may be the ultimate work in the "gotta dance, gonna die" subset of movies where people pursue their art (or their section of show business) against all sane advice that it's killing them. In fact, Bob Fosse lived eight more years before exactly the pattern of insane work and a bad heart outlined in this film claimed him. The only other film he made in that time is *Star 80*, an oddity, without the exhilaration that was Fosse's sole reason for living. If Fosse had died in middance on *All That Jazz*, it's hard to believe that his producer and close friend, Daniel Melnick, would not have honored his star by filming and including his fatal attack.

The story, scripted by Fosse and Robert Alan Aurthur, is that of Joe Gideon (Roy Scheider), a man cutting a film about a comedian (the reference is to Lenny Bruce) and putting on a stage show, driven by the battling rhythms of the dance and his own heart. He smokes hard. He works harder. He has a history of angina. What adds to his particular condition is his chronic habit of fucking his female dancers—and that, of course, is as dangerous a celebration of the heart as eight-hour days of dance rehearsal. Thus, as he rehearses new dancers, Joe is watched by Audrey Paris (Leland Palmer), his ex-wife. He beds a young dancer (Deborah Geffner) and is discovered in bed by his "steady" girlfriend, Kate Jagger (Ann Reinking, a Fosse girlfriend). In life, Fosse had three wives, all dancing partners—Mary-Ann Niles, Joan McCracken, and Gwen Verdon—and others.

The ultimate female figure in *All That Jazz* is Angelique (Jessica Lange), the "Angel of Death" and a sardonic commentator on his own coming demise. Scheider does a superb job as Fosse, grasping the exact fusion of mortality and attraction. The film has a very high-production look—photography by Giuseppe Rotunno, production design by Philip Rosenberg, and fantasy designs by Tony Walton. There is also a lot of good music, assembled from here and there. What is missing is the sense that Fosse has some great work in hand, and here we face the dilemma of the choreographer and the dancer.

We take it for granted that Fosse moved to the beat in a very special way. We do not doubt the influence of his dance styling on *Chicago, Cabaret*, and *Dancin'*. But did he ever manage to take over or conceive of an entire musical? *Cabaret* is the closest thing on film, but it has this wide gulf between the stuff inside the club and the love story beyond that. Fosse obviously had an immense ego; making *All That Jazz* almost requires the man to blind himself to the distress of children and family. And there is a kind of self-glorification that really needs choking off in a film set in a broader context. But you know that people in the business—and maybe, above all, people who spend their lives dreaming of getting a break—watch *All That Jazz* once a month. It always ends the same way.

All the King's Men (1949)

A new *All the King's Men* arrived in 2006, and the world wondered *why, why?* Yet in the years since the first version, we have had opportunity to respect the destiny of Southern governors—Jimmy Carter, Bill Clinton, George W. Bush, to say nothing of Lyndon Johnson, who may be a better fit for Willie Stark, the central figure in Robert Penn Warren's novel, which had an astonishing reputation once for quality and which led to a movie that won Best Picture in its day.

It was hard to think that the makers of the remake (producer Mike Medavoy, writer-director Steven Zaillian, actor Sean Penn) had spent very long with the original, or that anyone now can judge that the Robert Rossen film of 1949 ever recovers from the limits (or is it the assurance?) of Broderick Crawford as Stark. When he first appears, he's a quiet, calm family man with firm convictions and little political style. Foreseeing what is coming (the whole reputation of being made in the image of Huey Long), one might hope for ambiguity—until there is a finger-licking close-up of Stark chewing a chicken leg, lost in a revery of fried chicken, and plainly capable of anything except good acting.

What now seems cripplingly trite and convenient is the way Stark's progress toward taking over an unnamed Southern state is offset by Burden's Landing, the enclave of old money and high-mindedness where Stark seems more than ever the hollow ranter. This place consists of a noble doctor, a pure judge, a lovely Southern belle, and the film's narrator, Jack Burden, an outcast from privilege who has gone away to be a newspaper writer.

We can suppose that Jack is a radical, searching for a new kind of leader, and there's something about the dark weakness of John Ireland that is right for the role. But Jack is a stooge of a character, and an observer who sees the humbug in Stark very early. So his "agony" of disillusion is specious and his corruption is unfair.

There's little sense of the countryside or the South. But cinematographer Burnett Guffey fills the frame in packed compositions with sweaty faces and avid eyes—and that's where we come to Mercedes McCambridge as the political manager, Sadie Burke. She talks of being a smallpox victim and having a hard face as a result, and there are mirror scenes where she ruminates on her lack of beauty—Joanne Dru is the film's forlorn saucer holding that milk. McCambridge is sharp, frosty, always thinking. You'd say she steals the film, if there was enough to steal.

So it won Best Picture, though Joseph Mankiewicz won the writing and directing Oscars for *A Letter to Three Wives*. Crawford and McCambridge won Oscars, and Ireland was nominated. Why did Rossen not get Best Director? How about, he didn't deserve it? Nice try. I suspect he lost because by 1949–50 he was blacklisted and marked down. If only this limp picture left any reason for the forces of reaction wanting to destroy him.

All the President's Men (1976)

Even Ronald Reagan opined that the movie of *All the President's Men* lost Gerald Ford the 1976 election—and I suppose you can argue that Rocky Balboa and Jimmy Carter were the two great mavericks of the bicentennial year. On the face of it, you would not think that the Carl Bernstein–Bob Woodward book that tracked their *Washington Post* campaign against Richard Nixon's Watergate would make a compelling or coherent movie. After all, it was a very tangled story, calling for a host of minor parts, and everyone knew the ending in advance.

But then William Goldman delivered one of the most clarifying screenplays in Hollywood history, and Alan Pakula directed it with a paranoid subtext that whispered, Look, just because righteousness and reporting won the day, don't relax or begin to feel comfortable. What the film as a whole did was to say, Look, Washington is men and women like these, all busting their guts to be successful. So it's dirty tricks and shabby honor. It's like show business: Anything could happen, and it probably will. It's in this movie that we met for the first time such figures as Karl Rove and Scooter Libby, George Stephanopoulos and James Carville. In other words, the undergrowth of a city and a system had been indicated, and that left no room for comfort.

So it's a film noir with a happy ending, which goes against a lot of rules. On the other hand, it's also two cub reporters looking like major movie stars. My guess is, it's a better film without Robert Redford and Dustin Hoffman, but that was becoming a truism by then, and Redford was a coproducer getting the movie made. Still, imagine Robert Walden and Stephen Collins (who are in the picture already), and I think it feels braver and more unlikely. It's so hard in this era to believe that Redford could be denied, and he's so unlikely to offer any evidence of hunger.

Therefore, it becomes a maze that's a treat to follow. Alan Pakula directs every last detail out of it, and one has to suppose that he's the root of the quite exceptional casting. But consider the work from these people: Jack Warden, Jason Robards, Jr., playing Ben Bradlee as if he were Babe Ruth, Jane Alexander (Oscar nominated), Meredith Baxter, Ned Beatty, Martin Balsam, Nicholas Coster, Lindsay Crouse. I come to Hal Holbrook last. His Deep Throat is superb, wintry, bleak, and plainly corrupt down to his esophagus.

Gordon Willis did the photography, which runs from his customary noir gloom to the hospital-like brightness of the *Post* office. George Jenkins in turn built a set that had real journalists fooled.

The movie was a big hit, which may have toppled Ford and may have built up a false sense of security in liberals. For many others, I suspect it was a textbook on how to get what you want in Washington. *Rocky* beat it for Best Picture and Best Director—enough to let anyone know that the United States was insane. The only Oscars the film won were for Robards and for Goldman's script.

Alphaville (1965)

Eddie Constantine was forty-eight in 1965, but he looks like a thousand-year-old lizard in *Alphaville*. And it was a great piece of casting in which this iconically weathered face and presence could get away with being just a little flat in delivery—after all, he is talking to a computer, so it is a certain politeness to seem stilted. But in raincoat and fedora, with a face like the surface of the moon, he is ancient, prephotographic, absolutely emblematic. And it's as if Jean-Luc Godard and actress Anna Karina had seen how, to accommodate Lemmy Caution's offer of love, her Natasha Von Braun needed to be simply the most winsome face, eyebrows curled like quotation marks, reading Paul Éluard's *Capitale de la Douleur* as if it were a street guide.

And so precinema meets silent cinema in a film where the reigning voice is disembodied—the endless, merciless Godardian brilliance of Alpha 60 himself, the being so sage, so embodied in time, and so mint in condition that Lemmy and Natasha can inhabit the most vulgar of comic books that cinematographer Raoul Coutard can find in Paris by night. For this portrait of the future was committed to doing no more and no less than filming contemporary Paris in the most passive or obedient way. The sci-fi comes not just in the drab seductresses who linger like dust in every hotel corridor, or the swimming pools where state assassinations seem like rough swimming lessons. But this is a film where modern office architecture is comment enough on the various processes of dehumanization.

It begins with music (by Paul Misraki, an important deepening of Godard's tone or attempt) and with Alpha 60's warning (a mixture of doomsday Kubrick and the society for the preservation of John Ford): "There are times when reality becomes too complex for Oral Communication. But Legend gives it a form by which it pervades the whole world."

And what better register of diseased pervasiveness is there than this lovely, croaking voice-over—not just as in "superimposed on" but "above" and the natural position of "fucking us"? And it is heartbreaking—just as much as the sight of Gestapo marching on the Champs-Élysees—that Alphaville is Paris, for the New Wave had among all its moral principles the notion that Paris belonged to them. They claimed it as the Impressionists had done, or as novelists from Proust to Céline to Hemingway would. But every image of Alphaville says, See how the city has surrendered already, and see how resistance is futile.

In fact, we watch resistance fade: It is in the death of Henri Dickson, Akim Tamiroff's unshaved private eye, the man who still dreams of telling himself that the seductress on his lap is Madame de Pompadour. It is the ultra-Godardian impulse that he lovingly spells out the system of control, like a man who wants to be Alpha 60 and close those great reproachful eyes in Karina's face.

Amadeus (1984)

There was always a risk that a film made from *Amadeus*, the Peter Shaffer play, would seem like a gift album derived from it (with amazing location views of Prague, let's say, as a bonus) instead of a movie made in its own right. You almost feel as if you're walking out of the theater with a souvenir wig and your own piece of an autographed Mozart manuscript. You feel richer—and isn't that the state to which art has been reduced?

The play opened in London in 1979 and on Broadway in 1980, and it was a coup in that, just as *Rosencrantz and Guildenstern Are Dead* was offered as oblique, back-corridor access to *Hamlet*, so the fascinating story of Salieri got the benefit of having Wolfgang Amadeus Mozart in the middle distance as a bit of a buffoon. And in the increasingly decadent view of art as business in the 1970s and 1980s, the story of Salieri was a new modern classic. Because Salieri was the wannabe, the careerist, consumed in lust, duplicity, and intrigue, he was Tom regularly confounded by the helpless innocence of Jerry in those great cartoons. He was every gray eminence, from Ovitz to Eisner.

There's no problem about the play's being "opened up" to the full resources of décor, costume, and court panoply. A very pleasing illusion is conveyed—ersatz history—of being in Vienna at that time, smelling the wine and the shit, by a director, Milos Forman, who is a great *metteur en scène*, even if he can't always find too much that is personal in the material. Forman would do a *Valmont* that is actually better at the eighteenth century than *Dangerous Liaisons*. And the casting was surprising and delicious. It's not that Tom Hulce or F. Murray Abraham were unknowns (the previous year Abraham had been a lovely, sleazy Cuban gangster in *Scarface*). But Abraham's Salieri is like a parched man being given water; we can feel the dried-up venom becoming juicy and even fleshy again. As for Hulce, he is childlike, so that it's easy to miss his absolute certainty with just one thing—his music.

You could run the film for young people as an introduction to music, the creative process, and envy. As a whole, it feels as much like a Saul Zaentz picture as anything else—that is to say, the organization of a very good producer, a man who so mixes taste and economy that he could be Salieri himself. It follows from all this that Mozart is the true outsider or alien, a figure beyond understanding or polite company, an urchin. Of course the film won Best Picture, Best Screenplay, and Best Actor, as well as several other craft awards—eleven nominations and eight Oscars, including a nod for the superb photography of Miroslav Ondricek and a win for the art direction by Patrizia von Brandenstein and Karel Cerný.

The cast also includes Elizabeth Berridge, Simon Callow (who was the London Mozart), Roy Dotrice, Christine Ebersole, and Jeffrey Jones.

Amarcord (1974)

Americans especially loved *Amarcord:* In 1974, the Academy gave it Best Foreign Film, and the year after, Fellini was nominated for it as Best Director. Compared with American films of the mid-1970s, it was so optimistic, so serene in believing that all things shall pass. Yes, there were scenes of life under the Fascists, and they weren't very pleasant. But the great floral head of Il Duce himself was a thing of fun, of dream almost. The word *amarcord* means "I remember," but the mood of the film is more that of someone saying "I wonder," trying to forget harsh times or ugly truths.

More or less, it's the memoir of Titta (Bruno Zanin), an eager teenager, as he recalls his life in a small seaside town in the Fascist period. There's no war yet. The local cinema can show Astaire and Rogers and Gary Cooper. A year passes with natural and unnatural ceremonies: Fascist parades, snow falling, big-bosomed women giving Titta their nipples to suck—unlikely bits of theater. It's an episodic film, although I do think there's a conscious effort to suggest that fascism is an adolescent ideology. But nothing hints at why fascism had come to Italy, or at the process that would remove it. Fellini knew that bad time, of course, but *Amarcord* is a case of leaving nostalgia uninspected. Equally, it's a movie that did nothing to disturb or chasten those thousands of Americans who spent their carefree summers in Italy.

Written by Fellini and Tonino Guerra, it is a display of charm done without much shame. It reminds us, perhaps, of Fellini the cartoonist, watching life go by and turning it into lively comic sketches. Everyone wants sex or romance, and there is one quite marvelous sequence where the dreams and desires are embodied in the passing of a great liner, the *Rex,* a Fascist achievement but a string of lights on the moonlit ocean and the very best show these people get. (You can feel the idea for *And the Ship Sails On.*)

But there's the point. Fellini once was a real social observer and storyteller. Here he is a mere collector of material. He has withdrawn enough from story to give up its urge to judgment. So *Amarcord* discourages history or political thinking. The Fascists came like the snow or the blossom; you shrug and wait for the next season. It's startlingly devoid of drama or self-criticism. And it begins to look very old-fashioned.

Of course, the two hours it takes slip by without friction. Fellini can make a scene in his sleep—but does he have to? And with Giuseppe Rotunno as his cameraman and Nino Rota doing his music, the film is never short of prettiness. Then look at pictures of Fellini as a real kid in Rimini and you're struck by the sharp, hungry face and the desperate look. You know it wasn't quite like *Amarcord,* and you long for the real thing.

American Beauty (1999)

On a lofty view of American suburbia, the dreamy voice begins, "My name is Lester Burnham. This is my neighborhood. This is my street. This . . . is my life. I'm forty-two years old. In less than a year, I'll be dead." It is an opening as good as that of Joe Gillis lying facedown in the swimming pool in *Sunset Blvd.*, and in a way it is the same story: that of how the dream didn't quite work out in practice.

The screenplay was by Alan Ball, a successful series writer for television, and it found its way to Sam Mendes, the English theater director, looking for a first film. Mendes, who generally had great difficulty reading scripts, read it several times in a row: "The strange thing was that at each reading the script seemed to be something else. It was a highly inventive black comedy. It was a mystery story with a genuine final twist. It was a kaleidoscopic journey through American suburbia, and a hugely visually articulate one at that. It was a series of love stories. It was about imprisonment in the cages we all make for ourselves and our hoped-for escape."

That's not an unfair description of the film that emerged, and I think it's a just account of film in America reaching a complexity beyond that of Billy Wilder or Frank Capra or any of the American classical directors who might have been engaged to direct this film. *American Beauty* is not so much a fixed genre as a novel for the cinema. Nothing would seem out of the ordinary in a police report or a newspaper story, yet it's the virtue of the film that we realize how far every mundane incident is spiked by uniqueness.

Though the tone is willfully serene—and Kevin Spacey's narration as Lester is vital to this—*American Beauty* is a film in the school of *Bigger Than Life* or those fifties melodramas that knew something profound was out of joint in America. In the decades after—the age of civil rights, Vietnam, Nixon, the end of the Cold War—it was easy to think that that fracture would heal. It didn't. Ordinary happiness is itself suspect in the very nation that values it most—indeed, that insists on it. This gentle but very sharp comedy is one of the films that returns to that subject.

Mendes directed like an expert, though he gave lavish praise to his cameraman, Conrad Hall, for letting things be so smooth. The score, by Thomas Newman, was Satie-like and a very important guide to the film's equivocal mood. And the playing showed what years of theater experience can lead to: Kevin Spacey dropped his supercilious manner and seemed very human, Annette Bening was magnificent, and there was a string of fine supporting work from Thora Birch, Wes Bentley, Mena Suvari, Peter Gallagher, Allison Janney, and Chris Cooper.

American Gigolo (1980)

No one was ever short of reasons for laughing at the poise of *American Gigolo,* yet it seems to me a fabulous, nerveless walk on the high wire, with Richard Gere managing at every turn to indicate the chic of his clothes. There is one shot where a greased drawer in Julian Kaye's Los Angeles home slides open to reveal a chorus of sleek Italian designer shirts—the silent cry from the shirts is every bit as choral and liturgical as the response from a real choir in a religious piece. In other words, the wire being walked here is that in which high art turns into high camp. If you find that distasteful or far-fetched, then I can only assume that you have never lived in contemporary Los Angeles. Apart from everything else—and there is a lot of everything else—this is one of the knowing L.A. classics in which Lies Allowed begins to turn into Lassitudes Anonymous. (It all speaks to the influence of the great Italian designer Ferdinando Scarfiotti on director Paul Schrader.)

Julian Kaye is Richard Gere, and vice versa, and welcome to the realm of daft perfection. It was to have been John Travolta as the L.A. male prostitute, but for some reason that lovable guy ducked the show—leaving Gere in the part, one that did a great deal to establish him and to make clear his resemblance to flake. I have been hard on Gere in the past (if not quite hard enough), but I do allow a few occasions when he is good—in this film, *Internal Affairs,* and *The Hoax*—and then there is no one like him. It took courage to be an "American Gigolo" (one of the great high-concept titles), an expensive stud with stylistic aspirations who gets caught up in a very nasty murder case and nearly finds himself the fall guy but for the love of the fine wife of a senator, modeled by Lauren Hutton—and if more in our Congress were married to women like Lauren, dare I say that this country would be in a more wholesome condition?

Paul Schrader directs from his own script and puts his every love and desire into the picture, so it thrills to the pulse of disco music, voyeuristic sex, Robert Bresson, the L.A. light, the Polo Lounge at the Beverly Hills Hotel, driving on the freeway in a convertible, the "privacy" of Palm Springs, and the infinite blossom of corruption in southern California. It is often like an advertisement (shot with exquisite taste by John Bailey), and it delights in streamlining moderne-ism, and the sultry swish of the passing moment.

The whole thing is poised on an edge where collapse or public mirth are equal possibilities, yet it survives and brings its fatuous Sirkian plot to a lovely finale. Within the delirium of clichés and pretension, something absolutely true strides forward, personified by Gere's lounging walk and his shameless attitudinizing. This was a new kind of riveting trash, and it has a fluency that Paul Schrader's stop-start career has seldom regained. But if you want to know about America in 1980, then go to *American Gigolo,* and *Raging Bull.* There they are, on the far shore of AIDS, just wondering if would-be hoodlums might be seen in public wanting to do disco and wear the right shirt. Go for it!

American Graffiti (1973)

American Graffiti is still fun, and still an honest teenage picture from a time when teenagers kept their fun and their anguish decently to themselves in the certainty that they weren't worth a hill of beans anywhere else. And they were right. There is a shy charm to *American Graffiti*, like a note to parents that says, "Don't worry. We're having fun. Everything will be OK." It may not work out that tidily in practice, though it does here. Going away to Vietnam is the biggest danger the kids face, and the picture never thinks to ask the parents, "Why will we be in Vietnam?" Indeed, the parents don't exist. But the kids are fresher and more appealing than so many other movie teenagers in that they know they know very little.

So let's call the town Modesto, where George Lucas (born in 1944) was himself raised in years of American splendor when a kid could have a dynamic set of wheels, the blonde coasted by from time to time, and the sound track kept coming because Wolfman Jack was playing everything from Frankie Lymon and the Big Bopper to the Beach Boys and Del Shannon. It is 1962 (just before the Beatles), and we meet the gang. There is romance, racing, nostalgia already (these kids are backing into the future), terrific jokes, and a dead-on accuracy in Lucas's control that ought to have given someone the shivers as early as 1973.

Coming out of the University of Southern California, Lucas had been the quiet kid, with Francis Coppola the talker. It was no surprise that as Francis leaped ahead with *The Godfather*, George bombed with *THX 1138*, a gloomy sci-fi picture about a world short on trust, warmth, and rock and roll. George does not like to bomb, and *American Graffiti* was a shift to something he knew—and something he guessed would sell. Francis was his godfather, acting as producer (with Gary Kurtz) and telling the studio to leave the kid alone. Gloria Katz and Willard Huyck joined Lucas on the script. Walter Murch did the sound mix. Verna Fields and Marcia Lucas were the editors. And Haskell Wexler (an old friend) was "visual consultant"—the photography itself is credited to Ron Eveslage and Jan D'Alquen, but today it's regarded as a Wexler job.

The film cost $750,000, grossed nearly $50 million, and keeps on earning. It is, in my opinion, the best film Lucas has ever made, a delight and by now a movie that can safely be shown to children. The only pretentious thing about it is the title—though it's a very good title, too. As to life, it is sober, modestly hopeful, and quietly beautiful in observing the rapid pinball of hopes and dreads. But surely once upon a time "Modesto" must have meant that kind of place.

The cast is a who's who, or by now a who was that: Paul Le Mat at the center as Milner, Ron Howard, Richard Dreyfuss, Charlie Martin Smith, Cindy Williams, Candy Clark, Mackenzie Phillips, Harrison Ford (as Bob Falfa), Bo Hopkins, Kathy Quinlan, and Suzanne Somers as the blonde in the T-Bird.

An American in Paris (1951)

Art for art's sake? A way of reviving the tourist trade? A conspiracy on the part of Impressionist art dealers? One more curious episode in the career of Vincente Minnelli? Or a tribute to the great influence of Powell-Pressburger's *The Red Shoes,* a film that had its biggest initial response in America? It's worth noting, I think, that the M-G-M film has its self-contained ballet sequence—in just the same way as *The Red Shoes.* Well, not really. *The Red Shoes* is a dance film, of course, but it is an opera, too, and a trembling melodrama. Its ballet sequence is a model for the whole film and for its sense of the war between love's passion and art's rapture. It is the core of a film that is really about the most important things in Michael Powell's life.

Whereas *An American in Paris* is about the allure of art and its prestigious decorative display. It's as empty at its heart as the love affair between the Gene Kelly and Leslie Caron characters is flimsy. Does that seem unfair, or beside the point? The answer may rest in how great our demands are for the musical. Is it a "pure" genre—one where dance, music, décor, and movement are everything—or does the story matter? I know that *The Red Shoes* and *Silk Stockings* move me, that the story of *Singin' in the Rain* and *Funny Face* have always interested me. Whereas, with the Minnelli film, the title says it all. It is a film about a situation, not a drama.

Still, this was plainly the most important production from the Arthur Freed unit at Metro. Minnelli would direct a film in which design was vital. The photography was by John Alton and Alfred Gilks; Orry Kelly, Irene Sharaff, and Walter Plunkett did the costumes—with exquisite taste borrowed from so many Impressionists, but essentially from the spirit and color clashes of Toulouse-Lautrec; Cedric Gibbons and Preston Ames did the art direction. On the other hand, Gene Kelly was the lead and composed the dances. The music was by George and Ira Gershwin—not just the big ballet number, but "'S Wonderful," "Our Love Is Here to Stay," and Georges Guétary's "I'll Build a Stairway to Paradise," which has its fans.

Nominated for eight Oscars, it won six, including Best Picture, but not Best Director, and one for Alan Jay Lerner's screenplay, as generous a nod as the script is hard to find. I know how much Minnelli cared about this subject, but I feel none of the commitment that is so resonant in *Lust for Life.* I'm not sure that the most interesting aspects of the film aren't those involving the superbly melancholy Oscar Levant. And of all the great M-G-M musicals, I wonder if any of them is now looked at less often than this. In so many polls of our great movies, *Singin' in the Rain* has replaced *An American in Paris* as the big one—yet *Singin'* was not even nominated for Best Picture.

An American Romance (1944)

Time and again with King Vidor, we witness titanic and contrary storms. It is the conflict of mother love in *Stella Dallas* and the mother's feeling that she must sacrifice for her child. It is the uncertainty as to whether a film is about me or mine—the egoism that drives Lewt and Pearl to die just out of reach of each other's arms in *Duel in the Sun*. It's the difference between the overwhelming social togetherness of *Our Daily Bread* and the haunting solitude in *The Crowd*. And it's why King Vidor is, at his best, exhilarating and desperate at the same time. Like Howard Roark in *The Fountainhead*, he is a builder who may tear down his own construction.

An American Romance was undertaken at M-G-M, Vidor's home studio, but several years after the death of Irving Thalberg, his natural patron. It was Louis B. Mayer who allocated a couple of years and at least a couple of million dollars to the archetypal story of an immigrant who makes his way by means of steel. It was a film that would have elements of documentary (it used or reassembled factory production lines), yet it would be as gravely beautiful as anything made by the Soviets in the 1920s.

As Vidor saw it, "I read the lives of Andrew Carnegie, Steinmetz, Knudsen, Walter Chrysler, and many others who had arrived in this country as poor immigrants and through democratic opportunity had worked their way to the top. I would have the immigrant Stefan marry a schoolteacher in Minnesota, who would bear his children when they moved to Chicago. These children would go to high schools, colleges, play football. Then their children would say: 'My grandfather came from the old country, but my father was born in America.' This is what I believe has made America strong, this constant process of rebirth and refining of its cruder basic ores. I would attempt to make metals and men analogous."

The first draft was written by Norman Foster and John Fante (who were on the Orson Welles staff). Thereafter, a dozen people worked on the script, always guided by Vidor. It concerned Stefan Dangosbiblichek, who comes off a boat from Europe in the 1890s with $4. He walks to Minnesota to get a job in the Mesabi mines. He becomes Steve Dangos. He marries. He goes to work in the steel mills, and he rises to become a tycoon. He works for a safe automobile; he is against unions. But his ups and downs are settled by the Second World War and its intense appetite for steel.

It was Vidor's hope to have Spencer Tracy as Steve, but the studio gave him Brian Donlevy instead. Donlevy is fine, busy, truculent, touching—but he is not a given, not immense, not a star. And Vidor believed that his plan to treat Steve's inner life lightly needed an actor who could imply depths.

Just as he came to make the picture, Vidor took up painting. This inspired a Technicolor not seen before, in which the natural colors of earth and minerals and the hues of factories dominated. Harold Rosson did the photography, but it's clearly the inspiration of Vidor, and thus begins the dynamic beauty of a film as much about earth and machines as anything else.

Vidor's cut was 151 minutes. Mayer said he loved the film, but the studio cut it to 122 (it is not clear whether the longer version survives). Even at the shorter length, this is an amazing lost treasure, vital to the turbulent career of Vidor and a partner to *The Magnificent Ambersons* in a Dreiserian view of the American factory, its glory and its cultural drag.

Le Amiche (1955)

In the early 1950s, Michelangelo Antonioni made a series of broken romances: *Cronaca di un Amore* (1950), *La Signora Senza Camelie* (1953), and *Le Amiche* (1955). They were plainly departures from neorealism, even if they used a traveling-camera style that was reminiscent of Roberto Rossellini in the same years. The films owed something to Jean Renoir, and something to their literary origins. But in hindsight, they are most fascinating as a preparation for the breakthrough that occurred with *L'Avventura, La Notte,* and *L'Eclisse.* Much depends on memory, for the films are not easily seen nowadays. I suspect that they are impressive but flawed, and I believe that *Le Amiche* is the best.

It comes from a short story, "Tra Donne Sole," by the noted Italian novelist Cesare Pavese. The screenplay was done by Antonioni, Suso Cecchi D'Amico, and Albe De Cespede. It is set in Turin, where Clelia (Eleanora Rossi Drago) has just returned to open a branch of the fashion house she has been working for in Rome. She meets a group of friends: the spiteful socialite Momina (Yvonne Furneaux), Mariella (Anna Maria Pancani), a potter named Nene (Valentina Cortese), and Rosetta (Madeleine Fischer), who has just attempted suicide. The action of the film covers the setting up of the new salon, Clelia's love affair with Carlo (Ettore Manni), chief among the workers doing the decorating, and the eventual suicide of Rosetta.

At the end, Clelia will return to Rome. The novel was altered here and there: For Pavese, Rosetta was the victim of overall boredom, but in the film she suffers from unrequited love. For the first time, Antonioni plunged into the sensibility and the company of women in a group, and in the 1950s on the art-house circuit the film was esteemed for its feminine psychology and its instinct for the bitchy behavior in a female group. To that extent, the very animated performance of Yvonne Furneaux (an actress who rather roamed around Europe) was thought to be central to the film. Seen now, however, the chief artistic interest is in the physical or photographic deployment of groups and the spaces between people. If that sounds cold-blooded, it helps suggest Antonioni's very cerebral approach in the fifties. But you have only to think of Renoir to know that the spaces between people can be the signs of affection or misunderstanding.

The set piece is a long sequence on a beach—a kind of party—in which small groups form and break up. This was clearly a prefiguring of the long sequence on the island in *L'Avventura* and a mark of obsession with the ways in which people touch and do not touch in meeting and parting, and how those things can be read as signs of boredom or dismay, or of intimacy. With Antonioni, more than nearly any other director, those gaps are the focus of the film more than what is said and what is done. And they are the things we see and feel.

L'Amore (1948)

By 1948, Roberto Rossellini was entangled with Ingrid Bergman—he had made commitments to her as a person and as an artist. Above all, when she identified him as her and the world's best hope of uncovering the truth in existence, he said yes, that's me—and this is what I will do for you (*Stromboli* was only a year away). At the same time, personally and professionally, Rossellini was still deeply involved with Anna Magnani and making a testament to her bravura skills and her old-fashioned preeminence as a diva. I don't think any other term serves to embrace her two nonstop performances from *L'Amore,* or to avoid the notion that Rossellini was ready to do just about anything to get ahead. In years to come, Ingrid Bergman must have longed for her new man to find material for her as rich as *L'Amore.*

Just 80 minutes long, *L'Amore* is in two parts. In the first, Magnani does the part of the Woman in Jean Cocteau's one-person play *La Voix Humaine,* in which a society woman talks on the telephone with her ex-lover, imploring him to return. It is set in her bedroom and bathroom, and the only other living creature is her dog. The hopeless attempt to prevent the lover from marrying another woman ends with the woman knotting the telephone cord around her neck as a prelude to suicide—or had Rossellini just seen Edgar Ulmer's *Detour*?

Rossellini and Tullio Pinelli converted the play into a film script, and Robert Juillard photographed it. The art direction is by Christian Bérard. Magnani is extraordinary, not least in the relentless ingenuity with which she dispels the very pat self-pity of the situation. The play is a vehicle for an actress, of course, yet in a way it's an albatross around her neck, too, because her strength becomes overpowering. It is a model, obviously, for why the poor man has felt compelled to leave her: because she will not shut up or stop performing.

The second episode is more intriguing by far. It is called "The Miracle," and now Magnani is Nanni, a simpleminded peasant woman, a goatherd, who is accosted and seduced by a vagrant (Federico Fellini), whom she mistakes for Saint Joseph. As in the first part, the man doesn't really speak or contribute beyond impregnating the chatterbox idiot. Fellini worked on this script, and Aldo Tonti did the photography.

It's not that the two parts don't work together. They are stories of unrequited love and of a talking woman who hardly hears or notices the lack of response from the man. Yes, together they seem to worship Anna Magnani, yet there is also a streak of misogyny apparent. Who would really want to be trapped with either woman? And a trap is what the whole film feels like. Rossellini is reported to have signed over all income from the film to Magnani—it may have been a way of getting rid of her. But the scream of performance and theatricality is intense, and realism seems a very long way away.

L'Amour Fou (1969)

If ever anyone has the courage and the time to write a great chronicle of the French New Wave, I suspect that Jacques Rivette's *L'Amour Fou* will emerge as the climax and crisis, the moment when it becomes clear that the load that had been carried by Truffaut and Godard had passed to the least likely of all of them. Rivette had made *Paris Nous Appartient* slowly. He seemed so much more withdrawn from the hurly-burly than Godard. Then he had prolonged censorship troubles over *La Religieuse,* adapted from Diderot and starring Anna Karina, but shocking to the French authorities. The film was banned. It was delayed. And still, it was thought to be rather esoteric—or a good deal less shocking than was promised.

At that point, Rivette made his magnificent documentary on Jean Renoir and then, with Georges de Beauregard, the producer who had defended him on *La Religieuse,* he made *L'Amour Fou*—without the least sign of contrition or compromise. *L'Amour Fou* was and remains deeply shocking in the old-fashioned sense: It is about two people, lovers once, who tear each other to pieces. If you care to put it that way, you can say it is a simple story. Sébastien (Jean-Pierre Kalfon) is rehearsing a production of Racine's *Andromaque.* His wife, Claire (Bulle Ogier), is cast in the leading role of Hermione. But she walks out. She says she cannot endure the invasive pressure of the television crew that is filming the rehearsals—though this filmic attention (not uncommon in the sixties, with the decade's rage for vérité shows) is only a metaphor for Rivette's own filming. For, in truth, Kalfon and Ogier were actually working together on an *Andromaque* for the stage at the same time. The fusion of latencies in the words *rehearsal* and *performance* had never been so complete or so deranging. For we see the love between Sébastien and Claire reduced to tatters. At the end, they destroy their own apartment. There were stories of a nearly helpless and dangerous turmoil in the real actors. Don't forget Renoir's intuition about life and theater as a wrestling match. For him that was often tricky yet humane and funny. For Rivette, it is the dark night of the soul, and something he can't take his eyes off.

He produced a film of 4 hours and 12 minutes. I have not seen it in years (and it is hard to see), but I suspect that it is the most intense ordeal Rivette has ever made. Beauregard protested: This was far too long for the material. He begged for a shorter version. Rivette obliged but insisted that duration was central to the agony. He was undoubtedly correct, and in the end the audience proved that: They preferred the long version, they ignored the short one. It is a landmark in modern film and in the medium's anguished treatment of love and performance. And it was a sure measure that, for a moment at least, the most precious ground in movie belonged to Rivette. The quiet one was ready for boldness.

Anatahan (1954)

At the age of sixty, Josef von Sternberg took himself to Japan to make a perfect film. Such an announcement is in character, of course, but what did he think he had been making before? *Jet Pilot* had been shot but not yet released; *Macao* (1952) had been released under his name, but some of it had been reshot by Nicholas Ray. He had not had a proper release since *The Shanghai Gesture* in 1941, and that is his most louche, perverse, and insolent Hollywood production.

Was *Anatahan* a formal experiment? Yoshio Osawa and Nagamasa Kawakita appear to have issued the invitation on behalf of Daiwa Productions. Sternberg and his family were exquisitely entertained in Japan, and members of the royal household attended his lectures. Of course, the subject of his film had been chosen in advance. But as the director knew, what does the subject matter when such an intense style will be brought to bear? He could have added that, since he spoke no Japanese, all communication would have to be through translators. That would have meant trouble to many practitioners, but to Sternberg it was simply a refinement of purity.

The film was made in Kyoto, a proper feature film of 92 minutes about the juxtaposition of a group of sailors and a married couple on a jungle island long after the Second World War is over. Sternberg was the producer, the director, the writer, the photographer, and the narrator of the film, though it's notable that Japanese talent was also credited in all departments except that of direction. It was not filmed on a deserted island. Indeed, the essential characteristic and beauty of the venture is that it is all done on sets, with the trees and foliage of the jungle constructed and rendered synthetically. I remember it as an intense film, very beautiful, of gazing faces and spied-upon scenes, with the light playing upon a jungle of cellophane. It was said that Sternberg regretted being compelled to use real water—everything else was artificial.

The film was not released in America for years. It was butchered in Britain. But in France it was received with awe and wonder. Such reactions are perhaps just extensions of Sternberg's complete ownership of the project. He was only sixty, and the film is that of a man in complete control of his medium. A day may yet come when *Anatahan* is rediscovered—though I would be quite happy to continue to think of it as a mythic film, an ideal to which everyone else might aspire.

Sternberg comes down to us as a monster of folly and arrogance, largely because of the tone of his book, *Fun in a Chinese Laundry*. But the proof was there on the screen. Films were about light, a large enough subject, surely, that human nature should wait its turn. Equally surely, the great waiting face is that of his Marlene. Not hers. In herself, she was some kind of German woman, dull, bourgeois, good-natured, generous, actual, physical. Whereas Sternberg taught us to see that she was also a ghost—eternal, enigmatic, ungraspable.

Anatomy of a Murder (1959)

Not the least delight of this magnificent film is the discovery that way up in Michigan's Upper Peninsula Edward Kennedy Ellington is playing piano at a local tavern—as well as pumping one of the great scores into every pore of this picture, like heat insulation for those cold climes. The swoon of music when we first see Lee Remick's "raped" wife is not just delicious and appropriate, but a sly warning to all members of the audience to behave like jurors.

The jazz is there for Paul Biegler (Jimmy Stewart), a country lawyer who would just as soon go fishing or listen to the "Black and Tan Fantasy." Stewart is droll and lovable, but be careful—he's actually as sharp and cold as the knife he uses to gut his fish. And he sees what we see: Lieutenant Frederick Manion, as cool and insolent as the young Ben Gazzara himself, and Laura Manion, who would flirt with a fire hydrant.

The trial that ensues is a test for us all. Panties are involved—panties ripped off in a brutal sexual act or tossed aside with sexy enthusiasm. But as Joseph Welch's judge quietly insists, get your laughing over with: "Panties" are going to come up, and a man's life, maybe two men's lives, may hang on them. The fact that this judge is played by the man who first rebuked Joseph McCarthy on television may have faded away somewhat now, so gather the children in a circle and explain to them how Otto Preminger, our director, is identifying not just heroes but a full respect for the law. You could add that Preminger was himself the son of a great Viennese jurist.

After that, stand back: even in Michigan, and in black and white (shot by the unsentimental Sam Leavitt), your kids can enjoy Stewart and George C. Scott fencing in court, and the point will dawn on them: that the law, sir, is a game, a kind of ping-pong, in which good players usually come through. But still we are a society that believes in the law. And so this model courtroom melodrama is also an honest testament to America and its brave attempt to spread a little justice around.

As always in such things, Preminger's camera style prefers deep space and groups of people, so that we have to decide where to look while clinging onto every word. The one sentimentality in the film, perhaps, is that northern Michigan ends up seeming as Athenian as Ford's Monument Valley terrain. (Preminger has too much taste to get into redneck life.) Still, it is no lie to honor a country and a system that can produce such things as George C. Scott's sotto voce, Stewart's injured innocence, Eve Arden, panties, and Duke Ellington's music yarning away in the background like a wiseacre in some Faulkner story.

It's not going too far to call this film perfect—not just as a passing show, but as a tribute to reason, irresistible impulses, and that rare gambling game that was the young Lee Remick. Enjoy.

Andrei Rublev (1966)

Imagine a movie life of Shakespeare. How can film capture the sixteenth century? Is that era determined by how far a man can walk? In which case you could do Shakespeare with a steady tracking camera and a heartfelt sense of duration. Or was the sixteenth century a matter of how many violently disparate ideas a Shakespeare can hold in his head? In which case you need a charged montage scheme, endlessly tidally energized and forever leaping at poetic allusiveness.

How would they have made films in Russia in the fifteenth century? It seems to me that Andrei Tarkovsky was as much fascinated by such questions as by the difficulty of knowing for sure what the painter Rublev did or what he was like. After all, research is too far away. So what Tarkovsky does in this truly epic film is to redevise incidents from the painter's life that amount to the trials and ecstasies of any painter at any time. Above all, he ponders: Shall an artist make art, or must he attempt to be involved in the most obvious and painful political dilemmas of his age? Does it matter? For if his art is so strong, even if he puts it aside, won't the art continue to make him? I don't think it's going too far to say that *Andrei Rublev* was an experience that determined the way in which Tarkovsky lived his own life.

Scripted by Tarkovsky and Andrei Mikhalkov-Konchalovsky, the film tracks the life of a great icon painter. The Russia behind that life is tormented and tempestuous: It is like the four movements of, say, Shostakovich's Tenth Symphony playing simultaneously. Having befriended a mute girl, he kills to save her life—and then vows to end his art. But then he observes and participates in the casting of a new bell, and he begins to work again.

Shot in 1965–66, the film was not favored by Soviet authorities. A version played at Cannes in 1969, and there was a 185-minute version released in Russia in 1971. Two years later the film was at European festivals. And now there is a 220-minute version, thought to be complete. The photography is by Vadim Yusov and the music by Vyacheslav Ovchinnikov. Anatoly Solonitsyn plays Rublev. Irma Raush is the mute girl, and Nikolai Burlyayev is the bell-caster.

Obsessed with rain and fire, saintliness and abandon, the film is a celebration of a pagan age when no cause or claim has authority. Just as in the later Tarkovsky films, apocalypse is like a hungry dog exploring the land, and disasters and horrors crowd in on the exquisite beatification of life. The camera races along at ground level and then soars up to magisterial points of view. Of course, Tarkovsky would probably have clung to that flux whatever his circumstances. My opening reference to Shakespeare is not casual, however. Tarkovsky's epic stance reveals his single handicap: the lack of humor and the way in which that slows his grinding pace. One doubts whether there was ever a Tarkovsky film that he didn't itch to lengthen.

Angel Face (1952)

Night in Beverly Hills. An ambulance hurries to a home on a hilltop. A woman (Barbara O'Neil) is half-gassed. It looks like attempted suicide, but she says someone tried to kill her. The ambulance driver, Frank (Robert Mitchum), is leaving the house when he hears a sad piano playing. We thought it was part of the film's score, but now we see the piano is being played by Diane (Jean Simmons) in the drawing room. They talk. She is on the edge of hysteria. He slaps her face. She slaps him back. That's not in the ambulance driver manual, he says. And she looks up at him from beneath her helmet of black hair and gives him Jean Simmons's best smile. Now he's really in trouble.

Angel Face is RKO, with a script by Frank Nugent and Oscar Millard from a story by Chester Erskine. Nugent was John Ford's screenwriter, but the look on Jean Simmons's face is far from that kind of woman. This picture is called *Angel Face,* but Diane is dangerous, so it's reassuring to discover that Ben Hecht went over the script before Otto Preminger shot it. Hecht knew perverse psychology, and he and Preminger had already done *Whirlpool* and *Where the Sidewalk Ends.*

The first trick to this story is to see not just that Diane is crazy, but that Frank—the ambulance driver who wants to open a shop for sports cars—is a chump, despite being played by Mitchum. Diane's father is Herbert Marshall playing a novelist who hasn't written a word since he married O'Neil. To say the least, there's a rivalry between the two women. But the angel is as manipulative as she is beautiful. Her wings may look white, but they come with the "Death" label attached.

That's the story onscreen. Offscreen, Simmons had been hired by Howard Hughes when she came to America with her husband, Stewart Granger. Hughes wanted her, and bought her contract from Rank. But she wasn't playing. So he kept her under contract and gave her nothing to do—until he found this little study in alluring evil, which she was obliged to play in order to end her contract. Preminger never falls for his own star, but he photographs her (by Harry Stradling) in a way that helps explain why Mitchum and others are suckered by her. It's a rich portrait of a femme fatale in which the young woman is driven by an insane selfishness.

A lot depends on that piano melody, and it's one of Dimitri Tiomkin's best. Apart from that, just study the objectivity in the framing, the breathtaking beauty of the photography, and the importance of automobiles—yet again, Frank knows cars, but not in the way Diane has learned. Did Hughes like the film? We don't know. But Simmons is brilliant. In 1952, she brought an intelligence and a sexiness to Hollywood that were ill rewarded by her being turned into a routine leading lady. In Diane here, you can still feel Estella from *Great Expectations*—the kind of girl men make idiots of themselves over.

Angels with Dirty Faces (1938)

The manufacture of gangster films in the 1930s was a steady source of problems with the censor at the Breen Office. Sure, the gangsters nearly always died in the end, but there were sharp parents at Breen who knew that kids loved the spectacular death-falls as much as the scenes where the hoodlums were cleaning the streets with a Thompson. The censors knew that a lot of young testosterone went to Cagney pictures to have a good time. And so, as a concession to moral caution, the pictures often employed an idea of two pals, or brothers even, one who went straight and the other directly to hell. The epitome of this plan is *Angels with Dirty Faces*, a picture founded on the childhood friendship between Rocky Sullivan (Jimmy Cagney) and Jerry Connolly (Pat O'Brien). Rocky becomes a low-down dirty rat (with high style), while Jerry ends up a priest (with a rugged manner).

It began as a story for First National by Rowland Brown, meant for Cagney in his rebellion against Warners. But then peace was made, so Warners took on *Angels.* Hal Wallis always saw it as a vehicle not just for Cagney and O'Brien, but for the "Dead End Kids," the gang led by Leo Gorcey that had featured in William Wyler's *Dead End.*

And here is the shameless point of the story, as finalized in the script by John Wexley and Warren Duff. In his terrible career, Rocky has won the admiration of some local kids whose own futures may be in the balance. So, as the time comes for Rock to test the electric chair, Father Jerry takes him aside, and in the name of friendship (and the hint that Rocky was a Catholic once, too) he wonders if on the way to the death cell Rocky could put on an Oscar show of cowardice to lose the kids' support. At first the Rock snarls and sneers. But when the dawn comes, in shadow play (thanks to director Michael Curtiz), Cagney cringes, howls, and generally carries on like someone who has just read the scene in *White Heat* where Cody hears his Ma is dead. Father Jerry gives a grateful look toward heaven, and Leo Gorcey and the boys see the light—don't be a gangster, be an actor.

The inner meaning is so comic and so unabashed that this is one of Hollywood's great lessons about its own power of fantasy—as well as an inadvertent comedy. Anyway, the Breen Office was left helpless. No one likes censorship, but you have to feel for the Breen boys and their awareness of the complete unscrupulousness of what they were up against.

Cagney is as unbridled as you would guess, and O'Brien is doing Spencer Tracy—there's a soft, gay, Irish light in their eyes, which only reminds me of another fantasy that didn't get settled. Curtiz directs with terrific panache. Hal Wallis was always trying to get him to cut back on those little camera movements, and now they are the best thing in sight. Also with Humphrey Bogart, Ann Sheridan, George Bancroft, Gorcey, Huntz Hall, and the boys. Can you imagine the reaction the film would get now in a decent juvenile hall?

Anna Christie (1930)

Eugene O'Neill's *Anna Christie* opened in New York in 1921, with Pauline Lord as Anna—though the play's first title was "Chris Christopherson" (Anna's father). Chris has not seen his daughter since she went away as a child to live with relatives in Minnesota. But she was raped there, and so she became a prostitute. She comes home and meets a sailor named Matt. The play ends in some uncertainty as to whether Anna will be there waiting for Matt when he returns from a voyage. The human drama is offset by many soulful references to the sea and its affinity with fate.

There had been a silent-movie version, with Blanche Sweet, but the property was then considered by Irving Thalberg to become Greta Garbo's first talking picture. "Garbo Talks!" the posters would shout. Garbo was very wary of opting for sound. She had delayed it as long as she could. But many advisers guessed that sound would help her enormously. Garbo possessed a voice that suited her face. It was deep and low, and—this is vital—it had a pacing that matched the change of expression in her eyes. Still, in the end, she persuaded M-G-M to make two versions of *Anna Christie*—one in English, one in German—because of her feeling that she would be more at ease in the German language.

The English version was done first, with Clarence Brown directing from the Frances Marion screenplay. George Marion played Chris (as he had done onstage), Charles Bickford was Matt, and Marie Dressler made a comeback as Marty, the drunk. Garbo and Dressler got on very well—there is an uncanny feeling of sympathy between them—and Clarence Brown declared that Garbo's instincts about speech made her even better with sound. He admitted that he sometimes accepted her judgment on a scene or a take. That wasn't just polite talk. From her first line—"Gimme a visky, ginger ale on the side—and don't be stingy, baby!"—she was made. Critics adored the deep contralto voice. And *Anna Christie* was an event. Both Garbo and Brown were nominated for Oscars.

William Daniels shot both the English and the German versions, but Jacques Feyder (who had just directed Garbo in *The Kiss*) was hired to direct the German. It is 8 minutes longer than the American, and Anna's clothes make her work more obvious. Garbo's friend Salka Viertel took over from Dressler, and Hans Junkermann played Matt.

Two things resulted: Garbo's stardom was assured, even if in time the pace of her talking might become a touch monotonous—she was no more suited to comedy vocally than in the inner room of her own mind. Marie Dressler was immediately acclaimed by M-G-M. Her days as a comedy sidekick with Polly Moran were over. She was now central, and so with *Min and Bill*, *Tugboat Annie*, and *Dinner at Eight* Dressler was a star again. Indeed, at sixty, she was the most popular actress in the nation. When Garbo looked at Dressler, was she wondering whether she could or would get away with being that ancient?

Annie Hall (1977)

Around 1977, a wave—something—swept over American filmmaking. Some called it feminism and pointed with a weird mixture of pride and wonder at the new sensibility. *Annie Hall* won Best Picture—and seemingly that must be about a woman. Another nominated film was *Julia*—see the pattern? And then there was *The Turning Point,* which was susceptible to the label Can a woman enjoy career and life? Lurking, though less noticed, was one of the most profound of films: *Three Women,* an orgy of female consciousness, under the name of dream. Martin Scorsese even made a picture—*New York, New York,* perhaps his finest—in which a woman qualified as a leading character. In the next few years, there were other major American movies that in their titles and their selling lines seemed to stress this new deal for women: *Coming Home, An Unmarried Woman, Norma Rae, Coal Miner's Daughter, Tootsie* . . . well, no, not exactly.

It passed.

And really, *Annie Hall* is a misnomer. The film should be entitled *How Alvy Singer Learned to Forget Annie Hall and Keep Worrying About Himself.* Which is to say the film itself was a rotten trick. It won Best Picture, with Oscars for Woody Allen as director and writer, and for Diane Keaton. Now, I treasure Ms. K and would happily surround her with Oscars if it was in my doing—I would have given her one for *Reds*—but I have to say that the statuette for *Annie Hall* was a public love letter, a mash note. She is not actually allowed to act in the film, in part because she is not given a character, but chiefly because she is put in a weather system where her silky sails can only fill with the cold wind of Alvy Singer. After all, the song is his.

Ostensibly, it's a film in which a twice-married, self-preoccupied neurotic sucks a sunny California girl into his gloomy orbit and sets her tasks in order to free him from the witch's castle on which he holds—no, grasps—a 999-year lease. In other words, he is not letting go. The film is full of jokes and funny observations. It has great scenes. But it is not a story or a drama. It is a comic's sad monologue filled out to the dimensions of a movie (93 minutes) in which the impenetrable, impregnable self-regard of Alvy fends off a delightful woman. This is not quite feminism. Indeed, it is a kind of celebration of male infantilism (otherwise known as the movies).

Marshall Brickman and Woody Allen wrote it, Woody Allen directed it, and you can guess who plays Alvy Singer. The picture charmed the masses, for it seemed like a turning point at which Woody went from comic to comic artist. Events have proved otherwise. Gordon Willis shot the film. Ralph Rosenblum edited it. Mel Bourne did the art direction. The whole thing is very hip, very American New Wave, and disastrously empty. Diane Keaton sings "It Had to Be You," and many filmmakers might see then and there the way the film had to go—into the *Annie Hall Songbook.* Also with Tony Roberts, Carol Kane, Paul Simon, Janet Margolin, Colleen Dewhurst, Christopher Walken (very good), and Marshall McLuhan (looking a bit like Gary Cooper as a professor).

À Nos Amours (1983)

There's a scene just before the middle of *À Nos Amours* where Suzanne (Sandrine Bonnaire) comes home late and finds her father (Maurice Pialat) still up. They talk. Suzanne is said to be fifteen. Her sex life has begun—she is responding to the muddle of her home life by sleeping around. Note that Pialat, the director, plays the father himself and that he cast his real wife, Evelyne Ker, as his wife. I stress that because the acrimony between the two parents is hard to take, or to deal with, and the thought that a real couple—even if their love is over—could enter into this lacerating contest is hard to credit. Is there anything people will not do for a movie? Is there anything they should be stopped from doing? In other words, *À Nos Amours* belongs in part in the theater of embarrassment.

Yet the scene between the father and Suzanne is absorbing, tender, and extraordinarily detailed. It has at least three components: one, the assigned roles of father and daughter and the background of family history we have seen; two, the actors, a man in his fifties and an extremely attractive girl (I don't mean to say that anything happened between them, but it is absurd to think that the possibility did not exist); and three, the director and the kid he has discovered, the strange mixture of hope and envy that exists in that kind of relationship.

I feel confident that Pialat would have encouraged Mademoiselle Bonnaire to embrace all three states of being, because as an artist he relied upon that candor and authenticity. Indeed, *À Nos Amours* was a minefield and an ordeal from which many parents might have preferred to shelter their daughter. Needless to say, in this instance, the gamble was successful in that Sandrine Bonnaire was clearly going to be one of the great actresses of our time. Fierce, funny, very sexy, and as smart as a wolf, she was a match for the rest of the family. She was a life force.

À Nos Amours won the César for Best Film and the Prix Louis Delluc. Two years later, Bonnaire won a César herself for her role in Agnès Varda's *Vagabond,* which could be construed as an extension of the part here. Bonnaire has done great work since, but there is nothing like the debut, even if she made hers very young. And surely one of the life-affirming virtues in cinema is that it reiterates the greatest thing in real life: meeting a sensational new person. Of course, the novelty is never repeated, and few people can survive familiarity, but when you see someone startling for the first time—Dean, Depp, Kidman, Bonnaire—it means so much. We fall for them (one way or the other). Our affair with the medium is renewed: Look, it has done it again. Most profound of all, we feel better again about life, and the way an ordinary meeting can reenergize us. And that's exactly how Pialat is in that scene. You can feel him saying, My god, how lucky I am, and alas, how old I am.

Apache (1954)

You can see *Apache* as one of the films that began to examine Native American life and history responsibly, or you can see it as an important stepping-stone in the career of Burt Lancaster. There was a novel, *Bronco Apache*, by Paul I. Wellman, that traced the last days of a rogue Apache warrior who refused to live on the reservation. Robert Aldrich and Joseph Losey had teamed up to purchase the rights (though apparently Aldrich had paid for them), so when Losey went off to Europe blacklisted, Aldrich took on the project. But it got made and financed through United Artists, largely because Burt Lancaster liked it and the opportunities it allowed him in the great career surge that followed *From Here to Eternity*. So it was a Hecht-Lancaster production, with Harold Hecht as the official producer and Burt getting his way.

James R. Webb did the screenplay, which doesn't sound quite right. Webb was conventional in his work, and *Apache* was a strikingly new kind of film—not just in the way it really explores the independence of its hero, Massai, but in the authentic toughness of Apache life, which makes him a good deal more "savage" than the Indian figures in films like *Broken Arrow*. Maybe Losey left some marks on the script, maybe it's Aldrich—or Burt, wishing to be rugged and rough to his women—but this is an austere and uncomfortable view of Native American life. (It's worth noting that that attitude would be delivered fully, and with far greater severity, decades later in *Ulzana's Raid*, which is Aldrich and Lancaster again.)

It's easy to see what Burt enjoyed: He wore a black wig, and his blue eyes seldom smiled. He had a lot of running, hiding, hunting, and fighting to do in the hard rock of the desert Southwest, and *Apache* is among other things a tribute to a buffed athlete who never wears a shirt. In addition, he treats his wife (Jean Peters) with a brusqueness that may be based on research, but may have been to Burt's taste, too.

Everybody on board, Burt included, was of the opinion that Massai should die. The logic is plain, and the integrity of the character is hardly going to settle for a quiet farming life. But that's what United Artists insisted on—and that's the point that was redeemed only in the death of the rogue chief in *Ulzana's Raid*.

Never mind: this is an important and impressive Western for its time, and a valuable attempt to correct the old code of being a redskin. A star had never before dared such a role, and maybe only Burt could have identified so readily with Massai's triathlete robustness. The supporting cast includes John McIntire (as the one white man who respects the Apache), Charles Buchinsky (or Bronson), John Dehner, Paul Guilfoyle, Morris Ankrum, and Monte Blue. Rather surprisingly, it was a big hit. To this day, it makes a fascinating double bill with *Ulzana's Raid*.

The Apartment (1960)

Gradually, in the course of the 1950s, Billy Wilder picked up the reputation of being a comedy director. Yet that was far from an adequate description of a naturally amusing mind allied to a very dark view of human nature. Plainly, funny lines aside, *Double Indemnity* is no more of a comedy than *The Lost Weekend;* and while *Sunset Blvd.* is loaded with ironies, its situation is as macabre as that in *Ace in the Hole.* Still, *Some Like It Hot* was hailed as one of the funniest films ever made—though it was not acknowledged by the Academy for its exhilarating mix of tones. So Wilder seems to have felt the need to reestablish himself as the surveyor of a cold and heartless world.

The Apartment (written with I. A. L. Diamond) turns on C. C. Baxter, as likeable though as neurotic as Jack Lemmon, yet deeply compromised—for Baxter is ready enough to loan the key of his apartment to figures in the corporation where he works to be ingratiating and to get ahead. And one of his superiors, Sheldrake (Fred MacMurray), is carrying on an extramarital affair with Fran Kubelik (Shirley MacLaine), the cheerful but vulnerable elevator operator in the building where Lemmon works. How is Baxter going to live with that compromise when Fran is driven to the brink of suicide and he has to look after her—because she tried to kill herself in his apartment? Or pose a larger question: Is Lemmon a heroic actor or a fumbling wretch?

Shirley MacLaine has said that the script was only a sketch when they began, and that Wilder and Diamond let the two leads improvise a good deal to flesh out scenes. On the other hand, this was a fairly sumptuous production. Alexander Trauner was hired to do the sets for the office and the apartment, and despite black-and-white photography, it was filmed in Panavision. The picture cost $2.8 million (the same as *Some Like It Hot*), and the photography by Joseph LaShelle looks rich. There was also a good score from Adolph Deutsch.

The picture did very well, with first-run earnings of $8 million, along with a spectacular cleanup at the Oscars, including best picture, director, story and screenplay, editing, and art direction. Lemmon, MacLaine, and Jack Kruschen were nominated, but nothing. In hindsight, I have the impression that *The Apartment* feels very sour, with an unconvincing happy ending tacked on. Its world (like that of *Psycho*) is unrelievedly bleak—Sheldrake, for instance, is a very cold-blooded fellow, which would shock a new age used to MacMurray's benevolence on TV in *My Three Sons.*

Wilder seemed to have hit a peak. He was only fifty-four, but he would never win another Oscar. Of course, the awards aren't everything, but I fear that Wilder never quite regained his instinct for what would work, or what he could get away with. There are brave and interesting films to come, but they seem more and more detached from their times. And less and less amiable.

The Apartment has other good performances, from Ray Walston, Edie Adams, and David White.

Apocalypse Now (1979)

In its day, *Apocalypse Now* was perceived as a warning to American foreign policy and ambitious moviemakers alike: Don't go up the river, for there is no decent way of coming back. You know the setup, and you know vaguely that it comes from Conrad's *Heart of Darkness:* how Captain Willard (Martin Sheen—after Harvey Keitel dropped out, no questions, please) must proceed up a Vietnamese river to locate the rogue officer, Colonel Kurtz (Marlon Brando), and eliminate him with prejudice. Kurtz was perhaps the most brilliant officer of his generation, and Francis Ford Coppola was the great American director of the 1970s.

It seems like an unambiguous mission. But no one knows exactly where Kurtz is. And in the Philippines, where they filmed, the production had disastrous weather, enough to destroy sets and stretch every dream to the point of nightmare. Francis himself suffered all of this, along with the extra dismay of breakdown in his private life. In 1979, his wife, Eleanor, wrote a book about this, *Notes,* one of the best and saddest books on the making of a film. And then, when Brando arrived for what was anticipated as a short shoot, he was underprepared and overweight. The delays went to the depths of the director's soul. There are people who know Coppola who believe he was never quite the same again.

The picture was attacked, long before it opened, as a model of Hollywood excess and vanity. When it did open, there was amazing spectacle, but it was not always clear what the film believed it was about. The jungle was savage and beautiful (Vittorio Storaro). The music (from the Doors to the Stones by way of Wagner) was hallucinatory. Some said the film "got" the Vietnamese experience perfectly, but at the end, is Kurtz mad or sane? Sometimes in a movie, if the action stops in a crisis, you can't tell dementia from wisdom. Would it have been easier to have had Robert Duvall (superb and feisty as Kilgore) as Kurtz?

It was a film that just needed to be over, and it was a story that had different endings even in 1979. Then, decades later, Coppola determined to reedit the picture, and so he made *Apocalypse Now Redux,* which retained the French plantation scene, established Dean Tavoularis's work as designer, and let us see Aurore Clément in the love scene. I think the addition (and there are others) helps the picture, though it is finally a movie in which you must choose your own meaning. There are fine performances in small parts: G. D. Spradlin, Harrison Ford, Larry Fishburne, Sam Bottoms, Frederic Forrest. It is a film made in such a way that druggy witness may be the best way to see it. And still, I'm not sure that the versions of the film are as frightening or as human as *Notes.* The script had begun with John Milius, and the final narration was much influenced by Michael Herr. But there are people from the movie who felt that the whole thing grew in its own darkness, like some dire jungle infection for which there was no cure.

Applause (1929)

Rouben Mamoulian sounds like a made-up name now, but if it was invented (or improved), then pay heed to its rhythm and its flow. Mamoulian is out of fashion now, his reputation dwarfed by people remarkable for their coarseness. But he was a master at a crucial moment. As his name itself suggests, there could be movement in sound. More than that, with the grace of sound, movie drama was coming into a new life that would alter everything. The visual was no longer a dictatorship and no longer as insecure and bullying as most dictatorships.

Mamoulian was born in Tiflis in 1897, Russian, but Armenian. Raised in Paris and Moscow, he studied at the Moscow Art Theatre with Yevgeny Vakhtangov and then went by way of London to America. He directed theater in Rochester, New York, and in 1927 he made a striking New York debut when he mounted the folk play *Porgy* (a few years later he would direct the opera *Porgy and Bess*). He was not shy about presenting himself as fastidious, brilliant, and a genius, and it was not long before that reputation got him hired by Paramount. And so he came to do his first film, *Applause,* working at the Astoria Studios in Queens, New York.

Applause came from a hackneyed novel by Beth Brown, scripted by Garrett Fort, about an aging vaudeville singer, Kitty Darling (played by the torch singer Helen Morgan), who has a daughter, April Darling (Joan Peers), she tries to keep from following in her mother's footsteps. It is trite material, and that may have inspired Mamoulian to be bold. When he arrived at Astoria, it was to find no less than three producers hovering over his project—Monta Bell, Jesse Lasky, and Walter Wanger—to say nothing of a studio dominated by the sound recordist (Ernest Zatorsky) and his estimate of what could or could not be done.

Mamoulian knew his film history well enough to realize that the camera movements of the late 1920s had been stopped dead in their tracks by microphone jitters. He had a setup where he wanted the tracking camera to start on a long shot, come into a close-up, and then go back to the long shot. It was meant to catch the interplay of mother and daughter, the mother singing and the daughter saying her rosary. (At the same time—just like life! In silent film there is a dreadful habit of things happening one at a time.) The crew went crazy. Nothing could be done. Cinematographer George Folsey said the camera could not track; the mike could not record two distant strands of sound. Nonsense, said Mamoulian—he was gambling. Put the camera in a box, and have men push it. Use two mikes, one for the daughter and one for the mother. Hilarity! What do you do with two sound tracks? asked the experts. You marry them, said Mamoulian, guessing: you mix them.

And of course he was right: Sound was a new fluidity that might bridge cuts or opticals, a constant that allowed the pace of film to quicken to the speed of thought. This was crucial, and I do not mean to say that *Applause* is a great film or that Mamoulian was the only man alert to such breakthroughs. *Applause* is very antiquated and weepy, even if Helen Morgan is something to see. With confidence, Mamoulian took the unit out into the city streets, into real places. He realized that sound could be recorded or controlled, that sound was poetry as well as a synapse. The appalling rigidity of silent film and the moral and literary freeze that went with it were over.

The Army of Shadows (1969)

Context changes so much. When *L'Armée des Ombres* appeared in Paris (in September 1969), sympathy for or interest in the Resistance was waning. *Cahiers* condemned it as "Gaullist art." The age of Pompidou was beginning. Marcel Ophuls was busy making *The Sorrow and the Pity*, a profound survey of collaboration more than resistance. Jean-Pierre Melville's film seemed old-fashioned. Admissions dropped nearly half a million from his previous work, and that almost certainly prevented the film from getting an American release. A lot of time had to pass. It was not until 2006 that the film played properly in America—and, in a country that was for the first time wondering about its own tyranny, did very well. Manohla Dargis of the *New York Times* wrote that it might be the best film of the year.

Of course, Melville had himself served in the Resistance, and he took as his basis for the film a celebrated novel by Joseph Kessel (published in 1943). It is the story of a group of men who are working for the Resistance, and it's only proper to observe that their hostility to the police (the Gestapo, the Vichy forces) makes them resemble the several circles of criminals Melville had filmed earlier. But these men are stronger, far less given to betrayal, and they do what they do for altruistic reasons, which they hardly expect to live to see fulfilled. Indeed, Melville's film is rather darker and more pessimistic than even Kessel's novel.

It was filmed in Paris, in the South of France, and in London, and Melville staged a small coup in that he had a fine shot of German soldiers marching on the Champs-Élysées—technically still against the law. It's a world in which strangers, or shadows, come together under code names, in which brothers may not know that they follow the same bleak service, and in which sometimes you murder your own people to prevent the risk of their talking. The threat, of torture and helpless betrayal, hangs over the whole enterprise, and part of the film's grip, I find, comes from the certain understanding that even the Paris one loves and admires was once chilled by this terror. The excursion to London—where Adrien Cayla-Legrand appears as De Gaulle himself—is odd and not very English. But I can believe that it is the way these haunted Frenchmen saw London.

France in the war is a great subject, and one that the French have been reluctant so far to film. The wounds are deep, and the urge to forget is very strong. But here, in Bertrand Tavernier's *Safe Conduct*, and of course in *Hiroshima Mon Amour*, the story emerges. On the demerit side, there is the quite dreadful *Is Paris Burning?*, a film that one would like to forget belongs to René Clément, who once made the somber *La Bataille du Rail*. The great cast of *Army of Shadows* includes Lino Ventura, Paul Meurisse, Jean-Pierre Cassel, Claude Mann, Simone Signoret, Paul Crauchet, Christian Barbier, and Serge Reggiani.

L'Arrosseur Arrossé (1895)

We take it for granted now that the Lumière brothers were dutiful sons and fond brothers—after all, their name means "light," so why should they not serve as windows to that transmission, patient, impartial, and lucid? Except that they were brothers, too, and don't we know that it is a short step from, "Well, wouldn't it be nice if he had another little fellow to play with?" to *The Master of Ballantrae* or Michael giving Fredo the farewell kiss? So *L'Arrosseur Arrossé* begins to make you wonder about Auguste and Louis, and it cannot help but guide us to the edge of an opening sentence in some great revenge epic.

Of course, the Lumière brothers do seem to have been a bit sly. When Georges Méliès approached them with a view to purchasing their invention, *le cinematographe,* they are supposed to have gone all wide-eyed and told him that it had no future. Well, if they could not yet see Méliès's wild dreams, they surely saw a business of their own. In the next few years, they compiled a catalogue of over a thousand items, almost all of them matters of fact and visual observation, but from all over the world. Yet they went further: some of these famous events were staged or improved. And others were created—like a short version of Faust and the Joan of Arc story. It was not until 1900 that Louis Lumière (the stronger figure of the two) abandoned the shooting of fragments and concentrated on equipment.

That does not take away from the pioneering occasion of December 28, 1895, when the brothers took over the Grand Café on the Boulevard des Capucines in Paris and showed their bits of film to an audience—over thirty people, it seems. On the whole, they had simply shot available things: workers leaving their father's factory; a baby being fed; a train drawing into the station at La Ciotat. The fragments are calm, removed, but trembling with authenticity—you feel the light and the sudden trick that is being played with time where a shot or a "snap" may become emblematic. And so, all at once, humble duration is a sea of metaphors.

But they went even further. They filmed in one unbroken shot a little ruse or escapade. A man is watering his lawn with a hose. Behind him, a joker, a trickster, the spirit of Peter Lorre, steps on the hose. The flow of water is blocked. The puzzled idiot looks at the nozzle. The foot is removed. Face full of water! You can say it's just innocent fun in the noon light of some meadow near Lyons. But don't you at least consider the follow-up: an international, *touristique* film in which the joker is pursued round the world by the soaked citizen? (Think of *The Duellists.*) After all, we have laughed at the joke just as we may have flinched at the splash of indignity. But we are part of it all. And somewhere way down the line—it may take over fifty years—a man with an empty nozzle (think of Javier Bardem in *No Country for Old Men*) is going to stumble toward us, pained, wronged, and driven by the pain to murder but asking us what it is we want of him. Story is as long and twisty as hose. It goes on forever.

Ascenseur pour L'Échafaud (1958)

A couple of years before the New Wave, Louis Malle's *Lift to the Scaffold* (its English-speaking title) is perhaps more readily understood as in the Melville school of the mid-1950s: as a very neat, tricky thriller, poker-faced and with a sting in the tail. On the other hand, its luminous night shooting on the streets of Paris is by Henri Decae, and its assurance that if, on those streets, you have the harrowed, haunted face of Jeanne Moreau when she was twenty-nine, looking for someone, then what more do you need? I stress the actress's age because I have known people who have met her in later life and come tottering away, gasping about what she must have been like in her twenties. Well, this is what she was like—she made you want to make a movie. What would its subject be? Just photograph that face and wait for things to happen. You don't need anyone to tell you that Louis Malle must have been in love with her.

Moreau and Maurice Ronet plan to murder her husband, and they nearly pull off a perfect crime but for a stalled elevator. Ronet was handsome and tough in those days, and the chemistry is so deep and quick it doesn't need to be dwelled on. After that, it's a film about frustration and missed timing, and about the way small vagaries of life can spoil the outline map made by intelligence. This theme is not deeply felt, not nearly as deeply as the mounting pain in Moreau's face. But there are many moments in great film where the greatness comes from the God-given and the film's simple acceptance that that is what we want to see. A woman on the real streets of a city after dark was a rare sight in movies in 1957. After all, so many of those streets had been sets, like the one where Joan Bennett appears in *The Woman in the Window*. But being able to use the real Paris brings you the sinking cold, the damp, the wind, and the fact of strangers giving you their insolent scrutiny. So the face toughens just that little bit, and at twenty-nine Moreau had a face where the toughness and the pathos (not to say the eroticism) were in perfect balance. So that sequence could go on a lot longer. And in a way it's as much thanks to the development of Tri-X stock as it is to the vision of Decae.

There's someone else looking, and when I remind you that it's Miles Davis, you may conclude that that rather bloody-minded genius did not look for anyone. But he went into a studio with his trumpet, and he improvised over the scenes of Moreau on the street. The combination is exquisite, and it suggests a method that has been used too seldom. More than that, you want Mademoiselle Moreau to come around a corner and bump into the growling voice and the Satanic readiness of Miles himself. What do I play? Davis might have said. Just look at me, she tells him.

Ashes and Diamonds (1958)

His name is Maciek, and there is a nearly American narcissism in the way he observes himself and plays scenes. He wears dark glasses in the daytime and says they are a souvenir from the sewers. This places him as one of the Polish partisans who fought for the Warsaw uprising in 1944, the events depicted in *Kanal* (1957), the previous film by Andrzej Wajda. It was never quite clear how determined he was about the sequence, but there were three films—*A Generation, Kanal,* and *Ashes and Diamonds*—about coming of age in Poland during the war. It seems to me that *A Generation* is the purest, *Kanal* the most intense, and *Ashes and Diamonds* the most interesting.

If you need it, here is the reminder: The Allies went to war in Europe to save Poland from Nazi takeover. Yet here we are in May 1945, the last day of the war, and Poland has not been rescued. It is a matter of judgment or taste whether it has survived. But Maciek and his colleague are in a small town in Poland, under orders from the Polish émigré government in London, to assassinate the local official who is ready to make peace with the Russians. The Nazis are gone from Poland, along with the Jews, but Poland is in the Soviet sphere of influence. Another tyranny is coming into place. And Maciek—so young, so vivid he is nearly girlish—is the last assassin, well aware that his task is futile, but acting out the part like someone in Dostoyevsky and ready to convert himself into one more glass of vodka. There is a spectacular scene where he lines up those glasses—the lost heroes of the resistance—and sets light to them one by one. And in his attitude, he is tragic but ironic. He has to die, for he is nearly mad.

The film covers twelve hours or so in the small town, much of it in the ramshackle hotel where the target of the assassination lives. Maciek meets a girl there, a barmaid (Ewa Krzyzewska), and they become lovers of a doomed sort. But the photography is tender and lustrous, and you can see how far Wajda has come in his trilogy, even if the characters in *Ashes and Diamonds* are the most gripped by doubt and anxiety. The action has set pieces—Maciek dying among sheets hanging on a line and then on a trash heap—and there are glaring symbols from time to time (an upside-down crucifixion, the white horse of Poland). But the trilogy is a powerful work, and *Ashes and Diamonds* is the romantic treatment of Poland's final failure.

The film owes a lot to its Maciek, Zbigniew Cybulski, an actor who could hardly deny the impact of James Dean and Marlon Brando on him. Alas, Cybulski was killed in 1967, in a rail accident. He was only forty, and he had been born in the Ukraine. But he resolves that this film will be existentialist, ironic, and rueful, and he survives his own mannerisms as easily as Dean ever did.

The Asphalt Jungle (1950)

In the late 1940s, there were several American neo-realist crime pictures, shot on the city streets and determined to reveal the tough, unglamorous life of a cop—*The Naked City* was one of the best known. *The Asphalt Jungle* sounds like the same kind of thing, a lament for used-up shoe leather and lost illusions. But it's John Huston, and it's a bit different. The W. R. Burnett novel (1949) that he sold to M-G-M was a conventional piece, narrated by a police officer, very much along the lines that a postwar city was a jungle for hoodlum apes.

Huston wasn't the only director who might have turned the emphasis around, but he sees the criminals as colorful monkeys, full of character and charm, trying to make their own sort of living in difficult times. Indeed, Huston—who kept company with diverse and fascinating circles—opined once that crime was just "a left-handed kind of activity," nothing you could really condemn, but a vagary in human nature and understandable if you realize what a raw deal the would-be criminals have had.

It was shot beautifully in Los Angeles by Harold Rosson, with a harsh-looking image (you feel the asphalt from the first sequence, where boorish cops are trying to hustle enigmatic criminals). There's no doubt where the sympathy lies as the film assembles its gang for "the job." There's Dix Handley (Sterling Hayden), a "hooligan" but not bright, a guy who longs to live among horses. There's Gus (James Whitmore), the laconic barman, who can be expected to stash guns and drive the car. Throw in an expert safecracker, Calveri (Anthony Caruso), and Alonzo "Lon" Emmerich (Louis Calhern), the crooked lawyer who has a sick wife and "some sweet kid," Angela (Marilyn Monroe), on the side. There's Cobby (Marc Lawrence), a pro and a turncoat. And there's the Dutchman, Doc Erwin Riedenschneider (Sam Jaffe), a brilliant manager of jobs who can't keep his imagination off girls.

And, more or less, we like them. Dix is the hero, with a girl named Doll (Jean Hagen). Lon is made very sympathetic by Calhern, and his scenes with Marilyn are lovely, wistful and horny. But Doc is the gem, the little artist, doctor of something or other but expert in perverse human nature; it's his luck that, when his escape is nearly made, he will be picked up because he lingered just a few seconds too long to watch a pretty girl (Helene Stanley) dancing to a jukebox.

The film was scripted by Huston and Ben Maddow, and everything ends up all right. The cops "win." A suicide kills himself offscreen in just the poetic touch that would have appealed to the character. Dix gets his by a horse meadow. And Huston's self-mocking toughness has carried off the switch to perfection. By the way, he got this job only after he managed to beg off doing the monstrous *Quo Vadis*. Working on a sweet picture or one that stank could be just luck. And that's how Huston sees the jungle operating. John McIntire is the police commissioner with a routine sermon on the wicked enemy, but he knows those are the guys Huston prefers.

I have to gulp at the thought of just five hundred words for *L'Atalante,* instead of a book. This is not so much a masterpiece as a definition of cinema—and thus a film that stands resolutely apart from the great body of films, even most of those in this book. *L'Atalante* is the end of director Jean Vigo's life, yet it is the dawn of so many possibilities in cinema and a manifesto for a kind of personal cinema that may destroy the filmmaker in the process while leaving his name like a memorial. It is the French New Wave, yet it is *l'amour fou* as well, surrealism and magic all done in a camera style that hauntingly evokes and then surpasses a thing called gray reality.

That may be the best place to start in a short tribute, for the camera was in the hands (chiefly) of Boris Kaufman, a man whose career reached from *The Man with a Movie Camera* (made in 1927 by Boris's brother, Denis, known as Dziga Vertov) to *12 Angry Men* and other pieces of New York naturalism. Now, how could anyone see or feel ghosts or spirits in Sidney Lumet's jury room, yet how, as this old barge passes slowly by, do we not see all the spirit forms of romance in *L'Atalante*?

Is the difference just France in the 1930s and America in the 1950s? I think not. Vigo is a poet, and it would not have been possible for anyone on his film to miss the way in which every image was both a sufficiency and a metaphor. In America, it has always felt natural and comfortable to assume that if you photograph something, then you come away with the exact appearance of that thing; all the more credit, then, to everyone from Diane Arbus to Samuel Fuller, who guessed that the truth was more open. But in France, the inwardness of the image is not questioned, and that is the fundamental thing that makes it easy (or necessary) to treat French film as an attempt upon art, as opposed to entertainment.

The story is as simple as it can be. Two men work a barge, Jean (Jean Daste) and *le père* Jules (Michel Simon). They are like Ishmael and Queequeg, except that Jules has something of Ahab, Long John Silver, and Jonah's whale in him. Jean finds a woman to marry (Dita Parlo), and after a brief, stark ceremony, the wedding procession walks back to the boat and the barge moves on again, plus one. The love falters. The woman goes away. The man searches for her. And all the while Père Jules is a monster of eternity, bestiality, and death, all those things the lovers fear and ignore.

Desire makes the story work, and the film is waterlogged with longing, from the couple's need for "happiness" to Jules's urge for outrage. This kind of rural life seems unshakeable, yet the film is filled with vulnerability and the immanence of loss as it shifts our gaze from Miranda to Caliban and sees that they may be siblings or in allegiance. The essential music is by Maurice Jaubert.

Atlantic City (1980)

Sally (Susan Sarandon) works at one of the casinos in Atlantic City. She is a waitress at the shellfish counter, but a part of her day is devoted to lessons on how to speak French and how to be a deft croupier. Her teacher is Joseph (Michel Piccoli), a worldly Frenchman. He promises her a future in Monte Carlo. But at the end of the day, Sally smells of fish, so she comes home and washes her arms, her neck, and her breasts in lemon juice. In the dark, across the way, Lou (Burt Lancaster) watches this show. He is handsome but elderly, a minor player in the numbers racket who tries to dress like an old-fashioned gangster. Then Sally's sister, Chrissie (Hollis McLaren), arrives in town, very pregnant, with her husband, Dave (Robert Joy), and a load of stolen cocaine. Soon enough the real gangsters will come looking for their stuff. Lou nurses Grace (Kate Reid), his lover from way back, who came to town, took third place in a Betty Grable look-alike contest, and stayed around.

The dreams are fanciful, the past is another country, and it's winter in Atlantic City, which hasn't quite made it yet as a major American resort. But these lives get tangled, and for a very short season Lou is able to behave as a gangster might have done once before, and Sally becomes his doll. It's a light, whimsical film, fond of its dreamers, and just a touch generous to them all. It's an interesting question as to whether director Louis Malle would have been quite as forgiving if he had had French characters. Does he see America as morally looser, or more adventurous? At any event, the characters we'd happily see gone are disposed of, and those who have earned a night or two of wayward bliss are given it.

In truth, it's a French-Canadian film, despite the setting. Denis Héroux produced it out of Montreal, with Malle's brother, Vincent, from Paris. The special flavor comes from John Guare's screenplay, full of ingenuity without ever abandoning realism. It was shot by Richard Ciupka, with clever design work by Anne Pritchard and costumes—Lou's tendency to white and gray is splendid—by François Barbeau. Michel Legrand was in charge of the music, though there are extracts from Bellini and Paul Anka.

It would make a fine double bill with *The King of Marvin Gardens*, and Bob Rafelson would have every right to claim an extra toughness. Yet *Atlantic City* got five big Oscar nominations: Best Picture and Best Screenplay, as well as nods for Malle, Lancaster, and Sarandon.

The supporting cast includes Al Waxman, Robert Goulet, Moses Znaimer, Angus MacInnes, and Wallace Shawn. It's a sweet picture, and not a bad example of the calculator in Louis Malle. He was a bit like Lou, acting tough and experienced but prepared to settle for a lucky bonus here and there. This is five nominations better, and several degrees more facile, than *The King of Marvin Gardens*.

Attack! (1956)

In the mid-1950s, Robert Aldrich made a run of films that easily explains why so many smart French filmgoers thought he was the crack shot among younger American directors. I'm thinking basically of *Apache, Kiss Me Deadly, The Big Knife*, and *Attack!* In subject matter, they cover the waterfront, though thematically one can see emerging a kind of demented heroism, a warping ordeal in which the braver or more forthright the hero becomes, the more doomed he is. That said, it's possible to see *Attack!*—the least known of the four now—as the most characteristic.

It comes from a play, *Fragile Fox*, by Norman Brooks, and despite the opening-up in some harsh combat scenes, no one could miss the staginess of the format. During the Battle of the Bulge, a few American soldiers huddle in shelled buildings or dugouts in a mountingly hysterical analysis of courage. Aldrich once said, "Basically it's an antiwar film. You start from the cliché 'War is hell' and you try and refine that into a personal statement of the unnecessary heroics that induce people to get into a war-psychology. And reverse the war-psychology into saying that it's a pretty ugly business. The Defense Department refused cooperation and it looked for a while as though it wasn't going to be made. But we devised methods to make it look reasonably acceptable and realistic and went ahead."

You can see the Defense Department's point of view; for as scripted by James Poe, this is a film about the fear of fear, and the way command power can manipulate military operations to benefit public relations. Thus, though Eddie Albert plays a devious and cowardly officer (and does so superbly), the real villain of the piece is Lee Marvin's cocksure colonel, one of his very best bastards, and the kind of self-promoting officer we have become more familiar with in military operations since *Attack!* In passing, I should note the obvious influence of this colonel and the film's overall mood on Stanley Kubrick and *Paths of Glory*.

But *Attack!* truly is a Jack Palance film, and one of his best. His character dies some ten minutes or so before the end of the picture, but there are several glimpses of his face thereafter, caught in the horrific moment of death, deepened by rigor mortis and by Palance's none-too-subtle Christ-like stance. These shots make it clear that he was an actor with a death mask rather than a face. That is not a flippant comment. *Attack!* sends his character to the cross, and Aldrich trusts the actor to deliver the inner dread and exultation in the crisis.

It's an Associates and Aldrich film, which means Joseph Biroc did the photography and Frank de Vol the music. Together, they made something claustrophobic and special, a true portrait of the madness in war. The supporting cast includes Robert Strauss, Richard Jaeckel, Buddy Ebsen, Strother Martin, Steven Geray, and Peter van Eyck. In hindsight, it's stunning that *Attack!, Men in War*, and *Paths of Glory* were overlooked while *The Bridge on the River Kwai* was hailed as an important statement on war.

Au Hasard Balthazar (1966)

Over the credits, a Schubert piano sonata pauses for the braying call of an unseen donkey—had Robert Bresson turned to comedy at last? Or to what a donkey helplessly stands for? After all, Bresson can cast his pictures and carry out their direction by being abstemious over personal expressions and those habitual yieldings toward sentimentality that others are prone to (call them smiles or frowns). But a donkey! Can anyone film a donkey without summoning up that unquenchable (if absurd) affection for any placid animal beset by man, kind or unkind? When the horrid teenage boy in the leather jacket ties newspaper to Balthazar's untidy tail and sets fire to it, how are we to prevent or restrain our hatred of him, let alone our moral disapproval?

Somewhere in the French countryside, a donkey is born. It is not clear at first whether he is central to the film or a mirror to all the human characters he meets. But I think he is intended as a saintly example, ignored by some and likely to vex and anger others. He grows up, cared for by a young girl (Anne Wiazemsky, frozen-faced but still closer to an actress than Bresson had been before). He works for the baker, carrying panniers of loaves around the area—that is the time of the tail-burning. He is beaten by cruel people. He does tricks in the circus. He falls sick and is nearly "put down." He attracts a strange, Christ-like vagrant. But, like any animal, he is at the mercy of fate or providence. And as we watch him more closely, so he becomes like a pilgrim, making his way toward death, on a hillside surrounded by sheep.

No, Disney did not seek the remake rights, though that idea is probably less absurd than Cary Grant's redoing *Bicycle Thieves*. The ending of *Au Hasard Balthazar* is, I find, moving in ways that exceed Bresson, just because this saint is a donkey. We do not know how to look at such creatures without abandoning scrutiny or objectivity. It's not that Bresson's austere style—with quick dissolves here, going from one time to another without connecting the two—ever comes close to a kind of *Black Beauty* for donkeys. But one look at those large, sad eyes—why do I call them sad?—and we are suckers. Donkeys may be as withdrawn as Bartleby, but they can't help their affinity with get-well cards.

The photography is by Ghislain Cloquet; it was his first Bresson film, though he would do *Mouchette* and (I have to admit it) Jacques Demy's *Donkey Skin*. The music is by Jean Wiener, when it is not Schubert. And the supporting cast includes Walter Green, Jean-Claude Guilbert, and François Lafarge. The film is also notable for the attention Bresson pays to teenagers. He was to become increasingly drawn to and troubled by the anger or confused feelings of young people, no matter that his purity of style still manages to suggest a cinema made in the eighteenth century.

Autumn Sonata (1978)

At the time, much was made of the meeting—at last—of Ingmar and Ingrid Bergman. But Ingrid might have anticipated a chilly atmosphere. She was ill already. This would prove her penultimate film—she died in 1982—and it is a very testing challenge on some aspects of being Ingrid Bergman that had slipped by in all the celebration and scandal. So Ingrid might have guessed what Ingmar would have waiting—and no one was more preoccupied with issues of parental responsibility than Ingmar.

So Ingrid plays Charlotte, a world-famous concert pianist. Her longtime lover and musical associate, Leonardo, has just died. One day, she gets a letter from her daughter Eva (Liv Ullmann), who lives in the Norwegian countryside with her husband, Viktor (Halvar Björk), and her spastic sister, Helena (Lena Nyman). So Charlotte comes on a visit and is startled to find Helena, for, as the mother, she had years ago put Helena in an institution. Eva has quietly elected to look after her.

That is the beginning of Charlotte's stay, a time in which the mother listens to the daughter play Chopin and feels bound to correct her playing; and in which, in a long middle-of-the-night encounter, all the old unresolved issues are made clear. What it all comes down to is that Charlotte has put her career and her art above her own children, and that Eva, at least, has suffered in resentment and loss because of it. In all his talk, it is quite clear that the film—if obliquely—is relying on our knowledge of Ingrid's life. The Leonardo figure (though he appears in flashback, played by an actor) is plainly an allusion to Roberto Rossellini.

It is a film of faces and interiors, done in color and shot beautifully by Sven Nykvist, and as such it is a model for the very late period of Bergman's ventures, like *Faithless* and *Saraband*. It is very powerful because of that deep concentration on words from the heart and because of its lack of interest in any other diversionary subject. Still, it is not as good as the later films, in part because it does seem set up and reliant on Ingrid's willingness to go through this ordeal. She is wonderful in the film, and one cannot doubt that after all the adventures of her career she remained a great Swedish actress, utterly at home with Ingmar's grilling. But it says something else about Ingrid's masochistic narcissism that she will sit still for this. In a way, the film needs the voice of Leonardo—or some figure more lively and generous than Liv Ullmann's Eva.

Still, Ingrid was nominated for an Oscar—her sixth nomination—and it may be that she found great comfort finally in returning to Scandinavia. As for Ingmar, it was easy at the time to think that this might be his farewell, too, for it gave no sign of the warmth that was still to come flooding into his vision. So Charlotte's guilt is not really questioned, even though Ingmar's own life had been a steady symphony dedicated to unremitting work and art.

L'Avventura (1960)

An excursion is promised—it will be an adventure. Anna (Lea Massari) has invited Claudia (Monica Vitti) for the day. Claudia sees that Anna is uneasy. Perhaps her love affair with Sandro (Gabriele Ferzetti) is in trouble. Perhaps it is just a passing phase. But Anna is moody, impulsive. With a party of friends, they take a boat and go sailing to an island near Sicily. (The film was actually shot on Lipari and in Milazzo, on Sicily's north coast.) It is summer, but it is a gray day, overcast, beautifully photographed by Aldo Scavarda. The island has steep, rocky cliffs. The sea beats against the rocks. People realize that Anna has disappeared—or is it that she is simply no longer there? Presence is a curious thing in the cinema. Just because we are seeing Ilse and Victor talking in the Café Americain does not mean that Rick has ceased to exist. Or does it?

The others search for Anna. They wonder if she has had an accident. They cannot conceive how she could have departed from the island. But she was uneasy. There was something about her that signaled a readiness for her own adventure, or departure. Was it simply a mood, or something more substantial? The question hangs over the search, which director Michelangelo Antonioni conducts with every respect for place and space. Sandro is a disappointed architect; he sees things in terms of physical reality. And Antonioni has one of the great camera styles, built on respect for moving in space. Yet somehow Anna has defied that idealistic continuity, the context. She has vanished.

Famously, *L'Avventura* was booed at Cannes. Some people said it was the cerebral, pretentious version of the boredom or the spiritual dismay being addressed so much more journalistically in the contemporary *La Dolce Vita*. But *L'Avventura* was far more important in terms of the medium moving forward, and far more undermining in its suggestion that, well, if a character who was there has gone away, you have to get on with life or the film. You can search for her. You can search all your life, if you wish, and searching is an impulse in film's form, because the looking goes on. Or you can forget, try to forget, and then wake up one day, bored, and never notice that forgetting has occurred. So Claudia will slip into the empty place the film has created. She will become Sandro's girl, and in that way she will come to understand the uneasiness that Anna was feeling.

So *L'Avventura* is a very simple story, an idea from Antonioni himself, scripted by the director, Elio Bartolini, and Tonino Guerra. It turned out to be the first film in a great trilogy—*L'Avventura, La Notte, L'Eclisse*—a landmark in film history, stories of love and lack of presence that keep nagging away at happiness. You can see the films separately, but they are three versions of one concern and one moment in upper-class Italian society. And they are three attempts by Antonioni to believe in the radiance of Monica Vitti. Also with Dominique Blanchar, Renzo Ricci, James Addams, Dorothy De Poliolo. *La Dolce Vita* now is like an old shoe, ruined, found on a beach. *L'Avventura* is a fresh footprint, still warm.

The Awful Truth (1937)

In just a few years at the movies, Cary Grant and Irene Dunne go from *The Awful Truth* to 1941's *Penny Serenade*. Now, *Penny Serenade* is in this book, and I think you ought to see it—if only to gain a better appreciation of *The Awful Truth*. It's not that *Penny Serenade* is awful, but it's the one where Grant and Dunne have a baby who dies and so they adopt—and then, Lord help us, they are in danger of losing that child, too, because they're short of money and Grant's on the irresponsible side.

There are tears in *Penny Serenade*, and I regret every one of them. The funny thing is that in *The Awful Truth* Grant and Dunne play a married couple (Jerry and Lucy Warriner) who don't have any children. They have a dog instead, Mr. Smith, a wire-haired terrier, and when they divorce, custody of that dog is a serious issue. But they don't cry over it, and I have to say that if I were a child, I'd far rather go with the Warriners than into *Penny Serenade*. The why of it is quite simply in the Warriners being grown-up about things. Our best comedies are about grown-ups and the way talk may keep them growing.

The Awful Truth is Columbia in 1937, a script by Viña Delmar (an interesting writer, also on *Make Way for Tomorrow*), directed by Leo McCarey. The Warriners live stylishly and on the expensive side. And there are indications that they carry on a little on that side: He has been somewhere for two weeks, and she was out all last night. Not that when they divorce, anyone else suddenly emerges, demanding to be loved. They are in love already—a fool could see it. Still, Lucy does get talking with Dan Leeson (Ralph Bellamy), who is in Oklahoma oil—and gets the most terrible shakedown for just showing his nose and offering banal good cheer. He works for a living, and the Warriners have never stooped to that.

But Dan Leeson is the kind of stooge that can be quite useful in comedies of remarriage—for that is where we are going. Jerry and Lucy want the fun back in their life together, and their life together does go on, despite the judge's separation order. They think about each other. They are better at talking than most people—throw in telling tall stories and getting away with them. They also have Mr. Smith. They have divorce, too, which in their hands resembles a tricky new dance, or a way of falling over each other in public.

Yes, films like *The Awful Truth* present a blithe portrait of wealth and of divorce. But like most of our vital comedies—and this is one of them—it is rooted in the mystery of marriage and the desirability of two people's being together. So she is slightly smarter than he is—but he was smart enough to choose that. Grant and Dunne do it here without a trace of neurosis or yearning. It's a professional relationship, like dancing, and it turns out brilliantly, a film in which people chat for 92 minutes and every conceivable matter has been dealt with. And that is one of the heights of optimism in American life and film.

Baby Doll (1956)

Had informing loosened Elia Kazan's screws? Had he lost his mind? "*Baby Doll* was a lark from beginning to end"! Had humor slipped into this most earnest body of work? For some reason (could it have been an urge to get better acquainted with Carroll Baker?), Kazan began writing this script himself from a couple of Tennessee Williams short stories. It had a glowing central image: Baby Doll Meighan (Ms. Baker) in a grubby white slip in her crib, maybe sucking her thumb—nineteen and as yet unrelieved of her virginity, despite marriage to Archie Lee Meighan (Karl Malden), with a horn as large as the actor's nose. But Archie Lee had agreed to wait until his bride was ready. And in his frustration, he had burned down the cotton gin of Silva Vacarro (Eli Wallach)—an Eye-talian, an outsider and not one of us. Whereupon, Mr. Vacarro comes looking for revenge and ponders the most suitable way to take it.

Kazan tells how he coaxed a reluctant Williams to watch a rehearsal at the Actors Studio, and when the playwright saw Carroll Baker, he agreed to go to Mississippi with the unit to touch up the dialogue, if he could have a swimming pool. So everyone got something out of it, including Ms. Baker, who got a splashy start to her career. (Truth to tell, she was already twenty-five.)

So the film was shot in Benoit, Mississippi, with Boris Kaufman doing the photography and Richard and Paul Sylbert in charge of the tattered décor. This was a time when America was discovering the real South, thanks to movies, and it was usually impoverished, hot, sticky, and sex-obsessed. Or was that just the directors? Anna Hill Johnstone came up with the various child's night garments worn by Baby Doll. Kenyon Hopkins wrote the music. There was a speech consultant to make sure you couldn't quite understand everything the Southerners said.

And as far as can be determined, it is a comedy on sexual paranoia. "Many people said it seemed like a European movie," said Kazan—the final insult to the South. Karl Malden seems to have been given sweat pills. Eli Wallach plays it like a fine young cockerell. And Carroll Baker exhibits a kind of stunned vacancy that suggested she might have been up all night. As Kazan noted, it was Cardinal Spellman who came to the film's rescue—"a contemptuous defiance of the natural law," the great man announced. Who had thought it was that funny? Of course, the cardinal had not seen the film. "Must you have a disease to know what it is?" he demanded. Meanwhile, all over the world, the horizontal stills and posters of Carroll Baker in her crib became a model of lewdness.

It was the actress's great moment. She did *Giant* and a few other pictures. She was very sexy in *Station Six Sahara* for Seth Holt, and she actually played Jean Harlow in the sixties. But for a giddy moment she established that there were two things over which most of America lives in a cloud of ignorance: sex and the South.

Baby Face (1933)

Lily Powers (Barbara Stanwyck) is discovered living in Erie, Pennsylvania, and the first tough attitude in this punchy little movie is that that's no place for a human being to be. Which is not common. Hollywood usually flattered and idealized the outlying provinces in the great dream of small towns and countryside that are in fact alien to nearly everything Hollywood cares about. And in 1932–33, Erie must have been tough. Lily is prepared. Her father runs a bootleg-liquor operation, where she turns the occasional trick to give the customers something extra. She is hard-faced and soft-dressed, if you know what I mean, and while Stanwyck was always pretty, there is no denying the cynical edge on this film. She hates her father and sees no way out of her bitter life. But then the father is killed in an accident—his still blows up. And Lily moves on, ready to deserve her surname.

What follows is what has brought *Baby Face* back into circulation in those gleeful festivals that seek to celebrate "Pre-Code" toughness and candor in American pictures. Lily has an elderly gent who advises her with bromides about a woman's natural power. So she decides to sleep her way from entry level to penthouse in a skyscraper business organization. This is accomplished with speed and verve and a target-shooting amusement that reaches its peak when the young John Wayne proves to be one of her horizontal stooges—though he plays a very decent guy.

But at the top, Lily meets Courtland Trenholm (thrill to the name—played by George Brent). And he is on to her. He knows her game and transfers her to Paris. But then it turns out that this is so that he can romance her all the better. He marries her! The company goes bust. There is a brief moment in which she says, Tough luck, Courtland. But then something happens—it's that old Pre-Code cowardice. Lily suddenly snaps to. Decency surfaces. She sells her jewels. She hurries to Trenholm's side. Because—can you guess?—she loves him.

In other words, Baby Face becomes a Wise Woman, which is not as good a title. If we wonder what such a picture was trying to do, it's important to realize that the story came from no less than Darryl F. Zanuck, the head of production at Warners, and Gene Markey, who would produce some pretty sappy pictures while doing his best at being married to Joan Bennett, Hedy Lamarr, and Myrna Loy. Was the picture a gift to Stanwyck, or the throwaway joke of two Hollywood guys? And how did they look at themselves in the mirror with that excruciating happy ending?

Alfred E. Green directed, and it is only 76 minutes. If it looks hard-bitten today, I suspect it's because of how little we get the real robustness of the early thirties. It's not actually daring in things done or seen. The crucial stuff is offscreen—though you can't wipe away the merciless look on Stanwyck's face.

Baby Face Nelson (1957)

Director Don Siegel always claimed that *Baby Face Nelson* was a horrible film to make because he was allowed only $175,000 to do it; because Mickey Rooney was the most unpleasant person to work with he ever knew (there was good competition); and because Rooney was itching to take the picture over and finish it according to his splendid vision of a little man with a big gun. So this minor masterpiece escaped by the skin of its teeth, and—just like Brando on *The Godfather*—Rooney sold off his percentage on the picture before it went big.

What Siegel saw was that Rooney, at thirty-six, was a great star on an unstoppable downslide, a mixture of energy, remorse, and hatred for the world that was the perfect recipe for a psychotic gangster. And because of that lucid, not very fond, understanding in an onlooker, we have one whole picture that *gets* Mickey Rooney and that may be offered as an alternative to the nearly insane fragmentation of his life and work.

According to Siegel, there was a script ready to go—by Irving Shulman—so bad that the director said, Let it go. So he hired in an old friend, Daniel Mainwaring (who had just done *Invasion of the Body Snatchers* for him), and gave him two weeks to come up with something better. They then had seventeen days for Hal Mohr to shoot it, and on the last day, working against the clock, Siegel said, he did fifty-five setups.

The result is a uniquely American action film in which the central figure is hero and villain, where he is permitted to do anything he can think of, because we all know that he will be eliminated finally. What a hundred years of this has done to American ethics is another matter. But it has led to an outburst of national energy and frenzied desire that is as interesting and threatening as a Charlie Parker solo or a Jackson Pollock painting. With three minutes or a frame to fill, Parker and Pollock go crazy. Rooney does the same. He behaves as badly as he can think of—and he was a natural master at delinquency.

So this is a far more searching and challenging film than, say, the liberal humanism of *12 Angry Men* (made in the same year) and so painfully anxious to draw America closer to enlightenment. Of course, the irony is that Henry Fonda's thoughtful paragon, never sweating on that hot day, may be defending someone as gleefully guilty as Baby Face.

There is never a dull moment or a still frame, and Siegel offsets his helpless worship of Rooney with a number of fond glimpses of rare character—thus Carolyn Jones as the girlfriend and Sir Cedric Hardwicke relishing his own slumming as a crooked doctor. More than that, this is a noir B picture with a gallery of the great small-part actors: Ted de Corsia, Emile Meyer, Tony Caruso, Leo Gordon, Jack Elam, Dabbs Greer, John Hoyt, and Elisha Cook, Jr.

The Bad and the Beautiful (1952)

Producer John Houseman once said he never had a picture that went as smoothly as *The Bad and the Beautiful.* (He didn't realize then that David O. Selznick was considering suing the project for defamation in its treatment of the egomaniacal impresario, Jonathan Shields.) Houseman said the idea came from a treatment by George Bradshaw about a life in the theater obviously based on Jed Harris. Houseman thought, Suppose it was a Hollywood story; and he got production head Dore Schary interested, too. At which point Houseman asked Charles Schnee (he had done *Red River*) to write a script.

As the story begins, Shields (Kirk Douglas) is in disgrace. He has betrayed everyone he ever knew. But studio manager Harry Pebbel (Walter Pidgeon) tries to rally the old loyalists: a director, Fred Amiel (Barry Sullivan); a writer, James Lee Bartlow (Dick Powell); and a movie star, Georgia Lorrison (Lana Turner). This allows for a tricky flashback structure that recounts the ups and downs of the Shields studio. The "witnesses" still dislike him, but in the artful last scene, having all said "no" to a new picture with Jonathan, the three heads are clustered around one phone as he makes his pitch.

We know what will happen—whether it should or not. *The Bad and the Beautiful* is true to Hollywood in having its cake and eating it. For yes, it says, there's a lot that goes on here that is "bad," but don't forget that these people are "beautiful," or if that doesn't quite fit, then what they do is beautiful. Whereas *Sunset Blvd.* could see damage in film, the attitude of *The Bad and the Beautiful* is, if you've had a good time, forgive and forget. It's strange, for Houseman was both insider and outsider, a real professional but able to see things amiss in the system.

Vincente Minnelli directed everything with flourish and inside jokes, and there is a bravura sequence where Lana Turner nearly kills herself in a car crash. This is shot by Robert Surtees, who won an Oscar for his work.

The casting was easy once Metro had agreed to borrow Kirk Douglas—and this lovable rogue is pretty close to Kirk's self-image. In addition, Gloria Grahame was hired to play the writer's Southern wife—and she won a supporting actress Oscar for it. If anything, the supporting cast is more fun than the leads, with Gilbert Roland, Leo G. Carroll, Elaine Stewart, Paul Stewart, and Ivan Triesault, plus Louis Calhern as the voice of Georgia's father (a Barrymore-like figure).

The Bad and the Beautiful was a second-thoughts title. They were going to call it *Tribute to a Bad Man,* but the studio said that was a Western. And so they all begged the question of whether Shields is a bad man. Fifty years later it's not as easy. In the latest *King Kong,* for example, Jack Black says, "You can trust me—I'm a movie producer!" and the house comes down.

The film got six nominations and won five, including for Schnee's script, but nary a nod for David Raksin's lovely score, music that is now redolent with the swoons and wistfulness of old Hollywood.

Bad Day at Black Rock (1954)

When Dore Schary took over as head of production at Metro-Goldwyn-Mayer, he was determined to put a few tough, liberal projects into the bland program. And no one has ever questioned that *Bad Day at Black Rock* was his idea, though he did have a story called "Hondo" (by Don Maguire) as a basis. But when a few house producers proved unavailable, Schary elected to handle it himself. He got Millard Kaufman to do the screenplay (it was Oscar nominated), and he hired John Sturges to direct.

Bad Day is the story of a minor government official who gets off the train at a whistle stop—it's Arizona or Nevada. He has something to deliver: a medal won by a son dead in the war—a Nisei, or Japanese American, who fought for the American forces. But in this small, very isolated desert community, the man's father has suffered in the war as many Japanese did—he lost his property and his life. It's a simple, emphatic story that fits the terrific élan of the title and the stark approach of Sturges. And it comes in bright desert colors shot by William Mellor.

Spencer Tracy had more or less agreed to play the government man, but he felt the guy needed some problem in his life, some handicap or flaw. It was Schary's notion that the man had lost an arm in the war, and so *Bad Day* shaped up as Tracy, with one arm tied behind his back, up against a very menacing trio of Hollywood heavies: Robert Ryan as the man who really runs the town and Lee Marvin and Ernest Borgnine as his thugs. At that time, those two had serious credentials for glowering brutality, and the set-piece fights that ensue are a little like the battles in *Shane*, where pint-sized Alan Ladd disposes of the much bigger Ben Johnson. (Ironically, in the Oscars Tracy was beaten out by Ernest Borgnine, for *Marty*.)

The community is filled out with Dean Jagger, Walter Brennan, John Ericson, and Anne Francis, and it clearly benefited from the Mojave locations and the decision to use CinemaScope. So the parable works like a well-oiled lock. The only trouble is the complete absence of ambivalence or doubt and the clear-cut opposition of good and bad characters. Part of the problem is that the characters in the small town are Hollywood types, not the kind of people who actually inhabit the hinterland. Truth to tell, the anti-Japanese racism in America during and after the war was more extensive than this clean-up operation suggests. What the film needs is a real touch of redneck recalcitrance and tranquil bigotry.

So it's notable that while *Bad Day at Black Rock* was proffered as a radical political statement, it really offended no one. Its plot doesn't get at the embedded, vested interests that could be challenged only at the challenger's peril. For Schary and his like it's a comfortable feel-good film, as opposed to a genuine exploration of social and political trouble. If only fear of the foreigner had been the kind of job a one-armed Spencer Tracy could take care of.

Badlands (1973)

When people lament the decline of the Western, they overlook such pictures as *Badlands,* made in the early 1970s but set in the late 1950s, and precisely describing the effect of the great Western spaces on Americans. Indeed, the picture takes its title from the classic labeling of an empty part of the nation, then reexamines what "bad" could mean as it tracks a strange young killer whose self-dramatics place him as an outlaw in the empty quarter. In other words, the Western will endure for as long as young men like this are captivated by the legend of heading off into space with a gun.

The film is based on the real case of Charles Starkweather and his underage girlfriend, Caril Fugate, who went on a senseless killing rampage in Nebraska and Wyoming in 1958. (That story is told more fully in the 1993 TV film *Murder in the Heartland,* with Tim Roth.) Kit Carruthers (Martin Sheen) is working on a local garbage crew when he sees a newcomer in Fort Dupree, Holly (Sissy Spacek), just arrived from Texas. She is fifteen; he is twenty-five. Kit pays court, but her father (Warren Oates) rejects him, with the result that, casually and without real malice, Kit murders the father in front of the daughter. She is not much put out and soon enough runs away with Kit.

This was a first film, and really in its time a model of unexpected independence—written and directed by Terrence Malick, an Ed Pressman production, a film that used "Love Is Strange" by Mickey and Sylvia as well as Erik Satie and Carl Orff's "Musica Poetica." It is a film about modern delinquency, where acting out has nearly lost touch with the damage of murder, but it is a film about wild children going off on a great picnic trip, too. They live in the sparse woods. They kill people they meet. And Kit can always talk about himself as if he is a movie he's making.

The calm, or the tranquillity, of the violence is often hallucinatory, and you can surely feel some very big artistic aspirations in Mr. Malick, not just to the Western and the Dean-age daring, but to the Jungian meaning of fairy tales and the clear knowledge that Malick and Kit were both wayward geniuses of a kind—interfere at your peril.

With the music and the sweet, semi-abstract span of the photography (by Brian Probyn and Tak Fujimoto), one can feel the draw of surrealism and the banal cruelty of the actions. The rampage stands comparison with the killing of the Clutters in *In Cold Blood,* yet here Kit's unsteady grasp of the nightmare in what he has done is both intriguing and frightening.

Coyness and the matter-of-fact go close together. Holly's voice-over is artless and natural, yet I can imagine it being studiously rewritten. And the ending, with Kit recognized by state troopers as a Deaner, is too tidy. But that very patness helps us see how far the "Badlands" are not real country but an imagined place. Altogether, this is one of the most exciting American debuts on film, and a picture lamentably let down by the more recent artiness of Malick.

The Bad Seed (1956)

There's no denying the power that remains with this hideous melodrama and its horrible assurance that nature takes priority over nurture. *The Bad Seed* had been a minor Broadway sensation in 1954 as a Maxwell Anderson play, adapted from a novel by William March. Mervyn LeRoy was knocked out by it, and he bought it for Warners, determined to use the original cast. He then got John Lee Mahin to do the screen adaptation, and Mahin was an expert with melodrama as well as a natural conservative. The result is not for the squeamish, for social workers or child psychologists.

For Rhoda (Patty McCormack), aged eight, is horrid, despite her pretty dresses and her blond braids tied as tight as ropes. You see, her grandmother was a notorious murderess, and these urges get passed along. When her father (William Hopper, who had only just got over having Natalie Wood as a daughter) goes to war, Rhoda gets a little out of line, and her mother (Nancy Kelly) can't help but notice. The mother is the central role, and Kelly is actually heart-stopping in the scene with her father (but her adoptive father), where she learns the nature of the crooked family tree.

There are several allegedly learned voices gathered in this shameless "play" to say why, yes, these things can happen—notably Evelyn Varden as Mrs. Breedlove, a know-all amateur psychiatrist. And Rhoda is just a nightmare. The legend persists that Patty McCormack (who was actually eleven) gives a great performance. She does not. Instead, she has two looks—the oily smile and the mean frown—and it's up to us to say which is more hateful. She doesn't act, and the character of Rhoda is not explained or made remotely plausible; in fact, she's like a visitor from sci-fi land, sacrificed to the social determinism that believes in bad-seed tosh like this. Apply the idea to matters of race, and you can see what this is really about. So the picture is a portrait of America in the 1950s, and that is far and away the most scary thing. There are no real relationships between any of the characters, and there is not the least sense of shared ideals beyond those of cliché. In all of this contrived fever, Nancy Kelly insists on delivering a very careful and deeply felt performance, the mad logic of which is to send her unfortunate bearer of the bad seed to suicide, just as if she was carrying a fatal virus.

I won't say more about the disgusting contrivances of the last fifteen minutes, except to say that God takes a hand, all's-well-that-ends-well gets a look in, and there are credits in which the actors appear on the dreaded set as themselves—this includes Kelly spanking Ms. McCormack on the bottom in an inadvertently comic and suggestive prank. It's ghastly, but not to be missed.

Mervyn LeRoy does nothing to get in the way of the portentous text, or to detract from two very good supporting performances—from Eileen Heckart as a mother whose little boy has incurred Rhoda's wrath, and from Henry Jones as the handyman who is on to Rhoda from the start, because he's badder. The film did very well, alas, and Kelly, McCormack, and Heckart were all Oscar nominated.

Bad Timing (1980)

Bad Timing counts as a British film in that it was made for the Rank Organisation. But the delivered picture shocked the old bakery operation, so they removed their logo (Billy Wells banging the gong). You could say it's an American film in that Art Garfunkel and Harvey Keitel are both American, while Theresa Russell's character, Milena Flaherty (Joyce meets Musil?), is said to be American and is played with an American accent and a naggy American urge to get to the bottom of everything. However, I see no real doubt about it: The picture is tourist Viennese, for good and ill.

Milena has been having an affair with Dr. Alex Linden (Garfunkel), a psychoanalyst. In despair, she tries to kill herself. She is rushed to the hospital. Inspector Netusil (Keitel) is brought in to investigate. The blood at the end in attempts to save Milena's life is a part of the art direction: All along, she has been a girl who wears strident mauves, begging pinks, or assertive reds. (Art direction by David Brockhurst; photography by Anthony Richmond.) She is, I suppose, the sexual principle in that she lives to fuck, without undue regard for loyalty or conventional movie methodology. And, of course, she is the director's wife.

Theresa Russell is not a great beauty or an extraordinary actress. There is even a disconsolate, slightly depressed air to her, as if she is aware of these shortcomings—but what can she do about them? On the other hand, she is fiercely sexual, quite unashamed and untouched by coyness. And the fact is that the amazed lust and reverence Alex feels for her is not too far from the way in which Nicolas Roeg's film and camera observe her. This is where Vienna comes in, for we are on the home ground of Klimt, Schiele, and Freud—it's a wonder, but not a note of Mahler is heard. And in what is a very heady (if not pretentious) film, the history and its look are inhaled not just as atmospheric décor but as a sort of explanation for the people. We see some Klimt and Schiele in galleries, and the tesselated look of one and the sprawl of the other are taken to be the origin of the profuse disorder in the apartments. More or less, sexual expression here equals untidiness, and Alex and Roeg watch with the same bated breath to see all the unexpected ways in which Alex and Milena can do it.

The script comes from Yale Udoff, a playwright, and it says far too much while delivering too little. I wish Roeg would trust animal action more and intellectual justification less. As it is, the most profound thing is the kind of exhausted affection for Milena/Russell that grows as the film progresses. Rank was upset because Alex delays calling medical help for Milena in order to have sex with her potential corpse. That's not an improper or unlovely resolution of their desperation about each other. It's justified. It works. Until explanation steps in—and that's where Garfunkel is helplessly wordy and inferior next to Russell's defiant belief in action. Still, the attempt is remarkable. The film does not reach the bottom of sex, but as to the bottom of Ms. Russell, we are home. It also has Denholm Elliott—alas, if only there was more of him, for he watches what he can with a look of Ophuls on his face.

La Baie des Anges (1962)

The first shot: dawn on the promenade at Nice. We see a woman wearing white—it is Jeanne Moreau. And as the camera begins to move rapidly away from the woman and ahead, we hear a rising crescendo of music, by Michel Legrand. It is the "passion" music that goes with the gambling sequences in this astonishing film. I love the whole picture, and the sardonic, reptilian aura that Moreau tosses out with a glance. But the opening shot is one of my favorites. The music is exhilarating, yet the figure diminishes, receding but staying visible because there is no one else around at that time of day. And the light and the loneliness are as undermining as the music is momentous. Somehow, in a single shot, Jacques Demy has caught the contradictoriness of gambling in a film that understands its subject so well, it never stoops to moralize or see the consequences. You have only to see that gambling is just a metaphor for living, and you have a film close to perfection. And this opening is not just arresting but maybe the best shot in the film. How sure are you, or how fatalistic, if you're going to play your best card first?

Of course, I am talking about a fusion of action and music such as we saw in Demy's *Lola,* with the white Cadillac and some phrases of Beethoven—and still to come is the ecstatic, discovered genre of his *Les Parapluies de Cherbourg,* where a very simple love story rises with Legrand's music. Demy and Legrand—it is one of the best marriages in film history.

The story is so modest: A handsome but timid young man comes to gambling, and he meets Jackie (Moreau), a woman who has been doing it all her life, someone in whom haggardness and radiance go on and off like the light. You could say she is bipolar, and I do not mean to hide the nearly sublime portrait of that very grave condition that the film presents. But Demy sees gambling as akin to faith in life itself. The plunging and surging of fortune—the almost immediate shifts from no money for coffee to the best hotel room in the city. And Moreau's woman swings round on a dime in this room and asks, "Quel luxe?" as if she hardly notices the good fortune or the extravagance.

The casinos look like churches, and not by accident, for the most daring or insolent thing about this film is the way it sees gambling as a spiritual adventure. Of course, in Monte Carlo or Las Vegas that is not always so; the sordid, the grim, and the absence of pity await most gamblers, just like the damage to their friends and relatives. But winning is a proof of life, and art, and everything. It is like the vision, the command, and the actress willing to walk the length of the promenade on her own that gets you that first shot. This is very dangerous territory, and it would be a terrible mistake not to see that Demy's people walk the high wire without a net. But if you don't get that opening shot and aren't changed by it, there is always gardening or embroidery.

The Baker's Wife (1938)

Marcel Pagnol (1895–1974) was his own man, with his own studio, but today he has an odd worldwide reputation that does not seem to waver. In the 1980s, director Claude Berri made two very successful films, *Manon des Sources* and *Jean de Florette,* in a ravishing color that Pagnol never used and with stars a lot prettier than Pagnol preferred. But the movies were taken for granted as "Pagnol," and six thousand miles away, in Berkeley, California, Alice Waters opened her restaurant, Chez Panisse, as a tribute to the world and the culinary interest of the filmmaker. In time, Chez Panisse was joined by the smaller Café Fanny. The restaurants are open to more than filmmakers, of course, but the northern California movie set love the place.

Pagnol was born and raised in the harsh south of France, near Marseilles, and he was a schoolteacher for several years. But once posted to Paris, he tried out some of his plays in the big city. *Topaze* and *Marius* were acclaimed, and so Pagnol returned to Marseilles, opened a modest studio there, and began a local film industry that flourished in the years before the war. *Marius, Fanny,* and *César* made a trilogy, bound together by the great actor Raimu. *The Baker's Wife* was made quite late, but it was one of Pagnol's great hits, and it survives as a very enjoyable comedy.

Raimu plays the baker in a small town. He has a young, pretty, but not thoroughly satisfied wife (Ginette Leclerc), who runs away with a handsome drifter (Charles Moulin). The baker is distraught, and his bread suffers, whereupon his regular customers determine that, for the sake of continued good eating, they must do whatever it takes to repair the marriage. The story comes from an incident in the novel *Jean le Bleu,* by Jean Giono, and Pagnol, as was his habit, translated it into a screenplay. Georges Benoît photographed it, keeping generally to interiors, with a few sunbathed exteriors of the countryside. However, Jean Renoir, who went to the Pagnol studio to make *Toni,* was far more observant of the real location.

Pagnol was unashamedly theatrical. He liked good talk and comic acting, and his films have been remade time and again, in France and elsewhere. John Barrymore did a remake of *Topaze* in the 1930s; and Joshua Logan's *Fanny* (1961), with Maurice Chevalier, Charles Boyer, and Leslie Caron, actually does as good a job as Pagnol's even if it is prettified. In other words, the world has been kind to his movies, and it enjoys his idyllic portrait of romantic troubles being manageable enough to be handled by the interests of gastronomy. It was François Truffaut who shrewdly observed that the quite cunning real-life dramas of, say, Vittorio De Sica came directly from the work and ambiance of Marcel Pagnol, who appreciated country people so long as they were characters, good talkers, and great cooks.

Ball of Fire (1941)

Sam Goldwyn often bemoaned the fact that "his" Gary Cooper pictures seldom made money, or not as much as when the star was loaned out. So he begged the writing team of Charles Brackett and Billy Wilder to find a vehicle for the big guy. And Wilder remembered a treatment he had written with Thomas Monroe in which a learned lexicographer meets a showgirl. They did a screenplay and called it *Ball of Fire*. The story now turned on an encyclopedia project that had come to "Slang," so the compilers seek an expert—enter a young showgirl trying to get away from her mobster associates.

Whereupon Cooper himself—who had just enjoyed doing *Sergeant York* and sensed a big hit there—suggested Howard Hawks as a director. Goldwyn was not happy: He didn't get on with Hawks, or his $100,000 asking fee. But he agreed to it all, because Hawks admired the script—"It's *Snow White and the Seven Dwarfs*," he explained to Wilder. That doesn't get you a shared credit, warned Wilder. The role of the showgirl, Sugarpuss O'Shea, was touted for Ginger Rogers, but she was not interested. Carole Lombard said no. Betty Field and Lucille Ball were tested. And then Cooper suggested Barbara Stanwyck.

As a Goldwyn production, the film was given everything, including Gregg Toland as cinematographer, Perry Ferguson as art director, and Edith Head to do Sugarpuss's costumes. Cooper complained as the shooting went on that the rapid, intellectual dialogue was a stretch for him. So lately, as Alvin York, he had been a religious Tennessee boy. Yet the marvel about Cooper was that, just as in life the cowpoke could look like the most elegant man in *Vanity Fair*, so if he got comfortable with his lines, he could seem Ivy League or man of the West.

Filmed August through October of 1941, *Ball of Fire* stands as a fine example of merry escapism as war clouds draw close, with Hawks having a lot of fun getting Stanwyck to remind the professors of the shorter words in the dictionary. She is saucy, naughty, and as quick as a shortstop. The guys doing the dictionary are as fanciful as the gangsters, Joe Lilac (Dana Andrews) and Duke Pastrami (Dan Duryea). Indeed, there's a cheerful attitude to the interchangeability of all human pursuits that foreshadows *Some Like It Hot*—especially if sex is kept in mind as the number-one pursuit. Cooper was easily funny with a saucy girl without ever forcing the humor. His character is named Bertram Potts, so Stanwyck gets to sigh, "Oh, Pottsy," and make it sound very sexy. The group work by the dwarves is nicely done; they are Oscar Homolka, Henry Travers, S. Z. Sakall, Tully Marshall, Leonid Kinskey, Richard Haydn, and Aubrey Mather.

The picture was released days before Pearl Harbor, and it was exactly the high-energy, blithe escapism that clicked with the war spirit in those first days. After all, what did the title mean, except that America in its innocent exuberance fired off entertaining explosions? "It was a silly picture," Wilder would say. "But so were audiences in those days."

Bambi (1942)

Felix Salten had done a novel for children about a fawn growing up in the forest. (None other than Whittaker Chambers translated it!) Disney bought the rights to it in 1937 with an eye to a feature film, but it was five years in the making, delayed by a traumatic strike at Disney, the onset of war, and the meticulous preparations Walt insisted on for this picture. He sent artists and researchers to the woods of New England. He even installed a small menagerie in Burbank so the draftsmen could study animal movement. In Maine and elsewhere, researchers undertook immense field projects on rainfall and how it splashed, and countless brilliant photographs of water on foliage, spiders' webs, and so on were sent back to California. As a result, *Bambi* is the Disney picture with the most exhaustive animation of nature. The movements of the deer are anatomically as exact as anything done by George Stubbs. And the forest is probably the most realistic setting—even if idealized—that Disney ever attempted or achieved.

None of which conveys the extraordinary drama of the film. For Disney was faithful to the Salten novel—which meant that Bambi's mother would die. One of Walt's own daughters protested this detail, and parents ever since have had their qualms over *Bambi*. It's all the more striking, therefore, to remember that *Bambi* came out in 1942, by which time death was an altogether more disturbing prospect to most Americans. No one is quite sure now how thoroughly Walt weighed this. He was a man for detail more than the big picture. But no viewer raised on the film would ever question its tragedy and its feeling for a developing disaster in the fire scene. I can recall Lassie running from the Gestapo, and Bambi and Faline running for their lives, and I know which was the more alarming.

But the skill of *Bambi* is to open in an infant's world: This is the forest made of perfumed rain and balmy banks. It is the place of Thumper. The father deer is hardly seen. But as Bambi grows, so his life becomes tougher and the vague threat—of man as the real enemy in the meadow—becomes more testing. It's the book, said Disney. But thousands of American hunters believed they were being attacked, and protested.

It does come closer to a point of view than anything else Disney ever tried, and it seems blind of a critic like Manny Farber to protest the loss of fantasy without seeing the parable on maturation. Unlike so many Disney projects, *Bambi* is about coming of age and discarding childhood. It's about watchful male deer (scouts) keeping the forest safe. Was there a political undertone? I suspect Walt would have been amazed at the suggestion, but that does not mean it is not there. *Bambi* may be the most beautiful film Disney ever made, as well as the toughest ordeal for any of his characters. In the course of under 70 minutes, the world changes.

Bande à Part (1964)

The "kids" in *Bande à Part* are all too old—they're in their mid- to late twenties. But that hardly matters, because the kids in American films are usually too old. It's one of the things that kids enjoy about them, because they're being flattered for their alleged maturity. And in this case, you have French people, old enough to be dead, who are determined to be like American kids. They have no careers. They hang out together in the suburbs. They go to cafés and dance the Madison, like jerks who always knew they could be Rogers and Astaire.

There are three of them—Odile (Anna Karina), Arthur (Claude Brasseur), and Franz (Sami Frey)—and Odile lets it out one day that maybe the aunt she lives with has some money hidden away. They resolve to steal the money. It seems like a game or a dream, and the air of making it all up as they go along leaves uncertain to the end what has happened. Yes, there has been a robbery, but it was a robbery on film. The daydreaming idleness of the outsiders' life has risen gently to the level of action. But it's only a movie. And, in truth, it's a chance to witness the shallow friendship of the three—the odd way they amount to a trio by doing things like their two-minute tour of the Louvre. They are not so much real people as an attitude. Nothing ever happens at the movies, after all, nothing except the frenzy on the wall.

As his basis, Jean-Luc Godard took a novel, *Fool's Gold,* by Dolores Hitchens, which he then stripped down to its bare bones. He cut out all the psychology and meaning: He wanted to concentrate on the trio, the dream of action, and the odd way in which they know their action (if taken) will likely end the trio. It's like Sherlock, Jr.: He can be a detective if he steps into the film—but then who'll trust the film running on, because the projectionist has vanished?

Shot in a few weeks, in black and white, by Raoul Coutard, this is one more work in imagined cinema, which still played at international film festivals and got worldwide distribution. It is *Funny Face* meets *The Big Combo.* It is part of a game of Trivial Pursuit in which, drawing two cards—film titles—you act them out, ideally doing the whole film in two minutes. Above all, it loves and defends the sense of fiction in the chill, damp winter light, the readiness, the fuse that could go off at any minute. And it would not hurt if the "kids" were really children or if they dressed and talked like infants. For they are three small laps in one chair reading a large adventure book and climbing into its pictures. The result is so slight and so momentous that it's strange, and as always it is a throwaway commentary from Godard on the nature of film. Utterly beautiful, yet threatening some dire change. How long would Godard be content with this playfulness? When it was clear that he was not one bit a playful guy?

Music by Michel Legrand (very helpful to the dream). Godard does the narration, his harsh voice cutting to the bone. Agnès Guillemot edited. Also with Louisa Colpeyn, Danièle Girard, Ernest Menzer, Chantal Darget, Michèle Seghers, and Michel Delahaye.

The Band Wagon (1953)

I know a number of people who love musicals for whom *The Band Wagon* is the peak of that art. One reason is that it is a story about "putting on a show," about the theatrical enterprise and the efforts of a gang of people to provide a few moments of fun, magic, and elegance. It's about doing musicals, a genre that maybe at its best has so little content you'd be an idiot to go looking for it. Especially if you've got the chance to hold the screen for a few minutes with "Dancing in the Dark," by Arthur Schwartz and Howard Dietz. This is one of the select dances the desert island comes equipped with. It's Fred Astaire and Cyd Charisse on a set that represents a clearing in Central Park. It is twilight, and they both wear white. Her dress is yards of some silk that swirls and hangs like waves in thick air. They scarcely touch, yet they have the loveliest unison you ever saw. Michael Kidd did the choreography, and you'd better see it before you die.

Anyway, there are characters in the film—played by Nanette Fabray and Oscar Levant—who are like Betty Comden and Adolph Green, cobbling together the script for this film. And Fred Astaire and Jack Buchanan are the two egos—one shy, one glaring—trying to dominate the show. Just like life.

This is the Arthur Freed unit at M-G-M at its best, and in a routine product. This isn't *An American in Paris;* it's everyday work, and maybe more appealing because of that. Vincente Minnelli directed. Cedric Gibbons and Preston Ames did the sets. Harry Jackson photographed it.

There are set pieces, like "The Girl Hunt" ballet, where Kidd got Fred to do staccato moves and somehow the show had him in white and Cyd in orange against a crushed plum and dusky blue scene. Cyd was dubbed by India Adams, but you can't dub dancing, and you can see that between them Kidd and Charisse have persuaded Fred to loosen up. Then there's Fred and Jack doing "I Guess I'll Have to Change My Plan." There's Fred at the depot, "By Myself." There's the "Triplets" number, which I never have liked, but I find I wait for it every time.

Not even Freed said the Arthur Freed films were going to save the world or qualify for a Nobel Prize. No one said they were important. But did Hollywood ever do anything so odd so well? There really is something about the idea—so long as you don't stress it—that putting on a show is the best thing in the world for your disasters and dreads. I find myself torn over whether musicals should or should not be "about" anything. But *The Band Wagon* is about itself, and how a country may have had three hundred years of bloodshed and idealism, *Moby-Dick* and chewing gum, but a couple of minutes of "Dancing in the Dark" can make it all seem sensible.

The Bank Dick (1940)

W. C. Fields (1879–1946) is the kind of figure who can come off badly in a book like this. How easily one can imagine him squeezed out by yards of Fellini and Ford, or trying to invite Ingmar Bergman for a drink. After all, in this compendium of superlatives in film, what is a Fields to do but wish for some tidy two-hour anthology that had all his best routines and moments. Surely that is the video fate awaiting those stars of whom it is said that they really only ever made one film, stretched out over the years—as if Dietrich with Sternberg or Wayne with Ford didn't come under the same category. With Fields, moreover, you might strike boldly and go for a single, sublime film, like *It's the Old Army Game,* with Fields's "Elmer Prettywillie" beholding Louise Brooks's "Marilyn," all directed by Eddie Sutherland and produced by the William LeBaron who would hire Preston Sturges.

But then I wake up from a nightmare where Fields is poking me with a pool cue because I have neglected to direct you to the very sound of him—squashed, aggrieved, plaintive yet drawling, the very voice of sober soliloquy dismissed by a busy world. You have to have the man's sigh, as wounded and as solipsistic as my dog's as he signals sleep and luxurious farting. I am wary and fearful, and I have discovered that, whereas today's children will stay awake for the Marx Brothers (they are enthralled by Harpo), they simply cannot penetrate the lifelike sounds of breathing and dismay (to say nothing of the failure, the old age, and the fulfilled misanthropy) to get Fields. How can a culture founded on "Have a nice day" conceive of Fields, or the way he would have lashed out in attack at such an opening insult?

I am going with *The Bank Dick* because it was a film, at Universal, where Fields had come as close to freedom as makes no difference in the mind of a man convinced of eternal imprisonment. It is the one where he may be hired as a bank guard. It is the one where he is Egbert Sousé, with Grady Sutton as Ogg Ogilby, suitor for his daughter's hand. Edward Cline directed, and the studio tried to rewrite the script, even to honor the Breen Office's worry over the Black Pussy Saloon. But Fields wrote it all, and in a way it is Fields's masochistic glee that is energizing all the appalling women, children, and sober men who make his life so painful.

Milton Krasner shot it, and it is good to think of him going on for years afterward, doing things like *Bus Stop* and *The Seven Year Itch.* Imagine Fields with the real Marilyn. Imagine Fields in *Persona,* or *Belle de Jour;* imagine him as Nicole's father in *To Die For*—there is not a picture ever made that is not enlightened by his presence. I do not mean "improved," merely, or suddenly exposed to a surreal light. I mean not a picture that is not led gently and sadly toward life's impertinence by Fields's attendance. One mouth says "Rosebud," and Fields's answering lips say "Wild Turkey."

The Barefoot Contessa (1954)

There was a time when this was taken very seriously as a picture—and not just by all the well-shod Hollywood actresses who aspired to be reappraised as barefoot Gypsies. Even François Truffaut, who had acclaimed its sincerity and daring, wasn't quite sure what it was about. I regret to say that I think it was about the delusion—shared by Joseph L. Mankiewicz and others of his generation once they got the warm air of French praise in their lungs—that they might be Thomas Mann, or at least Somerset Maugham. So, I'm afraid to say, it's about the Movies and the World, and the terrible dread in smart practitioners that maybe their own heartless depravity is set to crush all the wonderful Maria Vargases in the world. Because Maria is really intended as a noble savage, a sedate version of King Kong.

Of course, by 1954, Mankiewicz was such a guarantee of Oscar nominations that it's striking how badly this gloomy romance fared—though Edmond O'Brien, overacting outrageously (as Oscar Muldoon!), did get the supporting-actor award. Even so, in the early 1950s hardly anyone made what is now the real comparison (and the killer): that if you want Humphrey Bogart in a picture that rips the mask and some of the rotting skin off the face of Hollywood, then it exists in *In a Lonely Place*. How strange it is that Hollywood managed to make such an exposé and still ignore it. How bizarre that the dogged Mankiewicz, lining up lines for his characters, could pass as a great filmmaker.

Nor should the critical eye excuse the film's very strange awareness of "Europe" as a place where Ava Gardner, fully made up, can exist in patient poverty. The many would-be actresses of Spain, Italy, France, and all points deeper must have died laughing at the fatuous portrait of "simplicity." As for Ava's "flamenco" scene, why be surprised at its torpor? Ava could be sexy, but she had her pace—languid—and nothing jolted her out of it. Please note, too, the effete prince (Rossano Brazzi), the decent Englishwoman (Elizabeth Sellars), livid Continental vice (Marius Goring), and the very ugly American producer (Warren Stevens). How can anyone believe that *Contempt* is only ten years later—accurate while crazed, and so very unsettling?

The only real romance in the picture is the one involving Ava, Technicolor, and cinematographer Jack Cardiff—though even there, *Pandora and the Flying Dutchman* feels bloodier and more out of control. The look is impressive sometimes (the funeral scene, outdoors, with umbrellas like crows), and so it's worth stressing that Technicolor itself was not long for the world—it was thought to be too naïve! If only we could have mustered a similar system of rebuke for films like this. It may be added that Mankiewicz probably never made another decent or sane film after it—*Guys and Dolls* may just pass inspection. But *Suddenly Last Summer* is plainly the payoff to *The Barefoot Contessa:* a comic case of Art-thritis.

Barry Lyndon (1975)

At 185 minutes, this is Stanley Kubrick's longest film, and many would say his emptiest. But it has an exquisite look, not least in its use of candlelight, with special lenses made to capture its flutter, and various other degrees of dusk and dawn, twilight and firelight. You see, in the late seventeenth and early eighteenth centuries, the light was natural, or it was candle. On the other hand, the unlucky inhabitants of that age didn't know what photography was, let alone a director who could take years to watch beards grow. All of which is an admission that this was the first film I can ever recall falling asleep at. I daresay I was under unusual strain; still, I was shocked at the time and took it for a nearly objective proof of Kubrick's own lack of interest. Whatever century, we like to think that the characters in pictures are too pressed to fall asleep. And nothing ever alters the fact that Barry Lyndon himself is no one to care about, and 185 minutes is a long time to register that absence.

As Thackeray described the character in his novel, Lyndon was a self-interested knave who rose and fell by the same pattern of bullying, dishonesty, and luck. Ryan O'Neal, who plays him, seems quite prepared to leave any judgments up to us. On the whole, he would prefer not to be involved. It's hard to resist the way in which—given this character and the work's aloofness to him, given O'Neal's intractability, and Kubrick's own impassivity where human feeling is at issue—the film sought a narrator, so that the story might take on just a little of the curvature of arc, as opposed to a flat line. So Michael Hordern's narrative is the most natural reservoir of sentiment in the film.

Of course, all this time, "period" is prevailing, like sultry weather in which no one has the energy to do anything. John Alcott did the photography, and Ken Adam is in charge of the design—though he takes advantage of places like Corsham Court, Stourhead House, and Castle Howard. The very pretty and authentic clothes are by Ulla-Britt Söderlund and Milena Canonero. There is music from just about every composer of that era you can think of, with some Irish traditional music played by the Chieftains.

Living in Britain, subject to its natural resources and its television, Kubrick not surprisingly felt drawn to the eighteenth century as a kind of board game on pragmatism and cruelty. But why did he fix on Thackeray's novel? And how is there not more gathered moral force and human energy in the telling?

The one strength of the film is its supporting cast. The more O'Neal glowers and glares, the more likely it is that a scene will be rescued by Marisa Berenson, Patrick Magee, Hardy Kruger, Steven Berkoff, Gay Hamilton, Marie Kean, Diana Koerner, Murray Melvin, Frank Middlemass, André Morell, Arthur O'Sullivan, Godfrey Quigley, Leonard Rossiter (who would have been better as the lead), Philip Stone, and Leon Vitali.

The Battle of Algiers (1966)

Gillo Pontecorvo's *The Battle of Algiers* has its ups and downs. Oh, it only looks like a documentary, some opponents say, so don't miss how far it is rigged, or contrived, or set up—as if movies have not always been an insouciant mixture of honesty and sham, of photograph and theater. Then there is the ebb and flow of history, the times when it seems a little hard to stomach the way the film may have been used as a training manual by insurgents. Then time passes, the insurgents win, and it seems all the more evident that *The Battle of Algiers* understands the cruel logic of these events.

Pontecorvo's picture covers the mounting turmoil of the 1950s in Algeria, with the emergence of the FLN in 1952, the increased severity of the white colonists' resistance, and the eventual compromise or betrayal that brought De Gaulle back to power and that settled the future of the country. As such, it is a story of street fighting, guerrillas, and suicide missions opposing an organized army, led with more or less brutality and less and less understanding of guerrilla warfare.

In 1965, it was quite natural that Pontecorvo should employ the practices of cinema verité, and it's to his credit as a dramatic filmmaker that they make so tidy and forceful a picture. Indeed, the inevitability of what is going to happen is handled with great restraint, and in many ways the film resembles Otto Preminger's *Exodus* of 1960, which says, Put your partisanship aside, look and see, and isn't it plain what will happen? The Israelis pioneered fighting techniques that were inherited by the Palestinians. What Pontecorvo had on his side was the nature of the Casbah—a tradition that went back as far as *Pépé le Moko*—and a great eye for sharp, frightened, hostile faces. The paramount immediacy of the film is in those faces and the way the casting went to types and known political sympathies.

Beyond that, everyone behaves badly, beyond excuse or vindication. In the same way, it is quite apparent that the insurgency will win, for armed soldiers in civilian situations look archaic, foolish, and like targets. It is no way to handle an army, or a military purpose. In short, insurgents are defeated only by the politics that can provide what they want without seeming to give up the ghost.

The film doesn't enlist sympathies, even if Pontecorvo was of the left. Instead, it shows armies to be dinosaurs, the monsters of the past, increasingly abject in an age when anyone can carry a bomb or know the rudiments of torture. After that, films like this—films that re-create live terrorist incidents with suspense and character—are helplessly on the side of the lone-wolf terrorists. That a film like *The Battle of Algiers* was available through most of the years of Vietnam and all of the time of Iraq only demonstrates the ruinous stupidity that overtakes armies when they do not have political control of their work. One day, every "soldier" will realize that it is his destiny to be an insurgent.

Battleship Potemkin (1925)

In the ice pack of the Cold War, at Brussels in 1958, *Potemkin* was voted by an assembly of film critics as the greatest film ever made. Considering the films made in just the late 1950s, that vote is a measure of how little critical thinking was going on. Only two years after the Hungarian uprising, the Brussels result spoke to aging, left-wing attitudes that could not forget (or place) the excitement of Soviet cinema of the twenties. But the dynamic of Sergei Eisenstein's cinema—of drastic composition and editing fusion—had been displaced (thanks to Murnau, Renoir, Welles, Mizoguchi, Ophuls, and so many others) by fluidity, movement, and duration. There was also the feeling, pointed out by critic Pauline Kael, that "great as [*Potemkin*] undoubtedly is, it's not really a likable film."

Of course, that can promote the argument "Be careful what you think now, because in fifty years the opinion may look foolish." But *Citizen Kane*'s dominance in so many best-film polls is sixty-five years old now, and while many people recognize something unproductive in always approving *Kane*, still, that film is no less impressive or intriguing than it was in 1941 or 1962. And there's a key point: Starving sailors and massacring people on the Odessa harbor steps are not nice things. We hardly need "great cinema" to convince us of that. Yet the spectacular visual and rhythmic nature of *Potemkin* began to seem formalistic (the Soviet criticism) or too satisfied with technique to notice the slaughter. On the other hand, Charles Foster Kane is a muddle of a man over whom we still have mixed feelings.

But Eisenstein and his colleagues were working in Russia in 1925, with the horror of tsarism recent enough to demand remedy. And Eisenstein was an illustrator of astonishing power. Moreover, in seeing cinema as a matter of so many angled compositions or "shock shots," he was locking himself into an editing style that was always cutting away and that would never appreciate real time or space. In fact, this issue was being solved in German cinema, where expressionistic composition was already giving way to contextual camera movements (you can see that in Fritz Lang and F. W. Murnau).

It's not that Eisenstein was entirely without influence. Alfred Hitchcock had a very similar melodramatic way of composing and framing, and Hitch and Eisenstein did their real work with pen on paper—storyboarding. (Hitch was more interested in people.) The storyboard brought to life is Eisenstein's real achievement, and you can find him in such odd places as the paintings of Francis Bacon and the history of the graphic novel. But in the history of cinema, he was a dead end, and the way *Potemkin* lasted as a sacred cow is still a measure of how far in the rest of the world the movies followed quite different subjects, like love and money. *Potemkin* is about being right, and it was important in that it came to a people who hardly knew they existed. So being right was the first step to being wrong, which is usually the most testing state of peoples, and people.

Beat the Devil (1954)

I suppose that a great documentary on the making of *Beat the Devil* might be more entertaining than the real thing. The shifting party that attended its making is rare even for the romance of European coproduction. But the film we have is close enough to the notion that a movie is seldom as foolish or as entertaining as the record of its making. So the first advice on watching *Beat the Devil* is to see it as John Huston's laughing observation of the crack-up in the picture business and the first shuddering intimation that films are going to be made anyway—that chaos, lack of preparation, narrative disorder, and willful mistake are no deterrent. It's as if Huston had glimpsed this truth: that the urge to make a comic caper movie is enough—there's no need to labor over the real thing, no need to take it seriously.

A great deal of the comedy, I think, rests in the way this was in part a Santana Production. In other words, it was part of Humphrey Bogart's desire to make a packet of money for himself. Huston was his friend, I suppose—they had certainly been through a lot together—and you can feel Huston's stifled mirth all through the picture that Bogey is seeing his fortune dry in the sun while trying to maintain his cool, surly manner.

Where did the film come from? From a novel by James Helvick (a pen name for Claud Cockburn); from a script by Truman Capote, more or less written a few hours ahead of the shooting; and from Huston's give-up-the-ghost grin. Is that why Huston teases David O. Selznick (never far away from the set) by giving Jennifer Jones blond hair and a sense of humor? (With Selznick she might have had the first but never the second.) And is Gina Lollobrigida actually meant to be sexy, or the impossible sexy Continental star who walks behind her own breasts the way a gangster chief follows his bodyguards?

The alluvial wealth of the picture rests in its supporting cast. Above all, Robert Morley and Peter Lorre together are like Lorre and Sydney Greenstreet, except that there is the extra comedy of Morley's serene social disapproval of Lorre, which never comes close to preventing the infection of madness. Then add in Edward Underdown and Ivor Barnard—one stupidly dangerous, the other lethally stupid.

And yet . . . I have to say that the pleasure one finds in *Beat the Devil* can die in the throat, if only because there is too much despair here. It's as if, by 1954, if you please, enough knowing people had got the sure sense that it was all over, that more or less everything that followed was going to be a camp version of some lovely, foolish memory of the golden age. That anxiety has not yet been dispelled. Equally, who is to say that every film fan is not now as daft and as isolated as the Arab prince who hungers for word of the great Rita Hayworth?

Being John Malkovich (1999)

In the enchanted village of Manhattan, Craig (John Cusack), a man who performs with puppets, takes a job at Lester Corp., on floor 7½ of an office building. He has been pushed into this by his wife, Lotte (Cameron Diaz), but Craig falls in love with another worker, Maxine (Catherine Keener). Because the floor is only half a floor, it has low ceilings. It may be the regular crouched stance that helps Craig discover a door and a hole that lead into the head of the actor John Malkovich or, as the credits insist, John Horatio Malkovich. Craig takes that trip, and for fifteen minutes he is in the head of our most mannered and supercilious actor. Then he is ejected somewhere on the New Jersey Turnpike.

This is the setup for perhaps the most startling and innovative American film at the end of the twentieth century, written by Charlie Kaufman and directed by Spike Jonze. And maybe best of all, it is what you want to make of it. I proposed the enchanted village of Manhattan in that this story covers the territory from fairy story to Kafka. Nor is it accidental that the central figure is trying to make a kind of puppet play (operating from the outside) in which he is led to see the possible advantages—and insanity—of internal possession. So this is a film about acting as much as pretending, and it is truly a kind of critical essay on John Malkovich to which Malkovich has loaned himself with an absence of ego that is all the more striking in view of his work. Critic Jonathan Romney asked us to consider what the film would have been like had it been *Being Jeremy Irons* or *Being Charles Dance*? Or *Julian Sands*? Mr. Romney is our kind of subversive.

Well, with respect to those gentlemen, I think "A good deal less," is the proper answer, just because this film dwells exquisitely on the gulf between the languid hauteur of a John Malkovich we have learned to get along with onscreen and this very patient, long-suffering head that permits a great deal of coming-and-going traffic without more than a sigh. And again, it is Kafka-esque, the literalism of being inside someone's head and hearing the different timbre of sound effects from inside, as opposed to outside.

I daresay there were some audiences, happily accustomed to the mainstream fare of the day—say, *The Insider*, by Michael Mann—who wondered how a whole film could simply be this odd, show-offy, and pretentious? After all, what kind of insiderism, really, was this, next to the metaphor of "insider" in which Russell Crowe informs on a tobacco company? But the alleged and massive sanity of the Michael Mann film is all very well. Everyone acts in his own interest in that film, until you realize that the film exists only because millions of people are smoking—an irrational, neurotic behavior. *Being John Malkovich*, on the other hand, goes to great lengths to make a fantasy factual. It seems to me not just more alarming than *The Insider* but a great deal funnier. And it's only when peril gets neurotic, and comic, that people start to smoke.

The Bellboy (1960)

For ten years, from 1946 to 1956, Dean Martin and Jerry Lewis were the most successful double act in American show business. They had met in 1945—Dean Italian, from Ohio, a crooner; Jerry Jewish, from Newark, a comic—when they shared little more than ambition and going nowhere. Though it never translated adequately to film, they were inspired together. In part, they were the straight guy and the idiot. In part, without really knowing why, they were hugely successful when they had not been—and that meant a lot of money. But it was a live act in which the cool (and very good-looking) Dean would eventually crack up at Jerry's antics. And when that happened, they were not just home; they were brothers. They liked each other—and that is not always true in double acts.

In nightclubs and on television, this act was a sensation of the late 1940s. They would sometimes run on for hours if the mood took them. But soon enough, a clash developed. Dean was truly cool, lazy, casual, a natural—he could get a laugh just like that. Jerry was a worrier, a fusspot, and a tyrant, and he was endlessly concerned about getting "it" right. And being in charge. He wanted to rehearse, while Dean thought just being up there together was enough. Dean found Jerry's excess of sentimentality overpowering and fake—he knew that Jerry the crier could be a killer, too. Jerry thought he was doing everything: Dean said Jerry on his own would be too much for any sane audience.

Brought together by Hal Wallis at Paramount, they made seventeen films that are lackluster and tend to confirm Dean's faith in spontaneity. So they broke up (rather than kill each other). Dean became a pretty good actor, a world-famous singer, a stage drunk, a member of the Rat Pack, and an increasingly sad and lonely man. Jerry, in going solo, started the muscular dystrophy telethon, a monstrous exploitation of his own emotionalism. But he never really had a solo live act. Instead, he became not just a director of films, but an auteur—by which I mean that he was regarded in France as a genius, and he developed a taste and a knowledge for talking about film that had no equal.

The Bellboy is the first film he directed, and in many ways it is a harking back to the history of silent film. Set at the then fairly new Fontainebleau Hotel in Miami, it is a series of set-piece routines in which Jerry plays a bellboy. They are physical bits of business, conceived and carried out with a total allegiance to the camera. In that vein, Jerry had a very successful career through the 1960s, but then his taste for material became mawkish, and young audiences apparently deserted him. Despite much ill health (he seems like a creature of illness in so many ways), he soldiers on, and I suspect he has little more than half a dozen ideas a day. But *The Bellboy* is a masterpiece of visual comedy in which Jerry is still a simpleton while the mind that sees the jokes is a mathematical genius.

Belle de Jour (1967)

Why not? By the mid-sixties, years famous for their fusion of love and radicalism, it was time for the bourgeoisie to have a discreet look at sexuality. What happens? Well, it is exactly like the box that the Japanese man brings to the brothel. Do you remember? He has a box, which opens, and when it does, we see nothing but we hear the intense whirring of . . . a scorpion on a leash or a demented dildo? After the film was released, and famous, director Luis Buñuel reported that at all manner of social events he was approached by a great range of women—society ladies to tramps, the rich and the poor, the beautiful and the ugly—and without fail all of them wanted to ask him about it. "Well?" they said. And when he replied, "Well, what?" they all asked, "What is it inside the box?" And the maker of the box answered, "Whatever you want it to be." We are talking about desire—which is not necessarily the same as love, and certainly not marriage.

Séverine (Catherine Deneuve) is a well-to-do woman married to Pierre (Jean Sorel), who is pretty but boyish. They have a friend Husson (Michel Piccoli)—rather sinister, a little too odd and intimate—who implies that he knows things about Séverine. He suggests an establishment where she might gain rather more satisfaction than comes from her marriage. But when she realizes the place is a brothel, she is shocked at first (isn't she?) and frightened away. But she tries again, and she wins the favor of Anaïs (Geneviève Page), who runs the place. They make an arrangement.

You see, Séverine is really only free in the afternoons. In the evening she must be home for Pierre. But she could work as a "belle de jour," couldn't she? I ask these little questions because the great delicacy of Deneuve's extraordinary performance is that she hardly seems to have the choice; she is, after all, a wife, in whom obedience is a treasured asset. So she does what she can, what she must, and it is left to us to gaze on that very beautiful, polished face and deduce where frenzy meets necessity.

In time, she encounters "ugly" clients, not just the Japanese man, but a lout, Marcel (Pierre Clémenti), violent, dangerous, and hopelessly in love with Séverine. Marcel cripples Pierre out of vengeance, and Séverine cares for her husband until Husson tells the helpless man the truth.

The film comes from a Joseph Kessel novel and was scripted by Jean-Claude Carrière, in his second collaboration with Buñuel. But this film is in very pretty color: it is a world of interiors such as the bourgeoisie cherish (design by Robert Clavel, photography by Sacha Vierny). The color is a key part of the glossy stylization being practiced here; it goes with witty dialogue, starry players, and a dainty perfection in performance. But do not be deceived. The deepest, dirtiest questions are being asked in the age of feminism—like what do you desire? Do you need to see your husband crippled by a monster from the gutters? It's whatever you want it to be, and one of the very few great films.

Made so soon after the end of the war, in a French countryside that was liberated, *La Belle et la Bête* is as much of a tribute to being fancy-free as *Les Enfants du Paradis*. And to the extent that it coincides, roughly, with the first wave of Disney feature films, so this Jean Cocteau movie is a signal that, yes, there are films that any child and any adult can see together, with profit and pleasure. For although Cocteau's film is filled with natural miracles, and no matter that it has a Beast who might have been too fierce (or too subtextual) for American cinema to authorize, I have yet to meet a child who can't handle the film. They know they can trust the storyteller.

This was Cocteau's first full-length movie and his first film work since *Le Sang d'un Poète* (in 1930). André Paulvé was the producer, and although the resources were modest (as outlined in the published diary Cocteau kept on the filmmaking), the film succeeded marvelously in using very simple and economical special effects: mercury mirrors, reverse action, arms appearing out of black satin drapes, and so on. The gorgeous photography was by Henri Alekan, and it is still a matter of delight for most viewers that the world it depicts can turn into something else with so little fuss.

Cocteau wrote the script himself from the fairy story, and he made the basis of reality a Vermeer-like Loire Valley. That's where we find Belle (Josette Day) at first, along with Avenant (Jean Marais), her rather obtuse boyfriend. But once we enter the enchanted lair of the Beast, Marais blooms under the fantastic makeup designed by Christian Bérard. This Beast is leonine, capable of anger and repose. He has been wounded. He has suffered. And his glance at Belle is decidedly erotic. Yet children understand it all, without alarm or sniggers. They have been lifted up by the enchantment of the film.

René Clément helped on the film with technical matters. Bérard did all the art direction as well as the Beast mask. Marcel Escoffier designed the costumes, and Georges Auric wrote the music. The rest of the cast includes Marcel André, Michel Auclair, Mila Parély, Nane Germon, Raoul Marco, Noël Blin, and Christian Marquand.

The secret to it all is that Cocteau set out to make a film that would stir adults; along the way he discovered the child's imagination, too. So it's an extraordinary and very encouraging fusion of pictures for kids and the surrealist art tradition, yet totally true to the diffused but heated sexuality of the original tale. It's also the best opportunity that would ever come the way of Jean Marais, statuesque and handsome but waiting to have a little bit of the big cat pumped into him. Further, the realistic basis of the film and Alekan's approach to magic are so very down-to-earth and practical. What keeps the film modern and dreamlike are things like Belle's way of moving without effort or friction, and the very adult, Freudian understanding of symbols. Children at the movies require no special care or condescension. They expect genius.

La Belle Noiseuse (1991)

About one hour into this 240-minute Jacques Rivette masterpiece, the painter Frenhofer (Michel Piccoli) takes up a pen and begins to draw. We hear the scratching on the paper, and it is like his imprisoned soul coming back to life. I should say that the shots of hands working—drawing now, painting later—use the hands of Bernard Dufour. So the figure of Frenhofer is intriguingly mediated; after all, when Marianne (Emmanuelle Béart) takes off her clothes to be painted, it is Mademoiselle Béart. You can see.

In that first hour, we are in the Cévennes. Béart and her boyfriend, a painter, have come to visit Frenhofer. He lives in one of the great houses in the history of film fantasy, with a studio at the end of the garden. But Frenhofer is uneasy. He has not painted for a few years; he was doing a picture, *La Belle Noiseuse,* of a "nutty" young woman, and he stopped. Now he lives in the house with his wife (Jane Birkin), and he waits. He decides he would like to try drawing and painting Marianne.

She is angry. She tells her boyfriend that he has pimped her into this situation. She knows she is going to have to take off her clothes and be seen. But the next morning she is awake before her boyfriend, and she goes to the Frenhofer house to present herself. Silently, but in consent, the painter takes her to his studio and—here is the joy of a film taking its time—there is a scene of ten minutes or so in which the painter simply fidgets in his studio, killing time and making an opening for art, moving things, getting old pens and inks out again, angling his desk, just working his way into the situation of being an artist. It is the start of an enchantment that takes us into the hand and the being of a painter.

I used to think that *La Belle Noiseuse* was a lovely, elegiac work from an aging artist, a reverie on the process and on Mademoiselle Béart. But it is far more than those things. It is a symphony on the sexual transaction in art—there is usually something like this at work, and I think there is no question but that making art or life is every bit as biologically positive and hopeful as having sex. It is a reminder that, as a rule in any Rivette film there is a work of art in development: the plays in *Paris Nous Appartient* or *L'Amour Fou,* the unwinding of the inner movie in *Céline and Julie Go Boating.*

And so, in this case, in the painting of the nude body there is the astounding intimacy and the distance at the same time, the notion that you are never more alive than when making art though you're always an observer. It is an old-fashioned view, perhaps, a Renoir view—but earlier in his career Rivette had made a long documentary film, *Renoir, le Patron.* This is the culmination of that work. Piccoli shows how great an actor he is. Jane Birkin gives one of the most touching performances you will ever see. And Mademoiselle Béart is defiantly herself and naked for the duration of, say, *Run of the Arrow.*

Ben-Hur (1925)

Lew Wallace's novel *Ben-Hur* was published in 1880. In 1899, it was presented onstage in New York in a dramatization by William Young. There were real horses on treadmills; William S. Hart played Messala, and Edward Morgan was Ben-Hur. One of the people behind the production was Abe Erlanger, and it was Erlanger and Florenz Ziegfeld who formed a syndicate to bring *Ben-Hur* to the movies. To that end, they sold the property to the Goldwyn Company in return for the ludicrous reward of 50 percent of the gross! Thus, when Goldwyn became part of the M-G-M merger in 1924, this was one of their properties—though it was spelled out in the merger that no one from Mayer would share in its profits.

But very soon, Mayer and Irving Thalberg would be called upon to rescue the company from this monster. At first, Goldwyn had put June Mathis in charge of the whole thing. She had attempted a script, hired Charles Brabin to direct, and cast her lover, George Walsh, in the lead. They had all gone off to Italy together to research locations and soak up the Roman atmosphere.

The results were disastrous. Louis B. Mayer horned his way into the mess (through Marcus Loew), renegotiated the profits arrangement, and began to consider options. Relations with the Fascist film authorities in Italy were not good. The building of sets and the hiring of labor presented many problems. Brabin's footage was inept, and no one reckoned that George Walsh could carry the film. So Mayer took a closer hand and gradually eased Mathis out. A great deal of the material shot in Italy was abandoned. Carey Wilson and Bess Meredyth were to redo the script. Fred Niblo was the replacement director, and Ramon Novarro was now cast as Ben-Hur.

It was only after Mayer went to Italy (with his family) and watched the shooting of the battle of Livorno that the enterprise was ordered home. There was a real crisis in Italy. Mayer fell ill and had to have all his teeth removed. Later on, Thalberg had a heart attack. Niblo was bullied and harassed, and several other people came in on the direction. With a final cost likely to be $4 million, Mayer pulled production back to Los Angeles, and the actual chariot race—high spectacle, with twelve chariots, each with four horses—was shot in L.A. in October 1925.

At one time, the Mathis project had called for a 250-minute film. It came down to 140 minutes, but they had spent 214 days shooting. A lot of the most exciting effects were handled by B. Reeves Eason, with Karl Struss in charge of photography. The cast also included Francis X. Bushman (as Messala), May McAvoy, Betty Bronson (as the Virgin Mary), Carmel Myers, and Nigel De Brulier.

The film lost money, but probably only about half a million. So it was regarded as a triumph of executive decision, with the showmanship of the great chariot race.

Has anybody made a voluntary decision to see Heston's *Ben-Hur* in recent years? I understand the possibility that it may appear on television, in the way clouds slowly pass across the window space. And maybe the film stays on for a few minutes before the viewer realizes what's happening. I know it was nominated for twelve Oscars and won eleven, a record that has been tied but not topped. But does anyone really check it out for all that craft? I think it's more likely that any rentals come from attempts to track Gore Vidal's malicious but unforgettable rumor that Stephen Boyd's Messala and Charlton Heston's Ben-Hur had a feeling for each other, but that only Boyd was aware of it.

Vidal posits this suggestion because he did a good deal of rewriting on the picture to add something to Karl Tunberg's original screenplay—that was the single nomination that went unrewarded. And all of this came from General Lew Wallace's novel, written presumably on those rainy New Mexico evenings when he didn't have Pat Garrett to dinner. It's about boyhood friends who become deadly enemies, and it's about the Christ who reaches out a hand to help Ben-Hur at an especially bad moment in his life.

Ben-Hur climaxed a wave of religious epics in the 1950s, and I suppose the trend speaks to a real devoutness in the nation. If only those films' directors had anything like vision or faith in their minds. It remains one of the great ironies of film history that Hollywood was making this kind of heavenly-choir bombast at exactly the time when Robert Bresson was directing some of the most genuinely spiritual films ever made.

William Wyler could be a pretty good director, but he was wry, wary, and down-to-earth. Nick Ray, by contrast, made a film about Christ, *King of Kings*, that is vivid with his own belief in belief. *Ben-Hur* is 212 minutes long. The rare passages of excitement, like the chariot race, are delivered by unit directors Andrew Marton and Yakima Canutt. If only they had been given the whole project. You have to sit down and breathe deeply, because it is my duty to tell you that *Ben-Hur* won Best Picture—defeating *Anatomy of a Murder.*

Wyler won his third Best Director Oscar. Charlton Heston won for Best Actor, beating out Jimmy Stewart in *Anatomy* and Jack Lemmon in *Some Like It Hot.* Hugh Griffith beat George C. Scott in *Anatomy* to win the Supporting Actor Oscar. The terminally boring cast also includes Jack Hawkins, a lady named Haya Harareet, Martha Scott, Sam Jaffe, Cathy O'Donnell, and Finlay Currie. What else is there to say, except that these immense Biblical protestations are as profound and ignorant an intrusion on the life of what we call the Middle East as our several wars and invasions. And very likely there is a muscular connection between those two insults. Finally, it is justice of a special kind that the film Hollywood chose to honor the most is now forgotten and unseen. The attempt by the Academy to impose an academic standard failed.

Berlin Alexanderplatz (1980)

So Rainer Werner Fassbinder, having made more than thirty-five films in fifteen years, committed himself to direct *Berlin Alexanderplatz* for Bavarian television. More or less, it would run for 933 minutes, and it would require a shooting schedule of 200 days. Fassbinder agreed and said that he would promise to come off drugs for the duration, to facilitate the production. In the event, he shot it in 154 days. And he died in 1982, having resumed his drug habit.

In the nature of things, it is not easy to see the whole of *Berlin Alexanderplatz*. It is harder still to see it as a movie in a theater. There were complaints when it was released that some of the TV imagery was too dark to be seen clearly. Still, this is the climax of Fassbinder's tumultuous career and one of the landmarks in realist film. It's easy in this day and age to say that we have "everything" we ever wanted to see at hand, whereas the ideal viewing circumstances for every project are much harder to achieve. Fassbinder is at a point where he is dismissed in many minds because of his fertility—how can the newcomer sit down and see all that work?

The TV show is based on Alfred Döblin's novel, published in the years 1927–29. Fassbinder had read it as a youth, but it was only just before the television show that he read it again—reviewed his own work—and decided in effect that it was the basis for everything he had done. In that sweeping gesture, you have a taste of Fassbinder the idealist, as well as the analyst, the man who saw that Döblin's stress on the whore-pimp bond was beneath nearly all of his own work. And so he adapted the novel for the screen himself (noting and appreciating Piel Jutzi's film from 1931). It's the saga of Franz Biberkopf (Günter Lamprecht), who comes out of prison resolved to go straight. But his friendship with Reinhold (Gottfried John) leads him back to pimping. He sells Nazi newspapers. He runs a team of girls. He loses an arm. He falls in love with a whore, Mieze (Barbara Sukowa). The girl is murdered. He is shut up in an asylum.

Xaver Schwarzenberger shot the series in color. Juliane Lorenz edited it. Peer Raben did the music. Helmut Gassner led the design team. And the cast also included Hanna Schygulla, Franz Buchrieser, and Claus Holm. The result is sordid, tough, but amazingly authentic—and a crucial material for anyone researching Berlin in the late twenties.

It's clear that Fassbinder was surprised and distressed by the poor reception on television; he had hoped to make a definitive work. And so it is hardly surprising that in his last years he was planning a separate movie version—not cut from the TV show, but begun again. This time, Gérard Depardieu would be Biberkopf, Fassbinder would himself have been Reinhold, Isabelle Adjani would have been Mieze, and the rest would have included Jeanne Moreau and Charles Aznavour.

The Best of Youth (2003)

Marco Tullio Giordana's *The Best of Youth* was a sensation, all over the world. Its virtues are many, but I suspect its impact is more significant than its achievement. It was a 423-minute series made for RAI, Italian television. As it was aimed at domestic consumption only, it took a little time for critics and writers to spread the word. Eventually, however, it had theatrical releases in many other countries in shorter versions, and there were places where it played for weeks on end, like a cult film. Audiences knew it by heart, and yet in most cases they were not aware of all the details in modern Italian history to which the film refers.

The Best of Youth (written by professionals, Sandro Petraglia and Stefano Rulli) covers the years from the 1960s to the 1990s, following several members of the generation born right after the war. In other words, these are the new Italians, people who had to find out whether they could make their own lives and their nation's starting at Italy Year Zero. Key figures include Nicola (Luigi Lo Cascio), a medical student who will become a psychiatrist; his brother, Matteo (Alessio Boni), who becomes a policeman; Giulia (Sonia Bergamasco), who joins the Red Brigades; and Giovanna (Lidia Vitale), a magistrate who opposes the Mafia.

The approach is realistic, detailed, and humane but not auteurist. Giordana is a good director, but some of his feature films are a good deal more personal than this. He shoots simply, directly, with a lot of close-ups, and in a self-effacing way that lays every stress on his story and his characters. If you're going to like this, he seems to say, it's because you will believe in the world I establish. In other words, it is simple accuracy to say that *The Best of Youth* is an example of the economy and effectiveness of TV storytelling.

That needs to be established because I believe the audience's "discovery" of the film—a real phenomenon—was in no way the grasping of something new or radical. It was a way of saying, Look, here we are, and we still treasure good stories well told. I'd never make the claim that *The Best of Youth* is a great film. But it is absorbing, sympathetic, and good-natured. It tries to show us decent people in a coherent way. And in 2003 and the years immediately after, all over the world, significant numbers acclaimed the achievement and, it seems to me, passed an oblique verdict on so much of modern moviemaking, where cruelty and obscurity in subject matter show a disinclination to entertain.

There's another conclusion worth making: that in most countries of the world we have had excellent TV dramas, some far longer than *The Best of Youth,* that dwarf the achievement of the "movies" of the time. These are group works, in most cases, even if *The Sopranos* always relied on a "creator" like David Chase. But how many can say that the great achievements of *The Godfather* tower over the lives we have led with the Soprano family?

The Best Years of Our Lives (1946)

In 1944, for $20,000, Sam Goldwyn asked MacKinlay Kantor to consider writing something on men coming home from the war. It turned into a verse novel about three men, *Glory for Me*. It struck Goldwyn as something different. Then William Wyler, himself back from a tough war, read it and said he'd like to do it. Goldwyn persuaded Robert Sherwood to try a screenplay. At first nothing clicked, and then, on the point of giving up, Sherwood saw a way to do it. The script he wrote was far too long, but Goldwyn promised they wouldn't change a word.

Wyler wanted Gregg Toland to shoot it, and Toland noted how the war had altered Wyler: he cut down on his old camera movements. Now he wanted simplicity with depth—naturalism as far as the eye could see—and Toland delivered. Goldwyn had thought of Fred MacMurray and Olivia de Havilland to play the older couple. They turned him down—third-banana part, said MacMurray. So Goldwyn went to Fredric March and Myrna Loy instead. Teresa Wright would be their daughter, and she would fall in love with Dana Andrews as his marriage to Virginia Mayo broke up. One of the trio had lost his hands, and Farley Granger was the first thought. But Wyler wanted to look at real veterans, and they found Harold Russell in a training film, joking about how he'd lost his hands in a fight with TNT. Cathy O'Donnell would be his girlfriend.

They shot for more than a hundred days, and they kept every bit of social criticism from the script about the way the bank was ready to make quick deals with new entrepreneurs while shafting the veterans. They treated the difficulties as honestly as they could, and they fought the Breen Office on its starchy attitude toward adultery and affairs. They found a real graveyard for bombers where Dana Andrews could have his great scene remembering the battle. And Wyler recalled his own return and put Loy and March at different ends of a corridor in an unexpected reunion. These are heartbreaking moments in a nation's history, decently put down as fiction but resonant with the real thing. They had Hoagy Carmichael doodling piano in the bar. They got a score from Hugo Friedhofer. They did it all and hardly changed a word.

Daniel Mandell cut it, and it came out at more than 160 minutes. Too long, they all said. Goldwyn said they'd preview it and cut it down from the audience reactions. Not to worry. They ended up at 172 minutes and a budget of $2.1 million. It wouldn't be cut. The audience drank up every scene.

In its first year the film grossed $10 million. It was nominated for eight Oscars and won seven: Best Picture, plus statues for Wyler, March, Russell, Sherwood, Friedhofer, and Mandell. No, it's not the best American picture ever made. But if you are interested in the complex relationship between being American and the nation's movies, you can do no better than start here. It was a moment when the realpolitik, the sense of duty, and the romance of movie storytelling went hand in glove. And it was a war that needed that much good luck.

Bhowani Junction (1956)

What a subject: the British in India. Yet how few films there are on it, let alone good pictures. David Lean's *A Passage to India* seems to me inept and awkward. There are cheerful inventions like *Gunga Din* and *Lives of a Bengal Lancer.* On television, there was *The Jewel in the Crown*—without rival as drama as well as historical commentary. And there are moments from Merchant Ivory and even Satyajit Ray. There is *The River,* which may be as true as anything to a certain blinkered English colonial life, so kindly treated by Jean Renoir's forgiveness. And then there is *Bhowani Junction.*

Nobody could or has ever tried to claim the picture as a success. Its director, George Cukor, regarded it as one of those projects ruined by the studio—and he was something of an expert in that kind of suffering. On the other hand, it has the look of India (in excellent CinemaScope) and the feeling of heat, polite or blunt prejudice, and impossible, fine-grained distinctions of mind-set and character that leave one marveling at the endurance of modern India as any kind of entity. And there is Ava Gardner.

It all comes from a John Masters novel, with a script by Sonya Levien and Ivan Moffat. Not that they worked together. Originally, I believe, the picture had a straightforward narrative from the point of view of the half-caste girl, Victoria Jones (Gardner). But then there were previews where the picture got knocked about and audiences didn't like Victoria—maybe because she was half-caste, maybe because she had several affairs. So Moffat reordered the picture in a way that put it under the narrative thumb of the English colonel (Stewart Granger), one of Victoria's men.

This has several bad results. It's awkward as a flashback story, with too much voice-over telling us what to think. It makes Victoria look more promiscuous. And it hurts what is otherwise a pretty good performance from Granger. What's left? Well, a very intriguing story that shows the seething impossibility of India, great photography from Freddie Young, and George Hoyningen-Huene's color advice. All of which leads to maybe the most beautiful Ava Gardner we ever had. It's also clear that she saw this as a unique chance. There are moments of her in distress, with India coming apart at the seams in long shot behind her, that are impressive and moving.

The supporting performances are wildly variable: Bill Travers is terrible and Lionel Jeffries is a cliché, but Francis Matthews and Marne Maitland are outstanding. And then there are moments where Granger and Gardner together are like grown-up lovers from a better film. But at M-G-M in 1956, Cukor—a loyal servant to the studio system—had no power, and no trust from above. He had clearly been aroused by India, and by Gardner, too. Cukor had wanted Trevor Howard in the Granger role—there was a time when every film wanted Howard instead of their male lead. By now, it's just a dream, but this is one of those films where we want everyone to try again.

Bicycle Thieves (1948)

First things first: The original Italian title to this film is *Ladri di Biciclette*, which can only be translated as "Bicycle Thieves." However, a stupid orthodoxy prevails in the United States, where, on its first release, the picture was called *The Bicycle Thief.* That contradicts the very thing that anyone moved by the story takes away from it: that in the world it shows, there are thousands of bicycle thieves because of the terrible economy.

Consider the story: Ricci (Lamberto Maggiorani) is one of so many men in Rome looking for work. He has a wife and a son to support. One day he finds a job. It is to ride around the city pasting up posters for American movies; the image he labors over is Rita Hayworth from *Gilda*. But he has no bicycle, because his wife, Maria (Lianella Carell), pawned it. So she pawns bedsheets to redeem the bicycle, and Ricci is off. But every time he puts up a poster, he leans the bike against a wall. We know what will happen. And once the bike is stolen, Ricci is left with his young son, Bruno (Enzo Staiola), to lament his fate, to search for the thief and his bicycle, to get soaked in the rain, to exemplify poverty. In the end, Ricci is driven to try to steal another bike for himself. But he is not a good thief, and he is caught and disgraced in the eyes of his son.

The film came from a novel by Luigi Bartolini and a screenplay by Cesare Zavattini, who was a key figure in what became known as the Italian neo-realist movement. A true humanitarian, Zavattini maintained the social realism in Vittorio De Sica's work and kept its sentiments on the left. That surely helps explain the impact of the film: *Bicycle Thieves*, though ignored by the Italian film business and funded by De Sica himself, became a hit in America and the rest of the world. It made real money. It was referred to often as a model of postwar poverty in Europe and What Had to Be Done. It inspired David Selznick to think of an American remake—with Cary Grant as Ricci! The screenplay was nominated for an Oscar.

And, of course, the film is moving, even if the attempt on our heartstrings is so blatant and so much at odds with the thing that is really striking and beautiful: the sense of the streets of a great city where nearly everyone is having a hard time. Although De Sica used nonprofessional actors, that does not mean they were not actorly. They feel theatrical (in both the good and the bad senses—eloquent, yet arranged). The nature of the fable is obtrusive, whereas the atmosphere of the streets is stunning. And that was what was really new: the untidy infinity of life made to seem like the crowd, or all of Italy. For De Sica was a very talented film director: He saw the grayness and heard the faraway sea of bicycle bells ringing. *L'Eclisse* was taking shape.

So we are all likely thieves now, or if times get hard enough—because we are urban creatures. That's what the film says, and why it needs its due restoration to *Bicycle Thieves*.

The Big Combo (1955)

These days, the urge to make film noir respectable and festival-worthy is so chronic and academic that it's hard to find a noir that is as nasty and pretentious as the genre once wanted to be. The characters should be not hard-boiled, not entertainingly cynical—they should be odious, without any chance of redemption. But the film, while low-budget and hurried, should have streaks of vulgar intelligence. You should be able to convince yourself that it was made by a hood who had read some books in prison and was insufferable because of it. The picture should be suffering from a proper neglect, so that its sourness seems to be turning rank in front of our eyes. Some deterioration in the film stock would help, some harshness that enhances the mannered photography. The trouble is that nearly every candidate has now achieved cult status, so that some archive has fondly restored the film and rot has been stopped.

So be it. Still, I'd like to propose Joseph H. Lewis's *The Big Combo* as a work that should be lost or withdrawn to ensure that people start desiring it, and I support the attitude of Philip Yordan, its writer, who, when asked if he liked *The Big Combo,* said no and moved on.

It's a story of two men, a cop and a mobster, who are essentially very alike. Played by Cornel Wilde and Richard Conte (the sort of marginal actors and heavy presences that do well in noir), they have the same cynical attitude to life and the law, and the same sadomasochistic view of the woman they love (or need), who is played by Jean Wallace. Wallace (1923–90) was a beauty of an especially somber kind, one that is the more lovely for not being much of an actress. In her time, she was married to both Franchot Tone and Cornel Wilde (she died just a year after he did). She is photographed in *The Big Combo,* by John Alton, as if she is the Virgin come down among men. She is bathed in light, a thing she hardly notices, but it brings a wan spiritual quality to the film that exactly fits the kind of pretension I like to see in a noir.

So this nasty little crime film is actually made in a spirit busting for a prize. But Lewis is content to go through the motions here, never touching the real humanity of his far better *Gun Crazy.* But whereas that is a truly strange, unbalanced film, this is a hack job looking to get by on "class." And Jean Wallace is a weird icon of class caught between two snakes. There is clever use of a hearing aid to build sadism, and the cast also includes Brian Donlevy, Lee Van Cleef, Robert Middleton, Earl Holliman, and Helen Walker. Just don't let the word get around.

Bigger Than Life (1956)

It's touching to see how often in his first years in Hollywood James Mason inspired a rare kind of movie by launching into friendship with a director on the cusp of the system. There was his alliance with Max Ophuls, and then there was the meeting with Nick Ray that made *Bigger Than Life*. For this is one of the finest pictures of the 1950s, a diagnosis of mounting alienation and madness in a very ordinary guy: an idealistic, small-town teacher.

The idea came from a *New Yorker* article, "Ten Feet Tall," by Berton Roueché, on some of the deluding side effects of the new miracle drug cortisone. Mason produced the picture, and Richard Maibaum and Cyril Hume did the screenplay, though Ray's close friend Gavin Lambert did some doctoring work and then Clifford Odets added one or two scenes—scenes that Maibaum found overreaching, and a part of what he called Ray's muddying it up.

There may be something in that. Ray, Mason, and Odets were all creative people wounded by the system, and bitter about past compromises. Given a good subject, like this one, such talents are always likely to go for broke. And some people find *Bigger Than Life* overstated in that end-of-the-world mood that could overtake Ray. Equally, I think you have to see how in the 1950s a safe director would have made this too tidy, too pat. The hero, Ed Avery, is a man tormented by the feeling that he might be a colossus, and so the film needs to rise to that inflated stature.

I think it does, because of the benign but epic fury in Mason, but also because of Ray's further pursuit of design as an element in the melodrama. The compositions and the color schemes evident in *Rebel Without a Cause* and clearly inspired by CinemaScope are here again: Joe MacDonald was the cameraman; Lyle Wheeler and Jack Martin Smith did the décor. These are studio names, people who presided over sedate pictures, and I think we have to see Ray himself having a tremendous impact on the production design. David Raksin delivered one of his best scores. And the cast includes Barbara Rush (as the wife), Walter Matthau, Robert Simon, and Christopher Olsen.

Mason is brilliant and very moving, and yet one has to ask—is he right? For he seems both English and patrician, and soon enough Mason's liquid eloquence would be interpreted as a sign of villainy. Yet Ed Avery is mainstream America. I can see how Mason wanted to play the part, but I wonder how much more striking the story might have been for American viewers if it had penetrated closer to home, with someone like William Holden in the central role.

Who can tell? *Bigger Than Life* did little business in its day, but it is now established as one of Ray's most important and dynamic films. Of course, there was too much Ed Avery in Ray for him to stay stable. He had his own addictions and inner storms, and so the career was always likely to go off course. But *Rebel* and *Bigger Than Life* show how plainly he saw manias building in America.

The Big Heat (1953)

I saw an essay the other day that argued that *The Big Heat* was driven by the selfishness of the Glenn Ford character, Detective Dave Bannion: He lets his wife be killed after he's had warning; he helps bring about the death of Debby (Gloria Grahame), his unexpected ally; and he generally carries himself with an immense self-righteousness that begins to lose sight of the lesser feelings of others. But I'm not sure that that reading is missing from Fritz Lang's simple yet layered film. Indeed, Lang takes pains to show how far every action has a consequence, and I do not think he has any illusion about the fate of this widower cop who has tasted revenge and extreme violence. In the context of Lang's work, Bannion has become a dangerous man. That's what the big heat—the pressure—has done to him, and to the city at large.

The Big Heat is the kind of picture easily placed at the fountainhead of the modern police story, with one exception: Ford's integrity does seem to put the wicked city to rights—until you think how extensive the Lagana organization was, and how thoroughly it had infiltrated the police department. Lagana (Alexander Scourby) is gone, along with Vince Stone (Lee Marvin). But that only leaves a vacuum, and the one thing *The Big Heat* needs today to be a masterpiece—as opposed to a brilliant, lethal exercise—is the hint that Ford's cop is no longer sound.

Still, as far as it goes, this movie charts the stepping-stones of pressure: a suicide; the widow becomes a blackmailer; Ford is pressured; his wife is killed. There is hot coffee on the heater. Vince sees it and, in his temper, hurls it in Gloria Grahame's face—thus her famous molten look really turns to marred plastic. And so, in turn and in time, from the dark, she will repay the gift and make the sneer on Marvin's face as permanent as scarring.

I think we know that Ford is going to pursue evil to its lair; we know that his determination will not be cheated or bought off. But that only makes his resolve more ugly or warping. And so, in a movie that seldom fails to show cause and effect, we have to ask ourselves what is happening to our Dave Bannion. Is he growing braver, or more desperate? Is he out to build a new city, or destroy himself? Isn't his menace to the Lagana gang a matter of his not caring?

It follows that because the human action is mathematical, with equations showing the thrust of dynamic forces, so the style of the film is geometric—a series of tense diagrams where the figures of the people pass like scraps of clothing blown by a great wind. This is no city, or all cities. It is another version of metropolis, or M, where structures are alike. And it is Bannion's sentimentality, or hope, that you can make up your mind to be good. He does not see that, instead, he is impelled by vengeance and its sure erasure of nobility.

The Big Lebowski (1998)

When you think about it, the most inexplicable and forlorn thing about Elliott Gould's Philip Marlowe in Altman's *The Long Goodbye* is that he is still a private detective, for heaven's sake. This doesn't take anything away from the importance of Gould's drifting, muttering, swinging guy—this Marlowe is a pioneering apostle of not really caring, even if you're in a movie. But who, by the early seventies, would trust ten cents on the methodology or ideology of the private eye? The world had gone to hell, and hand baskets were about all America made. However, if we can muster the belief, and if he could summon the necessary resolution (perhaps with the Nina van Pallandt character—just a suggestion), then here, wandering up on the millennium as if it were a split spare, we have the Dude, Jeffrey Lebowski, big in his dreams and in his scruffy sneakers, and dragged into a semblance of the private-operative stance thanks to a mistaken-identity routine, when thugs mistake him for the real Big Lebowski, and end up pissing on his rug.

This is the Los Angeles where a midweek bowling league can be the center of some guys' lives, and *The Big Lebowski* is a movie about the kind of life that would be burned at the stake before it admitted to being impressed at being in a movie. As such, it is one of the Coen Brothers' most coherent and endearing satires on movie existence, shot through with a genuine affection for the kind of no-hopes who people this world and who hold off silence and horror by the steady beat of "dude" talk. It is all the more pleasing that the film came nowhere near any Academy Awards, or such, yet it has surely passed into the slacker pantheon of those millions of people—homely guys, especially—who suspect their lives may never amount to anything (unless fate provides for them in the form of some hooligans pissing on their rug—it's enough to sustain the rug business when rugs are, actually, pretty far-fetched).

Could the film have been made without Jeff Bridges? We doubt it, because Bridges is the weary saint of that brigade of great American actors who will never get an Oscar—or not until the day comes when honor falls on his casual shoulders (in which case let us hope the award itself is called "the Dude").

So maybe this is for acquired tastes, or maybe taste is just something we all have to work hard at acquiring—and where better but in the groves of failure, shabbiness, and La Cienega? It is a key work of late-twentieth-century culture (whereas a lot of more vaunted things aren't), and we love everyone involved—not just Jeff, but John Goodman, Julianne Moore, Steve Buscemi, Philip Seymour Hoffman (we remember him when he wasn't ubiquitous), Tara Reid, Peter Stormare, John Turturro, and the magnificent Sam Elliott. Above all, we like this one because its tattered dignity and straight-faced hilarity served to take the superior smirk off the Coen Brothers' faces (Joel directed, they both wrote it, and Ethan produced).

The Big Parade (1925)

Two pictures, *The Big Parade* and *Ben-Hur,* secured the place of Metro-Goldwyn-Mayer as the maker of prestige productions in the mid-1920s. Not that the pictures were alike: *Ben-Hur* lost a lot of money (though the crowds seeing it didn't realize that), and *The Big Parade* made a fortune. It had been Irving Thalberg's idea (just as *Ben-Hur* was a project that always had Louis B. Mayer attached). On a trip to New York, Thalberg had seen the play *What Price Glory?,* written by Maxwell Anderson and Laurence Stallings. He was deeply impressed by Stallings, who had lost a leg in France during the war, and he invited him out to Hollywood. When Stallings arrived, he had a five-page outline for a movie.

Thalberg assigned King Vidor to the project, and Vidor, screenwriter Harry Behn, and Stallings went back east by train as Vidor dug into Stallings's memories. The film would be the story of James Apperson (John Gilbert), the drifting son of rich parents, who goes to France in 1917, meets a French girl, Mélisande (Renée Adorée), loses his two best friends, and is wounded in the leg. He goes home when it is over, but he can't find it in him to renew an old romantic relationship. He realizes that his destiny lies in France, and so he goes back to find Mélisande.

The picture was shot around Los Angeles and in Texas, with John Arnold doing the photography and Cedric Gibbons and James Basevi the design. The studio had considerable volunteer support from Army contingents, and so there are scenes of massive troop deployment that came relatively cheap. According to the studio, the film cost only $382,000; Vidor claimed it was cheaper still. But Vidor was given every indulgence by Thalberg. He shot one scene of troops on a curving road, decided it needed a straight road for better effect, and restaged the whole thing.

The Big Parade is more martial and less tragic than we now feel the Great War was. This may be an American perspective—it may just be the urge to deliver an unprecedented spectacle. Still, it shows an American imagination being drawn to Europe, and not just because of a love relationship. The film made John Gilbert a big star, in part because of his manliness or even the romantic scenes (he teaches Adorée to chew gum), but because of the sense of an older, sadder, wounded man. There's no doubt that Vidor had learned a lot just from listening to Stallings, and even if in 1925 the film was more important in terms of M-G-M's future, still, there is some sense of a world calamity.

The cast also included Hobart Bosworth as Apperson's father, Karl Dane and Tom O'Brien as his fallen comrades. There was an original music score by William Axt, and the picture ran 141 minutes; audiences complained that they couldn't get transport home when the last show ended. It ran two years at the Astor in New York and grossed $1 million at that one theater alone. The studio reported a profit of nearly $3.5 million.

The Big Red One (1980)

When *The Big Red One* opened in 1980, director Samuel Fuller was sixty-eight. He had been nursing the project since his involvement with the First U.S. Infantry in the Second World War. Fuller had won medals, and he had survived, and he had become a moviemaker able to liberate so many of his memories of warfare. Thus, in *The Big Red One,* the Sergeant (Lee Marvin) makes the last killing of that war, unaware that a cessation had been declared four hours earlier. For Fuller fans, that seemed familiar and unduly mythic after the brutal opening of *Run of the Arrow,* in which Rod Steiger's loner fires the last shot of the Civil War.

Run of the Arrow, although benefiting greatly from Steiger's unsuitability as the lead, still feels like a work conceived the night before and then shot in a matter of a few days. Whereas *The Big Red One* has always felt like respectability triumphing over experience. I wonder how many of the classic age of American movie directors really needed lengthy preparation or extended meditation. Or did that uncommon advantage make them ponderous sometimes, too deeply premeditated, when urgency was a keynote to their style and their desperation?

Over the years, *The Big Red One* has grown. In 1980, it was 113 minutes long. There had been budgetary restrictions; the film had been compelled to shoot in Israel, as opposed to North Africa and Italy; and there were reports of episodes that had been cut, one involving Fuller's wife, Christa Lang. At first, it seemed that Fuller was pleased with the 113-minute version, but then the story emerged that the film had been taken away from him and that the release version was the work of another. Fuller's preferred cut was four and a half hours.

In Fuller's book *A Third Face,* published in 2002, five years after his death, he proclaimed himself deeply attached to the epic length and hopeful of a director's cut someday. He sounded ominously close to the self-importance that is derided in his best films. He had got posterity: "My longtime dream had finally come true. That *The Big Red One* now existed, even in an abridged version, was miraculous and, without any doubt, my most important achievement. Future audiences and film historians will judge it for themselves. All I ask is that they be given the opportunity to see the movie I lived, wrote, directed, and edited with my heart and soul—the entire four-and-a-half-hour movie—before they render their final judgment."

In 2004, thanks to the efforts of Richard Schickel, a "restored" version was released at 158 minutes long. I think it merely extends the problems of the first version: a grandeur and nostalgia that are in part autobiographical but also the result of a Sam Fuller who has listened to too much critical commentary on himself. *The Big Red One* enlarges vanities in Fuller, and it loses his crucial sense of survival at all costs. Fuller's own real war was a just war. But the Fuller who worked so hard in the 1950s knew that such thinking was humbug.

The Big Sleep (1946)

The chemistry uncovered in *To Have and Have Not* had to be repeated for the screen, even if Bogart and Bacall had their own setup eventually to be known as marriage. And although Howard Hawks may have felt jilted, or outmaneuvered, there were those who knew that the chemistry had started in his mind. And so, in due course, Raymond Chandler's *The Big Sleep* was sufficiently realigned so that it could be a series of sneering, needling, loving set pieces between actor and actress. The result is the best example we have of snapping backtalk as a metaphor for sex.

Not that this movie is unkind or unfaithful to Chandler. The esteemed trilogy of screenwriters—Jules Furthman, William Faulkner, and Leigh Brackett—guessed how decisively Chandler worked in scenes: Open a door and you met a shot; ask a question, and you got a tougher question back; and why should life not be a puzzle if the air of mystery is stealthy and seductive enough? It's pretty clear that, on first impression, no one could make sense of the Chandler plot or care about it. If Hawks was right, you just made each scene so damn interesting no one bothered, and then at the end you eliminated several people and had your guy and his girl upright but writhing, like the smoke from two cigarettes.

But we know now—thanks to the discovery of a print released to the U.S. forces ahead of commercial release—that there was pressure to explain it all. And the explanation is so tedious it seems unkind to the troops. So it was abandoned, and suaveness was allowed to reign. After all, confusion is in the mind of the beholder, and if Bogart elects not to notice it, then it's not really there.

So this is Philip Marlowe coming to the Sternwood house, where the General gives him his job, and Vivian and Carmen give him a feel. The chase will involve two bookshops, one fake, the other a paradise for bookworms. There are suspect photographs. There are Agnes and Joe Brody. And finally there will be Canino and Harry Jones. You don't have to follow it all any more than you need to follow a road at night: You do follow it, but you don't care where you are going. Meanwhile, Marlowe and Vivian play a very high-class game of tennis whenever they meet, and this dread noir world keeps rocking with laughter. *The Big Sleep* is a mystery, a noir, a love story, and an absurdist comedy—and when Bacall sings "And Her Tears Flowed Like Wine," it's a musical. It's whatever it pleases. It's about as much fun as anyone could have in 1946.

Sid Hickox photographed it. The music is Max Steiner. The art direction is Carl Jules Weyl. And the rest of the cast had better be in heaven (or some other closed court) ad-libbing fresh takes till the end of time: John Ridgely, Martha Vickers, Charles Waldron (Sternwood), Dorothy Malone (at the Acme Bookstore), Peggy Knudsen, Regis Toomey, Robert Steele (Canino), Sonia Darrin (Agnes), Louis Jean Heydt (Joe Brody), Elisha Cook, Jr. (Jones), and half a dozen knockout girls to get you from A to B. Forgotten your alphabet, Marlowe?

The Birds (1963)

Alfred Hitchcock was far better suited to small worries than big ones. In which case, I think it is wiser to see *The Birds* not so much as an alarm being raised about birds—or any creatures, winged or not—taking over the world but, rather, a nagging revery on why Jessica Tandy and Tippi Hedren have such similar hairstyles. In which case, *The Birds* was an uncommon amount of investment and time spent on real seagulls, special effects, and even painting the passing circumflexes of aggressive crows onto the film stock.

Look at it this way: Mitch Brenner (Rod Taylor) finds Melanie Daniels (Hedren) in a San Francisco pet store. He is attracted, so is she, but their flirtation is not quite natural—it begins to reveal the cracks of insecurity. So Melanie follows Mitch "home" to Bodega Bay, where he lives with his mother, Lydia (Tandy), and there's a schoolteacher in the town (Suzanne Pleshette) who's obviously a burnt-out flame from Mitch's past, frightened off by the mother and by Mitch's reticence about going beyond Mother's wishes. May I say in passing, or remind you, that *The Birds* followed *Psycho* in Hitchcock's career, a film much concerned with ways in which the mother-son relationship can get tangled.

And Melanie and Lydia do have the same hairstyle—a front wave swept up off the head, with little vertigo curls at either end. And the mother is unhappy about Melanie, just as Mitch is nervous about claiming her while Mother is disapproving.

That is when the birds start to attack—and, by implication, it is what drives them. This all comes from a Daphne Du Maurier short story (set in England, with simple farming people). The script is by Evan Hunter, though he and Hitch did not get on too well as the project advanced. Once the birds take wing—with classically Hitchcockian shock effects tinged with comedy, as when the birds gather on a playground monkey bars—the movie is a prolonged and very taxing ordeal, in part because birds are spiky, alien, unpredictable, and ungraspable. And the climax of the ordeal is one in which Melanie (and even Hedren herself) is subjected to a kind of onslaught or rape—hell to film, and traumatic in impact. So a stricken Melanie becomes the child of the mother.

We know now that this strange drama was exacerbated by Hitch's infatuation with Tippi Hedren, in many ways the inevitable outcome of his lifelong adoration and torture of actresses. It is also instructive that *The Birds* comes after the huge success of *Psycho,* so he was unbridled, and the film was more abstract than anything he had done before. It was also his last unflawed film.

So it's an extraordinary, very troubling picture—not just because of the irrational hostility of the birds, but because of the deep-seated neurotic explanations for their aggression. It is as if Hitch had at last elected to act on his most insightful reviews and had admitted sexual insecurity as his subject. All in all, it's not just a brilliant if rather academic film, but something tinged with embarrassment—ours: We wonder if we should be watching. And these birds attack the eyes.

The Birth of a Nation (1915)

Do we need to see it? Yes, of course. But should you see it, or sit down with it, unprepared? No. *The Birth of a Nation* is a piece of history. It's like the site of the Battle of the Little Bighorn in eastern Montana. You can't honestly walk the ground and reexperience the battle, but in recent years archaeologists have dug up bullets from the old war, and in their gathering places they have worked out the story of what happened. It's not quite decent or American, but it involves beleaguered groups of Custer's Seventh Cavalry shooting themselves rather than face the wrath of Crazy Horse. And, of course, years later, once the lesson was learned, the Sioux were nearly wiped out.

The Birth of a Nation is claptrap, racist, and wrapped up in the worst kind of melodrama. So lesson one is simply how much show business atmosphere influenced early (and all later?) filmmaking. It is the work of an unreconstructed Southerner, made at a time when it was automatic for white extras to put on odious blackface to become "the other." And do not forget or let anyone fail to mention that the huge audience response to *The Birth of a Nation* led to a resurgence in the Ku Klux Klan and to a rise in the incidence of lynchings in those parts of the United States where that was considered sport.

Is it also a galvanic gathering of countless small inventions in cinematic storytelling that D. W. Griffith and others had been working over for five years or so? Yes. And is it a momentous gamble on the part of the theatrical business to exist and flourish as something above and beyond the riot of nickelodeon arcades? Yes. And did it directly lead to the development of fortunes that would very soon bankroll what we call the studio system? Yes. So, beyond doubt, is this a turning point in the evolution of the capitalist enterprise and the modern storytelling known as movies? Yes.

Are there still passages of authentic excitement? Yes, the battle scenes, the rapist chase scenes, and even the pondered killing of Lincoln all quicken the pulse. On the other hand, Griffith was always working by the mundane mathematics of 1 + 1 = 2. He put shows together in steady accumulation. I don't think he grasped the incendiary, surreal, internal dynamic of psychic outrage or delight in editing. So the film now seems slow, methodical, and merciless, like Scott dragging sledges across the South Polar plateau.

Yet reading and research tell us so much more. The way Woodrow Wilson was sent out of his mind by it only hints at the public frenzy. The stories of Louis B. Mayer crooking Griffith on the New England take is a manual for industrial procedure. And by 1915 there were works in other arts of such majesty, fineness, and profundity that it was easy to conclude that this new lightning was what would keep the public frenzied and fed, as opposed to enlightened. All the important questions are there. So, yes, you should see this appalling movie.

The Bitter Tea of General Yen (1933)

The Bitter Tea was the movie that opened New York's Radio City Music Hall, on January 11, 1933, only a few months after the debut of Josef von Sternberg's *Shanghai Express*. Despite passing references to the Chinese as "all tricky, treacherous, and immoral," Frank Capra's film is actually much more sympathetic to China, chinoiserie, and another way of thinking than the Sternberg picture. It is altogether a fascinating picture and one much helped by a knowledge of local history.

The project was set to be filmed by Herbert Brenon, with Constance Cummings in the lead role of Megan Davis, the fiancée of an American missionary in China, who becomes infatuated with the Chinese warlord General Yen. The source was a novel by Grace Zaring Stone, and there was a script by Edward Paramore, Jr. But either Brenon fell out at Columbia or Capra edged him out. He wanted the project for himself, and for the lead he was drawn to cast Barbara Stanwyck—the woman who had rejected Capra after a love affair that lasted through *Ladies of Leisure, The Miracle Woman*, and *Forbidden*.

In fact, Capra made changes in the script so that the General drinks the poison tea rather than rape Megan or lose her. The balance of their relationship—starting in her frozen distaste but then going through a fevered dream sequence (not in the novel) in which Yen is both rapist and rescuer—leads to several long dialogue scenes, not always well written, but very daring for 1933. I think it's possible that Stanwyck was troubled, and that she is a touch too prim because of her awareness of Capra's private agenda—for he was surely trying to win her back. So Stanwyck tries to be the missionary when everything in the film calls for a creeping abandon in Megan. When I say everything, I mean above all Nils Asther's Yen, one of the most attractive figures in early sound cinema—witty, fatalistic, and very smart.

Columbia threw money at the film. It has great impressionistic scenes of warfare and chaos, as well as sumptuous palace interiors where the décor is immaculate. Most of the film is nocturnal, and Joseph Walker's imagery is lustrous and erotic—in addition, Capra's eye for angles is acute and still modern. He frames action beautifully and always on a diagonal line to the key to a scene. In all, Columbia is reckoned to have spent $1 million on the picture—and still no Academy attention. It only played eight days at Radio City. Women's groups protested the love story, and the film was actually banned in Britain and the empire.

Of course, the interracial love is not conventional, and Asther lifts the film into a range of feeling that still works today. There are also fine character studies by Toshia Mori (in what you might call the Anna May Wong role, but much better) and Walter Connolly as an American moneyman who works with Yen.

The Bitter Tears of Petra von Kant (1972)

In a claustrophobic apartment where the white shag carpet is beginning to grow up the walls to claim the baroque murals, to the rhythm of Pandora's Box and in the vile scheme of Trucolor turned toxic, it's Rainer Werner Fassbinder's stunned day in the life of Petra von Kant. I think it's stretched out half an hour too long at 124 minutes, though without some boredom it might not quite be itself. But it still works, both as a flagrant slowed replaying of daytime soap opera and the world of Douglas Sirk, and as a macabre projection of how people like Petra see themselves. In other words, this is a camp reappraisal of a certain type of melodrama, but it's real, too, from the moment Petra wakes up in a sweat of congealed face cream, calling for orange juice (that being the color blood takes on in this chemistry). There's a lot of poker-faced humor in the approach, but it's crazy for anyone to think that the hectic Fassbinder did not care deeply for people. As just a parody, this would be ninety minutes too long.

So it's Fassbinder on a single set, filming his own play (based on one of his failed love affairs), getting the whole thing with the sweet camera movements in ten days, hustling cinematographer Michael Ballhaus to set up his lights in one hour instead of four. Petra (Margit Carstensen) is a fashion designer. When she wakes, the silent Marlene (Irm Hermann) is there already—seamstress, draftswoman, body servant, and sounding board for the endless, soured narcissism of her boss. A friend, Sidonie (Katrin Schaake), comes by, and she prompts the visit of a young model, Karin (Hanna Schygulla), as potential meat for Petra's table. The designer has been married to men, but there's no question where her real tastes lie. The central passage of the film is a prolonged sojourn with Karin in which their exotic harem costumes come and go like mood changes and in which Karin finally faces the tyrant down with her own power game. Whereupon, Petra is left with her mother and her daughter (they seem almost the same age and the same person—feeble adjuncts), brought to ground, lying in the carpet clinging to the telephone waiting for Karin to call like the woman in Jean Cocteau's *La Voix Humaine.*

Petra is very frightening and quite empty. Her clothes are fabulous, but Fassbinder hardly pauses over them. She does design as a way of getting at other women's skin, and the claustrophobia of the piece is cannibalistic. But as a professed homosexual, Fassbinder photographs the women and their skins the way Pabst shot Lulu in *Pandora's Box.* There are two-shots of Carstensen and Schygulla that are drunk with lust. An air of vampirism (at least) hangs heavy in the apartment and is supported by nude, hairless mannequins that have been drained of blood. And yet these women pulse with life, and Carstensen would never give a better performance. It is only when you reflect upon Fassbinder as the crazed yet very controlled anthologist of styles that you see how bizarre the fastidious extremism is here. Fassbinder made too many films for his own good. People could not keep up. And he has gone completely out of fashion. But *Petra von Kant* is unique and sensational—even if it could have used a few more lugubrious pop songs as commentary.

Bitter Victory (1957)

It can be argued that this may be the last occasion on which Nicholas Ray withstood his own willful disintegration enough to make one of his whole films. There were great sequences still to come, marvelous passages. But the fact remains that *Bitter Victory*—even with Curd Jürgens and Ruth Roman—is close enough to perfect, especially in the full-length version that is now available, which makes clear the full contrition and wretchedness in the Jürgens character and the absolutely bleak regard that the film holds for the job, team spirit, and "the war."

Of course, many would have said that the Libyan desert begged for color as well as CinemaScope, but Ray does brilliantly with the wide screen and a black and white in which, for most of the time, the sun itself seems wounded. And so two officers lead a desperate mission behind German lines, two men who love the same woman. Ray had wanted Montgomery Clift for the Jürgens role, and suppose, instead of Ms. Roman, that he had had an English actress—Elizabeth Sellars or Dorothy Tutin or. . . . Well, it's no use now. Let's just say that Jürgens is better than you fear, while Roman serves adequately in a world where women have an automatic rather than an earned exchange rate.

And of course it says so much for Richard Burton—his career hardly the most illustrious in movies—that he holds the pain in place without having to exert himself. Was this a providential meeting of mutually inclined self-destructives? Whatever the answer, Burton is quite simply the most intelligent and fatalistic of all Ray's doomed heroes, and by far the most tranquil about it. If only they could have kept each other alive and interested a little longer.

Meanwhile, the commando raid is exemplary, and it shows how far Ray had command of editing as well as sequence shooting. And the film becomes itself on the journey back, with a gallery of English grotesques in the platoon, none better than the Punch-like Nigel Green, who has a madness to him that could have come from private whisperings from Ray himself.

The set piece in which Burton's Leith kills one wounded prisoner and then tries to save a dying man is unmatched in even Ray's work for its tragic tone, and the effect here is greatly augmented by the magnificent music of Maurice Le Roux.

There are people who categorize *Bitter Victory* as an antiwar film, but that is a disservice to Ray's pungent, agonized intelligence. He knows that war is circumstantial and accidental, a fog bank under which we do some of our worst acts. No, *Bitter Victory* is antipeople—that is the real savagery it contains—and it is one of those films in which Nicholas Ray was able to set aside all traces of comfortable, saving "optimism." He was a natural pessimist, and in this strange war film (made without a trace of anti-German feeling) he found the necessary cover for his real raid on the human spirit. I recall a time much closer to World War II when it seemed possible that *Bitter Victory* would date. Instead, its severity increases.

Blackboard Jungle (1955)

So maybe you had to be there at the time, but *Blackboard Jungle* was an extraordinary event. Coming at the same time as *Rebel Without a Cause,* it seemed to establish one ominous thing: that high-school students were so old, something must be wrong in the system. Sidney Poitier was thirty-one, Paul Mazursky twenty-five, James Dean twenty-four, Vic Morrow twenty-three, Corey Allen twenty-one. Only Natalie Wood and Sal Mineo were the right age. But if "kids" were getting that old in high school, surely something was holding them back.

The film was director Richard Brooks's adaptation of an Evan Hunter novel about delinquency eclipsing teaching in some New York City high schools. Brooks took the project to Dore Schary and M-G-M at a time when that regime was allegedly pushing back the flap on the envelope. Well, Schary jumped as if stung. In his autobiography, *Heyday,* he said he was gung ho to do it, but he admits that he soon had pressure from the MPAA to lay off—at the very least to have a coda in which the tough teach (Glenn Ford) comes on and says, "You think we have a problem? You should see the schools in the Soviet Union!"

Brooks persisted: He felt he had a true subject, and he smelled authentic box office. With Pandro Berman as his most unlikely producer, and with Russell Harlan shooting it in black and white, it is a tough little picture in which Ford (as Richard Dadier—terrific play on that name) comes to a high school and finds trouble. It's an all-male school (which avoids a lot of problems), and one in which the racial problems have had a shot of amnesia. Still, Dadier has to enlist Sidney Poitier finally to quell the unreachable Vic Morrow—and, as so often, Morrow was frightening and very good.

There's lots of pungent detail: Richard Kiley as a teacher in tears when the kids smash up his Stan Kenton records, Margaret Hayes as a teacher who courts rape, Emile Meyer as the school enforcer, Louis Calhern as a world-weary veteran, John Hoyt as the fascistic school principal, and Anne Francis as Dadier's pregnant wife. In fact, M-G-M did roll out the troops. Yes, I'm sure it's funny now and dated, but the exposed nerve was real. For its time, this film had a raw, gritty feeling not present in the more affluent circles of *Rebel.* It's TV series like *Welcome Back, Kotter* that really lied about the school system and that pre-1939 thing known as education.

All of this was good rabble-rousing stuff in a film that needed to be made. But the reason the film exploded is on the sound track. On the radio, Brooks had heard a record that flopped but that seemed to him urgent, rowdy, and just the music for his dangerous kids. It was Bill Haley and His Comets doing "Rock Around the Clock." Given a second chance, that record went wild, and the future had begun.

Black Legion (1937)

Between *The Petrified Forest* (1936) and *High Sierra* (1941), Humphrey Bogart made twenty-eight pictures. I pick those two because *The Petrified Forest* was the first important notice he got, while *High Sierra* introduced the character that would make him famous. All of a sudden you see what a business it was that he was making something like five pictures a year, hardly knowing where he was going or who he was meant to be. Bogart hadn't found that moment where the insolent kid stands in the doorway and feeds him the kind of lines he'd have been dreaming of—if he'd been that good a dreamer. But then the world clicked into place, and he became Bogey.

One of those twenty-eight is *Black Legion*, and it's a film so few Bogart fans know, you have to wonder why. You won't believe it got made. There was this writer-producer at Warners, Robert Lord, who had been to the University of Chicago and Harvard and written for *The New Yorker*. And he wrote the story for *Black Legion* about an ordinary guy, a factory worker named Frank Taylor (Bogart), who loses a promotion to a man named Dombrowski. Frank starts to listen to a rabble-rouser on the radio, a man who preaches "America for the Americans," and he joins the Ku Klux Klan. And it's not a sanitized version of the Klan. It's a version based on research, one that uses the same language in initiation oaths as the real Klan. And this was not too difficult to find out in 1937, because in rural areas the Klan was very active. Its membership was up because of the Depression, there were gangs of white-supremacist bikers, and there were lynchings.

Hal Wallis, the production chief at Warners, backed it. Lord guided it into being. Abem Finkel and William Wister Haines did a screenplay from Lord's story, and Archie Mayo directed the picture. Mayo was not a strong director, but give him strong scenes and he could be very effective. *Black Legion* would be a scorching crime drama, and a frightening picture of an ordinary guy's shift toward fascism, even if the Klan wasn't a pressing reality in society. But Warners made the film and took on the risk of local attack. And it is possible that Bogart does some of the best acting of his career, good enough to help explain the violence of *In a Lonely Place*.

And in all the great wave of nostalgia we once had for old movies, and especially those of Humphrey Bogart, isn't it interesting that *Black Legion* is seen so seldom? Yet it survives—and Lord got an Oscar nomination for his original story. George Barnes photographed it, the art direction was by Robert Haas, and Bernhard Kaun wrote the music. The cast includes Dick Foran, Erin O'Brien-Moore, Ann Sheridan, Robert Barrat, Helen Flint, Joseph Sawyer, Addison Richards, and Eddie Acuff. Henry Brandon—the actor who would be Scar in *The Searchers*—played Dombrowski.

Graham Greene wrote: "The horror is not in the climax when Taylor shoots his friend dead, but in the earlier moment . . . when he poses romantically with his first gun." There's a Fascist in every kid, and this one gets life imprisonment.

Blackmail (1929)

There is a great production still from *Blackmail,* taken at the Elstree studio, with Alfred Hitchcock standing beside Anny Ondra, the German actress hired for the picture. There are a couple of feet between them, yet they are worlds apart. Alfred—fat, tousled, villainous, very intense—has his whole being focused on the earphones he is wearing. He could be listening to a message about the end of the world—or the start of a new one. And Ms. Ondra is simply speaking, emoting, uttering. He may be hearing her, but he is infected with some far more potent virus.

Hitch was a graphic artist, a designer, a man who always liked to storyboard as much as possible. But he was like a dog in heat with sound. The meeting tells us a lot about Hitch's appetite for novelty and technology, and it alerts us to his hearing, too—not just talk, effects, and music, but the stealth of room tone, the pressure of ambient sound. He was a gossip with story, and gossips can hear a guilty sigh.

Blackmail was overtaken by sound, so there was a half-and-half version as well as one with full sound. It's the story of a police detective with a girlfriend who finds herself compelled to knife a rapist rather than surrender. Her fellow gets the investigating job. It all turns out OK in the end, of course, though Hitch favored a "depressing" ending, to mirror the film's opening, where the detective locks his girl up and then meets a colleague in the washroom. They're washing their hands, men of the world. "Seeing that girl tonight?" the friend asks. "No, not tonight," says the hero, "I'll just be going home." Casual, macabre, official duty smothering private life—it's a sign of things to come.

Anyway, Charles Bennett and Benn Levy did the script from a play by Bennett. Jack Cox was the cameraman. Yet obviously, the fun and games was with microphone and earphones. Above all, Hitch fashioned a scene where the guilty girl (Ondra) comes home and the talk becomes a blur, with the word *knife* becoming sharper and more emphatic the more often it's used. It's no way to treat a good word, and a sign of a certain dottiness in Hitchcock. Far more interesting, Anny Ondra spoke English poorly, so Joan Barry stood just out of frame, speaking the lines that Anny was mouthing. Now, that is a real dream.

But the film is well worth seeing, if only because you see a master getting the hang of a new trick. The story is very silly, and nothing in the movie compares with Hitch's telling Ondra a dirty joke (it happened to be filmed) and seeing her reaction. That inadvertent intimacy was the way to go with sound, and Hitch soon caught on. With Sara Allgood, John Longden, Charles Paton, and Donald Calthrop.

The Black Stallion (1979)

There was a type of film once, far more common than it is now, that parents and children could see together in perfect company. That does not mean they see or feel the same things. For instance, as a little boy follows *The Black Stallion*, it is delightful that this crusty, fussy little man—his name is Henry Dailey—should materialize to train the great horse and its kid rider. He is such a character. Whereas the father (and the grandfather) are weeping gently over the Las Vegas chance and the rare suitability—that the actor playing Henry is Mickey Rooney.

It is 1946 (though it could be anytime). A boy, Alec (Kelly Reno), and his father (Hoyt Axton) are on a ship sailing the Atlantic. Also on board is a magnificent, high-strung horse, a black stallion, guarded by Arabs. The ship sinks. The boy and the horse wash up together on the shores of a desert island. They become friends. They are rescued and restored to Flushing, New York, where the boy's mother (Teri Garr) lives. The horse finds Henry. The dream develops that the stallion should race. He is taken up by radio hypester Jim Neville (Michael Higgins) and called "the Mystery Horse." There comes a big race where the stallion goes up against Cyclone and Sun Raider at Santa Anita.

The story, from a book by Walter Farley, was made into a script for executive producer Francis Coppola by Melissa Mathison, Jeanne Rosenberg, and William D. Witliff. Carroll Ballard was hired to direct—and Ballard is one of our great directors of wild life and boyish romance. The burnished photography is by Caleb Deschanel. Aurelio Crugnola and Earl Preston did the art direction. Robert Dalva edited. Carmine Coppola wrote the music. The producers were Fred Roos and Tom Sternberg. I do not always go so deep into credits, but Sternberg, a friend, once captivated my young son at the dinner table—a son who had to have the film's race sequence played every day—by showing him a statuette of Bucephalus that figures in *The Black Stallion*. Real people make movies.

You don't have to be Wittgenstein to see that horses are glorious. Or Mozart to know that a final race can settle every speck of drama available in the show. You don't have to be Tolstoy to see that a boy—or anyone—given a story at a certain age may be saved and set free by it, and at the same time charged with the deepest kind of responsibility to tell story. You don't have to be Degas to recognize that in nearly every sequence here there is emotion painted in light. An Olivier, I daresay, would stand back from this film and have to admit the raw genius of Mickey Rooney. I don't know what happened to Kelly Reno—I hope he's well and happy somewhere. And I certainly don't know what happened to Mickey Rooney—but I believe in him, and I think that's all he ever wanted. And the horse, Cass Ole, where is he? Riding in the sky with all the others—with Tom Mix's Tony, National Velvet, Sea Biscuit, and Barbaro.

As for me, you can have all the Indiana Jones films if I can keep thirty minutes of *Blade Runner.* I prefer, and find so much more pathos and interest in, Harrison Ford when he sometimes wonders not just whether his girl is a replicant but whether he, Rick Deckard, might be one, too. The place is Los Angeles. The time is 2019—not that long to wait now in a city desperate to escape the past. Deckard is hired to find and eliminate a group of escaped replicants—this in a place of immense skyscrapers, whispering holograms, endless rain, and a street level of trash, garbage, and spicy-noodle stands.

The story comes from Philip K. Dick's novel *Do Androids Dream of Electric Sheep?*, translated to the screen by Hampton Fancher and David Peoples. There are Dick experts who complain at things left out. I don't know Dick (you knew this already), and I love what is left in: not just the strange mix of tawdry and trash in the future world (production design by Lawrence G. Paull and Syd Mead), but the profound uncertainty as to which people have "integrity" and which do not. In the most direct sense, Deckard has to know or guess, and he lives with the mystery as to whether Rachael (Sean Young)—the inventor's daughter, and "special"—is someone he can love or may have to kill. (The vexed career of the glorious Ms. Young was never as well served as here.)

So the agent's grim progress by way of one replicant after another—Brion James, the staggering Joanna Cassidy, the amazing Daryl Hannah, and the truly noble Rutger Hauer—is not just his task, but seemingly the destruction of the most vivid people in the film. It's hard to ascribe all of this to a director as detached and versatile as Ridley Scott, yet this was the first occasion on which I felt that Scott is so good a director he could handle nearly anything. He is our Michael Curtiz—and we still don't quite know who Curtiz was.

Jordan Cronenweth did the photography, with much help, including Douglas Trumbull in charge of special effects. This was one of the first films where "special effects" seemed to be blooming in the credits list and invading the screen in ways that tested and deceived the eye. So it's nice to remember at the end that a few shots were donated by Stanley Kubrick from *The Shining.*

The word *clone* was not really current in 1982, despite the career success of Ronald Reagan. But *Blade Runner* was ahead of its time and as poignant as any sci-fi film I know just because of its sense of fragile identity. It is a superb piece of future-making and a film noir that bleeds over into tragedy. Ford has never been better—there was always a gruff reject in him waiting to be discovered—and Scott takes his hint from Deckard's gaze in creating a world that is soulless already as it sails into its future.

The cast is faultless, and mention should be made of Edward James Olmos, M. Emmet Walsh, and William Sanderson, and of Joe Turkel as Dr. Tyrell, the evil genius—wasn't he a barman somewhere, too?

Blade Runner was not nominated in the year *Gandhi* won Best Picture. That is the only mention of *Gandhi* in this book.

Blanche (1971)

The dream persists that the U.S.A. discovered animation and is still a rich source for such material—more and more, this parable seems like a paradigm of the history of film itself. So the first thing to say in this unusually broad entry is that American animation has already been reduced to the most circumscribed and unchallenging forms possible. *South Park* is an important recognition of depraved childhood in America, yet it takes pride in ultra-primitive animation. Pixar produces work of far less interest and takes a similar pride in "sophisticated" new animation techniques that are numb and barren next to the profuse, insane detail of *Bambi.* So *The Simpsons* can pass as standard American animation—which amounts to a severe shorthand technique that permits quick work but which is far less droll or touching than the films of Nick Park.

Of course, Park's work is sculptural, as solid and chewy as the contents of an old confectionery shop. As such, it alerts us to the potential—and the history—of animation as a way of working with objects, puppets, dolls, or parts of solid objects. It is the difference between a lovely set of cels, fluid with motion and duration, and a Joseph Cornell box that may come to life (or is it death?).

In these terms, animation is preeminently an Eastern European art, in which no one dares take it for granted that animation is material for children. I do not mean to attack or vilify children, but surely in America by 2008 we need no more warnings in the religious insistence on being brutish and youthful? It may be too late and thus the willful reduction of adult material or adult habits of thinking may prove far more thorough in ending our world than any amount of misplaced science.

Nevertheless, this is an entry that stands for the pursuit of grown-up animated films. As such it honors Jirí Trnka and the magic-lantern tradition as much as Jan Svankmajer and the Quay Brothers (please see *Street of Crocodiles*). But I am taking as my golden moment, the collaboration in Poland and then France of Jan Lenica and Walerian Borowczyk—above all films like *Once Upon a Time, Dom, Solitude,* and Borowczyk's solo film, *The Theater of Mr. and Mrs. Kabal,* a surrealist masterpiece.

Borowczyk is an extraordinary case—he died in 2006 in the ignominy of pornographic pictures (he did *Emmanuelle V*). But he is a genius, and I have chosen his live-action film, *Blanche*—set in a thirteenth-century world of castles and enclosing chambers, a fairy tale and a horror story (and starring his wife, Ligia Branice), but aglow with the eerie sensation that live action barely masks the skull and the boxlike framing of animation. It is obsessed with sex and freedom—like most great cinema—and it cannot take its eyes from the way in which these "living" images in film are dead and dying. But it is in great animation that we find the fulfilment of this paradox—that what we call "still life" is known in France as "nature morte."

Blow-Up (1966)

Forty years later, *Blow-Up* brings back so much: the way skirts went up a couple of inches a season; the certainty that sooner or later we were going to get to see pubic hair in a respectable film; the way in which kitsch was turning into antiques; the prolonged study of the Zapruder film; the cult of insolent-looking kids who were suddenly artists and photographers; and the certain knowledge that that street in London's Stockwell area was painted red long before Michelangelo Antonioni came along—because it was advertising a motorcar sales yard. So don't tell me *Blow-Up* is too cute for its own good. I know that it was there, the very moment the world changed. I would add that forty years later it remains a deadpan delight—witty, sexy, nasty, tricky, and one of the best movies to use in teaching film studies that anyone has ever made. Plus an Antonioni film that lets you laugh sometimes.

Thomas (David Hemmings) is a photographer and a cult in town. Poor soul, he's bored already shooting birds who'll do anything, or tramps in a halfway house. So he goes off to this darling park in suburbia (as long as I live I won't forget the breeze in the trees in that park), and there he photographs Vanessa Redgrave, deep in uneasy talk with a man. She sees him stealing her appearance, and she's very hot and bothered. She begs for the film. He tricks her. She comes back—takes off her top, smokes a joint, and rocks to the music—and again he tricks her. But he's interested now—like Jefferies in *Rear Window*—and in a long, sustained sequence he turns his pictures into a storyboard, and he begins to think he saw a murder committed in the park.

The film comes from a short story by Julio Cortázar, and the screenplay was done by Antonioni and Tonino Guerra, with Edward Bond touching up the English chat. Assheton Gorton did the sets, Herbie Hancock the music (with the Yardbirds), and Carlo Di Palma shot it. Jocelyn Rickards did the very cool clothes.

It's not as grave a film as the great trio (*L'Avventura, La Notte, L'Eclisse*). It's not as bluesy as *The Passenger.* But there are so many admirable things: the refusal to like Thomas or show any sympathy for him, the infatuation with appearance and the way it trains you to see, the chilly wit about what you can trust, and the ability to keep a genuine thriller going alongside a strange black comedy. When Antonioni went to America for 1970's *Zabriskie Point,* the gravity and foolishness upset the whole enterprise. But *Blow-Up* is a perfect bubble and a film of huge charm.

Granted that he was probably not directed, David Hemmings is dead right. Vanessa is bold and foolish and herself. Sarah Miles is in a daze and a crochet dress. The rest includes Peter Bowles, Veruschka (as the ultimate fuck me–photograph me model), Jill Kennington, and a whole line of birds all the way down to Jane Birkin (she's the one with the pubic hair).

The Blue Angel (1930)

Having worked successfully with Emil Jannings in Hollywood on *The Last Command,* Josef von Sternberg was requested to go to Berlin for Ufa to introduce the great German actor to sound. It was a lofty invitation, not an ejection from Hollywood, and it surely denoted some warmth between director and actor. And yet. The vehicle was *Professor Unrat,* a novel by Heinrich Mann, published in 1905 and of far larger scope than the film they would make. In the book, the girl has a child from a previous lover. That helps explain the marriage. And then, when the professor is humiliated, he becomes a gambler and a politician fighting society. It might make a good movie.

Sternberg was clear, however, and Heinrich Mann was his ally: They would tell the story of the humiliation of the professor. I think in hindsight it's fair to say that Sternberg had in mind an exposé of not just Teutonic grandeur and pretension but the hubris of one kind of acting. He meant to crush hallowed silence. And the key step in that process was casting Marlene Dietrich as Rosa-Frohlick, or Lola-Lola as she is called. According to Sternberg, Dietrich was one of those who believed she could not do the part and might ruin the film. I doubt that. I suspect a bond and a glance had tied director and actress together quite early. She was soon his accomplice. Along the way, the title *Professor Unrat* gave way to *The Blue Angel,* the name of the cabaret, and Sternberg's intuition that the moody gaze of a chanteuse could pierce the bubble of great acting was proved.

At every step, Sternberg gently but firmly reproached Jannings for overacting and allowed Dietrich to absorb attention. Professor Rath could have a great scene—but then Lola-Lola drew up her thigh. Dietrich is heavy here, and her tawdry costumes don't do much to glamorize her. What's more, she is hardly ever given close-ups or the shots Sternberg would perfect with her at Paramount. But her louche, ironic attitude is years ahead of Jannings's humbug. So we become accomplices in the professor's degradation.

Carl Zuckmayer and Karl Vollmöller have their names on the script, but I suspect it was Sternberg. Günther Rittau was the photographer. Otto Hunte did the sets, some of them quite pointedly expressionist. And Friedrich Hollander was taken on for the songs—he had played piano for another contender for the lead role, Lucie Mannheim.

Even then, the Germans didn't quite get it. Sternberg had advised Paramount to sign Dietrich, but Ufa had an option. They let it go, even after they had seen the picture! So then she signed with Paramount. Joe went home first, but Marlene gave him a book to read on the boat, *Amy Jolly* (the basis of his film *Morocco*). She stayed for the premiere, received huge ovations, and took the next boat. With sound it had become possible to look at someone else busy emoting and just consider their folly in silence, with maybe the hint of a sigh. Underplaying was born, and with it the quality of experienced smartness. The monotonous virgins of silent film vanished like the wicked witch of the West when she got wet.

Blue Velvet (1986)

Once upon a time in a town called Lumberton (and it was a very nice town where the fireman waved as his truck went past), there was this boy, Jeffrey Beaumont (Kyle MacLachlan), and Jeffrey's father had been struck down in the prime of life—as can happen. And on a piece of open ground in the town, Jeffrey found an ear, cut off from the rest of a human being. He gave it to Detective Williams (George Dickerson), like a good boy. And the detective's daughter, Sandy (Laura Dern), told Jeffrey her dark imagining that it might have to do with Dorothy Vallens (Isabella Rossellini), the mysterious nightclub singer. So Jeffrey, like a boy detective, and like a boy, stole into Ms. Vallens's apartment and watched her and waited for her. And she was ready to punish him when she found out, but she gave herself to him instead. . . . Dorothy sings "Blue Velvet," and she has lost a son. And Jeffrey loves her suddenly so much (though not in the way he loves Sandy) that he will do anything to help her. But then there is Frank Booth (Dennis Hopper), who already protects and menaces Dorothy, so there is hardly room for Jeffrey. And Frank has been stricken out of a dream in the way Jeffrey's father was struck down.

What's a boy to do when it's 1986 already and the fairy-tale world of Lumberton is so close to the most alarming horror film you were never allowed to see?

Blue Velvet was David Lynch's breakthrough film, whether he wanted it that way or not. All of a sudden, the art-school strategies of *Eraserhead* were erased and in their place—as naked as Rossellini at the end of her tether—was Freudian casebook served up with chocolate-fudge surreal toppings. With many other Lynch films before and since, it was not possible to explain the obscure inward action. But with *Blue Velvet* it was impossible not to try. It was as if Luis Buñuel had made *Un Chien Andalou* in such a way that it lodged directly into the public consciousness. Jeffrey was defending everything we had, and Jeffrey was a brave kid. But he was just a stripling in a dark place where eternal ogres strode and sang our favorite songs. This was Beowulf at the International House of Pancakes.

And it emerged seemingly from nowhere, with the blind imprimatur of Dino de Laurentiis—not just a vision, not just a masterpiece, but as American as *Casablanca* (though less safe). Lynch wrote it and directed with an implacable assurance that he has never quite matched since. Frederick Elmes photographed it like a new Grimm. Alan Splet did the vital sound design, with so much poisoned breathing. Patricia Norris did the production design. And Angelo Badalamenti wrote one of the enduring movie scores.

The human figures are indelible. There does not seem to be any acting in sight. But as well as those named already, there is Hope Lange, Dean Stockwell (don't let anyone tell you about Dean Stockwell—just see him), Brad Dourif, Jack Nance, and Priscilla Pointer.

Bob & Carol & Ted & Alice (1969)

There they were, four in the bed. It was one of the essential self-publicizing images of the late 1960s—like Goldie Hawn in bikini and body paint on *Laugh-In* or the LOVE dress on the cover of *The Medium Is the Massage* (Marshall McLuhan). Though, really, when you think about it, that nervously merry quartet is a harbinger of the early seventies and of teenage sexual liberty spreading to the thirty-plus generation.

Long before Photoshop, the four are sufficiently shy to look as if they might have been put there one at a time—Elliott Gould, as if caught unawares; Natalie Wood, hoping to say, Well, I don't see the fuss in all this, everyone knows I've been around; Robert Culp, wearing beads and sturdily not looking at the camera; and Dyan Cannon, in a dressing gown, hunched up, as if a mouse (or Cary Grant) could be chewing her toes. No, they're not having, or thinking of having, the most abandoned time, no matter that they all four feel the duty to do so. They're just hoping the picture won't outlast them. Of course, it will.

If you're like me, you may not remember much more about the movie than that shot. But as I study it, I feel the thing I always like in Paul Mazursky, the director: his kindness, or the wry good nature that could see caution and abandonment going hand in hand. He wrote the picture with his regular cowriter, Larry Tucker, and it's full of nuanced talk and behavior—a little like a Jules Feiffer cartoon brought to life, though without Feiffer's sense of the abyss being so close at hand.

And at the same time, for people who were thirty in 1970 (and who therefore felt in grave danger of missing the whole thing, the con called free love), this was a film that probably coaxed reluctance into a few absent-minded swappings and a generally looser sense of sex. But Mazursky was wise enough as a dramatist to know that only a part of us wants that looseness. The rest cries out for security, habit, and ownership. So in the history of sophisticated sexual comedy (which comes to an end not long after this film), *Bob & Carol et cetera* is a nice, enjoyable portrait of the tricks we play on ourselves.

In another way, of course, the poster still serves as a dead end. Yes, Hollywood could now put four more or less naked and very attractive people in the same bed. It could even get some of its stars to go at it. But the movies are at a loss when it comes to such wrestling—we don't know what the minds are thinking; we surmise that the whole sport is a fake. So, really, four in a bed with a little bit more showing than Ms. Wood was prepared for (she wears a Pentagon-issue bra) is fine and dandy, but the people have got to keep talking to be interesting. And to judge by our movies now, people are deaf when they have sex.

Bob le Flambeur (1956)

The title means "Bob the High Roller," and it promises a famous and delightful film, albeit one that goes a touch too sweet in its ending.

Bob is in his fifties, and Roger Duchesne makes him a rather shabby-looking Burt Lancaster (the picture would play nicely with *Atlantic City*). He has been a thief in the past and done time, and now he survives as a gambler. Which means he is hard pressed. He lives in one of the ugliest apartments ever filmed—but Sacré Coeur looms above it. He picks up a Bardot-like girl (Isabel Corey), but never complains when his young male protégé takes her over. There's a café owner he set up in the past: She adores him, but Bob's a gambler, so he deflects her signs of availability and waits for the big break. One day he gets the idea to rob the casino at Deauville.

This is Jean-Pierre Melville making one of the pictures that inspired the New Wave. There is an opening tribute to Paris, so full of gray vistas that it seems like *Les 399 Coups*—why not? Both are photographed by the great Henri Decaë. The atmosphere of Pigalle at dawn is matchless, and this love of the city actually helps explain what keeps Bob floating. He is kind, honorable, sad, and deeply romanticized, whether Melville knows it or not. For much of the film, this bargain is acceptable and very entertaining, but as the Deauville caper reaches its climax, the different tones are jarring. You see, Bob the bad gambler has his greatest night at the tables waiting for the robbery's 5 a.m. deadline. So he has cartons of money to go in the trunk of the police car that will carry him away. Enough for a good lawyer? someone wonders. Enough to sue the cops, he promises.

At that point, I fear, pleasure chills a little, and one cannot help but remember Melville's allegiance to John Huston's equally gray but truly sour *Asphalt Jungle*, where when the job goes wrong everyone ends up badly. My own feeling is that the ending needed to be worked out more carefully in script form and then shot more slowly. It feels rushed, and too close to a fairy story. I can easily imagine the ghost of Melville turning to me with Bob's pained face and saying, "Come on—a fellow needs a hit now and then!"

This is true, and it's always hard to challenge the sight of a gambler winning on film—after all, this is a medium about desire and dreaming. But Melville can be a great artist, and this film is so good for 80 percent of the game that it deserves better. The relationship with the cop is marvelously done. Howard Vernon is wonderfully laconic in a couple of scenes as the moneybags. I love the black jazz band in the nightclub. And Melville the tragic fights a long battle with us and himself over whether we're ever going to get a proper look at Isabel Corey's breasts. (Rest assured.)

Body and Soul (1947)

In the years just after the Second World War, the boxing picture seemed like a way of using a recognized genre to make fresh, daring statements about man's inhumanity to man, thus *The Set-Up*, *Champion*, and *Body and Soul*. The action in the ring was more brutal and realistic than ever before, and there were stories from *Body and Soul* of James Wong Howe on roller skates, using a handheld camera to get into the action. But, in addition, on this film, at least, the idea of boxing was taken up by some brave left-wing artists of real talent to dismantle a corrupt society. And so *Body and Soul* was a work from the new company Enterprise Productions, and an opportunity for the screenwriter Abraham Polonsky to give voice to his forebodings about what money was doing to a society.

Polonsky told the story of how he was visiting Enterprise (in the persons of producer Robert Roberts and John Garfield) and mentioned that a friend had just given up on a biopic about boxer Barney Ross, Jewish and an imprisoned drug addict. On the spur of the moment Polonsky sketched out how it could be done, and he was hired. It would be the story of a man who trades his soul to be a boxing champion. It was a crucial advance on Clifford Odets's *Golden Boy* (should he box or play the violin?). In *Body and Soul*, the question is whether the hero is a sportsman or a licensed killer.

Robert Rossen came on board as director, and it's fascinating that there was a clash over how the film should end. Rossen wanted the logic to persist. The boxer, Charlie Davis, should be killed by the gangsters after he has broken their deal to fix a fight. It was Polonsky who wanted and wrote the rat defiance of Charlie, holding on to his girl and challenging the mob, "So what are you going to do? Everybody dies!" Quite soon, this dispute was caught up in blacklisting issues, but it really had been Polonsky who felt impelled to give what he called a happy, proletarian ending in which the bum does the right thing.

You can feel these tensions throughout the film, along with the urge in a new company to have a hit and/or to make a trenchant, radical picture. Polonsky was a very good scriptwriter, but Rossen had been a writer, too, and a Communist, and I think it is the direction now that feels most daring. Above all, this is in Garfield himself, who has given up the rough kid of the 1930s for a real inner hardness. And you see it in his relations with his mother, the foreboding, gaunt Anne Revere, and in the girlfriend, Peg (very well played by Lilli Palmer).

The rest of the cast includes Hazel Brooks, William Conrad, Joseph Pevney, Canada Lee, Lloyd Gough, and Art Smith—all very good. Francis Lyon won the Oscar for editing, and nominations went to Garfield and Polonsky. It stands overall as boxing for real—with the baroque expressionism of *Raging Bull* still to come.

Bonjour Tristesse (1958)

Otto Preminger had discovered Jean Seberg when she was an inexperienced seventeen-year-old from Iowa for his film of *Saint Joan*. In fact, Seberg does a good job in that film but could not save it from seeming talky and static. The story then goes that, rather than give up on his own reckless choice, he put her in *Bonjour Tristesse,* which "everybody" regarded as a disaster. Everybody? Well, the darkest view on the film came from screenwriter Arthur Laurents, who bet Preminger that she would never be any good and lived to collect. If you've seen *Bonjour Tristesse* and have some doubts about the usually very smart Laurents, ask yourself how it was that Seberg suddenly became riveting in *À Bout de Souffle,* enchanting in a run of French films, and magnificent in *Lilith.*

Bonjour Tristesse flopped at a time when Preminger had little training for flops, and so the actress took a lot of the blame. Whereas the rather brittle Françoise Sagan novel makes a remarkable film, about a teenage girl who grows up as she destroys her playboy father's relationship with perhaps the first mature woman of his life. Shot by Georges Périnal in an intriguing mixture of black and white (the present) and color (the past), *Bonjour Tristesse* is a rare picture of a spoiled child who infects the world with her malign selfishness. It is a very challenging part, and there are scenes of Seberg regarding herself in a mirror that take one straight back to the power of Preminger's *Angel Face.* Indeed, in many ways it is the same character, and the Viennese director shows himself an expert at pathological behavior.

The setup is the more intriguing in that we become thoroughly caught up in the romance between Raymond (David Niven) and Anne (Deborah Kerr). Preminger makes humane and touching characters out of these people—and far better than the book—manages to show their fondness for Cecile (Seberg), no matter the damage she does to them.

Set in Paris and the Riviera, and filmed there and in London in CinemaScope, this is one more of those films that put the lie to the canard that Scope was ill suited to intimate space. In addition, a great deal is gained from the melancholy score by Georges Auric and the designs of Roger Furse. As so often with Preminger, the romantic attitudes of the characters are beautifully summed up in their use of space and movement; indeed, the link to *Angel Face* is borne out in the resemblance to the earlier *Daisy Kenyon* and *Fallen Angel.* Far from heavy-handed, Preminger sometimes showed a lightness and a sympathy with the woman's point of view that remind one of Max Ophuls.

The supporting cast includes Mylène Demongeot, Geoffrey Horne, Walter Chiari, Martita Hunt, Roland Culver, Jean Kent, Juliette Gréco (who sings the title song against Saul Bass titles), David Oxley, and Elga Andersen.

Les Bonnes Femmes (1960)

In the first flood of the French New Wave, it was not easy to place director Claude Chabrol. I'm not sure if it has become any easier over the years. With Eric Rohmer, he was the author of a striking book on Hitchcock. In print, he had made fun of big subjects and Stanley Kramerism—of generalization. Yet here was *Les Bonnes Femmes (The Girls),* apparently a cross section of young women in Paris in 1960 as seen in a quartet of women working, or waiting, in an electrical appliance store. Yet as time goes by, *Les Bonnes Femmes* seems one of the most mysterious and involving films of that heady period. It may even be a film that haunts Chabrol—seventy-six now, very active, but perhaps a creature of habit. And whereas *Les Bonnes Femmes* is very much about lives on the edge of a prison called habit, its mercurial, detached eye is acidic and new still.

Chabrol had made a couple of films already, *Le Beau Serge* and *Les Cousins*—strong, tidy, rather moral (almost Rohmer films). *Les Bonnes Femmes* was startlingly different: Its women were all pretty, or more, but they were foolish, limited, and small-minded, without any hint of condescension or malice in the filming. They were girls with their dreams. Jane (Bernadette Lafont) can't see beyond guys. Rita (Lucile Saint-Simon) is so set on marriage, she doesn't see that her fiancé is an idiot. Ginette (Stéphane Audran) has a dream of being a singer, but the public act is something she wants to keep secret. And Jacqueline (Clotilde Joano) dreams of a dark stranger—and gets him (Mario David).

Chabrol wrote the script with Paul Gégauff, and no one is romanticized in any way. Sometimes there is a hint of the girls as feeble insects, but that is always offset by the fond ways they are photographed or perceived—by Henri Decaë. And of course Paris, or the passing street, is very much a part of this film, even if Chabrol's Paris is closer to Jacques Rivette's than François Truffaut's.

The four also make a circle, a *ronde,* and the film is content to see the wheel turn without passing judgment—except to say that women, without a god, are desperately deprived in their choices. Not one shot is feminist here, yet in hindsight you can see where Chabrol's feminism came from. There isn't really a decent or worthwhile man in view! Or one without violence.

Later on, Chabrol took up other guises: He could be Hitchcock, he could be a connoisseur of inner subtleties, he could be sardonic and even a little grotesque. But none of those moods really matches the glassy slippage in *Les Bonnes Femmes,* the way Chabrol seems to say, Just let a little time pass, and beauty will age just as placidity will be surprised. It's a film Robert Bresson might have made if he had been more willing to admit to a liking for light, camera moves, and the look on a woman's face. Of course, in 1960 the film was called unpleasant and misanthropic—it's neither. But it sails close to that cold wind. And it's more disturbing than anyone can explain.

Bonnie and Clyde (1967)

This is one of the most influential films ever made in America, in that it took an archaic genre—the 1930s gangster film—and reinvigorated it for the moods of the sixties. It was an antiestablishment picture, a love story, and a ballad for sexual fulfillment, a parable about getting people to take notice of you and being famous in America, and still it was a gangster picture. It was reaching out for everything it could get, and nothing was quite the same afterward. Sex and violence, the willingness of Miss Bonnie Parker to give good head, and the presidential smirk on Warren Beatty's face were all smeared together in a strange triumph, all the stranger in that it was only by being shot to pieces that these two lovers really got it on together.

At the outset, two young writers, Robert Benton and David Newman, had been so impressed by the new French films that they wanted to write an American picture in which the mood changed as swiftly as it did in Truffaut. Benton was from Texas, so he knew the Bonnie and Clyde story. The pair offered their first script to François Truffaut—he doubted that his English was good enough. Then it went to Jean-Luc Godard (think of his *Pierrot le Fou*). Only then did Warren Beatty hear about it, and he knew it was right for his debut as a producer. He brought Arthur Penn on board, and when the picture went off on location to Texas, Beatty enlisted Robert Towne to do rewrites all night. Beyond that, I think you would have had to be there to say where it all came from.

But Penn was an electric director of actors then, and passionate with violence. Beatty saw the film as a story about celebrity. Benton and Newman had wanted C. W. Moss (Michael J. Pollard) as the third in the outlaw bed, and while that troubled Beatty, he liked the notion that Clyde was sexually squeamish. And when in doubt, they gave the picture a violent gear shift, so laughter came so close on the heels of violence that the audience was captivated. Of course, Warner Brothers was bemused. It thought the film was a disaster. And on a first opening it did poorly. But Pauline Kael came in with a passionate plea, and the film took off like a rocket in London. Truly, the novelty was so great that the audience had to feel their way in.

Penn shot *Bonnie and Clyde* as skirmishes, indoors and out. There's not a flat or plain scene, though the mood is on its private switchback and the mounting sense of doom is scary and deserved. The film felt like an escaped wild animal, and in the finale you feel the beast being put down and getting laid.

Beatty and Dunaway cling to each other like Fred and Ginger. Michael Pollard was inspired casting. Gene Hackman and Estelle Parsons are Punch and Judy. But don't forget Gene Wilder and Evans Evans, Denver Pyle and Dub Taylor. Dede Allen did the brilliant editing job. Burnett Guffey, an old-timer, delivered fabulous, sensual color photography. Theadora van Runkle did costumes that became mass market. Dean Tavoularis made his debut as a great art director. And the wheels on the cars went *plink, plank, plunk* to that banjo music.

Boogie Nights (1997)

Perhaps the first point to make is how remarkable that it took the "respectable" motion picture business so long to try the shadow world of pornography as a subject. Then recollect that in Paul Thomas Anderson's brilliant and very poised film there is hardly any "real" sex—I mean the kind of happy, relieved, self-discovering sex that couples tend to have in most of our movies. In other words, the manufacturing of industrial sex has eclipsed the authentic thing. That is a truth with one exception, and it's crucial: in the midst of the porn production, Little Bill's wife seems utterly unimpressed by the hard-core celluloid job. She just wants a small closet where she can rut away with anyone and everyone. And when Little Bill glimpses that, he is devastated by the horror and kills everyone involved—himself included.

What are we to make of that, especially those of us who have unmistakably used movie sex as a vital part of our sentimental education? It sometimes seems to me that one of the most fascinating things about sex in the movies—and no one can deny the creepy affinity that exists—has been to educate a large public in how to regard and exercise sex in an age when its widespread use became not just possible but a source of enjoyment (and indeed, in some cases the epitome of all pleasures). And so, for the period up until the ruin of censorship, sexuality was, like horror, a thing all the more potent for being so reticently shown. And then moviemaking (the respectable pursuit) had to ask itself what it was doing when Amber Waves and Dirk Diggler (or figures like them) could do it in the long shot and the close-up in the same half hour, with little more feeling than that of vague family fondness (and that rather distant warmth is maybe the most shocking and disturbing thing in Anderson's film).

So this was an amazing choice of material, long before one faced the actual depiction of life at the Jack Horner studio. And while Anderson shows the virtual disintegration of the Horner approach, and the savage re-education of most of its witless members, still the film leaves open the larger question: is sex a real physical thing, or is it always in the head?

All of which omits to say how very funny so much of *Boogie Nights* is—the sexual smoothness of Rollergirl (Heather Graham), for instance, is entirely human yet lodged in the annals of satire. And Mark Wahlberg is so undeveloped in most other respects that his humungous proportions in one part amount to a cartoon triumph of comedy. Burt Reynolds is sublime as Horner—it is a very telling sign of the passing of one cultural era to another that Warren Beatty declined that role! For the rest, the Anderson stock company was taking shape: Julianne Moore (more stunned than stunning as Amber), John C. Reilly, William H. Macy, Philip Baker Hall, Philip Seymour Hoffman. (Does the guy only hire triple-decker names?) No, there's Don Cheadle, Alfred Molina (terrifying), Robert Ridgely, and several others.

Some films are just for seeing, and some are for talking about. You could run a seminar on the nature of film after *Boogie Nights*.

Born Yesterday (1950)

I don't mean to suggest that *Born Yesterday* alone could protect the Constitution from those who mean it harm. Still, it is hard to imagine within the confines of, say, *The Godfather* or *The Sopranos* a Billie Dawn–like character, whose sharp memory and developed conscience could bring down a Harry Brock and his corruption. After all, the movies have taught us to think of Billie Dawns as corpses found on urban wasteland in the opening sequence of foreboding pictures. So it's worth stressing that *Born Yesterday*, the play by Garson Kanin, was a triumph in the age of HUAC.

The play opened in February 1946 and ran for 1,642 performances. Harry Brock was played by Paul Douglas, Billie by Judy Holliday (after Jean Arthur backed out), and her teacher Paul Verrall by Gary Merrill.

Harry Cohn bought the play for Columbia, with Holliday set for the lead and George Cukor directing. A script was done by Albert Mannheimer, but everyone involved agreed that it hurt the play. So Kanin was hired on to doctor it, on the understanding that he would receive neither pay nor credit (which helps you see that Brock was Cohn). In fact, Kanin managed to open up the one-set play and arranged several scenes in and around Washington, D.C., to good effect. Broderick Crawford was natural casting for Harry after his success in *All the King's Men*, and William Holden was given the part of Paul—thus, in 1950, Holden had two films in which it is his delicate task to get divas to see the world straight (the other was *Sunset Blvd.*).

Of course, it is Holliday's film, and Cukor and Kanin (with Ruth Gordon) had prepared the way for this with Judy's scene-stealing debut in *Adam's Rib*. Yes, Holliday was a comedienne, but Cukor always understood that that quaver in her voice was real feeling—and might even be pain. It's tempting to compare her with Marilyn Monroe, who might have done a decent job as Billie in the hands of a Cukor. But Marilyn's emotionalism was vague. Holliday was always pitch perfect. She is a little like Meryl Streep in her accuracy, and both can be accused of overcalculation. But what's clear is that an intelligent if muddled woman existed behind Holliday's terrific acting, whereas Marilyn had a way of doing "dumb" to ward off any penetrating assaults (or the question of what was inside her). I think she might have grown tedious in *Born Yesterday*, whereas Holliday always understood the play.

The film is still a delight, despite some obviousness once the setup is digested. And it works because the underdog is so appealing. Holliday won the Oscar for Best Actress, defeating not just Bette Davis and Anne Baxter in *All About Eve*, but Gloria Swanson in *Sunset Blvd.* It was as if the Academy had asked itself, Which would you prefer in elected office?

There's a remake, not just depressing and stale but without any sense of the politics as real issues. Melanie Griffith was reasonable as Billie, but John Goodman and Don Johnson were helpless as the guys.

Le Boucher (1970)

Have you noticed that butchers regard it as their right, and even their duty, to flirt lightly with their women customers? It is as if the cutting of bloodied flesh is too potent or magical to be accomplished without a word. The husband has provided, of course, but the woman will cook the meat, converting rawness to tenderness. And the butcher—the man whose apron is heavy with blood—has the special cut just for her. It was a dangerous exchange, and in our food markets now the meat is precut, wrapped in plastic. It needs only to be taken away. Anonymity has done it all. But I remember butcher shops where there was sawdust on the floor and the handsome butchers had a private word for every woman.

This is the background to Claude Chabrol's magnificent and mysterious *Le Boucher*, set in the savage beauty of France's Dordogne region, a part of the world where food is taken very seriously. There is a schoolteacher, Hélène (Stéphane Audran). She certainly seems omniscient enough to be a great teacher, but she is not local. She wears Parisian makeup. She smokes in the street. She is quite content—I mean, she has no apparent neuroses—but she is from a more sophisticated place. And she knows that the butcher Popaul (Jean Yanne) is in love with her to such an extent that he is bound to betray himself.

Popaul was a soldier once, and the butchery he was exposed to then has wounded him. It requires some steady bloodletting. You might assume that his work satisfies the urge, but no; Popaul is a killer, a murderer, and like a loyal dog, he almost lays clues about his guilt at the feet of his mistress. She knows he is the killer—doesn't she know everything?—and yet she has discounted the possibility that he might have to kill her. Or is she perhaps tempting fate? Does she look at him with that serene insolence to see if his knife could carve her?

Le Boucher is proof enough of Claude Chabrol's intelligence, and his ability to let psychic depths unfold on the strength of very little action. It is only the first step of awareness to say that these two people need each other—that they are in love. But what is the balance of the desire? And is the film a tragedy or a work of ironic aplomb? It's a picture to be seen repeatedly over the years, one that trains us to observe carving style and table manners. There's a way in which it makes Hitchcock—the obvious model or point of reference—seem rather coarse.

It's not that Chabrol was always this good, but the point should be made that he is an expert, chronic entertainer and a very intelligent man. I think his work is variable, along with the degree of his caring. But somehow on those hot, dusky evenings in the Dordogne, when Stéphane Audran was still his wife, he knew he was at the brink of something wonderful and monstrous.

Boudu Sauvé des Eaux (1932)

At the end of Jean Renoir's *La Chienne,* Legrand the failed lover and successful painter saunters away: He will not be blamed for killing his Lulu, but he cannot take credit for the pictures that are starting to sell. Allow that a year, or a generation, passes—perhaps it's only a day. Now he is Boudu, gentle, amiable, yet dangerous, Paris's subtle answer to King Kong, a tramp, or a bearded leaf carried by the wind or the current. Every poetic tie is possible, because Boudu is once more Michel Simon at the height of his creative power.

In many ways, the mood of *La Chienne* has simply moved a notch or two up on the social scale. We are in the household of Monsieur Lestingois (Charles Granval), on the banks of the Seine. He is a bookseller, with a wife (Marcelle Hainia), a housemaid (Sévérine Lerczinska), and time to watch a splendid hulk of social rejection, Boudu, who then opts to enter the Seine. Boudu seems mildly suicidal, though he has an ineffable, unsinkable buoyancy that makes drowning seem very unlikely.

In a splendid clash of heroism and awkwardness, Lestingois rescues Boudu and takes him into his home. This is exactly the kind of good-natured disaster to which Lestingois is prone. The same is true, I think, of Renoir as a whole, with whom motive or intention so seldom comes home straight and true. Irony, chance, accident are all prepared to do their creative mixing. It follows that there is a wryness, or ambivalence, in the film's view of benevolence or the social responsibility that foreshadows politics. Renoir was only five years away from his Popular Front period, but Boudu is a warning note about making your charitable attitude to a tramp too earnest.

Boudu is savage, priapic, uncontrollable. It's not just that he will seduce wife or maid—and Simon now is as naturally lecherous as he was shy in *La Chienne.* He will butcher his new friend's books. He will polish his shoes on the tablecloth. He threatens madness in the tranquil foolishness of the Lestingois household. He has to go back to the river. Long before Renoir's journey to India, it is clear that Boudu is the river, the eternal fluidity that is a metaphor for passing time in which all anecdote and morality swim along.

The camera moves from side to side, it gazes through dusty space, it links one room with another, and it tracks the back-and-forth of meetings. Film by film, you feel Renoir's camera like a pen that is shaping the prose of classical cinema, the way that seeing equals description. That is why these very small pictures, sketches shot off the cuff, remain as fresh and piercing as great short stories. The American remake of *Boudu, Down and Out in Beverly Hills,* has so many of the elements in the original, just none of the air that holds them together and not a glimmer of the lyrical sadness that knows Boudu is, quite simply, not civilized.

The Boy with Green Hair (1948)

In the postwar breakup, they started making pictures that were like fairy tales. You could call *The Boy with Green Hair* a fable (it came from a magazine story by Betsy Beaton), in which green equals Red: Before the film started production, its producer, Adrian Scott, was subpoenaed by the House Committee on Un-American Activities, and its two writers, Ben Barzman and Alfred Lewis Levitt, were named in proceedings. Dore Schary invited Joseph Losey to come to RKO to make the picture when Losey was at M-G-M doing very little.

Losey set to work and would later blame himself for letting the metaphor grow. In the original script, the green hair stood for racial prejudice, but as they developed the movie, its message became inflated until it stood for a vision of peace. At that point it took on aspects of being a kind of children's crusade venture. Indeed, RKO sold it as that after their new owner, Howard Hughes, had done his best to iron out the message.

So it's a story set in small-town America, a place Losey associated with the bigotry of the country. He had wanted to go on location—even to his own hometown of La Crosse, Wisconsin—but the studio said they couldn't afford that. Losey did manage to keep Ben Barzman on the set, but the loss of Scott was severe: He was regarded as a great producer-writer after *Crossfire*. He was replaced as producer by Stephen Ames, a businessman and a Technicolor stockholder. But that worked out well, for Ames supported Losey in every situation where he wanted Technicolor to try something they weren't used to.

George Barnes did the photography, and the sets were by Albert d'Agostino and Ralph Berger, though Losey used John Hubley to consult in the overall design. Losey had wanted to use 16 mm and blow it up to 35 mm, and that would have come close to halving the budget (about $900,000, eventually). As it is, the picture looks the way it should—like a kid's vision of the world.

The studio added a song to the sound track—"Nature Boy," written by Eden Ahbez—and while a Nat King Cole version of it became a hit, the song did little to clarify the film's subject. You still meet people who saw the film as kids and are still wondering why the boy's hair turned green!

Dean Stockwell was hired as the boy, and though Losey found him difficult and suspicious, he gives a fine performance. Losey had wanted the Irish music-hall performer Albert Sharp as Gramps, but the studio had Pat O'Brien with nothing to do, so he got the job. In other lead parts, RKO supplied Barbara Hale and Robert Ryan. Ben Lyon's son, Richard, got a part, and the cast also included Walter Catlett, Regis Toomey, Charles Meredith, David Clarke, Billy Sheffield, Dwayne Hickman, and the young Russ Tamblyn.

Brazil (1985)

In the midst of Ronald Reagan's America, Universal—*Brazil*'s American distributor—gave every indication of being unwilling to release this huge, untidy satire on a crushed state. A battle ensued in which critics Kenneth Turan and then Jack Matthews fought for the film, and its director, Terry Gilliam, went on many American talk shows (sometimes with the earnest Robert De Niro) to speak on its behalf. The subsequent book by Matthews is well worth reading as a portrait of studio indecision. But of course Universal had to be careful: Though it only shared in the investment with Fox (distributor in the rest of the world), the movie had cost $15 million at least. And movie companies are so fastidious.

Well, the fuss has passed, and *Brazil* now stands as the prototypical example of the tricky career of Terry Gilliam. Yes, he had done other things before, like the Monty Python films and *Time Bandits* (which was a hit). But *Brazil* was a departure and probably the most personal picture he had done to date. It was a *1984*-ish fantasy about a country—Brazil, or what you will—in which antique industrial mechanics had come to the aid of modern thought control in a most ingenious and alarming way. In turn, this was a very good vehicle for Gilliam's teeming visual imagination, but an inadvertent demonstration of his problems with narrative.

It was not an easy picture to set up. But Gilliam fell in with producer Arnon Milchan and writer Tom Stoppard and, despite fundamental differences of approach, they got a screenplay—which Gilliam then offered to Charles McKeown to be improved (or to spell out those things that Gilliam "understood" about the material but had difficulty conveying).

Twenty years later, after a series of Gilliam pictures in which the same problem of communication has shown through, one has to be a little wary of taking sides. *Brazil* is a visionary picture, often hilarious and frightening. Could it have been more coherent and more forceful? I think the answer is yes, and I don't necessarily accept the argument that "coherence" is always going to impede or hobble "vision." Terry Gilliam, I suspect, is an artist whose glorious talent may work best when he is executing everything himself. Put him down in a collaborative medium, and his chronic problems will recur. You can take the side of the artist or the system—or you can understand that one of the most severe tests in moviemaking is communicating clearly with strangers. That local test is a harbinger of the great directorial challenge: getting audiences to feel what you see.

But *Brazil* is a major work, in which inventive exuberance is often at odds with the filmmaker's wish to make grave and tragic points. Gilliam loves to do "art"—it's like exercise, and it may be that he needs a very firm controller. The film is photographed by Roger Pratt, with production design by Norman Garwood (though I think a lot of its beauty comes from Gilliam, who sought out antique industrial buildings and turned them to modern use). The cast includes Jonathan Pryce, De Niro, Katherine Helmond, Ian Holm, Bob Hoskins, Michael Palin (brilliant), Ian Richardson, Peter Vaughan, Kim Greist, and Jim Broadbent.

Breathless (1960)

And so, after five short films and nearly a decade of writing on film, Jean-Luc Godard came to make his first feature film with a studied, aggressive, and dismissive new ease. Notably, he came a little after François Truffaut and Claude Chabrol, and he had both of them on board as helpers and guarantors of talent. But he had a producer, too, Georges de Beauregard, who said he was ready to help. So Godard cashed in on a promise, and Truffaut wrote a four-page outline about a young Frenchman and an American girlfriend who had had a summer together and shot a motorcycle policeman. With four pages from Truffaut (whose *Les 400 Coups* had been a hit at Cannes in the spring of 1959), Beauregard put up 500,000 francs (about $48,000). In return, he got Chabrol the job of "artistic supervisor." A quarter of that budget was immediately passed over to Jean Seberg, the Otto Preminger star who had lingered in Paris after *Bonjour Tristesse* and who had married a young Frenchman, François Moreuil. Jean-Paul Belmondo came after that, and must have been paid far less—the first reason for his savage scowl.

The two are like comic-book icons. He is razor thin and deeply tanned, in odd assorted clothes, smoking all the while, yet not inhaling—he leaves clouds of smoke wherever he goes. He is Bogartian, stopping at mirrors to perfect the mannerisms of a star only two years dead, but his lifestyle is that of the Bogart before the images he adores. For Michel Poiccard, alias Laszlo Kovacs, is impulsive, wanton, urchinlike, and given to antic, sensationalist behavior and runic, intellectual commentary on himself. Driving recklessly in the South of France, he finds a gun in the car he has stolen and shoots a cop. It is all very casual: We see the deed in the dappled, late-afternoon light, but it feels as remote as a column filler in an old newspaper.

Then he's in Paris with her—"New York Herald Tribune," Patricia Franchini cries out, cropped, flirty, tee shirt and jeans, the American doll, with false eyelashes, perfect makeup, and Berlitz French. He tells her she is a tramp in words she doesn't understand, and it is clear immediately that a Godardian misogyny—a dread of romance—keeps them apart. But they talk and they play bedroom games, and they play a kind of hide-and-seek with continuity errors and jump cuts. Young people in a movie had never looked like this: It was cool, and whether Godard would ever admit it or not, it had a deep debt to Americana (the film was dedicated to Monogram).

They shot fast with hardly any lights in August and September of 1959, with Pierre Rissient as assistant director. At night they used Ilford HPS, a new stock, and there it was, tossed on a plate like a fried egg, the new Paris, the thing that held so many New Wave films together—their love of that bitter city. Raoul Coutard shot it (he was Beauregard's man), and his astonishing skill was vital. So were the broken fragments of jazz by Martial Solal, and the laconic antiaffection that cut 2 hours and 15 minutes down to 90 minutes almost at random. That's how the new editing worked. *Breathless* was a sensation, but it was nothing yet. Hardly a millimeter of Godard's heart had been revealed.

Bride of Frankenstein (1935)

Just as Henry Frankenstein is seeking to create fresh life after death, so Universal—with a hit on their hands—struggled to think how the monster (dead at the end of the 1931 original) could live for another day. So they cut his last death scene from existing prints and trusted that the public would forget. John Balderston and William Hurlbut took on the new script, in which a mate should be found for the monster. James Whale was the director again—no one seems to have doubted that requirement—and he sought a little touch of respectability by having the same actress play both the bride and the figure of Mary Shelley in an 1818 prologue.

Boris Karloff was also taken for granted, and the point of the sequel was to squeeze more value out of his pathetic personality. This time, against Karloff's purist instincts, the monster would talk, smoke, and whistle a tune. As for the bride, Whale looked back on his circle of friends in London and picked Elsa Lanchester: bluestocking, cabaret artiste, and the wife of Charles Laughton. (When Laughton saw the film, he praised his wife's pretty pointed ears.)

Whale himself devised Lanchester's look: the electrified hairstyle standing straight out from the head, and the body swathed in white muslin—a mummy, but sexy. Lanchester said she learned her character's frightening, hissing way of speaking or uttering from the swans in Hyde Park. There was less of Henry Frankenstein (in part because Colin Clive had become an unpredictable alcoholic), though the teenage Valerie Hobson was cast as his ladylove. To beef up the "human" cast, Whale introduced Dr. Pretorius, "necromancer, scientist, and grave robber," and cast Ernest Thesiger, one of the most open and self-mocking homosexual actors in the English theater. In his way, Thesiger is every bit as exquisite and far-fetched as the monster, and his wit brought a great deal of personality to the film, just as it was the first hint of smart skeptics making these horror films.

Then there is the old blind man (O. P. Heggie) who takes in the wandering monster and teaches him smoking and music. Theirs is a wondrous odd-coupledom, and a partnership in which Whale's own gay proclivities may be read. The new film had a rather lighter, more conventional photography, from John J. Mescall, as well as a complete and original orchestral score by Franz Waxman. In so many ways, Whale and Universal were bent on carrying the myth toward a new kind of reality—satirical, yet still frightening. But after this second film (another success), the story slipped back toward the gruesome and the crude. The idea that the monster might be a parody gentleman was forsaken, as if too alarming for the audience. But here, for a moment, we can see the monster and his bride as the ancestors of so many grotesquely happy pairings in television sitcoms. (Don't all private worlds look a little odd eventually from the outside?)

It is a sad reflection on Elsa Lanchester's originality that this fierce beauty is probably the best-known work she ever did.

The Bridge on the River Kwai (1957)

The Cold War was especially bleak, and nuclear testing in the atmosphere recognized no limits. So the middle-brow idea gathered that war was a very bad idea and a cruel tease to the hopes of those who might promote it. And so *The Bridge on the River Kwai* says, Suppose that British prisoners of war detained in the jungles of Burma were ordered by their captors to build a rail line and a bridge. Then suppose that a British commander began to take pride in the good work of bridge-building. Soon enough a commando strike force is organized to go upriver to eliminate this curious kind of Colonel Kurtz from Surbiton.

When Sam Spiegel discovered the French novel, by Pierre Boulle, writer-director Henri-Georges Clouzot held the rights. Carl Foreman wanted to write it, and Spiegel got involved by finessing the blacklisted writer. Howard Hawks was considered as a director, but he judged the project poor box office—let the English do it, he said. And that's how David Lean, essentially a director of small, literary films at that point, came into the reckoning. It was Spiegel's special talent to get Columbia to fund the picture at about $2 million, despite the opposition of Harry Cohn.

As it turned out, it's intriguing to see the modest "irony" of the material opened up into an epic. That supposes two levels of action: the events at the camp, including the effective torture of Colonel Nicholson (Alec Guinness) by the Japanese, and the team (Jack Hawkins, William Holden, Geoffrey Horne) coming through the jungle.

Foreman did the script with Michael Wilson. Jack Hildyard did the color photography, most of it in Sri Lanka, and Malcolm Arnold did the music. Like many British war films, the direction is very stiff, or fixed—it's as if war immediately deprived Brits of their ironic faculty. Equally, the bridge building is rather routine, though the film does develop an unusual struggle of wills between Nicholson and the Japanese camp commander (Sessue Hayakawa). One trouble is that the eventual meeting is only being delayed, though Nicholson's stubborn response is clearly predictable. Still, by 1957, the British prisoner-of-war-camp picture was so clichéd a genre that it is very hard to know how anyone really behaved. But there is a huge gulf between Holden in this film and the Holden in 1953's *Stalag 17*.

The finale does have a classic tension, and it actually uses the space at the foot of the bridge very well. As to what the whole thing means, the film's attitudinizing is so much stronger than its logic. It was an enormous hit. Although, at $2.8 million, it had gone badly over budget, it would earn over $65 million eventually. Nominated for eight Oscars, it won seven: Best Picture, Best Director, Best Actor (for Guinness), plus screenplay, music, photography, and editing awards. The only loser was Sessue Hayakawa, but it was plain in this movie that his side's point of view was less pressing.

Brief Encounter (1945)

This is a film in which two married people meet at a railway station and fall in love, a film that ends with the woman of the pair and her dull, decent husband embracing after she has "been a long way away." The other man, a doctor (Trevor Howard), is going off to Johannesburg with a wife and two sons (none of whom is ever seen), and I cannot detect any evidence that the woman (Celia Johnson) is going to follow him. Except in her heart and her dreams. And that is exactly the point about a pair of "lovers" who never actually make love, but who meet at the railway station, have lunch, go to the cinema, and sometimes drive out to the country to stand together on a humpback stone bridge. They are unlucky, if you like. Their dutiful lives have been interrupted by a tempest of feeling—a most unfortunate encounter. Or is it the light of their drab lives?

Brief Encounter does not go away, or date, even if it was always on the edge of self-parody and coming at the end of a war where adultery and divorce had begun to get under way in Britain, as anywhere else. It is a film with two warring winds: the heady romanticism of Rachmaninoff's Second Piano Concerto, played by Eileen Joyce, and the precision and the grim clerical correctness of the railway system, where the trains come on time and the refreshment-room liquor license is scrupulously observed. Of course, each wind has its opposite: Ms. Joyce has to play the Rachmaninoff correctly; and in the railway station, the stationmaster (Stanley Holloway) will smack the barmaid (Joyce Carey) on the bottom when he gets a chance. It's a theorem of order and explosion, yet the one thing the film omits (and it would be telling) is ruinous bomb damage in the provincial towns where the action plays. Didn't that disorder edge lives into madness?

The words are Noël Coward's (it derived from a one-act play, *Still Life*), and just as surely as Coward loved the prim clichés of the middle class, so he is a harbinger of Pinter. Coward, David Lean, and Anthony Havelock-Allan did the script. Coward was a producer, too, and Ronald Neame gave a big assist. Robert Krasker shot it as a film noir: The majority of scenes are nocturnal, etched in shadow, and leaning toward the resolution in *Anna Karenina*. Trevor Howard and Celia Johnson are heartbreaking—I can't quite omit the fact that she resembles my own mother. So I wonder about lives I ignored as easily as the stupid husband. And finally this, for what it's worth: Lean was a Quaker, raised on order, and he went through wives like Len Hutton losing batting partners in Test matches against Australia.

So is this a call to madness, or is it the last and gravest insistence on duty as part of the just war? It is a movie that waited for the lampooning of Monty Python and others. Yet it is an experience that survived that assault. Are we here to keep ranks or to explode them? I don't think Lean could make up his mind, and the anguish shows in Celia Johnson's face as if she were Sophie with her choice.

Brighton Rock (1947)

You can't really talk about *Brighton Rock* without giving away the ending—but that's because the ending they went for sells out the picture. Not that the filmmakers are to be blamed. On the contrary, they filmed the book faithfully, only to see the official censor in Britain step in to correct their work.

Graham Greene's novel was originally published in 1938, and it's important to stress that its world is that of the thirties, when Brighton was a raffish, exotic place, smart yet tawdry, in a country otherwise set in gloom. It features the romance and the marriage of a boy gangster, Pinkie, and a girl, Rose Brown. He marries her to prevent her from giving evidence in a possible murder trial. But the relationship is complicated in that they are both Catholics with an unusual sense of the nature of guilt. It may have been to escape that odd overlay that John and Roy Boulting (director and producer) sought a treatment from the fashionable playwright Terence Rattigan.

The result was reckoned to be far too pleasant, with a weird happy ending. So the Boultings then turned to Greene and asked him for a screenplay of his own. Greene obliged, and above all the resultant film catches the tense mood of the seaside town and rival gangs. Without too much trouble, it became a postwar film, coinciding with the cosh and razor gangs that were prevalent in England after the war. But Greene, naturally enough, included all the Catholic references. To be brief, Pinkie, on his way to death, leaves the very innocent Rose with a recording made at a pier stall. What it actually says is to this effect: I want you to think I love you . . . but I hate you. This is true to Pinkie's evil, and it is a shocking conclusion. The British Board of Film Censors could not endure it, and the Boultings were compelled to reshoot the ending so that the record sticks and repeats on "I love you." Does everyone feel better?

The greatest failure of this ending is that it betrayed the startling performance by Richard Attenborough as Pinkie. He was twenty-four at the time, though he looked younger. But it is a fearsome performance, one of several throughout his career. Carol Marsh plays Rose, and it is, in truth, a very tough part, chiefly because Rose is more a symbol than a real teenager. Hermione Baddeley is Ida, the woman who helps track Pinkie down, Greene felt she was too theatrical, but I think she works. The rest of the cast includes William Hartnell, Nigel Stock, Wylie Watson, Alan Wheatley, and Harcourt Williams.

The American version was not censored (the film was called *Young Scarface*). That gives you the idea of how it was sold and removes the great difficulty of explaining the sticks of jaw-breaking confectionery known as Brighton rock.

Bringing Up Baby (1938)

The shooting of *Bringing Up Baby* lasted ninety-one days, which was some forty days over schedule and ridiculous—unless they were having fun. People at RKO were shaking their heads in a gloomy manner long before the film opened. The overages to Cary Grant and Katharine Hepburn had pushed the budget to nearly $1.1 million, and the wiseacres knew that no Hepburn film had a chance of recovering that. Moreover, they pointed out, in a fairly simple (if insane) story involving a few people, a leopard, and a dinosaur skeleton, how could it have gone forty days over schedule? So the film, which grossed $715,000 in the home market, was doomed. It was a loser and a contributor to Hepburn's reputation as "box-office poison." Yet maybe it's the most fun ever had in Hollywood.

I am writing this entry shortly after having attempted *Greed*—and I feel driven to some comparisons. *Greed* is a famous ruin (if that's what you want to see) that lost about the same amount of money as *Baby*. Yet *Baby* survives—which is a plus. What's left of *Greed* is still, I think, a momentous film. And that is often put down to Erich von Stroheim's rebellious daring. He defied the studio system because he wanted to tell the Truth. But look at *Baby* with wise, fresh eyes, and I think you will have to agree that its sentiments and its philosophy are more daring than those in *Greed*. Indeed, it says that life is lunacy, so that the diligent reassembly of a dinosaur skeleton (the pursuit of knowledge) means very little compared with getting your bone into a warm box. Having fun. And the film survives. And it is just a touch funnier than *Greed*.

This is not an attack on *Greed* but an effort to suggest that Hollywood is seldom more usefully serious than in its best comedies. You can dismiss *Bringing Up Baby* by saying it is "only" screwball and by pointing out that leopards hardly happen in Connecticut. The advice to people to have fun of a certain kind in 1938 may be judged frivolous, or it may be the acme of common sense. But do not be deceived: Within the magnificent frolic, the inspired and inventive dementia (that's what needed an extra forty days), *Baby* speaks about life, energy, and the equation of the two. And when David Huxley (Grant) admits to Susan (Hepburn) that the collapse of his skeleton, his engagement, and his rather grim, glued-together life hitherto has been "fun," something profoundly American and movie-ish is being offered. It's up to us whether we take it or leave it.

Dudley Nichols and Hagar Wilde did the script. Russell Metty photographed it so that no one could miss the noir gathering in the Connecticut woods. The support players are Charles Ruggles, Walter Catlett, Barry Fitzgerald, May Robson, Fritz Feld, Leona Roberts, and George Irving, with Jack Carson and Ward Bond, as well as a dog and a leopard. The entire venture was overlooked by the Academy, but it still feels as if it was made last night.

Bring Me the Head of Alfredo Garcia (1974)

This is the last real film by Sam Peckinpah, and probably the least known—early reviews were so bewildered and so affronted by its violence and its singular interest in Mexico. But this is the last film sustained by a large parable-like arc in which honor surpasses money, and in Warren Oates's clear impersonation of Peckinpah himself it is a tribute to a dying breed. That had always been the termination point in Peckinpah's legends, but here he finds the duality of Mexico—ancient and primitive, yet lit up by progress—his perfect setting. Death is there from the start: Alfredo Garcia will never say a word. His head is just one more Mexican artifact, provenance unknown but suspicious.

A Mexican boss, El Jefe (Emilio Fernández), has a daughter who has been made pregnant by Alfredo. The boss offers a million dollars for the seducer's head. Two businessmen take up the quest, Quill (Gig Young)—though Quill says his name is Fred C. Dobbs—and Sappensly (Robert Webber). In turn, these men offer $10,000 to Bennie (Warren Oates), piano player in a bar, to find Alfredo. He goes off with his doomed girlfriend, Elita (Isela Vega), because she used to know Alfredo, too. Many corpses later, Bennie will die a spectacular death, having forgotten to carry away the million dollars.

Bennie is driven by the loss of Elita, one of the most poignant and complex heroines in Peckinpah's work. But behind Bennie's dark glasses, his cheap patter, and his shark's grin, he has always known that the whole search for Garcia was a pretext. Deep back in the film there is an ideal world. It consists of a love relationship, some good drinking, a car on the open road. But Bennie knows that its benefits have been corrupted, and he forms a bizarre, ghoulish brotherhood with Garcia and his severed head. It is the only secure male partnership in this testament of a director who has given up on everything.

Scripted by Gordon Dawson and Peckinpah, the film has Helmut Dantine as executive producer and as one of the gangsters. The death wish had overtaken Peckinpah by now. He would mouth any lie to get his money, and then he would revile the system. Bennie is forced to watch his girl be raped. He is buried alive. He is blown to pieces. But he delivers the head and, in effect, does it for free.

Coupled with macho attitudes, this fatalism can easily win enemies for Peckinpah. That's how this picture was dismissed. But you have to study the passing beauties it uncovers (photographed by Alex Phillips, Jr.) to appreciate Bennie's torched appetite for life and the pain he feels for all the opportunities that have passed. Peckinpah was drunk on spirits just as his pictures are drunk on the fading light. And drunkenness leaves one terribly vulnerable to being juvenile. But in a cinema that so often makes an idiot of itself over strong men, Peckinpah had no rival in fashioning wasted trash who trusted no one but themselves and knew that worse times were coming. It's not just his hero that is dying; it's the prospect of any more honest films.

Broadway Melody of 1940 (1940)

It is too much to ask a film to be perfect, or even good, most of the time. The process is so inherently flawed that we must be prepared for twenty minutes of fragrant sunshine in an otherwise overcast afternoon. It is enough to remember the day by. And it is another lesson: Be alert, for your life's sake. You must see, otherwise the thing may go unnoticed. So if you happen to be writing Mahler's Eleventh Symphony on that afternoon, don't miss the 19¼ minutes of perilous sunlight as the gray clouds prepare their fatal attack.

But with films, it is our habit to say that this one is good, that one a masterpiece, whereas maybe the most truthful approach would say that in John Frankenheimer's *I Walk the Line* there are two or three minutes when the look on Tuesday Weld's face is from some other film, a film made by William Faulkner, while the rest is, well, decent filler. I think once we got into that way of looking, we could all build an anthology of moments while admitting that elsewhere a film rests or glides downhill. So, in *Broadway Melody of 1940* (a 102-minute picture), there is 9 minutes and 43 seconds of "Begin the Beguine."

It is a Norman Taurog film—good for you, Norman. Suffice it to say that out of some very silly plotting maneuvers, Fred Astaire and Eleanor Powell (his partner after Ginger but, alas, for only one film) come together. The movie is black and white, and the beguine sequence (music by Cole Porter, of course) builds as follows: A soprano sings the song, giving tasteful vent to its exotic atmosphere. Then Fred and Eleanor appear in the mid-distance, he in a Latin dance costume, she in a long white dress, to do the beguine. The movements are sinuous, Latin, and very romantic. And we steadily see them reflected in the dark, lacquered floor. There is then a brief interlude as four women pick up the song, and then it happens.

Fred and Eleanor come back, in the foreground now—he's in a white tux, black tie; she's in a swirling white frock that stops at the top of her calf. Now it's a flat-out tap version of "Beguine," one of mounting speed and exuberance, with a gaiety and an energy so great that if you'd been Hitler in 1940, you might have looked at this and called a halt. Fred and Eleanor had no artillery, no cavalry, no infantry. But they had the assurance to do this dance as if in the front parlor, for millions of people. And as it ends, there's a quite enchanting moment where the dancers stop and Eleanor's loose white flower of a frock keeps dancing for a second and a half.

The film was made at M-G-M, and I will not weary you with the story or claim that Eleanor Powell was an actress of any great note. George Murphy is the second male lead. And it is heaven. I see no reason why there couldn't be a small corner in your house where this scene is playing on a loop all the time. After all, if you had a Rembrandt, you'd put it on your wall for as long as you could see, wouldn't you?

Brokeback Mountain (2005)

In the summer of 1963, two pretty simple cowboys—Ennis Del Mar (Heath Ledger) and Jack Twist (Jake Gyllenhaal)—get the assignment to herd sheep on Brokeback Mountain. We might be on the brink of one of the unasked questions in Western mythology: How boring was it to be a cowboy? Well, so boring that they start to have sex—though these are guys so simple and so strict in their upbringing that they discount love from the outset. They are fucking the nearest thing in sight.

Back in "civilization" (small-town Wyoming), they revert to type: Ennis marries Alma (Michelle Williams); Jack goes back to Texas and marries Lureen (Anne Hathaway). They have family lives. But the two cowboys, once separated, are in love, even if they hardly know a way to express it. Over twenty years, they have a few seasons together, and then Ennis learns that Jack is dead. The story is about an accident, but in fact Jack was killed by a homophobic gang.

This comes from a story by Annie Proulx, which is terse, tight-lipped, and fatalistic; there is less "love" in the story than there is in the movie. Ms. Proulx is a very fine writer, in part because her own sensibility is so violently at odds with that of the Wyoming she describes. Not that the story is an attack on Wyoming. It's more a matter of don't be too surprised if these things happen to you. It's a kind of writing that doesn't need two earnest, good-looking, and very smart young actors as the boys—and if you don't think they're smart, look again and see how much they can load into underplaying.

What that means is that *Brokeback Mountain* doesn't work for me as a movie. Why? Essentially because the yearning it invokes is so great that there's no reason why these two thwarted lovers don't quit Wyoming and go off to Los Angeles together. Still, there are those who feel that the script (by Larry McMurtry and Diana Ossana) and the direction (by Ang Lee) are so profound that the social importance of the film's subject carries all before it.

But what is the subject? That gays should be able to live as they like? That these two guys need to distinguish between love and satisfaction? Or that the general level of education in Wyoming is a disgrace? Proulx's story is a splinter pushed under the skin. Lee's film is a raft on which poor boys may sail to freedom. My own guess is that good movies should not have such a reliance on timber, whatever form it takes.

Rodrigo Prieto did the photography, and you will hardly be surprised to hear it's like an ad for Wyoming. The acting is heartfelt, though I feel the actresses come off best, with far easier roles. As for Lee—who has begun to look less like an artist lately—I feel only his detachment. My guess is that ten years from now this will look like a very odd picture.

Broken Blossoms (1919)

If you want to give a young modern audience the chance to appreciate D. W. Griffith, let me suggest passing over *Birth of a Nation* or *Intolerance*. Show them *Broken Blossoms* instead. But go carefully: With too many films like this, there's not enough air to breathe. For it is cliché and melodrama raised to the level of tragedy.

Apparently, it was Mary Pickford who first suggested to Griffith the best-selling book *Limehouse Nights*, a collection of lurid stories by Thomas Burke. When Griffith read the book, he was struck by one story, "The Chink and the Child," in which a wretched twelve-year-old girl, constantly abused by her illegitimate father, the boxer Battling Burrows, is taken in and cared for by Cheng Huan, "The Yellow Man," lonely and sensitive, who lives in London's Limehouse district and treats the child with a rare, exquisite delicacy. In the story, he kisses her. He contemplates her. But then Burrows finds out, and he descends on the scene of tranquillity. He beats Lucy to death. Then Cheng shoots the boxer and dies himself.

Griffith took this story, dropped the kiss, and raised Lucy's age to fifteen. Even so, this is one of the first films in which the erotic charge in violence, the brooding affection in voyeurism, and the quality of torture are significant parts of the action. It is said that Griffith thought first of casting Carole Dempster (his girlfriend) as Lucy, but it is hard to credit that as a serious consideration. Lucy is a role not just crying out for Lillian Gish but almost unplayable by anyone else. Why? Because Gish's own nature did not bring a sexual interpretation into play, and it is only if the scenes with the Chinaman are played as worship that they are tolerable. Equally, George Fawcett rehearsed in the role of Cheng Huan before being replaced by Richard Barthelmess. It is one of the great performances in silent cinema—spiritual, transcendent, melancholy—and hopelessly racist in ways that barely disguise the breathless sexual content in the prolonged scenes where Cheng Huan "attends to" Lucy. The kiss in the story was logical and proper, but it would have closed the film down.

That is one source of tension. The other is the quite shocking violence that Burrows (Donald Crisp) inflicts on the girl, a response in which the loathing is once more driven by smothered sexual feelings. The scene where he shuts Lucy in a closet is unbearably claustrophobic, so powerful that we want to escape the film. And it is a moment—the first in film history?—where you cannot miss the natural ties between the medium and cruelty. Billy Bitzer shot the film, but the still photographer, Hendrik Sartov, brought an artistic soft focus to many shots that is revoltingly beautiful. It's the same old riddle: This is a film of such power, you begin to question the ethics of power—and the absence of any room left for thought by the enclosed tragedy and its reliance on cliché (as opposed to character). Anyone more imaginative than Gish might have shuddered to see the use being made of her.

Bugsy (1991)

Bugsy is what you might expect from Warren Beatty: a PBS tribute to the gangster as American entrepreneur, and an opportunity for this fatally shy actor to make one of our flashier scoundrels seem like a figure from Ernst Lubitsch. Of course, if you challenged Beatty that the picture is weighed down with sedateness and gentility, he would widen his eyes and wonder, "How can that be? I got Jim Toback to do the script."

But Toback (that insouciant maverick writer-director, the enfant terrible of his own gossip) has seldom been able to do a picture about a man fucking every woman he sees or gouging enemies' eyes without putting Mahler or Beethoven on the sound track. He is the Ph.D. hoodlum, the Harvard Rimbaud, that Warren always needed—and this film grows rather more out of their wary admiration society than from any notion that it would be sensible to work together.

Just like *The Godfather* and *Goodfellas*, *Bugsy* is a movie that aspires to the boy's dream of being a gangster—don't forget that Michael Corleone, given his choice, would rather sit in a deep chair, model superb silk suits, and droop just an eyelid to let minions know that so-and-so needs a knife in the back of his neck. And so the execution of Elliott Gould in *Bugsy* is done far away off camera, with shots ringing out like a loon in the night. It's a pastoral killing.

It's Beatty's fond idea that Ben Siegel is really a great producer gently rising to his lifetime's challenge: to found Las Vegas as the infinite money laundry his pals need. And Beatty does the visionary scenes with boyish passion—it's like Clyde Barrow getting to be famous. Like Saul on the road to Tarsus, he sees the idea of the Flamingo as a burning bush waiting to go neon. And like the incredibly poor manager he is, he turns the surefire plan into an immediate disaster.

There is no cohesion—Beatty is as polite as Irving Thalberg most of the time, but then ready to be a quivering psychopath. (Do you like my quiver? I got it at Cartier.) The conception needs to be more satirical, more of a battle between Toback's pretentious violence (which can be awesome) and Barry Levinson's supposedly hip managerial style as a director. So Annette Bening is sometimes at a loss—but why not? The film never decides whether she is the swindler skimming away so much money or Ben's true love. Really, the only way to play the love story is with Bugsy as the chump taken for a ride. But as you may recall, it was on this film that Warren and Annette found love—and that's another blanket that takes the life out of their warm bodies.

Ben Kingsley is Meyer Lansky—it feels like Sir Meyer Lansky. Harvey Keitel is Mickey Cohen. Bill Graham is terrific as Lucky Luciano. Joe Mantegna proves that George Raft was a nonentity. Ennio Morricone copies some of his old music. The film got ten Oscar nominations in major categories and won nothing big. More or less, after this Beatty gave up work for marriage and family. It's all very middle-class.

Bull Durham (1988)

It will emerge eventually that this book has omitted dozens of baseball pictures, from *Pride of the Yankees* to *Eight Men Out*, from *Field of Dreams* to *Fear Strikes Out*, from *The Winning Team* (Ronald Reagan as Grover Cleveland Alexander) to *The Pride of St. Louis* (Dan Dailey as Dizzy Dean). The essential reason for this neglect is that, as any real follower of the game knows, it has become a television pastime in which we follow not just the game itself but its off-the-field spin, and the general attempt to suggest that these narrow-minded geniuses are great guys. Sport has to be live. The spectator must wait for the ball to go through Billy Buckner's legs or for Zidane's astonishing chipped penalty to score in the 2006 World Cup final. Movies remake everything—and this is fine, because they allow us to improve on the past, on what we did and how fine we were (it is a dreamscape). But you cannot re-create sporting incidents without humiliating your players and trashing their ease.

Bull Durham is a little different, in part because writer-director Ron Shelton (who came close to a serious baseball career himself) went to the minor leagues for his setting: the second circuit of small, spiffy ballparks in provincial cities, where there is none of the nonsensical pay scales, the agenting of idiot players, or the fatuous spin put on their ugly souls. In the minor leagues, you have nothing to do but play the game for the love of it. This is in North Carolina, where you can still feel how far baseball was a country game.

Shelton is so good on the atmosphere that we pardon him his settling on just three players (and his relative exclusion of blacks and Hispanics—since 1988 even the big game has become increasingly Hispanic). The one is Bull himself (Kevin Costner), the catcher, the rugged philosopher (far closer to Gary Cooper than the fellow in *Pride of the Yankees*), who is trying to control and direct Tim Robbins, as wild a pitcher as you're going to see. That much is routine. But then there's Susan Sarandon as the team follower who takes it upon herself to educate one of the players in sentiment, feeling, and all those things that may be important when the career is over. What a great game it would be if some government grant provided for a Sarandon (circa 1988) to soften the hard edges on so many obnoxious players.

This film is a modest pleasure, but it has enough of the real thing to be persuasive. At the same time, one has to make some gesture to Kevin Costner's beyond-the-call-of-duty commitment to baseball. *Field of Dreams* is pure fantasy, but one of the great male weepies and one of the most cockamamie pictures about rural life. Then there is *For the Love of the Game*, in which Costner delivers the title as a veteran pitcher and wins his girl around again. Of course, the family life of sportsmen varies, but sometimes it reaches deep into the field of horror. Just think how often the baseball bat is a weapon in American movies.

Bullitt (1968)

You can imagine Clint Eastwood (who was born in Oakland, California, and raised in the Bay Area) looking at *Bullitt* and asking himself, "Where was I?" Take a rebellious but absolutely steadfast cop. Put him in San Francisco, and suggest in his own minimal lifestyle that he is a liberal of that era. But then establish his conservative credentials in terms of his attitude to the law in an age when criminals are finding more and more loopholes. Throw in the vexation of city bosses who exploit the law-and-order issue for their own campaigning. This kind of on-the-street cop has superior officers for whom he has a grudging respect, but in so many respects, he is a lone-wolf operator. He is not doing it for the money, nor for the girl. He isn't even committed to the switchback circuit established in San Francisco—not as long as they let ordinary motorists clutter up the Grand Prix circuit.

Steve McQueen nearly let *Bullitt* go. "I never liked cops in my whole life," he once said. "I figured they were on one side of the fence, with me on another." But this was a film made for McQueen's own production company, Solar. Though his friend Robert Relyea was credited as executive producer, McQueen made all the important decisions, including the hiring of Englishman Peter Yates to direct (McQueen had seen and liked Yates's *Robbery*) and the script (by Alan Trustman and Harry Kleiner), taken from a novel, *Mute Witness*, by Robert L. Pike. It was McQueen who picked San Francisco (just to get away from Warner Brothers), who chose Jacqueline Bisset (there must have been a reason), and who discovered on a midnight motorcycle jaunt in the city that there were hilltops where a vehicle actually took off.

Bullitt and Delgetti (McQueen's close friend, Don Gordon) are given the job of looking after a crook turned state's witness, to keep him alive for the trial. Congressman Walt Chalmers (Robert Vaughn)—*hiss!*—is leaning on them hard to get this done. But whaddya know: Someone inside is working for the outside (a good reason why Frank Bullitt doesn't talk to too many cops), and the witness is offed. Or was he the witness? Don't worry. If you can't follow the plot, the cars will soon be coming over the hills like seabirds looking for fish.

Scholars in San Francisco will tell you that the great chase scene is an immense cheat: One location cuts into another with impossible aplomb. Who cares, if you're producing the film yourself and driving is what you really like and you know these ten minutes are going to be the money scene. The picture went way over budget, and it probably cost $1.5 million. Nuts, it had rentals of $19 million, and who took the biggest part of the $19 million? Well, probably Warner Brothers, but they had a battle on their hands.

So it's daft and essential, and only a few nondrivers don't watch it every couple of years. Also with Robert Duvall, Simon Oakland, Norman Fell, and George Stanford-Brown.

Bus Stop (1956)

The wisdom is out now that this is Marilyn Monroe's best film. No, it's not as good a picture as *Some Like It Hot,* but for Wilder, Marilyn was there without quite being in or of the picture. Whereas in *Bus Stop* she is intrinsic; she is vital to the structure and the feeling; it's a movie about her.

A lot of this comes from writer George Axelrod, who managed to be infatuated with Monroe while holding the opinion that she was clinically nuts. He wanted to take care of her, and he reckoned in all honesty that in adapting William Inge's play, he had improved on Inge. The play had opened in 1955, with Kim Stanley as Cherie and Albert Salmi as Bo, the cowboy she meets at a bus-stop diner in Kansas.

Once Axelrod and director Joshua Logan knew that they were doing the film with Marilyn, they acted accordingly. After Axelrod's first draft, he worked with Logan to make Cherie a better fit for Marilyn,but they knew that the long dialogue scenes would be a grave test for her confidence. She never really questioned lines, but she had a terrible time remembering them. So Logan sometimes did dialogue scenes with an assistant directly feeding lines to the actress. They never cut, and they edited the conversations together later.

In addition, I'd guess that newcomer Don Murray presented very little threat to Monroe—she was better with actors who didn't intimidate her. He was raw, and very effective in Bo's dumbness—for once Marilyn was not the dumbest character onscreen. More than that, her tatty costumes and the film's garish color scheme were very flattering to her. Marilyn was not naturally tidy, just as she didn't often keep a trim figure. So blowsiness suited her, and Cherie wasn't set up as a sexpot—she was a person.

The set piece added for the movie was the song "That Old Black Magic," and it was Logan's kind decision to film it live—Marilyn is actually singing—instead of in a playback where she is miming. He guessed that the miming would be a technical ordeal. And he found that in really singing, she flowered. It is perhaps her best passage in film, and proof that she excelled in songs.

Betty Field played the diner's owner—onstage it had been Elaine Stritch—and the rest of the cast includes Arthur O'Connell, Hope Lange (who later married Don Murray), Eileen Heckart, and Hans Conried. It would be argued that Monroe never again handled dialogue scenes with such skill, and certainly there were occasions when her problems with simple script brought films to a standstill. Maybe Logan and Axelrod were unusually tender spirits. Maybe the role of Cherie was one that pierced all the barriers Marilyn liked to set up. Still, it's a film in which she seldom puts a foot wrong, where she seems central instead of just a dirty joke or a curiosity.

Butch Cassidy and the Sundance Kid (1969)

Both made in 1969, *Butch Cassidy* and *The Wild Bunch* end in immense shoot-out battles south of the border, where our guys get it. Except that that's not quite right. In Peckinpah's film, the bunch are shot to pieces in the Mexican village, leaving just Sykes (the old-timer) and Thornton (the hunter). But in George Roy Hill's film—or should we say the Paul Newman–Robert Redford friendship schtick?—the two guys are saved from fragmentation and death. They become a frozen still photograph, preserved in the aspic of legend. It would be interesting to hear a few Peckinpah characters watching a movie with an ending like that.

So we print the legend and shuffle aside the facts; the disease gets a bigger hold on us. Even in 1969, the apparent fondness for the Western in *Butch Cassidy* was tongue-in-cheek, a touch camp, and the very thing that was going to leave the genre stranded. You could argue that the film was a few smart, modern fellows having fun with the idea of making a Western—so William Goldman does a script that cunningly links period and immediacy, just as George Roy Hill pulls out every modish way of "placing" the past. As for Newman and Redford, well, they're obviously pretending, aren't they? They're protected against the damage of believing in that stuff. So they're updating it. That's why Katharine Ross can look pretty much as she does in *The Graduate,* and why Hal David and Burt Bacharach can throw in "Raindrops Keep Fallin' on My Head," just so we don't forget that this is 1969, when the hits kept coming.

And the whole thing was very pleasant, as easy on the eye and ear as Newman and Redford lost in the hope that they were doing something for the ages. Maybe they were: The film has an entertaining sheen, a painless ease, that keeps it in the repertoire. But I think its very success made it harder to do authentic Westerns, and in the eye of history I'm happy that *The Wild Bunch* stands beside it as an example of a great American movie—one that smells of corpses, not cologne.

Strother Martin is in both films, you may observe. In *Butch Cassidy* he is shot down just after he has proclaimed, "I'm a character," and it is an unkind rebuke from a film that wants everyone and everything to be a self-captioning version of the legend. Whereas in the Peckinpah film, Martin is an odious, all-too-plausible man, brimming with a character we despise. It's a crucial difference.

Butch won Oscars for its script, the Bacharach score, and that song, all of which are smart and fake, and for Conrad Hall's photography, which is far more creative even if it did begin to show that "magic hour" might be a marketable commodity (available as a spray in the Sundance Catalog). As for Newman and Redford, they were given fatal encouragement to stop thinking and start posing.

Cabaret (1972)

Cabaret, Sally Bowles, and Christopher Isherwood go on and on, but somehow it never comes out quite right. *Cabaret* was a 1966 Broadway opening (more than 1,100 performances) in which Joe Masteroff adapted the play *I Am a Camera,* by John Van Druten, itself adapted from Isherwood's writings about Berlin in the early 1930s. But *Cabaret* was a musical, with music by John Kander, lyrics by Fred Ebb. Hal Prince produced, Jill Haworth was Sally Bowles, and Joel Grey was the master of ceremonies at the Kit Kat Club. In 1951, in *I Am a Camera,* Julie Harris had played Sally Bowles. That was filmed in Britain in 1955 by Henry Cornelius, with Harris playing Sally again.

The thing about *Cabaret* was to place as much of the action as possible in the club, in lurid, expressionistic settings that were like George Grosz in Matisse colors. And whereas the real model for Sally Bowles had been a modest performer in some pretty low dives, the Kit Kat now became a spiffy place, and Sally was . . . well, she was Liza Minnelli in the film, a star who could hardly claim to be going unnoticed. Indeed, it's much more likely she'd be the talk of the town. But in the 1950s, Julie Harris's Sally was a far more pathetic character than Isherwood had ever intended.

What's missing in all these adaptations is the plain fact of Isherwood's ego and homosexuality. Few lives have left less to the imagination. Isherwood pursued the lower levels of Berlin entertainment, looking for rough trade. Sally was just one of his acquaintances. And all the while, of course, Germany was falling apart, getting ready for you know what.

Producer Cy Feuer hired Jay Presson Allen to do the screenplay and urged her to restore as much of Isherwood as possible. But the form of the musical, and the urges of the chosen director, Bob Fosse, resisted all her efforts. Sometimes you can think that Christopher (or Brian) (Michael York) is actually in love with Sally. His gayness—not to mention the shabby gayness favored by Isherwood—is hardly allowed to challenge the box office. And nothing can detract from the power of Joel Grey. He is not just the best performer in the club. He could be a Nazi spy, an informer. He could be Goebbels in disguise.

That said, the film is very effective. Bob Fosse evolved a dance style that has nothing to do with Germany in the thirties, but that is sexy and insolent—and it matches the songs with their delight in money. Indeed, the film is more sinister every time you see it, as if Fosse's cheerful ignorance of politics was letting fascism seep under the door. Liza was hugely striking in 1972. Now her limits show through. It took *The Godfather* to beat *Cabaret* as Best Picture, but Oscars went to Liza, Fosse, and Grey (none of whom ever made as big a splash again). Meanwhile, the story of Isherwood remains to be told.

The Cabinet of Dr. Caligari (1920)

Caligari is alive and well. It is astonishing (I think) how many cultural historians and German experts still read Siegfried Kracauer's *From Caligari to Hitler.* But even if Dr. Mabuse deserves to be in that title somewhere, the notion of an affinity between an asylum chief and a certain dictator is neither stupid nor useless. The public likes that kind of melodrama, and "Caligari" is still a familiar term in certain households. Better still, *The Cabinet of Dr. Caligari* remains an extraordinary film. It's still very easy to feel the startling impact it had upon the first age of film buffs as the Great War ended.

Whether it is Griffith or Feuillade, Sjöstrom or Chaplin, we think of the first silent films as almost desperate for the light. That was the only way to film, so pictures went outdoors or shot in "studios" with glass roofs. An inevitable tradition of realism was struck up just because of that reliance on nature. But *Caligari* represents a theatrical tradition: that theater lights are strong enough to film by, that it might be possible to make and film a world that is the opposite of "natural," one that expresses inner states of being. In fact, I'm not sure how far expressionist décor was prevalent in the theater anywhere except in Germany. And one thing to say about *Caligari* is that it represents a complete interaction of film and theater talents.

It came from a script by Carl Mayer and Hans Janowitz. Some murders occur in the town of Holstenwall. Francis, a student, suspects a local fairground impresario, Caligari, and his somnambulist, Cesare. Francis's lover, Jane, is abducted by Cesare; Francis follows them to an asylum to discover that Caligari is installed there as a therapist.

Erich Pommer produced and Robert Wiene directed the film, but the most exciting element is the décor—jagged, nightmarish, distorted, the expression of a deranged sensibility—and that was done by Hermann Warm, Walter Reimann, and Walter Röhrig, stage designers crossing over to the movies (Warm would work on Carl Theodor Dreyer's *Passion of Joan of Arc,* and Röhrig was a key part of F. W. Murnau's team).

Of course, the characters are real actors, but Wiene was prepared to treat costume like décor, and he used nearly impasto makeup to suggest ghostly spirit. He also ordered movements that owed a lot to dance; this is especially true of Conrad Veidt's Cesare, a seductive figure of doom. But you can also see it in Lil Dagover's Jane, Friedrich Feher's Francis, and Werner Krauss's infernally untidy Caligari.

There is more. The story had a frame to it, in which Caligari was a supposedly benign master of the asylum and Francis and all the others were inmates. So the film was like a Freudian case, a sign that madness could be healed. No one has ever been satisfied with this smiling act. Caligari ranks as a deeply sinister figure (all the more so for controlling the action) and the movies' first mad psychiatrist.

Cabin in the Sky (1943)

It was in October 1940 that *Cabin in the Sky* opened on Broadway, a "musical fantasy" with book by Lynn Root, lyrics by Jean Latouche, and music by Vernon Duke. The show didn't run too long, but it was famous for dances by Katherine Dunham and George Balanchine, and for art direction by Boris Aronson and assisted by Vincente Minnelli. So Minnelli was invited to M-G-M by producer Arthur Freed, and after a few isolated warm-up sequences on other films, he made his debut with the Hollywood film of the all-black musical.

Joseph Schrank did a screenplay from the stage show, maintaining the story of Petunia Jackson asking God to spare the life of her wandering husband, Little Joe. Joe is given six months to redeem himself, and he has the Lord's General on his side, as well as Lucifer Jr. scheming against him. Joe nearly ruins his chances, but at the last moment God is touched by Petunia's pleas.

Ethel Waters kept the lead for the screen version, but Dooley Wilson was replaced as Little Joe by Eddie Anderson. Rex Ingram kept the part of Lucifer, and in the movie the young Lena Horne made a striking appearance singing "Honey in the Honeycomb," one of the original Vernon Duke numbers. The other songs from the stage show are "Cabin in the Sky" and "Taking a Chance on Love" (both sung by Waters and Anderson).

Harold Arlen and E. Y. Harburg wrote some extra songs for the movie, notably Ethel Waters's heartfelt number "Happiness Is a Thing Called Joe." In addition, the Duke Ellington Orchestra appeared in two Ellington songs, "Going Up" and "Things Ain't What They Used to Be." Louis Armstrong is there, too, though he seems a little lost without a really strong part.

Compared with *Carmen Jones* (1954), say, *Cabin in the Sky* is folksy and condescending, yet it is one of the first films to treat a black myth seriously. Moreover, in some of the numbers, under Minnelli's guidance, you can see the ethos of the new musical and the urge to cast human nature as fantasy and romance. Minnelli had designed many shows at Radio City Music Hall, and in doing *Cabin in the Sky* he was trying to develop a potential he had seen in Ernst Lubitsch's *Love Me Tonight,* in which character came out of song, dance, and décor. He had the greatest difficulty working with the studio art department, because those people had become very fixed in their realistic way of doing things. Right from the start, therefore, Minnelli saw the need for dream in his style, and the dream was a way of escaping the harsh black stereotyping.

In short, there were from the outset two approaches in the Metro musical: the kind of deliberate, athletic realism that Gene Kelly and Stanley Donen preferred, and a theatrical stylization that Minnelli had picked up on Broadway. There's no need for this difference to be resolved, with either side victorious. *Cabin in the Sky* looks much better, however, if you see it as a dream—almost certainly a white person's dream.

Camille (1936)

If you look at Greta Garbo's *Camille* today, you can act smug if you are so inclined. You can say, Well, of course, they could do that kind of nonsense in 1936, but you couldn't do it today. I think you'd be right—no one in Hollywood, at least, now has the daring or the wisdom to do this story with such breathtaking simplicity and brevity. They'd build it up; they'd camp it up. Whereas all Garbo does is murmur to herself, Well, of course, it's about someone who dies for love—what's more natural than that?

There had been a lot of Camilles in picture history: Sarah Bernhardt, Clara Kimball Young, Theda Bara, and Nazimova had done it (the last with Rudolph Valentino as Armand). But after Garbo, people stopped doing Camille because she had nailed it, because no one was reckless enough to go near her gravity again, because no one could comprehend the simplicity with which she died finally—like a flower deserted by the light.

Yes, it's the story of Marguerite Gautier, derived from Alexandre Dumas, of a courtesan of a certain age who falls in love with a ravishing young man, gives him up under the pressure of respectable society, and is then briefly reunited with him before her death from consumption. Today, as the film's director, George Cukor, observed, women tend to be consumed with their own liberation, not self-sacrifice. But look around you in life, look at the stories of Colette, look at Cherie, and you may realize how often young men suck their romantic education from older women and then abandon the women. It remains an everyday sort of thing, tragic and inevitable. And all Cukor did was to insist on the truth of the situation and permit Garbo's great work.

Cukor gave a lot of credit to Irving Thalberg, who had nursed Garbo's career personally—and who died during the filming. They labored over a script. Frances Marion and James Hilton produced wordy stuff, and then Zoe Akins delivered a script that worked on the principle that the less Marguerite had to say, the more she was going to feel. Time and again, Garbo found modest physical gestures (restrained but seething, Cukor said)—just look at the swoon that is actually her death. How does an actress make the death in *Camille* a surprise except through genius? The bittersweet expressions on her face are by now the idiom of classic cinema. Everyone went to school on her.

You can say that Cukor merely attended to her performance. But consider that Max Ophuls attends to his actresses out of affection while a Joseph Mankiewicz, say, does so from strict duty. You can feel the difference, and you can feel Cukor especially in the treatment of Robert Taylor, telling him it's all right to be so beautiful—let it shine—because, truly, you are in the film to be a face looking at her.

The film was photographed by William Daniels and Karl Freund—how did they collaborate?—with brilliant décor and costumes and fine support from Lionel Barrymore, Henry Daniell (very good), Elizabeth Allan, Laura Hope Crews, Lenore Ulric, and Jessie Ralph. This is Hollywood at its best.

Cape Fear (1962)

No one could seek to suggest that J. Lee Thompson was a better film director than Martin Scorsese. Everyone can see that Scorsese's *Cape Fear* (1991) is a subtler film than the original, with far more complex character studies. But I will stick with the first film, because it is trash honestly done, whereas the Scorsese version is a tangled mess of violent urges and improving attitudes. And, finally, I think that Robert De Niro's Max Cady is a superb master class given by a great actor, whereas Robert Mitchum's Cady is the Beast.

You know the story. Gregory Peck is a lawyer, as decent a man as Peck would lead you to anticipate. He lives in Florida with his wife (Polly Bergen) and an early teenage daughter (Lori Martin). Then Max Cady comes back into his life, a prisoner Peck once had to defend—but not too strenuously, because in his heart he knew that the only safe place for Cady was inside a maximum-security prison or at the bottom of the swamp. Cady vows to be avenged, to hurt Peck where he is most vulnerable.

This all came from a John D. MacDonald novel, *The Executioners*. The 1962 version was scripted by James R. Webb, and it settles for emphatic characters. But in 1991, with Wesley Strick doing the screenplay, Scorsese took the very reasonable course of enriching the motivation. In the remake, Nick Nolte plays the lawyer, and it is clear that he is lazy and unprincipled. He did let Cady down, and he has betrayed his wife (Jessica Lange) in affairs. So the threatened household is far more insecure. Above all, the daughter in the remake (Juliette Lewis at her best) is a theater student who thinks Cady is her new acting teacher. They have a couple of brilliant and very frightening scenes together that actually suggest a quite different menace: that Max really woos the daughter away from home.

The Scorsese picture is in color, photographed by Freddie Francis. The Lee Thompson is in black and white, handled by Sam Leavitt. And given the much more restrictive censorship of 1962, the first film is far more suggestive and far more reliant on Mitchum. This is Harry Powell from *The Night of the Hunter* without the comedy. This is the man who allegedly wandered the country as a drifter before he became a movie star. This is the man who could be flat-out frightening in his mature life by letting you see the contempt he felt for your world. When Mitchum takes off his shirt and goes into the water, he is a sea beast, hot and lusty in ways no sophistication can match. The threat in his watching Polly Bergen and Lori Martin, the gloating over them, is unequivocal and unlimited. It is hideous, and it lets us feel the darkness that has so often been romanticized in Mitchum's heroic roles.

Thompson films it straight and well, and he gets good supporting work from Martin Balsam, Jack Kruschen, Telly Savalas, Barrie Chase, and Edward Platt. He is plainly gripped and alarmed by his own story. Scorsese is far more spectacular. He shows off by giving Peck and Mitchum cameos. He takes the original Bernard Herrmann score and has Elmer Bernstein redo it. Scorsese is not afraid. But he should be. For *Cape Fear* is an authentic confrontation with paranoia.

Carefree (1938)

Alas, by 1938, *Carefree* wasn't the best working title. At last, the blithe gulf between the world of wealth onscreen in the Astaire-Rogers musicals and the economic realities of the time was exposed. *Carefree* was number eight in their series. It cost $1.25 million, nearly three times as much as *Flying Down to Rio* and about $300,000 more than *Shall We Dance?* Production costs were building, perhaps, but above all, Astaire's salary was mounting. He was paid $10,000 for *Flying Down to Rio;* by *Carefree* he was up to $100,000.

Who can say he wasn't worth much more? Fred Astaire was an art and a genre unto himself, not to mention a business. If his pictures had happened along in the 1970s, say, he would have been their owner. His wealth would have been at a quite different level. Yet for RKO in the 1930s, he was the pressure that was making "his" pictures untenable.

More serious, *Carefree* was said to have lost money: Its total income was $1.73 million. With marketing costs added on, it was left in the red on its first run. *Shall We Dance?* (1937) had earned $2.16 million. In other words, the audience was in decline. Just as Ginger Rogers was pressing for solo pictures where she got more acting opportunities, so it seems that the public was jaded. (Note, too, that *Carefree* was 80 minutes, instead of 116 for *Shall We Dance?* and 105 for *Swing Time.*)

Carefree also had one of the best ideas behind an Astaire-Rogers film: him as her psychiatrist. The script was by Allan Scott and Ernest Pagano, from a treatment by Dudley Nichols and Hagar Wilde, from a story by Guy Endore. The songs were Irving Berlin, and they include "I Used to Be Color Blind" and "Change Partners." The latter involves a fascinating dance sequence in which Fred is like the hypnotist while Ginger is the sleepwalker. That was edging into fresh territory, and maybe the novelty put some audiences off.

Hermes Pan did the dances, and it's notable that Astaire was more willing to cut closer shots into the objective, full-figure coverage. Mark Sandrich directed. Yet something was amiss—almost like the irresistible germ of change for its own sake nagging at Preston Sturges, the inability to leave well enough alone.

Of course, Ginger Rogers succeeded in her ambition: She became an actress, won her Oscar. It was Fred who was stranded. He never really found a formula for a different kind of film, just as he never surrendered his own meticulous standards. So his search for partners began, meeting with as much success as failure. The trouble was that his rather vague charm never found another personality. Fred had to prove the lesson that if you do something better than anyone else has ever done it, you may lose your following.

The pair made only two more films: first, *The Story of Vernon and Irene Castle* (1939), which had about the same business history as *Carefree.* You can blame the studio and Rogers's urge for independence. But the end of the partnership must also be credited to Astaire's inability to find a fresh format. Just over the horizon was a young, athletic, very male dancer—Gene Kelly. And ten years later, *The Barkleys of Broadway.*

Carmen Jones (1954)

Carmen Jones appeared on Broadway in 1943, prompted by Oscar Hammerstein's urge to give the Bizet score modern lyrics. It was the classic opera set in a cigarette factory in the American South, done with an all-black cast. It wasn't quite *Porgy and Bess,* but it was a big hit, and eventually Otto Preminger managed to bring it to the screen at Twentieth Century Fox.

Harry Kleiner did a good screenplay for the musical, and it was always Preminger's intention to make it a dramatic film with songs. His Carmen was Dorothy Dandridge, a fascinating if tragic Hollywood story, and Preminger's mistress. The soldier, Joe, would be Harry Belafonte.

The production went to the South, and Sam Leavitt did a great job photographing the open spaces and Edward Ilou's sets in CinemaScope. A young Herbert Ross worked on the dance numbers, and they involve a dynamic moving-camera treatment from Preminger in which the energy of the players pushed against the limits of their world. Of course, the actors could not do the singing themselves, so Dandridge is dubbed by Marilyn Horne, Belafonte by LeVern Hutcherson, Diahann Carroll by Bernice Peterson, and Joe Adams by Marvin Hayes. But the dubbing is done so well that there is not the usual feeling of dislocation in the performances. The cast also includes Olga James, Brock Peters, and Pearl Bailey, who does sing "Beat Out Dat Rhythm on a Drum," to tremendous effect.

Dandridge delivers Carmen sultry and insolent—she is still one of the best Carmens offered on film (in all forms of song, dance, or overacting). She was Oscar-nominated as Best Actress, the first time a black performer had been so rewarded for a lead role. That she lost to Grace Kelly in *The Country Girl* (maybe Kelly's worst performance) only adds to the chagrin—she could at least have lost to Judy Garland in *A Star Is Born.* Dandridge was dead by 1965 (aged forty-two).

Five years later, Preminger took on *Porgy and Bess,* another great score. He was given more means, and he had Dandridge again and Sidney Poitier in the leads, with Sammy Davis, Jr., as Sportin' Life. It is a far inferior film, moving slowly and somehow managing a much faker view of black life. But there the matter stands. Apart from *The Wiz* (misguided in every way), we have not really had a black musical since, and it certainly doesn't even have to be all black—no matter that in our culture black music has been so dominant in the years since.

Carmen Jones still has creative excitement attached to it, and the feeling that a breakthrough was being accomplished. Moreover, it is set in a real South, whereas *Porgy and Bess* was in a picture-postcard landscape that the Gershwins had chosen to idealize. What a treat it would be if somehow we could muster the ambition to do the life of Louis Armstrong, say, as a largely black enterprise. Blacks in the South are among the great untold movie stories to this day.

Un Carnet de Bal (1937)

Julien Duvivier (1896–1967) ended badly on a long run of undistinguished films, including the worlds of Don Camillo. He had gone to America during the war and made those two odd episode films, *Flesh and Fantasy* and *Tales of Manhattan* (in part, surely, because enough people had fond memories of *Un Carnet de Bal*). But when Truffaut met Duvivier in 1966, the old man was complaining about bad reviews. A few years later, Truffaut found that in Japan *Poil de Carotte* was still cherished, while in Hollywood there was a great but unidentified actress who longed to have the waltz music from *Carnet de Bal.*

Carnet de Bal is a dream for the late-middle-aged. Christine (Marie Bell—who was actually only thirty-seven) is recently widowed. She wonders if she chose the right man. Then she finds the dance card for a great evening long ago, and she resolves to rediscover the men who seemed to be contenders that night. She's lucky in finding them, a little less fortunate in that she becomes the constant in an episode film in which a number of strong actors have their moment with her: Harry Baur (who has become a priest); Raimu is a town mayor; Pierre Richard-Willm is an Alpine guide; Louis Jouvet is a fatalistic nightclub owner; Pierre Blanchar is an epileptic doctor; and Fernandel is a hairdresser. It works very pleasantly, with just one problem: We don't really learn a great deal more about Christine in the process. If you think of *Kane,* it is a marvel how many fresh sides of Charlie slip out as the film proceeds.

There is a revelation (of sorts) that works beautifully: We realize that the dance itself—which has become momentous in Christine's mind—was actually a very humdrum affair. But even that touch is spoiled in that the Maurice Jaubert music cries out with nostalgia and tenderness. How did that music figure at so minor an event? All of which is a pity, for the dance card as a way of reentering the past is very promising, and the contrast between how youth felt and middle age recollects is one of those things that could be the driving force in many more films. It might be a great idea to have some senior French filmmaker of today recall Cannes in the spring the New Wave broke—and then to confront the reality.

Duvivier wrote his own script, though with a string of collaborators—Henri Jeanson, Yves Mirande, Jean Sarment, Pierre Wolff, Bernard Zimmer. The camerawork was done by Philippe Agostini, Michel Kelber, and Pierre Levent. The sets were by Paul Colin and Serge Piménoff. The cast also includes Françoise Rosay.

At the 1937 Venice festival, *Un Carnet de Bal* won the Mussolini Cup for the best foreign film. It certainly doesn't stand up as well as *Pépé le Moko,* and dance cards don't really exist much anymore. But any knife that can find its way into complacency's past is valuable—it may turn out to be a scalpel. Perhaps it's just that *Carnet de Bal* illustrates the astonishing fertility of scriptwriting in the 1930s.

Carrie (1952)

Mention *Carrie* in most American movie circles, and it is assumed that you are talking about the Brian De Palma film from 1976. And that's fair enough, for that prom-night bloodbath struck a new young generation as just what a movie was for. The final grasp out of the grave's ground is one of our favorite nightmares. However, for those who have learned from experience that life is so much grimmer and less melodramatic than De Palma knows, the 1952 *Carrie*, by William Wyler, is the movie to tremble at. I'm not sure there is a better American movie about an ordinary man's unnoticed downfall.

Sister Carrie was Theodore Dreiser's first novel, written and ready in 1900, when the author was twenty-nine. It was actually held back until 1912 because the publisher believed it was too shocking and too outspoken on the way in which simple romantic/sexual energy carried people so close to disaster. May I add that it is a great novel, and one that really requires a remake? It is the story of a young woman from the country with vague theatrical aspirations. She comes to Chicago and is taken up by a traveling salesman, Charles Drouet. But she then meets George Hurstwood and has him fall in love with her. He is secure, married, well-to-do, and far older than she is. But he cannot resist her youth, both as sexual renewal and as a restored hope in life itself. Their affair proves fatal: Hurstwood is ruined, though Carrie becomes a success onstage.

The movie is not as tough as the novel (that could be the excuse for a remake), but it is so severe and unsentimental that it was a real box-office failure at the time, no matter that it displays Wyler's genius for examining the middle class, their feeble romanticism, and the way in which the unsympathetic world can turn on them. This is the toughness that made *Dodsworth* one of his best films, and it is something you can feel in *The Letter*, *The Heiress*, and *The Best Years of Our Lives*. Wyler was seldom an inspired filmmaker, let alone an artist of beauty. But he was loyal to his actors, and he had an innate sense of unpleasant truths that is often interesting.

It has to be admitted that Carrie is played by Jennifer Jones, and that several other actresses of the time might have been better. But Laurence Olivier is Hurstwood, and this is one of his finest performances, deeply American, doggedly self-destructive, yet gentlemanly at every step. If you have doubts about Olivier, see *Carrie*. His work there is a triumph. There are other good performances, from Eddie Albert and a very nasty Miriam Hopkins. Hal Pereira contributes a series of very good sets, admirably filmed in black and white by Victor Milner. David Raksin's score helps bring out the tragedy. A remake? It is so unlikely. But think of it with Julia Roberts and Robert Redford, with a script as tough as Dreiser.

Carrie (1976)

This is the authentic bucket-of-blood film—pig's blood, as it turns out. That is what is awaiting Carrie White (Sissy Spacek) as she walks onstage to become prom queen at the high-school dance. And, as is so often the case in American films, this is high school and Spacek is at least twenty-five. Of course, the film assumes that her problems in school have to do with a fiercely overprotective mother (Piper Laurie, encouraged to rant and exhibit signs of Gothic fixation) and Carrie's ignorance of her own menstrual processes. The film begins at the hysteria with which she greets her first period. And the prom night ruse is a cruel game, led by bad girl Chris Hargenson (Nancy Allen, also twenty-five).

I know that this is Middle America as dreamed and dreaded by Stephen King, but still I marvel at so many kids who seem to have been left behind by the educational system—is the film perhaps a secret call for rescue? The only thing that offsets the humiliation of Carrie is the small matter of her telekinetic powers. No, they're not exactly explained, but I can easily think of ways they might have helped her get through school. Instead, of course, they serve to crucify her mother—all too late in the day. With the best will in the world, it's very hard to imagine how Carrie has put up with this Mom when she can do her kind of knife tricks. But Carrie is a curious character—all-powerful when she has to be, but otherwise a creature huddled in paranoia.

Carrie was scripted by Lawrence D. Cohen, who is definitely not the person who became Larry Cohen, the maker of his own domestic horror pictures. But this was clearly the film that carried Brian De Palma over from intriguing offbeat pictures (like *Sisters*) to bucket movies. It caused a small sensation when it opened, and people who should have thought harder and longer rushed off some glib commentaries on the "craft" to be found in creepiness—photography by Mario Tosi, art direction by William Kenney and Jack Fisk, music by Pino Donaggio, and editing by Paul Hirsch. And in fact, I haven't mentioned the best thing in the picture—and the biggest kicker of pure fright—but you have to stay till the end for that.

It seemed pretty clear to me in 1976 that De Palma was an interesting minor talent, ready (if not determined) to sell out to reckless exploitation but with a quite subtle taste for cruelty. Nothing has altered that view or the surmise that, drained of its hysteria and with real kids of the right age, *Carrie* might be a very interesting picture about the real impact of menstruation. But it's also true that *Carrie* gave a kind of credibility to those willing to take garish horror pictures seriously.

The cast also includes Amy Irving, William Katt, John Travolta, Betty Buckley, P. J. Soles, Sydney Lassick, Stefan Gierasch, and Priscilla Pointer.

Carrington (1995)

Sometimes, a certain kind of Brit—to say nothing of Americans relying on *Masterpiece Theatre* to keep their heads above the rising flood—can believe that he is and was a part of Bloomsbury. Or at the very least, a distant relationship is vaguely perceived, like the principle that the tube can take you from Balham to Russell Square. There have been so many books, documentaries, and dramatic impersonations of those alert, prickly minds, their Edwardian fashions, and their wild gardens. We believe we saw Virginia Woolf herself plunge into her cold river, dragged down by stones, and we did little to rescue her, no matter that she wrote with Nicole Kidman's hand.

In this atmosphere the wit and wisdom of the Bloomsburyites stands in for the loss of religious faith with which their era coincides. There is a scene in *Carrington* where people on the southern shores of sweet England hear the artillery bombardments in Flanders. I don't know if that was possible during the war, but I can see that it seemed essential afterward and was part of the rather flippant way in which these smart people observed the end of civilization, even if one of them, J. M. Keynes, had a plan for ending the economic crash.

Carrington is the best film about this moment and group, in great part because it has the sense to concentrate on a fringe figure, Dora Carrington—would-be painter, would-be lover, and suicide. It is very much the work of Christopher Hampton, who wrote the script and directed the film and who was so intent on doing good work that he hardly noticed the extent to which Carrington was a downer perhaps, a self-dramatist for sure, a minor figure maybe, but the opportunity for Emma Thompson's finest acting in film. The reason to see it is Thompson's loyalty to a confused and confusing woman, a chump among so many paragons, yet one who exposes a great deal of their self-serving fakery.

The film has another rock to stand on: just as it is adapted in part from Michael Holroyd's biography of Lytton Strachey, so Strachey is its other central character—fey, coy, hilarious, selfish, lovable, hateful. It is a very thorough portrait and the best thing Jonathan Pryce has ever done. You can take it for granted that in the matter of country houses and sylvan picnic glades, the film is beyond reproach. Similarly, there is hardly a costume that might not have graced the Victoria and Albert Museum. There is nudity, too; this is a properly sensual film. Nevertheless, its strength is a kind of biographical integrity: we believe that these lives were as we see them—and that leaves no room for evading the final tragedy.

Denis Lenoir photographed the movie, Michael Nyman wrote the music, and Caroline Amies did the production design. The cast also includes Steven Waddington as Ralph Partridge, Samuel West as Gerald Brenan, Rufus Sewell as Mark Gertler, Penelope Wilton as Lady Ottoline Morrell, Janet McTeer as Vanessa Bell, and Jeremy Northam as Beacus Penrose.

Casablanca (1942)

It's a war picture, it's a love story, it's a bit of a musical—and it's a café picture. You have only to think of *To Have and Have Not* to see how many genres can coexist (like all those refugees) under the roof of a café picture, an uneasy haven close to the battle lines, a place where every supporting actor can have his or her moment.

There is an excellent full-length book on the making of this one picture (*Round Up the Usual Suspects*, by Aljean Harmetz), in which you can follow the many uncertainties that attended this extraordinary hit and lasting classic from Warners. And every doubt and shift in direction is worth recalling when one recalls the lustrous, phenomenal "rightness" of the picture. The lesson here is that—in classical cinema, at least—doubts can be rendered feeble in the face of the certainty of the medium.

Casablanca began as a play, *Everybody Comes to Rick's*, by Murray Burnett and Joan Alison, set in Casablanca and inspired by seeing Jews attempting to escape from Vienna. Warners got the play (unproduced) on December 8, 1941, the day after Pearl Harbor. The play and the names of the characters are very close to the final film (though Ilsa was originally called Lois). The three credited screenwriters were the Epstein brothers and Howard Koch, not that anyone was sure who did what. Asked his opinion, the very good producer Robert Lord reckoned that Rick was "two parts Hemingway, one part Scott Fitzgerald, and a dash of café Christ."

It's true that many other contract players were considered for the leads, but Hal Wallis always saw Rick as a Bogart part, and in the end the chance of borrowing Ingrid Bergman from David O. Selznick outweighed thoughts of Ann Sheridan, Hedy Lamarr, or Michele Morgan. While Warners paid $20,000 for the play and $47,281 to six writers (including Aeneas MacKenzie and Lenore Coffee), they paid $73,400 to the one and only director, Michael Curtiz. The total cast salary bill was $91,717. In other words, a huge stress was put on Curtiz pulling this all together—and I think criticism should follow the money lead. The visual panache (photography by Arthur Edeson) is extraordinary and very subtle. The framing and the movements are golden.

Yes, the casting seems inspired: not just Bogart and Bergman, both with bruised, masochistic strains, but Paul Henreid sporting a concentration camp scar, the impeccable Claude Rains, as well as Peter Lorre, Sydney Greenstreet, Conrad Veidt, S. Z. Sakall, Dooley Wilson (singing "As Time Goes By"), Madeleine LeBeau, John Qualen, Leonid Kinskey, Helmut Dantine, and the divine Marcel Dalio.

But the screen was not enough. The film was released as the Allies took Casablanca—a just war breeds perfect publicity. It cost $878,000, and the first domestic rentals were $3.7 million. It won Best Picture, Best Director, and Best Screenplay. It stands for brave movies in a just war. It may be America's great moment: hard-boiled, soft-centered, and with a dream coinciding with the real.

Casino (1995)

Casino for me is a test case. When I first saw the film, I recognized that it had astonishing prettiness, fluidity, and a musical line. I had a good time, though I was wary: It seemed to me I was being encouraged to fantasize about being a gangster—and I fear that for Martin Scorsese (a great filmmaker, not equaled in his age for raw talent), that was a beckoning dead end already fully explored in *GoodFellas.* Why would we spend so much time gloating over (and almost singing along with) the lifestyles of the rich and vicious if Scorsese and we were not deeply vulnerable to the myth "It must be fun to be a gangster"?

I am not giving up that uneasiness, or its application to Scorsese's career as a whole. I believe he has allowed himself to become monopolized by young hoodlumism. But I have to add this: Over the years since it was made, I have found myself watching *Casino* endlessly—not always the whole film, but half an hour here or there, passages, riffs, routines, "numbers" if you like—and I think that references to music are vital. I can hardly do that without asking myself why, or at least admitting that I just love the sensation, in the same way that I listen to certain pieces of music over and over (for example, *Sweeney Todd,* some Sinatra songs, Mahler symphonies, Lester Young). And so I think that the thing I called "prettiness" first (and there is a put-down in that word) is beauty: It's sheer love for the expressive flow of film, especially when musicalized (and I am at the point of seeing *Casino* as a new musical).

But it is more than that. I think I like *Casino* as much as I do because of two eternal, frustrating ties: the one between Robert De Niro and Sharon Stone, and the other between De Niro and Joe Pesci. The latter is something we have seen before in Scorsese (in *Raging Bull* and *GoodFellas,* but in other films, too, like *Mean Streets,* where "brothers" move apart). In *Casino,* Pesci's infernal zest actually overpowers De Niro's fusspot meticulousness (the scene where De Niro folds his pants in the office is sublimely telling).

Then there is Sharon Stone's Ginger. There are not really that many interesting women in Scorsese's work, and that is one of his gravest handicaps. But Stone will not let Ginger be overlooked. She gnaws at the film like a mongoose with a grip on a cobra's neck. She is incessant, forlorn, trashy, and human. And she actually conspires with Pesci to undermine De Niro's perfect manager figure, a negativism that rises to the level of tragedy.

More than that, the film has so many inspired scenes—like the car blowing up, the desert digging, the analysis of how a casino functions. Plus, everything involving James Woods, Don Rickles, Alan King, L. Q. Jones (superb), Dick Smothers, and Frank Vincent is to see again and again.

Casque d'Or (1952)

By general consent, this is the masterpiece of Jacques Becker, one of the most popular men in the French film industry and someone who often rated friendship as the finest thing in life. It's a love story set in the Paris underworld in the late 1890s, the bond between Marie (Simone Signoret) and Manda (Serge Reggiani), and there's ample reason for saying it was the best thing either one of them ever did. Signoret was a beauty on a very rapid arc—to see her at her best was a matter of only a dozen years or so—and in *Casque d'Or* the title refers to her hair, a golden helmet, put down on top of an insolent and sensual gaze. It's the keynote of the film, a measure of a real love story told without any sentimentality or any concession. For these characters are lowlifes—they are, I think, the predecessors of so many Jean-Pierre Melville pictures—who will do what they have to to survive.

François Truffaut reckoned that the film was as if done in one line or motion, with absolute assurance. Jean Renoir thought so highly of it that, in his *French Cancan,* he had an aside where a look-alike version of its three central characters are sitting at a café. The *Casque d'Or* script was done by Becker himself, with Jacques Companéez and Annette Wademant, and the film was a production of the Hakim brothers. Those famously sleazy producers loved movies about the underworld, and it's pretty clear that they believed they were the heroes. The story ends badly here—the guillotine plays a part—but it leaves us in no doubt about the erotic glory that came first. Becker was always a very natural director, and there are some open-air love scenes that deserve their place in the history of erotic cinema. Of course, it goes without saying, too, that the film is a cheerful advertisement for that lowlife Paris we all cherish. Pauline Kael turned a bit prim over it. She said it felt touristy—but that's like complaining that Monument Valley in the Ford films asks, "Wish you were here?" Of course it does: It is a great part of movie magnetism that we want to be there. In the picture.

Robert Le Febvre did the photography. Marguerite Renoir edited the film. Jean D'Eaubonne did the great sets. The costumes were by Mayo, and Georges Van Parys wrote the music. I think it's agreed that the overall re-creation of that rich period in Montmartre was never done better. The cast also includes Claude Dauphin as Leca, the gang leader, as well as Raymond Bussières, Odette Barencey, Loleh Bellon, Solange Certin, Jacqueline Dane, and Gaston Modot.

When *Casque d'Or* opened, it was a failure in France. But in Britain Signoret won a prize for her acting and her undeniable sensual presence—legend has it that's how she got her Oscar part in *Room at the Top* a few years later. But she never looked better than as Casque d'Or.

The Cat Concerto (1947)

It's 1947, so who's surprised that it's another noir picture? There is this cat—dressed to perfection, looking like aces—and it is his big night at somewhere like Carnegie Hall. He's black and white, just like the keys on the piano. He has no name, but you know he's a Mr. Perfection, and you know that he's had the years of training and the master classes. And you know that, despite his claws, he has a fingering technique that is strictly for virtuosos. Except that he has this fatal flaw, that little crack in the enamel, the hardly detectable fissure in the golden bowl. You can call it neurosis or big-night nerves or just the certainty that something is going to go wrong. Think of him as doomed. Who wants a cat's life?

So he starts up on the "Hungarian Rhapsody" by Liszt, and everything's going hunky-dory and keep your sofa cushions plump. But what do you know—there is a mouse who lives in this Steinway, and he is woken up by the hammering on the keys. Once the mouse sees that the player is the cat he sets a furious, loving obstacle course for him. And that's how *The Cat Concerto* becomes a routine about keeping up with hell. I know, it's M-G-M and Technicolor, but this is the great American film about the highest artistic dreams leading you to madness.

Tom and Jerry came into being at Metro with the meeting of William Hanna and Joseph Barbera, two of the many loose-end ideas and gag guys in animation. They teamed up with Fred Quimby and soon enough—in 1940, in fact—they had *Puss Gets the Boot*, about a nice middle-class household presided over by a big black housekeeper, and sporting a cat and a mouse. It is the cat's being and destiny to be tormented by the mouse and it is the mouse's purpose in life to overcome nature and defeat the cat—so that the cat keeps after him. In *Puss Gets the Boot*, the mouse frames the cat for smashing the household crockery so that Black Mama throws him out. So it began, so it would always be. The cat leads a dog's life.

With Scott Bradley doing the music (very important in *The Cat Concerto*), Hanna and Barbera had a winning formula. For several years in the 1940s and thereafter they made as many as six T&Js a year, and they turned the animation Oscar into their private possession. The gags were brilliant. The situations often imitate the plots of movies—*Heavenly Puss* is a takeoff on *A Matter of Life and Death*. And the two guys were crazy about their play. Later on, the cat (Tom) turned lean, mean, and driven, but at the outset he was good-natured enough, with a lovely smile. It was just that he was too stupid to do anything except behave like a cat all the time. The mouse (Jerry) is the epitome of spunk and courage and the nerve that lets a flyweight handle a dinosaur. Hanna and Barbera became a factory, and huge on television, but they never again recaptured the lyrical battleground of cat and mouse or the sweet way in which the mouse always won.

Cat People (1942)

In less than a month, producer Val Lewton's new unit at RKO shot *Cat People* using bits of sets from *The Magnificent Ambersons*. The film ran 71 minutes and cost about $134,000, it grossed over $2 million, and the studio was saved again. Cheap horror, B-picture horror, had made a sweet marriage with maybe its most enlightened and fastidious entrepreneur. Indeed, Val Lewton was so artistic, and so smart, that he grasped this rare insight: You don't actually show the frightening thing.

Irena (Simone Simon) is a fashion designer, born in the Balkans but living in New York. She is afraid that she is the descendant of cat people; she is also sexually frigid. It was Lewton's intuition that neurosis could be the engine of horror or some heightened fantasy. She marries Oliver Reed (the upright, neutral, unthreatening Kent Smith), but she is too alarmed to consummate the marriage. He might be too if he understood exactly the kind of cat he has at home.

Lewton gave the film to director Jacques Tourneur, who had worked in France with his father, director Maurice Tourneur, but who was an unknown quantity in America. At first, RKO thought Tourneur was failing, but all they were seeing was Lewton's scheme of reticence, shadow, and suggestion. It was only when the film previewed that the studio realized they were on to something. (And Tourneur did so much good work—*I Walked with a Zombie, Out of the Past, The Flame and the Arrow.*)

The Lewton method is still a model: artistic restraint and fiscal moderation going hand in hand, reveling in the natural suggestiveness of film itself. On *Cat People*, DeWitt Bodeen did the screenplay, Nicholas Musuraca handled the photography, Mark Robson was the editor, Albert S. D'Agostino and Walter E. Keller were art directors, and Roy Webb did the music. This was essentially the team that Lewton would use on the series of films that followed, though he had other directors, including Robson and Robert Wise. But Tourneur's profound understanding of sequence construction was Lewton's greatest asset, and it needed only a face like that of Simone Simon (or Jean Brooks in *The Seventh Victim*) for the audience to have a handhold on the dream.

But Lewton was both very intelligent and highly neurotic, and the tone of his movies is rooted in that combination and in the overall feeling that quite subtle or intricate states of mind could be conveyed through violent states of denial. And so in the great works of horror, just as in the best of surrealism, there is a creeping awareness of narrative arcs that are the imprint of repressed emotions. And *Cat People* has the added advantage of being set in a modern New York; the exotic or period settings sometimes diluted the strength of these fables. To this day, the idea of films of suspense derived from urban neuroses is intensely promising; Hitchcock is only the most obvious example of directors who benefited from this pioneering work. Paul Schrader's remake of *Cat People* (1982) was laughed at, because its sex was flagrant instead of repressed. But Schrader understood the secret, buried link between neurotic behavior and horror, and his *Cat People* could have been very interesting if all its characters had slipped from numb coldness to the wild overheat that lurked in Nastassja Kinski.

Caught (1949)

It is hardly possible nowadays to see Max Ophüls's *Caught* without pondering the muddled legends on how it was made—and why. On the one hand, you have this begging romance about a rather easygoing (empty-headed) model named Leonora Eames (Barbara Bel Geddes), her gaze full of those silly, romantic dreams that afflict women, who finds herself not just wooed by but married to Smith Ohlrig (Robert Ryan), a millionaire without feeling, the kind of husband who behaves in such a way that the wife is going to wonder whether he's just "Oil rig" misspelled. So she can't take the misery any longer, and she runs away and finds a job as receptionist at the clinic of a small, hardworking medical partnership—half of which is Dr. Larry Quinada, all of whom is James Mason—in a poor neighborhood, where the dedicated docs work late. And this girl never even pauses to ask, Is she lucky or what?

On the other hand, the film apparently grew out of Ophüls's pathological loathing of Howard Hughes, a lifetime's experience acquired on the wretched *Vendetta* project. Thus, Ophüls approaches the screenwriter, Arthur Laurents, and tells him, Don't bother too much with the book you've been assigned (*Wild Calendar*, by Libbie Block); make this film the blackest portrait you can of that evil Howard Hughes! Well, why not? So many films have been made by great or graceless men attempting to portray their own story, why not a piece of character assassination like this? Except that word gets back to Hughes himself—the walls have ears, et cetera—and Hughes, in a passing whit of fimsy, calls in Robert Ryan and says, I hear you're playing me—in which case, let me give you a few pointers.

Of course, what we're outlining here is the picture of a world so demented that it passes understanding that it should be taught at decent universities, let alone that Ph.D.'s should be given for advanced knowledge in it. Something else remains to be said: *Caught* is a treat. Somehow all the mixed motives have conspired to make a love story noir in which the rawness of the material makes a rich contrast with the sophistication and warmth in Ophüls's way of looking at people.

Arthur Laurents is on record as saying that he couldn't see what the fuss was about where Ophüls was concerned. In which case he should look more closely at the rapturous passage of the film where Leonora joins the Quinada practice—look at the spaces, the light, the movement of the camera (there is a dance sequence that is ravishing), and the overall way in which Mason (who loved Ophüls) begins to convey to Leonora that she is in another world.

Photographed by Lee Garmes, *Caught* has passages where the cinematic density lifts the whole project up. There is also music by Frederick Hollander. To my eyes, Robert Ryan is just like Robert Ryan in a rather clichéd role, but Mason is the heart of the film. Good support from Curt Bois, Frank Ferguson, and Art Smith.

Céline and Julie Go Boating (1974)

It is summer in Paris. Julie (Dominique Labourier) is a librarian, sitting in one of those pretty, small parks, watching the cats watch her. She has a book of magic, and she mutters a spell. Whereupon a creature, Céline (Juliet Berto), appears, in a rush, dropping things, unaware of the scene she is making. Céline is a magician, and you can wonder what a librarian and a magician might have in common, save for the feeling of being mystified by what the other does. Well, they become friends or accomplices, no more suited than those other great couples held together by an ampersand, like Laurel & Hardy. And Céline tells Julie about a house where something rather nasty is going on. Meanwhile, summer continues, and Céline and Julie chat and get into silly adventures.

But the idea of the house weighs on them. It is a very pleasant place, rather secluded and apparently unoccupied. Julie enters the house and is thrown out, as if by force. But she has a candy in her mouth, and when she sucks on it, she gets brief flashes of imagery of the life inside the house. Gradually, the two of them enter the house. And they discover . . . it is still summer, very nice, and the cats are about in the small, pretty parks.

When they are in the house Céline and Julie go unnoticed. There are people in the house—three adults (Barbet Schroeder, Bulle Ogier, and Marie-France Pisier) and a little girl, Madlyn (Nathalie Asnar). The two young women cannot work out what is happening in the house—how would they know that this action, "Phantom Ladies Over Paris," comes from a couple of Henry James stories? But they do realize that Madlyn is at risk. You see, something like a movie is playing continually in the house, and over the course of a few visits Céline and Julie begin to piece it together. The adults in the house are trying to win Madlyn for her money. Someone must rescue the child.

In advance of *Céline and Julie,* Jacques Rivette had made his immense conspiracy film, *Out One,* at over twelve hours. I think that experiment in duration had cleared the way for this unusually epic encounter with a dream. It is 192 minutes. It is a film in which we often feel time pass, though never with anything other than fascination or suspense. For what it builds to is a parable on film-watching itself, as "Phantom Ladies . . ." becomes increasingly like a *Fantomas*-style serial breathed back into life. The script is credited to the cast, to Eduardo de Gregorio, and to Rivette himself. The original 16 mm photography was by Jacques Renard, and Nicole Lubtchansky did the editing.

I don't think there has ever been a portrait so fond, so oblique, so touching, or so funny of what happens to us at the movies. The humor and the taste are exquisite, yet very commonplace, and the airy conception is rooted by the very physical behavior of Labourier and Berto. Their delight as the story inside the house begins to look more and more like an RKO film noir is that of people who are finding their way home. And so it all ends in a pretty little park, so that it can begin again. Continual showings.

The Ceremony (1971)

I had seen *The Ceremony* once, when it came out—that might have been 1972 in England—and I remembered two things: the anguish of the picture and a kind of collective image on a wide screen of family faces hovering around a coffin. I knew I treasured the film, or the uncertain memory of it, but I guessed that it must have detailed bearings on modern Japanese history that left me helpless. So I thought, as I watched the film again and began to remember it, that it was like a family from Faulkner or Greek tragedy. We do our best. I could not identify the film in its Japanese context, and I have seen enough Japanese films to know that, much as I admire that national cinema, it is based on precepts that are strange to me.

So, for this book, I looked at the film again—on DVD, whereas I saw it in a cinema the first time. All of this touches on what seems to me a huge and enveloping topic: the ways in which we remember and forget films. Anyway, on second viewing, Nagisa Oshima's *The Ceremony* looks like a gripping film, full of that embattled struggle with the world that is so notably absent in the work of Yasujiro Ozu. Oshima, of course, is from another generation. He was born in 1932, and so he was a child during the Second World War. In fact, I know now, he was of samurai descent, and this is the ruinous story of a family like his own, dominated by an autocrat, a man whose life was pledged to the supremacy of the emperor and who began to collapse when that institution was reduced to ordinariness.

The film follows Masuo Sakurada from childhood in 1947 to 1971. He and his cousin Ritsuko (female) are journeying to an island of exile where another cousin, Terumichi, has committed suicide. It was a family dominated by the grandfather, Kazuomi, to the extent that many of his "grandchildren" are actually his own children because of incest and the virtual rape of others' wives or mistresses. It is a place of torment, where Masuo begins to realize that his love for Ritsuko may be made impossible by their being brother and sister.

I'm still not sure of every reference in the film. And the picture is one where the new viewer might be helped by a family tree. But what is clear is Oshima's sense of disgust and horror at what has been done to his family by the rule of the grandfather (this character is fearsomely well played by Kei Sato). Oshima's use of interior space, distended by the wide screen, is akin to looking at Ozu's tidy groupings and ripping them apart with the savage truths that formality is trying to deny. Oshima is a more troubled man than Ozu, but he is the best example of Japanese self-criticism in the era since the war. He has many other films well worth watching: *Diary of a Shinjuko Thief*, *Boy*, and *In the Realm of the Senses*, a movie that explores his considerable awareness of sex. But *The Ceremony* still seems to me his masterpiece. It has a chilly score by Toru Takemitsu, and it is very well photographed by Tsutomu Narushima.

The Champ (1931)

There are anomalies within *The Champ* that transcend its obvious sentimentality and help remind us that it is a King Vidor film (yet not one of his own favorites). Andy Purcell (Wallace Beery) is a failed boxer, a drunk, who is deluded into believing in his own comeback. He lives in Tijuana with his son, Dink (Jackie Cooper, ten when the film opens). But quickly we discover that Andy is divorced from a society woman, Linda (Irene Rich), who is now married to Tony Carlton (Hale Hamilton). The Carltons are well off financially, and they are well intentioned. They like horse racing, but they do not seem to be running liquor or organizing prostitution. So what divorce court gave custody of Dink to Andy? Come to that, how in the world did Andy and Linda ever get married?

Well, you'll tell me that in 1916, briefly, Beery was married to Gloria Swanson (when he was thirty-one and she was nineteen). Still, the narrative structure of *The Champ* establishes the Dink-Andy bond before we ever meet Linda, and demonstrates that the kid is looking after the father as well as he can under the circumstances.

On the face of it, you could see a lot of ways the story could go. Linda tries to regain custody. Dink grows increasingly independent. And a very intriguing clash is set up between the impoverished "warmth" of the Champ's household and the pristine coolness available with Linda. Instead, the story introduces a beloved horse and the problem of its ownership, which sends Andy back into the ring again in a desperate and potentially disastrous bout with Manuel Quiroga (Frank Hagney). This fight takes place, and against all odds, Andy wins. But he has a heart attack and dies, and Dink is taken away by Linda.

The script was by Leonard Praskins, from a story by Frances Marion. Gordon Avil did the photography, and the film is interesting among other things for location work in Tijuana and Agua Caliente (frequent movie escapes in those days). But what is most interesting is not Andy's punch-drunk stalwart sentiments so much as Dink's attitude to the world. Jackie Cooper was the toughie among child stars—Mickey Rooney before the Mick. But he was very good and very grown up, and he makes it clear that he prefers life with the Champ. Indeed, when his father dies, he goes nearly frantic; it is a superb, alarming piece of work, and it shows what a rich character he has become.

And so it's one of the few films where a sequel, or a follow-up, would be interesting. The Carltons are good people, but it's possible to see Dink unhappy or restless with them and compelled to move on. He has the courage, the aggression, and the unshakable basics of Andy. He has found a liveliness in life or a reality in existence that a much more genteel middle-class setting cannot grasp or contain. And that is Vidor, homing in on the elemental and the essential.

Wallace Beery won the Oscar, which is fine, but it's a sign of how widely the film was misread.

Chariots of Fire (1981)

Chariots of Fire is crowded with the names of yesteryear, so the credits make sad reading. Dodi Fayed was executive producer, David Puttnam was producer, Hugh Hudson directed, and Colin Welland wrote it. The cast includes Ben Cross, Ian Charleson, Alice Krige, Patrick Magee, Lindsay Anderson, John Gielgud, and Brad Davis. I know, some of that company are with us still, doing quiet good works. But *Chariots of Fire* rang with the promise and the warning that the Brits were coming, and yet Ian Holm is about the only stalwart professional on the picture who still has credibility.

It's asking a lot to have a film build toward ten seconds of dash and blur—the shortest great event in sports theater, the Olympic 100 meters—and last in the memory. Still, *Chariots of Fire* won Best Picture in its day. It's the story of an age of sprinters left standing after the First World War—Londoner Harold Abrahams (Cross), son of a Russian Jew; Eric Liddell (Charleson), the Scottish child of missionaries, lean as a greyhound and far more devout (though not a great talker); and Jackson Scholz (Davis), American college boy—who come together at the Paris Olympiad of 1924.

Welland wrote the script with a view of athletes that made a nice mix of awesome ability and gestures toward real life. So Abrahams, as a Jew, is looked at just a little askance—don't even ask why there are no black runners in these races (they were inventing jazz). And Liddell misses glory when the crucial heats of his event are moved to Sunday; he doesn't run on Sundays, you see. It's hard to see why, in 1981, anyone really thought this was a movie, instead of just an odd story. But such mean thinking had no vision yet, of young British colts striding out on the training sands to the inspiring sounds of Vangelis (otherwise known as music—and winning an Oscar).

Whether that coup was Puttnam or Dodi Fayed doesn't really matter. It was a high-class production for the uncertain eighties, and it made so stirring a trailer and TV ad that people just had to see the picture. Of course, once they got there, in their seats, they found that quick races hardly sustain serious interest. So the picture is pumped up with romance, religion, and the struggles of a professional trainer, Sam Mussabini (Holm), to be taken seriously. In turn, that character improves and strains the film, for imagistically and spiritually it wants to believe that the young men just run, for God's sake (or not), so that training seems technological and nearly unfair (as well as foreign).

But winning a race only works if, say, you know the boy rider and the Black Stallion love each other. As it is, the race is an excuse for certain shallow observations on England, all at the level of TV movies. The trouble is that the Olympic Games (like most sporting events) have become the province of live television. And the only way to get ten million people to watch the final of the 100 meters is if it happens now, in one shot.

Charulata (1964)

The creative relationship between director Satyajit Ray and poet Rabindranath Tagore (1861–1941) is as intense as that between Ray and his cameraman, Subrata Mitra (b. 1930). And so Ray's response to Tagore's fascination with liberal tendencies in India finds its expression in the enclosed light in which Mitra sees the precious provincial community of *Charulata*. The title comes from the name of the wife, who hardly knows how imprisoning her comfort is. The time is around 1880, in Bengal. Charulata's husband is rich and settled, fond of his English pipe and half in love with the England of Shakespeare and Gladstone. He dreams that Gladstone's Liberals mean better by India than do Disraeli and the Conservatives, and he runs a progressive newspaper, *The Sentinel*, to voice his self-satisfied, provincial thoughts.

To inhabit *Charulata* for twenty minutes is to realize how rich a context Ray had—and how difficult it was for modern Indians or Europeans to pick up on all his references. Yet the density of hypocrisy and muddle is vital to the way the husband likes to sprinkle his Bengali with English phrases, and the way his visiting brother-in-law plays "God Save the Queen" on the piano. The husband is hardworking and earnest, but the brother-in-law is an intriguing mix of fop and poseur: He sings, he writes for literary magazines, he flirts, and he practices indolence. He is barely respectable, but in the innocent gaze of Charulata, he may be the lesson she needs in feeling, expression, and love. She does not quite fall in love with the brother-in-law, but she falls for his version of love, and she realizes that the security she has with her husband is far short of love. Indeed, she writes for the literary magazines, and she is published, but she cannot draw her husband's attention to that much independence.

Meanwhile, Mitra studies these hothouse creatures in deepening close-up. They live in their overdecorated salons and their overplanted gardens. You feel a shortage of air itself. Yet the faces are beautiful, and Mitra's austere black-and-white photography turns them into icons likely to be undermined by fresh ideas. For instance, there are views of Madhabi Mukherjee as the wife in which new ideas seem to grow at the pace of aging or disillusion. The Western viewer may be inclined to think of Chekhov (or Renoir), but I'm sure that we need only a better knowledge of Tagore to see where it all comes from.

The mood changes. The precious stillness is broken by small acts of dishonesty. The brother goes away, and Charulata is left to face the question of whether she can continue to grow in his absence. This is one of the best films about feminist awakening, and it comes as a sweet but belated measure of satisfaction to see that it was made in the same year as Carl Dreyer's *Gertrud*. *Charulata* won the Silver Bear at Berlin, while *Gertrud* was hooted off the screen in Paris.

The Chase (1946)

There has to be room in collections like this for films as unlikely, vagrant, and thoroughly *maudit* as *The Chase* (1946), even if it means firing that large, heavy, and ominously respectable *The Chase* from 1966, the one where Marlon Brando is the sheriff of a depraved Texas town who is beaten to a pulp by the vicious citizenry. We shall not miss that *Chase* too much—concentrate instead on pulp, a vital ingredient of so many American cooking processes.

First of all there is a novel, *The Black Path of Fear*, published in 1944 by Cornell Woolrich, perhaps the most inspired and haunted of all the American noiristas, a man who lived with his mother in a shabby Manhattan hotel and wrote stories to frighten himself. It became a United Artists picture, produced by Seymour Nebenzal, who had worked on *Pandora's Box* and *The Testament of Dr. Mabuse* before leaving Germany, and who would help to produce *Mayerling, Hitler's Madman, Summer Storm, The Chase*, and then the remake of *M*.

Nebenzal, neurotic but talented, entrusted the screenplay for what became *The Chase* to the astonishing Philip Yordan, a mythic figure among American screenwriters—a real talent but a masquerader (he is credited on *Johnny Guitar, Men in War, The Black Book*, and *El Cid*). Yordan grasped the frenzy of the Woolrich novel and did it justice. And so this strange film proceeds accordingly:

Chuck Scott (Robert Cummings) is just out of the Army, a damaged man. In his hazy half-life, he takes a job as chauffeur to a gangster, Eddie Roman (Steve Cochran), but straightaway he starts to fall in love with Roman's pale, mysterious wife, Lorna (Michele Morgan). He escapes with her to Havana, but then retribution catches up and gangsters kill Lorna so that Chuck will be framed. Then a pop goes off in Chuck's head and he wakes to find everything was a dream, except that he is still a chauffeur in love with Lorna. Can he avert the old ending as one version of his life chases another?

The director of the film is Arthur Ripley, another strange fellow, the writer for comedian Harry Langdon and then the maker of increasingly arty trash—his career finished with *Thunder Road*, that sultry fantasy about Robert Mitchum in moonshine country. In addition, *The Chase* is beautifully photographed by Franz Planer (who did *Liebelei*, *Letter from an Unknown Woman* and *Criss Cross*).

The Chase is a great demented rapture, so close to dream as to make no difference. It is also one of the truest reflections of the world of Cornell Woolrich and his amazed mixed feelings over death. I could add that it also stars Peter Lorre as a sadistic gangster—one Lorre scholar actually called it "the strangest film Lorre ever made"—but then you'll be getting really angry that no one has told you about it before. Yes, Robert Cummings is entirely miscast in the lead role. And yes, it really needs Lorre as the desperate hero for a queasy sort of reality to loom into place. But you can't have everything.

The Chelsea Girls (1966)

Early in the 1960s, everyone was rethinking "cinema": what it was, where it had been, and where it was going. Surely there was an obituary sense in that concern. It was as if in the late fifties television had stolen the crown of urgency and purpose (the thing called audience) from the movies, and the cinema had made a few glorious swan songs that summarize the changes in fifty years and the achievement to date: *Lola Montes, The Golden Coach, Ugetsu Monogatari, Vertigo, Some Like It Hot, Rio Bravo,* et cetera. And surely you can see a sweet sisterhood between Angie Dickinson in that last film, asking us to consider what black tights might do for her, and, let's say, Viva in *Blue Movie,* trying to decide whether she has really been screwed or not.

In other words, if you gather together all the startling summaries on the medium offered around 1960—from Godard to Kael, from Hitchcock to McLuhan—don't forget to include Andy Warhol. In what he did and did not do, in his slogans and signs as much as his films, Warhol changed the ground. Few people adored Hollywood as much (or were so prescient in seeing that nostalgic reverence for it had turned camp), and no one at that time was so radically cannibalistic about why and how we were prepared to eat the signs of fame and beauty and turn them into excrement. Moreover, in so many ways Warhol sought to remove the "extra" of cinema—the vibrato, the pathos, the shivering shakes he saw—that it was so expressive it should play "flat" as if for the Lumière brothers, in 1895. Once the camera has made that intrusion upon nature through appearance, it should be that films mean anything (and nothing). They just are. Thus, all films are great and boring.

If I choose *The Chelsea Girls* to stand for Warhol, it's not because he ever reckoned to make one film that captured all his thoughts, as in a masterpiece. I pick it because it is a film subject to the theater of performance, for it plays as it projects, and such things as "timing" or "cross-reference" can be taken any way you like. Quite literally, if you have the elements of the film, you can play it your way.

Beyond that, the stunning originality of life unwinding is unerringly a riddle over fate and freedom—was this directed or planned? Is it theater or life? The "vision" of people just talking may be boring, but it is also a primitive occasion. Let the camera be chained. Let everything be filmed "in absentia"—it may look as "beautiful" as Bob Williams. Don't worry too much about the craft of it all, and don't waste our time getting the acting right! Warhol never once felt that an actor could go wrong or right. It's enough for them to be there. Warhol knew that he was a kind of last emperor—not just of America's cultural supremacy but of art's gimmick and film's gotcha. He is the force that lets us see that the world has become an act. It is a very bleak vision, notwithstanding his own lazy insolence and the empty assurance that everyone looked terrific. It no longer photographs.

Un Chien Andalou (1928)

"Once upon a time. A balcony. A man is sharpening his razor by the balcony. The man looks through a window at the sky and sees . . . A light cloud passing across the face of the full moon. Then the head of a young woman with wide-open eyes. The blade of the razor moves toward one of her eyes. The light cloud now moves across the face of the moon, the razor-blade slices the eye of the young woman, dividing it."

Anyone who has ever tried to teach film knows that scene, and without being identifiable as sadists those of us who have used the seventeen-minute "silent" film have invariably chosen to show it without warning. The talk of the dead sheep can come later, after the panic attacks that were still very common in the 1970s (when some students had seen Vietnam). I hope they happen still, because if ever outrages like this lose their power to shock then maybe the movies can fold up the tent.

If I were teaching anything on film, I'd come to this blade of a film very early and I'd say, Look, here we are at the moment when the lifelike dream went complete and industrial. We are at the start of sound and the complete fantasy, all done under the easeful guise of the lifelike. But here we are, in the same year, in Paris (with bits of Beethoven, Wagner, and a tango) as this "silent" short caused such a stink and showed the other way to let film work upon ourselves as complete dream, an apparition in which the lifelike is the ability of the ghosts to smile and be polite. Thus, the man on the balcony (Buñuel himself) wears a striped shirt, without a collar. And when he, or another he, comes to hold the young woman's eye open, he has a striped diagonal tie, too, not evident in the fuller shot.

Continuity gives way to consciousness. It's just the first lesson looking at dreams, along with the realization that we have to explain or respond to the carved, burnished head of the man in the moonlight—is he a thug or a lover? Next lesson: Every question of analysis contains its own answer. He is both. See everything. Use everything.

Within minutes of the cloud and the moon, a young man (Pierre Batcheff) sees the woman (Simone Mareuil):

"The man with the determination of someone who feels sure of his rights, goes over to the young woman and, after staring at her lustfully with rolling eyes, grabs her breasts through her dress.

"Close-up of the man's hands fondling the breasts which appear through the dress. The man's face has a terrible look, almost of mortal anguish, and a stream of blood-flecked saliva begins to run out of the corner of his mouth onto the naked breasts. The breasts disappear to become a pair of thighs which the man kneads."

It is only seventeen minutes—you can afford the time, even if no one can take the risk lightly. This is the start of Luis Buñuel, of course, not just a great career, but the most naked indicator that the history of movie is the history of whether or not we can come to terms with sexual existence. And don't think that's a foregone conclusion. Its half-brother, cruelty, gains every day; there are people who would rather do torture than fuck. We are hardly more mature than we were in '28, and maybe sex and cinema both need to be put back in their sleeping bags and locked in the cabinet. The Andalusian dog may have passed us by.

La Chienne (1931)

La Chienne is Jean Renoir with sound. In fact, *On Purge Bébé* was his sound debut, a test taken on to prove that he could handle *La Chienne.* As he explained it, the film was an attempt to make a *naturaliste* tradition: It was filmed in and around Montmartre, in natural light, employing as much slang and untidy talk as possible, yet somehow having the camera soar as if it were a butterfly.

Monsieur Legrand (Michel Simon) is a failure. He works as a cashier in a large store. He is married to a very unpleasant woman (Magdeleine Bérubet), who regularly finds him failing in comparisons with her first husband, a soldier killed in the war. He is also a Sunday painter, unknown to the art world. One night, on the streets, Legrand sees a drunken pimp, Dede (Georges Flamant) roughing up one of his girls, Lulu (Janie Marèse). Legrand sees Dede off and takes the girl home.

One thing leads to another. Legrand falls for Lulu—in a very casual way, this is a deeply erotic film, with Legrand's humble innocence exposed to flesh and rapture for the first time in his life. Of course, Lulu and Dede milk the foolish man. They draw off his money. They have their eyes on the cash box at his store. But Legrand establishes Lulu in a small apartment. There are stairs leading up to it; there is a courtyard and windows on the far side of the yard. This is the vision of Jean Renoir coming to life.

Things go well for Legrand for a moment. He paints. He loves Lulu. And he bumps into that supposedly lost soldier, the first husband. He sees how his dreadful marriage can be nullified. But, of course, his fall is also assured, and one rainy day he finds Lulu in bed with Dede. Legrand is crushed.

I cut now to a passage in a letter from Renoir to Dudley Nichols in the hope of an American remake of *La Chienne* (Cary Grant wanted to be Legrand!): "Legrand tells Lulu he will take her away, far from Paris, and from Dede. They will live together in the country, he will paint, and they will be happy. Lulu is lying on a bed cutting the pages of a book. Street-singers are outside. Whilst he paces up and down in the room their voices reach him through an open window. He is trying to understand what's going on in the girl's head. And suddenly he understands she does not love him, has never loved him. He tells her so, and it makes her laugh. She cannot stop. And this laugh is so exasperating that he kills her with the paper-knife."

So much is there: If only she hadn't wanted to read, if only the window had not carried a song, if only people weren't destroyed by love. It is tiny, intimate, and messy, and it is so much more profound and ironic than even Ernst Lubitsch's *Trouble in Paradise* a year later (or Fritz Lang's Greenwich Village remake of *La Chienne, Scarlet Street,* from 1945). This is Renoir in the 1930s, the decade that had no minor films.

Chimes at Midnight (1966)

For years, it seemed, the one part for which Orson Welles had been in training was Falstaff. But it was as long ago as 1939 that he had first done the play *Five Kings*, his own free adaptation of the Shakespeare texts, telling the story of Sir John Falstaff and what Welles always thought of—with a fat tear in his eye—as "Merrie England." At the age of twenty-four Welles had been Falstaff, while Burgess Meredith (seven years his senior) had been Prince Hal. But the obsession lasted, and grew.

And so in the winter of 1964, on locations near Barcelona and Madrid, Welles brought Falstaff to film, using his old *Five Kings* script, which draws from *Richard II*, the two parts of *Henry IV*, *Henry V*, and *The Merry Wives of Windsor*. It's a masterpiece in which some of his modern carelessness—sound issues, continuity, and so on—are easily eclipsed by the emotional intensity. This is the film Major Amberson is seeing as he gazes into the flickering firelight. And although Welles was "only" fifty as he made the film, there's no doubting what the midnight bell means, or what the necessary rejection by Hal stands for.

Of course, the egocentrism has not abated one bit, because Orson *is* Falstaff. He is the fat, boozy magician who has lost his touch. This is happening to him—and even Shakespeare knew that Falstaff dies of a broken heart. Moreover, though this film is pledged to the lovely, nostalgic view of England when it was Arden, sentimentality is crushed at every turn. Chivalry makes a few gestures, but the battle scene, done in mud and treachery, has the Somme and worse in mind. The merriment exists only in the minds of men, together with their capacity for hurt.

The photography was by Edmond Richard (he had done *The Trial* with Welles), and even in Spanish winter light it has exquisite moments, along with the castles and mountains that are not quite England—but who cares? Welles credits himself with "Costumes," and the crew is all Spanish. But Spain was a country Welles loved, and it shows.

Placed in Europe, he was able to hire a remarkable cast. Keith Baxter is great as Hal, and it's clear he was very close to Orson. John Gielgud makes an austere Henry IV. Jeanne Moreau is wonderful as Doll Tearsheet. Margaret Rutherford is Mistress Quickly, Norman Rodway is Hotspur, Marina Vlady is his wife, Alan Webb is Justice Shallow, and then there are Walter Chiari, Michael Aldridge, Tony Beckley, Fernando Rey, Andrew Faulds, José Nieto, Jeremy Rowe, Welles's daughter Beatrice (as a page), and Paddy Bedford. Ralph Richardson is the narrator.

The film opened at the Cannes Festival in 1966 and played none too well in the following years. But in the gradual reappraisal of Welles that started in the seventies, *Chimes at Midnight* has been accepted as a late masterwork, as well as a reminder that if doing things in a proper, classical manner is what appeals to you, why, Welles could do that, too. But he had it in mind to be independent, experimental, an island, a Prospero as much as a Falstaff.

Chinatown (1974)

Tell me the story again, please.

Very well, there was this detective in Los Angeles, Jake Gittes, as honest as he could be after years with the LAPD. But he had had trouble in Chinatown and so retired into independent operation. Then he was set up, and you have to realize that he was sought out in just the way that Scottie was in *Vertigo*. Someone picked him to receive the story that Hollis Mulwray was having an affair. Trace it back and you'll see it was all a cruel design. Jake Gittes did his best, but he was as much damage as he was good, because he fell in love on the job with a woman who was such trouble it smelled like gangrene. And so, finally, the bad man, Noah Cross, was left in charge, and they led Jake away to some hiding hole and they whispered in his ear that it was all "Chinatown." I really don't see why you love the story so much.

It was a story that Robert Towne, an Angeleno, dreamed up for his pal Jack Nicholson to play. And another friend, Robert Evans, would produce it at Paramount. But Evans thought that Roman Polanski should direct, and Polanski battled with Towne over the script—it had to be clearer and tougher. Towne had had a gentler ending, with less death. But Polanski knew it was a story that had to end terribly—so no one forgot. The director won, and the picture worked with its very bleak ending.

What's more, the picture worked in every way you could think of. Faye Dunaway was the woman, and she was lovely but flawed and incapable of being trusted. John Huston was Noah Cross, and the more you see the film, the better you know that that casting is crucial, because Cross is so attractive, so winning, so loathsome. And the rest of the cast was a treat: Perry Lopez, John Hillerman, Darrell Zwerling, Diane Ladd, Roy Jenson, Burt Young, Belinda Palmer, and the others. John Alonso shot it. Richard Sylbert was the production designer. Sam O'Steen edited the film. Jerry Goldsmith delivered a great score. The craft work, the details, are things to dream on. We are in 1937. And don't forget Polanski's own little bit of being himself.

So it's a perfect thriller, and a beautiful film noir in color. Moreover, if you care to look into how William Mulholland once brought the water from the Owens Valley to Los Angeles, it is a piece of local history. But with this extra aspect—that accommodation of the history of southern California itself, and the fable of how sometimes power and corruption make life and the future possible—you also get another reflection on filmmaking in that world: It is that you can do very good work, work so full of affection and detail and invention that you can live with it over the years, but in the end the system will fuck you over and someone will whisper in your ear that you are not to mind, because "It's Chinatown."

And that's how it worked out. There had been a trilogy in the reasonably honest mind of Robert Towne. They let him make the first part near enough to his own dream so that he would always know it could have been. And then they crushed him on the second (*The Two Jakes*)—blew it straight to hell—so no one had the heart ever to ask about the third.

El Cid (1961)

The films made in Spain in the early 1960s by the producer Samuel Bronston were an uneasy bunch. *55 Days at Peking* marked the professional demise of director Nicholas Ray, and *The Fall of the Roman Empire* had a melancholy and a sense of inevitable historical disintegration that were not well suited to Anthony Mann. In Ray's hands, *King of Kings* was a striving for belief from a man notoriously lacking in confidence. The only one of the four films that seemed promising, and accurately assigned, was Mann's *El Cid,* which now stands as one of the last authentic epics in American film history.

Perhaps it helped that very few in the audience knew the legend of how the Spanish warrior hero had cleared the Moors out of Spain in the eleventh century. But if the energy was fresh, the opportunities provided by Spain—in landscapes and castles—was immense, and there was a fairly tidy Cold War message, in that the Moor chieftain (Herbert Lom) easily seemed like a forerunner of Fascist threats. Today, that ease is gone, of course, and *El Cid* is rather awkwardly anti-Islamic in its basis.

The screenplay, by Philip Yordan, emerged from his purchasing a draft that Fredric M. Frank had written years earlier for Cecil B. DeMille. All Yordan did was make sure that trials by conflict fell at regular intervals, and that the epic tale was underscored by a thwarted romance between the Cid and Jimena. It was then up to Bronston to get Charlton Heston and Sophia Loren for those roles. What Mann brought to the task was an unclouded conviction—from first to last he believes in the nobility of the Cid—and an imagination ready to make the story as good-looking as possible.

El Cid had outstanding art direction from John Moore and Veniero Colasanti, in which sheer prettiness and historical plausibility ride side by side. The photography was by Robert Krasker in 70 mm, and it is notable for some lucid winter scenes as well as the finale on the beaches near Valencia. The great Yakima Canutt was on second unit, and Mann was still a tremendous director of intimate fight scenes—no matter that they involved heavy armor and swords as tall as men.

With music by Miklós Rózsa, *El Cid* begins to gather together all the arts of storytelling with the skill of *The Adventures of Robin Hood.* And, in truth, it is an epic that does not disappoint and that draws excellent, earnest performances from its two leads. But the richness of the film is in its supporting cast and the care that has been taken with so many smaller roles, not least Geneviève Paige, Raf Vallone, John Fraser, Hurd Hatfield, and Andrew Cruickshank, all of whom work as if in a small, intense drama. Today it's fanciful to think of that kind of money being employed on such a story (though *El Cid* had rentals of $12 million, three times what it had cost). Far more important, I don't think there are other actors, directors, or writers who could approach the monumental narrative with the same enthusiasm and faith.

The Cincinnati Kid (1965)

In the early years of the twenty-first century, various forms of poker became very hot on television. A special under-the-table camera let us see the undeclared cards, and the rest was chips and sweat. So it's nice to give cultural credit to the influence of a silly but entertaining film, *The Cincinnati Kid*, which gave as good a clue to poker on the small screen as *The Hustler* had done with pool.

It all began life as a Martin Ransohoff production, with Sam Peckinpah set as director. Ring Lardner, Jr. did his job on the screenplay and spent a week in read-throughs with Peckinpah and the cast, making adjustments. The film began, but Peckinpah went off and shot a scene in which the Rip Torn character was in bed with his mistress—well, Sam cast a black girl, and in 1965 that was still trouble. So Ransohoff fired Peckinpah. Norman Jewison was brought in in his place, and he claimed the right to have a fresh script. To that end, Terry Southern was called on (he and Lardner never met), and Southern shifted the setting from St. Louis to New Orleans.

So the Kid is this very hot young poker player: because it's Steve McQueen in the part, he's also ultra cool. To prove himself, he's going to have to beat the grand old man of the game, Lancey (Edward G. Robinson). All of this comes after the Kid, through arrogance, has let slip his sweet girlfriend (Tuesday Weld) and taken up with no-good Ann-Margret. The warning here is pointed. Ann-Margret is playing a scarlet woman in a silent film, whereas Tuesday gives every hint of lasting all through the week. So the Kid's lack of judgment in love prepares you for who will win the card game. Still, the confrontation of two owls' faces over the cards is well handled, and it was a delight to see Robinson in such fine fettle. One-on-one, there were few people who could surpass his concentration.

Apart from this, the Southernness is laid on like fudge sauce on a bourbon sundae. But there is a lot of local color, including Cab Calloway, and there are excellent supporting performances from Karl Malden, as the dealer and Ann-Margret's haunted husband, and from Joan Blondell, as "Lady Fingers," a relief dealer. One look from Edward G. and we know where she got that nickname.

Of course, the film did very well and was a vehicle in the irresistible rise of Steve McQueen, a man who seems to have been likeable in those precious gaps between "Action" and "Cut" and nowhere else. Robinson gives so much more to the film, not least that gentle, shy conversation with the cards, that wonders if the vehicle is his.

As for poker, with interest so high now, we might be in for a run of such pictures. So actors, beware: The greatest faces tend to come in second, after the face cards.

Cinema Paradiso (1988)

In the year 2007, readers of *The Guardian* in Britain were asked to vote for the greatest foreign-language movie ever made. *Cinema Paradiso* was a resounding winner. And I suppose there is a way in which that title, and this subject matter, seem to ride on a perfect United Nations film, a movie to show E.T.—actually, judging by E.T.'s voluminous tear sacs, I think he has seen it somehow, somewhere. Perhaps he left his home in a brave attempt to forget it.

So here is the story. In a little town in Sicily, not the prettiest, not the worst, there is this little boy. His name is Toto (Salvatore Cascio), and he is the prettiest: He won poster boy with heartbreaking smile two years in a row. He has a darling mama but no father, so he spends his time in the projection booth at the Cinema Paradiso, where the projectionist, Alfredo (Philippe Noiret), is a kindly fellow. I know, Noiret is French, and you wonder how he got the job in a Sicilian town. You also may wonder why he has only one 35 mm projector, not two, so he doesn't get to make change-overs.

Well, one day nitrate film stock bursts into flame and Alfredo is blinded. Whereupon Toto takes over the job, though the old man is paid. Toto grows up, everyone gets older—you have seen this movie before? Toto as a teenager meets a lovely girl, Elena—a knockout. But her father thinks Toto unsuitable. So they break up. Alfredo urges Toto to go away—become a film director. He goes. He becomes Jacques Perrin—he becomes even Giuseppe Tornatore, maker of this film.

Alfredo dies. Toto comes back to town. Mother is very forgiving over how little he has seen her. But on the streets Toto sees—of course, it is Elena. And so Toto is eventually reunited with her (she is now Brigitte Fossey, not a bad deal for all concerned). There is a very romantic scene in a car as they talk, and the whole muddle of the past is worked out. And then—nice timing, huh?—as they pull the old Paradiso down, Toto sees a montage of the screen's great kissing scenes.

In fact, Tornatore made a long version, and it flopped in Italy. Then a 123-minute version goes to Cannes, wins the jury prize, and later gets the Oscar for Best Foreign Picture. An international hit. Whereupon Tornatore rereleases the 174-minute version, which has all the grown-up Elena stuff and lots more chocolate sauce. What is missing is who this crybaby film director is, why he treats his Mama so bad, and what?—was there a war in Italy and fascisti and all that nasty stuff? *Cinema Paradiso* is mercilessly made, as a pump for tears. And it is so moving, you want to cut the projectionist's throat. It has many film clips, of course, from Renoir to Antonioni, and a little boy's face as seen through the booth window is a winning effect—the first dozen times you see it. After that, you're on your own.

Citizen Kane (1941)

In his retreat, his castle and kingdom, a man is dying. Sooner or later, he will utter his last word. Does he spend hours and a year deciding what it should be, or is it just any word that occurs? In this case, whatever process arrives at the word, it is delivered with intense emotion, as a kiss for us or the camera, the mouth in full close-up, like the ship for life's voyage. "Rosebud," say the lips—like a Man Ray mouth, floating in time and space. And with that expiration, death seems to occur. A glass ball, holding a small house and a snowstorm, slips from the lifeless hand and cracks open on the hard floor.

Is it that noise, or the word, that brings a nurse in from outside? We never know, but we see the door open in the shard of broken glass. We realize that the word was not a call to the nurse: it was the man's gift to us, his legacy.

Yet somehow the world seems to know that he said "Rosebud" as he died. It is just that no one knows what "Rosebud" might mean. But the word is enough to convince journalists—the newsreel people—that they do not know what this man was about, this Charles Foster Kane. "Rosebud" is a secret. It is also the best hint he could leave to make sharp minds like theirs beagles in the hunt. A man named Thompson is assigned to go off and talk to everyone in Kane's life to find out what "Rosebud" meant. I bet it'll be something very simple, says his editor.

And so Thompson sets off in his journey to talk to a former wife, a righthand man, a lost friend, a mysterious butler. Did you ever hear him say "Rosebud"? Thompson asks. No, never, they answer—it could have been . . . well, something he lost. A man with everything is likely to remember anything he lost.

One man, the butler, says he heard the word—he was close to the nurse on that last night. But no, he doesn't know what it meant. And so the search is at an end. The newsreel people are at the warehouse full of Kane properties. Most of it has a date with the incinerator; the stoves are alight already. The reporters leave. The camera stays. And so we are there as a workman picks up a rough sled from the nineteenth century, a kid's toy, and takes it to the furnace and throws it in. And is it the camera looking, or just our need to know? Is it enquiry's just end of our pact with Kane: We heard the word; we find the answer. But as the sledge begins to burn, we see its trademark, "Rosebud," before it starts to burn away. In the instant of discovery, the clue begins to be destroyed.

Beyond that, it is up to us to decide whether "Rosebud" is a true measure of fondness for and loss felt over those days in Colorado when Charlie refought the Civil War, cried "The Union forever!" as his parents broke up, and played in the snow when his world was all white, before the darkness came in? Or is "Rosebud" just a trick in a game, a sweet sidestep, a feint, a way of saying, Well, life has to be about something, doesn't it, so never mind the serious things, let it be about "Rosebud" and the thought that once there was a hope and a calm and a play, though it only came to be noticed when all those things had been pushed aside in life's dark. It's up to us.

City Lights (1931)

Chaplin thought of a clown losing his sight. The clown has a daughter, and he amuses her by pretending to be blind. But Chaplin realized this might be mawkish, and so he developed the notion of a lovely girl, a humble flower seller, who wins the love of the tramp. But he believed he needed more plot. So he created a similar kind of second level in the tramp's life. The tramp becomes part of a rich man's game: The millionaire entertains the tramp whenever he is drunk but ignores him when sober.

In Chaplin's *My Autobiography,* and in all the other biographies, there is not a complete answer to what the combination meant to him. He had a very technical side: He was keen on filling time, and he wanted familiar routines—the clash of rich and poor had always been a stock-in-trade. He loved the sentimentality of what the heart feels and the eyes don't see. So the tramp would save the girl's eyesight and then, when she could see, she would not notice him.

I suspect that Chaplin could develop these twin ideas only by not relating them in all the ways that are available. In other words, the intellectualization of his art could have stripped it. He had to depend on situations where, in effect, he was all the people—or they were parts of his teeming soul. And it's quite clear from what happened on *City Lights* that he felt the potential of these setups without grasping the detail. That's why the schedule went well over five hundred days (on an 86-minute picture!), with many of those days spent waiting for Chaplin as he thought about what he wanted. Yet any simple analysis on his part, that his two plots were versions of one idea, could have ruined it.

So love and money (Charlie's warring passions) came together in a film still being made when Wall Street crashed in October 1929.

He was wanton in his changes of mind. So he fired Henry Clive (who had also done the sets) as the millionaire and replaced him with Harry Myers, no matter that that meant reshooting a lot of material. He never warmed to Virginia Cherrill, his discovery for the blind girl, and had terrible trouble getting her to be as exquisite as he believed the girl should be. He came very close to firing her. And in the famous last shot, of himself with a flower in his teeth, watching the girl ignore him, Charlie was all parts, all in one. It is monstrous, great acting, cannibalistic, and one of the most potent shots in film history.

City Lights opened in an impoverished world, still silent except for music, and it did immense business. Chaplin had made it his enterprise, and in the end he likely profited by $5 million—extraordinary money in those days, and his greatest success. To this day, the film is worth every penny, and it is the amazing mirror of his very mixed-up ego. You could argue that there isn't another movie that so addresses the appeal of films to poor people in a world where the only other recourse would be violent political action.

City Streets (1931)

Although *City Streets* deserves to be remembered as director Rouben Mamoulian's second film at Paramount, and a far more drastic experiment with sound than *Applause,* quick history says it is one of the few times Dashiell Hammett had his name on a picture as a screenwriter (as opposed to author of the source material). This is true: Hammett wrote a story, someone named Max Marcin did some adapting, and Oliver H. P. Garrett turned it into a script—though I suspect that all three men raised their eyebrows to see what Mamoulian had done with it. In fact, Hammett wrote to Lillian Hellman that he found the film "pretty lousy, though Sylvia Sidney makes the whole thing seem fairly good in spots. She's good, that ugly little baby, and currently my favorite screen actress."

Well, that's a note of authentic sadism, plus the discovery that even distinguished authors go to the movies to look at the girls and dream about them. The story is Gary Cooper in his country boy mode: he is "the Kid," a guy who works in a carnival and falls for Nan Cooley (Sylvia Sidney), the daughter of a racketeer. Alas, the Kid gets drawn closer to a life of crime, and soon he's in prison. None of which is very interesting, though Paul Lukas and Guy Kibbee give good performances as gangsters, and there is a natural chemistry between Cooper and Sidney.

The film is important and still worth seeing because of two things: the ways in which Mamoulian explores the possibilities of sound, and the wonderful chemistry he has achieved with cameraman Lee Garmes—himself one of the most artistic of Hollywood photographers and someone famous for searching out new ways for film language to work. So, just as Mamoulian had begun in *Applause, City Streets* goes all over the city (New York) and Garmes delivers a tone poem to the place that deserves lasting attention. And, of course, the visuals are now all the more eloquent in that the film is conceived of as a sound symphony. Mamoulian uses voice-overs with flashbacks in a way not done before. He turns dialogue into abstract noise with just certain words or phrases sticking out. He begins to build the sound track with talk, music, effects, and atmospheric sound in the way indicated in *Applause.*

Paramount must have had mixed feelings: The experiments (and they don't all succeed) smothered the story too much. Mamoulian himself might have replied, Why not take a year to shoot all manner of sound experiments before embarking on a piece of material? Of course, that was too sensible or long-term for the factory, and so Mamoulian began to get the reputation of a technician, not terribly interested in material or story. Mamoulian never got an award from the Academy (or even a nomination). Warners got one for *The Jazz Singer,* and in 1959 Lee de Forest got an honorary award for his pioneering work with sound. Sound was irresistible, but Mamoulian was one of those who knew why.

Claire's Knee (1970)

In the matter of Eric Rohmer, with so many films that are reflections or variants of each other, it would be too easy to take them all—or to leave them all behind. You could argue that few directors came so close, so regularly, to meeting their own ambitions. And I must confess that I have sometimes found myself in the middle of a Rohmer film, content but utterly lost, because I was thinking about something else altogether. And I can't help feeling that there was a moment, at the end of the 1960s, when Rohmer mattered most. He seemed to turn a corner, one in which the physical became mathematical—it is like the right angle made by, let us say, a knee at the moment when it shifts from being part of a body to a shape in a theorem. I know, for myself, it is Nabokovian.

So here we are in a village near Annecy in the summer. Jerome is visiting from Stockholm, where he is cultural attaché. His marriage is all planned; he is only waiting. He is Jean-Claude Brialy, the classical figure among young French actors. He meets an old friend, Aurora (Aurora Cornu), a novelist, and they both agree, playfully, to see him as a character. He meets Aurora's landlady, Madame Walter (Michèle Montel), and her teenage daughter, Laura (Béatrice Romand). Aurora tells Jerome that Laura loves him. He doubts this but is too provoked to ignore it. He kisses the girl. She rebuffs him—she was merely looking for a father figure. But then Claire (Laurence de Monaghan) arrives—a little older (seventeen?), moody, nearly a woman, but burdened with a stupid boyfriend. Jerome realizes that the boyfriend is unfaithful. Caught in a storm, he tells Claire this. She is distraught. He comforts her—he touches her knee. He tells Aurora, proud to have made it as a character. He goes away to be married.

There it is, a little summer adventure, all shot in the amiable light by Nestor Almendros. There is no music, no adornment, no frame—except for Aurora's way of judging everything as worthy of a story or not. It is intensely erotic, no matter that Jerome remains gentlemanly, kind, and civilized. I hope the touch may help Claire become a good woman, just as it may make Jerome a more mature husband.

This is a world where people talk a great deal more than they do things, and it seems to me entirely true to the condition of summer holiday and life at large. It's also a deeply suspenseful film, and a wholehearted immersion in the absurd—after all, even in 1970, was it a criminal offense to touch a girl's knee? No, but perhaps it was a singular failure of the human spirit to let it go unattended. Rohmer is one of the kindest of film directors, and that is a quality that doesn't crowd our heroes' lives. Aurora Cornu, I believe, was a novelist, but she was also one of the thirty or forty special women Rohmer found over the years for a film. Indeed, Rohmer was a tender wolf, so much more gentle than Roger Vadim, and so much more nurturing.

Cleopatra (1963)

Long before this monster of its own doom dragged itself (243 minutes) across the wide screen, the picture had been stifled by its fuss and furor. So what chance does a real queen of Egypt have when trying to emerge from the embrace of Elizabeth Taylor—not just notorious for her $1 million salary (the first for a woman), not just near death as the project foundered in Britain, but then so much the subject of the film that she managed to turn her Antony into her guy. No wonder, then, if, despite all the research on period and costume, she and Burton manage to look like a couple from mid-America enjoying themselves at Caesars Palace, the soon-to-be opened and innovative theme casino in Las Vegas.

It's not that Elizabeth Taylor is bad in the film. She was always, beneath all the fuss, a professional and a smart actress who knew her range very well. But that meant she was shrewd enough to know there was little point in doing *Cleopatra* as a thinking person's epic. Sooner or later, it's sex and the asp; it's desert scenery, old palaces, and battles; it's gold leaf, doing your wanton act, and being drawn in a chariot by a hundred seminaked Nubians. It's spectacle, and yet the strange rescuing decision made by Darryl F. Zanuck as the film spun out of control was to make it intelligent.

The whole thing had begun as a Walter Wanger production, with Rouben Mamoulian directing. Sets were built at Pinewood in England, and Cleopatra herself caught a mighty chill that turned to pneumonia. She didn't perk up until she got to Rome, with Joseph L. Mankiewicz in charge. While he made the script literate, she waited on an authentic Egyptian throne with her then husband, Eddie Fisher (snatched from Debbie Reynolds), and then along came Richard Burton. Imagine the forlorn task of Mankiewicz trying to make these sex-and-publicity freaks sound Shavian. (Of course the Shaw version, *Caesar and Cleopatra,* had been done years earlier, and with Claude Rains and Vivien Leigh, it was a small delight. Leigh looked feline, sexy, crafty, dangerous, and something you could wrap up in a carpet.) Whereas Liz already had more bulk than flimsy clothes were kind to. Her eyelashes needed cranes!

All you can say is that the film got done—for $44 million more or less. It earned $26 million, and on an intelligent film plenty of people can see that those figures don't match. Worse by far was the unstoppable gulf opening up between publicity and reality. The picture business had always been for barkers and come-on artists—Wait for next week! Wait for *Gone With the Wind*!! We did, and we judged that the wait had been worthwhile. But the years of publicity and paparazzi on *Cleopatra* could not hide a sluggish, dull film without wit, beauty, sex, or blood. Yes, it does talk a lot, and at last Mankiewicz's smart talk began to sound dead on arrival.

You have to see *Cleopatra* if you have any remote interest in film history, but it is better to read the Joe Hyams and Wanger book on the mishaps along the way. Rex Harrison was Caesar, of course—why can't Caesar be more like an Englishman? The only people to emerge with credit are Pamela Brown and Roddy McDowall, but that's not quite enough.

The Clock (1945)

At Dartmouth College, I discovered that the archive possessed a 16 mm print of Vincente Minnelli's *The Clock,* a 90-minute movie, on two reels of equal length. That's what gave me the idea. We aligned two 16 mm projectors side by side. Reel 1 was loaded onto the first projector, playing forward, with sound. Reel 2 was put on the second running backward from the end of the film toward the middle, without sound. The two images played side by side.

What did it accomplish, beyond a method of screening films in half the normal time? Well, it introduced a new mode of film—in reverse—so stunning, so lovely, so surreal, that it helped eyes appreciate all the same lyrical, kinetic things in forward motion, things to which we become so accustomed that we grow blasé. Movies are about movement. Second, it became apparent that they have an internal structure—master shot, close up, reaction, et cetera—that plays over and over again. Films are narrative machines. And as the two parts converged an exhilarating artificiality became clear in which momentum surpassed meaning.

The method seemed not just fair but enlightening with a picture based on meeting and time, and on the rapidity with which a meaning—"love"—could be conveyed in that time. A girl and a soldier meet by chance under the clock at Penn Station in New York. They fall in love, and though he has only forty-eight hours left on his leave, they will be married before he goes off to war.

Next point of view. This very simple story was beset by chaos. M-G-M had cast Judy Garland as the girl, despite the mounting difficulties of working with her. They had a script, by Robert Nathan, derived from a story by Paul and Pauline Gallico. Jack Conway was going to direct; he collapsed. Fred Zinnemann replaced him—the Zinnemann who had just made *The Seventh Cross.* But Zinnemann was quiet, introverted, logical. He couldn't see why you had to tell Judy you loved her all the time. After ten days, Judy had lunch with Minnelli and explained the situation. On *Meet Me in St. Louis* she had done her best work for him. They had been nearly in love, but they knew he was gay.

Judy asked him to take over. Zinnemann was ready to resign. The studio had the Penn Station set built and $200,000 spent. So Minnelli came on board, and the tenderness, the charm, and the love were back. You can see it in every foot of this lovely little film. But they were trapped. Judy moved in with Vincente. They got married. It was Hollywood perfection. No, of course it couldn't last—though Liza came out of its odd egg, looking startled.

By the way, Robert Walker (the soldier) behaved like a champ. He was going crazy at the time, because his wife, Jennifer Jones, was dumping him for David O. Selznick, the producer who had discovered her.

The art may look natural, but this is not an easy life.

A Clockwork Orange (1971)

With *A Clockwork Orange* (if not before), a problem came to the surface with Stanley Kubrick, a matter very like one's response to Billy Wilder: If the artist doesn't like people or humankind, then how long can it be before his films take on a sardonic mannerism where cruelty is hard to tell from style? It seems to me part of Kubrick's analytical eye for intelligence that he tends to see people in terms of the mistakes they make. This is lucid sometimes, but so cold. Think of the Peatty marriage in *The Killing*, the paranoid state of the army in *Paths of Glory*, the madness running society in *Dr. Strangelove*; think of the shells of beings in *2001*. *Lolita* is the one film where we have a chance of liking the people, and surely that comes from the irresistible thrust of Nabokov, a novelist sometimes challenged for his chilly control and supercilious omniscience.

Having lived for much of a decade in England, Kubrick was undoubtedly affected by English issues. *A Clockwork Orange* came from Anthony Burgess's virtuoso novel, with an invented language for its teenagers, but it also reflected England's horror of personal violence, along with its seeming indifference to bureaucratic or institutional force. The world of the film is very stylized, but you can feel the mean streets of England, where young people have grown steadily more callous. Burgess did not want to work on the film, so Kubrick took the script on himself, and he kept faith with the novel.

In many ways, this was his fullest film to date. The air of the near future allows a great surge of invention in the décor and the costumes, and Kubrick took color to heart for the first time. John Barry did wonderful work with the production design, and the costumes by Milena Canonero—especially the droogs in white, a codpiece, and a bowler hat—have passed into international culture. John Alcott did a superb job with the camera and with lenses that regularly stretched real space to bursting.

But there's something else new to Kubrick here, which is the zest, the desperation, and the dread of Malcolm McDowell as Alex. McDowell was so alive then, so passionate and gloomy, so nasty and saintly. He breaks through Kubrick's restraint—he makes the film love him in a way that had never occurred in Kubrick before (it would happen again with Jack Nicholson in *The Shining*). Moreover, Kubrick's old fondness for supporting players came through in the use of Patrick Magee, Michael Bates, Adrienne Corri, Miriam Karlin, and Philip Stone (as Dad).

The film was deservedly controversial. The rape, to "Singin' in the Rain," was too gleeful for many. To this day, there are tender souls who should not see that scene. Several moral guardians wondered aloud whether it was dangerous. Of course, in some ways this question was at the heart of the film's theme—and that put censors on their guard. But in England crimes followed that Kubrick felt were copies of acts in his film. So he censored it himself. He had control of the film in Britain, and for the last two decades of his life he would not allow it to be shown there.

Close Encounters of the Third Kind (1977)

It was whispered in advance of *Close Encounters* that Steven Spielberg's film was going directly to the "third kind," in that Spielberg did not really do human closeness. He did man meets truck or man meets shark, but not intimacy. But then, as he prepared the film, he started seeing Amy Irving, and he had Paul Schrader as his first screenwriter because Schrader brought some spiritual quality to the idea of man meets lights in the sky. There were many bridges and a lot of water to come: Schrader claimed no screen credit in the event—though later he felt a little tricked into that generosity. But when all was said and done, *Close Encounters* was something new for Spielberg in that it concerned very ordinary people convinced that they had seen and felt something momentous. What's more, the momentous was not threatening or disturbing.

I don't know if I believe in UFOs, said Spielberg, but I believe in people who believe in them. And he had three characters, from humble roots, who know what they have seen: Roy Neary (Richard Dreyfuss), a blue-collar guy from Muncie, Indiana; Gillian Guiler (Melinda Dillon), a mom; and Barry (Cary Guffey), her son. As Schrader withdrew as scriptwriter, any and every writer Spielberg had access to came in with six cents' worth: Matthew Robbins, Hal Barwood, Jerry Belson, and others. And by then Spielberg was doing the script himself, albeit as a kind of popular survey.

But the marvel of it all was the light show, and the way toys and machines assumed a new life as the lights passed over them. Roy becomes the victim of common obsession: He makes shapes out of mashed potatoes that imitate the mesa where the alien craft may land, and like a driven pilgrim, he goes there. There's no question that the film worked, and works, because its sci-fi elements were locked into very basic human behavior. Vilmos Zsigmond (with a host of others) was shooting the lights, with special effects by Douglas Trumbull. But the picture had a lovely emotional kick and a feeling for the childlike in adult characters.

The materialization of François Truffaut as Claude Lacombe, the professor who speaks to the aliens in sound waves, was a good deal more far-fetched, yet Truffaut's lack of fluent English placed him quite nicely somewhere between humans and aliens. It worked too. And thirty years ago, when we were just babes, the climactic light show was awesome. Hear those notes and we are humming. If anything else was clear, it was that Steven Spielberg had grand ambitions, few of which had yet been spelled out. The film was an immense success, and it's still a good deal more emotionally satisfying than you'll expect. The power of renewal and repeated surprise was clearly a vital part of Spielberg's being. Don't forget, this was the same year as *Star Wars*. Look at the two pictures again, and the lesson is obvious: Spielberg believes in people—his capacity for close encounters is growing. Also with Teri Garr, Bob Balaban, and J. Patrick McNamara. The picture ran 135 minutes, but a later TV version was 10 minutes longer. The phrase "director's cut" was first heard.

Close-Up (1989)

Propose to the average American citizen that one of the most fertile and appealing national cinemas of the last fifteen years has been that of Iran, and a look comes into his eye that perhaps he is about to be made a fool of. At the very least, I suspect, his brainwashed state of thinking on things Iranian will anticipate the possibility of some guerrilla filmmaking operation, in the mountains and in great peril, challenging one part of the "empire of evil." That is the simpler response. There is another already, accompanied by sighs and groans and the general understanding that we—the citizens of the greatest of all nations, the citizens of the saved—have helped to make fools of ourselves.

There is one available mercy: *Close-Up* may or may not be among the finest or the most characteristic Iranian films, but a large part of its subject and its impact is to make us more tolerant of foolishness, especially the sort that we insist on wearing as we make fools of ourselves. *Close-Up* is that rarity—a film made in gentle irony, straight-faced wonder about the vagaries of human nature, and a patience and faith that believe all these things can be worked out. Not very much happened. The film is not very long. But it is as if we have been on the sidelines at the odd events that will inspire a story by Gogol or a report by W. G. Sebald.

The story goes like this: A man, unemployed, is arrested for attempting to impersonate the lofty Iranian director Mohsen Makhmalbaf—a real person, albeit as much of a legend in his own time as Stanley Kubrick. (Let us agree to agree: There are some film directors who somehow gather this kind of mystique.) A rich family, the Ahanhahs, bring the charges in the hope that the great director will come to their house and make a film about them! And we have to admit that there are people who nurture the absurd notion that it might be fun or prestigious to be in a great man's films. There is talk of fraud and even planned burglary. In fact, those fears seem groundless. The fellow simply wanted to be the great man. He is sheepish about it now, on the downslope of discovery. And, of course, the more shy he becomes, the less plausible he is as a director.

All that Abbas Kiarostami has done is follow the incident and its amiable, long-winded trial with a documentary camera that keeps teaching us to see how much of the pose, or acting, there is in all of us. For as the story unfolds, we realize, more or less, how much of life is taken up by rather modest acting. Life would be so much simpler and clearer if people acted better. But no, they falter, they fumble for words, they seem ill prepared. *Close-Up* has no obvious directorial style. It is as if Kiarostami—or someone hoping to suggest him—had simply observed the outward signs of fraud and asked us to pass judgment. All of which begins to suggest some traces of culture in Iran as ancient and intricate as one might suspect.

Colorado Territory (1949)

You can expect to hear in every commentary that Raoul Walsh's *Colorado Territory* is a Western remake and relocation of his 1941 movie *High Sierra,* with Humphrey Bogart and Ida Lupino, adapted from the novel by W. R. Burnett. But a rather more interesting possibility is that this very strong, tough Western—shot in a deliberate and severe black and white by Sid Hickox—was intended as something of a correction to David O. Selznick's lurid *Duel in the Sun* (1946), a picture that—in the eyes of some Western fans—introduced enough hysteria and sexual overtness to make strong men and women flinch. Walsh was not the man to point fingers or preach, but I think it's possible he felt too many tough decencies had been squandered in *Duel in the Sun.*

So the admirable Joel McCrea is Wes, an escaped convict who would like to go straight but is led by fate toward his own destruction. Dorothy Malone is the girl he helps and might marry, but she is too feeble for him. Colorado, an untamed girl with Indian blood, is his more natural mate—and Virginia Mayo always found an extra vitality for Walsh.

But the best thing about the film is the way its landscape changes from pastoral and gentle to austere and rock-ridden as Wes moves further away from any chance of survival. This is a film with a strong feeling for the implacable natural savagery in so much of the Western landscape, and of the few men who will find themselves only within it. Cliffs or mesa walls tower over the human figures and make a superb contrast with the laconic courage and self-sufficiency of McCrea.

When the lovers recede into the bleakest terrain, we know what awaits them, but Walsh rejects the sadomasochistic tangle that exists between Lewt and Pearl in *Duel in the Sun.* He satisfies himself with one strangled but instinctive reaching for contact on the part of Wes. It is an eloquent and touching moment, and it reveals the depth of Walsh's faith that emotion can remain as the subtext signaled by telling gesture. He was not persuaded by a cinema that went deeper. Indeed, I suspect he thought that to go deeper was to grovel and humiliate yourself.

Joel McCrea now looks about as epic and unquestioning as Harry Carey in his silent films for John Ford. And McCrea was the kind of actor who could do a *Colorado Territory* or a Preston Sturges picture with the same shy good nature. He wasn't going to stoop to acting, because he reckoned that acting looked pretty silly next to the glories of this landscape, or the dance in a Sturges picture. He was the kind of actor who stood up to be photographed, and Walsh and Sturges alike took amazing richness from his determined simplicity. For what happened was that, in his calm and quiet, the viewer begins to feel increasing subtlety and doubt. McCrea trusted that if he believed in his material, then the integrity would work. And so it does. He kills and he makes love with the same sweet shyness.

Come and Get It (1936)

Edna Ferber's novel *Come and Get It* was published in 1934; it dealt with Wisconsin lumber people over two generations. Sam Goldwyn bought the screen rights for $40,000. The key role is Lotta, a barmaid who marries a lumberman and then has a beautiful daughter (another Lotta) on whom another lumberman, Barney Glasgow, lavishes money and opportunity. Howard Hawks had signed a contract with Goldwyn (against his better judgment), and he was penciled in to direct the Ferber novel.

Edward Chodorov wrote one script, not much liked, and then Jane Murfin did a better version. Miriam Hopkins and Virginia Bruce were both talked about for Lotta, but Hawks kept looking. He put Jules Furthman on the script, and then he saw a Bing Crosby musical, *Rhythm on the Range,* with Frances Farmer in it. Hawks was married, to Athole Shearer; she was pregnant for the third time. But he seems to have turned discovery into an affair with Farmer. In his words, she was the most beautiful and the best actress of the many he "discovered." She was hired on at a pittance, but eager for the opportunity. Edward Arnold was cast as Barney, Joel McCrea as the young male lead, and Walter Brennan as the man who marries the first Lotta (Farmer). They were filming with Gregg Toland as cameraman.

You can see for yourself, still: Farmer is dazzling. But Hawks was apparently using Furthman to take the script further away from Ferber and make it more of a showcase for Farmer. It was then that Goldwyn became angry and aggressive. The facts are hard to pin down now, but as William Wyler finished *Dodsworth,* Goldwyn fired Hawks and told Wyler to finish the film. Wyler was not happy about it, and Frances Farmer took it into her head to loathe him. There is a point in the film where something seems to have happened, and it may well be that Hawks was making something for Farmer that would have infuriated Ferber. On the other hand, when Hawks got an idea like this, it was wise to go with it. There is a frankness and a humor in Frances Farmer that is stunning: she was like Carole Lombard with Katharine Hepburn's intelligence.

Wyler felt uneasy about the whole venture and wanted no credit. The Directors Guild was as yet not recognized by the studio. So Goldwyn agreed to give both men credit. The problems had pushed the budget over $1 million. Goldwyn sometimes claimed he had made a new picture; this is nonsense. The outline of a Frances Farmer vehicle is clear and unalterable. The Hawks plan shaped the existing footage, and as far and away Farmer's best film, it furnished the tragedy of her decline.

Richard Rosson deserves credit for directing the tree-felling sequences which Rudolph Mate shot. Walter Brennan won a supporting-actor Oscar. Richard Day was the art director. The cast also includes Andrea Leeds, Frank Shields, Mady Christians, Mary Nash, and Clem Bevans.

The Conformist (1970)

When it opened, *The Conformist* contained many lessons that modernist filmmakers were eager to make gospel. Above all, it asserted that private and public politics were as one: When Clerici (Jean-Louis Trintignant) advanced on an assassination attempt, a putative seduction, or merely a furtive backtrack to pick up his forgotten hat (that closing lid on his being), all purposes were in his scuttling motion (he moves as Gregor Samsa might—and decades later it is Trintignant who seems to own the film). Surely it was a proof that cinema was ready to come of age if one gesture contained all those dimensions of meaning.

After the flagrant abruptness and fragmentation of the French New Wave (which had been a huge influence on Bertolucci), *The Conformist* harkens back to a stylistic sophistication of the 1930s, a sinuousness, and a way with light, décor, and clothes that brought back memories of Max Ophüls, Josef von Sternberg, and even Mitchell Leisen. But, of course, *The Conformist* was set in the thirties, so it was natural for the movie to use reflections, separating walls, mirrors, and depth of focus.

Then there was the fruitful integration of so much artistry in the film's very pronounced look—not just Bertolucci, but Vittorio Storaro as lighting cameraman and Ferdinando Scarfiotti in charge of production design. This brilliant unification of resources had a very strong impact on Coppola, Scorsese, Schrader, and others. In time, Storaro and Scarfiotti became figures who did work in America, and there's no doubt that the look of *The Conformist* (and its underlying faith in the emotional content of imagery) was a vital infusion for American film.

It was also Bertolucci's wish to match Jean-Luc Godard, I think, that made the structure of *The Conformist* so ostentatiously difficult. In later films, Bertolucci gave up on that structural crosscutting and the obliqueness of omissions—he became a much more conventional storyteller. And *The Conformist* still works best, I think, in the motif of delayed or evaded pursuit that is built on Gastone Moschin's assassin (he reappeared in *The Godfather: Part II*), the sinister black car used, and the stealthy waltz in Georges Delerue's music (indeed, Delerue shows many signs of wanting to bind the broken structure back together again). That car trip could be the basis for every flashback. But as it is, the incidents are so scattered that the film becomes needlessly obscure.

There's another problem: The association of fascism and Clerici's suppressed gayness now seems hopelessly glib and naïve and a part of Bertolucci's urge to see sex in everything. That works very well in terms of the wife—flirty and mediocre, and beautifully played by Stefania Sandrelli. But Dominique Sanda's wife/lover/whore/lesbian is too tricky and infinite and good to be true, or credible.

Never mind, *The Conformist* is a great film, very beautiful and deeply disturbing, and that last look from Trintignant, over his shoulder, goes into the past and the future simultaneously and speaks volumes on his dread need not to be noticed.

The Conversation (1974)

Two young people are strolling in San Francisco's Union Square at lunchtime, talking. They might be lovers, but they seem suspicious of the air and the passersby. Why is a mime artist following them? We see and hear them by means of a network of surveillance systems, set up by Harry Caul, the best bugger on the West Coast. It is his job. He hires himself and his equipment out to rich clients, no questions asked. All Harry does, it seems, is record stuff in the air, stuff that is out there. And in many respects, Francis Coppola's film was a bow to the techniques and the ingenuity of modern security agencies, just as it is a showcase for the brilliant editor/soundman Walter Murch, who had been an associate of Coppola's since college days in Los Angeles.

The setup is beguiling. Caul is austere, ungiving as a person or a lover, withdrawn. Yet he is loaded with the possibility of guilt. It's interesting to note how far *The Conversation* turns on conscience and its agony, whereas *The Godfather* is most novel and perhaps most modern in the absence of that very thing. But Caul feels he is a failure. Such an invader of other people's privacy, he cannot muster or depend on a private life of his own. And so he begins to wonder why he is recording this young couple in Union Square, and he believes that he may be a distant accomplice to a murder.

The paranoid mood works very well, apart from one crucial implausibility: We simply cannot credit that the alert Harry Caul would accept the plant of a souvenir pen at a trade show and then be distraught when it turns out to be a microphone that has recorded his own intimate conversation.

In addition, the key line from the set-piece bugging is altered in tone to accommodate its second, later reading. It is not the same line. These touch-ups hurt more than you might think in a film full of atmosphere and worry but desperately tidy as it unfolds.

We know that Murch really completed *The Conversation* in postproduction, as Coppola was compelled to move on to *The Godfather: Part II*, and Murch has a tendency to bury impulse in the very precise working out of everything. So *The Conversation* can feel like the tightening of a diagram, as opposed to the gradual trapping of the viewer in its moral dilemma. Still, as a thriller it has a remorseless, building tension that is hard to shake off. It's only in the inevitable comparison with Michelangelo Antonioni's *Blow Up* that one is bound to recognize the limits to this game.

Gene Hackman is superb as Caul, and there are other fine performances: from John Cazale as Harry's assistant, Allen Garfield as his rival, Elizabeth MacRae as a floozy, Harrison Ford as a young suit, Robert Duvall (briefly) as the villain or victim, and Frederic Forrest and Cindy Williams as the young couple, looking too pale and amiable to be dangerous.

The Covered Wagon (1923)

The year 1923 was a big one in film history. *The Ten Commandments* (with its modern story and the Biblical epic) and Lon Chaney's *Hunchback of Notre Dame* were rival contenders for box office. But no picture did as well as James Cruze's *The Covered Wagon.* Costing $782,000, it supposedly grossed $3.8 million in the United States alone. It's a measure of how far in the silent years certain films were advertisements for a way of life. After all, producer Jesse Lasky had encouraged Cruze to shoot the film in Utah and Nevada, terrain unfamiliar to most Americans. The West had been sold to the world first in pulp fiction and still photographs; and the first moving pictures had a similar impact.

So people interested in the history of American realty may want to see *The Covered Wagon* (and try guessing where it was shot). For those of us interested in the development of the movie, alas, it's not a great deal more than a marker in time—it's hard while watching it not to keep longing for the way *Greed* identifies a certain landscape (or cityscape) and makes it luminous in our sense of the nation developing. The emblematic use of Death Valley in Stroheim's film means so much more than the moralistic distinction between gold-beset California and arable Oregon in the Cruze picture.

The Covered Wagon came from a novel by Emerson Hough, and Jack Cunningham adapted it for the screen. Two wagon trains meet and join forces in Kansas City as they take on the hazards of the West, crossing rivers, up and down the mountains, fighting those red Indians, and surviving winter. There's a very tedious love story along the way. Tully Marshall plays scout Jim Bridger, and Guy Oliver is Kit Carson. Karl Brown did the beautiful landscape photography, Dorothy Arzner edited the picture. Hugo Riesenfeld wrote an original score, and a young Delmer Daves worked in the props department. The cast was J. Warren Kerrigan, Lois Wilson, Alan Hale, Ernest Torrence, and Ethel Wales.

Whatever its reputation, *The Covered Wagon* is not to be compared with *The Iron Horse* (1924), John Ford's tribute to the building of the railways. Still, it is remarkable that the Western was not a front-rank genre in the silent era. Of course, there were personality cowboys, from William S. Hart to Tom Mix. But it was not really until the late 1930s that the Western acquired prestige and the confidence to pursue uniquely Western stories as opposed to clichéd material.

Yet again, *Greed* is the signal film, the indication of a fascination with stories about the West, a territory and an idea that was developing at almost exactly the same time as the movies. Stroheim's picture, and the Frank Norris novel it was based on (*McTeague*), see the West as a living, changing place. Too many early Westerns settled for exotic backdrop and seemed to be made for people who were not likely to go to the real place. What *Greed* guesses is that the West is the real America, as distinct from the European footprints left on the East Coast.

Cover Girl (1944)

It was during the filming of *Cover Girl* at Columbia that Rita Hayworth and Orson Welles were married, sneaking away from the set one morning (September 7, 1943) without telling studio boss Harry Cohn or her family, the Cansinos. It may have been one of the happiest moments of her life, though Cohn was leaning on her not to appear in Orson's evening tent show for servicemen, where he cut her in half. He wanted her fresh for the musical and never guessed that it was Orson who was keeping her fresh.

The film was a musical based on fashion and the new way in which pretty girls were getting the cover or not. Arthur Schwartz (the composer) was the producer, Charles Vidor would direct, and Virginia Van Upp did the screenplay—she would go on to do *Gilda* with Rita (though it seems that Sidney Buchman had the first idea for the film). Columbia got Gene Kelly on loan from M-G-M to play opposite Hayworth, and they cast the comedian Phil Silvers as their pal. The songs were by Jerome Kern and Ira Gershwin, and the musical highlight of the picture is "Long Ago and Far Away," done by Kelly and Hayworth, even if Martha Mears was dubbing the song.

The other highlight, and a large reason for Kelly's taking the assignment, was the "Alter-Ego Dance," in which Kelly dances with himself. This was a very complicated number to design and rehearse, and it was the first occasion when Kelly gave his assistant job to Stanley Donen—although the two had worked together onstage in *Pal Joey* and *Best Foot Forward.* Charles Vidor chose to take a very superior attitude toward their collaboration, and often left them to it. The choreography also involved Seymour Felix and Jack Cole, and it showed that Hayworth was by now a glorious dancer, as much at ease with Kelly as she had been with Fred Astaire in *You Were Never Lovelier* and *You'll Never Get Rich.*

Allen M. Davey and Rudolph Mate did the photography, Fay Babcock did the sets, and Jean Louis the costumes. Clothes and magazines play a big part in the picture; the cast included leading models of the day, like Anita Colby and Jinx Falkenburg, as well as Otto Kruger as an editor and Eve Arden as his wisecracking assistant. Indeed, Arden tends to steal the picture.

The film was a hit, and Cohn was as pleased as he was upset to lose some of his power over Rita. Imagine if she had had a voice, or could have acted as well as Eve Arden. And surely there were times when Ms. Arden said to herself: If only I looked like that. The ironies of such juxtapositions are a source of tragedy. Rita and Orson were together such a short time, and happy only a part of it. For her, it was an extraordinary coup, to be taken seriously by such a man. And when he grew bored, one can argue, her dismay and depression were under way.

Cria! (1976)

In a gloomy Madrid house, the nine-year-old Ana (Ana Torrent) comes downstairs at night, urged out of sleep and into awful discovery. The night is in color, but splashes of Gothic shadow creep up to the vulnerable white of the child's nightgown. She hears sounds from a living room: whispers of adult lovemaking, which, separated from grown-up bodies, seem closer to superstition than suspicion. It is her father and a girlfriend: In an ecstasy that seems remote and insubstantial to the child, the father chokes and dies. Ana regards his body, arrested in grisly spasm. She looks at the glass of milk she poisoned and he drank. She takes the glass to the kitchen to wash it. After a while her mother comes in and says, in a matter-of-fact way, It is late, time for you to be asleep. It is a fond mother, neither alarmed nor surprised, but as sure of pain as Geraldine Chaplin's drawn features.

This lucid beginning is not quite what it seemed. The heightened state of waking and the child's adoration have conjured back a mother who died some years before. It is not a happy family, even if Ana and her two sisters are as busy as birds in the rain. The father was a philanderer: His affairs and handling of every woman within reach broke the mother's health, or so it seems to the single-minded Ana. She has taken on herself the suffering of the mother; she sees her in the house and talks to her, without expressionist devices or trembling music. This is everyday haunting as natural as a child's dependence on her mother. Imagination easily disarms reality, and the tiny witch is not maddened by her powers.

Now, this has been done before: The exposition is a blend of *What Maisie Knew*—the child who witnesses adult depravity—and all those fantasies in which a child's invented playmate monopolizes her. But director Carlos Saura adds another level of emotional grace. There are unadorned close-ups of Geraldine Chaplin looking into the camera and describing her childhood. But this Chaplin is not the mother who died young—it is the child Ana, now grown up and reporting the childhood we are in the process of observing. The impact is haunting. Pale faces and dark eyes begin to rhyme; time is turned inside out; and the formal device is a rare surge of feeling in which loss entwines with a deeper continuity. We appreciate a little later how far Saura's expansion of the relationship has enhanced affection with imaginative energy, and made a history of the female role in the sad and happy remembrance of daily life.

What does it all mean? Well, that this is an allegory about Franco's power too obscure for any Franco to see the point. It is also an understandable confession of Saura's infatuation for Geraldine Chaplin. And in the delicate, fragile ping-pong of two characters with eyes alike, it is the affirmation that film is a dream. The film ends in light and happiness. You can tell yourself that every dark item was imagined—as if you can ever forget imagination.

Cries and Whispers (1972)

When we sometimes hark back to the early 1970s as a supreme moment of cinema, it is all very well to invoke *The Godfather, McCabe and Mrs. Miller*, and *Mean Streets*, but let us not forget the accompanying intensity of *The Discreet Charm of the Bourgeoisie*, *Céline and Julie Go Boating*, or *Cries and Whispers*. *Visknin-gar och Rop* (to give it its Swedish title) is 91 minutes long. It may have cost $100,000. It has period costumes and color but a small cast. And surely it is among the greatest films ever made—not just because of Ingmar Bergman's long, uncompromising journey as an artist, but because of the feeling that there in the early seventies his own talent and that of his family of collaborators was at a perfect pitch. And it is a moment when a film like *Cries and Whispers*, removed from so many of the urgent realities of 1972, seemed somehow to reach out to all of life and to speak as the medium of the moment.

Agnes (Harriet Andersson) is dying in the house where she was born and raised. She is attended by her two sisters, Karin (Ingrid Thulin) and Maria (Liv Ullmann). Yes, the allusion to Chekhov is obvious, but critics also identified the influence of Ozu in the essential stillness of the picture and its patient scrutiny of a family lost in their different levels of discourse—literally the cries and whispers, the outward show of feeling and the repressed inward confessions. For what is extraordinary about this film structurally is the ease with which its moments of family observation are interwoven with fantasies or scenarios that are the individuals' attempts at explanation or vindication.

There is an American tradition—stronger now than it was in 1972—that the cinema is not meant for this inward intensity, that a slow death and the pain of family relationships are not the material of movie. Give people something to cheer them up—and *The Godfather* in many ways was a bracing, rousing movie. Historically, there is much in favor of this argument: Life is hard enough, and the movies are an escape and a consolation. But then you listen to Bach or Mahler or Beethoven's late quartets; you look at Bergman or Ozu or Mizoguchi, and it is hard to argue against the supreme truthfulness of this family portrait, the terrible sense of injury and loss, with the accompanying recollection of some shared joy. *Cries and Whispers* is as full of pain as a deathwatch, but it ends in a sense of a time when three sisters were as one in a summer of joy.

One does not hear of *Cries and Whispers* playing too much these days. And Ingmar Bergman—who died in 2007—is amazingly forgotten. Shame on us. This is one of the great films of an unrivaled film artist. It is Bergman's finest use of color in expression—the photography is by Sven Nykvist. As for the actresses, what can one say except that they are like his old lovers and his new children? If you have any doubts about the cinema—and you should—this is one of the films you have to see. (*The Sting* beat it for Best Picture.)

Le Crime de Monsieur Lange (1936)

Amédée Lange (René Lefèvre) is one of Jean Renoir's great romantics. Thin, pallid, properly dressed with a little bow tie, he is tongue-tied and halting, except when he is writing the stories of "Arizona Jim," tales as bold and expansive as the American West the Frenchman has never seen. These stories are the best-selling product of a small print shop and workers' cooperative, not just based in a Paris courtyard but embodied by it. Renoir had used courtyards before, and the views and the camera movements that flourished there had been laid down long before this remarkable collaboration with the Popular Front. It was as if Renoir—a little deaf—had been asked, "Will you make a film about the people, about the group?" To which, of course, he had replied, "I always do."

So he joined with a real collaborative, and agreed to write the script with Jacques Prévert. That was the important innovation, for Prévert—a poet and wordsmith—adored playing with words, whereas Renoir in the past had been at pains to ensure that his characters spoke naturally. So here we have socialists, typesetters, and people of the people uttering puns, epigrams, and the well-rounded sentences of theatrical talk. Yet it works.

The politics may be as naïve as Arizona Jim, but the particularity of the films clings to these actors and that place. The women—Florelle, Nadia Sibirskaïa (a classic exploitable virgin), and Sylvie Bataille—are closer to stage archetypes. But the triumph of the film is, perversely, its great capitalist, exploiter, and outsider to the socialist spirit, Batala (Jules Berry). One of the greatest scoundrels in Renoir's work, he is also the one given the most dynamic dispatch as the entire cooperative and building seem to join in the fabulous circular tracking shot (photographed by Jean Bachelet) in which he is finally executed.

At the time—and when Renoir joined in the clumsier *La Vie Est à Nous,* in 1936—some remarked on the way politics had taken over the director's mind. But in hindsight, *Le Crime de Monsieur Lange* looks like one of those happy minglings of theater and cinema that Renoir would develop in the 1950s. So, as early as 1936, it is fascinating to see the great realist prepared to enjoy theatricality and take advantage of it. Equally, the film's score, by Jean Wiener and Joseph Kosma, is the first hint of something like performance or dance taking Renoir's fancy.

In just a few years, it is true, Renoir would lose a lot of his faith in joint action and solidarity, at least in France. *La Règle du Jeu* (1939) is a film in which politics are in tatters and the old struggle of servants and masters has turned into tragicomic operetta. Whatever will be will be, and woe betide the doctrinaire spirit. But in sharing this very lively socialist unit with us, Renoir easily enlarged his own style and began to see the shapes of theater in all of life. Was he aware of that at the time? Probably not. But it is in the nature of Renoir's policy and method that you may have to look for some time before you see. The single great consistency is his searching gaze.

Crimes and Misdemeanors (1989)

The idea persists that *Crimes and Misdemeanors* is one of Woody Allen's more serious, novelistic movies. Equally, I recall the time when expressions of disaster were to be seen on the faces of Allen admirers as he slipped from *Annie Hall* to *Interiors*. To be blunt, I'm not sure that Allen has demonstrated the muscle, the warmth, or the true humor to be taken that seriously. I know he's a comic, a stand-up once, and often the author of very funny lines, but I'm not sure that he is amused by life, in the manner of Preston Sturges, Howard Hawks, or Jean Renoir. Sometimes his comedy seems like sniping opportunism rather than a profound, extensive attitude that functions across a wide range of experience. The thought endures that gravity for Woody Allen is a matter of being himself—and therein lies solemnity, not anything akin to the novel, or what he reports as finding in Tolstoy. We are accustomed to having to deal with his ongoing reference to Ingmar Bergman. And Ingmar was not really a stand-up. Still, before agreeing to Allen's seriousness, I would like to see a humor as interesting as that in Bergman.

There are several stories in the pattern of *Crimes and Misdemeanors:* Judah Rosenthal (Martin Landau), a married man, has been having an affair with Dolores Paley (Anjelica Huston), but she is "difficult"—she wants something more lasting; she wants Judah to leave his wife, Miriam (Claire Bloom). Ben (Sam Waterston), a rabbi, is going blind. Cliff Stern (Woody Allen) is making a slow, verité-like documentary film about "life" and another about his insufferable, more successful brother-in-law, Lester (Alan Alda). Judah asks his brother, Jack (Jerry Orbach), to get rid of Dolores. It all fits in theory, yet none of it fits in practice. And I'm bound to wonder about Allen's method: Write the script, cast it, let his players see only their "bit," and give them very little direction. Contrast that with the method of Mike Leigh, whose actors assemble and arrive at parts through a long process of rehearsal or improvisation, all under the encouragement of Leigh. There is a huge difference in felt reality. Allen's method is hurried but superficial. He works all the time, yet lazily and privately. Without criticism or collaboration. I don't think he ever really explores his worlds. And so—for instance—the central murder in *Crimes and Misdemeanors* is never more than a gesture.

The Allen approach has become very refined, and on this film he had Sven Nykvist as photographer and Santo Loquasto as designer. But does it look good or interesting? No. I think generally it looks like TV drama, without much character or texture. Again, the apparent obsession with filmmaking is accompanied by an actual indifference.

People say that actors long to be in Woody Allen pictures, and I suppose that's true. But do they really benefit from it, or do they just say the lines? It seems to me that in this film nearly every figure suffers to some degree from Allen's latent dislike of people. The contrast with Sturges is very revealing. Sturges loved actors—it's the only word—whether the overlooked Joel McCrea or a dreamboat character actor like Eugene Pallette. You can feel Sturges laughing at his people—and that's why the movies are more than comedies. But in Allen you feel him as a sunken figure watching from a distance, unwarmed, unpleased—and that's why I seldom laugh.

Criss Cross (1949)

You can find commentaries on Robert Siodmak's *Criss Cross* that say it's OK except for the "miscasting" of Burt Lancaster as the weak ex-husband who comes home from the war and falls for his no-good ex again as sure as fate. Whereas almost the thing I like the most is that curdled weakness in Burt, the sneer that's directed at the self, that knows what a masochistic idiot he is. So imagine you have an OK film with this superb, piercing use of Burt Lancaster as his own worst enemy.

Steve Thompson (Lancaster) comes home to Los Angeles, to the small family house in the Bunker Hill area, and straightaway this picture delivers one of its major minor virtues: a first-class sense of the old downtown Los Angeles, with the elevated railway, the steps, and the houses pushed into the hillside. It's background, of course, but there it is, laid out as an invaluable architectural record (second unit photography by Paul Ivano). Steve is restless. He wonders about the old place, the bar, and what happened to Anna (Yvonne De Carlo), his wife. Very soon, he's back at his old habits, though now Anna is married to Slim Dundee (Dan Duryea), a vicious dandy who wears silk and talks like the feel of lingerie.

The evocation of the interior L.A. is as good as the exteriors. In the daytime the bar is half-empty. No one there remembers Steve. But at night it's a jumping place, with great Latin music supplied by Esy Morales and his orchestra. And then we get a sight of Anna dancing—and apart from realizing what a great dame De Carlo was then, you suddenly notice that her dancing partner is a very young Tony Curtis, looking like gold dust.

Well, Steve gets hooked into the Dundee gang, because Anna lets him believe she still cares—and he's so helpless and narcissistic that he believes her. There's an armored-car robbery and a lot of double-crossing, with a finale in a little house in San Pedro where you can see the sun setting. Burt is on the slide all the way, but there's a brilliant scene in a hospital where, all smashed up, he begins to realize that the amiable guy visiting him (John Doucette) is there to finish him off.

I don't mean to overload *Criss Cross* with significance. But the craft can bring tears to your eyes. It's from a novel by Don Tracy, but the script was by Daniel Fuchs, one of the best writers working in Hollywood. Franz Planer did the photography, Bernard Herzbrun and Boris Leven were the production designers, and the music is by Miklós Rózsa. Siodmak had no superior at this: With *The Killers* (which *Criss Cross* resembles in some ways) you have Siodmak as one of the great natural noir directors and the clearest diagnosis of Burt Lancaster anyone would ever make.

The rich cast includes Stephen McNally, Percy Helton, Alan Napier, Griff Barnett, Joan Miller, and Curtis, so happy to be there you feel like shouting out, "Give that kid a line!"

Crossfire (1947)

It started as a novel by Richard Brooks, *The Brick Foxhole*, which deals with homophobia in the U.S. Army. That was a little tough to take in 1947, so for the film, the "problem" was switched to anti-Semitism. All this in a movie that would become a gathering place for people who were blacklisted: The producer Adrian Scott, the writer John Paxton, and the director Edward Dmytryk would all be named as unfriendly witnesses. Never mind. This low-budget RKO venture was nominated as Best Picture (it lost to *Gentleman's Agreement*, an error that tells you all you need to know about the Academy). It also got nominations for Robert Ryan and Gloria Grahame as well as for Paxton's screenplay and Dmytryk's direction.

The film is a sort of whodunit, with three Roberts in the leads. But since Robert Young is the evident good-guy cop, and since Robert Mitchum is doing his very coolest work as a laconic bystander, it's hard not to guess that the jaw-grinding, fatally anxious, and ingratiating Montgomery (Ryan) is the bad guy. But as if to compensate for lack of surprise, Ryan makes him as nasty as possible. Nevertheless, this would be a more intriguing film if motivation was more muddled and if everyone else didn't regard hating Jews as worse than talking and chewing gum at the same time.

That may sound ungrateful as a commentary on a truly enterprising B picture that is made with confidence and skill. But the more you see it, the clearer it is that the fabulous lighting (photography by J. Roy Hunt) is trying to distract you from rough edges in the scenario and a somewhat smiley-faced attitude to the good old Army. So the daring is as isolated as the offense, if you see what I mean. There's an underlying assurance that places like the Army are sound and true—and I'm not reassured.

What is best about the film is its effortless command of the city at night and the way frightened, hard-up people live; time and again, the real breakthrough in American noir is to give you the texture of working-class life. In that respect, I don't think there's any real doubt that the most striking scenes in the film are those that involve Gloria Grahame and Paul Kelly in a relationship that smacks of Jim Thompson. If the rest of the film could have been securely rooted in that alarmingly vague and unreliable mood, then *Crossfire* would be a masterpiece instead of a worthwhile curiosity.

All that said, there remains Robert Ryan, acting a touch too hard, I think, but still a remarkable performer, so far ahead of his time you sometimes marvel that he was employed. In life, Ryan was liberal, decent, and troubled. Onscreen he could be the least sentimental villain America has. It's as if somehow this actor had access to levels of psychosis not available to others. And it's still both troubling and intriguing. This is not his best work, but *Crossfire* could hardly function without Ryan's commitment to his own idea of black malice. Here is an actor who seemingly had no wish or need to be liked. He makes everyone else look soft and complacent.

The Crowd (1928)

Beginning with sweeping crane and tracking shots that traverse Manhattan skyscrapers, and ending on a long, emerging crane shot that starts on our reunited family at the theater and then shows them as part of a large audience, King Vidor's *The Crowd* is a monument to populism, to the little guy refusing to be small, to some ultimate alliance between society and show business—and to the very mixed feelings that make Vidor so remarkable and American a director.

There is not a sweeter Hollywood story than the one Vidor tells of how he bumped into Irving Thalberg on the lot and Irving asked, What next? So Vidor proposed the ordinary guy, his battle in life. "Why didn't you mention this before?" says Thalberg. And Vidor admits he's just thought of it. Vidor thinks of a first title, *One of the Mob*, but then he goes for *The Crowd*, with a boy and a girl, ordinary people, barely making out—this in the year before the Crash. Thalberg says make it, and it costs more than half a million dollars. But it makes a small profit, and there it is still, one of the great silent pictures, and a tangle of issues. A few people said it would outlive *The Big Parade*, and they were right.

It's the John and Mary story, two good-natured young people. They meet. He's a friendly dreamer. She's a doll who chews gum on the first date. She is Eleanor Boardman (Vidor's wife, and a great beauty working hard to look "regular"), and he is James Murray, a clown but a sweetheart, a natural actor who became an alcoholic and was dead at thirty-five—a man Vidor never forgot, and an eerie shadow to John in the film.

John is a clerk at the Atlas Insurance Company, one among hundreds, who dreams of his ship coming in. He and Mary have two children, a boy and a girl, and live in a small flat. He writes advertising slogans for a hobby, and one wins $500. They celebrate. They call the kids to get their gifts, and the little girl is killed in a street accident. It nearly breaks the family up.

The mixed feelings: Well, begin with the shots of skyscraper architecture, meant to show the alienating world in which the little man may be crushed—they could be buildings by Howard Roark from Vidor's *The Fountainhead*. Vidor has faith in the individual, but only if he succeeds. John lurches into self-pity, he nearly kills himself—and you feel Vidor's loathing of that despond. But Vidor can't or won't admit the politics that can save the little guy, whether the socialism (of *Our Daily Bread*) or the welfare state that Vidor's innate conservatism resisted. The ordinary guy and the crowd is still the American story in 2007, and Vidor is a chaotic mix of populism and self-reliance. *The Crowd* is a "simple" film in some ways, but its fable story is just the surface in a profound battle of ideas that neither John and Mary nor Vidor can settle. But Boardman and Murray give it a naturalism that is so energetic. Vidor wanted to do a sequel—and we long to see it.

Cutter and Bone (1981)

Santa Barbara is a place much favored by retired movie people (Robert Mitchum lived there) but seldom used in movies. More's the pity, for it is sweet, attractive, pleased with itself, rich (and poor), decadent, and probably corrupt. *Cutter and Bone* (also known as *Cutter's Way*) is a small, insidious film noir set there, and a picture that has nearly vanished from sight these days. Our loss. One day a campaign has to be launched to retrieve the many intriguing films made by Jeff Bridges that went nowhere. He is among our best actors, and very bold and searching in the material he does. But there are those in the business who tend to write a picture off if Bridges is in it.

Richard Bone is one of his key parts. Handsome, lazy, compromising, vulnerable, he "works" as a yacht salesman and a gigolo—you can guess where his heart is. His friend Alexander Cutter (John Heard), who left an arm, an eye, and a leg in Vietnam, is alcoholic, brilliant, and bitter. Of course, he and Bone are a perfect mismatch: Each one grinds on the other's nerves. Cutter's wife, Mo (Lisa Eichhorn), worn out by his diatribes, is aware that Bone lusts after her but disdains him.

Late one night, Bone sees or thinks he sees a body being dumped. He begins to think the guilty party may be J. J. Cord, a leading figure in Santa Barbara society. Bone would let it go, but Cutter is too angry and desperate for that. He latches on to the incident and says that he and Bone have to solve the case. Their pursuit gets into very dark waters.

The picture comes from a novel by Newton Thornburg and a very good script by Jeffrey Alan Fiskin. The film was directed by Ivan Passer, one of those Czechoslovakian directors who came west with Milos Forman in the late 1960s but whose careers never settled down in Hollywood or thrived like Forman's. The moody cinematography is by Jordan Cronenweth, and the music is by Jack Nitzsche. What Passer does so very well here is leave us in real uncertainty as to whether this plot is real or hokey. But Cutter has resolved that his life depends on its being a chance to confront evil and all his own bad luck.

Heard is the revving engine of the film. Bridges drifts and looks at his mustache in shiny surfaces. He really is so easy an actor. And then there's Lisa Eichhorn—quite wonderful and tragic as Mo, and soon to disappear from view. These days, I don't know what she does, or Ivan Passer either. But I can easily believe that someone like J. J. Cord still has Santa Barbara under his thumb. So don't expect the world from *Cutter and Bone*. But if you're ever in the mood for a thriller that will wake you up after too good a dinner, this is it. Also with Nina van Pallandt as a woman of Santa Barbara.

Daisy Kenyon (1947)

Daisy Kenyon (Joan Crawford) is single, in Manhattan, a designer. She is having an affair with Dan O'Mara (Dana Andrews), a success, a man-about-town, and a married parent. Dan carries all before him, calling everyone "honeybunch" and reckoning that he can arrange or fix anything. But then Daisy meets another man, Peter Lapham (Henry Fonda), a man messed up by the war but wanting to be a boatbuilder. So it's a triangle film, apparently conventional, except that Daisy comes to see that both these men are feeble and immature next to her. It ends up a classic case of the woman's picture, in which women everywhere are encouraged to put less reliance on men.

Add to this promising recipe the fact that it is an Otto Preminger film, made by a man alert to ambiguity and human weakness. He made it at Fox, on a screenplay by David Hertz taken from a novel by Elizabeth Janeway. Enormous production values come from the photography by Leon Shamroy and the music by David Raksin. Moreover, this was a loan of Crawford to Fox right after *Mildred Pierce* and *Humoresque*.

In her book *From Reverence to Rape*, Molly Haskell argued that *Daisy Kenyon* was an example of the "choice" in a situation where the idea of choice was actually spurious. And I think that's what concerns Preminger—the notion that through intelligence and independence, a woman might argue herself out of this allegedly confining dilemma. And it's in the persistent observation of small things in the men—cheerful dismissal from Andrews, mounting depression in Fonda—that Daisy is required to make decisions for herself.

As always with Preminger, this way of assessing people is borne out in small movements within the frame—the way they meet, how they regard each other, what they notice in the world. Daisy's apartment building is a fascinating contrast in how her two men behave and move—very basic things, not unduly underlined in the script but staples of performance.

The quality of the acting is remarkable. Crawford is restrained, ironic, wry; Fonda is lofty, high-minded, and a little pompous; Andews is smart but compromised. As so often, Preminger had the ability to show us parts of stars hitherto unseen. Much the same applies to the genre, the woman's picture, which in this case begins critical of the men but discovers redeeming features. In fact, it's the wholeness of life that is being treated—*Daisy Kenyon* could almost as easily carry the names of either of the two men.

And, ahead of his time, Preminger brought a Manhattan realism to the picture. When the O'Maras go out to the Stork Club, we see the real figures of Walter Winchell and John Garfield passing by. Yet Preminger uses that very sequence as a measure of privilege and boasting in his two men. The cast also includes Ruth Warrick, Martha Stewart, Peggy Ann Garner, and Connie Marshall.

Les Dames du Bois de Boulogne (1945)

Begun in 1944 in German-occupied France and not released until 1945, *Les Dames du Bois de Boulogne* is a great film in danger of being neglected simply because it does not fit tidily into the mainstream of Robert Bresson's work. You can see the problem. Bresson is hard to grasp and harder to teach. Yet a stylistic gravity (and a way of seeing) that begins with 1951's *Diary of a Country Priest* applies to all the later films. So let *Les Dames du Bois de Boulogne* slip? Or recognize that Bresson did once deal with melodramatic emotion, and though in later films he rigorously tames that wildness, it does not go away—Bresson characters are wild but imprisoned. And in *Les Dames,* there is less of the prison apparent, and far more theater.

It was taken from a story told in Diderot's novel *Jacques le Fataliste et Son Maître*. Bresson did the bones of a screenplay, which was then given to Jean Cocteau for the dialogue. Cocteau's work was exemplary. He seems never to have disputed Bresson's line or intention, but the dialogue is luminous—some of the best in French cinema. In turn, this lets us feel the eighteenth century and a tough-minded Lubitsch-like world. But the story itself may remind people of Choderlos de Laclos.

Hélène (Maria Casares) has lost the love of Jean (Paul Bernard). In her pride, she claims it doesn't matter, because she no longer loves him. This is not true. So she plots vengeance. She finds a cabaret dancer, Agnès (Elina Labourdette). She is poor, and she lives with her grasping mother (Lucienne Bogaert). Hélène gives them some money so they can set up a better establishment. She then sees that Jean meets them and falls in love with Agnès. Only then does Hélène reveal that Agnès and her mother are no better than prostitutes—that's what "les dames" in the title refers to. But the cruel plot fails.

It is not just Casares's baleful look (something Cocteau would employ for his own purposes) that makes Hélène so hateful; it is almost the pressure of the Occupation. And for a long time it looks as if her control is faultless. So it is very much a film about class and money and the things money can buy. The décor is resonant. The camera moves with purpose. And there is a lot of very good acting—even if several of the players complained that Bresson controlled them to the tiniest detail. Later that control will show or be felt; here we feel the restless nervous energy of the people.

Philippe Agostini did the black-and-white photography. Max Douy was the art director. Jean-Jacques Grünenwald wrote the movie music. The result is enclosed and rather claustrophobic, and you may judge that the eroticism is all at the level of chess. But the instinct for both cruelty and grace is remarkable. *Les Dames* was not a great success, but it quickly became a cult film. Bresson had to wait six years to do his next film, but he was a marked talent.

The Damned (1969)

Deep into *The Damned,* you see Ingrid Thulin, as pale as white chocolate, shooting up, and you see Dirk Bogarde howling with grief. Ostensibly, his problem is that his position as managing head of a family-owned steelworks is being undermined by the rise and fashion style of the loathsome Nazis. Believe that if you will; my guess is that the very fastidious Bogarde could only get himself to cry out loud by asking the question, "How did I get into a piece of shit like this?"

Oh, those dysfunctional families at the movies! And, oh, the decline that set in with the Duke of Modrone, otherwise known as Luchino Visconti. The action begins more or less in 1933. What will happen to this family business as power shifts in Germany? Well, along with the immense pondering by the prince in 1963's *The Leopard* over what he's going to do with "progress," it's good to know that the onetime Marxist Visconti was still grappling with such issues in 1969, even if the film did end up looking as if Monty Python might have made it.

It's the crashing vulgarity that is most surprising here, after years and films in which Visconti had practiced the poise of aesthete and connoisseur. It's the grisly summoning of so much camp homosexual iconography, and the worry that Visconti had gone nearly mad denying himself that life for so long. It's the way women become cyphers so quickly: Claudia Cardinale in *The Leopard* is warm, ripe, in a dusty cherry-red dress, but Charlotte Rampling here is a study in gray and green (the hues of tooth decay), so thin she nearly disappears when she turns sideways, and without a glimmer of pleasure in life (or humor onscreen).

This family is rich and powerful, and their sense of downfall should come gradually, whereas these ghosts know they're damned, doomed, and dull from the outset. It's not just that they deserve what's coming—they are ready to inhale it, like opium. I suppose that's part of the point of it all, and I daresay Visconti would have said that he employed all those swift, ugly sock-it-to-me zoom shots because they might have been a Nazi invention. (He should have studied Leni Riefenstahl and made the style war so much more absorbing.) In the same way, many of the men are sweating all the time, though the atmosphere of the film is midwinter. It's the flop sweat of moral terror, don't you see? Yes, we saw it and we tried to look away.

Of course, real history suggests that the intricate compromises by which old Prussian industry (and aristocracy) went along with the Nazis might make a very good and valuable film. But that would require an approach to depth of character that is way beyond Visconti's rush to get to the Götterdämmerung stuff quickly. And, to quote an Eric Idle bit, "Ooh, you do look damned, misses!" "Well, I should think so, I've been in makeup since four o'clock!" Thus the approach that makes Ingrid Thulin look dead while still alive (a hint that Bergman had been managing for years without resorting to makeup).

Dance with a Stranger (1985)

Her name was Ruth Ellis. She shot one of her lovers, and in 1955 she was hanged for the offense, the last woman ever executed in Britain. In the recent film *Pierrepoint,* she is shown for a moment laughing in the face of her executioner, and that insolence is said to be enough to destroy the nerve of the somber Albert after more than six hundred drops. That's not how *Dance with a Stranger* ends, and it's likely an invention, but it is a kind of tribute to the silly bravery of Ruth Ellis as established in this film.

Ruth (Miranda Richardson) is chilly, brittle, sexy, but very limited. She's pretty and sparkish enough to want a "good time" out of life. But she's not smart enough, or classy enough, to make it for herself. So she's a hostess in nightclubs, a whore, with a ten-year-old son. In her heart of hearts, she knows life is either a drawn-out disaster or some sudden mishap. And she has just about enough foolishness and bravado to go for the melodrama. She has a lapdog already, Desmond Cussen (Ian Holm), a small, clerical man, ready to be mocked by her if he can have her occasionally—this is a perfect portrait of the besotted man. But Ruth is hanging out for bigger game, and her eyes light on David Blakeley (Rupert Everett), rich, flashy, casually cruel, utterly patronizing toward her but ready to fuck her now and then. She is his Desmond.

In all this, Ruth tries to keep her dignity and her tight attitude toward life intact. She has a dream of being marriageable—I doubt she ever laughed at the hangman, if only because she can hardly smile at herself. She is the sort of woman who expects to be pleased and surprised every time she looks in the mirror. She is also the means of a prodigious performance from Miranda Richardson, then twenty-seven and making her debut. What makes the film work so well is her refusal ever to play for sympathy, allied to her obvious understanding of the idiot Ruth Ellis could be in her own cause. And the whole thing works beneath a bone-white china look that is eerie and frightening.

The film is ably directed by the versatile Mike Newell, but—after Ms. Richardson—its greatest asset is a very thoughtful screenplay by Shelagh Delaney, the author more than twenty years earlier of *A Taste of Honey.* The script gets the class differences exactly, and shows how far they ran the show in the 1950s. For that reason alone, you can see why Ruth might kill someone—and her David, always off to Goodwood or Silverstone for motor racing, is the perfect target. He's someone who must have known Tony in *The Servant.*

The picture was photographed in rather bitter color by Peter Hannan. The production design (scrupulous and shabby) is by Andrew Mollo. Richard Hartley wrote the music. Pip Newbery did the big A-line costumes. But the flame of bleached body is all Ms. Richardson. Holm and Everett are wonderful supports for her, but they seem to know that they're watching something out of the ordinary. The rest of the cast includes Stratford Johns, Joanne Whalley, Tom Chadbon, Sally Anne Field, and Lesley Manville.

Dancing Lady (1933)

Dancing Lady is one of those pictures that had more meanings than anyone involved in it could articulate. It was an M-G-M film, made under the influence of the success of *42nd Street* and featuring the growing romance between a stage director, Patch Gallagher (Clark Gable), and a young dancer, Janie Barlow (Joan Crawford). Louis B. Mayer wanted it for Crawford, and he asked his son-in-law, David O. Selznick, newly arrived from RKO, to produce the picture.

Then something odd happened. Fred Astaire was about to start his contract at RKO, so Selznick asked him if he could give a few days to *Dancing Lady* as a guest star. Apparently, RKO offered no protest: The studio then was headed by Merian Cooper, who was very friendly with Selznick. M-G-M offered to pay for the Astaires' honeymoon to sweeten the deal. And Fred would appear as himself. Still, it is odd.

Johnny Considine was associate producer, Robert Z. Leonard was the director, and the screenplay was by Allen Rivkin and P. J. Wolfson from a novel by James Warner Bellah. Oliver T. Marsh was the photographer. The lavish costumes were by Adrian, and Merrill Pye did the beautiful moderne sets. The songs were by several hands: Burton Lane and Harold Adamson, Jimmy McHugh and Dorothy Fields, Nacio Herb Brown and Arthur Freed, and Richard Rodgers and Lorenz Hart.

Astaire would say he was grateful for the experience and for all he learned—not least the need to avoid Joan Crawford in the future as a dancing partner. Crawford had been a dancing girl, of course, and she was as enthusiastic as she was beautiful. But she had the habit of doing the same dance—a flapper stomp—to every song, and she manages to look garish (in "The Gang's All Here") next to Astaire and very sexually aggressive. How far Astaire rationalized that is hard to say, but it does point to his need for a partner who would not question the artistic and sexual quality of his dancing. People say Ginger Rogers gave him sex, but perhaps she had the tact to refrain from asking that leading question.

Meanwhile, something very like chemistry was developing between Gable and Crawford. He is her dominant man, and she is the slut he is made for. They had already done three films together, including the impressive *Possessed*. But here they are beginning to make heat—no matter that Crawford was apparently nursing some feelings for her other costar, Franchot Tone. The film repeatedly puts Gable and Crawford in clinches, with a big kiss only at the end, and you feel that Selznick knew what was happening. He had wondered out loud whether Joan could play this part—maybe it was Jean Harlow material—and that had provoked Crawford to greater extremes. She wears clothes (or not) as well as any star. She lets her hair go wild. And she gives such a sense of easy maturity that the awkward dancing is all the odder. Meanwhile, Fred looks on like the man in the moon.

Dangerous Liaisons (1988)

Pierre Choderlos de Laclos published *Les Liaisons Dangereuses* in 1782. It was an epistolary novel in which former lovers and companions in depravity—Valmont and de Merteuil fall out over a plot: Valmont must seduce the virtuous Madame de Tourvel without falling in love with her. It was filmed poorly in 1959 by Roger Vadim—despite Gérard Philipe and Jeanne Moreau as the handsome leads—updated to a modern ski-slope world, with a jazz sound track. Then the ingenious Christopher Hampton made a stage success of the work in London in the 1980s, and that led to his collaboration on the film with director Stephen Frears.

Frears and Hampton do the story in wigs and costumes, yet with very knowing modern actors in the roles. What results is a brilliant entertainment and a crowd-pleasing film, as droll and modern as Ernst Lubitsch but not too interested in the elegance and the unkind mathematics of the Laclos original. So the staginess of the Hampton script carries over very well: You almost expect John Malkovich and Glenn Close to come down to the footlights at the end, toss their wigs and their characters at the audience, and embrace like fellow players who have had a ball and provided one for us.

Frears is a connoisseur of sexual gamesmanship and romantic folly, as he is of acting, and the same expertise unites the two ways of being. So Frears throws châteaux, coaches, clothes, and fauteuils around in the spirit of an indoor rugby match, and nakedness, embarrassment, and triumph are all stages of the game. Glenn Close is lovely and bitchy, John Malkovich is superior and wicked, and Michelle Pfeiffer (as Madame de Tourvel—it really is the stooge role) tends to be teary-eyed and hurt. So the screenplay won an Oscar, along with the art and set direction (Stuart Craig and Gérard James) and the costumes (James Acheson). Everyone else was nominated, except for Malkovich, which really wasn't very sporting, for his bored elitism is the very spirit of the whole thing. The supporting cast includes Swoosie Kurtz, Keanu Reeves (rather encouraged to be stupid?), Mildred Natwick, Peter Capaldi, and a very young, very bare Uma Thurman.

It happens that only a year later, yet another film from the material appeared: *Valmont,* directed by Milos Forman and scripted by Jean-Claude Carrière. Of course, coming in not just second but last, the Forman picture did little business, but it is the best of the three in terms of getting Laclos. For this time the story has been done icy cold, with scalding sex and a true sense of the viciousness of the eighteenth century. Nothing takes away from the fun of the Frears version and its adroit instinct for audience gratification. But if you ever get the taste for a drier wine, without a cherry in the glass, try *Valmont,* which has terrific performances from Annette Bening (excellent as Merteuil), Colin Firth as Valmont, Meg Tilly, Fairuza Balk, Siân Phillips, Jeffrey Jones, Henry Thomas, and Fabia Drake.

Dark Victory (1939)

Which films would you take on your honeymoon, have on a desert island, or treasure in prison? The parlor game less often played is what film would you prefer to have playing as you die? Well, *Dark Victory* has to be a candidate. If you recall, Judith Traherne has worked it all out, the way her blindness surely signals the approaching finale. Husband and friends are out of the house. She has just Martha, her housekeeper, and her dog, Terry—and in the script she does take Terry up to her room as she prepares to die. Indeed, the last shot of that sequence was to be Terry lying on the floor, his head stretched out on his paws. In the finished film, however, Judith is absolutely alone. No dog sees her fade away. Was it the SPCA?

Dark Victory had been a play in 1934–35, by George Brewer, Jr., and Bertram Bloch. It starred Tallulah Bankhead and was a disaster—but dying onstage is far harder than doing it in the movies. Anyway, several people remembered the play and kept dreaming of a movie, notably David O. Selznick, who owned the rights for some time and had thoughts of doing it with Janet Gaynor or Carole Lombard. Another prospector was Casey Robinson, who seems to have written a script and offered it to Warners. That's when Warners began to ease the rights away from Selznick. A third fan was Bette Davis, who ignored Jack Warner's amiable "Who's gonna pay to see you die?" (he had come close himself sometimes) and backed her own hunch that it would work.

At last Warners got it, and David Lewis was eager to produce it. Edmund Goulding was hired as director. Casey Robinson was installed as writer, and he made the point that the success of the story depended on Dr. Steele—he urged that Spencer Tracy be offered the part that eventually went to George Brent. Davis was the leading candidate for Judith, though Kay Francis was a contender.

The great difficulty about the film today is that we know so much about it, not least that unexpected death (through a brain tumor) is coming to Judith Traherne. More than that, we are all hypochondriacal medical experts. So many hospital shows have made us very knowing and very sharp about what death looks like. And it's not quite the sweet spectacle that cinematographer Ernest Haller achieves in the film. In fact, the cinema has externalized death relentlessly: Death is being ripped apart by bullets; it is the riotous death scene of great acting ("Is this the end of Rico?"); it is the endless ingenuity with which people in films meet explosion and collapse. But the inner moment is so empty. That's why death and sex are so difficult to film, and it's why what happens to Judith Traherne is more a kind of socialite sainthood, all done in the church of Max Steiner's splendid, unquenchable music. And just as Robinson foretold, George Brent is very good. But Geraldine Fitzgerald as Judith's friend is even better. In addition, you get Humphrey Bogart trying to be Irish, Ronald Reagan trying not to cry, and the dogs trying to get screen time.

David Copperfield (1935)

You can argue that this adaptation of Charles Dickens is one of the most influential films ever made. It established that a classic novel could be adapted with decency and tact—thus 800 pages became 135 minutes, and few grumbled at the omissions. In turn—in ways that would come to affect the BBC in its serializations of so much period literature—the notion arose that with good costumes, authentic furniture, an army of supporting actors, and taste, then, yes, the world of Dickens, or whomever, could be brought to the big screen.

In this case, the urge and the enthusiasm (if not the taste) came from David O. Selznick, who loved the book and all it represented, and who was prepared to visit England and let the Dickensian world seep into the picture. It came from Hugh Walpole's discretion and delicacy over the screenplay—and his realizing that to some extent Dickens had lost interest in his own novel. But, above all, I think, we owe the picture to George Cukor's instinct. As he wrote: "There was the problem of re-creating Dickens' characters, making them slightly grotesque, at times caricature, yet completely human—as Dickens did himself. It was a difficult thing, making these people funny and frightening at the same time. You achieve it partly by the casting but also by deciding on the style of the playing. The outward semblance is important, too, and here we were guided by Phiz, who did the original illustrations. And somehow I think we managed all that."

Fair comment? I think so, just as I marvel at *Mutiny on the Bounty*'s getting Best Picture that year. The *Bounty* story now feels slow and predictable; somehow we know that what transpired on that unlucky ship was more complicated. Whereas *Copperfield* is a benign meeting of so many craft talents: the script; photography by Oliver T. Marsh in velvet black and white; Dolly Tree's costumes; the sets by Cedric Gibbons, Edwin Willis, and Merrill Pye; and even some montages by Slavko Vorkapich.

And then you have to list the glorious characters: Edna May Oliver as Betsey Trotwood; Lennox Pawle as Mr. Dick; Lionel Barrymore as Dan Peggotty; Basil Rathbone as Mr. Murdstone; Roland Young as Uriah Heep; and W. C. Fields as Mr. Micawber, cast after Charles Laughton had been intimidated by the role. Fields is Fields, of course, always ill dressed but insouciant, never quite drunk or sober, unusually fond of children here, and—as Cukor saw it—exactly the near monster (kind or unkind) that a child perceives. Dickens guessed something of profound importance: that in studying adults and passing from fear to equality, we achieve adulthood. And that is why, onscreen, Dickens needs his young characters, who guide our reaction to the larger world.

It follows that Freddie Bartholomew is not just perfect as David—he is the eyepiece for the movie. Alas, when David becomes grown up (Frank Lawton) and makes mistakes with the women in his life, the film falters. But Dickens was never too impressed by falling in love, or much interested in writing about it.

Dawn of the Dead (1978)

Here are the rules of the game: Unfortunately, the world is subject to mounting attacks from the zombies. The zombies are the dead, but they have been given another, desperate, slow-motion life in which they seek their food: normal, living humans. You will know the zombies by the lurching, exhausted manner of their attack, and from their very messy mouths—they have no table manners. They can be made dead as dead by a shot to the brain. And they're back after the phenomenal success of George A. Romero's *Night of the Living Dead* (1968), the classic exposition of the threat, done in black and white with no stars. Educated at Carnegie Mellon, Romero was a devotee of the Pittsburgh area and the associate of collaborators first encountered in college.

I am fond of *Night of the Living Dead*, and I recognize the great danger of such talents becoming unduly sophisticated as success swells their budgets. *Dawn of the Dead* is in color, and clearly better funded, and there are Romero purists who sniff at it a little because of those advantages. But the budget allows Romero to use the mall, and I have to say that *Dawn of the Dead* is a superior shocker, finally, by virtue of the allusions made possible by the way four vigilantes allow themselves to be besieged by zombies in a huge Pennsylvania shopping mall. The constant menace of a noxious embrace is underscored by the prospect of a lifetime supply of everything being available within arm's reach. This is coupled with the natural schlock poetry that compares the zombies and the mannequins—dead already, but perfect or idealized figures. It's not that Romero really convinces as a social critic, but the extra glee cinematically is giddy and stirring. The shock is piled on, and the viewer can draw his own conclusions about the "ethics" of the zombies or the vigilante integrity of those armed freedom fighters who are defending the consumer society. Let's just say it works. There is a note of social pessimism, but it is saved from solemnity by the sheer magic of the juxtapositions and by our increasing sense of the zombies as children helplessly following in our footsteps. Romero has never gone this far, but I think his approach cries out for a film in which children are the ultimate zombies, the hungry, questioning ones.

The fragile eco-balance at the mall is destroyed when a gang of bikers come hunting zombies—and then the world is at risk again. Michael Gornick did the photography. Romero wrote the script and edited the movie; Dario Argento is credited as a script consultant and as composer of some of the music. Once again, it seems a good deal more fun to play the zombies than the living guys, though naturally the zombies are expected not to laugh as a way of showing their hunger. We are accustomed by now to regard Romero as a slick primitive and one of the best "local" filmmakers in America. Of course, what's more intriguing is just how much his vision fed the borrowed tastes of Hollywood.

Day for Night / La Nuit Américaine (1973)

Not every moviemaker really loves the process of making pictures. It can be exhausting, strenuous, and likely to take away from insight or concentration. You have to have answers for everyone on set, from the neurotic actress who thinks she loves you to the union shop steward who wants to make an idiot or a scoundrel of you. There are directors—not least François Truffaut's adored mentor, Alfred Hitchcock—who declared that the real art and joy was making the storyboard, conceiving all the visual ideas. After that, being on the set was a bore and a chore.

But there is a sustained passage in *Day for Night,* called "Cinema Reigns," in which we have no doubt that for Truffaut the process itself was heaven—a sweet weather. And for every time something does not work—there is a very funny passage with a cat that does not deliver the goods—there is the ritual of readiness and preparation that is exquisite and spiritual. Indeed, you can feel in this film how far, for Truffaut, the fragments of life reordered as film were religious and blessed: *Day for Night* is therefore one of those movies that can be used in any introductory class on what it feels like to make a movie if you want to feel good.

Indeed, I think it's very telling that whereas films like *Sunset Blvd.* and *The Bad and the Beautiful* are concerned with the atmospherics and treachery that surround filmmaking, Truffaut is so dedicated to the work—to tracking shots, to the background fuss that assistant directors control, to the lights and the sound—that you can appreciate the zeal that hardly sees the larger consequences. And so, truly, there are very few films that are as technical and educational as this and that survey the background—the betrayals, the infatuations, the location romances—with such steadfast indifference.

It is a bonus that most of *Day for Night* was shot at the Victorine Studios in Nice, thus providing us with a documentary on that hallowed ground in practice. Of course, the charade is much enhanced by Truffaut's own presence—rather grim and a little deaf—as the director, and in his dreams of a childhood encounter with a locked cinema where *Citizen Kane* is playing. This is not just reverential but fond, not just confessional but intimate; and it inevitably leads us to look back on Truffaut's emotional role as the leader of the New Wave (he was so much more winning than Jean-Luc Godard) and as someone we lost far too early. As in any profound study of a passion, you see that the life is nearly irrelevant.

Pierre-William Glenn did the photography. Truffaut, Suzanne Schiffman, and Jean-Louis Richard wrote the script. Georges Delerue did the lovely music. And the very appealing cast includes Jacqueline Bisset (never prettier), Valentina Cortese, Jean-Pierre Aumont, Jean-Pierre Léaud, Nathalie Baye, and just about everyone else Truffaut knew or could meet (including Graham Greene as a moneyman).

Day of Wrath (1943)

As Carl Dreyer's *Day of Wrath* proceeds, it is easy to think that its subject matter is far from us. At the outset, we have the language of the Day of Wrath spelled out as we see a medieval manuscript. And it may be tempting, at times, to think that because this film was made in Denmark under Nazi occupation, it is a reference to that terror and the place of testimony against others that it encouraged. But the film is more searching than that.

On a beautiful day in May 1623, with blossoms on the fruit trees, an old woman is put to death as a witch in a small Danish community. There is not the least objective evidence of her wrongdoing beyond the fact that she grows herbs. Under torture, she makes no accusation against others and no admission. But just before death, in anger and a spirit of revenge, she tells the pastor, Absalon, that his young wife, Anne (Lisbeth Movin), may be driven by the devil. As the old woman is burned at the stake, the flames are nearly lost in the sunlight.

Life goes on in the pastor's house but for one change: His son by a first wife, Martin, comes home. Martin is actually older than Anne, and almost without signs, a love affair develops between them, like plants growing in the sun. They go off to the secrecy of the birch woods and make love. But Absalon's mother hates Anne—the bride is so young and has an obvious power over Absalon because of it.

Absalon hears Anne laughing—it is a piercing moment, the laughter offstage and the old man's face stricken by the novelty of what he hears. It is, if you like, the first brush of stroke. He questions Anne, and suddenly she cannot tolerate the dishonesty. Yes, she loves Martin, and they want the old man dead. His hand starts to shake, and the stroke hits him. But then, at the funeral, Absalon's mother charges Anne with being the devil's work, and despite her fear of what will happen, she admits to it all. Martin backs away from her as if now he doubts his own life and prefers to believe in the devil.

Filmed in austere black and white (the photography is by Henning Bendtsen), with long takes and simple adjusting camera movements, it is like Rembrandt on a strict budget. The psychology becomes shockingly modern at the end. Surpassing not just the seventeenth century but Nazism, it is a record of the way sexual guilt and exploitation can turn into thoughts as delusional as those of witchcraft.

The men in the film are restricted in their performance: They are upright, impassive, ludicrously burdened by their privilege and spiritual weight. But the women are the life forces. The old woman burned is one of the most pathetic figures in film, Absalon's mother is a monster we long to see damaged, and Anne is, quite simply, a modern woman trapped by male thought control. With only nuances and gestures, Dreyer is able to let us see Anne as a minx and a saint, a witch and a figure of sanity and responsibility. The influence on Bergman is huge, but no less is Dreyer's achievement here.

Days of Heaven (1978)

Days of Heaven, Terrence Malick's second film, is a small period noir story as if seen through the immense cultural telescope of documentarian and historian Ken Burns. It becomes an epic of the prairies in which every blade of grass and every insect has been blessed by Walt Whitman and Exxon Mobil. The result is fascinating and beautiful but perilously given to pretension. In the decades since, it has come to seem like a dead end, even if it is the work of one of the most cultivated men ever to get his hands on a mainstream American film.

Three kids break out of the factory furnace of Chicago in 1916: Bill (Richard Gere); his kid sister, Linda (Linda Manz); and Bill's girl, Abby (Brooke Adams). They travel south by train and come to Texas, where they find work on the ranch of a man known only as the Farmer (Sam Shepard). He is a gaunt, shy man, and he falls for Abby. Bill encourages this so that they will be looked after. The Farmer marries Abby. Bill still has her, but then Abby falls in love with the Farmer. So Bill goes off with a circus troupe. He comes back. There is a great plague of locusts and a fire set to kill the locusts. Bill kills the Farmer. Then the three are pursued, and Bill is killed.

Without doubt, the most striking, dramatic thing about the film is the narrative by Linda. This is a version of Holly's voice-over in *Badlands,* but it is bolder because Linda is younger while her voice is more philosophical. Manz gives the best performance in the film, yet it lends a sunset sheen of magical improbability to everything. That is magnified by the lustrously beautiful photography of the landscapes (by Néstor Almendros and Haskell Wexler), which becomes euphoric or religious in the plague and fire sequences. The beauty is overpowering, symphonic, and enough to leave the meager human action far behind.

It is hard to say, finally, what this odd film is meant to mean—for the expressive powers of the visuals are intoxicating yet empty. (To illustrate this point, I'd refer to *The Thin Red Line,* Malick's next film, where the island of Guadalcanal is so elemental, so beautiful, so God-given that it is a very minor distraction that there should be a war going on there.) Not for the first time, a really promising director seems to have fallen in love with the cinematic and lost all sense of where he was going because of it.

So what does the title mean—granted that the story makes a small hell in which the one man who loves and works the land dies? Is it an idyll, simply? Is the film saying we are unfit for this land or these days? Or is there an adolescent irony at work? None of these answers is sufficient. Meanwhile, *Days of Heaven* remains one of the great visual experiences in American film, and a warning that film is more than visual.

Days of Wine and Roses (1963)

As I write this, a top Hollywood personality, Mel Gibson, has just been charged with driving under the influence. There is talk that he will be entering serious rehabilitation, which usually means a clinic, and there have been stories that Gibson has had a drinking problem for years. It may be a smokescreen to excuse his other problems—notably his anti-Semitic talk. But anyone who spends time in Hollywood recognizes that the great strain of the business, and of flourishing in it, does drive some people to drink or other addictions. In which case, it is interesting that I can quickly think of only three movies that deal with the issue: *The Lost Weekend, Days of Wine and Roses,* and *When a Man Loves a Woman.* But if Hollywood is scared of the subject, let's note that *The Lost Weekend* scooped the big prize, while *Days of Wine and Roses* took in $4.3 million and got respectful Oscar nominations for both Jack Lemmon and Lee Remick.

Days was done for television originally, in 1958, as a Playhouse 90 production, written by J. P. Miller and directed by John Frankenheimer. In that version, Cliff Robertson and Piper Laurie played the young couple, and Charles Bickford was the girl's father. For the big screen, Frankenheimer stepped aside—he was at the busiest time of his career—and Blake Edwards took over the direction. Jack Lemmon was apparently very keen to play Joe Clay, and he recommended Lee Remick for the part of Kirsten Arnesen, the girl he marries. But Bickford was retained in the role of Kirsten's father, Ellis. The strength of the material is to show an honest love affair—with marriage and an appealing daughter—while still knowing the insecurities that will lead to drinking. Kirsten has never quite grown up, while Joe is in a muddle over the career rat race. He introduces his wife to drink and then lives to see her destroyed by the curse.

The film was photographed in black and white by Philip Lathrop, with art direction by Joseph Wright. The playing is expert and deeply touching, and the subtlest thing about the film is the idea that if these two people loved each other less, they might be able to haul themselves out of trouble.

In many ways, the domestic situation and the love story take this problem picture much closer to ordinary life than *The Lost Weekend* could ever be. And, of course, this film has a tragic ending. The Academy steered clear of the picture, and the only Oscar it won was for a rather sickly sweet song, written by Henry Mancini and sung by Andy Williams. The tune is still well known (it's a kind of torch song in its structure and tone), and one can't help but feel that it was meant to muffle the bleak effect of the picture as a whole. Rest assured, the problem lives on, especially in show business, where the chronic urge to be thin puts more emphasis on drinking than eating.

The Dead (1987)

The occasion of *The Dead* is replete with its own stories: Of how John Huston came to what would be his last film in an advanced state of emphysema. Of how he re-created the Dublin of 1907 in the blaze of summer in a studio near the Magic Mountain amusement park, in the hills north of Los Angeles, importing a rich cast of Irish players for the dinner. And of how the dying man bent himself to the noble task of filming the James Joyce story faithfully and surely, if only as a way of staying alive.

What happens? There is a dinner party in a Dublin house. A number of lives are sketched in, along with the self-consumed society of a provincial city that fancied itself. Huston's son, Tony, wrote the script with his father, and I don't think there's any fault to be found with it beyond its helpless condition of not being the story itself. Wasn't it nominated for the Oscar in the same kind of futile respect?

The craft work was very solid and careful: Fred Murphy did the photography in muted color—I'm sure he'd have preferred black and white, but what was anyone to do about that? Stephen Grimes did fine production design, lovingly furnished. Roberto Silvi edited the film. Alex North did some music, content to develop music of the period. And Dorothy Jeakins did the costumes and got an Oscar nomination. Put all of that together and you could quite easily believe you were in Dublin at the time—a thing that film can do, and will. Which is all very well, except that James Joyce, who was in Dublin, had the uncanny ability to be everywhere else or to use words that roamed in time.

The cast is fine. I can believe that Donal McCann as Gabriel and Anjelica Huston as Gretta are married, and content or not, in the way of the narrative. I took great pleasure in watching and listening to the others: Rachael Dowling, Cathleen Delany, Helena Carroll, Ingrid Craigie, Dan O'Herlihy, Frank Patterson, Donal Donnelly, Marie Kean, Maria McDermottroe, Sean McClory, and Colm Meaney. And what with all of them, there is the air and the sniff of Dubliners and there is the story of "The Dead."

But what there is not and never will be is the great rhythm of the Joyce story, the writing, the imagery (such as anyone would be an idiot to try to reproduce), and the sense that literature can give of the past and the memory of it. To tell the truth, it's not a very good film. To be fair, for all its faith, it's pretty empty next to this:

> A few light taps upon the pane made him turn to the window. It had begun to snow again. He watched sleepily the flakes, silver and dark, falling obliquely against the lamplight. The time had come for him to set out on his journey westward. Yes, the newspapers were right: snow was general all over Ireland. It was falling on every part of the dark central plain, on the treeless hills, falling softly upon the Bog of Allen and, farther westward, softly falling into the dark mutinous Shannon waves. It was falling, too, upon every part of the lonely churchyard on the hill where Michael Furey lay buried. It lay thickly drifted on the crooked crosses and headstones, on the spears of the little gate, on the barren thorns. His soul swooned slowly as he heard the snow falling faintly through the universe and faintly falling, like the descent of their last end, upon all the living and the dead.

You see, it was about then that, seeing there were eager souls who could never do the writing, God invented film and so on. And I suppose it was a kindness. But it showed what an idiot He was.

Dead Calm (1989)

Dead Calm would be just a suspense film about people on boats, taken from a novel by Charles Williams—as such, it did inspire one of Orson Welles's unfinished films (the one with himself, Jeanne Moreau, Laurence Harvey, and Michael Bryant). Purists might wish for the Welles film, but the *Dead Calm* that exists—complete—is no small thing, not with Nicole Kidman in it, as large and freckled as life.

Not that her being in the film really stands up to any test of reason. She was twenty when she made the film—a rare achievement, yet a disqualification, too. After all, as the film opens, her husband (Sam Neill), a naval officer, comes back from a voyage, expecting to be met by wife and child. But something has happened, an accident in which the child has been killed, a child of four, which suggests that Nicole's character, Rae, was a freshman in high school at the time of the marriage.

As part of her convalescence, she and the husband go on a substantial voyage on his yacht. She seems to be getting better. But when she takes a swim off the yacht, she wears a one-piece black bathing suit. The appeal of Ms. Kidman's body is not in doubt, and I'm sure that there were some basic censorship regulations that applied—but isn't it remarkable that the wife would not swim naked in that situation? The restraints cannot help but beg to be interpreted. They hint at some limit—some polite barrier—in the marriage (Neill is twenty years older than Kidman). In other words, you can't show anything in a movie without having the audience interpret it—so you might as well have a reason for everything.

The story here is very simple. The couple see another yacht in the distance, seemingly out of control. Then a young man—Billy Zane—makes his way to them in a small boat. He is near collapse, but he says that people died on the other yacht, apparently of some kind of poisoning. He falls asleep. And then Captain Sam decides to go over to the wallowing yacht to see what really happened. Should he go? You know the answer—and you can tell without seeing it that his going amounts to another kind of neglect of his wife.

He finds a lot of trouble on the boat—an engine that doesn't work and people who have been murdered. Whereupon Billy Zane wakes up and makes off with Nicole. What will he do to her? Can Sam follow them and keep up? Ms. Kidman on camera acts like a brave and resourceful young woman, even if in her efforts to slow Mr. Zane she just about lets him rape her. Or is that it?

The Phillip Noyce picture is content to be a suspense story, so the matters of character—the questions—are ignored. That doesn't mean they are settled. So *Dead Calm* is fishing for subtext. There are many other ways in which it might proceed, and Nicole's gaze seems to have seen most of them. The trouble with a great "discovery" (in fact, Kidman was already well-known in Australia) is that she can leave your movie looking a bit simpleminded.

Death in Venice (1971)

Here, in the course of one film, you can measure the shift from one man intent on making a masterpiece to something like a monstrous parody created by the Monty Python boys. So be careful when you set out with a masterpiece in mind, and think several times before taking on a work as slight yet pregnant as Thomas Mann's 1912 novella in which Gustav von Aschenbach, writer, aesthete, and connoisseur, takes himself off to Venice in a time of cholera. (We know from the décor that this is the Europe of just before the First World War, and it is part of the film's gloom that it slots in with that cliché of fatefulness.)

Aschenbach is of a certain age—probably a little more than fifty, the age at which Dirk Bogarde played the role—in love with youth as he himself loses it. But as if to greet or taunt the man's repressed sexual urges, a boy, Tadzio, appears, and he is like a watermark in the film. Tadzio is tall, slender, blond, classy, and he feels as Swedish as the actor, Björn Andrésen. I hope Mr. Andrésen is leading a quiet, fruitful life somewhere—it must have been a tough assignment for recovery. For although everything in the picture adores Tadzio, Mr. Andrésen has no idea why and not very much to offer. He is a passive, lofty kid, rather bitter about being photographed, but safely kept at a distance. And as Aschenbach's desire is thwarted, Dirk Bogarde's performance becomes a study in torment, degenerating to the point where his mascara begins to run in the rain and the tears.

Death in Venice still has many admirers, some of whom seem to believe that the Mahler in which the film is washed (the Third and the Fifth Symphonies) must have been written by Visconti himself, inspired by his own footage. Some viewers find the stress on the costumes pretty and significant (Piero Tosi was Oscar-nominated for them); others can only think how quickly white shows the dirt.

The quality in this quality production is like waterlogging. In some films it is Venice that sinks; here it could be the movie, wallowing more and more as the buildings loom larger. Ferdinando Scarfiotti did the art direction, and Pasquale de Santis did the photography. The cast includes a number of distinguished actors with very little to do or say: Mark Burns, Marisa Berenson, Silvana Mangano. It's notable, I fear, that at Cannes *Death in Venice* won only a special 25th Anniversary Prize. Yes, a director had come out of the closet, but with such a burden of poshlust and production values that one longed for the age of discretion.

You need only go back to Visconti's *Senso*, done in Venice in 1954, to see the loss of emotional reality and the sacrifice of storytelling to lassitudinous self-regard. *Death in Venice* is a very bad film, made with such clarity and vulgarity that one can at least be grateful for its educational warning value—it is an embroidered banner indicating a vast minefield.

Deep End (1971)

Mention *Deep End* in informed movie circles, and everyone thinks you mean *The Deep End*, the 2001 picture (with Tilda Swinton, directed by Scott McGehee and David Siegel) a remake of Max Ophüls's *The Reckless Moment.* I like *The Deep End*, and it came close to making this selection. But I am here to tell you that *Deep End*, made thirty years earlier by a nearly forgotten figure, Jerzy Skolimowski, is a better film.

It was always a film that asked its admirers, Well, where am I from? Its makers were Polish, if Poles in exile. The money came largely from West Germany. But the two leading players were English, and so for me the film felt English if only because of the lovely, guttersnipe voice of Jane Asher as the enigmatic female figure. I hasten to add that Ms. Asher was a classy bird in her own right. In putting on the south London voice, she was acting—and acting so well it's a marvel and a disgrace that we don't know her from other films.

Mike (John Moulder-Brown) is sixteen or so and just out of school. He gets a job as attendant at a suburban swimming pool—indoors, Victorian, tiles, old-fashioned, but a strange meeting ground for sexy kids, fitness freaks, and those outsiders who live a life of municipal facilities. He has to avoid the lubricious advances of another attendant, the voluptuous towel lady (played with high comedy by Diana Dors)—and he falls for a schoolgirl, Susan (Asher), who comes to the pool to be seen, to wear a swimsuit, to flirt with her teacher (Karl Michael Vogler), and to act as the mysterious threshold to life for Mike.

Jerzy Skolimowski (born in Warsaw, 1938) had made *Identification Marks: None, Walkover, Barrier,* and *Le Départ.* He was a dynamic and dangerous figure. There was something of Godard there, as well as Polanski. But could he function outside Poland? *Deep End* was a test of that, written in collaboration with two other Polish exiles, Jerzy Gruza and Boleslaw Sulik. The picture was photographed by Charly Steinberger and the important art direction was done by Max Ott, Jr., and Anthony Pratt.

None of which necessarily prepares one for so lyrical or violent a parable about sexual awakening. From the seedy mood of the bathhouse to the electric potential of the two lead actors, *Deep End* is mundane and surreal together at every instant. Its ending is savage and comic. Its passage is erotic and deeply unsettling. *Deep End* is not too far from a major film, and its neglect is representative of the way Skolimowski has slipped into obscurity. There were later films—*The Shout* and *Moonlighting*—based in England. But Skolimowski has fallen silent (he acts in *Eastern Promises*). So it's important to stress that *Deep End* is a film worthy of Vigo. There are images of Jane Asher—of her and her image (see the film)—that deserve a place in the history of erotic cinema.

The Deer Hunter (1978)

At the time of this controversial film's release, there were complaints that the North Vietnamese had not employed Russian roulette. It was said that the scenes in Saigon were fanciful or imagined. And it was suggested that De Niro, Christopher Walken, and John Savage were too old to have enlisted for Vietnam (Savage, the youngest of the three, was thirty). Three decades later, "imagination" seems to have stilled those worries. It is not necessarily a comfortable conclusion, for Michael Cimino has gone far away from making movies since the famous disaster of *Heaven's Gate*. Never mind; you still need to see *Heaven's Gate* and decide for yourself, and *The Deer Hunter* is one of the great American films.

In Clairton, Pennsylvania, Michael (De Niro), Nick (Walken), and Steven (Savage) are soon to go to Vietnam. Before then, Steven is to marry Angela (Rutanya Alda). At their prolonged wedding, we meet other friends: John (George Dzundza), Stan (John Cazale), and Nick's girlfriend, Linda (Meryl Streep).

After the wedding, the guys go off on a deer hunt—in country impossibly far from Pennsylvania. It proves to be a rite of passage in which Mike declares his ideal of the one-shot kill.

At this point, we are an hour into a picture after a first movement that is long, slow, and ominous, and a second that is short and electric. The structure might come direct from Shostakovich's Tenth Symphony, for immediately we plunge into the close confines of horrible imprisonment by the Vietcong, of torture and Russian roulette. The three guys are involved, and they escape. Steven will lose his legs. Nick vanishes into the hinterland of Saigon.

Michael returns to Pennsylvania. He becomes involved with Linda, though nothing really can happen between them. He decides to return to Saigon, and he finds Nick, who has made a tormented career out of Russian roulette. Michael tries to save Nick, but the urge to self-destruction is too great.

You have to feel the musical structure, marked out by two songs—"Can't Take My Eyes Off You" at the wedding and "God Bless America" at the close. You have to respond to the brilliant visualization of every moment, the photography by Vilmos Zsigmond. And you have to understand the existentialism of acting. Within it all, this is a story in which the stupid male pride of America bows to stronger forces and more elastic philosophies. It is a picture in which a small survey of manhood reveals desperate, tragic, and inadequate characters; in which women hardly know how to make their presence felt. It is redneck America. Yes, it is a film about America's Vietnam that will outlive the wounds and memories of that war. You have to see it, finally, as an aghast realization about the violence in America—and so it becomes the companion to *Heaven's Gate*.

The Deer Hunter is one of the few American films that work like a novel. It is unsettling, yet it is mysterious. It is as if the deer in the mountains and the steel furnaces are in possession of some inner knowledge that explains the Dostoyevskian gambling in Vietnam. Far more than *Apocalypse Now*, this film smells of Conrad.

Deliverance (1972)

If you go down to the woods today, you'd better not go alone . . . but how many friends will you need to keep you safe? America has not often used its cinema to explore the society of the hinterland—I mean the deep, rural places, off the highways or the air routes, where life goes on, determined to be undisturbed or dragged into the bright light of civilization. And that neglect has led to a widespread paranoia in the urban, educated places—that the country is a hideaway for barbarism of a kind that deters casual visiting.

It's a fascinating question for historical research how far this initial wariness prompted the hostilities with native Americans in the nineteenth century, and the view of the South that has grown up since the Civil War. So I think it's worth saying that young, able Americans from all over the country do go exploring in Texas, hiking along the Blue Ridge of Tennessee, or kayaking on the great rivers of Appalachia without facing worse than the natural dangers and the endless hospitality of the locals.

That is not what *Deliverance* was ever about. It comes from the novel by James Dickey, published in 1970, about four city guys who plan a river adventure. It turns out badly. They are held up by rednecks. There is a rape. There is murder. Only three of them come through, and they are shattered—as are we. In the hands of director John Boorman this is a terrifying, compulsive movie, as successful as it may be misleading.

Boorman made friends with Dickey, who delivered a screenplay that is a solemn, not unpretentious work of literature in its own right. It begins: "Black screen. I would like this to be sustained for a while, perhaps even a bit longer than it is in most cases, so that the audience becomes very quiet, wondering if something might not possibly be wrong."

The only thing wrong was that directors—even those as smart as Boorman—don't respond happily to such guidance. The two fell out, and Dickey had to leave the shooting—though he plays the sheriff very nicely. Boorman did not betray his cause, even if Vilmos Zsigmond's outstanding photography does not fully catch Dickey's troubled apprehension of nature.

The film is not for the queasy. It is rough and scary as hell: The rednecks—Bill McKinney, Herbert Coward—are nightmare stuff, and the rape is not done discreetly (I don't think it can be). But Boorman's real quest is to see how the men shape up, how the macho Lewis (Burt Reynolds) cracks and how the more thoughtful Ed (Jon Voight) becomes the leader or the one left guilty. Ned Beatty is very good as the chief victim, and Ronny Cox is the one who dies. There is also the meeting with a boy (Hoyt Pollard) who plays such wild banjo that it is as awesome as the power of the river and the intractability of its natives. This is a film of frightening power—just like America. But is the power and its fear accurately imagined?

Desire (1936)

For a moment in the mid 1930s, Paramount thought to put Ernst Lubitsch in charge of all production, as if he might touch and bring magic to everything. Second thoughts crowded in, and Lubitsch was quite quickly replaced with William LeBaron (the executive who did so much to get Preston Sturges his start as a director). Still, here—from 1936, with Frank Borzage directing—is one of Lubitsch's productions. Almost certainly, it was a picture he had intended doing himself; the erotic suggestiveness of jewels (especially when slipped into a pocket) is not just his touch but nearly a trademark. Lubitsch had a way of looking at necklaces as if they were private parts—and I don't think I need to spell out the place of the pocket in such transactions.

Please notice Paramount's cheerful indifference to Spain in 1936 (the studio had just done *The Devil Is a Woman,* which unsettled diplomatic relations). Tom Bradley (Gary Cooper) is a Detroit engineer who takes a vacation in one of the company's top cars. He elects to drive from Paris to Spain, which, according to this film, is still available for blithe romance. But Madeleine de Beaupre (Marlene Dietrich) is on the road, too, with a pearl necklace that is not hers. At the customs post, going from France to Spain, she slips the pearls into Tom's pocket, just in case. Well, romance is under way, and since theft has played cupid to this couple, there will be unusual problems in sorting out honesty.

This pleasant nonsense came from a play, *Die Schönen Tage von Aranjuez,* by Hans Szekely and R. A. Stemmle, which had already been filmed in Germany, with Brigitte Helm in the Madeleine role. Lubitsch got a new script worked on by Edwin Justus Mayer, Waldemar Young, and Samuel Hoffenstein, and he reckoned to reunite Dietrich and Cooper; one suspects that he looked back over the Sternberg films and saw the Cooper-Dietrich chemistry as one of the few things worth pursuing commercially and creatively.

Dietrich, one has to say, seems liberated after Sternberg, and there is no doubt that she had a terrific Berliner fondness for Lubitsch, not to mention a yen for Cooper. He is adroit at playing the simpleton who lets her run rings around him, until the rings have her tangled. Meanwhile, she gazes at him with the awe of simple lust—a quality too neglected in films. And it helps so much that they have a similar pace, with Dietrich's amused gaze nestling in Coop's elongated responses.

What did Borzage do? Well, he shot it all, with Charles Lang and Victor Milner doing the photography. But in addition, he has the gravity to know how far to make "love" an ennobling little prison for a couple (as when Madeleine is pretending to sleep). Borzage did love, whereas Lubitsch was always looking over his shoulder. Borzage could concentrate, and that skill is very kind to the two stars and to the flimsy story.

The film is justly famous for its luxe costumes (by Travis Banton), and its art direction (by Hans Dreier and Robert Usher) is definitely Spain before hostilities commenced. Frederick Hollander did the music, with a song, "You're Here, I'm Here," for Marlene.

Destry Rides Again (1939)

Don't forget that, in advance of *Stagecoach* or *Red River*, someone had seen the possibility (or is it the need?) of spoofing the Western. Originally, *Destry Rides Again* had been a novel by Max Brand about a droll, yarn-spinning cowboy who brings law and order to a gunslinging town (named Bottleneck). As such, it had been a Tom Mix picture in 1932—but in that version, the hero's true love was his horse. By 1939, enough people at Universal were convinced of the chance of a new version of the story, but this time the horse would be a woman. Better still, it would be Marlene Dietrich, in an attempt to revive her American career.

Producer Joe Pasternak presided over the managerial confusion as many more people than those credited offered script pages. But there was a safety net: If they didn't know what to do next, Destry the cowboy would tell one of his shaggy horse stories, or the saloon girl, Frenchy (Marlene), would sing a song. All of a sudden, Jimmy Stewart (Destry) found that quavering, drawling, make-it-up-as-you-go-along storytelling style that he traded on the rest of his life. His high voice became manageable and sleepy—and all at once charm oozed out of the spindly kid. No one needed a map, especially not Dietrich, who fell upon her costar in gratitude and respect. She gave no trouble to the cameraman (Hal Mohr) or the director (George Marshall), and she took sensible comfort in having Frederick Hollander to write a few songs for her—notably, "See What the Boys in the Back Room Will Have," which she never abandoned.

The chemistry between Stewart and Dietrich was classic Americana—homespun outwits Continental sophistication—but Marlene had the good sense not to contest it. And Stewart knew he was a lucky guy. So, along the way, the outlines of the Western were satirized, or spoofed (if you prefer that American word). Marshall deserves credit, too—throughout his career he exhibited the ability to make gentle fun of familiar genres. Dietrich hadn't made a film in two years—not since *Angel*—but this got her a contract with Universal, where she was happy making eyes at big, rough American men like John Wayne and Randolph Scott.

Other songs (lyrics by Frank Loesser as well as music by Hollander) were "Little Joe, the Wrangler" and "You've Got that Look." The supporting cast included Charles Winninger, Mischa Auer, Brian Donlevy, Irene Hervey, and Una Merkel (with whom Dietrich has a drag-out catfight of the sort that men always appreciate).

The picture began shooting days after Hitler invaded Poland and was in theaters by the end of November, thereby adding to the pleasing illusion that in 1939, amid such troubles and uncertainty, Hollywood could hardly put a foot wrong. A real flop in 1939 might have killed Dietrich as a star. *Destry* set her up again as an amused and amusing woman—one who could sing to the troops and deserve their affection.

Detour (1945)

People marvel that Edgar G. Ulmer's *Detour* was shot in six days, but six days can be an awful long time. Imagine six days with this film's female protagonist, Vera (Ann Savage); it's enough to bring on thoughts of doing away with yourself. How easily the ugly circumstances of *Detour* the story seem to supersede the film. It is a reality that travelers might tell warning tales about.

Al Roberts (Tom Neal) is making his way west to be with his girl, Sue (Claudia Drake). In Reno, he recalls her in a brief flashback—it is all we will ever see of her—singing in a nightclub. She went west to make her name; he would follow when he was a success. But he can't wait for that, and now he is nearly in California.

A man, Haskell (Edmund MacDonald), says he will give him a lift to L.A. They drive through the night, and Haskell tells him about a woman he picked up—not a hitch-hiker, but a waiting curse. Al drives, and while he's doing so, Haskell dies. Al fears he will be blamed. So he dumps the body and takes Haskell's car, his money, and his identity. He picks up a woman, Vera, and he realizes she is the woman Haskell talked about. She realizes that Haskell is dead and assumes Al has killed him. She dominates him. She gets her teeth into him.

They go to L.A. and then San Bernardino. They are holed up in a motel. They read that Haskell had a wealthy father. Vera tells Al he will pretend to be Haskell to get the money. But before that can happen, Vera goes into another room to make a phone call. Hating her, Al pulls hard on the cord, then harder. He finds he has strangled her. He never has had any luck. A cop picks him up. "No matter what you do, no matter where you turn, fate sticks out its foot to trip you." It's a more persuasive refrain than the song Sue was singing at the start, "I Can't Believe That You're in Love with Me."

Edgar G. Ulmer was Viennese. He had designed for Max Reinhardt and F. W. Murnau, and he came to America in 1930. He began directing in 1934 and worked for thirty years, usually on B pictures. He seems always to have been hanging on by his fingernails, yet he was plainly very smart and highly talented. Half a dozen of his pictures (*Ruthless*, *The Naked Dawn*, for instance) are still classics of the underground that existed before "independent" film came along. He was interviewed, and he talked like a pirate king. Yet how did he survive? And how is a film like *Detour* endurable? I don't mean that in a derogatory way. The film is a portrait of hell, and brilliantly done. It was made for Producers Releasing Corporation, with Leon Fromkess as producer. The credits on the picture say that Martin Goldsmith wrote it from his own novel. Benjamin H. Kline did the photography. The film runs 67 minutes.

Tom Neal ended up badly: he was involved in violence and did six years in prison. Ann Savage is alive still and sometimes appears at special showings of *Detour*, an old witch who hardly seems to grasp what she has done. *Detour* is preserved now, famous and taught, but it only shows that there may be plenty of films as good, as ugly, and as disreputable waiting to be found in the gutter.

In the second half of the nineteenth century, the Parisian Claude Roc goes to stay with the Brown sisters. They are Anne and Muriel, and they live in a gray-stone house on a clifftop; it seems to be Wales, and it is idyllic, not just as the three parties slip in and out of love but simply in terms of place, the air, and the color of the light. The summer is a mix of shyness and impulse, set against the idea of a young French author staying with a pair of Bronte-esque sisters. Words are everywhere, in the narration (delivered by François Truffaut himself) and in the form of letters passed among the trio like nervous glances.

My feeling that this is Truffaut's essential film comes from several things. One of them is the fascinating, suspicious relationship of film and literature, for there is a steady uncertainty over whether this work will lean toward one or the other. Another is the friendship between English and French characters, as uncommon in film as it may be in life, but surely worth thinking of for constant neighbors. Then there is the absorbing study of sisterhood. I'm not sure if the intuitions and the rivalries of sisters have ever been caught better onscreen. And this is to say nothing of the love affairs themselves, the heady notion of passion and the characteristic resorting to and fear of a natural, unbreachable solitude in people.

The film comes in various forms. It has been called *Two English Girls* and even *Ann and Muriel*, and it has different lengths to watch out for. But this confusion captures the uncertainty over how far Claude or the girls are the center or the key observers of the story. The interplay is fascinating, very fast, and entirely satisfying. And in the odd history of film and literature, this film has a special place that turns on the original novel by Henri-Pierre Roché (the author of *Jules et Jim*, too).

Truffaut did the screenplay with Jean Gruault. The radiant color photography is by Néstor Almendros, and the rich, expressive sets are by Michel de Broin. It comes as no surprise that the music is by Georges Delerue. As never before or since (apart from Jean Eustache's *The Mother and the Whore*), this picture digs into the acting persona of Jean-Pierre Léaud—we see the posturing and the pride, the solitariness and the brusqueness, and they all fit together. Truffaut's perseverance with Léaud is an oddity, and who knows how happy the man was being an actor. But this is a full, rounded performance. Even so, the towering stars of the film are Kika Markham (as Anne) and Stacey Tendeter (as Muriel). We are accustomed to Truffaut's special skill with actresses. We also have to recall his being helpless with the English-speaking Julie Christie in *Fahrenheit 451*. Yet here, with English actresses, he seems to know that they are the poles of a major film. It's all the more poignant that, beyond this one, the two women hardly had any other career.

The Devil Is a Woman (1935)

The game was up. Even before *The Devil Is a Woman* began, Paramount announced that this would be the last time Marlene Dietrich and Josef von Sternberg worked together on the studio's payroll. Sternberg would say later that he did not intend the very pointed title, that his chosen title—*Capriccio Espagnole*—was overruled by Ernst Lubitsch in his new capacity of head of production at the studio. On the other hand, just to compare the images of Marlene in *Morocco* and *The Devil Is a Woman* is to see an extraordinary journey in fondness. In *Morocco* Dietrich is so soft, so enticing; but in the later film she is a painted mask, dark, sardonic, and cruel. It is very hard not to see this as a baleful, albeit respectful, farewell by a beaten man. Moreover, Marlene had a long and eventful career ahead of her, whereas Sternberg became almost instantly both forgotten and mysterious. Cut adrift from Paramount, he never had the same command of resources again.

The Devil Is a Woman is based on the book *The Woman and the Puppet*, by Pierre Louys. John Dos Passos is credited with the screenplay, but scholars suspect that most of it was done by Sternberg—and as if to make it a one-man show, or a private room, he apparently did the cinematography himself, too, with the young Lucien Ballard as his assistant. It is a story of Concha Perez, a woman who plays every man in her life off against all the others. Her victims are played by Lionel Atwill, Cesar Romero, and Edward Everett Horton, and there is not one relationship that seems remotely wholesome or plausible. Indeed, Concha is a temptress by profession and a liar by instinct. She is the bleakest portrait of female purpose in the world that Sternberg ever allowed himself.

The Spanish government chose to be insulted (in that the setting was Spain), and it would have barred all Paramount product if the film had not been withdrawn. It did little better in countries not offended. Stylistically the movie is brilliant: The look of it is very severely black and white, as if done in Spain's real heat. Yet the emotional temperature is icy and unforgiving. The dark humor evident in *Morocco* and even *Shanghai Express* is gone, and the mannered style that Sternberg loved always needed an undercurrent of humor.

If you want more on that, go to Luis Buñuel's *That Obscure Object of Desire*, derived from the same material—not much less impressed by the behavior of men, but made with a kind of acid tenderness that burns even as it comforts. It's a dead end to the Dietrich–Sternberg story, and it surely points to the latter's arrogance and intractability. She really wasn't his kind of woman, no matter that in looks, gesture, and affect he had made a creature so lovely that her monstrousness clogged his heart. Their story is one of the great tragedies in screen history, and anyone touched by it should see all seven films the pair made together (I have restrained myself to just five of them in this book).

Le Diable au Corps (1947)

Claude Autant-Lara was one of those directors regularly roasted by the young critics in *Cahiers du Cinéma* in the 1950s. François Truffaut, for one, wrote, "I have always deplored his tendency to simplify everything, make it bland. I disliked the coarseness with which he 'condensed' Stendhal, Radiguet, Colette. It seemed to me he deformed and watered down the spirit of any work he adapted." The criticism is well made, and I think it still stands the test of time, but it is hardly fair to the impact left by *Le Diable au Corps* in the years just after the Second World War.

Raymond Radiguet wrote the original novel at the age of seventeen. It was published in 1923, and Radiguet was dead a year later. That spared him a good deal, for *Le Diable au Corps* was about the passionate love affair between a schoolboy and the wife of a soldier. It was based on an event in Radiguet's own life, and for years after the author's death the woman protested that Radiguet had greatly exaggerated—or wished for—the physical side of their relationship.

To give Truffaut credit, I can easily imagine his making that the focus of the film: a woman, still young, who becomes the figure in a scandal because of the way she was depicted in a kid's novel. The author dies. The woman's husband abandons her. Society settles around her in a mixture of horror and respect. She wonders who she is. Yes, it's a more interesting idea than the novel itself. But still, it's churlish to turn one's back on the film that was made.

Autant-Lara got Jean Aurenche and Pierre Bost to adapt the novel, and they worked faithfully enough. The coup was in the casting: Gérard Philipe was the boy (the actor was actually twenty-four), while Micheline Presle was the wife (she was the same age). Those were the days when filmgoers from America and Britain believed that the French cinema was the only one actually allowed to do sex. That spirit should proceed with caution: *Le Diable au Corps* is very good on the storm of feelings in these two, but it is not unduly candid or open erotically. In fact, Philipe has the tougher task by far, and he really does make us believe he's a teenager.

Called *The Devil in the Flesh* when released outside France, the film was an art-house hit. It had been made by the regular unit that Autant-Lara employed: Michel Kelber on camera, René Cloëric doing the music, Max Douy on production design, his wife, Monique Dumas, on costumes, and Madeleine Gug doing the editing. It was enough to establish Philipe as a romantic lead, and it promoted Micheline Presle into a few unhappy years in Hollywood.

I'm sure the picture worked because of the young leads and because such secret loves always flourish in war. The subject was remade in 1986 by Marco Bellocchio (a better director) and with startling sexual candor. Maruschka Detmers actually delivered a blow job—but the audience acted as if they'd seen it all before.

Les Diaboliques (1955)

The study of movie genres is often so narrow. Thus, even Carlos Clarens, in his excellent book *Horror Movies* (1968), excludes *Les Diaboliques* because it is "a pure puzzle, a thriller (however black) that employs the apparatus of terror in the context of the detective story." Well, we didn't see the same film. While it is true that Charles Vanel plays a detective in *Les Diaboliques*, a man who clears up the whole problem, I know that my dreams, my waking fears in a large, dark house, were left untouched by that rescue.

The setting is a wretched school in the provinces of France, a place where the sun never shines. There is a schoolmaster (Paul Meurisse), a sadist and a tyrant to the school and his family. He has a wife (Véra Clouzot), whose dread of him is sharpened by her heart condition. He has a mistress (Simone Signoret), who eventually seems to take sides with the wife because the schoolmaster is so loathsome. They plan to kill him. They think that they have accomplished this. We believe it. But then there are signs that it may not be so. Is he about to return? Will he come as vengeful ghost or disfigured self?

The director is Henri-Georges Clouzot, one of cinema's most dedicated misanthropes, and the story comes from a novel by Pierre Boileau and Thomas Narcejac (the team that also inspired Hitchcock's *Vertigo*—Hitch loved *Diaboliques* and showed it to the *Psycho* crew). Still, I think the dank mood of the film—and it is far more about atmosphere than puzzle—comes largely from Clouzot's way of seeing and feeling the world. It is there in the wan light, the shabby décor, the feeling that all the characters could be unclean or diseased (as well as hopeless). It is in the air of prison that hangs over the school, and the way its swimming pool—dark, clotted, poisonous?—is like the sump pit of creation. (Drowning is a special horror or trick in this film.) And the menace is calculated in terms of whether it may bring on a fatal heart attack in one of the characters.

Horror dates so often—not here. That alone is a sign that the purity of the puzzle has nothing to do with the insidious, infectious growth of the film in your mind. For it grows out of an authentically bleak and nasty attitude toward life, and the unkindness is in every word or glance, not just in the constructs of the mystery plot. You can see the film many times and still be able to recall how, in your teens, the necessary descent at night down two flights of stairs to the cellar to get coal, with lights that did not always work, was enough to send you back to that school.

The story was remade in America three times: once with Sharon Stone and Isabelle Adjani, and most effectively of all as *Reflections of Murder*, with Tuesday Weld, for television. But no American setting can seem as imbued with toxic feelings as the one Clouzot created. Horror, for Carlos Clarens, maybe, is a way of goosing yourself. But for Clouzot it is the discovery of a dread that has always been there, in us.

Dial M for Murder (1954)

Here is one of those Hitchcock films where objects mean so much. The key, for instance: This is a story of several latchkeys floating through the ether. It's a drama waiting for the dressmaking scissors on the table. And, of course, the telephone. Trust Hitchcock to make a picture in which dialing is a moral ordeal. In the great exhibition "Hitchcock and Art" that Dominique Paini designed for Montreal and the Pompidou, the recurrence of these objects in Hitchcock was much alluded to, and in the end their hard, guilt-inflicting role surpasses the many ways in which *Dial M* was out-of-date even in 1954.

It was from a play by Frederick Knott (he would do *Wait Until Dark* a few years later) that had been a hit in London and New York, and Hitch hired Knott to do the screenplay, if only because no one else could grasp the movements of that key or comprehend the convoluted ways in which, once upon a time, a fellow might have his wife killed. Nowadays, it can happen in a twinkling of irresistible impulse. But Tony Wendice (Ray Milland) creates etiquette problems for himself with his lovely wife, Margot (Grace Kelly).

They have no children. They have a very nice South Kensington garden flat. Yes, he has money troubles. Still, if Tony wants to kill Margot, I suspect that Tony has got a gay spirit locked in his closet with all those old tennis rackets (he was a Wimbledon player once). It's true that Margot is having a minor fling with Mark Halliday (Robert Cummings), but the day when Ray Milland can't outvolley Bob Cummings will be a long time coming. And really, Margot is so lovely, so fragrant, and so stupid—what more does a man about town want?

Well, Tony hires a rogue (Anthony Dawson) to do the wicked deed, in the apartment with a stocking. A phone call will trigger it all. But Margot is so plucky she is leaning back in last gasp when her hand strays to those scissors and plunges them into the small of his back! For reasons that only Mr. Knott could get away with, Margot will end up about to be executed for murdering the rogue, unless. . . .

This is very stagy, but so it should be: Nearly everything takes place on the one set. After films like *Notorious* and *Under Capricorn*, this was a leap backward (though it was a hit). But you can see Hitch taking on fresh life as he looks at Grace Kelly. Victimized blondes were his meat and drink, and you can feel the hunger. Ray Milland does a very suave job as a Fred Perry type who has run out of cash. Bob Cummings is the ball boy, and John Williams gives a nice little performance as Chief Inspector Hubbard, who will explain it all. When you realize that *Rear Window* was coming up next, you see how deftly Hitch could step from the Iron Age into the eighteenth century. But only because he had Grace on his arm.

Diary of a Chambermaid (1946)

A book like this is composed of choices and selections in which the author sets out his allegiances. At the outset, coming to Jean Renoir, I wondered whether I might not be compelled to include everything; and from the 1930s, I have nearly done that. But there are so many worthy claims to be considered, and so rationing has to be accepted as policy. It hurts most when we come to Renoir in America. Every one of the films he made there is distinctive and personal. Yet the greatest admirer of the man has to admit that those films are flawed (*This Land Is Mine, Woman on the Beach*) and perhaps, just because of their virtues or their attempts, unbalanced or misguided. So where does the choice fall? It would be nice to go for the "most American" picture—*The Southerner,* say? But I end up with the "most European," *Diary of a Chambermaid.*

There was a novel, by Octave Mirbeau, a rather naughty French classic, of life in a great house as viewed from the servants' quarters. It had been turned into a play, and it was from that play text that Renoir and the actor Burgess Meredith made a screenplay. This was nothing less than Renoir's weary discovery in the United States that his only possible way to work was to find friends and be encouraged by them. So it was the comradeship of the director with Meredith and his then wife, Paulette Goddard, that led to this film. Their other ally in this was Benedict Bogeaus, a Chicago real-estate agent who had come to Hollywood in the early forties with hopes of being a producer. He had just made *The Bridge of San Luis Rey* and *Captain Kidd,* and he later would produce *The Macomber Affair* and *Slightly Scarlet.* So he was not a nonentity—and Renoir thought highly of him.

Diary is a strange film, on nineteenth-century sets that often seem not quite finished—or tending to the abstract. Eugène Lourié designed them, and he had worked on *La Règle du Jeu.* All he did here was to make artificiality more pronounced, but that gave original viewers a hard time. American crews, Lourié thought, sugarcoated the sets—they wanted to feel they could live in the film. Another Frenchman (though based in Hollywood), Lucien Andriot, did the photography, and Michel Michelet wrote the music.

Still, Renoir was of the opinion that it was Meredith's script that gave the film its flavor. It was by turns harsh and playful, gentle and, as Truffaut said, "ferocious." It is a script that understands the madness of the household and the difference between waywardness and folly and absolute evil. In 1946 there was so little ability in an American audience to respond to those shifts in mood and tone, but today it's much easier to see how the truly frightening and the childlike sit side by side. And that's where this picture is truly Renoir: in grasping the precariousness of existence.

Meredith and Goddard are the children, if you like, but then don't forget the degrees of vacancy or malice in Hurd Hatfield, Reginald Owen, Judith Anderson, Florence Bates, Irene Ryan, and the most foreboding figure of all, Francis Lederer as the vicious manservant, Joseph.

Diary of a Country Priest (1951)

"An hour ago, my life seemed in order," says the countess to the country priest in the course of their scorching conversation. Be careful, or be hopeful, for some spirit could visit you with the same suddenness. There is always a moment with this film when one is weeping for the glory of the cinema, only to realize that the tears are for some larger or more extensive possibility. The cinema cannot be good without subject matter. But if you are open to subject matter, then you may forget the cinema.

This is an adaptation of a novel by Georges Bernanos, written for the screen by Robert Bresson himself. Let me speak about the method: We hear the narrative voice of the young priest (Claude Laydu) as we realize that he is reciting his diary entries—black ink on graph paper. The words, written and spoken, are like prayer, which he admits he finds so difficult. This is his first parish. He is proud, yet he is so humble he hardly eats. Another reason for that is the stomach cancer that is killing him. He is an invalid seeking validity, and this struggle is imprinted second by second on the face of Laydu.

On the screen, in a sunless French countryside, we see the priest's slowing journeys to visit parishioners. There is a grand house, with a count and a countess. The count is having a love affair with the governess. This has mortified his wife and his extraordinary, raging daughter. The priest is an innocent in such a crucible, but he seeks to be their confessor. This takes the form of fixed-frame imagery, hugely enriched but offset by off-screen sounds—the raked gravel during the debate with the countess, for instance. It turns on the faces of the people and the severity and beauty of what they say. The photography, by Léonce-Henri Burel, is in a spectrum of grays. It seems objective and drained, but as you stay with the film, so its reverence for faces and objects grows.

The film is 115 minutes, and it is nothing less than the progress of this priest toward death. His debates with the people in the big house are added to by talks with a neighboring priest (André Guibert), a very different kind of man, older, less extreme and austere, played by a psychiatrist friend of Bresson's. There are views of the film that address the insignificance of this country priest and his failure. I do not see it that way. His encounter with the countess is a triumph. That with the daughter is more open-ended. And if this priest dies, he has never been deflected from his own path.

The balance of his success and the film's is the ultimate question. For there is both pride and humility in the film—though I think it is striking, and a serious omission, that this country priest hardly meets poor people. He is an intellectual. He is a priest in a film. He is a performed character—even if Laydu was not a professional actor. That struggle is not resolved. You can see the film over the years, and I can only say that art's triumph seems to matter a little less on every viewing.

Diner (1982)

If I tell you that *Diner* was a directorial debut and that it is set in Baltimore, the hometown of writer-director Barry Levinson, then it is clear this is a picture where the title says it all—and despite the many surface energies, all doesn't amount to enough. Yes, it's a lovely, small film, and it stands up well enough, but more than twenty years later the question is tough to handle: What was Levinson's "promise" offering us? Or, to put it another way, has he ever made a picture that is substantially more challenging, or satisfying?

Levinson was nearly forty when he made *Diner*, and maybe that hints at a slightly middle-aged take on a subject that lives or dies on the silly immediacy of being caught between school and a career in a town where life does not change too much. After all, the Colts are still in Baltimore at the time of *Diner*, and a potential marriage to one of our lads hangs on whether the bride-to-be can pass a searching exam on Colts history. It's true to the film's tone that this sort of device is known to be misogynistic and insane but is not disowned by the picture.

Of course, *Diner* always depended on two things: the film's complete sympathy for the guys who chat away the years in the diner, and the immediacy of the young actors who play the parts. There are newcomers in the film who would go on to have modest careers—Steve Guttenberg, Daniel Stern, and Paul Reiser—though all of them have faded away by now. Of those, Stern looks the most helpless, Reiser the most perverse, and Guttenberg the prototype of Ben Affleck. Which leaves the gems of the film: Kevin Bacon and Mickey Rourke.

Bacon, playing a giggly drunk, does the most interesting piece of acting, and in hindsight one gets a better sense of how his performing character might develop. But the star is Rourke. I was startled on reviewing *Diner* at just how musical and dreamy he is—not in the rather flat set-piece scene, the popcorn bag in the movie dark, but just in the way he talks to the guys. There was a sweet gentleness in Rourke then, a lyricism, that may remind us of the later Johnny Depp. But equally you can see how challenging Rourke was in terms of casting. He wasn't tough, macho, or punk. He was a poet, if someone could lay down the length of his lines.

And in many ways a similar question still hangs over Barry Levinson. Professional, humane, likeable, deft, funny—so many welcome attributes, but so little real character. He has been back to Baltimore, of course, and some might say that he still does better with group studies of the lads. All of which brings an odd poignancy to *Diner* and the way promise can get lost in America.

Dinner at Eight (1933)

When David O. Selznick moved over from RKO to M-G-M, *Dinner at Eight* was there waiting for him as a present. The play, by George S. Kaufman and Edna Ferber, had opened on Broadway in October 1932, and it had been regarded as a victim of the worst of the Depression—the situation in early 1933 as Roosevelt had to close the banks briefly. But with remarkable speed it was set up as a picture, with a screenplay by Frances Marion and Herman J. Mankiewicz and some additional dialogue from Donald Ogden Stewart. George Cukor, Selznick's favorite, would direct, and he shot the whole thing in twenty-four days (including time for a visit by George Bernard Shaw and the Long Beach earthquake of March 10, 1933) for a release in August.

In large measure, that haste was made possible because Metro was a streamlined studio under orders to please the boss's son-in-law. William Daniels did the high-key "rich" photography. Adrian designed the costumes, and the art direction was by Fredric Hope and Hobe Erwin. The story is what it sounds like: a high-class Manhattan dinner party, one designed to show the clash of old and new money and the several degrees of opportunism at work. It was never a deep play, but Cukor pointed out that it's a setup in which everyone is trying to fool or betray someone.

It was obvious from the outset that the cast would be high-powered (a key reason for shooting it quickly and tidily). Billie Burke is Mrs. Oliver Jordan, the hostess of the party. Marie Dressler is Carlotta Vance, the faded beauty. Jean Harlow is Kitty Packard, wife to Dan Packard (Wallace Beery), who's reluctant to accompany him to Washington on his new job to help fix the country. John Barrymore is Larry Renault, a former matinee idol. Lee Tracy plays Renault's agent. Lionel Barrymore plays Oliver Jordan (planning to leave his wife). And there were roles for Edmund Lowe, Madge Evans, Jean Hersholt, and Karen Morley.

The film is funny still, nowhere more so than in John Barrymore's every moment as Renault. Playing a version of himself, close to the brink of humiliation, he was always eager for more, and he relished Cukor's ideas about getting mixed up with an intransigent stool in his suicide scene. But the pièce de résistance is a conversation between Dressler and Harlow.

"I was reading a book the other day," says Harlow.

At which Dressler is caught between a totter and a hesitation—as if that Long Beach earthquake happened while they were filming. The reaction is magnificent. But then Dressler asks what the book was about.

"How machinery is going to take over from every profession," bleats Harlow.

"Oh, my dear," says Dressler, "that's something you need never worry about." In fact, Harlow's one problem on the film was wearing all white in a white room—somehow the dark arrowhead of her pubic hair showed. It had to be bleached. All in twenty-four days. Cost $375,000; profit nearly a million dollars.

The Dirty Dozen (1967)

I think you'd have to include *The Dirty Dozen* in this book if only on commercial grounds. With first-run rental income of more than $20 million, it was a huge hit as well as a dreadful example of how a certain kind of cynical adventure film could be set up on a parcel of alleged but second-rate stars. The most telling comparison is with *Attack!*, only ten years earlier, and a film filled with such pain, such candor about combat, and such precise character studies that *The Dirty Dozen* seems grotesque in comparison.

Yet here is Lee Marvin (so good as the manipulative colonel in *Attack!*) as the very detached commanding officer who is given the task of rounding up a bunch of prison scum to go on a suicide mission against a Nazi stronghold. The film is in two blunt parts: recruitment and training, and then the mission itself. And suddenly, it's as if war had become no more than a pretext for cheap, vulgar entertainment—whereas *Attack!* is a movie seemingly made by men who had been to war themselves and who had their own dark stories (Lee Marvin for one). In its look and its sense of period, *The Dirty Dozen* is slovenly and second-rate, devoid of cinematic interest or tension.

It comes from a novel by E. M. Nathanson and a script by Nunnally Johnson and Lukas Heller. But Robert Aldrich is the real author, and that is an admission that this remarkable director of the 1950s had become a desperate, stop-at-nothing survivor by the sixties. The real cynicism of these movies is borne out by the revival of Aldrich the artist in the seventies, with films like *Ulzana's Raid* and *Hustle*.

The Dozen are lurid, unrestrained, and unwholesome—no, that's not a description of their criminal record so much as a tribute to their dire acting styles, all over the top and all cheerfully proud of their dirtiness. Aldrich may have felt that he was tuning in with the antiestablishment mood of the late 1960s. See the film and try that stupid explanation. Anyway, the hired men are Jim Brown, John Cassavetes, Charles Bronson, Donald Sutherland, Ralph Meeker, George Kennedy, Telly Savalas, Clint Walker, Trini López, and Ben Carruthers.

The raid is something of an anticlimax, in that it has to be more conventional, but it is equally stupid, notably in the "run" in which star football player Jim Brown delivers a lot of explosives. Still, the nastiest thing in the film is the use of Robert Ryan as a fusspot officer who is trying to spoil the Dozen's fun. There is a veiled antigay thrust in the role and a scurrilous muckraking that shows the decline in Aldrich. Justifiably in *Attack!* he had had to make do without Defense Department support. Here, he never comes close to deserving it.

The cast also includes Ernest Borgnine and Richard Jaeckel, men who had seen Aldrich at his best. Did everyone chuckle and forget the humiliation as they realized the hit they were embarked on?

Dirty Harry (1971)

Once upon a time, *Dirty Harry* was to be set in New York and Frank Sinatra was to play Harry Callahan, whose dogged pursuit of a serial killer offends the ethical code of police conduct and the Miranda rules. You can see and hear Sinatra doing it—even "So, do you feel lucky, punk?"—but he would have been casual, laconic, soiled by the city and sour from contempt. The thing about Clint Eastwood's Callahan is his tweed jacket, his upright stance, his tousled surfer beauty, and the anger in the man that the world has got to this grubby state. Norman Mailer once said that the film felt like a Western. That fits the way Eastwood strides through and ignores the world, and it gives his anger a faint edge of the nineteenth century.

John Milius worked on the script with Terrence Malick at an early stage, and apparently he had an opening where Harry addressed the audience (or an assembly of cadets), ranting about the modern dilemma of the police. It was too close to *Patton*—so said Eastwood once he came on board. It was then that Harry Julian Fink, Rita Fink, and Dean Riesner were hired and the film got the opening of San Francisco on a sunny day, with the first killing, a girl shot dead in her rooftop swimming pool.

Don Siegel came onto the project as director because of Eastwood, and it's fascinating to note the way they were left and right wing in their attitudes. But Siegel found Andy Robinson to play the killer, Scorpio—young, long-haired, perverse, as wordy as Harry was taciturn, and potentially loathsome. Bruce Surtees did the photography and caught the bright light of the Bay Area, and Siegel enjoyed using some unlikely locations, like Kezar Stadium. Lalo Schifrin wrote the music.

It's important that Harry is a loner—as Eastwood saw him, a sad man—who has already lost his wife and who wonders if he is bad luck for partners. But the fury is Eastwood's own, I think, as the killer is likely to get off on a technicality and as Harry goes after him as a private mission. The audience backs this because we hate Scorpio, and there's no doubt that this picture was crucial in the elevation of Eastwood as a popular hero in the age of Reagan. Pauline Kael called *Dirty Harry* a fascist film, which was going a lot too far and only played into the hands of the wry Eastwood, who could arch a Clintish eyebrow at so highbrow a word.

But Clint/Harry is already a free agent operator. So his wars with authority (Harry Guardino and John Vernon) are obligatory and perfunctory. And there's no doubt that as he throws away his badge, he is filled with disgust for liberal America. The film had rentals of more than $50 million, though, so the badge was retrieved. There would be five more Callahan pictures, plus *Tightrope*, in which even Clint seemed to agonize over his character.

The Discreet Charm of the Bourgeoisie (1972)

Once upon a time, in *Land without Bread* (1932), Luis Buñuel knew how to raise the howl of protest, the terrible cry of rage at hunger in the world. But the history of his career is the distillation of rage, until he is able to isolate that mundane irritation that still afflicts the well-fed when they have to wait. The discreet charm of the bourgeoisie is their polite handling of their sense of futility and dismay. (Of course, it is also one of those sublime titles that applies to the medium as a whole.)

So you take a handful of the "right" people (and their melodious names are worth repeating): Henri and Alice Sénéchal (Jean-Pierre Cassel and Stéphane Audran), an ideal romantic couple in their mid-forties, her false eyelashes making a nice rhyme with his sideburns; the Thévenots, Paul and Delphine (Paul Frankeur and Delphine Seyrig); the slightly rebellious Florence (Bulle Ogier); as well as a bishop (Julien Bertheau) and an ambassador, Rafael de Acosta (Fernando Rey), a man absolutely smooth enough to be running consignments of cocaine in the diplomatic pouch (or behind his mustache). They are stars, starry, superbly dressed, though in a pleasingly old-fashioned style. They are the people you might expect to meet at a French dinner party, even if you had to walk there on the open road, surrounded by the corn, the buttercups, and the aimless blue sky. And, really, as a group, these people are not demanding or difficult. But they would like their dinner. Something simple, if necessary: a soup, homemade from stock; a piece of meat with the blood showing; a salad glistening with oil; and something sweet, a pie of sliced apples and ears; and of course the appropriate wines.

Alas, everything from small misunderstandings to major eruptions of civil disturbance keep getting in the way of the proper marriage of these pilgrims and their meal. And as the interruptions mount, a profound panic breaks through, so that even when the would-be diners are at the point of a gun, a hand can't help but give itself away by reaching up for a slice of pink lamb, still warm. Sooner or later, a meal becomes a massacre.

This is Luis Buñuel, collaborating on a screenplay with Jean-Claude Carrière, working for that ancient producer Serge Silberman, with Edmond Richard doing the very pretty color photography, sets by Pierre Guffroy (the film is full of pieces of furniture one might give an arm for), and editing by Hélène Plemiannikov.

Here was a tranquil international art-house hit, rising like a soufflé above any suggestion of censorship, anti-Americanism, or unpleasantness, but gently acting like acid on the tender meat of bourgeois self-protection. The film got an Oscar nomination for best script (it lost to Jeremy Larner's *The Candidate,* another sign of how steadily the bourgeoisie looks after itself). The cast—who also include Michel Piccoli, Maria Gabriella Maione, François Maistre, and Milena Vukotic—are as beautiful as white marble statues. This is the work of a great filmmaker in his classic period.

Distant Thunder (1973)

It is 1942, and we are in a Bengal village. A girl bathing in the river sees fighter planes pass overhead, and she says to herself that they are as beautiful as cranes. A profound film is about to unfold. Ganga is a young Brahmin who moves from village to village as a doctor. He is about to set himself up as a teacher—why not? He is educated, he is a Brahmin, and he has a sweet wife, Ananga. They are the local class. Ganga notices that the price of rice is mounting, and he supposes it is the war. It is still only 1942.

This is a major work by Satyajit Ray, written for the screen from a novel by Bibhuti Bhushan Bannerjee and photographed in color by Soumendu Roy. Of course, the famine advances. The value of rice goes mad, and Ganga's calm and class are left helpless in the panic. Biswas offers him rice because of Ganga's caste when the official report is that the store is empty. Then the store is truly empty, and Ananga does manual labor for some rice—no matter that that breaks the caste laws. The value of money goes. Rape becomes a currency, nearly. The famine rages, and Moti, an untouchable girl, dies outside Ganga's house. He decides to bury the untouchable. He and Ananga take in starving strangers, and she tells him she is pregnant.

The vulnerability of people aches out of the film, and even though Ray was telling the story thirty years after the events, he supplies a chilling title at the end of the film, all the more shocking to people who know no Indian history: that five million people starved to death in the Bengal famine of 1943.

Not that anger or recrimination really figure in this film. It's a Chekhovian study of country life in ghastly times, and it has the warmth and curiosity to see something of value in nearly all the characters, just as it observes the discipline and fatuity of caste without any apparent disturbance. And whereas Ray had filmed the poverty or the hard times of Bengal before, by going back to the years of World War II, he was involving Western audiences in a new way. For we know "our" war reached India, and we may have a friendly image of brave, fierce Indian troops who served the Allied cause. But in India, one year there was a minor rice problem and the next there were five million dead. And just because the human context is so lucid and understandable, the political implication is one that cannot be shrugged off.

It is said, still, that Satyajit Ray was a European Indian, in that he was raised and trained in London ways, and that he made movies aimed cleverly at the European art-house market. But why not? There are stories—like that of the five million—that deserve to be heard. As for Ray's "humanism," it is just another form of colonial patronage (or condescension), laying claim to an authentic artistic vision as a European heritage. Ray is one of the supreme directors.

The Diving Bell and the Butterfly (2007)

Movie gathers up "the disasters of life" with insatiable greed, yet it misses the dead ends that so many people have to face. I write—this is my last entry for the book—in a season in which slaughtered barbershop customers are converted to meat pies, where a bizarre figure of Death stalks the Big Bend country of Texas, and where the fierce struggle for oil promises "there will be blood." Yet few of us actually give up the ghost to those ingenious gas-cylinder guns that can leave a hole in the world big enough for golf balls. My life has depended on concentration, attention, and choice in nothing more dangerous than words, and the terminus in life I fear the most, I think—I *know*—is stroke or some gentle smothering of whatever minor faculties I have.

Julian Schnabel's mercurial picture *The Diving Bell and the Butterfly* is a study of that risk, and because it has such a lifelike and accurate sense of death and loss, it is a film that shines with the immanence of life. It is based on a real story, that of Jean-Dominique Bauby, once the editor of French *Elle*. We see, briefly, the flashy spasms of his magazine and his work—we know the ceaseless activity and the importance of image. But then Bauby is stilled by a stroke that leaves him paralyzed except for one eye. He can see. He can hear. He can comprehend. And he will learn to communicate—he invents a language through the device of blinking his eye. At the same time, Schnabel, a painter in his other life, can see the wreck of Bauby and imagine the point of view from within as his other eye is sewn shut to avoid infection. This is the most claustrophobic shot I can recall in the history of cinema.

So what does one eye see—apart from its own wretched handicap? Well, there is the slow business of rehabilitation and learning language again. That ends in the way Bauby will write a book. There is also the way in which memory and the new, fragmented moment conspires to keep Bauby in love with life—whether he is looking at the thighs of a woman or the sweep of long grass in the sun and the wind.

We are here to notice things, I propose—for if we do not notice, then we and the things might as well not be here. So we remember and try to guard the things worth loving—the thighs, the grass—and yet our feebleness leads to forgetfulness. Whether it is by stroke or just the gradual erasure of loss, we lose the precious things. At the end of Bauby's life, this film incorporates the closing music from *Les 400 Coups*—sparse, stricken, yet alive—and I should say that as I heard it, and remembered it, I was in love with the thing I can only call experience. And lost in doubts over how often the movies have sought to bury those precious sights and sounds in the ceaseless catalogue of bizarre ways in which we die. A slight touch, a stroke, can turn out the light. But before then, did you see?

Dead on Arrival, or "I don't think you understand, Mr Bigelow. You've been murdered." Frank Bigelow (Edmond O'Brien) is a lawyer from the desert country, looking forward to a weekend in San Francisco. He reckons to get away from his small-town girlfriend and live it up like a traveling salesman on a spree. San Francisco is alive with parties and available women, and Bigelow never dreams of the risk.

He goes to a terrific-looking jazz club on the waterfront (if only such clubs still existed!), and someone slips him an unusual drink. He starts to sweat (this is Edmond O'Brien). He has a stomachache and intimations of mortality. He's in agony. He hobbles into a doctor's office and learns the truth. He has been given a radioactive poison, and his hours are numbered. There's a shot famous in film noir of a darkened room and the X-ray with a livid, glowing block of poison. So Frank decides he has to find out what happened to him and why.

This fabulous setup came from a story and script by Clarence Greene and Russell Rouse. Within a few moments, Bigelow is reduced from a cocksure tourist to a furious bundle of mortified energy and ruined body, searching to work out why he has to die. In truth, the answer to that puzzle is a lot less satisfactory than the mystery itself, but that's a weakness with plenty of film noirs. And there's no denying that the desperation here is both alarming and faintly comic—there is room for a little more surreal humor. Leo Popkin produced. Rudolph Mate directed, with Ernest Laszlo as his cameraman, and the film is as visually arresting as it is startling. There are wonderful sequences of Bigelow running down Market Street in San Francisco, half-crazed because of what he has found out about himself. You can imagine that the pounding score, by Dimitri Tiomkin, leaves no doubt about the general level of panic. The intrigue that unfolds only proves that lawyers like Bigelow should stay out in the sticks. San Francisco looks racy and exciting, but the point of the film is to stress that it's too sophisticated for its own good.

The supporting cast is very good, so often with these noir pictures, the unusual setup relies on exaggerated character studies to sustain interest. There's Pamela Britton, Luther Adler, Beverly Garland, Lynn Baggett, William Ching, Henry Hart, Neville Brand (punching Bigelow in that glowing stomach), Laurette Luez, and Jess Kirkpatrick.

The story has been tried again, most notably in a 1988 remake by Rocky Morton and Annabel Jankel that starred Dennis Quaid and Meg Ryan. But now it only seemed fanciful and implausible, because there was no grasp of the atmosphere or the hectic style that noir needed if we were to suspend disbelief. Once that disbelief goes, not a lot is left—noir was always a genre poised on the brink of style without content.

Doctor Zhivago (1965)

Everything about *Doctor Zhivago* reeks of middlebrow compromise; nothing is direct or authentic. And the crucial point to be made about David Lean is that, once upon a time, within the framework of Dickens adaptation or enclosed romance, so much in his films was particular and local. Indeed, you can hardly measure 1940s Britain better than through the strangled emotion of Trevor Howard and Celia Johnson in *Brief Encounter*, and yet in *Zhivago* Lean asks an Egyptian to be a Russian and trusts that we will abandon all doubts in the shimmer of exoticism. It is all part of a condescension and willful ignorance that has separated Britain (and the West) from real knowledge of other parts of the world.

Having despaired of the way producer Sam Spiegel regularly screwed him out of money on successful pictures, Lean looked to Carlo Ponti to back a film from the novel that had won Boris Pasternak the Nobel Prize (then rejected by the author) while becoming a test case in the Cold War. Robert Bolt writes the screenplay, in a vein that will become the basis of BBC adaptations of classic novels: where being faithful means keeping the incidents while omitting the cultural air that the characters breathe. So the Russian Revolution is an aberration in *Zhivago*, not an understandable and tragic response to the despotism of Russia. So it's easy to have Yuri Zhivago and his loved ones as the wounded figures in the history of modern Russia, and far too easy to make black-hearted villains out of the other characters. So, finally, the sentiment of interrupted love affairs takes precedence over the core of poetry or the meaning of Russia. *Doctor Zhivago* is an epic that could be set down in any country. Just give the external events different names and remember the heart of *Brief Encounter*: that a thwarted-love story is richer than one that lasts.

Freddie Young (replacing Nicolas Roeg, after disagreements) did the photography for Panavision 70 mm, and it is beautiful, but worse than that, things are arranged in order to be beautiful. Over the years, spectacle rises up and drowns Lean. John Box did production design, Terence Marsh art direction, Phyllis Dalton costumes—and all are talented and well funded, which usually means Oscars. The music is by Maurice Jarre, and "Lara's Theme" became one of the hits of the swinging sixties.

The performances, as always in Lean, are secondary to the casting: Omar Sharif, Julie Christie, Geraldine Chaplin, Tom Courtenay, Alec Guinness, Siobhan McKenna, Ralph Richardson, Rod Steiger, Rita Tushingham, Adrienne Corri, Geoffrey Keen, Klaus Kinski, Jack MacGowran.

The film was defeated for Best Picture by *The Sound of Music*, but it won Oscars for Bolt, Young, and most of the craftsmen. It had cost $15 million, and its first-run rentals were $43 million. This time, Lean himself was to earn as much as $10 million in the long run. Let Pauline Kael have the last word. The film ends with a pretty, forgiving rainbow over a Soviet dam, as if to say, Well, it all worked out for the best. Asks Kael: "Would Lean and Bolt place a rainbow over the future of England?"

Dodsworth (1936)

Deprived of all knowledge of its credits, one could easily guess that William Wyler's *Dodsworth* had been photographed by Gregg Toland. There are a lot of very artfully composed images of people arranged in deep space that seem to prefigure the work the director and cameraman would do a few years later. In particular, look for a scene in happy Naples when the lead, Sam Dodsworth (Walter Huston), has at last escaped his very spoiled wife (Ruth Chatterton) and found his true love (Mary Astor). Dodsworth is set on a new life—but then the telephone rings. It's Vienna, which means it's *her*. The use of spatial relationships and full figures moving in the frame is quite beautiful. And the film was shot by Rudolph Mate, a fascinating semigenius figure (he filmed *The Passion of Joan of Arc* and made *D.O.A.*).

At any event, *Dodsworth* is a very sophisticated film for 1936—a real social study as opposed to a romantic comedy—and one of the most telling portraits of marriage in American film. It comes from a Sinclair Lewis novel, published in 1929 and turned into a play by Sidney Howard in 1936. Incidentally, it was Howard's brilliant script for this film (being faithful to a novel while cutting a lot) that inspired David O. Selznick to give him the *Gone With the Wind* job.

Huston had played the role of Samuel Dodsworth onstage, and it was a touch of great sanity to have him do the film. For Dodsworth is central but not handsome, not even strong (he's curiously indecisive and passive for a successful businessman), but Huston brings the detailed observation of supporting acting to a lead role. And you feel the picture shift as a result. It is no longer a study of stars but an examination of muddled people. Just watch for the way Huston uses Sam's limp, and the change in physical stance—for all the gruff, forthright manner, this is an insecure man, and Hollywood did not often bother with them in 1936.

While the wife, Fran, could easily be loathed—she is frivolous, selfish, thoughtless—Ruth Chatterton makes her familiar and understandable. The scene where Maria Ouspenskaya tells Chatterton she isn't right for her son (played by Gregory Gaye) is a classic. And then there is Mary Astor, as Mrs. Cortright, the other woman. She never looked better than here, and there is a shot of her standing in a far doorway in a midlength dress that is to die for. Astor and the film are so decent that we say, Yes, Sam deserves her—but will he be brave enough to take her?

Richard Day won an Oscar for very good sets—and this is really a film about traveling people, in transit, trying to find themselves, so the sets are important. As for Wyler's work, he is devoted to his players and surely responsible for the very unusual feeling of a picture about grown-ups. Also with David Niven, Paul Lukas, Spring Byington, and Grant Mitchell.

Dog Day Afternoon (1975)

It's August 2, 1972, and a branch of the First Brooklyn Savings Bank is under siege. One of the secretaries has been on the phone to her husband. Finished, she turns to Sonny (Al Pacino) and says, "He wants to know what time you'll be through?" That's very true to the spirit of New York living theater: Sonny had resolved that this was going to be his big day, but now a bit player is horning in with a smart line and his priorities. Do we need to be told that this all happened—or something more or less like it? Or is it simply very close to that sense of bursting street theater that was so self-conscious in New York in the 1970s and that really bespeaks a general public who have already been on television a few times and who are addicts of the Gore Vidal principle—that you can't be on television or a minor celebrity too often. Face it, there are no minor celebrities.

In *Dog Day Afternoon* (it is very hot and humid), three men hold up the bank with guns. One of them runs away, leaving Sonny and Sal (John Cazale) in charge—and they begin to negotiate about how to get out. The bank has a manager (Sully Boyar) and a female staff who recover their nerves enough to keep up a back-track of chatter. The police are in the form of Moretti (Charles Durning), and the FBI are around (James Broderick). It's dangerous, clearly: the guns could go off. But the great strength of *Dog Day Afternoon* is its ear and instinct for comedy. The film is based on a magazine article by P. F. Kluge and Thomas Moore, but Frank Pierson's script goes out of its way to give everyone a point of view. Indeed, in a way, it's everyone's big day, and they all rise to the occasion in the daft spirit of people who reckon they have a duty to television—so don't talk small talk.

Sidney Lumet directs and makes it the most ribald and unexpected of his police procedurals—how is everyone going to proceed when the whole thing is like an improv? It's at that thought that you may begin to get the feeling that the whole thing is an acting workshop in which Al Pacino is experimenting with that energy that was so repressed in *The Godfather*. I enjoy it, but I think everyone is a touch too colorful for comfort.

The producers were Martin Elfand and Martin Bregman (a major ennabler or indulger of Mr. Pacino). Victor Kemper photographs the film in a rough newsreel way, and Dede Allen is the editor. The most credible performances come from John Cazale (the one victim of the day) and Chris Sarandon as Sonny's transvestite "wife." Again, the gayness is more schtick than reality, but Pacino's Sonny is auditioning. Pierson's script, I think, deserves better, a performance more from life. Pacino was exploring his own larger-than-life charm. In truth, it's not an especially ambitious film, but it got a parcel of Oscar nominations (including Best Picture), and it won for Frank Pierson's script.

Dogville (2003)

You must realize, reading this book, that it's all a game. The notion that some films are literally and objectively "better" than others is a kind of smoke that encourages everything from the Academy Awards to the outside prospect that reading this book may improve you. One of my publishers once had the idea of a star system for the films, to spur you on. I responded that if anyone read what I said, they knew what I felt. Moreover, the pinnacle of all ratings systems, the steady nomination of *Citizen Kane* as "the best film ever made," is a damaging nonsense that has probably stopped people from seeing or thinking about *Kane*. All of which is a prelude to saying that as a more or less paid-up member of the auteur theory, I dislike director Lars von Trier a lot, but I love his *Dogville*. You see, you have to keep looking, because you never know when some hack is going to glimpse the grail. Even his own.

Why do I love *Dogville*? Let me count the ways.

1. As one who cherishes theater every time I see a film, and who loves the history of the stage breaking into film, I am thrilled by *Dogville*'s bold, radical, yet faintly camp reversion to a soundstage (or a rehearsal room), with areas marked out on the floor where the buildings are to be placed. The vision of a frontier town like a board game (or a construction kit) is delicious.
2. Further, the actual state of such infant communities as Dogville, Montana, is often so rigid, so doctrinaire, that this way of presenting the place is witty and inventive. Note, in this respect, that I am going along with the view of *Dogville* as a cruel anti-American satire—and a good thing, too.
3. The wild range of the casting here is akin to abandoning casting (or getting it wrong deliberately). It's a way of saying any actor can play any part. It's Brechtian and refreshing, and I think it's a way to break out of the dire confines of naturalism. So Lauren Bacall as a dour Ma Ginger, Paul Bettany as a lily-livered Tom Edison, and James Caan as The Big Man are all refreshing.
4. Although the film is too slow, there is a true narrative arc, a fable, like the moon's passage across the night sky. And surely Nicole Kidman was exactly right as the nice lost girl/witch/femme fatale who can set that arc moving just by slipping from one persona to another.
5. Above all, *Dogville* is a real contribution to the Western in its depiction of a fiercely ingrowing community terrified of the space it has challenged and the violence it is prepared to undertake. I can't think of another Western so acute or understanding of how the people who have gone there to sit in their little enclosures have ruined the West.
6. And because I'd never seen anything like it before, or found any movie that had such a charming offset between grand fateful design and small daily advances. The great point of America is that it can furnish a brilliant, if not radiant, display of its own complete failure as the land of the free and the home of the brave. This is the land of chains and the home of the afraid—which often feels much more like life.

La Dolce Vita (1960)

Some people believed that *La Dolce Vita* was a turning point in world cinema. Some said it was Thomas Mann meets Eurotrash. Some admitted that it was just Federico Fellini at his old game of pleasing the bourgeoisie with a gesture toward daring. Fellini got a Best Director Oscar nomination. And it occurs to me now that this film is actually *I Vitelloni* transferred from listless beach towns to Rome and replacing hapless young guys with the gossip-column elite of the Western world. In other words, both are films about the boredom of boring people. As for the turning point in world cinema, may we say that 1960 is also the year of *Psycho, Shadows, L'Avventura,* and *Breathless*?

By now, as if writing was a unique burden, Fellini had cultivated the Italian system of group writing, so he was aided and abetted by Ennio Flaiano, Tullio Pinelli, and Brunello Rondi. They got a collective Oscar nomination for Best Screenplay, though no one doubts that it was Fellini's vision to portray a great modern city (rooted in antiquity) where the various whoring professions of the day (the moviemakers, the journalists, the scandal photographers, the academics, the politicians, and the intellectuals) were all mixed in with the oldest one. As a measure of its depth and seriousness, the film ran 175 minutes, nearly twice as long as previous Fellini films. As a balance, less happened in overt script terms. You might think that cinematically a lot is happening, but if you're of that hopeful persuasion, you have to go to Antonioni to find the new texture of modern cinematic event.

Nothing happens, except for flatulent set pieces, epic reaches of symbolism, and teary-eyed larger metaphors. Thus you get Anita Ekberg in the Trevi Fountain, an upside-down Christ statue arriving by helicopter, and the little girl on the beach whose Mona Lisa smile urges Marcello to keep trying. Otello Martelli did the photography, and Piero Gherardi won an Oscar for the art direction. Nino Rota wrote the music.

The cast was headed by Marcello Mastroianni as the fatalistic, observing conscience—Fellini himself, surely—and this was the picture that made Mastroianni a star and ensured that he could get away with doing very little. For the rest, the film involves Ekberg, Anouk Aimée, Yvonne Furneaux, Magali Noël, Alain Cuny, Annibale Ninchi, Walter Santesso, Lex Barker, Jacques Sernas, and Nadia Gray.

The film was conveniently open to all interpretations. You could say it was a satire on the failure of any moral objections to grip the slippery sheen of self-indulgence. You could even say that it was a placid Catholic contemplation of the vague need for forgiveness. But in the end, no answer seems forceful enough to carry through the sheer monotony. When orgies are dull and obscure, as they are here, it means that a kind of laziness, moral as much as physical, has taken over. Yet, as it happened, *La Dolce Vita* coincided with the decline of censorship and thus gave serious weight to the thought that we would soon be seeing shocking things such as we had never dreamed of before.

Not yet.

Don't Look Now (1973)

Horror, it seems to me, is a painful and erroneous genre if one enters the dark tunnel chanting that label and expecting to be frightened. Almost inevitably that experience ends in disappointment and the historical evidence that no genre dates quicker than horror. But suppose wise heads ignore the label. Suppose they whisper to you, Well, here's a nice little story in which coincidence seems to get out of hand. Suppose it's a mixture of a love story and a mystery; suppose it's just one of those quiet surmisings about the habit in life for supernatural echoes to begin to shiver the surface of the water.

Don't Look Now is exactly what cool intelligence can do with horror, so long as it fights shy of using that word. Tell yourself that it's a family story. John and Laura are very happily married—there's never a hint here of that kind of glib sermonizing that says all their troubles come from marital unease. On the contrary, slap bang in the middle of the film, in one of those luxe but pressingly tight hotel rooms you find in Venice, they enjoy what may be the best married sex scene in the history of the movies. If you believe in that sort of magic, surely they have conceived in that silent frenzy, so stringently cut against shots of them dressing, or reassembling, afterward.

But perhaps you believe in other kinds of magic? A daughter has drowned in the pond in their English garden. They go to Venice in part to recover, and also because John is helping to restore a church there. They meet two English sisters, one of them blind, and it is the blind one who tells Laura that she has seen the dead daughter—not to worry, she's happy. If only the couple could take that advice. But, in grief still, and in Venice in winter, they succumb to fiction and to wondering. John sees a strange, childlike figure in red in the maze of side streets. He thinks it could be his daughter.

From a story by Daphne Du Maurier and a script by Allan Scott and Chris Bryant, this is a film that does not give up its cold grip. Yes, you can write it off, finally, as occult nonsense—except that nothing occult has happened, just the weakness of sensible people for believing in such things. *Don't Look Now* deserves a place in any survey of films impressed by the cinema's irrational force. But it works as a story of rotten luck hitting undeserving people. And I think in the end what it comes close to meaning is the lure of the death wish that calls itself luck.

This is Nicolas Roeg's best film by far, beautiful, grave, and forbidding. In so many ways it takes its atmospheric suggestions from Venice itself. Hilary Mason and Clelia Matania are perfect as the sisters, but the film belongs to the wounded good nature in Donald Sutherland and Julie Christie, just as it clings to our inability to stop believing.

Do the Right Thing (1989)

When I think of *Do the Right Thing,* the first thought I get is just the look of Bed-Stuy on the hottest day of the year in Ernest R. Dickerson's gorgeous, overheated color photography. You think you're in another country, the way Jonathan Demme can hit you for a moment. And there's a terrific, rowdy feeling in the film for Brooklyn as a black city, down next to New Orleans, except that the people are so much faster with their mouths and ready for the big switch to be hit. I don't know still exactly what Spike Lee meant—and he is the kind of guy who can look at you with droopy eyes, listen to what you got, and tell you that's exactly what he meant. But if you look at the movies Oscar-nominated as Best Picture in 1990—*Driving Miss Daisy, Born on the Fourth of July, Dead Poets Society, Field of Dreams, My Left Foot*—there isn't one of them I'd rather see than *Do the Right Thing.*

Yes, that's right, it didn't get nominated. Spike did get a nod for the script, yet I'd have to say that the script is, in this case, the most archaic thing in the film, and the sure sign of some desperate need to tie it all together at the end. What is special about *Do the Right Thing* is the life, the look, and the movieness of it all. But what can you say when a lace doily of a movie wins Best Picture and *Do the Right Thing* doesn't get nominated, except that the Academy is a club where people can get very sentimental over how good they are to their chauffeurs.

Do the Right Thing is *Street Scene* with soul food. And it's not just that you feel you are there. On the contrary, Bed-Stuy never looked like this—but this is a designed, photographed place as fresh as Jacques Demy's Cherbourg. And Lee, who, in my opinion, is not the greatest shot maker in the world as a rule, has got a deep perspective eye excited by the look. The screen is teeming with action and relationship, even though it's a very theatrical place where three old cats sit out in a Carib sun gossiping about it all.

It's the drama that is problematic, the fixing of everything on Sal's pizza place (Lee had wanted Robert De Niro for Sal at first rather than Danny Aiello—that could have made the trigger tighter still). The opportunity for direct talks on race and everything is too blatant, too easy, and too loaded. I wish the film had moved away from that direction and toward a loose, dancing form where the characters went into song. The daily life and the small incidents were more eloquent than the set-piece melodrama.

Never mind; this is an exhilarating movie, full of pleasure and surprises. The rich cast includes Ossie Davis and Ruby Dee, Giancarlo Esposito, Richard Edson, Bill Nunn, John Turturro, Samuel L. Jackson, Rosie Perez, and John Savage. Not least: on a budget of $6.5 million, it had a U.S. gross of $27.5 million.

Double Indemnity (1944)

James M. Cain (who knew a good deal about movies) once said of Billy Wilder's *Double Indemnity*, "It's the only picture I ever saw made from my books that had things in it I wish I had thought of." He picked out the ending and the framing device of the movie—the way Walter Neff (Fred MacMurray) is telling the story on the office dictaphone for his boss, Barton Keyes (Edward G. Robinson). But he might have added that sensational early scene where Walter calls at the Dietrichson house and there's Phyllis (Barbara Stanwyck), upstairs, in a towel and a sweaty shine from sunbathing. When she comes downstairs she is dressed, and she wears that anklet that catches Walter's eye the way a hook gets a fish. Very soon they're into that counterpunching flirtation that isn't in the novel and that you could easily attribute to Wilder's cowriter, Raymond Chandler. But everything listed here is part of Wilder's grinning fascination with nasty, sexy people and his huge respect for Cain's basic story. Because what you get in *Double Indemnity* is two scorpions, fucking and biting at each other. And you can do that in 1944—a big year for morale—because you've got Barton Keyes, the man for whom insurance is a church.

Wilder said it was producer Joseph Sistrom who sold him on *Double Indemnity*, which was published in 1943. For years, Cain's earlier book, *The Postman Always Rings Twice*, had been deemed unfilmable, but Sistrom thought they could get away with *Double Indemnity*. And Wilder sat down with Chandler to do the script, because Wilder, it was thought, had no experience of the American hard-boiled school. Then it turned out that Chandler knew nothing about movies. So the two classics knocked against each other badly, yet a smooth script emerged.

And Wilder was off. He had John Seitz as his cameraman, and he told him to show the dust hanging in the sunlight as well as the night as real night. The sets, by Hans Dreier and Hal Pereira, are quite beautiful, and the insurance office has a formal power not to be missed. When Walter is dying and Keyes tells him he won't make it to the elevator, it means something.

The casting is of a kind that changed Hollywood. Stanwyck was a little reluctant to be so nasty, but then she saw that it made her. Fred MacMurray simply looks a better and better actor as the years pass, and there are volumes to be said about a man who hates himself even while he's trying to look so good. But still, it's Keyes who holds the film in place, and Edward G. Robinson is a fussy little treat, nagging away at detail and looking for his matches. When he says, "Closer than that, Walter," at the end, you can see that his heart is broken, because he put his trust in Walter and now he has lost faith in himself. Like many things in Wilder over the years, there's just enough of a hint of something between the two guys that you notice it. It's like Stanwyck's anklet, or the angora sweater she wears. There are no holes in the sweater or the film, but you can see through them both. At the time, it didn't do too well: five big Oscar nominations but not a prize.

The Double Life of Véronique (1991)

Tony Soprano comes into a diner in suburban New Jersey and sees himself already sitting at a table alone, waiting. It's hardly a surprise. It's a place he frequents, and so he might easily be there already. In *The Passenger*, Jack Nicholson slips out of his own life and picks up that of a man who has died in the next room in a north African hotel; no one seems to notice the difference. We are all of us double lives in the age of film and photograph, likely to be held up to judgment against a still picture we don't recall being taken. The Jekyll and Hyde game is so enchanting now that we have pretty well given up on the old moral scheme, that Jekyll was a humanitarian and Hyde a beast. Once Hyde comes out into the open, you see he's so like Jekyll it's amusing.

And so Véronique, a beautiful, dark-haired French girl, goes to Crakow on some kind of trip. There is a demonstration in the city square, so the people in her tour bus have to be rounded up quickly to be driven to . . . safety, is it? Is that the place? As Véronique takes still pictures as the bus wheels and turns, she does not notice—photography can be a way of not seeing—that the beautiful, dark-haired girl in the square watching the bus resembles her. And she does not know that the girl's name is Veronika.

That's the setup for Krzysztof Kieslowski's *The Double Life of Véronique*, in which the Polish woman—possessed of an eerie, extraordinary singing voice—dies as she sings in Poland, and Véronique, trying to find her way through life in Paris, feels the shadow trip her. Of course, this is a film of our era. It identifies the theme or the cutting strategy of so many films, from *Short Cuts* to *Magnolia* that lives apart are lives together now. It is that old Poe-faced Borgesian notion of the double at work, but it is the infinite hope—the last desperate gamble?—that all our lives are linked, so there is no such thing as a stranger.

This is Kieslowski's best film, even if not entirely free from his awkward mixture of moral tales and the look of *Vogue* magazine. We can never forget the beauty of Irène Jacob in the two roles here or the sepia-enriched color photography (by Slawomir Idziak). The movie looks and feels sexy and modish in ways that actually curtail its huge thematic interest. Still, there are passages of authentic rapture and mystery, and I am grateful for the innocence of Jacob when the knowingness of Juliette Binoche might have dominated, embalming the chanciness of it all.

As it is, Kieslowski's aim seems to be to free Véronique for her own life, to have her happy. And, of course, if the scheme is valid, then it opens us all up to more complex and more interesting things—not least, whether resemblance is a key or the infinity beyond the locked door. The film is greatly aided by the music of Zbigniew Preisner, and it suggests that we are not far from a moment when composers might start to make films.

Le Doulos (1963)

The other day I saw Robert De Niro's film *The Good Shepherd* (2006), which I believe is based on the career of James Angleton, a man sometimes described as a master spy and subsequently revealed as a chronic mess. For about the first thirty or forty minutes of the film, I found it impossible to follow, or discern. Then, gradually, it became clearer—and less intriguing. What I am getting at here is something that is vital to Jean-Pierre Melville's *Le Doulos*, a classic of its kind, but a film that can break down philosophers with the simple request "Tell me the story."

Le Doulos comes from a novel by Pierre Lesou, published in 1957. All I am going to attempt to say is that it is about two underworld figures: Faugel (Serge Reggiani), a thief and a convict; and Silien (Jean-Paul Belmondo), a thief and an informer. Melville wrote the script himself and sometimes claimed that every item of the story did actually fit together and in place. There is a book on Melville by Ginette Vincendeau that breaks the plot down over several pages and then assumes that it has explained it all.

But explanations are so tedious. We learned that lesson—didn't we?—on *The Big Sleep*. In the course of the making of that film, several of the participants admitted that they didn't quite grasp the story. The worry worked its way back as far as Raymond Chandler (the writer of the book), and he agreed that it didn't fit. Then, late in the day, sensing a deeper anxiety, Warner Brothers added a long explanation sequence to the film. I'm still not sure that that dreary passage works. Who can tell, when it swiftly relinquishes the attention that the film had commanded until that point?

Le Doulos is brilliant and commanding. And I daresay that if anyone ever cracked its story and could reassemble it in the dark, then people would stop seeing the picture. How general a principle lives within this theory? I can think of plenty of instances where confusion over the story prompts viewers to dissatisfaction with a film, or even to walk out on it. So the lesson is not just "Be unclear and they will be hooked."

Still, there are stories that are more in the telling than the analysis. In the same way, there are situations in life, like the relationship between one's parents, that enthrall us forever, or until some kind of misery or terminus intrudes. We know the facts of those stories, but the why remains inscrutable. Yet because it is our story, we cannot lose the habit of wanting it told. I suppose we want the story to go on forever—we want our parents to live forever, no matter that it may have been a hard time.

Le Doulos led Melville into an obsession with obscure stories, and I'm not sure it was always good for him. It's there in *The Army of Shadows*, where the chaos is held off because we know (or hope) that some of these people were honorable. In the crime setting, no such hopes survive. And when people lie all the time, they become like counters in a game. Whereas the game is always better with people—and people sometimes tell the truth. They cannot lose the habit.

Dracula (1931)

There had been horror before *Dracula* in American film—after all, one of the great stars of the silent era is Lon Chaney, whose conviction—allied to his imaginative appetite for his own warping, crippling, and deforming—leaves him frightening still in many films. Moreover, we should remember that Chaney died in 1930. But for that, he was the obvious candidate for the two films that introduced the sound horror picture from Universal: *Dracula* and *Frankenstein.*

There had been a stage play of the Bram Stoker novel with Hamilton Deane in the title role. It was an immense success, and when it came over to Broadway in 1927 it acquired a strange Hungarian actor, Bela Lugosi, who had done supporting parts onstage and in the movies. He was three years in the play eventually, taking it on tour, and sufficiently unstable to have reached the conclusion that he really was Dracula.

In 1931, Universal decided to film it. (There were reservations about the story, apparently. Carl Laemmle, Sr., had the feeling that people didn't want to be frightened and upset. It was his son who stuck out for tightening the screws.) Tod Browning was the director, and he had a script by Garrett Fort that was based on the play (by Deane and John L. Balderston) far more than on the novel. Dudley Murphy did some additional dialogue. Perhaps the key assignment was that of the photography—to Karl Freund, who had recently arrived from Germany, where he had done Murnau's *The Last Laugh* and some of Lang's *Metropolis.* Freund would become a great Hollywood cameraman—*Camille, Key Largo*—before ending up as an authoritarian master at Desilu.

All seemed set, and the movie was a tremendous success, opening on St. Valentine's Day and being advertised as "The Strangest Love Story of All." It's too late to complain. Lugosi's harsh Hungarian voice announced, "I—am Dra-cu-la," and the myth was afoot. No matter that it's Browning and Freund (which ought to be magic); the film is really rather stodgy. The cast includes Helen Chandler, David Manners, Dwight Frye (very spooky as Renfield), Edward Van Sloan, and Frances Dade. Seen today, I fear that Lugosi is just a preparation for Martin Landau in *Ed Wood.* In other words, the hint of camp is in there at the outset—not just in Lugosi's "I drink—wine." We never feel that anyone making the film had seen *Nosferatu.* And I'm not sure that Browning was ever convinced by the subject—as he clearly was by *Freaks* and many of the Chaney pictures.

Never mind those reservations. The film had a million in rentals, and it set Universal on a firm course. Dracula and his relatives keep crawling out of their coffins. The trend is clear. Over the years, as if to satisfy the female instinct about Stoker's point, the count has become more handsome, more irresistible. A key step in that development was Christopher Lee in the Hammer film *Dracula* (1958). But Frank Langella's 1979 version—though pioneered onstage—still left question marks.

The Draughtsman's Contract (1982)

Peter Greenaway had been known before this film (and since) as a determined member of the avant-garde, experimental, formalist, and intensely intellectual. But *The Draughtsman's Contract* caused a stir in that, while retaining some of those austere traits, it also stepped over the line into a kind of British mainstream: It was a country-house mystery, it exploited dandified seventeenth-century elegance, it had a good deal of sex, and any tasteful home would have been happy to have it on its walls. In addition, it was jointly funded by Channel 4 and the British Film Institute for about £300,000. As it happened, *The Draughtsman's Contract* was a hit in many countries. Moreover, Greenaway elected to shorten his first four-hour cut to 108 minutes, which seemed to take advantage of provocative material.

A handsome draughtsman, Mr. Neville (Anthony Higgins), is hired by Mrs. Herbert (Janet Suzman) to do twelve drawings of her house at Compton Anstey. This work is to be done while her husband is away. Payment is to include hospitality at the house and access to Mrs. Herbert's bed. What follows is a puzzle and an intrigue: Why the strange contract? How will it all come out? Is something far more sinister going on at the house?

The film exhibits many of Greenaway's concerns with pure form, numeracy, line, and artificiality, but you can't offer a British audience adultery and antiques without prompting their greedy enthusiasm and their wish to be in at the kill. The picture was shot by Curtis Clark, but there was a lot of rostrum work with drawings, too. The art direction was by Bob Ringwood, and Michael Nyman wrote the music. It was not quite clear how far this had been Greenaway's intention, but a beguiling mixture of mystery and experimentation came together in a movie that flattered the audience's intelligence and connoisseurship. As with high-toned advertising, it was difficult to resist the allure of acquisition and the sigh of digestion.

In Britain especially, Greenaway paid for his success and the faint aroma of mixed motives. Opponents argued that he was never much interested in the content; he had taken advantage of it here to help get a hit. This argument arose again, with far greater fury, in 1989 over *The Cook, The Thief, His Wife & Her Lover,* in which really gruesome violence was allied to sex and eating in very arresting ways. *The Cook* settled the matter for many people that Greenaway's alleged human interest was usually a sham. But in that film Greenaway used bigger stars (Michael Gambon, Helen Mirren), and the sex was so flagrant and gloating as to be objectionable. There were also charges, with some reason, that he was himself unduly excited by cruelty. So what? If films are really supposed to give up on the delicious task of tricking and offending us, how long can this pious behavior last? The film's mystery comes down to the wish to make an heir. Well, art cinema and exploitation have just the same horny urge to secure property. And we are the property.

Dr. Jekyll and Mr. Hyde (1932)

Who could be surprised at the screen appeal of *Dr. Jekyll and Mr. Hyde*? There's no need for murder and mayhem to feature in the transaction. It can be simply the difference between sitting in the dark and singin' in the rain—the spectator is Jekyll, and the man on the screen is Hyde. Robert Louis Stevenson's 1886 novella, *The Strange Case of Dr. Jekyll and Mr. Hyde,* began being filmed nearly as soon as the medium existed. There were at least seven versions before this, the Rouben Mamoulian classic, and the most recent had featured a very showy performance from John Barrymore. But when Paramount decided on this remake, they went for a prestige production.

Samuel Hoffenstein and Percy Heath did the script, Karl Struss was the cameraman, Hans Dreier was in charge of art direction, and Mamoulian was the director. Fredric March had the title roles, Miriam Hopkins was his girlfriend, and the rest of the cast included Rose Hobart, Holmes Herbert, Halliwell Hobbes, Arnold Lucy, Tempe Pigott, and Edgar Norton. Moreover, in the very impressive transformation scenes—done apparently in unbroken takes—there were tricks that were never revealed but that may have employed different-colored makeup that came in and out of view.

The picture was a hit—it had over $1 million in rentals—but it was not Oscar-nominated for Best Picture, no matter that Fredric March shared the acting Oscar that year with Wallace Beery in *The Champ.* March is good, but you get the feeling that there is some restraint being exercised. The thrust of the film was that Jekyll needs his alter ego so he can find sexual satisfaction, but maybe censorship was pressing on that nerve. One has the feeling that March's prize is owed to the makeup people above all. One longs for him to be bawdier and more dangerous.

The story was remade at Metro in 1941 by Victor Fleming, with Spencer Tracy in the lead. He huffed and puffed and changed his face, but it might have been subtler to play it drunk and sober. The intriguing thing about that version is that Ingrid Bergman and Lana Turner swapped parts, so Ingrid played the slut and Lana was the nice girl (I bet you can guess which one came off better).

The greatest performance in the role, I think, is that of Jean-Louis Barrault in Jean Renoir's *Le Testament du Docteur Cordelier* (1959), made for French television and not easy to see. Barrault does not do a transformation, as I recall, but his Cordelier is a man of such wanton, lurching movements as to be frightening and yet a remembrance of Boudu (but, of course, the tramp and the middle-class man is just another enactment of Stevenson's seminal dream).

A word should also be added for Stephen Frears's *Mary Reilly* (1996), where John Malkovich plays the two roles (but which is more frightening?) and Julia Roberts does wonders as the housemaid who realizes what is happening.

Dr. Mabuse the Gambler (1922)

You can argue that this onslaught from Fritz Lang does not deepen the intrigue of the Norbert Jacques novel on which it is based. There is not yet the darkening political undertone that distinguishes 1932's *The Testament of Dr. Mabuse.* But this is a thriller that plays well over three hours in its two parts, in which the narrative energy never flags. Nor is the film ever let down by visual imagination. The English critic Tom Milne argued that *Dr. Mabuse the Gambler* does not rival the earlier Feuillade pictures, especially for their haunting exteriors. It's a fair point. At the same time, I challenge anyone to point to more plot material being delivered per minute of screen time in 1922 with such conviction or atmosphere. Quite simply, in the development of early cinema, the control of complicated information, the delivery of moral point of view, and the accumulation of fascinating urban atmosphere is unrivaled.

Dr. Mabuse (Rudolf Klein-Rogge): "Who is he?" asks another character. "Nobody knows. He is there! He stands over the city like a huge tower!" In this, his first incarnation (delivered to screens just a year after the novel's publication), Mabuse is an exponent of psychological power who shows his command in gambling, mind games, hypnotism, telekinesis, and so on. His genius is to have such a powerful, staring eye that he takes over the weaker minds of others. His targets are the rich, especially those who are prepared to gamble away their wealth at the gaming tables or on the stock exchange—that sharp comparison is itself a good deal beyond the economic wisdom of most American films at that time. Mabuse is sexy—he likes to seduce important women—and he can even add an undertone of sexuality as he overpowers men. He wants to take over Edgar Hull (Paul Richter) and Count Told (Alfred Abel), but he is opposed in everything by State Attorney von Welk (Bernhard Goetzke).

It was all filmed at Babelsberg (now part of Potsdam) in 1921–22. Lang collaborated on the script with Thea von Harbou—they married not long after the film was released. That's worth stressing, because there is a giddy, exhilarated whirl to the action, with many sexual encounters. Lang would say later that he was out to show the depravity of postwar Germany, but in truth there's a glittering delight in the debauchery and the collapse of lives, and an absolute fascination with so many ways of yielding to irrational power. The interest in psychology that one might expect in the German-speaking world is still pitched at the level of a kind of masochistic madness, a vision of weakness in which the "villain" Mabuse is often more ambiguous than that position allows.

The photography was by Carl Hoffmann, the art direction by Otto Hunte, Erich Kettelhut, and Karl Vollbrecht. Above all, filmed largely on sets, this epic introduces the themes of enclosure and claustrophobia in Lang. They will be better handled later, but this Mabuse ends, insane, in a locked chamber. The place is the symbol of his mania, but the world of the films thrills to the geometry and the trap. From the outset, Lang loved his Mabuse and reacted to him. That guilty secret is still there. *Dr. Mabuse the Gambler* doesn't quite mean what it claims—but that is modernism.

Dr. Strangelove (1964)

Months after the death of John Kennedy, and not much more than two years after the October missile crisis, *My Fair Lady* beat out *Dr. Strangelove* for the Best Picture Oscar. Rex Harrison beat out Peter Sellers for Best Actor. It's all a measure of Hollywood's urge to look the other way—but I'm still not sure that *Dr. Strangelove* has worn very well.

The subtitle—*How I Learned to Stop Worrying and Love the Bomb*—was much employed as the film opened, if only as a way of suggesting that this was a gentle, ironic comedy and a public entertainment instead of an utterly bleak satire made without hope or much amusement. Moreover, this was the second "American" film in a row that Stanley Kubrick was making from a strictly British vantage point. Rather more than might have been wished for, the film had an anti-American undertone, or a vein of English comedy that sees America as a land of buffoons. In so many ways, that comes from Peter Sellers's triple act (as a British Air Force flier, as the American president, and as a mad scientist who has invented the Bomb).

Kubrick and Peter George were working on George's book *Red Alert* and getting nowhere, though Sellers had signed on to play as many as four roles. So Terry Southern took over, working in the car on the way to the studio with Kubrick. There were disputes over the writing later, but it's pretty clear that the satirical approach was all due to Southern. I'm not so sure now whether it feels like a funny film or a much more serious work struggling to find the right tone.

There's something resolutely facetious and schoolboyish in the humor. It seems to grow out of British Radio's *The Goon Show* and an adoration of Sellers the mimic that goes beyond reason. This indulgence of Sellers had already helped to spoil *Lolita,* where he had been permitted to improvise in ways that betrayed the commitment of James Mason—noble yet insane, eloquent but demented—as Humbert.

The real imaginative energy in *Strangelove* was going to Ken Adam's brilliant, futuristic sets (all made at Shepperton) and the attempt to create a world that was the manifestation of the daft bureaucracy in the nuclear-secure operation. This clash, or gap, between the tone of the action and the awesomeness of the physical world is not uncommon in Kubrick, but it is ruinous, and it sometimes enforces the inescapable feeling that his England is not the America that haunted him. His decision to be in England may have been made for strong personal reasons, but I think it did great damage artistically.

That said, here is a film alive with daring, a chilly black-and-white look (by cinematographer Gilbert Taylor), and very funny supporting performances from George C. Scott as Turgidson, Sterling Hayden as Ripper, and Slim Pickens as the ultimate pilot of the Bomb. If Preston Sturges had taken on this story—we can dream—the one thing I'm sure of, and that underlines Kubrick's limits, is that there would have been a woman in a lead part. Of course, I can't say for sure that Sturges would have left us laughing. But it's quite clear that Kubrick removed no one's worry.

Drunken Angel (1948)

Because it's still only 1948 in Tokyo, it's no surprise to see and feel a strain of Japanese neo-realism. There's nothing angry or aggressive in this film, but notice how Akira Kurosawa keeps showing us a city in ruins, with stagnant water stirred only by mosquitoes. Tuberculosis is everywhere, and as the film makes clear, this is a disease that can be stopped. But the doctor is a drunk, embittered at the way his treatments are so often neglected and mocked by the class of minor gangsters that seems to have taken the city over.

But look at *Drunken Angel* from a different angle and you have to ask yourself whether Kurosawa had been open to all of the best American noirs of 1947—or has he somehow intuited or predicted their tough angularity, their use of shadow, the jazzy dance halls, and the whole nature of the young yakuza who has TB and who is played by Toshiro Mifune (at the age of twenty-seven).

Put the package together and *Drunken Angel* is a remarkable picture. Kurosawa had made several films before this, but this is the one on which he felt he had become his own man and was able to work without interference. So it's important that he met Mifune here, of course, but just as important a presence is Takashi Shimura (as the doctor), who would be the leader of the *Seven Samurai* and the clerk in *Living*. Shimura is gruff, contradictory, alcoholic, but altruistic. He is a mess, but one of the most moving characters in world cinema, trying to make sense of things after the war.

Mifune is clean-shaven, thinner than he would later be, dressed in padded shoulders and striped ties. He is languid and lethal, with an air of Robert Mitchum to him. Yet there are moments when he lets us see the vulnerable boy dressed up as a yakuza, and Kurosawa gives us a very logical course for the character as he ultimately challenges a more mature and corrupt gangster.

I prefer *Drunken Angel* to the period adventure of *Rashomon*. I think the characters here mean more and that the film grows out of a Japan that all the cast and crew were struggling with. If you think of noir as an international wave—and we have to, for it is postwar despair—then *Drunken Angel* is as disturbing as the best films, as well as a proof of Kurosawa's astonishing facility and dexterity with Western techniques. He does several mirror shots, for instance, that are not underlined but are as lucid and subtle as Sirk or Ophüls.

One lesson is to stay interested in the modern Kurosawa, the one who doesn't need samurai costume and manners. The photography is by Takeo Ito, and it ranges from urban desolation to fevered-dream sequences. The script is by Kurosawa and Keinosuke Uegusa, and there is a gallery of good work from actresses Michiyo Kogure, Reisaburo Yamamoto, and Chieko Nakakita. The other lesson is not to kid ourselves about having discovered the limits of Japanese film. Indeed, as I write, Mikio Naruse is opening at the National Film Theatre in London for the first time.

Duck Soup (1933)

Duck Soup is all credentials: Leo McCarey directed; Herman J. Mankiewicz produced it; Bert Kalmar and Harry Ruby wrote it; Ansel Adams photographed it, mostly at magic hour; it was Marcel Proust's favorite Marx Brothers film; the Duke of Windsor watched it constantly in his years of exile. Are you believing this? Where does that get you? It was the poorest performer of all their Paramount films—there was a time when the University of Chicago economics department was stocked with people who'd done their Ph.D. on "*Duck Soup* and the Collapsing Cash Nexus" and similar titles. In other words, how could you expect a dazed, defeated, demoralized, and de-walleted population to go to see a film that mocked government when the folks were waiting for a New Deal?

In case you can't place the film, this is the one where Mrs. Teasdale (Margaret Dumont) will give the nation of Freedonia $20 million if Rufus T. Firefly is appointed its leader (and if she gets the fire in the fly). Aha, you may say, such cynicism and manipulation in the affairs of modest third-world nations was far more likely the cause of public despair. Enter Trentino (played by that very respectable actor Louis Calhern), the ambassador from Sylvania (before it was in the TV business), and soon we are on the brink of world war. But why remind the public of that?

Like many Marx Brothers films, *Duck Soup* has the suspicious air of a few set pieces strung together with Christmas lights and pretending to be a whole film. And why not? Hollywood was learning with talk and plots and so forth that the manufacture of whole films (as opposed to scene anthologies) was a dirty job, even if you were being paid for it. There has never been a better answer to the question of what holds this film together than glue. The essential ethos of the Marx Brothers (this is Irving Thalberg talking as he prepared to ship them off to Culver City) is to make their fragmentation seem natural. So Thalberg foresaw Marxian nights with a film program continually interrupted by little scenes from Marxist groups. This was a principle applied fully on the BBC years later with the arrival of Monty Python. The show might be over, but still somehow the other programs—the news, Gardeners' Question Time, England v. Pakistan—could not but take on a Pythonesque flourish. This could have revolutionized TV, but the Python boys (who had been to university) asked for ghostly residuals.

Anyway, *Duck Soup* has the extended routine where Chico (as Chicolini) and Harpo (as Pinky) harrass Edgar Kennedy. And it also has Groucho and the mirror, which is enough to persuade you all to get every bit of polished glass out of the house.

If you find you like this sort of thing, you'll be glad to know that *The Cocoanuts, Animal Crackers, Monkey Business,* and *Horse Feathers* once existed. There was a moment—we call it sound—when the Marx Brothers made the trip from vaudeville to Hollywood, and it's like Neil Armstrong stepping down onto the moon and landing on a banana peel.

Duel in the Sun (1946)

This astonishing film began life as a novel by Niven Busch, based on some modest "psychological" principles. When it became a best seller, Busch himself proposed to produce the movie, and he was thinking of John Wayne as Lewt and Hedy Lamarr as Pearl, the half-caste. But then David Selznick got wind of the enterprise and reckoned that Pearl might be the role that would display his beloved Jennifer Jones as a sex bomb. Very soon Busch was gone and the Selznick production was under way—it would be bigger than *Gone With the Wind*.

It isn't. But what is it—apart from the painful evidence of a producer making an immense home movie about his rather naïve sex life? Selznick hired an old friend, King Vidor, to direct but then interfered so much that Vidor quit the film. William Dieterle became director (uncredited), and an entire backstory involving Pearl's parents—Tilly Losch and Herbert Marshall (a marriage that called for a Buñuel)—was incorporated.

I suppose it's a Western—there are cattle, wire fences, shoot-outs, and cowboy clothes. But it is more significantly the story of how Pearl is torn between gentle Jesse (Joseph Cotten) and rampant Lewt (Gregory Peck). In fact, Peck is far better than one might anticipate, and he is easily the most beautiful person in the film. There were sex scenes shot and cut, but it's still not clear whether this was because they offended censorship or stretched Jennifer Jones's "abandon" too far.

All that said, the film is of a weird piece, with everything overdone, growling-beast music from Dimitri Tiomkin, a solemn narrative by Orson Welles, and a color scheme that is like the entire Kalmus family with fatally high fevers. You almost expect one of the lurid sunsets to catch fire in the projectors. It is beautiful, silly, and sexy, and for sure the film needs some kind of visual madness.

I credit Vidor for the color, and we know the director conceived the sadomasochistic ending in which, fatally wounded, Lewt and Pearl reach out for each other across burning rocks. In the end, there is a ludicrous heat between them. As bystanders, the film has Lillian Gish, Lionel Barrymore, and Charles Bickford (very good), and no one is more adrift than poor Joe Cotten, who really gave years of his life to domineering men.

The film cost at least $5 million, and it made that back—a tribute to advertising plans that called it "Lust in the Dust" and to the way Selznick formed a distribution company for this one film. So he took in cash but made a loss. At the same time, to slip past the bad reviews he foresaw, he released the film in a rush, multiple bookings years ahead of that scheme of the 1970s. Nothing worked. The film was a famous laughingstock, and deservedly so. But the violent color can still choke the laugh in your throat.

The Duellists (1977)

When Ridley Scott's first film opened, the excellent critic Tom Milne warned, "Picturesqueness tends to be the downfall of *The Duellists.*" And it was painfully obvious that Scott had been not just raised but marinated in television commercials. Image after image from this picture (photographed in unending magic hour by Frank Tidy) seemed like advertising shots for the town of Sarlat and the Dordogne, Napoleon brandy, dark chocolate, truffles in autumn leaves, saddle leather, polished steel, and the dressing of beautiful women in 1810 frocks (all removed in time). The prettiness was delirious and inane and so showoffy as to risk the film's being damned. But then the truth began to dawn: The obsessive handsomeness—claustrophobic, fusspot, morbid even—was a wondrous consort to the maniacal, humorless relentlessness of the story. It worked. It still does. Though you feel like a stuffed goose liver after seeing it.

In 1800, Lieutenant Armand d'Hubert (Keith Carradine) of the Hussars is ordered to have a Lieutenant Gabriel Feraud (Harvey Keitel) confined to barracks for fighting a duel. Feraud takes offense and challenges d'Hubert to another duel. They fight and Feraud is wounded, but then the war carries them off in opposite directions. And so it goes on until 1816 (and the royalist restoration), with the ridiculous duel being renewed at intervals with an intensity that shows no sign of matching the aging in the combatants. Feraud is the madman in this. It is his brittle honor that demands death or satisfaction (though Feraud is innately dissatisfied and forever wronged). D'Hubert is more normal, more lazy, more inclined to forget. But he knows that nothing will appease Feraud—not even death, really. And so the two lives wait on each other.

The film comes from a story by Conrad, "The Point of Honor," and in this film the obsession is at least as funny as it is crazy. But obsession lends itself to film so easily. It is as if the destined plod of human journey and motive are allied to the succession of frames and the persistence of vision. I do not mean to be fanciful, but revenge is a topic that seems to breathe in film, and I do not think the daft reliability of madness in *The Duellists* would work as well on the page. Gerald Vaughan-Williams did the screenplay. Peter J. Hampton was art director. Ann Mollo did the set decoration and Tom Rand the costumes. William Hobbs deserves credit for the fights.

Keith Carradine is not quite right (he's too hip, too American), though that does make him seem more trapped. But Harvey Keitel is magnificent. This may be his greatest part. There are also several amused, languid men—Albert Finney, Edward Fox, Robert Stephens, Tom Conti—and a series of amazingly lovely women: Cristina Raines, Diana Quick, Gay Hamilton, Jenny Runacre.

Sir Ridley Scott goes on, and he is a grand and versatile entertainer (*Alien, Blade Runner, White Squall, Black Hawk Down*) yet always likely to go on a prettiness binge.

Earth (1930)

You will have seen nothing like *Earth*, and so it is tempting to accept the words that come with the preservation of such films. And so the advice, or the warning, offered with Alexander Dovzhenko's silent film is that "the story itself is secondary to the visually stunning and incredibly moving images." I'll come to the visual in a moment, but the story is not secondary. Made in the Ukraine, *Earth* is a propaganda film in which the machine from God is a rather crude tractor that may transform the working life of the peasantry in the area. One character, Basil, loves the tractor. After its first day of work, he literally dances in the village street in ecstasy. These are long shots at twilight, where the dust he kicks up is like gold, and the joy of the man is too directly dance-like to be resisted. Then he is killed—because the resistance to the tractor and to the larger organization of the farm system is very large. There will be a battle.

And so this ecstatic 69-minute movie is an attack in that battle, and while I know far too little about the best way of farming the Ukraine, I have a most uneasy recollection that eventually millions died in the decision. So the story is vast, and part of its message is the question of how reliably this transcendent, poetic imagery can be trusted, or how far Dovzhenko has loaned genius and beauty to a harsh cause.

That said, you have never seen land, sunflowers, apples, and burnished faces like these before. Dovzhenko does not often shift his frame (though he does track sometimes). He makes this film out of edited "stills," in that the first composition in a shot lasts. But the rhythm of the editing is akin to the vitality of the images. At the very start a peasant dies like a man turning the last page of a book. Do people ever die that simply? I am convinced from seeing and feeling *Earth* that, yes, sometimes they do—and that perhaps they did in the Ukraine, where growth was the essential machine until the tractor came along.

And once you yield to the power of form and light—to the shots of shiny grass waving in the wind; to the oxen, shot from a low angle as if they were battleships—then *Earth* is like a draft of water or sweet juice on a hot day. Are the people idealized? Yes. But without any feeling of contrivance or exploitation. You feel Dovzhenko loves these people—and one of the faces is that of his wife, Julia Solntseva, one of the great beauties in the history of film.

Danilo Demutsky did the photography, and I defy anyone not to see and feel the passionate enthusiasm of early Bolshevism in it—it is like Dziga Vertov's *The Man with a Movie Camera* (1927) in its direct transmission of wonder at how the world looks. That does nothing to alter the very forceful storyline of the film. But in things like the mourning of a wife—naked and helpless—there seems no veil or explanation needed. Let's just say that Dovzhenko was from the Ukraine, the son of a peasant, and that his film was denounced by some authorities for being reactionary. Now you have to see it.

Eastern Promises (2007)

Gracefully, like a sweet assassination, as *The Sopranos* withdrew itself from our world—and perhaps gave a hint that the Italian mafia might be stale—here comes David Cronenberg's *Eastern Promises* with the twenty-first-century version of offers not to be refused. The Russian mafia have landed, and with their wicked curved knives (ideal for opening an oyster or an enemy), with the deadpan cool that can stub out a cigarette on their own tongues, to say nothing of the wintry panache of Viggo Mortensen, we are equipped with a new villain we love to hate. And, as far as one can tell, this band has so much more footing in reality than the old Italian romancers.

Eastern Promises is a very sly title for so magnificent a bloodbath, every bit as "academic" as *A History of Violence*—and look where that textbook approach ended. So maybe the first thing to be said is that, having gone down the long, clammy, and very unpromising backstreet of *Spider*, David Cronenberg seems to have looked in the mirror, noticed his gray hair, done some basic math, and asked himself whether he was compelled to make intractably private films forever . . . or could he start to have some fun? I know that Cronenberg for years gave off many hints of being above and beyond fun. His early work is fascinating, but his two Viggo Mortensen films seem to owe as much to Cronenberg's shift in direction and identity as they do to the actor's lazy-eyed patience, as in, I won't kill you—just yet.

Just like *A History of Violence*, *Eastern Promises* believes in narrative suspense and the moral content of astonishing action. The story is set in London. Naomi Watts, a hospital midwife, delivers a baby, and the mother, a teenage girl, dies. The doctor finds a diary and a clue that leads to a Russian restaurant in London. It is owned by Armin Mueller-Stahl, one of whose employees, Mortensen, has the task of looking after Mueller-Stahl's unstable kid. Is the whole thing one great web of conspiracy? Yes. Will things culminate in Mortensen naked but for many tattoos fighting for his life in a Turkish bath? Yes.

There's a way in which the latent familiarity and the brutal shock of situations place this film in a genre tradition begging for exploitation. We might even get real Russians in the cast before long! The script, by Steve Knight, is very knowing, save for one concession to making us feel good. It would be unfair to point it out in advance, but you'll see it and you'll flinch. Never mind; this is noir material as fresh and foul as the insults on the lips of Chelsea F.C. supporters.

Mortensen becomes a major star. Naomi Watts demonstrates her readiness to be secondary, and rather more tired than beautiful. Mueller-Stahl goes straight into the hall of fame for polite monsters. And it's very nice to see Sinéad Cusack and, above all, Jerzy Skolimowski, in supporting roles. Vincent Cassel is outstanding as the unstable kid.

East of Eden (1955)

Several things have to be accepted at the outset. This is not Steinbeck's novel—it covers only the "modern" section, and it omits altogether many people's favorite character, Lee, the Chinese house servant. It is also a James Dean film, as if, for both artistic and commercial reasons, director Elia Kazan realized what he had in his hands and elected to side with Cal Trask, the Cain figure. Because of that, both brother Aron (Richard Davalos) and the father, Adam (Raymond Massey), suffer as characters or as objects of our sympathy.

What's left is a parable about the adorability of the Cain character—and, of course, there were reasons at the time for Kazan to see himself as a bad boy, a betrayer, a Cain. The Trasks live in the farming country of Salinas: Aron is a good boy with a very nice sweetheart, Abra (Julie Harris). Cal is a slouching, sly dark spirit; he feels unloved, awkward, and afflicted. Adam is a prig, upright, doing his best—and only readers of the book know that he lost his wife, Kate (Jo Van Fleet), in part because of her waywardness but also because he was a domestic tyrant.

The time is the brink of America's entry into the First World War. Adam is pursuing a quixotic attempt to freeze farm vegetables. The shrewd Cal, seeing war on the horizon, plants beans to make money. He gives that money to his father as a gift and a sign of love, no matter that his father—who serves on the draft board—is horrified at having to send young men to their death. There is a strange reversal in family affairs. Adam has a stroke. Abra turns to Cal. And Aron, lost, goes off to war.

I have heard stories about young people today finding Cal a self-pitying bore. They have a point. But that's a reading that altogether misses the extraordinary emotional force of the film in the 1950s, and the way Cal signaled the kind of outlaw kid from the sixties and seventies. You can see Dean acting if you resolve not to be involved, and there's no doubt about his cunning, his wolfish unfairness. But to maintain that resolve is more than I can manage. There were some of us for whom Dean in this film was the determining and turning-point performance of the 1950s.

Let me add that the film is also a sign of real art coming to Kazan. The color and the Scope (by Ted McCord) are very eloquent—for example, in the whole sequence in which Cal goes to Monterey on a foggy day to find his mother. And Jo Van Fleet gives one of several very fine supporting performances, along with Burl Ives, Albert Dekker, Lois Smith, Timothy Carey, and Barbara Baxley.

Paul Osborn did the drastic adaptation and did it well. James Basevi and Malcolm Bert did the art direction. And Leonard Rosenman wrote a new kind of score, identifying with Cal as much as Kazan did in every shot. Dean is still amazing, but so is Julie Harris, who was older than Dean (thirty to his twenty-five).

Easy Living (1937)

Jean Arthur opened six films in a twelve-month period, from April 1936 through March 1937: *Mr. Deeds Goes to Town, The Ex-Mrs. Bradford, Adventure in Manhattan, More Than a Secretary, The Plainsman,* and *History Is Made at Night.* This was the factory system at the height of its powers, when someone like Miss Arthur was expected to be as fresh as the first rose. Her contract with Columbia allowed her to do some outside films, and she told studio boss Harry Cohn she wasn't going back unless her material improved. So she told Paramount she'd do a picture for them. About the same time, a screenwriter and nightclub owner took a story by Vera Caspary and turned it into a screenplay called *Easy Living.* His name was Preston Sturges. In her first scene, Jean Arthur was riding down Fifth Avenue on an open bus when a fur coat, thrown from an upper window, fell on her head. At last—a touch of class!

Arthur's character is named Mary Smith, and she is a very ordinary, decent, nice girl. But once she has a fur coat—though she seeks its rightful owner—she has moved up in the world as surely as it fell down. The assumption follows that she is loaded, important, and not entirely nice. She is probably somebody's mistress. Mitchell Leisen got to direct the film, and he had the smart urge to leaven the wordplay a little with slapstick. After all, if you're on a Fifth Avenue bus one minute and in a world of fur the next, anything ought to be able to happen. The result is one of the great screwball comedies, quietly—for 1937—nursing a whole set of questions about how much money, or its reputation, has to do with "easy living." It's a sweet, collapsible phrase; after all, it can mean dissolution, not far from Berlin in 1923, or just living with an easy state of mind. If you paired the film with *My Man Godfrey,* you'd have a beautiful portrait of money in New York—as well as a very happy audience.

Edward Arnold is the rich man who tossed the coat. Ray Milland is his son, with whom Mary Smith clearly sees a way ahead. There is a great scene where Mary is shown a hotel suite that is deemed worthy of her fur coat—it is a small palace designed by Hans Dreier and Ernst Fegté—and as she explores its shining white dimensions, she collapses in a chair and just says, "Golly!" It is one of the sweetest moments in Jean Arthur's career, but it is also a desperate American attempt to keep its wits in the face of plenty and luxury. It's a scene that should have played every day at the HUAC hearings as those beavers in defense of our nationhood searched for Red influence in our movies.

The fur coat and the other clothes are by Travis Banton, Ted Tetzlaff did the photography, and the cast also includes Luis Alberni, Mary Nash, Franklin Pangborn, Barlowe Borland, and William Demarest. You can see the later Sturges stock company taking shape, and you can feel his naughty hand treating the stock market like a wobbling blancmange.

Easy Rider (1969)

In the late 1960s, the Roger Corman organization had made a number of "biker" films, including *The Trip* and *The Wild Angels*. Peter Fonda was on the road to promote *The Trip*. One night in a Toronto hotel, he was looking at a photograph of himself and Bruce Dern in that picture—he may have been on his own trip—and got the idea of a road picture, of two bikers and a drug deal. He called up his pal Dennis Hopper and outlined the film. "You direct it," said Fonda. "I'll star."

Roger Corman was interested, but two things stood in the way: He wasn't sure that Dennis Hopper could direct a whole film (history has hardly proved him wrong), and he was nervous about a picture that so clearly advocated the selling of drugs. So he hesitated. Whereupon Jack Nicholson told Hopper and Fonda to take their baby to BBS (Bert Schneider, Steve Blauner, and Bob Rafelson). They sat down with Schneider and said it would cost $325,000. Schneider wrote them a check on the spot, for *The Trip* and other biker pictures had earned serious money.

You might not guess this from the film, but there was a script. It is Terry Southern's position that he wrote most of it—for $350 a week and no points. Hopper and Fonda shared in the writing credit (and hogged the points), but Southern said it was he who took out the barnstorming, trick-riding part of the treatment and made it a drug-deal picture. He also strengthened the role of George Hanson, the lawyer who rides along with them, based on William Faulkner's Gavin Stevens.

So there it was, ready to go. But Dern (a man dogged by bad luck) turned down the Hanson role, wanting more money. Then the part went to Rip Torn, but he had another commitment and a short temper. So Jack Nicholson ended up in the role that altered his career.

It was a road shoot, lasting seven weeks, traveling from Los Angeles to New Orleans. László Kovács did the photography, and the cast included Luke Askew, Luana Anders, Phil Spector (as the connection), Karen Black, Toni Basil, Robert Walker, and Sabrina Scharf, as well as people met on the road. The editing was assigned to Donn Cambern, but it was done by a committee that included Hopper and Fonda, Bert Schneider, Jack Nicholson, and Henry Jaglom.

About 130,000 feet of film came down to 95 minutes. The film went to Cannes. It won a prize for New Director: and it earned $17 million on its first run, and maybe $40 million in total. As such, it launched the careers of those attached to the film. It allowed BBS a couple of creative years. And it undoubtedly encouraged the system to think of offering opportunities to young directors, actors, and writers. It established Nicholson as the new master in a rare American tradition, heroic yet comic.

And it is unwatchable—unless you are benefiting from the illegal substances it advocates.

L'Eclisse (1962)

Consider the extraordinary coincidences of 1962, like Luis Buñuel's *The Exterminating Angel* and Michelangelo Antonioni's *The Eclipse.* Do they just exist together in the same year, or do they have anything more in common than being shot in black and white? I know that the Antonioni film is set in the busy city of Rome, where the stock exchange goes wild and there is always the insect life of traffic on the streets, whereas *The Exterminating Angel's* action—or should we say the opposite of action, the ingrowing nature of the film?—occurs at a large house in a quiet Mexican suburb on Calle de la Providencia. That is where the social event is set, the one from which—mysteriously—the guests are unable to depart.

So I wonder, is it just possible that *L'Eclisse's* two young Italians, Vittoria and Piero (Monica Vitti and Alain Delon), who had been scheduled to meet on a certain street corner, or at a Roman intersection—is it possible, when they do not meet, that they are among the company irrationally but quite definitely detained, or withheld, at the Calle de la Providencia?

This may sound more like a game than criticism, but there are profound ways in which great films are more like one another than like lesser films. In other words, there is a point in film's hierarchy where schemes like Western or Romance or even Noir fall away, tired and useless, and the only genre left intact is the name of the author. And then, even though Buñuel is famously a surrealist while Antonioni maintains a kind of baffled respect for reality (the shots of the city at the end of *L'Eclisse* are documentary-like; indeed, the longer they go on without our characters arriving, the more grossly banal they become). Still, the ellipses in great artists quite easily reach out to hold hands, and I mean it in all seriousness when I say that the rendezvous in *L'Eclisse* has been prevented by *The Exterminating Angel.*

Now, ostensibly *L'Eclisse* concerns the meeting of a beautiful but hesitant young woman—shall we just say Monica Vitti—with a young wolf of success, a man of money, disguised as Alain Delon. It is about the chance of some kind of relationship developing be-tween a creature who lives in her imagination and a man who counts nearly everything that is precious to him—thus, she has two eyes, two breasts. And since this is Antonioni arranging figures in a cityscape (photography by Gianni Di Venanzo), then this is less a movie narrative than a visualized novel in which space, light, movement, and gesture are as factual and as evocative as words. We are talking about probably the most heightened or searching kind of movie ever made. We are talking about a masterpiece.

But don't rely on narrative suspense. What will happen to these two people is rewarded by their sustained absence and by the prospect of the city's carrying on without noticing. The year 1962 was also the year of the Cuban missile crisis, and when the streetlamp comes on at last, as dusk comes in, you can easily think of it as some kind of explosion. For the failure to meet is now achingly metaphysical, a warning. As the critic Seymour Chatman has proposed, it is a whole society or a whole civilization that cannot meet.

Ed Wood (1994)

Edward D. Wood, Jr. (1922–78), was famous in his shadowy lifetime as perhaps the most eager and probably the least talented director around. He made films like *Glen or Glenda* (much interested in sex change) and *Plan 9 from Outer Space* (a stranded vehicle for the dying Bela Lugosi). There was a good-natured college cult over his films, which played in the sixties and the seventies. *Ed Wood*, quite simply, is a tender, trusting film about this guy, lit up equally by director Tim Burton's sense that passion is more than talent and by Johnny Depp's fabulous, wide-eyed absence of self-awareness in the central role.

The picture is derived from a book, *Nightmare of Ecstasy*, by Rudolph Grey, and from a screenplay by Scott Alexander and Larry Karaszewski, and I think it's fair to say that there is a great deal of well-digested research, without the least attempt at the kind of cutting judgments that are so available. In other words, treating Wood on his own terms—and making this in some ways like a Wood picture—is the challenge. That said, apart from the overall control of Burton, a huge debt is owed to the rare black-and-white photography by Stefan Czapsky, which lets one think of Wood's own murk-and-milk lighting while offering a thing of beauty in its own right. There is also very good work done in production design (Tom Duffield), art direction (Okowita), set decoration (Cricket Rowland), and costumes (Colleen Atwood).

The film sketches in its own backstory but concentrates on the making of *Plan 9*, and thus it hinges on Bela Lugosi, acted with deep, slow relish by Martin Landau (he got an Oscar for it) and much helped by the lurid makeup work from Rick Baker. Yet in a way, Lugosi is an easier role than Wood himself and some of those bright idiots he had for company. Depp was still young doing *Ed Wood*, and a dozen years later he is a huge cult but still a question mark as an actor. This film ought to have stopped that chatter. He gives an inspired and inspiring performance—you can see how Wood believed in himself and had won others to that cause. Great credit goes also to Sarah Jessica Parker, Patricia Arquette, Jeffrey Jones, G. D. Spradlin, Bill Murray (as Bunny Breckinridge), Mike Starr, Max Casella, Brent Hinkley, Lisa Marie (as Vampira), and George Steele.

But I have to give a special nod to Vincent D'Onofrio, who has a single scene as Orson Welles. There have been plenty of Welles impersonations onscreen (including those by Orson himself), and I think it's clear that he is a great temptation and a severe challenge as well as a diatribe against it. D'Onofrio's version is a moment that accepts Wood as a fellow pilgrim in an absurd quest. And it is so close to Orson Welles that it is a tragedy to let the actor and the chance of a biopic go. You feel that if only D'Onofrio could have been Welles—and Welles Ed Wood—then who knows? Things might have worked out more kindly.

8½ (1963)

Forgive this observation, but if you're undecided about what film to make, 135 minutes is rather self-indulgent on the worry. But then you'd have to consider the argument as to whether Federico Fellini—full of art-house celebrity and restless facility—didn't turn to self and selfhood as opposed to story or subject. I know that seems ungrateful when you consider the unique and endearing insouciance/lethargy/fraud/boredom that Marcello Mastroianni turned on for this role—to say nothing of the photography (by Gianni Di Venanzo) that produced sophisticated blacks and whites like the layouts in a great fashion magazine. (It's not that you admire the clothes in this film—you want to purchase them. A boutique in every lobby would have cleaned up!) And surely, after the brooding disquiet of, say, Antonioni, there were more Italians than just Fellini who saw the charm in having the greatest problem in the world be what will you do or wear next?

But Antonioni—give him his due—hovers over spaces filled with mystery, whereas the gravure look that Fellini perfected here has an instantaneous accessibility that shuts out subtexts, doubts, or inner meanings. What you see is what you get—and what you see is Fellini reveling in the ironic self-centeredness of a whole film in the way Guido (Mastroianni) dreams up the harem set piece to give equality to all the competing (and betrayed) women in his life. So the considerable bitterness and justice of his wife (Anouk Aimée) can be shrugged off as high-strung nerves.

On the other hand, I agree with anyone who observes that as Fellini gives up on the charade of being interested in anything except himself, his style becomes richer and more mellifluous. It's not that *8½* could or should go on forever, just that it feels as if it does. Whereas there was an authentic conundrum awaiting him after the specious *La Dolce Vita:* What should he do next? The matter of pressing subject was waning, and it was one among many signs that film was losing its grip on him. So Fellini turned to celebrity, with some wry grace but still as wholeheartedly as far more painfully vain directors.

Now, there is talk about his life as an ongoing circus or party—but we know those parties we cannot remember, and after a few years we gaze in dismay on the hundreds of nights they consumed. This was an act Fellini could turn on anything—his *Rome* was to come. He could as easily have made a film about his shirts or shoes. For myself, I don't think another real movie for him comes after *8½*, and I include *Amarcord,* which is something like *My Youth,* yet in a way that has forgotten how to notice pain. So the word *Fellini-esque* crept into being at almost exactly the moment when it had come to mean much less than ever before.

But Di Venanzo's photography changed the world. And Nino Rota had the oil to add to every dish. Also with Claudia Cardinale, Sandra Milo, Barbara Steele, Rossella Falk, and Madeleine LeBeau. The script was by Fellini, Tullio Pinelli, Ennio Flaiano, and Brunello Rondi.

Election (1999)

By tradition, we are supposed to be more afraid of Rosemary's baby, Damien in the *Omen* films, or even Patty McCormack in *The Bad Seed.* But a more frightening idea could be that the gravest threat comes from our own young, possessed by a fierceness that we never commanded and hardly understand. And this is a type you can find out there nowadays, a pert child of the 1970s born again as a new conservative of the nineties with a special vendetta against the fatal untidiness of the sixties. I give you—please take her, and throttle her—Tracy Flick.

Not many people remarked on it at the time, but the central character in Alexander Payne's smoky *Election* was this good girl turned very nasty—and it was clear by the end of the film that Payne saw Tracy moving on to Washington, D.C. She is a character who deserves sequels—the next part could be her becoming a media voice, a sexpot who brings brimstone and treacle to moral ambivalence. But we had not seen this type before, even if Katharine Hepburn had drawn close to it in films like *Alice Adams* and even *The Philadelphia Story*—the toxic nerd.

Maybe I am praising Payne too much. His work has been inconsistent, to say the least. But at this moment, I would rather be generous to a new comic talent than able to recognize authentic misanthropy in another David Fincher. And *Election* is a dazzling comedy in which the pain is as intense as a bee sting in the eye, or an early knee in the groin to the promising career of civics teacher Jim McAllister (Matthew Broderick), the lightweight who chooses to go up against the dread Flick. It is his job to run the school-president election, and in a reasonable if not just way, he knows that for the good of Carver High, Tracy Flick must not win. We know that in most circumstances she has lost, for her idiot rival, the big penis, has been so softhearted as to vote for her. So Jim fixes the election, and he is going to be an outsider for the rest of his life. While Tracy . . . ? Who knows?

Payne wrote *Election* with Jim Taylor, working from a novel by Tom Perrotta. The supporting cast is solid, but everyone on the film knows that the satire is flying because of the sails in Reese Witherspoon's self-satisfied cheeks. And this was only her second great show. The first came two years earlier, when she was only twenty, in *Freeway*. That remaking of the Little Red Riding Hood tale makes Red so much more dangerous than the Wolf, and thereby inaugurates what might be a new volume of American moral tales in which murder and mayhem are done in the names of the old clichés. Ms. Witherspoon was bound to grow older, and lo and behold, in *Walk the Line* she was adorable and sexy. It's quite possible that she will be a curiosity. In which case, there's all the more point in insisting that in *Freeway* and *Election*, Reese Witherspoon was on the point of taking over. The Republic is so vulnerable.

Éloge de l'Amour (2001)

It's notable that when this film got a release in English-speaking countries (and it was Jean-Luc Godard's first such opportunity in fourteen years), it was called *In Praise of Happiness*, which is not quite the same as an elegy to love, even if it may offer more comfort to a middlebrow audience.

In Paris, Edgar (Bruno Putzulu) is preparing some creative project on love that will observe meeting, passion, breakup, and reconciliation. He is auditioning various people for parts. He meets a young woman (Cecile Camp) who seems capable of playing the lead. But before the event, she kills herself—there is suicide in her family. This event is played against an incident from a couple of years earlier, when Edgar travels to Brittany to visit a historian (Jean Lacouture) about the history of the French Resistance. An elderly couple live nearby; they were the "Tristan and Isolde" circuit once, and they are in the process of trading the rights to their story to a "Steven Spielberg." Their granddaughter Berthe is helping with the contracts.

The Paris sequences are shot on film, but in black and white. The Brittany scenes are done in beautiful color video. That contrary decision, it seems to me, is part of the still Godardian effort to make us reflect on what decisions have been made. And there are very gloomy issues here (often found in his early films) about how television has reduced the cultural gaze of individuals and society simply by letting it seem that our choosing to look or not hardly matters. And the reason I include *Éloge de l'Amour* is not because I am certain of its masterpiece status so much as because of a response to its belief in my title, *Have you seen . . . ?* For instance, Berthe is kept a scarcely visible figure—shadowy, with her back to us, obscure—if for no other reason than to make us look in every way we can at her.

The satire is scathing. I don't think any Steven Spielberg was involved with this couple, but the idea of a movie with William Styron doing the script and Juliette Binoche in the lead is all too credible. (Mademoiselle Binoche will be telephoning personally once the contract is signed!) Whereas the valiant couple from the Resistance, grandmother and grandfather, are homely and sunken, and who knows how well they remember the actual betrayal of the past? He turned her in under Gaullist instructions?

So "happiness" is hardly at issue. Instead, we have a dense and truly difficult film document in which we are invited to consider the verity of so many clichés: the Resistance, the value of reporting, books and films, and even the notion that Edgar and Berthe may be in love. Like the best of Godard in the old days, this is a "story" that perpetually questions itself, and if there is an elegy to love buried deep inside, it is not necessarily of comfort. This is the world of a filmmaker—and it is blazing and beautiful—but it agonizes over the question of whether film has turned us in.

The Elusive Pimpernel (1950)

Alexander Korda had done a version of *The Scarlet Pimpernel* in 1935, directed by Harold Young. It had Leslie Howard as Sir Percy Blakeney, Merle Oberon as his wife, and Raymond Massey as Chauvelin, the French official who is pursuing the Pimpernel to stop his efforts to save aristocrats from the guillotine. Then Korda asked the Archers—the British filmmaking team of Michael Powell and Emeric Pressburger—to do him a remake, no matter that the status of aristos had altered in fifteen years.

It was their first idea to take the rather flimsy Baroness Orczy story and turn it into an extravaganza, a kind of movie operetta. They even flirted with the idea of doing the whole thing in song. (Can you picture a version of the Pimpernel story as if done by Jacques Demy? Of course you can.) But Korda was nervous: He had seen the thing work as an adventure story, and he flinched at Powell's vivid accounts of a fantasia. So the novelty was cooked at a lower temperature. No songs. Not too much music. Yet what remained was Powell's inclination not to take the adventure too seriously and to make everything look as blatantly pretty as possible. What we do have, still, is a version of the Pimpernel story that could be set in the Brighton Pavillion and that might be painted by Dufy.

David Niven was to be Blakeney, and that was fine. He was a demure swashbuckler, after all, with great humor and poise and the nerve to play over the top. Chauvelin would be Cyril Cusack (after first thoughts of Marius Goring), and he does a lovely job: malicious, suspicious, sly but stupid. The great problem occurred with Lady Blakeney. The woman was French, said Powell, so let's have a French actress. Korda was all for Margaret Leighton, who struck Powell as the stiffest kind of stage actress. He found Madeleine LeBeau (she sings "La Marseillaise" in *Casablanca*), but Korda was adamant.

So the Archers team went to work, Christopher Challis doing the photography, Hein Heckroth the sets, Brian Easdale the music. Powell called the result a mess and a navet—a turnip. He is too hard on himself. The open-air shooting—the English countryside, the Normandy shore, Mont St. Michel—is lovely. Niven and Cusack are first-class, and there is a great sense of champagne and fun, as well as a supporting cast dressed and behaving like the Harlequins rugby club on a weekend trip to France: Robert Coote, Edmond Audran, Charles Victor, David Hutcheson, David Oxley, Patrick Macnee, and Terence Alexander, along with Danielle Godet, Arlette Marchal, Gérard Nery, and Eugene Deckers.

As with the Archers' *The Small Back Room*, this film deserves rediscovery. But in hindsight one can see their tastes diverging from British feelings in the 1950s. Powell and Pressburger rate at the highest level in the 1940s, but they were blessed by being in step with the audience. To be out of step is to be like Josef von Sternberg after *The Devil Is a Woman:* The art is perfected, but the business is a wreck.

Empire of the Sun (1987)

It really was the case that the young J. G. Ballard became lost in Shanghai as the Japanese attacked at the start of that theater of the Second World War. For the boy, the city was half-playground, half-wasteland before he found himself the Artful Dodger of a prison camp and chief imp to the languid yet thoroughly evil Basie (John Malkovich). So, yes, this is a war story and a prison-camp movie in many ways, but what makes it sublime is its adherence to the boy's vision. He is "safe" at the end, I suppose, yet he is on the edge of a breakdown, too. And in this great ordeal, the Japanese are bad enough, but still Basie is his Fagin figure, the most understanding fount of evil.

Steven Spielberg talked to Ballard and suggested Tom Stoppard as screenwriter. Ballard was uncertain at first, but then eager to say what a fine decision it was. Stoppard made an arc of the book and simplified the narrative without subtracting from the richness or character. Above all—and I give Spielberg much credit for this—the emotional life of the boy remains central. This is a fearsome story of innocence exposed, in the violence and cruelty he has to see as well as in the lingering on the threshold of a sickly sexuality in the form of Mrs. Victor (Miranda Richardson—so good, you long for more of her in the film).

The camp is very well re-created, not just in terms of design (Norman Reynolds) and photography (Allan Daviau), but as a place of small, vicious advantages and constant hardship. Jim (Christian Bale), the boy, is so desperate for someone to admire that the reptilian Basie becomes a laconic angel in his eyes; the rapport between Malkovich and Bale is uncanny, for this is not a common situation in life or film. Bale is widely recognized as a very good actor now, but here, as a novice, he is flat-out brilliant. You feel his giddy impulse and Spielberg trusting it. And, of course, Malkovich was already on his way toward a kind of louche genius.

David Lean was in Spielberg's mind, but this is far subtler than Lean ever managed. They shot in China and built the camp in Spain. But remember "the Sun," both as the metaphor for Japan and the promise of the Bomb that ends the war. So much of this movie contrives to be hellish and radiant at the same time—and that is authentic vision, even if it began with Ballard.

The film did not do very well, which I take as a proof of its lethal awareness of moral peril in a strange place. It came out the same year as *The Last Emperor* (which is fine but old-fashioned in comparison). *Empire of the Sun* is a great work through and through. It received few Oscar nominations, yet for anyone with a sense of film I think it was the first clear sign that Spielberg the showman was an artist, too.

Also with Nigel Havers, Joe Pantoliano, Leslie Phillips, Robert Stephens, Emily Richard, Rupert Frazer, Paul McGann, and Takatoro Kataoka. (When Spielberg was auditioning child actors, a guy named Liam Neeson was hired to read lines with them.)

Empress Yang Kwei Fei (1955)

I wonder, did Max Ophüls ever see a film by Kenji Mizoguchi? In any event, in 1955, Mizoguchi and his team went to Hong Kong to research their new project, *Empress Yang Kwei Fei.* It was a story set in China in the eighth century, and a third of the financing was coming from the Shaw Brothers company in Hong Kong. The hope was to find a visual style or the materials of décor. But they found that Hong Kong had nothing, and so they returned to Japan and began an immense amount of research, not just on Chinese history but on the particular look of things: fabric, porcelain, skin, and hair. For, apart from other innovations, this was to be Mizoguchi's first color film, in Daiecolor.

The story is ancient but kept alive in Chinese culture by more modern writings. Indeed, it was a favorite tale of wistfulness and yearning, and there is little question that Mizoguchi understood that tone exactly.

The emperor (Masayuki Mori, the expert swordsman from *Seven Samurai*) is a recent widower, and he is neglecting his affairs of state. An Lushan (So Yamamura), a coarse general, thinks to find him a new wife, and he notices Yu Juan (Machiko Kyo) working in the kitchens; he says she looks a lot like the emperor's first wife. He promotes her, and in due course she becomes Empress Yang Kwei Fei.

They are happy together for a time, but the country is in turmoil. An Lushan is at odds with the rest of his family. The people are confused and angry. An Lushan puts soldiers in the field. Disorder reigns. And so the idea is offered that Yang Kwei Fei must be to blame. She was a tool of An Lushan's family. She must be scapegoated. And the emperor is too restricted by protocol to save the woman he loves. We see a noose set up. We see her robe and her slippers left on the floor. And then her earrings fall in the dust. We do not see the execution, but there is some sense of calm returning.

Hiroshi Mizutani was in charge of design, and Kohei Sugiyama did the photography. This is a film of enclosing interiors, long corridors made for rules and ritual. We see very little open air or country. It is as if the world is a work of decorative art, full of soft, pastel colors. But the beauty it cherishes is also a reflection of the imperial helplessness. It is rather less art for art's sake than art as an abdication from responsibility. And a living person is sacrificed because of it. The lack of natural backgrounds and the very formalized story have put some people off—this is an artificial tragedy, whereas in Mizoguchi's *Ugetsu* and *Sansho* the tragedy is full of spilled life. But the abdication is a measure of fatalistic love and duty, and of the terrible lack of freedom in this China for even an emperor. You may recall the climactic episode of Ophüls's *Lola Montès*, in which Lola goes away rather than bring about the end of Ludwig's reign. *Empress Yang Kwei Fei* and *Lola* are films from the same year, filled with the impossible balance between authority and despair, beauty and prison.

Les Enfants du Paradis (1945)

As you grow up with film, people will tell you that you must see *Les Enfants du Paradis* (*The Children of Paradise*), and they are right. The virtues of this policy are many: First, you will encounter the vision and the style of Marcel Carné, a small master of film at the very least, and terribly neglected nowadays. You will see the beauties possible in black and white and in a world made through art direction, on sets. You will learn to love Paris. Above all, you will encounter the theater—and one of the most absurd, self-denying heresies prevalent among filmgoers is to disdain the theater.

In Paris and in Nice (at the Victorine Studios), in 1943, despite the many local difficulties, Carné set out to make a movie about French theater (or show business) of the 1840s. And though I doubt that it was the original intention, as the film grew it became the embodiment of French patriotism under occupation and, to a degree, the spirit of resistance (though later Carné would suffer charges of having been a collaborator). In any event, the first screenings came after the Liberation, and they helped the picture feel like a brave flag. A similar thing happened in Britain with *Henry V*.

The filming is itself the subject for a film. Vichy regulations at the time declared that a movie could not be longer than 2,750 meters (5,000 feet). The script (a masterpiece of wit and eloquence) was by the poet Jacques Prévert (who had been Carné's associate on many films). Roger Hubert was the director of photography. Alexandre Trauner was in charge of art direction, and his achievement is as outstanding as the task was difficult. This is a 3-hours15-minute film, full of sets and clothes. The music was by Maurice Thiriet and Joseph Kosma.

The film is a panorama of theatrical enterprise, from the lowest street performers to the loftiest actors, and Prévert's screenplay is a masterpiece that keeps everyone in action, or in mind, at the same time. Moreover, the warmth and kindness of the film is not easily separated from the fluency of the style, the movement of the camera, and the use of space. It is the simple truth that Renoir or Ophüls would have been proud to sign this film.

The cast is a record of Paris under the Nazis, and one can only regret that some of the players did collaborate, while some were falsely accused of it. It is hard when actors are held up to the standards of human beings. But "les enfants" include Arletty as Garance (very close to the spirit of France), Jean-Louis Barrault as the mime Baptiste, Pierre Brasseur as Lemaître, Marcel Herrand as Lacenaire, Pierre Renoir (Jean's brother) as Jéricho (it was to have been Céline's friend Robert Le Vigan, but he took cover after the Liberation), Maria Casares, Étienne Decroux, Fabien Loris, Léon Larive, Pierre Palau, Marcel Pérès, Albert Rémy, Jeanne Marken, and Gaston Modot. Bless them all.

Les Enfants Terribles (1950)

At the time it was made, fights and controversies hung over *Les Enfants Terribles*. Director Jean-Pierre Melville and novelist Jean Cocteau were not on the same wavelength politically. Melville had been in the Resistance, while Cocteau had been a cultural figure in occupied France. There was also dispute over control of the film. On the first day on set, Cocteau—having just shot his own *Orphée*—was heard to say "Cut" at the end of a take. And when he sought to make changes in the script he and Melville had worked on together, Melville retaliated, "No changes. I signed on to do Cocteau's novel."

Enough time has passed for the film to be seen as a masterpiece, and as something really made by Melville. But what is masterly is the delivery of a rare, ambiguous atmosphere—that of teenagers who refuse to "grow up" and seek to inhabit a pretend world in defiance of adulthood. It is a natural thing, charming yet dangerous: You see it obliquely in *Rebel Without a Cause* (a far more prosaic film in many ways) when the three kids play "house" in the deserted mansion. I am bound to say that part of the fascination of *Les Enfants Terribles* lies in the way this precious, theatrical world may have as its corollary, in the lives of most teenagers, the cinema itself. (This was treated very well in Bertolucci's *The Dreamers*, from a Gilbert Adair novel that consciously plays off *Les Enfants Terribles*.)

The place is Paris, just after World War II (it was the 1920s in the novel, published in 1929). Paul and his sister Elisabeth (of a certain, vague age) take refuge from the world in an apartment. Paul is ill: He has been wounded in a fight with Dargelos, a schoolmate, whom he loves. They play games, and in time they are joined by Gerard and Agathe. Gerard falls in love with Paul, and then Elisabeth. But Paul is drawn to Agathe, who looks like Dargelos. Elisabeth tries to rule the group, but the tensions are too great, and in the end both Paul and Elisabeth die. It is their secret alternative to adulthood.

A synopsis can make it sound confused, yet the flickering of attraction is so close to adolescent experience, so secretive and exultant, and so subject to power plays. The film's intensity begins in the exquisite gray imagery by Henri Decaë and by Émile Mathys's work on the prop-room sets. But it's the faces that are haunting, above all Nicole Stéphane as the empress figure Elisabeth. Cocteau's lover, Éduard Dermithe, is Paul (Melville fought this casting). Renée Cosima plays Dargelos and Agathe, and Jacques Bernard is Gerard.

Just as fascinating is the harmony or the counterpoint between Cocteau's voice as a narrator and the lovely, simple camera movements that are characteristic of Melville. One has to say that the world is not one to which Melville will ever return, but was there another occasion when Cocteau's vision was delivered with such strength and such intimations of a lost life? Enmity is not the worst breeding ground for a great film. Love and friendship may be deceptive and overrated.

The English Patient (1996)

The English Patient is the kind of picture that some people say David Lean used to make. It starts as something very small and particular—a lovely stone found in the desert. In this case, it is an adulterous love affair and its gamble with tragedy. Gradually the film lets its natural scene expand, or open out, and we see the desert and the relationship of Africa and Europe, the war, modern history. The key is the direction. Start small and grow. Whereas *Lawrence of Arabia,* say, is about the size of the desert, offered with the hope that some seed, some precious stone, will be there at the back of the cave. But working that way, it is far easier to discover . . . nothing.

Beyond that, *The English Patient* was in every way a triumph. It took a novel, by Michael Ondaatje, that even, or especially, its greatest admirers said could not be filmed—should not be tried. But encouraged by the novelist and by his producer, Saul Zaentz, Anthony Minghella embarked on an outstanding job of adaptation. And the key to Minghella's work, dramatically, was separation (I suspect it is his true subject): the way the world can organize itself so that beloveds are forced into their imagination, the natural home for love. And so we have a patient, terribly disfigured, Count Lazlo de Almásy (Ralph Fiennes), and a nurse, Hana (Juliette Binoche). And as she treats him flashbacks uncover, unflawed still, his love for Katharine Clifton (Kristin Scott Thomas).

Then, on the point of shooting, the picture's financing fell apart, because the committed parties believed the venture had no chance of success. Saul Zaentz then took it to Miramax, where the Weinstein Brothers (not without a tough bargain) took it up, enabled it to be made as Minghella wanted, and carried it through to modest but happy box-office success and a cascade of awards, including Best Picture, Best Director, and seven other Oscars.

This is also a film that believed in craft of the highest order, thus superb photography by John Seale (and Remi Adefarasin), editing and sound by Walter Murch, production design by Stuart Craig, costumes by Ann Roth, and a score by Gabriel Yared (with inspired use of popular songs).

At a key point in film history, David Lean believed that "epic" had to be for everyone, yet his films are hollow. Minghella, it seems to me, has seen that this is a myth: Nothing is for everyone. Works of choice rely on discrimination. But the epic genre—so long as it is founded in love, and probably unhappy love—can be for enough people for the venture to be worthwhile.

The playing is as modulated as the construction: Fiennes is mysterious, damaged, and charming; Scott Thomas (a limited actress) is artfully used; Binoche was a revelation; and there is terrific work from Willem Dafoe, Naveen Andrews, Colin Firth, Julian Wadham, Jürgen Prochnow, and many others. Not an easy film—but why should films be easy? Not a difficult film—how could so much revelation be obscure?

The Enigma of Kaspar Hauser (1974)

Maybe no other director has the genuine, mad fascination for marginal creatures that has compelled the career of Werner Herzog. Through fiction and documentary alike, in Germany and now living in America, for more than thirty years he has been obsessed with those figures who stand upright, make noise, but do not seem fully aware of the pedantic human code—thus from Kaspar Hauser to Klaus Kinski to Grizzly Man. One can't help feeling that Herzog, a most amiable man, is secretly wistful that he came into the world complete, unflawed and unburdened. Or is he keeping some secret?

Kaspar Hauser is based on fact, or history's taste for story. In Nuremberg in 1828, a sixteen-year-old appears. He has been kept locked up all his life, but now he wants to join the cavalry. He is a savage, in the sense that he has had no education. He is put in jail, and the inexorable attempt on his being and soul begins. He learns some words. He is put in a circus. A wise teacher takes him on. Kaspar becomes unhappy. He is attacked. He is murdered. The autopsy reports that he had brain damage.

Coming just a few years after François Truffaut's *The Wild Child* and a decade after Arthur Penn's *The Miracle Worker*, Herzog's film afforded easy distinctions: Truffaut and Penn had been at pains to prove the educability of their outsider figures, but Herzog sees *l'enfant sauvage* as a disconcerting comment on all our alleged codes of intellectual and sentimental order. In the sane way, years later, Herzog understood very well that the vainglorious white expert on bears in *Grizzly Man* was insane and self-destructive while the grizzly was simply the "other." In short, Truffaut and Penn both love society and uplift, whereas Herzog is not as convinced.

Of course, it matters a great deal in these arguments that Herzog was using not an actor but Bruno S., a real reject of society and a youth of uncertain disposition. Was Herzog exploiting Bruno? The question could not be avoided. And his answer was that there must be an authentic inner spark—no matter how damaged—in someone like Bruno, which was reason for making the film. That argument became a great deal more complicated if one paused to consider whether Klaus Kinski was acting mad, like a fox, or was someone who was both mad and an actor.

In an opening dream sequence, beautifully shot by Klaus Wyborny, Kaspar (we presume, we do not see him) is floating on a lyrical river, being stared at with mounting hostility by people. And I think that that "civilized" reaction is what amuses and bewilders Herzog. There is enough of the anthropologist in him to see that one abnormality is much like another. So how do we make rules that must be observed?

Most of the film was shot by Jörg Schmidt-Reitwein, and edited by Beate Mainka-Jellinghaus. For me, this is one of Herzog's most successful films, but some sign that his lifelong pursuit of the same type of specimen has not always avoided monotony.

Erotikon (1920)

Mauritz Stiller's *Erotikon* is the earliest film in this book that the modern viewer has to watch with a modern sensibility—by which I mean, in the fear that you might miss something. Yes, it is a silent film, made in Sweden, with clothes and décor of the period—and very handsome clothes, I might add. But concessions need go no further. For it is a story about four absolutely modern people: a professor of entomology, his admiring niece, his distracted wife, and her romantic interest, a sculptor. It is a film about love, marriage, outside attraction, and flirting. And just as it accomplishes a neat ironic flip in its arrangement—two couples change partners—it leaves you in no doubt about the stability or permanence of the new partnerships. Flirting, curiosity, being alive—call it what you will—leaves these people as vulnerable to looking at fresh faces as any of us. Why has Cupid wings? is a question asked in *La Règle du Jeu* (though it comes from Beaumarchais). The answer: to fly away again.

So the extraordinary refreshment of *Erotikon* after the American silent film is the freedom from guilt or gloom in people moving on. Moreover, the game is played with degrees of irony, impishness, teasing, and sheer naughtiness in which—most notably—women take the lead and men reclaim that stodginess that is so often theirs in life. Watching this film is like watching real people alive today, and hardly a line or a situation comes without at least a double meaning. And so whether Professor Leo Carpentier (Anders De Wahl) is lecturing on tree beetles or the characters are attending a strange theatrical performance, it is taken for granted that the "act" reflects upon their lives and behavior.

Quite simply, these are sophisticated people with complicated feelings such as were seldom allowed on the American screen before sound. The legend goes that Ernst Lubitsch and Charlie Chaplin (as the latter filmed *A Woman of Paris*) were as much impressed with Stiller as was Louis B. Mayer when he recruited him for Hollywood. But the legend is mealymouthed. Stiller is avant-garde in 1920, with a camera style that is beginning to use space, levels of action, doorways and windows—there is even a mirror shot—to give action a greater feeling of physical reality. There is a close-up of a woman at the piano, from a slightly raised angle and just a little askew, that is giddy with emotion—and Stiller repeats it to help us get the point.

Erotikon comes from a play by Ferenc Herczeg, and the screenplay was done by Gustaf Molander, Arthur Nordén, and Stiller. The photography is by Henrik Jaenzon, the art direction by Axel Esbensen. The acting is the strength of the film, and by far the central performance is Tora Teje as Irene, the professor's wife. She is fickle yet firm in herself, witty but capable of being hurt. She is a flirt who knows she is playing with her life. I don't think a woman had been better in a movie up to this point in time. Also with Lars Hanson and Karin Molander—who was between marriages to Gustaf Molander and Lars Hanson.

E.T. is the model for American culture circa 1980. In trying to give identity and a look to his magical creature, his E.T., sometimes known as Puck, Steven Spielberg followed an old Disney concept: that people love the look of a baby, the wide brow, the clear, pure eye. So he pasted together a baby's face with a photo of Carl Sandburg's eyes, and the mixture of baby and sage was exquisite. Later he added the forehead of Hemingway, the mouth of Albert Einstein, and a voice derived from Debra Winger.

One could surely go further in reading this film for all tastes. Not only does it presuppose an alien world likely to be friendly to ours (to have seen the same movies), but it also hints at a world where parents may have failed, but never mind, the children can carry through. You can see that as a testament to the young, the newcomers, the fresh blood of pioneers—or you may be disturbed by the feeling of such trust and confidence being placed in the young, the ignorant, and those all too ready to lead them. For example, *E.T.* would be a very much more worrying (and interesting) film if E.T. himself had just one scene where he was less than perfect and a little inclined to play with children in the way that American kids came to play with their plastic E.T.'s.

Spielberg would also say that it was the experience of making the film that left him wanting to have children, and that he regarded the story as a precious trust not to be overexploited. Well, something happened along the way. Someone seems to have been convinced that this was a very big picture, if only because it does flatter its child characters so much by placing them as the figures most likely to see and understand E.T. And while E.T. can get high, he is too high-minded for any real wickedness, or even naughtiness. He does suggest a world of pretzeloid gods that is slightly stronger than even the societies Spielberg has seen in America.

Of course, Spielberg was still working, thinking, and changing, and you have to see *E.T.* as a further digestive process added on to *Close Encounters*—as well as a final rejection of aliens as interesting characters. So it settles for being a fabulous entertainment, one that says, "Nobody's afraid of Steven Spielberg," after a few films that had been pretty scary. Melissa Mathison wrote a script from Spielberg's idea. Allen Daviau photographed it and gave a nice enchanted air to the forest. Carlo Rambaldi designed the creature E.T., and it's a marvel in an age of robots that every house doesn't have one by now.

What does it mean? I don't think it means a thing. Which is rare in Spielberg's work and may account for his respectful attitude to *E.T.* Predictably, John Williams did the music, and the fun was enormously enhanced by the earthiness of the kids, Henry Thomas as Elliott and Drew Barrymore as Gertie. Peter Coyote was the figure of authority required for a little suspense. The film cost $10.5 million, and the worldwide gross now stands at $756 million—is that Carl Sandburg smiling, or Ernest Hemingway?

Europa '51 (1952)

The first fifteen minutes or so of this film offer a tour de force. Irene Girard comes home to her apartment. She is a socialite, beautiful, wealthy, but driven to keep up with her social calendar. She is late for a dinner party in her own flat. As she gets ready, she barely has time to notice or talk to her twelve-year-old son, Michel. Her husband, George, is part of her hectic life. The boy goes to bed as the dinner party begins. Then the maid brings word: The boy has had a fall and has a broken hip. But at the hospital, the word comes out: The boy had tried to kill himself. He dies.

Of course, Ingrid Bergman is Irene, and in the English version (it was filmed simultaneously in Italian) that made her delivery haughty, Knightsbridge, self-centered. But the loss of her son destroys the old Irene. She briefly listens to a friend, a Communist newspaper editor, Andrea (Ettore Giannini), who tells her there are so many sick children, most of them too poor to be helped. Irene gradually descends from her social privilege. She tries to help the poor. She hovers between Communism and God, and it may be that she has become a saint. But her husband and her family turn on her for her desertion of her own class interests, and she is committed to a mental institution. The film closes with her face—tearful but beatific—gazing through the bars of her prison.

As social parable and woman's picture (and it is both), *Europa '51* seems to me by far the most successful of the films Ingrid and Roberto Rossellini made together, more moving than *Journey to Italy* and more natural and fluent in its overall acting style. It was written by Rossellini, Sandro de Feo, Mario Pannunzio, Ivo Perilli, and Brunello Rondi, and the picture was produced by the triumvirate of Rossellini, Carlo Ponti, and Dino De Laurentiis. The presence of the last two may account for the strong narrative push. The photography (very good in the realist tradition, yet nearly noir in some lighting) is by Aldo Tonti, and Renzo Rossellini wrote the music.

It can easily be argued that the politics are naïve, but nothing lets us forget the biting impact of that opening sequence, where selfishness and lack of caring have accounted for the desolation of a child. The shift Bergman makes from that cold Irene to the troubled, far quieter saint is a great piece of acting, and she gets real help from Alexander Knox as her husband and Giulietta Masina as a humble wife and mother.

Europa '51 actually asks, What can be done with the impoverished of the world to prevent more wars? It may be that nothing has helped that dilemma more than the increased prosperity of our societies, but Irene is a test-case figure in the debate among socialism, religious faith, and some agnostic, charitable impulse. The film was badly reviewed, but in hindsight one wonders why. Bergman makes a legitimate and truthful journey from boredom and carelessness to commitment. It is a movie that resonates with the deep-seated urge for moral reform after the war.

Eve (1962)

As Joseph Losey was filming *The Damned* on location in Dorset in 1961, producers Robert and Raymond Hakim sent him the James Hadley Chase novel *Eve* and asked if he was interested. The Hakims already had Stanley Baker and Jeanne Moreau signed on for the lead roles, and Losey always felt that Baker had suggested him. It was the story of a writer in Hollywood who falls for a courtesan, and Losey liked it, though he wanted to change the setting from Hollywood to Europe. The Hakims agreed to that, and a deal was made.

For Losey—as artist, exile, and unhappily married man—this was an intensely personal project, and I think it's fair to say that an insecure man saw the property as a chance to explore female domination (which did not appeal very much to the Hakims). Losey proposed Hugo Butler as his scriptwriter, but the two old friends (*The Prowler*) no longer got on. Butler wanted things cut-and-dried and may have flinched at the weakness of the main male character. Losey was constantly drawing his own feelings into the script and making the character self-destructive. So Evan Jones was hired instead, and things improved. But the Hakims did not like the script. The project nearly foundered then and there, but a group meeting of all parties went through the script, and a version was agreed on.

It was now set in Venice and Rome. Tyvian Jones (Baker) has stolen a book his dead brother wrote and claimed it as his own. He takes up with Eve Olivier (Moreau), and she plays all his guilt and weaknesses. There was some early shooting in Venice at film-festival time (done by Henri Decaë), and then Gianni Di Venanzo came on for the main shoot. Richard MacDonald was art director, and old buildings and paintings were used as commentaries on the story. It was Losey's original intention to make a sound track with Miles Davis and Billie Holiday recordings, but in the end Davis was dropped, the Holiday cues were greatly reduced, and Michel Legrand did a score (one that Losey admired).

Losey's cut ran 155 minutes. He cut that by twenty minutes under pressure, and then the Hakims hacked it down further to 115 minutes (or less—prints vary). Their treatment of the film was appalling, and the issue may be confused in some eyes. But one day the truth will be revealed: that *Eve* is an extraordinary film, absolutely novel in its view of male humiliation and of this monstrous queen-bee figure who rules her world. Moreau never did anything stronger or more dangerous. Baker is brilliant and tortured. And this was before Losey did *The Servant.*

Although Losey fought with Di Venanzo, the look of Venice (especially) is unsurpassed in film, and the camera movements are both formal and emotional. The cast also includes Virna Lisi, Giorgio Albertazzi, James Villiers, Riccardo Garrone, and Lisa Gastoni. In short, this is one of the great lost films of all time and one of the most revealing works by Losey.

Exodus (1960)

Starting the end of the 1950s, in a bold but deliberate way, Otto Preminger addressed some of the eternally contentious issues of human government: Does the law behave justly (*Anatomy of a Murder*)? Can nationalism compromise with enemy nations (*Exodus*)? Is there a system of government that functions fairly (*Advise and Consent*)? Can a church exist without destroying the privacy of faith (*The Cardinal*)? That anyone should mount such a campaign exposes the awkward mix of intelligence, didacticism, and chutzpah in Preminger. Still, the achievement of the films is considerable. Just because the problems uncovered in *Exodus* have hardly improved in more than forty years that's no reason to forget or reject the picture and the overall feeling that intelligence and good drama can convey the conflicting points of view in a great crisis.

The key to the work is to trace the way in which the prolonged partisanship of the Leon Uris novel has passed through the hands of screenwriter Dalton Trumbo and then through Preminger's subtle mise-en-scène to make a study in ambivalence. Yes, the central characters in *Exodus* are Jewish (or Zionist), and the film's central task is to show the foundation of the Israeli state. But this is not a film that makes a travesty of the Arab or Palestinian point of view. There are good and bad men on both sides. One day there will be exhaustion, and perhaps from that something like compromise. But to take the title of the great Chris Marker documentary on Israel, *Description of a Struggle*, so the Preminger epic—filmed in Super Panavision 70, and 212 minutes—is actually far more objective and balanced than anyone had reason to hope. Forty-eight years later, it can be shown without apology. Forty-five years before *Exodus, Birth of a Nation* appeared—and it could hardly be shown in 1960.

All that said, there is a problem, which is Paul Newman's rather bad-tempered attitude toward the film. One can see all too clearly that he did not feel easy playing Ari Ben Canaan. But he might have realized that an epic does deserve a committed energy at its core, such as Charlton Heston gave to several films. On the other hand, Eva Marie Saint is excellent as the American nurse through whose eyes the story is revealed.

The Ernest Gold music is as strident (though it won an Oscar) as Sam Leavitt's camerawork is intimate and intelligent. Time and again, Preminger uses depth of focus and reframing movements to enlarge the scope of an argument. And, for the most part, the supporting acting is as rounded and tolerant as the overall sense of context: Ralph Richardson as the British general, Peter Lawford (rather overdone as an officer), Lee J. Cobb, Sal Mineo (very good; he was nominated for Best Supporting Actor), John Derek (surprisingly good), Hugh Griffith, Gregory Ratoff, Felix Aylmer, David Opatoshu (outstanding), Jill Haworth, and Marius Goring.

The Exorcist (1973)

Nothing dates worse than horror. It was not that anyone was bound to "believe" in *The Exorcist* in 1973—though I think it was apparent even then that the film was taking dangerous risks with anyone who had a heightened but unstable (is there a difference?) level of faith. Of course, the film was a giveaway even then: It simply would not have been made if director William Friedkin or anyone else concerned (including the novelist William Peter Blatty) had actually recognized and honored an extensive and authentic religious faith in their potential audience. If you credit God, *The Exorcist* is hideous—if you believe in horror, it runs the risk of being fun. The chance to be that "horrific" was a signal that we had lost our faith—and thus, by implication, the only believers left in society were extremists, the outrageous, or the crazy. And we expect them to fend for themselves.

Nevertheless, there was an inventiveness in the ingrowing claustrophobia: the way the wintry Georgetown scenes give way to that cockpit of a room where the battle over Regan's body will take place. The special effects were startling and very frightening, and we were still an audience unfamiliar with that very unsettling way of doing films. And there was a chemistry between the rather numb puppy-fat of Linda Blair and the infernal voice of Mercedes McCambridge that came from within her. Going into the film in 1973, one expected an ordeal—and one was not disappointed. You had to hang on to the ride.

Then in 2000 the film was rereleased, with ten or so minutes of allegedly more explicit material—and audiences were rocking with laughter. I suppose in part that was because the film had an ominous reputation for horror that a new generation of kids found they could handle with ease. Add in the acceleration in disbelief that had set in during the years since 1973. But now the threadbare purpose and the absolute absence of a real interest in fear (or its meanings) was naked to behold. The film had been exploitation—and once that atmosphere had subsided, leaving just the scaffolding, then the naïveté of the filmmakers seemed embarrassing.

In the end, I think, it may be more disturbing if a child looks on the world with just a hint of unkindness or insanity than if her head spins and she vomits green bile and walks upside down on her hands and feet like a beast. What can Satan do that we don't do anyway? The devil, in other words, is in the fine details of human behavior, as opposed to the lavish warping of nature that marked *The Exorcist*. And once the technology of this enterprise becomes central, then the lack of imaginative commitment leaves one very cold.

Not that anyone lets the 1973 film down, except for how Friedkin and Blatty betray their own suspense. Linda Blair works hard, along with Ellen Burstyn and Kitty Winn, and you can sometimes feel a trace of dread in Jason Miller and Max von Sydow. As for Lee J. Cobb, I just feel he's wrong. Of course, the *Exorcist* story goes on and on, and I fear that it is well past self-parody now, but the cinema's capacity to goose us has become as stupid as an uncle who has only one trick to try out at parties.

Exstase (1933)

We see several keys tried in a lock, and then a husband carries his bride over the threshold. He is a middle-aged man. He wants to get his tight shoes off. He rearranges things on top of a dresser. He is a fusspot. She is played by Hedy Kiesler, twenty perhaps. She wants much more than her shoes removed. She will sprawl on the marriage bed. But nothing happens. We never learn why this marriage was undertaken or why the man will take no steps to consummate it. But it is apparent already that Ms. Kiesler is especially beautiful and that the Czech director, Gustav Machatý, has an eye for composition that is fascinating. Although it is 1933, the film is in many respects like a silent: There is a little dialogue, in German, but it is badly synchronized. We are on the brink of a sensation in film history.

There is an almost immediate divorce, whereupon the girl, Eva, runs off to the open countryside. She is riding a horse. She comes to a lake and tears off her white suit to go swimming naked. Then her horse runs off and finds a gang of engineers working. One of them follows the horse back to Eva, but only after she has run naked across the meadows. She and the engineer are attracted, and very soon they are in each other's arms. That's when the most beautiful passage of the film occurs. She is lying down, her arms over her head, but it is clear that she is having an orgasm.

Hedwig Kiesler was the daughter of a Viennese banker, and she had been in a few films before Machatý discovered her for *Exstase*. The film became a scandal, not least in the eyes of Fritz Mandl, a munitions millionaire, who now married Hedy. He tried to destroy every print, but then she divorced him and moved on toward Hollywood, where she would be Hedy Lamarr. Machatý made only a few other films, and his 1931 *From Saturday to Sunday* is outstanding.

It's clear that he had been influenced by Soviet cinema in his framing and his vision, but it's hard to see that *Exstase* has any other point beyond saying sex is good and suggesting that Hedy is great at it. The nudity is utterly natural, and I'm not sure that Hedy was ever again as relaxed onscreen. Considering all the restrictions that came in in 1933, the orgasm scene is as startling as it is explicit. What is Eva thinking of? Well, it looks as if thought itself has yielded to sensation, but there are stories that even then Ms. Kiesler was planning developments in radar, et cetera, that would later win her government praise.

So *Exstase* is one of those talked-about films that fully repays the wait and the search. It is brimmingly sexual and not at all dirty. Machatý is a subject for further research—but so is Hedy Lamarr. She ended up so oddly, as an old-lady shoplifter in Florida, suing her own ghostwriters for stories they told in her "autobiography." We need a movie of *The Hedy Lamarr Story*—but is there anyone lovely enough to try the part?

The Exterminating Angel (1962)

Do you remember the cinema as a child? Wasn't it the first great chamber you had ever known in which there was no natural light, or windows? (Incidentally, just consider how that absence prepares us for the brightest light and the biggest window of our lives.) Do you remember in the absolutely packed circumstances of, say, *Rear Window* that first, tingling feeling of being unable to get out, certainly as long as the show continued? (By the way, do you see how the "rear window" at the movies must be that small rectangle of glass through which the projector pokes its searching finger?) In other words, do not be too surprised if the lifelong filmgoer develops a certain claustrophobia. And don't look vacant when people wonder what on earth *The Exterminating Angel* could mean.

At a very nice, rather well-to-do establishment on the Calle de la Providencia ("a wealthy district"), society people gather for an event. It is somewhere in South America, yet all the obvious European niceties are being observed. People wear evening dress. Dinner is expected, with drinks and small talk. But then when that hour is approached when people might be expected to leave, to go back to their homes, an inexplicable and irrational inability to quit overtakes them. We see no booby traps over the doorways, no firing squads waiting in the courtyards. There is nothing like a ravenous mob ready to eat the well-fed guests after the party. Still, collectively, they cannot muster the energy—or is it the belief—to be out of the place.

Luis Buñuel did the script, from a treatment by himself and Luis Alcoriza called "The Castaways of the Calle de la Providencia," (which originally came from an unpublished play by Jose Bergamin) and it is quite true that this becalmed soirée turns into a kind of desert island in which people succumb increasingly to privation and neurosis. The picture was made in Mexico, and the esteemed Gabriel Figueroa was in charge of the photography, in which anxious gloom steadily usurps the bright light. Jesús Bracho did the art direction, and it is another mark of the film that the physical splendor of the house decays like a place abandoned.

In my opinion, this is the first of Buñuel's modern masterpieces: serene, sardonic, sinister, witty. It is a movie in which the comedy and the menace are hand in glove. Buñuel no longer seeks to shock or shatter the bourgeoisie. Instead, he invades their confidence in one of their central rituals, the party. And, of course, he declines always to stand up for a meaning. The Spanish version of the film actually had a title warning against that search. With English-speaking viewers, saying that would only provoke them. Of course, it is the multiplicity of meanings that is important. But this is a great film, and the first clear proof that in marrying stylishness and bourgeois tastes, Buñuel had become his title.

With Silvia Pinal, Claudio Brook, Antonio Bravo, Enrique Rambal, César del Campo, Luis Beristáin, Augusto Benedico, and Jacqueline Andere.

Eyes Wide Shut (1999)

This is the last film of Stanley Kubrick—indeed, he died so soon after delivery of his cut that the legend quickly grew that he intended doing more things to his movie. But it's hard at the end not to see the substantial gulf between the man who knew "everything" about filmmaking but not nearly enough about life or love or sex (somehow, over the years, those subjects did get left out). Not that the film lacks intrigue or suggestiveness. Mastery can be felt. It is just that the master seems to have forgotten, or given up on figuring out, why mastery should be any more valuable than supremacy at chess or French polishing.

Bill and Alice Harford live in the Manhattan that can be built at Pinewood studios. He is a doctor; she is mother to his child. They also look like Tom Cruise and Nicole Kidman, who at that time were probably the most contentious romantic couple in the world. They go to a god-awful party, and in a very mild way they both flirt with strangers. What other things are such parties for, except immense business deals and the arrangements for assassination, all done over the pool table?

Later, Alice admits to Bill a sexual fantasy from her past (the fleshing out of a passing and innocent encounter), which then turns into a vivid blue-and-white movie in Bill's mind—the first sex Stanley had ever shot, I think. This haunts Bill and sends him closer and closer to infidelity, a bizarre chain of events, ending at the kind of Long Island orgy you've always been warned about, where—possibly—a woman is killed. Or did she die of ennui?

Eyes Wide Shut comes from Arthur Schnitzler's *Traumnovelle,* and Frederic Raphael has written an engaging and funny book about how he was called in to do the screenplay with Kubrick. It is the first clear cross-fingers over the fate of the film.

It took an eternity to make: Harvey Keitel and Jennifer Jason Leigh shot a lot of film, only to be replaced. There are several piquant supporting performances (do we know this pattern?), from Todd Field, Sky Dumont, Rade Serbedzija, Leelee Sobieski, and Alan Cumming; there is a ponderous contribution from Sydney Pollack. Cruise seems out of his depth in every instant, and very uneasy, whereas Kidman seems alert, wicked, and emerging from storage.

There was a film to be made, I suspect, in which Kidman (in savage, comic disguise) was all of the temptresses sent to lead Bill astray. And Bill should have been Jim Carrey. I am not being facetious. The terrible fake dread in the picture cries out for comic explosion—*Alice in New York*?

Of course, *Eyes Wide Shut* is immaculate: Les Tomkins and Roy Walker did the décor, Larry Smith was the lighting cameraman, and Marit Allen did the costumes. The music is diverse, highbrow, and rather boastful, like an intellectual's *Name That Tune.* It is a shock to find that the film is only 159 minutes. Every frame feels like a prison.

Eyes Without a Face (1960)

The strange career of Georges Franju (1912–87) is in danger of being forgotten. So let us stress first that he was cofounder, with Henri Langlois, of the French Cinémathèque (film archive). In addition, he was a celebrated director of documentaries in whom it was easy to detect the vision of a poet: *Le Sang des Bêtes* (1949) is ostensibly about the industry that slaughters animals for meat, yet in truth it concerns the cruelties we elect to ignore. *Hôtel des Invalides* (1952) was intended (by its sponsors) as a record of the French war museum, yet in Franju's hands it is a warning against war itself. Those and other documentaries made it clear that Franju was obsessed with everyday uneasiness.

Eyes Without a Face, or *Les Yeux Sans Visage* (it sometimes goes under other titles, like *The Horror Chamber of Dr. Faustus,* that show the business's efforts to pass it off as raw horror), is one of the cinema's great evocations of the tragedy of isolation. Dr. Génessier (Pierre Brasseur) is a sophisticated cosmetic surgeon living outside Paris. He has a beloved daughter, Christiane (Edith Scob), whose face was ruined in a car crash suffered while he was driving. And so, as a sideline to his regular work, he makes it his business to kidnap beautiful young women, remove their faces, and give them to his daughter.

This story came from a novel by Jean Redon and was adapted for the screen by Pierre Boileau and Thomas Narcejac (the team responsible for the book behind *Vertigo*) and Claude Sautet, who also worked as an assistant director on the film. Pierre Gascar did the dialogue. Of course, the setup does resemble that of *Frankenstein,* and Pierre Brasseur's Génessier is another brilliant, arrogant scientist who is overstepping ethical considerations. With his assistant, Louise (a grim Alida Valli), he hunts for victims in a Citroën, prowling a nocturnal Paris superbly photographed by Eugen Shuftan.

But the film shifts toward the lyrical as it identifies Christiane as a hopeless beneficiary of all this mayhem. Edith Scob was more a beauty than an actress, and she wears a mask most of the time, but the image of her in a flowing white gown, in command of her father's Doberman pack, is one of the most moving and ambiguous sights in horror films. I don't think one can claim that *Eyes Without a Face* transcends the horror genre. In some ways it is not as subtle as Franju's *La Tête Contre les Murs* (1958), about a man who is sent to an asylum by a strict father (Brasseur again). But the two films could easily play together as a haunting package on fathers who have betrayed and damaged their children. And *Eyes Without a Face* finally wonders what is beauty—if it is exceptional, then perhaps the hideous will qualify? Are we sure we know one from the other?

Made almost entirely at night, in Shuftan's lustrous black and white, *Eyes Without a Face* has production design by Auguste Capelier and a great score by Maurice Jarre. It also stars Juliette Mayniel, François Guérin, Alexandre Rignault, Charles Blavette, and Claude Brasseur.

The Fabulous Baker Boys (1989)

The Fabulous Baker Boys is increasingly hard to explain or understand as the years pass. On the one hand, it is rich entertainment; a fascinating glimpse of another way to make a musical; one more proof that Jeff Bridges is the essential, if still unknown, actor of modern American cinema; and the most serious testimony in the agonizing question, Whatever happened to Michelle Pfeiffer? One other thing: The film is unmistakably an example of the kind of picture nobody would make nowadays. Yet the pleasure in watching it does not diminish.

The Baker boys are Jack (Jeff Bridges) and Frank (Beau Bridges). They have a double act that Beau, the fusspot, has managed to screw into the ground or into the safe but diminishing entertainment circuits of the Pacific Northwest. But Jack, it is clear, is moody with crushed aspirations of being Seattle's Bill Evans. As their act sinks a little, they think of taking on a girl singer. There is a very funny audition passage where we get to realize how dreadful and copycat girl singers have become. Then in walks Susie Diamond (Pfeiffer), untidy, a mess, but a singer who could be playing the old Keystone Korner in San Francisco. It is cloud-cuckoo-land that this girl is looking for a job. But it is only another kind of cloud-cuckoo-land that Michelle Pfeiffer has never been used this way again. She can sing. Right, you may reply, but she could act once, too, and find herself in terrific pictures. There's so much she seems to have given up.

The movie was written and directed by Steve Kloves, and it still leaves one with the feeling that Kloves ought to be making a couple of films a year, in the way that Michael Curtiz did once. Yes, you know what's coming in *The Fabulous Baker Boys,* and it's not brain surgery. But you have lost faith that anyone can deliver it so sweetly.

Jeff makes a lot of a thinly written part, but be careful what you wish for: If this were the real Bill Evans, it would be a horrible tragedy, whereas what the film does deliver is a Diamond in the rough. Beau Bridges is a good example of a little goes a long way, and it's not quite plausible that Jack has stuck around so long.

Dave Grusin did the real piano playing. Michael Ballhaus does a superb job as cameraman, and William Steinkamp did the editing. The supporting cast includes Ellie Raab, Xander Berkeley, Dakin Matthews, Albert Hall, and a comic Jennifer Tilly. But it's the Susie Diamond show, and while everyone remembers the fully choreographed "Makin' Whoopee" on top of a piano, Pfeiffer also sings "Feelings," "More Than You Know," "Can't Take My Eyes Off You," "Ten Cents a Dance," "The Look of Love," and "My Funny Valentine" as if they'd just been written. Time was when the thought of Michelle Pfeiffer was as thrilling as the sound of Carole Lombard, but something clouded her sun or moon, and that red-rimmed sadness in her eyes took over.

A Face in the Crowd (1957)

This is another of Elia Kazan's rather paranoid visions of the South—it was shot largely in Arkansas and Memphis—when deep down he seems to be most hostile to television and a kind of acting that has abandoned responsibility. So it's a tricky film to handle, especially since its central character and villain, Lonesome Rhodes—surely ugly enough in the movie—helped launch the career of the "lovable" Andy Griffith on TV.

At the outset, Lonesome is a dormant force, discovered by Marcia Jeffries (Patricia Neal) and turned into a radio personality clearly founded on Will Rogers—a raconteur, a homespun philosopher, and a casual political guide. But there's a point in the film, never really explained, where Rhodes becomes a monster seemingly directed by much larger political forces and set on a national career. You can say that the warning is clear and that there's a natural arc to the rise and fall of Rhodes, but the film seems a touch too tidy or tame in the way it wraps Rhodes up instead of leaving America looking like a flock of sheep he surveys.

The film is based on a short story, "Your Arkansas Traveler," written by the screenwriter, Budd Schulberg. Schulberg is a writer who caught fire in the 1930s, and this exposé has a certain touch of Preston Sturges to it—of sheer idiocy rampant—until Lonesome's career is tangled romantically with the Patricia Neal character and the way he dumps her for that cute drum majorette played by Lee Remick. What the film now lacks is the formation of an entourage like the group that carried Ronald Reagan to power.

Of course, *A Face in the Crowd* came only five years after Kazan's "deal" with the House Committee on Un-American Activities, and it could be described as a bold comeback. But in truth there is muddle over comedy and melodrama and a failure to sustain an overall satiric drive. It's the ordinary characters—as played by Neal, Walter Matthau, and Anthony Franciosa—who are least surely defined. Whereas when Lonesome gets his hands on the song "Vitajex," the exhilaration is brilliant and terrifying, in that it points to a way in which we like to bamboozle ourselves. It also lets the wild energy in Andy Griffith seem dangerous and infectious.

So leaving Lonesome as a ranting wreck, unaware of his own oblivion, is too easy or cute. Neal may save herself, but only at the cost of Lonesome's thundering on, ready to treat America in the same way. And Kazan could probably have been sharper in showing how a ham actor comes to believe in his own performance and is lost to reality. We need to see a second part in which Lonesome becomes someone like Lyndon Johnson: verifiable and understandable, yet out of his own control. There are good supporting performances from a range of Southern actors, and Harry Stradling does his best with the camera, trying to match the harshness of TV coverage before color with the noirish interiors of Lonesome's world.

Faces (1968)

After 1959's *Shadows,* John Cassavetes had two adventures in conventional film-directing, *Too Late Blues* and *A Child Is Waiting,* that ended badly. He was still acting: *The Killers* and *The Dirty Dozen,* and *Johnny Staccato* and other things on television. But this left nearly ten years between the first screening of *Shadows* and the opening of *Faces. Faces* began life in 1964 as a script (around two hundred pages) that Cassavetes had written and that he was using in "rehearsals" as he tried to assemble a cast. There was thought of doing it as a play, but that shifted to a 16 mm film. It's a very simple setup: Richard (John Marley) is married to Maria (Lynn Carlin). He picks up Jeannie (Gena Rowlands), and Maria has an affair with Chet (Seymour Cassel).

The action covers twelve hours, but the shooting filled the first half of 1965. The cast and crew assembled at the Cassavetes house; they had dinner; they started to rehearse and improvise; and then gradually the camera came into use in long takes. Cassavetes was far more concerned with the actors than the shooting. Al Ruban, a novice, became director of photography; but he was given very little instruction as to where to put the camera or how to light the scene, so he did what he could to follow the action. They regularly shot until the ten-minute magazine was empty. And they ended up with about 150 hours of film, which Cassavetes and Ruban then edited.

The film cost about $225,000, though no actors were paid until the profits came in. The final cut was 130 minutes, but there had been much longer versions. The method—letting the scenes develop slowly—was such that the film could have been twelve hours or longer. For there is this conundrum about *Faces:* It is fiction, written and shot, yet it aspires to a reality that resists shaping, form, or anything other than duration.

As a portrait of middle-aged people who are "successes" (Richard is financially secure), it is grueling, depressing, and yet so filled with truth and good acting that it's very worthwhile. It's rather as if the characters from a Nicholas Ray film of the 1950s had assembled, without plot, and just begun to interact in ways that would uncover their unhappiness and alienation. What is depressing is the odd feeling that film's helpless recording process is only hammering the despondency home. And making it self-dramatizing. *Faces* is always said to have been a family experience, yet clearly for Cassavetes family was a very unhappy place.

At first screenings, the film was poorly received. But at the Venice Film Festival, John Marley won the acting prize. In New York, critic Andrew Sarris prevailed on Richard Roud to show *Faces* at the New York Film Festival, and it won admirers, Martin Scorsese for one. Pauline Kael said the acting was so bad it was embarrassing. But the film was talked about, and it got a release. Seymour Cassel and Lynn Carlin were nominated for supporting actor and actress Oscars. The film took in $8 million in rentals, an astonishing coup, and a figure that now looks so large as to be questionable. The year 1968 was a troubled time, and *Faces* is part of the proof.

Fahrenheit 451 (1966)

There is a fascinating diary on the making of this film, composed by François Truffaut under increasing stress and published in the journal *Cahiers du Cinéma* in English. The melancholy of the journal comes from the mounting alienation between Truffaut and his star, Oskar Werner, the man whose career had been so boosted by Truffaut's *Jules et Jim* (1962) and who was now looking for a route to stardom. But as the filming goes on, Truffaut is increasingly dismayed at the vanity of his old friend and more and more intrigued by the beguiling actor Cyril Cusack, playing the fire captain. Unfortunately, Cusack's character is the film's villain, and so the ironic humanity of the captain is an asset Truffaut can never turn in at the bank.

You can see the appeal of Ray Bradbury's novel about a future world that hunts down books as the germ of subversion. And Truffaut does a lovely job, in snow-touched woods, with his resistance community of freedom fighters who are memorizing the text of books so that they can pass them on to the future. The film does look good, and cameraman Nicolas Roeg does very well by the primary colors of this tyrannous state, especially the fire-engine red. The music is by Bernard Herrmann, and if it is not quite as good as he managed on *The Bride Wore Black*, still, it helps the picture.

The obstinate problem is with the leads. Werner looks lost far more than self-aggrandizing. It's as if he didn't understand the dynamic of a suspense film and how far that demands a kind of coded response in his face. Truffaut said he was far happier with Julie Christie—but really, it doesn't show. She has a rich opportunity in two roles: the automaton wife and the resistance fighter. It hardly seems possible to fail, but Christie—never an especially intelligent actress—seems to be working without direction.

This suggests another problem: Truffaut never learned to speak decent English. In his own language, especially in these early years, he had a terrific rapport with his players, a kind of intimacy that shows in every small movement of a face. But is it possible that he simply couldn't get through to actors who had no French? In turn, this reminds one of the considerable trouble French-speaking directors have usually had with English-speaking casts. Jean Renoir's American films are more worthwhile than *Fahrenheit 451*, but is it possible that his actors were striving to hear his nuances? A concomitant of this problem is this question: How many of the French critics who adored American cinema always grasped the exact intonations and idioms of American dialogue? *Fahrenheit 451* is an interesting curiosity, but it helps show the gulf between the two cultures.

Or was it that Truffaut had such a deep-seated prejudice against what he called "Anglo-Saxon cinema" that he inevitably began to manufacture problems for himself? It's strange and comic, for here is the man who—apparently—heard every bit of innuendo and superciliousness in the talk in Hitchcock films. Or was it that the pictures in those films told him how to hear the words?

Fallen Angels (1995)

I was in a video store, Le Video in San Francisco, renting Wong Kar-Wai's *Fallen Angels.* There were two guys behind the counter, very young, and as they noticed *Fallen Angels* passing through their system, one said to the other, "That's my favorite Wong Kar-Wai." The other guy was eager. "Does it have two stories?" he asked. "I don't know," said the first guy, "I've never seen it all."

Fallen Angels indeed, and somehow this seemed to me not just classic Wong but a scene from his work in an age when even Nicole Kidman will tell you he is one of the most important and innovative directors around and that she longs to work with him.

I include *Fallen Angels* because I like it very much and believe you should see it. However, I am bound to point out that the finale of the writing of this book happened to coincide with the deaths of Ingmar Bergman and Michelangelo Antonioni reported on successive days. I welcome Wong Kar-Wai (who will be fifty in 2008) to this community, but I am not prepared to be jostled out of the hot-shittedness of his work to the point of disloyalty to Bergman and Antonioni. Wong Kar-Wai is innovative, brilliant, and beautiful in ways that had made Jean-Luc Godard lose patience with himself by the age of forty. Even then, Godard had possessed an instant sense of gravity only assisted by his poker-faced wit. There is the smeared color of Wong's handheld, wide-angled shots that makes kids squirm like eels in the water of Hong Kong. It is a riveting, elastic vision. He knows that it's possible to watch his images in a trance of delight—with or without drug assistance. But to be so prepared for such limited pleasure is a warning sign of boredom that should not be ignored.

You will say that this is not exactly welcoming or enthusiastic. But again I insist: Look at *Fallen Angels,* look at the balletic flex of the mass killings and the stone-faced diligence of the girl who cleans up for the killer afterward. And ask what has happened to ballet or diligence. The rhythms, the sour color clashes, the overwhelming carnality of it all, are akin to the feeling of looking into a wok as noodles, sprouts, and human worms change color in the cooking. This is a very talented director who gives every sign of being ready to dump talent in our laps—and no more.

There is a second story in *Fallen Angels*—so often Wong slams ingredients together to make a menu and a sweet-sour explosion. The second story is of a son and a father, and in ways that are hard to itemize but inescapable as you see it, the father becomes a figure of pathos and tragic reach. The film does not build from that. The two stories do not interact (as events in *Magnolia* do); they are simply a gesture toward the world being an impossible crowd of situations.

Alas, I think that fame has bred self-regard in Wong Kar-Wai. I do not see him getting better, but I want you to see *Fallen Angels* as expressive of a moment when he was on the point of becoming an artist and not just a hot-shit cook.

The Fallen Idol (1948)

One day in 1947, producer Alexander Korda and director Carol Reed were together, wondering what Reed might do next. Korda had a bad cold. Before going off to bed, he gave his friend an old Graham Greene story, "The Basement Room," to read. Reed liked it and went to Korda's bedroom to tell him so. Straightaway, Korda got Greene on the phone and fixed a lunch for the following day. Greene arrived at the restaurant and asked Reed, "Well, how do you see it?"

The story was about a little boy living in a large house—an embassy perhaps. His parents are always away, so the boy grows close to the butler. But the butler is part of an unhappy love triangle, and there's a murder. It turns out that the boy, the man's great admirer, is the one who gives him away. Greene and Reed agreed that that ending was too bleak. But suppose the boy just feels the butler is a murderer and tries to save him but nearly ruins him because of his lies?

The two men felt they'd reached a workable compromise—but I'm not so sure. And it makes an intriguing point about endings. Greene's ending in the story was very pessimistic, but the salvation in the movie feels contrived and fake. For me it has always spoiled the film. A year or two later in *The Third Man,* Reed, Greene, and Korda, still together, delivered that great ending where Alida Valli never wavers or pauses but just keeps walking past Joseph Cotten in the cemetery because he's dead for her. And it was Greene who, in later publishing the novella of *The Third Man,* had the two characters reconciling and walking away hand in hand.

So *The Fallen Idol* has a large problem. Never mind; it's three-quarters of a wonderful film. For the embassy they found an empty house in London's Belgravia, and then set designer Vincent Korda and cameraman Georges Périnal brought it to life as the place where the boy, Phillipe, plays. And the film, for the most part, is seen through the boy's eyes.

The grown-up story is the butler, Baines (Ralph Richardson), his odious wife (Sonia Dresdel), and the foreign girl Baines loves (Michèle Morgan). And Reed is very good at letting us feel both the boy's vision of it and a darker adult perspective. Indeed, the boy, Bobby Henrey, is the switch that turns the film on. Reed found the kid and grew very close to him, and it's a new kind of child acting—full of plausible appeal, but showing how a child can get everything wrong, too.

I suspect the audience could have taken the tough ending. A good enough film raises our expectations, and it should be wary of cheating itself. Richardson is sublime, Dresdel is vicious, Morgan is saintly, and there's a range of good character work from Denis O'Dea, Jack Hawkins, Dora Bryan, Walter Fitzgerald, Bernard Lee, Karel Stepanek, Joan Young, and Geoffrey Keen. But Henrey is the secret heart of the picture.

Fanny and Alexander (1982)

As broadcast on Swedish television, this is a 300-minute work. The theatrical release outside Sweden was 189 minutes, and the DVD release we have is close to 200 minutes. So Ingmar Bergman, the master of the 90-minute film, has relaxed with the onset of memory and a splendid veteran status that began saying with this film that this might be his last full-length work. I do not begrudge the length when Bergman's appetite for detail and people remains so sharp, but there is a great contrast evident between the detached style of *Fanny and Alexander*—inward pauses, long shots, slowly unwinding action—and the dramatic severity of the earlier work.

Fanny and Alexander is, if not directly autobiographical, then the work of a man opening himself up to the notion of the adult being fed by the child. But in *Wild Strawberries,* Bergman took on a structure that had the same interest in the past. What is most striking here is the greater warmth with which that past works on the present. That owes something to the confident use of color and to a mounting interest in décor, but also to the older man's realization that despite every hazard, so many people come through more or less intact. Especially in Bergman's early work, there was a feeling of damage set up by early life. But here we feel strengths in the family, in tradition, and even in life itself that can restore balance and hope.

One other point: With *Fanny and Alexander,* it becomes impossible to overlook the influence of Dickens on Bergman. I am not just talking about the focus on children and their surviving hardship and threat. Nor even the Vergerus episode here, whose tone so resembles that of *David Copperfield* with the Murdstones. Instead, I am thinking of the abiding example of the theater (the grandmother of Fanny and Alexander is an actress, and at the end she is thinking of a comeback in Strindberg's *Dream Play*). The theater is seen as a model of life and a means of entertainment for all, in which the individual may lose his or her own neurosis. Surely this is Bergman's great lesson from life: that work in performance can turn real pain into a manageable process.

The pacing of *Fanny and Alexander* is magisterial, yet the experience of these children sustains the grandeur. The importance of place and routine is plain. And—this is no surprise—the acting is both collegial and idiosyncratic: Erland Josephson as the Jewish uncle is a Micawberish creation; Jan Malmsjö makes Bishop Vergerus hateful; Ewa Fröling is one more Swedish beauty as the mother, Emilie; Gunn Wållgren is the grandmother; and, among so many other good performances, I would pick out Harriet Andersson, scarcely recognizable but wicked as Vergerus's maid.

It's fair to say that the ease of working here has gone a touch too far. Just as Bergman's earlier pessimism could seem forced, so here the benevolence is a degree too much, too cozy. It's a small cavil. Bergman proves himself a visionary of old age, the saint of lives that may think they are settled.

Fantasia (1940)

If you had to compile a book about the decline of the American empire, there's a long list of things that many Americans hailed as triumphs but that turned out to be unmistakable proof of disaster. Take *Fantasia.* In the late 1930s, Walt Disney had the thought for a new "Silly Symphony" in which he would supply an animated story to go with Paul Dukas's symphonic poem "The Sorcerer's Apprentice." The idea was nifty and not a bad match for the music. It was Mickey Mouse as the mischievous apprentice who is finally packed off by the sorcerer's magic and a pack of swatting brooms. (You may still judge that this is the best thing in *Fantasia,* one section that gets the tone right.) Leopold Stokowski and the Philadelphia Orchestra were doing the music, which meant that the piece was costing $125,000, a lot more than was ever devoted to a Mickey short.

Roy Disney pointed this out, and Walt's grandiose response was, Let's do a whole movie like this. Stokowski (who evidently foresaw a lot of publicity for himself and his orchestra) said, Why not? Well, *Fantasia* ended up at 116 minutes at a cost of $2.28 million. The final selection was the Dukas, Bach's Toccata and Fugue in D Minor (done to abstract animation), Tchaikovsky's "Nutcracker Suite," Stravinsky's "The Rite of Spring," Beethoven's *Pastoral* Symphony, Ponchielli's "Dance of the Hours," Mussorgsky's "A Night on Bald Mountain"—and why not Schubert's "Ave Maria" as a finale?

The whole thing was introduced and narrated by musicologist Deems Taylor. If only it had had the calm common sense of Benjamin Britten's *Young Person's Guide to the Orchestra.* What happened—and I think it was predictable—was that the better the music, the more trashy, second-rate, and absurd the pictures seemed. I'm not sure if the history of Hollywood has so naked an example of the unbridgeable gulf between high art and low art. Moreover, the vulgarity of *Fantasia* has to be set beside the degree to which Disney's suffocating example has worked to deny alternative approaches to animation in America. There is a kind of animation as well drawn as painting, as adult as real drama, and as capable of dealing with experience as, say, Svankmaier and the Quay Brothers.

Nor is there really any reason to think that a child might be drawn toward "classical" music by the film. Disney had no respect for, and very little understanding of, how music worked. He wanted it to be accessible, malleable, and ready for translation. So when he gets to Stravinsky and Beethoven, the onscreen result is hideous and distracting. Nor did the American public respond to the picture—it was a flop and showed Disney's lamentable failure to grasp his own achievement. That the picture was a monument of animation hardly matters—the drawing was often brilliant, but always "house style" and impersonal. The Academy nevertheless awarded certificates of praise to Disney and his top people and to Leopold Stokowski.

Fantômas (1913)

Louis Feuillade, born in 1873, was the son of a wine dealer. He did military service in the cavalry, and he worked variously as a writer, an actor, and a bullfight critic—remember the matador with his cloaks and capes. In 1906 he started writing stories for the infant movie industry in France, and by 1910 he was the director-creator of immense, energetic serials, the standard short-form suspense material offered to a returning audience. What we know about him depends to a great extent on what has survived (thanks to the Cinémathèque Française). It is simply not possible to take an overview of his career, or even to be sure that Feuillade was ahead of his time and his peers. There may have been others. But in our present state of film history, Feuillade is rated as a pioneer, and even a genius. Whatever decision the viewer comes to, he is the first true director, chronologically, to appear in this book.

We do know that *Fantômas* was a sensation in Paris. It was a serial of just three episodes, made by Gaumont, taken from the novels of Pierre Souvestre and Marcel Allain, in which Fantômas was a masked figure, the Master of Crime, who teases and torments a policeman named Inspector Juve. The criminal organization led by Fantômas is infinite, and although the characters are wildly far-fetched, they are grounded by being filmed in and against the actual streets of Paris in 1913 (before the war began and regulations against filming were imposed).

Several things emerge from this setup and are notably distinct from similar serial adventures of the day in the United States: The serial in America is always in defense of law and order (before the onset of any censorship), yet in France the films are allowed to glamorize and eroticize the criminals and take pleasure in the way their infinite, and even magical, resources help them avoid capture. The criminal urge is recognized as something the public nurses. The mystical power of Dr. Mabuse in the German films just a few years away is certainly borrowed from the Feuillade pictures. Second, the view of Paris in the background is not just an invaluable physical record but a haunting mixture of real and surreal. And the photographic quality helps underline the deliberate siting of fantasy actions in real places. What's more, as time went by and Feuillade felt emboldened—even in war, as security was a blanket that could be used to smother his cloaked characters—he hired increasingly daring players and designers. Just as Paris was drawn into his work, so it partook of ideas and people from the avant-garde.

The Feuillade serials that followed—*The Vampires* (1915), *Judex* (1916), *Tih Minh* (1918)—are exhilarating, playful, profuse, and ingenious in their plot invention, and sinister in their notion of the disease of crime invading the stable structures of society. America caught the virus in the gangster films of early sound—the idea that we could have fun saying hallo to some hoodlum's little friend—but in the silent era Feuillade was without rival or peer at letting the black cloak confound morale. For the first time, it was hard to tell entertainment from subversiveness.

Fargo (1996)

At last, the proof that in the well-known phrase "Prairie Home Companion," the word to mistrust was "Companion." Yes, Fargo's cold enough to prompt a good deal of cuddling for comfort—and Marge Gunderson is pregnant—but the idea of trusting anyone ever again is so much less pressing than that lonesome cold. After all, what is Jerry Lundegaard doing but getting his own wife put up for ransom to get himself out of some tricky fiscal difficulties?

Fargo is just 97 minutes long, compact and efficient (cost $7 million; earnings $24.5 million), a sort of "the gang's all here" of American independent film, and a quiet knockout. When the snow is that thick, you won't hear a body or a Douglas fir fall, just the hush being underlined. But the tonal range of the film is what is leaving puffs of breath in the air. From one moment to the next this film is gruesome, bloody, and "Oh, no!" as well as so funny you wish those starchy voices would stop talking for a second.

Not even their loved ones would accuse the Coen Brothers of consistency, and for myself I gave up long ago hoping for a "straight" picture from them—one they believed in and expected us to treat with the same respect. On the other hand, there are times when their sense of pastiche strays out of play on that side of the field: *The Hudsucker Proxy, The Man Who Wasn't There, The Ladykillers.* These are rather grim occasions, so we must all recollect those days when the pastiche and the pistachio are perfectly in balance: *Miller's Crossing* (where the levels of satire do not impede the Dashiell Hammett force of the original) and *Fargo,* where absurdity and revulsion are hand in hand.

The wintriness of it all is beautifully captured by Roger Deakins, and the production design by Rick Heinrichs is hideous in just the right way. Out-of-date disco music burbles on throughout the film. And as always, the Coens did everything else—the venerable Roderick Jaynes is once more credited for the editing, but I think that's only a way of paying some of the blackmail money for a matter that really should not be discussed any further here.

Many people treasure every stammering self-contradiction from William H. Macy as Jerry, but I would add the real moral shading that remains. He is a scoundrel, and in the end amiability is as nothing. Steve Buscemi and Peter Stormare are to die for, literally. I adore Harve Presnell as the father—he feels and we feel he should be singing his lines. And the cast is right all the way down the line. But is that enough for Frances McDormand as Marge, probably the smartest cop on the American screen in the 1990s? Well, some have contemplated charging the Coens with kidnapping—with shanghaiing a wife (Joel's) and sister-in-law so she can only appear in their films. They have made grudging concessions over the years. Still, I would work her till she drops. She got the Oscar, and I hope she's allowed to have it two days a week at least. The screenplay won, too.

Fatal Attraction (1987)

There was a short era in which Michael Douglas was our Joan Crawford. He resembled Joan because he yearned to be a man to the full, a career man, a man with independence, and yet a man who was sometimes carried too far by the zeal of his identity. Thus, in Adrian Lyne's *Fatal Attraction,* he was Dan Gallagher, a happily married man and a publisher. Of course, we ought to have caught that clue: It was already too late for a man to be happy and a publisher. Let us simply say, then, that Douglas was ideally cast, with a wife, Beth (Anne Archer), and a child and a job that expressed the cutting edge in his strong gaze. (I am not being ironic or facetious: Just imagine for a moment being the son of Kirk, looking in the mirror as a child and seeing the daft, helpless rhyme but knowing that Kirk will always outstare you.)

Anyway, wife and child go off to Long Island (God's gift to adultery). And it's not long before Dan's imprint gets a new employee: Alex Forrest (Glenn Close), whose hair is done by the woman who did the Bride of Frankenstein, and who is just the kind of temptation that is too much for Mike. They have a wild night in her loft apartment that involves things like sitting in her sink with the water running. This may not sound fantastic, but Mike does "fantastic" every bit as well as Joan did: "I know this is wrong, but I have to do it."

Fatal Attraction was written by James Dearden as an enlargement of his own short film, *Diversion.* Dearden gets the screenplay credit, but we know that Nicholas Meyer did a good deal of work uncredited, and we know that the producers, Stanley Jaffe and Sherry Lansing, Lyne, and everyone else was in great confusion as to how to develop the setup and end it.

Alex turns out to be unusually needy. She says they are in love—and it did look like movie love. She says she wants Dan. She says she understands him—and you can believe that. Until that point, the story is so interesting it could take many different endings. After all, a solid marriage has been undone. Why shouldn't mad sex have its fling? Suppose these scumbags are in love? The film rather shrinks from its feminist brink by having Alex turn nuts, as screwed up as her hair, and dangerous. The film then becomes a mere suspense melodrama—though not a bad one.

It works because Glenn Close eats the film up and because it gets at a true and beloved weakness in Michael Douglas. A man I know said it was every man's worst nightmare, which suggests that too many men in the 1980s were worrying about the wrong thing. But there's no doubt that the movie hit the adulterous portion of the nation right in the privates. Everyone was nominated for an Oscar except Mike—but he was winning that year in *Wall Street:* it cost $14 million and did $70 million in U.S. rentals.

Fat City (1972)

Whenever you hear someone telling people about the great run of films America made in the early 1970s, and they get to the list, and they begin to feel fatigue, just wait for a pause and say, "And *Fat City*. John Huston's *Fat City*." At that point the kids frown, and they admit they've not seen *Fat City*. "Right," you say, "and you never even heard of *Fat City*!"

People were saying that Huston hadn't had a good film or hit since, well, since too long. Then producer Ray Stark gave him the go-ahead to do a low-down boxing picture. Huston picked Leonard Gardner to adapt his own novel, set in the hot towns in California's San Joaquin Valley, about two boxers: Billy Tully, on the way down, and Ernie Munger, on the way up. If anyone had read Gardner's book apart from Huston, they'd have known it was a big downer. At first, there was thought of Marlon Brando as Billy, but he wasn't interested, so Stacy Keach got the job. Jeff Bridges was then cast as Ernie after an "audition" where all he had to do was meet Huston in the Prado, look at some pictures, and chat.

The result, filmed largely in Stockton (design by Richard Sylbert), is probably the most honest boxing picture ever made, with lovely shabby color photography (by Conrad Hall) that looks like paper used to wrap a burger. Huston had several real fighters around to help (Jose Torres, Curtis Cokes, Sixto Rodriguez), and he liked to put his actors in the ring with the pros sometimes so that we'd feel we'd seen the real thing. In addition, Huston was not well; this was one of the first films where he was reported sitting on the set with an oxygen cylinder as his squeeze. Added to which, Stockton is the sort of location that many directors would pass on.

Still, we haven't got to the thing that people recall about *Fat City*, which is Susan Tyrrell—fat, boozed, blowsy, and so good as Billy's would-be girlfriend, so out of her mind with hope and depression, so used, so soiled, so lifelike, you could conclude that every movie ought to be done again. Candy Clark is also very good as the girl in Ernie's life.

And it's a film with a moment. There was a 2 a.m. call at a café in Stockton. The crew set up. Huston seemed to be asleep. "All of a sudden his eyes bolted open, and he said, 'I've got it. Have you ever been at a party when for a reason everybody just stops? When all of a sudden it's all a tableau? You're alone in eternity for a moment?' "

The cameraman said they could do it as a freeze-frame. No, said Huston, "I want the cigarette smoke to continue going. I don't want it to look like a stock frame. I just want everybody to stop."

As Bridges put it, "Everybody thought he was in a trance, receiving messages from god knows where." And he really hadn't made a good film for years.

Faust (1926)

Faust has been with us for centuries as a mythic narrative model. We have it as drama, opera, ballet. It fits every medium. And it is, surely, the underlying impulse in so much movie history: that of a genius who is given the world—limos, blondes, and terrific money—in return for his talent. Indeed, you can get yourself into a state of mind that reckons nearly every interesting movie ever made is a version of the Faust situation: *Citizen Kane* (we will give you everything, young man, but see how everything only reminds you of loss); *The Godfather* (so you want to be head of the family—prove it by destroying the family); *Sunset Blvd.* (so you want a screenwriting job—here it is); *City Lights* (you want the blind girl to see—all right, but then she won't notice you); *Sullivan's Travels* (you asked for reality?).

So it's intriguing that the direct assaults on Faust have been very few, and more remarkable that if you want a movie that "does" Faust properly, you need to go back to the F. W. Murnau version, which is eighty years old. It was made for Ufa, and in fact it was Murnau's last German picture. A month after *Faust* opened in Berlin, its director was in Hollywood. Lotte Eisner suggests that the first thought at Ufa was to have *Faust* directed by Ludwig Berger; that plan involved Conrad Veidt as Mephisto and Lillian Gish as Gretchen. But Eisner says that Emil Jannings was determined to play Mephisto and reckoned that Murnau was his most likely supporter.

Murnau worked from a script by the poet Hans Kyser that went back not just to Goethe but to older versions of the legend. And we know that Murnau did a lot to amend that script and that he brought into the film its extraordinary romance with light. From the outset, as we see the great bat of Mephisto over the German city, this is a film that thrills with light and shadow and the ravishing ways in which light can be diffused. It's clear from the film that just as the Devil was dark, so Faust meant light to Murnau—and the conflict operates in those terms. This makes it (thanks to the photography of Carl Hoffmann) one of the most intensely beautiful of the silent films (yet one that needs good prints if it is not to seem blurred and misty to a ludicrous degree).

The sets are by Robert Herlth and Walter Röhrig, and they are, once more, surfaces for the light. So it's intriguing to see Murnau's *Faust* and *Sunrise* together, for the latter is the same light and dark but as if those spirits had sprung from man alone, without divine assistance. Gösta Ekman plays Faust, and Camilla Horn replaced Gish as Gretchen. That is a place to remind the reader of a brilliant 1982 documentary, made by Hedda Rinneberg and Hans Sachs, in which the elderly Ms. Horn watches scenes from *Faust*. Her responses are not just those of an actress and Narcissus. They give a powerful sense of how a German audience in 1926 read *Faust:* as legend, as horror story, and as modern morality play. (It was not that they didn't have another real-life version about to open.)

This book is not meant to include documentary films, and *F for Fake* may fit under many people's definitions of documentary. After all, isn't it at least an essay on the matter of fraud, as witness the forged masterpieces of Elmyr de Hory, the Clifford Irving autobiography of Howard Hughes, and many events in the career of Orson Welles himself, not least the furor in 1938 over the radio broadcast of *The War of the Worlds*? This is a nonfiction film in which Welles offers to tell the truth for just so long before he yields to his chronic destiny—storytelling—with an amazing shaggy-dog tale that seems to implicate Pablo Picasso and Oja Kodar.

More than that, with its three-card swiftness of hand, its constant editing stealth, and the several moments in which someone or other looks at us with an arched eyebrow and asks, "Are you believing this?" there is none of the comforting gravity of documentary. This is the work of a man who, very early on, made the best newsreel obituary there has ever been, for a man who never lived. Documentary for Orson Welles is like a magician going before an audience, his hand on his heart, beginning with "Ladies and gentlemen . . ." And expecting to be believed. Documentary is the routine examination of the sleeve, and the history of sleeves, as a nudging reassurance that of course there's something up there even if you can't see it. Magicians hardly deal in documentary, for it is against their religion to give evidence on how the tricks are done.

In fact, the film doesn't give you enough time to really judge the value of de Hory's paintings, just as it doesn't allow you enough of Irving's book to decide whether it was impressive—and a fake autobiography could still be a valuable biography. So Welles is gracious and friendly to the other magicians without ever quite taking them under his black cloak. His own magic, in this film and all the others, is what we treasure, and all he is doing really is to tell us to believe in story because it's the most effective way of getting at truth. That's why Welles always knew that *Citizen Kane* was a game when it came to talking about William Randolph Hearst or Chicago financier Harold McCormick or any of the others who may have been Kane's inspiration—but a profound, predictive truth in the case of George Orson Welles.

There's something else to be said about *F for Fake*, which is that by the early 1970s, there was perhaps no better way of doing fresh fiction than as pseudodocumentary. The comparison with Nabokov's *Pale Fire* is telling, for that fraudulently academic presentation of a poem was itself a whole world done in fiction. But there are other comparisons still: with Jean-Luc Godard's *Histoire(s) du Cinéma*, with Chris Marker's great CD *Immemory*, and with that Borgesian construct, the library itself, in which all the history books are just witness to story. His story.

Fingers (1978)

In 1978—having done the script for Karel Reisz's *The Gambler;* written a book, *Jim,* about a white guy breaking into the life of football star Jim Brown; and teaching here and there—Harvard man James Toback burst into screen life with a momentous directorial debut, *Fingers:* truly violent, visceral, disturbing, and destructive of calm. In hindsight, Toback's relentless and good-humored self-promotion has tended to dilute his own rawness, just as his material and his method have come to seem more calculated. He became a character instead of a demon. Truly, to be an enfant terrible past the age of forty can be very awkward—and Toback had given sweeping guarantees about never making it past forty. So I have to say that the great promise of *Fingers* has not been fulfilled. But *Fingers* was always far more than promise. It is a shocking, great film that gets under the skin and beneath the schooled nervous system of America.

Jimmy Angelelli (Harvey Keitel) is an aspiring concert pianist. We see his audition at Carnegie Hall, and it is a disaster, because Jimmy is Jekyll and Hyde. On the one hand, he is his mother's son—she is Manhattan wealth and culture, as well as a stern taskmistress and someone he can never please. She is Marian Seldes. But for his father, Ben (Michael V. Gazzo), Jimmy collects underworld debts and applies brutal pressure.

Question: Is this mixture of artist and hoodlum a dysfunctional problem or is it actually a split-level paradise such as Toback—and others—adore? *Fingers* comes on as if the duality is a great ordeal—one multiplied when Jimmy meets a pale, dreamy girl, Carol (Tisa Farrow), who is also one of the kept women of Dreems (Jim Brown), an intimidating black stud. So the film, I think, is the fairy story of an educated white Jew who is drawn intensely to everything he has been told to hide from: wild women, violence, blacks, trash music, and existential outlawry.

The whole thing plays out in Manhattan, dynamically filmed by Mike Chapman against a sound track that goes from Bach and Chopin to the Chiffons and the Drifters. *Fingers* came early on in the history of American independents, and it had a terrific influence, because it did everything with such panache, wicked amusement, and greedy appetite. It's not for every taste, and it is certainly not for Dr. Jekyll's polite society—but isn't that why the doc experimented?

Made for a little over a million dollars, shot very fast, and just 90 minutes long, *Fingers* is a magnificent example of pulp cinema and one of the best things Harvey Keitel ever did—he went naked in this one long before we'd become depressed by his body. Brown is as thunderous as he was on the football field. Tisa Farrow and Tanya Roberts are sex switches. Marian Seldes is steel, and Michael V. Gazzo leaves us wondering why he wasn't used far more. Also with Danny Aiello, Ed Marinaro, Georgette Mosbacher, Carole Francis, Lenny Montana, Dominic Chianese, and Tony Sirico.

Fires on the Plain (1959)

Kon Ichikawa's film begins, before its credits, with a blunt, head-on discussion between an officer and the central soldier (Eiji Funakoshi). The soldier has tuberculosis. He has no chance of surviving on the battlefield. But there's every chance he'll be taking crucial rations from soldiers who might endure. He is therefore an outsider, a wanderer—and in great part Ichikawa's remorseless classic is a study of this scarecrow who can hardly coexist with any of the human groups on offer.

The place is the island of Leyte in the Philippines. The time is February 1945. Whereupon I can begin to hear modern moviegoers in their splendid isolation saying, Oh, you mean the kind of films Clint Eastwood made in 2006—*Flags of Our Fathers* and *Letters from Iwo Jima*? Well, of course Eastwood's two pictures concerned the desperate battle for Iwo Jima (all the more senseless in that it was simply an atoll airfield) and the equally ugly attempt by propaganda to make the Iwo Jima flag-raising stand up for fund-raising, too. But do I really mean to tell you that Japan itself had already taken on this kind of subject—with all the extra conviction and horror you might expect in a people who were there—at the time?

Ichikawa was a very versatile director: He could go from the epic canvas (as here) to close studies of inner obsession. He never makes Leyte look as tragically beautiful as, say, Mizoguchi might have managed. Needless to say, he never does those huge-screen-and-five-hundred-landing-craft shots that Eastwood's special effects can manage. But if you want to shudder at the look on gaunt faces considering and reflecting on cannibalism, then *Fires on the Plain* is the only film. Eastwood's Iwo Jima battle film is awfully like a Warner Brothers job from 1945 in which all the roles have gone Japanese while actually being informed by Western codes.

Fires on the Plain is universal in its antiwar message, but it begins and ends with Japanese experience. There is an American soldier briefly on view (with dialogue by film scholar Donald Richie), and we see how Filipinos are reacting to the use of their land. But essentially this is a story about a company that no longer has even combat as a unifying force. Their story is ordeal, honor, and starvation, with the shocking realization that honor means so little.

Flags of Our Fathers, it seems to me, is an intelligent and pained study of the stupid deceits in "victory"—a film well worth making. Whereas *Letters from Iwo Jima* is an academic exercise from a guy who has always done shoot-outs pretty well. On the other hand, *Fires on the Plain* is about the end of humanism, and Clint Eastwood is still too content with himself to notice that post has been passed. This film comes from a novel by Shohei Ooka, with a script by Natto Wada. The black-and-white photography is by Setsuo Kobayashi.

The Firm (1988)

No, this is not your 1993 *Firm* with Tom Cruise; this is the 1988 *Firm* with Gary Oldman, the one that Alan Clarke made. For the most part, Clarke made his films for British television, taking social situations that interested him and just boring in with a mixture of documentary authenticity (so the acting was like fresh blood) and a camera technique that was in love with Steadicam and this idea that a camera could walk in anywhere and see something special. It was a method that included being friends with writers and actors, and knowing them so well that he could lean on them to do more or do better. So the whole film became a test of daring, just as it was for the BBC or ITV later (would they dare to show it?).

The Firm grew out of what was happening in British soccer—in particular, the violence at games or around the grounds on gamedays, and the special reputation for "bother" that British fans were getting in Europe. Mrs. Thatcher said it was all unemployed kids fighting; keep them out of the grounds and everything would be all right. But *The Firm* is based on a darker knowledge: that the trouble is coming from gangs of older men, people with jobs and families, who just love the aggravation they associate with soccer and who have a general contempt for their society that is neither unfounded nor inexplicable. In part, it's because the society has never been able to reach them.

The script was by Al Hunter. David Thompson produced for the BBC. But "Clarky" was very much in charge out on the streets, filming adventures and accidents, encouraging his actors to improvise and to be dangerous. Bex Bissell (Oldman) has a wife (Lesley Manville) and a couple of kids, as well as a decent job in real estate. But Bex's life—his soul—is entirely caught up in the mounting rivalry between two gangs of football thugs. It ends, as it should, with a killing—not so much as a demonstration of a sick society but as a warning as to what heedless energy will do.

Oldman has never given a better performance than he does in this 70-minute film, and you should remember in the quarrel scenes he has with his wife that Oldman and Manville were married at the time. The rest of the cast includes Phil Davis (a mainstay of modern British film), Andrew Wilde, Charles Lawson, William Vanderpuye, Jay Simpson, and Nick Dunning.

Clarke (1935–90) died far too young, and it's very hard to say that BBC drama is as tough or threatening without him. There are several other Clarke films I thought of as well as *The Firm*—like *Elephant*, *The Road*, and *Scum*—but in the end I went for this one because it's grit in your face after the talcum powder of the Tom Cruise *Firm*. If you want to see Clarke's influence, you can find it in Gary Oldman's *Nil by Mouth* or in Tim Roth's *The War Zone*.

Fists in the Pocket (1965)

Born and raised in Piacenza, in a strict Catholic, bourgeois home, Marco Bellocchio went to art school in London and came back a scourge to his own class in Italy, a man infected by Buñuel and Dostoyevsky in equal measure. His debut film, *Fists in the Pocket,* was one of the great crossover films in Italian history, abandoning the conventional bourgeois ethics and stability for something (or anything) new and dangerous. It's one of the sharpest films of the decade in its attack on the family.

Four adult children live with their blind mother. Augusto (Marino Masé), the older brother, is in charge, but he's indolent, cynical, and greedy. He has two younger brothers, Leone (Pier Luigi Troglio), who is sweet but retarded, and Alessandro (Lou Castel), epileptic, brilliant, dangerous, and a giddy maker of mischief. Then there is their sister, Giulia (Paola Pitagora), who is unstable. As the story develops, Alessandro comes to believe that only one thing can save their ignominious status: a kind of collective suicide—and he can handle it.

Bellocchio establishes this dysfunctional group at the dining table. There is no central experience or direction. People read books. They sink into their own dismay. The cat prowls the table stealing food. People conspire behind each other's backs. There are sudden outbursts of temper and violence. It is like mealtime in a prison or an institution, and while the audience can guess that Alessandro is ill, we are still drawn to his insulting, aggressive, yet wildly funny mockery of the others. He has the last energy in the family, no matter how destructive he may be. The older brother, by contrast, is like a bored guard over the disarray.

And Lou Castel was a sight to behold as Alessandro. With a lot of James Dean's brusqueness, he was a Swede who had to be dubbed into Italian for this film. He never enjoyed a settled career, but everyone who loves *Fists in the Pocket* gives him credit for his wayward instincts.

Bellocchio wrote and directed, Alberto Marrama did the photography, Gisella Longo was in charge of art direction, and Ennio Morricone wrote the music. The style is rough and jagged, with a lot of long lenses used on intimate scenes so that focus is shallow and ordinary household objects jut into the frame with menace. The emphasis is very emotional or psychic, and a reminder that in years to come Bellocchio would work closely with his own analysts.

In the mid-1960s, this was as striking a debut as Bertolucci's, and it was reckoned that Bellocchio was a great director in the making. That promise has not quite been fulfilled, but nothing takes away from the stormy mood of *Fists in the Pocket* and its helpless scrutiny of a family living like isolated animals. There was a sequel of a kind, *The Eyes, the Mouth* (1982), with Castel again, Angela Molina, and Emmanuelle Riva. For anyone struck by the first film, pursuit of the second is to be encouraged.

Five Easy Pieces (1970)

Not many films before *Five Easy Pieces* had made such a bold assertion as saying, Look, that American down there—Bobby Dupea (Jack Nicholson), apparently an oil-rigger in California—is a self-imposed exile from an intense, tender, and musical family in the Pacific Northwest, or somewhere that looks like it. It's not just that he could have been a contender; he might have played piano recitals in hushed halls for the quiet reverence of just a few. But something in Bobby couldn't take the claustrophobia or the intensity, and so he hit the road to be the very opposite of what he had been raised to be. It is the same dynamic as figures in James Toback's *Fingers*, but that came seven years later. Still, it's a reflection, I think, of Nicholson, a quiet man who loves to be extroverted, and of director Bob Rafelson, studious, Jewish, Ivy League, very bright, who likes to be called Curly, roam the world, and behave like an adventurer.

Of course, Bobby isn't really happy or right anywhere he goes. He had Karen Black as a girlfriend at first, and her every word grates on the fine soul he hoped to lose. In the Northwest he sure would like to have his brother's consort, Susan Anspach, but she sees the horror of his self-betrayal and gives him back all his old guilt as if she were a member of the family. At the end of this film, Bobby is on the road again, ready to abandon every tie. It seems to me an open question whether he is going to become a vagrant or an outlaw. Maybe he settles the dilemma by being an actor.

Rafelson was working from a terrific script by Carole Eastman—terrific not just in its construction but in so many scenes of astonishing dialogue, like the chicken-sandwich set piece in the diner, Bobby's long speech to his silent father, and the lacerating way Anspach dismisses him. Rafelson has no more reason to trust an artist than an oil-rigger, and it is part of his great appetite that the film also has several other fascinating but mysterious female presences: Lois Smith as the sister, Sally Struthers as the sensational motel fuck, and Helena Kallianiotes as the witch picked up on the road.

The picture was made for BBS (Rafelson's company with Steve Blauner and Bert Schneider), and it was so cheap it turned out to be a significant hit—and an example of the new kind of movie. The rest of the cast includes Ralph Waite, Billy Green Bush, and Fannie Flagg, all excellent. And there are absolutely piercing incidents, like Bobby climbing onto a freight truck, starting to play the piano it contains, and being carried away as if forever. Deep down in this film there's an ear for the nagging call of getaway and escape, of not doing the obvious or the sensible thing, of being American and unknown; and it may be that just as it let Nicholson flower as an actor, so it is a prediction about what would happen to Rafelson. For here in the early seventies, with this and *The King of Marvin Gardens*, he makes his mark and then drifts away.

Flesh and the Devil (1926)

By the end of 1926, the case for Greta Garbo was not quite settled. The publicity was working, and *Torrent,* her first M-G-M film, had done well enough. But on the second, *The Temptress,* Mauritz Stiller was fired and the picture lost money. Irving Thalberg and Louis B. Mayer decided on *Flesh and the Devil* as her third—and now they would do the obvious thing: cast her opposite John Gilbert. Neither star was happy with the setup. Yet again, Garbo was asked to play a married woman, Felicitas, who has an affair, who ignores her husband and wins the love of two friends, Leo (Gilbert) and Ulrich (Lars Hanson).

The story came from the novel *The Undying Past,* by Hermann Sudermann (the novelist also behind Murnau's *Sunrise*), with a screenplay by Benjamin Glazer. Clarence Brown would direct, with William Daniels in charge of the photography—clearly this was a venture to which Thalberg was paying the closest attention. Garbo resisted for two days, and then she turned up for work. Once she and Gilbert were photographed together, the future was clear.

Of course, people had been kissing on the screen for what seemed like a thousand years, and some did it better than others. But the screen kiss was a formal gesture; it was a narrative device—these two people in the story are in love. The audience appreciated that but felt a deep, unsatisfied yearning. They knew in their shy hearts that the kiss meant something else: that these two people were going to make love. And I think it is very important, all over the world, that the movies had a destiny to meet in which they pleased the millions who had an idea of what being in love was but who were inflamed by the idea of sex. Just look at the title Metro gave the film, and at least understand the instantaneous recoil, the horror, in so many churches and churchy people. One thing over the edge was in prospect—abandonment. Could the public handle it? Could order survive with such intense private pleasure?

Not without go-betweens, and that is how we need to think of Garbo and Gilbert. This is how you need to see *Flesh and the Devil* and the way, within moments of their meeting, Felicitas takes charge of Leo and starts to kiss him as if his very head was a vessel full of life. The kisses are openmouthed. The lovers become horizontal. But she is the dynamic force in the transaction. Their first scene was more shocking and expansive than the first meeting in *Last Tango in Paris.*

And here is the key: When Brown had enough, he said himself, he simply made a gesture to tell his camera crew to stop and move away, to leave the stars still kissing—the fire was theirs to put out. They were in love; they were lovers. Shortly thereafter, Garbo moved into Gilbert's house on Tower Grove Drive. The picture opened early in 1927 and was the first sensation of the year. It cost $373,000 and earned $1.25 million all over the world. Do not underestimate the surge of energy in all directions: that kiss, that sucking, that moisture, had to be heard. The rest of the film hardly mattered.

Floating Clouds (1955)

Mikio Naruse made *Floating Clouds* in the year that produced *Love Is a Many-Splendored Thing*—from Twentieth Century Fox, with Jennifer Jones as the Eurasian doctor and with that thunderous theme song by Sammy Fain and Paul Francis Webster. It's a chance collision, perhaps, and in all likelihood Naruse knew as little about Henry King's picture as King cared about Naruse's. Yet the films are not dissimilar: Both are love stories in which the central relationship is fated not to be. You can blame it on the prior arrangement of the world and its lives, or you can put it all down to the bad luck of people.

Love Is a Many-Splendored Thing is not in this book, yet it seems to have been what America wanted in 1955. Although it indulges its interracial love affair temporarily, it does not want to go so far as to license it. And in casting Jones opposite William Holden, it allows the racially inclined fantasist to take the story whichever way he likes. And while love can be so many things, by night and day, the thought that it really is this many-splendored thing is more than a little unsettling. The bombast of the song leaves an unfortunate feeling that love is a kind of American or fascist or consumerist duty, when in truth a lot of people seem to get through life without being ambushed by it.

Yet here's the other thing that is very important to this book: Naruse's *Floating Clouds* was apparently a big success in Japan at just the time (the mid-1950s) when Japanese films by Kurosawa and Mizoguchi were making their way to the West, yet it took fifty years before the efforts of James Quandt of the Cinémathèque Ontario and the Japan Foundation managed to bring *Floating Clouds* to the West. For myself, I only caught up with it during the writing of this book, and I have to say that I find it heartbreaking, beautiful, and deserving of a place. But what of other Naruse films I haven't seen yet or other directors who are not set up on tracks that bring their films to the West? There has not been a moment since the 1960s when foreign-language films have faced such difficulty in finding an American audience.

Floating Clouds—which you will have a tough time finding—is based on a novel by Fumiko Hayashi (who worked a lot with Naruse in his last years), with outstanding photography (black and white) by Masao Tamai. It is the failed love story of a couple who meet during the Japanese occupation of Indochina in 1943: Tomioka (Masayuki Mori), an engineer with a wife at home, and Yukiko (Hideko Takamine), a secretarial worker. They fall in love. They return to a ruined Japan. Their feelings remain, but they are not strong enough to overcome the hard life. The greatest irony of all in the comparison with *Love Is a Many-Splendored Thing* is our difficulty in resisting the idea that this defeated fascist state—the country that produced *Floating Clouds*—may be the more modern and mature of the two.

Floating Weeds (1959)

It is not often the case in the work of Ozu that the occupation of characters matters too much. He seems to have felt—as many people do in real life—that job decision, or fate, was out of the hands of the individual. So people find their identity in his films in family status more than career position. Which makes it intriguing that Ozu was drawn to the subject of *Floating Weeds* twice in his career. Of course, it is not so surprising that a man who had worked with actors all his life should find acting interesting, or vulnerable. But such is the case. And what is most remarkable of all is that Ozu goes beyond Western artists in his calm reflection on whether the emotional decisions of actors can be trusted or are helplessly affected by the actor's readiness to be someone else.

Floating Weeds is the story of a group of traveling players—in Japanese, "floating weeds" is what they're actually called. Komajuro (Ganjiro Nakamura) is the leader of the troupe. The company is not good. They play the provinces in poor locations. They just about manage. Sumiko (Machiko Kyo), the leading actress, is his mistress. Their status together is like that of the company as a whole: a kind of suppressed sadness holding a system together. They have come to a town where Oyoshi (Haruko Sugimura) lives. Long ago, she and Komajuro had a love affair. There was a child, Kiyoshi (Hiroshi Kawaguchi), and the father is known as the young man's "uncle." But the mistress learns the secret and is so angered that she sets up an actress (Ayako Wakao) to seduce the young man. The father hates to see his son with an actress. He doesn't trust "players." But then he sees that the young couple are really in love. He wonders whether he once was in love with the mother.

It is fascinating to see how the company does its work and prepares, and it is as always a matter of deep satisfaction to see how Ozu identifies human connection or proximity. He does not glamorize togetherness. He likes separate shots of people, still, without camera movement. His imagery is full of depth and crowded compositions; we have to study the story in terms of spatial bonds and juxtapositions. Yet talk isolates people, and Ozu prefers to view them from a distance, objectively, without a need for sympathy or approval. He is saying, You must look very carefully if you want to distinguish between what an actor does and what his character is. In other words, in all of Ozu's films, he is gently posing the question: Can you trust an actor, or can you only be moved by him? And then he is asking us whether our dilemma in real life is any different. What follows is a situation of utter simplicity that becomes incalculably complex. And it is in the face of the complexity that most Ozu characters accept their lot rather than try to intervene in life. This attitude is significantly shifted away from the Western code of being held responsible for what we do—and of making our own lives. Ozu suggests instead, Be responsible for what you see—be affected yet silent. And that condition takes us very quickly to helplessness, or the feeling of being powerless with fate. How do we think we know other people—is it just from watching actors?

Foolish Wives (1922)

Just think of the situation first—it might be something for Melville or Preminger. Three people live in Monte Carlo, allegedly an exiled count and his two female cousins. They are imposters, gamblers, and tricksters, with their own incestuous possibilities. They live as if wealthy and carefree, but they are on the edge and desperate. They are living by their wits, trying to take advantage of the decadent bourgeoisie who are addicted to Monte. It will all end badly. But will they destroy themselves or others?

This is not too far from an adequate synopsis of Stroheim's *Foolish Wives,* a film of which we have no more than a third of what he intended. His New York premiere seems to have been for a 210-minute version, yet the AFI restoration in the early 1970s was about 75 minutes. There are mixed accounts of how the film fared, though physical ruin speaks to the way several states made butchered versions to appease the fierce moral attacks (the fan magazine *Photoplay* called it "an insult to every American").

The film is famous for Stroheim's relentless attempt to rebuild Monte Carlo in California, a plan enhanced by the outstanding work of designer Richard Day but clearly rooted in Stroheim's aesthetic: The audience had to believe they were there. The vast sets accounted for more than $350,000 of the final $1 million budget. But that same year the entirely fanciful film *Robin Hood* cost more, and the public was thrilled by the result. *Foolish Wives* was a bolder and more aggressive venture, because its theme was so critical of mass society and its protagonists were such fringe figures.

It's also true that throughout his career Stroheim courted popular dislike by himself playing one of those outsiders and by gloating in his own offensiveness. A subtler type—an actor like Richard Barthelmess, say—might have made the cynicism so much harder to dismiss. And in atmosphere and mise-en-scène, Stroheim is often far ahead of the melodrama (this is true even in *Greed*). If only he had trusted his eye for nuance more, and if only he had been prepared to make his characters at least as appealing as the outsiders and gamblers who figure in Hemingway's *The Sun Also Rises*—which comes only three years later.

So today, the viewer cannot do much more than survey the wreckage and see how un-American and naturalistic Stroheim was, and how easily his situations could be relocated to modern America. Suppose New York and a great hotel had been used instead of Monte Carlo. Suppose our new version of the film was set in Las Vegas.

The extraordinary photography is by Ben Reynolds and William Daniels. There was an original score by Sigmund Romberg (now mostly lost). And the cast includes Robert Edeson, Patsy Hannen, Maude George, Mae Busch, Al Edmundsen, and Cesare Gravina. Here is the first sign of an American art made in defiance of its paternal industry and as a challenge to most Americans. It's a film about a moneyed society where there is no other god—and America has not yet signed off on that bleak definition.

Forbidden Games (1952)

A line of refugees winds over a bridge and through the French countryside, strafed by large formations of German fighter planes. The parents are killed. The pet dog is killed. But a little girl survives. She is taken in by a farming family, and she makes friends with a little boy from that household. They start by burying her dead dog, and then they organize a private graveyard for animals, stealing crosses from the more official burial grounds. They are found out, and the little girl is sent away for adoption. The last shot is of her, in tears, as she hears the name of her young friend, "Michel," being called out.

Forbidden Games was a big event in its time. It won the Academy's award for Best Foreign Film; it won the top prize at Venice, and another prize at Cannes; and it was a considerable box-office success. Of course, this was a time when relatively few adult films had children as central characters. Today the film is not always quite believable, and in part that's because it tends to be shot in an adult style rather than from the children's point of view. We know a good deal more now than we did then about a child's regard for death, and today it feels a touch too convenient that the orphaned girl shifts her feelings to animals so quickly and tidily.

René Clément, the famed documentarian, made the film from a novel by François Boyer and collaborated on the script with Jean Aurenche and Pierre Bost. *Forbidden Games* seems to have come from a very genteel conception, compared with, say, Roberto Rossellini's *Germany Year Zero,* made a few years earlier. The French film may be too self-consciously "adorable," and no one could fault the two children—Brigitte Fossey and Georges Poujouly—for prettiness or charm. Moreover, once the film is under way it's hard sometimes to remember that this is a France at war.

These are serious criticisms, in the face of which you have to realize how many good and sane people were deeply moved by the film—and by its winning guitar music by Narciso Yepes. The photography is by Robert Juillard, and it does seem to be set rather farther from Paris than that line of refugees might have reached.

I suppose *Forbidden Games* was interpreted as an antiwar film, and certainly its unusual emotional force had to be given some meaning. But the "games" are very private, or enclosed, and I'm not sure how much the rest of us can make of them. It occurs to me that the film could have a very different meaning if we were clearly living under German occupation, in a city, with soldiers evident.

Brigitte Fossey had an ongoing career as a teenager and a young woman, without really making a great impact. She was always pretty and appealing. It might be a stronger film if the children were less perfect.

Force of Evil (1948)

In all the upheavals that were occurring in American cinema in the years after World War II, no film is as vibrant or beautiful as Abraham Polonsky's *Force of Evil.* Many films made in those years incurred the charge of being made under a "Red" influence, of being critical of the structure of the U.S.A. In most cases, such charges were somewhere between ludicrous and wishful thinking. But of *Force of Evil* one may utter the exultant, championing cry: "This is it—the real thing! This is a thing that tears the capitalist sickness of the country to shreds." And it was released by Metro-Goldwyn-Mayer, with Mr. Mayer in charge.

Polonsky was one of the most brilliant young men ever to get into American film. Born in 1910, he had served with the OSS in World War II and then returned to Hollywood. For Enterprise, he had written the boxing exposé *Body and Soul* and received an Oscar nomination. But he wanted to direct, and the actor John Garfield made that possible by committing to this picture. It came from a novel, *Tucker's People,* by Ira Wolfert, about the numbers racket. Polonsky took the book and turned it into a classic film, great parts of it written in blank-verse dialogue that is so striking still, it is a joy to sit and listen to the movie. Moreover, the elegance of the talk makes a beautiful and very suggestive contrast with the squalor of the material.

Joe Morse (Garfield) is a Mob lawyer who works for Tucker, king of the numbers game. There is a plot whereby on July Fourth the number 776 will win. This will break most of the small, independent banks and allow Tucker to take them over. But Joe's brother, Leo (Thomas Gomez), runs such a bank, and Joe tries to save him from being busted. This confrontation of family and efficiency, coupled with Joe's falling for Leo's secretary, Doris (Beatrice Pearson), will bring the whole house tumbling down.

For a cameraman, Polonsky had George Barnes (a Hitchcock veteran). After a few days, Polonsky asked him why all the footage looked so pretty. That's how we do it, said Barnes. So Polonsky argued and asked Barnes to look at Edward Hopper paintings. "Ah, single-source lighting!" said Barnes. "Why didn't you say?" And so the picture has a stark look that is exactly attuned to the rigor of the talk. More than that, in just 78 minutes, it manages to be a complete portrait of corruption and its destruction. Of course, it is served up as the end of the Mob—and we all want that, don't we?—but there has not been a picture since, not even *The Godfather,* that spells out the essential systemic quality of organized crime. It is being organized that makes it distinctly American.

In time, Polonsky was savagely blacklisted. But this is among the greatest directorial debuts we have. It is also Garfield's most astringent and least sentimental work, and he is matched by Gomez, Pearson, Roy Roberts, Marie Windsor, and Howland Chamberlain.

Forrest Gump (1994)

I wonder whether the mental condition of Forrest Gump in 1994 (going from simplicity to sublimity) did not approximate that of Ronald Reagan as he sank from office into Alzheimer's? In other words, the curious mixture of handicap and optimism in Gump rang a bell, not least in the conclusion that that was what American politics had sunk to. Of course, there was fantastic skill employed in the picture. Eric Roth's screenplay was artful to a degree, especially in the coddling of sentimentality, mindlessness, and an unconscious reactionary spirit. Indeed, within the "life is just a box of chocolates" theory lay a wish to simplify everything—to home in on common sense and human nature—that was really a reliance on conservatism in any crisis. The comparison with Reagan is not made idly, for that virtual president would have enjoyed the estimate that political alignments were specious, finally. In the end, you were American or not, pals or hostile. Beyond that lay the old bugbear—You'd better be American (or agree with me)—that was the hard iron hand George W. Bush would enclose in a Reagan glove.

As yet, American leaders cannot quite rely on, or expect, the widespread phenomenon of Gumpism. Though we may come to it. But here was a simpleton's story told with great charm and adroitness, and with the early signs of a digitized technology that could have Gary Sinise as a legless Vietnam vet without a flaw or a seam showing, without awkwardness or loss. The naked charm and the veiled authenticity were uneasy traveling companions—yet you can see the same mix of openness and secrecy (or lying) in the kind of administration a Reagan aspired to. Above all, the personal charm of Tom Hanks in the lead was calculated to disarm the audience's critical faculty. It was the Reagan method again: ordinariness and likeability taken to a lowest common denominator that cannot be challenged. Gump is too naïve to be cunning; would that the same could be said of his creators. Hanks had risen gradually to the eminence of a kind of Jimmy Stewart. If only Robert Zemeckis or other directors had risen to his support in the way of a Capra.

The curiosity is that the Hollywood that made *Forrest Gump* almost certainly considered itself vaguely liberal, and probably voted Democrat. But the allegiance is so unreliable when the custard philosophy is hiding or denying the real muscular differences and antagonisms of politics. But *Forrest Gump* was worse than that. It was the ongoing dream that this America was doing very well, despite every external and internal indication that American identity was cracking at home along with its influence abroad.

It happens that this is the fourth entry in a row I have written in which there is the same clash between sumptuous cinematic power and intellectual emptiness—*GoodFellas*, *The Silence of the Lambs*, *JFK*, and *Forrest Gump*. And I fear that it shows a condition in American culture whereby our "art" has become helplessly subservient to our insecurities. We have been telling profound lies to ourselves, with sublime oblivion and the flourish of empty good nature. "Have a nice movie!"

Fort Apache (1948)

Fort Apache is the first film in John Ford's cavalry "trilogy," and though it is set nominally in Arizona and filmed in southern Utah (in Monument Valley), it would seem to be set in Montana, scene of the Battle of the Little Bighorn—known in Sioux history as the Battle of the Greasy Grass, because the summer grass was so slippery underfoot. You can say that Ford was prepared to play around with factual details for the sake of the pictorial, for movie, but bear that looseness in mind as we proceed. *Fort Apache* is not just casual with its facts; it is mad for epic and legend.

The film centers on a version of Custer's Last Stand. Lieutenant Colonel Owen Thursday (Henry Fonda) arrives at his new posting, Fort Apache, with his daughter, Philadelphia (Shirley Temple). He is lofty, stern, by the book, and in love with military glory. He behaves badly in the community. He resists the implications when his daughter falls in love with a mere sergeant-major's son. He strikes an unfortunate contrast with the more natural, amiable, and discerning Captain Kirby York (John Wayne), and he insists on treating the Indians as stupid hostiles.

Thursday makes an ass of himself in small ways and large, but in the final, disastrous event, he leads his men into massacre. In the aftermath of that, while there is no disputing Thursday's rash judgment or his mistake, the film endorses the attitude of men like York in rallying to the legend: that Thursday was brilliant and courageous, that he took a loss so the white man's destiny should be fulfilled, and that the view of him as a hero should be preserved. This is done because it is the Army way, and good for the Army—and because, it is assumed, America depends on this notion of valor and service.

This is a crucial incident in Ford studies, and it is returned to in *The Man Who Shot Liberty Valance*. Let me make an analogy. It may yet emerge that at Abu Ghraib and Guantánamo, American forces (allowing that term to cover the military and security agencies) used torture and other malpractices in interrogating suspects. If that is so, then the truth must come out. There is no kind of Rumsfeldian "code" worthy of being protected. In other words, it is not enough for the film to admit Thursday's mistake quietly while holding to the legend of military duty. We do need the facts, whether they are that the cavalry's mission against the Indians was to make the West open for white free enterprise, or—as has been discovered on the site of the Little Bighorn—that in the last stand many men in Custer's Seventh Cavalry shot themselves rather than submit to the "horrors" of Sioux dispatch, a sign of the immense racist gulf between the two sides—the gulf that made for their war.

Fort Apache was written by Frank Nugent from the James Warner Bellah story "Massacre." It was photographed by Archie Stout. James Basevi was the art director. The cast also includes John Agar, Ward Bond, Irene Rich, George O'Brien, Anna Lee, Victor McLaglen, Pedro Armendáriz, Guy Kibbee, Grant Withers, and Movita Castenada.

Forty Guns (1957)

Pointedly, *Forty Guns* is set in Tombstone, Arizona, in the early 1880s—that is Wyatt Earp territory. The Battle of the O.K. Corral occurred in that frontier mining town in 1881. And the Earps were a trio of brothers who tended to wear severe black clothing. So here is Sam Fuller, writer and director, introducing us to Tombstone and three Bonnell brothers, dressed in black. Is this a polite way of handling the Earps? Not at all; this is Fuller taking a given in Western history and turning it into a savage comic-book analysis of sex and violence. As he said himself, this is not a Western setting out to enlarge our sense of history, but a film in the psychodynamic tradition of *Duel in the Sun*, *The Furies*, and *Johnny Guitar*. When anyone uses a gun in *Forty Guns*, phallic energy is out to hit us in the face.

Alas, the people who love the Western because of its encouragement of guns tend to be humorless and very guarded in their sexuality. The blatant symbolism of *Forty Guns* did not speak to the uncovered energies in the genre—but *Duel in the Sun* was written off as ridiculous more than ten years earlier. To this day, it remains very difficult for a film to take on the equipment of the Western genre and deal with sex. So *Forty Guns* has survived as a part of the rowdy, maverick tradition of Sam Fuller. It still comes as a shock to those fantasists who have never fired a gun themselves—as if it had broken the rules. But isn't it more likely than not that the urge to sex was vital and imperative in the history of the Western? In John Ford's *The Searchers*, the violence of Ethan Edwards can be interpreted as a kind of terrible sexual suppression in a man who cannot love his sister-in-law and may want to kill his niece; in that light, the film could be a sexual opera—and cannot be understood without hearing that music.

Fuller's picture opens famously with one of the longest tracking shots in the history of film, and don't think tracking shots aren't phallic, either. It's led by Jessica Drummond (Barbara Stanwyck), the local boss and rancher empress, introduced in a way fit for Sternberg. Her kid brother, Brock (John Ericson), is a hoodlum, based in Fuller's eyes on the gang from *Rebel Without a Cause*. The Bonnell brothers come to town, and Griff (Barry Sullivan) is as attracted to Jessica as he hates Brock. Her former lover, the feeble sheriff (Dean Jagger), hangs himself in humiliation. And we are headed for a climax to match the opening when Brock uses Jessica as a shield against Griff, only to learn that the gun has its answer to everything.

Joseph Biroc's camerawork makes a feast out of the tracking shots, yet I wonder if *Forty Guns* finally doesn't look a bit too conventional. Does it need the lurid color of *Duel in the Sun* or the more aggressively expressive décor of a different kind of film? It's a picture that might work better on a stage than on a prairie. But that decisive artistic boldness within the Western is hard to come by. Even artists as reckless as Fuller feel a duty to real horses and dust. The West is a legend (of course), yet we believe we know how it must look.

42nd Street (1933)

The great thing about the early Warner Brothers musicals is that they look like the gangster pictures out of the same studio. The story here is inane, absurdly convenient, and filled with a certainty that in show business no one ever gets hurt—even if Bebe Daniels breaks her ankle and can't go on, that's a good thing, because it teaches her that she ought to be with George Brent. And how was George ever going to get that across? Without anything to sing or dance, without even his mustache, he sometimes gets left out of some cast lists. But then look at the picture, look at the shadow the false eyelashes leave on Ruby Keeler's taut face—it's like a scar. The light in the pictures lets you know that showbiz is plenty tough; it's just that these kids will never blink.

And never forget that *42nd Street* was a Darryl Zanuck production. The happy-go-lucky story line is juxtaposed with increasingly fanciful dance numbers from Busby Berkeley that take the show over and lift it toward some new genre. If only, you feel, Zanuck had put Berkeley on a real gangster picture and told him to do the shoot-outs as production numbers! Imagine those flowering O's of girls' legs with Paul Muni blasting the petals away—she loves me, she loves me not.

Never mind, *42nd Street* hasn't dated yet. Every time Warner Baxter comes on as the desperate producer, fighting ill health and worrying whether or not he has a show, you feel for him. And the film was an original, not a stage rip-off. Rian James and James Seymour did the script from a story by Bradford Ropes. Lloyd Bacon directed, but Zanuck was in charge, and it has his quick-switch temperament, going tough, going soft on a dime. The show has to go on, and when Bebe gets up limping, Ruby Keeler just happens to know the part back to front. Baxter has a little trouble getting Keeler to act, but he asks her if she's ever been in love and gives her an express-train kiss. She never even blushes! Or acts.

The songs are by Harry Warren and Al Dubin, and they're peachy in themselves, but then Berkeley gets to work. It's not just that he did the set-piece routines with that astonishing aerial eye for orgasm. He could take a silly number like "Shuffle Off to Buffalo" and make you smile. Plus, Berkeley could never get enough shots of girls in their underwear or nightdresses or Joan Blondell pulling on her stockings. He was like Howard Hawks in that he knew how to toss in a little eye candy as a guy has to walk across the stage.

Dick Powell is a shameless mugger. Bebe Daniels is really very interesting (especially on "You're Getting to Be a Habit with Me"). Ginger Rogers is clearly itching for a break, yet she stands up and tells Baxter no, she's really not ready for the big time, give it to Ruby instead. Sol Polito photographed it. Guy Kibbee, Ned Sparks, and Una Merkel do the laughs. As to the irresistible, that's us, having a ball.

For Whom the Bell Tolls (1943)

The great drama in advance of the shooting of *For Whom the Bell Tolls* was who would play Maria, the Spanish peasant girl with cropped hair, the victim of gang rape in a Valladolid prison, who would be brought back into loving flower by Robert Jordan, Ernest Hemingway's hero from academia who also knows how to blow up a bridge. "Everyone" wanted the part, especially any actress who could claim a drop of foreign blood. So it was a surprise when the role was awarded to Vera Zorina, the Norwegian-German ballet dancer who was then married to George Balanchine.

A worse surprise hit Paramount as the first rushes came in from the Sierra Nevada location, north of Sonora. Zorina couldn't cut it. Whereupon David Selznick moved in with even stronger pleas on behalf of his contract actress Ingrid Bergman. He knew Ingrid was desperate for the part. She shot a test at Paramount (without letting her hair be cut) and waited. She was doing stills at Warners for *Casablanca* with Paul Henreid when Selznick called—Henreid treasured her cry of animal appetite on getting the good news. Selznick was well fed, too: He got $90,000 from Paramount for her services, nearly three times what he was contracted to pay her.

On the face of it, this was a major event: a best-selling novel from the country's leading writer, a sweeping love story that would become the great advertisement for sleeping bags, and a suitably anti-Fascist war story. Sam Wood was directing. Dudley Nichols had done the screenplay, very faithfully. And Gary Cooper was up there in the mountains in a leather jacket and a fedora waiting for his girl.

There are virtues to it all: Cooper and Bergman are plainly crazy about each other, Ray Rennahan's winter Technicolor shooting is superb, the locations are admirably Spanish, and the supporting cast is exotically foreign—even if no one was exactly Spanish. But in Wood's hands, the 130 minutes seem longer than the actual numbers. When it comes, the final attack on the bridge is exciting, but the uneasy days and nights in camp go on too long, and the flashback is awkward. You can't help feeling that Huston or Hawks would have given the film more edge.

Never mind: It was nominated for a Best Picture Oscar (it lost to *Casablanca*, of course), and it had rentals of more than $6 million. Cooper, Bergman, and Akim Tamiroff were all nominated. The Victor Young music is soupy and sad. But you do want to be in the sleeping bag with one or the other of the leads. The supporting cast is Tamiroff (more or less Russian), Katina Paxinou (Greek—she won the supporting Oscar), Arturo de Córdova (Mexican), Joseph Calleia (Maltese), Vladimir Sokoloff (Russian), Mikhail Rasumny (Russian), and Fortunio Bonanova (Italian).

This is arguably the most faithfully filmed piece of Hemingway ever, and the most successful. But that's not saying too much. The Hemingway style has never been captured on film, just as the Hawks style in the very cheeky *To Have and Have Not* has never been equaled. Great writers should take the money and run, or hope to be introduced to the actresses.

The Fountainhead (1949)

Having walked away from David O. Selznick's *Duel in the Sun* because of the intolerable competition between director and producer, King Vidor somehow agreed to make the movie of Ayn Rand's *The Fountainhead*. And so the director of *Our Daily Bread*—one of the most genuinely Communist pictures ever made in the United States—turned to the massive right-wing positivism of Ms. Rand. And what emerges, of course, is that the one is not so far from the other. In America, ideologies come and go, but personal passion—the confidence that the whole thing is about me—is what matters. Never forget that Charles Foster Kane, hailed as communist and fascist in his great obituary, had another title for himself: "American." What matters about *The Fountainhead* is that it is a King Vidor film, and one of the great examples of his towering achievement in trash.

Some say Howard Roark, the architect, was based on Frank Lloyd Wright. That immediately gives him an interest in pure design that is frivolous. Roark is a creative ego who designs buildings only initially for the good of society. His real purpose is to make a battleground with the craven forces of approval, and to assert his creative rights over all their treacherous second-guessing. He would as easily destroy a building as erect it. And surely the elements of movie in *The Fountainhead* help this scheme. Real buildings are obstinate; in the movies they are décor tents inflated or razed in one cut or dissolve.

So Rand involved herself in the production. She wrote the script, and then she stood up for Gary Cooper as Roark, instead of accepting Vidor's choice, Humphrey Bogart. That sounds like *Duel in the Sun* again. But pause a moment: In keeping her own baby talk and violent narrative energy, she served Vidor and left him to discover the cinematic expression that makes the dialogue seem natural. And in rejecting the more "intelligent" actor, the one who might have been better with the talk, she helped us see that Roark is more a force than a mind. Cooper is iconic, full of savage grace and grudging of conversation. Bogart was smart enough to sneer at the film's hysteria. Cooper never noticed it.

After that, it's like looking at the first film ever made. You can believe this is primitive cinema in which psychic thrust lies naked in the imagery, like a sword in a bed. There is no inhibition, and the viewer settles in after a few minutes. The exaggeration relies on the constant, penetrative accuracy of the imagery. You don't need to have Roark, the drill, and Dominique (Patricia Neal) explained. The film ravishes us. We might cry rape, but we have paid our money. And the risk of Rand's hysterical intellectualism is grounded by all the rock and stone, and by the impassive, unwavering Cooperism. What really shows Vidor's intelligence (a quality he was apt to mask) is the wit and cunning in the playing of Patricia Neal, Raymond Massey, Robert Douglas, and even Kent Smith. This is a film that reaches a point where it cannot make a mistake. That is the essence of Rand.

The Four Horsemen of the Apocalypse (1921)

Our first instinct is to say that the original *Four Horsemen* was the crucial Rudolph Valentino film, the one that lifted him out of obscurity and ensured five years of stardom. This is true, but it is the secondary truth. The real point about the picture is that it is Rex Ingram's vision, that Ingram is one of the spectacular directors from the silent era, and that this (rather more than *The Big Parade*, four years later) is the most moving statement on what war had done to the world.

The novel, by Vicente Blasco Ibáñez, was published in 1920, and despite its awkward set up—an Argentinean family sends cousins to fight on both sides in the Great War—it became a best seller. June Mathis, the head of the Metro script department, was not deterred by the evident expense of filming it—she smelled a big picture, and the deal was done for $20,000 against 10 percent of the profits. Moreover, Mathis was put in charge of the production: She would hire the director and do the casting. She opted for the Irishman Rex Ingram. He had nothing big to his credit yet, but Mathis believed that he had the eye and an epic sense of story. Between them, they settled on Rudolph Valentino to play Julio Desnoyers, the playboy who grows up during the war. Indeed, it was only after seeing Valentino try the tango that Ingram revived a dance sequence from an earlier film and built it into the sensational first appearance of Valentino as a star—in gaucho pants and a flat sombrero, effortlessly sexual in the dance and entirely commanding. When the scene played for real in the big picture, Valentino was a made man.

But Rudy only started at $100 a week, and *The Four Horsemen* cost $1 million. Photographed by John Seitz but truly visualized by Ingram, the picture built village and battlefield sets north of Los Angeles. The terrain was wrong, but nothing previously had revealed the terrible devastation of that war. Consider: The picture cost at least three times the budget of *The Big Parade*, and the reality of the war was magically lifted to the mythology or mysticism of the four horsemen themselves. And what makes the film work so well is that the sensuality and selfishness in the personal story are exposed and reeducated by the lessons of the total war. So it isn't just that Valentino was hot and sexy; he is also deeply thoughtful and tragic in the way he changes.

Alice Terry is the female lead; she was Ingram's wife and one of the great beauties in silent film (when you could get away with mere beauty). Moreover, she had real chemistry with Valentino. Other parts are played by Pomeroy Cannon, Josef Swickard, Brinsley Shaw, Alan Hale, Bridgetta Clark, Mabel Van Buren, Bowditch Turner, Nigel De Brulier, Jean Hersholt, and Wallace Beery. The film runs 131 minutes, and it seems to me in a class of its own for the time. Ingram was a real director, and it is to his credit that he understood both the war and the droop in Valentino's sad eyes. And somehow he bridged the gap.

4 Months, 3 Weeks, and 2 Days (2007)

The young Romanian director, Cristian Mungiu, had been gathering stories to make a panorama movie about life under Ceauşescu. But as he felt it taking shape, it seemed too comic in its general tone—and that was the last description that fitted those days. So he put aside that script and turned to one particular story that he had heard. A young woman, Gabita (Laura Vasiliu), needs an abortion—four months, et cetera, is how far along she is. Such a thing is illegal and difficult and expensive. She turns to a friend, Otilia (Anamaria Marinca), to help her. It began in Mungiu's mind as the story of two women, but as the picture advanced it became the story of one woman, the friend.

Otilia makes the arrangements, booking the room in the hotel—a shabby, official place, beset by petty regulations. The abortionist arrives—a mysterious, very tough man, not stupid but as hard as his trade and a scold to the women. And when it is clear that the women don't have enough money for him, why, he takes the extra in sex with the friend. We do not see this, but imagining it in the next room may be worse. And if the abortion works "tidily" then it is Otilia's job to dispose of the remains and to act as if nothing untoward has occurred.

Time and again, Mungiu exerts intolerable suspense through very long takes and relatively fixed compositions. The best example of this is at a dinner party that Otilia has promised to attend; there she has to wait before she can phone Gabita—still in midprocedure in the hotel room. Half a dozen figures fill the frame and the table in an unrelenting composition, with Otilia trapped in the center—the meal and the smalltalk play back and forth, and we await the telephone call or the news.

It is only when Mungiu has done that kind of thing several times that you realize how far he is a stylistic master (at a very early age), Bressonian in his reluctance to let people escape attention. The same severity applies in the long discussion with the abortionist, and it is enough to make the small anecdote seem like a trial by ordeal. This is as draining as an epic.

4 Months . . . won the Palme d'Or at Cannes and I suspect that it presages an important career. It is only in hindsight that one realizes the two huge questions that overhang the whole story without ever being directly addressed: Is it a good or bad thing to have an abortion? And were the days of Ceauşescu a monstrous deformation of the human spirit or just hard times that ingenuity, courage, and dogged perseverance can survive?

That those questions have been bypassed, or deferred, is the ultimate measure of Mungiu's intelligence—for he knows that the cinema is far better suited to the actual inspection of what happens in the passage of time than to the trite coughing up of an answering message. The cinema is a study of action, and action is behavior. The behavior of people under Ceauşescu is so fully laid out, we do not need to be given a "meaning" to go with it.

Frankenstein (1931)

Frankenstein, or the Modern Prometheus was published by Mary Shelley in 1818, and it was clearly a philosophical speculation (despite the atmosphere of horror) on the scientific responsibility in the possible remaking of life. While the *Dracula* story goes to the heart of neurosis, *Frankenstein* is always going to concern our future. That's why it's worth stressing the common error made with the story: that Frankenstein is the name of the monster. Not so: it's the name of the scientist.

By the time the project came to Universal's attention as a film, the novel was in the public domain. Carl Laemmle was all for leaving it there, but his son, Carl Junior, saw both its relevance and its appeal, and Dad let him go ahead. The studio bought the rights to the London play by Peggy Webling. They put John Balderston on the script, and then Garrett Fort and Francis Edward Faragoh. They were encouraged by the Frenchman Robert Florey, who was hopeful of directing the film. Indeed, Florey actually shot a test (though without a monster), and that's what persuaded Universal to assign the film to James Whale.

In turn, Whale cast Colin Clive as Frankenstein, and it was Whale's assistant, David Lewis, who noticed Boris Karloff in Howard Hawks's *The Criminal Code*. At one time, the part had been set for Bela Lugosi, but could the monster be that small? It was one of Whale's triumphs that, with makeup artist Jack Pierce, he created Karloff's look as the monster, with an enlarged skull. It was Faragoh's thought that the monster should inherit the brain of a vicious criminal (it's interesting to think of the whole genre if he had had the brain of Emerson or Herman Melville).

Whatever the audience wants, or expected, Whale makes this a whole drama—it's just that Clive's high-strung doctor is no longer as sympathetic as he might have been. He plays in a frenzy, and so much could be different if he was calm and thoughtful—some real scientists thought Clive helped establish the mad scientist cliché. Is the monster frightening? Well, once maybe, but not anymore. In seventy years, we have learned to see and hear the wounded humanity in the monster, and we can only revel in the great contribution Karloff was able to make to film history. He was a decent man and a serious actor, but truly his other work would not have made him famous.

There is a theory that Whale (who was gay) felt especially drawn to the monster. I think that's foolish, and an offense to Whale's professionalism in playing the horror for all it was worth. But in the haunting scene with the little girl at the lake, it's clear that Karloff wanted to play it more gently than Whale wished. Never mind; the material here is strong enough to invest horror with genuine ambiguities. In the years to come, it is far more likely that we might see a great film inspired by *Frankenstein* and man's quandary in designing life.

The film was a huge success—much more than *Dracula*—and may have earned $5 million in rentals.

Freaks (1932)

Is it possible? Could that small, slender, very good-looking guy have been some kind of freak—even if the freakishness didn't show? I mean, he was a perfect little man, except for his bad heart and that certainty in everyone who ever met him that he wasn't going to live very long. What did that do to him? There he was, being rational, sensible, practical, making sure the film-studio machine ticked over, and all the time he's saying to himself, "Will I wake up tomorrow?" The more I think about it, the more I like the idea of a movie in which there is said to be a monster in the studio. All likely leads are tested out. But no one ever suspects that the monster, the hideously deformed creature, is that paragon of law and order, Irving Thalberg. Until in one scene, where he's alone, he takes his head off and tops his body up with acid.

Far-fetched? Well, remember if you will that the very first production done at Metro-Goldwyn-Mayer after its merger was *He Who Gets Slapped,* in which Lon Chaney—and Irving and Chaney were very close—plays a man who has lost his science research and his wife, and as a result his face has been shocked and set in a hideous expression. Some see it as a grin; some believe it is horror. And then there is the reported fact that, over *Freaks,* Irving Thalberg said, "If it's a mistake, I'll take the blame."

Was it a mistake? I don't think so. Consider the case of Pauline Kael, who—somehow—was taken to see the film as a child and came away scared out of her wits by any malformation or oddity (and Pauline was small, very small). Then she went back as an adult and saw that the whole creatures in the film were the ugly ones. The freaks were warm, amiable, and tender. And so they are—not that it's that brilliant a coup to see that they might be. But the film of *Freaks* (credited to director Tod Browning) seems more modern still. I agree with those who say it might be Luis Buñuel, because its achievement is to subvert the anticipated order of things.

The screenplay was by Willis Goldbeck and Leon Gordon, working from a short story, "Spurs," by Tod Robbins. And it's a matter of how real-life people, beauties some of them in the circus, interact with the freaks. Money comes into it, and Cleopatra (Olga Baclanova), who marries a midget, Hans (Harry Earles), for his money. The film was shot by Merritt Gerstad, who did several of Browning's horror films, but the modernity here is a matter of the very straightforward style. Nothing is exaggerated; nothing is set up in a world of shadow or dementia. There is no souped-up music cuing us to the freaks' ugliness, and there are no italic close-ups. It's just a simple, cruel story told in 64 minutes. And it ends with Cleopatra reduced to the look and squawk of a chicken.

The other real people are Wallace Ford, Leila Hyams, Roscoe Ates, and Henry Victor, and then there are freaks—Siamese twins (kiss one and the other gets the thrill). The film cost $316,000 and lost more than $150,000—yet it plays somewhere all the time, when many of the M-G-M "beauties" of 1932 have been forgotten.

French Cancan (1955)

It was the simplest of ideas, and it seemed to coincide with the way, at sixty, Jean Renoir was thinking back to the old days. It would be the invention of the cancan, of French music hall, in the era when Paris belonged to his father, Pierre-Auguste Renoir, and his fellow painters. It would be his third film in color; it would be an excuse to celebrate some of the great artistes of the variety stage; and it would be a chance to make a film with Leslie Caron, the young French actress, already a Hollywood discovery, and the basis for Renoir's play *Orvet,* which he did with Caron in 1955. But Caron could not make the film (*Daddy Long Legs* and Fred Astaire called). So Renoir let his eye wander, and Françoise Arnoul was cast as Nini, the Montmartre laundress who will become the star of the cancan.

The impresario was based on the real figure of Ziegler, the founder of the Moulin Rouge and the character played by Jim Broadbent in Baz Luhrmann's *Moulin Rouge.* Renoir changed the name to Danglard, hired Jean Gabin to play him, and created a character who is a discoverer of female talent, who cannot stop moving forward in search of someone new. Each fresh discovery disturbs Danglard's company, but each new girl is a star, and so the company advances. Yet, within the enormous lighthearted energy of the let's-put-on-a-show film, there are plain signs of the damage done to people. Nini has a jealous fit when she realizes she has been supplanted by Guibolle (Lydia Johnson), and that's when Danglard and Renoir tell her to get on with it, to be professional, to see that instability is just a part of show business. Dance your heart out. There are some people—Gypsies, show people—who are good for nothing else.

What else? The prettiest sets of Paris in the late nineteenth century, made by Max Douy; the fabulous color photography by Michel Kelber; the salute to the trio from Jacques Becker's *Casque d'Or;* the chance to see such performers as Edith Piaf, Patachou, and Philippe Clay; the soulful eyes of Gianni Esposito as the prince in love with Nini; the immense force of María Félix as Lola di Castro, eating just carrots and steak, and nearly taking Arnoul's head off in their big fight; and the delirious froth and leaping of the cancan itself (choreographed by Claude Grandjean). Never filmed better.

French Cancan looks like one of those films in love with show business—with the bonus of its affections for the Impressionists' world. Yet it's profound as a demonstration of how for some people theater is a more lasting reality than life. Nothing can match the ecstasy of Danglard sitting backstage in his great chair, his foot tapping to the pounding dance and the gasps of wonder from an audience as the girls let everything go. I wonder if anyone at the age of sixty has ever made so lively a picture—or one that so subtly observes the loneliness of great performers?

The French Connection (1971)

When a movie opens, it is far easier to fall for its specious suggestions about its own purpose. And so *The French Connection* once could be passed off as a desperate study in the fight to keep "foreign" drugs (like surrealism, coffee, and Godard) out of New York. It followed that the rather informal police techniques offered by Gene Hackman and Roy Scheider were, if not forgiven, at least understandable. And so the film fell, apparently, into the category of movies in which we said to ourselves, Gee, don't we expect a lot of our cops—not just keeping us safe, upholding the Constitution, and being starry, but holding a movie together in the age of the ACLU.

Whereas it seems clearer now that what the film is really saying is, Look, how else are monstrous infants going to avoid growing up but by being cops? That's what allows them to dress that way, to stay up all night in a cold car eating junk, to talk like louts and vermin, to terrorize the streets with reckless car chases and unrestrained gunplay. The message of the sequel—that these kid kops will make perfect addicts—is already implicit. So the film is really saying to every kid in the audience, Let's rock and roll. That there is nothing remotely cool or hip in these Ubus only offends the Marcusian notion that rock is somehow a redemptive form.

So the French connection is a French drug dealer, but it is also the trashy-profound idea of director William Friedkin that the French do these things better. The title is an homage to the New Wave and to the alluring dandyism of the Frog himself, Fernando Rey, whose true cool remains a remote but mystical quest for our New York urchins. That's why the subway chase with Rey is actually a prolonged, absurdist seduction scene in which his last wistful wave is to the film as well as to Popeye Doyle (there's a lot of gay longing).

Isn't it easier now to recognize—and enjoy—the uninhibited grunge of this project, the enfants terribles–like gestures of the cops, and the poetry of the bumping bass notes in the piano? It's worth recalling that the film beat *A Clockwork Orange* for Best Picture at the Oscars that year—and why not, for this is really droogs in action without those decadent color schemes that Kubrick found in swinging England. No, *The French Connection* looks as real as names like Sal Boca (Tony LoBianco) and the "actual" cops in small parts, watching these actors with a mix of disapproval and longing. But in time those names become blunt words in a picture that is giving up law, language, and humanism. Brecht would have loved it, because here rogue cops are really taking over the city. Censorship (that pretty dream) stood on, helpless, and for a moment the saturnine, reptilian narcissism of Friedkin was a living terror. It all collapsed soon enough, but *The French Connection* remains to be seen as a jazzy dance of death. Civilians have been warned.

Frenzy (1944)

Here is a question for film buffs: Who was the first great screen actress to bring beauty et cetera to the work of Ingmar Bergman? Marks of distinction go to those naming Nine-Christine Jönsson in *Port of Call* or Doris Svedlund in *The Devil's Wanton,* but my real target is Mai Zetterling in the film that is Bergman's first writing credit, *Hets* in Swedish, *Frenzy* or *Torment* in English translation. It was directed by Alf Sjöberg, and I would be happy if this book encouraged more people to recognize him as an important director, albeit a rather lost figure.

Sjöberg was born in Stockholm in 1903. He acted with the Royal Dramatic Theater there and became Sweden's outstanding stage director—even Bergman acknowledged that. Sjöberg directed his first film in 1929 and was at his peak in the forties and early fifties. That's when he did his version of *Miss Julie* (with Anita Björk), as well as *Iris and the Lieutenant, Barabbas,* and *Karin Månsdotter.* And *Frenzy.*

Frenzy is set in the Sweden of 1944 (a neutral country), in a high school. Alf Kjellin plays a boy who falls in love with a young girl, played by Zetterling, who was nineteen at the time. Stig Järrel plays a sadistic teacher, named Caligula by the class but clearly rooted in fascism and looming over the lives of the students. Ingmar Bergman was the author of the screenplay; he was twenty-six at the time, immensely ambitious, though a long-haired outsider, looked at askance by his contemporaries yet oddly favored by young actresses, who believed he saw deeply into them. As Bergman did *Frenzy* he accepted a key job as director at the Hälsingborg Theater.

Frenzy attracted international attention. Kjellin got a Hollywood contract (using the name Christopher Kent), and he would appear in a few American films. Mai Zetterling won a contract with J. Arthur Rank in Britain and had a longer screen life than Kent, as a Swedish sexpot in British films. She then became an interesting director. Sjöberg died in 1980, eclipsed by Bergman.

I wouldn't dispute that Bergman is by far the larger figure. But that's no reason to neglect Sjöberg. The disappearance of his *Miss Julie* from critical appraisal is a bewildering thing. And *Frenzy* is not just a sinister, disturbing film but a clear influence on Bergman for several years and at least one source of his guilty obsession with sexual discovery. There was a time, in the late 1940s, when Bergman did a script for David O. Selznick: It was *A Doll's House,* with a happy ending, meant for Dorothy McGuire and Robert Mitchum. And that Bergman seemed ready to think of moving beyond Sweden. It was years before he saw the role that country would play for him as a remote fastness—ultimately in the form of the island of Faro, which the master could hardly leave. But Bergman was both an actor and a character working out the story of his life.

Frenzy (1972)

The Birds, Marnie, Torn Curtain, Topaz . . . that was the run of Alfred Hitchcock after *Psycho*, a succession of films that made even his great admirers begin to feel he'd lost touch or suffered fatigue at last. *Frenzy*, the next film, is a very special case, a mess, or a problem picture. Yes, Hitchcock was reported as often weary, or world-weary, during production. There were those who said that, returning to London in the early 1970s, Hitch could see only the place he had known in the twenties and thirties. So *Frenzy* is, in one way, a grindingly old-fashioned film. Yet there are bits of nastiness in it as startling as anchovies, things that seem to indicate his resentment at the way censorship had changed in the last few years. So the film needs to be watched with many concessions to the director's age, but then look out for the gotchas.

The source was a novel, *Goodbye Piccadilly, Farewell Leicester Square*, by Arthur La Bern (the author also of *It Always Rains on Sunday*). It's about a mad killer of women and the Air Force officer who is suspected of the crimes. The killer was Rusk, a man who obtained sexual satisfaction only in murder. The wronged man, Blaney, was an ex-hero, a drunk, and a man full of violence and unease. But this promise evaporated when Hitch hired playwright Anthony Shaffer to do the script and started pushing for deliberately archaic dialogue. Hitch and his writer did not get on very well. And Shaffer regretted that the script was clichéd, full of holes, and a throwback to older films. There was also a note of gruesome humor, much of it borrowed from the novel, but enough to make everyone wonder how the film would play in terms of taste. Universal paid for it all (just over $2 million), but it was shot entirely in London, with Gil Taylor as cameraman.

Turned down by Michael Caine, Hitch went with Barry Foster as Rusk and favored him far more than he did Blaney (Jon Finch). Indeed, Blaney feels like the morose outsider, while Rusk is the life and soul of the party—animated, cheeky, funny. He also plays a man in the fruit and vegetable trade (the work of Hitchcock's father).

The tone shifts violently. There is black humor that turns hideous; there are cooking scenes, involving a police inspector and his wife (Alec McCowen and Vivien Merchant), that seem out of control. The killing of Barbara Leigh-Hunt is really disturbing, sexually exploitative of the actress, and dark with cruelty. But then the shot that signals the killing of Anna Massey is done with an elaborate, floating crane that is exquisite—even if it seems out of place in this cut-and-dried film.

Frenzy is never stable or consistent. Much of it comes close to comic in its failures of tone. But then there are scenes that remind us of Hitchcock and suggest the frenzy he was feeling then. Far from a work of nostalgia, or a fond tribute to England, this is a piece of grotesque cinema, trying to be offensive and leaving us with the idea that Hitch feels uncomfortably close to his killer.

From Here to Eternity (1953)

They said it couldn't be filmed in the early 1950s—and in a way, they were right. If you want a full version of the James Jones novel, published in 1951, you need to go to the 1979 miniseries made for television, where the largest thing that emerges is that none of the five leading characters is as vivid or upstanding as they seemed in 1953. For instance, Sergeant Warden is a drunk and a mess, and the Donna Reed role really is a whore, and a pretty stupid one at that.

But they did make the film. Daniel Taradash brought in a screenplay that took an 800-page novel down to 118 minutes, cleaned up the language, and made the characters some of the most commanding in American film drama. Buddy Adler produced it. Harry Cohn stuck with it. And director Fred Zinnemann steered a way past all the rocks. He sat through the rage for Aldo Ray as Prewitt (Ray was far closer to the character in the novel) and clung to the idea of Montgomery Clift's brightest moment. He had the luck to lose Joan Crawford and the brilliance to cast Deborah Kerr. He trusted Burt Lancaster—though Burt made Warden a paragon compared with William Devane's earthy performance in the TV film. And Zinnemann got Sinatra instead of Eli Wallach for Maggio—let's not begin to argue how that happened.

The screenplay's focus on the action is a fine example of that mathematical art, and certainly for 1953 the texture of life in the military felt right to a middle-class audience that had never been there. Indeed, the treatment that Prewitt is subjected to was nasty and disturbing and enough of a shock. Of course, that still leaves a stunning gulf between real Army life and the public's notion of realism—which says a huge amount about the quality of our movies from the golden age.

Above all, this complicated romantic story is so wonderfully aimed at December 7, 1941. The sudden collapse of urgent personal stories in the name of war is what is most impressive about this picture, and most true to the mood of 1941. In a world war, millions of ordinary people put their lives and dreams on hold. In turn, the quality that a nation brings to its war is exemplified in part by the stubbornness of Prewitt and Maggio and the expertise of Sergeant Warden at getting things done.

So the failings of this film do not date or endanger it. Prewitt is still blowing taps. Donna Reed is still there like a poor boy's dream of calm. Burt and Deborah are rolling on the Hawaiian beach in a huge ad for the islands. Ernest Borgnine is fearsome and hideous. Thirteen Oscar nominations. Eight wins—including Best Picture and a statue apiece for Zinnemann, Reed, Sinatra, Taradash, and cameraman Burnett Guffey. Definitive popular cinema.

Funny Face (1957)

You can say that everything works on *Funny Face,* from the clever way director Stanley Donen integrates the title song and the darkroom development of pictures of Audrey to the artful playing on the reputation and style of Richard Avedon, the fashion photographer on whom Fred Astaire's character, Dick Avery, is based. But the heart of the film is the authentically touching rapport between Astaire and Audrey Hepburn. In the 1950s, she did pictures with several older men—Gregory Peck, Gary Cooper, Humphrey Bogart—but *Funny Face* is the most innocent and magical, because Audrey is so moved by being close to Fred. Once upon a time, Ginger gave Fred sex—but Audrey brings him assurance and pleasure. It's not that we really contemplate their marriage after the film stops, but we settle for the winged fantasy of their being together for an hour.

Leonard Gershe did the screenplay, working from a Gershwin musical that was never produced—not from the 1927 show called *Funny Face,* with music by George, lyrics by Ira, in which Fred and Adele Astaire had one of their triumphs. Gershe and Donen capitalized on Paris (tourism was still an infant business) and the current fad for existentialism, which is actually quite funny, and which serves the place of Marxism in *Silk Stockings.*

But the inspiration of the film is to make the fashion business its engine, and I think we respond to the uncomplicated adoration of clothes that Donen, Avedon, Audrey, and costume designer Edith Head had in common. (Don't forget that in 1957, fashion glory was another concept about to have meaning for the middle class.) Of course, the film's confrontation of hostile worlds—the mind versus clothes—is another version of the battle between lingerie and hair shirts in *Silk Stockings,* and thus *Ninotchka.* And in that battle, it's worth saying that Audrey's wide eyes stand up for reading in a vigorous way.

Then there is VistaVision (originally) and Ray June's photogravure color—so much of the time, the imagery seems still wet from the developing tray. The dances are not complicated, but Audrey had once been a dancer, and she acquits herself very well in motion, if not always up to the high standard of "How Long Has This Been Going On?" in the ravaged bookstore. And then there is the gaiety and utter conviction of "On How to Be Lovely," and Kay Thompson's moment of revelation on film—not just her encapsulation of every fashion editor from Carmel Snow to Diana Vreeland, but the exuberant "Think Pink," with its total self-confidence and the near certainty that tomorrow will be green.

Funny Face is a love story that blends two fragile fantasies (the idea of being Fred and Audrey); it is a love letter to Paris; and it is one of the last great musicals, taking its songs from here and there, but reminding us that in the great age of popular art in America called the movies, the joy of it all was sustained by a few geniuses like George and Ira and Fred, all born to the theater but in love with movies. Let's see it tonight.

Fury (1936)

It was director Fritz Lang's story, told in later years, that after he had hung around a good deal at M-G-M waiting for a project, somehow a short treatment, "Mob Rule," by Norman Krasna, was found for him. The studio regarded it as a C picture, Lang said, about a man who is nearly lynched for a crime he did not commit and who then returns as if from the dead to punish those who acted against him. The studio records suggest it was an A picture, that producer Joseph L. Mankiewicz had wanted to direct it himself, that he developed the script with Bartlett Cormack and offered it to Lang.

There were arguments. Lang wanted the man to be a lawyer. No, said Mankiewicz; an ordinary guy, a John Doe. It seems clear that at first in America, Lang had difficulty grasping the possibilities of a John Doe; he was still living in an atmosphere of the crowd and great men. Lang wanted elements of race in the story. The studio wouldn't have it. There was even an idea that the man's girlfriend (Sylvia Sidney) would fall for the lawyer investigating the case. That is gone, too, though maybe it lingers in glances.

It is also fairly clear that Lang had serious arguments with his star, Spencer Tracy, and with his cameraman, Joseph Ruttenberg. Lang was far from the easiest guy to get along with—after *Fury* he did not make another film at M-G-M until *Moonfleet* in 1955.

So it's important to stress that, despite working within the studio system, Fritz Lang made something utterly uncommon and un-Metro-like out of *Fury*. It is a blazing indictment that doesn't feel like America. Lang is still recoiling from the sudden, exposed energies of the mob in Germany. Yet if *Fury* is not quite America, it's close enough to teach America a lesson. "I could smell myself burning," says Tracy's victim. And he delivers the line with a terrible harshness that makes this a rare political statement in American film. Above all, in its view of people—the collective of ordinary guys—there is an accumulated loathing. You can see how far Lang fears and anticipates the crowd.

Tracy is immense, still, and dangerous. In Sylvia Sidney, Lang found the great face of his early American films. And the supporting cast is very rich: Walter Abel, Bruce Cabot, Edward Ellis, Walter Brennan, Frank Albertson, George Walcott, and Arthur Stone.

Reviewing the film in England, Graham Greene smelled the burning, too: "I am not trying to exaggerate, but the brain does flinch at each recurring flick of truth in much the same way as at the grind-grind of an electric road-drill: the horrible laughter and inflated nobility of the good citizens, the youth leaping on a bar and shouting, 'Let's have some fun,' the regiment of men and women marching down the road into the face of the camera, arm in arm, laughing and excited like recruits in the first day of a war."

In that shrewd view of excitement, we have the unexpected discovery that Lang in America may be as harsh as he was "at home."

Gaslight (1944)

Once upon a time, it was alleged in Britain that it was a crime when Metro-Goldwyn-Mayer, intent on filming the Patrick Hamilton play *Gaslight*, was trying to buy up and destroy every print of the 1940 British film, directed by Thorold Dickinson. Of course, there should have been room for both, and now that the Dickinson film has been recovered—and despite the fascinating, morbid cruelty in Anton Walbrook's performance as the husband, a man who secretly yearns to be exposed and punished—still the George Cukor version, done at Metro, is a more satisfying picture.

The play was a great success in London and on Broadway, where it was called *Angel Street*, with Vincent Price as the husband. But the Hamilton text is set in a very short time period, and as it begins the husband is already a terror and a needle to the wife. He is driving her crazy, or rather he is arranging events to make her feel uncertain about her sanity—hence the new use of the word *gaslighting*. What does he want? Oh, just some vulgar jewels that are somewhere on the property or in the attic.

To see the Dickinson film nowadays is to get the idea that *Gaslight* would work without the jewelry; in other words, it is just for sport, to pass the time and vent his malice, that the husband is trying to drive his wife mad. As such, there is more than a hint of Pinteresque intimidation to come in Hamilton's setup—and Hamilton is at his best when dealing with unmotivated dislike or ill feeling.

What makes the Cukor film more sophisticated and genre-pleasing is that Charles Boyer and Ingrid Bergman really do seem like lovers at first. The American film backtracks to trace their romance, and that has the effect of shifting the balance of the old play: Hamilton was interested in, and half admiring of, the husband; the Metro film is clearly a vehicle and an ordeal for the wife—and thus it was no wonder that she might end up in Oscar territory. But Ingrid Bergman's victory is also a reflection of her own profound attachment to sadomasochistic feelings. She was at her best as a victim, and there is no doubt that we shudder for her stability, especially when she is caught between the unkind stealth of Boyer and the insolent sexuality of Angela Lansbury as the maid (a brilliant performance). But I think Bergman secured the Oscar because of the resolve and the fierceness with which she then tortures Boyer.

Of course, I have so far omitted Joseph Cotten's Scotland Yard detective, which is no attack on Cotten—always a valiant actor and often priceless. But this character is a sham and a waste of everyone's time. If only Hamilton had found a way for the wife to solve and surmount her own problem. But I don't think he ever liked women enough, or trusted them to be strong. So the melodrama lumbers along toward a stupid happy ending. Even in the Cukor film there is every evidence that marriage is a nightmare to be avoided at all costs.

The General (1927)

The world does not deserve Buster Keaton—yet he does not complain. He is devoted to his beloved, Miss Annabelle Lee, yet what does he get in return? Simply her haughty-miss assumption that if he's not wearing the gray yet (the nation is at war—civil war), then surely he must be a coward and not worthy of her attention. Let me tell her something: when it comes to attention, she's hardly a starter if she considers that a man of such indifference and sterling, engineer's impartiality might even feel the breeze of a cannonball on his smooth cheek. This is a man who lives inside his own head (the only safe place to be), for whom that noble locomotive *The General* is the embodiment and the projection of all inward thoughts of purpose. And a train can be a hero in war. It can defy your civil war just by continuing to keep to its schedules.

As for North and South, Johnny Gray (Keaton) works to a quite different discipline: He is yin and yang (surely you know that restrained face from the great films of Ozu and Mizoguchi). It is not that Buster has no feelings, or even that he has risen above such things like a theoretical physicist. But he adheres to a code in which it is vulgar to express feelings. The other point of reference is Bresson. Time and again, as you watch images of Keaton, simply repeat to yourself some of the runes from Bresson's *Notes on Cinematography:* "It is not a matter of acting 'simple' or of acting 'inward' but of not acting at all," say, or "Put your models through reading exercises, designed to equalize the syllables and do away with any intentional personal effect."

So Keaton is in the nineteenth century again, not detached from history or even being old-fashioned but because he loves the past as a secure view. It is a serene, flawless America you see. He really does not notice or bother with the war. No, the war is simply a mishap that is blocking (or missing) the sweet utility of trains. And you could say that in his innocent way Buster does draw history's attention to this. He may even look forward to another war, where knights ride their trains like immense jousting lances.

The General is a story of mechanics and engineering in which Buster alone seems to grasp the way gears, wheels, and locomotion work and have purposes of their own that mock the disposition of armies on a battlefield. You see, Buster, in his sweet way, is quite mad. He doesn't really want the girl—just the idea of her. And he doesn't honestly understand how a war could be decided, not when war can cause *The General* to topple into a wooded gulch (somewhere in Oregon, they say), like a drugged King Kong.

So, really, the mystery with Keaton is whether we are going to go along with the cover story—that these are comedies—or have we the courage and the resolve to see that the films are demonstrations of order in an age of chaos? I am not being unduly fanciful. If you just watch Keaton and respond to his great masked desire, it is delicate order he wants. And deserves.

Gentleman Jim (1942)

Boxing and the movies grew up together. In the days when big title fights roamed the West, keeping ahead of the law, one side of the ring was often set aside for the camera stand from which the fight would be recorded—and the movie then played around the country. Today we seem to have ground boxing down to the level of pulverized fraud, but as recently as Leonard v. Duran, Spinks v. Tyson, and the great days of Ali, the television income from a fight (network or pay-per-view) was what kept the purses fat. One of David O. Selznick's first assignments was a film to promote Luis Firpo in such a way that he would seem to have a chance against Jack Dempsey.

James J. Corbett (1866–1933) was not exactly a gentleman—he was the son of a San Francisco livery-stable owner—but he was a "scientific" boxer. What that meant, in a nutshell, was that he was likely to employ a dodging skill that might avoid getting hurt and damaged but which placed his own punches as his brutal opponent tired. The previous type—the fighter—had reckoned it was natural to get hurt on the way to hurting your opponent more. Courage and strength would beat skill, and in those days fights were fought to a finish. Corbett was the pioneer of a way of boxing in which a man could win on points, wear boxing gloves instead of going bare-knuckle, and talk coherently twenty years later.

Corbett, after his retirement, appeared in *Gentleman Jack*, a "play" that concluded with an exhibition fight. Raoul Walsh's film *Gentleman Jim* is derived from that play, though it was given a smart script by Vincent Lawrence and Horace McCoy. Of course, it hinges on the 1892 fight in which Corbett defeated John L. Sullivan for the heavyweight championship of the world—in fact, *Gentleman Jim* was meant for release on the fiftieth anniversary of that turning point in boxing history.

Walsh had spent time in San Francisco (where the film is set) with Jack London, and he was eager to get the mood of the place. I suspect that the script inflated the role of Corbett as a social figure in part because that was how Errol Flynn wanted to play the role. But in the confrontation of Flynn and Ward Bond (who plays Sullivan), Walsh found one of his loveliest arrangements for sparring heroes. Naturally enough, Bond comes on at first as an Irish braggart, but after his defeat he delivers his belt to Flynn in a scene that is one of the most beautiful pieces of hallowed sentiment in American male cinema. According to Walsh, everyone on the set was moved—and you can expect the same.

Flynn loved his role, and though he was not a heavyweight, he is magnificent stripped to the waist. Sid Hickox photographed the picture, and the period feeling is very well done. The boxing scenes are likely a lot cooler than the real thing, but it was still felt that audiences were unready for the violence—*The Set-Up*, *Body and Soul*, and *Champion*, just a few years ahead, were far rougher.

Alexis Smith plays the ladyfriend (a sure sign of social aspirations), and the cast also includes Jack Carson, Alan Hale, John Loder, William Frawley, Minor Watson, and Arthur Shields.

Gentlemen Prefer Blondes (1953)

Was there ever a movie in which Miss Marilyn Monroe looked more relaxed, or closer to having a good time? You have to wonder what happened. Howard Hawks was a famous womanizer, but it's hard to think of him mustering the patience to endure all the takes that soured Billy Wilder's milk of human kindness on *Some Like It Hot*. It's all too easy to think of Hawks flirting with Marilyn, and being bewildered and dismayed that she couldn't volley a little repartee back at him. Was he uncommonly benign? Was she in between crises? It's a serious question for biographical research, and the chance of puncturing the gloomy legend that Miss Monroe scarcely had a calm or merry day in her life. Of course, you could argue that that naughty grin of hers came from something, or you could just say that when a girl sees she's got Charles Coburn, George Winslow, and Marcel Dalio in one film looking after her, she feels safe.

Gentlemen Prefer Blondes is an American classic, originally a novel by Anita Loos, funny but deadpan, about a girl from Little Rock getting ahead, and getting jewelry too, in the new age of jazz and movies. It is a superb satire on movies and their world, and it was such a success in print that it sparked a 1926 stage play where June Walker played Lorelei Lee. That led to a 1949 stage musical, where Carol Channing was first seen by the world as Lorelei. The show had music by Jule Styne and lyrics by Leo Robin, including such songs as "Bye Bye, Baby," "Diamonds Are a Girl's Best Friend," and "A Little Girl from Little Rock." Three years later, Fox brought that musical to the screen, with Hawks directing a screenplay by Charles Lederer.

It's a very relaxed film in which the numbers get a lot of care. There are terrific compositions in pink, black, red, and diamond in lavish Technicolor (photography by Harry Wild), with sets by Lyle Wheeler, Joseph Wright, and Claude Carpenter. There is the very adroit partnership of Marilyn with Jane Russell, who was still one of the most attractive women on the screen. Their singing voices blend very well, and Jane has a genuine affection for Marilyn—you can see it and feel it, and I'm sure it's as helpful as anything else. When the two of them turned, in full costume, to the flourish of Jack Cole's choreography, something called glamour was in full sail.

Still, I treasure the film for the more intimate scenes. Marcel Dalio is an inspired mess as the judge in the court scenes, and the idea of Charles Coburn simply beholding Marilyn Monroe is always a touching version of the dreamer and the dream. But the scenes between Lorelei and Henry Spofford III (Winslow) make the most tender romance in the picture. Let me just say that in the original Spofford was an adult. It was Hawks's idea to use Winslow and to make him a three-hundred-year-old child.

Germany Year Zero (1948)

At some moment in the late 1940s, Ingrid Bergman and Roberto Rossellini were proposing a picture to Sam Goldwyn. They were not married yet, but they were locked in scandal, so that they were almost bound to work with each other. Goldwyn was encouraging. He had a soft spot for Ingrid, and he admired the director's *Rome, Open City.* He liked the story Rossellini was outlining. But then something troubled him, and he asked if he could see another Rossellini picture. Sure, said Roberto—I've just finished *Germany Year Zero.* That blew it.

After the film played, there was silence in the screening room. A couple of days later, Goldwyn called Ingrid and said, "I'm sorry, I can't do the movie. I can't understand the man: I don't know what he's doing, what he's talking about. He doesn't know anything about budgets; he doesn't know anything about schedules." Alas, Ingrid had to agree—and they weren't married yet.

Germany Year Zero was scripted by Rossellini, Max Kolpé, and an uncredited Sergio Amidei. It's the story of a German boy, Edmund, who lives in the ruins of Berlin after World War II. In a way, Rossellini was acting on the experience of his colleague Vittorio De Sica that the neo-realist approach worked very well if you had a child as an appealing central character. That was the model for De Sica's *Shoeshine.* But the child in *Germany Year Zero* is one of the most intractable and unappealing of movie children. Yes, his life is very hard and he is scrambling to survive. But Edmund is a little Nazi still. He hungers for a revived Reich, for Nazism brought back, and in the most sinister passage in the film he sits amid the rubble of the city listening to a recording of Hitler. Had enough yet? Well, finally, this boy will kill himself.

Of course, this is not quite all. What is remarkable about the film is the way a moving camera traces the boy's grim life. Even in the ruins and with very limited means, Rossellini and his cameraman, Robert Juillard, achieve astonishing passages of sheer movie direction in which the city is sometimes like a desert island, sometimes like a madhouse. The boy may be insane. He never comes close to that natural appeal shared by most children. Bergman herself pointed that out, and Rossellini confessed that, once in Germany, he had been so consumed by anger and rage that he could do nothing but make the boy hateful.

So *Germany Year Zero* is a truly terrifying film—to see the basic element in life, the emblem of hope and innocence, so warped. It makes a very candid, brutal film, and in many respects there may be no other movie that comes so close to the devastation of postwar Europe. The boy himself, Edmund Moeschke, was not starved or deprived, but he has such a hard, closed face. The first time I saw *Germany Year Zero* I couldn't be sure whether it was a feature or a documentary. That was Rossellini's aim, of course, and Ingrid Bergman might have taken the ambiguity as a warning. But no one who has seen the film will ever forget it.

Gertrud (1964)

Coming just four years before his death, the stillness and intensity of Carl Dreyer's *Gertrud* and the seeming lack of cinematic vitality dismayed many festival audiences who wanted to acclaim the maker of *The Passion of Joan of Arc*. It was hard for them to see how far Dreyer had advanced. And it was a puzzle—in the age of Godard, perhaps—to realize that a succession of formally arranged two-shot conversations could be as absorbing or as painful as the heightened close-ups from *Joan*. More than forty years later, *Gertrud* looks like one of the great films, an assault on bourgeois morality and compromise, and a plea for passion even if the quick gaze found little of it in the film.

As the story starts, the marriage of Gertrud and Gustav Kanning (Nina Pens Rode and Bendt Rothe) is over. They sit in the same spaces, but she cannot look at him. And it is clear already that her search for love is frustrated by the fact that Gustav—soon to be appointed a cabinet minister—wants to maintain the decorum of having a consort. There is a chilling visit from Gustav's mother—to collect her allowance—that outlines Gertrud's future.

She is leaving for an affair with a far younger man, Erland Jansson (Baard Owe), a composer, possibly a great talent, but a selfish young man, a determined wastrel, someone waiting to use Gertrud. Their town is visited by a great poet, Gabriel Lidman (Ebbe Rode), a man in middle age. Once upon a time he and Gertrud had been lovers. She was ready to give up everything for him, but she found a scrap of paper on Gabriel's desk on which he had written how woman's love and man's work are mortal enemies. So that was the end of their affair, and it cannot be regained now. In the end, Gertrud decides, even at her age, to go to Paris and enter the Sorbonne. In the coda, she has gone from blond to white hair. Axel (Axel Strøbye), her sponsor in Paris, is with her. But she has published a book on Racine, and she plans her end. A simple headstone will say "Amor Omnia," and the grass and the anemones will grow over her grave. The door closes on the small house where most of the action has taken place.

Gertrud comes from a play by Hjalmar Söderberg. It is not only gradual and measured. In fact, it is four encounters that stress the same thing: this woman's refusal to compromise. It is just that with every repetition the consequences and the feeling grow deeper. There are very long takes and simple, theatrical arrangements of characters, yet this is a movie, a photographed thing in which reflections in a mirror and a final, very wide angle come as comprehensive statements and insights. Dreyer's control is immaculate, but it never seems to diminish the freedom in which Gertrud acts. So the film is destined, and recited as much as spoken, but it feels like the utterance of liberty.

Henning Bendtsen photographed it with a flashback and dream—and with a restraint that exactly suits the power of Nina Pens Rode in the central performance.

Giant (1956)

When I think of *Giant* in hindsight, the years and the acres of the Benedict story are as vacant as a Texas horizon. Yes, I can recall Rock Hudson and Elizabeth Taylor, his paunch sagging, her hair turning blue and gray, and I suppose that the film attests to the gradual, erosive way in which parents set in privilege become more open to doubt—or is it tolerance? I can conjure up a very melodramatic scene in a diner where Hudson is beaten up because he has brought a Mexican-looking kid—his grandson—into the place and expected decent service. I know that Dennis Hopper and Carroll Baker are Benedict children, the one trying to be a doctor who serves the Mexican people and the other flirting with that awful Jett Rink.

I daresay that screenwriters Fred Guiol (whoever he was) and Ivan Moffat (whom I knew as a faded English gent dining at Hamburger Hamlet, suave, funny, and noble) did a very clever job in bringing the immense Edna Ferber novel—it was a paperback too big to hold—down to a mere 201 minutes. I know that George Stevens (who did so many better films) won the Oscar for Best Director. It's just that I can't remember anything that happens in the film, apart from moments in the sea of size and the larger thought (or hope) that Texas might stay another place (this was seven years before Dallas became a cursed place everyone knew). It's a film that passes like the Atlantic in the night as you fly to England—it must be there, and yes, if you woke, there it was, still unwinding on its screen. But all I can recall is that awful Jett Rink.

Jett is the unschooled hoodlum cowboy who has a scrap of land that, when he has looked at it long enough with his longing and his desire, erupts with oil. There is surely the inadvertent subtext in the film that, because by virtue of class, precedent (her marriage), and mere taste he cannot have Leslie (Elizabeth Taylor), Jett sits alone, day and night, masturbating his land until it comes and he is the new Texas. Not just a rich, black kid (Dean was wreathed in oil, and I can imagine he bathed in it before the scene), slamming big old Bick in the stomach and racing off to be the real, new Texas—to be Howard Hughes, even. I still see James Dean's Rink the old man as one of the cleverest portrayals of Hughes on film: all power and no character.

No one is ever going to go back and watch all 201 minutes of *Giant* again. (God help us, there may even be a restored version at 221!) But every scene with Dean and every glimpse of Mercedes McCambridge as Luz, Bick's rough sister, are like awkward, unsettled, unhealed real movie. Dean fought with Stevens, it's said. I should hope so. And I wonder if there were moments in the life of George Stevens (himself an upstart once) when he marveled at how he had buried a real movie in this fatuous legend of size.

Gilda (1946)

The posters proclaimed, "There NEVER was a woman like Gilda!" but they might just as well have addressed the barbed novelty of the picture itself. There are so many ways in which it breaks uneasy ground. Ballin Mundson (George Macready) runs a nightclub-casino somewhere in South America during World War II. One night on the waterfront, he uses his "little friend" (a sword cane) to rescue a down-and-out tough, Johnny Farrell (Glenn Ford), from thugs. Is it friendship that begins between them, or more? Whatever, it seems excessive when Mundson sets Johnny up as his close friend and assistant. It is notably unclear what kind of film this is so far, and we are left with Ford's weak grin and Macready's scarred authority gazing at each other.

Then Mundson goes away and returns with a wife, Gilda (Rita Hayworth). Suddenly, we are in a Rita Hayworth picture, yet we have backed into it. Gilda is beautiful, a little wild and reckless. She knew Johnny "before" and seems ready to resume the affair, but he is shocked and scathing toward her—cruel, as if he would prefer to disown her. Johnny stays loyal to Mundson and to his idea that Gilda is trash.

We realize that Mundson and his club are a front for Nazi operations. He goes missing, presumed dead. Johnny now runs the casino. He marries Gilda, but only as a way of keeping her confined in case Mundson returns. She takes her revenge by performing at the nightclub—this is the famous "Put the Blame on Mame" routine, which serves as a vicious rebuke to Johnny's caution and masked gayness. Of course, in the last twenty minutes, the plot clears itself up magically, so that Johnny and Gilda may be left in some semblance of starry union. Except that nobody who treasures *Gilda* can ever believe a word of it.

For Columbia, this was a way of getting Hayworth back to work after the Welles marriage. And the film was arranged as that marriage died. The key executive at Columbia was Virginia Van Upp, *Gilda*'s producer, who gave a final rewrite to the Marion Parsonnet script from a story by E. A. Ellington. Is that where the twisted gender confusions come from, along with the flagrant portrait of a natural woman, a libertine, too sensual and honest for these crouched male figures?

There's no clear answer, just the self-loathing in Ford's performance (very unusual in that actor), the sardonic superiority of Macready, and the savage abandon of Hayworth. Photographed by Rudolph Maté and dubbed by Anita Ellis, she was at her greatest in the key number, wearing black satin (by Jean Louis) and long gloves, with hair to her shoulders. The whole film is fascinating, but the celebration of Gilda is quite remarkable. The design is by Stephen Goosson and Van Nest Polglase, and the supporting cast includes Joseph Calleia, Steven Geray, Joseph Sawyer, Gerald Mohr, and Ludwig Donath.

The film was a huge personal success for Hayworth, yet it trapped her, too, in ways she hated. Ever afterward, she said that men went to bed with Gilda and woke up with her. Charles Vidor directed, and "Mame" is as great a musical commentary on a poisoned relationship as the Cyd Charisse dances in Nicholas Ray's *Party Girl*.

The Girl Can't Help It (1956)

There are so many reasons for putting *The Girl Can't Help It* in this book: as recognition of its director, Frank Tashlin; as some gesture toward the rock-and-roll picture; as one more sign of the swiftness with which pastiche overtook movies in the late 1950s; and as a way of remembering Jayne Mansfield, who was not just a more thoughtful version of Marilyn Monroe but a comic commentary on—nearly an animated version of—the extraordinary fantasy of her own body. Not to mention the stupid innocence of the title and its way of arguing that no one was ever to blame for the thing later revealed as sexual exploitation.

The Girl is plainly a new version of *Born Yesterday*. Agent Tom Miller (Tom Ewell) is hired by slot-machine king Fatso Murdock (Edmond O'Brien) to make a rock star out of his girlfriend, Jerri Jordan (Jayne Mansfield). Of course, Tashlin and cowriter Herbert Baker didn't want to make Jerri a corruption-busting democrat. She is already well-enough developed to be the constant object of humor, or ridicule. In fact, Ms. Mansfield had a bust measurement of forty inches, and whereas the more normal thirty-five, say, could look enormously attractive on someone like Monroe or Novak, those few extra inches take us into the area of the grotesque and the stricken American embarrassment that greeted it.

Mansfield was educated and educable. She studied at the universities of Texas and California, and she was often heard to talk sense in ways denied to Monroe. And though she had serious ambitions to be an actress, she seemed to have had that other "intelligence," the one ready to compromise with fate and allow herself to be portrayed as a cartoon character. Thus the infamous moment in this film when she holds two bottles of milk up to her breasts and says that she reckons she is qualified for motherhood. She was in pictures for a decade, and acted quite well once or twice, before age added to her excessiveness and she was treated as only a joke. She died in a car crash aged thirty-four, and in the process she was decapitated. The national comedians were hushed—waiting to hear if maybe other "comic" parts had been lopped off, too.

I'm tough on the director for the way he treated her, but that doesn't mean that Tashlin (a key figure in the career of Jerry Lewis) wasn't very funny and smart with human talent that was "over the top." Nor does Mansfield operate with any self-pity.

Funnier now, in most ways, is the attitude the film and Twentieth Century Fox took to the new music. The fact that Tom is an agent allows the film to be a parade of rock acts, filmed in color and CinemaScope and covering a bizarre range: Fats Domino, Little Richard, Gene Vincent & His Blue Caps, the Platters, the Treniers, and Julie London, who is said to be playing "herself" and seems uneasy. The cast includes Henry Jones, John Emery, and Juanita Moore, not to forget Tom Ewell, who found a short-lived glory as the limp straw meant to stir the big blond drinks of Americana.

The Glenn Miller Story (1954)

There's a sweet irony in the way in 1954—with rock and roll sounding faintly, like drums beyond the horizon—the Glenn Miller sound reached its last great swan song—"String of Swans," if you like. And there is absolutely no irony at all in the film's credo that big-band leaders are the sweetest guys in the world. Some spectators still hold the opinion that the loss of Miller was the most devastating blow to American sentiment and coziness in the entire war.

That *The Glenn Miller Story* proved so enduring a favorite (rentals of $7.5 million, twice those of *Singin' in the Rain*) has to do with these strokes of luck, but it owes more to the sweetness of the music and the cunning with which Jimmy Stewart could take on the martyr-to-be insouciance of this guy who just longed to put a clarinet on top of a sax section. There are those who look at the hard-jawed face of the real Major Miller and divine a strict manager, a fusspot perfectionist, and something other than the world's greatest sweetheart. It doesn't matter, for just as the Miller band stayed together long after "swing" had collapsed, there's little doubt that this cuddly movie ensured the band's longevity.

Of course, the picture was made by Anthony Mann, who in the same period was revealing a much tougher, nastier Stewart in films like *The Far Country* and *The Naked Spur*. So the subterfuge of it all, and the view of Glenn as a guy who deserved his own music, is plainly from cloud-cuckoo-land. It's not until Scorsese's *New York, New York* that we get a bandleader as coldhearted as that profession requires.

But this picture is more than postwar nostalgia or merciless syrup pouring out of the "Little Brown Jug." It is also a fond account of genius slowly surpassing all its obstacles; the scene in which Miller hears the way to do "Moonlight Serenade" is worthy of *Amadeus*. Beyond that, the treatment of the military band, and the scene in the English hospital where they keep playing through an air-raid, amounts to one of the great martial moments in American film. Indeed, Mann loves this music as much as he does the landscape in the Westerns. The affection is in the detail.

June Allyson is the sweetheart and the wife, and I have to say that she and Stewart manage to be fur on flesh in a quite excruciating and shameless way. (I have a strange dream of a Hans-Jürgen Syberberg movie in which Adolf Hitler watches *The Glenn Miller Story* and kills himself as it ends.) There is also a version of "Basin Street Blues," with Louis Armstrong, that could leave a wide-eyed mind wondering why and how America has ever had a race problem. So this is phoney-baloney, but you can know the picture shot by shot and the deceit still works. There's a clue here to the power of music in films that no one wants to hear or admit.

The Godfather (1972)

So many things are on show here—how a pulp novel, adapted by its author, Mario Puzo, and by the director, Francis Ford Coppola, becomes a landmark. Then there is the miracle that the same picture could be one of the great American films, an immediate and widespread critical success as well as the most successful picture ever made in America. Don't forget that for a few years *The Godfather* was our box-office champion, just as it became a model for many people seeking to be glorious (and impassive) but rich in Hollywood. And notice how it stands for a brief era when the details of our evil could be inspected without moral relief being insisted upon. Michael Corleone is the hero. He is the boy meant to be saved from the family's life but who himself rescues the family in a crisis. He is the outsider drawn into the hallowed interior darkness of Don Corleone. That is a place created by photographer Gordon Willis and designer Dean Tavoularis but that ultimately is the celebration of a Nixonian efficiency, of the many dirty means serving the vital end of family obedience and extended power. It is the movie that half realizes how far its hopeful novelty has become a new tyranny.

I say "half realizes" because I doubt anyone could claim that the intent or meaning of the film is clear. After all, we identify with Michael through the oldest tricks of the medium; we become his soldiers and supporters. In that sense, the influence of Bertolucci's *The Conformist* was enormous, for that was the breakthrough film in which a would-be decent or ordinary fellow becomes an accomplice to every weakness he dreads in himself. And it's worth adding that *The Godfather* carries on the tradition of a world of the sick spirit rendered in décor and light that was established in *The Conformist* by art director Ferdinando Scarfiotti and cinematographer Vittorio Storaro.

Control is the film's grail, but that does not mean it is always palpable. Indeed, *The Godfather* goes through several stages, like a movie testing the styles of the forties and fifties, before it climaxes in the astonishing fusion of baptism and slaughter. That is an editing solution to some narrative confusion, but it is also a passage of exhilarating nihilism, so shocking that it may have stranded Coppola for the rest of his artistic life. He could hardly be ordinary again, no matter how hard he strived.

Of course, Coppola was uneasy at first as the director. A replacement was ready. But the picture made him strong, and in turn the cast became his family. There is no need to praise the inspired casting or the flawless performances, but still it should be stressed that this is a story about Michael, and Al Pacino's is the guiding performance, that whispers to all the others. Compellingly entertaining, *The Godfather* is still as beautiful as it is mysterious. No other American classic so repays repeated viewings. How odd that American film offered this last song of vindication just as it delivered its most foreboding message: the corruption of the state. For years, Hollywood films were happy and positive; now it has grasped eternal unease. Has the America that followed been fit for "movies" or songs, or is it just too sunk in its own dismay?

The Godfather, Part II (1974)

Why should Paramount not make a sequel when the first film had been so successful? Equally, no cynic of remakes would have doubted the eventual truth: that the second film would do much less well. Not that this history deterred a third film one day, a minor work not to be mentioned in the company of the first two. Still, the phenomenon for the critic is that *Part II* is in many senses the bolder work—not just filling in the story gaps from Puzo's novel but building an explanation of how this America came about and of how desperate innovation grew into the most baleful and conservative measures. Notice how far this transition—the shift from hope and arrogance to fatal gloom—repeats the emotional journey of *Citizen Kane*, that earlier film full of warnings about being a success in America.

But there's something else that needs to be said: that the darkest attributes and the chilliest manners of the Corleones are dwelled on here with gloomy relish. The darkness that Gordon Willis created for the first film was authentically Italian, walnut brown, churchlike. But the darkness here is more mannered. Its wearers begin to stroke it and admire its sheen. There are prolonged shots of Michael in his solitude that are reverential as well as crushing. There is a depressive quality to the film, especially as it can find no way out of its labyrinth. In other words, the film cannot come up with a way for the Mafia to be ousted, or for their sardonic nihilism to be disproved. And you feel the weight of despair settling on Francis Coppola himself, like earth falling on a coffin.

At the same time, there are vivid set pieces, beautiful flights of movie: the recreation of Havana and the Sicilian passages, with Robert De Niro feasting on the small acting ploys that Marlon Brando had established in the first film. There is the classic Senate committee of investigation. There is Lake Tahoe in winter as the perfect setting. And there is the eventual tragedy of Fredo—not just John Cazale's great performance but the brother who clearly stands for Francis Coppola in his childhood.

I praised few names for the first film, so let's do justice here: to Fred Roos for casting; to Dean Tavoularis for design; to Walter Murch for sound; to Robert Duvall, Diane Keaton, Talia Shire, Lee Strasberg, Michael V. Gazzo (not just brilliant but a late replacement for Richard Castellano), G. D. Spradlin, Richard Bright, Dominic Chianese, Gastone Moschin, and so on.

We think of the two films as one now, and that's a measure of how far Coppola took the opportunity of the second bite to amplify the first flavor. The two films have been reassembled to run in chronological order, and that has allowed many small gems to come back. But still, there is a grandeur in the two films on successive nights, on a huge screen in Zoetrope prints. Try to convince yourself that we have done better in the thirty years since and counting.

Both films won Best Picture Oscars. Altogether they were nominated for twenty-two Oscars and won nine.

God Is My Witness (1992)

The movie enthusiast adores the idea of India—but the reality is overwhelming. And so we sail on blithely in the hope that the Indians may learn to make films such as we would expect from them. After all, their civil service is based on British models of trial and error, logic and system, so why shouldn't they approach movies in the same way? So, it would be possible to compose a book like this with a nice handful of "Indian" films. Start with *The River* (that model of hope) and then offer three or four by Satyajit Ray—something from the Apu trilogy, *Charulata, Distant Thunder,* and so on. I had applied this pattern—and I believe in the Ray films—but I was nowhere near India.

The Ray films come from "his" India—Bengal and Calcutta—and they are in every sense a minority taste in India. Yet for decades now, India has been the unstoppable source of film supply. You want a thousand films? The industry based in Bombay—or Mumbai—turns out that many a year. In a week, India sells seventy million tickets; in a year it gathers an audience a billion more than the audience in America.

God Is My Witness—directed by Mukul Anand and starring the vacuously pretty male star Amitabh Bachchan—is one of those films (just one), an example of what the world laughingly calls "Bollywood." In that label there is not just condescension but the recognition of a kind of unduly sweetened melodrama with censorship, of profusion and excess with an odious daintiness of ultimate moral character, that seems painful and restricted compared with our own great tradition of melodrama. In turn, apologists for Bollywood point to a film like *God Is My Witness;* you may say it's ridiculous, but wasn't the tug of war between desire and practicality ever so in the great melodramas of Stroheim, Borzage, Murnau, Stahl, Sirk, and so on? Look at Hollywood again, and can't you see the mad mythic genres, the white lies, and the captivating charm?

So is it just Ray and/or Bollywood? No. Over the years there have been worthy films, essays in greater realism—*Mother India* (made by Mani Kaul in 1957), the films of Mrinal Sen, and those of Shyam Benegal, the really heroic figure in that he works more or less within Bollywood while striving to present his audiences with fresh and challenging narrative material.

At the same time, in 2007, a young American, Tim Sternberg, made a short documentary, *Salim Baba,* about a man who gives small movie shows in the Indian city where he lives—odds and ends of old film spliced together for a broken-down projector. A snatch of that "film" is like stolen smoke. For us, it is an experience from the 1890s, but in India, it is still happening. Lumière and Méliès might be working with the nuclear bomb as their light in a culture that happens to be centuries older than ours while still primitive by comparison. A thousand new feature films a year!

Going My Way (1944)

Going My Way doesn't play much these days, no matter that it won the Oscar for Best Picture of 1944. It beat *Double Indemnity* and *Gaslight,* evidence that God was even then making a world for the righteous. But a world for those who feel good about themselves and their prospects in a next life doesn't necessarily have much to do with religion. It's more a matter of insurance. The numbers suggest that the United States is a country rich in religious feeling. There are many crowded churches and many parts of the republic where literal reading of the gospels can intimidate local lawmaking. There are even states where some inclination exists to abandon the teaching of evolution. So why doesn't *Going My Way* play?

Frank Butler and Frank Cavett wrote the screenplay, from a story by the producer-director Leo McCarey, in which Father O'Malley (Bing Crosby) is a priest who writes and sings songs and who employs that tactic to win over a disapproving father superior (Barry Fitzgerald) and a gang of local kids. (McCarey took pride in telling the story of a cardinal who had said the film was "gently disrespectful.") Under a false name, the priest sells his songs to a music publisher, thereby gathering funds for the church. Wouldn't you know it, a girl he had known—just a little—before he put on the collar is now a top singer, and she gets the Philharmonic involved. All of this is unloaded with exactly the lazy charm that Bing Crosby had so much difficulty mustering in real life. Ah, but that's another story altogether, as Barry Fitzgerald would mutter.

Buddy DeSylva produced the picture. Lionel Lindon and Gordon Jennings did the photography. Hans Dreier designed the sets. And the hit song—written by Jimmy Van Heusen and Johnny Burke—was "Swinging on a Star," performed by Bing and the Robert Mitchell Boy Choir. Of course, Van Heusen and Burke didn't actually write the bits from "Silent Night," the "Ave Maria," the "Habanera" from *Carmen,* or "Too-ra-loo-ra-loo-ra" (allegedly an Irish air).

The picture had domestic rentals of more than $6 million. It won Oscars for Best Picture, Best Director, Best Actor for Crosby, and Best Supporting Actor for Barry Fitzgerald. "Swinging on a Star" won Best Song. Paramount and McCarey were so giddy with glee that they went straight into a sequel, *The Bells of St. Mary's,* in which the Bingle comes to the aid of a run-down parish led by Sister Superior Ingrid Bergman. In this one, Bing sings "Aren't You Glad You're You?" (a song that I have been told nearly made it into *Double Indemnity* . . . yet they lie). *The Bells of St. Mary's* was nominated for Best Picture, too. It didn't win and may be best known now as the movie Michael and Kay have just seen in *The Godfather* when he hears about the shooting of his father (not a good day).

Leo McCarey could be a sublime director of comedy, as well as the touching *Make Way for Tomorrow.* He had a grand theory of "incidents" making movies, with one incident leading to another, and he understood human nature in real and practical terms as a sort of evolutionary process. But not here.

The Gold Diggers of 1933 (1933)

There was a time, while preparing this book, when I felt sure I was going to go for *Footlight Parade* in this spot—the spot being a second Warner Brothers/Busby Berkeley musical after the inescapable *42nd Street*. After all, *Footlight Parade* has James Cagney in a masterful role and three Berkeley routines—"Shanghai Lil," "Honeymoon Hotel," and the truly delirious "By a Waterfall." But it happened that Turner Classic Movies (as so often) came to my aid by showing all three films in a row one night. Of course, part of what I am saying is just to observe that all three films came out in one year—the first year of FDR and in many respects the worst year of the Depression—and they have a nerve that simply refuses to be depressed. (The RKO musical is coming up, but it never risked the political attitude of these films.) Let me add this: that Darryl Zanuck inspired them all, and that somehow he, Berkeley, and the attitude at Warner Brothers leave you with the fever dream that the three films are a great fruit-stand of breasts offered to the camera.

Anyway, I determined that *The Gold Diggers of 1933* had to be included. For here is a film that opens with the puppy-fat insolence of Ginger Rogers singing "We're in the Money" and closes with the magnificence of Joan Blondell starting off the "Remember My Forgotten Man" number. Mervyn LeRoy directed the film, but it seems clear that Busby Berkeley did both these numbers, and you have to wonder how far he ever bothered to reconcile them—or to attempt it. For the first number is brazen, hedonistic, and mercenary, no matter that the coins themselves have become the girls' guarding clothing—each girl has three coins to cover (or price) their erotic zones. Couple that in-your-face symbolism with Ginger's screw-you stare, and you marvel how a studio reckoned an audience would or could take it in 1933—and it is the direct opening.

But you get your payback with "Remember My Forgotten Man," which may be the most radical, progressive, and outraged number ever put onscreen in a Hollywood picture. It has a gallery of female voices and images, ranging from an old woman in a rocking chair to Blondell and the black singer Etta Moten. All of which turns into studio shots of First World War soldiers marching in the rain and then coming back shattered and wounded. And that is the finale. We never go back to the story. "Forgotten Man" rises to the height of its criticism, and the film is over. It's breathtaking. You wonder in hindsight why Zanuck, Berkeley, LeRoy, and the others were never called by HUAC.

Gold Diggers is a 96-minute movie, written by Erwin Gelsey and James Seymour from a play by Avery Hopwood. Sol Polito photographed it. Harry Warren and Al Dubin did the songs—there's "Pettin' in the Park" and "I've Got to Sing a Torch Song," too. The cast includes Dick Powell, Ruby Keeler, and Warren William.

The Golden Coach (1953)

The ship from Europe comes bearing the Viceroy his greatest prize in life: a golden coach. But on the same ship, Camilla and her boyfriend, traveling players, have discovered that that coach is the most comfortable cabin on the ship for spending the night with a friend. It is a real carriage, but it is a stage, too, and *The Golden Coach* is the movie above all in which Jean Renoir identifies the ongoing pulse of theatricality. There are shapes in life, repeated and sometimes learned from, and they are the DNA of drama and story. Of course, the discovery was there long ago, in *La Règle du Jeu,* when a house party of friends and lovers could hardly stop themselves from falling into the routines of burlesque, melodrama, and even tragedy.

The Renoir of the 1950s does not really want to know about tragedy—he has paid his dues there already. So this picture in some Spanish South American country in the eighteenth century is a "romp" that hardly notices poverty, plague, or prejudice. You could rip it apart on those grounds, but that would be to miss the high comedy of a vivacious actress pursued by a viceroy, a bullfighter, and her own man. Who will win her? The audience, of course, the only people to whom any actress can ever hope to be faithful.

Renoir wrote the script with Renzo Avanzo, Giulio Macchi, Jack Kirkland, and Ginette Doynel, from a play by Prosper Mérimée. Bravo. Credits are a fine thing, like contracts and insurance certificates. Claude Renoir did the gorgeous harlequinade of photography. Mario Chiari was production designer, and I would guess that if the director was ever in any real doubt over what to do, he simply played himself a little Vivaldi.

The Golden Coach is the first film in a trio—*French Cancan* and *Elena and the Men* are the others—which all say the same thing: that the show must go on. But it harks back to Renoir's *The River* and to much earlier films in its awareness that the show is not just a play people write and perform but a design in nature, a wish to catch the light, a phrase of music, and the look on a woman's face.

It is a radiant film, an easygoing masterpiece, a game if you like, a fond cage for its own monster, Anna Magnani, and for Renoir's vision that he, his father, his nephew—who knows how many more—straddled a hundred years with no greater urge or purpose than to say, "Stop the light! Look at that! Have you seen . . . ?" In the end, it is like the daily miracle of seeing a baby born, with 90 percent of his or her nature there already in the smoky eye, or seeing a curtain go up and realizing that people who are just names in credits have prepared a world and a life for you there, like a great hotel room, like a *carrosse d'or.*

Anna Magnani is often shy, pensive, tender, and often not. Also with Duncan Lamont (very good), Odoardo Spadaro, Riccardo Rioli, Paul Campbell, Nada Fiorelli, and Dante. And so, it is 1953, and here is the last Renoir in the book chronologically. You see: I left some out to show you how balanced and judicious I can be.

Goldfinger (1964)

Goldfinger was the third of the James Bond movies, from a novel published in 1959. This is hardly the place to get into the complicated backstory to Bond onscreen, and I doubt that the films have enough intrinsic interest to justify the effort. (I am proposing to let this one film stand for the entire franchise.) But history makes it clear that Bond hesitated in going to the big screen. Ian Fleming's first novel featuring the character, *Casino Royale*, was published in 1953, nine years before the film *Dr. No* was released.

Nor are the books really like the movies. Fleming's Bond is more English, more conservative, bleaker, and less funny. Somehow, somewhere along the line, a series of books about a fantasy agent in the British secret service became the Bond franchise: spectacular, international, sardonic, cool, and essentially apolitical, with Bond as the kind of remorseless womanizer who never feels a thing. Did Ian Fleming make this shift? Was it Harry Saltzman and Cubby Broccoli, the producers? Was it the directors of the films and Sean Connery? Was it screenwriters Richard Maibaum and Paul Dehn? Or was it Kevin McClory, a curious writer and Irish adventurer, once a buddy of John Huston's, who waged a legal battle over the years with Fleming and film studios and who actually has a credit on *Thunderball*?

Goldfinger would trace the attempt by the villain (Gert Frobe) to rob Fort Knox. The first draft was written by Richard Maibaum, then Paul Dehn came on board to do rewrites, and finally Maibaum came back. The sets were by Ken Adam; the director was Guy Hamilton. I credit the two men in that order because décor and gadgets were becoming increasingly important to the franchise. Indeed, cars (product placed, of course), technical gimmicks, and special effects were gradually swamping any realities of espionage, let alone politics. The Bond films came into being in the Kennedy years (and JFK's listing of one of the books in his bedside reading helped), but they went out of their way to look and feel very different from the political realities of the 1960s (so many of which would have been beyond a rugby team of Bonds).

But by the time of *Goldfinger*, the sexual innuendo of the series had become more blatant. Thus the piquancy of Goldfinger's spy girl (played with mischief by Shirley Eaton), who, having yielded entry to Bond, is covered in gold paint—her sex like Fort Knox. Then there is the bizarre character of Pussy Galore (Honor Blackman), as if Bond could subvert even the lesbian urge.

This is also the film with Oddjob (Harold Sakata) and his hat, and the brief threat to Bond's privates from a laser beam. It beggars belief that these films go on and on when you recall that lasers once were the cutting edge of technology. *Goldfinger* has a worldwide gross of $125 million (on a $3 million budget) and its success ensured a steady stream of the films, all held in place by Sean Connery's icy sadism and every schoolboy's notion that a pun is the essential riposte to international affairs and inhuman conflict. Music and theme song by John Barry, sung by Shirley Bassey.

The Gold Rush (1925)

With Douglas Fairbanks one day, Chaplin was looking at still photographs of men trekking through deep snow on their way to the Yukon gold rush. He had also read something about the fate of the Donner party in the earlier California rush. And so the pictures and the legend of cannibalism stewed in his mind, and the result was *The Gold Rush,* not just one of the great silent comedies but a very telling nightmare on the immense disturbance of reality that was caused by gold. Chaplin's routines are often self-contained, but there is a pervasive amazement or alarm throughout his work that nature and human nature can be so violently shifted by the discovery of a silly thing called wealth. This playing dice with fate is far better handled in *City Lights,* but it is there in *The Gold Rush* and in the way Chaplin stressed the matter of needing to eat to survive when gold is inedible.

The influence of the still photographs was enough to persuade Chaplin to find real snow, so he scouted Truckee, California (in the Sierra Nevada), and did a great deal of shooting there, having to build roads in the process and shivering in the tramp's costume in the authentic cold. A major problem arose with his casting of Lita Grey as the music-hall girl. But when he got Grey pregnant and was obliged to marry her, he dropped her from the picture and brought in Georgia Hale.

Of course, the set pieces are the heart of the film, notably Charlie's dance with the dinner rolls; his application of haute cuisine to a boot in order to make a meal for Big Jim (Mack Swain), with Charlie sucking on the nails to get the last "meat"; and Jim's hallucinatory vision of the Tramp as a hen, fit to be roasted, with Charlie imitating the herky-jerky movements of that bird. Then there is the superb extended nightmare of the cabin on the brink of a precipice, where safety is put at risk by the slightest movement. You can argue that the comedy in the film is isolated and concentrated in numbers that are like dances in musicals. But they all contribute to the dread of madness; and in turn, the transformation of life and fortune during a gold rush is regarded as something beyond reason.

Rollie Totheroh shot the film, on location and in the studio. Chaplin amassed over 230,000 feet of film, which he edited down to 8,500 feet, or about 82 minutes. (In 1942, he went back to the picture, shortened it by about ten minutes, and introduced a score.) When it opened, it was on its way to rentals of $6 million, with Chaplin himself keeping about $2 million in personal profit. Today *The Gold Rush* is still very funny to the newcomer and intriguing to anyone who knows it well. Kenneth Lynn, a Chaplin biographer, has suggested that Charlie was influenced in part by knowing of Stroheim's attempt in *Greed;* this is very likely, and it may explain why the two films play together so effectively.

Gone to Earth (1950)

The short business relationship between Alexander Korda and David O. Selznick was as hilarious as it was vexed. And it ended in huge litigation, from which there were eggcup results. Perhaps it was all because the two men—wonderful and impossible—were so alike. It hardly matters, since their history together produced *The Third Man* and *Gone to Earth*.

Korda owned the rights to a Mary Webb novel, *Gone to Earth*, about a strange country girl, Hazel Woodus (Jennifer Jones). She lives in Shropshire in the late nineteenth century (which feels closer to Shakespeare's time than ours). She is bound to a pet fox, and you don't have to be trained as a Freudian to see that the wild animal's life embodies her sense of herself. Romantically, she is torn between the prim parson, Edward Marston (Cyril Cusack), and the squire, Jack Reddin (David Farrar), who is red-blooded, brutally selfish, and devilishly attractive. Marston believes it is heretical and absurd to love a fox, whereas Reddin sees the creature as the proper quarry of the local hunt. The film ends with a heartfelt chase scene across fabulous country where the greens, the browns, and the reds are rainbow strong.

Mary Webb's material is unashamedly melodramatic or heightened, and Michael Powell, the director, was heard to wonder whether it was even filmable. The answer is yes, but only if the filmmaker was as imbued with melodramatic symbolism and emotional extremism as the author. What equips Powell is his sense of place (he never filmed nature or landscape better), his instinct for color (this is one of the greatest Technicolor films ever made, and a sign that British Technicolor at this period was better than American), his fairy-tale sense of character, and the fact that he got to work with Jennifer Jones.

That was not easy. It was during the trip to Europe for *Gone to Earth* that Ms. Jones and David Selznick were married, after the collapse of their previous marriages, years of tortured indecision, and some suicide gestures by Jones. You don't have too far to go at this period to find Jones struggling as an actress (*Duel in the Sun, Terminal Station*) while her real life was close to crazed. But Powell treated her professionally, and Hazel won her unsteady heart. There are passages in the film where you can believe the girl is possessed by the same deep Celtic or gypsy imagination that figures in Powell's *I Know Where I'm Going*.

As for the surrounding world, Cusack seems pained by the simplicity of his part, but Farrar exudes a scent of leather, tobacco, and earth, and the supporting cast is outstanding: Sybil Thorndike, Edward Chapman, Esmond Knight, Hugh Griffith, George Cole, and Beatrice Varley.

Selznick did not like or understand *Gone to Earth*, so he exercised his contractual right and tried remaking the film. He hired Rouben Mamoulian to direct. There was some more shooting. He recut and added a narrator—all under the heading of *The Wild Heart*, and inexplicable compared with the original.

Gone With the Wind (1939)

We know it worked, but why? Margaret Mitchell's novel, published in 1936, was an immense best seller in an age when that counted. Kay Brown, Selznick's literary scout, insisted that he buy it—no need to read it first. On top of that, by decision and helpless accident, the Selznick organization pumped up public interest in the project in hysterical ways. Today that interest could easily prompt disaster; in 1939 that was unlikely, because the public was so much more innocent.

The picture opened in December 1939 (premiering in Atlanta), as the American public was reckoning on how long before it found itself in a war. The war in the movie was mild by comparison with 1939–45, but it seemed relevant to the audience and recent to most Americans. In the same way, they may have been ready to relinquish a great age and culture that had lasted since the coming of sound: the American romance. So perhaps *GWTW* was a farewell as much as a fulfillment.

Sidney Howard wrote an amazingly clear and effective script. Selznick did everything he could to bury it in rewrites. But in the crisis of January 1939, as he fired the original director, George Cukor, Selznick rediscovered the early script and trusted it. Victor Fleming was brought on board as a director to get it done. The balance then was perfect: Fleming had the drive, and Selznick had the vision.

The film marked the full arrival of glorious Technicolor. In design (William Cameron Menzies) and photography (Ray Rennahan and Ernest Haller), it had a look that struck 1939 as burningly real but that was actually profoundly romantic. And the faux-Southern look carried all the way through, like a pulse. It was there in Max Steiner's music—music, as in the Tara theme, that has come to stand for Hollywood itself.

Clark Gable was so perfect that his indifference and laziness hardly mattered—they actually give Rhett a glow of amiability.

Vivien Leigh was the miracle, the ultimate reward for insane casting hopes that had nearly ruined Selznick's venture.

Olivia de Havilland and Leslie Howard did subplot without rancor or envy, and they gave the audience an "ordinary" couple to admire.

Hattie McDaniel and Butterfly McQueen (if you can credit this) actually made a great stride forward for black players and black characters. McDaniel was the first black actor to win an Oscar, yet she was not allowed to go to Atlanta for the opening.

This was almost the only time in his life that David Selznick won an important gamble: The film cost $4.25 million, and it is still earning money. And Scarlett O'Hara and David O. Selznick were alike in believing they would survive and flourish. Long before the theory of authorship in American movies, Selznick established that in his time and at his studio producers made the films. It all came undone later. He ruined himself, and he gave up his ownership of the film that had both made and destroyed him. This brought untold grief and damage to most people in his circle. But the film—having been made—ignores those things and now dares America, Hollywood, and the picture business to be as grand or as lucky again.

The Good Earth (1937)

Pearl S. Buck's *The Good Earth* was published in 1932, and it won the Pulitzer Prize for fiction. It was an earnest if patronizing attempt to comprehend the life of the Chinese peasantry, in which those peasants were reproduced very much as they might have been played in a Hollywood movie. At the time there were a few Asian actors (like Anna May Wong), but when the film came to be made at Metro-Goldwyn-Mayer, both lead parts were taken by Austrians.

Though he was dead before the film was released, Irving Thalberg had been its mastermind; indeed, the film must take some credit for dispatching him. M-G-M bought the screen rights, and the project was at first entrusted to director George W. Hill and his wife, screenwriter Frances Marion. As Marion worked on the script, eliminating any elements that might offend the Chinese government, her marriage to Hill broke apart because of his syphilis. (He would die in 1934, only thirty-nine, an apparent suicide.)

The plan was to film as much as possible in China. Hill was sent there to get as much footage as possible. He worked with the consul general in Shanghai and even had interviews with Chiang Kai-shek. But he had to return because of illness. In the end, the studio gave up on China after offending everyone in sight. So the picture was rearranged to be shot in California. The script was reassigned to Tess Slesinger, Claudine West, Talbot Jennings, and Marc Connelly, with Sidney Franklin directing—in fact, it seems certain that Victor Fleming and Gustav Machatý shot some parts of it. Thalberg put Albert Lewin in charge as producer, and he engaged Karl Freund as director of photography.

The central role of the farmer Li went to Paul Muni, and his wife, O-Lan, was Luise Rainer. That casting and the departure from China had left many bad feelings. Though the studio was eager to repair fences as best it could, its enormous ignorance about what China and the Chinese were like shows in the film, an idealization of peasant life that might have been set nearly anywhere in the Third World. The acting is heartfelt but empty epic, with strained accents and makeup struggling to be exotic and understandable at the same time. Far and away the best things are the landscape shots and especially the locust-attack montage, which Freund and Slavko Vorkapich contrived with coffee grounds in water.

To be sure, the result was a "big" picture, 138 minutes long. It cost $2.8 million and lost money eventually, despite strong reviews and big audiences. It got a Best Picture Oscar nomination, but lost out to another Muni picture, *The Life of Émile Zola*. Muni was nominated for *Zola* but not for *The Good Earth*. But Luise Rainer won her second Oscar in a row, for playing O-Lan—Graham Greene thought her acting great and heartbreaking. The rest of the cast included Walter Connolly, Charley Grapewin, Jessie Ralph, and Tilly Losch.

GoodFellas (1990)

Was *GoodFellas* an attempt to stand up for the "working class" elements of the Mob, stripped of the sham dignity and gravitas associated with *The Godfather*, or was it just Martin Scorsese's helpless yearning to get in on the act himself? There's no doubt about the momentum and exuberance of *GoodFellas.* It rushes down its slope like a great musical or a wild comedy, exhilarating in its sense of "movie" and sometimes finding an exact balance of film fluency and character. For instance, the terrific, serpentine, Steadicam tracking shot by which Henry Hill and his girl enter the Copacabana by the back exit is not just his attempt to impress her but Scorsese's urge to stagger us and himself with bravura cinema.

The comparison with a musical is not far-fetched. These Mafia hoods do not sing and dance, yet their routines are constantly musicalized by Scorsese's jukebox of hits. I don't see that as just a way to fill in period atmosphere on the sound track. It is a subtle moral legitimization of what we're seeing. And here is the really tricky point about *GoodFellas,* and about where Scorsese has gone: Does this film have a secure attitude toward the lives of its guys, or is it giddy with its own ability to ride along in their slipstream?

It's all very well to say that the point of view of *GoodFellas* is from within the group, so this is how small-minded career criminals see themselves. Frank Pierson's 2001 television film *Conspiracy* does much the same thing for the Nazi leaders at the Wannsee Conference. Yet that film leaves no doubt about the evil of that group and the grisly camaraderie—the jokes, the cruel asides, the little nods of tacit understanding—that accompanied the evil. The GoodFellas may not be as evil by an absolute standard, though they murder, steal, and undermine the concept of law and justice in their society. And what emerges from Scorsese's film is a trembling, increasingly cocaine-dependent ambivalence.

One has to add the sinking realization that, time and again, Scorsese returns to this boys' world and its fearful isolation from adult values. Nowhere is that clearer than in his indulgence of the Joe Pesci character—hilarious, yet so dangerous he could be a Nazi thug. It's as if Scorsese cannot bring himself to disown this demon, and movement, vitality, mad humor, music, and contempt for women are the ingredients of the lifestyle of the GoodFellas.

The film is superbly done, from the screenplay (by Scorsese and Nicholas Pileggi, based on the latter's book *Wise Guy*) to the beautiful photography by Michael Ballhaus and the sets by Kristi Zea, at the same time grotesque and exactly right. The acting is like the music. These guys really are singing, and it's irresistible when they're most familial—as in prison (their paradise of an existence): Pesci, Ray Liotta, Robert De Niro (very frightening), Paul Sorvino, Lorraine Bracco, Frank Sivero, Tony Darrow, Frank Vincent, and Samuel L. Jackson.

A film made by a master, but a man who is lost—and *Casino* is still to come.

The Good, the Bad and the Ugly (1966)

Clint Eastwood had to go to Italy to find his river to cross. He had done some movies, and he was a star in the TV series *Rawhide,* but he was not a movie star. Then he agreed to go to Italy to do *A Fistful of Dollars* (1964) for Sergio Leone. He did it for $15,000 and coach airfare. *For a Few Dollars More* followed in 1965. And these films did well in Europe (though they had not opened in America yet!). For *The Good, the Bad and the Ugly*—which Eastwood had said would be his last Leone picture—he would get $250,000, a Ferrari, and 10 percent of the profits in the Western Hemisphere.

Clint was nettled that on this picture there were to be three leads—not just himself as the Stranger and Lee Van Cleef as Angel Eyes, but a new role: Tuco, a kind of urchin outlaw. Gian Maria Volonte passed on the role, and Eli Wallach got it instead.

Like the first two films, this one was shot cheaply, using locations around Burgos and Almería, Spain. The budget on the third film was only $1.3 million, which included the cheroots that Leone insisted Eastwood smoke and that were always close to turning his stomach. But on this film, Leone had a new cameraman, Tonino Delli Colli, who went for a less harsh look and indulged Leone's taste for imitating the compositions of great paintings. So, depending on your taste, it looks better or sillier than the first two pictures. In addition, Ennio Morricone had done the score in advance, and there's no question that Leone had it in his head as he shot certain scenes.

The story came from Leone and Luciano Vincenzoni, and as on the first two pictures, it was a flagrant yet sluggish anthology of scenes from Westerns. But whereas *Butch Cassidy and the Sundance Kid* (only a few years away) was very cool, very hip and superior (as if *The New Yorker* had opted to run a Western story), Leone's film was exaggerated, coarse and arty. The violence was different, largely because it was so isolated by silence, and the cynicism was new: The West had become a gutter, and even if Clint was ostensibly "the Good," he was mercenary, cold-blooded, insolent, and cruel. He also had a scene with a prostitute that was cut in the American version of the film. But Leone was not superior to the Western; he adored it—no matter that he gets the genre and its historical reality so wrong.

It was only in 1967–68 that the "trilogy" opened in the United States—three pictures in the course of a year—to unimagined success. In a way, the nearest comparison is with the James Bond pictures, for truly the Western had been subjected to a camp but brutal dislocation. These were fever-dream Westerns, but they helped close down the prospects of the real genre. *The Good, The Bad and the Ugly* had $8 million of rentals in the United States, and it fixed Clint's image: angry, cold, narrow-eyed, hearing his own music. You could put him into a police force, but he was still a loner. It was his future. Nowadays, in its odd mix of the garish and the flat, the trilogy is clearly the origin of video games where echoing gunfire merges with Morricone's music and the blood is poured like tomato sauce.

The Graduate (1967)

The Graduate is supposed to be one of those films that straddle prehistory and modern times, and I think it's the case still today that the picture takes such old-fashioned genres as the coming-of-age movie, the love story, the screwball comedy, and even the fatal love story and taps them gently to see if each gives off a different musical note or the same wounded bleat. And for the first half of the movie, there's no doubt that everything is coming up new and strange in movie terms. Ben (Dustin Hoffman) has just graduated from college. Allegedly the world waits for his decision—will his future be plastics or not. The world is a series of acrid *New Yorker* cartoons, and Hoffman plays Ben without affect or identity. And then he meets Mrs. Robinson (Anne Bancroft), the mother of a potential girlfriend (Katharine Ross).

Mrs. Robinson seduces him—she will claim later that he raped her. But as we see it, in intimidating camera angles and finely cut close-ups that do not quite show anything naughty, it's not just that she is the deeply depressed aggressor. Before her, Ben was not really there. He takes her to a big hotel for sexual liaisons. He sleeps with her—this is clear. And it is clear, too, I think, that she is very disturbed. But the film is so arranged, as an information system, that we never see Ben asking himself about that. In other words, his acquiescence is so passive as to absolve him from responsibility. And this is a very big problem if we are being asked to consider *The Graduate* as possessing any kind of emotional reality.

Of course, it all comes out, at which point *The Graduate* becomes an impossibly dreamy frustrated romance story in which the daughter is said to be Ben's one true love, despite her being embodied in the famously pretty but quite empty Katharine Ross. She is a Berkeley student who seems to be wearing false eyelashes in her every scene. The way Ben tracks her, up and down the coast—and don't forget Simon and Garfunkel driving him on in the background—is not just rosy and silly but nearly as demented as the affair with the mother. In other words, Ben has no judgment, no soul, but he has a romantic horniness that falls for every woman he meets.

Now, the film is very astute, if not cunning: You know that from the Simon and Garfunkel score and the odious way in which second-time director Mike Nichols keeps zooming all the time. More problematic, the script by Buck Henry is full of great lines and situations (in one of the best of which Henry plays himself)—and a nearly complete reluctance to make them coherent. So *The Graduate* seems to me a mess, a film that cries out for thorough reconstruction and critical debate. I think it's a cold, heartless entertainment, never more ruthless than when dumping charm on us. As a start, it is a fair indication of how long it would take Mike Nichols to find character, and it still raises the question of whether Hoffman could ever get at simple truth within his intricate, self-serving flatness.

Still, for the moment it is said to be one of everybody's favorites!

La Grande Illusion (1937)

So here is the Renoir who had flirted intensely with the Popular Front, noticing the small but distinct gap between a man and an aristocrat. How does one film of only reasonable length, often so casual and easygoing, have so many nuances and so many large statements (including its title) without ever seeming portentous? And how, in the great light of Hollywood, was it possible to make a film, set in the past, that assuredly spoke to 1937 without overdoing the bleakness or the hope? There are American films of 1937 striving to be on the same shaky pulse—like *The Good Earth, You Only Live Once, Dead End, Make Way for Tomorrow*—but *La Grande Illusion* is simply there, candid, cheerful, sad, alert. No wonder Hollywood gave it a Best Picture nomination, but the prize went to *You Can't Take It With You,* strenuous, radiant, archaic.

It is war, and we see French officers taken prisoner: Lieutenant Maréchal (Jean Gabin) and Captain de Boeldieu (Pierre Fresnay). We see a German air ace, Captain von Rauffenstein (Erich von Stroheim). Even as the film begins, if you know the basics of film history, you ask yourself, "Renoir and Stroheim on the same picture?" It is like Joyce meeting Shakespeare. But, of course, it was a job like any other, with Stroheim fussing a little at first and then doing as he was told. Together, they made a great line from 1919 to 1937, becoming strong and clear—the tradition (or is that just another illusion, too?).

Rauffenstein is crippled, and every bit as imprisoned as his French guests. Every man has his prison, as well as his reasons. Attempts to escape are obligatory, and so eventually Rauffenstein will have to fire a fatal shot in the night air, and he and his victim, like daft experts, will assess its difficulty, its fineness, one dying, one broken. Then think of the comradeship in the camp, think of the mise en scène—the depth, the movement—when the inmates fall silent to see one of their fellows dressed up as a girl. Think of Gabin and Marcel Dalio as they escape, in a hideous quarrel and a helpless reunion. Remember the geranium in the fortress. I offered it once as an example of plants in movies. Why not? It is still growing.

La Grande Illusion is a portrait of companionship, the company made by war, and one of the illusions is that that bond may solve war. Another is that war solves anything, or that the fatalistic conscience sees that and abandons war. War is full of stupid human hope. It keeps coming, like the urge for sex. So *La Grande Illusion* is just a prison-camp picture in which the organization of men lets lives wither and waste. "In 1937," said Renoir, "I was told I had made the greatest antiwar picture—two years later war broke out."

Written by Renoir and Charles Spaak; photography by Christian Matras; design by Eugène Lourié; edited by Marguerite Renoir; music by Joseph Kosma. The roll of honor should include Dalio (as Rosenthal), Julien Carette, Gaston Modot, Jean Dasté, and Dita Parlo (who comes like fresh milk in the last part of the film). But the roll of honor is open: Everyone who sees the film is included.

The Grapes of Wrath (1940)

Here are some dates on *The Grapes of Wrath:* the novel was published in April 1939. Nunnally Johnson had his script in by July 13, 1939. John Ford started shooting it October 4, 1939. Picture opened January 24, 1940. Yet no one could say the film seems hurried. What that high speed indicates is, first, that Darryl F. Zanuck was behind the film as he had seldom been before. He wanted to see it—and to be seen for it. Second, that Johnson's script was hardly altered in the course of the shooting. Third, that John Ford shot a complex picture with absolute authority and command of detail. And finally, that the editing, under Zanuck, was full of conviction. There was less than a year between the novel's publication and its opening as a film.

Within that context, it is nice to know this story: that Henry Fonda and Jane Darwell were more than ready for their last scene together, the farewell, with his assurance about being present in every detail of life. The two actors had seen their moment ahead on the schedule. Then Gregg Toland had to rig a small light for the match in Fonda's hand. And Ford fussed with a few other extras he invented and kept them waiting. Then he did it—one take, and Ford walked away.

The Grapes of Wrath came from the heart. Steinbeck felt the impulse and wrote the novel quickly. Ford and Zanuck approached it in the same way. And Toland shot it on his way to *Citizen Kane,* with sets by Richard Day and Mark-Lee Kirk. It's not clear how far Ford himself had researched or seen the Dust Bowl, but he was moved by the script because of the way it reminded him of Irish stories. Time and again, Toland adds a mood of Dorothea Lang and the WPA. Ford got it right. It's hard to draw much of a distinction between his movie and Walker Evans's work on *Let Us Now Praise Famous Men* (1941, but planned years before)—there is an epic, pictorial quality in both, and maybe in the Ford you can see the faces of actors sometimes. But he delivered the message.

It is remarkable that America was overtaken in the space of a year by two sensations like *Gone With the Wind* and *The Grapes of Wrath*—and they are together part of the country's tribute to the Depression and having survived it. The cast includes John Carradine, Charley Grapewin, Dorris Bowdon, Russell Simpson, John Qualen, and many others from the Ford family.

The movie was nominated for seven Oscars, including Best Picture, but it won only for Ford himself and for Jane Darwell as supporting actress. That meant she beat Judith Anderson as Mrs. Danvers in *Rebecca*—a nonsense, but no greater than *Rebecca* beating *The Grapes of Wrath* for Best Picture. Sixty years later, *The Grapes of Wrath* still looks like an earnest and touching attempt by the film industry to honor years of national hardship and sacrifice, and Fonda's Tom Joad is timeless and true and a key warning of how a society may make outlaws out of its best material.

Grease (1978)

Grease is here not just because any large machine needs lubrication, nor even because of its stupefying success on stage and screen. It is here because I like it, and because it showed how camp attitudes could resurrect the good-natured ethos of old musicals and rearrange the universe so that being in high school was really equivalent to being in a musical. And once you're there, you can see that its being from *Romeo and Juliet* (*West Side Story*) or a Jungian analysis of fairy tales (*Into the Woods*) are bonuses. Just being there is all right, too. Making a musical doesn't need to be literary or distinguished. And so at last we found a way of making peace with the lovely "emptiness" of the Astaire-Rogers films. Singing is as good as talking; dancing is better than dying.

The stage show, by Jim Jacobs and Warren Casey, opened in 1972 and ran for 3,388 performances. In other words, rock and the modern pop industry were old enough for satire and nostalgia. And here is a musical where the extra distance or remove of the screen was better than the stage. *Grease* is one of the first films where watching it is like being a clerk at a video store, or having access instantly to all the films ever made. "Look at me, I'm Sandra Dee" is only the most obviously self-referential song. "Hopelessly Devoted to You" is a witty reflection on "rapture" songs. The whole idea of a couple torn between being Elvis and Ann-Margret or Troy Donahue and Sandra Dee is what the film is about. And with all these silly role models knocking around, there's no need for real character. Sandy and Danny (the lead kids) are Barbie dolls, and we can change their clothes and songs to suit our mood.

The movie was produced by Robert Stigwood and Allan Carr. Bronte Woodard wrote the script, helped a good deal I suspect by Carr. Bill Butler photographed it. There was a discolike feeling of songs running into each other and a kind of kid-Fosse dancing directed by Patricia Birch. Randal Kleiser directed (he would never really do anything again). Of course, the casting was crucial: John Travolta is Danny, and in Travolta the idea of a James Dean–like aggression or menace is a hoot. Danny is cuddly, gentle, and cute; in turn, Olivia Newton-John's Sandy manages to be the safe sweetheart who puts on tight pants and foxy makeup. Their combined gestures toward sexiness are full of charm and sweetness and the essential coded promise of never needing to grow up.

The songs are not very good, but they work. They're like instant juke-box selections in a diner from high-school days. No wonder *Grease* is such a favorite high-school production. The supporting cast is full of jewels: Stockard Channing as Betty Rizzo, Kelly Ward as Putzie, Jeff Conaway as Kenickie, Didi Conn as Frenchy, Eve Arden as Principal McGee, plus Frankie Avalon, Joan Blondell, Sid Caesar, and Edd Byrnes. The stage success was matched. *Grease* on film got nearly $100 million in rentals.

The Great Dictator (1940)

It seems that Alexander Korda was the first person to suggest that Charlie Chaplin take a shot at playing Adolf Hitler—or, rather, a common man mistaken for the Nazi leader. The screenwriter Konrad Bercovici actually provided Chaplin with a six-page treatment in which the little fellow—a barber, perhaps—is mistaken for the Dictator. Always claiming originality, Chaplin settled out of court with Bercovici and used most of his ideas. And as the film took shape, it was a simple case of mistaken identity attached to a sermon. At last, Chaplin accepted sound, so that he could address the world. Artistically, that was disastrous: The "silent" comedy of *The Great Dictator* remains wicked and subversive, while the sermon brings the film to a halt.

Biographer Kenneth Lynn established the lie in Chaplin's *My Autobiography* where he claims to have been motivated by Hitler's invasion of Russia. In fact, the Nazi-Soviet nonaggression pact occurred just before filming started and had a crushing effect on the Popular Front in the United States—but still Chaplin proceeded without any challenge to Russian cynicism. It would be an item in the case against him as a Red sympathizer.

More than ever before, Chaplin went beyond his set group of actors: Jack Oakie was cast as Benzino Napaloni, the ruler of Bacteria; Henry Daniell would be Garbitsch (a version of Goebbels); Billy Gilbert would be Herring (Göring). Paulette Goddard would be the barber's girlfriend, Hannah (named after Chaplin's mother); and Charlie would play both the barber and the Dictator, Adenoid Hynkel. Karl Struss was hired as director of photography.

There were complaints and threats from Germany about the use of figures from life, but no one in America stood in Chaplin's way. There are comic set pieces—most notably the balloon ballet, and stuff with Oakie—that deserve to be in any anthology on Chaplin's genius. But the atmosphere of the film is odd. The Nazis look and sound like Americans. The landscape is glaringly wrong. And in the long speech where the barber addresses the world, the shading was fatal. For the speech does not quite attack Hitlerism. It complains at changes in modern life that were apolitical but that had long been part of Chaplin's naïve creed:

"The way of life can be free and beautiful, but we have lost the way. Greed has poisoned men's souls—has barricaded the world with hate—has goose-stepped into misery and bloodshed. We have developed speed, but we have shut ourselves in. Machinery that gives abundance has left us in want. Our knowledge has made us cynical; our cleverness, hard and unkind."

The intellectual community found fault with the film, saying it lacked a refined argument, but in 1940 the masses devoured it and were moved by the cheeky affinity between a humble barber and the monstrous Hynkel. The deflating satire came from the English tradition, though it was one that America knew well. So the film may be misjudged as arrogant and crude. But no one else in Hollywood dared do it—and, as if inspired by rivalry, *The Great Dictator* is Chaplin's bravest moment. It took in $5 million and was his last great hit.

Great Expectations (1946)

There have always been reasons for admiring *Great Expectations* in the English canon. For years, the BFI used the sequence where the boy Pip encounters Magwitch in the desolate marshlands as a perfect example of editing. Well, maybe, though today it is impossible to avoid the calculation of that effect and far more tempting to concentrate on the décor, whether it is real marsh or a movie creation (a set with a glass painting). The awesome feeling of the child's dread is far more in the setting than in the cutting, and so *Great Expectations* is more interesting as an example of atmosphere than of Lean's academic cutting (he was an editor who became a director).

The film is much more of a travesty or a cartoon than Lean's *Oliver Twist,* but *Great Expectations* is so much larger as a novel, and Pip is a character beyond the earnest approach (and the age) of John Mills. In so many films of Dickens, it helps to have the central figure as a child. Onscreen, it is hard to miss that Mills's Pip becomes self-satisfied, a bit of a snob and a simpleton. We make so much more allowance for the children. It doesn't matter that they don't quite act; indeed, it helps. And Pip suffers helplessly in every scene he shares with Alec Guinness's Herbert Pocket. Was Guinness a thief or an innocent? Just watch the way he comes upstairs in his first scene, and then revel in the pious kindness with which he corrects Pip's coarse manners. You could say it's Dickens's fault—he was so uninterested in plain heroes.

Of course, I haven't mentioned the things most people actually remember about the film: the world of Miss Havisham, and the astonishing fact of Jean Simmons as Estella. I can never quite believe that the Havisham scenes were not affected by Cocteau's *La Belle et la Bête* (made the same year). The diagonal of the great table is the same, and the enchantment is built on the same kinds of magic trick. It's atmosphere again, and Martita Hunt's performance is actually rather posed and prim compared with the icy haunting of Wilfred Shingleton's art direction.

But what could Hunt do without Jean Simmons—in fact, a robust seventeen, but the personification of serene childish spite. Her scenes with the young Pip remain a lovely rendering of the bitter hopelessness of childhood crushes—and a fine study in Dickens's notion of malicious beauty. It's a hopeless task for Valerie Hobson, trying to be the grown-up Estella. It's a marvel that Lean's genius—and his undoubted instinct for sexuality—didn't insist on Simmons making the shift to adulthood herself (though maybe Estella would then have to come closer to *Angel Face*!).

So what is left? *Oliver Twist* is by far the better film, but largely because that Dickens could have been writing for the movies and because the story of a foundling child is so much more concentrated. The real loss of the movie *Great Expectations* is that, a few scenes apart, it is proof that Dickens was an artist and Lean an illustrator.

The Great McGinty (1940)

It was *The Biography of a Bum* at first, but years later someone at Paramount claimed that "bum meant something awful in Australia," and so the film became *The Great McGinty*. But linger a moment for a character: Edmund P. Biden, to be known as Preston Sturges. There he was in the 1930s, somewhat adrift as a writer—a playwright and a scenarist—with an itch to direct, no matter that he was assured that the profession was unseemly in a gentleman and entailed getting up absurdly early. Still, the Bum (inspired by political stories he had heard at the knee of an old judge) tickled him enough to think directing might be the light: "It was to be my entering wedge into the profession, my blackjack. After that, it was simple. It only took six years."

There is the insouciance of the man you must come to love if this book will mean anything to you. With a meager five-hundred-word allowance, I cannot trace all the Bum's ups and downs. But eventually the Sturgeses had William LeBaron of Paramount to dinner. Louise Sturges did wonders with every course, and LeBaron sat back at last and said that if Sturges could make a meal like that, then surely he could make a film. Such is the lot of wives. Such was the attitude of executives toward their own product.

So Sturges became a Paramount worker: $10 for the script (ten times his asking price) and a humbling sum to direct. (If he ate that well, he presumably had private means.) Sturges reworked the script and faced a great dilemma in a scene where he had to show that McGinty had never taken sexual advantage of his young "bride" (taken on for political face). The solution—walking into the linen closet to speak to her instead of his bedroom—may have alluded to some of Sturges's own romantic escapades, and it showed how far he had the Lubitsch touch, as well as the greatest drop shots Hollywood has ever known.

McGinty was his debut, and I will not scold observers who regard it as a warming up, but the Sturges style was there, along with his taste for loyal and steady crewmen and eccentric actors. William C. Mellor shot the film; Hans Dreier did the art direction, Frederick Hollander the music, Edith Head the clothes. The central players—Brian Donlevy as McGinty and Akim Tamiroff as The Boss—were backed up by Muriel Angelus, Allyn Joslyn, William Demarest, Arthur Hoyt, and Louis Jean Heydt.

In 1940, a year of general election in the Greatest Democracy God Had Yet Permitted, it is encouraging to observe the open treatment of a political system where a vote has the bargaining power of about half a bowl of warm soup. McGinty is a nonentity, voted into office, who tries to go honest, and the film was once meant to carry this moral motto: "I propose to show that honesty is as disastrous for a crook as is knavery for the cashier of a bank." At a mere outlay of $400,000, there is wisdom indeed for a great nation on the Cusp of Crisis.

The Great Train Robbery (1903)

Edwin S. Porter was born the year before Charles Dickens died—and died the year that *Citizen Kane* opened. He was a gunnery officer in the Navy and then a collector of varied careers, nearly all of them dependent on technical expertise. As such, he was taken on by the Edison Company with the task of trying to invent an effective projector. It was in that pursuit that he started to make short-story movies, a model of the emerging narratives that turned the wonder of spectacle into stories with character involvement, suspense, and a tidy moral ending. He was a giant in his day and then a forgotten man for at least twenty years before his death. But amid the hundreds of titles he made, or produced, there is *The Great Train Robbery*.

This is a 12-minute piece, coherent in nearly all respects, about a plan to rob a train and the eventual capture of the robbers. It manifests elementary screen geography, approximate cutting on action, and a respectful fondness for the long shot. It is the cinema before Griffith, and the state of play that allows us to think of him as a master, a magical possessor of insight as an engineer who saw ways of making the stream of cut images more fluent, speedy, and compelling. Thus, the only reason to look at Porter nowadays is as a sign of his times and a measure of how history was working itself out.

This holds until the very end of *The Great Train Robbery*, when something extraordinary happens. A "cowboy" (or an actor so dressed) comes before the camera in medium shot (it feels like a big close-up) and fires a six-gun into the camera. It is not clear that he is recognizable as one of the characters from the story just ended, because those faces are not really identifiable. Moreover, in possessing or embodying a type of shot not used in the rest of the film, it feels like an afterthought or an insurrection. And its impact is stunning. Is he meant as a flourish or a kind of company logo for "cowboy adventures" or "nickelodeon shoot-'em-ups"? Or is he just some deep-seated energy or adventure inspired by the process of the film that says, "Give it to the audience. Give them what they want. Shoot them in the face!"

The wealth of secret knowledge implies that worthy people watch, and what they long for is immense. Does it whisper to us that, yes, in our dreams the robbers can win because isn't that what we want? Film may be—even in 1900—an infant capitalist venture, set to make a fortune out of law and order. But somehow it knows and wants to reach out to our wildness, too—the thing that is burning in the dark. In *The Story of Film*, Mark Cousins points out how Scorsese has Joe Pesci do the same thing at the end of *GoodFellas*—a woeful defense of law and order, and a thrilling admission that we are there for the violence and the mayhem.

The Great Ziegfeld (1936)

It's a black-and-white picture, but it comes complete with Overture, Intermission Entr'acte, and Exit Music. Still, the film is a sketchy biography of Florenz Ziegfeld, the impresario who had died broke in 1932. Today it's a tough grind, with fascinating moments. William Powell holds it together as Ziegfeld, his hair turning gradually grayer, and he has all the famous attributes: the eye for girls and staircases, the extravagance with gifts and cables, the love of spectacle, and a reckless charm where pretty girls and creditors were concerned. Of course, at three hours, the film has to be packed with dull numbers that may or may not be faithful reproductions of the Ziegfeld style. They feel far more like "production values" in a rather anonymous but expensive Metro-Goldwyn-Mayer picture that seems like an antique now because it didn't go for color. Hunt Stromberg produced it and Robert Z. Leonard directed, and that leaves it a struggle with cliché and famous show business attitudes.

So we see Flo move from Chicago to New York. We see the evolution of the Follies. We see the marriages to Anna Held and Billie Burke. We see the impact of the Crash. Ziegfeld may easily have been a scoundrel or an obsessive in life, crazed for his art, a constant womanizer; in the movie, he has his flutters, but he's a decent and honorable guy and a grand father, and it's easy to see why his wives love him.

Metro clearly threw money at the subject. There were five different photographers: Oliver Marsh, George Folsey, Karl Freund, Merritt Gerstad, and Ray June. There's a tremendous revolving spiral set (designs by Cedric Gibbons and Eddie Imazu). The music (rather conventional) is by Walter Donaldson.

Myrna Loy does very little as Billie Burke, but Luise Rainer gives a heavily underlined performance as Anna Held. Why she won the Oscar is hard to answer these days. She seems terribly coy, poignant, and overdone, and her celebrated telephone scene (quite short) is nearly laughable.

On the other hand, there's a scene where Ziegfeld is caught in a dressing room chatting to Will Rogers, and it's a small gem, with Rogers explaining how his wife is encouraging him to just walk onstage and chat to the audience. Then Fanny Brice is announced, and it's a rare chance to see the great woman herself—very funny, and singing "My Man." William Demarest and Dennis Morgan appear without being credited, and Morgan actually sings "A Pretty Girl Is Like a Melody." And I have a hunch Eve Arden makes a brief appearance.

That the film won Best Picture in the year of *Dodsworth*, *Mr. Deeds*, and *A Tale of Two Cities* may be the ultimate tribute to Ziegfeld. Apart from Rainer's victory, Powell was nominated—but for *My Man Godfrey*, and to give him his due, he plays the two films pretty much the same way. With Frank Morgan, Virginia Bruce, Reginald Owen, Ernest Cossart, Nat Pendleton, and Ray Bolger.

Greed (1924)

You can talk of *Greed* as a ruin, if you are inclined. That means despairing of a commercial system that would let a nine- or ten-hour monster survive as more than 140 minutes of rare sensation. It is part of the culture of ruin that points to a little gathering of memorials: like Rick Schmidlin's reassembly with the use of stills, which amounts to four hours; like Herman G. Weinberg's book *The Complete Greed*, which prints a lot of those stills. Some people even mention Frank Norris's novel *McTeague: A Story of San Francisco*, published in 1899. And then there is *Greed* itself, quite plainly a masterpiece, a model of a kind of psychological realism that shocked and horrified most people, because it gave them no one in the film to like.

There is the point: *Greed* proposes a movie that might read and feel like the great realist novels until Stroheim used the visionary trigger in film to show the characters' inner states—and then, as they became more dependent on loneliness or madness, greed or desire, fear or violence, as they became more like us, we shrank back from them even more forcefully. All that is there still. And even if hardly a single Stroheim film is intact—do you see a strategy there? do you feel he was not responsible for it if he is responsible for everything else?—what does that mean except that he made ruined films? That is his comment on the film industry. That is his lesson. Learn to regard so many films as ghosts of themselves.

So Stroheim had had his falling-out with Irving Thalberg at Universal over *Merry-Go-Round*. He went to the Goldwyn Company and made a deal to do Norris's novel. He would write and direct it himself, the story of McTeague the dentist and his friend Marcus; of setting up in San Francisco; of meeting and marrying Trina, who steals his money so that he murders her; and of the final meeting in Death Valley, where the two men find gold at last. But too late.

Stroheim shot the film in 1923, in real locations and interiors whenever possible. William Daniels, Ben Reynolds, and Ernest Schoedsack were his cameramen. Richard Day was the art director. Gibson Gowland played McTeague, Jean Hersholt was Marcus, and Zasu Pitts was Trina. The schedule was said to be nine months, and the cost of production $470,000. That was not a ridiculous sum.

But as the director cut his film, Goldwyn entered into the merger with Metro and Mayer established in 1924. By a narrative stroke that Stroheim the fatalist must have relished, he was back under the command of Thalberg again. There was a dispute. There were screenings of the full-length *Greed*. Some fairly smart people saw it and judged it heavily overdone. So a cut *Greed* was released, and you can say it is a bastard version of its proper self. There is no doubt that M-G-M betrayed themselves by throwing away the cut material, though that was standard practice at the time. Otherwise, they behaved like a movie studio, like the kind of place that sold pictures for a living. And all one can say about *Greed* is that it is essential, frenzied yet under control, and one of the great indicators of film and its future. It is still very hard to make pictures about people the audience does not like—but, remember: At the movies, the audience is afraid of the dark. It wants comfort.

The Grifters (1990)

Jim Thompson is one of those hard-bitten writers who seems to have been made by and for the movies. And in recent years there has been a craze to do his material. Yet he's tricky. He has a very literary force. His self-pitying characters often say things that actors find challenging. *The Grifters* had an odd history. Once upon a time, Martin Scorsese was going to direct it himself. Then he decided to produce, with Englishman Stephen Frears directing. There had been several screenplays that didn't work before Frears found a writing partner in Donald E. Westlake.

The story is of three loners, all working the grift, in southern California. Grifting is small fraud, anything from tricking a barman over the change to fixing the odds in a horse race. But it is also any crime. And the starkest thing about its story is the revelation that every criminal is a loner. There are old ties, family bonds even, but this is the world of cold mistrust. You can rely on no one. We see that quite early on in the way the mother, who makes a technical mistake at the track (Anjelica Huston), is brutally punished by a man (Pat Hingle) she has known for decades, a man who is fond of her.

But that rebuke is only the model for what happens as her son (John Cusack) becomes sexually involved with a freelancing girl (Annette Bening). Every family tie is invoked, but the terrible imperative of survival makes loners of them all. So it's a film that starts with the very merry and very sexy display of Bening (never better) and then sinks toward what is Huston's most severe performance. All in all, it's hard to think of an American film about the criminal life that is less sentimental or more impressive.

There are several great supporting performances—Henry Jones, J. T. Walsh, Michael Laskin, Charles Napier, Stephen Tobolowsky—but the most striking thing is the way the lead figures are seen in the same way as the supports. There is an unusually good score by Elmer Bernstein—droll, melancholy, macabre even—that is a very good guide to the way the tone gets darker as the film goes on.

It's interesting to wonder whether an American director would have kept this as such a scathing character study. You feel that Frears likes or at least pities all these people, and you can see how an American toughness might have dismissed them all until *The Grifters* felt like *Detour* or a Sam Fuller film. But this is a film about family ties that just don't count enough in a world where dishonesty has made for a terrible privacy.

This is easily the best of the films Frears has made in America, the best Jim Thompson adaptation (rivaled only by Bertrand Tavernier's *Coup de Torchon*), and just about the best of Huston, Cusack, and Bening. Put that package together and it's a compelling film—if short of ultimate power.

La Guerre Est Finie (1966)

As he made *La Guerre Est Finie,* Yves Montand was forty-five—it is the age Tom Cruise is now. How can this be? For instance, I think you could get away with having the Montand from *La Guerre Est Finie* serve as the father to the Cruise from *War of the Worlds.* Are we on the brink of some odd condition of nurture (or nature) that increasingly separates Americans from Europeans (or non-Americans)? Is it that Montand, born in Italy and raised fairly poor during the Depression, ended up looking older, more worn, more tired than an American boy born into the Great Society? Or is it a matter of experience? I am not picking on Montand or Cruise in this argument. The outlines of the question apply to a whole range of other actors. And that's why one notices a terrible, perhaps fatal, handicap—that of American actors to grow older, or to seem more loaded with experience and doubt. The last American lead actor who had that mixture of being good-looking but exhausted was William Holden—who is a long way from the faded boyishness of Warren Beatty and Robert Redford.

That is an aside to remarks on the resonance of Montand as Diego Mora in *La Guerre Est Finie*—a Spaniard, a veteran of the battle against Franco, and still an agent in the commitment to overthrow the dictator. It is not that Montand was a great actor, but he was a mighty presence, and his seeming so much more mature or resigned than his actual age would permit is vital to this deeply affecting film. Its subject is an agent who knows his old war is no more. After all, Franco had changed Spain, even if fascism remained. Diego can foresee the kind of transition to democracy that occurred when Franco at last died. The war is over. The battles of the late 1930s—losses then—are now to be re-registered as victories.

But Diego is committed to taking the grave risk of going back when he knows he may be arrested. And the dilemma is beautifully personified in his two love relationships: he has lived with Marianne (Ingrid Thulin) for several years—they have a searching affection, and the same history; but he enters into an intense, very physical affair (the most erotic ever filmed by Resnais) with Nadine (Geneviève Bujold), a student, a very smart girl, and exactly the radical Diego might have been twenty-five years earlier. This is far from old sex and young sex. It is not even quite fidelity. For Resnais manages to film and edit the sex as if aware of the complicity, and the joint effect on Diego.

In short, this is a very sophisticated thriller about character, written by Jorge Semprún (who would do *Stavisky*) and worked on by the usual Resnais team: photographer Sacha Vierny; music by Giovanni Fusco; production design by Jacques Saulnier. It is also a striking example of the viability of political cinema, for this is a study of ideas and practice in which every private gesture carries a larger meaning. Inexplicably neglected today, *La Guerre Est Finie* is another Resnais masterwork. Also with Jean Dasté and Michel Piccoli.

Gun Crazy (1950)

There are times when the sheer knowingness, the terrible omniscient superiority of people like Mitchum and Jane Greer gets in the way of a film noir. So it's easier to believe of *Out of the Past* that these two sleepwalkers are more in love with death than each other. That's a pity, and it's the moment to renew your acquaintance with the terrific, ragged unlikelihood of the lovers in Joseph H. Lewis's *Gun Crazy,* John Dall and Peggy Cummins.

Though it's an 87-minute B picture, produced by the King Brothers, *Gun Crazy* has literary antecedents. It first saw the light as a *Saturday Evening Post* story by MacKinlay Kantor (the writer who started *The Best Years of Our Lives*). That turned into a two-hundred-page script, written by Kantor and Millard Kaufman. Kantor had had in mind a thorough social survey of violent youth, and he never spoke to Lewis again after the director shaped it up for a movie. But Lewis improved it: for the finale, when the young lovers are in the swamp, he cut out the sight of the cops closing in—now, they are just heard and felt by the young people. In nearly everything he did, Lewis honed in on their emotions.

Bart Tare (John Dall) is a strange kid—he is good-natured and sensitive, but he loves guns in a way he can't explain. He goes to reform school. He goes in the Army. Then he meets Annie Laurie Starr (Peggy Cummins), a trick-shot artist in a show where she wears Wild West clothes. They aren't a match, except as shots, and that's what turns them on. It is a sexual kick at first and it sends them on a modest crime rampage. Then the feelings deepen. They pull off a bank job and then rob a meat-packing plant. They kill people almost as a way of affirming their own love. And it is a love story, no matter that Dall seems gay while Cummins (offered as Canadian) is a petite blonde from Prestatyn in Wales whose brief career with Fox was just about over.

There was a thought that this sexual edge showed too much, and the picture was called *Deadly Is the Female* at first, but *Gun Crazy* is better, because it admits to their real passion and it gives them the equal weight they deserve. Above all, the picture is handled with terrific verve by Lewis: very bold framing, deep focus, and a single-take bank robbery seen from the back of the car. These are wildly exciting and easily encourage the comparison with *Bonnie and Clyde*—though nobody on that much bigger success seems to have known about the Lewis film.

It's also a source of Lewis's success that these kids are Wild West characters, and it helps that the film is set in unnamed rural parts of the country. Russell Harlan shot it and the cast also includes Barry Kroeger, Anabel Shaw, Harry Lewis, Morris Carnovsky, Stanley Prager, Nedrick Young, Mickey Little, Russ Tamblyn, and Don Beddoe. But it's Dall and Cummins who last in the memory, and who give unexpected proof that once in a while miscasting is golden.

Gunga Din (1939)

On every picture that involves a lot of location work, a scout has to go out into the territory and find economical, accessible, and lovely places where the filming can be done. In the case of *Gunga Din*, RKO would have sent someone out to discover a manageable northwest frontier or Khyber Pass sort of country. As far as I know, they found places on the eastern face of the Sierra, near Lone Pine, a glorious world of immense mountains and near desert. And if someone asked me to close my eyes and say "Gunga Din," I think I'd see those places first (superbly marked out for action by George Stevens), especially the sequence where the British army is marching into the jaws of ambush, but Gunga Din (Sam Jaffe) climbs to the top of a shining tower and blows the alarm on a bugle—saving the day and winning his place in regimental history.

It comes from a poem by Rudyard Kipling, of course, and it's a nice touch of the film to include Kipling as a supporting character (something picked up years later in Huston's *The Man Who Would Be King*). The script was by Joel Sayre and Fred Guiol, but only after an adaptation by Ben Hecht and Charles MacArthur. Actually, in view of Hecht's soon-to-be-intense Zionism, it's good to see him so wholeheartedly on the side of the British army here. Is *Gunga Din* racist?—yes, of course it is, with many extras in body paint as the revolting Indian hordes and Eduardo Ciannelli turning in a classic, leering, and roaring performance as the rascal in charge.

I don't think it matters. The story concerns a trio of British soldiers—Cary Grant, Douglas Fairbanks, Jr., and Victor McLaglen—and it would take a very stern taskmaster to disown them. They are sui generis, to be sure, and the movie is steeped in mindless imperialism. I don't think it could have been made with the same panache and innocence in 1946, only because Indians and Asians had figured so much in the recent war.

So this is Hollywood on the brink of its future—George Stevens would never again be as lighthearted. It's fast, funny, adventurous, and spectacular. And Sam Jaffe is more than touching as the water boy who longs to be part of the team—he is a new kind of hero. Would I like to be introducing it to an audience of the Taliban? No. Could I defend it? No. But I come from a culture that sees the black humor in that predicament, and the Taliban do not.

Gunga Din was a routine film—it was not nominated for anything, nor should it have been. But its confidence, its brio, and its fun have hardly faded. If anything, the rest of the world is left with just one objection: not that the film and its follies were uttered, but that America has become so much gloomier and more self-conscious a country, always testing its own motivation. Joan Fontaine is the pretty female lead, and the cast also includes Montagu Love, Abner Biberman, Robert Coote, Lumsden Haire, Cecil Kellaway, and Reginald Sheffield as Kipling.

Hail the Conquering Hero (1943)

This was the end of Preston Sturges at Paramount—and, as you might suspect, it is one of his most brilliant and disconcerting pictures. Woodrow Truesmith (Eddie Bracken) sits alone in a nightclub drinking. Enter six Marines, just in from Guadalcanal. Woodrow buys them a beer and tells his story: He was a Marine once, but then hay fever ruled him out. So he stayed away, writing home about being a Marine hero, while actually laboring in a shipyard. He told his girlfriend Libby (Ella Raines) to give him up because he'd found another girl. The Marines give him a uniform, an "honorable discharge," and they take him home to Oak Ridge, California. Hail the Conquering Hero! His mother's mortgage is paid off. There's going to be a statue of Woodrow. He could even be mayor!

It's typical of Sturges that he should expose the mechanics of heroism at just the moment when real heroes were returning. And it's not just that he shows a system vulnerable to the spin and deceit of public relations. Rather, he marvels at a country where flatulent concepts like heroism, honor, and duty can get so out of control.

Of course, the truth comes out, and Woodrow is a little like a fallen hero in a Capra film, half expecting to be lynched. But his girl now realizes that he always loved her and the public won't let him go. As one character observes to him, "Politics is a very peculiar thing, Woodrow. If they want you, they want you. They don't need reasons anymore; they find their own reasons." And truly it is that wanton, irrational energy that Sturges is seeing finally, and being dismayed by. This is a country determined to go crazy over someone—anyone. It's the first serious warning about the loss of judgment in American public life, and it's the shrewdest estimate in Hollywood of what the war was doing.

They used the old sets from *Miracle of Morgan's Creek* on a project kept within safe budgetary limits. John Seitz was cameraman. Hans Dreier did the art direction, and the music came from Werner Heymann, with Sturges himself writing a song. The cast included William Demarest, Bill Edwards, Raymond Walburn, Jimmie Dundee, Georgia Caine, Al Bridge, James Damore, Freddie Steele, Jimmy Conlin, Arthur Hoyt, Harry Hayden, Franklin Pangborn, Vic Potel, and Chester Conklin.

In her first days of shooting, Ella Raines was not very relaxed. The Paramount people (notably Buddy DeSylva) grumbled and wanted her removed. But Sturges stood by his choice, and defended her in a big studio battle that extended to the question of why Sturges preferred his old familiar faces. There were those who thought it threatened the end of Preston Sturges. His new contract was being negotiated, and Sturges asked for a two-week window after every production during which he could leave. He had been a gold mine at the studio. But Frank Freeman resisted the two-week gap, and everyone was too stubborn to make a compromise. Sturges probably knew he could make a better deal elsewhere, but in fact he never had as fruitful a setup. If you're inclined to like the man, then his self-destructive loyalty to Ella Raines is as touching as the way Sturges's heroines love their guys.

"The only amazing thing about my career," wrote Sturges, "is that I ever had one at all."

Halloween (1978)

Haddonfield, Illinois, 1963. Michael Myers, aged six, kills his sister, Judith. Cut forward to 1978. Dr. Sam Loomis (Donald Pleasence), while driving to the asylum, tells a nurse that Michael hasn't spoken a word since. Dr. Loomis thinks Michael is evil. So guess who is lurking in the dark at the asylum gates to steal the car and drive off? And guess where he's headed? From the outset, there is a sweet, practical innocence about *Halloween,* coupled with the "I-dare-you" spirit of campfire stories told about the night that horrors walk the suburban streets of the Midwest. So there's one joke in having Donald Pleasence (not always the sanest actor in sight) as the doctor in charge—and there's another in him having the name of the John Gavin character from *Psycho* (the guy who actually captures Norman Bates).

Meanwhile, in Haddonfield, three comely teenage girls—Jamie Lee Curtis, Nancy Loomis (is the name why she was cast?), and P. J. Soles—are reckoning what to do on Halloween night. They're too old to trick-or-treat. But two of the girls hope to get their treats indoors with their boyfriends. It's only Jamie Lee who counts on a night of dutiful babysitting, and who isn't ready to give herself away in sex yet. Jamie Lee is on the virginal side, but, children, if you want a steadfast babysitter who will protect you against everything, pick a virgin.

Of course, Michael Myers, in a mask, will stalk Haddonfield this night. Those casual fun-loving girls will pay the price for hoping to be entertained, and Jamie Lee, with old-fashioned pluck and ingenuity, will stand up to Michael Myers and the heavy pressure of terror. It all rises to a demented climax and a fearsome scene where Michael seems to have trapped Jamie Lee in a closet. But then Loomis appears. He puts a bullet in Michael. The youth plunges to the street. Survivors draw breath. They look around, and Michael's corpse has gone. The sequels want him.

Halloween is simple, good-natured, and sturdy in its conservative morality, a part of which is the certainty that the mentally disturbed are going to be dangerous until the end of time. Written and directed by John Carpenter and produced by Debra Hill, it was made for peanuts and it had rentals of $18 million. It needs the gutsiness of Jamie Lee Curtis and it made her a quasar if not quite a star. As photographed by Dean Cundey, it is quick, moody, and evil-minded in the way of smart high school kids. We are a long way from real evil or the meaning of horror. But the series would run to eight films, and it would inspire so many other horror franchises for horny teenagers. Carpenter was a good director of action, and the editing is on to every trick in the goosing repertoire. In hindsight, there's regret that Carpenter's talent didn't flower. But, as Dr. Loomis might have put it, if America is prepared to pay you a small fortune for putting on the frighteners, be a public servant.

Hamlet (1948)

In taking on *Hamlet* (with the J. Arthur Rank company paying for it), Laurence Olivier was under some pressure to cut the text. His film is 155 minutes, whereas the Kenneth Branagh version (1996) is 242 minutes. The Branagh is in color, too, but still I think it is a less powerful film. The Olivier cuts (including Rosencrantz, Guildenstern, and Fortinbras) are forgivable, and the black and white is a happy, noir accident. For, actually, Olivier resorted to it only because he was having an argument with Technicolor and was determined not to give them the pleasure. As a consequence, this Elsinore (mounted at Denham) is a deep-focus labyrinth, and a far more satisfying place than might have been achieved by palatial color. Indeed, the place looks as if it is being filmed as an impressionable young actor's remembrance of Xanadu.

Olivier cut the text himself and generally followed the approach of his 1937 production at the Old Vic. Naturally enough, Vivien Leigh had been eager to play Ophelia, but she was too old and so the part went to the very young Jean Simmons. After much uncertainty, Gertrude was awarded to Eileen Herlie—though Herlie was twelve years younger than Olivier (and six years younger than Leigh). Herlie is the most serious limitation on the film's cast, and it's a marvel that Olivier nowhere comments on the possibility of casting Vivien—perhaps it would have crushed her vanity, though "Mummy" was one of his pet names for her. Basil Sydney is Claudius, and he does well enough, but in hindsight one regrets that the sexual tremors are not more apparent in that triangle. Olivier was sexually minded, and the treatment of Ophelia and lying between her legs actually involved some cutting when the film reached America.

What really works is the blond Olivier prowling the dark corridors and delivering most of the essential speeches. Yes, the play is curtailed, but Olivier as an existential hesitator is very effective and the engine to what was a crowd-pleasing film. *Henry V* is a bolder film, and truer Shakespeare maybe. But the success of delivering a decent *Hamlet* was greater still, and this is a landmark in Shakespeare productions onscreen, the proof that anything can be done.

The capper on that effort, of course, was winning Best Picture (*The Red Shoes* was Rank's other contender that year). Olivier also won the Oscar for Best Actor, and other statuettes went to Roger Furse for art direction and Carmen Dillon for sets. The picture had cost £574,000 (way over budget), but in time it broke into healthy profits with rentals of $3.25 million in the United States alone. It was during the filming that Olivier was knighted.

Felix Aylmer is Polonius, Terence Morgan is Laertes, Norman Wooland is Horatio, Peter Cushing is Osric, Patrick Troughton is the Player King, Anthony Quayle is Marcellus, and Stanley Holloway is the Gravedigger. The music was written by William Walton, and the picture was photographed by Desmond Dickinson.

Hamlet (1964)

Everyone does *Hamlet* now—and it's hard to be empty with that play, though it easily goes wrong. It wouldn't amaze anyone if Tom Cruise had a go, or Johnny Depp. I'm sure people whisper the poison in their ears. We have Mel Gibson and Branagh, and we can take the vanity-plates quality to such works. So it's arresting to see a *Hamlet* made not for the central actor, but for us all, in the certainty that this play speaks to us and our society as well as any ever written. The film made by Grigori Kozintsev is like a very high-class state theater rendering of the play. Yet it's a real movie, too.

So it's interesting to note that Kozintsev had dreamed of doing a *Hamlet* since 1923: He had planned an abridged mime version with the Factory of the Eccentric Actor. That failed, but in 1954 at the Pushkin Theatre in Leningrad, Kozintsev did a version (employing the new literary criticism of Jan Kott) that was clearly the basis for this film. So this is not just Hamlet's dilemma but the portrait of a diseased Denmark, a place where the unstable prince's pretending to be mad may hasten the symptoms of real illness. Compared with Olivier, therefore, Innokenti Smoktunovsky is not so much a lone romantic figure as a victim of group malaise.

This is ensemble playing in a scheme of black-and-white CinemaScope not nearly as atmospheric as the Olivier version but more stark, and in many ways more intriguing. The sets are beautifully matched with real exteriors of stormy seas, rocky cliffs, and forlorn castles. This is a *Hamlet* for which the "where" matters a great deal and seems to bear out the failure of so many personal relations.

The text comes from a translation by Boris Pasternak, and since the film is only 140 minutes (13 minutes shorter than the Olivier version), it's the more impressive that this version includes so much and yet makes the family story so gripping. Great speeches are shortened, yet everything is done to compress the drama—there's more Ophelia than usual, a lot of the players, but a brief appearance by the Ghost. The photography by Jonas Gritsius is outstanding, and I have to say that I think this is the most compelling of the film *Hamlets*. A great deal of the martial mood and the sense of warped destinies is supplied by the exceptional music by Dmitri Shostakovich, who had known and worked with Kozintsev since the film *The New Babylon* in 1929.

Of course, the poetry is lost, or distanced, though the sepulchral Russian voices seem very well suited to this interpretation. For Kozintsev, *Hamlet* becomes a political play. Olivier was striving for a Freudian portrait. The play can handle all comers. But for anyone searching, and unaware, Kozintsev's *Hamlet* and his subsequent *King Lear* are major works. Grant, too, that this severe, restrained *Hamlet* is the same year as the unrestrained *I Am Cuba* and it's easier to feel the vitality in Russian film waiting for the age of Tarkovsky and Sokhurov.

Hangmen Also Die! (1943)

Bertolt Brecht arrived in Los Angeles from Finland in July 1941. No one had done more to help that journey than Fritz Lang (he had heard so much about Brecht from Peter Lorre). So, in the New World, the two men walked their dogs together. Lang enthused about the ideal society of California. Brecht reckoned that it was just high capitalism. In fact, both men needed a job, and it came in the form of producer Arnold Pressburger (a Czech), who urged a resistance story set in Prague. Then, on May 26, 1942, Reinhard Heydrich, the Nazi chief in that area, was assassinated in that very city. In addition, Pressburger suggested a quisling character in the story who might be tricked into helping the resistance.

Lang and Brecht worked on the script on the beach. Brecht had a deal for $8,000—Lang had a contract for $50,000, which included $10,000 for his script contributions. So they didn't exactly get on: Brecht's script tended to be didactic; Lang was looking for a story line. Eventually, Lang brought in John Wexley to smooth the script out. And Brecht liked Wexley at first—Wexley spoke German. They were going to call the script *Trust the People* (not exactly a Hollywood code). But then Brecht got the impression that he was being eased to one side, and Wexley made it clear that he would claim primary credit.

The whole thing is a drama in itself (or a novel), and it ends with Brecht in fury and contempt, suing for anything he can think of and going before the Writers Guild. Yet, as Lang admitted later, there were clearly several scenes (involving Walter Brennan's character) that only Brecht could have written. What Brecht lamented was the casting of the story in Hollywood conventions, the use of regular studio actors, and an overall absent-mindedness about the Jewish question.

Prague was built at the General Services Studio, with William Darling as art director and James Wong Howe as cameraman. It's good-looking, but you can smell budgetary limits, as opposed to a setting that ought to be nightmarish. Worse than that, there are too many placid or well-fed American actors—Brian Donlevy, Brennan, Anna Lee, Gene Lockhart, Dennis O'Keefe—who simply don't convey the desperation in the resistance situation. Brecht saw Hollywood details everywhere, and he wanted many more refugee actors in the cast (including his mistress, Helene Weigel).

In the end, Wexley won the Guild arbitration and got the screenplay credit, while Lang and Brecht shared story credit. The general press reception was as good as it was predictable. This was a major war-effort movie: It concludes portentously with "This is NOT The End." But the critic Manny Farber, for one, found the picture awkward, and truly, granted the thriller aspects of the material, as well as the presence of Lang and Brecht, it is not the film it might have been. But the score, by Hanns Eisler, is marvelous, and in the supporting cast you can find Lionel Stander, Margaret Wycherley, Alexander Granach, and Hans von Twardowski as Heydrich.

A full ten years after *Happy Together,* even his greatest enthusiasts begin to wonder aloud whether Wong Kar-Wai can deliver the masterpiece he seems capable of—let alone the string of masterpieces such as easily identify Mizoguchi and Naruse. Those masters took the family group, and the secret antagonism of men and women, as their subject. Wong Kar-Wai is cooler and more modern, and *Happy Together* is about two gay men who have gone to Argentina together. Wong said it was a way of missing the fuss that attended Hong Kong's change of status. But in truth this film has very little political context or interest. It's far more a model picture of the new loneliness where a person can go nearly anywhere he can think of.

So, although this picture stresses "Together" and has the pop song as a final theme, it's most impressive as a picture of two boys alone and together. They are gay lovers, to be sure, but it's a competitive love, struggling for dominance or authorship. And it's no surprise when the film separates the pair before the end and has one of them talking about the other. I think Wong Kar-Wai is more interested in that lone attempt to make sense than in a truly integrated existence in Buenos Aires.

That said, Wong Kar-Wai has a great eye and ear—one of the characters is impressed at how different people sound, and the film as a whole responds to salsa and tango as well as the permanent mistiness of the Iguazú Falls. These are guys who work in cheap restaurants, and domesticity as a whole is countered by the steady habit of eating out. They are not the best educated kids in the world, though they are street-smart and hip. They could be in any café you care to name and they could talk to anyone. But their rhythms are different, and Wong is a master at getting things like that: The one (Tony Leung) has an inward resource that the other (Leslie Cheung) simply lacks—and in the end the film does cleave toward introspection and a voice that wants to define the impact of company and assess it in the framework of intellectual solitude.

Very little happens—hardly anything in the way of story. Yet we know these guys and their limits, and we see that one of them has at least a nostalgia for the literary or intellectual placing of things. Who knows whether Wong Kar-Wai will ever work that out for himself. The very quick, deft photography is by Christopher Doyle, Wong's regular coworker, and they are certainly happy together.

You could call this postcard cinema—or is it e-mail? Messages voiced in the shared night by two guys who wonder whether their existence and travel can challenge marriage, say. The tone is wistful, elegiac, and steadily interested in the world. But I'm not sure whether Wong has the nerve or the need to face the old challenge to make masterpieces—the habit that Kenji Mizoguchi and Naruse nearly took for granted. It's odd, because he has the skills.

A Hard Day's Night (1964)

In the terrible history of the movie exploitation of young singing sensations, there is no pity and little joy. Consider, for instance, the astonishing vitality of one Elvis Presley and the malignant spirit that insisted on his films being so bland, so enervated, so absent of all the things that made Elvis remarkable and dangerous and sexy. Once upon a time, the cinema was to celebrate those antisocial forces, but with Elvis they served as a plaster cast to keep his body and his spirit still. You could argue that *Performance* approached the bristling flower of Mick Jagger with far more panache. But Jagger is an actor in that film, and not the Stones. So I think it's time that Richard Lester received proper praise for finding a movie form that was wildly flattering to the Fab Four, generally smart and hip with film's possibilities, plus a reminder that having a real director might not hurt.

It has to have helped that there was no one in an intermediary position (like Elvis's dreaded and bogus Colonel Parker) who could come between the boys and the camera to "control" the image. And then it meant a lot that the Beatles were a very cool, hip collective who had already essayed the style of the film in their attitude to press conferences. So when, in their first days of glory, the lads were asked what it felt like, they brushed such idiocies away with studied vacancy, insolence, surreal irrelevance, or "you tell us." And I think that Alun Owen's script for *A Hard Day's Night,* as well as Lester's visual approach, took off from the press conferences and the Harold Lloyd–like idea of the boys forever trying to escape their mob. Thus, their private sport in the playing fields scene—shot near Isleworth—is a kind of "away from it all" reverie. And their entire imitation of a running, jumping, and standing still film (one of Lester's earlier works) is part of their canny reluctance to be pinned down in the white heat of narcissism. They looked great, of course, by 1964, but their whole manner is to say, This is pretty stupid, isn't it?

The film had to be packed with songs, but Lester took that problem head-on, and used it as an excuse for no story. The very worst thing about the Elvis pictures is the attempt to restrain the dynamo with story when it is quite plain that he is ready to do anything and anyone. And that's what the Beatles are like in this film—though their sexual aggression has been "handled" well enough to make the film friendly to very young children.

Yes, there was a lot more to the Beatles, as time would tell. But granted that movie exploitation was inescapable, I think everyone comes away from *A Hard Day's Night* with credit and aplomb. *Help!,* done two years later, is full of color and money, and the luxury shows to no good effect. The nice thing about *A Hard Day's Night* is that feeling of a silly sensation that might not last long enough to get the film out. Also with Richard Vernon, Wilfrid Brambell, Norman Rossington, John Junkin, Anna Quayle, and Victor Spinetti.

The Hard Way (1942)

Sometimes a story or a script starts to be talked about in Hollywood long before the cameras turn over. It was like that with *The Hard Way*, a Jerry Wald story about a woman, Helen Chernen, who tries to kill herself in the first sequence (just what Wald would do in *Mildred Pierce*). Why? Because, she says, she has given her own life to promote the career of her kid sister, Katherine (Joan Leslie), in show business. The rumor was that the story was based on real figures in Hollywood, but nobody could pin down those origins. Wald hired Irwin Shaw to do a screenplay, and then Daniel Fuchs and Peter Viertel were asked to do a polish. Meanwhile, the lead role, Helen, was thought of for Ginger Rogers, Rosalind Russell, and Olivia de Havilland, before it found its match in Ida Lupino.

She was twenty-three and clearly an out-of-the-ordinary actress, but her father was dying and she was suffering from exhaustion. From the outset, she was drawn to the part and the opportunity, and of course she was herself from an intense show business family. But for those very reasons, maybe, she resisted the material and the bitchiness in Helen. She said she found the role very difficult to play, and some observers reckoned that the stress of the part was adding to her illness. There were times when she was too sick to come to work, and Warners even considered replacing her with Ann Sheridan.

But that seems to have given Lupino a steel edge, and it persuaded her to do the part without conventional makeup. Let Joan Leslie look lovely as the younger sister—there should be no question but that Helen was too tough or grim to have a show business career herself. In short, she made it through, despite her father's death, and she gives a performance that many people reckoned should have had some recognition from the Academy. She did win the New York Film Critics award.

Vincent Sherman was the director, and he did a very good job. James Wong Howe was the cameraman, and at a moment when Warners tried to reassign Howe to another picture, Lupino begged for him to be retained. The film stands up very well in the severity of its portrait of the necessary lack of compromise in show business careers, to say nothing of that kind of surrogate success that emotionally feeds a person the public never sees. It's hard to think of any film of this period that is less sentimental in its view of the business—and nowhere is this more true than in Jack Carson's fine performance as a very feeble guy who gets pushed around.

And yet, oddly enough, Ida Lupino didn't catch fire. Indeed, she remained a bit of a secret for most of her career. But when she started to direct herself, in the 1950s, it was not difficult to see the influence of *The Hard Way* on her pragmatic approach to untidy emotions.

Heat (1995)

It is the assumption of *Heat* that everyone in its Los Angeles is pressurized by the unlikelihood of survival. Time and again, small overtures of decency or ordinariness are chopped off by this ceaseless yet nameless tension. In the end, the most natural explanation is that this fever derives less from some bleak analysis of victory or money than from the remorseless, despairing beauty of Michael Mann's style. This is a world without boredom, rest, or humane reflection. What passes for philosophy is only the preening of cats for whom it is always night, and always the battle—even if you're having a friendly and lunatic cup of coffee with a soulmate in a diner. Or it's show business.

Vincent is a top cop, Neil is a taker-down of big scores—they are also Al Pacino and Robert De Niro, and in that contest of wary if kindred champions (father and son in *Godfather II*), it is vital that they could swap roles. Thus Mann's facile concept: that cops and thieves are alike, forged in the heat, equally ready to give up common attachments in real life for . . . well, for movie, I suppose. The real point of *Heat*, granted Mann's exhilarating prowess, his unmatched capacity for holding the screen, is that so sweet a movie justifies the flagrant absurdity (and worse) in the idea. If you can't stop watching, Mann might say, then the fix is in, just like the master bolt in a machine. Nothing else intrudes in the dire but delectable equation in which the horror of life is made cinematically exquisite.

That sounds pathetic and disturbing, and someone has to stand up for the stupidity of the fundamental premise—that cops and thieves are interchangeable, and that the idea of these men being ready to give up all "family" in thirty seconds if the heat comes down is adolescent and fascistic. But fascistic cinema can be engrossing—as witness Leni Riefenstahl's days and nights in Nuremberg. And Mann is the hapless possessor of something like genius—or mastery—or is it more accurately perceived as the ability to make surface so alluring that we no longer think of substance? *Heat* is a skin—taut, alert, buffed—like the look of a great athlete or a new car.

On the other hand, *Heat* has nothing less than a love of Los Angeles and a remarkable ability for holding many lives and subplots in balance. The structure is as intricate as that of *Magnolia*, and in the interaction of lives Mann is at his most intelligent and demanding. It follows that there is not a bad performance, and not a character crying out for autopsy, or mercy-killing. (There is a profound alienation from life itself.) Just look at Val Kilmer, Tom Sizemore, Natalie Portman, William Fichtner, Jon Voight, Tom Noonan, Diane Venora, and even Ashley Judd, to see a faultless hiring of players as well as an unerring ear for movie talk. It is 172 minutes, too long, yet it could be longer. We could watch this ease for days at a time—or until the realization that making movie movie is not enough, and may be the medium's most disastrous digression.

Heaven's Gate (1981)

It was all too easy in 1981, and for years afterward, to say that *Heaven's Gate* had gone out of control. *Final Cut,* the excellent, pained, and nearly confessional book by Steven Bach—one of the United Artists executives who took the fall in the film's disaster—gave an exactly plausible account of where and how control had been given up. That book remains one of the most frank and alarming descriptions of the film business written from the inside. Bach takes on a good deal of the blame himself, which makes it fairer for him to point out the arbitrary outrages by Michael Cimino, the writer-director who had been hired as a savior by United Artists and who was given every indulgence allowed to a great artist. So I am not saying that *Heaven's Gate* might not have turned out better with more modesty and an urge to compromise on all sides.

Still, in the four or five times I have looked at it since 1981, and in the most recent reviewing, where fate spared me the prolonged opening scenes at Harvard (actually Oxford), so that I began as James Averill comes to Wyoming on the train, I thought it was close enough to a real film to leave no worthwhile gap.

Of course, it is not impossible to have a good film that destroys not just itself, but its business enterprise and many settled ideas of what makes a movie. More or less, *Greed, Gone With the Wind, Citizen Kane,* and *Apocalypse Now* all build that pattern. But there is a rich American tradition (Melville, James, Ives, Pollock, Parker) that seeks a mighty dispersal of what has gone before. In America, there are great innovations in art that suddenly create fields of apparent emptiness. They may seem like omissions or mistakes at first. Yet in time we come to see them as meant for our exploration.

So I'd like to stress, in *Heaven's Gate,* the uncertainty that exists wherever we look—and which at first seemed so offensive in so big and expensive a film. Spending that much, why not establish the emotional facts in the triangle of Averill-Ella-Champion? Yet as I see the film again, their yearning glances, those things unsaid, the very doubt, become as fruitful as the wide open landscapes of Wyoming—beautiful, dangerous, extreme, inhuman. Wouldn't it be something if Cimino had found a way of looking at his characters that was affected by the scale of the place?

That may be enough to persuade you to look again. But have a large basket for the other virtues: Vilmos Zsigmond's heartbreaking photography; the music—a prelude to Ken Burns and films like *Cold Mountain* but still not surpassed; the eastern European faces and the savagery of Wyoming; the murderous violence; the perfect parable for control and the lack of control in using the great spaces. And the very title—*Heaven's Gate,* and hell's journey. Yes, it was a disaster, but disasters are ten-a-penny. It is also a wounded monster.

Isabelle Huppert is luminous—although nearly everyone warned Cimino not to use her. Kris Kristofferson has some of the stature of silent Western stars. Christopher Walken is the eternal lost Kid—lethal and loving. And there is fine support from Brad Dourif, Sam Waterston, and a John Hurt who hardly needs to be there.

The Heiress (1949)

Some people would rescue the slightest work if it could be called "film noir." But they miss so much. Go to the late 1940s, the heyday of the genre, and try to find a picture with worse things to say about human nature and the traps people make for themselves than *The Heiress*. The end is breathtaking: The wretched Morris Townsend (Montgomery Clift) is beating helplessly on the door of number 16, unable to escape his shallow calculating soul, and excluded for the rest of his life. Catherine Sloper (Olivia de Havilland) is making her way upstairs. She has eliminated white lies and embroidery from her life. She is set in a living rigor, determined to be the bleak, despicable woman her father saw. But coming close now to the cruelty of her father, Austin Sloper (Ralph Richardson), who has gone upstairs to his bed to die—unless we get to him first, for Sloper has a case for being the wickedest character in American film, prepared to tell his daughter that she disappoints him utterly. Is *The Heiress* not a great film noir—or could it be that Henry James was degrees wiser and sadder than Edgar Ulmer or Joseph H. Lewis?

James's novel, *Washington Square*, was published in 1881. In 1947 it reached Broadway as the play by Ruth and Augustus Goetz, with Basil Rathbone as Sloper and Wendy Hiller as Catherine. Two years later, William Wyler came to make the film as his first freelance film after leaving Goldwyn. The Goetzes did the screenplay and seem to have missed an Oscar nomination for it only because they had done such thorough work already for the stage. Harry Horner's sets made the house come alive (and won an Oscar), and the dark velvety photography (with a lot of deep focus and staircase angles) is by Leo Tover.

Of course, it is all James; Wyler and the Goetzes were simply translating his conception. But anyone watching decades later will be startled by the meticulous hatefulness in Richardson's Sloper, all done with a gentle touch and a light voice, but showing the offense he has taken at being given a plain daughter. The moment when Sloper, a doctor, puts his own stethoscope to his chest to discover fatal illness is so chilly and narcissistic it is breathtaking. Richardson was nominated only as supporting actor—a nonsense (he lost to Dean Jagger in *Twelve O'Clock High*).

Montgomery Clift is Morris, and you can see him flinching at the character's duplicity—a hint that Clift would turn down Joe Gillis in *Sunset Blvd.* Then there is de Havilland, winning her second Oscar. She is hunched and dark in shyness at first, and then made older and deeper in her voice by revenge. It is a great performance. Credit, too, to Miriam Hopkins, Betty Linley, and Ray Collins. As for Wyler, is this simply professional, exact, accomplished—or great? The play may be tidy, but Wyler lets the beasts show in father and daughter. Grant Wyler this, *Carrie, The Little Foxes, The Letter,* and *The Best Years of Our Lives*.

Aaron Copland won the Oscar for his fine score.

Hell's Angels (1930)

Howard Hughes made his first airplane flight in 1920, at the age of fifteen—it was one of the sensations in life he most enjoyed, and it is likely that he actually died in the air, on the way to futile medical assistance in Houston, where he had been born. It was after the success of his movie production *Two Arabian Knights* (1927, Lewis Milestone) that he first conceived the notion of *Hell's Angels,* a flying epic set during the First World War.

"Story" is a strong word for what is left, but it's the arc of two brothers, Roy and Monte Rutledge (James Hall and Ben Lyon), Oxford men who join the Flying Corps. At the outset, Marshall Neilan (who was going to direct) worked up this story line. But Neilan was fired as director, and when his replacement, Luther Reed, went, too, he suggested that Hughes might as well direct it himself. Would nobody ever ask?

Hughes was a kind of toy-collecting little boy as well as a grown man, and as he prepared for the film he is said to have spent over half a million dollars on eighty-seven aircraft from the 1914–18 era. From October 1927 onward, Hughes was shooting scenes—a great many of them aerial over the Mojave Desert—with a camera crew headed by Tony Gaudio but including many others, notably Elmer Dyer. Many planes crashed, and it is alleged that three men were killed in the shooting.

Not that a coherent movie had emerged. But suddenly Hughes realized that as he had been working sound had arrived. He could not possibly offer a film full of planes and battle without sound. So in a way he started again. He hired Howard Estabrook and then Joseph Moncure March to write a new script—one that could be spoken—and he dropped Greta Niessen because her Norwegian accent would never work as the English girlfriend. Ann Harding and Carole Lombard were both considered for the part but it went instead to Jean Harlow—a sign of what Hughes was looking for. James Whale was hired to direct the new dialogue scenes, but he reported that Hughes might just as well have not bothered. At one point Whale cracked and told Harlow that even if he could tell her how to act he couldn't help her be a woman.

Hughes did not seem to be interested personally in Harlow—very soon, he would drop her contract. But neither could he recognize the flatness of her delivery. His ear was all attuned to aircraft engines and the bravado of boyish talk.

No one knows what the film cost, because no one trusted Hughes. He claimed $4 million, just enough to have beaten *Ben-Hur.* But it was likely no more than $3 million. Whatever, it grossed about half that in America. Of course, Hughes could afford to lose money on the film, and he was personally thrilled by many of the dogfights and the overall feeling of being in the air. But the regular, human scenes just went to prove his great difficulty at hearing people. The cast also included John Darrow, Lucien Prival, Frank Clarke, Roy Wilson, and Douglas Gilmore.

Henry V (1944)

No matter that the wretched French had to stand in for the Germans, *Henry V* was a self-bestowed flag of honor in approaching victory in late 1944. The British went to see it—and this writer was taken along as a child—to be a part of the party. It was like being held up on a south London street corner as Winston Churchill was driven past in a 1945 limousine, just before he was voted out of office in a landslide and the most significant Labour government in history came to power.

So I am suckered by the Olivier *Henry V*, especially by the burden of having hardly understood a word when I saw it. I could not know then that the first part, with its painted backdrops of fifteenth-century cities, was in debt to *Les Très Riches Heures du Duc de Berry*. And I did not really notice the lovely shift as it goes to the green fields—the Technicolor green—of Ireland. I can only remember the complete assurance with which victory came to the British, and the breathtaking idea that "history" might be as immediate as the rush of arrows in the air and the hallucinatory message that page boys' faces were burning like waxworks as the French set light to the English camp.

So the Olivier *Henry V* is not just a matter of taking pride in one's country, but of discovering the medium. I had no notion how daring it was to build a Globe Theatre and have the camera plunge down into its O to discover the nervous actor waiting to be a king. But ever since, I find, I have exulted in backstage stories and take it for granted that works of the imagination should lift a modest hem and let the public see the legs of how the thing is done.

I have heard people say that the Kenneth Branagh version (1989) is honest, worthy, robust, brutal, and probably truer to history—or to the early fifteenth century. And maybe there is no gainsaying the version of *Henry V* you were born with. I am helplessly loyal to Olivier, who, even when I was four, was spoken of as an ordinary man more regal than kings. And truly, I think that the transition from the theater and its feeble props, to the Giotto-like flatness of cities, to the steeplechase rough-and-tumble of knights in armor was a just reflection of the Chorus speech, "O, for a muse of fire that would ascend the brightest heaven of invention."

And don't forget that Olivier was himself in the process of discovering cinema, of how a great soliloquy could be just a voice-over on scenes of a noir camp, and realizing that music like that of William Walton spoke for chivalry as well as Shakespearean verse. There is even the possibility that the final scene, with the princess (Renée Asherson), helped break millions of British people in to the idea that a foreign language—French—might be possible, or speakable.

There is also the splendor of artisan acting—Leslie Banks, Robert Newton, Leo Genn, Esmond Knight, Ralph Truman, Max Adrian, Robert Helpmann, Freda Jackson, John Laurie—all those voices sounding as if recorded in a small back room made of oak.

He Who Gets Slapped (1924)

When it was finished, *He Who Gets Slapped* so impressed the sales force people at Loew's, Inc., that they asked to have the picture held back until the Christmas season. By all accounts, this was the first project started after the merger of Metro, Goldwyn, and Mayer. And it's fascinating that it was, principally, a Lon Chaney vehicle. Production chief Irving Thalberg had grown close to Chaney at Universal, and now the great actor was freelancing. So Thalberg made his move—a handsome young man opting for a famous monster.

Of course, there was another reason for Thalberg's interest. The role of the bareback circus rider ended up with Norma Shearer. The story goes that Thalberg had seen a short film she made but had been unable to track her down. It was only when established at M-G-M that he was able to find the Canadian actress, who was then twenty-three. She had made a lot of films, but nothing as a star. This was a big promotion for her, not just because of the prestige of a first production, but because John Gilbert had been cast as the young male lead. Almost as an act of will, Mayer and Thalberg had determined to promote Gilbert—whether he liked it or not.

The material of *He Who Gets Slapped* was extraordinary. It came from a Russian play by Leonid Andreyev about a leading scientist (Chaney) who loses his wife and his vital research to the same man. This shock fixes a dreadful look on his face—somewhere between hilarity and horror. His only recourse to this is to go into the circus as a clown! That's where he meets and falls for Consuelo (Shearer). As a clown, he is a figure of deliberate humiliation, and of course in the romantic triangle he is the loser.

Carey Wilson was hired to do the script. Cedric Gibbons built the circus sets, and Victor Seastrom was assigned to direct—this was Victor Sjöström, who had sought to escape a slump in the Swedish film industry by joining the Goldwyn Company. He adjusted to American studio conditions very well and shot the picture in a month for just $172,000. He seems to have turned a good rapport with Chaney. When the picture opened, it turned a profit of about $350,000, which kept Seastrom at the studio for several years and led to his being admired intensely by Lillian Gish.

Not that M-G-M was gentle to him. Mayer saw that he had a contract with Goldwyn that gave him $10,000 a picture plus a percentage of the profits. But Mayer persuaded the Swede to take another $10,000 up front and give away the profits. "We'll never be able to work them out anyway," Mayer had warned. And so an eager artist fell for money in hand against a portion of the business.

Thalberg was delighted. He pushed Gilbert hard and he started to date Shearer. She got a good studio contract in 1925, and in 1927 the actress and the mogul were married in high Hollywood style. A paradise was in the making, but by 1936, Chaney, Gilbert, and Thalberg were all dead and Shearer was stranded.

High Noon (1952)

People make faces at *High Noon* a lot nowadays, but I think they're being snobs. Yes, there are things I don't get about the picture (and we'll come to them), but it's easy to see why it works. When three gunslingers ride into town just to wait at the depot for the noon train, something's working—it's the long stretch of straight line (found near Sonora); it's Lee Van Cleef and Robert Wilke as two of the heavies, before anyone knew who they were; and it's that song, "Do Not Forsake Me, Oh My Darling," written by Dimitri Tiomkin and Ned Washington, and sung by Tex Ritter. Let's put it this way: That song is a lot better and lot more relevant than "Raindrops Keep Falling on My Head."

Fred Zinnemann read the script and knew it was a masterpiece. I think he meant that for 84 minutes, or whatever it took, everything was going to be inevitable. Will Kane (Gary Cooper) is sheriff of the town and he's retiring—on his wedding day—and on the day an old enemy gets out of the penitentiary. That's who the guys are waiting for at the depot—it's going to be four against one. So Kane asks around for help, and no one in the town is ready to step forward.

The script was written by Carl Foreman, and by the time the shooting began he'd had to leave the country because of the House Un-American Activities Committee. All of which has led to the interpretation of the film that, when the chips are down, your friends don't want to know you. Howard Hawks famously sounded off against *High Noon*, saying, Why ask for help from amateurs? Stick to what you've got. And he made *Rio Bravo* as a corrective. Which is fine, but *High Noon* works—though it might work better if Kane kept refusing help. I'm not sure, now or then, that the unwillingness to fight is fair to American civic spirit. Most Americans will fight anyone. Though I can believe that a man like Kane would prefer to do it alone.

Anyway, it's not a film to see more than once. Because if you know how the suspense comes out, then you want to know so much more about how and why Gary Cooper (age fifty-one) has just married Grace Kelly (age twenty-four). And why doesn't he want to get to Las Vegas with her as fast as he can? A remake could have him tell her nothing about the problem but take her to a hotel room and give her the best 84-minute honeymoon she ever had and then go and shoot the bad guys and come back to a drowsy Grace for more.

Because I don't like her being a Quaker and then helping in the fight—and I don't like her itching to run away, either. When Cooper looks at Kelly (and apparently this is what happened in life), he knows it's his lucky day even if he's got the forty bandits or the seven samurai at the gate. So Cooper got an Oscar, Tiomkin got one for the score and one for the song, and Elmo Williams and Harry Gerstad won for Best Editing. Also with Katy Jurado, Lloyd Bridges, Thomas Mitchell, Otto Kruger, Lon Chaney, Jr., and Harry Morgan.

High Sierra (1941)

High Sierra is a key step in the transformation of Humphrey Bogart, and it is clear now how large a part John Huston played in that. It was a novel, by W. R. Burnett, published in 1940, whereupon Huston wrote to Hal Wallis urging that it not be a conventional gangster picture. "Take the spirit out of Burnett, the strange sense of inevitability that comes with our deepening understanding of his characters and the forces that motivate them, and only the conventional husk of a story remains." Within a few days, Huston was plunging ahead on the screenplay, where he did his level best to make Roy Earle rather less the "Mad Dog" killer referred to in the press than a sad, isolated figure, living somewhere between law and order. And it was thanks to that new status that the Bogart we would love was able to emerge.

Paul Muni was the first casting idea, but he turned it down—and so did George Raft. That's how Bogart got it, after he had made a personal plea to Wallis. So Huston's Earle is a guy sprung from prison after eight years of his sentence. It's plain that he is being freed because of underworld influence, and to pay back that good turn he has to commit to doing one more job. Very soon, he's on the run again, with a yearning to "break out" of this pattern.

He finds a girl, Velma (Joan Leslie), a cripple, and he puts money toward an operation for her. But being healed does not sweeten her nature, or improve Roy's chances. She turns nasty and confirms Roy in his bleak regard for society. He has only two friends: a dog, Pard; and Marie Garson (Ida Lupino), a gangster's moll who becomes his loyal friend. As the police close in, Roy is forced deeper and deeper into the Sierra and his own melancholy. But in the process, he abandons the conventional snarling of gangster talk. This is the guy who, on first being released from prison, goes to a park and feels the grass under his feet.

This was a Mark Hellinger production, directed by Raoul Walsh and released in January 1941 (well ahead of *The Maltese Falcon*, where Bogart's tough manner at last could reside on the side of the law). He was turned from being a nasty, vicious slugger into a wise, world-weary counterpuncher, and it suited Bogart's sense of himself. Walsh deserves some credit, and Howard Hawks later would add humor to the mix. But John Huston had won the act's confidence, and seen how his sardonic grin would play. And so the rat became our hero.

The black and white was shot by Tonio Gaudio, with art direction by Ted Smith and a score by Adolph Deutsch. There were some who objected to the softening of the gangster character, but Earle is killed in the end and that "inevitability" has been there from the outset. Vigorous supporting work from Alan Curtis, Arthur Kennedy, Henry Hull, Henry Travers, Jerome Cowan, Minna Gombell, Barton MacLane, and Cornel Wilde.

Hiroshima, Mon Amour (1959)

In the dark, bodies in a bed. Are they lovers, or are they dead? That crystalline coating they wear, is it the sweat of their affection? Or is it the first sign of another affliction—call it radiation? Is that why they shine—or is shining simply the glow that says "ready for story"? Ready for history, too. She is French, from Nevers. She is an actress come to Hiroshima to make a film about peace. He is Japanese, and they are becoming lovers. They call each other by the place-names they have—Hiroshima and Nevers—and we recall the first shock this great film ever gives us, the astonishing title, and the cinema's insistence that the epitome of disaster and the most treasured thing can be put side by side. Not just can be, but must be. Have there been lovers since 1945 who have woken in the middle of the night and not sometimes felt the litany of names somewhere in their darkness and warmth—Auschwitz, Treblinka . . . It is the start of a poem.

Alain Resnais's feature film, his first, after so many films that altered the nature of documentary and introduced "essay," came as the New Wave came. But it was hardly a young man's film, or even a picture that was jostling to be on the crest of that wave. It was a fine reminder to young people that just as they got their breakthrough, so another film might change the landscape.

The lovers in Hiroshima, Elle and Lui, Emmanuelle Riva and Eiji Okada, are completely free from any of the terrible burden, from *Sayonara* and the like, of "Gee, you Japanese are strange . . ." She comes in from the balcony with him asleep in the bed still and she sees his arm twisted oddly, and she is back in Nevers in 1944, cradling the body of her German lover. She was in *Le Silence de la Mer*? Not quite, for her love affair was fulfilled so that she had the stain of German blood on her face once and then her hair cropped and her own blood where she was beaten up. She loved an official enemy, an ordinary soldier. Yet she survived. And people survived in Hiroshima, too. Or did they?

So it is a love story, a story of three loves—call it four, because she is not quite the same person at twenty and thirty-five. It was written for the screen by Marguerite Duras and then directed by Resnais, and I think it is true that Resnais submitted to the great beauty and authority of the text—for it is poetry uttered as law, erotic and geological at the same time. And if it is Resnais's greatest film, then I think it should be said that the script is vital. It is not really a story so much as a process, to be seen over and over again, photographed by Sacha Vierny and Takahashi Michio, with exquisite music by Giovanni Fusco (the piano motif) and Georges Delerue (the desperate lyrical passages). Henri Colpi was in charge of the editing, though you know that every hesitation comes from Resnais.

There is a scene in a public place where an old Japanese woman sits between the lovers on a bench—like a passerby looking at Romeo and Juliet—that is one of the greatest things ever done. But so is the whole film.

His Girl Friday (1940)

In 1928, a play, *The Front Page,* written by Ben Hecht and Charles MacArthur, opened in New York (Jed Harris directed). It still plays all over the world, the story of a Chicago newspaper editor, Walter Burns (Osgood Perkins in the play), who tries to stop his ace reporter Hildy Johnson (Lee Tracy) from quitting—to get married. It was filmed decently in 1931, by Lewis Milestone, with Adolphe Menjou and Pat O'Brien in the leads—and less well by Billy Wilder, in 1974, with Matthau and Lemmon.

Somehow or other, the idea occurred to Howard Hawks to try it with the reporter as a girl—and if you did that, suppose they had been married, but now Hildy was divorced and about to marry a decent, reliable guy. Hawks said the idea arose impromptu, at a dinner party, with a girl reading Hildy's lines. Maybe. Whatever the history, Hawks got Charles Lederer to do the necessary rewrite, and thus we owe "Bruce" to Lederer—the insurance man from Albany, galoshes and umbrella, and one of American film's most joyous insults to its own mainstream. Morrie Ryskind was also hired to do some rewriting (uncredited).

Hawks had always seen Cary Grant as Walter, but it's fascinating to note that half a dozen actresses turned down Hildy before Rosalind Russell accepted the part. Of course, people knew Hawks, but *The Front Page* was a modern classic and maybe the shift seemed perilous. Ralph Bellamy agreed to play Bruce and went along with every sly dig that the guy was so dull he was like that fellow in pictures—Ralph Bellamy.

We are talking about a picture that received not a single Academy nomination, and we are talking about one of the glories of American film. More than *The Front Page* ever dreamed of being, this is a relentless comedy of talk, action, and bad manners; it is a loving tribute to the newspaper business filled with contempt for the ethics of those who work the business; and it is possibly the greatest of the sublime comedies of remarriage made in Hollywood.

Think of it as a game. With seconds to spare, Walter learns that Hildy is off to marry Bruce. Now his every wile and invention goes into preventing that marriage, keeping Hildy as a writer, but retaining her as his girl. They bicker, they swap insults, they fight—they are in love in the Hawksian world. For the process of skirmish is the same as wooing. It's only gradually, as you relish the film enough, that you realize this game will have to be played over and over again. Walter will never be the reliable guy Hildy wants. They will break up time and again, so that they can get back together. Indeed, you realize why Hildy came to the office to say good-bye: It was her signal, "play ball."

Joseph Walker photographed the entirely interior picture, and it looks like noir coming to life. The supporting cast includes Gene Lockhart, Helen Mack, Porter Hall, Ernest Truex, Cliff Edwards, Clarence Kolb, Roscoe Karns, Frank Jenks, Abner Biberman, John Qualen, and Billy Gilbert as Pettibone.

Bliss.

History Is Made at Night (1937)

Sometimes chance lets us know a little extra about the making of some movies—and it's the little extra that tells the truth. *History Is Made at Night* was a Walter Wanger production in which Charles Boyer and Jean Arthur would be giddy lovers. Wanger had slipped into the belief that Gene Towne and Graham Baker were brilliant new screenwriters. As far as we can tell, Towne and Baker were on to a good thing, or they were working on their gardens. Suffice it to say that the script was in chaos after an opening in which a humble waiter, Paul Dumond (Boyer), and a shipping magnate's wife, Irene Vail (Jean Arthur), run away together after, apparently, Boyer has accidentally killed the lady's chauffeur. Her husband, Colin Clive, arrives to discover the corpse and quite correctly elects to pursue his wife.

Frank Borzage was directing, and he was keen to do his thing in the romantic scenes—there is a barefoot dance number, for instance, as well as a chemistry between the leads that had some onlookers persuaded they were an item. At this point, the young Joshua Logan was hired to do some "additional dialogue" work. He teamed up with Arthur Ripley (neither man is credited on the picture) and saved it. Ripley saw that it needed a "man kicks dog" scene, as follows: When Clive the husband finds the chauffeur, the wretched man comes round—he was only unconscious. Whereupon Clive hits him with the poker and blames the murder on Boyer!

Logan's memoir (*Josh*, 1976) is discreet about what happened with the rest of the film. Its admirers note the abrupt shifts in tone and mood—from melodrama to screwball to romance to epic—but allow that the love story acquires an enchanted quality "all its own" in which the waiter and the millionairess discover many truths about life. So let us—fond and dutiful believers in the factory system—remember that sometimes the factory was a madhouse where momentum and the habit of doing one damn stupid thing after another was all that kept a film going.

History Is Made at Night ends up with the sinking of a *Titanic*-like ship and Boyer and Arthur being reunited in a lifeboat. The rest is a matter of Colin Clive being nowhere near cool enough for Boyer and Arthur. When the lovers talk, it is all whispered innuendo and her breathless reply. It is a fusion that begins as radio—and you only have to hear lovers pass two or three lines to explode the myth of silent lovers gazing at each other. Talk is the sexy thing. The balance of two voices—that is casting.

The photography was shared by David Abel and Gregg Toland. Alexander Toluboff did the art direction. The cast includes Leo Carrillo, Ivan Lebedeff, and George Meeker. One reference book refers to the "seamless" direction of Frank Borzage, and the film with its cute title is regularly included in the list of Borzage masterpieces. But the truth is less tidy and convenient, and it suggests that many films survive only because they had a doctoring job in the nick of time.

A History of Violence (2005)

It begins like *Out of the Past* and it ends as *Back to the Future.* Tom Stall (Viggo Mortensen) runs a diner in Millbrook, Indiana. This is classic small-town America, a hidden place, like Bridgeport, California, in 1947, a wonderful place to live—if you are dead already. He has a wife, a honey, not just the mother of two good children, and a lawyer, but Maria Bello—one of the most attractive women in American film. Yes, it's lovely—including the playful sex where she dresses up as a cheerleader—but it's not quite a movie yet, is it?

Then hoodlums and murderers pass by—it is chance—and Tom, just like flipping a burger, disposes of them. This is vivid movie; it is the flash of violence, a thing that requires angles, cutting, and the way in which purpose finally chases the sadness out of Mortensen's eyes. For Tom Stall knows what it will mean—he can't delay history any longer.

The next visit is Ed Harris as a guy named Carl, someone who knows "Joey Cusack" and remembers how Joey took his eye out. Carl is hideous: he is violence in the flesh, and he is a great supporting actor threatening to take over a film. He rides "Joey" about the past, and in the end Tom has to kill Carl, too—so it's a good thing Joey is there and remembers how to do it. The Stalls' son turns violent. Tom and his wife have sex again and now it's sex noir—rough, urgent, nasty. Haven't the movies always taught us that sex is our act—we play it our way?

It's very important that this film isn't called *Joey in a Corner* but *A History of Violence.* In other words, it sets us up to receive not quite a graphic novel but an academic paper, and the marvel of the film is that David Cronenberg knows how to bridge those two styles. So, from the outset, Tom is just a touch too moody, and he's a laboratory experiment. The film comes from a comic-book fiction by John Wagner and Vince Locke, and Cronenberg did the script with Josh Olson, so that the picture feels a little Edgar G. Ulmer meets Bresson.

Tom tells his wife that he had a revelation and gave up violence. But clearly it is there still, the dregs of DNA or a cultural style left by so many movies. If ever there was a picture that needed a sequel this is the one. For after Tom has gone back to Philly, to his brother (William Hurt—of a scummy brilliance) and to triumph, who says the machine stops there? Who says he goes back to Indiana? He is the ideal brother to take over the violent business—his job interview eliminated the incumbent.

The precision and cold advance of this film are beautiful and enthralling. The use of actors is supremely intelligent. The photography (by Peter Suschitzky) is so restrained as to make you scream. That's what it comes to: the math textbook tone and the material of trash—one of the best American films Canada has yet provided.

The Hit (1984)

There's always been an engaging side to Stephen Frears that says, Really, there's no need to make quite so much fuss about filmmaking—it's not that complicated and needn't be as strenuous or as earnest as many make it. In that light, *The Hit* is a kind of summer holiday movie in which some English attitudes and actors go to Spain for a few weeks to relax. But more than that, the Frears who had been raised in very good British traditions—low-budget television, documentary realism, and slices of uneventful life—seems to have realized on this project that he deserved an adventure.

Written by Peter Prince, *The Hit* has the notion of some iconic London underworld figure who has grassed ("We'll Meet Again," the crooks sing in court as he gives damning evidence). He goes off to southern Spain, boredom and ease, but he knows what's coming: John Hurt and Tim Roth, two versions of nastiness, one educated, one not. They pick up the grass (the urbane Terence Stamp) and have to take him back to London, and apparent doom. They acquire "spitfire" Laura del Sol along the way, and why not? It would be a solemn attempt on this genre that didn't include an unpredictable sexpot ready to scratch anyone's eyes out. And the final touch of aplomb is that the Spanish policeman who makes a hunt of it all should be the very same Fernando Rey who had lately done drugs in New York and been humiliated in *That Obscure Object of Desire*.

The Hit is merry, spiteful, full of event, pretty to look at and listen to (Eric Clapton did some of the music), and it is quite an important step in the modern adoration of the criminal class in the new English film—you can see how much *The Hit* must have inspired *Sexy Beast* and other such pictures, even if Frears would always be too modest or ironic for, say, the unrestrained beastliness of Ben Kingsley in that film. Not that there isn't enough to make enjoyment in Stamp, Hurt, and Roth. This picture did a lot to rescue Stamp from the inglorious coproductions to which his beautiful vacancy had led him. He found a comic edge in this character, just as Hurt for once was sober, lethal, and efficient. As for Roth, this was a movie debut, and it was evident that his promise would go far.

Finally, the intriguing point is the question of where Stephen Frears is most at ease. He has tried Hollywood, and had a few bruising experiences. He has proved himself, early and late, dealing with cycling clubs or 10 Downing Street, an expert eavesdropper on British society. *The Grifters* is a brilliant American film. And he found a nice part of himself in Ireland. In all that traveling, *The Hit* seemed to give him confidence and the urge to stretch his legs. It also revealed a dry, unsentimental fondness for character that could easily live on either side of the line of the law. *The Grifters*, for instance, could be called *The Dreamers*—and equally *The Hit* is *A Hit*.

Hitler, a Film from Germany (1980)

Was it a dream? If so, was it a nightmare of horrors, or a torrent of wonderful things? I am writing this essay in the first days of 2006, at a time when the filmgoer is supposed to be making his or her "top ten" list for the past year. Not for the first time, I find myself hard-pressed to recall films of the first quality. For instance, in 2006 there was a film called *Babel*, by Alejandro González Iñárritu, that proposed the novel platitude that we are all of us in one world, so that a shot fired in one continent echoes in another. And *Babel* is, I suppose, getting on for three hours in this blind mission. Yet people marvel and complain that this *Hitler* is seven hours long. Why complain, if something like a terrible and tormented century has been conveyed in just one night's sleeping space?

Hitler may have exhausted its maker, Hans-Jürgen Syberberg. Being *Hitler* clearly had the same impact on Adolf. I met Syberberg only a few years after the film when he was still engaged on immense enterprises—like *Parsifal*—though nothing could compare in scope and power with *Hitler*. And Syberberg, a man of great charm, admitted without coyness to his own greatness and to the way he tended to tower over other filmmakers. It was all true, undeniable, and if any filmmaker had eyes, ears, and mind open, it was apparent that *Hitler* was doing everything in the space of one night. I mean "everything" in that it was digesting and presenting two histories: that of the world, and that of cinema. And if most people in Germany saw the work on television, then there was no getting away from the implication that television could hardly carry on afterward. Just as there must have been the intimation in 1941 for smart people as they saw *Kane*, that it's all up—we can't make movies anymore, so *Hitler* seems to declare a moratorium on television. For its great stew of news, entertainment, and commentary has made the poisoned Kool-Aid for the world. Talk about an educational experience!

Of course, television and film go on, though it becomes harder every year to believe that anyone in the process, filmmakers or viewers, really expects to be changed any longer. And the truth to this profuse but controlled anthology of Hitlerisms is that the epic theatrical form that Syberberg has put on film is finally a way of discovering the Adolf in every audience. Susan Sontag—whose commentaries on the film are vital—observed that Syberberg had converted Hitler into a filmmaker. The film was called *Our Hitler* in America—fair enough, clever enough—but another viable title is *My World* when the possession is Hitler's.

You can discuss every strand of the history in the film—the actual events or the sickening way in which the circumstances of his doing and our watching indicate a terrible fascism in the nature of film itself. So Syberberg may be "over," in the way some volcanoes are. But his orgy took film to its limits, too, and it is why the idea that we still make great films is a kindness, like telling our children everything will be all right—instead of "all right" will be everything.

Hoffa was a horrible failure: having cost $42 million, it earned only $24 million in the domestic market. There were plenty of explanations to choose from—the public had it in its head that Jimmy Hoffa, president of the Teamsters Union, was a bad man who deserved whatever he got. Beyond that, there was a widespread feeling in Hollywood of why draw attention to unions by making pictures about them? If God made a mistake, have the tact to leave well alone. And what was with this lugubrious narrative setup where Jimmy and his sidekick are waiting all day long at a roadhouse for destiny to arrive. Are they idiots, or what?

But then look at the stirring, nearly Soviet way in which director Danny DeVito can use a single, developing camera movement to shift from a small gathering of dissidents to a great surge of protest. The feeling for labor and union cohesion is extraordinary, and it's in the mise-en-scène, the life and breath of the film. Again, look at the suspended, wordless scene where Hoffa returns from a great battle in a crowd of other people and the battered madonna figure of Karen Young attends to him—the suggestions of a love affair, but also of how her character is his conscience, are uncanny and beautiful. Look at the high comedy of the deer-hunting sequence. In all the union gatherings there is an implicit comedy of shady men being dumb boys together. This is a movie fully aware of how a great hero in labor can become corrupt, but faithful to the significance of unions in the history of so many American industries. The picture never excuses Hoffa or sentimentalizes him, but in its overall attitudes and in Jack Nicholson's tough Irish snarl—don't explain, don't complain—it leaves us fully aware of what happened.

Edward Pressman produced this out-of-the-way project and David Mamet's script is probably the best he has ever done for the movies in that it is loaded with humor and compassion. Stephen Burum did the photography, and he rises to every great challenge DeVito throws at him. But there's the point to stress: This is a very well directed film, with a bold, forthright vision that could easily fit a much bigger name.

As for Nicholson, he was at a point where people were beginning to think he traded on just being Jack. But this is so tart and fresh a performance, so wiry, needling, and so set on an aggressive or unfriendly manner. It's an irony that the people who did Nicholson's makeup on Hoffa got nominated but not Jack himself, though it's very clear that the makeup is a natural extension of attitude and thinking. DeVito plays the chief sidekick. Armand Assante has the right empty panache as the mobster, and then there are a host of beautifully judged performances: J. T. Walsh, John C. Reilly, Frank Whaley (the onlooker?), Kevin Anderson (as Robert Kennedy), John P. Ryan, Robert Prosky, Natalie Nogulich (the wife), Nicholas Pryor, Paul Guilfoyle, Karen Young, Cliff Gorman.

Hold Back the Dawn (1941)

We open on a working film set at Paramount: Mitchell Leisen is directing Veronica Lake and Brian Donlevy in a scene from *I Wanted Wings*. An unexpected visitor slips in, George Iscovescu (Charles Boyer), and at the lunch break he insists on telling Leisen his story. Iscovescu (a ballroom dancer) had found himself in Mexico trying to get into the United States. He is warned by the authorities that the "Iscovescu" quota is short of places. But his dancing partner, Anita Dixon (Paulette Goddard), tells him there is a way. He would have to marry an American woman. He looks up and there is Emmy Brown (Olivia de Havilland), a schoolteacher, leading a class day trip to Mexico.

Like a cad, George woos Emmy, who proves a simple and gullible woman. When he tells her he loves her, she wants to believe him. They are married. Emmy takes the kids back to California, while George refiles for immigration. Then Emmy returns—for her honeymoon. She is a changed woman already, but Anita tells her about the real George. Emmy pretends not to be upset, but she goes back to the United States in distress and is hurt in a car crash. George sneaks over the border to be with her. They are in love now, and he wonders if Mr. Leisen can help their cause by telling their story.

And *Hold Back the Dawn* turns out to be their story and a Mitchell Leisen picture from Paramount. It is one of his best (it was nominated for Best Picture), an adroit mixture of romance and social commentary coming from a film community that knew real stories of people denied visas and working papers (Billy Wilder's included). It came from a short story by Ketti Frings (based in fact), and Arthur Hornblow produced it for Paramount, with a script by Charles Brackett and Wilder. Later on, Wilder would often complain that Leisen had spoiled or softened his scripts, but it's easier to see how the Wilder of the 1940s might have made this a far nastier film. Whereas Leisen really liked people more than Wilder did, and knew the story had to have a happy ending and a reformed heel.

It was treated as a big picture. Leo Tover shot it, and he had a noir feeling. Robert Usher did the excellent sets (the picture is notable for its time in not making fun of Mexico or its people), and Edith Head made the clothes. De Havilland handles the shift from naïveté to beauty as the emotionally awakened woman (she got an Oscar nomination), and Boyer enjoyed playing the heel with a heart. But it's the development of warmer feelings, and the sly growth of love, that marks Leisen, and as so often he uses an excellent supporting cast to build a community of needy people. Goddard is spunky and funny. Rosemary DeCamp excels as another refugee, and Walter Abel is outstanding as a lawyer. Also with Victor Francen, Nestor Paiva, Curt Bois, Eva Puig, and Madeleine LeBeau. Music by Victor Young.

Holiday (1938)

It's a nice trick question: What's the most sophisticated film Cary Grant and Katharine Hepburn made in 1938? And the answer is *Holiday*, which is really a new subgenre (of enormous promise) in which someone says, "Is this a comedy?" and the answer goes, "Only if you're laughing." As a piece of material, *Holiday* is very serious: It's what are we going to do with life—is it a burden or a duty, or a holiday? Having its origins on the happy side of the Great Crash, *Holiday* is one of the most inspired ways of asking the rich in America, What are you going to do with it all? I first saw the film with Ivy League undergraduates in the late 1970s, and the sweet way in which their merriment turned quiet was to know just the questions these kids were asking themselves.

So *Holiday* was a play by Philip Barry that opened in 1928 (there was a 1930 movie, with Ann Harding as Hepburn—very worthwhile). In the play, Johnny Case (Ben Smith) is a success made from not much who is about to marry one sister, Julia, only to find that the other sister, Linda, is closer to him in philosophy. It's important that Case is not of the monied class. He is an American newcomer. And his dealings with the sisters are a prototype of the comedy of remarriage: It's also a pattern for the two sisters in *My Man Godfrey*.

The play did well enough (and a young Katharine Hepburn understudied in it), but this movie is a decade later and by then a lot had changed. The Depression had isolated the old rich and made their good intentions suspect. So Case now is not as wealthy—indeed, he's an ordinary sort of fellow, and it is therefore just a little suspect that he has won the heart of the other sister to begin with.

The movie was scripted by Donald Ogden Stewart and Sidney Buchman, and it was mounted at Columbia, with nearly everyone out on loan. That may have added to the verve of *Holiday*, and George Cukor said it was one of his favorites in which he loved exploring Barry's penetrating points made as light comedy. Grant and Hepburn developed their bond from *Sylvia Scarlett*—and the way they like each other's oddness is vital. He does some physical comedy and she lolls around in mock solitude. In a quiet way, it's very physical. Lew Ayres may never have been better as the smart, sad brother. Doris Nolan is so good as the jilted sister—and men were crazy about her. But then you've got the effortless byplay of Edward Everett Horton and Jean Dixon as Case's friends. Horton was often made fun of by the movies so it's good to see his decency. As for Jean Dixon, why did someone never make a movie that was just Dixon reflecting sotto voce on the action of idiots and bringing the house down?

Holiday was, in a way, a routine picture. Can you credit such brilliance as a routine thing? Can you really hide from the grandeur of smart comedy in all the Hollywood forms—or miss what has been lost?

Yes, they made *Bringing Up Baby*, too!

Hope and Glory (1987)

Now that the film is in the past nearly as much as the war it describes, John Boorman's *Hope and Glory* is called warm, nostalgic, and a tribute to survival and conservatism in another age. But that's not quite what it is. My sense of the film (especially the first part in more central London) is of the surprise, the marvel, and the spontaneity of the great fireworks show. People die in this blitz, to be sure. There is sudden damage. And the explosions are amazingly large. But still there's a feeling for the great, unsignaled playtime of the war, especially for the kids—and John Boorman would have been seven in the summer of the Battle of Britain.

Of course, the idea of a movie about the home front is so obvious, we have to wonder why it took so long. Everyone who was alive then, or half remembers the reality, remembers being told that the civic mood was benign and supportive as it would never be again. There was a neighborliness and a willingness to help others that simply defied all set British notions of privacy or solitude. In truth, Boorman's Rowan family lives in the suburbs—it is not quite the London we see ablaze in Humphrey Jennings's classic documentary *Fires Were Started*. This is not a target area, then, but somewhere the Germans might look to dump bombs on their way home.

But the great skill of the photography (by Philippe Rousselot) and the production design (by Anthony Pratt) is to suggest domes of blast and glare, pits where buildings have gone and the sky is a mess of searchlights and balloons. The kids are warned to stay in and keep to the shelters, but the light show is too beckoning—and bombing soon made a community of ruined but barely guarded houses where rats (boys and the real ones) could go in search of plunder.

The family is disrupted—there is an American boyfriend, and you see once again how quickly societies can change once in combat. But the second part of the film retreats a little to the Thames-side home of the grandfather (Ian Bannen), a man who is protecting everything possible against the damage of war. As for the kids, most notably Bill Rowan (Sebastian Rice Edwards), they exult in the adventure and they hardly notice danger in their wild unpredictable glee. The Germans are mentioned, but they are not vilified, not even when one kid is shot down (and played by Boorman's son).

The cast also includes Geraldine Muir, Sarah Miles, David Hayman, Sammi Davis, Susan Wooldridge, Jean-Marc Barr, Derrick O'Connor, and Annie Leon. The music is by Peter Martin. Ian Crafford edited the film, and Shirley Russell did the costumes with loving care (and every coupon she could find). Boorman was Oscar-nominated for the script and for directing, and the film won a Best Picture nomination. It is also, I suspect, the closest Boorman has come to an international hit—what's more, despite its subject, it is one of the most lighthearted and cheery of his films.

The Horse's Mouth (1958)

Question: For what film did the same person receive an Academy Award nomination for adapted screenplay, and the Volpi Cup at the Venice Festival for best actor? Answer: Alec Guinness in *The Horse's Mouth,* playing Gulley Jimson, perhaps the most explosive, cantankerous, and ungraspable artist ever presented on film. Jimson is the central figure in a novel by Joyce Cary, and one who so won the affections of Guinness that he felt compelled to do the screenplay and promote the making of the film.

For, in truth, this film is not very English—it has no respect for artists or their table manners. Instead, it believes in Jimson as a genius but a rascal, an unreliable, dangerous, and thoroughly uncouth figure. Among geniuses he is in the category of Renoir's Boudu or Salieri's Mozart, and it always seemed a bit of a shame that Jimson's paintings for the film were done by a painter named John Bratby, a kitchen-sink realist of modest achievement in the 1950s. Just think what more the film might mean if it had Lucian Freud nudes as its set pieces, some of Francis Bacon's trapped figures, or a few of Stanley Spencer's visions at Cookham.

Guinness is fiercer than he usually allowed himself to be, and I'd guess that that release is part of the appeal. Even so, some English audiences were pained by the film's vulgarity, its clear suggestion that Jimson lapped up sex like hot soup, and the idea that so barbaric and antisocial a figure might be doing valuable pictures. Jimson scrounges and looks for walls that may bear his murals. To that end, he is a kind of terrorist—gruff, unshakable, and devilish.

Guinness's old friend Ronald Neame directed the film and showed not for the first or last time that he was a deft filmmaker, with humor and a good eye. Arthur Ibbetson did the photography. Anne Coates edited the picture, and Bill Andrews was in charge of the art direction. The music included extracts from Prokofiev's *Lieutenant Kije* suite—whimsical, jaunty, insolent, and suddenly suffused in glory.

It would be no shock if Michael Powell had done the film, for it really is a lovely piece of English eccentricity and one more proof of how versatile Guinness could be onscreen. He needed to play men with secrets, and Jimson qualified very easily. More than the other great English theatrical knights, Guinness knew the potency in film of characters who seemed out of reach, or beyond improvement. Gulley Jimson is not a man you'd take home.

The excellent, rather scruffy cast includes Ernest Thesiger, Renee Houston, Kay Walsh (once wife to David Lean—and Nancy in *Oliver Twist*), Mike Morgan, Michael Gough, Robert Coote, Veronica Turleigh, Reginald Beckwith, and Arthur Macrae.

The Hospital (1971)

It plays very little today—perhaps because the mechanics of hospitals as well as the sociology date rapidly. But on looking through the list of Academy Awards, one finds that for 1971, George C. Scott got a Best Actor nomination for *The Hospital,* while Paddy Chayefsky won Original Screenplay for it. So long as your health is good enough to preclude the need to go to a hospital soon, this has to be on your list. I have heard stories of audience members who laughed at it so violently that they ruptured parts of themselves and so faced exactly the kind of treatment they had learned to dread.

Dr. Herbert Bock (Scott) is chief of medicine at a city hospital. His personal life is in chaos, but he tries to keep sane by doing a decent job. The hospital for which he is responsible is only a mirror of his personal chaos. The benign attempt to bring comfort and healing to the unwell is steadily ridiculed by the inept performance of this hospital. What goes wrong is the result of bureaucracy, clerical confusion, human error, and chance. That this panorama is not just funny but hilarious owes little to clowning or slapstick (though sometimes a doctor and nurse will screw in a patient's bed) and everything to the tenor and language of Chayefsky's screenplay. The great realist and miniaturist of the 1950s (*Marty*) has become a satirist on a broad canvas, but a writer of such explosive humor that I far prefer him sour to sweet.

It turns out that Dr. Bock's hospital houses a serial killer, the father of a very strange, English-sounding, hippie-prophet, Barbara Drummond (played with such sensual élan by Diana Rigg that the problems of the character vanish). They become lovers, and she is all for taking Herbert off to the woods to a very simple life. But Herbert is used to urban chaos, and in the end he stays and presumably has plans either to reform the hospital or to put up with it. That he will likely die in one of its beds seems certain—from natural causes or avoidable error is the only open question.

This is a formidable comedy, absolutely apart from those TV series that do good work dramatizing the procedures of a hospital while assuring you that the staff are human (*ER* and so on). This is a grand satire on liberalism and every attempt to have a health policy for a race of animals that are error-prone, self-destructive, and doomed. Arthur Hiller directed. Victor Kemper photographed it. But you can ignore such things. This is a film about a man hoping to fall silent—for his scathing eloquence is the measure of the hopelessness of his hopes. Here is proof, if you doubted it, that Scott was the actor of his generation. As for Chayefsky (with *Network* still to come), he was a kind of genius. Also with Barnard Hughes, Nancy Marchand, Stephen Elliott, Donald Harron, Roberts Blossom, Frances Sternhagen, Robert Walden, and Richard Dysart.

House of Bamboo (1955)

More or less, no one in that other world—the respectable domain of arts and leisure—has ever heard of *House of Bamboo,* let alone seen it. So the first thing to say is, get yourself the chance to see it: Ideally, that means on a big screen, where the CinemaScope photography can be seen and felt. The camerawork is by Joe MacDonald, who was an expert at Twentieth Century Fox and who therefore had to photograph far too many dull, worthy films. I do not give him credit for *House of Bamboo.* The passion for form in the picture, for dynamic, changing compositions, and for the unique way in which Japanese interiors can have paper walls that instantly rip apart to reveal fresh shapes—all these things are Samuel Fuller, and Fuller alone, and they are his greedy eye for the marvels of form that arise whenever different races try to live together. Years ahead of his time, when it looked like miscegenation more than friction and misunderstanding, Fuller was attracted to interracial stories. Thus, the alleged innovations of, say, Ridley Scott's *Black Rain* (not a bad film) all fall away if you have seen *House of Bamboo* first. And it was made thirty years earlier.

So when you look at the film, the first thrill is just to witness and inhabit Fuller's command of the screen and the image. And, truth to tell, he was so restless, so quick, so inquisitive, he can leave even Nicholas Ray and Anthony Mann looking overcomposed. But then go further into the trite story of a rancid loser (Robert Stack) who has to act as nasty as he can to penetrate the austere, samurai-like circle of former American soldiers who have made a crime syndicate in Japan. Especially, take note of Robert Ryan's cold, intellectual, and cripplingly organized boss. As a rule, Fuller liked to give his own energy to lone wolves (Steiger in *Run of the Arrow* and Widmark in *Pickup on South Street*). But here, Stack's character fulfills that function and then leaves fresh ground for the meeting with Ryan (Sandy Dawson is the character's name), who is an unusual figure in Fuller's work, just because of his cerebral detachment.

What does this meeting mean? Well, some observers have remarked on a half-buried homosexual bond, and that is one of the few things from which Fuller really did flinch. Yes, his guys can love each other, like links in a chain or man and dog. But man to man troubled him, I suspect, and so in many of his films there is a bond that remains closeted—though Fuller generally was all for ripping aside every sham and tearing down every door. Of course, Ryan is invariably a haunting presence in most of his films—but he stands in *House of Bamboo* for what is a new world for Fuller, one in which nearly every problem could be thought through. And all of a sudden, the role of women in Fuller's films seems limited, conventional, and apologetic.

How Green Was My Valley (1941)

Richard Llewellyn's best-selling novel about life in a Welsh mining village presented Hollywood with many problems. The novel was a story of family, but set against a background of labor strife in which the miners fought a losing battle with the coal-mining industry. In a project taken on in the first years of war, Twentieth Century Fox had grave reservations about making Britain look bad, and time and again Darryl Zanuck gave the order: Stress the family story and play down the labor issue.

As so often, Zanuck took a very direct, personal hand. There had been first thoughts of shooting in Wales itself, but war and the weather reports killed that. There were also early scripts, by Ernest Pascal among others, that proved disappointing. Philip Dunne was asked to report on the script and thus he got the job himself. He devised the flashbacks and the voice-over and worked very closely with William Wyler, who was scheduled to direct and who prepared the picture in detail. The script Dunne wrote was too long, and it seems that Zanuck himself did the final editing. Meanwhile Richard Day was building a Welsh mining village on the ranch at Malibu. But the budget was too high, and Wyler was thought to be extravagant, so at the last moment John Ford was brought in to direct—he had the reputation not just of being very good, but of filming economically.

The film that resulted is not just esteemed. It won Best Picture in the year of *Citizen Kane*, and it collected several other Oscars. I have to say that no one who knows Wales has ever had this respect for the film. Day's large set was pretty to its tiptoes, idyllic and breathing with the proper nostalgia (it won an Oscar). But in no way did it resemble a Welsh mining community, places where the weather, the overcast, and the poverty have done so much to take away prettiness.

But the inner prettiness—the sentimentality—of the family story is every bit as big a problem. This is a weepie with coal dust in your eyes, as well as an uplifting but distant view of mining that is not willing to examine the economics closely for fear of giving offense. Yes, the family life was strong, but the truth in many places (and it's a truth written on headstones since 1941) is that the nation exploited coal and its workers heartlessly and left a place of poverty and eyesore. To the prettiness of the film's village, I would just respond "Aberfan"—a place of disaster unknown in most American minds.

So it's coherent and touching, but shot through with a fatal wrongness—the fact that the almost all cast are from everywhere but Wales is part of this. Roddy McDowall is excellent as the child, and he was bold casting for the time. The cast also includes Walter Pidgeon (Canadian), Maureen O'Hara (Irish), Donald Crisp (Scottish), Anna Lee (English), Sara Allgood (Irish), Barry Fitzgerald (Irish), and Rhys Williams (Welsh!). It's said that the film cost $1.25 million and it had first-run domestic rentals of $2.8 million. So it worked—but, of course, next to *Kane*, it looks like Victorian homily.

Humoresque (1946)

Joan Crawford had just done *Mildred Pierce,* and her reward was a big new contract at Warners. So she surprised her producer, Jerry Wald, by saying that she'd heard of *Humoresque* and wanted to do it. Wald explained that the story really centered on the young violin player from the slums, Paul Boray. Her part, the woman who becomes his lover and patroness, the one who drowns herself finally, was secondary. "But it's delicious!" said Joan, and she was right. She was playing her age in a sensible way. She guessed the film would end up hers, and she saw that she and John Garfield together could be like La Motta and Robinson.

It's probably a good thing that neither star knew exactly how the film came into being. A couple of years earlier, Clifford Odets had been hired to work on the George Gershwin biopic, *Rhapsody in Blue.* He had written miles of script that couldn't be used, so the studio reckoned to marry it off to the outline of a 1920 *Humoresque,* taken from a Fannie Hurst short story. Barney Glazer was doing this marrying, and he had one big query for the studio: Should the fiddle player's background be Italian or Jewish? In the end they settled on Italian, which meant they used Paganini instead of a Hebrew lament.

Of course, Garfield was at a disadvantage: He had to act while he was playing the violin. He worked hard at it, but in the end they came to an arrangement where the nimble digits of Isaac Stern came up out of the darkness to do the fingering on a violin attached to Garfield's chin. This ensures a very noir look in the music scenes, and leaves one hungering for the dialogue between Stern and Garfield.

For her part, Joan had the clothes designed by Adrian and the dead-on notion that when she looked at Garfield playing the violin she was imagining his hands elsewhere. It works. The love story is clichéd and sultry in just the right mix, and director Jean Negulesco seems to know exactly the kind of high-tone trash he is dealing with. In essence, this is a fancy equation in which the gutter-urchin genius and the Park Avenue hostess can each get their rocks off through a little noisy art. Without this exchange, who knows whether New York—let alone the movies—would ever have survived?

The film is greatly enlivened by the supporting cast, notably Oscar Levant as Garfield's piano player and as the film's comic relief. He has many droll lines, most of which it's easy to imagine he wrote himself—like "It isn't what you are, it's who you don't become that hurts," which could have been Levant doing his own epitaph. One day, looking at Garfield with his arms pinned, at Stern reaching up to finger the strings and himself on piano, Levant suggested they all go on the road. The rest of the cast includes J. Carroll Naish, Joan Chandler, Tom D'Andrea, Peggy Knudsen, Ruth Nelson, Craig Stevens, and little Bobby Blake as the child Garfield.

The Hunchback of Notre Dame (1923)

Victor Hugo's novel *Notre-Dame de Paris* is a root of cinema, made five times already before what we like to think of as the classic Lon Chaney version. But what does the old story mean? You can easily draw a parallel between the Hugo and *King Kong*, with the monstrous, hallucinatory "beast" being revealed as a tender soul filled with love for our heroine. But Kong hiding out on Skull Island is far removed from Quasimodo reigning in the upper reaches of the stronghold of the French Catholic Church or—as Hugo put it—the heart of Paris itself. How does Quasimodo fit with the Church—as its terrible bastard son, or as a warped Christ figure? Is his mere existence in the great cathedral enough to start us thinking that the Church is a corruption and a failure? Does Quasimodo die to save Esmeralda, or to protect all of us under the roof of the Church? In the considerable gaze of the handicapped—hardly focused when Victor Hugo wrote—what does it imply that Quasimodo should die? Don't we, rather, wait on the day when the hunchback comes down from the roof and reveals himself as a wise man?

This Universal version, directed by Wallace Worsley, was a colossal undertaking. Notre Dame was a copy of the original on a 6,000-square-foot lot that was meant to show eight blocks of surrounding housing. Edward T. Lowe, Jr., did a script that was faithful to the outline of the book, and nothing was spared on the costumes. Still, the reason for doing the film was the imagination of Lon Chaney, for whom Quasimodo was an obvious part. Chaney is said to have needed three and a half hours a day just to put on the makeup: the great glaring eye, the mouth full of broken teeth, the idiot tongue poking through the mouth, and the hump itself—allegedly forty pounds of rubber. It is one of his great triumphs, yet Quasimodo remains surprisingly upright, noble, and masculine. Everyone always remarked on Chaney's prowess with his makeup kit, yet there are roles—and this is one—where the actor is always recognizable and where the pained experience of Chaney shows. He was the man of a thousand faces, but he had a great face and it is that of someone who has seen and survived horrors. In much of Chaney's great work, we long for him to speak, to tell us about that world he has known.

Worsley's direction is not very inspired—it's as if, early on, the way to use Chaney was to let him guide the film. And this Hunchback could use the real space of the cathedral better—the monster could be more agile. His strange sexiness lies there. And in the best versions of the story, Esmeralda usually reaches a kind of fascination with her dark dream. Charles Laughton is too masochistic perhaps—we feel his beast loves the whip by now. Years later, Anthony Hopkins caught the intelligent man. What a film it might be if Quasimodo had become the leader of the vampyres, say, a revolutionary figure ready to save Paris. Quasimodo and his brother, Boudu? Imagine a Quasimodo who works with the Resistance. It goes on. Depardieu could do it—but Belmondo, too.

Hustle (1975)

In thirty years, the Eastman Color has gone rancid, and *Hustle* never looked like anything except routine 1970s product. But it's also Robert Aldrich, in Los Angeles again, twenty years after *Kiss Me Deadly*. And it's a picture that says nothing has improved. At every turn, the story and the way of doing it gives off the smell of humiliation, compromise, and graft—it's somehow a drab measure of those times that Burt Reynolds was a big star in 1975, and there he is playing a loser who has to listen to his call girl live-in, Nicole (Catherine Deneuve), making out over the phone with clients. But would he "look after" her? No, he can't afford it. So the world goes round and everyone does the hustle.

Aldrich is working this time from a script by Steve Shagan, and he may have had doubts about it. A girl's body comes ashore at Malibu. It could be a drug suicide, but there's semen in every orifice, and there are hints she knew a big-time lawyer, Leo Sellers (Eddie Albert). Reynolds and Paul Winfield are cops and partners and they investigate in a city where it's hard to tell whether the chief of police (Ernest Borgnine) is more or less corrupt than Pasadena-based Sellers, who is also one of Nicole's clients.

The plot is intricate, and there's a large slice of routine in it, as well as Burt's dream of taking Deneuve to Rome one day. The casting is strange but effective: Reynolds is trying to get an Oscar; Deneuve is wondering about Hollywood. She's at ease and he's struggling. But this is not a picture where dreams come true. Far more effective—and carried in the mordant dialogue as well as the chic-ugly interiors—is the constant feeling of lives that the occupiers have sold out.

So many elements of *Kiss Me Deadly* are missing—most of all the naked idiocy of the comic book, the strut of Mike Hammer, and the yearning for the end of the world. But still, *Hustle* has a special squalid pessimism and the casual sadomasochism that runs through it like dried blood, or semen. There's a much better film here, I think, if the corruption is like a fur coat, and Nicole is an endlessly tradeable commodity in the sick city. But the frequent references to old movies and songs is a sign of Aldrich's awareness that the code was cracked years ago. There's about as little love for L.A. here as any film shot there can boast.

It's a letdown for Aldrich, but still it's a mark of how dark he could be when he felt hopeless. And, needless to say, it's something that got made in the 1970s which no one would dream of doing now. The Aldrich team is on board (Joseph Biroc on camera, Frank De Vol doing music, Michael Luciano the editor), and they must have winced to see the look of *Kiss Me Deadly* turned so sour. But if you want a film to show the ugliness of America at that moment, this is it. These days, of course, in a remake, the Reynolds carved out of plastic would play the Eddie Albert part. It doesn't bear thinking about.

The Hustler (1961)

By the time of *The Hustler*, no one had much reason to anticipate fresh works from Robert Rossen. He had been blacklisted. He had produced films as obscure as *Alexander the Great* and as heavily labeled as *Island in the Sun*. *They Came to Cordura* was a painful, studied piece on heroism. Some people remembered that *All the King's Men* had been a bad film, whatever its reputation. So there was little on the credit side but *Body and Soul*.

What made *The Hustler* as surprising was the discovery that a pool table could hold us riveted for hours and that it was the natural cockpit for drama. All of that came from Walter Tevis's novel, but Rossen had absorbed not just the game—he had learned character and real conflict from reading it. Thus the greatest pleasure: that at last someone had elected to make a picture about the handsome weakling lurking in Paul Newman. Nothing is as key to *The Hustler* as the moment where the George C. Scott character announces, "This boy's a loser!" But that leads us to the maturity that can handle someone like Scott in a movie.

Eddie Felson (Newman) is a pool demon and a hustler who is playing on the small-time circuit. The focus of this film is how he lives up to two challenges: meeting Bert Gordon (Scott), who offers to manage him in the big time; and falling in love with Sarah Packard (Piper Laurie), so much more of a woman than Rossen had ever tried before.

The Hustler is one more of those beautiful films done in black-and-white CinemaScope, and the format suits the table just as the lighting revels in the grungy world of hotels, diners, and pool halls. The photography is by Eugene Shuftan, who had worked most recently for Franju. His contribution is enormous and must have offered hope to a design team that included Harry Horner and Gene Callahan. Rossen and Sidney Carroll did the screenplay, and this has to count as by far Rossen's best and only major work. An intriguing question was how far his maturity had to do with the onset of an illness that would soon kill him.

In theory, Eddie comes through—he grows up. In reality, he remains a loser, because the smirk of superiority and the grimace of self-pity in Newman are flip sides of one coin. Rossen had a theory that actors needed to find themselves in a part (he said that's what happened with Broderick Crawford on *All the King's Men*). In which case this picture was an ordeal for Newman—or was he pushed harder than usual by Laurie and Scott, both of whom are arresting and frightening in equal degrees?

The other immense force in the film is TV comic Jackie Gleason as Minnesota Fats, the reigning pool champion. Gleason never mugs, never seeks a laugh. He seems filled with respect for the project. There are also good performances from Myron McCormick and Murray Hamilton and a grave score from Kenyon Hopkins. Dede Allen edited, and Willie Mosconi, another pool champion, was the technical adviser. Not that Newman and Gleason play a poor game.

I Am a Fugitive from a Chain Gang (1932)

Seventy-five years after it was made, *I Am a Fugitive from a Chain Gang* is still a slap in the face, exemplary as dramatized journalism, and enough to move any audience to anger and grief. You could redo it today, though the "I" would likely be a black character now. It remains a country where awkwardness is shut away and forgotten, or executed. America is still terrified of its own outcast energy. And every year, there are press stories of someone—old, retired, established, the Count of Monte Cristo—who is found out to be not what he said, but a fugitive from the thing called justice.

The credits say, produced by Morgan Wallis, executive producer, William Koenig, directed by Mervyn LeRoy. None of which helps much. Of course, it was a Warner Brothers picture in the years when that studio was winning a reputation for doing crime pictures, or gangster movies. Yet this is an anticrime movie. It's a tribute to all those unknown, unattained "I" figures in the prison scenes from big, violent pictures. The executives' names don't mean much. Mervyn LeRoy is considered a lightweight—he did *Random Harvest, Madame Curie,* and *Little Women.* But in the early 1930s he had a reputation for hard-hitting stuff: *Little Caesar, Three on a Match,* and *Hard to Handle*—one of the best "routine" Cagney pictures. So LeRoy was something then, but it's more than likely that he was driven by the production chief at Warners, a name linked to good, honest work: Darryl F. Zanuck.

This is what happens: James Allen (Paul Muni) comes back from the First World War. He gets a job in construction in the South, where he is tricked into joining a holdup. He is given a ten-year hard labor sentence. He serves on a chain gang and escapes after a year of brutality. He runs away to Chicago and sets up under a false identity. But his landlady finds out. He has to marry her. When he finds another woman, the wife informs on him. He is sent back to the chain gang. He escapes again. He meets his true love. "How do you live?" she asks him—for he is like a beast. "I steal," he says—and it is stark and straight into the camera, like a shot or that slap in the face.

It was scripted by Howard J. Green and Brown Holmes and taken from a book, *I Am a Fugitive from a Georgia Chain Gang,* by "Robert E. Burns." That was an alias, actually paid by the studio—despite legal objections. Sol Polito did the photography, Leo Forbstein handled the music, Jack Okey was the art director.

Paul Muni would soon enough earn the reputation of being a ham. But he is as big and human as "I" requires. It is a simple, raw performance, and it soars because of sound—because he can speak and think at the same time. It is a modern film because of that. In fact, it has survived far better than *Little Caesar.* The cast includes Glenda Farrell, Helen Vinson, Noel Francis, Preston Foster, Allen Jenkins, Berton Churchill, Edward Ellis, and David Landau.

From the first shot, as a transcendent camera tracks over a black molasses sea and comes to an island where the palm trees seem frosted, or like ghosts on the shore, *I Am Cuba* is a giddy piece of self-expression desperate to go to any extreme it can think of. There are plenty of underwater shots, and for the rest it feels like swimming through humid air or thinking of sex. As the film progresses, you may be reminded of *Que Viva Mexico* as done by Oliver Stone, or *Touch of Evil's* delight in rancid frontier passages. Every obvious point of reference is stylistic and personal to the point of self-indulgence, and yet there's no way to describe the film except as a rhapsody on the themes of Cuban vitality and liberty. For this is a film in four movements that goes from the decadent fleshpots of Havana under Batista to the gathering of insurrectionaries in the mountains. You know the judgment you're meant to pass—but you want it all, as in a holiday of the senses.

The history is as astonishing as the film. It was made in 1964 (i.e., just two years after the Cuban missile crisis) as a coproduction of Cuba and Russia, but with a Russian crew. The script was by the Cuban Enrique Pineda Barnet and the Russian poet Yevgeny Yevtushenko, and the film was directed by Mikhail Kalatozov (director of *The Cranes Are Flying* and *The Letter That Was Never Sent*). Both countries regarded the frenzy of its filmmaking with alarm: In Cuba it was written off as *I Am Not Cuba,* and in Russia it was dismissed for stylistic formalism. Nobody wanted to know. But then in the early 1980s, Bill Pence and Tom Luddy secured a print for the Telluride Film Festival—and all of a sudden audiences and filmmakers were going crazy for its orgy of imagery. In time, the officials behind the film found some compromise, and they yielded to its great success—though Yevtushenko was always a little bitter about being involved with such "kitsch propaganda."

In truth, the film is far more radical and lush than Kalatozov's other feature films. You have the feeling of a Soviet crew surrendering to the light of Cuba, the music, the bodies, and celebrating them all in some of the most sinuous and dream-ridden shots of all time. It adds up less to the politics of Castro than to a profound, tourist poetry with many hints at the underground marvels to be seen and heard in Cuba. The film feels drugged, with movement and skin tones as its chief stimulants. And just as it is a very difficult film to convey, or to imagine before you see it, so it hardly subscribes to the matter-of-fact strain of "documentary." Cuba is a dream. You can argue that it takes the visual beyond the point of reason and that the film is finally a kind of musical cry on behalf of Cuba and those drunken poets who love the place.

David Sherwin and John Howlett wrote a script called *Crusaders* in 1960. It was about life in a British public school. They sent it everywhere they could think of, and Seth Holt saw it and felt that Lindsay Anderson might be the director for it. If Anderson was interested in directing, Holt would produce. Anderson met with the writers and gave them notes toward a new draft. Holt and Howlett fell away, but Sherwin and Anderson gathered steam, in part because they both loved Jean Vigo's *Zéro de Conduite* and saw it as a model. The script was becoming more epic, more surreal, less English, less authentic. But the spirit of anarchy was moving in it.

But then Albert Finney heard about it. Rich from *Tom Jones,* he had formed a company, Memorial Enterprises. His partner, Michael Medwin, went to New York and persuaded Charles Bluhdorn of Paramount to front $600,000 to make it (this despite the fact that Paramount in London had already turned it down). Sherwin then came up with the title *If,* from Kipling, and Anderson added the three dots.

They used Cheltenham College—Anderson's old school—for the basic exteriors, and they went to work with Miroslav Ondrícek, filming it in color and black-and-white (the latter because he was uncertain about the color image inside the chapel). They found twenty-four-year-old Malcolm McDowell to be the sixteen-year-old imp of rebellion, Mick Travis. Anderson was said to be never happier than on the film, and it is the one project rooted in a credible situation that reaches his dreamed-of lyrical and surrealist manner. Moreover, it is rare among public school films in that it has a true loathing of its subject, and not a glimmer of a tranquilizing nostalgia. Stephen Frears was an assistant director on the film, and it's worth noting that his film *The Queen*—funny as it is—turns full circle and finally evokes sympathy for the benighted monarch, leaving republicanism stranded. *If . . .* leaves no stone unturned—literally, it uses machine guns upon the enemy. You can call that a dream, but you can smell the death.

The film won the Palme d'Or at Cannes, despite being disowned by some British authorities and called a disgrace to the nation. It even made money. McDowell was never more natural, or more likely to make it as a movie star. The cast also included David Wood, Richard Warwick, Robert Swann, Christine Noonan (in a great sex scene), Arthur Lowe, Graham Crowden, Peter Jeffrey, Mona Washbourne, and Simon Ward.

Forty years later, the English public school survives (and is still largely a place of privilege). The three dots that Anderson added to the title can stand for the threshold to fantasy, or an encouragement to everyone to keep hoping that the walls come tumbling down one day. Lindsay Anderson, meanwhile, a prickly, insecure talent, but someone who was an English example for a couple of decades, never made a film again that felt so right or such a happy mixture of wrath and absurdism.

I Know Where I'm Going (1945)

Joan Webster (Wendy Hiller) is a modern young woman who is engaged to be married to Sir Robert Bellinger, the head of Consolidated Chemicals. Ostensibly this is the brave new world that was supposed to follow the war, uniting big business with a smart young mind. Suffice it to say, Bellinger never actually makes an appearance—we do hear him, crackly on the radio, unable to get there yet, and it is the voice of Norman Shelley, so blimpish that he would play Pooh and Dr. Watson on radio in later years.

The big thing in *I Know Where I'm Going* is the "there," the Scotland of the islands, the Celtic archipelago, the fringe where hard common sense joins hands with myth and magic. Joan makes her way north, and on the train she has one of those Powell-girl dreams in which the landscape is a tartan rug shifting like the sea. (It is a part of the mythology here that the land has attributes of the ocean—including storms, calms, shorelines, and whirlpools—Michael Powell and Emeric Pressburger do not make a travelogue in this film so much as an evocation of the allegorical forces in water.)

In the north, Joan finds a new world that is an old one—and as so often in the Powell-Pressburger films the great new challenge comes in standing up to an old order or tradition. Sir Robert actually owns the lands that once belonged to the Lord of Killoran, Torquil MacNeil (Roger Livesey), who has fought the war at sea—as opposed to consolidating chemicals. He was so broke that Bellinger got his property. But there will be a fair exchange: for Killoran will get Bellinger's wife-to-be.

They went north—to Mull and Tobermory, actually—with Erwin Hillier doing the black-and-white camerawork. But Alfred Junge then re-created many parts of Scotland in the studio on sets, in a story where the characters must survive tests and ordeals (as in fairy tale) to deserve the right to know where they are going. Indeed, the confidence of the title and its song are actually belied by a gambling uncertainty.

During the filming, Powell fell in love with Pamela Brown, who played Catriona, a girl led on by wolfhounds: He saw "a spectacular young actress with resplendent chestnut hair to her shoulders, and great liquid eyes full of disdain, that could dart a glance backwards like a nervous thoroughbred. She was tall, with a long back and lovely legs, crossing the stage with swift strides and a queer long gait as if she were a cripple and trying to hide it."

You can cherish cinema, and the piercing impact Brown makes, but Powell could put her in words, too. It's a film in which you feel the love for the people, so it's the place to remark on how superb Roger Livesey was for Powell. Hiller might have felt hurt, or shunned. In fact, her gradual discovery of instinct within common sense is still the engine of the picture. The cast also includes George Carney, Walter Hudd, Duncan MacKechnie, Ian Sadler, Finlay Currie, Murdo Morrison, C. W. R. Knight, Jean Cadell, and a young Petula Clark.

Illustrious Corpses (1976)

This is the last part of Francesco Rosi's informal trilogy of the 1970s in which he gradually allows the tide of paranoia and uncertainty to invade every institution of society. With *The Mattei Affair* and *Lucky Luciano,* he had taken real cases and historical figures to demonstrate the difficulty of any investigative process emerging with reliable truth. And here, in the finale, he stages a completely fictional inquiry in which finally society concludes that the leading investigator had gone mad. Thus, his death ends the process and his unsoundness leaves us free to ignore his findings.

It comes from a novel, *Il Contesto,* by Leonardo Sciascia, with a screenplay by Rosi, Tonino Guerra, and Lino Iannuzzi. The setting is Italy, but without the usual points of identification preferred by Rosi. Instead, this is set in a Lang-like city, granted that it has the architectural elements of antiquity. But the photography—by Rosi's regular, Pasqualino De Santis—has a quite different approach: The real is now primed to be the décor of theater.

When a public prosecutor is shot dead, Inspector Rogas (Lino Ventura) is engaged to find the answers. But Rogas quickly guesses that the murder—and then the murders—involve a more thorough attempt against law and order. Rogas is being pressured by, and growing suspicious of, everyone—a judge (Alain Cuny), a chief magistrate (Max von Sydow), and a minister of justice (Fernando Rey). The casting indicated in this hierarchy speaks less to realism than the discreet charm of authority, and as always with Rosi there is straight-faced humor that is held back only by the sequence of crimes.

Indeed, there are moments when *Illustrious Corpses* is reminiscent of both Luis Buñuel and Jean-Pierre Melville, and one feels the hardened realist in Rosi yielding more and more to style and feeling less certain of his old political allegiances. Moreover, as style builds, so paranoia becomes harder to defy or forget. The more accomplished the filmmaking, the easier it is to feel afraid of the grand design of conspiracy. And the ending to this film seems to indicate something close to despair in Rosi—it is him listening to the Italian version of "It's Chinatown." In other words, it's nothing that an honest man can alter or deter.

This undermining atmosphere works especially well on the potent, earthy, and plainly strong Lino Ventura as the chief investigator. He is iconic, a man as used to violence as to thinking for himself. And Ventura brings with him the air of much experience in difficult noir situations. Yet his strength will be dissolved and his likeability left for little. Equally, the prosecutor killed at the outset is none other than Charles Vanel, eighty, and very near the end of an illustrious career. Gradually, Rosi had worked himself away from figures of rugged probity to the brittle, none-too-full charmers such as Gian Maria Volonte who played in several of his films. It is as if we no longer deserve the star system.

Imitation of Life (1934)

There was a time in the study of film when most people had seen Douglas Sirk's *Imitation of Life* (1959) before they caught up with the original version, by John M. Stahl. Indeed, it seems to be the case that Sirk himself put the Stahl aside until he had done his work. With good reason: for what was clearly a story filled with social criticism in 1959 was a blithely racist film in 1934 in which the silliness of the romantic plot was washed up on the shore of American opinion, without any treasure of satire glinting in it. Not that the ignorance or indifference in the original is without interest.

It comes from a Fannie Hurst novel, published in 1933, with writing for the screen that involved a credited William Hurlbut and a host of uncredited people, including Preston Sturges. Bea Pullman (Claudette Colbert) is a widow with a daughter, Jessie. She has a hard time coping. A black woman, Delilah Johnson (Louise Beavers), comes to the house, looking for work. Delilah has a daughter, too—Peola. Bea asks her to move in as housekeeper. It all clicks, and Delilah makes the best pancakes anyone ever had. They start to sell the mix locally.

Time passes: The girls have grown up (they are Rochelle Hudson and Fredi Washington now). But Peola is passing for white at school. A newcomer, Elmer Smith (Ned Sparks), suggests the pancake mix is good enough for mass marketing. A company is formed, but Delilah refuses the 20 percent offered to her because she just wouldn't know what to do with it. So quietly Bea puts some money aside for her. Don't ask how much—charity is a private act, and Colbert trusts her own taste in such matters. Bea meets another man (Warren William). The man goes for Jessie. Delilah dies. Big funeral. Peola owns up.

It sounds a lot like an idea James M. Cain might be trying out, and one can suppose that he studied the original novel carefully. What is startling about the 1934 version is Bea's sublime but relaxed air of superiority, which includes the idea that 20 percent is an equitable payoff for the mix, that a vague bank account will suffice instead, and that Peola is really being pretty "uppity" trying to horn in on white lifestyle. Truth to tell, Colbert's self-regard fits this rather ugly superiority in ways that keep the picture working.

And yet, it is a picture about the friendship between a white woman and a black—and clearly they are intended to be seen suffering from the same problems with "pushy" kids who overshadow the mothers' lives. But Hurst and Stahl alike seem to see the title and the idea of "imitation" or mirroring as ironic or comic—not as a first attempt at social criticism. Sirk in 1959 dropped the pancake mix to boost the melodrama. So his Delilah (renamed Annie) is simply a servant. And there irony strikes at last: for equality of the races is so much assisted if the Delilahs have a respectable bank account. Still, the 1934 *Imitation* was nominated for an Oscar as Best Picture. That was before supporting acting was recognized, but if it had been, then Louise Beavers might have got the first "black" nomination.

Imitation of Life (1959)

In 1958, Lana Turner's fourteen-year-old daughter, Cheryl Crane, stabbed her mother's lover, Johnny Stompanato, and killed him. She went free because it was said that she was defending her mother against attack. Turner was not much short of forty, and Universal sprang to her rescue by putting her in a remake of their 1930s hit, *Imitation of Life,* a story of mothers and daughters, one couple in the theater, the other their servants. Douglas Sirk was the natural director at Universal for such material.

It all turned out a great success, and Turner's career was prolonged by the box office. The real oddity is that Sirk, only fifty-nine when it opened, made it his last American picture. In fact, he fell ill, and that got in the way of later, more independent ventures. His producer on the film, Ross Hunter, would carry on, but never again with Sirk's critical intelligence.

Some have surmised that Sirk was preparing to leave America and that he added hints of summing up to what he guessed would be a smash hit. For himself, he was most interested in the racial contrast and in the long friendship between Lana Turner's actress character and her housekeeper, played by Juanita Moore. But the strength of the film is elsewhere, in Susan Kohner's great performance as Moore's daughter, a girl who can pass for white and who elects to lead that duplicitous life. And so Sirk took the old Fannie Hurst melodrama and turned it into a critique of racial identity in America, with Kohner giving one of the most desperate performances in his work.

He had his reliable team of craftsmen: Russell Metty on camera, art direction by Alexander Golitzen, and costumes by Bill Thomas. The color scheme is fiercely controlled, and, as usual with Sirk, the fine aesthetic control of so many hysterical scenes is the heart of the picture. John Gavin is Turner's romantic interest, and he is a quieter version of Rock Hudson (if that is possible). Sandra Dee is a dead spot as Turner's daughter—and that's a big omission when the contemporary audience was sniffing scandal.

But I can't help feeling that illness or the decision to move on has damaged *Imitation of Life.* It's as if Sirk leaves the mechanism to look after itself, instead of building the mood of romantic madness in the detail. So the old lesson emerges: that trash—or material that is so defined—is just as demanding of artistic control as much loftier stories.

Of course, this genre—the women's picture or the weepie—did not have far to go in movies. Television would soak up that audience, especially in daytime serials. And so Sirk can look increasingly camp as time passes. It's a regrettable trend: So many of the lies in our way of living are accessible through the women's picture—as witness the startling force and rather academic beauty of *Far from Heaven.* But it was not clear whether that was a remake, a parody, or the rehabilitation of a genre. Sirk's best work stays fresh, and it can still stimulate ideas.

The Immortal Story (1968)

"It is very hard on people who want things so badly that they can't do without them. If they can't get these things, it's hard. And when they get them, surely it is very hard." These are the words uttered by Levinsky (Roger Coggio) after his master, Mr. Clay (Orson Welles), has died. They lived together once in Macao, where Clay was a rich and powerful merchant installed in a mansion. But Clay is troubled by the thing others call "story." He is a man of dry accounts, money, and ledgers. He can look up the facts of his life. Story disconcerts him because it is not factual or reliable. So Clay decides to put a story to a test.

This is Orson Welles, shooting in 1966, for a first showing on French television. The project is the 58-minute "Immortal Story" by Isak Dinesen. Working for ORTF, on a limited budget, Welles does the screenplay and assembles the barest hints of art direction to convey Macao and the period. The story that troubles Clay concerns a young sailor and a rich man's wife. So Clay uses Levinsky to hire actors: Jeanne Moreau is Virginie Ducrot—she will serve as the wife; and Norman Eshley is Paul, a young, blond sailor.

Clay is warned that to meddle with the story is very dangerous. And so it comes to pass: The sailor couples with the wife of the merchant. Clay dies—though the character does not die in the story. The sailor leaves a large seashell and Levinsky puts it to his ear. He thinks he has heard the sound before. But where?

The Immortal Story is very restricted as a film, perhaps because ORTF said it had to be, but perhaps because this Mr. Clay is already enormous and chair-bound. He cannot go out into the world. Reports of it come to him. Willy Kurant did the photography, in Eastman Color—so it is Welles's debut in color. André Piltant was the art director. The music consists of haunting pear-shaped pieces by Erik Satie, played by Aldo Ciccolini and Jean-Joël Barbier. In color and framing it stays simple, but deeply eloquent.

What is stirring and suggestive is all the ways in which it seems to be self-referential. Clay is Kane-like, enthroned but unable to move finally, with life coming before him as a play or a movie. Moreover, it is a ritual that he thinks he can control or direct. And the seashell is made to resemble the glass ball in *Citizen Kane,* just as we are surely set up to think of a story's ungraspability tormenting a man who wants to be master of the form.

Welles was only a little over fifty, yet *The Immortal Story* has a grandeur or finality in which no kind of irony is allowed to enter. I used to love this film, because I felt it was a superb, ominous prediction of its maker's own passing. But as I have passed that age myself, so I am less happy with its finality and pomp. I think it is a picture that shows the fatal lack of humor in Welles, and the surfeit of vanity. Still, it is rare and you should see it.

In a Lonely Place (1950)

From the same year that offered *Sunset Blvd.*, a really scary movie about that paranoid place. There are some remarkable violent men in American pictures. Let's just note the ones in great romances: There's George O'Brien in *Sunrise;* there's the hero in *Carousel,* Billy Bigelow; there's Montgomery Clift in *A Place in the Sun*; and there's Dixon Steele (Humphrey Bogart) in *In a Lonely Place.*

Steele is a screenwriter—a bitter, depressed man, a bit of a drinker, a failure with women though still attractive, and inclined to lash out under pressure. Why is he like that? The film never really offers an answer, though we are left to conclude that his place has something to do with it, for he is a creative man in a town where creative people are asked to take poison to be part of the club. Then, two things happen to him: He meets a woman, Laurel Gray (Gloria Grahame), who might save him; and he becomes a suspect in a murder case. No, he didn't commit the murder, but in the course of their uneasy affair Laurel realizes that he has a terrible murderousness inside him and she wonders if she can really share that lonely place with him.

It comes from an excellent novel by Dorothy B. Hughes and a screenplay by Andrew Solt and an adaptation by Edmund H. North. And it is both thriller and love story, one genre cracking into another like eggs breaking. It was directed by Nicholas Ray, and the depth and self-hatred of his personal thrust is made clear in the casting of Gloria Grahame, who had been his wife but from whom he was splitting as the picture came to be made. Grant, too, that Bogart and Bacall were in an uneasy foursome sometimes with Ray and Grahame and you can feel how much of Bogart's nasty manner here comes from firsthand observation.

In Billy Wilder's Hollywood picture of 1950, all the madness is borne by the slender frame of Norma Desmond. You could say Joe Gillis is crazy, or broken, too, but Wilder lets him tell the story in his hard-boiled way. Whereas in *In a Lonely Place,* everyone has some of the damage taken in, and no one gets away unscarred. Of course, McCarthyism isn't mentioned in the film, so we're left at liberty to read that into the malevolent climate, too.

Robert Lord produced, Burnett Guffey shot it in black and white, and you feel acid in the air—not a hint of glamour. Robert Peterson did the art direction, and there's a good song, "I Hadn't Anyone till You," sung by Hadda Brooks. But it's Ray who brings menace and mistrust to nearly every composition. This is probably the best work Bogart ever did. Grahame stands up to the withering scrutiny. And there are fine supporting performances from Frank Lovejoy (as the cop), Carl Benton Reid, Art Smith, Jeff Donnell, Martha Stewart, Robert Warwick, and Morris Ankrum.

The Incredible Shrinking Man (1957)

It's a simple split screen—today we hardly think of such things as special effects. But it is one of the most stirring movie images I have ever seen. The full figure of a man is struggling to close a door, except that he is pushing with all his might against maybe the bottom six inches of the door. And in the open gap we see a cat—maybe only a kitten—five or six times bigger than the man, its paw reaching in to hold the door open, its claws like hooks the size of the man's head. This is *The Incredible Shrinking Man,* written by Richard Matheson, directed by Jack Arnold, and it is one of the things movie was made for.

Richard Matheson was just thirty when he wrote the novel *The Shrinking Man.* It's about a middle American sunbathing in his garden as some unlucky cloud of nuclear radiation passes over. He starts to lose size, an inch a week. The crisis is so stunning and so comic, there's no real attempt at psychological realism. His wife is troubled, tender but then bewildered. How many husbands can lose an inch a week and keep their dignity? He has to hide from the cat and from spiders. He lives in a doll's house and a matchbox. And so on.

The novel becomes wonderfully detached and philosophical—you know Matheson had read his Kafka. You realize that true love, a happy family, and a purpose in life really do lose their point if you can't see your husband or hear him crying for help. It was a project at Universal, produced by Albert Zugsmith, scripted by Matheson, and directed by Arnold in an utterly straight, humorless manner. That may have been Arnold's natural style, but it amounts to genius. This story needs no tragic music or underlining. It is just one of those processes in life that change everything. And yet suddenly, and despite economic art direction (by Alexander Golitzen), the house becomes a Himalaya range to the man. And as befits this great fable, there is no rescue, and no end. Universal did put a bizarre title at the end about how God loves even zero. But the gods we know at the movies have to see something first.

The cast is unimportant, though Grant Williams as the man is perfectly OK—the story needs a dull everyman figure. He also catches the inadvertent courage of the man. But the greatness of the film belies the studio's addition of the word "Incredible." Not only is it credible. This is a film that might persuade you to keep a small easy-use ruler in your pocket just in case. Of course, in the real America most of us grow larger—and that has its own set of tragic or absurd consequences—but the beauty of Richard Matheson's story is to make us afraid the other way, and to let us see how, in the right light, the plain circumstances of our own homes may be as horrific as Kurtz up the river.

The Informer (1935)

The Informer was once taken for granted not just as a masterpiece, but as a landmark. In *The Film and the Public*, published in 1955, Roger Manvell spoke of "the near perfect unison of theme and structure." He liked the way the fateful action occupied a single night in a fixed place—the one in which Gypo Nolan sells an IRA companion to the British authorities for £20. How he boozes away the money and comes to contrition. Manvell admired the creation of a nocturnal city through just a few lamps and pieces of wall. He liked Victor McLaglen. In the end, surely, that is what it comes to. It is his response to McLaglen that lets Manvell compare the impact of *The Informer* with *M* or *Odd Man Out*.

It is my impression these days that not even the most steadfast Ford fans really want to see *The Informer* again. So it needs to be stressed—as a warning to us now, with our intemperate passions—that *The Informer* won John Ford his first Best Director Oscar (this in the year of *David Copperfield*!) as well as Best Actor for McLaglen. Max Steiner won for his music, Dudley Nichols for his screenplay. With trepidation, I went back to *Sight & Sound* for winter 1961–62, to find the new top ten films. *The Informer* was not there. Not even Manvell had voted for it. Ford was not among the top twelve directors. The only ones of his films to get a vote were *The Grapes of Wrath*, *Wagon Master*, and *The Quiet Man*. Is it possible that enough people had had the chance to compare *The Informer* with what history said about it?

It comes from a play by Liam O'Flaherty, and the supposed unities of time and space praised by Manvell seem to me an obtrusive staginess founded on the idea that this night we will witness a soul in the process of self-flagellation. The sets are by Van Nest Polglase, and the photography is by Joseph August. It may be that we lack prints good enough to show the quality of their work, but I have never seen *The Informer* as anything other than maudlin self-pity trapped on a stage.

Perhaps *The Informer* needs to be opera, with someone like Verdi writing for a great tenor whose flights of liberty are always restrained and brought crashing down by the form of the music. In song, it might be possible to miss the crushed sob, the slobbering whimper, the self-satisfied snort of McLaglen. When I say I do not like him, I mean I hate having to watch him. That may be in part distaste for the treachery of Gypo Nolan. I don't think so. Treachery is surely intriguing. Rather, it is the righteous self-pity I find so offensive, and the failure of the man to notice himself quietly in a mirror when he has a stage at his disposal.

The Informer is truly a silent film, one of those universal statements much loved in Germany and Russia and supposedly the begging opportunity for grand acting. But when the lack of restraint in playing is so flagrant, then I think the undisciplined nature of the character is nauseating and overwhelming. Ford became a decent director of underacting—Harry Carey, Henry Fonda, John Wayne, and so on. He is bearable and even interesting when his characters stay masked. But when he decides to show us everything, I have had enough after a couple of minutes.

The Innocents (1961)

Henry James's novella (it is a hundred pages) *The Turn of the Screw* appeared in 1898. He called it "a very mechanical matter . . . an inferior, a merely pictorial, subject & rather a shameless potboiler." It's good of him, so soon after the appearance of movies, to drop that hint about the pictorial being a touch vulgar or second-rate, and it can be taken as his adroit way of suggesting that the kind of hysterical people who "see" things may come into their own as and when a medium gets under way that literalizes the seeing.

Alas, it's too late now to think of taking Henry James to the movies, though it is fascinating to think of James as a film critic. Imagine him on the "physicality" of Malkovich and Kidman in *The Portrait of a Lady.* Life will probably be too short—and a good thing, too, I hear you saying. Nevertheless . . .

. . . as you find yourself in the dark, with just the lovely but alarmed face of Deborah Kerr to light up the dark places in Bly House, don't say I didn't make the suggestion. We hardly know if Henry James went to the movies (there is no truth in the suggestion that he died during a screening of *Intolerance*), let alone what he might have thought about it all. But *The Turn of the Screw* (which has tempted dramatists in so many forms) does have a Grand Guignol frisson to it that cries out for movie. That's what Truman Capote thought when he was approached to do the screenplay. He loved the novella and enjoyed the work, though the powers that be found it necessary to hire William Archibald and then John Mortimer to do a little polishing.

The film is faithful, in a fashion. Miss Giddens is the governess coming to Bly House—though in the novella she is not named, and stays as just "I," like another newcomer at a moody house. Their uncle has hired her to look after two young children, Miles and Flora. Miss Giddens has the help of a friendly housekeeper, Mrs. Grose (Megs Jenkins), but she begins to realize that the children have been affected—and maybe more than that—by the evil of a former employee, Peter Quint (Peter Wyngarde), and his lover, Miss Jessel (Clytie Jessop), the previous governess.

The film was directed by Jack Clayton and photographed by Freddie Francis in black-and-white CinemaScope with reverence and with a clear interpretation: that Miss Giddens is sexually repressed and that the horror she finds (with its allure of sexual possession) is something she needs to find. It's a reasonable modern interpretation: these days we reckon that governesses are more deadly than evil itself. As James might have observed, the problem with a thing being pictorial is that it becomes fixed—it is one thing and not all the others it might be. Whereas the blessing of reading is the possibility that lingers, the way in which we are encouraged all the time to see things in so many different ways. So *The Innocents* is not very frightening, or not as perilous as the novella. But chances are that any day now someone else will try it again.

In the Heat of the Night (1967)

One night in a small Southern town, a man is killed. A lone black man is picked up at the railroad depot and arrested. He's brought before Sheriff Gillespie and it turns out that the black is from Philadelphia. "What do they call you up there?" asks Gillespie, and the black replies, "They call me *Mr. Tibbs.*" Yes, it's a fetching hook, but don't lose sight that—seven years later—this is *The Defiant Ones* again, a plot device that chains a black and a white together until they make friends.

It came from a routine thriller novel by John Ball, and the appointed screenwriter, Stirling Silliphant, saw it far more as an opportunity for creative narrative than a sermon from the mount. It's a clever trick that leads to a fundamental antagonism between two guys who have to solve a crime together. And with Sidney Poitier still playing the black man, and with Rod Steiger as Gillespie, there was no trouble with the audience getting the message. As Silliphant has made clear, you don't really get points for messages so trite and obvious.

Quincy Jones delivered a good, jazzy score. Silliphant wrote the scenes as tight as he could. And Norman Jewison did an expert job at keeping it running predictably. In turn, it was well edited by Hal Ashby. The supporting cast included Warren Oates, Lee Grant, Scott Wilson, Larry Gates, Quentin Dean, James Patterson, Anthony James, and William Schallert.

There's no reason for a professional job like this not to work. But then you have to reckon with the terrible way in which the film was overpraised for its hollow political correctness. It won Best Picture and Best Actor for Steiger (Poitier was not nominated), and it won for Best Adapted Screenplay. Ashby also won for the editing. The travesty in those results is that *Bonnie and Clyde* lost out: Warren Beatty as Best Actor, Benton and Newman for their original screenplay—and Dede Allen was not even nominated for editing. You can say that *Bonnie and Clyde* was too daring, that it pushed too many uncomfortable buttons. But not to notice the depressing, safe rectitude of *In the Heat of the Night* leaves the Academy looking foolish and helpless. There was also the consideration that *Bonnie and Clyde* did more than twice as well at the box office.

Meanwhile, the movie of *In the Heat of the Night* simply spread a false but comforting view of the South, one in which deft storytelling could heal all wounds. There was even a TV series in the 1980s, with Carroll O'Connor as Gillespie and Howard Rollins as Tibbs, in which those good old boys just worked together and Americans were supposed to believe they had imagined racial problems. Whereas *Bonnie and Clyde* was a film that opened up new social and political realities and opportunities. In a country as diverse and seething as America, there is no good way for movies to be as comforting and reassuring as the Academy would like them to be.

In the Realm of the Senses (1976)

It seems so unlikely—Ozu meets Norman Mailer—and it was a film for which its maker, Nagisa Oshima, had to work in France to challenge Japanese censorship. At home, he could not have made the shots of exposed, erect penises and open vaginas let alone the obsessive sexual coupling that is the film. So he shot in France (aided by the French producer Anatole Dauman), and then found that the infamous film had trouble getting a proper release in many parts of the world. Yet to this day (and even with Michael Winterbottom's admirable *Nine Songs* greedy to be seen), *In the Realm of the Senses* deserves to be judged as a lucid, tender yet completely arousing film about the sex urge.

There is an important prologue, too often omitted from accounts of the film: Sada (Eiko Matsuda) is a beautiful young woman come to work at the inn of Kichi-zo (Tatsya Fuji). Before she has met the boss, an old tramp claims to have known her once. She is touched. She offers him some sexual consolation—thus his is the first penis in the picture and it is as young, vigorous, and handsome—or not—as that of Kichi-zo. The universality of the sexual act and its indifference to appearance are established already—and their meanings are a little at odds with the ravishing beauty of Oshima's lovers.

Sada and Kichi-zo become sexually insatiable for each other. The Ozu-ish camera has to get quite low and angle itself a little more accurately than is usual to observe all the penetrations. The pleasure is acted? Who knows? Certainly the question arises, for there seems to be a complete sexual immersion on the part of the two people. And that leads directly to the question of whether sexual pleasure relies on acting or has deeper roots. This is underlined by the many situations in which the couple are so overwhelmed as to allow others to watch them—like us?

We believe in their love: the playing achieves an astonishing tenderness that makes all the nakedness that much more shocking. But they are on a futile quest. Sex exhausts them. She becomes radiant, he grows tired. Habit does intrude on the explosive freshness. And so the lovers gravitate toward their own finale: death as the game they want—with the penis that she has cut off as the memento mori.

Thirty years after it was made *In the Realm of the Senses* still has an erotic charge that leaves most rival films seeming feeble. Oshima was as interested in the politics of sex as in the heartfelt coupling, and he is—like all of us—in love with a process that may be as disillusioning and as separating as it is orgasmic. In contrast, *Last Tango in Paris* seems a very contrived, sheltered film, just as those American sex films—even the pornography—from the new age lack Oshima's critical intelligence. This is a landmark picture because it begins to suggest that the cinema has finally lost its great obsessive quest. "Are they really doing it?" drifts into the larger question, "Is anyone convinced?"

In the White City (1983)

In the 1970s and '80s, a genre came into being that one might call a "film festival movie." As a rule, it was a European coproduction; it was artistic or adventurous, and it was not likely to sustain a high audience in any one country. But it was the sort of film that easily filled out the program at the growing pack of film festivals. Some were better than others; many were much worse. It's just that without the circuit of film festivals I'm not sure they would have been made. And some of them were almost poetically about people out of their element, in strange cities, muddling along with the language, beginning to wonder if their identity was slipping.

One of the very best of these films is Alain Tanner's *In the White City*. It was a Swiss-Portuguese coproduction, though there was some English money in it, too. It was in at least four languages—Portuguese, French, German, and English.

Bruno Ganz is a seaman on a tanker ship that comes into Lisbon. He gets off the ship to go exploring. He never says to himself or the film, "Ah, Lisbon, what a beautiful city," yet this picture (photographed by Acácio de Almeida) does bring out all the intricacy of the old city, with winding streets and alleys on several hillsides overlooking the Tagus. He stays in the city. He finds a small hotel and rents a room. He even starts an affair with the maid there (Teresa Madruga). He has a wife or another woman back in Germany, and we see her—disconsolate and bitter—receiving his letters. He is robbed. He is even stabbed a little later as he goes after one of the robbers. Time collapses on him. Sometimes he barely survives, but he pawns a Swiss watch for 5,000 escudos, and some whiskey.

Much of the film is silent, except for the natural sounds of the streets and the saxophone music of Jean-Luc Barbier. The man has a small movie camera: He films himself and the things he sees. But the drifting life in the white city is taking its toll. He becomes utterly rootless, free but lost, and you could argue deep into the night what the film is suggesting about internationalism and the breakdown of personality. It is very beautiful, and Ganz is the ideal actor for this kind of thing—stalwart, inward, yet full of tiny nuances and signals, a man to be watched, and a man content to have very little action. He is sympathetic, and yet we would not be astonished to discover something awful about the man. We are getting down toward a human zero where anything is possible.

And quite clearly, it's something that only film could have done. To see him strolling away his life in Lisbon is lovely, calming, yet disconcerting. You feel the charm and the stealthy terror in letting yourself get lost. Plainly, not too many people were ever expected to see the film. And no one was too disturbed about that limited plan. So, let's do it, they said. And watching the film is very close to the weightlessness that can hardly remember which festival you're at today.

Intolerance (1916)

What happened in the mind of D. W. Griffith? He had labored so hard to make *Birth of a Nation*—it had seemed that he would never raise the money or persuade an audience to pay attention. The film had stirred up controversy with its support of the old South and a new Klan. It had indicated the viability of something to be called the film business. As a work of art, it had several passages of beauty and a new, narrative intelligence mixed in with strident, alienated detachment from the mood of 1915. And so the next year Griffith tried to make a film that made it clear he understood everything. He would call it *Intolerance*, and the title was meant to sum up man's inhumanity to man as well as some people's misunderstanding of *Birth of a Nation*. *Birth of a Nation*, for good and ill, had been an authentic epic. *Intolerance* just asked for admiration.

As if the effort of organizing one story had been too much for him, Griffith made *Intolerance* an episode film. This was the more crushing a disaster in that one of his four episodes could be cut clear of the wreckage to make a remarkable picture. I mean the "Modern Story," which had been planned as a separate film and which is still very exciting in terms of its cross-cutting in the attempt to save the boy from the gallows. This episode is what Griffith did best: brilliant, modern suspense, geared up to rapidity—whenever Griffith let himself slow down he was yielding to bathos.

But then there are three other episodes: the "Judean Story," leading up to the Crucifixion; the "French Story," which is the massacre of the Huguenots in 1572; and the "Babylonian Story," set in 539 B.C., with the Persian siege of the city.

The Babylonian episode includes the fabulous sets built in Los Angeles—and yes, there is that crane shot where the camera even moves a little over the set. It is stupendous, yet it goes nowhere—and that is such a model of the film's self-destructive frenzy. The crosscutting, self-interrupting format is wearisome (the film originally was three and a half hours). The sheer pretension is a roadblock, and one longs for the "Modern Story" to hold the screen.

Virtually everyone in Hollywood worked on *Intolerance*. There were assistant directors like Stroheim, Tod Browning, and Woody Van Dyke. Billy Bitzer and Karl Brown photographed it. There was a painful linking device, Lillian Gish sweetly rocking the cradle of history. And there are many worthy performances: In the "Modern Story," Mae Marsh as the heroine, Robert Harron as the wronged boy, and Miriam Cooper (the best thing in the picture) as "the Friendless One." In the "Judean Story," Howard Gaye as the Nazarene, Bessie Love as the Bride of Cana, and Stroheim as a Pharisee. In the "French Story," Eugene Pallette as Prosper Latour, Josephine Crowell as Catherine de Medici, Constance Talmadge as Marguerite de Valois, and Joseph Henabery as Coligny. In the "Babylonian Story," Constance Talmadge is very vivid as the Mountain Girl de Alfred Paget is Belshazzar, and George Seigmann is Cyrus.

Anyone concerned with film history has to see *Intolerance*, and pass on. The film cost a little under $400,000, and it did badly. One guesses that Griffith was as surprised by failure here as he had been by triumph on *Birth of a Nation*.

Into the Woods (1991)

I have done this for my children and just as often for myself: I load the videotape of the New York production of *Into the Woods* and sit back. You could say that I am watching the live recording of several performances in the New York run of that show. But, these days, I watch many movies in exactly the same way—though seldom with the same mix of emotions or an equally inspiring belief that moving imagery, drama, narrative, and music can still work wonders. In other words, the fierce "purist" separation of film and television seems increasingly wasteful and misleading. It is often true that television seems unable to become a resplendent visual medium. Things are rarely beautiful on television. But only a fool can say that television doesn't these days beat big brother at narrative ingenuity, dialogue, and daring content.

The real point is to address oneself to how the genius of Stephen Sondheim is conveyed. But just as there are a few outstanding figures in the arts in the age of cinema who have managed not to be deeply involved in film—Balanchine, Ellington, Nabokov, Sondheim—so it is fatuous and self-abusive for the serious hedonist to deny himself *Into the Woods* because it is a mongrel. My biggest dilemma was whether to opt for *Into the Woods* or *Sweeney Todd*, a "play" with music that has already enjoyed several different versions. (I took both.)

Not that I mean to make unusual claims for the "film" of *Into the Woods*. What exists on tape is the *American Playhouse* version of the original 1987 Broadway production, "directed by James Lapine," who had also written the book. Lapine himself may wince at a few awkward moments when "coverage" was fudged—in the same way the sports crews that film great games admit that they "miss" certain moments. And one could easily enough imagine a movie movie of *Into the Woods*—by Baz Luhrmann, say, or even Mr. Sondheim—that starts afresh, employs far more elaborate sets, and is like a fairy story as rendered by Cocteau rather than a fairy story tenderly dissected on the stage.

In the end, the paucity of Sondheim movie movies has to indicate his love and preference for the stage as a grid—and this tape can only approximate the live delight of seeing actors and actresses "play with" the anthology of fairy stories that makes the show and makes its very special acid wit. Rather than do *Moby Dick*, Welles went to an amateur attempt at it—because he saw more meaning there. And that is the way to read Sondheim's shows, I think, as the bits and pieces of movie with the suspended disbelief like a ball that is being kicked around.

Into the Woods is an "attempt" to show the structures of fairy story and modern romance. It is as tricky and delicious a mix of show and show business as *The Golden Coach*. It is one of the masterworks in American culture and it is—quite simply—miles ahead of nearly all American movies made since 1987. If you doubt that sweeping statement, see it and get yourself a broom. If this is musical theater, then let us expand the definition of film enough to take it in.

The Intruder (2004)

Claire Denis was finishing one film, *Trouble Every Day,* when she happened to read a book by Jean-Luc Nancy, a philosopher, in which he described the "intrusion" of having had a heart transplant. Where does it come from? What does it bring? Where does its new life take you? Of course, you can be cold-blooded about it—you can say the heart knows no more history than a spleen or a metacarpal—but who can write a page of personal prose without using the heart as a measure of authenticity? What follows with *The Intruder* is a dense, enigmatic film, one of those movies open to infinite interpretation, yet a breathtaking example of modern cinema (and one that reflects Denis's early admiration for Jacques Rivette).

Louis Trebor lives alone in the wild countryside of the Jura. He is played by Michel Subor (Godard's *Le Petit Soldat* and the commandant in Denis's *Beau Travail*). He is a loner, he is tough, and you can argue whether he has a heart. But his real heart lets him down so that he needs a transplant, and the old and the new both leave him in quandaries of desire. What is his past? He has traveled. He has sown his wild oats. He may have been a criminal, cruel, ruthless—he has a Swiss bank account and the instincts of a killer. He has Subor's tanned, strained face: This is a man of rare ambition and hope.

Lest *The Intruder* seem too tidy, let me add that it has scenes in Geneva, Korea, and Polynesia as well as on the French-Swiss border. There is a murder and a search for revenge. There is a failed search for one son in a film that begins to persuade us that it could find a son anywhere. And throughout this, the style of the film goes from iron—to match Subor's face—to silk, a material that can be folded in so many ways without ever picking up a crease mark. In other words, the manner with which *The Intruder* works is to accumulate possible plots as it goes. Only a few are actually explored—and the richness may make some viewers uneasy. But the openness is also a tribute to the poetry of the world. If it had just a touch of humor this might be a masterpiece.

As it is, I find it Denis's most intriguing and rewarding film, and I should point out the contributions made by the photography of Agnès Godard and the music by Stuart A. Staples. Then consider the magical footage from *Le Reflux* (1962), an unfinished film—set in Polynesia—that Subor made with Paul Gegauff. Then the film is full of fiercely animated people, many of whom might be the center of larger movies. We only glimpse them, but we feel the expansive rooms behind them—Grégoire Colin, Florence Loiret-Caille, Katia Golubeva, Lolita Chammah, and Béatrice Dalle—to say nothing of some of the best dogs seen in recent cinema.

Invasion of the Body Snatchers (1956)

A doctor, Miles Bennell (Kevin McCarthy), comes back to the small town of Santa Mira, where he lives. Santa Mira is tucked into the hills of California, a little sleepy, fairly prosperous, and white. He finds that several of his patients have unusual symptoms: People are reporting that some of the others in their lives are not quite themselves. You mean they're sick? asks the doctor. No, comes the answer, just different. And so begins one of the best parables in American culture, the least crowded with special effects, but probably the most important sci-fi film of the 1950s. If you care to tell yourself this is the future rather than now.

It was a Walter Wanger production, directed by Don Siegel, with a script by Daniel Mainwaring adapted from a story in *Collier's* by Jack Finney. And what it leads to is the entire population of Santa Mira being taken over by lifelike, yet lifeless imitations. Think of *Bigger than Life* (in the same year), and this is plainer than life—plus an excellent double bill. The oddest device in the story—it could be comic, yet it works very well—is that the bodies in waiting come in the form of pods. As the person sleeps, so the pod takes on final resemblance. In the big sleep, the one replaces the other.

Siegel turned this into an 80-minute suspense thriller, beautifully handled and judged—the moment when the doctor's girlfriend (Dana Wynter) falls asleep is really heartbreaking and scary just because Ms. Wynter was always lovely but a touch hollow. And the cozy world of Santa Mira is very well used as the background.

At the time, there was wide debate as to whether the pods were a metaphor for Communists or anti-Communists—and in a way that confusion says it all about the 1950s. Seen now, the film's focus has shifted and deepened: The pod people are those who would give up critical thinking, and human difference and flaw, for the smooth custard of uniformity. For that reason alone, it may be that every generation will want to redo its own *Invasion*. Thus Philip Kaufman did the story in the 1970s in San Francisco, and did it very well, with a lot of humor before the dread struck home.

I think the original is the best version, just because originality counts for so much, but it has to be said that Don Siegel—a self-effacing director—was a very smart man. The diagnosis of 1950s America here is balanced, cool, and adroit. Allied Artists found the finished film too frightening. It had ended with Miles in freeway traffic shouting, "You're next!" at cars and at us. The studio asked for a framing device where Miles goes to an L.A. hospital and is told that everything is going to be all right. Just rest, he's told—as if anyone ever felt happy about falling asleep in a hospital! The cast also includes King Donovan, Carolyn Jones, Larry Gates, Jean Willes, and even Sam Peckinpah in a small spot.

The Iron Horse (1924)

As he ranged far and wide in the making of *The Iron Horse*, the story of the transcontinental railroads, and as he naturally enough imitated some of the drinking habits of the railroad workers, John Ford found himself in Truckee, in California, just over the border from Nevada. There he bumped into Eddie Sutherland, known as one of the funniest and fastest-living Hollywood directors. Eddie was in Truckee because he'd been visiting a film set—fellow called Chaplin doing *The Gold Rush*. So Ford and Sutherland took over Chaplin's room at the Summit Hotel, emptied it of all furniture, and filled the room with liquor bottles—empty ones. There's something lovely about it—the way these kids were telling new stories of the West and having such a grand time doing it.

The railroads were a natural subject (and one that they keep going back to): how the Central Pacific and the Union Pacific railroads went all the way from Chicago to Sacramento and met up at Promontory Point in Utah on May 10, 1869. No group was more numerous in the labor gangs than the Irish, and Ford had relatives who had been there and had told him stories. But it was entirely Fordian to dream up the idea of having a young Abraham Lincoln (played by Reno businessman Charles Edward Bull) bless the union and smile over the introduction of so potent an artery. Indeed, Ford found ways of bringing in Buffalo Bill and Wild Bill Hickok and just about every other thing in the West he fancied. The result is a merry picture, very good-looking and more entertaining than *The Covered Wagon* from the previous year—but still a picture that only Ford maniacs and Western buffs can sit through.

Charles Kenyon and John Russell did the story, which is also bound to include a hero (George O'Brien), a railroad scout searching for the man who killed his father. Then there's the romance which Fox believed Ford had neglected. So they took miles of close-up of the heroine (Madge Bellamy) and stuck it in wherever they felt the picture needed a sweetener. George Schneiderman was in charge of the handsome photography, with Burnett Guffey as his assistant (years later Guffey would shoot *Bonnie and Clyde*!). Ford's brother, Eddie, was assistant director, and the story is that they had some terrific fights along the way.

But Eddie was hard-pushed, looking after 5,000 extras, 2,000 horses, and 1,300 buffalo—and keeping them apart. The shoot lasted ten weeks, in part because of blizzards and the need to find the best vistas, but maybe because of the bottle situation—these were Prohibition years, but a film crew has always been a traveling town with its own laws. The picture cost just under $300,000 (less than half the bill for *The Covered Wagon*), and Fox would get rentals of $2 million. The cast also included William Walling, Fred Kohler, Cyril Chadwick, Gladys Hulette, James Marcus, Francis Powers, J. Farrell MacDonald, George Waggner (as Buffalo Bill), and John Padjan (as Wild Bill Hickok).

In 1927, and for a few years in that vicinity, Clara Bow had a case as the prettiest, the sexiest, and the nicest girl in Hollywood. *It* is a fair example of the very cautious limits to what the town could do with her—at least, on the screen. There are darker stories about how she was used in private, and they gather together the other rumors that Clara was mentally unbalanced. You'd never guess it from the screen: She has spunk, common sense, kindness, and practicality. And as with every girl that attractive, we want to know a lot more.

It is silent, and it is in many ways an exploitation of Elinor Glyn's unremarkable divination that "It" was attractiveness plus—you could say it was sex, but in the American context it was more likely stardom, fame, or the thing that got you noticed. So the first sadness of the Bow films is the way her own cheery nature is used to mask or divert her sexuality.

In *It,* she is Betty Lou (not quite Lulu), who works in a big department store as a clerk and is candidly out to hook her boss, Waltham (Antonio Moreno), a dandy who looks half-afraid that Clara might devour him. Things are going well, and Clara has had Madame Glyn's seal of approval, but then there's "a terrible misunderstanding." This kind of plotting dogged Clara Bow's films—if only sometimes she had the right and the will to do the wrong thing and let the world shape up (like Mae West).

But Betty is mistaken for the mother of her roommate's baby. (Gary Cooper has a small part as a reporter, leaning in the doorway and writing down the dirt. If only Clara had said, "I want him!") So she's a scandal now, and she quits her job. But is Clara down? No way. When she learns the truth from Montgomery (William Austin), Waltham's swish assistant, she vows a little gutsy revenge. She'll get Waltham to admit he loves her and then she'll slap him in the face.

So Betty gets herself on Waltham's next yachting trip—the boat is called the *Itola*! And it all works out the way she predicted, except that love intervenes. The boat has a collision and people are thrown overboard. Betty is soaked to the skin, and very nice, too, and it's all going to be OK. Clarence Badger directed, and Elinor Glyn added her flashy signature to the script.

Bow was bursting for more, yet Paramount never really turned her loose. The kind of uninhibited sexuality that Louise Brooks delivered—in Germany—was always going to be out of Bow's reach. You wonder what someone like a Sternberg or a Lubitsch even would have done with her. In close-up, she seems quick, thoughtful, and understated. Yet no picture ever really took her up on those offers. So *It* is just another version of a babe who wants to marry well and settle down—as opposed to having a life, a job, and a choice fit for a man.

The Italian Straw Hat (1927)

René Clair (1898–1981) was more than a star—he was one of those people who was cinema, at least until the 1950s. He was a hero, too, and a perfect cineaste: He had made his own puppet theater as a child; he had driven ambulances in the First World War, and been invalided out. He wrote poetry and acted a little, and he began as an artistic and experimental filmmaker—*Paris Qui Dort* and *Entr'acte*. Then as silence turned to sound he made a handful of exquisite comedies. He went to England and America and returned to France after the war. In his day, he was held in glory for *The Italian Straw Hat* (an international classic of silent film), *Sous les Toits de Paris, Le Million,* and *À Nous la Liberté.* And yet he is now as thoroughly in eclipse as any great name I can think of. And it's a puzzle, for he seldom seems to have given offense.

The Italian Straw Hat "is very simply one of the funniest films ever made and one of the most elegant as well" (Pauline Kael, 1966). It comes from a play by Eugène Labiche and Marc Michel, first produced in 1895. It is a farce, in which the horse of a young groom eats a young woman's straw hat as the groom is driving to his wedding. It turns out that the young lady with the hat was enjoying a romantic interlude with a friend. Now she must find a new hat to prevent her husband from being suspicious. And so, our would-be groom is diverted from his own wedding to preserve the illusion of another. Eventually, he will conduct the entire wedding party on a citywide search for just the right Italian straw hat.

Clair was both a Parisian and a fond historian of the movies, and the re-creation for this film (sets by Lazare Meerson) is a very fair approximation of what the city looked and felt like in year 1 of the *cinématographe.* In addition, the chase framework and the race against time permit a steady stream of ironic observations on the middle class, propriety, and marriage. Clair wrote and directed, and was plainly in love with audiences, laughter, and the new language of film. Yet he has been steadily dumped upon over the years as an inflated reputation hardly deserving of the place in film history that was once granted to him.

So let me say that *The Italian Straw Hat* now plays as more sustained hilarity than many things by, say, Chaplin or Keaton. In great part that is because it is not a comedy about self-pity or solitude, but a complete social observation in which the maturity of the gaze knows there is no need to spread the jam of sympathy or villainy on individual characters. Kael was right. This plays. It would be perfect accompaniment for a children's party—or a wedding reception. It was redone in 1937 at the Mercury Theatre as *Horse Eats Hat* (with Joseph Cotten as the groom—and with music by Paul Bowles and Virgil Thomson), and it was one of their greatest successes. It is still available.

It Always Rains on Sunday (1947)

The title, spoken with a sigh, is so expressive of English pessimism and the conviction that bad luck is dogging one's steps. The weather is beyond intervention, and it is far from religion. It is not necessarily a statistical reality so much as an emotional assertion about the way the one day a week that "lowly" people had off is traditionally marked by overcast skies and picnic-killing rain. Life in Britain in the late 1940s was, in some ways, tougher than it had been during the war. A camaraderie had existed then. Victorious, the British reclaimed their solitude or shyness. And the victors were rationed for years as they walked past unhealed bomb sites. That is the mood of Robert Hamer's *It Always Rains on Sunday,* a picture that uses all the eloquence of film to express the standard British idea that belief in film fantasy is absurd.

Rose (Googie Withers) is a barmaid in London's East End. She lives with her husband, George (Edward Chapman), an older man, and her stepchildren. She is steady but not happy. The marriage fulfills none of her need for love; indeed, she has learned to suppress that feeling, and never talks about it. Suppose she had gone with her former lover, Tommy (John McCallum), so much more daring and exciting than George, but in prison because of it. And then one day, she finds Tommy sheltering in the air-raid shelter (the war lives on) in the back garden. She takes him in, for he has escaped from prison. Without telling anyone in the household, she hides him and tries to smuggle him to freedom. But Tommy sees the danger he represents. He goes off, and he is captured. Rose tries to kill herself, and recognizes that family life will go on.

This was an Ealing film, derived from a novel by Arthur La Bern with a screenplay by Hamer and Henry Cornelius. A good deal of it was shot in the Bethnal Green area, with Douglas Slocombe doing the photography. In fact, there were reviews that remarked on the film's gloom and set it in contrast with the "cheery" attitude of East Enders. No wonder the melancholy Robert Hamer sank a little and ended up an alcoholic. He is best known for the brilliant, sardonic period style of *Kind Hearts and Coronets,* but this is from his heart and it helped build the remarkable quality of British filmmaking in the years after the war. The one gesture away from strict realism is the score, by Georges Auric, which is a mordant link with the tradition of film noir in France. But *It Always Rains on Sunday* is a reminder that in noir it was possible to express a country's sense of itself—a prospect less often envisaged in America.

The acting is outstanding, and a tribute should be paid to Googie Withers and John McCallum, married in real life, and happy exiles to Australia in the 1950s. Withers is the lead in another Hamer period piece of the same era, *Pink String and Sealing Wax,* and her sad, tight face was the image of numbed desire.

It Happened One Night (1934)

Night Bus, they were going to call it, full of foreboding. The people around Frank Capra at Columbia were convinced it was going to turn out badly. But *It Happened One Night* is one of the most important pictures ever made in America—not least, but not only, for the great boost it gave to Capra. For one thing, it was a comedy that turned out to be a big picture—and that still goes against the grain in Hollywood. For this would be the first occasion on which the Best Picture Oscar went to a comedy. More than that, the early sound comedies were very often pictures about the rich or the faux rich (like *Trouble in Paradise, City Lights*, and even the Marx Brothers movies). *It Happened One Night* smelled like a news story—it need not have been a comedy—in which the class distinctions of America were bridged as a newspaperman met an heiress, and proved smarter than she was. In other words, it was a comedy that spoke up for the common sense, the wit, the ingenuity, and the romantic readiness of the ordinary man. You could call it "sexiness," and it transformed Gable's fortunes and licensed his cocky grin.

The first thought was to borrow Robert Montgomery and Myrna Loy (two of a kind), and it's fascinating that the chemistry that worked was a mismatch: Clark Gable and Claudette Colbert—he was loaned by M-G-M for peanuts in an effort to discipline him. Colbert was the proof that Columbia could get real stars. They were different cuisines; they were hard work versus snobbery, real life against being spoiled—and this was 1934, a moment when such clashes meant a lot. It was Capra and his writer, Robert Riskin, who really saw that potential.

It came from a magazine story by Samuel Hopkins Adams, and it was budgeted as a film for $325,000! Colbert was apparently "snooty" on the shoot, while Gable enjoyed Capra. But Capra knew the chemistry, and there were sexual jokes on set just as there was her hitchhiking technique (the raised skirt) and the absence of his undershirt. Joseph Walker shot the picture, and the supporting cast included Walter Connolly, Roscoe Karns, Alan Hale, Ward Bond, and Jameson Thomas.

When it opened, in a country where many theaters had gone dark because of the hard times, *It Happened One Night* was the model of show business success and the tough, teasing deflation of the rich by guys like Gable. It had rentals of around $1 million, and it undoubtedly changed the business's expectations of comedy. In hindsight, it's a mystery that Gable and Colbert were not reunited until the lackluster *Boom Town*.

Capra was gloomy about the Oscars, because he had been rejected before. Moreover, the Academy was in some chaos over rival acting unions early in 1935. But the sweep achieved by *It Happened One Night* was authentic—Best Director, Best Writer, Best Actor, Best Actress, Best Picture. This success would not be repeated until *One Flew Over the Cuckoo's Nest*.

It's a Wonderful Life (1946)

It's a wonderful life—except for what you can't get out of your head in the early hours of the morning, when you can't sleep. How many of us have gone to bed imagining we were Jimmy Stewart in *You Can't Take It with You* or *The Philadelphia Story* and woken up as George Bailey watching our sweet little town, Bedford Falls, pass by as some poisoned Pottersville? You may be checking the title, and asking yourself, Is this really one of America's most heartwarming pictures he's talking about, our Christmas picture, or has the printing system gone awry?

There is a great tradition in the American movie of our heroes packing their bags with our imaginary energy and going out into space, adventure, and the new. It is Charlie going to Gold Rush country. It is the great land race in *Cimarron*. It is Kit and his girl loping into the Badlands like wild deer. It is Rick and Louis strolling off into the fog together at the close of *Casablanca*. And then there are the films about people with too little courage or risk for the dream: It is the Smiths who stay home in St. Louis; it is Dorothy getting "home" again; and it is George Bailey.

He stayed in a backwater. He denied himself so much challenge, and in its place he took security, a sweetheart for a wife, a respected job at the savings and loan, the state of being trusted by a few people. But then there is the risk of that going sour, because Uncle Billy lost the crucial deposit. And Potter will move in . . . and George, in that despair known most intensely in Frank Capra films, where the young men have the DNA of being haunted by guilt in their souls already—George may kill himself.

Yes, it turns out all right, thanks to an apprentice angel, Clarence, thanks to Christmas and it's being a movie. But you can feel the ordeal and the agony, and you know what I mean when I say it's also a film noir itching to get out and infect the small-town assurance. You know more. You know that since 1946, the United States has come to resemble Pottersville far more than Bedford Falls. The rural idyll of security and self-sufficiency didn't work. America was too desperate to get ahead. So as the years pass, this would-be charmer becomes a little more disturbing.

But what else from 1946 still bears watching in the same suspense—as if your life depended on it? So *It's a Wonderful Life* deserves "Isn't it?" as a coda. But the film is coming into its meaning and the vision of Pottersville is grim and obstinate. Who can forget it? Stewart is on the cusp of prewar and postwar. The cast is listed in our hearts: Donna Reed, Lionel Barrymore, Beulah Bondi, Thomas Mitchell, Henry Travers, Frank Faylen, Ward Bond, Gloria Grahame, H. B. Warner. Script by Frances Goodrich, Albert Hackett, and Jo Swerling from a story by Philip Van Doren Stern, "The Greatest Gift"—surely modeled on *A Christmas Carol*.

Ivan the Terrible (1945/1958)

Despite its immense research and the effort to re-create the world of Tsar Ivan IV (1530–84), it's very difficult now to extricate this film from the history of another great Russian leader, Josef Stalin (1879–1953). Moreover, the fantastic graphic style or artistry of Sergei Eisenstein has so dated that it may be easier to view the film (to read it) as a disguised account of Stalin more than a reliable portrait of Ivan the so-called Terrible. At the very least, a great deal of backstory is required.

Eisenstein had come home from the United States and from Mexico in 1934–35, under a shadow, if not in disgrace. The Mexican venture was depicted as an abortion by the authorities, and the director had none of his footage. He was attacked by party officials, and his attempt to film *Bezhin Meadow* (from Turgenev) ended in disaster and severe criticism from Boris Shumyatsky, the production chief under the Soviets. But he had another chance with *Alexander Nevsky* (1938), and it was reckoned that he had redeemed himself by making a conventional, heroic epic, free from excesses of montage and unequivocally patriotic—it's stately and exotic, but it's in Michael Curtiz territory. *Nevsky* is old-fashioned and simplistic by Eisenstein's standards, but it worked, thanks in part to a score by Sergei Prokofiev.

Thus, in the early 1940s, a remade man (it seemed), Eisenstein planned a three-part *Ivan the Terrible*. The research lasted two years. Starting in 1943, part one was filmed at the Alma Ata studios in central Asia. It premiered early in 1945 and was regarded as a magnificent fusion of history with the current war effort. The photography was shared by Eduard Tisse (exteriors) and Alexander Moskvin (interiors). Prokofiev did another score and Nikolai Cherkasov played Ivan in a story that showed the child coming to power, being defeated, but rising again to unite Russia.

Part two (*The Boyars' Plot*) was filmed in 1945 with the same team, and with the addition of garish color sequences. But in part two something in the ideal Soviet story went astray. Ivan's court is now a hotbed of conspiracy, of plots and secret police. It is also rife with homosexual feelings. It's not hard to see why Stalin and those close to him felt uneasy with the film. It was not released. It was said Eisenstein had suffered a heart attack—and he died in 1948 (he was only fifty). It was 1958 before the film was released.

Since then, *Ivan the Terrible* (like Eisenstein as a whole) has gone out of fashion—which is another kind of secret police. Pauline Kael said *Ivan* was no more than a collection of staggering stills, and it's not that she's wrong. Eisenstein was out of his element doing propaganda, and yet the totality of his imagination is beyond dispute. If he had done graphic novels, he would be a cult. But Eisenstein has reached a nadir now that needs rediscovery, and we ought to start looking at *Ivan the Terrible* again, if only in the spirit of history. After all, we love stories of the artist up against the system if they are our artists (and our system). Eisenstein may have been an imagist prodigy battling many things in movie's nature. But he was a designer of genius, a brave homosexual and a hero who had been turned away by America when he sought authentic American fun and the chance to have an affair with Mickey Mouse. A life of Eisenstein would have been a lot more energizing and complicated than a tribute to John Reed.

I Walked with a Zombie (1943)

No one says there is a war going on (when nurses are as valuable as artillery shells), but everyone knows in *I Walked with a Zombie;* everyone knows what fate is. So a pretty nurse Betsy (Frances Dee) comes to the island of Haiti. She has been hired by a planter, Paul Holland (Tom Conway), because his wife, Jessica (Christine Gordon), is unwell. How sick is she? Well, Paul somehow feels that he's responsible—and people know about responsibility. But the Haitians think that Jessica has been made into a zombie (the walking dead). As screenwriter Curt Siodmak put it in talks with his producer, Val Lewton, the woman "lacks vaginal warmth." Meanwhile, Jessica has a half brother, Wesley (James Ellison), who loves Jessica, blames Paul for the problem, and longs to walk with Jessica into a sweet, welcoming death.

This is an RKO production, a 68-minute picture, the film Lewton and director Jacques Tourneur made after *Cat People,* and it's like that pioneer work in its tidy folding in of schlock manners and quite advanced literary ideas. Lewton dreamed of making *Jane Eyre* in the Caribbean, and in the end of this film Betsy does get her man after Wesley has found a way to be with Jessica in death. In other words, the deep and illicit romantic yearning is accomplished through the apparatus of a "silly," atmospheric horror film. Not that the zombie-ism is played to the Haitian hilt. The film sees voodoo going on and accepts what the natives believe. It is more interested in the stealthy heat of the night where white dreams can turn into shadows. And the result is uncanny: The ridiculous suddenly becomes beautiful and arresting. A Freudian interpretation is entirely possible: that Jessica is unmoved by Paul, that the marriage has never been consummated, so that both people exist in a kind of virginal prison.

This emotional intelligence seldom penetrated the A pictures of the era, just as the patent fantasy of the story (the nurse wants her boss) was rarely worked out in so open a way. *I Walked with a Zombie* was marketed as a horror picture, but really it's not that. It's a dream in which the studio Haiti (art direction by Albert S. D'Agostino and Walter E. Keller) is a set of scrims and screams and the acting styles reflect this: so Tom Conway is effete and languid, while Frances Dee is strong and direct. The whole thing is done in J. Roy Hunt's photography—those day-for-nights where every frond and finger throws a shadow. To add to all of this, Lewton hired a real calypso singer, Sir Lancelot, who strolls through the action offering a Feste-like commentary on it.

Just as the basis of *I Walked with a Zombie* might easily be redone now as a story of romantic aggression overcoming dead marriage, so it would be fascinating to know whether this suggestive *Jane Eyre* was seen by Jean Rhys as she came to write *Wide Sargasso Sea.*

I Was a Male War Bride (1949)

With a title that smacks of Ed Wood and several scenes where characters talk earnestly of "female troubles," it's a marvel that this picture earned over $4 million at the domestic box office, especially since (as Howard Hawks's biographer, Todd McCarthy, admits) it is a film that alienates young male viewers not accustomed to seeing their heroes so relentlessly exposed to frustration and humiliation. On the other hand, Cary Grant reckoned that it may have been the best comedy he ever made.

As they discussed Hawks making a contract with Fox, Darryl Zanuck suggested that the director might film *Twelve O'Clock High*. But Hawks was against doing another war picture, or one that took the war too seriously. There was another idea knocking around Fox, a true story, about a Belgian, Henri Rochard, who had married an American nurse and was only allowed into the United States as a "war bride." It seemed promising.

Leonard Spigelgass had done a draft, and Hawks asked Hagar Wilde and Charles Lederer to rewrite it—stress the humiliation, he told them, and think Cary Grant in the role. It says so much about Hawks that four years after the peace, the war was for him an opportunity for farce in which man's real enemy was military bureaucracy.

On paper, it's a small picture, but Hawks and Fox had the notion to shoot on location. The reason for this was tempting and had nothing to do with veracity: The studios had cash in Europe that they couldn't withdraw, because of currency restrictions. So going to Europe to spend it seemed politic. But as Hawks would discover, the cuisine and the hotel facilities were not what a movie director was used to. The European method ended up expensive and unsatisfactory, and a lot of the unit got sick along the way.

But the script was brilliant, and enough to send the Breen Office into a panic. Some cuts had to be made, alas, but Hawks actually ignored the Breen advice and just trimmed in the editing. They filmed in Heidelberg and Bremerhaven and then at Shepperton. Norbert Brodine did most of the photography, but Russell Harlan filled in on sick days.

Hawks had thought of Ava Gardner opposite Grant, but he decided she couldn't deliver a joke, so he picked Ann Sheridan as the female lead, and this is the film that leads us to regret that she was often neglected by her own films, for she is very funny and still saucy in uniform. (You have to remember that the Army dressed its women with the hope of burying sex appeal.) Just to look after himself, Hawks cast his own girlfriend, Marion Marshall, as Sheridan's girlfriend. The cast is rounded out by Randy Stuart, William Neff, Eugene Gericke, Ruben Wendorf, Lester Sharpe, and Ken Tobey.

This is the film where Grant has a couple of scenes in drag, but otherwise it is a delicate, dirty-minded comedy about that seldom treated but ugly scar on the face of just and honorable wars—that they get in the way of our sex lives. Meanwhile, *Twelve O'Clock High* survived without—as far as I recall—a single joke.

I Was Born But . . . (1932)

The "but" is a crucial conjunction in twentieth-century art, and it's so remarkable to see it raised in Japan, in 1932, in a silent film. For here is the essential declaration that yes, of course, life is great or fun, "but"—with the question being, Is there something in life inherently deceptive or treacherous to the high purpose—or are we letting it down, by compromising? Of course, with the movies, we are talking not about a Rilke elegy so much as the mass medium of the age, the attempt to embrace all the people, most of the time. And Yasujiro Ozu's title here is like adding to Capra's, in 1946, *It's a Wonderful Life, Isn't It?* By the end of the twentieth century, you may decide, there was more robustness in that skepticism than there was in cinema itself. But it is so striking to see the mood arising in Japan—where, like simpletons, we believe a different system prevailed.

As invariably, with Ozu, it is a family story. A father and mother and their two little boys, Ryoichi and Keiji, move from the country to a suburb of Tokyo so the father can be closer to work. It is a measure of his stepping up in the business. The boys have a hard time at first at their new school. They long to have a radio. They play truant and forge reports, But they are found out and their father tells them to improve. They settle down and then one day they see home movies—a crucial sign of technology breaking down the old order of secrecy—taken by the father's boss in which Father has to clown around to amuse people. He makes faces. He is humiliated. His sons are outraged and they go on a hunger strike. It doesn't last. Life goes on. The boys have had a first lesson about the way their society is a hierarchy where freedom exists only in carefully defined levels.

You can make *I Was Born But . . .* sound like a sociological treatise. In fact, as scripted by Akira Fushimi and Geibei Ibushiya, and with the plucky vigor of the two boys, this is a comedy of manners with a darker lining to it. Indeed, you can easily pick out Ozu's future mystery (or is he resigned to it?), that life's plan is so often subverted by petty distinctions and by the ordinary unkindness of others. Ozu seldom sees this as malice. Rather, it is just that others do not have one's own point of view. It is in every human justification being valid that the great confusion begins—this is surely Renoir. And just as Renoir has a free camera style where any character can take over the mise-en-scène, so Ozu's style is complete and withdrawn, covering all points of view. In other words, the unity of style and meaning is shared—look at *I Was Born But . . .* and, say, *Boudu Sauvé des Eaux,* and Renoir is more unsinkable just as Ozu may be more pledged to a society founded in order. But the two pictures of life are so close. And if Ozu is so resigned, then why is there such a growing pain in his films? Meanwhile, it's hard to think of children in an American film of 1932 being treated as such grown-up minds.

J'Accuse (1919/1937)

The story behind *J'Accuse* is matchless. Abel Gance (born in 1889) served in the French army at the end of the First World War. An accident at a gas factory nearly killed him, but Gance insisted on returning to the front because he had conceived the idea of an epic, antiwar film. And the story goes that he shot real battle scenes in the last months of the war that easily outstripped any other contemporary war picture. Shot by Léonce Burel, *J'Accuse* became a sensation. It had a strange, but very Gancean subplot in which two soldiers, in love with the same woman, become deadly rivals. One of them, Jean Diaz (Romuald Joubé), becomes the "Christ of the Trenches"—himself just saved from being buried, he calls on the dead to rise up and walk at the end of the film. They are skeletons in uniform, and they revisit the land where they died to see if their deaths were worthwhile. At the same time—and this is Gance again—those scenes are amazingly vivid and unbearably melodramatic. The French military hated the film, but the public was overwhelmed by it.

So then history takes a turn, and in 1937, Gance decides to remake his own film. The second film repeats and abbreviates the action of the first, with Victor Francen in the role of Diaz. Francen is a blessing: Not only does he have a strong, somber face, he is a natural underplayer, and thus works against Gance's excesses in a very intriguing way. Once more the trench scenes are outstanding and hideous (they surpass the horror of *All Quiet on the Western Front*).

Then the action moves forward: Diaz has survived, though in unlikely ways—he is the woman of that triangle from the first *J'Accuse*, but since he promised a dying husband that he would not tell the man's wife that he loved her, the new relationship suffers. What's more, his deep pacifist feelings have driven him into . . . technical work on inventions that will assist war.

Gance is still taking the whole matter very seriously, and it's not that he can't do something on the screen that is amazing. The first half of the second *J'Accuse* is essential viewing. The second half comes close to helpless self-parody. But, of course, it ends with the big finish reprised: with the dead walking and warning the France of 1937. The film was actually dedicated "to the war dead of tomorrow, who will doubtless look at it skeptically, without recognizing themselves in its images."

At those words, the silliness of the project falls away. Gance was a fabulist and a self-romancer (he could as easily be Napoleon as a Christ of the Trenches). But he believed, and when he is flowing he is a torrent and an immense filmmaker. *J'Accuse* is history (the real thing), a document of its times in which the last images—of the soldiers rising from the dead—wipe the smile off the face of any winning side.

By the time it was over, the shooting schedule and the budget on *Jaws* had doubled. Seven million dollars for no major stars and a rubber shark. By now, you likely know the film inside out, and you know it well enough to be sure that many individual passages still work, still bite, despite familiarity. And rubber. So be assured: On the eve of opening some people reckoned it was a disaster at which audiences would soon be laughing. Never happened. Instead, they jumped. Initial rentals were over $120 million. The movies were changed, again. And again it could happen tomorrow.

There was a novel, by Peter Benchley, based on a four-page outline delivered in 1971, with an advance of $7,500. But the Bantam paperback bid on the book was $575,000. People don't go to the beach in summer to be terrified. They want to be entertained. But suppose one fits the other?

Richard Zanuck and David Brown bought the screen rights for $150,000, and they got Benchley to do the screenplay with Carl Gottlieb. As a director, they had in mind Steven Spielberg, twenty-seven in 1974, who had just made *The Sugarland Express* for them, a small, offbeat picture with a modest audience. But they had seen *Duel*, Spielberg's TV film where a truck chased a man, and no one laughed.

There would be three brave men who went after the shark, and the casting was Roy Scheider, Robert Shaw, and Richard Dreyfuss—the local cop; a veteran seaman; a marine biologist. The shark was ready to eat them all and it started with a beautiful girl (Susan Backlinie) who goes midnight skinny-dipping on a Cape Cod–ish beach and gets the biggest sexual surprise of the 1970s.

The shooting was a nightmare—photography by Bill Butler, camera operator Michael Chapman—and truth to tell, a lot of the film looks scrappy and scruffy. It didn't matter because the balance of action scenes and calm was exact and because when the action came Spielberg's concept and the editing (by Verna Fields) were decisive. Then they put the John Williams music on it, with that infernal theme signaling the shark itself.

The guys are terrific, and when Robert Shaw delivers the long speech about the *Indianapolis* (which he may have written—John Milius, too), then we are in a comic-book *Moby Dick* that could not be bettered. The climax is everything required. The audience is cheering when it is not moaning with terror. And it means nothing at all—not even the half-baked social criticism of the resort town that would rather not frighten tourists away. It is zero to the power of ten.

And that model became the basis for the new cinema of the young as people like Lew Wasserman (in charge at Universal) realized that kids would come back time and again to see such thrills. In time, the computer would be the new gas in the thrill-making. But popular cinema was back. The young demographic was in charge. And the bright days of the early 1970s were shutting down.

La Jetée (1962)

I feel cursed, or end-gamed, sometimes in that this book is a survey of fiction films. As a result, I have had to omit several pictures which seem to me close to the core appeal of all cinema—films like Humphrey Jennings's *Fires Were Started;* Alain Resnais's *Night and Fog;* some of the works of Marcel Ophüls. But I found a little comfort in that I could, honorably, include one film from Chris Marker, who is the grand master of the essay film. For his 29-minute movie from 1962, *La Jetée,* is a story. Indeed, it may be our perfect commentary on the special way in which photographic images work with time to make the explosive equation of moving film.

Marker's picture is placed sometime after the end of the Third World War. The surfaces of the earth are hopelessly contaminated from the war. But some survivors exist in the underground galleries beneath Chaillot in Paris. It is like science fiction, isn't it? And this small community has a plan or a hope to escape the ruined earth, though the only possible journey will be by way of time. One man is selected because he has an especially intense memory—and this threatened culture believes in (it clings to) the intensity of memory. You see, it's like a great romance.

He remembers this: "Orly. Sunday. Parents used to take their children there to watch the departing planes. On this particular Sunday, the child whose story we are telling was bound to remember the frozen sun, the setting at the end of the jetty, and a woman's face."

He is not clear what happened, but he knows he saw a death there. In twenty-nine minutes, Marker tells this story—of the man's training and journey—through the medium of still, black-and-white pictures, which he took himself. The man practices immersion in memory, as if it were sleep, and fragments of that other time begin to cohere. But only as stills, the bits and pieces of culture—the relics, the fragments, the remains. In other words, by being still, they cannot overcome the resemblance to death, to stillness. These pictures are still-lifes but that is dead nature.

And then, for a flicker or so (you must keep awake, no matter how tempting dreaming is), you have to see this. As I say, for a flickering, and you know what I mean by a flickering—like the flutter of a match coming alive—we are looking at the young woman and she is alive, existing in time and duration. Time passes through her like the sky through our eyes. She is living, pulsing, watching us. Then it goes.

I will not tell you the rest of the story, but if you love these stories where the film moves, and if you see *La Jetée,* you will know what I mean and why I include it here. For breathing duration is life itself, and at the end of the nineteenth century we identified it, we could use it, we trapped it. It may even be the case that we started to destroy it. No, *La Jetée* is not a comedy—though the young woman looks at us as if she expects an amusing remark.

Jet Pilot (1957)

A book like this occasionally sails within sight of a fair, friendly shore where "cinema" may be a sensible medicine passing into the collective body of society as sweetly as orange juice. Then a mist comes up, a contrary wind, and we are all at sea again. In other words, do not discount madness as an essential condition of movie, the thing that binds the hopes of filmmakers and the dreams of the audience. Take *Jet Pilot,* not a good film, but unavoidable in its proud air of folly.

A monument and a *monstre sacré* of the 1930s, Josef von Sternberg had been "resting." Since the insouciant delirium of *The Shanghai Gesture* (1941), he had done a 12-minute documentary, *The Town,* he had been seen on the troubled sets of *Duel in the Sun,* and he had taught at the University of Southern California.

Then he was approached by Howard Hughes to make *Jet Pilot,* a sort of *Ninotchka* in the air, with John Wayne as an American flying ace trying to tame Janet Leigh as a Soviet pilot. Sternberg was prepared to accept because Jules Furthman was already hired as writer and producer—and Furthman had been screenwriter on *Shanghai Express* and *Blonde Venus.*

Let Sternberg say what happened next: "A little stumbling block became evident at the very outset. I was first asked to make a test—not of an actor or an actress this time, but to prove that I could still direct. Having devoted most of this book [I am quoting from *Fun in a Chinese Laundry*] to the problem of directing a film and its etiology, it would be out of place to mention that doubts about my ability to direct are not shared by the author of this work. One does not lose a skill that has been mastered. Not wishing to make my talent a subject for controversy, I thought it advisable to consider the curious proposal a test of my temper rather than a test of ability, and therefore offered no objection, not even bothering to observe that directing a film was not the same as climbing a tall steeple."

Sternberg goes on to claim that he directed a sixth of the film in two days on his test—though in black and white, not the color intended for the final version. This was 1951 at RKO, where Winton Hoch did a great deal of the photography, and John and Janet did their honest best, while Howard Hughes, presumably, meant to make an anti-Communist, pro-flying film.

Sternberg was not even fired. But after the wrap, Furthman did a lot of rewriting and redirecting. The film was not released properly until 1957, and it is wildly silly, beautifully unbelievable, and immensely entertaining—especially if you begin to wonder what Wayne and Leigh were saying between takes. Yes, it does suggest that mastery had slipped. But be careful. Mastery means being in charge. In 1953, with far less means, Sternberg made *Anatahan,* which is not just a masterpiece, but—as he might have said—worthy of him.

Jezebel (1938)

As he drew closer to having *Gone With the Wind* as a finished picture, David O. Selznick took a very condescending attitude toward Warners and their *Jezebel.* He chose to believe that it had been a venture taken on to spite him, especially after Selznick had declined the package deal of Errol Flynn and Bette Davis for Rhett and Scarlett and gone with Clark Gable, some money, and Loew's distribution instead. Selznick even offered to do a quick edit on the Warners picture to save them embarrassment. In fact, Warners had had *Jezebel*—a play by Owen Davis—since 1935, or before Selznick had ever heard of Margaret Mitchell.

Not that there aren't always resemblances beneath the fevered skin of melodrama. Julie Marsden is an ambitious self-centered demon, and Southern, just like Scarlett O'Hara (Northern women are seldom as languid and serpentine). The word *bitch* is easily employed to describe the pair of them—and with the same mixture of disapproval and delight. But there were those at Warners who advised against doing *Jezebel* just because they did not see how Julie could be made sympathetic. In time, the script—pushed along by John Huston—did introduce a change in her. Her selfishness yields and is replaced by self-sacrifice. But it's all melodrama and nobody really argued with Bette Davis in her estimate that Scarlett O'Hara was made for her. So Davis got her compensation with Julie Marsden, one of whose big moments is appearing at a black-and-white ball in a scarlet dress (though in a black-and-white film).

William Wyler was borrowed from Goldwyn to direct, and he trusted the screenplay that Huston had produced. Ernest Haller did the photography and Max Steiner the music (exactly the team that would do *Gone With the Wind*). Wyler infuriated the studio by his endless retakes, and there were stories that he was imposing this routine on male lead Henry Fonda because both Wyler and Fonda had been married to and divorced from Margaret Sullavan—of course, Sullavan herself could have played Jezebel (or Scarlett).

This brings to mind the notion that by the late 1930s, the bitch type was gaining in popularity—as if women had grown weary of their own demureness onscreen. *Gone With the Wind* and *Jezebel* (Southern epics in successive years) established the screen vitality of the woman as ruthless romantic go-getter. And the Best Picture in the following year—*Rebecca*—is further proof. For the dead Rebecca, the bitch, is so much more powerful than the "I" character played by Joan Fontaine.

Wyler went nearly four weeks over schedule. But the picture came in at a tidy 103 minutes, and nobody really complained about the lack of color. Davis won her second Oscar. Fay Bainter won a supporting Oscar. And both Henry Fonda and George Brent did reliable jobs as the men in Julie's life. The cast also included Donald Crisp, Spring Byington, Henry O'Neill, and Richard Cromwell. In being a big hit, *Jezebel* seemed to make it less likely still that *Gone With the Wind* could flourish with similar material.

JFK (1991)

For those old enough to remember November 22, 1963 (and the next killing, on Dallas police premises, two days later), it's not that any of us were ever complacent about the *Warren Report.* It was an inadequate mess; it was hurried; it was pressured by the need for political stability and reassurance. And it became gasoline to paranoia. But it needed a lot more than Jim Garrison to make the argument. There are fine, searching books on what happened—and there was even a second official examination (the Stokes report) that concluded that there probably was some kind of conspiracy—or more than just Lee Harvey Oswald meaning mischief that day in Texas.

And so we come to Oliver Stone's *JFK* and its pride of place in a lamentable line of American films made with extraordinary skill and panache, but so carried away by that power of film as to ignore the forces of logic, argument, and responsibility. It's not just that *JFK* is earnest, sincere, and crackers. It is that film is no way for a sane society to come to terms with such issues. Historically, it's very hard to see that *JFK* shifted the lassitude of a bored, ignorant nation. Above all, it leaves a fatal gap between the dogged whine of Kevin Costner's Jim Garrison and the flagrant overemotionalism of Oliver Stone. Watching this film is painfully close to watching a decent man go crazy.

And after you've dealt with the director's cut (205 minutes as opposed to 188) and after you've gone through *JFK: The Book of the Film,* it's still hard to resist the feeling that Stone's doubts about what happened stem from his hurt feeling that President Kennedy would not have allowed the Vietnam War to swell and persist. Whereas the evidence on both sides of that issue is balanced, and Stone's fecund paranoia over political motivation can hardly trust the good sense or moral rigor of any individual. What thrives in this film, after all, is the feeling for everyone's instability—for the suggestiveness of possibility. And that is no attitude for judge or jury.

That said, there are amazing virtues: The script by Stone and Zachary Sklar is immensely ingenious at cramming in all the detail along with its banal storyline; the editing by Joe Hutshing and Pietro Scalia is delirious, and a sign of new editing fluency that had come with video editing. Robert Richardson's photography is beautiful and corrupted at the same time, riveting and yet seeming to dissolve in front of our eyes; and the film is full of smart performances (as well as some that are terribly overdone)—I'd note Kevin Bacon, Tommy Lee Jones, Gary Oldman, Joe Pesci, and Donald Sutherland (all to the good); and Jack Lemmon, Walter Matthau, Ed Asner, all too much, with Costner and Sissy Spacek clinging to a very tenuous central story.

It's a disastrous film by a talented and concerned man, and a terrible warning of film's limits and its helpless weakness for melodrama once those limits are ignored.

Johnny Guitar (1954)

It's very difficult to approach *Johnny Guitar* as the result of any kind of sensible process. Far more acceptable is the thought that in concept it was fanciful enough to be camp—not an honest story, but one of the first deliberate, or helpless, exploitations of the collected clichés of movie and moviemaking. Yet I'm not sure that Nicholas Ray, or anyone, really deserves credit for that breakthrough. Far more likely is the explanation that this wayward project got into such a mess that it came out looking as if it had been made by the surrealist movement of the 1920s, or S. J. Perelman after a hard season with the Marx Brothers. We rejoice in *Johnny Guitar*, and we may speculate forever on what happened. But don't lose sight of this moral: that by 1954, even, the movies had sniffed the chance of giving up the ghost.

There are far more stories about the film than there is story in it. According to Philip Yordan, its credited screenwriter, none other than Lew Wasserman was to blame for it. Joan Crawford was his client. Nick Ray was his friend—more to the point, Ray was the good friend of his wife, Edie Wasserman. So Wasserman persuaded Republic to do a Joan Crawford Western, based on the script that Roy Chanslor had written from his own novel. It was only when the unit had moved to Arizona that Wasserman called Yordan and asked if he would go down there to rescue a disaster. Crawford apparently had said the script was such shit she would walk off. In the aftermath, as the film became notorious, several hands took credit for salvaging ideas. But it was probably Yordan who elected to make Crawford the "male" role, to pose Crawford and Mercedes McCambridge as bitches in heat, and to overplay everything whenever in doubt.

I have heard Ray scholars and enthusiasts claim that the love story is "poetic" and from Ray's heart. I think such talk is nonsense and damaging. The one thing I don't doubt is that Ray determined to shoot the film as if in a fever, instituting a savage color contrast, and turning small moments into set pieces. Of course, he may really have had a fever—or been drunk. But thanks to Trucolor and Harry Stradling there is a demented symbolism to the color scheme and an overall feeling that lipstick is made of blood.

In the same way, the mishmash of real location exteriors and a very mannered art direction in interiors (by Hal Pereira and Henry Bumstead) is genuinely exciting—like garish color photographs touched up with expressionist gesture. In all of this, Crawford plays everything three or four inches beyond the hilt, and struts around—in black riding clothes or a white wedding dress—like a lost cake ornament. Sterling Hayden has a languid air that seems to say, or hope, that all this will pass, and Mercedes McCambridge has smelled the chance of being the craziest person in the whole goddamn picture. The supporting cast includes Ernest Borgnine, Scott Brady, Ben Cooper, Royal Dano, Ward Bond, Frank Ferguson, and John Carradine.

Journey to Italy (1953)

This was probably the film that began the end of the stormy relationship between Ingrid Bergman and Roberto Rossellini. But that may only be a way of saying that it was made at their crisis. Did it really end things, or did it instruct the couple in moving forward? It's not certain that there ever was a "script"—George Sanders told stories of being given scraps and fragments on bits of paper—but Rossellini had a story, from close to home. Alex and Katherine Joyce are English. They have been married long enough for it to go stale. They come to Italy. Headed for Naples. Meaning to see a piece of property they own. As they travel, their marriage suffers further. Until, finally, they are separated during a religious procession. They pause—they will try again.

Nothing Rossellini and Bergman had done had prospered, and so by this time the director was compelled to get a big actor as a guarantee for the film. George Sanders may have been the best or the worst choice. An actor of neglected depth, he had become used to playing suave villains. He despised himself and his much-married life. He was depressed, lonely, and fastidious. He was quickly driven mad by Rossellini's improvisations. He collapsed with Ingrid (they had played together in Hollywood): "I can't go on. I can't do this commedia dell'arte and invent and get the lines at the last minute."

Ingrid was far more familiar with her husband's methods, and more innately drawn to improvisation, but she was just as sure that the method was fruitless. And so, in many ways, Rossellini was filming the real alienation of his players and trying to harness it to the story of a man disillusioned and a woman desperate in her search for something new. But does he deserve credit for that? At its best, Rossellini's style develops long takes and fluent camera movements to formulate context and when the wife sees the ruins at Pompeii and sees the lasting embrace of old feelings, there is something profound or yearning in the movie.

It is said, for instance, that the name "Joyce" had been used out of homage and with a view to making a great love story. *Journey to Italy* is not that, and it is the very dry remains of what had been a great scandal. Yet *Cahiers du Cinema* would vote it one of the greatest films ever made, and for people like Bertolucci it became an emblem of personal cinema. I think the ordeal of director and actress is historic and instructive, and I can see a hope or an attempt in the picture that is not to be denied, but it is very hard nowadays to watch it in the spirit *Cahiers* and its best writers found. I think it's much easier to be embarrassed on behalf of Bergman and Sanders, and to hear the forlorn jokes they exchanged. But as a story, this is probably the least of the films she and Rossellini made together—less powerful than *Stromboli,* less alarming than *Europa '51,* and less delivered than *La Paura.* Those European years were so full of hope for so many, and so disastrous commercially. It is a great subject for a movie.

Here is a film that as late as the 1950s was regarded as an impeccable French classic, and which could have been employed in the argument that the French invented film noir on the screen, and not just on the page. Referring to it as a key film in history, in 1955, Roger Manvell spoke of the ideal blend in "Prévert's feeling for spiritual defeat and Carné's hard sense of locality and character." Isn't that a tidy definition of noir, as well as a good account of French apprehension on the eve of war?

But then something happened. In part it was the necessary rediscovery of Jean Renoir, something much encouraged by the New Wave and its allegiance to Renoir, and in part because of the story that Marcel Carné (despite *Les Enfants du Paradis*) might have been something of a collaborator. The facts of that case are dubious, but even if there was more to the suspicion I can see no reason for forgetting the bruised radiance of *Le Jour Se Lève,* and other Carné films of that pregnant period. *La Règle du Jeu* is the greater film, but we have room for both, and Marcel Carné today has slipped to the status of forgotten master.

The story, by Jacques Prévert and Jacques Viot, is simple and mundane: Jean Gabin is working class, rough but decent; he falls in love with a florist (Jacqueline Laurent); but the girl is entranced by a wicked small-time showman (Jules Berry); so Gabin takes some comfort with the world-weary woman (Arletty) who is assistant to the showman. Gabin kills Berry, not really to win his girl but in a vain effort to cleanse the world. And so he is holed up in a house under police siege. As the dawn rises, he will be killed himself, but as the night passes he flashes back over the events that have brought him to this situation.

As so often with Carné, this is a world—morbid in its soul, yet lifelike in detail—that is built on sets: The designer was Alexander Trauner, then at the start of his career, but already expert at balancing the physical and the metaphysical aspects of claustrophobia. Trauner's work is harnessed to the immaculately somber black-and-white photography of Curt Courant (who had done *Woman in the Moon* for Fritz Lang and *La Bête Humaine* for Renoir). The music is by Maurice Jaubert, who was Vigo's composer, and that makes clear how richly the different streams of French film run into one river.

Rightly so, people remark on the glittering malice of Jules Berry's performance and its rare, disconcerting mixture of cruelty and charm. Yet Arletty's may be the voice of the picture—so casual, so accepting, so candid, and so fatalistic: This is the voice of France in 1939. But Gabin is the active heart of the film and *Le Jour Se Lève* made him a great star. In the American remake, *The Long Night* (1947), by Anatole Litvak, Henry Fonda is the hero and Vincent Price the murdered man. But that picture was heavy and depressing, whereas *Le Jour Se Lève* has a tormenting strain of hope—the final French irony.

The Joyless Street (1925)

After *The Saga of Gösta Berling,* Mauritz Stiller brought Garbo to Berlin. He was in a very agitated state, receiving contract offers from many quarters (including America already) and apparently accepting them all. Yet he was broke, and living at the Esplanade in Berlin on credit. It's hard to think that he had any other destination in mind except Hollywood, and he assured Garbo that she would go with him. But while they hesitated, in Berlin, they got an offer from G. W. Pabst to have Garbo in his new film. It would be called *The Joyless Street,* a bleak portrait of how, in Vienna, decent girls could easily slip into prostitution because of the pressures of inflation.

Pabst's advisers warned him that Garbo was just a beauty, no more. But he looked at her closely, and his genius "lay in getting to the heart of a person, banishing fear, and releasing the clear impact of personality which jolts an audience to life." Who said that? Louise Brooks, much later in life. But Brooks had by then learned that Pabst looked at the eyes and was ready for everything else to be still.

The Joyless Street is pretty raw melodrama, but couched in terms of the urban misery of Europe in the 1920s. Garbo is Greta Rumfort, a woman who nearly succumbs, only to be rescued by an American lieutenant. There are two plots, the Greta story and the Maria Lechner story—Maria is a famous courtesan and she was to be played by Asta Nielsen, the preeminent seductress in European cinema and at least twenty years older than Garbo. The script was by Pabst and Willy Haas, and Guido Seeber was the cameraman. But Stiller drove a hard bargain: Garbo and Einar Hanson (a Swedish actor as the lieutenant) got $4,000 each, the same as Nielsen.

Stiller wanted to be on the set, and Pabst entertained him at first. Seeber had to admit that Garbo looked less impressive in the first footage than she had done in *Gösta Berling.* It was Stiller then who said, Use Kodak film instead of Agfa—the German style of using faces was harsher than that in Sweden, and Stiller began to teach Pabst a more romantic look. Indeed, he urged Pabst to use a slightly slower motion in the close-ups—it masked a nervous tic Garbo had, and it gave a lingering, extended sense to the feelings. It made the eyes slower and more momentous.

Having learned all that, Pabst asked Stiller to leave the set, and he then showed Garbo what directing could be. Stiller had been bold, authoritative, brilliant. Pabst preferred to whisper to his actress privately. She listened. Her eyes enlarged. She said she learned the world from Pabst. And *The Joyless Street* is a powerful melodrama, lit up with psychological naturalism. It was a major event in Europe, alerting governments to the social misery on the street. And it was a secret turning point in film history. Pabst asked Garbo to stay in Germany. But Louis B. Mayer arrived in Berlin, and the deal with Stiller and Garbo was done. People asked Mayer had he seen *Gösta Berling*—but had he seen *The Joyless Street* was the bigger question.

Judge Priest (1934)

The marriage between Will Rogers's homespun philosophizing and John Ford's reactionary assurance is sweet indeed, and *Judge Priest* remains so entertaining one might sign on for the restoration of the Confederacy, Jefferson Davis, and D. W. Griffith, too. The setting is rural Kentucky in 1890, a benign, summery place where Rogers is the widower Judge Priest, a man with loose grammar and extensive kindness. So he has Hattie McDaniel as his housekeeper, and there is a lovely moment when they sing together, in call and response, and the pleasure of two expert players wraps up most awkward questions about race and condescension.

For the charm of Rogers and Ford is not in doubt. The film is so relaxed it takes your breath away. There are long shots where folks just amble around and wait to think of something to say. Then there are fade-outs where Priest's wise sayings drift on for several seconds over the darkness. As for Rogers, he is nicely made into a real part, not just his radio voice being photographed—though he does sometimes chat straight to camera.

Still missing his wife after a couple of decades, still mixing a little fishing with the law, Priest is just what the name says—a surrogate for that idealized Catholic father figure to a community that exists largely on summer heat, booze, dreams of the old South, and thinking about nothing. That's how Stepin Fetchit just about gets away with his show of comic imbecility. How some film commentators can behold without a shudder this demented paradise built on racial prejudice is another matter.

Action does not matter too much in this leisurely life (though the script has the names of Dudley Nichols and Lamar Trotti on it). But there is a case and a trial that makes up the second half of the movie. It is a set piece that allows Francis Ford's spitting in the spittoon act—ping!—as a deflating joke on Berton Churchill's windy rhetoric. There is also an awkward flashback to the war as Henry B. Walthall (no less) gives character testimony on behalf of the dour, laconic Gillis (David Landau).

Justice and history are alike here in that very rosy spectacles are required for all forms of looking. The general hope that such court proceedings celebrate common sense sits very oddly beside the ongoing statistics of lynching in the South—even in dear old Kentucky. But Priest here is a clear god for Ford and an antecedent of Lincoln and every other unschooled lawman in the Ford canon. Did Ford believe this was in some way "true" to the Kentucky of 1934? Was he merely wallowing in nostalgia? Or is this a kind of Brigadoon where all realities have been suspended?

As you may guess, the film is outrageous, shockingly racist, and serenely opposed to all forms of progress or argument. At the same time, it feels like a yarn spun on a porch in the late afternoon sun, and it reminds us of how closely and mysteriously allied such storytelling ease can be with the blunt lineaments of fascism. All the problems of Ford are here, in 1934.

Jules et Jim (1961)

Here was something new in the New Wave. It was not just the spontaneous decision to film a piece of life as lived in 1960, with time (just about) to find actors and give them something to say, albeit breathlessly. This was a period film in which a careful research was made of newsreels and the corners of Paris that still felt like the eve of 1914. It had costumes, an old-fashioned movie star (Jeanne Moreau goes from Brooks to Garbo), and a novel to be based on. It was a film such as France had made in the thirties, the forties, and the fifties. Except that it was new, so quick, so darting, never settling, seldom letting old-fashioned sentiments have their sway. It was an hysterically modern film, guessing the sexual freedom that was about to dawn in the sixties. And it was not just a New Wave hit (like *Breathless* and *Les 400 Coups*), but the kind of film that "everyone" went to see. It broke records, and it allowed for some future deals that were fanciful. But ask anyone alive then to list the films that were the New Wave and they will answer *Jules et Jim,* and they'll likely say the names in that peremptory, provocative, gambler's way that Jeanne Moreau could offer with her enticing smile. Truffaut said women were magic. The film added: beyond understanding.

It came from a novel by Henri-Pierre Roché, about two friends, one French (Henri Serre), one German (Oskar Werner)—they love the same mercurial woman, the war comes, and the losing side wins Catherine. But the matter is never quite settled. Affairs cross over, beds are swapped—this was the sixties part of it—and in the end Catherine is a dark flame ready to burn herself or anyone else.

François Truffaut did the script with Jean Gruault, and it is faithful in outline, yet terrifically jazzed up by film. Truffaut was hardly letting a sequence exist or settle. His system was fragmentary, arbitrary, rule-breaking. Shots didn't "match" or keep a steady beat of promise and delivery. And yet there was a classical voice-over—from Roché—that spoke to Truffaut's love of literature and order. This battle is the life of the film, and if in doubt Truffaut seemed to imply that Catherine (or Moreau) was question and answer enough. He made a rough medley and then there was a shot of the enigmatic woman surveying it all, and passing it.

It was shot in black-and-white CinemaScope by Raoul Coutard with the newsreel pieces stretched like dreams. That violence worked beautifully, and it was all deeply if not lyrically expressive of a life too full and turbulent to be measured—and again that appealed to 1961 as much as the sleeping arrangements. All the while Georges Delerue's net of music, fragile but hopeful, tries to hold it together.

Today? It looks brittle, nervy, too rapid to face its own doubts, too hurried to let deep feelings emerge. But the exhilaration has not turned sour or stupid because the lethal intimacy of Moreau insists on command—so that she can blow the whole game up. I think she inspired the film—and she knew it. Without Moreau, the New Wave is a paddling pool.

Julius Caesar (1952)

What's not to like? A strong story, a good script, a fair cast, and a valuable moral. I'm only half tongue-in-cheek, because in truth the virtues of this Shakespearean translation begin in the idea of making a small, workmanlike story about men and power. You only have to imagine the extra resonance of the Mercury Theatre version of 1938, clearly aimed at modern fascist dictatorships, to see how M-G-M's Rome is a safe removal at a time when Hollywood was unusually beset by political anxieties. But there's not a hint of *Quo Vadis*—only a year earlier at the same studio—and, thank God, this is a toga story in which God takes a snooze and the power drives of plausible men are studied instead.

The black-and-white photography is by no less than Joseph Ruttenberg, the sets are by Cedric Gibbons and Edward Carfagno, but the picture is resolutely un-good-looking. Of course, Joseph Mankiewicz lends his notorious blind eye to that, seeming quite content to make a picture full of talking heads. And the whole thing is just two hours long, which leaves it the perfect aid for kids who are studying the play at school.

Marlon Brando's Antony has always been the star attraction, if only because at the time his shift from mumbling to full-scale Elizabethan verse came as a surprise. But this Antony looks good and doesn't overdo the Machiavellian streak. It's a fine performance, even if—to these eyes—it has to bow before the real movie acting of James Mason (as Brutus) and John Gielgud (as Cassius). They are both very good (until they put on helmets)—good enough to let us feel the shade of "Good night, and good luck" creeping in. (If only these Romans smoked.) Louis Calhern is terrific as Caesar, and Edmond O'Brien is Casca. Yes, you can believe your eyes—that's Deborah Kerr as Portia (last seen tied to the stake in Rome in *Quo Vadis*) and Greer Garson as Calpurnia.

The film is decently plot-driven, and you have to wonder whether—a mere ten years later—Mankiewicz didn't hunger for some of this merciful momentum as he was laboring with *Cleopatra*. The smothering element in that epic, of course, is the banality of the dialogue. The great lesson of Shakespeare is that—given their best wishes—everyone would speak in sixteenth-century English.

It's hard to imagine Shakespeare being done with less imagination—and let's not forget that the Welles versions of *Macbeth* and *Othello* are streets ahead of this as pieces of cinematic reimagination. But John Houseman (the producer in 1938 and 1952) had worked with Welles, and he had seen the benefits in a very plain way of doing things. Brando could have learned so many lessons. He could have accepted Gielgud's invitation to go to London and do theater—*Hamlet* included. Instead he claimed a prior engagement: scuba diving. And this is a Julius Caesar in which you can imagine that Marc Antony is dreaming of a perfect wave.

Jurassic Park (1993)

In the 1980s, already, the cult of the dinosaur had begun. Science and natural history museums had life-size models of T. rex, et cetera, skeletons or fully clothed in reptilian hide, where movement overtook the beasts. Come up on T. from behind and the system went into effect: he whirled around, a growl came from the machine, and his dead eye fixed on you. It was a lot of fun, and the rather naïve mimicry of museum technology was soon surpassed by triceratops in your lap. The key movie in the process came from Steven Spielberg and DreamWorks, though before that it was a best-selling novel by Michael Crichton in which—if I remember correctly—just a little DNA preserved by chance could bring back the imaginary thrill of *The Lost World*.

Of course, the real breakthrough was in the digitization of computer-generated imagery so that a drawing of a dinosaur could be animated to produce lifelike locomotion. It was Muybridge again and flicking the pages fast enough to get the feeling of the naked woman opening an umbrella—except that in this case it was a prehistoric creature chasing theoretical movie stars (in the very same year that Spielberg had the Gestapo chasing Jews—a short film on crosscutting could easily show the similarity of the dynamic).

Was it amazing? Yes, it was, and instantly dull. I would dare point out that the invention of the movies themselves was sometimes regarded in the same way. For instance, Virginia Woolf, who lived through their very invention, and who was a person with a considerable interest in narrative, character, and what we may call the depths of being, noticed quite quickly that the cinema was both miraculous and boring. *Jurassic Park* contains wonders (along with the threat of greater ones yet), but it still comes down to Lord Attenborough as a benign but daft master of creation.

Whereas, in 1912, Arthur Conan Doyle wrote a novel, *The Lost World,* in which four men—two scientists, a game hunter, and a journalist—go off to explore a plateau in South America where the past has been preserved. I recall it as a reading experience to treasure, amply informed with scientific research and Doyle's great energy, and founded upon four interesting and very different characters. It also had the great idea—later employed by *King Kong*—of one specimen at least being brought back to civilization (or the Royal Albert Hall).

Jurassic Park does not really have characters. One reason why the animals are the hit is that they know melodrama drives them. The people here are puffy and vague with explanations of silly points of view. They are Sam Neill, Laura Dern, Jeff Goldblum, and so on, and they seldom achieve rapport with a monster (in the way Naomi Watts does in the third *King Kong*). It was a sensation when it opened (budget $63 million; gross income $914 million), but I doubt today that one kid would lift a fat thumb in its favor. Show me marvels—before I sleep.

Kameradschaft (1931)

Before the First World War there was a French mining disaster at Courrières so drastic that German miners from only a few miles away had come to help their colleagues. In 1931, G. W. Pabst saw it as a splendid opportunity for the widespread liberal sentiment that former foes should find common cause, and so he made a film, set after 1918, in French and German versions, simultaneously—*Kameradschaft* in the German version and *La Tragédie de la Mine* in the French.

Shut up in the dark of the movies, we are prey to claustrophobia—a great deal of suspense or horror depends on it, not to mention trapped submarine movies, locked-room ordeals, and collapsed mines or people who simply cannot muster the will to leave a dinner party. *Kameradschaft* in all its versions was a major event at a time when most of the world mouthed such easy opinions as "It must never be allowed to happen again." The "it" in that case was a renewal of military hostilities—not the chance that in a tragic disaster different countries should aid each other. The really heartbreaking story on this point of view would be a movie about Christmas Day 1914—the first Christmas of the Great War—when, apparently, British and German soldiers sang carols across no-man's-land and then came out into the open to share Christmas dinner and play a game of soccer. And then, when Christmas was over, they went back into their trenches and picked up their guns. That incident is at least as human as the basis for *Kameradschaft* and a good deal sadder.

But Pabst had strong international support—it was a very easy endorsement. His script was written by Ladislaus Vajda, Karl Otten, and Peter Martin Lampel, after an idea from Otten. The photography was by Fritz Arno Wagner and Robert Baberske, and the magnificent and extended mine-shaft sets were by Ernö Metzner and Karl Vollbrecht. Indeed, if the mines in France had been made as securely as the sets for the movie in Germany, maybe the disaster could have been averted.

There was this side to Pabst: He had made *Westfront 1918,* too, a heartfelt plea to sensible people about the foolishness of war. But all people are sensible until they are not, and it's intriguing that the Pabst films that have best stood the test of time are the ones that see and feel the internal confusions in people—*Pandora's Box, Diary of a Lost Girl, The Joyless Street,* and *Secrets of a Soul.* Pabst had lived in Vienna and read Freud: Contradictory passions were meat and drink to him, just as they are more fruitful material for films than sane and pious ideas that win the support of every right-minded person in the abstract. So the film ends with miners from both sides telling each other that "gas and war are the only enemies." But the conversation is flat and captionlike, and it shows Pabst's odd reluctance to explore talk. He loves the underground noises as communication is attempted, but he's far less inspired at having "enemies" talk like potential friends.

Key Largo (1948)

What they did to Maxwell Anderson's play *Key Largo* is a sign of how high and mighty they reckoned they were. And it was John Huston who did it. *Key Largo* opened on Broadway in November 1939. Its central figure is King McCloud (Paul Muni), who urges his group of men to desert during the Spanish Civil War because the cause is lost. Beset by guilt, back home in America, McCloud determines to visit the families of his lost comrades. So he visits one family in the Florida Keys and finds them under threat from gangsters. Cynical, at first, and detached, he feels compelled to join in the fight and is killed saving the family.

It was a Warner Brothers picture, with Jerry Wald producing and Huston looking to end his Warners contract. Richard Brooks was the assigned writer, and he and Huston agreed that the play—in blank verse—was a bit of a bore. Huston challenged Brooks to find some way of making it interesting. So they made the hero a veteran from World War II coming to the Keys to meet the family of a fallen comrade. That's how they smuggled in a love story. But he discovers that the hotel the family runs is held up by gangsters waiting for a payoff. So it's that old wartime spirit against modern criminal corruption.

The writers had been to the Keys to soak up atmosphere and gamble, but Warners preferred to shoot almost all the picture in Burbank. So they were fortunate to have Karl Freund there to cook up the stormy atmosphere, inside and out. Freund concentrated on the fleshy tones, the sweat and the threat of a hurricane, and he did wonders in photographing the chief gangster, Rocco (Edward G. Robinson—smoking a cigar in his bath), who looks, in Huston's words, "like a crustacean out of its shell." There's also a hushed moment when Rocco leans into Lauren Bacall's ear and whispers filthy sexual suggestions, not heard, but spelled out in the grossness of his face and the tremor of her mare's nostrils.

The gangster is based loosely on Lucky Luciano, and he has a mistress, Gaye Dawn (Claire Trevor), whose fallen status is touching. There's a moment when Rocco makes her sing "Moanin' Low" to get a drink—and then denies it. The Floridians are Lionel Barrymore in a wheelchair as the father of the hero, and Bacall as his widow. The other hoodlums are Thomas Gomez, Marc Lawrence, Harry Lewis, and Dan Seymour, and Jay Silverheels can be seen playing an Indian. The guy back from the war, McCloud still, is—of course—Humphrey Bogart.

In fact, Huston allows Bacall and Bogart to be overshadowed. They get very little warmth or fun. They have only a few routine stiff-upper-lip scenes. There's far more attention on Rocco and Gaye, no matter that Robinson was reluctant to hit up the old clichés. But he is very good and the best source of energy in the film. In his book, Huston recalled *Key Largo* getting a Best Picture Oscar nomination. It didn't—that was *Treasure of the Sierra Madre* (a far better movie). But Claire Trevor did win for Supporting Actress. Max Steiner did the score.

The Killers (1946)

The Hemingway short story (written in 1926) hangs there in the night like a cold moon: Two thugs hold up a diner, intending to kill Ole Andreson when he comes in to eat his usual dinner—this in a small town, nowhere, but Nick Adams is there to see it all and remember the thugs' poised talk and the sinister rhythm of their stay. They depart and Nick goes to warn Ole. But the Swede is impassive. Sooner or later, he seems to say, he's going to get it. So where should he go to be safe? That cold moon is going to be watching. You eat your dinner and wait your time, and in the end the gunfire will come as a relief after the grating menace of the way the thugs talk.

So what happened, and how is the Swede so young and healthy and so down in the dumps that he'll take what's coming? Very seldom before had a full film thought to take off from the germ of an earlier story, and even if Anthony Veiller and an uncredited John Huston aren't Hemingway, they made a pretty good shot at the backstory. So good that when you see it laid out you're going to say, Well, I could have guessed that. Because according to the noir standards of the day, the Swede—he's no longer Swedish in the movie, he's Burt Lancaster—fell for one of those beautiful girls the whole world knows you can't trust, Kitty Collins was her name, and Ava Gardner got the part.

The Hemingway story, strangely, remains more visual, and more of a movie, just because it isn't explained. You can see the tense hour at the diner so well, and William Conrad and Charles McGraw are matchless as the double act, the killers. They don't kill anyone in the story, but that's why you take them seriously. That, and the scarring impact they make on the conventional or undeveloped mind of the law-abiding Nick, the kid who needs to work out where and what these dark angels came from. And how they learned to talk like ruined comedians.

So the plot of *The Killers* feels mundane and pedestrian, even if Edmond O'Brien does a busy and vaguely plausible job as the insurance investigator who needs to know. And cameraman Woody Bredell busts his britches to give you every noir effect in one movie and to convince you that, sure, he read the Hemingway story and he really "saw" the whole thing. *The Killers* is a classic movie of its kind, and really no one ever did such things better than Robert Siodmak or with a more equable, self-effacing manner. If there was an inch more of ego in Siodmak he'd be far more famous. As it is, it's just that he made half a dozen fascinating and near-faultless films. He gets the masochistic fatalism and somehow he got the burstingly robust Burt Lancaster to see it, too, and to settle for living in the sad sigh that always lurked in Burt's voice and his hurt eyes.

But if you really need to think highly of the film, don't reread the story.

The Killers (1964)

Why would I rather see this, the 1964 television remake, in drab red-sauce color, than the magnificent Siodmak-Bredell original? Well, you can call it perversity, and I can hear the dirty-minded whispers that this guy could never resist five minutes of *Police Woman* just because Angie Dickinson was in it. We'll come to that. Meanwhile, I have a nice high-minded and quite intellectual answer.

The TV *Killers* never set out to be a classic, whereas the 1946 film felt loaded down with class from the start. And whereas in the original, Burt Lancaster is an undeserving victim for the killers, in the later version no one is going to fret at the thought of John Cassavetes getting offed. One tense grin from Cassavetes and he was living on borrowed time, and in this picture he plays a nasty, self-centered idiot who has notions of being a tragic hero. For myself, I admire the way Roman Polanski took one look at Cassavetes's tragic side and cast him as the devil's henchman.

But the real coup of the TV version is the boldness that realizes it's a story about the two thugs—Conrad and McGraw in the original—two heavy suits who seem doomed to drive the highways of America, waiting their time at unappetizing diners with their lethal small talk for rosary beads. And for TV, director Don Siegel (a very smart guy whenever he was under absurd pressure) had Lee Marvin and Clu Gulager, in love with each other and their Beckett-crossed-with-Benny backchat. They are the center of the film, and that is enough to excuse the inert texture of the '64 *Killers*. There really are matters of content in stories that have to be honored. And what the 1946 movie never grasped (it's there in the title!) was that the two visitors were the kick.

In the TV version, they become the engine of the film, just as they are—if you like, or even if you don't like—crusaders on their mission. And Siegel is decisive about it: He knows in the end that once his killers become characters then they have to die too—don't minimize the impact this film had in establishing the "Lee Marvin" image in the fragile mind of Marvin himself. You can still see how much he loves every step and grunt of his journey, and here at last a new type is emerging in noir, the dutiful killer.

With that established, you can turn to the incredible casting of Angie and Ronald Reagan as the vicious lovers who do such dirt on poor John Cassavetes. Here are bedmates from opposite ideas of the bed, and we can feel how they grate and nag on each other so that finally—in one of the few authentic gestures of his career—Reagan reaches out and slaps Angie. That scene could last a lot longer without any referee I know intervening. But when Reagan and Angie are "together," I can't think of a more persuasive proof of how much winning and money mean in America.

The Killing (1956)

The horse is named Red Lightning. He will be shot on the far turn. At the same time there will be a staged fight in the racetrack bar. The cops will go to the bar, attention will go to the far turn. And that's how a heist operation will take sacks of money out of the racetrack, the sacks tumbling through the air so a crooked cop can put them in the trunk of his car and get away. The whole thing should work like clockwork, because Sterling Hayden has planned it all out and hired the perfect men for every job. Except that there are no perfect men.

So, long ago, when he was hardly out of *Look* magazine as a red-hot journalistic photographer who did human interest the way some lawyers follow ambulances, Stanley Kubrick had a debut film to knock your eyes out. It still does the trick, with a grinding voice-over commentary and lovely little switchback flashbacks. Jim Thompson is alleged to have done some of the dialogue, and you hope he did the sour back talk in the Peatty marriage—that's Elisha Cook as George and Marie Windsor as Sherry, about as humanly interesting as chop bones left overnight on a plate. There was always a way Kubrick had of snapping human vitality just at the instant where you felt life was going to be replaced by a fresh corpse, still warm and fragrant. You can smell Sherry's lipstick and George's flop sweat.

The Killing is extremely cut-and-dried. Intellectually, Kubrick's scenario allows the need for chance, but you feel he has had that fusspot little dog in training all the time so it will escape its owner and run out onto the tarmac, so the luggage handler swerves and the big suitcase bounces on the ground and—bingo!—there's the money eddying around in the slipstream of a patiently waiting jet. In other words, Kubrick knows luck or chance about as well as he knows true love or warmth in a woman.

But the panache of the film is irresistible, and Kubrick finds time to dig up a lot of hard-luck stories in his strange male cast—from Jay C. Flippen, never more wheedlingly gay, to Timothy Carey, a fuckup with his gun and his perfect parking place, about the last hiring a real boss would ever make. Never mind, we love them all—Vince Edwards, Ted de Corsia, Joe Sawyer, and Kola Kwariani, who tosses cops around as if they were dolls. And since reason dictates that the film can't be simply the Peatty hell, and since 1956's taste would have forbidden a glimpse of their congealed sex acts, then it's no bad thing to have enough diverse characters to make the 84 minutes slip by.

But that doesn't give enough credit to Sterling Hayden's fine Johnny Clay, diligent, patient, a diplomat, a manager, a dreamer, the guy who had it all worked out. It's only after a good dose of guys like Johnny that you understand why and how the only people Kubrick ever trusted were flat-out crazies, like Jack Torrance.

Kind Hearts and Coronets (1949)

Start obliquely: How nice it is that the photography on *The Servant* (in which a sharp eye cannot miss the ooze of social putrescence) was handled by Douglas Slocombe, the very man who had photographed *Kind Hearts and Coronets* nearly fifteen years earlier and given it such mourning undertones—never say that photographers do not have themes or motifs. For while there is a sturdy English defiance of deep truth that says, Oh yes, *Kind Hearts* is a very funny film, don't let yourself settle for the jollity. Yes, it is funny, but haven't we learned yet that good comedy is a very serious matter, and generally the most confounding and subversive way of dealing with important issues?

So, let us be clear, coming to its climax in the year 1902, *Kind Hearts and Coronets* is insurrectionary and quite prepared to murder the members of the upper class if political reform can find no other way. This is an immense celebration of the upstart spirit and the way a "Louis Mazzini" raised on Balaclava Avenue, in southwest London, can take Chalfont Castle by the inspired process of killing off every prior claimant. Nor should it be missed in this story that our Louis (the magnificent Dennis Price) is altogether the best-spoken and most aristocratically behaved person in sight. I think it's also essential to note the degree to which Price and Louis resemble or invoke Oscar Wilde (who had died in 1900).

In 1949, probably, very few people read *Kind Hearts* clearly enough to note that Louis was gay—though nowadays I think Price's performance can leave little doubt, just as it is evident that the film enjoys the charms and the menace of womanhood. This attitude is not malicious, or politically incorrect, merely competitive—and the only reservation in the film, I think, is that in all his gallery of D'Ascoynes Alec Guinness doesn't get the chance to be an attractive young woman, a sexpot.

Of course, it was directed and cowritten by Robert Hamer (the other writer was John Dighton), and it is high time that Hamer—uneasily upper class, secretly gay, publicly alcoholic—be recognized as one of the most impressive of English directors from this rich period. And in the context of Hamer's work as a whole, with its interest in the working classes and in murder as a social resolution, it's easier to see the contempt within the satire of *Kind Hearts*. At the time, and thereafter, the film was known for Guinness and his eight D'Ascoynes, but next to the subtle playing of Price, Guinness was surely meant to address the English fondness for feeble impersonation and indulged eccentricity. So one of the ironies to the movie is its being known as a Guinness picture.

Joan Greenwood is ravishing as Sibella, but I think it's worth saying that Greenwood's breathy underlining of herself always had a suggestion of female impersonation—in other words, this is woman (treacherous, intelligent, greedy, and dangerous) such as confirms every gay suspicion (and delight).

Let me go further: If ever a movie deserved a sequel, this is it. Left on the steps of Pentonville, free, while recollecting his memoirs, the look on Dennis Price's face is exquisite: He is an idiot, for once; he may be doomed; and yet—he is a writer—and writers long to be read.

King Kong (1933)

Some people are afraid of Kong, but me, I'm afraid of Carl Denham (Robert Armstrong). He is the reckless, fearless showman who is prepared to leave Skull Island and its civilization in tatters if he can bring Kong back to New York as the eighth wonder of the world. And the more you look into the history of this phenomenal cultural event, the less interested it seems in large monkeys and the more helpless it is with Denham.

In the 1920s, increasingly, there had been an interest in film crews that went to wild places and came back with documentary footage. Flaherty had started it, but Ernest Schoedsack and Merian Cooper carried it on with films like *Chang* and *Grass*. Of the two, Schoedsack was the explorer and Cooper the showman—though it unduly restricts Cooper to call him that. Merian Cooper was an air ace and a man of many parts, and one of those parts was to succeed David O. Selznick as executive in charge of RKO.

Cooper had the idea for *King Kong*, and it was to turn on a figure half Cooper and half Schoedsack—a ranting producer/hunter. But the artistic thrust to the idea was that the beast they would find would be manmade in a film of special effects. So the work went on to write a script (Cooper, Edgar Wallace, James Creelman, and Ruth Rose all helping), but at the same time Willis O'Brien began to consider the special effects that would make the whole thing filmable in the studio.

The importance of that process is to see Kong as a dreamed creature, a large stuffed toy, a crudely animated model, engaged in fights with dinosaurs and the pathetic attempt to hold Fay Wray in his paw. And so it worked out that Denham rescues Ann Darrow (Fay Wray) from poverty and takes her to Skull Island, teaching her how to scream as she sees "it" along the way. The true stooge in the show is Jack Driscoll (Bruce Cabot), Ann's boyfriend—and clearly a bolder version of the comic-book legend would have Denham revealing the monster and his own beast to Ann and seeing which gets the bigger scream.

The camerawork was shared by several people, and Cooper and Schoedsack directed it all, but it's the dynamic of Denham and the extraordinary inventiveness of O'Brien that carries the film along, all on the chest-pounding score of Max Steiner.

Two remakes have not crushed the spirit or the naïve intensity of the original—it towers over the slick, much longer color versions. *King Kong* is an unstoppable 110 minutes, without an ounce of irrelevance or small talk, crammed with classic situations—from Ann staked out for Kong, to Kong staked out for the theater audience. Everything on the island is savagely racist and deliriously exciting. Everything in New York makes you long for the simplicity of the island. And in the last set piece, the planes attacking Kong when he is the roaring Christmas star on top of the Empire State, how can we not see the prophecy of what is called 9/11? Eternal proof that sometimes America can make a trash movie that might have moved Lear.

The King of Comedy (1983)

Rupert Pupkin (Robert De Niro) may be one of the most original, and alarming, creations in the work of Martin Scorsese. Bearing a massive, unfocused good nature rather in the way a parade float might be carrying an ICBM, he charges through American media society of yesteryear armed and crippled with his certainty that the celebrities—above all Jerry Langford (Jerry Lewis)—know him in the way he knows them. Rupert is crass; he dresses very badly; he hardly listens to people who are talking to him; and he could bring the world tumbling down. He leaves us longing for the days when Travis Bickle was the most dangerous fellow you might meet out there on the streets.

It is part of Rupert's lethal good nature that he believes he could be the King of Comedy, and, when all is said and done, after he has practiced a little genteel kidnapping and ransom, and been on the show, it looks as if he could make it. In that sense, he is Travis's brother—for Travis does find the providential shoot-out situation where he can become a celebrity, the taxi driver who gives riders a thrill and who always gets the right change and a healthy tip.

The King of Comedy passed at the time as a one-off venture, a jeu d'esprit—until it was realized that there was little "jeu" in Mr. Scorsese and a very guarded esprit. *The King of Comedy* meanders and wallows sometimes. It lacks that lip-smacking thoroughness that Scorsese finds for gangsters, as if Scorsese didn't entirely understand Rupert himself. But the problems and the doldrums are forgivable because there is a black comedy of embarrassment in much of the film that is enchanting and liberated compared with the tight, anal way in which many Scorsese jigsaws fit together so that they squeak.

There are so many unexpected things—like Rupert's ghostly home life: Are there other people there, or is he in some institution already? Then there are the women—the decorous, dainty Shelley Hack, forgotten now, but tripping up to the reception desk with dulcet lies. There is even the receptionist, who I seem to remember was Mrs. Winkler (the producers are Chartoff and Winkler). There is Diahnne Abbott with nothing to do. And then there is Sandra Bernhard, whose existence in life and cabaret might otherwise have gone unnoticed in film. This proves she existed and was very weird and wondrous.

And so we come finally to Jerry as Jerry—Jerry Lewis as Jerry Langford, the sort of Carsonian figure this story needs, except that Langford has been in Carson's seat half his life and is nothing but polish. It is a glorious performance, worthy of a book by Wittgenstein, the nonentity everyone knows. There is a sequence where he walks the street—in public, waiting to be mobbed, but not quite—that is perhaps the gentlest, finest comedy Lewis ever did.

Paul D. Zimmerman wrote it, and I'm not sure that Scorsese ever understood the script. But the film seems more barbed and cuddlesome every year. I love it. But when the Terror really comes, it will be like Rupert Pupkin.

The King of Marvin Gardens (1972)

Although it has persistently drawn less attention than *Five Easy Pieces, The King of Marvin Gardens* still seems to me Bob Rafelson's most intriguing picture. If I had to answer why in one word it would be brotherhood. The idea of bipolarity acted out in two brothers is obvious, but the question as to whether David Staebler (Jack Nicholson) is more creative, more rational, or even more stable than his brother Jason (Bruce Dern) is endlessly provocative.

It was a BBS production, with Rafelson acting as producer and director, working from a screenplay by Jacob Brackman that seldom lets us relax in our feelings about the material. So the long, opening story by David only gradually becomes an actor on a radio show. For the most part it seems to ache with the actor's sincerity—it is a tour de force of self-effacement in an actor identified with pleasure. So David emerges as a retiring person: a man who needs the dark security of the radio studio and a certain freedom from test or criticism. He can only be true by making it up—by turning the world into his sad novel. It is a part of that process that Nicholson seemed older, heavier, drabber, and so much less hopeful than ever before.

By contrast, Jason is the showman, the confidence man, the performer, the rabid dreamer and schemer who has some immense plan that will get them all out of the cold East Coast—Atlantic City and Philadelphia—and away to Hawaii. He is a developer, even if the concrete is not yet set in his own mind. And he is exactly the kind of madman who gets movies made—quite subtly the film is a story about the relationship between a producer (always in the light) and the member of an audience (nursing his dark).

The brilliance of the plan for brotherhood is casting Dern and Nicholson—longtime friends, colleagues, and contemporaries—at the moment when Nicholson was beginning to accelerate and to leave Dern far behind. It goes without saying that the parts could have been swapped, without any loss. Nicholson thrived without Dern, but you can almost hear Dern complaining that Jack lost his integrity in doing so; these two guys lived with a dream, that each one kept the other honest.

Of course, there are two girls, too—Ellen Burstyn, not just magnificent, but the pivot of drastic action, a woman made raggedly self-abusive by her situation; and Julia Anne Robinson, wan, mysterious, seductive, and not long for this world. The women prompt the breakdown in the brothers' world and the end of their rhythm, and it's one of those rare films that really gets at the fear and loathing of women in American men. László Kovács did the lovely winter photography, Toby Carr Rafelson did the art direction. Bipolarity has become a huge subject since 1972, but this great film opened up the metaphor for us all. It's a rare thing to see two people so dysfunctional who manage to keep going just by bouncing off each other.

Kings of the Road (1976)

While driving on the autobahn one day, Wim Wenders saw two trucks staying side by side for miles as the drivers chatted to each other. One is wary of challenging the movie director looking for inspiration, but it's a surprise they weren't locked together on the CB radios that are so vital a part of Jonathan Demme's *Handle with Care* (1977). Never mind, Wenders saw the chance for a road movie in which Bruno (Rüdiger Vogler) travels the line of the "wall" between West and East Germany servicing projectors in dying movie houses, and one day picks up Robert (Hanns Zischler), who can hardly believe the solitude and the monotony of the life.

Kings of the Road is nearly three hours long—time enough for those qualities to sink in. Wenders said in interviews that this was a movie about men who just preferred to hang out with other men. They are not gay. They are not exactly antiwomen. It is more that they like to shelter from exactly those people who might ask them about such matters. But it could mean so much if the relationship between the two men were just a little bit more thorough or pleasing. Three hours and hundreds of miles gives them time to talk, but the talk—it seems to me—is enough to make us want to get off the truck. Is it that being a man involves being bored, without complaint?

Wenders is credited with the script, though he has said that he and the actors really improvised it together as they traveled. And there's an opportunity for a lot of pseudo-tough pronouncements about women and the influence of America on Germany and Europe. And Wenders is smart enough to be critical and penetrating. But we know now that the American road—as celebrated by Kerouac and Sam Shepard—is more to his taste than the German highways. He has a real taste for boring or silent men and can find a nearly spiritual haven there in a film like *Paris, Texas*. But that's in part because of his devotion to American music and movies and the underlying faith that—just like in *Detour*—a hell of a situation is just around the corner.

Kings of the Road is photographed by Robby Müller and Martin Schäfer in a solidly realistic tradition that extends to black and white and, shall we say, long-held shots where not too much happens. The editing is by Peter Przygodda. The most interesting point now, I think, is Robert's interest in words and language, and the most entertaining point is the near-slapstick sequence on silent comedy. But if so little in the way of shaped drama is to be allowed into this journey, then it soon cries out for incident and diversion. There could easily be a story in truckers who become separated from their world to an unhealthy degree—and even dangerous because of it. But that's the American scenario at work—it's the impulse that spurred Spielberg's *Duel*. And I have to say, finally, that Wenders allows himself to find more atmosphere in his books of still photographs than he permits in his movies.

Kiss Me Deadly (1955)

How could it be, working within the bounds of commercial cinema when many were still nervous of seeming to step out of line, that Robert Aldrich delivered a work of such scathing, brimming satire that was still so embedded in a "safe" genre (the old noir game) that there was no need to laugh out loud (that sort of giveaway could be incriminating still)? After all, you could say to any investigator, aren't we simply watching your standard, brutalizing L.A.-private-eye-meets-gangsters stuff? And look, whereas the "literary" basis for all this—Mickey Spillane—has routine in-and-out sex passages every fifty pages or so, the dolls here stay as inert and insolently comic as household appliances—refrigerators, ovens, or flush toilets.

Kiss Me Deadly remains a miracle of tact and tone, real yet surreal, set in a city that is more than ready for the kind of atomic apocalypse that waits in the big, locked box—itself so close to the tantalizing object of desire in the game shows that would soon invade TV. "Open the box!" you can hear yourself yelling, just so that the severe photography by Ernest Laszlo can give us the stark beauty of a ground zero in Santa Monica.

It is not enough to say that Aldrich was great for a moment, and coarse thereafter. One really needs to know the exact circumstances of chance, opportunism, and devious luck that got this film made. For example, did Ralph Meeker's Mike Hammer comprehend his own muscle-bound strut, or did Aldrich just let him go with it? Is there another film in which noir violence nuzzles up against real evil so suggestively? Remember the girl's hanging legs and the idea of pliers? How do we forget the staircases, the steep streets of the old city, the sudden, punitive hurts that are inflicted and the bravura madness of "Va-va-voom!"

The women are to die for, ranging from the subcompetent but stacked Maxine Cooper to Gaby Rodgers, who is, arguably, so knowing a creature, so fixedly cruel and desirable, that a case could be made for keeping her out of pictures forever afterward (that did seem to be the policy, alas). And still I haven't mentioned Cloris Leachman's desperation, and how I know she's naked, raw, and violated under that raincoat.

If you have to know the story line, it's just that a phallus named Mike Hammer (it's hard to type this stuff without cracking up) gets caught up in an intrigue which will end with a box full of atomic fire. Oh, I see, you say—it's a film noir! But that satisfaction only demonstrates the ruinous state of noir criticism, when it is enough for a film to be saved or not saved. *Kiss Me Deadly* is so much more—a black comedy, a serious case of coitus interruptus (because the Spillane sex scenes never come), and the sheer rapture of stupidity and moral self-confidence going hammer, hammer, hammer on the eggshell world until it blows up.

Magnificent. And should there be a comma in the title?

Kiss Me, Stupid (1964)

Kiss Me, Stupid stands directly in the path of anyone intrigued by the question as to whether Billy Wilder was more interested in making us laugh or throw up. It is also a fascinating picture in the awkward history of Hollywood in the 1960s, desperately trying to keep up with moral standards on the slide. No one doubted that Billy Wilder had always had an eager, dirty mind. But for years he had taken it for granted that he had to keep it out of his pictures. But now, by 1964, was smutty becoming fashionable? He was moved yet angry, and here he lunges at bad taste the way Hitchcock in the same years wanted his own sex and violence to be more disgusting.

At first, everything was promising. *Kiss Me, Stupid* came from a play, *The Dazzling Hour*, by Ketti Frings and Jose Ferrer, that had failed in the 1950s. Wilder and I. A. L. Diamond restaged it completely. The story now was as follows: Dino is a nightclub casino singer stranded in Nevada—in the town of Climax (let double meanings reign). This excites Orville Spooner, a songwriter, and his lyricist friend, Barney Milsap. If only they could get Dino to sing one of their songs. They think to detain Dino in Climax, and they recognize his steady need for sex. So they hire a local hooker, Polly the Pistol, who will pretend to be Mrs. Spooner and keep Dino interested.

As a first step, Wilder got Ira Gershwin to come on board: Orville and Barney's songs would be some of those Gershwin songs the world doesn't know—because they flopped. He got Alexander Trauner to do the sets for what was a Panavision film. Trauner toured Nevada, reckoned that all construction there was temporary, and worked accordingly. Then there was the cast: Dino tickled Dean Martin, no matter that it was very close to his real bone—indeed, Martin's production company came on board with funds. Polly the Pistol would be Kim Novak—casting that sort of said, Well, aren't you Marilyn Monroe now? Felicia Farr would play Orville's real wife. And Peter Sellers was cast as Orville.

Wilder was plainly intrigued by Sellers—he was already lining him up to play Dr. Watson. He loved the mimetic skill and the emptiness behind it all. But Sellers was exhausted and just married to Britt Eklund—this in itself sounds like a Wilder joke. He did not enjoy the way Wilder kept an open set and a partylike mood. In short, he had a heart attack so bad he had to be taken off the film—and was replaced with Ray Walston.

The result is a fascinating but uneasy film. It got a C for condemned from the Legion of Decency, and it did very badly. On the other hand, it deserves an important place in any series prepared to take on the breakdown of America as its theme. The nastiness goes all the way through—so often Wilder tried to throw syrup on his own bad moods. This is disturbing, often very funny, and finally sad and touching.

Kiss of Death (1947)

The material of *Kiss of Death* can easily make a dull film—as witness the 1995 remake by Barbet Schroeder, with David Caruso as the hero and Nicolas Cage as the villain. It's just another story about a criminal, stirred by thoughts of family, who informs on his old cronies. It came from a script by Ben Hecht and Charles Lederer, when they were top-of-the-line, even if they were presiding over a factory of screenplays and many minions. It was directed by Henry Hathaway, who deserves to be regarded as a confident professional, and who would handle several of Fox's documentary-type thrillers in this period. It was well photographed by Norbert Brodine. And it had a routine Fox cast, with Victor Mature as the hero, the underrated Coleen Gray as his wife, and then Brian Donlevy, Karl Malden, Taylor Holmes, and Mildred Dunnock.

And only there have I come anywhere near what this film is about. Ms. Dunnock plays an elderly woman, a wheelchair case, who is pushed down a staircase—in her chair—by Tommy Udo (Richard Widmark).

Widmark was already thirty-three, from Sunrise, Minnesota. He had taught drama at Lake Forest College, and he acted in radio in the early 1940s. But he had not made a film before *Kiss of Death*. Let me add one other thing, based on personal encounter, albeit many years later. Richard Widmark (who died in March 2008) is among the gentlest, most amiable, decent, and modest men I have ever met. It would be hard to detect a strain of cruelty or malice in him. I would trust him under the worst circumstances of storm, plague, and natural disaster, with old ladies and young puppies alike.

Yet Tommy Udo—remembered by people who cannot recall anything else about *Kiss of Death*—is one of the most frightening people ever revealed on the American screen. It is not just that he is a thug, a villain. He is plainly sadistic—whatever emotional life he has is fueled and gratified by inflicting pain and suffering on others. Nor is this a grim, silent process. No, the pleasure he has is greeted with glee, with immense giggling fits of supremacy, with a simply evil reversal of all human values.

Widmark played Udo in a fedora, a dark suit, a black shirt, and a light tie (and when he dies in the gutter, we see white socks—a dandy). It is my memory (I only saw the trailer of the film in 1947, before a mother's hurried hands shut out the view—the giggle was another matter) that he resembled the Gestapo look. I don't know how widely this was appreciated at the time, or even how calculated it was by the filmmakers, but Udo was the imprint of the great evil.

He was nominated for the Oscar as Best Supporting Actor. He stole the picture. And for several years thereafter he had to be nasty onscreen. He became, later, a hero—though he could do anger and hatred still, at the drop of a Stetson. But he changed pictures, and our safe view of their evil characters.

The first thing to ask about this ravishing film is, why is it called *Klute*? Sure, John Klute (Donald Sutherland) is the character we meet first, the one who seems to drive the action when he is hired out of being a small-town cop to investigate the disappearance in Manhattan of a respectable citizen from that small town in Pennsylvania. But Klute is also numb, underdeveloped, not just a country boy but a recessive soul: Klute is a watcher, and maybe a voyeur—by which I mean someone who gets his deepest psychic gratification just from watching. And Klute's watching is what discloses Bree—Bree Daniels (Jane Fonda), a fairly successful call girl. Put it this way. Bree never made it as an actress, but when she's acting out sexual rapture for guys in from Pennsylvania and elsewhere she's a trick.

In time, Klute and Bree will find the answer to the initial mystery. They will identify the sex killer who murdered that respectable fellow. Yet not an atom of the dread that inspires the film will be abated. There is a stunning last scene, as Bree quits her apartment. She is going off with Klute, it seems. She takes a last call as the call girl and says she's going away. Will they marry? Will they endure? Or is Bree's acting instinct so strong that she needs the telephone like a drug—the film is full of phones, recorders, and voice-overs, the sinister nature of which blends exquisitely with Michael Small's minimal but indelible score.

Andy and Dave Lewis wrote it and Alan J. Pakula directed, and I think it's the best film he ever made because the paranoia at which he excelled is more intimate and concentrated than in any other film. The scenes where Bree hears someone or something on the roof of her building are so well done that repeated viewing does not take away their menace.

But this is truly a film about Bree and about the several ways in which being a psychiatric patient (talking about oneself), being a hooker (acting out), and being an actress (acting in) are overlapping or in a rhyme scheme. And the triumph of the film is the intelligence and the appetite with which Jane Fonda falls upon it. That she won the Oscar goes without saying, but this is one of the best movie studies of performance. The delicacy with which Fonda balances the real story of Bree and the larger implications is exemplary. No wonder Sutherland seems so numb watching her—she was a sight to behold.

Is it more than that? Well, yes, I think so. Pakula was not a secure or happy man. He had a lot of analysis himself. And this is, if you like, a tribute to a kind of urban anxiety that is uniquely American. And it says a lot, for that large atmosphere—the dark that surrounds Bree and Klute—is one in which every supporting role contributes. So Roy Scheider was never better than as a pimp, and there is excellent work from Charles Cioffi, Rita Gam, and Dorothy Tristan. Here is one of the most disconcerting works of the early 1970s.

Knave of Hearts (1954)

It is usually known as *Monsieur Ripois* in France, as *Lovers, Happy Lovers* or *Lover Boy* in America, and as *Knave of Hearts* in Britain, where it was largely shot. As you might guess, it is very hard to see it anywhere. Yet warm memory says this is a remarkable film, one of the most bittersweet on the compelling subject of womanizing. It comes from a novel, *M. Ripois and His Nemesis,* by Louis Hémon. Apparently, Raymond Queneau was the first person who saw a film in the book. He encouraged director René Clément to hire Jean Aurenche to write a screenplay. But Clément rejected that and assigned it to Englishman Hugh Mills.

It's the story of Andre Ripois (he's named Amede in the book), an attractive Frenchman who is living in London. He is married. But a divorce is under way and he is engaged in an affair with the wife's friend. Ripois is a kind of a virus of infidelity, except that he seems to love all women—as the film goes forward, we get flashbacks on previous affairs. The film was produced by Paul Graetz, who had produced *Le Diable au Corps.* For the English viewer, there were two heady wonders in the film: the impact of a great French actor (Gérard Philipe) on English women; and the way in which Clément saw or noticed a London that had seldom been featured in British films.

The film was photographed by Oswald Morris, and it has that summery grayness that became a keynote of his work. It was filmed in summer, and Clément and Morris together get that sultry, blossomy feeling of the city. It's often the case that visitors see the heart of a city better than natives, and *Knave of Hearts* had a big effect on how the British saw their great city. There's a scene where Ripois picks up Joan Greenwood on a bus—and all shot on a moving bus—that has a stinging freshness not seen in British film before.

But more than that, Graetz and Clément chose a range of English actresses not quite in the first rank, or the most obvious casting, but full of life—Valerie Hobson as the wife, the very beautiful Natasha Parry (Mrs. Peter Brook) as the mistress, Joan Greenwood, Margaret Johnston, Diana Decker. As for Philipe, he handles the English language very well and shows how easily he might have become an international star. But it's probably true that he misses the moral severity in Hémon's novel.

Ripois ends up in a wheelchair, dependent on women to push him around. But the character exists in outline of a handsome man who simply collects women for his own pleasure. Some observers at the time noted that Clément was possibly trying to remake *Kind Hearts and Coronets.* Maybe, but I wonder about another connection—with Tom Ripley, the amoral figure beginning to appear in the writings of Patricia Highsmith. Only five years ahead, a film appeared, *Purple Noon*—the first great attempt at Ripley onscreen. Alain Delon played Tom—and René Clément directed.

Kramer vs. Kramer (1979)

Ted Kramer (Dustin Hoffman) is an adverting executive. He and his wife, Joanna (Meryl Streep), have one son, Billy (Justin Henry), who is seven. Joanna decides to walk out, because she has no fulfilling life of her own. So Ted tries to take care of Billy, a child he hardly knows. But in the year that follows they make a bond and are getting on fine. Then Joanna comes back, feeling restored. She wants her son returned to her. Whereupon Ted loses his job because he's not concentrating. Lawyers and a judge come into play, and Joanna is awarded custody. But human nature and the legitimized cruelty of divorce are yet to be "righted" by this smug Hollywood story: Joanna relents and lets Billy stay with his father.

When the story is put like that, you may marvel that Robert Benton's *Kramer vs. Kramer* has the reputation for being a sophisticated study of modern divorce (as opposed to a Griffith film, where Dustin Hoffman plays Lillian Gish). Again, that lets us know how early 1979 was in the story of American divorce, which was seemingly the great raw bone of contentiousness that was being served up as popular entertainment. Some hope! *Kramer vs. Kramer* is loaded, prejudicial, softhearted, terribly upper-middle-class and Manhattan, and almost intolerably enlightened. In other words, don't have any doubts about it: Great family and personal damage is being done in the divorce courts every day. Above all, matters of relationship are being converted wholesale into arguments about money, the only measuring stick that is available to the courts.

Kramer vs. Kramer came from a bestselling novel by Avery Corman, and it departs from the statistics of divorce in all these respects: It has a divorce in which no one has been unfaithful; it serves as an unspoken rebuke to women's liberation; it never gets into money talk; it has a magical ending. And all of these mind-boggling departures function within what is hopefully regarded as a broadly accurate social statement, one that tries to take account of the child's point of view. Benton wrote it himself; Néstor Almendros photographed it. Paul Sylbert did the art direction. Jerry Greenberg edited. Ruth Morley did the costumes. And the music is lifted from Purcell and Vivaldi. So it looks like *The World of Interiors* and sounds like a PBS minidrama. The prettiness and the tidiness are oppressive and entirely at odds with the natural violence that is unleashed in divorce.

Hoffman is the kind of father whose acting is chronically self-centered. Streep is playing a character whose life is not properly addressed. Justin Henry is there to be adorable, and there are wise, "sensitive" supporting performances from Jane Alexander, Howard Duff, George Coe, JoBeth Williams, Bill Moor, and Howard Chamberlain. It won Oscars for Best Picture, for Benton, for Hoffman, for Streep, and for screenplay, and I suppose its inane studied gentility may have inspired many more people into divorce. So remember this: Sooner or later in divorce cases, everyone behaves as badly as Shelley Winters and Rod Steiger—and sometimes all the time.

The first delight in Curtis Hanson's adaptation of James Ellroy is the sheer density of plot. It is a while before we begin to sense where this story is going, but in that while we meet three very different cops: Jack Vincennes (Kevin Spacey), dapper, expert, mildly corrupt, and the liaison with a TV cop show; Bud White (Russell Crowe), brutish, violent, corrupt; and Ed Exley (Guy Pearce), handsome, the son of a cop, incorruptible, but a pain in the neck. And by necessity, all of them have their special private relationship with Dudley Smith (James Cromwell), captain of detectives, master of spin and presentation, the spirit of the city.

It's notable, and refreshing, that the script—by Hanson and Brian Helgeland—has opted for a quiet control, especially when compared with the crammed and hectic feel of Ellroy's writing. A lot of the novel has been put aside, yet the result is not just a rich sense of period, but a series of stories and characters all done justice. The one thing lacking is a larger sense of what the story might be about, of what it's saying about the nature of the policeman. Its ending is gentler than we have been led to expect, yet along the way there are large questions about what makes a good cop that don't necessarily fit with a public sense of duty.

So the film settles for texture and delivers it from the start. Dante Spinotti's camerawork is a tribute to noir without any kind of pastiche. Jeannine Oppewall's production design is faultless and a delight for the connoisseur of the shady city. Ruth Myers's costumes speak volumes in a world where young women can make a strange career if they look enough like a movie star. More might have been made of that, but it's characteristic that Helgeland prefers to settle for Kim Basinger being her real self rather than a girl lost in the simile of Veronica Lake. Hanson is not one for the mythology. Instead, he delivers a stunning story—never more so than in the final meeting of Vincennes and Dudley.

Spacey is pretty self-effacing as Vincennes. Crowe emerged as a new kind of lead actor. And Guy Pearce just about gets away with Mr. Priss. James Cromwell is the star of the picture, I think: His ambiguities are the bloodstream of the LAPD. He is the history and the startling present. Danny DeVito may overdo it a bit as the magazine publisher. But there are superb performances from David Strathairn, Ron Rifkin as a cowardly DA, Paul Guilfoyle (as Mickey Cohen), Graham Beckel and Darrell Sandeen as two soiled detectives, Amber Smith, Simon Baker, and actors playing Lana Turner and Johnny Stompanato. Basinger was the one Oscar winner—a kindness in a film crowded with better performances. (It won for adapted screenplay, too.) It's only on repeated viewings that *L.A. Confidential* seems more cautious than shocking. In the last analysis, Ellroy's horror has been not so much missed as shelved. Citizens of L.A. can sleep in confidence, more or less—which was never quite Ellroy's plan.

The Lady Eve (1941)

Charles Pike (Henry Fonda) has been two years up the Amazon—and it shows. He is an ophiologist, and surely those waters are rich with his chosen passion. Still, after two years of the serpent, it is about time he met Eve. Did I say that he is the heir to the Pike's Pale Ale fortune, the ale that won for Yale? And so he leaves by dugout and makes rendezvous with the SS *Southern Queen*, a luxury liner. Watching him come aboard is a most attractive father and daughter couple, "Colonel" Harrington (Charles Coburn) and Jean of that ilk (Barbara Stanwyck). They are cardsharps, and they smell a rich idiot in Charles. In a gorgeous scene in the shipboard dining room where Jean uses her face mirror to scan the crowd of women eyeing Charles, she flattens him with a fifteen-yard trip, but escapes any call and limps away to her cabin with the thoroughly flustered Charles, there to have him stroke her ankle and look into the eyes she has placed so close to his. Poor beer heir, he is only used to handling snakes. And this is one of the sexiest scenes in American film.

This is *The Lady Eve,* inspired by a shaggy dog story, "Two Bad Hats" by Monckton Hoffe, and advised upon by Albert Lewin (an uncredited associate producer) but spun as gold by Preston Sturges alone. Charles and Jean fall instantly in love, despite or because of being so unsuited? Surely love takes oxygen to its fire in unsuitability? Still, the colonel does take Charles to pieces at cards, and Muggsy (William Demarest), the Pikes' Luca Brasi, smells bad fish. So in time "Hopsy" (the motion of the beer) learns the truth, and turns solemn and furious over the dastardly scheme. It is all over?

It is just starting. Jean elects to educate her expert. She will masquerade as an English aristocrat, the Lady Eve, and go to Bridgefield, Connecticut, where the Pikes live. She is aided in this by a friend, "Pearlie," or Sir Alfred McGlennan-Keith (Eric Blore). Charles's father proves to be Eugene Pallette, a very reassuring discovery—for Charles might yet be a nasty, supercilious ophiologist (instead of a guy stirred by Stanwyck's ankle and moist gaze), but now we see he has sterling things in him. Lady Eve is a wow, though Muggsy suspects it's "positively the same dame!" A marriage ensues and it's only then that Eve has to admit her checkered past and her many lovers, teaching Hopsy his ABCs.

The Lady Eve is screwball, yet it is a fine romance, too, one in which the dense Charles has to learn to look at Jean/Eve and decide what it is he sees. Very funny, strangely erotic, utterly endearing, this may be the Sturges film that outlasts all others. Fonda is like Tom Joad as if he were Professor Joad's son. Stanwyck was in her harvest moon period. Charles Coburn is exquisite, and the cast also includes Melville Cooper, Martha O'Driscoll, Janet Beecher, Robert Greig, Dora Clement, Luis Alberni, Frank Moran, and others in the Sturges gang.

The Lady from Shanghai (1948)

Consider the possibility that, in order to avert and forestall real madness, Orson Welles "went mad." I am offering a man so brilliant, so self-centered, and so actorly that, just as he sees the real dread thing looming up, he determines to act the idiot. So long as he is acting, doesn't he have everything under control? No, I cannot prove this, not without asking you to consider *The Lady from Shanghai*.

Orson Welles was thirty-two, in the breakup stage of a second marriage, about to be the lost father to a second child. He had slipped in a few years from being wonder boy to washed up in the eyes of American show business. There may have been moments when he realized how close he had come in the hectic years to burning himself out. He was in Boston, with an enormous production of *Around the World in Eighty Days* that was melting money and proving very little except his empty audacity. And this is the story as he told it himself. He telephoned Harry Cohn (at Columbia) for urgent monies to save the show. And he told Cohn that he would do a picture for him. Just send $50,000. "What story?" asks Cohn. And Orson is on the phone in a hotel lobby from where he can see the bookstand (oh, happy days, when hotels had bookstores), and he reads out the first title that catches his eye.

If I do the crazy thing myself, by choice, am I really mad yet? Don't dismiss the case—it is the story of the scorpion and the frog. Perhaps it is just being in Boston.

Anyway, it happens, and Cohn says he must use Rita, too, Rita Hayworth, that second wife, if only because there will be frisson in putting the couple together. Does Rita wonder if this means Orson still loves her? (No one has ever suggested that she wandered away from their marriage.) Welles would say he wrote the part first for Barbara Laage, a new amour, but it's hard to watch the film without feeling the pangs of regret and revenge over the old one. It depends on how seriously Orson ever regarded a woman. As with the cooking of soft-boiled eggs, the margin is fine.

So here we are in Central Park, where an Irish seaman you'd need to be mad to hire, Michael O'Hara (I spy Orson), saves a lady in distress—that's Elsa Bannister—and soon he is hired to take the Bannister yacht over the seas—that's Arthur Bannister (Everett Sloane), a crippled lawyer, and his pal George Grisby (Glenn Anders), who is a crooked lawyer's straight man—as straight as a pretzel.

It's a film of explosions, and there's a great moment in the bright sun of Acapulco when Grisby talks lovingly about the Bomb to come—ultimate explosion. The other sunspots include Elsa's blonde hair, the insane upheaval of the court case, the madness of hiring a man to kill you, that sea dark with blood where the sharks fight, and the hall of mirrors finale where everyone is shooting themselves.

It was a failure, and it lost a lot of money—but those are sensible, practical objections to what is a glorious rotting mess, the dump outside town, always seething with fire. William Castle helped, with Charles Lederer and Fletcher Markle and several cameramen. The novel was actually called *If I Die Before I Wake*—that's what Orson said over the phone. And can't you hear *If I Die Before I Wake*—or *If I Go Crazy Before I Put On the Act*? It's the same exultant frenzy. So, please, dear God, don't ever let anyone clean it up the way "Orson really wanted it." It's the way he meant it already, a vital mess, like your last guts heaved up in your bed beside you. The last thing you see.

Lady of the Night (1925)

This film was only recently discovered and made available by Turner Classic Movies (generally a friend to all film scholars and moviegoers). It was one of seven films from 1925 that star Norma Shearer, and it comes from the recent Metro-Goldwyn-Mayer amalgamation under the heading "Louis B. Mayer Presents." But, of course, Irving Thalberg was already at the studio, and already taking an unusual interest in Ms. Shearer.

But in this case, each executive could have his movie star, for this is a story (by Adela Rogers St. Johns) in which Shearer plays two roles: Florence, a rich woman, with a veil over her hair; and Molly, a street girl, with a sideburn kiss curl and lips twice as large as Florence's. Of course, it is positively the same actress playing both parts, and, apparently, in the few scenes where they actually meet, a girl named Joan Crawford was the rearview stand-in. And as Joan might have said, she'd hugged the good girl and the bad in Shearer and didn't know which was which.

In truth, however, I think Shearer was more suited to silent acting than sound pictures. Born in 1900, Norma was raised in the silent "attitude." Even now, it is not that easy to conjure up her voice. And there is plenty of onscreen evidence to suggest that she worked her face more boldly when she could not speak. For instance, as Molly here Shearer has a vigorous gum-chewing habit that works very well. But it's hard to think of a talking picture where she feels as able to be as active. Again, when we first see Molly in *Lady of the Night*, it is a stark close-up in early morning light. The actress has only a little makeup, and the impression of a raw presence is startling and exciting. It suggests, too, that director Monta Bell—who did several pictures with her—was someone whose help she valued.

So this is a very effective melodrama—as played by TCM—it has a piano accompaniment by Jon Mirsalis which is proficient but routine. That tinkling piano and the color tinting of sequences seem to me debilitating "extras" in silent film that actually detract from the best things—like the black-and-white photography and the ability (clearly possessed by Bell) to give a quick, vividly composed shot, full of meaning, and to advance on it. But the sequencing here—the notion of dramatic development—never gets past the posing of essentially still shots and the taking up of brave close-up attitudes. In other words, silence stilled movement—in American films more than in European—and so Shearer is often left looking and feeling like a promising statue.

There's no question that Bell was a subtle director—but nothing to match *Applause* (which Bell produced and Rouben Mamoulian directed). So just as *Lady of the Night* increases one's interest in Shearer, still it points to a terrible limitation in the silent mode. The story is trite—as if the people working on the picture were still uncertain that it could be profound.

The Lady Vanishes (1938)

Although the prewar economics of a Gainsborough picture shot in Islington meant that many of the railway shots are toy trains, or a set on rockers, it's hard to argue that Alfred Hitchcock was encumbered or restricted at this stage of his career. Indeed, he had virtually pioneered the comedy suspense film and given a few hints already that—from his point of view—a big part of the fun was the way in which he could startle the suckers (us) and make them jump with "pure cinema." *The Lady Vanishes* has comedy or irony at so many of its sharpest points—a nun in high heels? a message fingered on a steamy window that will fade away? to say nothing of the idea of Michael Redgrave as some kind of musicologist swapping flirtatious insults with a very gutsy and sexy Margaret Lockwood (who said Hitch could only imagine doing it with blondes?).

Of course, there is an icy warning in this film—that even the most joyous English amateurism has no idea of just how deadly the mounting threat in Europe is. Sometimes, admirers claim that Hitchcock took his family off to America while still uncertain about what was going to happen in Europe. It's not possible to be so charitable after you've seen *The Lady Vanishes*, a picture that has no doubt about the German intent or the British vulnerability. Beneath the comedy and the despairingly fond regard for English eccentricity (especially in the Basil Radford and Naunton Wayne team, dreaming of cricket and hardly seeing the deadlier game), *The Lady Vanishes* is aghast at British complacency (the real butt of this attack is the Cecil Parker character, who can hardly believe he has been shot).

The script was by Sidney Gilliat and Frank Launder, who launched their own production team on the strength of it. It is deliciously organized, and it's a sign of how far Hitch himself always delighted in the crosscut from mystery to lucidity. He takes us on his ride with the teasing assurance that he can play us—for suckers first, and then smarties. And even in 1938, there was a kind of plot computer in Hitch's head that knew all stories had been told too many times before, and all referred to one another. In other words, intrigue is like a pack of cards in which every deal is fascinating and hard to bring home as a contract.

It's also notable that while Hitch is scathing of British dullness, he doesn't want to overthrow all the favored character types—so he relishes the notion of Dame May Whitty as a superspy, just as he appreciated the English capacity for game playing. Of course, there is real pain, too—sudden deaths, little bits of nastiness, and the real menace of Paul Lukas, quiet, polite, but too intelligent to be believed, and quite smart enough to pick English locks. Not that Hitch was single-minded about Germany: He had learned so much there and from the Mabusian atmosphere in Fritz Lang. But Hitch was also a comic, so as Lang and Hitchcock went to America, Hitch became a commercial genius, while Lang stayed desperately loyal to his cold art.

The Last Emperor (1987)

As a young man, and a friend of Pasolini's, Bernardo Bertolucci had been of the left wing. There must have been a time, therefore, if he had ever considered filming the Chinese Revolution, when his heroes would have been the great leaders, or even the people. Instead, in 1987, he made a true epic that rehabilitates a forgotten figure, Pu Yi, the child emperor, deposed as a young man, disgraced, and then put through the grind of thought reeducation, a nobody.

The Last Emperor won Best Picture, along with a chess set of other Oscars—and there's no doubt but that it does balance the personal and the national story with unusual delicacy. In that sense, it's the kind of epic that people say David Lean used to make, but which is actually so hard to find. What interests Bertolucci—who by now had emerged as far more the child of Freud than of Marx—was the indecision, the passivity, the powerlessness of Pu Yi. And by far the most beautiful passages of the film are those of his sexual education and later humiliation, as a figure so pampered that he hardly has identity, let alone character.

The great coup of the film (it was produced by Jeremy Thomas) was to gain access to the Forbidden City of Beijing, and there is no question about the magic of those scenes, and the extraordinary weight of history pushing upon Pu Yi. As a result, the rest of the film had no option but to maintain that very high level of décor. It does so, in a way that would delight the staff of any museum of Oriental arts. The fusion of camera style, with fresh-washed color (Vittorio Storaro), with the production design of Ferdinando Scarfiotti, Bruno Cesari, and Osvaldo Desideri and the ecstatic costumes of James Acheson amounts to a production value that is intoxicating, and which easily distracts one from the strange, wistful arc of the picture, which seems to sigh and say, "Poor Last Emperor."

It's not that his story isn't fascinating—and it's not that this nostalgic concentration on the "lost" (more than the last) isn't exactly in keeping with a reappraisal of the Bolshevik Revolution as the sad story of Anastasia. But the curiosity is that the very high style of *The Last Emperor* is easily mistaken for the verdict of history—so can a film that looks so good be wrong or irrelevant in its sympathies? Could Storaro and Scarfiotti be this good—this much themselves—re-creating the life of the peasantry?

The film was scripted by Mark Peploe and Bertolucci (with reference to the published autobiography of Pu Yi) and it is the story of a boy who becomes Bartleby, losing everyone and everything he ever enjoyed along the way, and hardly understanding the history he has figured in. John Lone is very appealing as Pu Yi, and it's clear that he felt the film was on his side. Joan Chen is very good as Wan Jung, his bride, and the whole sexual intrigue (involving Wen Hsiu and Kaige Chen—as the captain of the guard) is worthy of Sternberg, the model for the whole movie. Victor Wong is the grim interrogator, the only representative of the new order—absolutely excluded from the film's enchantment. Though Peter O'Toole exists in another private world for cyclists and seers as the British tutor.

The Last Laugh (1924)

Why is it called *The Last Laugh*, when the German title is *Der Letzte Mann*? Well, about 70 minutes in, the film admits that it should have ended there, with the doorman at the Hotel Atlantic reduced to the depths of humiliation. (And the film was shown at that length sometimes in Germany.) But then there's a coda in which fate takes a turn and the doorman (reduced to the status of lavatory attendant) becomes a millionaire simply because he inherits the fortune of a customer who dies in his arms. In other words, this very foreboding story of how fate can get you comes without cake, and with.

The film has an immense reputation in some history books, and there are good reasons for that. This is a landmark in fluent storytelling, in camera movements through elaborate sets, and even in the use of depth in the frame. But at some cost. Every piece of pioneering technique, alas, is offset by the antiquated concentration on humiliation, self-pity, and a style of acting that defies the naturalism of the camera technique.

So the hotel doorman (Emil Jannings) is too old to help lift the heaviest trunks. The manager sees this and quietly demotes the old man. Thus, he turns up for work next day to find a younger man in the job. Now, I suppose we are open to infinite cruelty in the hotels of Germany in the 1920s, but this line of action is very implausible, and it serves as the first instance of piling on. The doorman is monstrously pleased with himself at first—he is Emil Jannings, after all, and that seems to justify every lash the film serves up. He loses his job, his uniform, his makeup, his respect from his own family. And the great figure of the actor becomes stooped, shuffling, and very sorry for himself. He doesn't deserve it—and even if he did, are we ready to sit through so much attenuated torture?

I think it's true that screenwriter Carl Mayer controlled the film and suggested the naturalistic style. And director F. W. Murnau went along with it—often to stunning effect. The sets are seen cinematically, instead of as if for stage presentation. There are spaces beyond and within spaces. The very first shot has the camera coming down in an elevator. We believe we are in a hotel. The design by Robert Herlth and Walter Röhrig and the photography of Karl Freund enhance this and leave little need for titles. But then why is Jannings allowed to play in so old-fashioned and laborious a way? Played really quietly and inwardly (by Michel Simon, say), the doorman would be touching—but then he'd need more story, more home life, more substance. Murnau never made another film so emphatic or limited. As for Jannings, I suppose one had to be there—in the theater especially—to feel his power. As it is, he looks like a sacrificial victim, so it's easy enough to imagine some people dreaming of a comeuppance for him.

The Last of the Mohicans (1992)

One of the more neglected (or easily assumed) qualities of the Western is the physical commitment, the way in which largely unsupported human physiques had to stand up against the landscape, the weather, and the Iroquois hatchets. Time and again, Michael Mann gives us sumptuous shots of folds of mountains reaching into the distance. A novice might automatically think of the Rockies or the Sierra. But these hills are green and blue and mauve. They have eastern growth. They are "only" the hills of North Carolina. Yet it is a place in which, in 1826 (when James Fenimore Cooper published *The Last of the Mohicans*), a man, a family, a tribe, or a nation might have got lost.

We know Michael Mann now as a master of cityscapes, and above all Los Angeles at night—*Heat* and *Collateral* are unrivaled records of urban pleasure and disquiet. So it is proper to praise *The Last of the Mohicans* for the ecstatic locations—places where great action occurs, but places where the eye needs time and time again simply to revel in the narrow defile, the sheer slippery rock, the steepness of the place. And the immense, constant effort required of all men and women who seek to survive there.

But then you have to recall the athletic prowess of actors, above all the running and leaping that traverse these places, and the thud of moccasined feet on fresh earth. The sound throughout this picture is pristine, ominous, and beautiful; it is the deepest level of perception offered to the new land, and it is never marred by an exactly contemporary and poignant score (by Trevor Jones and Randy Edelman).

Magua (Wes Studi) is one of epic literature's fiercest villains, but we know that Mann respects Studi and likes him. So the exchange of looks between Studi and Jodhi May near the very end (just before she floats off into the abyss, like a sketch of waterfall) is so rich with hope and dread—it is a great moment, and so touching that Magua is hardly a villain anymore. He is a man who lives in this terrain, just like Hawkeye, Uncas, and Chingachgook. Indeed, the villains in Mann's mind are all those people—the soldiers, the settlers—who wear the wrong clothes for the terrain. That is not just stupidity but a failure in respect, and Mann knows that the great god of America was then and must be still not the kind of fellow who trades in stone tablets and Guides for Life, but Nature. I cannot praise this film enough or come closer to its spirit than to say it would not seem amiss if William Wordsworth passed by at some point, ducking astutely to avoid an arrow.

Daniel Day-Lewis and Madeleine Stowe convey a real sense of heat—I would have liked a moment in which the woman tossed off London clothes and made a costume out of nature. But the great truth in this Western—and it is something the genre too often avoided—is that it is a work of history, and of how America looked and felt in 1757.

The Last Picture Show (1971)

Thirty-seven years later, this feels like a great American debut (no matter that *Targets*, 1968, was actually Peter Bogdanovich's first feature film). So it's natural that Bogdanovich should bring his film historian's mind to bear: This is an update on what happened to the iconic Texas, just as the presence of Ben Johnson inhales some of the atmosphere of John Ford. More pointedly, there is a bittersweet contrast in the way the one movie house in this windswept town is closing down, and saying farewell with Howard Hawks's *Red River*. The extract we see is the dawn gathering before the cattle drive heads north. All too plainly, this new Texas lacks the exhilaration of that moment. The sweetness of legend has been replaced with heat and dust.

The film is adapted from a novel by Larry McMurtry, and he and Bogdanovich wrote the script together—with how much help from Bogdanovich's wife, Polly Platt, remains a fascinating question. It is also a coming-of-age story about kids in this arid world, helplessly devoted to thoughts of sex and love, and of the older generation, their parents, already crushed by the failure of the same hopes. So it is way beyond Ford or Hawks in its temperament. This is a French film made in the West, with few illusions and no concession to romance. People grow older here, but no one comes out of it too well. No wonder in 1971 if we rejoiced that a good film critic and historian was showing such touch.

It may be that everything fits a little too tidily—thus the discovery that the Ben Johnson character has had an affair with the Ellen Burstyn character—but this is small-town life, where the options are not crowded, and where memories linger in the strangest way. Indeed, here in 1971 was maybe the first Texas film anyone could recall that noted how small, mean, and provincial the place was.

And as if made under the sign of Renoir, *The Last Picture Show* is an ensemble piece: Timothy and Sam Bottoms are very good as the central brothers, the older one cursed by having to look after the kid; Jeff Bridges gives one of his key performances as Duane, the adventurous boy; Cloris Leachman is heartbreaking as the woman who grabs at a last chance of love, and feels better for once in the madness of it; Eileen Brennan is a delight; Ellen Burstyn delivers just the kind of extra class a bit of money allows in this world. Ben Johnson is immense as Sam the Lion, and the scene by the pond is among the great moments in American film. Then there is Cybill Shepherd as the daughter of the rich family—pretty, spoiled, and trouble.

It was nominated for Best Picture and Best Director, Johnson and Leachman won Supporting Actor Oscars. All earned. There was a sequel, *Texasville*, that was decent but minor. This is a great film, and its sadness has only mounted as Bogdanovich seems further away from matching it.

Last Tango in Paris (1972)

On a movie screen, vacant real estate can tip some people over the edge—especially if it's photographed by Vittorio Storaro and designed by Ferdinando Scarfiotti. And so, in 1972, one of the worst-dressed couples in modern film find themselves in the same empty space in Passy and they fuck. Except that since they do not actually discard those awful clothes, and since they go through the movie motions of sex, I'm not quite sure what is accomplished—or what the film as a whole is going to mean.

I feel I can start in this way because you all seem to know *Last Tango in Paris*, no matter that it predates *Star Wars* by a full five years. It was a sensation—which now gives it the burden of an ex-sensation. Some critics even proposed that it was the line in the sand dividing the saved from the unsaved. It is often presented as the Marlon Brando film that shows you what Brando longed to do if not just expected to be Marlon Brando all the time. Some people—even those who've seen it—still believe that it's the film in which two people really did it. To which one has to smile sadly and say, Oh no, people have worn clothes that bad and said silly things onscreen before. Indeed, there may be a mathematical bond between the two.

The real history of the picture is something one longs to know, and I suspect it begins in the special mixture of opportunism and real creative daring that is Bernardo Bertolucci. Coming off *The Conformist* (which is a great film, and deeply concerned with sexuality), he had some kind of notion for a man and woman who meet and exist for a few days as just a sexual couple. He wanted Jean-Louis Trintignant and Dominique Sanda, the couple from *The Conformist*, and people who seemed to register an unusual attraction and loathing onscreen. It was promising, though even in outline it seemed more important that they talked wonderfully than that they made us think people in a film had done it.

You see, people in a film are never going to convince us of that, even if the screen records pulse rates, nervous excitation, and sensory stimuli (all those wiggle lines beneath the writhing bodies). We think they are acting because we are watching—and we're right. But in talk, we can believe in people. The trouble with Marlon Brando and the long-suffering Maria Schneider (who is so much more interesting in *The Passenger*) is that we can't believe in a flicker of exchanged interest. Their whole thing is an assignment, and then you realize not only that Brando's sniff of interest changed the whole film, but that this may be the picture where he is really being Marlon Brando, hunching up in stupid self-pity and behaving like a jerk.

I am tough on the film because misunderstanding has championed it for far too long. There are great things—the décor, the framing, the occasional look of broken nobility in Brando, and the idea of strangers fucking. But it is hard to have two people onscreen for two hours and keep them as strangers. Great music by Gato Barbieri. Rather wishful use of Francis Bacon in the credits. Suggested retitle (*pace* O. J. Simpson): *If They Had Done It*.

Last Year at Marienbad (1961)

It was impossible to view *Hiroshima Mon Amour* without feeling the crisis of the world—not just the dread of world war, but the possibility of nuclear holocaust. That made for an earnestness, a respectability, a respect for the real, that was as gripping as the extreme formalism of the picture. So it came as a shock to many with *L'Année Dernière à Marienbad* that Alain Resnais was also fascinated by the rococo flourishes of a great eighteenth-century hotel, by the lavish costumes that Delphine Seyrig wore from one moment to the next, and even by the curl of her eyelashes that resembled the arc of the question mark in her every statement. Could Alain Resnais be this decorative?

So it was the more intriguing that there was a buried resemblance between these two opposite films. Just as in *Hiroshima,* a man and a woman haunted each other's steps, the one asking the other to remember that this had happened before, so in *Marienbad,* in the glassy hotel, the man suggests to the woman that they were there before, last year. It was as if the mood of *Hiroshima Mon Amour* had been extracted and served up again in a Douglas Sirk picture. But I think many viewers were disconcerted in 1961, and even led to doubt the gravity of *Hiroshima.* As a consequence, *Marienbad* has gone from being a sensation and a cult event to a film that is very little seen today. Alas.

The film was a collaboration between Resnais and Alain Robbe-Grillet, a notable novelist and soon to be a director in his own right. Robbe-Grillet's screenplay is very readable and ornate, but it is founded in his knowledge that the writer can only stimulate the cinematic process that "realizes" what the writer has suggested, "For instance, the author describes a conversation between two characters, providing the words they speak and a few details about the setting. If he is more precise, he specifies their gestures or facial expressions, but it is always the director who subsequently decides how the episode will be photographed, if the characters will be seen from a distance or if their faces will fill the whole screen, what movements the camera will make, how the scene will be cut etc."

So Resnais flowered where Robbe-Grillet was the ground, and he made a series of superbly cinematic renderings of the endless male questions to the woman. By contrast, Marguerite Duras (in *Hiroshima*) was far more drastic in defining action. Robbe-Grillet is a writer who objectifies all action in his intense, surface description of it. It was a beautiful match.

Sacha Vierny did the black-and-white Scope photography. Jacques Saulnier did the production design. Henri Colpi edited the film, and Francis Seyrig wrote the music. It was shot at the chateau of Nymphenburg, in Munich. Seyrig commands the picture as a swan does a still pond. The men are Giorgio Albertazzi and Sacha Pitoëff.

As an abstract film it is entrancing. But what is greater still is the subtle evocation of film as a process that exists in eternity—in other words, see the film more than once and its prior existence (last year) immediately becomes more meaningful.

Late Spring (1949)

It would be possible to write a book on the roles that actress Setsuko Hara played for Yasujiro Ozu. It is so much quicker, and more searching, to see the films. And that is a way of saying that these deceptively simple movies are prodigious in their complexity. Indeed, to watch *Late Spring* (the first they made together) is to enter into something like a novelistic process. In turn, novelists might answer that they would need more "action" or material than Ozu and his regular scenarist, Kogo Noda, provide. Not very much happens in *Late Spring* apart from the essentials. But as soon as you try to write down that outline, you realize the infinite range of the brief cutaways and the extraordinary power of cinema when Ozu is handling it.

Noriko (Hara), the daughter, lives with her widower father (Chishu Ryu). He is in his early fifties, she is in her midtwenties. She is attractive—but so is he, even if he has a little bit of the absentminded professor about him. They live in a house which we know from other Ozu films—a set of flat rectangular enclosures: It has the comfort of home, yet it is cramped and resembles a prison. Straightaway, we are asked to look at the house and its living drama—family life—and ask ourselves whether family is, simply, a fine thing, or an ambiguous institution.

Noriko does not seem interested in marrying, though she is friendly and fun with men. She is attached to her father—is this healthy, or not? An aunt (a frequent figure in Ozu, and blunter than his central characters) urges marriage and hints that the father has already started looking elsewhere. There is another woman in the father's life. They all attend a dramatic performance, and Noriko is plainly disturbed to see the interest between the other two. Is the father being selfish? Does he simply want to get the daughter out of the way? Is the daughter being immature and possessive, or is her realization of her love for her father unusually mature?

The daughter is edged into marriage, though she makes it clear that it is not what she prefers. We see it as a compromise, and we hope it will work out. And then we gather that the father has feigned interest in the other woman. He does not want to marry again. And after his daughter's marriage, he returns to the home, alone. He sits there and peels an apple and we feel that a great grief has come over him.

I have outlined the "action." Yet I'm not sure I have given away the story, for every viewer of this magical, very finely balanced film will take a different explanation of what has happened—and what we should think about it. Further, the synopsis is to be read in the full film against shots of the sea, of the trees, the trains—cutaways that place the action, along with the wistful music (by Senji Ito). Add in some of the great perfomances in film history, and *Late Spring* is the threshold of late Ozu, one of the most complex portraits of life we have to look at. But in Ozu the reciprocity of seeing and feeling was fraternal. The calm of the art should never mask the great inner turmoil.

Laura (1944)

Having had an uneasy patron-son relationship with Darryl F. Zanuck at Fox, Otto Preminger was given *Laura* to produce, with Rouben Mamoulian as his director—he even had Mrs. Mamoulian doing the famed portrait of Laura Hunt. Well, as shooting developed, Zanuck had complaints and somehow Otto managed to unload them at Mamoulian's door. "OK," said Zanuck to Otto, "you direct!" So he did, firing Mrs. Mamoulian's portrait along the way. If this all sounds like a little bit of Waldo Lydecker in the night, you are at least prepared for the high intelligence of *Laura* the movie and the way in which Clifton Webb makes Waldo Preminger's first tragic hero, nailed up on the cross of his own intelligence.

But in turn, that asks the question, What kind of movie is *Laura*? Well, it's a murder mystery, not just in terms of who did it, but even of who is the victim. The setup makes you think it's Laura Hunt. Dana Andrews is there from the start as the uncouth, depressive detective, a very important Preminger character and proof of his instinct for Andrews's rare moral lassitude. He's been fed so many stories about Laura that he's half in love with her before the magnificent set piece where he "lives" in her apartment at night, examining her underclothes, her perfume, and her letters, and finally lapsing into dream beneath that portrait (all of this to the David Raksin score—though Preminger had wanted Duke Ellington's "Sophisticated Lady").

And that's when the film really becomes a treat and very Preminger, for the detective now begins to hate his dream girl because she's so ordinary—the prediction of and comparison with *Vertigo* is uncanny and by no means in Hitchcock's favor. For Laura's noir look covers a comedy (the dialogue is brilliant) and a profound, nearly surreal romance in which desire is seen as more potent than any realization. And that's how and why Waldo—a connoisseur to the ferrule on the end of his cane—is really the center of the film, its sour heart as well as its best brain.

Moreover, as Andrews turns on Gene Tierney—because, in truth, she is a rather ordinary woman—he becomes a lot uglier. There's even a hint of a longing for torture in the grilling he gives her. The film ends up by wrapping them in love, but only with Waldo's flinching disdain. The critic Eugene Archer understood their real doom: "One can visualize their future—the tormented detective brooding into his liquor before the omnipresent portrait, while poor, unwitting Laura, the merest shell of his erotic fantasy, ponders her unhappy lot while washing his socks in the kitchen sink."

This is a masterpiece, so assured in its tricky style and its handling of Waldo (ramrod, but swish) that you wonder what brought Preminger to life just as you realize how complex his best films will be. The casting is as acute as the constant reframing of the camera in its resolve to keep as many people in frame as possible, including the vibrating spaces between them.

The Lavender Hill Mob (1952)

The starting point of *The Lavender Hill Mob* is when a man who wears a bowler hat meets a fellow given to bow ties. Already, in 1952, this spoke volumes about class and pretension, and it was a meeting of opposites enough to justify the word *mob* in the title, quite apart from any tongue-in-cheek allusions to American crime films in which breaking the law was like sex. In most British films, crime is just a Sunday outing.

Apparently Michael Balcon had asked T. E. B. Clarke to do a serious film about gold thieves. But Clarke was a man unto himself, born in 1907, Charterhouse and Cambridge, and dodging the rest of that career to become a *Daily Sketch* journalist and then a screenwriter. He did the fascinating *Champagne Charlie* for Cavalcanti; he then did *Hue and Cry, Passport to Pimlico*, and *The Blue Lamp* before *The Lavender Hill Mob.* Later on, when Ealing's little England movies had become more studied, he did *The Titfield Thunderbolt.* But he won an Oscar for original story and script on *The Lavender Hill Mob,* and he gave south London something to cheer about—its salubrious neighborhoods are not often celebrated in pictures (Julia Roberts did *Notting Hill,* not *Tooting Broadway*).

Well, the bowler hat and the bow tie have a naughty plan. The bowler hat belongs to a bank clerk who feels taken for granted. He sees a way to free the banking system of a quantity of bullion. Bow Tie then fancies that the gold can be rechanneled in the form of Eiffel Tower souvenirs. The subject became a comedy, and it sprang to life once Alec Guinness was cast as Bowler Hat and Stanley Holloway as Bow Tie. When I say that their little gang is augmented by Sidney James and Alfie Bass, I am talking perfection. Now four English types were together: the humble, the spiv, the rogue, and the straight. You can work out which is which—and although this film regards the enemy forces of law and order with generous indifference, you could see the same setup working as a resistance story too, resistance to being taken for granted. Years later, on TV, *Dad's Army* was a beloved hit show that worked on the same sly dynamic.

And Ealing could roll out the talent then: Charles Crichton directed and helped secure his reputation for subversive humor; Douglas Slocombe photographed it; and the young Seth Holt was the editor. There is even Audrey Hepburn in a walk-on part.

The Lavender Hill Mob was one of those films that impressed the world with English spirit as much as its humor. And it stands up very well. In the same year, *The Quiet Man* took a similarly fanciful view of the charm of the Irish. It stands up less well, and is somewhere between condescending and cloud-cuckoo. But *The Lavender Hill Mob* trusts Guinness's ability to bring distinction to a comedy by the simple process of acting as if in a serious film. This is and was the trick to Guinness and to a special kind of Englishness.

Lawrence of Arabia (1962)

It's tempting to argue that more than forty years ago, pitched midway between the Suez "affair" and the Six-Day War, *Lawrence of Arabia* could be forgiven for being a certain glance at history through English eyes. And so, more or less, the thrust of the movie is, My word! Just see how far one English eccentric could alter the history of the world! That's us Brits for you. And thus, T. E. Lawrence is presented as a mystery man, mercurial, ungraspable, a show-off yet shy, and almost as much a riddle to Robert Bolt and David Lean as he is to Jack Hawkins's Allenby at the memorial service early in the film. And in so many ways, Peter O'Toole's flamboyant, staring-eyed performance is a diversion from asking useful questions about Lawrence. Indeed, it takes refuge in O'Toole's frequent stance—well, isn't everyone a bit of a ham if you scratch the surface?

In which case, it's useful to spend a moment or two studying the real T. E. Lawrence: short, rather plain, stubborn-looking, reflective, but clerical. Alec Guinness is maybe the natural casting, and Guinness did play Lawrence on stage once. But in Lean's scheme of history he has to make do with being a silky saturnine Arab prince in *Lawrence of Arabia,* a warning sign of how little interest the film was prepared to show in Arab feelings, let alone the Arab point of view.

There may be patriotic defenders of Lean already reaching for their scimitars. So let me say that with Robert Bolt's schoolmasterly script (and Michael Wilson's help), with Sam Spiegel's great determination as a producer, and with the inescapable chemistry of desert and camera, *Lawrence* is spectacular enough to pass for a thinking man's epic (without the thought). Unfortunately for that argument, Otto Preminger had made *Exodus* two years earlier, managing to ignore the easy trick of desert "splendor" and grasping (Preminger was Jewish) that that part of the world was politics and then more politics, a place where everyone believes they are right and blessed and where everyone has behaved very badly when the opening occurred.

Lean and his cameraman, Freddie Young, did some things very well: the match light that gives way to immense desert; the prolonged arrival of the Omar Sharif character, as somewhere between magic and mirage; the raid on trains; the reverse angle attack on Aqaba. And then there is the music (by Maurice Jarre), which I find hackneyed and stately, but which many people think of highly. Certainly it is conducive to the leisurely epic that unfolds.

But in the end, I find O'Toole insufferably swish without ever really examining homosexuality. I despise the casting of Guinness and Anthony Quinn as Arabs (Jose Ferrer as a Turk is in the same line). And I lament that in this day and age the film gives very little insight as to how modern Iraq came into being—we need more of Claude Rains's character. (*A Dangerous Man,* 1990, with Ralph Fiennes, covered that far better.) Still, it had ten nominations and seven Oscars, including Best Picture. My guess is that already the reputation hovers like the desert sun over the shell of an empty film, one where the interest has evaporated. Ah, the desert! How fortunate England was to be spared such wastelands and their astonishing metaphorical value.

Leave Her to Heaven (1945)

It was not the kind of part Gene Tierney expected to be given—Ellen Berent in *Leave Her to Heaven,* taken from the novel by Ben Ames Williams, a portrait of a beautiful but dementedly selfish young woman. It was what Tierney herself saw as a "bitch" part, the kind of role Bette Davis played. And Tierney hoped she wasn't like that. But something in her made her go up to Darryl Zanuck at a party and tell him that if he gave her the part he wouldn't regret it. She was right. She is amazing as Ellen, in ways she never matched before or since. What does it mean? Well, you could point to the fact that in time Gene Tierney had serious nervous breakdowns of her own—there were great strains that went with being one of the loveliest women in the world, and she gave birth to a retarded child. But I'm not sure that was it. Let's just say that in any actress there builds slowly—and sometimes very politely—the energy that knows how to murder people.

Leave Her to Heaven is actually rather more than a "bitch" movie—it's a mad goddess creation. Because Ellen has something in her that doesn't quite see or admit her own calculations. She's like so many of us, not objectively privy to her own bouts of unreason. And that's the way *Leave Her to Heaven* is played. Jo Swerling did a very good script in which we never quite lose all sympathy with Ellen—no matter that one of her victims is a sick child, allowed to drown in a lake (Bass Lake in northern California) in quite hideous circumstances. That Ellen should still be understandable owes a lot to the Swerling script, to Tierney's natural warmth, and to John M. Stahl's direction. He seemed an old man to Tierney (he was fifty-eight!), and he was a master of silent films and of women's pictures from the sound era.

Beyond that, this is a very fine example of Technicolor as a source of unruly passion—the colors of hair, lipstick, and skin are like paint (as they nearly were in the Technicolor dye transfer system). If ever you need a proof of how Technicolor fueled films, this is the one to quote. The camerawork was done by Leon Shamroy, a true master, and he won an Oscar for it. The design was by Lyle Wheeler, and it involves some luxurious and spacious country houses as well as a staircase down which Ellen throws herself at one point.

The supporting cast includes Cornel Wilde (rather out of his depth), Jeanne Crain, Vincent Price, Mary Philips, Ray Collins, Gene Lockhart, Reed Hadley, Darryl Hickman, and Chill Wills.

Tierney was nominated for an Oscar as Best Actress, and she lost to Joan Crawford in *Mildred Pierce.* You can see why: Crawford had more than paid her dues; she had made a serious comeback; and *Mildred Pierce* is a valuable and important picture. But if you want a wild thrill one night, I know which way I'd go.

Leaving Las Vegas (1995)

Talk about moments. At one point in *Leaving Las Vegas*, Ben (Nicolas Cage) and Sera (Elisabeth Shue) go to a desert motel for a tryst. They watch television in the middle of the night in the open air by the pool: it's *The Third Man*. Why? The rights were free, said Mike Figgis, director; it was a favorite, and, "I also loved the idea of that zither theme in the desert mixing with crickets and coyotes."

In the middle of the buoyant 1990s, *Leaving Las Vegas* was the sort of film they were not supposed to be making. It was a film about alcoholism and hooking, uncompromising in its ugliness and sublimely without any concession to healing or conversion. This drunk starts the film as a screenwriter still in Hollywood, still recognized as a screenwriter. He seems at a low point. But he will get no higher—except for winning the love of a Las Vegas hooker who hasn't yet grasped all the dangers of being a freelance, of a certain age, with a self-destructive streak and insane hopes of making something better of herself.

This is a story of savage downward arcs, with a redemptive value of nil. It was shot on Super 16 mm, on a very tight budget. But it only cost $4.4 million and it would gross $31.9 million in the United States alone because there were enough people around ready to concede that this is the greatest Hollywood picture ever made about alcoholism and addiction.

Mike Figgis had been around for several years doing interesting work, often working on the music himself. But this was a breakthrough film with an intensity he has never regained. It came from an autobiographical novel by John O'Brien—who killed himself after selling the movie rights. Figgis did the script himself and then went on location with the crew. Declan Quinn did the photography—it's not hard to make Vegas at night look spectacular, but there are so many other darker moods here. Waldemar Kalinowski did the design, and Laura Goldsmith did the clothes—Sera's costumes are especially notable, "sexy" but repressed, too, and trying to hide a small weight problem. Figgis did the music and was part of a jazz ensemble playing it. There were also several songs sung by Sting and one, "Ridiculous," by Nicolas Cage.

Both lead players were nominated, and Cage won the Oscar—not unexpectedly, for his part is the showier of the two. But it is a true case of joint acting. The risks and the glories are shared, and Figgis deserves great credit for earning their trust on a small venture. Shue has never had such a chance again, while Cage is as flagrant with his talent as Ben is with life.

The picture is crammed with excellent small performances, or presences: from Lou Rawls and Xander Berkeley as two cabbies to Graham Beckel, Danny Huston, and Julian Lennon as three bartenders, and Figgis, Kalinowski, and Ed Lauter as three heavies. Also with Richard Lewis, Valeria Golino, Carey Lowell, Julian Sands, Vincent Ward, Mariska Hargitay, Laurie Metcalf, and Bob Rafelson.

The Leopard (1963)

If you want to know how the Sicilian aristocracy dressed and had dinner in the 1860s, this is the film for you—and I do not mean that facetiously. For what is most remarkable about *Il Gattopardo* is that the film's eye for table settings, porcelain, the color of the wines, and the costume of the ladies is only as strict and admiring as that of the film's central character, Don Fabrizio, Prince of Salina, the monarch of melancholy. He is Burt Lancaster to the eye, but in all other ways he is a surrogate for that duke of Modrone, Luchino Visconti himself.

Yes, it is Sicily again, but an island where the film is only interested in the wealthiest inhabitants, and the mixed feelings with which they are bound to observe the political process called the unification of Italy. Does it sustain for a film of 205 minutes—the proper length of *The Leopard,* despite several shorter versions with degrees of dubbing—or is it more realistically an attempt on the part of the director to imagine that he is there, being rained upon by every moment?

With Goffredo Lombardo as his producer, Visconti adapted the novel by Giuseppe Tomasi di Lampedusa, with the help of Suso Cecchi d'Amico, Pasquale Festa Campanile, Enrico Medioli, and Massimo Franciosa. Time and again, Visconti—and Italian cinema as a whole—employed this screenwriting by committee. And it's hard to guess what was done on *The Leopard* beyond the fond transcription of the novel, along with the studious researching of any bit of protocol, décor, and mannerism. The Technicolor photography is justifiably famous, and it was the work of Giuseppe Rotunno. The music was by Nino Rota.

It was a casting coup when Burt Lancaster was hired in to be the old aristocrat, and it's not that he does a bad job. What is more striking is the way Visconti himself has shifted so much in regard to his own work so that the would-be revolutionary is now a connoisseur of the manifestations of a dying order. Lancaster is handsome and elegant. He moves with nobility (he always did). But there are the beginnings of that camp regret in his feelings that will prove catastrophic with Dirk Bogarde in *Death in Venice.*

The Leopard won the prize at Venice in 1963, and its long version has a deserved reputation for style and detail. But in the end this is no more than *Masterpiece Theatre* made by a heartfelt conservative who can hardly accommodate the loss given up to history. The rest of the cast includes Alain Delon, Claudia Cardinale, Paolo Stoppa, Rina Morelli, Serge Reggiani, Romolo Valli, and Leslie French. The people move to order, like figures in a dance that the prince is observing. His artistic eye has so little awareness that his etiquette is as severe a restriction on liberty as poverty or the climate of Sicily. It's worth stressing that after *The Leopard,* Visconti moved increasingly—and without irony—into the self-protected worlds of solitary men of taste.

The Letter (1940)

It is a great opening, and vital evidence. On a rich tropic night somewhere in the Malay jungle (with the rubber trees oozing), shots ring out. A man staggers down the steps of a house pursued by a woman in a flowing housecoat. She puts six bullets into him and you know that if there had been more bullets in the gun he would have got all of those, too. She is Leslie Crosbie, the respectable wife of a leading English planter. Even with six bullets in the middle of the night, the authorities believe the matter can be dealt with. The man had just called by on a friendly visit and then he turned ugly. But there is a letter, from her, begging him to come.

At Warners, on the eve of *The Letter*, Joseph Breen warned the studio that it could hardly be done with decency. There was all that implied sex, there was a Chinese mistress, and the English would be offended. The Somerset Maugham play had been filmed in 1929, with Jeanne Eagels, and it had been a scandal. But producer Robert Lord and production head Hal Wallis were eager to do it again—and to have Bette Davis as Leslie Crosbie. The excellent Howard Koch was put on the script, and he turned the Chinese mistress into a Eurasian wife. For the rest, everyone very sensibly recognized that the sex was not required onscreen—just get the night and the weeping trees, clouds scurrying over the moon, Max Steiner's music, and Bette Davis's pinched, greedy face. It would work.

William Wyler came over on loan to do it. He wanted longer and more rehearsal than the studio could allow. He was a very deliberate worker. But he did the necessary thing: He entered into an affair with Davis. I am not being unkind, I think, in saying the film needed that—as many films did and do. For it all depended on Davis, and she needed a director to reassure her that this was not just trash but tragedy. It is a close-run thing. *The Letter* remains a great, bursting melodrama of the sort that hinges upon censorship saying you can't show the sex—and so the desire builds out of all proportion and it becomes a study in yearning and the way desire can wreck every civilized system.

Of course, the crime comes at the start, and the rest is the maneuvers that follow. But this is where the movie most excels. Herbert Marshall is the forlorn husband, taking Leslie for granted still. And James Stephenson is her lawyer, a man half in love with her until he realizes the loathing she deserves. So much of the best of the film is in Stephenson's way of watching her. And then you have Gale Sondergaard, in Chinese costume, as the widow taking her revenge.

Wyler wanted Gregg Toland to do the photography, but too much deep focus might have looked studied and in 1940 he had another job. So Tony Gaudio stepped in and did fine. Pauline Kael once observed that Steiner's music vulgarized Wyler's direction, but I think it just added the right juicy ooze. Wyler, Davis, Stephenson, and the picture were all nominated for Oscars.

Letter from an Unknown Woman (1948)

In 1946, Joan Fontaine married her second husband, producer William Dozier. They were eager to work together and came upon a Stefan Zweig novella, *Brief Einer Unbekannten*. Set in nineteenth-century Vienna, it's a woman's story of three meetings she has with a man: an encounter as a teenager; a one-night stand a few years later; and a final meeting where she writes him a letter telling her story. Of course, he does not remember her. It was not a simple part, in its progression from teenage years to maturity, but Fontaine was a very accomplished actress, and she felt she could do it.

How easily the project could have gone astray. Yet every decision was sure. They went to John Houseman to serve as producer—he had had his own fling with Joan earlier and he was devoted to her. Howard Koch was hired to do the screenplay (an old Mercury associate of Houseman's), and it was Koch who asked the others to see *Liebelei*, with a view to securing Max Ophüls as director. At that time, Ophüls had just had his ruinous experience on *Vendetta*, and he jumped at the Zweig material and saw it as the opportunity for his greatest picture.

They were filming at Universal, but they managed to have Franz Planer for the photography (he had shot *Liebelei*) and Alexander Golitzen to do the sets. There was some attempt to get Charles Boyer for the male lead, but he was unavailable and a little too old, so they cast Louis Jourdan instead in his signature performance—handsome yet a touch empty; romantic yet not entirely there. Houseman felt he lacked sex appeal, but that shortcoming serves very well as his defect of memory.

According to Houseman, Ophüls worked like a demon on the picture. He established a very good relationship with Fontaine, even though they hardly shared a language, and he took immense pains to correct and enhance the sets, as only someone who loved the Viennese tradition could. So this is the re-creation of a bittersweet city, perfectly attuned to the heartbreak of the central character, a place where we hear long dresses swish on marble stairs but the camera soars above the figures in angelic silence.

Of course, for Ophüls, movement was like life, and one reason for his attention to the sets was that they were places that a tracking, craning camera would have to work. At the climax of the film, he planned what Houseman calculated as a three-minute tracking shot, with many extras, the flying in and out of some décor, and an immense amount of rehearsal. Furthermore, Houseman feared that Ophüls meant to do it all without coverage or mercy. But he achieved the shot and then did two cover close-ups to appease Houseman. When the scene was cut, the close-ups allowed it to be half its length—but the exhilaration of the movement was there, and it feels like flight in the short life of a bird or a lover. This could be one of the great Viennese movies, and it's a thrill to think that it is in so many ways American.

Liebelei (1932)

As you follow the history of movie romance, you have to go through the years of strenuous silent proclamation—they are saying their hearts are broken. And then, in 1932, you get *Liebelei*—when you notice that your own heart has split. It is a story of two dragoon officers in Vienna before the Great War—they are played by Wolfgang Liebeneiner and Willi Eichberger. One night at the opera, they meet two pretty girls when the girls drop a pair of opera glasses from a box—they are Magda Schneider and Luise Ullrich. The one officer, Liebeneiner, is ending an awkward affair with another man's wife. He feels free as he finds out what real love can be with Christine (Schneider).

This comes from a story by Arthur Schnitzler, and it was adapted for the screen by Curt Alexander and Hans Wilhelm. As photographed by Franz Planer, this is a Vienna of nighttime or twilight, and there is an intoxicating intimacy to the way the quartet of young lovers drink and carouse together. They are officers and nice girls but the suggestion of regular sex is unmistakable—and I should say in all of this that Luise Ullrich (the blonde of the pair) is actually the more vivacious of the two girls.

Max Ophüls films them as if no one has been in love before—the very touching is stroked by the camera. There is a superb nocturnal sleigh ride in the snow, to be set beside a similar scene in *The Magnificent Ambersons*, and there is an altogether astonishing and timeless fluency in the ways moments are shot. Of course, fate intrudes. The jealous husband from the dead affair (Gustaf Gründgens) demands a duel of honor—and then Ophüls films that with just the other officer and his girl hearing the first shot and waiting for the second.

Magda Schneider (the mother of Romy Schneider) was a popular favorite, and she gets to sing as well as deliver a tragic speech when Christine has heard the worst news. It's almost the only failure in the film: a set piece for a star rather than a real, trembling response to life. Decades later, *Liebelei* hinges on the duel and its code of honor, and I think more could be made of that—even of a couple who went on the run from society, rather than submit to the archaic rulings on what has to be done.

Liebelei was made on the eve of Hitlerian success. Famously, Ophüls and his family had to leave Berlin as the film opened. Ironically, it was a great hit, enough to launch a big career. But Ophüls was on the run from very early on, and there is never anything as touching in his films as the eagerness (and then the fear of loss) with which lovers rush together. One way or another, Ophüls would not get back to "his" Vienna until *Letter from an Unknown Woman*.

The Life and Death of Colonel Blimp (1943)

Michael Powell was one of those deliberately naughty boys who had been daring rebuke all his life. So don't mistake the recklessness of doing *Peeping Tom* in 1960—just see it as part and parcel with offering *Blimp* in 1943 (and expecting the world to turn around for him in 1980,as it did—even the world has taste sometimes).

In the summer of 1945, when the Labour Party was elected to run the country (just months after parades to celebrate Churchill), many in the electorate were voting against "Blimpishness" in Britain. Blimp was a cartoon character created by David Low, an elderly military officer who believed in the old pre-1914 world, and in war by the Marquess of Queensberry rules. He was a High Tory archetype (you can read the tough version of the old boy in Evelyn Waugh's wartime trilogy, *Sword of Honor*). In the film, Blimp is honorable, kindly, decent, but helplessly old-fashioned. In truth, he probably believed in capital punishment, keeping the wogs in their place, flogging homosexuals, and a little charity for the poor. Powell and Emeric Pressburger do not stress the latter attitudes, but this is their hero for 1943. And their loyalty hurt. Churchill opposed the film and war shortages caused 40 minutes to be chopped out on first release.

That rationing brutalized the fond flashback structure Pressburger had devised, and thus the film on first release lost a great deal of its subtlety and warmth on two big gaps: that between Germanic and Anglo-Saxon; and that between the young and the old—you could just as easily throw in the ocean between the sexes in Powell's films, and the yearning scrutiny of every horizon, waiting for a redhead.

What emerges is a period piece, showing the losses of the first forty years of the twentieth century—not just the casualties, but the decline in manners and class loyalty. It is a tale of friendship between Clive Candy (Roger Livesey—it was to have been Olivier, but he could never have been warm enough) and Theo Kretschmar-Schuldorff (Anton Walbrook—a Viennese Jew as one of Powell's favorite, modest fascists).

As a drama, it is the most intricate the Archers ever tried: It really needs its length, just as it depends on two refugees—Georges Périnal and Alfred Junge—for its look. Its proper length is 163 minutes, and there it stands like a gentle rebuke to the carelessness that can allow war, or forget the deep bonds in friendship or the necessary adjustment in tolerance as we grow older.

The film has been restored and reminds me of another statement in this book: that in any war we hope to be on the side that made *To Be or Not To Be*—or *Blimp*. The friendship compares with the bond between Stroheim and Pierre Fresnay in *La Grande Illusion*. The French film, finally, is stronger because it knows one man may have to kill the other. But you could do only good by playing the two films together. Deborah Kerr plays several female roles, and you can feel the effect she had on Powell. Also with Roland Culver, James McKechnie, Albert Lieven, Ursula Jeans, and John Laurie.

Life and Nothing But (1990)

Sometimes actors who work from habit with the same directors pick up a way of speaking from their auteurs. It is nothing as direct as imitation or flattery. Rather, it is the simple equation of being. As the actor puzzles over his nature and direction, how can he mistake or be betrayed by the voice of his director? And so, now that Philippe Noiret is dead, it is easier to hear the eccentricity and the moral earnestness of Bertrand Tavernier in the actor's onscreen voice. Actors are like flowers, helpless beneficiaries of the rain and the rhythm that falls on their soil.

It is 1920, on one of the old battlefields. It is all a farmer can do plowing a field not to kill himself on a buried mine. There is a commission of graves and inquiry, and a major (Noiret) is its leading clerk—tracking as best he can the 350,000 missing soldiers, assessing corpses against photographs. Meanwhile, the official France is looking for the ideal corpse (for a ceremony at the Arch of Triumph) to be the "unknown soldier"—just make sure he's not German, British, or American. The dead have so many embraces in their informal burial.

Somehow it is characteristic of Tavernier that he should approach the history of the Great War—and he is, so often, a historian—from the perspective of the aftermath. The war goes on, though. Gas pellets are released. There are explosions. The relatives come in droves searching for any signs of confirmation. And the major becomes involved with two women: the ex-schoolteacher in the village (Pascale Vignal), searching for a lover, and an aristocratic woman who is looking for the remains of her husband (Sabine Azéma). He begins to wonder if the two women aren't searching for the same man.

Life and Nothing But has echoes of other Great War films—of *Paths of Glory*, especially, in a final singsong sequence where Tavernier feels far more hope than Kubrick heard. And it is true to Tavernier's misanthropic romanticism that a strange affection blooms between the major and the aristocratic woman. Moreover, the skill with which such things are seen in terms of the impromptu hotel arrangements and the starkly verdant fields is what makes the body of the film.

Noiret is an officer in his own army, too severe, too moral to belong to the official army. He is wonderfully expressive as a man who is both shy and romantic—and surely that's where Tavernier's own voice comes from. Noiret did so many roles for Tavernier, and for French film as a whole. He is a Spencer Tracy figure, and the major here is one of those roles that led him toward his own outsider nature. In the end, too, I think Tavernier is right. Battle scenes are so often misleading—heroic, tragic, but momentary. The slow, patient, and very awkward business of digging up the bodies can tell us so much more. Especially when a director sees how a gentle sidelight of love story is creeping into the scene.

The Life of Emile Zola (1937)

As Warner Brothers took it upon themselves to save French history from obscurity, they had the unfortunate experience of discovering that members of the Dreyfus family were still alive. And when they saw the script for this film, they had in all conscience to admit that Lucie Dreyfus's (Gale Sondergaard) stirring speech to Zola (Paul Muni) to take up the case never actually happened. Warners were not perturbed or made any the wiser. They knew that it *should* have occurred, and thus scenario triumphed over history; the screenwriters won Oscars, and Best Picture was awarded to this enjoyable but bogus affair.

How do we now reconcile ourselves to what happened, or to this, from the Warner Brothers files (it comes from the story editor): "Now, while it is true that our picture is exceptionally true to the spirit, the background, the meaning of Zola's character, life and times, it is also true that—but, only after learning the facts—we took great liberties in other respects. . . . Briefly, the picture of Zola has little in common with accurate chronology or factual history . . ." On the one hand, you can smile at the willful deceit and the hubris that saw "spirit" as meaning more than "facts." You can say it was only a movie. Though then you must at least understand that *The Life of Emile Zola* was a very prestigious set of lies—that's what Best Picture does for you. And then you have to admit, seventy years later, the helpless ignorance in educated Americans about history and the damage that can do to current events.

The studio liked the idea of *Emile Zola* because it was High Art, Paul Muni, and Relevant for Today. And Warner Brothers was probably the only studio in 1937 that would have been willing to charge anti-Semitism in the Dreyfus case. They also loved to do the art direction for the past, and they were always searching for such parts for Muni—*The Story of Louis Pasteur* had been a hit the year before.

So Henry Blanke (a good man) was the producer and William Dieterle was the director. The studio bought Matthew Josephson's book, *Zola and His Time,* and they entrusted the script to Norman Reilly Raine, Heinz Herald, and Geza Herczeg. The script is elementary and clichéd both as history and drama, and it bears out in every detail Hal Wallis's instruction to the makeup department: Make sure Muni still looks like Muni, despite the three-hour makeup session he has every day.

And we see Zola making his name with *Nana* (actually he had been famous years earlier) and meeting a real Nana; getting through the Franco-Prussian war; having visits from Cézanne (Vladimir Sokoloff); and finally doing the Dreyfus case. Anton Grot designed it. Tony Gaudio shot it. Max Steiner did the music. Joseph Schildkraut won a supporting Oscar as Dreyfus, and the cast also includes Gloria Holden (as Zola's wife), Morris Carnovsky as Anatole France, Louis Calhern as Major Dort, and Grant Mitchell as Clemenceau.

The Life of Oharu (1952)

It is a symbol, perhaps, or a measure of artistic nature. But quite early on in this film, Oharu, the young daughter of a samurai, meets a young page, Katsunosuke. The two make love, but are seen and stopped. Theirs is a fatal crime against caste: Katsunosuke is beheaded and Oharu is sent into exile. The time is 1686, in Kyoto. But the film is 1952, and Katsunosuke is Toshiro Mifune, the sensation of Akira Kurosawa's recent *Rashomon*, winner of a prize at Venice in 1951. Older and nettled, Kenji Mizoguchi now set out to make a film that would surpass *Rashomon*, and to that end he chose Kurosawa's star actor for a big love scene and early departure. It was a gesture toward Kurosawa, to be sure, but far more it was Mizoguchi's indication that he was more interested in making a film about women. Not only were such stories sadder; they had a far greater capacity for revealing the terrible travail of Japan.

In fact, the film opens twenty years or so later than this incident. Oharu is fifty and a prostitute—her fate is settled. It is in seeing imagery in a temple that she sets off on the several flashbacks that make up the film. A fascinating comparison can be made with the form of Ophüls's *Lola Montès* (just a few years later). Spelling out the incidents of Oharu's life makes her tragedy clear—but it shows how far, like Lola, she has become an actress or a self-performer.

She is hired to provide Matsudaira with a son—and then she is banished again for having tired the lord.

She has to work as a courtesan to give her father money—but she is fired for being too proud.

She marries and she is happy, but her husband is killed by thieves.

Living in a convent, she seduces a man in return for dress material.

She becomes a prostitute and is mocked for her age and ugliness.

She is sick. She learns that her father has died. But that long-ago son has become the lord—perhaps she can live with him. But then she is told she is the shame of the clan. She can see her son once, from a safe distance, and then she must go away again.

As acted by Kinuyo Tanaka, Oharu is an emblem of the abused state of woman in Japan. But this is more than long-suffering and endurance. Mizoguchi has made his heroine desirous and desirable. She always wants to fall in love. She never accepts the rules that condemn her, or hides her nature. She is a figure ready to give and receive love. Taken from a much more ironic novel, by Ihara Saikaku, this is one of the great Mizoguchi films, in which every situation is described in terms of deep focus, camera movement, and a world made by décor. It is a series of acts building to tragedy, but Oharu is not beaten or subdued. At the end, she is still in motion, a degree or so more resilient than Lola Montès even.

Lilith (1964)

If *The Hustler* was sharpened by Robert Rossen's illness, did *Lilith* flower with his dying? Not that the film has too many defenders—is it still the case that not many have seen it? Warren Beatty is known for disliking it, and even as good a critic as Andrew Sarris reckons it is as pretentious as profound. Alas—suppose Ingmar Bergman had made it, or François Truffaut, by which I mean one of those directors famous for his mad women, and not afraid of the asylum.

Beatty must have known what he was being lined up for. Although the novel (by J. R. Salamanca) begins with his character, Vincent, coming to a mental hospital as a new nurse, the title of the project made it clear that the number one female patient, Lilith Arthur, was the film's subject, as immediate as Jean Seberg yet as legendary as the name.

The screenplay was done by Rossen and Robert Alan Aurthur. For the second time, Eugen Shüfftan was in charge of the photography, and the design was credited to Richard Sylbert and Gene Callahan. These talents are vital, for the film has to make the asylum into a credible reality as large as the world.

Beatty's grievance may have come from the bond Rossen had to build with Seberg. How do you take on this subject without making a kind of rapture with your actress? This is Jean Seberg with long hair, never lovelier and never acting better. And there are complex dialogue scenes between Lilith and Vincent in which Seberg takes just about every point, reducing Beatty to his collected gestures of uncertainty and hesitation as a feeble response.

Seen today, the film is remarkable for the prescience of its casting: It's not just the excellent, vigilant Kim Hunter as Vincent's wary employer; or Peter Fonda as a disturbed patient; it's also a desperately tense Gene Hackman as one of Vincent's friends; Jessica Walter, James Patterson, Anne Meacham, and Rene Auberjonois in an overall cast that could be an Actors Studio party.

Of course, Lilith is a femme fatale, woman the devourer, a feminist godhead at a time when many men in film were fiercely addicted to the defense of manhood. I do not rule this out as a reason for the box-office failure of the film and its general critical neglect. So let me end, and urge you to see the film, with this from Jean Seberg:

"*Lilith* was for me at first the chance to try, in America, something in which I believed deeply with someone whom I esteemed very much; this film allowed me at last to leave my usual character, to do something other than what people usually proposed to me. That is to say in what degree the financial failure of the film affected us, Robert Rossen, who was already very ill, as well as me. We had truly given the best of ourselves, and that, for an empty theater. So *Lilith* was for me at once the most exciting of my experiences as an actress, and something rather sad."

Limelight (1952)

By the time he reached *Limelight*, Chaplin was in an autobiographical, and self-pitying, mode. And so this very strange story of an aging comedian who fears he has lost his touch contains long, intemperate discussions on the fickleness of the audience, without seeming to realize that a teary movie has stretched out to 143 minutes of old-fashioned melodrama.

His name is Calvero and he lives on film sets, though there is an attempt to place him in the London of Chaplin's own youth. As if drawn by his own melancholy, he notices that his neighbor, a young dancer named Terry, has tried to kill herself. So he saves her and then nurses her through some weird kind of nervous paralysis. The actress he cast as Terry was Claire Bloom, and everyone in the world noticed the striking resemblance between Bloom and Chaplin's latest wife, Oona O'Neill. Then as Chaplin talked to Bloom, endlessly, about the backstory of the film, it became all too clear to the actress that she was a stand-in for Chaplin's mother, Hannah. In real life, she had gone mad, but in *Limelight* Chaplin was trying to tell himself a story in which he rescued her.

As if to underline the family ties, Chaplin found parts for most of his children, and he blithely incorporated speeches on many of his growingly grumpy attitudes about the modern world. Of course, it is still Chaplin, whose astonishing history commands not just respect, but interest. No one had so represented the movies like Chaplin. On the other hand, the self-pity is suffocating, and far too much of the sentiment now seems funnier than the set pieces of comedy—it's not for nothing that the film is sometimes called *Slimelight*.

Bloom observed that Chaplin treated her like a parent with a child, lecturing her on every aspect of life, and then expecting her to deliver complete imitations of his actions. There was so little room for her own talent. And in the famous "reunion" with Buster Keaton in the final benefit show, it is plain that Keaton has no option but to do as he is told. Of course, he was in no other position, whereas Chaplin was still making a movie according to his own whims.

None of this is any excuse for what happened to *Limelight*. The feelings against Chaplin in America had been growing for several years (thanks to his sex life and his leftist talk) and the Immigration and Naturalization Service was calling him to be questioned. He was reluctant, and so everyone from the American Legion to Loew's blocked *Limelight*—it only took in $1 million. Very soon thereafter, Chaplin left America and lived the rest of his life in Switzerland. But he had been there years already in his head.

Technically, therefore, *Limelight* was not released in America for another twenty years, and so Chaplin and a couple of aides won an Oscar for the score ("I'll Be Loving You") in 1973. By then, the Academy and America had forgiven the man. But what is most instructive is the relative ease with which "genius," or a complete command of the audience, had dwindled to nearly nothing.

Little Big Man (1970)

Everything seemed perfect, even if much of the everything was bound to be a field of blood, ruin, and tragedy. Still, anyone could see in 1970 how *Little Big Man* was "made" for Arthur Penn. Considering how Penn had so artfully employed the local context of the Barrow gang (Texas in the years of the early Depression) to be eloquent about America in the late 1960s, it was a foregone conclusion that *Little Big Man* would be a decisive allegory on the Vietnam War. So when that duly happened (for the most part), there was at least a kind of anticlimax and rather more deadly, nothing like the gradual discovery of analogy that dawned on us as *Bonnie and Clyde* shot people to pieces.

Little Big Man was a novel by Thomas Berger, published in 1964, or at a time when literature, at least, was able to contemplate the fate of the Native American without benefit of analogy. It was a brilliant, picaresque novel, written in the voice of Jack Crabb, a 121-year-old Candide of Western history, an idiot-coward who had been there during Custer and the destruction of the Sioux and so many other things.

The novel was very literary (why not?), by which I mean that it did not try to be a movie or even a novel on its way to the screen. It was a book, telling a complicated set of episodic stories. The movies do not like old men. And Arthur Penn had established a need for his central lives to be in the balance. That is what he does well. Crabb's ancient wisdom suited Thomas Berger very well, but it was not right for a Penn picture. His characters go through great crises. They do not measure them decades later.

So the film cast Dustin Hoffman (a smart choice) and agreed that he had to be himself when young and this amazingly wizened figure, too. Calder Willingham was credited with the script, and that may be where this decision came from. But it made the urge to pass a verdict on America irresistible and obvious. So the terrible bloodletting in the picture—and the best of Penn is very violent—was not awesome, beautiful, or ambiguous, it was bloody depressing. Penn's depiction of Custer as a grotesque was both obvious and quirky, and it seemed like piling on in the age of McNamara and Westmoreland. None of that is as important as the casting of the witty, humane Chief Dan George as an Indian.

So the film wanders through time, and the Faye Dunaway section is a great deal less compelling than the rest—Penn needed to feel that actress as a sexpot about to boil over; Berger saw her as a comic slut. The two don't mix and so the film wallows. Harry Stradling, Jr., did the vivid photography, and the cast includes Martin Balsam, Jeff Corey (as Wild Bill Hickok), Aimée Eccles, and Richard Mulligan (as Custer).

The Little Foxes (1941)

Lillian Hellman's play *The Little Foxes* (the title comes from the little foxes that spoil the vines in the Bible), a melodrama about family and money, opened in 1939 and had great success, with Tallulah Bankhead playing the central role of Regina Giddens, who outwits her brothers and husband and gains control of the family cotton mill. As such, it is part of the widespread literary legend that the great families of the South are corrupt, greedy, and deserving of each other. The family history actually came from Hellman's own memories.

As the play fared well, so Sam Goldwyn decided to buy the rights. He was warned by an adviser that the play was very caustic, whereupon Goldwyn is supposed to have said, "I don't care what it costs." Still, as he hired Hellman to do a screenplay, she was encouraged to build some point of sympathy for the audience. So Hellman created a boyfriend for the Teresa Wright character. Then others thought this was a foolish distraction from the play's point. Meanwhile William Wyler was hired to direct, and Bette Davis was cast as Regina (for $385,000). At the same time, she was ordered to see the stage production, no matter that she said she wanted to be uninfluenced by the Bankhead performance.

Hellman said she was burned out on the script, and there was a period when Arthur Kober, Alan Campbell, and Dorothy Parker came on board to do a rewrite. It hardly mattered. Wyler and Davis would fight seriously because Wyler had some notion of Bette being different from Tallulah. But Bette insisted that there was no other way of playing the part. She's right: Regina is an exultant bitch and any attempt to make her more reasonable or appealing is loaded with mistaken estimates of the play. In the end, on the screen, Davis won out—though she never enjoyed the film.

The most interesting thing about it all in hindsight is Gregg Toland's photography. Wyler wanted the realism to control the melodrama, so he stressed the spatial continuities of the household. You can see depth and furnished distance. You can feel the way people may be spying and eavesdropping. And in one great moment from melodrama, the deep focus holds in place Horace (Herbert Marshall) having a heart attack, his pills—out of reach—and a disdainful Regina walking away upstairs. The photography works beautifully, but in a dryly mechanical way that only reveals the extra content in the imagery of *Citizen Kane*. On that film, depth is an offered reality already being undermined by madness. In *The Little Foxes* it is just the four corners of a plot of ground where a cutthroat game is being played.

Apart from Davis, many players from the stage version were kept: Charles Dingle, Carl Benton Reid, Dan Duryea, and Patricia Collinge. Teresa Wright is the daughter, and Richard Carlson plays the boyfriend. Nominated for nine Oscars (including Best Picture and Director, and for Davis, Collinge, and Wright), the film won nothing.

Little Women (1933)

In the first years of sound, the American movie studios went through the classics library like the shark clearing the shore in *Jaws*. And if the latter increased everyone's respect for sharks, then Hollywood in the 1930s laid down an attitude to literature that lasted until *Masterpiece Theatre* (and which faded into it without a bump). So it's fascinating that George Cukor—uncommonly literate among movie directors in 1933—had never actually read *Little Women*, and was happy to find it so good! And as the newcomer, Cukor had both David Selznick and Katharine Hepburn telling him what a nice surprise he had.

Louisa May Alcott's New England family novel was published in 1868–69, and it was clear that in the years of the Depression, the binding role and prestige of the mother had not altered one bit. I say that because, if you come forward to the 1950s and early '60s, it's equally clear that the mother has come under cultural suspicion—think of *East of Eden*, *Imitation of Life*, *Psycho*, *The Manchurian Candidate*. By contrast, there's so much vigor (as opposed to feminist conviction) in the role of mother and daughters. Cukor has admitted that Hepburn's Jo imported wholesale the atmosphere, the optimism, and the decency of her own New England family.

Of course, although he left RKO before *Little Women* opened, David Selznick was the driving force on the project—his own *Since You Went Away*, ten years later, was a *Little Women* for the war. The script was by Sarah Y. Mason and Victor Heerman (they won an Oscar for it), and it honors the episodic structure of the novel. Hobe Erwin did great work on researching the look of New England interiors, and Walter Plunkett dressed them according to the economy of a family where sisters were likely to share clothes. It's as if the stress on real talk that came with sound gave extra impetus to the value of research on the look of a time. Henry Gerrard did the photography.

Hepburn is the dominating figure as Jo, and Spring Byington is too conventional or soft for Alcott's mother, but the rest of the cast is outstanding—Frances Dee as Meg, Joan Bennett as Amy, and Jean Parker as Beth, and with Edna May Oliver, Douglass Montgomery, Paul Lukas, and Henry Stephenson.

There have been two remakes—in 1949, with June Allyson, Elizabeth Taylor, Janet Leigh, and Margaret O'Brien as Mary Astor's daughters; and in 1994, directed by Gillian Armstrong, with Susan Sarandon as the mother, and Winona Ryder, Claire Danes, Samantha Mathis, Trini Alvarado, and Kirsten Dunst. That last version is very good and faithful, but I think the Cukor version was clearly the one that has been vital in our history. As with all remakes, you have to consider the cultural necessity (and what happens to it) as times change. What Cukor knew was that the period right after the Civil War was as insecure and anxious as the early 1930s.

The Lives of Others (2006)

The Stasi got up and quit their desks in 1989, when the Berlin Wall came down, but *The Lives of Others* resurrects an approach to film that goes a good deal farther back. This is an intricate plot, about cross and double cross, where the viewer has to listen as hard as Wiesler (Ulrich Mühe), a Stasi surveillance man and the gradually emerging protagonist of this subtle story. He is part of a system that records the activities of all likely subversive elements in East Germany. He has a frozen face. We know he is a skilled, if not cruel, interrogator. He seems to be an unquestioning member of the state, a part of the atmosphere of dread that hangs over the country, unsmiling but complicit in the rampant confusion at higher levels.

I know this crisis in history is over, but that doesn't mean its threat is gone. Indeed, it may be the countries on the winning side in 1989 that are now most likely to bug the phones of possible enemies, or just those who disagree with the party line. So, this is a movie about integrity and courage, viable in the age of *Casablanca*, but so much more complex and true to life than that great entertainment.

And this is a debut feature, written and directed by Florian Henckel von Donnersmarck. Wiesler seems dedicated to listening. For eight-hour shifts, he listens to the recorded conversations of suspects, making his written reports. He is a prized and trusted operative. A chief target is the writer Dreyman (Sebastian Koch), a playwright who gets drawn into writing an essay for *Der Spiegel* on the exceptional and unreported number of suicides in East Berlin. Another target is Christa (Martina Gedeck), Dreyman's lover and one of the best actresses in East Germany. As the story unfolds, we see human weakness and betrayal, and then a stunning, poker-faced coup by which the just go free. Building its tension gradually, *The Lives of Others* (not the best title, I admit) becomes increasingly gripping. And it is so clever a film that as soon as it's over you want to see it again. There is an exceptional score—romantic but sinister—supplied by Gabriel Yared and Stéphane Moucha, and the central performances are outstanding.

Above all, I think, *The Lives of Others* reaffirms not just the idea of liberty but the affinity between espionage and the methods of film. Surveillance and bugging are processes that fascinate us—in part because they come close to imitating our closeness to the events in film. But surveillance is addictive, and it can result in a bleak, pitiless, and destructive use of a great medium. There are surveillance experts who would intrude on—and destroy—every intimacy. What is so striking about Donnersmarck's film is the firmness with which he insists on a moral compass sitting in watch over surveillance's constant theft. The malice and the pity exposed in this story are general, and the power of allegedly free states is as effortlessly enriched by surveillance technology as those of the restrictive and the mean-spirited.

Living (1952)

If I tell you that the first shot of *Living* (or *Ikiru*) is an X-ray of stomach cancer, advanced, you will say you know this film already. And you do. Television has made countless movies of the week about some kind of ordinary person who discovers that he or she is dying—it is cancer, or a tumor, or a bad heart. That is tough enough, but there's an extra degree of pain to it all in that the people believe their lives have been empty, or wasted. What have they done for fifty or sixty years except go to the movies and live with their unhappiness? And if I tell you that Mr. Watanabe, the subject of the X-ray, is going to rally his spirits enough to make a small park for city children, you'll say, That's right, I've seen that one! And you have, many times over fifty years, for this story line has become a chestnut of diagnosis and treatment. The person will die, but they will have done something.

I cannot and will not even try to tell you that the story had not been tried before Akira Kurosawa's *Living*. But *Living* is the modern basis of this small genre. And I need, above all, to persuade you of its freshness when it was made. Very little real reflection had been started anywhere on the difference between life and movie life. *Living* grew directly out of the neo-realist moment, the postwar feeling that films need not be reserved for heroes, for sergeants who went up the beach at Iwo Jima. You could make a film about an ordinary person. He could lack charisma, starriness, courage, good luck—all the things that all of us lack. He could be struck down by fate or misfortune or illness. And he might rally. As if his story had never happened, or been seen, before.

What I'm trying to suggest is that the history of the movies is the chronicle of changing taste and new ideas. There are films—like *Bicycle Thieves*, like *12 Angry Men*, like *Living*—rooted in a sense of ordinariness that quickly become a new orthodoxy. At that point, they can be drastically reinterpreted as simpleminded, sentimental, obvious, and flattering to all of us. It's like seeing a great new ad: It works for two days, say, and then it becomes the postmodern version of that ad, peeled away by familiarity and contempt.

But you can't see *Living* as it was made in 1952—not anymore. So do the best you can. Go to a movie theater where *Living* is playing, and just sit there and resist it if you can. It is for later to argue how or whether it "fits in" with Kurosawa's career, or whether it simply enlarges his opportunism. Just resist it if you can.

Takashi Shimura plays Watanabe—he would be the leader of the Seven Samurai in two years' time, a bold, assured, physical champion, and a wise, amiable leader. Watanabe is none of those things—and Shimura gives one of the great performances in film history. But if you feel the actor, honor this principle—that he has made the famous story new for you. Now it is 1952, and you are a wreck.

Lola (1961)

Black-and-white CinemaScope, the full frame, into which sails a white Cadillac convertible. The ocean. A man gets out of the car, a blond dressed in white with a white cowboy hat. Beethoven on the sound track, the Seventh Symphony. With the motto, "*Pleure qui peut, rit qui veut* (Chinese proverb)" and then the dedication—*À Max Ophüls*. It is one of the magical openings in film history: *Lola* by Jacques Demy. What are we to make of the dedication? In part that this Lola in Nantes is cousin to Lola Montès, the subject of Ophüls's last film, made only a few years before. That the style of the film may develop the poetics of the moving camera and passing time. That woman as helpless, chronic performer will be the subject. Yet nothing prepares one for Demy adapting the glorious studio style of Ophüls to the casual, home-movie manner of the New Wave.

Lola (Anouk Aimée) is a cabaret singer in Nantes. She lives with her little boy. The father went away a long time ago, to go to the South Seas or Hollywood, to be on some big screen. And just as Lola has won the love of another provincial boy, Roland (Marc Michel), so her man will come back from Pago Pago or Bird of Paradise. Which frees Roland to go at least as far as Cherbourg.

There was something in Demy that probably aspired to having his every film be attached to all the others (remember we shall see Lola in Los Angeles in *Model Shop*), and characters reappear along with phrases in the Michel Legrand scores—to say nothing of their lamenting optimism. So the other female characters here that Roland knows—the mother and the daughter (Elina Labourdette and Annie Duperoux) are just as elegant and nervy as Lola. In Demy's films, or on his carousel, mistakes are subject for guilt or gloom only so long as the people don't notice the momentum that carries them forward. Feelings change. Moods shift. Luck comes and goes—gambling's call was there before we had even heard of *Baie des Anges*. Lola has never given up on her old bet, never deserted the table. In a way, the gamble is what keeps her young, romantic, and silly—and Anouk (not always the supplest of actresses or the one to step away from solemnity) is so giddy and impetuous you love her too.

It is a musical, of course, not just for the cabaret scenes and Lola's song there (words by Agnès Varda) or even because of the Beethoven, but because Demy had already identified Legrand as his dramatic composer. Demy knew already that every line of dialogue was waiting to be sung—and perhaps that was the best direction he ever gave his actors.

Raoul Coutard did the camera work, and the movements are lush and streamlined. Bernard Evein did the décor—and in time Demy would be fascinated by design. But in 1961, you could see that Demy had something of Ophüls and something of Minnelli. The real wonder was in seeing how much Demy there was, too.

Lola (1982)

Yes, you can imagine that when Rainer Werner Fassbinder, only a year away from his early death, determined to make a film called *Lola* he was harking back to *The Blue Angel* (1930) and to what had happened to Germany in the intervening fifty years. So it's wise to begin with a comparison. In *The Blue Angel,* Professor Rath is destroyed, and Lola-Lola (we may surmise) is headed for somewhere like Hollywood. The sexual imperative accounts for her rise and his fall. Thus, the loss of integrity equals destruction of self. Well, that's nice and tidy, isn't it?

But Fassbinder the maker of violent, modern theater, the survivalist (and the relentless consumer of cocaine), sees things very differently. Von Bohm (Armin Mueller-Stahl) comes to the small city where the action takes place as the new building commissioner. Note, straightaway, that Fassbinder wastes no time on illustrious teachers as models for society—the man in the vortex and the feeding trough of the new Germany is the building commissioner. Schukert (Mario Adorf) is wary—he is the corrupt city gangster, the boss and the lever, and the owner of Lola (Barbara Sukowa), star singer and prize whore at his club, the Villa Fink. Schukert seeks to delay and spoil Von Bohm's reformist energies by having the man meet Lola. They become lovers. They are eventually married. But Schukert gives Lola the Villa Fink as a wedding present, and then continues his affair with her. Von Bohm is still the building commissioner. In Fassbinder's world, you do not get off so lightly as having a "fall" allows. You stay in office and you make your reports.

One of the most interesting things about *Lola* is that, despite Fassbinder's personal disintegration, this is one of the most fluent and stylish of his films. Indeed, just as with Buñuel, it's remarkable to see how the early radical was falling in love with the medium of film itself. Whereas with Buñuel that process took decades, Fassbinder had so little time it was accomplished in a few years. But in color scheme and in its very articulated camera movements, this is a film with a relish for the rotting spaces in a corrupt system. The continuity in time and space in *Petra von Kant* was an ordeal, but here it's a process—the coming to a decision. The savage compressions of the early films have been abandoned. Some thought this amounted to decadence in Fassbinder, but you only have to live with this reworking of *The Blue Angel* to get the bitter satire and the inability to sustain heroes. Indeed, as the stylishness mounted, Fassbinder's feeling for people and conventional eroticism was becoming more implacable.

The script for *Lola* was done by Fassbinder himself, Peter Märthesheimer, and Pea Fröhlich. Xaver Schwarzenberger did the very accomplished photography. Helmut Gassner did the production design—and more effort and money was going in that direction. The cast includes Matthias Fuchs, Helga Feddersen, Karin Baal, Ivan Desny, Elisabeth Volkmann, Hark Bohm, Karl-Heinz von Hassel, Rosel Zech, and Christine Kaufmann.

Lola Montès (1955)

Made two years before Max Ophüls's death, *Lola Montès* invokes the idea of some butterfly that discovers the most demanding and balletic movements in the air just before it expires. A tired man might have had reason for settling, but Ophüls's camera here is moving to stay alive, and in the circus scenes it has a circling motion—circles round a still thing, or reverse circles around another *ronde*—that is beautiful and heartbreaking at the same time. You have the feeling of a destructive performing energy having been summoned.

And that is entirely suited to the framing scenes, the *cirque du minuit* in New Orleans. Lola Montès, about forty, has been engaged by an impresario/ringmaster (Peter Ustinov) to be the stricken centerpiece in tableaux of her scandalous life. It is all done in a circus ring, and at the end, after Lola has again survived the dire plunge into a small pool of water, she sits like a frozen empress selling her kisses at a dollar a time to a line of men that stretches out to meet us, the ultimate audience.

There are those who say that Martine Carol was not the actress to be Lola, that she was not vivacious enough. Perhaps. Casting is a grand game that goes on forever. (Vivien Leigh? Danielle Darrieux? Ingrid Bergman? Judy Garland? Marlene Dietrich? Simone Signoret? Every suggestion is ravishing. Because nearly every one of those women would have understood Lola Montès.) But Carol was beautiful, of the right age, herself touched by notoriety and in her rather drained way a suitable player of the exhausted, sick, depleted Lola Montès. So I do not believe a problem shows—and I am not afraid of the possibility that Lola is a very sad, unsentimental person compared with the fevered legend of her which the apparatus of circus and the glorious formal enactment (the ritual) of Ophüls's tracking shots only enhances.

To be an actress, or a performer; to put on a show; to turn life into a circus or a mise-en-scène; to see beauty dying—these are some of the motifs to be found within this dazzling film. The circus gives access to flashbacks—scenes from her life all the way from the teenager on the boat back from India, through the liaison with Liszt, to the bittersweet romance with Ludwig of Bavaria (Anton Walbrook). It is based on the real woman, yet the film is free to invent and adorn. And in its use of color, décor, CinemaScope, movement, and music, it is the swan song of Ophüls's very troubled career. Of course, we have it incomplete—110 minutes as against 140 originally. It is enough.

Christian Matras did the photography. Georges Auric wrote the haunting score. Jean D'Eaubonne was in charge of the design. Madeleine Gug was the editor. Ophüls and Jacques Natanson did the script, with Annette Wademant and Franz Geiger. Also with Oskar Werner, Ivan Desny, Will Quadflieg, Henri Guisol, Lise Delamare, and Paulette Dubost. Ustinov speaking quietly to Lola as she wonders if she can jump again is among the most pained and precious moments in cinema. It is every director asking every actress to be public, because he loves her in private. And the one erases the other. For the butterfly knows that there is only one exit. One of the essential films, despite misguided abuse on its release—deeply influential on the New Wave.

Lolita (1962)

In electing to do *Lolita,* Stanley Kubrick put himself forward in the small field of those contesting for the title of the most intelligent/the most stupid film director in the world. In another decision that could be taken either way, he elected to live and work in England. So, on the one hand, to take on the Vladimir Nabokov novel and its weird best-seller status was a way of claiming sophistication and literary learning. Equally, to suppose that a film of *Lolita* was either necessary or possible was also a display of idiocy, pretension, and vainglory. Yet you can tell how far flattery, self-delusion, and compromise were afoot when you know that Nabokov himself was persuaded to do a screenplay for the picture. Indeed, Nabokov seems to have been thoroughly wooed by young Stanley.

The Nabokov screenplay is published separately, and it is an intriguing document—but this was plainly rescripted by Kubrick, and perhaps some others. Tuesday Weld was certainly considered for Lo, but the nod went to Sue Lyon, an unknown. Peter Sellers—a man for whom Kubrick felt little reservation—was to be Clare Quilty; Shelley Winters would be Charlotte. And James Mason was Humbert. To this day, the film remains of interest because of Mason and his voice, his tenderness and his folly. He does seem like a man of high learning. He does also seem profoundly in love, and sure as an actor that he is handling a great work. Kubrick is not often interested in ambiguity in his heroes, and I feel that Mason delivered things that are beyond his director.

So what do we have? Sellers is grotesquely conceited and fussy in a role that needs deadly simplicity. Shelley Winters is right and smart. Sue Lyon is not bad if you like sixteen-year-olds (which is not what the novel is about). The decision to film in Britain—when *Lolita* is one of the great roaming tours of Americana—is demented. But Ossie Morris delivers a nice, gray black-and-white look that encourages one to listen to the words. Also on the sound track is a naggy, silly, cute, but actually quite enticing score (Nelson Riddle and Bob Harris) that I can never get out of my head and which I now associate with the great book.

In all the extensive silliness called the Novel and the Film that goes on in academia, you should simply work on *Lolita*—the book and the film—and with as much pain as you think fit make it clear that anyone prepared to take literature seriously and to read novels like *Lolita,* hoping that a film on such a book will turn out nicely, is akin to hoping the Jews didn't suffer too much. And there is a torment in that process, too, which is that we do not possess a recording of Mason just reading the entire novel aloud.

Such a thing was done with the remake: Jeremy Irons read the whole book on tape. He is not bad, though the second film repeats the inaccessibility of the book. But Irons believes he is reciting a tragedy. Mason knew it was a dangerous rapture.

London After Midnight (1927)

Do not be encouraged too much. Tod Browning's *London After Midnight* remains a lost film, one of the most famous and most sought-after films that have vanished in the industry's famous neglect of its own material. It seems to have been one more of those very short films made at M-G-M, with Waldemar Young as the screenwriter (he was a Stanford graduate who would go on to work for DeMille), though in this case he adapted a novel by Browning, called *The Hypnotist*.

The film was a couple of minutes longer than *The Unknown* (made in the same year), but it has vanished. However, I am including it in this book not just because absence has stimulated thoughts about the picture, but because the resourceful Rick Schmidling has made a reconstructed version based on stills from the production as well as titles from the original (he did the same with *Greed*). In other words, he has pioneered a new medium: the illustrated film script, all done in stills. Ron Haver employed this method in lost sections of the 1954 *A Star Is Born*, and it is up to the viewer to say how well it works. History is helped, but drama pays the price, I fear.

Anyway, *London After Midnight* is London at the turn of the last century with murder afoot in the streets. Lon Chaney is presented to us as a grim, upright police inspector on the trail of the criminal. Then we discover that a vampiric figure is also on the streets. He is stooped. He wears a top hat with long hair hanging down beneath it. He has huge, protruding eyes and a mouth made savage by enlarged teeth. There was no way that the audience of the time could not recognize this as another Chaney part (one for which eyes and mouth were painfully stretched by wire). In other words, the actor's versatility dispelled the intrigue and diminished the "horror" of the vampire's appearance.

It's worth saying that when Browning came to remake *London After Midnight* as *Mark of the Vampire*, he had the good sense to separate the two roles (Lionel Barrymore and Bela Lugosi). But *London After Midnight* may be the first use of the vampire figure in an American film, and it is fascinating to wonder whether Browning or Chaney had seen the Murnau *Nosferatu*.

The Schmidling reconstruction has only a limited number of stills, so it is obliged to use many of them several times. But it pans and scans across the surface of a still, and it uses a sinister music track. So it's interesting to wonder why Schmidling didn't go all the way and have the titles spoken on the sound track, instead of printed. Surely this would have made for a more compelling film, or one that came closer to fear. As it is, the titles only draw attention to the way in which so much acting was a signal of impossible talk: You either take the risk of people missing sense, or you employ this woeful slowing and rearticulation. It leaves *London After Midnight* as a museum piece—but nothing takes away from the haunted look of Chaney as the vampire with Edna Tichenor as his daughter.

Lonesome (1928)

In the last twenty-five years, at festivals and in academia, *Lonesome* has been recognized as the surviving piece from a strange, maverick director, Pál Fejös (1897–1963), and also as one of those key films made in the moment of sound's arrival, and deeply expressive of a new urban wistfulness being discovered by cinema. Thus, elsewhere there is *Sunrise, The Man with a Movie Camera,* King Vidor's *The Crowd* and *Street Scene, People on Sunday* (made in Berlin by that group of young beginners), as well as Gustav Machatý's *From Saturday to Sunday* . . . and *Lonesome.* Fejös's previous film—*The Last Moment* (1928)—is tantalizing in various descriptions, yet apparently lost for all time.

It was on the strength of that hit that Universal invited Fejös to make *Lonesome.* A machinist (Glenn Tryon) and a telephonist (Barbara Kent) meet on a bus to Coney Island. They have a day out amid the entertainments. There is a little talk between them—utterly banal small talk—but Fejös films everything in the real places of summer holiday and moves his camera constantly to convey the flux of feeling in a strangers' meeting.

Just as in *People on Sunday,* say, or Dziga Vertov's work, there is that uncanny feeing of being there, of documentary, while at the same time the movements of the characters and the camera build a fascinating and complete fictional mood. As in so many films of this brief era, you feel the excitement of the artists as they begin to appreciate the seamless and fantastical command of a total reality that is coming into being. Scott Eyman has said that *Lonesome* is not as searching as *The Crowd,* and I think that's correct. Moreover, its brief dialogue scenes have to be listened to tongue-in-cheek. But the anticipation of what is at hand, for the medium and its makers, is extraordinary, and it may leave the viewer all the more open to an interaction of sound and presence. In other words, I suspect writers and directors felt the potential depth of scenes opening up—for example, the talk scenes where Fejös is too fresh to bother with them much. After all, the very title aspires to a generalized inwardness that is not really possible under the restrictions of strictly silent pictures. Because a picture plus sound equals more than illustrated action. It is action itself. It is drama and context.

In fact, the couple in *Lonesome* are not really such strangers. It turns out that they live in the same building—so loneliness is an urban condition that can be altered or reappraised. In short, *Lonesome* is a film more pregnant than delivered. *Broadway,* done in 1929, was another big picture. Fejös stayed active through the thirties, though he went to Europe and was generally disappointed and frustrated. He ended in documentary (in Siam and Peru!)—but *Marie,* made in Hungary in 1932 (and shown at Telluride in 2007), is enough to prove a talent who had gone way beyond *Lonesome.*

The Long Day Closes (1992)

Liverpool, 1955–56, before the Beatles. An empty street, it is pouring with rain. This is not a real street, but the set of a street. The camera has a life of its own (a crane and a track), and it moves down the street like age advancing. We see posters for movies. We hear brief flourishes of their voice or music on the sound track. *The Robe. The Ladykillers. The Happiest Days of Your Life. Meet Me in St. Louis.* We enter a house, and there is a boy of eleven. His name is Bud. And he says to his mother, "Mam . . . Mam . . . Can I go to the pictures, Mam?"

It is the start of Terence Davies's *The Long Day Closes,* and it is one of those tender moments when film goes to the pictures (if it can get in): I think of Truffaut's dream in *Day for Night* of that locked, barred place where *Citizen Kane* has shown; or the picture house in a windswept Texas town where *Red River* is the last film that is ever going to play. "Can I go to the pictures, Mam?"

Terence Davies was born in Liverpool in 1945, and for the first part of his life, he made films about that experience. There was the trilogy—black and white, 16 mm, done as student films, paid for by scratching and saving and miracles; there was *Distant Voices, Still Lives,* which centered on a violent father; and then there is the reward, *The Long Day Closes,* which is just Bud and Mam and the pictures, and the paradise of American grandeur in raining streets.

You need to see all those films in order to get the proper sense of the boy growing up and emerging from one church (Roman, florid but harsh) to another—the unrestricted fantasy hedonism of the movie palace. But I include *The Long Day Closes* here because of its ecstatic sense of good fortune. Of course, Davies was a boy becoming a man at a time when "the cinema" was not sure where it would go. That doubt has become so chronic now, it has altered the experience. These days, Mam has so many other things the boy could do. And in the last decade, I fear, Davies (a superb talent) has found it very difficult to get the work he deserves (his excellent and unremitting *House of Mirth* went unnoticed).

The Long Day Closes was made by the British Film Institute and Channel 4. Olivia Stewart was the producer. Michael Coulter shot it in ravishing color. Christopher Hobbs was the production designer. There is not a lot of story in the film. Rather, it is a quiet passion, a religious celebration of the dark and the light that lives there. One day, maybe, we will need *The Long Day Closes* if only to say to children, There, that is what it was like and how it was done. And they will look back at us in horror—at being the descendants of people who could not be trusted to look after something.

Leigh McCormick is Bud, Marjorie Yates is Mam, and the cast includes Anthony Watson, Nicholas Lamont, Ayse Owens, Joy Blakeman, Denise Thomas, and Patricia Morrison.

Long Day's Journey into Night (1962)

Who said this?: "After such an experience, I don't see how one can niggle over whether it's 'cinema' or merely 'filmed theatre.' Whatever it is, it's great." Eugene O'Neill's *Long Day's Journey into Night* was not meant to be produced for decades after the playwright's death. But his widow overrode his instruction—and we are in her debt. The play opened in New York in 1956, with Fredric March, Florence Eldridge, Jason Robards, Jr., and Bradford Dillman. The film came six years later, directed by Sidney Lumet, with Ralph Richardson, Katharine Hepburn, Robards (again), and Dean Stockwell.

And it is still a great experience (it was Pauline Kael who offered that verdict). It's easy to say that this is because it's a great play, or a searing ordeal, in the theater—but now we are watching in greater comfort and with all the advantages of close-ups. But very quickly this argument gets into a consideration of how film and theater relate. I have seen the final plays of O'Neill several times "live." I have seen *The Iceman Cometh* with Ian Bannen and Kevin Spacey as Hickey—and I have seen the television version, where Lee Marvin played Hickey. It's enough to think that O'Neill lends himself to the screen. But he doesn't. There are many bad films of O'Neill. There is also the enforced habitation of O'Neill's places—the house on Long Island, or the bar. Being there is part of the sense of group or family.

But one thing emerges from the film of *Long Day's Journey*—though I am not quite sure what it means. In the film, Mary becomes central. I don't think that's because Katharine Hepburn was a better actress than those onstage. But whereas onstage the figures have equal force—like the figures in a weather house—in the film, Mary is the center or the wavering light.

If it's not Hepburn making that shift, is it Lumet, is it photographer Boris Kaufman, or is it cinema itself? I don't know the answer. But whenever a "family drama" has moved one at the movies, I think there's a case for putting on *Long Day's Journey* and seeing just how much deeper O'Neill goes. And it is O'Neill. My admiration for Lumet hinges on his doing the film in O'Neill's service.

But then there's another aspect to the play: It is a kind of history of acting in that James O'Neill (Richardson) was one of the great figures in nineteenth-century theater—and here he is, decades later and in another process, acting the part of himself. I'm sure O'Neill felt that, and I'd guess that Lumet was fascinated by the opportunity to look at the history of acting in America. So the play may change. Later productions may miss a lot—but Hepburn and Richardson are from the start of the twentieth century. They knew silent cinema and signaled acting. And now here they are, bringing a life into a look, like putting a tiger in a jewel.

Longford (2006)

There were five killings, of children and teenagers, and they occurred in 1963. A young couple, lovers and partners in sadomasochism, lured the children into a vehicle. Then they were killed—sometimes with tape recordings of their last pleas. The bodies were buried on the moors, near Manchester. The killers were Ian Brady and Myra Hindley, and in 1966 a court gave them life imprisonment. The court said Brady was "wicked beyond belief," but Hindley might reform if removed from Brady's influence.

That's what Frank Longford noticed—he was an aristocrat, devout, sixty, in the Harold Wilson cabinet. He had causes, like prison visiting. He believed that wickedness could be overcome, and he felt that most prisoners had a right to earn parole. That's how he got interested in Myra Hindley.

That's all you need to know before you see *Longford* (made for HBO), one of the most absorbing of the new British films, and the shot in which Longford (Jim Broadbent) searches in the visitors' room at Holloway Prison for Myra Hindley. He expects a blonde—in all the harsh press pictures, she had blonde hair—but in prison she has gone back to brown. She sits off to one side, a pariah, abused by other prisoners, fearful they will read her lips. Longford sits down, and before long he is telling her she has a nice smile—she does, though we have to judge whether it is Myra's or a smile from Samantha Morton, the uncanny actress. Is she seducing him, or just trying to be human?

Longford is directed by Tom Hooper and written by Peter Morgan (who wrote *The Queen*). It is a brilliantly made character study, a film over which finally we have to make up our minds. But don't be surprised if you have the rare feeling—without any scenes of overt violence—that you have looked evil in the face.

Brady and Hindley are in different prisons, but they write to each other. And as Longford goes to see Myra more often, so he gets an invitation to call on Brady (Andy Serkis, and as still and startling as Lecter in *The Silence of the Lambs*). Leave her alone, he tells Longford, she's mine. Don't trust her "reform," he says. It's all a trick.

Longford wavers. His wife, the author Elizabeth Longford (Lindsay Duncan), hates the involvement with Hindley. Until one day she reads Myra's letters and becomes a convert, too. The film is very balanced: It allows the possibility that a Myra might have been led and dominated by Brady, that she might be sorry and redeemed. But what is redemption? And how does a young woman survive in a prison situation where everyone hates her without being exceptionally strong, or prepared to play that part until the end?

Yes, it's a British story, and Longford (wonderfully impersonated by Jim Broadbent) is a very English figure—noble, lofty, but not too bright. I daresay that no government would ever have released Brady or Hindley (for fear of public reaction). But locking people up does not stop their damage. Anyone capable of imagining Brady or Hindley from this film can be reached by their wickedness. But then a film as grave as *Longford* makes the clash of hope and fear as piercing as eyes looking at us. And virtue requires that we recognize evil.

The Long Goodbye (1973)

Observers have commented on how Leigh Brackett was one of the writers on Howard Hawks's *The Big Sleep* (1946) and on Robert Altman's thorough autopsy of the Philip Marlowe character in *The Long Goodbye*. What did Ms. Brackett think about the way her earlier version (with comedy, heroics, action, and mood) was reduced to cat food (curry-flavored)? Not that Altman dislikes or disapproves of Marlowe. On the contrary, it's just that he is now something of a relic or a throwback, an amiable, decent, and very hip guy. And Altman cherishes those characteristics. He spends the whole film concentrating on the way Elliott Gould moves, murmurs, sighs, and allows silence or stillness to prevail. You may not be sure whether it's quietism or those brownies the ladies make across the way, but this Marlowe is swinging, even if his world is no longer within his control. The real goodbye in this picture is to the brilliant effectiveness of Hawks's character.

That said, the shift is easy enough, from the late 1930s to the early 1970s. In place of the magnificent, dandyish control with which Hawks defied darkness and chaos, Altman has a camera (by Vilmos Zsigmond) that oozes through the warm ice cream space of southern California, and a sound track where Marlowe's mocking title song (by John Williams and Johnny Mercer) wakes up every time the doorbell rings. And it's the richest part of Altman's L.A. that it is lovely and quite mad, or depraved, or corrupt. Take your pick. A private eye now is no longer a knight without armor who will go down the dark streets, et cetera; he's a wry, forlorn dude who needs shades in the sun and who tries not to do harm.

The ending is underlined: Terry Lennox, who started it all, is dead at Marlowe's hand. He passes Nina van Pallandt on the way in and out (with a hint of *The Third Man*), and the jukebox hits "Hooray for Hollywood!" As an explanation or a condemnation it doesn't stand up nearly as well as Marlowe's own gentle forgiveness of more or less everything. This is where Gould's dance through the picture is so utterly different from Bogey's prowling stroll in *The Big Sleep*, yet as great a performance.

The most unnerving thing about this is the "It's OK by me" as one damn thing after another comes apart. Just consider how marginal and how emotionally oppressive is Marty Augustine's scene with Jo Ann Eggenweiler. This is a comic reverie with one of the ugliest moments of violence in American film. It is also a fair summary of Arnold Schwarzenegger's contribution to film and to California.

Of course, long before, *The Big Sleep* had exploded genre expectations and let the pieces fall where they might. But here is one of the great American films of a bright new age that says, "No more genres for you, America. Just work it out." Gould is the film, but he gets terrific support from Sterling Hayden, van Pallandt, Mark Rydell, Henry Gibson, Jim Bouton, and Ken Sansom, the guard at the Malibu Colony who would let Charles Manson in just to get a chance of impersonating him.

The Lord of the Rings (2001–2003)

The Lord of the Rings is three films, but it is only one. It is an enterprise in which it is hard to resist recounting the business story first, for the business was handled with the precise, appointed acumen and good sense that we long for in our military campaigns. So, on the one hand, you can point to the dismay at Miramax after they had nurtured the project only to find that their owners—Disney—were alarmed by the scale of it all, and by the undoubted reaching for deeper, darker mystic values than Disneyfication was used to. So it's not going too far to point to *The Lord of the Rings* onscreen as a signal defeat for Disney. Will they ever be the same again?

It was in that gap that Bob Shaye thrust himself and New Line to be partners with Peter Jackson's own company and the pledged German money—so we have a co-production from Germany, New Zealand, and America. Nor is the German link mere business. If you want to find the roots of this astonishing epic, you need to go back to Fritz Lang and the *Nibelungen* (nearly eighty years earlier).

Grant then the magnificent decisiveness of the Peter Jackson/Fran Walsh plan: to shoot the three pictures in one immense process, and to do it at the end of the earth—in the God-given New Zealand—and at the cutting edge of digital image generation (also from a base in New Zealand). So a crew was lined up to handle the entire picture—Andrew Lesnie as photographer; Howard Shore doing music; and the effects houses required to devise a scheme of illusion for the entire film and its great series of battles. Walsh, Jackson, and Philippa Boyens had a screenplay that eventually offended very few fans of the original novel by J. R. R. Tolkien. Shooting lasted 274 days spread over a period of sixteen months.

The costs were simply divided by three, and so each film was assigned a budget of $94 million—for a total of $282 million—against which, in worldwide theatrical rentals alone, the three pictures earned $869 million, $920 million, and $1,118 million. Any one of the three would have been in profit on the total costs. And there was video still to come.

It was said, with absolute justice, that these rich numbers were sustained by the fact that three generations of any family could see the film at the same time, in emotional comfort. There were battles, violence, suspense, and fear. There were likeable central characters. There were hideous villains. Viggo Mortensen became a star as Aragorn. Elijah Wood and Sean Astin were fine as the heroes. Cate Blanchett and Ian McKellen added to their luster. Perhaps nothing was more influential than the computerized look—in this case a superb, pewterized undertone to everything that one can easily believe Tolkien would have loved. At the same time, there were those who felt that the lack of photography's light was building a drab certainty in the film that was oppressive and without oxygen.

All of this is a few years ago now. *The Lord of the Rings* was an extraordinary business achievement. But this evening if I had to watch something special from Peter Jackson, I'd prefer *Heavenly Creatures,* which I still think of as a work of art, whereas the Tolkien pictures are a regime undergone.

The Lost Moment (1947)

There is a film called *Aspern*, from 1985, directed by the estimable Eduardo de Gregorio, in which Jean Sorel plays the man who has come in search of ancient love letters. They are held, fiercely, by an old woman (Alida Valli), and then there is the younger woman (Bulle Ogier), who may be used in the plot to get the letters. I have never seen this film and I would like to, just as much as I would love to see a perfect film made out of the novella on which it is based, Henry James's *The Aspern Papers* (1888), one of those several works in which James somehow suggested he had seen and absorbed every movie that might be made for fifty years or so.

But there is another version of *The Aspern Papers*, and it is surprisingly good—the surprise is yours if you take the easy attitude that Robert Cummings and Susan Hayward are unlikely to be in the same intriguing movie. So, give it a try.

It was a Walter Wanger production, and in its time it was written off as being rather gloomily literary, whereas I think it shows the intelligence in Wanger that helped make pictures like *Scarlet Street* and *The Reckless Moment*. Despite the invitations of period, and Venice (where the old woman lives), this is a 1947 film noir, beautifully shot by Hal Mohr, in which we come to discover the dangers of trying to bring the past back to life. For the dry papers are love letters and we hardly know now whether their muse (in the grim form of Agnes Moorehead acting at least twice her age) is wistful over her own passion or loathing of it. Is the moment worth recovering or is it more safely lost?

The picture was scripted by Leonardo Bercovici—at very much the same time he worked on *Portrait of Jennie*, which has moments of nearly occult seductiveness as the past comes back. Martin Gabel (more an actor than a director) directed the film and he does not do enough to withstand the fits of melodrama in the material. But he also makes us feel not just a haunted house but the way in which past drama may be remade. In short, this is a film that leaves one thinking of things like *Vertigo* and *Celine and Julie Go Boating*.

I have the hunch that James would have admired it. Coming two years before *The Heiress* (which is a very fixed and unmagical story), this is the first movie that comes close to James's spirit. And Susan Hayward deserves high praise for the way she switches from a prim young woman to one who sometimes seems carried away by the romance of the letters. Cummings might have been recast—Montgomery Clift is the obvious choice. But Agnes Moorehead could have played any woman of any age. Anyone who loves her—and wishes there was more of her on film—will be stirred by this wolfish invocation of a dangerous past and a fatal future.

The Lost Weekend (1945)

The train trip, coast to coast, was four days and a boon to reading. (You also got to see "the dark fields of the republic.") Sometime in 1944, just after *Double Indemnity,* Billy Wilder traveled east, with Charles Jackson's *The Lost Weekend* as his reading. It was a best seller and one of the first accounts of alcoholism written as fiction but supplied with modern medical information. Living in a community of heavy drinking and self-delusion, Wilder jumped at the subject. He said he had the shape of the movie in his head by the time he reached New York.

Then he sat down with Charles Brackett to do the script. And here are valuable stories: Brackett's wife was a drunk; he had a relative who was a closeted gay—and in Jackson's novel, Don Birnam drinks for that very reason: He cannot face his own sexual nature. Furthermore, in March 1944, Myron Selznick died of alcoholism—and he had been Wilder's agent once. So the personal drive to do this film was out of the ordinary. Wilder even wanted a character actor to play Birnam—to take away glamour or starriness. But Paramount prevailed on him: A star would permit better identification—so they all agreed on Ray Milland.

With John Seitz doing the camera work again (he had done *Double Indemnity*), the picture went on location in New York. It even used Bellevue and incurred their wrath when the film came out. Moreover, apart from having Jane Wyman as the rather woeful girlfriend, Wilder went for a tough cast: Frank Faylen as the sanatorium aide; Howard da Silva as the barman; Phillip Terry as the brother; and Wilder's girlfriend, Doris Dowling, as the hooker. The bat and the mouse played themselves—and you have to stretch your imaginations to get the really loathsome kick in those scenes in 1945.

Then came hiatus. The studio didn't like the picture—they suddenly realized it was about the most common social disease in America. It was said that gangster Frank Costello offered Paramount $5 million to have the negative burned. There was no release date, and Wilder went off to a shattered Europe to do war work—especially a film on the camps. His marriage was breaking up. No wonder if he started drinking more.

He was back in the fall, and somehow the world had changed. Early screenings got good results—had the public grown up? Even the studio? Miklós Rózsa dumped the jazz score and replaced it with dark, violent music of his own using the wailing theremin (which he had pioneered on *Spellbound*). All of a sudden the downer picture had a tragic force—as well as an allowable positive ending: Birnam may be on the road to recovery. Then again, he is so weak.

The Lost Weekend was a hit, which surely says a lot for audiences then. It had cost close to $1.5 million, but it had rentals of $4.3 million. Maybe there was a backlash from the neglect of *Double Indemnity* (a better film), but *The Lost Weekend* cleaned up: Best Screenplay; Best Actor for Ray Milland; Best Director; and Best Picture (*Spellbound* won for score!). It's still deeply alarming.

Loulou (1980)

One of the great dangers to cinema is that audiences feel they've seen it all and (at least in their fantasies) done that. And by 1980, it was possible for people to be blasé about sex and violence—censorship no longer existed, did it? You could show whatever you could get actors to do—and the danger was clear already, that bored and cynical audiences sat back and said, "It's not real anymore. It's just actors pretending." And so a kind of class distinction opened up—you can see signs of it all over the world—between people who were sophisticated about sex and violence, and those who did it. *Loulou* is that sort of film.

You can easily reckon Nelly and André (Isabelle Huppert and Guy Marchand) have seen *Last Tango in Paris* and *The Godfather*. They've talked about these things, and sometimes the talk has spiced up their love life. He runs an advertising agency where she works. They go dancing one night and, irritated by André's manner and assumption of authority, Nelly lets herself be picked up by Loulou (Gérard Depardieu). He is a drunk, intimidating. *Loulou* means "yobbo" or "lout." He is a working-class character. He probably doesn't go to the movies. They become lovers.

One reason for that—and Maurice Pialat reveals it with a strange mixture of tenderness and grimness—is their sex. For Nelly, it is new and less gentle. It goes on so much longer. It exhausts and fulfills her. She doesn't know whether she's coming or going. But the attraction is more than that. She likes Loulou's wildness, the cheap hotel where he lives, and the life of minor crime into which she is drawn. Is it the danger, or the pursuit of disorder? She doesn't know, but it helps her resist every effort from André to win her back. How will it end?

The abrasive novelty of class disparity is very well revealed—for instance we see Nelly go from a studiously "nice" apartment to a dump (art direction by Max Berto, Jean-Pierre Sarrazin, and Alain Alitbol) without really being troubled. Pialat is as tough as he is fond of his characters: He pushed them to the limit, and there are excruciating scenes close to embarrassment. But he is a believer in the unpeeling of emotional nature, and he grasps a lot about how Nelly's mind works—Huppert easily supplies the rest. But Loulou is a chump. He doesn't get it or find something playful in the girl. Is it true to life, or just to story, that they begin to cross over?

This was a big hit for Pialat, a breakthrough, and it's still riveting—obviously for the most part because the three actors trusted him to observe them in extremis. Arlette Langmann wrote the script with Pialat, and the photography was done by Pierre-William Glenn and Jacques Loiseleux. Philippe Sarde did the music, with contributions from Larry Coryell and Hubert Laws. The cast also includes Humbert Balsan, Bernard Tronczak, and Christian Boucher.

Love Affair (1939)

There are two halves to *Love Affair*, and it has always been a great question as to whether they match—or are they separate parts each searching for a mate? But the question takes you straight to the tricky heart of Leo McCarey and to the matter of sentiment in American pictures. So it began like this: McCarey, at RKO, had a plan for a romantic story involving an American woman and a French diplomat. He had Irene Dunne and Charles Boyer lined up for it. But the French government went into a stuffy fit (now there's a subject for the film: U.S. screenwriter has to thrash out with French ambassador the proper way to do a love story).

Keep moving. McCarey apparently woke Delmer Daves in the middle of the night and said, I have to have a story to go with the title "Love Affair." So Daves thought about it, and lo and behold . . . on board a ship, Terry (Dunne) meets Michel (Boyer). He is engaged; she has a lover. They pick each other up in a quite delightful way—smart but vulnerable, expert yet awkward: It really is a love story.

They agree to meet six months later—on top of the Empire State Building. But on her way to that date, she is hit by a car and crippled. She conceals her injury from him. He decides she didn't care. The wonderful, elegant tone of the first part turns into every-line-loaded-with-misunderstanding. McCarey hired Donald Ogden Stewart to smarten up the dialogue, but of course he had his own method in that, too. He liked to come on set in the morning, doodle away at his piano while looking at the script until he found a point of departure—a line to improve. Then he and the actors were at it in improvs and rehearsals, nudging the text this way and that. Indeed, in the first half of the film, we feel we are watching the rehearsals as the characters comment on their own dialogue, improve it, mock it, and generally scrutinize its honesty. It's their shared way of working that lands them in love.

You can say it is the Hawksian method, but whereas Hawks loved play, in McCarey the search is on for real feeling. Boyer was not used to it, but he learned to like it—and Dunne was always a great comedienne.

Then there is the second half—same people, same cameraman (Rudolph Maté), but a different style and an essentially cockeyed situation in which self-pity and sympathy have replaced desire and intelligence. (Is this the decline of America?)

In 1939, the audience slipped over from one track to another without being derailed. It was a big success—with Maria Ouspenskaya, Lee Bowman, and Astrid Allwyn. In 1957, McCarey remade it himself, with Cary Grant and Deborah Kerr, as *An Affair to Remember*. Eighty-seven minutes became 115 (no small thing) and Grant—according to McCarey—played the whole thing for comedy: In other words, he couldn't swallow part 2.

Alas, in 1994, they tried yet again: Warren Beatty and Annette Bening in *Love Affair* (directed by Glenn Gordon Caron), and with Katharine Hepburn. Now neither part worked.

Love in the Afternoon (1972)

"Since my marriage," says Frédéric, "I have found all women beautiful." It is a line worthy of Lubitsch from the last of Eric Rohmer's six moral tales. And if Rohmer's tone is more modern and anguished than that of Lubitsch, still, the link between the two is touching to anyone who likes to see traditions in cinema. Although Rohmer and the moral tales seem to have gone out of fashion, this was and remains the climax to one of the great series in filmmaking. It is not simply a perfect, perilous film; it is also the vindication of the series of six.

Frédéric (Bernard Verley) is in a private business he enjoys. But he has gone beyond the hesitation that affected every other hero in the moral tales. He is married, happily, to Hélène (Françoise Verley). They have one child and another on the way. He is handsome, complacent, and just a little overweight from the bounty of marriage and tender cooking. He has a habit after lunch of falling into reveries. Early on, we participate in these extraordinary voyeuristic inspections of passing women. It is a male thing, perhaps; but it is the imprint of movies, too—for Frédéric watches all the girls go by and accepts a simple embrace from them in his dreams. (Note: The women he meets on the street are the women from the earlier moral tales—Françoise Fabian, Aurora Cornu, Marie-Christine Barrault, Haydée Politoff, Laurence de Monaghan, Béatrice Romand.)

Frédéric judges that this dream is safe—and no one seems to take anything too seriously. But then he meets Chloé (Zouzou), and we know straightaway that she is real: She is not perfectly groomed or composed, she feels raw and dangerous. And at first Chloé is simply someone to assist—the male has fond illusions of friendship that can be inhabited with some women (though he does not mention it to his wife). And before long, Chloé has become a needy, begging threat to his order and complacency. Love in the afternoon is the kind that usually seeks out the weakness in happily married men.

As with the rest of the series, Rohmer has his team: producers Barbet Schroeder and Pierre Cottrell; Néstor Almendros doing the photography; and this time there is music (fantasy requires wings) by Arié Dzierlatka. And, if I may say so, Eric Rohmer himself. There is a quality, a calm, in many Rohmer films that amounts to an abdication, almost, of the directorial function. We seem to be the privileged observers at so many special encounters. But the calm is agitated here, or striving, and it's hard to miss Rohmer's feeling that this film was special. You feel compelled to see the moral tales again. You are admitted to dark secrets about happiness—like the need for secrecy and dishonesty—that take us to the root of romantic comedy and its avid neighbor, tragedy. What did Rohmer mean by "moral tales"? The question was often asked. People wondered if they were being got at, preached to, educated? No, nothing so blunt. But you are shown an experiment, and yourself in it—and then the comedy exerts its toughest grip. You are in danger.

Love Me Tonight (1932)

When Rouben Mamoulian did *Porgy* onstage, in 1927, he had often confused his cast but dazzled onlookers with his sense of an overall rhythm—involving speech, music, sound effects, and movement. When the curtain rose on Catfish Row, he had tried to bring that scene to life with native, or Gullah, calls, no matter that his New York black actors had no idea what that language meant. And when he came to *Love Me Tonight,* five years later, he took all his earlier experiments and put them together in the sensational opening: "Isn't It Romantic?" beginning with Maurice Chevalier in the tailor's shop, going out onto the street, a train, and the gypsy camp before Jeanette MacDonald finishes it from the balcony. There had never been a musical item so fluid, so regardless of settings, and so much a guiding force of rhythm. And it was made possible because Mamoulian saw that you could record a number and then film it to a playback. Their energy was liberated.

As the story of a tailor (Chevalier) who falls in love with a princess (MacDonald), it owes more than its casting to Lubitsch. At the same time, this is the Mamoulian film in which even his scolds agree that the inventiveness worked as a whole instead of just a series of coups. It came from a play by Paul Armont and Léopold Marshand, and it was converted to the screen by Samuel Hoffenstein, Waldemar Young, and George Marion, Jr. But it's the wit of Mamoulian, the swinging hipness of the Rodgers and Hart score, and the sauciness of Chevalier and MacDonald that make it work. Of course, stage musicals would always require that performers sing and dance at the same time. But the speed and the streamlining of the movie musical were accelerated by *Love Me Tonight* and they became like spirits or arrows of desire.

Victor Milner did the photography, and Hans Dreier designed the sets. MacDonald does a great version of "Lover," and Chevalier does "Poor Apache" and "Mimi." Above all, the quality of fantasy and reality fused in a musical—it might be possible to have a fellow on a real street in the rain, doing a very complicated song-and-dance number, and looking as if he were in paradise. One of the loveliest things about sound was that the music, at last, came from the air—and not from that orchestra beavering away in the lamplight.

The cast includes Charles Ruggles, Charles Butterworth, Myrna Loy, C. Aubrey Smith, Elizabeth Patterson, Ethel Griffies, Blanche Frederici, Joseph Cawthorne, Robert Greig, Marion Byron, Cecile Cunningham, Tyler Brook, Edgar Norton, Rita Owen, Rolf Sedan, Gabby Hayes, George Humbert, and Bert Roach.

There seem to be prints in circulation of various lengths, so it's worth stressing that it was originally released at 104 minutes. It is still exhilarating to see *Love Me Tonight,* and when one recognizes that Mamoulian is also responsible for the stage debut of *Oklahoma!* and the movie of *Silk Stockings,* then surely he has to be acknowledged as a facilitator of one of our sweetest fantasies.

The Love Parade (1929)

As soon as *The Love Parade* begins, Ernst Lubitsch pulls the carpet from under sound's insecure feet: There's a conversation heard behind a closed door and then Maurice Chevalier appears and immediately talks to the camera. The technological battery is dumbfounded; Lubitsch is in charge again. And so *The Love Parade* is reckoned to be the first musical with a story—so long as you see that Lubitsch is tongue in cheek. Jeanette MacDonald is Queen of Sylvania and horny as hell—and MacDonald, despite being a "songbird," did a very hungry look, thank you. She wants a husband and then Chevalier arrives. He's a Count and she makes him a Prince so they can be married. But happy days and happier nights are intruded on by his status as "prince consort." A man needs a job, and so finally she has the sense and the sensuality to make him King.

Sylvania is from the studio that invented foreign kingdoms for *Duck Soup,* and royalty here is very much a way of measuring sexual passion. In other words, Jeanette's Queen is a Queen Bee, and every conversation she gets into is filled with sexual innuendo. It's uncanny to think that this is just two years after the moral system of silent cinema. It is as if the audience had been transformed, that they are suddenly expected to keep up with the innuendo of *The Love Parade*—which reaches some delicious, lewd places. Yes, it's Lubitsch in charge, but he was not alone—and this is a film that teases Chevalier about his French accent and generally takes a smartness in the audience for granted. Think of Farrell and Gaynor in *Sunrise,* say, and going to see this movie in a country movie house!

Supposedly the film came from a play, *The Prince Consort,* by Leon Xanrof and Jules Chancel, with a script by Ernest Vajda and Guy Bolton. Yet in truth it's so flimsy that Lubitsch might have dreamed it up in an afternoon. Hans Dreier did the sets and Victor Milner the photography. The songs are by Victor Schertzinger, with lyrics by Clifford Grey. They are not distinguished, but Lubitsch likes to shoot them in single takes when he can, and Chevalier and MacDonald seem perfectly relaxed under the primitive recording conditions.

There's a comic subplot, with Lupino Lane as Chevalier's valet and Lillian Roth as the Queen's maid. They have the best number, "Let's Be Common," and Roth is so pretty and saucy you wish that she could have done more pictures. Still, the movie wouldn't hold today if Chevalier were not amiable and MacDonald so naughty. The conceit of the story is that in every royal marriage when it gets dark the royal line and future depend on the sex. Chevalier and MacDonald leave no doubt about grasping that. You can argue that their facetious-filthy dialogue goes on just a little too long, but the chief impact is the wonder that Lubitsch should have done a talking picture with such wit and charm. Also with Edgar Norton, Lionel Belmore, and Eugene Pallette.

Loves of a Blonde (1965)

The thing that was immediately striking about Milos Forman's *Loves of a Blonde* was the way in which the helpless humor of three awkward, pudgy, balding reservist soldiers gazing at three bored, pretty girls at a tea room/dance hall turned into a quite ravishing sexual scene as the dark-eyed blonde, Andula (Hana Brejchová), has a heady romantic afternoon with Milda (Vladimír Pucholt), the kid who is playing tentative jazz piano at the dance hall. The same gray light, from cameraman Mirolav Ondrícek, washed over the soldiers' flat faces and Andula's body. And one day Ondrícek would photograph *Amadeus* and *Valmont*.

The Czech New Wave came quickly: It had only four years really before the slapdown in Prague, and after that so many of the naughty boys were off to Paris or New York. One of the scenarists on *Loves of a Blonde* was Ivan Passer. You could see the influence of the French New Wave, to be sure, but it was in the forlorn view of the middle-aged soldiers that Forman exhibited a sad, middle-European irony, something nearly Chekhovian. See the film again, today, and you want to know more about those very tin soldiers and how their world has betrayed them.

The story of Andula and Milda is very slight, and you can argue that throughout his work Forman sees the love affair as a very fleeting thing, and as a test of adaptability for all parties. But it's the freshness of real behavior here, and the fondness for unglamorous faces, that distinguishes Forman. Not much lasts here, whether under a Communist regime or something more open. The factory is the ultimate prison. People have to get along the best they can, chained as much by shyness and natural reticence as by the reports of secret police.

But Forman is a realist, and he recognizes that if you're going to dump a barracks of soldiers in a small town, then they've got to have some girls—otherwise, the humbug of soldiering will curdle in their veins. Forman does not have a lot of time for idealists: They make trouble—for themselves and for others. Even Mozart is beyond idealism. He is a bullet, propelled through stagnant space, giggling at his own momentum, and altogether too unusual to have any social lesson to be passed on.

Still, you can sniff the air of insurrection in a film like *Loves of a Blonde* and guess what a short future Prague communism has. The film is very simply made, with telephoto shots that encourage untrained actors to be natural. It follows that Forman and Ondrícek have a greedy eye for the giveaway glance—the pity and the self-pity alike. Of course, Forman became a New Yorker—whereas in odd ways Roman Polanski stayed a European. It's a fascinating comparison, for both men had grown up in tough places where they learned to measure freedom. Yet neither has made so big an issue about it. And for both men, there are invisible barriers in life—and in self—that may prove every bit as daunting as police barriers.

Lucky Luciano (1973)

Charles "Lucky" Luciano has been portrayed several times on the American screen—Bill Graham in *Bugsy,* Andy Garcia in *Hoodlum,* Angelo Infanti in *The Valachi Papers,* and so on—so that he begins to be one of those heroes of infamy, like Billy the Kid: No matter what fresh crime is added to his record, no matter how sketchy the proof, his luster increases. In the last scene of Francesco Rosi's superb *Lucky Luciano,* our guy goes to meet a screenwriter, and somehow the collision of fact and fiction brings on a fatal heart attack.

Rosi's film came just a year after *The Godfather,* and was assuredly made easier to deliver because of that success. Indeed, there was a version twenty minutes shorter for the U.S. market that cut out a lot of the Italian stuff. In addition, this was a picture for which former blacklisted writer Jerome Chodorov did the subtitles on the English version. Beyond that, the film was cast with a number of American actors—Rod Steiger as Gene Giannini, Vincent Gardenia as a military man, and Charles Cioffi (the villain in *Klute*) as Vito Genovese.

What interests Rosi most of all is the way, long before the movies, the Americans had seen Luciano as a mixed blessing. And so it is that the movie follows history in showing the release of Luciano from an American jail so that he may assist the Allied landings in Sicily during the war. The film leaves little doubt but that the very Americans who had prosecuted Luciano saw fit to rehabilitate him in the building of an antifascist resistance movement in Sicily. In turn, that led to the revitalization of the Mafia and its development of the drug trade in the years after the war. The weapons of mass destruction are something an agile democracy must know how to find when it suits them.

With a script by Rosi, Lino Iannuzzi, and Tonino Guerra, the wartime intrigue is handled with sardonic relish—in so many ways, the flourishing of the Mafia has been presented in the movies as one of those imperfect but amusing forces: Someone has to do it, someone has to let the luck fall on him, no matter that the real Luciano spent a good deal of his life in prison, or being hounded toward that destination.

As befits the maker of *Salvatore Giuliano* (1961), Rosi is of the opinion that no one knows the truth or the facts about a figure like Luciano, yet everyone walks in his sun or shade. These people exist to define our nature, our capacity for entertaining violence, and our dreams of conspiracy. And just as with *The Mattei Affair,* Rosi's view of the "gangster" is hooked upon the lovely, flashy, but shallow performance by Gian Maria Volonte and the implicit assumption that a man like Luciano was always so intent on impressing or intimidating people that he was akin to an actor.

That's where Rosi's characteristic fondness for documentary and epic hand-in-hand works so well—for theatricality is the document-level with a man like Luciano. The beautiful photography is by Pasqualino De Santis, and the rich cast also includes Edmond O'Brien and Charles Siracusa, the real Narcotics Bureau agent who devoted his life to curtailing Luciano's.

Lumière d'Été (1943)

The state of war universal in 1943 is not mentioned in Jean Grémillon's *Lumière d'Été*. Yet a malaise hangs over the strange, half-empty hotel in the desolate mountain area of Provence (it was filmed in Alpes Maritimes and at the Victorine Studio in Nice). It is a place that feels like the dead end of the world. The only activity going on there is mining, and the occasional distant blasts are the signal of some enormous panning operation that is sorting through the rocks and the stones for unnamed minerals. It is a house where Agatha Christie might have set a murder mystery—or Jean-Paul Sartre could have trapped hell. Not the least virtue of the production design is that the house seems to be starting to come apart—because of the remorseless explosions. That design work was done by André Barsacq and Max Douy, with the aid of Alexander Trauner (who was Jewish).

The script and the dialogue are by Pierre Laroche and Jacques Prévert—though it would be no surprise to hear of a stage play behind the film. A young woman, Michèle (Madeleine Robinson), comes to the house to make a rendezvous. She will attract three men: a pathetic failed painter, a maker of scenes rather than pictures (Pierre Brasseur); an engineer in a leather jacket who works at the nearby mine (Georges Marchal); and the indolent, vicious fellow who has been courting the hotel owner, a man who likes to do a little target practice with his rifle (Paul Bernard). The owner of the hotel is played by Madeleine Renaud.

There is something like a curse on these people, and I'm sure in original prints of the film, Grémillon and photographer Louis Page intended that the harsh light would stand for it. Alas, I have never seen a print that captures that severity. But the spitefulness and the boredom of the hotel people is mordant, Prévertian, and a contrast with the vigor and naturalness of the working-class people.

Grémillon deserves his following among French filmmakers, above all in that he was a documentarian who turned to fiction and knew how to find the "facts" of the world of his characters. So the mining operation here gets a good deal of attention, and it is like a kind of surgery that could be applied to the people. And yet, attempts to compare *Lumière d'Été* with Renoir's *La Règle du Jeu* seem ridiculous and damaging to the Grémillon picture. I can believe that Grémillon had Renoir in mind, and I can easily imagine that he intended the audience's sense of the war to explain the becalmed self-loathing of these people. But the dramatic activity is so much less than in the Renoir film, and the class perspective is thinner.

When *Lumière d'Été* has its big fancy-dress party it's a mistake. The atmosphere of the film has depended on so few people in so large a space. So where do all these extras come from? Where do they live? Our sense of the picture has been undermined.

Lust for Life (1956)

It's over fifty years old now, and I daresay that Vincent Van Gogh scholarship has moved way beyond the level of Irving Stone's melodramatic novel about the unhappy painter. The message of the title and the fixed bourgeois notion that ecstatic art should expect no fitting reward in this world are trite as well as erroneous. But *Lust for Life* is still Vincente meets Vincent, a delicate, very sophisticated Italian-American sensibility honoring the raw power of an uncouth Flemish genius. Minnelli lived to old age in Beverly Hills; Van Gogh shot himself in a cornfield at thirty-seven. The gulf does not matter. The movie is flooded with respect, and there are few moments as glorious as when Minnelli lets the CinemaScope frame become a wall of Van Goghs.

John Houseman was the producer, Norman Corwin wrote the script, Russell Harlan and Freddie Young did the photography, Miklós Rózsa wrote the music—and all of that work is the epitome of craftsmanship. Still, it was Houseman and Minnelli who set such stock in going to the real places of Van Gogh's life, from Holland, to Paris, and then gradually farther south in France. Without any didactic heavy-handedness, there is still the notion that the actual light and the real places are essential—because a painter is the creature of his world as well as its creator. That's why it is so telling that in *Lust for Life* there is never any concession to the old Hollywood notion that perhaps this driven artist might have been happy, too, and socially acceptable, with a little better luck, a few sales, and the right woman. Vincent is doomed from the outset, and that certainty animates Kirk Douglas's performance, in which finally the outward resemblance between the two men seems incidental to the inner affinity.

The largest gesture toward "entertainment" in the picture is Anthony Quinn's Gauguin, and, of course, Quinn won the Supporting Actor Oscar—Douglas lost to Yul Brynner in *The King and I*! Quinn is all very well, but his biggest lesson for Van Gogh would appear to be, Take your crises and turn them into grandiloquent ham.

Far, far better are the other supporting parts, nearly all of which are completely subservient to the film—Everett Sloane as the doctor, Pamela Brown as one of his women, and James Donald as the long-suffering brother, Theo. In the choice to root the film in the letters between Theo and Vincent the film made perhaps its soundest decision.

One other issue needs to be faced: Metrocolor is handled with great care and tact by the two cameramen, but still one can't help but long for Technicolor as the system that applied to Van Gogh best. The colors need to throb like wounds. We should come away from the film searching for dark glasses. Whereas Metrocolor, finally, is just a touch too tasteful. Still, as the years have passed we have had other movie Vincents—by Altman, Paul Cox, and rivetingly by Maurice Pialat. But it is justice, I think, that the Minnelli survives and stands at the heart of the group.

The Lusty Men (1952)

Rodeo riders have their season and their eight seconds on a bull. They take their prize money while they can, and soon they are arthritic from their fractures, hobbling round the circuit, picking up beer money. Producer Jerry Wald had read this sad outline in a magazine story by Claude Stanush, and he put Stanush with David Dortort to furnish a movie treatment. What the fellows hit upon was one cowboy in decline, Jeff McCloud, teaching another on the way up, Wes Merritt. Dortort did a lot of research, and for a moment Robert Parrish was going to direct it at RKO. Then he fell away and Nick Ray was the director for hire, reveling in the research material and the chance to film the back roads of the West, country he had explored in his time as a folk-music researcher. Horace McCoy turned it into a shooting script, and Robert Mitchum and Arthur Kennedy were cast as Jeff and Wes.

It was then that Howard Hughes, interested in Susan Hayward, looked for a way to get her on his lot. Wes has a wife, he surmised—Susan Hayward—and she is drawn to Jeff. McCoy and Dortort did hasty revisions to accommodate this new angle, and Ray managed to get Lee Garmes to bring mood to the tatty, nomadic world of rodeo.

It all sounds like a routine project, yet a bond formed between Ray and Mitchum, no matter that the actor was bewildered by Ray's introspective silences and his search for "motivation." And Mitchum found himself as a loser, a man who has wasted too much time and broken too many bones and promises to himself. But in a funny way it's the bourgeois drive of Susan Hayward's wife, Louise, that is most interesting, struggling to make a stable world out of the gypsy life when Jeff prefers to believe that nothing is going to last. And the harder Wes tries to be a star, the more surely Jeff and Louise are drawn together in their rueful, common understanding.

The Lusty Men is not the best title it could have had, for the machoism in these guys is short-lived. Wald wanted a happier ending, where Mitchum goes off with an old girlfriend (Maria Hart), but Ray could taste the tragedy he had on his hands and he held to the scripted ending where Jeff gets a fatal injury trying to recapture his past.

After the studio shooting (with excellent art direction by Albert D'Agostino to show the trailer homes), they went traveling with the rodeo circuit. That's when Ray and Garmes did some great scenes—the one where Mitchum goes back to his old family home (used in Wim Wenders's *Lightning over Water*) and the melancholy shots of the rodeo ring at twilight with the wind stirring up dust and hot-dog wrappers. And that's the secret to the film: for its conventional triangle story is brought to life by an eye like Walker Evans's and the actors' respect for the inner delusions of pipe dream. Insist on the full 113-minute version—shorter versions were released.

M (1931)

If you look at Fritz Lang's work as a whole then it is fascinating to see the hinge and the transformation represented by *M*—as his urban thrillers took on character and foreboding, as they moved from frenzies of pure (or genre-driven) action to the crooked path pursued by warped figures. Thus, it is as if the city itself takes on more tragic character once Hans Beckert is the subject of a film. It is not simply that he is a villain, or a dysfunctional hero. But he is a trapped figure for whom his own nature (hidden beneath that drab, draped overcoat) is just another version of the city where law and outlawry alike will join in the hunt for him. As if they cared! For surely, the plaintiveness in Beckert—and in Peter Lorre's bulging eyes—is that he has become a victim so that the vicious routine of the others' urban game (call it the system, or corruption) can go on as before.

The film was evidently based on Peter Kürten, the Dusseldorf killer, who was at large in 1930—though Kürten killed adults as well as children, and often burned the corpses. Lang saw Peter Lorre onstage (in Wedekind's *Spring Awakening*) and made his famous bargain: If Lorre would stay off the screen, Lang would give him a starring part one day. What part? asked the actor. To which Lang said he didn't know yet. I think it's plain that Lorre inspired Lang's killer far more than Kürten—thus *M* begins with the stricken childishness in Lorre, the high voice and the masochist eyes. In seeing Lorre, Lang had discovered a character vital to his work: the man terrified of himself.

Thea von Harbou took credit for the screenplay, though Lang and even a few others had significant input. Even so, the greatest power of the film lies in the way Beckert is seen, and heard. It is as if he is there, in the city, or at our shoulder, before we notice him. So the beautiful device by which a criminal who recognizes the "Peer Gynt" whistling plants a white chalk "M" on Beckert's shoulder is akin to this presence, and it is like that clammy sense of Beckert being close to us in the dark.

But then notice the exquisite views of this fabricated city—the high-angled shots of insect groupings, the web of framing devices, and the implacable architecture of the frame. The light is bright often, harsh and scathing, but it never has a hint of daylight or fresh air. Does that mean theatrical? Or cinematic? It's more than stage light, it's the consistent fog of city life where breathing itself draws the light through our lungs, with so little nourishment or solace. Photographed by Fritz Arno Wagner, and with art direction by Karl Vollbrecht and Emil Hasler, *M* is a masterpiece of prison's mood in everyday life.

Of course, it is Lorre's film (just as it became his curse), but notice the fine work by Ellen Widmann, Inge Landgut, Gustaf Gründgens, Fritz Odemar, Paul Kemp, Theo Lingen, Ernst Stahl-Nachbaur, Franz Stein, Otto Wernicke, Georg John, Rosa Valetti, and so many others. The sound is off and on, and that variation is oddly effective—again, it is as if the sound comes in with a heartbeat or breathing. (And they say Lang himself did the whistling.) What's the most disconcerting thing about *M*? Neither its killer, nor the cold paranoia. It is the beauty.

Joseph Losey made *M* at almost precisely the worst time: he was on the verge of being run out of America by the blacklist, and it was not likely that any new approach to the Fritz Lang material would be viewed sympathetically. Moreover, Lang himself was by then a Hollywood resident, as well as a deeply competitive soul. He got into a shouting match with Seymour Nebenzal (producer of both the original and the remake), and he volunteered his opinion that the whole thing was theft. That led to accusations that Losey had in some places copied the mise-en-scène of Lang's classic. That is simply not true. Nor is the subject of the two films the same.

It is true that Nebenzal sought to do a remake for Columbia. Further, when the project was offered to the censor, his response was that the only justification for doing the film was as a repeat of an historic masterpiece. So the Lang script had to be followed. But Losey saw the material differently: "The attitude of the film-makers and of society then [1931] was that a sex maniac or anyone guilty of sexual acts towards children was a monster to be hounded down even by the criminal underworld—who were in fact his peers—because he was worse than they were. This is obviously a pretty unenlightened and even old-fashioned view, and very few people would subscribe to it now. Most people realize that this sort of thing is a terrifying illness."

The shooting lasted twenty days and led to a film with long, intricate takes that should be 88 minutes—there are cut versions around which do damage to the sense as well as corrupting David Wayne's heartfelt performance as Martin Harrow.

The script was by Norman Reilly Raine and Leo Katcher, and there was additional dialogue by Waldo Salt. Don Weis was script supervisor and Robert Aldrich assistant director. John Hubley was the design consultant, and Ernest Laszlo did the black-and-white photography. The picture is set in Los Angeles (especially the old downtown) and there are some beautiful shots of steep streets, and of the Bradbury Building.

And then there is Wayne, an actor too often confined to comedy and a rather waspish manner. It was Wayne who made Losey eager to do the film, and it is Wayne's performance finally that answers all the carping. Stripped down by his confession, and feeling himself among alien beings, he is for Losey a model of the shattered soul—it might be anyone—who can now be found on city streets, ready to make an ordinary enterprise of a monstrous crime. If it is true that people no longer quite attend to the Lang version, because it is a classic, then Losey's film sets the real terror free again like a wild animal.

Along with the reconstruction of L.A. to match Lang's schematic view, Losey assembled a great cast of small-part actors: Howard da Silva, Luther Adler, Martin Gabel, Steve Brodie, Raymond Burr, Glenn Anders, Karen Morley, Norman Lloyd, John Miljan, and Jim Backus, many of whom were about to become victims of the blacklist.

Maclovia (1948)

In what a narrator describes as the most beautiful and tranquil part of Mexico, there is a lake and an island in the lake, called Janitzio. There lives Maclovia, a girl, an Indian, a virgin, the daughter of Don Macario, a modest landowner. Maclovia is María Félix, who was thirty-two at the time, stunningly beautiful, if a little past her virginity. It doesn't matter: sometimes virginity is a state of mind. *Maclovia* is an epic melodrama and love story, made by Emilio Fernández, "El Indio" (he was of mixed Spanish and Indian descent). Fernández is known as a broad actor in Peckinpah films—he is Mapache in Peckinpah's *The Wild Bunch*. He is also the great director of Mexico's golden age. *Maclovia* is a characteristic work, easily treated lightly, but still burning with romantic intensity.

Maclovia falls in love with José María (Pedro Armendáriz), and he is too old for the story, too. But for Fernández and his cameraman, Gabriel Figueroa, the pathos is over the top but utterly sincere. Forbidden to look at Maclovia, José María wants to write her a letter. So he goes to the village school and begs to be admitted. Gradually, he learns to write—*cut,* and there is Maclovia, at the same school, asking to be taught to read. Of course, this storytelling tradition works in part because of an uneducated audience and a very basic way of life. At the same time, these peasants wear white suits that seem washed every day, Félix's Maclovia wears false eyelashes and benefits from the beauty parlor. Why not? Once upon a time North American films worked at the same code—and Félix resembles the divas of the Joan Crawford era.

There is a loathsome army sergeant, the military power in Janitzio, and he wants Maclovia, too. José María attacks him and gets twenty-four years' imprisonment (Fernández himself got twenty years once for a shooting). We tremble to discover whether Maclovia will give herself to the sergeant to free José María. You'll have to find out, though I'll say that I think the very ending of the film should have been more violent, more tragic, more operatic, more everything.

The one participant who gives his all is Figueroa, a great cameraman to be sure and a master at bringing subtle shadows to the harsh light of Mexico—you can see here how he uses fishing nets to diffuse the light. And Figueroa took pictures the way María Félix strikes attitudes: they were a perfect match. You may find the knockout compositions overpowering after a while. Some American directors who used Figueroa, like Ford and Huston, came to that opinion. But, again, if you grasp what *Maclovia* is doing, then Figueroa is a vital source of its power. Félix could be funny and explosive (see her work in *French Cancan*). Here she is beautiful, in love and suffering. When she hears José María's letter to her, the film runs riot: there are at least ten different close-ups of her response.

Madame de . . . (1953)

If I told you the story of *Madame de . . .*, I could easily make light of it. It could be a silly woman who fancied she could do as she pleased. Then her husband gives her a pair of earrings. Now, you must understand, she is "comfortably" married. She and her husband look good together. But they almost certainly both have their secret affairs where they look good—or is it happy?—in their own eyes. I could be ironic about the story. The woman was reckless. She was spending too much. Some people in love are like that. So she pawned the earrings. It's all so trivial to start with, yet it turns into a tragedy that overwhelms Madame. It's just like a good horse and carriage: one minute you're making your handsome way to lunch or the opera, and the next you're in the gutter, broken. You believed you were immortal, when you were no better than an expensive watch.

La Ronde is the story of an entire society. *Lola Montès* is about the most famous courtesan of her moment. And *Madame de . . .* is about earrings. Yet, clearly, as the jewels change hands they are just the hard token of the soft hopes passed around in *La Ronde.* With Max Ophüls, as much as with any director, it is the pursuit or the circling, the impulse, that puts the camera in the air as if it were a butterfly in its short life between soaring and exhaustion. And maybe just because this is the smallest story that Ophüls did, it is the quintessential film, the one that knows the suddenness or the brevity of both happiness and disaster. After all, it's a tragedy to Madame de . . . , and a bit of gossip to you or me.

The film comes from a novel by Louise de Vilmorin. It was adapted for the screen by Ophüls himself with Marcel Achard and Annette Wademant. Fickleness was perhaps *the* Ophüls subject, but time and again, in different countries and diverse studios, he hired the same people. So Christian Matras was the photographer. Jean d'Eaubonne did the design. Georges Annenkov and Rosine Delamare designed the costumes. The music was by Georges Van Parys.

Danielle Darrieux is Madame de . . . . Charles Boyer is her husband. And Vittorio De Sica is her lover. The rest of the cast includes Mireille Perrey, Jean Debucourt, Serge Lecointe, Jean Galland, Hubert Noël, Madeleine Barbulée, Jean Degrave, and Léon Walther.

The film exists at 102 minutes, and seems perfect. Yet there's a story of a longer version, as much as 180 minutes, lost. We lost other Ophüls projects, too, like *La Duchesse de Langeais,* with Garbo and James Mason, and the story of Modigliani. Jacques Becker made that, with Gérard Philipe as the painter, and the film is dedicated to the memory of Max Ophüls, like Jacques Demy's *Lola,* like so many films. People ask what killed Stanley Kubrick. Don't rule out the horror of making *Eyes Wide Shut* and realizing that he was not Max.

Mad Max (1979)

Very few people guessed what *Mad Max* was going to be when the first film in the series opened. It looked like a biker movie, set in a future world, vaguely after the apocalypse, with Mel Gibson as its figurehead. The film was very badly released (with dubbing so you could hear what the Aussies were saying!) with very little promotion. But the audience loved the strange mix of biker action, futurism, and (shall we say?) Australia-rules fascism.

The first film was written by James McCausland and George Miller (who directed, too) and the photography was by David Eggby. Gibson played Max Rockatansky, a policeman (albeit one with an overriding urge to become freelance). It's when the nasty gangs on outback roads get his wife and son that Max turns Mad.

The second film, *Mad Max 2* (1981), known as *The Road Warrior* in the U.S., is a Kennedy Miller Entertainment production. George Miller is still making the film, but the script has been turned over to Terry Hayes (one of the best writers in Australia then), Miller, and Brian Hannant, and American Dean Semler has been brought in to do some photography. It's clear in *The Road Warrior* that the Third World War has come and gone and fuel oil is now the gold that runs the world. The setting and the talk were far more blatantly Australian. Mel Gibson had become a dress-up doll. And this was probably the liveliest film in the series, with a cast list that included the following comic-book characters: Feral Kid, Humungus, Curmudgeon, Quiet Man, Lusty Girl, and so on. Join the dots and you had a story. This time, there was no mistake about the financial cleanup operation.

Then in 1985 came the finale, *Mad Max Beyond Thunderdome*, in which Max comes to the city of Bartertown and finds Tina Turner waiting. It was a pretty good match. Again, Miller directed, and the ingenuity with homemade vehicles, rocking sound, and unconsidered violence was taken in whole—this was also the age of Rambo and the Terminator, and it was a great joke for Australians that maybe the wildest of these silly franchises was not even American.

Of course, there was another lesson, not lost on Mel Gibson, who has seldom lacked for confidence. It was that in the matter of violence, far-fetched plotting, and anything and everything in the name of home, family, fatherland, and so on, he could probably get away with whatever he elected to do. The sweet liberal spurs of outrage whenever he goes over the top with a car or a drink are so minor compared with the complete fantasization of liberty, vehicular motion, and bull's blood in the *Mad Max* films. He knows what we want. He proved it three times in a row. Alas, the odd talent of George Miller seems to have been left by the roadside. But a pattern for Australian confidence was laid down, and Mel Gibson had our number.

The Magnificent Ambersons (1942)

There is only one way to start—by saying that this might have been the greatest of American pictures, the clear and present expression of the tragedy that occurred in the land when such things as the motorcar, personal obsession, and "development" eclipsed the late-eighteenth-century republic. Just as Orson Welles sometimes spoke with reverence and nostalgia (as if he had been there) about the "olde England" behind *Chimes at Midnight*, so this is his bow to "olde America," and the surest sign of how much the very modern man loved the past.

I am speaking as if the movie we have—and are likely to have for the rest of time—is not our great tragedy. But it is, in two ways: as the masterwork on the screen, and as the story of its own ruin—a story that becomes George Orson Welles just as fully as the onscreen disaster is fit for George Amberson Minafer.

It was the second film of his RKO contract, made in the dismay that followed *Kane*, the exuberance with which Orson would depart for Rio de Janeiro and his South American adventure, and the more certain onset of war. It was from the novel by Booth Tarkington, published in 1918, and it developed from a radio version in which Orson had played George. For the film, Welles gave that part to Tim Holt, and chose to use himself as narrator. Thus we have the gravest twenty-seven-year-old reading the decline of the Ambersons into the national record. Stanley Cortez did the photography, and he was slower than Toland, apparently. But he had his own genius, and he was well suited to the deep continuities of space and time required by the old house and the placid naturalism of life there. The tragic spirit is in Cortez's light, whereas Toland's in *Kane* is often—appropriately—a light show. That is why people say *Ambersons* is more deeply felt.

This may be the greatest ensemble acting in American film: Holt—bumptious yet dull; Joseph Cotten, so ready to yield as Eugene; Anne Baxter in bud, then bloom, as Lucy; Dolores Costello, like old lace as Isabel; Ray Collins as Jack—so chipper, so brave; Richard Bennett, heartbreaking, as Major Amberson. And Agnes Moorehead as Fanny, coming unglued as her nephew stuffs himself with strawberry shortcake.

So, the film was shot by the end of 1941. Early in 1942 after throwing a rough cut together, Welles went away to Rio, leaving Robert Wise to edit the film and his manager, Jack Moss, to guard it. They tried. They cabled Welles, who was shooting miles of film and getting to know the ladies of Carnival. He stayed away. It was his momentous decision. And in his absence RKO previewed the film and shrank from raucous laughter in a crowd of kids. They intervened. It seems likely that Welles's version would have been 132 minutes. RKO released the picture at 88. Much of the closing material was gone. A studio ending was tacked on. Years later, the cut footage—the last hope of rescue—was apparently dumped in the ocean. The full film was lost—but its full meaning was vindicated.

Magnolia (1999)

I have already seen *Magnolia* several times since it opened, and it gets better and more complex on every viewing. I can see the frank structural debt to Robert Altman's *Short Cuts,* in its notion of several stories from one part of town that may slightly overlap but which reflect on each other and become more fascinating as the picture builds. But *Short Cuts* came out of the considerable experience, in life and art, of Raymond Carver and Robert Altman, and *Magnolia,* in blunt fact, is a young man's film where one has to give credit to the way thinking has made up for a sheer lack of life so far.

So it would not be surprising if *Magnolia* were a little schematic, and I suppose that the plague of frogs at the film's end could be read as an arbitrary intervention, and a way of drawing the proceedings to a close. Instead, I think the frogs are not just sublime and casual, but a very poetic, absurdist way of enlisting the universal. A wiser, less hopeful man would not have used the frogs. They come out of nothing but Paul Thomas Anderson's desperate belief in life.

There are five areas of focus: Jason Robards is dying, despite the care of Philip Seymour Hoffman and the terrible mixed feelings of his young wife, Julianne Moore. Robards's estranged son, Tom Cruise, is the commanding figure in a strident men's movement, but he is on the point of being reduced to zero by the patient inquiries of a young woman journalist. Melora Walters is a drug addict and a piece of refuse who finds a cop, John C. Reilly, falling for her. Philip Baker Hall is a TV game show host at the end of his tether, in part because of the guilt he feels toward his daughter, Melora Walters. And William H. Macy is a wreck in life, a former kid quiz-show champion.

It's easy enough to extract from that information the kinds of guilt or shame that hang over these people and which amount to a deep loneliness, no matter how crowded their frames are with other people. But that level of awareness is minor compared with the howling anguish of Julianne Moore at her own infidelities or the helpless vacancy left in Tom Cruise once he is brought back to the core of truth that all his life has been constructed to deny.

So it's obvious enough that the film relies on very good writing and astonishing acting. But then you'd have to allow for the mournful persistence of the Aimee Mann music and the steadfast adherence to context in Anderson's way of shooting. In the end, nothing so sustains this film as the sense of neighborhood, or the mathematical possibility of contingent lives and the way in which pain and grief and failure are shared things, like air, no matter that the economy may be lonely and capitalist. There's the real point of *Magnolia,* I think, the way in which Anderson shows us a common or shared place, and the undeniable achievement of contingency as a kind of politics.

Major Dundee (1965)

When *Major Dundee* opened it was under a cloud. Its director, Sam Peckinpah, disowned it, because of interference from the producer, Jerry Bresler. It was shorter than Peckinpah wanted, and there was a good deal of confusion apparent on the screen. But Andrew Sarris felt that "the suspicion persists that *Dundee* was a disaster on the directorial level long before the front office stepped in." Well, years later, a fuller version emerged, allegedly closer to Peckinpah's intentions, and Sarris seemed prescient. Not that *Dundee* isn't a fascinating picture and as much of a promise of what was to come as an indication that Peckinpah wore storm clouds instead of hats.

Bresler had approached Peckinpah (a second best to the already engaged John Ford) with a treatment by Harry Julian Fink. It was a Civil War story; it was a rogue Apache story; it was a Mexican story; and it was a prisoner-of-war story. Dundee was a Union officer who would free and enlist a bunch of Confederate prisoners to go after a rogue Apache warrior. This would lead them over the border and into Mexico, where they would end up fighting the French who were trying to suppress a Mexican revolution.

Charlton Heston was attached as Dundee. Peckinpah sat down with Fink, who then produced 163 pages of script on a third of the story! So Fink was fired and Oscar Saul came in. Peckinpah went location scouting in Mexico, and the more remote the place the better he liked it. Then, just as shooting was to begin, there was a power shift at Columbia (the studio paying for it) and the $4.5 million budget was cut back to $3 million. Out of reach, Peckinpah shot what he wanted and spent . . . $4.5 million. And so the clash was inevitable.

More than that, Peckinpah had gone for the violence. He took it into his head to rip away the golden legend of the cavalry as set down by Ford. To that end, he stressed confusions of leadership and the terrible violence of battle. There would be no heroes. The war was a storm that took on a life of its own—and Peckinpah was certainly reaching out for a metaphor for Vietnam. His cut came in at 160 minutes; the film was released at 124.

The trouble is plain to see: it's Richard Harris and the Confederates offering a view of chivalry and a war within the army. Whereas it might have been a film about a lost patrol, hacking away and killing, despite the loss of function. Harris is mocking the film. Heston is stalwart. And there are very good supporting performances from James Coburn, Warren Oates, Ben Johnson, L. Q. Jones, R. G. Armstrong, and Slim Pickens—a stock company taking shape. Peckinpah said it was one of the most painful things that had happened in his life—but it was early still. The photography, by Sam Leavitt, is violently antiromantic. The jittery music is by Daniele Amfitheatrof. Everything involving Senta Berger should have been cut.

Make Way for Tomorrow (1937)

Make Way for Tomorrow seems like one of those knockout fortune-cookie titles from the 1930s (tough but optimistic), like *Little Man, What Now?*, *You Can't Take It with You*, or *Gone With the Wind*. It sounds like the description of a bracing future, a challenge but surely good for us all. And there are characters in the film—the younger characters, the children—who might utter it in that way, albeit wistfully. Like "Time Marches On" as a warning to a lame horse. In truth, *Make Way for Tomorrow* is an extraordinary film for America—which may account for why you haven't seen it. *The Awful Truth* (the other film Leo McCarey made in 1937) is the one you know, the one that got Academy attention. It's a great film, daring, challenging, funny enough to make playboys and playgirls think twice. But *Make Way for Tomorrow* is so tough you can't believe it's going to do what it does.

Barkley and Lucy Cooper (Victor Moore and Beulah Bondi) have been married fifty years. The bank is taking back their house. They have four children, and they tell them the news: Cora (Elizabeth Risdon), Nellie (Minna Gombell), Robert (Ray Mayer), and George (Thomas Mitchell). In 1937 Beulah Bondi was two months older than Mitchell. One way of addressing that is to say that Beulah Bondi was an actress who frequently looked older than her actual years; she also wears aging makeup in the film. But the other is that in using Thomas Mitchell, McCarey was deliberately employing a "veteran" and favorite actor because George is a son who will do a wretched thing.

It is plain that Barkley and Lucy are deeply fond of each other—you could say "in love" if you are not shocked too much at the thought of that bounty being available for old people. And their children agree to their being separated. A time will come when George has to advise his mother that he has a rest home in mind for her. Watch that scene and remind yourself that McCarey is known for "comedy," for this is one of the unkindest and yet most understandable scenes in American film. McCarey films it as such yet he makes it ordinary and natural, too, and he lets the mother recover the son's shattered dignity. It is one of the great moments in American film, and it is dazzling and confounding to know that Mitchell won the Supporting Actor Oscar in *Stagecoach*, and was not nominated for his George Cooper. Why not? Because some acting is too truthful to be endured.

Did Ozu know this film?

Viña Delmar wrote the script from a novel called *The Years Are So Long* by Josephine Lawrence. William C. Mellor did the photography. Hans Dreier and Bernard Herzbrun did the sets. George Antheil and Victor Young wrote the music. I think it is the best American film about family betrayal, yet it is so good that it does not content itself with blaming the young. It is about life, and if it is seldom seen it is because we are not strong enough.

Malcolm X (1992)

Spike Lee's *Malcolm X* is 202 minutes long. It cost about $30 million and earned rentals of $19.4 million. Those are disappointing figures. But we live by the ethic of the marketplace, and in the history of film there have been more drastic disasters. I recall that Lee had great difficulties getting *Malcolm X* completed, so I don't think there's much room for charges of extravagance on the production. On the other hand, Michael Mann's *Ali* somehow cost $107 million—and grossed only $58 million. That's a gross figure as opposed to rentals: in other words, *Ali* lost far more money on first run, yet somehow or other raised a budget three times as high.

Was that because *Ali* was reckoned to be more likeable than *Malcolm*—especially to a white audience? Or was it because Michael Mann was white? We are on very tricky ground here, and Spike Lee, for one, would opine that we are being idiots if we don't recognize that a black director has a harder road to follow in "Hollywood."

Suppose you are inclined to judge that a lot of the audience would regard Malcolm X as an "unattractive" or unappealing movie hero. Then compare it with *Reds*, the John Reed biopic made by Warren Beatty. That film opened in 1981 (at 200 minutes) and it cost about $35 million. In other words, allowing for the time difference, *Reds* was a good deal more expensive. Yet it had rentals in the U.S. of only $21 million. But *Reds* was Oscar-nominated for Best Picture (generous, but OK), and it won for director (very generous). *Malcolm X* was not nominated in either category.

I am trying to keep this entry as factual as possible—to make a climactic point. But now I want to say that I believe *Malcolm X* is a better-made, more dramatically coherent film. Vittorio Storaro's photography of *Reds* is classical and magnificent, yet I think Ernest Dickerson's imagery in *Malcolm X* is more organic and dramatic and stirring. Let me go further: Warren Beatty's Jack Reed is a narcissistic gesture; Denzel Washington's Malcolm is from the soul. *Reds* is a liberal's nostalgia for days he has no real wish to reinhabit. *Malcolm X* is a record of the life and lies that formed Lee.

Malcolm X is important not just in showing the conflicting influences on a young black man in the mid–twentieth century. It also tracks the appeal to such a man of Islam, a subject that still hangs over the world. This is an extraordinary film, an exciting story, and a parable where every meaning is fresh.

There are outstanding supporting performances from Angela Bassett (as Malcolm's wife, Betty), Albert Hall, Al Freeman, Jr. (as Elijah Muhammad), Delroy Lindo, Theresa Randle, Kate Vernon, Lonette McKee, Tommy Hollis, Giancarlo Esposito, and Lee himself. The screenplay was by Lee and Arnold Perl, using *The Autobiography of Malcolm X*.

Male and Female (1919)

This is actually *The Admirable Crichton,* the play by J. M. Barrie which opened in 1903. An English aristocratic family and their butler are shipwrecked on a desert island, whereupon Crichton the butler—the devotee of common sense—becomes head of the family. Let us suppose that a gentle dash of social criticism was intended, still Cecil B. DeMille foresaw other revolutions contingent on the story—for instance, he imagined Gloria Swanson striding out of the surf after the shipwreck so that her tattered silk gown clung to her body. It was only when DeMille volunteered his title to exhibitors that they begged him to make a change. Films about admirals had no track record, apparently. So DeMille reconsidered and decided to call it *Male and Female.*

Of course, when you realize that it was made in the same year as *True Heart Susie,* you can see the divergent paths possible in cinema. An audience existed still for Griffith's respect for Lillian Gish, but a new force had come into being and it was eager to see as much of Swanson as possible. Jeanie Macpherson wrote the script, though the actors on DeMille pictures rarely saw a script—it was usually C.B. telling them a bit of the story and them acting it out.

DeMille elected to film the desert island scenes on Santa Cruz, a small island off Santa Barbara, and everybody went out there for a couple of weeks. For those scenes, Swanson was bedraggled first and then increasingly exposed as the sun beat down. But DeMille foresaw the charge of exploitation and therefore determined to have his star as near nude as possible as often as possible. So in her secure existence before the shipwreck she takes a ladylike bath where she is apparently nude. And then, just to add balance, after Crichton has read to the family from a book about Babylon, Swanson's character (Lady Mary) has a dream in which she is a slave girl and Crichton (Thomas Meighan) has become the emperor of Babylon. This required slave-girl costumes. The young Mitchell Leisen was hired to design them, and he used batik and beads, a lot of skin, and big built-up clogs so that the diminutive Swanson might seem taller.

Yes, it's shameless, but done with enormous zest and good humor. And suppose that DeMille was correct—suppose that sex was the best American antidote to any threatening signs of class distinction. Consider this account, by Swanson, of what Elinor Glyn told her:

"The Prince of Wales absolutely adored you in *Male and Female.* . . . You children don't realize what has happened yet, I know. But you will. Motion pictures are going to change everything. They're the most important thing that's come along since the printing press. What woman can dream about a prince anymore when she's seen one up close in a newsreel? She'd much rather dream about Wallace Reid. People don't care about royalty anymore. They're much more interested in queens of the screen, like you, dear."

The Maltese Falcon (1941)

In this case you can trust the lady. It was Mary Astor who observed, "It was Huston's picture, Huston's script. He'd had the wit to keep Hammett's book intact. His shooting script was a precise map of what went on. Every shot, camera move, entrance, exit was down on paper, leaving nothing to chance. Inspiration or invention." But spur-of-the-moment genius did have its opening: that's how Ms. Astor and Mr. Huston found time for a nice little affair during the shooting of *The Maltese Falcon.*

Warner Brothers had purchased the Dashiell Hammett novel (1930) when it came out for $8,500, and on the strength of that they'd ruined it twice already—*The Maltese Falcon* and *Satan Met a Lady.* But John Huston was a favored man at the studio. He had been writing his head off for them, and producer Henry Blanke asked what he would like to direct. Huston got the feeling straightaway that the studio was backing the offer. So *The Maltese Falcon* got its third shot. Early plans to cast Geraldine Fitzgerald and George Raft sank away, and Huston got Astor and Bogart instead, the latter at three days' notice when he was on suspension. So don't give up on paying your dues and having the luck. Huston was thirty-five.

Among many other things, he was an astute and regular reader. He knew Hammett had done so much of the work and had written a movie if the studio chumps would leave well enough alone. For his part, Huston storyboarded the whole thing and then went out and found Peter Lorre for Joel Cairo and Sydney Greenstreet for Casper Gutman. Even then, he read the book closely enough to realize that Spade and the dame are two of a kind—not very nice—but that Spade has a bleak sense of honor while she'll do anything. He also saw that Spade walks a fine line. He often seems to be in charge of everything, and with Bogart in the role, that could lead to sardonic superiority. But Spade can be rattled. You can get under his skin. And at the very end he isn't quite sure whether to be the man he wants to be or to trade everything away for Brigid.

So I'll grant that *The Maltese Falcon* is meticulously shot (without ever getting that locked-up Fritz Lang feeling). I'll allow that Lorre, Greenstreet, and Elisha Cook, Jr., are definitive supporting characters in the world of noir to come. And I'd add that it took a mercurial spirit to know that Greenstreet and Lorre would have such sly chemistry. But it's the love story that is riveting, by which I mean the way Mary Astor tells her tales, with deepening sincerity and fuckability (they are very sexy together), and Bogart's Spade chuckles and says, "Oh, you're good, darling!" More or less, I think it's the first film in which two characters go on a spin based on not telling the truth. It's something Hammett guessed, that the players felt, and it's the lovely crisscross of screwball and noir. It's one of the sweetest discoveries in American film.

The Manchurian Candidate (1962)

There's a fascinating group of pictures made in the late 1950s and early 1960s where American genre seems to have gone astray—*Some Like It Hot, Touch of Evil, Psycho, Rio Bravo,* and *The Manchurian Candidate.* It's not that that thriller wasn't a warning. Frank Sinatra certainly seemed to wonder whether Lee Harvey Oswald had seen *The Manchurian Candidate.* Yet no one, I think, ever took the whole brainwashing stuff seriously, with its stress on playing a little solitaire and the Queen of Diamonds, as anything except Richard Condon and George Axelrod's wild injection of screwball menace into an electoral comedy. In other words, aren't election campaigns comic enough already without solitaire?

There are sublime things in the picture: the dream in which a ladies' flower-club meeting slips in and out of brainwashing; the entire conceit of Laurence Harvey as someone not quite there; the furious, digestive satisfaction of Angela Lansbury feeding on all around her; and the dotty-meeting-cute scene between Sinatra and Janet Leigh on the train. Throw in director John Frankenheimer's gleeful portrait of television at work as a confusing miasma and *The Manchurian Candidate* is jumpy with stuff to watch (and laugh at). For instance, when Lansbury, playing Harvey's mother, gives him the full-lipped kiss we can't honestly say that that issue is explored—it's an instant joke, especially since we half know that Lansbury was only three years older than Harvey. Think if he had really begun to get the hots for her.

The notion that we are asked to accept—that the Iselins are Communists on their way to the White House as part of a Big Red Plot—is nonsensical, scriptwriting ingenuity, and an idea that deserves to be treated comically. The real sources of paranoia and menace in American politics are so much more alarming than the Iselins. If you want to worry, think of people as jittery as Sinatra's Ben Marco in any position of power in the Army.

Of course, Frankenheimer had an instinct that his film had to be played over the top. He took his cue from Harvey's natural-born zombie act and the amazing release in Angela Lansbury. And he never let the audience have time to reflect on the cockamamie plot. In the lamentable remake (by Jonathan Demme), the flat-footed time we have to think about it all kills the fun.

Axelrod deserves great praise: He was one of those writers who could hold the screen and the moment while letting a mass of resonance fill the theater. Lionel Lindon's black-and-white photography is tough and wintry, and the young Richard Sylbert did a great job on the décor. The film might have been better still if the crazy design had gone all the way through, like the streaky remnants of some hallucinatory drug. But in fact, as it nears its end, Frankenheimer turns pro and solemn, Ben Marco becomes active, and the film says, "Look, I'm a suspense thriller!" But that's not what we remember later.

A Man Escaped (1956)

Fontaine is a French Resistance fighter captured by the Germans. He is sent to a forbidding prison. Not that we have to see individual Germans. When Fontaine is in a car being taken to the prison with other prisoners, he thinks to make an escape. He runs, but the camera remains, fixed on his empty place in the back of the car. We hear the noise of feet and scuffle and then Fontaine is brought back, bloodied. Now he is handcuffed, too. But everything has been told in terms of his pace, his face, and off-screen sounds.

The "actor" playing Fontaine is François Leterrier; he has the face of a saint, and of a man who will go to any extreme to be free. It is a brave face yet a frightening face, and by now—1956—we are learning what to expect of Robert Bresson's faces. So he picks people who do not regard themselves as actors, but they have the most compelling faces we have encountered. The first principle of watching, therefore, is exaltation. Fontaine looks like Antonin Artaud's Brother Martin in *The Passion of Joan of Arc*.

The story of the film, its ritual, is his attempt to escape. With an old spoon, he is able to loosen panels in his door. With the wires in his bedstead he can make ropes, wrapping the wire in shredded clothing. He shapes hooks that will hold the ropes so he can climb up and down. Meanwhile, there are the sounds of executions. Prisoners come and go. Fontaine doesn't know how long he has. He washes his face. He has a pail of food. He walks in the yard and cleans out his latrine pot. He listens and waits. The film is a relentless study of his face—imprisonment has never seemed so intense.

Then, at the point of crisis, he acquires a cellmate. Is he an ally or a stool pigeon? Fontaine must make his decision. He looks at the boy: is he a lout, or another baffled saint? He makes his choice, yet he has no choice: the subtitle of the film is "The wind blows where it will." He is a man escaping. The camera just admits that he has to kill a German on the way out. But Bresson refuses to dramatize or humanize the event. It is past four in the morning. They have left their shoes and jackets behind. I am not spoiling it for you. The title tells you. Fontaine has fulfilled his duty again. He has escaped. And as he and the other man walk away, Mozart comes up on the sound track welcoming them, taking them in. Not that it is a film about Mozart.

It is a film about the triumph of the will—and obviously I choose those words very carefully. It is an acceptance of fate, too. But it is a fierce film, as well as utterly humble. And you can tell yourself that it is a French Resistance story, if you like. Photographed in black-and-white by Léonce-Henri Burel, based on an account of real events by André Devigny. Design by Pierre Charbonnier. Bresson's second masterpiece. There are books that say the "style" is "rigorously spare," and you know what they mean. But it is a symphony of a face in concentration and in excelsis. No effect is as special.

The Man from Laramie (1955)

After *Winchester '73,* Anthony Mann made four more Westerns with Jimmy Stewart: *Bend of the River, The Naked Spur, The Far Country,* and *The Man from Laramie.* If we only have space for one, which will it be? I grew up on them all, and it hurts to exclude anything, but I'll settle for the last if only because the story is the most interesting.

Will Lockhart (Stewart) comes to the West with a mission and a mule train. We're not sure at first what the quest is, but with Mann it usually involves some unpaid score from the past. Lockhart is driving pack animals, but when he puts them out on a salt flat he is viciously attacked by Dave Waggoman (Alex Nicol), the son of the local rancher. What follows is a reason for including *Laramie,* for it's one of the more startling pieces of violence in the Western. Dave shoots Lockhart in the hand—and Stewart is harrowing in registering the pain and the outrage.

He is reassured by Dave's father, Alec (Donald Crisp), and by the foreman, Vic Hansbro (Arthur Kennedy). But followers of Mann don't need to be told to watch Kennedy closely. It has been said that the story is a version of *Lear,* with Donald Crisp as the unbalanced king. That's going too far and it detracts from the quality of Crisp's performance. But if it's not *Lear,* it's still one of the subtlest stories in a Western.

The script is by Philip Yordan and Frank Burt, and taken from a *Saturday Evening Post* story by Thomas T. Flynn. Charles Lang photographed it, and it's the first Mann Western in CinemaScope. Yes, he had loved and honored the golden section, but the compositions here are alive and eager for the new screen shape, and there are several of the great traveling shots that Mann did better than anyone.

There isn't the feeling of betrayal that haunts *The Far Country* or the near breakdown of the Stewart character as occurs in *The Naked Spur.* But the eye for terrain, depth, and the splendor of trees is without limit. It may seem trivial or sentimental to say that Mann filmed trees better than anyone—but look at the movies long enough and you will know what I mean. No other director ever studied the details of a location or a landscape with more feeling. The place is always a character in Mann, and the unspoken bond between the hero and the country is the code of honor he adheres to. To see the same thing addressed or felt in, say, Michael Mann's *The Last of the Mohicans,* is to feel the artistic power of Tony Mann's eye and the political decisions attached to it. He should have been secretary of the interior.

The cast also includes Cathy O'Donnell (always touching), Aline MacMahon, Wallace Ford, Jack Elam, James Millican, John War Eagle, and Gregg Barton. From *Winchester '73* to *Man of the West* (with all the Stewart films in between), this is the last great campaign in the Western until Peckinpah comes along, and he was too drunk or too sad to see the trees.

Man Hunt (1941)

Geoffrey Household's novel *Rogue Male* is a thriller with real flavor and a book that has attracted several filmmakers—there is a version from the 1970s in which Peter O'Toole plays the hero as a far more authentic and high Tory sportsman than Walter Pidgeon dares in Fritz Lang's *Man Hunt*. But it's the story of a hunter-stalker in Europe in the late 1930s who actually has Adolf Hitler in the sights of his high-powered rifle near Berchtesgaden. He pulls the trigger, but the gun is not loaded. He has done the stalking as a lark and a test of skill. But he is pounced upon by Nazi guards and tortured. This is not a pretty scene, and it is all part of Lang's larger wish to persuade us that this enemy is not sporting. The man escapes, but he is on the run with a chance of uncovering a Nazi plot in London.

Dudley Nichols had done the script for Twentieth Century Fox and John Ford, with Kenneth Macgowan producing. But Ford declined and Macgowan saw Lang as the ideal person for the story. The film came out in the year the U.S. entered the war. Still, it's fascinating how much Lang gives it a period feeling—it could be occurring in the twenties, with Dr. Mabuse running the conspiracies. Richard Day and Wiard Ihnen did the sets and they're very good; even in open country Lang prefers to build the world rather than let nature or daylight get a look in. Arthur Miller did the black-and-white photography, and there is great stuff with streetlights, fog, the parapet of a bridge, and nothing else in the night. Alfred Newman wrote the music. It might qualify as a film noir if it dug deeper into the violence in the man—is he a natural killer, or just a sportsman? Could he have killed Hitler? Of course, Lang believes he is foreseeing a new world where everyone must be ready to kill.

Lang and Hitchcock went to school on each other, and it's interesting to compare *Man Hunt* with *The 39 Steps* in that both books were adventures told from the point of view of an English upper-class gent. Hitchcock believes that polish never fades, even if it goes down fighting. But Lang has seen a world that knows not to trust anything for lasting value. The Hitchcock hero retains his identity. For Lang, it can be the first thing to go. And in an era of stardom, Lang's anxiety was far more pessimistic than Hitchcock, though Hitch would go on to paint darker portraits of individual dread.

Walter Pidgeon does a sturdy job as the hero. Joan Bennett (in her first film for Lang) is excellent as the London tart who helps him (though Fox was uneasy about mentioning her job), and there is good work from George Sanders, John Carradine, Roddy McDowall, Ludwig Stössel, and Heather Thatcher.

Mannequin (1937)

Taken from a short story, "Marry for Money," by Katherine Brush, *Mannequin* is not just an unexpected working of feminist ground, but one of the most remarkable and admirable Joan Crawford pictures. She plays Jessie Cassidy, a hard-working seamstress in the city (it's New York). She lives at home with her family, and she knows full well that the money she turns over to her mother (Mary Philips) often ends up as booze money for her idle father and brother (Ralph Morgan and a crackerjack Leo Gorcey). Frank Borzage, the director, sees her coming home one night, so poor she has to walk, and trudging up tenement staircases in one of the best scenes of ordinary hardship.

Jessie has a boyfriend, Eddie Miller (Alan Curtis), a second-rate boxing promoter, a no-good, and she's kidded herself about their love. In fact, as her mother sees all too well, Jessie's life is going nowhere—so it's odd that those eyes are like headlights staring ahead for Joan Crawford's great beauty. But in a moment of weakness, she marries Eddie and is suckered by the apartment he's rented for them. She thinks it's all going to be OK. Then they meet John L. Hennessey (Spencer Tracy), a self-made rich man, someone who escaped the slums and went into shipping. It's clear that he adores Jessie.

Eddie wonders if maybe he and Jessie could have a "divorce" so Jessie could win Hennessey and take his money. Jessie settles for the divorce. She is magically transformed, not a seamstress now but a mannequin modeling great clothes (by Adrian). She marries Hennessey, and he does his best to win her—but she never loves him. And the point of the film is to heed her mother's advice: Be strong, be selfish, be the man, look after your own life.

It was an M-G-M picture, produced by Joseph L. Mankiewicz, scripted by Lawrence Hazard and with Borzage directing. But this is beyond the usual Borzage: he was all too good at making a secure dream world for lovers and he does it quickly a couple of times here only to shatter the dream in the steady working toward an idea of economic independence. So the film is beautiful in Borzage's normal way; in tough and sweet circumstances, he depicts external reality in terms of female emotion. But the plot keeps driving toward self-sufficiency and a kind of solitude that is rare in Borzage, but which glorifies Joan Crawford. There's a lush song, "Always and Always," written by Edward Ward, that got an Oscar nomination, but the inner sentiment of the picture is to say "maybe" and to leave decisions in the woman's hands.

And Crawford leaps at this new power. There's a story told that while the picture was shooting, Norma Shearer wanted to borrow the cameraman, George Folsey, for some tests. But Crawford came to her dressing-room door, dressed in her underwear, and told Shearer, "Not on your life!" It was an answer that had been ten years in the making.

Man of the West (1958)

Link Jones is a man of about sixty—if you look carefully you have to see that he is dying. This is not just because he is gaunt-looking. It is a matter of the inward anxiety beneath the weathered exterior. He takes a train, headed toward Fort Worth. He has a modest packet of money, enough to hire a teacher for the frontier community where he lives. The thing he fears is not just death, but the responsibility of carrying the means to improvement for his community. We never see this small town where he has a wife and two children. For the train is robbed. Link recognizes some of the outlaws as members of the infamous Tobin gang. He ought to remember this, for he was once himself one of the Tobins.

Man of the West was made three years before Gary Cooper's death, and it seemed strange then that James Stewart was not the central hero he had played so often for Anthony Mann. No doubt Stewart would have done a fine job, though he was seven years younger than Cooper. But just as Stewart would have been unlikely to catch Cooper's shyness at the railway depot, so Stewart did not seem as ready for the tragedy that faces Link Jones as he renews contact with his own past.

Of course, Mann had often used the idea of a lone Westerner who has an ugly past to live down. But he had referred to it quickly. With Cooper in this story, Mann seems far more struck by the wounds left by the past. So it's striking that while Link has a family, the film pushes him into a relationship with Billie Ellis (Julie London), the saloon singer who is on the train and who becomes his surrogate wife in the lecherous eyes of the Tobin gang. Thus, Link has to save his precious money, but he has to defend Billie against the threat of rape and ultimate defilement at the hands of Dock Tobin (Lee J. Cobb), the head of the gang and Link's father figure.

The film comes from a Reginald Rose script adapted from the novel *The Border Jumpers*, by Will C. Brown, and it has the framework of a fable, so that as Link goes after the gang, he moves into radically different scenery. The train is robbed in semi-desert. But the Tobins live amid softer greens and browns, in a poisoned pastoral country. And when the gang goes on its last great raid, it is, unwittingly, to a ghost town in another desert. The Tobin gang may be famous still, but they have gone mad, too—and it is plain that Link's departure has broken the demented Dock.

Man of the West is striking for its character study and for its rueful sense of consequences, and it has a savage sexual undertow not evident elsewhere in Mann. It is often disturbing (the forced striptease that prefigures rape was always noted for its nastiness), and it leaves little comfort at the end. But in the exhausted, ruined face of Cooper there is justification for the sweeping title.

The Man Who Shot Liberty Valance (1962)

There are Fordians who swear by this film, yet I wonder if they have really reflected on what it tries to say. It is a film that smells of soundstages. It goes back to black and white, as if the scent of the range had dried away. And, most fatal of all, it tries to have elderly stars playing young men. All of a sudden, the Ford ethos looks fossilized, yet there he is urging us to believe in the legend and call it fact. By 1962, surely it was plain to anyone that the movies had done terrible damage to a sense of American history with their addled faith in bogus myths.

The film begins in about 1910. Senator Ransom Stoddard (James Stewart) comes through the old frontier town of Shinbone on the train. He stops awhile and thus we go back to a past that must be thirty years earlier. Stoddard was then a law student who came to the town. He met his future wife (Vera Miles); Tom Doniphon (John Wayne), a rancher; Dutton Peabody (Edmond O'Brien), editor of the local paper; and Liberty Valance (Lee Marvin), the local rogue and intimidator. It was at that time, the legend goes, that the young lawyer faced down Valance and killed him in a gun battle that launched the lawyer's political career. But, no, it was not really so: It was Doniphon, under cover of darkness, who did the shooting.

Ford had a good team: the script was written by James Warner Bellah and Willis Goldbeck (who was also producer). William H. Clothier did the photography. But it's not just the thinness of the image that is disconcerting. James Stewart was fifty-four when he made the film, and really only cursory efforts are taken to make him look younger—in scenes when he should be in his twenties. It is altogether regrettable, for the law student who is not a man of action does not need to be middle-aged, too. Vera Miles, as Hallie, his girlfriend, is twenty years his junior.

It's as if Ford is no longer prepared to look at his own films—and, of course, that reticence is fatally close to the film's disinclination to honor the truth. The result is an excessive kindness toward the enfeebled ideals of old men. And there's a way in which Lee Marvin's honest aggression as Liberty seems preferable. Indeed, you can't help feeling that Liberty is a Peckinpah hero who has got horribly caught up in an elderly film.

The nostalgia has moments. The irony in the central situation is appealing. Woody Strode is excellent as Pompey, Doniphon's "servant." Strother Martin is a delight as Valance's sidekick. And Wayne and Edmond O'Brien do their duty. But you can't help feeling that history for Ford is the terrible obstacle of a man who refused to face modern times. Whereas the real history of how "legend" rescued anecdote is rich, funny, and vitally suggestive of the American character.

The Man Who Would Be King (1975)

John Huston had wanted to try Kipling's story of two English army sergeants who find a magical kingdom somewhere in Kafiristan since the days when he might have had Bogart and Gable in the leading parts. As a result, he had several scripts accumulated over the years, all of which told the same story—and why not, it's a good story and cuter still if you have Kipling as a figure in it, his mustache standing on end as he hears the tale. But by the time Huston found himself in a position to do it, the industry thinking was that Newman and Redford (very hot as a team in the early seventies) were the ideal casting. Don't let's forget, when obituary time comes, that Newman dropped the script and said, "They've got to be English. Connery and Caine!"

Thank God! For once those two get together, the heart of the film is impregnable, and a natural boyish humor emerges. I suspect that if he could have done it in 1945, Huston would have gone to the Sierra and fancied he was redoing *Gunga Din*. Bogart and Gable would have been fine, though there might have been too much time spent on lugubrious rival accents. By 1975, Huston had color (by Ossie Morris), location work in Morocco, and Mrs. Caine—the fabled Shakira—as Roxanne, the beauty who comes to Daniel Dravot in marriage.

Huston was always very proud of his sense of irony, and the Kipling is loaded with it as these two wastrel deserters become the lords of misrule up in the mountains—until they go too far. But I'm not sure that Huston knows what else to do with the Kipling story, which is not just a "fate is strange" piece, but a rueful examination of misunderstanding between the British and their then-subject peoples.

So it's an adventure story, plain and simple—without, I fear, the gathered punch of all the ironies that end *Treasure of the Sierra Madre* or *The Asphalt Jungle*. Never mind, Connery and Caine are certain they're having a good time and delivering the goods. Christopher Plummer is a treat as Kipling. And Shakira is beautiful, even if she looks as if she's served too much time as a hostess in one of her husband's restaurants—or listening to him telling us the simple secret of screen acting.

In other words, it's rather minor Huston. But if he had always wanted to do it, it must have been a relief that it turned out so well. Fabulous comic-book art direction by Alexander Trauner and a scene-stealing performance from Saeed Jaffrey as Billy Fish, the boys' interpreter. In his book, Huston says that it was the sort of thing where an assistant director—Bert Batt—was essential if you were going to get the camels and the tribesmen surging through the Khyber Pass looking pretty. Thank you, Bert—and let's hear more on the art of the A.D.

The Man with a Movie Camera (1927)

Ladies and gentlemen, I am about to cheat. I told you there would be no documentaries, and this was a considerable easing of my great problem: how to pick 1,000 feature films, story films, worthy of you and worth writing about, and with a chance of telling the story of the medium. My friend Tom Luddy looked doubtful. He said, "What are you going to do with Dziga Vertov and *The Man with a Movie Camera*?" I winced. I writhed. I worried. So it's in.

And here is the best reason I know. Suppose that you are a reader of this book, intrigued because you like watching movies, but a little intimidated because there are a good many here you haven't seen or heard of. You may very well not know the history: how Dziga Vertov (also known as Denis Kaufman) was an inspiring spirit and innovator in the field of newsreel in the Bolshevik era. You may not know or be excited by the Soviet urge that film could show the new country to itself as a mechanical marvel. Most important, let's say that you have young children who are monopolized by the screens that convey television, the Internet, and video games. You want to show them something that says "movie," and you have come to realize that "movie" is not really of your child's world. It's not quite like madrigals or belles lettres. But it's changed. Try *The Man with a Movie Camera.*

You will find that the child's lack of context or narrative guilt accepts easily Vertov's conceit of the cameraman as everyman—the proletarian hero who has the power and the camera knowledge to show us not just ourselves, but visibility itself. Of course, the film is full of tricks and editing but they are all as candid and innocent as someone warning you that he's going to cheat you. I have never found a child who was not sad when the film ended, who did not have hundreds of questions about the world being filmed and a new exhilaration with the whole process.

I will go further. This is only a very partial record of Russia in the 1920s, so filled with hope and beauty as to be out of its mind with poetry. In being out of its mind, the camera makes a first step toward story. In truth, this film is a utopian vision—it never was or will be as free from friction and other problems. Like *I Am Cuba,* looking at Cuba in 1964, it is far less about the real place than the profound desire to sing or shout out.

This could change your child and change you. With *The Passion of Joan of Arc* it is, I believe, the only silent film that needs no qualification or apology. It is perfect. It is new still. And it makes you love the world. If you have a child in such need—show them both films, *Joan of Arc* first, because they sort of know that story, and Vertov second because they need to be brilliant to see its story.

The Man with the Golden Arm (1955)

Literally, I can't have this wide-screen title go across my mind without the rattle and flat-footed menace of Elmer Bernstein's score going with it, plus the elegance of the Saul Bass titles—the train needs its smoke. It was said to be a jazz score, and Frankie Machine, the central character, does want to be a jazz drummer, like Dave Tough, but it's jazz according to Stan Kenton or those intellectual white bands that were a big part of the fifties. If it's Chicago, and I think it is, where are the black people? What I'm trying to say is that Otto Preminger's *The Man with the Golden Arm* was one of those 1950s films that said, There's a big, nasty world out there. With women like Eleanor Parker and DRUGS!!! (So we'll do blacks next time?)

At this distance, I neither know nor care whether the film is any good. It's just that, seen at fourteen or so, sneaking in under the intended barrier of ratings et cetera, this seemed so hellaciously and giddily adult as to be intoxicating. OK, you took DRUGS—which was a very bad thing—but then Kim Novak lay with you to keep you warm as you went cold turkey. All of which is patently fantasy bumping up against the harsh realities in life—and perhaps the lesson is that film has nothing to do with reality, and don't try pretending that it does.

So it came from a Nelson Algren novel of 1949 in which Frankie is a would-be drummer, an expert card dealer, and an arm aching for a fix. Walter Newman and Lewis Meltzer did the script, and producer-director Preminger had to accept that Machine no longer killed himself if the film wanted to get the subject of DRUGS onto the American screen. Of course, in real American life, Dave Tough was dead at forty from what the reference books call bouts of alcoholism. Jazz had quite simply mapped out the self-destructive struggle between liberty and order in American life, years ahead of social studies.

I still love the black-and-white photography by Sam Leavitt and the feeling that the whole street is one big set—because it was. And Preminger could film space, movement, and context as well as anyone. Arnold Stang is wondrous as the pal, Sparrow. Darren McGavin is one of the most odious suave drug dealers in American film. Kim Novak was a Molly that every boy dreamed of every night, whereas Eleanor Parker's Zosch was the kind of woman no one had met yet.

And then there is Frank—Sinatra—who craved to be in great movies until he got there and then grew bored with the whole thing. Maybe Sinatra really did act so fully as a singer that no other version of the art interested him. I don't care. Sinatra as Frankie Machine took over one's life for a season. His desperate face was the screw that held the CinemaScope in place. It's a total performance—no wonder DRUGS took off in such a big way in America. If only jazz could have ridden along on the same arrows of desire.

Mare Nostrum (1926)

Rex Ingram's *Mare Nostrum* is often hailed as one of the most beautiful of silent films. Alas, the more such praise is applied, the clearer it is that a fatal gap was opening up in the 1920s between visual spectacle and common sense or dramatic holding power. The screen was apparently a place where you could get away with nearly anything, if it was dazzling or hitherto unseen. At the same time, the public quickly heard alarm bells when plausibility was being tested. We still gasp at effects if we have not seen them before—and a moment later hiss if we feel they are unearned.

Of course, it's nearly always the case that when one notices "beauty" ahead of anything else in a work of art then the work is doomed and likely short-lived. Ingram had a painter's eye, it is often said—but, we have to add, a painter who would have been in his element thirty or forty years before he was working. The sort of empire Ingram enjoyed at Metro-Goldwyn-Mayer—with his wife, Alice Terry, as his unquestioned leading lady, and the Victorine Studio at Nice as his getaway—did not last long. The pictures came in too expensive, but worst of all they were archaic in their dramatic attitudes.

Mare Nostrum may be the most beautiful of all, no matter that it's ostensibly a portrait of naval warfare during the years 1914–18. That was a grim period, with Jutland and Scapa Flow as key events. Yet Ingram persuaded himself into a romance involving submarines and sailing ships in the Mediterranean. The source material was the novel by Vicente Blasco Ibáñez. An adventurer, Ulysses Ferragut (Antonio Moreno), is tempted into supplying the German submarines by Freya Talberg (Terry). She is shot as a spy and he is reunited with her in a watery grave. It is turgid nonsense, so far from the new "realism" in Army films like *The Big Parade*. Moreover, this much later in time it has to be said that Ingram's loyalty to his own wife leaves only one appreciative person: the wife. Ms. Terry was a beauty, but that condition had had a calming effect on her mind that may have warmed Ingram in life. It seldom helps on the screen. Yet Ingram hardly seems to have realized that his characters were responding to ancient and literary codes of honor in an age when war at sea was the business of mighty ships and fleets.

Willis Goldbeck wrote the script, Ben Carre was involved in the art direction (though Ingram apparently took on that key job himself), and John Seitz was the photographer—it's so telling that Seitz shot this and the exposé footage of *Sunset Blvd.* The cast also included Hughie Mack, André van Engelmann, and Álex Nova. *Mare Nostrum* cost £140,000—and Ingram said it earned £400,000. Tiny sums today, but it was enough for Metro to shut off its involvement with Victorine. The studio was becoming a factory.

Marnie (1964)

It's hardly possible to describe the psychosexual condition of the character Marnie without applying a similar scrutiny to Alfred Hitchcock. This was the first picture Hitch had undertaken since the career-spanning interview conducted by François Truffaut. And screenwriter Evan Hunter was a little perplexed to discover that Hitchcock was now tape-recording their conversations. Was he so much more conscious of posterity, or was he becoming impressed by his own fame? It had been his first determination that Marnie—a beautiful woman who is a chronic thief and sexually frigid—should mark Grace Kelly's return. We should note that this would have been a less merry Grace, something of a return to the haunted woman in *Dial M for Murder.*

Tippi Hedren was still there, under contract, as a standby, and no one yet saw any of Hitch's irrational interest in her. But Evan Hunter, while intrigued by the Winston Graham novel, was forever stuck on the scene where Marnie was to be raped by her new husband, Mark. Can't we lose it? he asked. Oh, no, said Hitch, painfully eager. In the end, Hunter was fired, and replaced with Jay Presson Allen, a novice. They got on, but Allen always felt the film was flawed. And by the time it shot, Hitch was pressing his attentions on Tippi Hedren in a way that shocked the actress—something of that horror surely helps the film. And it's not that the morbid psychology isn't felt. Marnie really is a wreck, and I'm not sure how much confidence we have in her recovery at the end. Rather there's a feeling of life as a slippery, canted slope—where things get worse.

So, to put it mildly, the sexual openness of the film is both gloomy and melodramatic—it's as if Hitch sensed that censorship was breaking down, but he was lost in the new liberty. There's also the chance that he felt both his new celebrity and his age and became obsessed with an actress, something he had played with all his life, but handled.

A lot of the film feels contrived—I think Hitch's knowledge of the real world was beginning to betray him. Hedren gives a very touching performance, but do we quite believe in Marnie's sexual hang-ups driving her to steal? Or care? Hedren feels like a victim onscreen, not a strong enough person to be interesting. In turn that makes Sean Connery's Mark unduly sadistic. It's a problem, and it's a film with many effective scenes fatally let down by occasional exaggeration.

The team is the same: Robert Burks on camera (for the twelfth and last time); Robert Boyle on production design. Edith Head doing costumes, George Tomasini as editor. Bernard Herrmann doing music—his last Hitchcock score. The supporting cast includes Diane Baker, Martin Gabel, Louise Latham, Bob Sweeney, Milton Selzer, Mariette Hartley, Alan Napier, and Bruce Dern.

The Marriage of Maria Braun (1979)

As he prepared to do *Berlin Alexanderplatz* for television (the biggest budget ever ordered in West German TV), so Rainer Werner Fassbinder horrified his colleagues by suggesting they could "squeeze" one more picture in before they started. He had this story in mind, *The Marriage of Maria Braun*. Fassbinder was a wreck. Peter Berling reported: "His skin . . . looked like the rind of a sweating Swiss Emmenthal cheese." But there was backing for another film because, for a moment, it seemed possible that the German favorite Romy Schneider might play the title part. But, once he'd met her, Fassbinder announced that she was a "dumb cow," and so he fell back on Hanna Schygulla, who had been out of favor since *Effi Briest*. The budget for *Maria Braun* was less than a million marks, but the filming doubled that in a nightmare of scenes, stoppages, and sulks, chiefly because Fassbinder behaved so badly. Of course, it would prove his greatest hit. By the time it was finished he was doing seven or eight grams of cocaine a day.

It's the story of a German woman who kills a black American soldier (Günther Kaufmann) during the war. Her husband (Klaus Löwitsch) takes the blame for her, and Maria gradually rises and becomes wealthy and powerful in the West German "miracle." The screenplay came from Peter Märthesheimer and Pea Fröhlich, but the idea was Fassbinder's and he was changing the script as they went along, turning Maria Braun—beautiful but coarse, a survivor but greedy—into the model of postwar Germany, and using Schygulla's vibrant sexuality as a way to the box office. The truly remarkable thing was that the film should never have been made, that Fassbinder forced it upon everyone and behaved monstrously—as if he expected and wanted someone to come forward and kill him—and yet it is a superb, comic-book satire on German success (it culminates in Germany's winning the World Cup, and the voices of most of the modern chancellors). And these things preside over Maria Braun's carnal puddle, stretching out to claim more and more.

Michael Ballhaus did the photography, and Helga Ballhaus did the design. The cast also included Ivan Desny, Gottfried John, Günter Lamprecht, Elisabeth Trissenaar, and Hark Bohm. But there's no doubt that Schygulla carried the film—in performance and as a poster image. Fassbinder's sexual tastes were clear, and there's more than an edge of contempt expressed for Maria. Still, those movies that have a female central character seem more coherent and expressive. It's as if his social satire was prompted or encouraged by having to work with actresses.

The Marriage of Maria Braun won the Silver Bear at Berlin and it then proved to be his greatest box-office success all over the world. At Cannes, a few months later, he was being pursued by distributors—even those from Hollywood—with gifts, bribes, and honors. The picture that begged not to be made. Such savage ironies were as vital as cocaine.

La Marseillaise (1938)

The height of Jean Renoir's emotional participation with the French Popular Front was 1936. That's when he supervised the making of *La Vie Est à Nous* with the support (if not more) of the Communist Party. He also launched a public appeal for funds (a franc each from a citizen guaranteeing a ticket to see the film) for a movie to mark the anniversary of the French Revolution. Alas, the ticket money raised was insufficient and so *La Marseillaise* did not appear for two more years, funded by CGT (the congress of French trade unions). But the film is fabulous and badly neglected. It traces the events from July 1789 (the storming of the Bastille) to 1792 and the defeat of the Prussian army.

No one would be tempted to call *La Marseillaise* an epic—and Renoir was afraid of it being labeled a "history film." Instead, he wanted to make a panorama of France in the moment of the revolution. So the key to his approach is to fix on the citizen army from Marseilles, to follow it on its untidy march north and to trace the composition of the song that every Frenchman knows. The film is deliberately casual, fragmentary, charming, and amusing—the capital-letter grandeur of history is shrugged away at every opportunity. As they are in all of his movies, Renoir's people here are too busy living to observe and caption their own significance.

Renoir worked on the script himself with Carl Koch, and Martel and Jean-Paul Dreyfus. André Zwoboda was the production manager. The photography was shared by Jean-Serge Bourgoin, Alain Douarinou, Jean-Marie Maillols, Jean-Paul Alphen, and Jean Louis. The production design—from palaces to common homes—was by Léon Barsacq, Georges Wakhévitch, and Jean Perrier. The editing was by Marguerite Renoir.

By the time Renoir made *La Marseillaise,* the Popular Front was breaking up and Renoir's interest in individualism was having to face the sad evidence that people could persuade themselves to love one another only for so long. So his revolution is full of wry observations of petty selfishness, of self-interest masquerading as team spirit, and of humble kindnesses in the people marked down for posterity as royalists and aristocracy. The great achievement of *La Grande Illusion*—his previous film—is the way men of different standing can still march side-by-side, in community and compromise. In other words, "revolution" is a big word for the small changes that Renoir sees. What's more important are the real spatial connections—the way people on the march mingle and chat, and the suddenness with which palace guards desert their defunct cause.

It's surely true that one big reason for doing the film for Renoir was the chance to cast his brother Pierre as Louis XVI—awkward, seeming lost, but decent and resigned to his fate. Lise Delamare is Marie Antoinette and Louis Jouvet is very good as Roederer. The rest of the cast includes Andrex, Ardisson, Nadia Sibirskaïa, Jenny Hélia, Léon Larive, Gaston Modot, and Julien Carette.

P. L. Travers, the author of the Mary Poppins books, was Australian, and her name was Pamela Lyndon Travers. Although the books are set in London in about 1910, they began to be published only in 1934, and so it's clear that from the outset they spoke of a secure and nostalgic time at the height of the Depression. Equally, the movie of *Mary Poppins* is one of those immense conservative successes that tried to withstand all the tides of change in the 1960s. And so, as kids in America felt the ground moving in '64 and '65, there was Mary Poppins and her umbrella as ways to achieve safe flight.

There were several Mary Poppins books, and there was no stage original for the movie. Instead, Disney supported Bill Walsh in his great belief in the books. He was a Disney veteran who had produced and helped write such live-action adventures as *Davy Crockett, King of the Wild Frontier* and *The Absent-Minded Professor.* He was associate producer on *Mary Poppins* and cowriter with Don DaGradi. They hired Robert Stevenson to direct it—and his career went back to *King Solomon's Mines* (1938), *Tom Brown's Schooldays* (1940), *Walk Softly Stranger* (1950), and *The Absent-Minded Professor* (1961). Stevenson was English and he may have been the one to suggest the Poppins books. But the real coup on the picture was the score, by Richard M. and Robert B. Sherman, which worked as modern music while keeping the flavor of the period. The Shermans had done some songs for Disney—on *The Absent-Minded Professor* and *Summer Magic*—but nothing really prepared anyone for the hit songs in *Mary Poppins*, or renewed that level of success later.

Edward Colman photographed the picture. Tony Walton did the sets and costumes; Walton then was married to Julie Andrews, the star. She was a stage success, of course, most notably in *My Fair Lady*, but 1964 brought her film debut as Mary Poppins, just as she was passed over for "her" role of Eliza in the movie of *My Fair Lady.* The subsequent lesson was emphatic. Andrews won the Oscar as Mary Poppins, and she exactly caught the balance of open appeal and period assurance—the nice way of being right. She also sang the songs as if she had written them—not just "A Spoonful of Sugar" and "Chim Chim Cheree" but "Supercalifragilisticexpialidocious" (which is the hip, swinging version of "Do-Re-Mi" from *The Sound of Music*).

Mary Poppins is genuinely pretty, and absolutely clear in its provision of a perfect nanny for everyone. Not that the parents are belittled. Mother is a suffragette, with a song to prove it. Father is a banker. And they are Glynis Johns and David Tomlinson. But the perfect match for Mary is Dick Van Dyke, whose charm did not always work on the big screen. It won the Oscar for music—*My Fair Lady* won for scoring. And the picture earned $31 million, two and a half times what *My Fair Lady* earned. Super!

Mary Reilly (1996)

Mary Reilly was a novel, written by Valerie Martin, that invented the character of an Irish housemaid who is employed in the London home of Dr. Henry Jekyll. She is a simple, innocent girl who has had a terrible upbringing—she has been terrorized by her drunken father (Michael Gambon). He has tortured her with rats, her greatest fear. So in a way the Jekyll house is a precious escape for her. But it is more than she has bargained for. Jekyll (John Malkovich) has his own intense work going on, in a laboratory from which the servants are excluded. But he is drawn to Mary—and she to him. And, when he appears in the house, the doctor's assistant—Mr. Hyde—has his way with her, too, no matter that she is deeply affronted by his direct approach.

A consequence: In due course both Julia Roberts and her director, Stephen Frears, received "Razzie" awards—the raspberry—for the worst work of the year. Less expected, perhaps: This is the best version of the Jekyll and Hyde story ever put on the screen—and it is a wonderful movie.

Ms. Martin has not exploited Robert Louis Stevenson. She has reimagined his book (1885) in ways that are not just proper, but flattering. So here is a version of the Stevenson in which there is a special sexual concentration on the "other" part of an orderly personality. It works not just in terms of the doctor and the brute, but in showing two sides to Mary herself: the good girl, and the woman who is tempted by feelings of romantic and sexual fulfillment. And so this Mary Reilly is both an example of the awed Victorian readership clinging to Stevenson's novella, and a real participant in the story of which Nabokov observed, "Excluding two or three vague servant maids, a conventional hag and a faceless little girl running for a doctor, the gentle sex has no part in the action."

Well, that vagueness goes in this film. Mary is as pale as the London fog or a concentration camp victim. She has a sharp fox's face (I think the idea of the rat is felt in her very look). In turn, that is a measure of Julia Roberts's commitment to the part. She has no anxiety about how she looks—ill, haggard, deprived, undeveloped, all of which have a sexual as well as a medical connotation. What is remarkable and delicate about her performance are the ways she lets Jekyll gently warm her—her sexual dream, with hushed sighs; her shattered response to a kiss; her tremulous intimation of her own sexuality.

To say that Malkovich's two men—both strong, one inhibited, one outrageous—are at her bidding is to convey the real creative line of *Mary Reilly*. Malkovich has so much more to do. But the film makes him Mary's mirror. The script is by Christopher Hampton and it is a great piece of work, the identification of the major film that awaits. But in turn, that film would not be ours now but for Frears's intelligence, the brilliant art direction of a team that included Stuart Craig, Michael Lamont, and Jim Morahan, and some of the dankest photography (by Philippe Rousselot) ever seen. I can see how this was less than commercial, but the neglect of the film by real critics is shocking. It cost $47 million and earned $5.6 million in the U.S. Cheap at twice the cost.

*M*A*S*H.* (1970)

There must be a great book to be written on how *M*A*S*H.* went through our culture, and one of its topics would be the radical difference between the tone of the movie (a mockery of team spirit) and that of the inspirational television series that followed. It would also be a history of back-door genius, or as Pat McGilligan puts it in his biography of Altman, "It came to pass because a pushy agent believed in Altman, because an iron-willed producer backed him to the hilt, because it was the best possible script, and because the studio was not entirely cognizant of what was happening."

It was a novel first (with the initials standing for Mobile Army Surgical Hospital) by Richard Hooker. It was seen by screenwriter Ring Lardner, Jr., who believed it might make a great movie. In turn, he showed it to Ingo Preminger, who came on board as producer, and then Preminger let George Litto—Altman's agent—read the script Lardner had done.

Despite first thoughts of shifting the action to Vietnam, Lardner stayed with the Korean setting. Many people liked the script, but fifteen directors—Kubrick and Lumet among them—were put off by the episodic nature and the sense of drift or "mash." That's how Altman got the job on a Fox film budgeted at $3 million. At first Fox had thought of Lemmon and Matthau as the two leads, but Preminger knew they had to be younger, hipper—Donald Sutherland and Elliott Gould. As it happened, Altman upset both the leads but that was part of his steady cultivation of all the minor players instead. For he wanted a film with no lumps, or stars, in the mash.

The script was filthy, profane, and awash with blood, all things that had to be negotiated. But nothing did that better than the way the two surgeons talked about anything except surgery while they were at work. Irreverence or antiestablishment thinking was the essence—and in fact this is the Korean War as seen through the druggy hopelessness of Vietnam. There's a fascinating period shift.

What goes with it is a new, slippery camera style—full of zooms, reframing (or bad framing), focus issues, and a sound track that moved in and out, picking up different or unexpected things all the time. The texture of the film was mashed, stoned, and dislocated. And yet it was beautiful, funny, and sometimes crazy. There was an ending with Hawkeye going home. But Altman dropped it and threw in a wild public address credits sequence—as if the film we've just seen is the movie of the night at the hospital camp.

Fox never understood it until it did $40 million in rentals. Altman was established not just as maverick, but as a stylist. And a host of new actors got exposure: not just the leads, but Tom Skerritt, Sally Kellerman, Robert Duvall, Jo Ann Pflug, Rene Auberjonois, Gary Burghoff, Michael Murphy, John Schuck, Bud Cort, and so on.

The TV show, on CBS, went from 1972 to 1983, with Alan Alda as Hawkeye and Gary Burghoff as the single holdover from the movie. Its success dwarfed that of the film: its final episode, with Hawkeye having a breakdown, is still one of the most watched things on the small screen. Yet the TV show was about a reverence (for the unit) that became more pious and more sweet as the years passed. Whereas the original mash is sour and astringent, and with a kick.

Master of the House (1925)

At first, as you watch Carl Dreyer's *Master of the House*—and it seems to be provided nowadays with the crudest kind of overdone piano accompaniment—you feel yourself locked into all the worst traditions of silent melodrama. We are in a Danish home, in fixed long shots, a place where the severe husband (Johannes Meyer) seems like the tyrant in charge. He is waited upon, hand and foot, by his wife (Astrid Holm). There seems to be no limit to his demands or his sense of entitlement.

But wait, a few things seem to be happening that break the Victorian mold: Sometimes this husband is seen with his back to the camera, and the effect is striking—for the film seems to say, What an idiot he is: and rather than grimace with the pain of long suffering, sometimes the very pretty Astrid Holm seems to toss her head as if she knows some other possibility; and then there is something else—Dreyer's long shots are not just habitual, the way of the medium, they are a gradual opening up of context and the larger frame in which the man's behavior looks worse and worse. In other words, there is a moral in the space.

Something really unexpected is coming: the man's aged nanny (Karin Mellemose), who comes back to the household and starts to assess the value of everything the husband demands as a price to be paid to the wife. The setting is plainly nineteenth century, and the whole thing comes from a play by Svend Rindom that he and Dreyer adapted together. But what follows is not just mountingly funny, but a feminist treatise in 1925 that completely outstrips the kind of suffering-wife melodrama that has been indicated. And as the picture progresses, time and again it is the full frame—the spatial suggestiveness of a whole apartment that Dreyer had built for the filming—that works against the husband's attitudes.

We do not expect a comedy from Dreyer, maybe. But what a revelation it is to see this as the film that preceded *La Passion de Jeanne d'Arc,* and what an insight into the gravity of that classic. What we have to face, at the outset, is that by the mid-1920s Carl Dreyer was as sophisticated an artist as Shaw—though morally and emotionally he is a great deal more piercing. Yet again, for those sympathetic to Stiller and Sjöström, here is evidence that the highest achievements of silent cinema were often Scandinavian.

Yet as far as can be judged, *Master of the House* was an enormous export success. For instance, its domestic attitudes and the comic touch had a very big impact in France. It follows from this that, like Stiller, Dreyer was in the process of developing a camera style that was close to that of Renoir and which prefigures the glorious achievement of *Gertrud.* Dreyer may have been austere and spiritual. What is more impressive is his breakthroughs in placing story, context, and meaning in revolutionary ways. *Master of the House* is a satire in the Lubitsch class and a clear forerunner of Ingmar Bergman.

The Matrix (1999)

We are in the kind of future city where the rain and the drab chic run together like salt in an open wound—it is a pace first established in *Blade Runner* and *Se7en,* and it speaks to the confidence and the good humor in today's young. On the sound track there is the rattle of Marilyn Manson and groups actually called Massive Attack and Lunatic Calm. You could get depressed but for the plain fact that a blithe empty-head like Keanu Reeves is thriving and the Wachowski brothers reckon they are about to make a bundle. There have been a lot of future noir films, and franchises, and at last the role of dutiful film critic is widely recognized as purgatorial. But *The Matrix* has an unquenchable cheek and chutzpah. When the Wachowski brothers went with the immense video package of the three films, they hired professors of philosophy and film critics and recorded their feelings as they reviewed the films. I was one of the critics. The three of us (add in Todd McCarthy and John Powers) trashed the great pretentious beast. But the brothers ran the track anyway. You have to love them.

Thomas Anderson, sometimes known as Neo and an anagram of One (as in "the One"), is a nocturnal hacker in our sad world. He is arrested by the multiple Smith (Hugo Weaving) and told to help arrest Morpheus (Laurence Fishburne), resistance leader of the struggle against the Matrix, "an artificial intelligence that rules the world"—you know the kind of guy. It's a battle in which Morpheus has one-liners from old fortune-cookie factories, the good guys wear long dark coats, and the girl, Trinity (Carrie-Anne Moss), favors soft-shiny black leather and catatonia.

Andy and Larry Wachowski wrote and directed it, and you know they have a lot of theories about what it means. Vaguely we know what it means: Matrix is destroying the world, sucking away its vitality (doesn't everyone have that feeling?), and Neo is going to have to find a new kind of martial combat to handle Agent Smith, who just turns into two or two hundred Smiths if you kill one of him. Bill Pope photographed the whole thing and the visual effects credits go on forever. These films are very expensive. But, lo and behold, they work: It is supposed to have cost $63 million, and it had a U.S. gross of $171 million. And that was only the beginning. There were two sequels and then there was the DVD.

Of course, you're going to say that the Matrix-like threat to human vitality actually operates on such different battlegrounds as the home front, the school, how people think politically, and so on. But we all know very well that no one has the least faith in those forums, not even the "and so on," and the Wachowski brothers know that a good, earnest teacher in a needy school might earn $50,000 a year. So our culture goes straight to the apocalypse and the big killing. And in its profusion of computerized effects, its monotone acting, and its assertion that people like Neo and Morpheus and Trinity are alive, the film is the enactment of its own warning.

The Mattei Affair (1972)

It's easy for Italians, as well as Americans, to believe that Hollywood owns the "Mafia" film, as well as that tradition of picture-making (it goes back as far as Capra, at least, the Sicilian) in which we begin to see the forces of outlawry as a dark mirror image of the people called "law and order." And it fits into the complex, and sometimes ironic, view of Francesco Rosi that these things sooner or later become synonyms for "Italian" and thus a constant fog or miasma as any Italian—artist or not—makes his way in the world. And so, Rosi has often explored other kinds of material, but the selection in this book, and others, inevitably homes in on those things that seem clichéd Italian. Let us just say that Italy is not only a founder of democratic ideals and rational government; it has also been a model for natural corruption and confused thinking.

Enrico Mattei was a left-wing oil tycoon killed in 1962 when his plane crashed on the way from Sicily to Milan. The pilot and a reporter from Time-Life were also killed in the same accident. (October 1962, of course, was the haunted moment of the Cuban Missile Crisis—and thus a prelude to the eternally uncertain mystery of who killed John Kennedy, and how and why.)

I make that reference because the Mattei affair remains an unsolved case. Rosi's film (scripted by himself and Tonino Guerra, with the assistance of Nerio Minuzzo and Tito Di Stefano) is a reconstruction of the main strands of Mattei's life, with evident allusions to *Citizen Kane*, in the realization that so many people had reasons for wanting him dead—the Mafia, the CIA, perhaps even aspects of the Left who may have felt betrayed by him. Indeed, one of the investigating journalists on the story vanishes when on the point of making a breakthrough discovery.

We know this modern paranoia from our own films, and Rosi leaves in a reference to the Corleone family just as he seems to have seen most of the relevant American political thrillers. But Rosi has his roots in Italian neorealism (he worked with Visconti on *La Terra Trema*), and he has a taste for the real places, for people playing themselves and for extras who are the voting public in the relevant areas. So this is not nearly as clear-cut or aesthetically decisive a film as *Citizen Kane* or *The Godfather*, films thirty years apart but done with the same bravura control so that the dream seems perfect and the heroes poised. As shot by Pasqualino De Santis, *The Mattei Affair* is far less tidy, but very suggestive. Indeed, ever since his groundbreaking mixture of legend and documentary in *Salvatore Giuliano* (1961), Rosi has pioneered a fusion of melodrama and naturalistic "coverage."

The result is a web of narrative, or is it intrigue? Remember, *plot* is a word with such different meanings, in which we are forever trying to find a solid ground from which we can judge the charismatic performance of Gian Maria Volontè as Mattei. So caught up in political theater, this Mattei has learned Kane's lesson—that you never know yourself whether your greatest allegiance is to truth or to performance.

A Matter of Life and Death (1946)

A Matter of Life and Death (*Stairway to Heaven* in the U.S.) could be a Stanley Kramer film, as if made by a young child. On the one hand, it involves the most direct, head-on confrontation with a large issue that could be imagined—in this case, the future of Anglo-American relations. On the other, it turns upon the resolution of a tiny, dreamlike situation—to wit, whether a downed bomber pilot can survive brain surgery or not. Granted the flex being exerted from either end, there are openings all over the place so that the film can absorb enchanted beach sequences that seem more surreal than natural; the blush on Kim Hunter's cheek; the working of a camera oscura; passing jokes about Technicolor—they're so starved for it in a monochrome Heaven that looks like a Moscow subway station. And so on: This is a film about a shattered mind and anything and everything can stroll in and out as the synapses flap in the breeze of concussion.

An English pilot, Peter Carter (David Niven), is shot down over the southern English shore. His last exchanges are with June (Kim Hunter), an American who is working for the war effort as a radio operator. He goes to a hospital headed by neurologist Dr. Reeves (Roger Livesey), and the crisis he faces in surgery is dramatized by a trial in Heaven where his right to live and Britain's virtue in American eyes are to be argued in a trial where America is represented by a slain patriot, Abraham Farlan (Raymond Massey). In the end, Peter lives because June is willing to die in his place—love conquers all.

No, it's not exactly the way Clement Attlee and Harry Truman discussed matters, but it is a film of sweeping boldness and confidence. Emeric Pressburger did the script. Jack Cardiff handled the Technicolor photography. Alfred Junge was the production designer. Hein Heckroth did the costumes. Reginald Mills was the editor. This was the core of the Archers team in those years, and this was a big production with large sets. However, Cardiff did replace Erwin Hillier, and that shift marked a new commitment to Technicolor. It was also important to Michael Powell's confidence that England looked far more heavenly than the appointed place.

The childlike story sustains a real knowledge of neurology and the American revolutionary era. The shift from real to fantasy was deft and comic most of the time, and in the best possible sense Powell always made his audience feel they were watching a movie, or a process that only film could manage. In turn, as Powell would have said, the movie was America's contribution to culture just as history, the countryside, and eager young people were Britain's. It's fanciful, yet it moves quickly enough for the question marks to be swept away by exhilaration. The cast included Robert Coote, Richard Attenborough, and Bonar Colleano as pilots, Kathleen Byron as one angel, and Marius Goring as one who lost his head in the French Revolution. Abraham Sofaer is the judge.

McCabe & Mrs. Miller (1971)

With two films in the early 1970s, Robert Altman established a poignant theme—that of the smart little boy who looked in most respects like a grown man, who, by dint of fantasizing energy, has willed himself up onto the screen and into the story. We are talking about a couple of the screen's perfect moments of self-reflection in which a director recognizes the thrust and the function of the movies—so men may kid themselves about their limits. I am talking about *McCabe & Mrs. Miller* and *The Long Goodbye*, two of the most beguiling films ever made in America.

McCabe was a novel, by Edmund Naughton, published way back in 1959. The rights had bounced around a lot and several scripts had been tried. The producer David Foster wound up with it in the late sixties. He fancied Altman to direct, with Elliott Gould in the lead, and he gave the script assignment to Brian McKay. Altman took that script over, which meant doing his best to edge McKay into obscurity. And it was Altman who said, Gould is not bankable, let's go for Warren Beatty—just off a thing called *Bonnie and Clyde*, which he had produced, too (so he was full of strutting McCabery).

Altman had had a falling-out with McKay, and he tended then to try to get rid of writers—so that everyone else could have a go. Altman rewrote. So did Beatty, and Beatty's line-slinger, Robert Towne. And then when Julie Christie was hired and the ampersand came into view, she was given rein to make Mrs. Miller a Cockney stand-up (in a lie-down mode). Then came rehearsal, with "script supervisor" Joan Tewkesbury writing it all down as fast as she could—if she could hear it, for amid all the one-upmanship people started improvising out of the corners of their mouths. It's likely that some of the best lines were simply forgotten.

And something of beauty emerged: the idea of McCabe in his derby hat seeming like the cock of the walk until Mrs. Miller comes along—someone who really knows the whoring business—and then the syndicate comes along. All of which leaves McCabe as an earnest idiot doing his best to stay in charge when everyone knows more than he does about how this fantasy works. Altman saw it as a love story in which the two people on either side of the ampersand are natural lovers but stay cut off by their situation and their differences in worldly knowledge. Then he got Vilmos Zsigmond to shoot it as from a helpless distance in a kind of druggy haze (I do not mean that Mr. Zsigmond was doing anything except beauty), and then he got Leonard Cohen to lay songs over it all, wall to wall, and if you can't hear it all or see it all, well, come back and try again. Anachronism? Anachronism is a new genre.

Beatty and Altman fought and each said, But for the other, what a film it would be. Christie curled up in her bleak privacy, and knew it was the film it could have been. Leon Ericksen did superb design on pine trees turned into homes, and then snow came down like heaven on the lovely shoot-out—the most wistful, dreamy climax in a Western. With Rene Auberjonois, Hugh Millais (superb), Shelley Duvall, Michael Murphy, John Schuck, William Devane, Keith Carradine, and so many others.

Mean Streets (1973)

Made very cheaply, with a bunch of friends, *Mean Streets* is the first of Martin Scorsese's "boys wanna be gangsters" films. Its impact was extraordinary, and a group of filmmakers rose on its panache and its biting immediacy. But notice one thing: Scorsese had had an invalid childhood. He was a nicely raised kid, who may have watched lurid events from his bedroom window but who never got into the kind of trouble that awaits Johnny Boy in *Mean Streets*. Thus, Johnny Boy is an idolized figure, based on Robert De Niro's great vitality and unexpectedness as an actor and on all the noir movies Marty had seen. One reason why he didn't get into trouble was that he spent so much time in the dark. So *Mean Streets* isn't life's experience, it's a distant view heated up by the history of the movies.

There is this gang: Charlie (Harvey Keitel), desperately ambitious to be a made man, trying to look after the self-destructive Johnny Boy and carrying on an affair with Teresa (an epileptic)—note, Teresa is Johnny Boy's cousin and I think we're meant to heed the possibility that Johnny Boy is literally crazy. Johnny Boy blows up a mailbox. He borrows money without intending to repay it. He gets into fights. He's on the edge. And Michael (Richard Romanus) is an idiot, a nag, a guy who might die for having not an ounce of Johnny Boy's impulsiveness.

We know it's going to end badly because Johnny Boy wears a stupid porkpie hat of the kind that brought doom to so many jazz musicians. Not for the last time, a real sense of jazz—of hectic lyric improvisation—haunts De Niro's performance, and I think it's interesting that by the time of *Taxi Driver* Scorsese had shifted his loyalty from Keitel as his lead actor to De Niro.

The color photography is by Kent Wakeford, and it's meant to be lurid and theatrical. Not to mention religious. Keitel (not compellingly Italian) is often in church as a Catholic in the film, and it's the occasion on which Scorsese refers to troubled devoutness more than any other. But the real thing is friendship and whether it can hold in a world where Johnny Boy is technically unknowable. The constant verbal teasing between the two leads is superb, and again it is musical. Not that there isn't music aplenty—for the first time, Scorsese made a radio sound track for the movie that has the Stones, Eric Clapton, the Shirelles, and opera, too.

Made when Scorsese was thirty, *Mean Streets* introduced a blazing new figure, but even then you could see the awkward strain of film buff and devil-may-care. So many things would fade away: the religion, the chance of a love story, but not De Niro and the great urge of boys at pretending to be gangsters. Who would have guessed, in 1973, before *Taxi Driver, Raging Bull, GoodFellas, Casino, Gangs of New York,* and *The Departed,* that this great director might be incapable of doing any other kind of movie?

Meantime (1983)

We're plainly meant to take this title two ways—*Meantime* is about an interim condition, that of unemployment, but it seems also to reflect a time of mean spirit in British public affairs, one in which only a fool could now regard the lack of work as temporary. More to the point, it was a comeback for a filmmaker named Mike Leigh who had made his debut with the aptly named *Bleak Moments*—grinding in its realism, yet devoid of hope or even fighting spirit. There was, and there remains, in Leigh an uncommon and often disarming awareness of the oppressed and pathetic in society—those who have given up, but who hardly notice their decision. There was a twelve-year gap between *Bleak Moments* and *Meantime*, a period in which Leigh worked in experimental theater and television. Indeed, *Meantime* was a film for TV, made for Central Television. It looks starry now in that it helped introduce Tim Roth, Gary Oldman, and Alfred Molina. Though in 1983, they seemed to be playing hopeless cases.

Leigh was a doctor's son from the Manchester area—in other words, he had seen humble suffering in his own lifetime, albeit from behind the more privileged walls of professional caregivers. I think you also have to say that Leigh was formed artistically by the failure of Labour governments in the 1970s and by the harsh administration of Margaret Thatcher. His subject was the underclass. His method was the steady cultivation of a company of preferred actors, encouraged to improvise their way to story lines. The result? Only Alan Clarke's films had the same sense of a downcast Britain—but Clarke himself was rowdy, violent, and energetic. Leigh was more intellectual, more watchful, and more anxious.

And so it is that his special ambiguity of tone emerged in which it is not always clear whether he is listening to the whinge and whine of the lower classes—or mocking them for their helplessness. By now, Mike Leigh is regarded as a maker of comedies—though *Vera Drake* is not really very funny, despite the comic load in a lot of its talk. Similarly, this story of two brothers and their father trapped in unemployment and one wretched East London flat is a portrait of hell, even if a lot of the lines are funny.

This book has films from either end of Leigh's career—and he deserves at least that, for his method and his dedication are unique and admirable, and the body of work is personal and deserving. But it's a bold spectator who jumps up to answer the question, Is Leigh a comic artist or a defeated listener?

He is at the service of his actors. But those actors end up sounding like Mike Leigh people. *Meantime* was photographed by Roger Pratt, and its cast also includes Marion Bailey, Phil Daniels, Pam Ferris, and Jeff Robert.

In its way, Leigh's ear for endless small talk is like that of Harold Pinter, and sometimes his conclusions are as frightening as Pinter's. The comparison with John Cassavetes is fascinating: both men seemed pledged to letting actors discover ordinary vitality. But at the end of the day, Cassavetes and Leigh are alike in offering us versions of people who are riveting yet caricatures of life.

Meet John Doe (1941)

Frank Capra was both a big hit and an earnest American by the time of *Meet John Doe,* and you can see the dilemmas opening up for anyone who wished to remain both. I find it hard to be entertained by the film now, because its ostensible ideas and its actual energies are so uneasy together. But that leaves it, unwittingly, one of the most exposed of American dreams, as troubled as the other great political film of the year, *Citizen Kane.*

Capra was three times winner for Best Director. Late in 1939, he and his writer, Robert Riskin, formed Frank Capra Productions. Riskin remembered a short story, "A Reputation," by Richard Connell, from the 1920s, about a clerk so dismayed by the world he announces he will kill himself. A movie treatment (by Connell and Robert Presnell) made its way to Riskin, who sent it on to Capra. The director jumped and told Riskin to start on the script—*The Life and Death of John Doe,* at first. Now the man was a drifter, an ex-ballplayer, Long John Willoughby. The suicide angle is a media hoax dreamed up by journalist Ann Mitchell, who is on the point of losing her job. Willoughby is built into a national hero, used by Ann's publisher D. B. Norton. Willoughby becomes so disgusted by the exploitation—a string of John Doe clubs for boys—that he really wants to kill himself. But he is exposed first and then the public turns against him.

The film was set up at Warners, who contributed $500,000; Bank of America added $750,000. There was a lot of time spent on the deal and Capra was vexed at having to do it all himself; he was casual about the money—yet he was very eager to come out well. It's a compromise not unlike the one in the story. Gary Cooper was cast as Willoughby and his dark, loner self is as important as his propensity for self-pity. Willoughby is a bum and an outsider, but ready to crack up. He is Capra's first helpless neurotic, a vagrant who might kill or be killed.

Barbara Stanwyck is quite brilliant as Ann Mitchell, a lively young woman who hasn't learned to think ahead enough yet. Nineteen forty-one is Stanwyck's year at the movies (*The Lady Eve* is there, and she shoots *Ball of Fire* before the year is up). She has real feelings of power yet she sees the dilemma of the movie, and guides "John Doe" to something like safety. But the idea of the despairing vagrant is so nearly out of control, and so close to unleashing fascist energies. The film ends with Norton being told he'll never beat the people, but the picture describes the people as dangerous, a mob ready to be tilted in any direction. In short, you feel Capra's idealism dissolving, and it's not comfortable. He was never again able to make a straight comedy. The haunting underside of populism had left him afraid of America.

The film did not do well. It was not nominated for Best Picture. Capra did walk away with a packet of money, but he closed down Frank Capra Productions. Ever since, the film stands there on the brink of America's war suggesting a population that has hardly begun to inhabit the real ideals of the Revolution and which is now at the mercy of its own size and power.

Meet Me in St. Louis (1944)

In 1944, people waiting for news or for no news sang songs. Would it be any wonder if unusually large emotions blew upon the embers of the "musical" and wondered if there could be a great fire? *Lady in the Dark*—the most ambitious stage musical of recent years—flopped as a film. Yet that sly fox *To Have and Have Not* is like a smart kid who whispers, Look at me in the right light, and aren't I a musical? And then there is the picture that may be the most satisfying story ever told as a musical in the history of the genre: *Meet Me in St. Louis*.

Take it at face value: It is a screenplay by Fred Finklehoffe and Irving Brecher from a kind of memoir novel, by Sally Benson, about family life in St. Louis during the year of the World's Fair there, 1903. The father (Leon Ames) is doing well enough in the bank to expect a promotion to New York, an event that the family regards with mixed feelings. To advance, to travel, to adventure—these are American urges, a part of the national optimism. But to give up the beloved house and its annual rhythm, that is also betrayal, loss, and the growing up that ends childhood.

This is a story with a crisis, and—of course—it is made for audiences in 1944. So it knows a lot about change, progress, the future, and the fears that clothe those states; it knows all the reasons for wanting to stay home, in a preserved world, the one that people left so recently. In the last great song in the cycle, "Have Yourself a Merry Little Christmas," Judy Garland sings, "Some day soon we all shall be together." Not quite all, we know that. But the togetherness is so powerful an ideal that maybe it can stop American progress in its tracks.

So, please be ready: The family album of the passing year is a framework for mounting crisis that Christmas will settle as Tootie (Margaret O'Brien), having heard her sister's plaintive song, the saddest Christmas song there ever was, will go down into the blue moonlit garden and smash the patient snowmen, because moving on and staying still are too much for her. In other words, this is a Chekhov play, and the reason why Garland is so touching is that she's trying to look after her sisters.

Now consider that the pretty sets on the M-G-M lot (under the charge of Cedric Gibbons) are the dream of all our childhoods. The Technicolor photography is by George Folsey and Henri Jaffa. The costumes are by Irene Sharaff. I do not know the wig maker who made the lush fall of Esther's amber hair. All these crafts accomplish the heat of summer in St. Louis, the mounting nightmare of Halloween (among the greatest dreams ever filmed), and the Christmas finale. The songs are by Hugh Martin and Ralph Blane and they also include "The Boy Next Door," "The Trolley Song," and the old classic, "Under the Bamboo Tree," that exquisite home musical dance with Garland and O'Brien.

Mary Astor is the mother. Harry Davenport is grandfather. Marjorie Main is the housekeeper. Lucille Bremer is the other sister. Tom Drake is the boy next door. Vincente Minnelli did it. If in any doubt about the journey, start here.

Melvin and Howard (1980)

Driving in Nevada is a good title for an existential novel. After all, it has huge extent and a few good roads with five-mile straightaways where you can let go. If you like driving and cars, Nevada is a friendly place. On the other hand, there are not many "theres" there, not many places worth getting to, or even noticeable. But if you have done much driving in Nevada at night, listening to music on the radio, or preaching, or *The Art Bell Show* with aliens knocking at your front door, *Melvin and Howard* is a perfectly natural film in which there might just be a bum needing a lift, and he could be Howard Hughes, so why isn't he likely to let you in on his will as a thank-you? The emptiness and the possibility are so very closely allied. No one would be surprised if it happened, not even if they'd driven half their life waiting for it. Real gamblers are never surprised when they win.

So *Melvin and Howard* is as sweet, hopeful, and generous as a ballad—there's no anger or resentment hanging over it. Melvin Dummar (Paul Le Mat) picks up a man in the desert and takes him to Las Vegas. The man says he is Howard Hughes (Jason Robards). Melvin's life is not doing so well, but neither is Howard's. Howard is at that long-haired point where he's living on the top floor of a casino, worrying over germs. Melvin's wife (Mary Steenburgen) walks out on him, taking their daughter. They divorce. Then the wife says she is pregnant and they get hitched again. She wins some money, but he is a spendthrift and so she leaves him again. It's the same old pattern until he gets a letter that is Howard Hughes's will with Melvin due an inheritance. That's when the lawyers take over and Melvin reckons it's all too much trouble.

All of this is, as they say, based on fact, or legend. Dummar did say he had a will. Bo Goldman wrote the script and Jonathan Demme directed it at the time when he had every reason to be the best hope among new directors. Demme and Goldman know not to press Melvin's case too far. It is its dreaminess that is most engaging. And then there is the way it fits into the odd mix of relaxed haplessness and chance—with game-show glory beckoning—that is so redolent of the new West where neon kids the moonlight.

It is this novelistic irony and the kindness that lets it ride that is so distinctive and pleasing, plus that sure notion that away from the coasts America is another country and every bit as strange as those Eastern kingdoms you hear about where people believe in things. That Demme is no more. I'd say the last clear sighting of him was in *Something Wild*. And it's a loss, one of our worst.

Tak Fujimoto shot this lovely Western light. Toby Rafelson did the production design for trailer living. Craig McKay edited it, and the music is a pretty medley of hits on the radio. The cast also includes Elizabeth Cheshire, Chip Taylor, Michael J. Pollard, Denise Galik, Gloria Grahame, Charles Napier, Pamela Reed, Charlene Holt, and someone named Melvin E. Dummar, coming in the back door for fifteen seconds' more fame.

Men in War (1957)

The story is that *Men in War* was a Sidney Harmon production, with a script by Philip Yordan, for which Anthony Mann took a platoon of actors out into the California hills, and just shot it without a single interior. It's a film about the Korean War, but the enemy are hardly named or seen as more than distant figures that leave the burnt grass trembling. By 2005, asking for the picture at a Pacific Film Archive screening, I found that no print seemed to be in existence. A Dutch television company owned the rights, but they had no material. All the PFA could find then was one good 35 mm print owned by a retired projectionist in Los Angeles. And this is the alleged art of film, and what had happened to an invaluable American movie.

The platoon is lost in open country under the command of a weary lieutenant (Robert Ryan). They come upon two other Americans: a shell-shocked colonel, driven by a devoted sergeant, the one man in view who seems made for war (Aldo Ray). The sergeant wants to remain alone, undisciplined, but the lieutenant insists on joining forces. And so the culture and ethos of the two men is put to the test—how do men in war behave if they mean to survive?

These men have no backstory, and little chance of a future. They are figures in Mann's eternally beautiful landscape photography, in which you can feel the beginnings of Japanese fatalism, a Mizoguchi, who sees that all men are shadows under the same sun. In the end, a few Americans make it to safety, though they are driven to use their flamethrower as darkness falls. This feels like a parable on weapons and commitment in which even the liberal lieutenant bows to the force of Sergeant Montana's flamethrower, the final answer to his own inarticulateness.

As always with Mann, the distant views are so lovely as to be mannered, and the fable on commitment comes close to being a homily. But as with Mann at his best, there is a profound identification with all the male figures and the minor disparities of bravery and resolve. I can hardly think of another film so unswervingly about war and yet so calm, so meditative, or so philosophical.

The photography, often with intricate moving shots, is by Ernest Haller, and there is an inane flourish of music at the end from Elmer Bernstein. The sound is actual, natural, and restricted and this music sticks out like a studio touch. You can say it's an antiwar movie, but the truth is graver. This is a picture about the necessary abandonment of other attitudes in war. As the film ends, the two leads toss the medals they have down the smoking hillside that has seemed so vital. In truth, *Men in War* is like a war memorial, made and built in the gravest helplessness.

Ryan and Ray are perfectly judged as opponents, Robert Keith is very good as the speechless colonel, and the grunts include Philip Pine, Nehemiah Persoff, James Edwards, Vic Morrow, L. Q. Jones, Anthony Ray, and Adam Davis.

Mephisto (1981)

Whenever the old riddles return on whether Leni Riefenstahl was good or bad, I feel the urge to reexplore István Szabó's magnificent and disgusted *Mephisto*. It's more than a mercy, it's a coup, that when this film comes to offer us its "leader" he is in no way a Hitler substitute—he's the General (Rolf Hoppe), not just a fan of Mephistopheles the character, but an expert on every nuance in the performance, and a man whose ultimate sense of power rests in wondering out loud why the actor, Hendrik Hofgen (Klaus Maria Brandauer), has such a limp handshake.

Szabó's film is based on a 1936 novel by Klaus Mann on the career of a real German collaborator, Gustav Grundgens, the actor who played the gangster chief in *M* and the husband in Ophüls's *Liebelei*. (Grundgens was also for a time the brother-in-law of Klaus Mann.) In the film (written by Szabó and Péter Dobai), we encounter Hofgen first as a provincial success—in Hamburg. He is a brilliant actor, a ruthless user of people, and one of those men so helplessly ambitious that even those most appalled by the spectacle are tempted to laugh at his shamelessness.

And bit by bit Hofgen rises: He goes to Berlin and wins the support of the General—though this general makes it plain at every step that he can as easily condemn and diminish as praise. The actor's life is crowded with women (including a black dancer, Karin Boyd), but he betrays them one after another in his effort to reach the top. And for Hofgen and Grundgens alike, Mephisto (opposite Faust) was the role by which the ascendant actor was best known.

So the reference to the Nazi regime is very clear. But still *Mephisto* works so well because it could be applied to any dictatorial and paranoid regime. Again, the story is best felt as one in which Hofgen gradually recedes from us—but only gradually. At first, his abilities, his energy, and his neediness are oddly appealing. We know we're going to loathe him very soon, but he is a great talent—or is it just that the role is battered by the full weight of Klaus Maria Brandauer's insatiable charm?

And this is where the full ambiguity of *Mephisto* sinks in. Brandauer is intensely physical, chronically devious—and in all of this he seems to love and beg for more of the close-ups that peer into his own greedy gaze. When *Mephisto* opened, Brandauer was famous only in Germany, and this spectacular film made him a star. Yet he was so personally difficult, apparently, that he became very hard to cast, or hold in a film venture. Several years ago, he was out of commission just because of this intense, problematic ego and his own inability to restrain his talent. It's a puzzle that adds enormously to the power of the film.

Lajos Koltai did the superb photography where Hofgen seems to be in a flaring emotional spotlight so much of the time. The supporting acting is first class: Ildikó Bánsági, Krystyna Janda, György Cserhalmi, Péter Andorai, and Christine Harbort, and the film does that first necessary thing for films of the Reich—it suggests the foul breath of these handsome people. It's a world in which you can't breathe for the stink.

In *Mépris,* Michel Piccoli (Paul Javal) is married to Brigitte Bardot (Camille). That means he is nine years older than she is. He is a scriptwriter who likes to keep his hat on, not because he has lost as much hair as Michel Piccoli, but because the Dean Martin character followed that strategy in *Some Came Running.* Piccoli's writer is working on a script of *The Odyssey* for a producer played by Jack Palance (Jeremy Prokosch) and a director who might be mistaken for Fritz Lang. The marriage is that odd sort where the wife apparently has nothing to do but take a bath or recline naked on the hotel bed all day. Bardot seems patient enough doing this. But we have known wives with a shorter fuse.

Now, in part, this was a contractual obligation. The producer, Joseph E. Levine, had ordered that Bardot must do a nude scene, so Jean-Luc Godard had reckoned to get it out of the way as quickly as possible. He arranges Bardot across the CinemaScope frame (it may have been her second nature by then), and he goes through a series of color filters as the couple talk for no other reason than to let you know the nudity is mediated and contrived.

One might argue that shades of "contempt" are being proffered here: toward Levine for his crass directive—as if Bardot's clothes might not be whisked away by providence; toward Bardot for tolerating this treatment of herself—is it crazy to say she would not let kittens be treated like this?; toward Paul for making such a trophy into a wife. And toward us, of course, for watching. But by 1963 Godard was already over the edge: he believed watching a movie (a Prokosch movie) was as great a ruin as making one. Yet he labored on.

A little later, Paul allows Camille to be alone for a short time with Prokosch. She believes he may have been making her available to advance his career. That she has so little self-respect or independence suggests a code of marriage belonging to the seventh century. Never mind: like many ultramodernists, Godard was old-fashioned in many respects. So the marriage breaks. Tragedy will follow. And a serene Lang will be left with *The Odyssey*—perhaps the least promising project Fritz Lang ever considered.

I am being a little facetious because *Le Mépris* is now so taken for granted as a masterpiece—and because I wish to show that it has many silly things wrong with it. Still, Godard's baleful feelings about the movies are no longer in doubt. He disapproves, and as he disapproves so he gives us yet more ravishing footage (by Raoul Coutard) from the roof of the villa (it had belonged to Curzio Malaparte) overlooking the Mediterranean (more spectacular than even Mlle. Bardot). With such grave camera movements and the music of Georges Delerue, *Le Mépris* has all the framework of a great film. But the little boy making it holds on to his disillusion the way older boys clutch their prick. It is beauty—but it is all over.

The Merry Widow (1925)

For every account of *Greed* that defines it as a battle between Erich von Stroheim (the director, the artist) and Irving Thalberg (the producer, the businessman), it has to be remembered that Stroheim's next picture was *The Merry Widow*—for which his immediate boss and the man who hired him was Irving Thalberg. Moreover, while the cost of *Greed* (all that shooting!) was $665,000, *The Merry Widow*'s budget was less than $600,000. Grant, too, that even before *Greed*, it had been Thalberg who fired Stroheim from *Merry-Go-Round* at Universal. So two things emerge: first, that Thalberg recognized some quality or potential in Stroheim; second, that the rogue director was hard-pressed to get directing work elsewhere.

Not that this silent *Merry Widow* was a pleasant experience for anyone. It was planned that pit orchestras would play the Lehár music—still, the songs are instrumental in the love story, and it's no wonder if Stroheim found screen time to turn toward a satire on the aristocracy in Montenegro (or Monteblanco as he called it). A story persists that Stroheim tried to introduce every perversion he could think of—but the film doesn't really substantiate that. The operetta romance is fully indulged: there are lavish sets by Richard Day, and lustrous photography by Ben Reynolds and William Daniels. The film had two major players—John Gilbert and Mae Murray—and it made a healthy profit ($750,000). Stroheim's treatment of the flimsy world in *The Merry Widow* is scathing and pungent, but there's every indication in public response that that went down better than Lubitsch's more wide-eyed reverence in the 1934 sound version (with Maurice Chevalier and Jeanette MacDonald).

I do not minimize the willful self-destructive in Stroheim, but the most intriguing thing is that if he could have "survived" a few years longer then the edge of his satire and his psychological realism could have been strengthened by talk. What Lubitsch did with sound is something that Stroheim might have trumped.

Yet it seems to be true that Stroheim let his relations with Mae Murray deteriorate. She was anxious to walk off the film and may have enlisted John Gilbert on her side. But the decisive incident probably occurred in Mayer's office. Thalberg was away, so Mayer had to deal with the Von. Mayer tried to persuade Stroheim to be less cynical in his view. Then Stroheim suggested that Sonia (the Murray role) was really a whore. "I don't make films about whores," said Mayer, his anger building. "But all women are whores," said Stroheim. Whereupon the toughie in Mayer lashed out and he is said to have knocked Stroheim off his feet. But the Von recovered himself and went back to work.

It's true that Tully Marshall plays a foot fetishist, and that may have upset Ms. Murray. But then look at the rapturous treatment of the key waltz—with its streamlined moving camera. That's something an actress might die for, an unrestrained romanticism. Also with Roy D'Arcy and Josephine Crowell.

The Merry Widow (1934)

You had to be there, maybe, for here is a subgenre that has faded away. Instead of this lightly veiled cherishing of aristocracy, with a developing cult of ballroom dancing, we get *The Queen.* So it's worth tracing the history of *The Merry Widow,* which premiered in Vienna in 1905, and then triumphed in New York in 1907. The book of the operetta was by Victor Léon and Leo Stein, and the music was by Franz Lehár. Although the story line does presuppose a European prince's need for money, it also takes for granted that every widow in sight (and most other women, too) are going to go wild for a prince who can sing and provide a palace. I suppose Rainier and Grace Kelly is the last time that trick really worked.

Metro-Goldwyn-Mayer owned the rights from the silent version (by Stroheim). That film had cost half a million and change and made a profit of over $750,000—without the songs. As such, it was the biggest hit Stroheim ever had. So a remake with Lubitsch in charge and Maurice Chevalier as Count Danilo was not to be argued over. It was their fifth film together and originally Grace Moore was to have played Sonia. But the studio insisted on Chevalier having top billing and Moore's dignity was too offended. Whereupon, the "natural" casting of Jeanette MacDonald went into effect. And she was able to deliver "Vilia."

Samson Raphaelson wrote the script for the movie with Ernest Vajda, and Lorenz Hart and Gus Kahn wrote some fresh lyrics to go on the Lehár songs. In order to give no direct offense to anyone in an anxious Europe, the original setting of Montenegro was changed to Illyria (where *Twelfth Night* takes place). Oliver Marsh did the photography (and he had shot the Stroheim version). The sets were by Cedric Gibbons, Gabriel Scognamillo, Fredric Hope, and Edwin White. Albertina Rasch did the choreography, and Ali Hubert and Adrian designed the costumes. The cast also included Edward Everett Horton, Una Merkel, George Barbier, Ruth Channing, Sterling Holloway, Donald Meek, Herman Bing, Minna Gombell, Akim Tamiroff, and Shirley Ross.

Thalberg was in charge of the production, and there seems to have been no hint that Lubitsch, Chevalier, and MacDonald were tired of each other yet. But there is something askew. It's as if in 1934 the intuitive Lubitsch can't quite see the reality of the Prince of Wales and Mrs. Simpson creeping up. Royalty was on the slide, and the gorgeous self-infatuated aplomb of Chevalier was beginning to date. It's hard to believe, but Lubitsch does the story without an ironic undertone. He does it straight.

So they shot for eighty-eight days. It cost $1.6 million and it lost money. No one quite knew it at the time, but this was the end of Lubitsch and Chevalier, though they nursed a dream of doing *Papa,* in which a father plots to end his son's love affair—and the girl falls in love with him.

Metropolis (1927)

Metropolis is everywhere now—you see it in "abridged" form with pop music accompaniment; it plays on the walls at fashion openings; would you be amazed to see it in a supermarket, the gloomy trudge of slave workers imitating the check-out lines? Have the Teletubbies done it yet? More or less, it has come to stand for cinema's attempt to be the macabre soothsayer of modern times—a role made all the easier in that no one ever seems to remember what *Metropolis* wants to mean. Perhaps there has always been a gulf between the proclamation of the last titles and the relentless respect for urban enclosure and trap in the imagery.

Once upon a time, film history had it that Fritz Lang and his wife, Thea von Harbou, were inspired to do the film by their visit to the United States, and New York, in 1924. In fact, that trip was to examine studio facilities. Lang and Harbou already had a script in hand as they made the journey. They had seen the future before they saw New York, but they were eager to report the latest tricks in set construction and epic-scale shooting to Ufa. For *Metropolis* was set in advance as the biggest film ever made in Europe.

This is its story: A future city-state is ruled by John Fredersen (Alfred Abel), who lives with his son, Freder (Gustav Fröhlich), in moderne penthouse splendor. But there is an evil genius, Rotwang (Rudolf Klein-Rogge), who advises Fredersen, and he lives in a warped house such as Hansel and Gretel might have found in the dark woods. Freder intuits that something is wrong: He has a vision of the slave labor being turned into virtual machines. And there is such a protest movement forming in the bowels of the city, led by Maria (Brigitte Helm). Freder takes her side, but Rotwang makes a robotic Maria who will preach depravity and destruction to the mob. The city is nearly destroyed—but finally there is a reconciliation: The heart and the head will work together. How this will work, or what happens to the economy of the metropolis, no one knows.

What matters is the dynamic geometry of the sets and the blocks of people, the way the foreboding message is carried in the imagery, and then the way in which the devilish version of Maria is so seductive. Karl Freund and Günther Rittau did the photography, with Eugen Schüfftan supplying some special effects. Otto Hunte, Erich Kettelhut, and Karl Vollbrecht were in charge of the design and Aenne Willkomm did the costumes. The movie shot for 310 days and 60 nights. And it cost 5 million marks (about $1 million). It was said that 30,000 extras were employed, and as you look at *Metropolis* today don't forget that the computer had hardly been thought of yet. This is a vast vision translated in theatrical terms. The story it tells can be lifted off, like a helmet from a skull, but the skull—the oppressiveness of the city, its labyrinth, and its suitability as a trapping place, are the message of the film. And when one Brigitte Helm becomes another, the essential virus in doubling had been let loose.

M. Hulot's Holiday (1953)

Such a pretty little beach—and apparently, it was at Saint-Marc-sur-Mer, near Saint Nazaire, in Brittany. You know the kind of place, with bijou boardinghouses looking out over the beaches and puppy rollers unwinding in the bright sun. With bathing huts and beach umbrellas like cupcakes. You feel, after the movie, that someone should put a polished glass dome over the place so that its light, its freshness, and its kindly humor may be preserved forever. It is where Hulot goes in the summer, though Hulot is clearly the kind of man who takes uneasily to the idea of holiday. He can never quite get it right.

Four years after his incarnation as the country postman in *Jour de Fête,* Jacques Tati was back in pants too short and a perky Robin Hood hat too small. He was an arc in the wind, his potbelly thrust forward, his head leaning back to have longer to look at things. He is a bachelor, plain to see, a good soul, but not naturally gregarious—not when he is so accident-prone. And as Tati observed the French, or the world, in the years after the war (with the last mines being swept from the beaches), he saw the innocent pleasure of seaside holidays and he made a film in which Hulot is never quite happily aligned with the other cartoon life in sight. But does Hulot complain? Not at all: he is tolerant, forgiving, and open-minded, and he is patient. He will come another year.

Meanwhile, any possible sense of lingering grievance or injury at bad luck is taken away by the serene sound track: not just the plaintive theme by Alain Romans (and the blonde in the boardinghouse, the pretty one, with hair done up as in a Dutch portrait of the seventeenth century plays it all the time on her record player); the seashell remoteness of natural sound effects; and then the muffled quality of every spoken word. It is as if Hulot is sinking into a summery swoon of deafness. But no one ever said anything worthwhile to him, so what's to worry over or regret?

The photography is by Jacques Mercanton and Jean Mousselle, and the open-air stuff is thoroughly enchanting—you can smell the salt, the sunblock, and the ice cream. The credits say that Tati wrote the film and needed three colleagues, Pierre Aubert, Henri Marquet, and Jacques Lagrange. Perhaps. I can just as easily believe that Tati sketched the whole thing out one afternoon, and touched it up as summer passed.

Of course, it was a comedy understood everywhere, and it was a breakthrough success for Tati. Today . . . ? Well, it is so benign, so clean, so airy in line and content. I don't think there is a drop of malice in the whole picture and so I have to wonder whether it could ever have been made. It is a last touch in the line of cinema that began with René Clair, and Hulot is one of the rare comic protagonists from the bourgeoisie. I suspect that Hulot has a small shop on the Left Bank, eccentric and distinguished, that sells stuffed creatures. That—or he is a secret agent.

Mickey One (1964)

Those were the days: just consider the assembly of talents—director Arthur Penn, just off *The Miracle Worker;* Warren Beatty in his most beautiful and ambiguous period; photography in black and white by Ghislain Cloquet (between jobs for Malle and Bresson); music by Eddie Sauter, but featuring the melancholy improvs of Stan Getz; a supporting cast that gathers Alexandra Stewart, Hurd Hatfield, Franchot Tone, and Jeff Corey; and a script by the brilliant, pretentious, paranoid Alan Surgal—the kind of script a kid does on spec, and which got taken up by some of the best people in town.

To call the film pretentious is hardly amiss, or less than flattering: this is the kind of daring experiment that a great industry should be able to make. It is also, let us note, the mood of Alan Pakula's more famous and successful paranoid movies, ten years earlier and far more jittery than velvetlike. Truth to tell, *Mickey One* is amazing and a huge tribute to the influence of the French New Wave on a mind as fertile and ambitious as Penn's.

The story is not meant to be clear, but Mickey is a comic and/or piano player, a nightclub stand-up, who now longs to hide because he believes the Mob or every They he can think of are after him because of a mysterious offense he has given. To say the least, this troubled soul relies on the very confused moodiness of Warren Beatty in the 1960s and his urge toward narcissism and reclusiveness at the same time. It is uncanny casting (since he was producer, too!), and no small tribute to the movie is the way Beatty dislikes it and has sought to distance himself from it. Yet he would never be more himself, both appealing and insufferable.

But as a fusion of noir and modernism *Mickey One* is hard to credit, even as you watch it. There are lurches toward symbolism and the ponderous dragging up of "meaning," but for much of the time the picture has a sinister, inane momentum all its own and quite stunning. George Jenkins did a great job on the seedy settings—this is a film made in "metropolis"—and for most of the time Penn trusts the weird serenity of the script and just lets it play. No doubt, his discussions with Beatty—in search of the core—were agonizing, but in fact Beatty's inconsistency as a player only feeds into Mickey's incipient breakdown. Alexandra Stewart's modest talent also serves to make the romantic setup more inexplicable.

It's beside the point to say that there are things "wrong" with *Mickey One.* The whole concept is outrageous, and the style-for-style's-sake is mannerism to an extreme. At the same time, I think it's relevant to say that only Arthur Penn would have tried it, but that Penn also is so generous and so curious that he refrained from imposing a starker line of control. So it's unique, wayward, and a film to see whenever you get depressed about the withering of the American imagination.

Midnight (1939)

Take your pick of these stories: Billy Wilder and Charles Brackett delivered a script for *Midnight* and it was "perfect." But producer Arthur Hornblow, Jr., felt the need to assert his own power so he called for a rewrite—from Ken Englund. The said Englund did his best, but Hornblow read it and agreed it was not as good as the original. "Who do we know," he asked, "who writes like Wilder and Brackett?"

"Brackett and Wilder?" said Englund.

"Excellent!" determined the producer. He passed the script back to the first two writers, and they retyped their original so that it would look different.

Or, the script came in and director Mitchell Leisen loved it but thought it was a touch too cynical. So he sat down with Brackett and Wilder and just made a few suggestions—at which Wilder hit the roof. All his life, he hated people who changed scripts. But he hated Leisen too, and that is more mysterious: Leisen was ahead of Wilder as a director; Leisen was gay, and he was a one-time designer. Whatever, Wilder put the word around that Leisen relied on good scripts (from Wilder and Brackett and Preston Sturges) and then tried to "improve" them.

It doesn't work out: There were good Leisen films written by other people—and Wilder did have a nasty edge. *Midnight* only adds to the dilemma, for here is one of the great screwball comedies, with Eve Peabody (Claudette Colbert) at its center, a smart mercenary on the make, far from likeable, yet acceptable within the general whirl of wit and competition that distinguishes the film. She meets a Hungarian cab driver, Tibor Czerny (Don Ameche) and is getting on well, but crashes a big party where she fastens on Georges Flammarion (John Barrymore), who starts flirting with her in order to pull his wife (Mary Astor) away from her lover (Francis Lederer).

But don't work too hard on who deserves the credit, because the fun moves too fast. Yes, it's a great script, but it's a great script rendered with terrific feeling and panache. Charles Lang photographed it (and it had a budget of over $1 million), Hans Dreier and Robert Usher did the sets, and either Irene did the clothes or Miss Colbert wore her own. So it looks funny and smart at the same time—a Leisen keynote—and only worth recalling when you realize that Wilder's eye could go blank.

Most people will settle for the fun of *Midnight* and the aplomb of the players. Claudette Colbert was never better, and if you feel what a steel blade she was behind the smile, what's wrong with that? John Barrymore is inspired, naughty, and irrepressible—you realize that he was a great comic actor. Mary Astor was so reliable that people take her for granted, whereas she was beautiful, intelligent, and sexy and all night long—ask George S. Kaufmann. As for Ameche and Lederer, Monty Woolley and Rex O'Malley, these are the supports who make so many fine movies work.

Midnight Cowboy (1969)

"Everybody's talking at me, I don't hear a word they're saying. Only the echoes of my mind." That song and the image of Dustin Hoffman and Jon Voight walking in Manhattan, his limp somehow joined at the hip with the other's stride, is one of the certain madeleine-in-the-tea memories of the late sixties. So it's a marvel to find that the Harry Nilsson song was not even nominated. But the song wasn't written for the film, and in the search they had discarded things by Joni Mitchell, Bob Dylan, and others.

John Schlesinger had had his success in Britain, most notably with *Darling*, which was nominated for Best Picture. It was when he came to the U.S. to open *Far from the Madding Crowd* (a failure) that he took root for the first time and considered making an American picture. A friend had recommended the James Leo Herlihy novel, and Schlesinger was fascinated by the characters of Ratso and Joe Buck. He got Waldo Salt to do a screenplay and Jerome Hellman came on board as a producer so United Artists (this was in the great era of Arthur Krim and Robert Benjamin) gave it the go-ahead and never interfered, no matter that the eventual X rating was predictable.

Jon Voight was very much Schlesinger's discovery, but Dustin Hoffman was urged upon him by Hellman. He encouraged Schlesinger to go to New York to spend time with Hoffman, and the actor was waiting in costume and character as Ratso.

The film is odd stylistically, like a lot of Schlesinger. On the bus ride there's a real documentary sense of passing life. But in Manhattan, there is too much feeling of the whole thing being very arranged, or Fosse-ized, that comes from the mannered and rather superior cutting. Nor was it exactly clear in 1969, despite the X, just how gay this subject was. In other words, I think Schlesinger was a little squeamish about New York and his own material. So it can be seen as just a very odd friendship—and since America is so "bizarre," perhaps that's all it is.

That said, it was a breakthrough film in that so many raucous and sordid things were handled so casually. Schlesinger was a little hurt that Hoffman didn't respond too much when the final film was seen, but I think that came from a fear that Voight's easygoing manner had stolen the film. Ratso is not really to be believed. It's a shameless piece of overacting—which is not to say that anyone else could have done it or would have dreamed of doing so.

So it opened as an X at 113 minutes, and then along came the R at 104. Far more important, it took Best Picture and Best Director and got nominations for Voight, Hoffman, and Sylvia Miles plus a win for Waldo Salt. All of that helped break down censorship, but the film is left in its cul-de-sac—an odd sidebar. Schlesinger remained far more at ease with British material.

A Midsummer Night's Dream (1935)

In a lot of history books you find this famous production of *A Midsummer Night's Dream* at Warner Brothers as "long awaited." I wonder. It seems to me more plausible as an overnight whim—as if Jack Warner and his wife had been to see Max Reinhardt's Hollywood Bowl version of the *Dream* and wondered, Why not a movie? Once it was agreed on, Hal Wallis and Henry Blanke jumped on it as producers, a budget of $1.5 million was approved, and the great Max Reinhardt was given William Dieterle as right-hand pro (in case he had any difficulties). The result got a Best Picture nomination, but it was not well received. Hollywood and the press were uneasy. There was no tradition then of gala movies and a lot of people were afraid of making fools of themselves. But this is really the only movie Reinhardt ever made, so we're left to the conclusion that the great man did anything he could think of to hold attention. It's not as if there's a palpable Viennese magic or mood at work.

But so much is creditable: Hal Mohr did a very good job at putting the dream feeling on film, and no one could wish for more in the big magic moments. Anton Grot created a version of little England and the forest that lends support to the photography. And everyone agreed that Erich Wolfgang Korngold did a wonderful job arranging the Felix Mendelssohn music dramatically. As for screenwriters Charles Kenyon and Mary C. McCall, they did their job decently without supplanting the reputation of Shakespeare. A little more shaky are the dance routines by Bronislava Nijinska and Nini Theilade.

There's common consent that Puck is the stand-out figure, with Mickey Rooney, thirteen at the time, gurgling and cooing like some nonhuman species. But I think the mechanicals do very well, most notably Jimmy Cagney as Bottom. Indeed, Warners was so impressed by him that they started thinking about him as Robin Hood—not the craziest idea. In addition, Joe E. Brown plays Flute (he and Cagney are very funny in the Pyramus and Thisbe pastiche), Frank McHugh is Quince, Dewey Robinson Snug, and Hugh Herbert Snout.

It's in the loftier parts that you encounter some problems with verse delivery and an overall indecision on "tone": Victor Jory as Oberon; Anita Louise as Titania; Ian Hunter as Theseus; Dick Powell as Lysander (he admitted later that he hadn't known what he was saying); Jean Muir as Helena; Verree Teasdale as Hippolyta; Hobart Cavanaugh as Philostrate; Ross Alexander as Demetrius; and Olivia de Havilland as Hermia—she had made her teenage debut in the Hollywood Bowl version.

So, was it meant to make Hollywood gasp at the class of Warner Brothers? A year later M-G-M did *Romeo and Juliet* (with notably less success) and then Shakespeare was allowed to rest until Olivier and Welles took him on. But you have to search hard for an American Shakespeare in the years since. So "long awaited" and long regretted may be more to the point.

Mikey and Nicky (1976)

Like a moon in the solar system of John Cassavetes, there is Elaine May's *Mikey and Nicky*. Apparently Elaine May had a play version of the story dating back to the days of her celebrated nightclub act with Mike Nichols. That means that the film was not much short of twenty years in "development," and generally I don't think that is good for a movie. Along the way, Peter Falk read the play and said he loved it. He would do one of the parts. In turn, that led to the casting of John Cassavetes in the other part. It is the story of two very minor gangsters in Philadelphia. Nicky (Cassavetes) believes he has offended the mob and is set for execution. So he wants to get out of town, and he enlists his old friend, Mikey (Falk), to help. But is it possible that Mikey is set to finger Nicky and present him as a sitting duck to the hired killer, Kinney (Ned Beatty)?

At some stage, Paramount gave the green light—this after May had directed *A New Leaf* (1971) and *The Heartbreak Kid* (1972). *A New Leaf* had been seriously reedited after May left, but *The Heartbreak Kid* was fresh and tart. The trouble with *Mikey and Nicky* seems to have been that May had been thinking about it so long, entertaining so many variations, that she couldn't make up her mind what she wanted.

Add that dilemma to the burning appetite of Falk and Cassavetes to turn it into an acting class for two improv-wild guys and you may begin to understand the problem. People on the film said that May was filming every scene over and over again. The schedule fell apart, and after a long period in Philadelphia the unit was reassigned to Los Angeles. Michael Hausman was the producer trying to hold it all together. But the film has three credited photographers—Bernie Abramson, Lucien Ballard, and Victor J. Kemper—as well as stories that Cassavetes shot some of it himself.

But it was not over. The editing process went on well over a year. May removed all the film from her studio cutting room to a hotel room, and then some of the stuff went missing—there was a story that May's psychiatrist had removed some of it to help her make up her mind. Anyway, two editors are credited—John Carter and Sheldon Kahn—but there are surely wilder stories. Paul Sylbert did the production design.

The film was buried by reviews and ignored by the public. Yet, like many of the Cassavetes projects, it has a seething intelligence at work that is reluctant to accept any formal discipline. It's not just that these two guys are unlikeable (they are). It's more that their situation is not very interesting. Had May lived with it all so long that she no longer saw it as a project or a story? All one can say is that this picture serves to enlarge the strange story of her undoubted but unresolved talent. The cast includes Rose Arrick, Carol Grace, William Hickey, Sanford Meisner, Joyce Van Patten, and M. Emmet Walsh.

Mildred Pierce (1945)

Warner Brothers was in a muddle over *Mildred Pierce* from the outset, and in many ways that was because everything James M. Cain wrote was always said to be "unfilmable" on grounds of censorship. The novel was published in 1941, and Warners flinched from the way in which Cain had told his story without "sympathetic" characters. It's easier to see now that that was his genius, and in *Mildred Pierce* he had deliberately moved away from melodrama and murder to deal with money and class, issues that fascinated him and which put him almost in the same league as Dreiser. So the book is very much about a divorced lower-middle-class woman and her difficulties in making it on her own. There is not a murder in the novel.

But there is a good deal of adultery, compromise, bad language, and sordidness, which is what Warners meant by it being unsympathetic. Perversely, this studio attitude introduced a killing, of the Monte character (Zachary Scott), in the attempt to make Mildred more winning or noble. Of course, this affected everything else, notably the role of Veda (Ann Blyth)—bad enough in the book, but hissable on screen. This process took time, and it went through a number of screenwriters, several of whom were so attached to the Cain original that they resisted the changes—notably the flashback structure with police station talk that came from producer Jerry Wald as much as anyone. So Thames Williamson did a treatment, and there were scripts from Catherine Turney and Margaret Gruen (at least) before Ranald MacDougall came up with the final version, which begins with the murder and finds Mildred on the waterfront at a point close to suicide. In all of this, Cain was amiable and supportive, but not inclined to write it himself.

In fact, the Cain view of money and self-respect survives the murder. Indeed, I think the compromise is acceptable, and I love the view of Mildred in southern California (with Eve Arden as her chum) trying to make a baking business. Director Michael Curtiz—that rich mystery man—is every bit as attentive to that job as he is to the melodrama, and I think a lot comes from the treatment of the character Wally (Jack Carson), sleazy but irresistible.

The studio worried over how to photograph Joan Crawford. They felt she looked better at M-G-M, the studio that had dropped her. But it's clear from that opening waterfront sequence that Ernest Haller had learned how to let shadow fall on her angry brow. It works, and the film is very well made. Ann Blyth would never be better, and the rest of the cast includes Bruce Bennett, Lee Patrick, and Butterfly McQueen. And today it's far easier to see it as a milestone in feminist cinema, as well as a triumph for Crawford.

Crawford won her Oscar—she was at home in bed, "ill," and they brought her the Oscar as medicine. And don't forget that Ann Blyth and Eve Arden were nominated for Supporting Actress, too.

Miller's Crossing (1990)

I am not a steadfast enthusiast of the Coen Brothers, and I have given up trying to explain the haphazard movements of their career. But the thing that nags me about their record is *Miller's Crossing*, a superb, languid fantasia on the theme of the gangster film that repays endless viewing. It is derived quite plainly from Dashiell Hammett's *The Glass Key*, although the script was done by the Coens themselves.

At the heart of the film's assurance are the dour, glum rhythms of Gabriel Byrne as the "hero" figure who happens to be fucking his friend's girl. The girl is Marcia Gay Harden, never better and so sexy that you understand why Byrne did not bother to debate the temptation. The friend is Albert Finney, charged with energy and booze in equal parts as the thick-headed crime boss who can't see a con if it's a cat curled up on his lap. This broken bond between Byrne and Finney is a good version of the relationship between Ned Beaumont and Paul Madvig in Hammett's novel. And it's a shared virtue of both works that they convey the disgust and disbelief in tough men that sees how they can betray each other over a piece of ass. Of course, it is a testament to Harden's ass that we never question the imperative of the ruinous equation.

The next thing to remark on is the way Canadian studios and locations give such a rich, satisfying air of period and place. We never know, or need to know, the city, but there is nothing shabby or secondhand in the décor, and there's an eagerness in the look of the film that speaks to a real love of space, furniture, light, and mood. The same pleasure vibrates in the very intricate story structure. There are some who find *Miller's Crossing* too clever by half, but I think that misses how far the Gabriel Byrne character recognizes the curse of intelligence that hangs over him and the duty it imposes—of always being driven to nose out the cons of others, while hoping that his own subterfuges are going unnoticed. It's kill or be killed and the air of life is smartness. Take it or leave it.

There's more, much more, and I think it centers on the "Schmatta" as played by John Turturro—queer as a coot, a dandy, a coward, and as brave as any coward who takes terrible risks. This could be the finest work of one of our best supporting actors. And don't forget that he stands out in a movie that includes the adorable Jon Polito and the very frightening Eddie the Dane (J. E. Freeman), not to forget a passing secretary, who is Frances McDormand flashing the camera a quick greedy eye as she minces by.

All of that said, after learning to love the crammed texture and its nearly constant inventiveness, it is the more baffling and disconcerting that the Coens seem so often prepared to deliver films that are enervated and without a single good reason for being made. Do they wake up at night wondering if they were ever really this good, or do they refuse to look at the film again?

Le Million (1931)

The camera sees a man and a woman at opposite rooftop windows. They say good-night and then the camera cranes and tracks over the roofs of Paris—and everything is a set, of course, by Lazare Meerson. It's a miniature city but one where nothing unpleasant could ever happen. So it's a film about money, but made by someone who doesn't really know what hardship feels like. We are in the world of René Clair, where a taxicab can't sound its horn without the orchestra picking up the phrase, and where a character's thoughts are soon carried along in recitatif. The people say they are poor, but they look like an affluent dance company, thank you very much. Truth to tell, the one thing Clair needed in these films was a stronger choreographic sense. For although *Le Million* has a lot of fun over the silliness of money and its pursuit, you don't feel much is at stake beyond the perfection of a soap bubble.

Never mind, it's instructive that Parisians loved these films in the early thirties and thought the use of sound was witty and elegant—it is, but sound can be so much more, so sound for Clair is like glass-blown silence. And in this one, Michel (René Lefèvre) and Prosper (Louis Allibert) have won the lottery—but where's the ticket? It's surprising, I think, that Michel claims the win instead of letting it be shared with Prosper; sharing, after all, is the visual motif of all those group shots that Clair loved where the light by Georges Périnal slips down on everyone equally, like blossoms in spring. (There is a very nice stage moment where Michel and his girl, Béatrice [a pouty Annabella], become reconciled while hiding behind the scenery as fat opera singers go on about nonexistent love.)

When it's over, you'll marvel that the search for the lost ticket took so long. Clair wrote the film as well as directing it, but he doesn't push himself into any really madcap situations and—compared with the screwball comedies in America—he doesn't want to say anything unpleasant about French society. So the people are without substance: Michel's poverty is alleged but not felt, and the plenty and stupidity of the society characters is just indicated. What appealed to Clair, plainly, was the idea of music carrying the action along—he must have died when he saw *The Umbrellas of Cherbourg*, but Jacques Demy gives so much body and weight to his romance.

Le Million is very fragile, but it's short and quick. The final scramble for the vital jacket ought to be crazier and funnier. You can imagine what the Marx Brothers or Buster Keaton might have made of it—and you feel the possibility that the madness will consume everyone, just like a panic or the cry "Gold!" So the film and its daintiness need more energy. But Clair's world is unique, and models like Lefèvre and Annabella adorn it prettily—not quite people, not quite puppets. They're toys that sing when you pinch them. Also with Raymond Cordy, Paul Ollivier, and Vanda Gréville.

Ministry of Fear (1944)

A man comes out of an asylum into a world that is at war. As he waits for the train to take him away, he sees a country fete in progress. He takes part in an absentminded sort of way, and apparently he guesses the weight of the cake—without ever knowing that the sweet mixture contains microfilm vital to the war effort. So begins the film that may yet be appreciated as Lang's greatest in America, more delicately poised over the razor's edge of war and madness, more lyrically given over to the abstract. It is from the novel by Graham Greene, published in 1943, and it does have a sequence in the improvised bomb shelter made out of a London tube station, but the film is not nearly as heavy on the atmosphere of London in the blitz as the novel. Which is not to deny that *Ministry of Fear* is actually more atmospheric than, say, *Hangmen Also Die* or *Cloak and Dagger*, films in which the history of the Second World War is more immediate but less dramatic. In *Ministry of Fear* we are back in those stage-made cities from the German period, where every building or doorway conforms to the architecture of dread and trap.

Ministry of Fear was written by its producer, Seton I. Miller, and made at Paramount. Henry Sharp did the photography, and the design is by Hans Dreier and Hal Pereira. Bert Granger did the sets, which ranged from the tube station to the country fete. And Ray Milland played the protagonist, Stephen Neale. Milland at this time was a very intriguing actor, handsome yet lacking natural confidence, and he has an intuitive understanding of how to be released from a madhouse, yet not necessarily beyond its care. The plot of the film is a series of irrational and unexplained forces striking at Stephen, yet inwardly Milland suggests no surprise. His madness has taught him that much.

For the rest it is a master class in Fritz Lang's use of entranceways and the barriers between spaces that can be elided by light and bullets. So the craziness of its world is opposed by a constant and precise physical geometry that is as beautiful as anything Lang filmed. And long before the end, that relationship of disturbance and visual grace is the music of the film, and its greatness as art. Do not come here expecting Englishness, Graham Greene, or a lucid espionage plot. Follow your eyes in all things, and see how the momentum of the film gathers. In the mid-forties as in the twenties and the sixties, Lang was one of the greatest compositional artists the movies have known, as well as a man who taught us to see the forms of framing. In the end, of course, the meaning of the framing is fatal or filled with dread. So even when this story ends well, the forms tell us to stay alert.

The excellent supporting cast—everyone edgy or eccentric—includes Marjorie Reynolds, Carl Esmond, Dan Duryea, Hillary Brooke, Percy Waram, Erskine Sanford, Thomas Louden, Alan Napier, Byron Foulger, and Eustace Wyatt.

The Miracle of Morgan's Creek (1944)

"Education, though compulsory," wrote Preston Sturges, "seems to be spreading slowly." He had the idea for *The Miracle of Morgan's Creek* back in the thirties. He eventually filmed it in 1942, but while there were few films with so frantic and inspired a take on the war effort, Paramount held the finished film up until 1944. And by then, Sturges was leaving the studio. It was the end of a perfect marriage. *Hail the Conquering Hero* was still to come, but Sturges was an independent, and he was lost. Meanwhile Paramount's comic output shrank to things like *Samson and Delilah*.

It had been Sturges's first idea that in a place called Morgan's Creek, a girl is pregnant by the banker's son. But he won't marry her. So she lives with a hermit and has sextuplets. Sturges wanted to do it with Betty Hutton and Harry Carey as the hermit, but he dropped the hermit and wrote a part for Eddie Bracken. As the story now stood, Trudy Kockenlocker (Betty Hutton) is determined to "kiss the boys good-bye" at a military dance. (Buy War Condoms as You Leave This Theater?) This is much to the ire of Papa Kockenlocker (William Demarest) and the woe and dismay of Norval Jones (Eddie Bracken), who loves Trudy. No matter that he is a feeble jerk who can't even get accepted by the Army. And so Trudy's six bright boys are attributed to Norval.

At last, Preston Sturges was setting aside New York and Palm Beach, as well as the society people he knew and loved. Morgan's Creek is a place that might frighten even the campaigning politicians as they pass through once in a lifetime. It is the home of madness, excess, and the frantic desperation to be American. It was Sturges's first great attempt to haul himself up on high and survey what the idiots had made of the terrain. Thus the foreboding comments on education and its prospects.

But since the comic invention was in no way moderated, this is surely the most frantic and headlong of all Sturges pictures, where laughter and distress over the folly of our fellows combine to produce a physical relief when the film ends. One measure of that is William Demarest being promoted to a leading part—a father fit to be tied. Another is the entire concept of Diana Lynn as his other, caustic daughter commenting on the action. And, for anyone who had thrilled to the stylishness of Fonda and Stanwyck, McCrea and Colbert, then the idea of Betty Hutton and Eddie Bracken bespeaks populist shock in Sturges.

John Seitz did the photography, Hans Dreier was the art director, Edith Head did the costumes. The Breen Office (censorship) was horrified at the idea of military men fathering six—though it seems to me hysterically patriotic. Sturges was even told to cut a scene where car brakes screeched because there was a need to save rubber. The cast also included Porter Hall, Emory Parnell, Al Bridge, Julius Tannen, Vic Potel, and many others.

As for the holdup—was there fear of respectable opinion? Even so, in 1943, here is a film that could have struck terror in the dead heart of Adolf Hitler. How do you defeat such idiocy?

The Miracle Worker (1962)

The cinema is a place that easily cheapens emotion. One of the most distressing experiences we ever find in its dark is to be in tears of sympathetic response to a situation which we know is trash. If we had time, or the sense, we would write books about that phenomenon, for it is remarkable and damaging, the way we have permitted our finest response to be exposed and manipulated. So it's important to cling to the memory of those works where the tears have been earned—by the plight of victims; by the magnitude of the human triumph; and by the notion that this is not just a story, but history, or her story.

Helen Keller was born in the South (she was alive when *The Miracle Worker* was made), and we still know her as a writer and a worker on behalf of the handicapped. She is a kind of modern saint and a beacon. That is not the subject of this film, or the William Gibson play that inspired it. This is the story of a savage child, a little girl who has made her disabilities into an armor, and of the teacher, Annie Sullivan, who rescues her. Indeed, as the title indicates, the focus of the film is on the teacher, and those most likely to be moved by it are those who have ever felt the marvel in teaching as a chance to change or uplift other lives. In that sense, it is a story brimming with hope, even if Penn makes it a story of lost wildness as much as achieved civility.

Penn had directed the play on Broadway in 1959, with Anne Bancroft and Patty Duke. It ran 719 performances, and in many ways the movie, produced by Fred Coe, was simply an attempt to film the production and the performances. But something happened. Penn seems to have fallen in love with film as he worked so that no one would ever accuse this picture of being stagy or think that the performances were set in aspic or classic reverence.

Penn creates the house, the yard, and the family who witnessed the miracle. He sees that the moving camera is essential to animate the fights between Annie and Helen—their great scene over folding a napkin may be the most violent scene in Penn's work. I know the film shot by shot, and I still marvel at its freshness and the danger.

Something else strange happened. Bancroft and Duke won the two acting Oscars. Penn was nominated as Best Director. But for reasons that are hard to see, the film was not nominated for Best Picture. This was the year *Lawrence of Arabia* won, and one can understand that impact. But among the nominated pictures were *The Longest Day, The Music Man,* and *Mutiny on the Bounty*—yes, the one with Marlon Brando. I doubt that anyone now sees those three, whereas I know people who re-view *The Miracle Worker* every year.

The Misfits (1961)

The Misfits is more famous as a cultural landmark than as a film. Yet it's worth remembering that it follows one of director John Huston's favorite subjects: horses. In turn, the best stuff in the picture involves the actors trying to rope and tame wild horses on silvery flats outside Reno, Nevada. Huston, at least, could look at a horse and see just the wild four-footed miracle. Yet somehow this aching movie is driven to see the horses as symbols of lost purity in America.

It's the sort of film that, maybe, a great writer and a famous actress might make on the upside of their relationship, when the poetry could be fed daily by the passion. Alas, Arthur Miller and Marilyn Monroe were over before this film was shot, yet Miller was doing his earnest best to find a role for his wife that might show how good she could be. And so a woman waiting for a Reno divorce gets herself associated with a gang—the last gang—of cowboys. It was a tough order and one that exposed Miller as a limited writer with a subject that needed at least a Willa Cather. But for Miller's name on the script, one wonders whether a pragmatist like Huston would ever have gone ahead, let alone honored the kind of dialogue that seemed more than pretentious in the rough open air.

Russell Metty's black-and-white photography captures the dry air of Nevada very well, and it makes the starry cast look pretty good. It's just that Miller can't deliver these people as real and ordinary—while Huston can't see that if they're not "grand" or "epic" then he'd be better off not filming them. Of course, the cowboys are a big trio—Eli Wallach (the most natural), Montgomery Clift (who is like his character from *Red River* after two stints at a Betty Ford Clinic), and Clark Gable, who was fifty-nine as if fifty-nine was the old man and the sea. It was shortly after the film finished that Gable died of a heart attack—some said it came from the exertions of the horsebreaking sequence; some pointed to the delays caused by Marilyn; others just noted that at fifty-nine Gable was like eighty. He's tough and tender with Marilyn, but she can't match him, line for line, smile for smile, in the way he worked. Her uncertainty seems like vagueness to him. And vagueness can give a guy a heart attack, too.

The best performance in the film comes from Thelma Ritter—but of how many films is that not true?

One might have wondered if Huston would fade away with the film. But he was probably the person least weighed down by the film's failure. He was a vagrant and a creature of chance. There would be worse films to come, but there would be *Fat City, The Man Who Would Be King,* and *Wise Blood.* Huston was like many gamblers: He never took too much credit for winning or losing.

Miss Julie (1950)

August Strindberg's *Miss Julie* was written in 1888, and despite its being a somewhat awkward length for conventional theatrical productions, it has been in the international repertoire ever since. Why not? It is a brilliantly tense tragedy about sex and class in which the aristocratic daughter of a great house flirts with the footman. The whole thing takes place on one hot summer's night, and it is a play that is difficult to produce without some impact. So it is all the stranger that the movie repertoire includes a phenomenal film of the play that is hardly seen.

Alf Sjöberg was born in Stockholm in 1903—in other words, fifteen years ahead of Ingmar Bergman. And Sjöberg was the master of the dramatic arts in that small country as Bergman came of age. Sjöberg was head of the Royal Dramatic Theatre, while on screen he did *The Road to Heaven*, *Frenzy* (which gave Bergman his first credit as screenwriter), *Iris and the Lieutenant*, *Barabbas*, and *Karin Mansdotter*. But *Miss Julie* was once the best known of his films—it shared the Grand Prix at Cannes in 1951 with Vittorio De Sica's *Miracle in Milan*.

The novelty to Sjöberg's *Miss Julie* is that the drama is extended by the use of flashbacks that play in the same frame and on the same sets as the night in question. This may sound awkward or contrived, but it works with silky ease and such strange, dreamlike resonance that it is remarkable that more films have not pursued the same strategy. For why should the one frame not contain different times? Why do flashbacks have to be so self-contained when in truth memory floods into every present moment?

The black-and-white cinematography is by Goran Strindberg, who was actually a distant relative of the playwright. The drama is centered on Anita Björk as Miss Julie and Ulf Palme as Jean the footman. For those who reckon that Ingmar Bergman must have used (and known) all the great Swedish actresses of the postwar era, Anita Björk comes as a welcome surprise (they worked together only once). A blonde, she was sexy, sad, intelligent, very quick in her reactions, and so compelling that she quickly got promoted to Hollywood. That move didn't take, but her Julie is utterly worthy of the part—there is no higher compliment. As for Palme, he accepts second place in the drama, but only because of a kind of bitter deference that marks the resentful servant class.

Very well reviewed at the time, *Miss Julie* ought to have found a place in the international repertory. If Bergman had made the same film in 1951, his widespread recognition would not have waited on *The Seventh Seal*. But Sjöberg and Björk are two first-rate figures who have been passed over in the film culture that allegedly now knows and gets to see everything. It is true that the play's concentration is dispelled, and I think it is true that *Miss Julie* works best with flesh, heat, and fragrance only a few feet away on a stage. But the elastic frame of Sjöberg's film could yet be a gold mine in filmmaking.

The Missouri Breaks (1976)

It was a famous failure in its day, part of the legend that Marlon Brando was so spoiled and so expensive and so hell-bent on destroying "sensible" film projects. It was also taken as a warning that the Western really was dead and that only idiots would be prepared to put two eccentrics like Brando and Jack Nicholson together and hope for coherence. There is also the notion that this was the start of Arthur Penn's decline, leading him astray from tightly controlled scripts and remorseless encounters with psychic ordeal.

In which case, how is *The Missouri Breaks* so amiable, beguiling, and seductive—as sweet as prairie grass—and how does it sustain such a foolish air of being a pointless ramble around the West, its clichés and marvels, and a band of actors who might have been born with their boots on (albeit the wrong way round)? It always seemed to me (I admit I am biased) that the nod early on in the film to Laurence Sterne and *Tristram Shandy* was the clue (the mad rancher Braxton asks his daughter to hand him down the book when he is vexed from having to hang rustlers).

This is the Western as picaresque, as shaggy-dog story, and—in a very Hawksian way—as a kind of on-set interview and improv with the various people assembled for the film (play it with *Beat the Devil*). There is actually a perfectly respectable theme to it all, if you need to have a theme: rich ranchers and landowners trying to keep away that indolent spirit, the wandering lout and his gang, inclined to steal a few cattle here and there, try growing cabbage, and steal your randy daughter. In fact, I trust screenwriter Thomas McGuane enough to guess that this is what the Breaks country was like in the late nineteenth century—or would have been like if enough people had read *Tristram Shandy*.

The gang is priceless, and the deaths worked out for them are as inventive as they are degrading—John Ryan, Frederic Forrest, Randy Quaid, and the superb Harry Dean Stanton, who has a lugubrious campfire chat with Nicholson that deserves to go straight to the anthology of great scenes. And I like Nicholson with Kathleen Lloyd, too, though she is a little Greenwich Village, I suppose.

But, really, it is Brando's film, and everyone knows this, Nicholson included (there are times when he seems content to watch—the rivalry does not show). As for Marlon, he is a wagonload of costumes, accents, personae, and tics. He is the regulator, yet utterly irregular. He is a great actor making sport in the long grass—he is a Boudu. And for me the film could go on forever. No wonder its dull reception crushed him. And remember that, despite every digression and divergence from strict order, he manages to make Robert Lee Clayton lethal and as scary as hell. So he talks to his horse! Conversation is too important to be entrusted to cowpokes alone. This is a sublime comedy and an uncommonly relaxed film, full of a feeling for nature and whimsy, caprice and cutthroats.

Moby Dick (1956)

Just seven years after *Twelve O'Clock High,* Gregory Peck is our commander again, but this time man management succumbs to destiny and the soaring metaphors of Herman Melville. In *An Open Book,* his autobiography (which was a little less than fully open), John Huston said, "*Moby Dick* was the most difficult picture I ever made. I lost so many battles during it that I began to suspect that my assistant director was plotting against me. Then I realized that it was only God."

That's a good joke, nicely Hustonian, and a fair measure of the level of this bold, romantic adaptation. I'm sure Huston had a large respect for the novel. Still, he was wise to make a boys' seafaring classic out of it. And it works, and would work again at the high school level. I can think of no better stimulus to a reasonable class to read and inhabit Melville than to see this film. Of course, there are tons of prose and barrels of sperm oil omitted, and there is no attempt to render Melville's deeper spiritual concerns. On the other hand, I don't think anyone seeing this film would walk away believing that it was just a story of a man's mad pursuit of a whale. Huston knew his great books (from B. Traven to R. Kipling to J. Joyce), and he never did an adaptation without knowing his limits and respecting the grandeur of the page.

So he got Ray Bradbury to make him a barebones script, and then he urged designer Stephen Grimes and cameraman Ossie Morris to find the right blanched look of eyes nearly blinded by the light and of paintings exposed to weather and time. Some said it was arty, yet in the Hustonian manner the art was practical and effective, too. You know from the start that there is a visual concept—that this material is being scanned by the blank eye of the whale and the equally uncertain gaze of God.

The unit settled in Youghal, Ireland, with a grand boat and they had merry hell with the weather—which shows. It was very hard to send expensive actors out in open boats in those conditions, and harder still to photograph the danger and the awesome battle with the whale. So awkward back projection obtrudes. Perhaps Orson Welles knew best in his stage play (done a year earlier in London), where actors simply swayed in unison to convey the pull of the sea. (Welles is here, too, of course, as a delightful Father Mapple.)

At the time Peck's Ahab was challenged as being, inwardly at least, too handsome, or too accustomed to his own nobility. Robert Ryan might have been more fearsome—as he was in *Billy Budd.* Better still, maybe Huston was his own ideal Ahab, though that could have stretched his rope past breaking. In *An Open Book,* the director maintains that time will recover Peck's qualities in the film—and I think that has happened. In the end, it holds up, enjoyable and very likely to send you to your proper place: the book.

The Moderns (1988)

We'll always have Paris? The hero's name is Nick Hart, said director Alan Rudolph—"Say it in French—'art.'" That may sound unpromising, a touch coy even, but do not be deceived. *The Moderns* is a wonderfully beguiling diagnosis of those afflicted by "art," and it is one of the great films about that other roasted chestnut, "Paris." Cue for the gloriously inane figure of Ernest Hemingway (Kevin J. O'Connor) to stride up to some innocent passerby with some turgid aphorism about the nature of Paris.

But go back to Hart (Keith Carradine) and his sketchbook, which entirely resembles the film he's in in his louche, absentminded way. He does cartoons for the papers and for money, but art's curse still hangs over him. And he is pretty good, some say as good as Cézanne, Matisse, or Modigliani. There he is in Paris, hanging out and drawing, when along comes an old flame, Rachel (Linda Fiorentino), who is now married to Bertram Stone (John Lone), a millionaire in condoms and looking to expand into art.

The rivalry between the two men will lead to an exquisite triumph of fake paintings (by Hart of course, a droll copier) that end up in New York's Museum of Modern Art while the vicious Stone destroys the real things, over which he thinks he's been duped. Rudolph wrote it, with Jon Bradshaw, and you could argue that in a world of any justice their script would be hanging on exemplary walls now. Alas, no, but we suffer a better fate: We get the movie in which love (the real thing and the fake) jostles with levels of authenticity in art and devotion to Paris.

The picture is a panorama of fakes in which really only Hart, the forger, stays honest. The delight of the screenplay is to keep this philosophical issue bubbling while bringing so many stray cats home for the night or a moment. The Paris was all made in Montreal, apart from a few dazzling montages of the old place. So we get passing eccentrics—Geraldine Chaplin, Wallace Shawn, Genevieve Bujold—on sound stages that are utterly acceptable as "Paris" because Rudolph and Bradshaw realize what an old whore the city is.

You can say the film is Altmanesque with its shifting circus of supporting players. But there's a more authoritative wit behind it all than Altman dared, and I suspect it comes from Bradshaw. This is a picture made out of infinite love for art, Paris, and love, but in a full awareness of how much all three have sold out to advertising in the modern age.

Just look at the sustained final sequence in which Hart and Oiseau (Wallace Shawn) quit Paris by train and come to New York, where Rachel will be magically discovered. The movement of people and of the camera in that sequence—with Bradshaw playing a small role as an idiotically confident MOMA guide—is a beautiful passage of film built around the score (by Mark Isham). If you take art seriously, let alone love, you have to see this film. And once seen it is with you forever, like Paris or short sight.

Modern Times (1936)

In 1935, a Soviet official, Boris Shumisatsky, visited Hollywood, and took time at Charlie Chaplin's studio to watch a work-in-progress, originally entitled *The Masses* but now set to be *Modern Times*. Later, in *Pravda*, Shumisatsky took it upon himself to say that Charlie had followed many of his suggestions on what to do with the film. And, of course, this story got back to the *New York Times* and was a formative influence on the notion that Chaplin had turned Red. Whereas anyone who worked with Charlie would have agreed that getting him to take any advice was the hardest thing on earth. Hadn't he even determined to keep *Modern Times* silent (or without talk) after the studio he built had been soundproofed?

Like many people—and Chaplin had toured the world—Charlie was distraught at the economic depression and the rise of fascism. He had seen automobile works in Detroit and he recognized the inhumanity in elaborate production lines—note, he had also appreciated the opportunities for comedy such as Buster Keaton had explored years earlier in *The Navigator*. He spoke out about such things in his naïve way, without acknowledging that mass production was part of an economy that might save the world. He never noted that movie was the industrialization of the image.

But he would make a film in which the Tramp fell foul of the mechanized production system—and made the audience laugh. There are union crowds in *Modern Times*, demonstrating and rioting, and Chaplin wags his finger at them disapprovingly. Still, the Tramp is driven to a breakdown by the system and he is largely rescued by the "gamin" (a role for his new girl, Paulette Goddard), and by far the most beautiful, tomboyish, and aggressive woman he ever put in a movie. And so the film ends with Tramp and girl disappearing down the endless road to the theme "Smile" (credited to Chaplin himself).

There was no talk, but Chaplin did want music, and he ended up hiring the very young David Raksin to help him. They fought a lot. Raksin was fired a couple of times, and he did not refrain from pointing out that the most autocratic boss he had ever heard of was named Chaplin. At the same time, Chaplin doubted that he would ever use the tramp character again: it was just that he did not know how to make that character appealing with talk.

The movie opened and had rentals of just over $1 million—in other words, it did far less well than *The Gold Rush* or *City Lights*. Why was that? Was the audience impatient with silence? Was the humor here too literally mechanical? Or was there the beginning of a movement against Chaplin in the public? Was it just that Charlie had been too big too long? You can take your pick, but I think it's true that the comedy is oddly detached from any theme. Machinery isn't the end of the world. Even Detroit was a scene of fresh opportunity for millions of ex-tramps.

Mommie Dearest (1981)

Joan Crawford died in 1977. Four years later, this film was a lurid hit that dragged campness into the mainstream and which has largely determined the ways in which succeeding generations regard Crawford. I don't mean to be pious about this. By and large, the children of Hollywood stars—whether natural or adopted—have had a very hard time of it, and surely they have some right to revenge and a chance to clean up. It may be that Christina Crawford (author of the original book) was abominably treated by a capricious monster. Yet she was rescued, she was spoiled, she was raised to lofty levels of spending—such as her book could maintain. I can believe that Joan Crawford was often an unhappy woman, mocked and patronized by her employers, and not easily given to the warm maternal touch that might have kept Christina sweet.

On the other hand, Joan Crawford once was ravishing; she was a sexpot, and a very good actress; and she survived through thick and thin. She deserves better of us than this very one-sided and horribly complacent demolition. I have to add that the enduring audience for *Mommie Dearest* has been gay, sardonic, and rather cruel. I can see how the history and iconography of Hollywood have gained that whiplash audience. But again, it is so much less than the full story. You have only to look at a few Crawford films to know that she was so much more interesting a person.

Mommie Dearest was scripted by director Frank Perry and producer Frank Yablans, with the help of Tracy Hotchner and Robert Getchell. It fixes on the period from 1939 until 1977, and of course that is sufficient to rule out the very tough years in which Joan Crawford made it from San Antonio to be an international star. Faye Dunaway plays the lead, and she offers an excruciating impersonation. She was not nominated for an Oscar, and I think the theory is plausible that she damaged her own career a lot by taking the part. There were plenty of people in Hollywood who knew bad stuff about Joan who still flinch from this merciless treatment.

By contrast, Diana Scarwid gives a very good performance as Christina. Howard Da Silva plays Louis B. Mayer without subtlety. But the film lacks a great deal in terms of atmosphere: it is far more Grand Guignol than a social commentary about the ways in which an ardent young woman could be altered by the movies that made her famous. This is a great subject, and we need as much sober work on it as possible. But *Mommie Dearest* seems like a forerunner of the new gossip press that builds flimsy figures into stars so that it can then rip them to pieces. It's far too late to expect an honest or thorough portrait of Joan Crawford. But everything we learn about the making of our stars suggests an uncommon ordeal and a rare mix of courage, stamina, and humor. What Christina Crawford never seems to get is how *Mildred Pierce* had told the story so much better.

Monkey Business (1952)

It was a treatment called, "Darling, I Am Growing Younger" by a newcomer named I. A. L. Diamond, and Howard Hawks liked it a lot. On the one hand, that interest was an admission of the clever setup: laboratory bent on searching for the secret of rejuvenation; a magical serum accidentally arrived at, and randomly distributed thanks to the chimpanzees who served as test cases. Of course, this was in the good old days when America's interest in rejuvenation depended on wonder drugs instead of on sheer stupidity. In those days people more or less acted their age, except that Howard Hawks had an extra-personal interest in the story to the extent that, close to fifty-five, he was dating a woman in her early twenties (this was Dee Hartford, a knockout who became Dee Hawks in 1953). Of course, picture people are different—or are they pioneers, full of the need to break unbroken ground?

The treatment was passed on to Ben Hecht and Charles Lederer and they turned it into a spiffy script that filled Fox with glee. Fifty-six years later and counting, it is a very funny film, a version of screwball as if done from lawn chairs at the end of a fine summer evening. What I mean by that is the gentlemanly air of expertise which starts right off with a bemused Cary Grant ready to begin the movie and the dry, caustic voice of Howard Hawks telling him, "Not quite yet, Cary." It's like Babe Ruth pointing to the spot. *Bringing Up Baby*—its clearest antecedent—is frantic and headlong, whereas in this picture Hawks and Grant seem to be enjoying themselves, rerunning a classic game from their own youth. And nostalgia may be the most active antidote to rejuvenation.

Ginger Rogers is the wife and she works hard and does fine, yet somehow you know that Hawks was bored by her. This is a married couple, a subject that Hawks seldom touched onscreen or allowed to interfere with his deep interest in seduction. So Marilyn Monroe gets a fuller run as Lois Laurel, the voluptuous office secretary who is eyed with the same interest by the chimpanzees and by Oliver Oxley (Charles Coburn), the old man who is putting up the money for this research and who plainly longs for the Viagra assist that will get him into Laurel's bush.

I would like to apologize for that, and I would, but apologies mean so little in the world of Hawks and, truly, the joke gets the level of innuendo as well as anything else I can think of. In other words, a Breen Office worth its salt would have burned this lewd and cunning picture and flogged Hawks on Pico Boulevard (outside the Fox premises). As it is, we are left with one of the most casual masterpieces ever made. That said, a film about these guys doing this picture while Howard was trying to act twenty-two (and Grant was chasing some youth) might have been heaven. Thank God, Howard Hawks had some vestiges of dignity, with Cary Grant along to keep everything professional.

Of course, it would be very hard to remake just because so many people now have learned to think young without any help from drugs, surgery, or religious conversion. Our immaturity has become entirely natural.

Monsieur Verdoux (1947)

The story goes that in 1941, Orson Welles gave Chaplin the idea for a picture called *The Ladykiller* based on the French mass murderer Landru. Chaplin snapped it up and paid Welles $5,000. He said it was an idea, Orson said it was a script. Go pick. Five years later, Chaplin had his script. He called it *Comedy of Murders*. He showed it to the Breen Office and they scolded him as thoroughly as they could. Charlie responded with venom. What the Breen people were doing was tantamount to limiting his freedom of speech. He easily read that response into the hostile attitude of many in the government. Yet an idiot would have known that the script raised problems for the Code on every page. And an innocent clerk in that office—if he or she existed—might have sighed and wondered how so benevolent an artist had come to this gloating portrait of cruelty.

Chaplin's answer was that the world was now into so much mass killing, who could measure the individual losses? He had been harried and harassed, and it is not too hard to portray Charlie as a victim by 1947. On the other hand, his tyrannical side had grown, his cruelty had built, and he had surely lost touch with what was or was not funny. When he hired Robert Florey as his assistant on the project, he was soon fighting with his own man, leaving Florey aghast that so much of Chaplin's art had atrophied. Far more than Chaplin realized, his spirit had turned to antisocial thoughts, to violence and to a sense of his own need for vengeance. I think there is no doubt but that he was so dismayed by the world's heartlessness that he felt compelled to make a satire on it. But his artistry and his own sentiments were now out of control. So it's hard not to feel the misanthropy in the film. As Roger Manvell said of late Chaplin: "These films are laments for the human soul lost in the devil's politics of our time."

Seldom does it feel like a comedy, and thus the genuine comic interludes seem forced or unreal. What holds us most in the film is Verdoux's quiet pessimism as he watches the "lost girl" become the mistress of an arms dealer. She tells him that life must go on, but Verdoux has a list in his head of those who deserve to die. And he is self-appointed to the task, the melodrama of which plainly thrills him. It is a film Adenoid Hynkel might have dreamed.

Rollie Totheroh shot it, and the cast includes Marilyn Nash, Isobel Elsom, Martha Raye, Irving Bacon, and William Frawley. It did terrible business in most of the world—only the French really approved of it—and it undoubtedly dictated the course of the next few years for Chaplin, notably his exile from America. It has to be seen, just as Chaplin has to be esteemed as the crucial figure in film history. You can easily conclude that Chaplin forgot the lesson of *Sullivan's Travels*—or that he needed someone as brilliant and modern as Sturges to direct this film. But *Monsieur Verdoux* is heartfelt. That is what makes it so troubling.

Monty Python's Flying Circus (1969–74)

My title refers to the original forty-five shows, undertaken by the BBC and all shown in Britain as part of the regular television programming before they had their debut in America. It's important to stress that subversive, institutional nature. Set up big in movie theaters, where they had many notable coups, the Python gang movies could never match the hallucination and the unraveling of that very silly thing—regular, steady TV—or the sense that "the right time" and British decorum had been taken over by program snatchers. To be sure, Python was funny, but never forget the underlying threat that a band of ruffians have taken over the institution of broadcasting. There is nothing as suggestive in television as that rumor, or innuendo—and Monty Pythonism was a version of anarchy always focused on the bland if benign totalitarianism of BBC television. "And now for something completely different"—indeed. I can think of no other program, show, or movie that so fruitfully drew upon the dynamic of interruption, the great risk but the great hope for a society where steady programming is the last imprint of the state and its drab plans for us.

The comparison with *Invasion of the Body Snatchers* is relevant, I think. For example, with the screening of the strenuous but misguided *The Invasion* in 2007, a profound truth emerged. Whereas in the mid-fifties it was all very well to play that story line with people good and pods bad, today the opposite view begs attention. Suppose that poddery is already in: as advertising, the "Net," regular TV coverage of everything; weather reports; stock market numbers; sports scores. Isn't it time by now for a pod that breathes poetry, error, and *l'amour fou* into this air-conditioned nightmare?

Make no mistake, the very elaborate technological enterprise of film and television cries out for insurrection—the Marx Brothers knew that (even if they were politically empty-headed) and so did the Pythons. Thus you have to start your assessment of their show by saying: If you had to devise an ideal TV network, the BBC would be very close to it—tolerant of diversity and minority tastes; risk taking; silly and serious; and with responsibility. All pluses for effort. But nothing takes away from the fact that a network cannot help but turn us into fish. In which case the primary thrust of a radical show must be to try to destroy the net and its tidiness. Nothing was as miraculous in Monty Python as the cockeyed view that regarded the rest of the evening's shows.

The boys were John Cleese, one of the great desperate clowns (as witness *Fawlty Towers*), Terry Jones (maybe the most directorial), Eric Idle, Graham Chapman, Michael Palin, and Terry Gilliam. Yes, they made "proper" films and some have moments of sublime filth and unreason. But the TV show was the thing and the shining example that the insane can not just take over the asylum but cleanse it.

The More the Merrier (1943)

Once war was under way, it was tough for people passing through Washington, D.C., to get a room, or even a bed. That is the basis for this delightful, and unexpectedly sexy, comedy, written by Robert Russell, Frank Ross, Richard Flournoy, and Lewis R. Foster (they shared an Oscar nomination and lost to *Casablanca*) and directed by George Stevens. But the story is not quite as simple as that. Garson Kanin met one of the four writers, Frank Ross, and Ross's wife, the actress Jean Arthur. She complained of the poor material she was being offered at her studio, Columbia. For $25,000, Kanin offered to write a script that Ross could then sell to Harry Cohn at Columbia. Indeed, when the key meeting came, it was Kanin who read the script aloud to Cohn, and won him over. Of course, the credits reflect none of this.

Arthur would play Connie Milligan, a young woman working for the government and of a rather clerical turn of mind. Connie is engaged to Charles Pendergast (Richard Gaines), a self-important bureaucrat. Better than that, Connie has a D.C. apartment. Half of which she has let to Benjamin Dingle (Charles Coburn), a millionaire who seems to be retired, but who wants to be close to the action. (He has a motto, "Damn the torpedoes. Full speed ahead!") Along comes Sergeant Joe Carter (Joel McCrea) from the Air Force, in desperate need of a place to stay. Thinking of Connie's sparse romantic life, Dingle lets Joe have half of his half.

It is a comedy of space and manners, in which as square footage goes through impossible stretchings for the war effort, so the cut-and-dried Connie becomes a looser woman whenever Joe is around. This was really Coburn's first opportunity to play a naughty if matchmaking old man—though he is not entirely immune to Connie's charms (Coburn was only sixty-five at the time). But he intrigues to bring Joe and Connie together, a task helped by the uncanny chemistry between them. Jean Arthur at this time was a leading comedienne, but a shy woman resigned to her reputation for being difficult. Meanwhile, McCrea told everyone who hired him that he knew he was their second choice. But it's about time to admit that McCrea had a wondrous charm, and fire-warning sex appeal.

Their great moment occurs in the doorstep scene, where Connie and Joe have just had dinner together for the first time. What follows was supposedly improvised: McCrea is gruff and taciturn, but he is feeling for her, and bit by bit the officious Connie is reduced to helpless womanhood. It ends in her seizing his face as if it were a jug of water and slaking her thirst. It is one of the great wooing scenes in American film, and a beautiful portrait of how in 1943 things could happen.

Ted Tetzlaff did the photography, Lionel Banks did the art direction, and there's a song by Leigh Harline. The rest of the cast includes Bruce Bennett, Frank Sully, Don Douglas, Clyde Fillmore, Stanley Clements, Grady Sutton, and Ann Savage. Jean Arthur was Oscar-nominated but not McCrea, and Coburn won the Supporting Actor Oscar.

Morocco (1930)

"Why don't you just marry her?" hissed Riza Royce von Sternberg to her husband Jo. This was 1930, in Los Angeles. Josef von Sternberg was designated in Marlene Dietrich's new contract with Paramount as her only director. Then Lubitsch, the fox, sought to shoot a cameo on Dietrich in a studio promotional package, but Sternberg had stepped in, argued the law, and done the segment himself with Marlene in a white tuxedo. It was a sensation. Next, Jo put his actress in an apartment across the corridor from the one he shared with his wife. That's when Riza threw her hissy fit, and Sternberg came back with, "I'd sooner share a telephone booth with a frightened cobra."

I know, you want to see that film now, with Riza launching a divorce and Jo spending hours and days with his discovery. He got her to diet (she had been pastry-plump in Berlin); he redirected her eyebrows; he had her work on her English; and then he got top stills artists in, and had her pose for new publicity pictures. According to Steven Bach's biography, Marlene thought they depicted the most beautiful creature on earth, but not quite her.

And so *Morocco* began, from a book called *Amy Jolly* by Benno Vigny, that Marlene had given to Sternberg. It's racier than the film, describing a high-class Parisian prostitute who follows the Foreign Legion to North Africa, does cocaine and lesbianism, and falls for a taciturn legionnaire. It's the story of a romantic sophisticate and a sexual expert (Amy) who gives up career, liberty, and her Parisian shoes to be a desert camp follower to Tom Brown, who likes her, and likes her yielding of all dignity to him, but who would never settle with her. Near enough, that's how Jo and Dietrich were getting on: he gave up marriage, dignity, and freedom; she respected and learned from his artistry, she surely let him in and out of her bed a few times when the schedule permitted, but she never settled with him.

So the series of their films was under way along with a complicated, and fairly absurd, sadomasochistic transaction which became the subject of the films. And Sternberg (who had once had much more interest in realism) shifted over to the ridiculous and the surreal. He reveled in the artificiality of this North Africa, the power of light and shadow to make a world (Lee Garmes on photography), and Jules Furthman's cryptic dialogue. Furthman coined a way for tough love to talk that deeply affected American pictures: It's the droll man letting himself be outtalked by an insolent woman, and it would be the making of Howard Hawks.

Gary Cooper got the Tom Brown role (over John Gilbert and Fredric March), and he was better than them. He can stand up to Marlene because he's as beautiful as she is. Her cabaret number, kissing the giggly girl in the audience, is revolutionary and still radiant with nerve. Adolphe Menjou is the other guy—and he looks just a little like Jo, as if to ask how can the man who made these gods actually exist with them?

In short, one of the most influential films Hollywood ever made.

The Mortal Storm (1940)

On the brink of war, Metro-Goldwyn-Mayer had several options to pursue: It could hope for the best, despite all reports coming in through its foreign departments, and it could look the other way, with fingers crossed; or it could adjust its own anxiety to that of the public. Not for a big studio the bold, personal confrontation of *The Great Dictator*, where Charlie seems to resent that another little man with a mustache is trying to take over the world. But a thwarted romance, as if to say, look, there is Nazism, which would break up families and prevent people from their heart's desire! Of course, you can read between the lines in *The Mortal Storm* (you can gather that the character of the professor is very likely Jewish). But this late in the day, the Hollywood message is clear: We would rather describe this crisis in terms of blocked romance than political causation and consequences.

It comes from a novel by Phyllis Bottome, adapted to the screen by Claudine West, George Froeschel, and Andersen Ellis. It begins in the German countryside in the year 1933, just before Hitler's electoral victory. Frank Morgan is the professor. His daughter, Margaret Sullavan, is in love with a young veterinary student (James Stewart). But the course of romance is threatened by the Nazi influence, which is seen—very much as it was presented at the time in America—as a strident call for order and reform. It splits the professor's family and then the professor is taken away to imprisonment. The question arises, Can the lovers stay where they are, or must they escape?

Director Frank Borzage does not shirk showing us the mounting brutality of fascist Germany, but those scenes are pained and clipped whereas the treatment of the lovers is lyrical and profuse. It is as if film itself were persuading Borzage of the justice of their cause. William Daniels did the photography, and he understood the exceptional screen chemistry between Stewart and Sullavan (at least friends in real life): Her hushed voice seems to draw him closer until he hovers over her like a guard. She is wiser; she knows and feels more—but he is her devoted student and she has found perfection in his innocence. Their love scenes are like holiday next to the brutal scenes of official interference.

Does it feel like Germany? No. Does it feel like a place where the police overshadow love's light? Yes. Should the American public have been content with this limited treatment? A much tougher question—and one that still deserves an answer as political situations facing America become so much more testing and ambiguous. But the face against the state is a classic cinematic answer (Carl Dreyer opted for it with Falconetti in *La Passion de Jeanne d'Arc*—and the cinema loves things that it can photograph). The cast also includes Robert Young, Robert Stack, Bonita Granville, Irene Rich, Maria Ouspenskaya, Gene Reynolds, Ward Bond, and Dan Dailey.

Mother and Son (1997)

We hear the sounds of a sea and birds calling. Darkness gives way to a shot of a young man and an old woman. It seems as if it may be a still, but then a ghost of a smile appears on the man's face. The woman is in bed, the man is on the bed beside her in something like the attentive position of a mother with a new infant. The woman, we will gather, is dying. The man is there for her; he is her son. They talk about dreams and it seems as if, so close at the end of life, they are having the same dreams. Then the woman asks to be taken for a walk.

Her son carries her out into a world of waving grasses, green and sere, like a young person's hair. There are blond tracks. There are trees and what may be white cliffs. The son carries the mother on her walks. Sometimes he rests with her beside the track, or in the grass, or in a birch glade.

The house is made of stone. There seem to be very few modern facilities there. No one else is in sight. Some admirers of the film have spoken of its sense of loneliness. But maybe they mean isolation. For there is a pact and closeness between the mother and the son that are the opposite of loneliness. Still there is no backstory or explanation offered. We do not know the family history, and I have heard some people deduce from the few words spoken that there may have been incest between the mother and son. I do not hear or feel it that way, but I cannot be sure.

The film is only seventy-three minutes long, and there are many long takes in it, time for us to feel the color, the composition and the inwardness of the whole enterprise. For I think the director, Aleksandr Sokurov, believes in an ineffable rapport between the landscape (including its texture and color) and the couple. And I think he is content for that bond to be classic, universal, and idealized. I don't think this is a particular story so much as a dwelling on the bond asserted in the film's title.

Critics say the film is painterly. They refer to Caspar David Friedrich. This is useful, and the stillness and the very muted colors are all tributes to the slow, imperceptible growth of nature—with the stirring of sea and wind as its music (though we do hear fragments of classical music far away in the distance). But there is something happening to the image. I cannot explain it, but I think that a painted glass or sometimes a distorting glass is being put in front of the lens—not to be puzzled over, but to take us ever deeper into the visceral nature of the dying. In some ways I am reminded of the opening of Dovzhenko's *Earth*, where an old peasant dies as if it was a very natural thing. The death here is regretted—the film is an act of mourning—but never disputed or argued against. The mother is Gudrin Geyer and the son is Alexander Anaishnov. The cameraman is Aleksei Fyodorov. *Mother and Son* is a masterpiece and in its tranquillity I think it surpasses even Tarkovsky (the most obvious influence). There is more Sokurov, including the one-shot *Russian Ark*. It's hard to think of him making a film not worth seeing.

The Mother and the Whore (1973)

I hope you won't be shocked by this, but people (even actors and actresses) are not always that good, or sophisticated, at kissing each other on camera, and going very much further, without becoming emotionally involved. I have no maps or diagrams to offer as evidence, but Jean Eustache's *The Mother and the Whore* is one of those films where one shudders at the vulnerability of the people. Is it that they are so very good as players, or so helpless as people? *The Mother and the Whore* trembles with its own damage, and delight. It is 219 minutes long—as long as *Gone With the Wind*—but not because it has an immense amount of story to tell. It is long because these people will talk themselves into silence over sex and love, and the uncertain hope that they can be kept separate.

The length is vital, not just because the spectator should be exhausted at the close of the film, but because it concerns lives that think they may go on forever—in other words, they catch youth at that tyrannical moment when it can believe it will never have to yield. So Alexandre (Jean-Pierre Léaud) does nothing but live in the St. Germain part of Paris, sitting in cafés, reading or arguing, and measuring the women in his life. He lives with Marie (Bernadette Lafont), divorced and a boutique owner (Lafont is six years older than Léaud). One day, Alexandre sets out to meet Gilberte (Isabelle Weingarten), an ex-girlfriend whom he abandoned when she got pregnant. Now he asks her to marry him. She refuses. Later that day, he sees another girl, Veronika (Françoise Lebrun), and he falls in love with her. As the affair builds, so Marie becomes more disturbed. Veronika tells Alexandre off in a most complete way, in language full of sexual contempt and violence, but she admits that she may be pregnant by him. He asks her to marry him.

The Mother and the Whore is not prurient or pornographic, but it is about people whose lives are more completely fulfilled in sex than anything else. It was also made in that fairly short interval between the collapse of movie censorship and the coming of AIDS. In other words—to quote Renoir's language from *La Règle du Jeu*—we are in that period when the collision of two epidermises (or more) and the friction of two fantasies was in the open, free and wild, and seemingly guilt-free—or at least free from all those guilts applied by society as braking impulses.

As I said, I do not know what happened during the filming. Yet I think that the quality of performance—the identification, the accusation, the vituperation—is as personal and as actual as the attraction being mimicked. This film puts us in the room or in the bed with the people. Above all, it puts us in the conversation. The impact is convulsive and complete. The feeling of complicity and touch is unique: you can ascribe it to Eustache for provoking and writing the conversation. But you cannot credit that these people are not speaking for themselves.

Mouchette (1967)

Mouchette has dark hair and a darker stare—she knows more than is proper for a child of fourteen. But does she know enough to be a character with more depth than, say, Balthazar, the donkey, in Bresson's previous film?

When the poacher rapes her in his hut in the woods, she does not know what "rape" is in any legal sense; she hardly understands the process that carries her from protest to acceptance. She only knows that the poacher—though he is an outcast, who suffers fits—is one of the few people on earth who offer her any tenderness. And it is not clear, finally, how far she realizes she is "committing suicide," or has she only come to see herself as a speck of vulnerability who might be carried off in play? So she ignores the responsibility of rolling down the slope and into the lake. But she practices the roll until she moves at speed, out of the frame—and we hear a heavy splash. Bresson does not show the splash—it is as if the rolling has carried Mouchette into peace and dream. And there is a suggestion that that splash would be too vulgar a piece of action in which, for a moment at least, the child or the actress would have to determine how to "receive" the water. In the rape, as it is, Mouchette's small hands clasp the rapist's back—and that is an unusual gesture in Bresson toward the inner life.

The film is taken from a novel by Georges Bernanos, *Nouvelle Histoire de Mouchette*, published in 1937. And it shows the decline of a girl living in poverty in rural France. She has a sick mother whose sickness has precluded family life. It means that Mouchette is not noticed. She is teased by the other children at school. But she is not stupid and not without appeal. Nadine Nortier plays her in the customary Bressonian manner, as blank as possible, but in her voice and bearing there are hints of intelligence and sensitivity that keep coming through. So it's easiest to conclude that Mouchette is misunderstood, and that her escape from the world is desirable.

But is that quite enough? Or has something been lost since the profound commitment of the priest and the escapee in Bresson. Those men were in terrible situations, but they were driven forward by spiritual energy. In contrast, Mouchette seems filled by lassitude or vacancy. And I wonder if a kid that resolute would simply roll down the hill—or would she fight back?

Of course, the film is meticulously made, with the gravest mise-en-scène and a feeling of making a mosaic of the 80 minutes—the stepping stones of Mouchette. But there are real people in the film—the mother, the poacher, the waitress, the shopkeeper—and there are a few very modest efforts to rescue Mouchette which seem to be resolutely ignored by the aesthetic of the film. In other words, Mouchette's dark gaze is greedier and more curious than the camera's calm. I think she yearns for a contact that has been forbidden her. And it is a first ominous note of stifling arrangement shutting out life.

Moulin Rouge (2001)

Moulin Rouge divides people like an old-fashioned God muttering "Loves me . . . loves me not" as he sorts the saved from the damned. For anyone who has contrived to read this book in such an order that *Moulin Rouge* comes last, or even in the last hundred, it may be clear before you say "Mou . . ." to yourself that I love the musical, I am very fond of the idea of Australia, and, if you want a third lost cause that flies my flag—try Nicole Kidman.

All those things aside, I love the history of film in the spirit of one who respects history as much as cinema, and so I cannot watch *Moulin Rouge* without thrilling to the tradition of Michael Powell pictures, of *French Cancan, The Blue Angel,* and *Lola Montès,* to say nothing of the work of Jacques Demy. Do not be surprised if, when the next great thrust forward by film occurs, it is borne on the wings of music, and if not exactly what Arthur Freed would have called a musical, still a melodrama in which the music and the story are not to be separated.

So yes, this is as postmodern or as camp as Montmartre in Sydney (or wherever they did it), and a turn-of-the-century romance requiring a medley of pop-rock love songs delivered with such excitement by Ewan McGregor and Ms. Kidman that they might have been high on something—and not just each other. The surge, I think, is show business, the chance of art or fun, and doing it for an audience. *Moulin Rouge* is a delight in that its creator, Baz Luhrmann, knows that the audience is the vital part of the process. And in this very silly working out of its love story it is, really, the audience that chooses the ending it wants.

The craft here goes very deep: to a screenplay by Luhrmann and Craig Pearce; to ravishing production design by Catherine Martin—the heart of this movie beats and flutters in its clothes and décor; the photography from Don McAlpine and Steve Dobson; the music arrangement by Craig Armstrong; costumes by Catherine Martin and Angus Strathie; choreography by John O'Connell. Look at the colors bolder than color in any contemporary film save for some from China. Look at the convulsive stagecraft—the inspired grasp of all the action in one great set. Listen to the natural melodrama of song. And feel the pressure of the film—it's that of a heart striving, and Satine, our heroine, will kill herself finally from overexertion. I know sane people who said the film was too busy, too much, and I can only respond, Look at the control. Feel the pleasure. You must see the frenzy of action, being, and performance, to say nothing of the innocence of such full-blooded pretending as Jim Broadbent (Zidler), John Leguizamo (Toulouse-Lautrec), Richard Roxburgh (as the Duke of Worcester), and McGregor and Kidman, who may never be as wild again.

Mr. Arkadin (1955)

It was called *Confidential Report* when it first appeared in 1955, and it did not open properly in America for another seven years. There could be no clearer measure of what had happened to Orson Welles in just ten years. He was no longer regarded as being exactly American, and he had spent much of the fifties based in Europe, roaming around, doing all manner of projects despite lacking the proper financial basis. So *Mr. Arkadin* has an insouciant air of what Welles might have done at a weekend house party if admirers asked him, Could you do a *Citizen Kane* again? And so the picture is hurled together with available talent (or the lack of it), with shortcuts and omissions where he didn't have all the footage he needed, and cooking the sound track as he went along. It's a kind of amateur tour de force, the work of a master who no longer has the patience or money to indulge in mastery. And as such it begins to show a new way of making films—fudge the preparation, shoot it fast and faster, and cut it together for the hell of it. These are New Wave energies in a movie that also seems bored with film.

Gregory Arkadin is rich and powerful and mysterious—he likes it that way because almost certainly his past is unsound. And don't forget the abiding rumor that Welles himself did write this as a novel first, though it seems more likely that disciple Maurice Bessy wrote it, just to cash in. Anyway, Arkadin hires a piece of Eurotrash, Guy Van Stratten (Robert Arden), to investigate his life. But as Van Stratten takes on this task, he begins to notice that the witnesses he discovers are being murdered. In other words, Arkadin is employing biography to make sure obituary stays blank. But Arkadin has a daughter (played by Welles' new and third wife, Paola Mori), and his very existence may depend on her reaction.

The attitude of the film is mocking yet ambivalent: Is Welles saying that *Kane* was just a bag of tricks, or is he putting himself more and more in the role of the magician? But the set pieces are intoxicating, and they include the story of the scorpion and the frog, with the final toast: to character.

To this day, there are different-length versions, to torment historians and critics. Jean Bourgoin did most of the photography, Welles himself was the art director; Paul Misraki did the music. The body of the film is made up of expert yet lurid cameo parts—Akim Tamiroff, Michael Redgrave, Patricia Medina, Mischa Auer, Katina Paxinou, Jack Watling, Grégoire Aslan, Peter van Eyck, and Suzanne Flon.

So there isn't really a story so much as the return to a myth. The tattered nature of the film, and the dispute over lengths and which version is most itself, seems to suggest the deliberate, provoking policy of making the remains of a film—to that extent, *Mr. Arkadin* is a prediction of those films Welles would leave behind, unfinished yet unmistakably himself.

Mr. Deeds Goes to Town (1936)

Mr. Deeds seems a character from the 1930s, until you think of George Soros, Bill Gates, Warren Buffett, or even Ross Perot. In other words, the rich American, the self-made man, who takes a fancy to help his less fortunate brothers, is a fixture in American public theater. And, as with a fictional version of the type—C. F. Kane—it is not always easy to know whether you're dealing with a communist or a capitalist, with altruism or manipulation. It's in such uncertainties that the word "American" comes in most handy. Without a birth certificate, Arnold Schwarzenegger eschews the "American" thing, but every time his uncontrollable Austrian accent assaults the word "Kalifornia" I think of him as a Capra creation.

The film came from a story, "Opera Hat," by Clarence Budington Kelland. Frank Capra and Robert Riskin got to work on it as a screen property, and it's fair to say that, from the outset, Capra, that awkward American success (in that he understood how badly many Americans were still doing in 1936), saw it as an examination of his own good fortune, or what Joseph McBride has identified as "the catastrophe of success." In other words, can you think of yourself as small-town American when you're as rich as the guys mentioned above? Or do you lose your credentials?

Longfellow Deeds is folksy. He plays the tuba, he is shy with women. He lives in Mandrake Falls, Vermont, and he writes verses for greeting cards. He is Gary Cooper—not so much the Westerner as the Northeasterner, and Vermont in 1936 was a good deal more isolated than most parts of the West. He inherits $20 million (a mythical sum) and reckons to give it to the poor. He comes to town with this mission and meets a smart newspaper reporter (Jean Arthur) who has a great time writing him up as a buffoon while he falls for her. In the end, an ingrate nation reckons he's insane and like most Capra chumps with good intentions he thinks of killing himself.

Graham Greene made a clever comparison with *Fury*, shown in the same year. They have the same attitude to the crowd—deep suspicion—but one film is made by an optimist and the other by a pessimist. I think that's true, and it's certainly clear that Capra could now make a film so that it hummed. But Deeds doesn't bear looking into. His wisdom is rural or cracker-barrel, and it barely keeps him from suicide. Just like Mr. Smith to come, Deeds wants hearts worn on sleeves. He will have nothing to do with compromise. Yet bargaining together is the means by which society can be reformed.

Deeds was shot by Joseph Walker on a budget of over $800,000—Capra was expanding. There is fine character work from George Bancroft, Lionel Stander, Douglass Dumbrille, Mayo Methot, Walter Catlett, Raymond Walburn, and H. B. Warner. It made a healthy profit and Capra won his second Best Director Oscar. But don't mistake the allegiance in the film's thinking to an old, rural, and Republican America, one mercifully free from government. In real life, FDR was having to be so much more practical than Longfellow Deeds.

Mr. Klein (1976)

Paris, 1942, under the German occupation. Robert Klein (Alain Delon) is an art dealer. We see him purchase a Dutch master from a Jew for a knockdown price. It is a chilly transaction. But then he goes home to find a Jewish newspaper addressed to him. It must be a mistake, another Robert Klein. He searches for this other man, to sort the matter out, but he cannot be found. He meets a lover of the other Klein, Florence (Jeanne Moreau), but he cannot locate the man himself. He believes he should take steps to protect his own name from any suggestion of Jewishness. He asks his lawyer, Pierre (Michel Lonsdale), to locate grandparental birth certificates. With his own mistress, Jeanine (Juliet Berto), he visits a cabaret where an anti-Semitic routine plays. The net of paranoia closes in. The police need to question him. Jeanine leaves him. Pierre offers to buy his business—at a knockdown price. Robert is taken to the Velodrome d'Hiver stadium where Jews are rounded up. Perhaps he will find the other Klein there. But Jews are being taken off in trainloads.

In a movie, it is enough for certain gestures of the surface to appear for an underwater current to be generated. Suggestiveness is everything, especially when you are looking at the beautiful, blank face of Alain Delon—yet again, the inspiration of a major film. Joseph Losey was at a loose end. The Proust film had fallen through, when he was sent the Franco Solinas script for *Mr. Klein.* He responded to it immediately, and he called Delon; the actor said he would do it if Losey would. And he guessed immediately that the mystery in Delon was perfectly suited to the enigma—Who is Klein? Is he Jewish? Or is he a fighter in the Resistance trying to cover his tracks? Who is out to get him?

The film is very cool, very frightening, and beautifully controlled. Yes, it played off Losey's acquired paranoia from the McCarthy days, but it drew upon his knowledge of Paris, too—this is one of the cruel Paris films. Alexandre Trauner did superb sets, full of a decaying bourgeois splendor. Gerry Fisher handled the photography. And the startling cabaret scene was done with Frantz Sakieri and a very unexpected use of Mahler.

I'm still not quite sure how far the French accept this as a French film—it has insidious things to say about the bonhomie of collaboration. But the journey of Losey, from *The Prowler* through *The Servant* to this Paris, is quite remarkable. And Delon's Klein, numb but deeply intelligent, cut off from society by some masquerade but then through the discovery of alienation itself, is extraordinary. The very skilled cast also includes Suzanne Flon, Francine Bergé, Jean Bouise, Louis Seigner, Michel Aumont, Massimo Girotti, Francine Racette, Roland Bertin, and many others. It is a film of frozen, listless faces, the perfect currency of occupation. And it's worth stressing that Alain Delon was himself one of the venture's producers.

Mr. Skeffington (1944)

By a nice touch of error, Bette Davis refers to this film in her memoir, *The Lonely Life* (1962), as *Mrs. Skeffington.* Of course, mistakes creep into the best of books. Still, it is charming to think of her costar, Claude Rains, attempting to persuade her that the film is actually called *Mr. Skeffington* (his part) only to be crushed by her withering eloquence. If Bette is in the film, how on earth should it not be treated as *Mrs. Skeffington*? Of course, this invented byplay could so easily be a scene from the film itself.

It's a saga about marriage, charm, and beauty—yet it's also one of the few American films that takes on the subject of Jewishness. It was a project close to the heart of the Epstein brothers, Philip and Julius. Not only did they write it, they produced it, too. As such, they undoubtedly let their feelings run riot. The final film ran 146 minutes, and Jack Warner was personally angry with it for being overwritten, with sequences so tied to previous sequences that it was hard to dislodge them. In truth, the story does not stand up to the length it was given. But assuredly the Epsteins could have said they were keeping faith with the outline of the novel it was based on.

Fanny is New York society, very beautiful and very brilliant, even if she thinks so herself. But when it comes to marriage, she has a problem. Her younger brother has behaved badly in the market. His debts need to be repaid and the only one of Fanny's suitors who will do that is Job Skeffington (Claude Rains), Jewish, and more brilliant even than Fanny. He mouths a lot of cynical wisdom about Wall Street, and there were those at Warners who objected to the project because it might be seen as an endorsement of all those fascist views on the Jews and their callous manipulation of the economy.

They marry, and Fanny resents her "dull" husband. A divorce is procured and still Fanny frets that their daughter is so plain. Job Skeffington is interned in a concentration camp. Which means that he comes back blind. Why? Well, Fanny has been seriously ill in the meantime and lost her looks (Davis plays these scenes with a sort of savage anticipation and dread)—but Job cannot see her to know the difference. He is the ideal husband, for he has always adored Fanny despite her paid-up status as bitch, snob, and hypocrite.

Vincent Sherman directed the film and did a fine job. Forty minutes shorter and it might have been a sensation. Some other actresses marveled that Bette went so far in depicting Fanny's ravaged looks, but Davis was as brave as she was vain. Meanwhile Claude Rains quietly delivers one of the most endearing and sophisticated performances in the history of the women's picture. If only courage had prevailed—think of the dry, comic Shylock he could have made.

Mr. Smith Goes to Washington (1939)

The junior senator of an unnamed Western state dies at an awkward moment. (In Lewis Foster's prompting story it was "The Gentleman from Montana.") For the Senate is about to hear a bill on a dam project in that state, a matter of considerable organized graft that involves the state's machine boss, Jim Taylor (Edward Arnold), and its senior senator, Joseph Paine (Claude Rains). In the hurried nomination of a new senator, the choice falls on Jefferson Smith (James Stewart), an organizer of boy rangers, the recent hero in a forest fire, and a handsome fellow who has been over every inch of his state, including the part where the grass bows under the wind, et cetera. He goes to Washington.

There follows a lull-like passage in the movie in which Jimmy Stewart does Washington and proves what a sweet clumsy innocent he is. There are adorable moments when the tough secretary Saunders (Jean Arthur), listening to him, begins to be altered by him. Then battle is drawn as Smith's plan for a boys' camp—wouldn't you know it?—requires just the same bit of land the machine has bought up for the dam.

I'm not complaining. Part of the pleasure—and there is much—of watching *Mr. Smith* is to admire the delicate craft of Sidney Buchman's script in which everything fits together. But there are warning signs: When Jeff says farewell to his loyal boys, there are tears in his eyes, and Jefferson Smith will cry a lot, just as he breaks down to a croak in the twenty-three-hour filibuster which is the set piece of the movie, and might be tense if Capra did not editorialize so much with approving smiles from Harry Carey as the president of the Senate (Carey and Claude Rains got Supporting Actor nods).

Jeff's grievance is that Washington has become a place of compromise. Well, let's think about it: Dams may have vested interests behind them, but dams, like Hoover Dam, changed the West and made life better for millions. And, yes, as someone says, there are a lot of other creeks where boys' camps could be sited. Washington is about the deals, the compromises, and the bargaining over such things—and it is American because practical democracy believes in compromise staying fair to the ideals. It does not hold by the shrill, teary idealism that makes Smith not just naïve, but a step toward fascism.

So the "boldness" of this film in 1939 is specious and a measure of how far sentimentality prevailed in Hollywood—of beautiful numbskulls like Jeff taking the high ground over Taylor (who acts like LBJ) and Paine (who looks like Harry Truman and sounds like the blessed Claude Rains). Has Jeff adored Lincoln all his life and not bothered to read about the practical politician who carried reform in his small change as well as his checkbook? So this is Capra-corn, brilliantly made, yet special pleading of a reactionary and dangerous kind. (Capra's radicalism is Goldwaterism written in invisible ink—and that is pretty much how Capra turned out politically.) I prefer to be governed by people like Paine (until the narrative catastrophe of the film's ending, which Buchman loathed and resisted—that kind of suicide attempt is so close to the spirit of assassination). Sentimentality leads to fascism quicker than compromise.

There is a superb Senate set (by Lionel Banks). The photography is by Joseph Walker and often quite noir—there's actually very little comedy in the picture, and Taylor's stripping down of Paine—"the silver knight," he sneers—is very frightening. Also with Thomas Mitchell, Eugene Pallette, Guy Kibbee, Jack Carson, and Beulah Bondi. It cost nearly $2 million, but earned twice that.

Mulholland Dr. (2001)

There's no sense in looking for a thorough explanation to *Mulholland Dr.*, and only madness would require a reading of it in which every last detail has been made to fit together. That has never been David Lynch's method, and this, plainly, is his scary valedictory to a kind of Hollywood and a movie atmosphere in which he feels he grew up. Moreover, to the extent that Lynch has a purpose in what he does, it is surely that we surrender as fully as possible to the helpless fluidity of the arbitrary and the ill-fitting. That's why the "Dr." in the title is a reference to dream rather more than to the moment-by-moment mapped-out coherence of either Mulholland Drive (a real place in L.A.) or the process of driving (arguably a unique state of introspection and public performance in that city).

But we are idiots in the dark, and even Lynch is quite fond of that status, so it is not unreasonable to ask for a thread. In which case, accept that this is a prophecy and a retelling of the legend in which the pretty blonde—this one from Deep River, in Canada—comes to L.A. to become an actress, a star, or a phenomenon. Yes, the film is full of other versions of this "Betty," including Ann Miller's landlady at the apartment complex where Betty finds a resting place and a casting couch. All the women are versions of this hopeless hope (and that is to describe the special look of Naomi Watts, who is so vulnerable as Betty). And all the men are variant figures on the set of dumb guardians that "movie" presents to the young woman trying to get in.

Of course, the DNA in this Los Angeles has been taken over by script situations: From the outset, as Rita is nearly shot up on Mulholland, she begs the coming outrage, "Don't do it. We don't do it this way." Life's accidental energy is always fighting scenario's tradition. And when Betty and Rita run the lines Betty has for a reading, they make huge fun of the stupid stuff. But then Betty takes the same nonsense and turns it into a terrific, unnerving sex scene, where every witness seems gripped by the melodrama.

Mulholland Dr. is very sexy—Lynch makes not the least effort to resist a steaming lesbian love scene—and every banal moment feels hinged to inexplicable violence or dread. Yes, the thrust of the picture is childlike and forbidding: this Hollywood is a very bad place—don't let your Bettys go anywhere near it, and trust in the monster around the corner. But Lynch has always nursed a provincial child who longs for a safe world. It is just that his numb organism is also invaded by an art-school sophisticate who has learned to be very cool with depravity and the disgusting. So *Mulholland Dr.* is the Hollywood we all treasure—the home of family entertainment with the extra kicker of the odious stag films made in the same place on the weekends.

Muriel (1963)

François Truffaut wrote that he had seen *Muriel* three times so far without liking it completely, and without liking the same things. And no matter that it was Alain Resnais's first film in color, it came after *Hiroshima, Mon Amour* and *Last Year at Marienbad* as a comprehensively "difficult" film, the one over which many people gave up on following Resnais's career. He became strikingly clearer in the next few films. He remains a great director. But—fittingly enough, in a film about bits of the past that slide away or are destroyed—*Muriel* became very difficult to see for years. It is therefore the mystery film in Resnais's own history, the one many people are curious about.

The central character is Hélène Aughain (Delphine Seyrig), a widow of about forty who lives in Boulogne—the city is very important, as is the experience of Hélène and other characters of having seen an old port city terribly bombed in the war and then largely rebuilt. So there are at least two cities there, the one of, say, 1939, and the one of 1963.

Hélène is an antiques dealer, though she is a gambler, too, at the casino. Her life has taught her you cannot rely on the past. A man, de Smoke (Claude Sainval), who owns a demolition firm, is her lover, and though he pulls things down we feel he wants to build her up. Then Alphonse (Jean-Pierre Kérien) appears, a failed restaurateur, and Hélène's first lover. He has a niece, Françoise (Nita Klein). In turn, Hélène has a stepson, Bernard (Jean-Baptiste Thierrée), who is haunted by the memory of an Algerian girl—Muriel—whom he helped torture during the troubles.

As can be seen, these characters are concerned with both physical salvaging and the emotional reconstruction of memory. The script is by Jean Cayrol (poet and novelist), and it insists on treating all the figures alike and from the outside. "Every person is a world," says Cayrol in the script to the film. You must then take into account the extreme editing style of the film: of very rapid cutaways to evoke the memories of a place, generally without the time or trouble taken to identify the places. The result was always a dense and difficult film to follow, and perhaps one in which Resnais made too great a demand on the audience. It is worth stressing that his subsequent relaxation, in narrative and in form, could be read as an admission of undue difficulty.

But Resnais is a great director, and I recall *Muriel* as a very demanding but emotional film, shot by Sacha Vierny and with a fine score by Hans Werner Henze. And in Seyrig's beautiful participation as Hélène we are eager to enter deeper into the film. I think it wants to explore recent memories, and it uses Algeria and Boulogne in the way that Hiroshima and Nevers are used in his first feature film. In hindsight, what is so striking about my memory of the picture is its ambition. Nearly everyone who "knows" *Muriel* will tell you how many times they saw the picture—and how many more times are still needed.

The Music Box (1932)

A simple player piano, tidily enclosed in a purpose-built box, has to be delivered to 1127 Walnut Avenue in Los Angeles. It is the sort of thing that happens every day, the small commercial exchange on which a great metropolis depends. In this case, the piano is a birthday present from a wife to a husband, a surprise, such as makes companionship endure. But in a land of free enterprise, where hope and ambition recklessly outstrip ability, you never know what you are going to get. It could be Mr. Laurel and Mr. Hardy, having gone into business as carriers on their collective funds of $3.80.

Like every great comic team, Laurel and Hardy are themselves a married couple subject to constant misunderstanding and the threat of violent termination. They are not really safe together, yet they are inseparable, and somehow this bond endures because of an ancient superstition that they are friends and eternal allies in the face of an unkind world. Yet every day, and every minute, they are made aware of not thinking or existing in the same way. Marriage, therefore, is the defiance of natural antagonism, and because—like all comic married people—they never address this problem, they are going mad. What I am describing can be presented in a different light—by Strindberg, say—and so I stress that the comic point-of-view is itself the last defense against terrible violence. But violence has to go somewhere, and in their case it must devastate the external world and its pianos.

One of the funniest jokes in *The Music Box* is the boys' eventual discovery from the helpful mailman that they did not have to get the piano up the steep staircase that leads to 1127 Walnut Avenue. There is a road that goes around the hillside to the top level in a manageable way. This is L.A. Suitably enlightened, Oliver and Stanley take the piano down the stairs, put it back in their cart, and make the journey by road. The wisdom contained in this joke, and its sadness, are of such an excruciating nature that it is kind of the short film not to draw attention to them.

Most of the other humor is up front, physical, and beautifully timed, and most of the appeal of the film lies in the gradual way in which a simple mission becomes apocalyptic. From small acorns, great oak trees grow (that is the business motto of these moving men), and in *The Music Box* we learn to yield to the gravitational force and appeal of destruction. We are enormous neurotics in life: We can't stand a scratch on our car, a leak in our house, or a typo in our wills. And we strenuously attempt to preserve order, tidiness, and newness. And then film came along with this insatiable urge to destroy and damage and leave ruin in its wake—even when it's your birthday. There's no need to be too solemn about the consequences of such silly fun as this, except to say that destruction is the natural end of man's plans. Comedy is hard; it is evidently painful sometimes; but most of all it is the finish for improvability and religion alike. And a good thing, too, for those dire frauds are fit to be removed. It is the great tidal force in film.

Mutiny on the Bounty (1935)

In 1935, there was only one way to play *Mutiny on the Bounty.* Captain Bligh was a vicious sadist, gross and awkward; Fletcher Christian—though he had to lose Clark Gable's mustache (naval regulations)—was tanned, urbane, a knockout and a natural leader of any insurrection against tyranny and overacting. This was an Irving Thalberg project, a very big film for Metro, with a carefully reconstructed *Bounty* even if it was put to no more test than the waters off Catalina. In the end, the picture cost close to $2 million and helped secure the wisdom that sea pictures were trouble.

It was based on a novel written by Charles Nordhoff and James Norman Hall, published in 1932, narrated in old age by a midshipman from the *Bounty.* It seems that director Frank Lloyd bought the rights for himself—he meant to direct it and to play Bligh. But somehow or other Thalberg talked him into this deal: Charles Laughton would be Bligh; Lloyd would direct and coproduce.

As was typical of costume and adventure pictures at Metro in those days, rather more effort went into the clothes and the rigging than into the story. So there's not much hint of Fletcher Christian and the crew as other than good-natured fellows bound to mutiny against the cruelty and mania of Bligh. The actors worked accordingly. Laughton turned himself into a monster of self-disgust—this Bligh hates the world, but we never doubt that the disease began in warped self-regard.

Gable declined to use an English accent or to be more than Gable. At first, he seems to have found Laughton a chilly fusspot, and there were times during the shoot when Laughton declared himself physically afraid of the robust Gable. This was Laughton's way of taking on a part and Gable's of remaining himself. In the end, they became friendly and Gable trusted that the script was on his side, so Laughton could act his head off.

It was scripted by Carey Wilson, Talbot Jennings, and Jules Furthman, and John Farrow helped. The confrontation of good and evil is not subtle or ambiguous. The only real dramatic interest lies in the depths and curlicues of Laughton's depression, and the way he rallies when cast adrift. It was as if he knew that he had found his most hateful role and the one that every impersonator would hammer at.

Studio boss Nick Schenck hated the film, but he was alone. It won Best Picture but not Best Director for Lloyd (that went to John Ford for *The Informer*). Laughton, Gable, and Franchot Tone all lost Best Actor to Victor McLaglen, and Laughton also lost Thalberg (his favorite producer). Nowadays, the generosity to *The Informer* looks very odd. *Mutiny on the Bounty* was a great hit, a film that passed into folklore: For decades, boys crouched, and lisped, "Mr. Christian!" as if they had had a whiff of evil.

Later films ruined the simple setup—notably Brando as a Fletcher Christian from Harrods. But Brando got into Tahiti and its women with a zest that is treated very tactfully in the 1935 film, despite the presence of "Movita" as an authentic babe of the islands.

Mutiny on the Bounty (1962)

Blame it on the 1959 *Ben-Hur.* What was Metro-Goldwyn-Mayer to do when that remake of an archaic monument turned into a hit and a Best Picture? They announced that epic remakes were now a policy, and they nearly destroyed themselves. The second *Mutiny on the Bounty* is still the best demonstration of the last days of Hollywood and the awful end of everybody. It is also a better film than legend would have it, so you can survey the death wish and signs of life at the same time.

From Canadian shipyards, M-G-M commissioned the building of a new *Bounty,* a third again as big as the original. They wanted it to look good, and in the end they sailed it along the west coast of the U.S.A. in a forlorn attempt to promote their picture. Not that everything looked ruinous at first. Marlon Brando had agreed to play Fletcher Christian and declared himself full of enthusiasm that the film's story would go on after the mutiny, for the chance at an English accent and for his deal—he got $500,000 plus 10 percent of the gross, $10,000 a week in expenses, plus $5,000 a day for every day over schedule. Plus script approval.

Carol Reed would direct. Trevor Howard would play Bligh. And Eric Ambler's screenplay would bypass the 1935 picture and go back to historical research, including Christian being more of a gentleman than Bligh, and what happened on Pitcairn Island when the mutineers found their Shangri-la.

The trouble began as Brando would call Ambler and Reed up to his house on Mulholland and lecture them about the script and its defects. Ambler quoted history and fact, Reed gently urged the needs of drama. Brando indicated that it was his picture, and even producer Aaron Rosenberg had to allow that this was so. At $3,000 a week, Ambler decided he was too old—and a troop of other writers started. This was an exact prediction of what would happen with Reed once shooting began.

Reed had an English cast lined up: Richard Harris, Percy Herbert, Hugh Griffith, Richard Haydn, Tim Seely, Gordon Jackson. They took sides (with Reed and Howard) and so the fictional hero of the ship, Brando, was loathed by everyone. And Brando started to take over the direction. Reed departed, Lewis Milestone (age sixty-seven) came in, and did his best. But as Brando took over a scene, Milestone wandered away. Where are you going? the producer asked. I'll see it when it opens, said Milestone.

The three-hour movie cost $27 million and earned $10 million (so Brando took another $1 million off that wretched gross). But somehow, Ambler, Reed, and Milestone left a portrait of the spoiled, sulky Christian as the mutineer who casts himself adrift by his actions. It's palpable that Howard despised Brando and in their last scene the dialogue is one actor telling another that he's an unprofessional lout. Inadvertently, Brando becomes a kind of Hamlet on the *Bounty.* Put that next to the vivid Tahitian color and a good score by Bronislau Kaper, and you can see a real movie struggling to survive. But by 1962, the system had smothered its product.

My Darling Clementine (1946)

It's a classic American story—ripe for comedy or farce as much as hero worship—how Wyatt Earp, gambler, businessman, all-purpose operator on the frontier, should come to have the Lincolnian resonance and easygoing gravity of Henry Fonda. Just after the war, turning to the Earp story, John Ford's head was filled with the legend of the O.K. Corral and Stuart N. Lake's alleged biography, *Wyatt Earp: Frontier Marshal,* published in 1929. The real history was ignored, including the way that in Earp's crowded, turbulent life he was a frontier marshal for just a few years, but always someone trying to survive and make a buck.

Winston Miller's script is a classic of hagiography, in which the Earps are gentlemen cowboys and not just rough opportunists. Tombstone appears to have shifted its geographical base to Monument Valley. And the Clanton family are low-down varmints, headed by that snake in the grass Walter Brennan and a vicious kid, John Ireland. The only departure from cliché is that Doc Holliday should be not an actor on a merciless diet but the burnished Victor Mature, as robust as any star (he would be snapping lions' jawbones in a couple of years) and aglow with the health of self-love. Ford gives him a large white handkerchief into which he may cough—or is he smothering laughter?

We know who wins it all, because every aspect of the film is fixed on who ought to win. The reality of a place like Tombstone, of its need to be controlled for business and law, is sadly neglected. It is somehow assumed that the Earps (Tim Holt and Ward Bond play Wyatt's brothers) were just a family born into the line of duty and service. They dress like cowboys, and they do entertain modest relations with ladies (as opposed to Doc's thing with Chihuahua—Linda Darnell), but they are clerics of law and order. We note how easily Ward Bond could slip over from Texas ranger to preacher.

The one extra is that passage in the film where Wyatt goes to a barber, lolls elegantly in a chair, and then walks himself up to Sunday meeting where we find real building going on in Tombstone. It's a moment of near authenticity amid all the Western conventions, and it cries out for something blunter than the decorous dance of Henry Fonda and Cathy Downs (who plays a girl called Clementine!). Much as one admires the sequence, and Fonda's awkwardness at the dance, the historian sighs for the real Wyatt Earp who was adding to upset in Tombstone by going with a Jewish actress supposedly the mistress of Sheriff Behan.

The photography by Joseph MacDonald is stark. Cyril Mockridge does the conventional music. Lyle Wheeler and James Basevi did the art direction, including the new church. Still, this Tombstone is a myth and a shrine, and never a place where now means now, with its share of fun and danger.

Years later, with *The Man Who Shot Liberty Valance,* Ford raised the question of truth or legend. But from films like *My Darling Clementine* there can be no doubt about which he preferred.

My Fair Lady (1964)

The musical adaptation of George Bernard Shaw's *Pygmalion* opened in New York in March 1956 and played 2,717 performances; it then moved to London and ran for another 2,281. Of course, there would be a movie, and the rights were sold by CBS and William Paley to Warner Brothers for $5 million. (But CBS was to get 50 percent of the gross over $20 million.) Seemingly, the transfer would be simple and tidy—the book by Alan Jay Lerner, the music by Frederick Loewe.

But on a project of such potential and investment, Jack Warner determined that he would produce the picture personally. His first move was to say that Julie Andrews (the toast of New York and London) was not a movie star. True, she hadn't made a picture yet. Lerner was horrified at the thought of dropping her. But it was serious: Warner would pay Audrey Hepburn $1 million to do the part, and be dubbed in the singing (by Marni Nixon). Warner then wondered about Cary Grant as Higgins with James Cagney as Doolittle. It was Grant who crushed that idea, and so the movie settled for Rex Harrison and Stanley Holloway repeating their stage roles.

George Cukor was hired to direct, and he was a sensible choice. So was Cecil Beaton to do the sets and costumes. No one could really anticipate that a war would develop between the two men and make the production more extended and troubled than was necessary. Beaton regarded Cukor as a Nazi! Cukor would say later that Beaton's sets were so difficult to build that Gene Allen did a lot of the work. Harry Stradling photographed the film. Hermes Pan did the dances. André Previn orchestrated the score. The supporting cast included Wilfrid Hyde-White, Jeremy Brett, Gladys Cooper, Theodore Bikel, and Mona Washbourne.

And really, it's all right, even if Rex Harrison takes over the show. It works. But it had cost $17 million in the end, and its rentals stopped at $30 million. Remember the CBS cut on the gross. It was profitable, but not by much. At the same time, Disney made *Mary Poppins* just to prove that Julie Andrews could carry a film. What happened? Well, the *My Fair Lady* score was overly familiar. The Shaw estate was against any changes in the play. Audrey was unhappy—and I think it shows. And Cukor's fight with Beaton did damage. But it won Best Picture. At last Cukor got his Oscar. Harrison won, and there were other Oscars for Stradling, Beaton, and Previn. But at 170 minutes, it seemed old-fashioned. When a show plays as widely as this one had, and when the long-playing record has sold in commensurate numbers, too many people in the audience were checking the film against a text in their heads. There was too little surprise or discovery.

My Man Godfrey (1936)

One may argue with the conclusion of *My Man Godfrey* (more anon), but is there a more beautiful beginning? I mean the credit sequence of the film, the lights of the titles with a Doré-like view of the Brooklyn Bridge and spilling down beside it the city dump (no. 32, actually), which looks like nothing so much as a landslide of diamonds. In 1936, the boldness of a dump worth millions was for the public to explain. But it is, simply, a stunning movie opening, and the prelude to that very noir sequence—though far too serious for noiristas to take seriously—in which the Bullock sisters come looking for a forgotten man. They are Carole Lombard (Irene) and Gail Patrick (Cornelia), and we need to catch all the subtexts between them, for these are sisters at war—the one wants the other to go mad. And he is Godfrey, gentleman resident of the dump, a habitué who says "bonsoir" to his fellows.

The film came from a novel by Eric Hatch, and it was scripted by Hatch and Morrie Ryskind. The director was Gregory La Cava. And we are dealing with one of the most amazing screwball comedies ever made, in which the poor behave decently and quietly and the rich are demented monkeys. As Eugene Pallette says, early on, there's nothing so special about an asylum—all you need is an empty room and the right kind of people. And the effervescence of the first half of the film is exactly that of a mob coming into a great salon, or champagne going into a fresh glass. The frenzy of characters as so many report from the scavenger hunt is beautifully handled—it is a dance, yet it is so close to real madness. And Godfrey will be engaged as butler to the Bullocks even if one sister (Patrick) means to torture and humiliate him, while the other needs him for her rescue.

Ted Tetzlaff photographed it with just the diamonds-on-black-velvet look he brought to *Swing High, Swing Low*. The women's dresses are exquisite, sheer and very sexy, and William Powell's butler is one of the handful of most elegant men ever to appear in American films. But for half the picture this is scorching social satire—you feel if it could go all the way, the house of cards might collapse. Did La Cava intend that? Or was there always the intention to play safe? Whatever, another narrative takes over. Godfrey and Irene (Lombard) are in love, and Godfrey, of course, is not quite what he seems. So, finally it is possible to forget the cannibalistic jokes and to see this crazed society reordering itself. If only La Cava could have found the necessary cruelty while keeping the wit—if only this Manhattan could be swept aside by a tempest.

Never mind, we are at a point here where within the legitimate confines of screwball comedy we have seen the end of the known world and the threadbare condition of its aristocracy. A film to treasure as it gambles away our capital—with Alice Brady, Mischa Auer, Alan Mowbray, Franklin Pangborn, and Jean Dixon.

Mystic River (2003)

Clint Eastwood easily seems like one of film's few aristocrats now (the Count of Malpaso Creek), so it's useful to remember his blue-collar Californian upbringing. And something vital of that pragmatic, survivor's toughness adheres, so *Mystic River* is, first of all, a study in Boston Irish toughies as good as has ever been done, leaving you in little doubt that the city that pioneered Independence can also be nasty, mean-spirited, and racist. But if you think back to the directorial career of Eastwood, if you go back to *Play Misty for Me,* you can see that that was a trick too dolled up with modish advertising airs and a misogynist panic to be a hip picture, whereas *Mystic River* is nothing less than a candid look at unhappy lives. There's no need—in my book—to read Eastwood as an artist, but very few filmmakers have shown such steady improvement.

So *Mystic River* is a tribal picture, really, about blunt, fearless savages who stick together even if three boyhood friends have turned out so differently. One day in 1975, one of them, Dave, was kidnapped and sexually abused—he turned out to be Tim Robbins in an ashamed performance of unhealed trauma. Another, Sean (Kevin Bacon), is a cop. And the third, Jimmy Markum, is a small-time kingpin, a local power and hoodlum, as well as maybe the best and most revealing part ever given to that uneasy mixture of sparrowhawk and fighting cock in Sean Penn.

It's a convoluted plot, a knitting together of past and present, that kicks off with the murder of one of Markum's children. It comes from a Dennis Lehane novel, with a good script by Brian Helgeland that requires labor and patience from the audience. Yes, it turns out very badly in a case and a context where the police have only so much power. But we are too ragged and brutalized by now to surrender the great white lie that the cops are going to clear everything up. In this world, nothing is designed to be tidy or comfortable. This is a part of the world and a reach of life where the nominal authorities know when to leave things alone.

It helps a lot that we meet the wives of these men: so Marcia Gay Harden is Dave's wife, crushed, conflicted in her loyalties, a liability to her own man; Laura Linney is Jimmy's wife—and this is one of those films where you have to admit that, as good as Linney can be when her characters are nice, she's a lot better when they're dangerous. As for Sean, his wife has left him (we hardly know why) but she has a habit of phoning him and staying silent on the other end of the line. So some get killed, and some lead shattered lives. Eastwood hardly seems like this sort of man now, but over the years his would-be gent has let fatigue show and allowed acid to eat away at fatuous self-polish. Larry Fishburne is excellent as the second cop, and the acting seems raised on unforgiving New England weather and Eastwood's sense of the underprivileged as people who must learn to look after themselves.

The Naked City (1948)

The movies have had an enormous and often unexamined impact on our everyday ideas and pursuits. But we should recognize at the outset that this is chiefly because they are a medium that releases pent-up or taboo longings. Nowhere has it been more persuasive or insidious than in affecting our attitudes to crime and love. Put the two together, and you can find yourself adoring the utterly unreciprocating and undeserving Michael Corleone, just as if you were part of his family. And *The Godfather* is only the most sophisticated version of the myth that wonders if gangsters aren't appealing, attractive, and imitable. But on the other hand, the movies have often fought to present crime as a kind of social overspill, as much the result of underprivilege, poverty, overcrowding, and hard luck as it is of inspired malignance. In that code, the cops are our soldiers and society's teachers, and all for a lousy salary.

Especially in the years after the Second World War, there was a surge of films that sought to show the realism of crime, and to do so in documentary terms. *The Naked City* is a characteristic film of that period. It was dreamed up by the producer Mark Hellinger in the thought that the urban police force was like the army—a regiment of decent men doing a hard job methodically in a way that deserved attention. As a result, the action and the camera went out on the streets—especially with such films made at Twentieth Century Fox. The look was realistic, yet the attitude to the police was idealistic. It would be twenty years before real study of police procedures resulted in the realization that some cops might be crooked.

The script was written by Albert Maltz and Malvin Wald, and Jules Dassin was hired as director. Cameraman William Daniels won an Oscar for the new gritty look, and editor Paul Weatherwax won another Oscar. There was a further compromise with "realism" in that Barry Fitzgerald was cast as Muldoon, the lead cop—you could argue that nobody behaved like Fitzgerald in real life, and he surely provided a lovable, eccentric hero. But the film was well cast all the way down the credits list: Howard Duff, Don Taylor, Dorothy Hart, Ted de Corsia, House Jameson, David Opatoshu, Arthur O'Connell, Paul Ford, and James Gregory.

The idea that there are eight million stories in *The Naked City* had a big influence. In 1958, ABC revived the title and Lieutenant Dan Muldoon (played by John McIntire) in a TV series that ran until 1963. Later, Horace McMahon took over as the top cop. It never went to eight million stories, but the collective genre of precinct stories includes such heights as *Hill Street Blues*. Let's just say we've heard most of the stories by now, and still don't have a coherent theory as to whether police or education is the best remedy for crime.

Napoleon (1927)

According to one of his great disciples, this is how Abel Gance addressed the crew of *Napoleon* in June 1924, the night before they began work:

> This is a film which must—and let no one underestimate the profundity of what I'm saying—a film which must allow us to enter the Temple of Art through the giant gates of History. An inexpressible anguish grips me at the thought that my will and my vital gift are as nothing if you do not bring me your unremitting devotion . . .
>
> The world's screens await you, my friends. From all of you, whatever your role or rank, leading actors, supporting actors, cameramen, scenery artists, electricians, props everyone, and especially, the unsung extras who have to rediscover the spirit of your ancestors to find in your hearts the unity and fearlessness which was France between 1792 and 1815, I ask, no, I demand, that you abandon petty, personal considerations and give me your total devotion. Only in this way will you serve and revere the already illustrious cause of the first art-form of the future, through the most formidable lesson in history.

Nearly three years later, *Napoleon*—the thing itself—opened in a definitive version that includes a triple-screen finale (i.e., a passage in which something like a CinemaScope screen is occupied by three side-by-side images which, as a rule, give different views of the same event). The movie is by turns rapturous and tedious. In the truest sense, it is based on an urge to be Napoleon—not to explain or understand the human phenomenon, but to glory in it.

At his best, Gance could animate a sequence like the childhood snowball fight. At his worst, he could lapse into a kind of unsleeping bombast and period detail. As for the Art and History business, make no mistake about it: If you wish to know all that you can about Bonaparte, then you must read books. You must do the work of research as it is available. But if you have neither the time nor the will for that, then you get Gance's *Napoleon* (which is oddly close to Gance's Gance. And with about the same amount of doubt or reflection).

The epic film is essential—yet it is minor, too. In 1981, thanks to Kevin Brownlow and David Gill, the film was restored and revived at 235 minutes in a labor of love and scholarship. This version was given a music track (in America) by Carmine Coppola and (in Britain) by Carl Davis—the Davis score is infinitely preferable, though I will repeat the plea made by Gilbert Adair (and derived from the screening policies of Henri Langlois) that silent pictures should play silent.

There have been histories of film that respond to all the fuss with clarion cries on the great and undying progressive impact of film. Alas, I see it differently. *Napoleon* is a film that makes painfully clear the medium's susceptibility to blowhards and their speeches. With Albert Dieudonné as Napoleon, Gance himself as Saint-Just, designer W. Percy Day as Admiral Hood, and Antonin Artaud as Marat.

Nashville (1976)

Why Nashville as the setting for this bicentennial panorama of America? Because Nashville would be a pretext for songs—and don't miss how far this movie is a musical, or one in which the narrative is set spinning in adjacent circles by the songs. But also because the songs encouraged ABC to think of an album to promote with the picture—and that's one reason why Robert Altman would get his actors to write the songs: so that he had few problems with controlling the rights. You may hear America, but Altman saw a means to a deal on a difficult picture.

Because his other vague intent was another set of circles—circles of activity (call them lives) all spinning in the same direction, many touching the outer edges of other circles. And offering comfort or friction in the touching as well as an overall pattern of the flux and order (the chaos and the rhyming) of so many lives all on their own yet in something like concert. It was a way of looking at society such as no American film had really tried before. So Nashville itself was almost irrelevant, and no one should regard this as an especially sympathetic approach to the country music capital of America. It's an open question, I think, whether Altman actually likes country music—and yet by the time of *Kansas City* there was no doubt about his attitude to jazz. (Of course, he had been born in KC.)

Joan Tewkesbury was charged with writing the first script, and she did crucial work in inventing characters and the kind of freewheeling, associative style of the film that let them meet. Altman said build the number of characters to twenty-four, with a killing at the end. The first script was 176 pages. Then Alan Rudolph tried to make a shooting script of it, and then Tewkesbury did another revision.

Of course, the music scene is a metaphor for show business (and filmmaking), and the self-conscious patriotism of the Nashville scene fixes on the hollow campaign for Thomas Hal Phillips (with Michael Murphy—as his agent—and Murphy would be Altman's Tanner, one day). The idea of Nashville as a place becomes a kind of great dome/mall where political messages are being delivered all day long to a population that is a cross section of a West full of dysfunctional families, escaping people, and returning madmen. As a view of America after two hundred years it is baleful. "We must be doing something right" is offered as a very weary hope.

The music made the film possible, but it becomes a labored crutch. The film could have meant more, I think, if the music had seemed from the heart and of the moment. *Nashville* is brilliant and audacious, but it just misses that Whitmanesque grandeur that it glimpses because so many of the people are trite. Still, it is perhaps the best ensemble cast in American film (until *Short Cuts* or *Magnolia*): Jeff Goldblum, Barbara Harris, Bert Remsen, David Hayward, Scott Glenn, Ned Beatty, Lily Tomlin, Dave Peel, Barbara Baxley, Henry Gibson, Ronee Blakley, Allen Garfield, Timothy Brown, Karen Black, Keith Carradine, Cristina Raines, Allan Nicholls, David Arkin, Shelley Duvall, Gwen Welles, Robert DoQui, Geraldine Chaplin, Keenan Wynn, and Richard Baskin.

The Navigator (1924)

The serene impartiality on the face of Rollo Treadway (Buster Keaton) is the clear glass to a rare sight in American film (or maybe film as a whole)—I refer to the vacancy or the brainstormed fit of the wealthy. So often, the wealthy are guilt-ridden and sinister in that they search the world for accusing or reforming urges. Or the rich are haughty and hypocritical (smiling upon the poor, treacling their pain numb). Whereas Buster knows that only one trinity properly explains inordinate wealth: absurdity, ignorance, and bad luck. And so Rollo—"Every family tree must have its sap"—is the arrangement of life to manifest wealth to the point of folly.

"I think I'll get married," he declares to the mirror and the silence when he sees a jolly black couple just married—in the back of a car. A truly inspired Keaton film might then follow based on Rollo's flawless logic that to be black and happy means you have to get married. He doesn't leap quite that far (though that collapse of logic is there waiting, or latent, in many of the films). So, instead, he gives us a beautiful shot of fine houses on the crest of a hill—it could be San Francisco, Pacific Heights—with a great arc of sky filling half the screen. Rollo comes out of his house, gets in the parked car, which then takes a chauffeured curve across the wide street to the house opposite where a girl/his girl/the girl (Kathryn McGuire) lives. It is not quite that she is the only girl in the world—just the only one Rollo has ever heard of. He goes inside, asks if she will marry him. Vigorously, she shakes her head—women are energetic in Keaton films. Whereupon he leaves the house, disconsolate enough to tell the chauffeur he needs a long walk. And then he walks back across the street to home.

And we are not even at sea yet, on the *Navigator*, with those long empty corridors and decks where Rollo and the girl pursue each other. (There is a faint sense of the Overlook Hotel in *The Shining*. And one can believe that Kubrick might have loved Keaton's withheld dismay at plans gone astray.) Having use of a ship, Buster reckoned to see it as a machine made for a thousand that cannot really cope with a couple. But his mind wanders so that there is a sequence with Buster in a diving suit on the bottom of the sea, and then frightening the wits out of some "natives." By the way, the ship, the *Navigator*, is in some tangled way the object of desire for the two sides fighting that little war over there—presumably the Great War, but handled like a tantrummy child by Buster's sense of perspective.

He directed this with Donald Crisp (so the credits say), working for Joe Schenck at Metro-Goldwyn-Mayer. Three people (including Clyde Bruckman) are credited with a "screenplay," but it's plainly a film without a plan. Indeed, Buster seems to wait to catch sight of a shot, a setup, or a plan (and the ship is one big, empty plan) before entering into it with his unique affinity for disorder.

Network (1976)

Elsewhere in this book, I challenge Sidney Lumet's impressive *The Verdict* for being a good deal less than it seems, and a victim of Lumet's excessive respect for tidiness. Above all, that respect shows in his reluctance to test or stretch David Mamet's complacent script. Consider in contrast, the profuse, explosive suggestiveness of Lumet's earlier *Network* and the spectacle it represents of Lumet clinging on for dear life to the flying reins of Paddy Chayefsky's reckless script, which only dares to be bolder as it encounters every difficulty.

What's it all about, within the inexhaustible satirical energy that lashes out at black power, the charisma of anchors, career women (the best thing Faye Dunaway ever did?), the sentimental faith in the good nature of the public, et cetera? It's about television, and I think it makes a fascinating contrast with Woody Allen's *Radio Days*, which is equally about radio and content to be a nostalgic tribute and a trusting celebration of the world of Allen's childhood. *Network*, on the other hand, has no doubt about the dangers of television and the way it has played into the hands of vile businessmen and the ever-available stupidity of the public.

This could sound like the warning description on one of the more radical movies ever made in America—and, in fact, that estimate is justified—but *Network* was a big hit, it received ten Academy Award nominations and it won four Oscars, including those for Best Actor (Peter Finch) and Best Original Screenplay. Of course, that was 1976, the bicentennial year, but a moment when the spirit and habit of American self-criticism was maybe more alive and well than it has been since. So this is not just a piece of bravery that survived, it is one of the reckless triumphs in American show business, a work of such heady eloquence that Hollywood hardly noticed how far it was biting the hand that fed it.

I suppose it seemed far-fetched in 1976, but Chayefsky the social critic was rooted in prophecy. *Network* is a film that, incidentally, warns us of the craze for dramatized conflict in television talk, the fusion of current events and the game show, and the coming surge in what we still call "reality TV"—you can't say we aren't inclined to trust our idiocy until the end. And it's proper to remind ourselves that Chayefsky had observed the modern history of television: He had been one of the pioneering dramatists in the age of live drama when we all took it for granted that the medium was very well placed and appointed to deal decently with ordinary lives—like *Marty*.

Network is, among other things, the record of how a kind of hysteria took over, and in that sense the ruin of the William Holden character—the way he surrenders family and weary love for the new sex—is a tragic account of men trying to keep up with changing times in the seventies. That is a type Chayefsky knew and dreaded in himself, and its greatest example is George C. Scott's doctor in *The Hospital*, a man who sees how far a once benevolent system has gone mad with bureaucracy.

New York, New York (1977)

There are Scorsese admirers who tend to put *New York, New York* aside—as if to say it was some kind of aberration, an infatuation alike with Liza Minnelli and drugs, a very difficult, untidy experience, and a film that proved to have little public support. And an unfortunate departure from Scorsese's natural métier (the gangster romance—or rather the film that romanticizes gangsterism). Whereas, not the least interesting thing about this film is that Jimmy Doyle is gangsterlike, yet denied any of the warm, supportive atmosphere of a gang. Because Jimmy is an essential loner. Add to that the film's uncommon interest in a female character, and the exceptional use of music as a dramatic element. In short, I love *New York, New York*, and if you are hurt or pained at mockery of gangster habits, let's settle for it being one of the most remarkable extensions of the musical.

Jimmy Doyle hits New York on VJ Day 1945. He is a saxophone player who goes through an extraordinary set of routines to pick up Francine Evans, a singer. She cannot drop him, escape him, or deny him. It may be that he loves her, or just that he needs to conquer her. But they become a couple. They marry, and they will have a child. Meanwhile, she is a singer in the big-band style, lovable and sweet, and he is a white saxophonist itching to get into the bop school. You can say they are incompatible, or you can conclude that Jimmy is so selfish, so alone, and such a chronic actor (or player) that he has no self to offer to anyone else. You can also say that this dilemma is as frightening as any of the crime situations in Scorsese films.

In the end, and as much because of musical styles as anything else, the marriage breaks up. Francine becomes a popular success and a Hollywood star while Jimmy is a cool jazz tyrant. There can be no reunion. Call it career, call it art—the musical drive ensures that these two people, "lovers" if you like, must go their separate ways.

Time and again, Scorsese uses musical numbers to spell out drama and character: the way Jimmy's style frightens the bandleader who hires them both (Georgie Auld); the dictatorial way in which Jimmy tells off other players in his own band rehearsals; the slinky, sultry liaison with Diahnne Abbott that precedes her doing "Honeysuckle Rose"; and the irony of the final production number, "Happy Endings."

The script was by Earl Mac Rauch and Mardik Martin; László Kovacs did the photography. Boris Leven did the outstanding production design. Irving Lerner and Marcia Lucas were the editors. Minnelli sings beautifully in a great range of styles and gives a lovely, stupefied performance. Indeed, the barrage of mannerism in Robert De Niro seems to have left her plain and simple for once. As for De Niro, he is so antic he is nearly deranged—but that's the point. And this is the most inwardly disturbing film from a director too easily persuaded to shock us with the stamp of violence.

Die Nibelungen (1924)

It speaks to the ambition as well as the solemn pretension of film in Germany, of Ufa and of Fritz Lang, that in 1924 he turned his hand to a two-part version of the Nibelung saga. It is as if, in America, Griffith, or someone, had elected to do . . . well, what? By virtue of being a freshly invented or discovered land, the United States had no mythic history. That Germany had this Norse and Gothic legend and felt it still, enough to pictorialize at the level of Andrew Lang's Fairy Books, tells us so much about what to expect from Germany in the next twenty years. It seems to have been Fritz Lang's idea, one that producer Erich Pommer jumped at. And naturally Lang's wife, Thea von Harbou, would write the script—hadn't she once played Kriemhild onstage? She delivered the script as a wedding present to Lang.

It's something more than just a "story," but Harbou had written for two movies: In the first, Siegfried (Paul Richter), the title character, wants to marry Kriemhild (Margarete Schön), but only after her brother, King Günther (Theodor Loos), has married Brunhild (Hanna Ralph)—and Brunhild will only marry a man who defeats her in combat. Through magic, Siegfried becomes Günther and defeats Brunhild. But before the double wedding, Hagen (Hans Adalbert Schlettow) exposes the trick and murders Siegfried. Kriemhild departs.

In the second part, *Kriemhild's Revenge*, Kriemhild marries King Etzel (Rudolf Klein-Rogge) and plans revenge. She invites Günther and Hagen to a banquet. There is an immense battle, which ends in conflagration and the death of all parties.

Photography was assigned to Carl Hoffmann, Günther Rittau, and Walter Ruttmann. Otto Hunte, Erich Kettelhut, and Karl Vollbrecht did the art direction, borrowing from paintings by Arnold Böcklin. The shooting lasted more than thirty weeks. There were training problems with a seventy-foot dragon that Siegfried fights. *Siegfried* ended up at 130 minutes, and *Kriemhild's Revenge* was 95 minutes.

Siegfried is by far the better-known film, in that it tells the Wagnerian story and uses filmmaking to assist in all kinds of magic. Its forest is a great expressionist creation, and the very studied unfolding of the legend is one of those unending monuments to silent cinema that cries out for speech and talk and humanity. The film is of historic interest, though there's far less feeling of Lang's lethal eye than in his contemporary crime films from the 1920s.

Kriemhild's Revenge is another matter. From the outset, it was the less seen of the two—in part it was too much of a good thing, and in the Nazi era it was actually withdrawn on account of its nihilism (or the remorseless execution of its plan). But it has to be seen. More or less, it is an hour of unrelieved combat, one of the outstanding action films in all cinema and a testimony to Lang's staggering violence, which so often he kept under wraps. That even the Nazis were shocked and exhausted by the film speaks to Lang's murderous energy. He could kill in ways undreamed of by other directors, and he could set a bloodlust howling with the rhythm of the slaughter.

Night and the City (1950)

Jules Dassin had made some promising thrillers in the late 1940s—*Brute Force, The Naked City,* and *Thieves' Highway.* But the ugly forces of the blacklist were conspiring against him. He had one friend, Darryl F. Zanuck, and the Fox mogul told him to get himself to London and start shooting *Night and the City* so that it would have to be finished. It was one more film to his bank balance, and his last American picture. Once in London, Dassin got a note from Zanuck: "You owe me one. Put Gene Tierney in your picture." There were worse compromises in those days.

Night and the City came from a good, tough novel by Gerald Kersh, with a setting in the wrestling business in London. The novel was well adapted for the screen by Jo Eisinger and Austin Dempster, and the central character, Harry Fabian, was made an American, trying to survive in this world. It was a perfect part for Richard Widmark in that Fabian, hounded by creditors, is cracking up and being pursued by heavies trained in the ring.

The whole movie was shot in London by "Mutz Greenbaum" (a pseudonym for blacklisted Max Greene). It has a lustrous noir look, and there is an astonishing scene where underworld news is spread from a car as it drives through the West End stopping at every news vendor. The look is very American, and one wonders how far Greene and Dassin had studied English noir films of the era—less melodramatic, more human and socially credible, more gray than black? One reason for asking is the expert supporting performance from Googie Withers (Robert Hamer's star on *It Always Rains on Sunday* and *Pink String and Sealing Wax*). Gene Tierney does her expert job as a beauty, but Withers as the girlfriend might have been better or more interesting. As it is, she and Francis L. Sullivan (Bumble from *Oliver Twist*) are perversely well-matched as club owners in the wrestling business.

It's content to be a story of fate closing in on Fabian, and the mounting hysteria in Widmark is a large part of the fun. But Dassin was clearly in love with London, and this is one of those films that helped a generation of English filmmakers realize what London looked like—or could look like. There's a fine, noir supporting cast—Herbert Lom and Mike Mazurki, for instance—and the bigger scenes (at the club or at the wrestling matches) have a terrific cynical panache. (Kay Kendall is seen briefly.)

Thereafter, Dassin was off the screen for four years. His new film proved to be *Rififi*, in many ways his most expert and profitable crime picture. What happened next is confused or like real life. Dassin stayed in Europe. He married Melina Mercouri. He made some poor films. Indeed, you can say he was never as good again as in the period 1948–54. But I daresay he was a happier man. There's a 1992 remake, with De Niro and Jessica Lange, directed by Irwin Winkler, and it's awful.

A Night at the Opera (1935)

Sooner or later, the United Nations is going to have to take it on—I had high hopes of Kofi Annan (he had the look of a brother)—as to whether Irving Grant Thalberg helped or hindered the Marx boys. It seems to me pretty obvious that that deliberating body's due respect is just morning dew until they buckle down to this one. (After all, isn't it more or less 1935—"I'll be seeing you," said Haile Selassie—that everything starts to go wrong?)

Duck Soup (1933) had been a failure, no matter that some purists regard it as the prize dish on the menu. The brothers by then were in their forties, and there were those who took the view that amid Depression et cetera there would be little sympathy for these elderly prophets playing the fool. However, Chico liked to play bridge with Thalberg and, while exchanging vulnerabilities, they had got into comic theory. The trouble is, said Thalberg, that men, and generally intelligent, educated men, like your films. Since anyone can see the future for that breed is dwindling in the republic, we have to get women to like your films, too. Three no trump, said Chico. Let's try romance, and songs, said Thalberg. And breathing spaces?

What's breathing space? asked Chico.

A hotel bedroom in Philadelphia? guessed Groucho later.

Thalberg gave them a good deal. He was prepared to hire writers—indeed, he apparently funded George S. Kaufman during his torrid affair with Mary Astor (I hope to see some UN enactment of these scenes). And he said they could have Sam Wood as a director. This may be the old Irving coming out a champ, for Wood was so humorless that he undoubtedly stimulated the boys to wilder flights of cruel fancy (there's a great title). And when they got Allan Jones and Kitty Carlisle as romantic leads, why they sent a dozen red roses from Jones to Carlisle—COD! Jones was heard to say his daughter wanted a cocker spaniel and the boys sent a Great Dane called Hamlet. The dog needed meat and—believe it or not—that is how Hamburger Hamlet got its start.

Duck Soup was 70 minutes; *A Night at the Opera* was 92. But you could relieve yourself in the breathing spaces. *Opera* has the Party of the First Part and the stateroom scene, and it's clear that when that didn't work onstage it was Thalberg who said keep it in—because the reality of the room is different on film. My friends, that is quietly brilliant, even if you can tell that someone in southern California with thoughts like that cannot be long for this world. The brothers never had a bigger hit than *A Night at the Opera,* and Margaret Dumont was there again, too, as if some bylaw had been passed to say that Groucho couldn't make a crack without that great lady present steadfastly ignoring the jokes—let alone the crack. And the brothers made more money themselves, and if you think that was a distraction from art ask yourself why Chico was playing bridge. Of course, Thalberg did die, and the brothers suffered because Mayer hated them, and Groucho often challenged Mr. Mayer. But don't kid yourself: Without this film, opera wouldn't be where it is in America.

Night Moves (1975)

From *The Miracle Worker* until *Night Moves,* Arthur Penn was not just a top director, but the one with the sharpest instincts for what was happening to America. He made films set outside the modern era, yet from *The Miracle Worker* to *Little Big Man* the metaphor was inescapable—he was dealing with now. Nowhere was that more true than with *Night Moves,* a compelling, twisty thriller and an increasingly bleak portrait of American ethical dismay at the end of Watergate and Vietnam. When *Night Moves* proved a flop, you could argue that it was because it was too uncomfortable for viewers, not that its director had lost touch. Yet *Night Moves* would prove to be the beginning of Penn's "decline." I put that word in quotes because he still seems so honorable and important, and because *The Missouri Breaks* is a delicious film. But a question remains: Did we lose Penn, or did he lose us? Is it even possible that he found it vital to start looking on the bright side?

From an original screenplay by Alan Sharp, *Night Moves* goes like this: Harry Moseby (Gene Hackman) was a football player, and now he is a private eye in Miami. Arlene Iverson (Janet Ward) hires him to find her runaway teenage daughter, Delly (Melanie Griffith—straightaway explosive). This leads Harry to the shabby world of movie stuntmen, one of whom, Quentin (James Woods), has been Delly's boyfriend. But as he makes one search, Harry blunders into realizing that his wife (Susan Clark) is having an affair. The main search leads to the Florida Keys and a trade in smuggled archaeological pieces from Mexico. But nothing turns out well. The intrigue and the mendacity mount. Harry is left helpless, a victim of intrigue and of every stupid Hollywood notion that a private eye can look after himself.

As so often with Penn movies, every task is top of the line: Bruce Surtees did the photography, the daytime color increasingly betrayed by night—this is one of the films that helped us realize there could be films noir in color; the production design is by George Jenkins; the editing by Dede Allen and Stephen Rotter; the music by Michael Small. Moreover, Penn's use of people is as tender and piercing as ever. The great cast builds an unforgettable gallery of unease and unreliability—in this, in addition to those named already, add the wolfish look of Jennifer Warren, Edward Binns, Harris Yulin, Kenneth Mars, and Anthony Costello.

Night Moves is gloomy, downcast, and grown-up. It's exactly what America deserved at the time: an unforced use of the thriller genre to show far-reaching dishonesty. Yet within a few years, the strain of such films had made the picture business cheer up. Surely we still—more than ever—need films made with *Night Moves*' reluctance to compromise about the Bush regime and its woeful empire. But the state of the nation and the state of its cinema are paths by now so far apart no one thinks of them being on the same map.

The Night of the Hunter (1955)

I recall the first time at Dartmouth College in the late 1970s when I tried showing *The Night of the Hunter* to Americans. The kids had no trouble with the film—though it scared them. But the adults (the senior faculty) found the picture silly and fanciful, and they remembered that it had done very badly when it opened—so badly, indeed, that Charles Laughton gave up all thoughts of directing again, no matter that he had a script from Norman Mailer's *The Naked and the Dead* all ready to go. So never forget that it can take nearly fifty years sometimes for a picture to go from crushing ignominy to being accepted at the Library of Congress as a work that must be preserved.

The producer Paul Gregory was working with Laughton on stage productions, and he thought to follow up on the actor's occasional feeling that he'd love to make a movie. They picked on a novel, by Davis Grubb, a remarkable work—Southern, in period, Gothic, haunted—about a mad "preacher" who goes after stolen money possessed by two young children. So he marries their widowed mother. He kills her. And he pursues the children across one of the great nightmare filmscapes ever made.

The plot thickens here. James Agee was asked to do the screenplay, and he delivered a work far too long and far too dependent on the literary power of the novel. Laughton was therefore compelled to redo the script himself. He hired the great Stanley Cortez to do the photography, and asked him to look at D. W. Griffith pictures to get that simplicity of vision that becomes fairy story. Hilyard Brown did the sets—and for the most part Laughton preferred sets to real settings, despite his attraction to Griffith. Walter Schumann did the music.

This was a rare team, but it would have been as nothing without the people. Robert Mitchum helped get the financing for the picture, but then imagine the depth of insight that could see through Mitchum's deliberate casualness and indifference over work and guess that he might be inspired, elemental, and quite monstrous as Powell. Shelley Winters (the widow) was a student of Laughton, so she was natural casting. But to go to Lillian Gish as the strict fairy godmother was intuitive in a way that almost lets us see Laughton the actor. Allow those leads, plus James Gleason, Evelyn Varden, and Billy Chapin and Sally Jane Bruce as the children. And still Laughton—famously inarticulate as an actor—had to know how to direct.

No, of course it doesn't look or feel like an American film of 1955, but at that moment it was essential that some movies begin to do things differently. *The Night of the Hunter* is not just a great film, it is among the great expressions of America's sense of childhood giving way to warped adulthood. Everything that was "wrong" about it, was right—because an artist had perceived the work as a whole and brought it home. It was the public that was wrong and no condition is more alarming.

Ninotchka (1939)

Ninotchka is a splendid example of sex in politics. The time is an unspecified moment in the late thirties. Ninotchka is a humorless commissar sent from Moscow to Paris to check up on three delinquent officials. "How are things in Moscow?" the trio ask. "Very good," she says. "The last mass trials were a great success. There are going to be fewer but better Russians." If you find that joke tasteless, you probably won't like *Ninotchka*—and you shouldn't go near *To Be or Not to Be*. After all, real people were appallingly tortured and slowly executed in the mass trials. Yet the jump to Soviet logic—fewer but better—is piercing political satire. And the film is setting Ninotchka up for her humorlessness to be "executed." She asks Melvyn Douglas, "Must you flirt?"

"I don't have to, but I find it natural." (This is the essence of Lubitsch: Let God stand up for nature.)

"Suppress it," she replies, and there the line has the politics of suppression and the sex of repression bouncing together. Don't forget that Billy Wilder did the script for Lubitsch.

What is less clear is why this large, charismatic, and powerful figure was let go by Paramount, and ended up at M-G-M. For the story is that Greta Garbo dropped by his beach house one day, uninvited. Ernst was touched, and he came out with that automatic endearment among Hollywood "friends"—"We have to work together." He had a meal ready. Garbo said, No, thank you, she wasn't hungry, but she would listen while Lubitsch told her the story. He got so carried away that he ate nothing. But Garbo was drawn in; she ate a hearty meal.

The idea had come from Melchior Lengyel—a stern commissar in America—but the script really emerged from the partnership of Wilder, Charles Brackett, and Walter Reisch. They came up with this idea: Garbo is sent West to recover three wayward and lesser officials who have been sent to stop the Grand Duchess Swana from selling her jewels. But the duchess is involved with a silky middle man, Léon.

Melvyn Douglas would be Léon, Ina Claire was the grand duchess, and the three naughty boys were Sig Rumann, Felix Bressart, and Alexander Granach—in his bureaucracies and minor roles, Lubitsch took delight in fusspot charm. William Daniels, a Garbo expert, did the photography. Adrian did the gowns, including a pre-Prada suit for lady commissars. The sets were by Cedric Gibbons, Randall Duell, and Edwin B. Willis.

The commercial key to it all was "Garbo laughs," and so she did. Of course, no one doubts that she is going to melt, but the lovely thing about the film is the way chat and smiles do the trick. She doesn't have to be convinced by some ponderous arguments over political destiny. Flirtation does it—the most egalitarian weapon. The film was a huge success in a very rich year. It was nominated for Best Picture, something Lubitsch had missed since *The Smiling Lieutenant,* and Garbo was nominated as Best Actress. But Lubitsch wasn't nominated as Best Director. He never won that award.

Nixon (1995)

Nixon has one of the great supporting casts ever put on film. How can you improve on James Woods as Haldeman, with his magnificent improv to Ehrlichman at the end of one scene, "You know who's next, don't you?"; or Paul Sorvino as Kissinger, his voice like Captain Queeg's ball bearings?; or Ed Harris, bristling and insane as Howard Hunt?; or David Hyde Pierce as John Dean?; or Mary Steenburgen as the harsh Mother Nixon?; or Bob Hoskins as J. Edgar Hoover, and Tony Lo Bianco as Johnny Roselli?; or J. T. Walsh as Ehrlichman, or Powers Boothe as Al Haig? To say nothing of the death's-head smile that holds Joan Allen's Pat Nixon in place, like nails.

It is a devastating portrait of a group and their queasy moment—and in hindsight it is so rich and intriguing that I think the only way to do the film would have been to omit Richard Milhous Nixon. Suppose he was always in the next room, at the other end of the phone line, or just off camera. He is the emptiness that inspires it all, the wall toward which all these shit-eating faces turn. But not quite there. Which would let us off the Anthony Hopkins hook.

Anthony Hopkins is a magnificent actor and a man who as he has aged has risen to greater challenges. But he doesn't get Nixon, and I think he's good enough as actor, mimic, and listener, to know it. He works like a demon. He sweats more than anybody in a film since Edmond O'Brien. He willingly becomes the face that is suffering a waking nightmare. And at every single moment, we say, Anthony Hopkins, know him anywhere. Of course, the problem is compounded by the way in which those of a certain age probably watched more of Richard Nixon on film and television than of anyone else alive. We know the Nixon voice, the moods, the smiles, the pauses, for even if Nixon famously lost the Kennedy debates because he was inferior as an on-camera performer, don't think that he was a slouch. Nixon liked being on camera a lot more than is often said. We saw him and we have taken his being into ours. Yet he remains very difficult for the impersonator.

And so Oliver Stone's three-hour *Nixon* is a fascinating picture in which nearly every scene and aside worked but for the looming mistake at the heart of it all. Of course, Stone is not a Nixonite, and he cannot help but tickle our paranoid fantasies with one or two quite far-fetched things about what Nixon may have done beyond all we think we know. And he does not show Nixon rationalizing it all (the David Frost Nixon). This is a portrait of a whipped, self-pitying loser.

The photography, by Robert Richardson, was beyond even his work on *JFK:* hallucinatory, beautiful, diseased—all those descriptions apply, and demonstrate the power of film to dig into the skin itself. It is a very fleshy, intimate film. You feel you can smell the stink of bad breath and the throb of bruised faces.

No Country for Old Men (2007)

Not for one minute does any viewer of *No Country for Old Men* feel that it's an anecdote, a crime movie, or just one report to file with all the other incidents that make up "the West" or border life. Equally, Anton Chigurh (Javier Bardem) is not simply an instrument of vengeance or retribution sent by some distant but powerful forces of order or disorder to punish the hunter Llewelyn Moss (Josh Brolin), who stumbled upon the remains of a broken drug deal and reckoned he had a chance of getting away with both the heroin and the case filled with $2 million. Nor is it that Sheriff Ed Tom Bell (Tommy Lee Jones) is going to be able to set the whole thing straight, as sheriffs were once supposed to do—his is rather the sweet, sad voice that may just be able to tell the story of slaughter and remain baffled by it.

No, this is a reiteration of the old myth that Death walks the land. That is why West Texas has that desert look, the scorched air, and the heat that leaves brave men listless. It's why Jones—himself from Texas, of course—talks in that languid, defeated way. There is no surprise in the story and it is not even that Chigurh has been hired, equipped, or paid to do his "job." What he does is his destiny, his solitary purpose—it is to bring dread and death into a place where man has demonstrated the limits of his folly, his defiance, and his ambition by trying to bring purpose. As if some minor drug deal could save this world from itself, or shift it an inch.

The film comes from Cormac McCarthy's novel, adapted with the utmost fidelity by the Coen Brothers—and then directed by them. The matter of fidelity lies not just in what happens and what is said (sometimes in soliloquy), but in the very narrow space left in the story for hope or pity or anything else besides the implacability of death's reach.

That sounds terribly bleak, but just as McCarthy lifts himself from despair by the burning clarity of his writing so the Coen Brothers have made this film as if Chigurh was after them, too. Much as I admire the film, I have to say that this tautness only exposes the slackness and the cute nihilism of so many of their films. But this is the real quiet terror alluded to in *Miller's Crossing* and *Fargo*, laughed off in too many other films.

Some may find Bardem's intense physical presence—loopy but staring; certain but so weird—a distraction. And surely Chigurh could have been played cooler and straighter. Bardem is a touch too lurid and wacky, and McCarthy's Death needs to be a clerical figure, ticking off assignments but never really getting off on them. He is not a serial killer, after all, he's encyclopedic. That's to be brooded on. Elsewhere, there are outstanding performances, from Woody Harrelson as a merely professional killer, Brolin as the ingenious outlaw, and Tommy Lee Jones, who seems to know that this and Melquiades Estrada are carrying him to the leadership among dismayed American old-timers.

No Man of Her Own (1950)

William Irish (or Cornell Woolrich) published *I Married a Dead Man* in 1948; it was a full-length novelization of a previous short story. Paramount bought the book, with Richard Maibaum producing and Mitchell Leisen set to direct. Maibaum and Leisen never got on well, no matter that this feels like ideal Maibaum material. Leisen showed the book to Barbara Stanwyck, and she told Paramount she had to play it. Sally Benson wrote a draft which Leisen rejected. Then Catherine Turney had a shot at it. According to Leisen, he did the script himself, but took no credit. According to Maibaum, it was all an unpleasant experience because Leisen didn't pay much attention to dialogue.

It doesn't seem that way in a film where the fragile plot is treated with loving care. Helen Ferguson (Stanwyck) is unmarried but pregnant. Her scummy lover, Stephen Morley (Lyle Bettger), has packed her off on a long train journey. On that train, she meets Hugh and Patrice Harkness (Richard Denning and Phyllis Thaxter). They are just married; she is pregnant. He is taking her home to meet his parents for the first time. The train crashes. Hugh and Patrice are killed, and Helen is misidentified as Patrice Harkness. And so she is taken in by the mother (Jane Cowl) and Hugh's brother, Bill (John Lund). It seems to work. Helen is made welcome. She is cared for. In time, she and Bill will fall in love. But then Stephen Morley turns up.

There's a great pleasure in recounting the narrative structures of Irish/Woolrich—the tidiness becomes fate. In Leisen's film, a happy ending is put upon the whole thing. The mother takes the blame for Stephen's eventual murder. Helen, Bill, and child can live happily ever after. And I like the film a lot, but I'm bound to say that the Irish novel is better still. Stephen Morley is killed, and the couple are left with guilt and uncertainty. The first-person narrative fears that they are going to break up one day and move on.

And that's where the quality of the film lies: the sense of a country where space beckons with ideas of escape, a second chance, a new beginning. In American culture, as opposed to European (and this is a force in many films), people are drawn outward, into that fresh space, toward new story. It takes a genius as strange as Woolrich's to identify that wanderlust with instability, madness, and desolation. So the book could be remade, with advantage, but even in Leisen's version the train is ordeal and hope for Helen, and her suspension of all other considerations when she realizes that she is being misidentified is sinister and exciting at the same time. And Stanwyck is just right as the woman who can make a new life for herself like a story. Any actress would be crazy for the part because it gets at what actresses do.

Leisen shoots it beautifully, with Daniel Fapp on camera and Henry Bumstead doing the design, Edith Head the clothes, and Hugo Friedhofer the music. It's one of those films in which we see how the example of acting has affected us all. It also has one of the best train crashes of all time.

North by Northwest (1959)

Living in San Francisco, I have had my fill of *Vertigo.* I mean, I love it to death; I admire it; I live with the deepest fears it invokes—which are not those of heights, but the ones that make imagination a prison. But the other day I woke up and realized, for the first time, that *North by Northwest* is better, because all the fears that this film touches on—a fear of trains, of blondes (above all of blondes who ask no questions), of inane national monuments and flat desolate fields—are rendered as comedy. You see, what I realized was that *North by Northwest* is only pretending to be a suspense thriller, an action-adventure picture or a road movie. It's actually a screwball comedy—and one of our greatest. And I have reached a time in life where I'd rather have a great screwball comedy than a profound tragedy. After all, tragedy is all around us and screwball is something only the movies can do.

Here's one demonstration. Don't you love the stupidity—the fond, yearning craziness—of a nation that will take an innocent, lovely mountainside and carve in it, larger than houses, the solemn faces of presidents? The mixture of authority over nature and childlike impulse! And then along comes a strange genius of another American form—movie—and he sees that this daft monstrosity can be employed for a desperate chase sequence where someone hides in Jefferson's nostril or a high heel trips on Washington's proud lip. Had I been a Soviet leader in '59—cold going on frigid—I'd have looked at *North by Northwest* and told my commissars, "Sorry, guys, the jig is up. They've taken the acme of patriotic realism and turned it inside out!" And isn't that a pretty good definition of screwball?

Anyway, this is the one where Roger O. Thornhill (ROT—we are warned) blunders into one embrace after another in his headlong run. This means catching a falling corpse at the UN, finding himself in bed with Eva Marie Saint and her flat, utterly available voice, darting into the cornfield and pausing briefly in a hospital room somewhere when the lady patient sits up and screams and corrects herself, "Don't go." The whole thing is in the cause of terribly important secrets, so vital that the film has the tact not to mention them. Just look at the stills of Cary Grant pursued by a plane and isn't it as plain as the plain—this is Keystone country, touched up by the hand of Sturges? And it is a great film.

Ernest Lehman wrote it, and for a talented writer who got himself into some awkward pictures, this must have been grace and reassurance: Just write Cary Grant straight against a rising disorder, and you have a film. Eva Marie Saint found herself. James Mason is divine. Bernard Herrmann is laughing to himself and saying, I knew I always wanted to do music for a comedy! Robert Burks makes it look like tourist country. And the immaculate cast includes Jessie Royce Landis, Leo G. Carroll, Philip Ober, Josephine Hutchinson, Martin Landau, and Malcolm Atterbury (the man at the bus stop on the prairie).

Nosferatu (1922)

When Cesare carries away the girl in *Caligari,* the hint was there already: Yes, it must be terrible to be abducted like that, but look at the way her long gown seems like roots drawn up out of the very ground, and isn't there something lustrous and sensual about it? Something cinematic? Come forward, to *Psycho* (1960), when at last—after forty minutes of having been grilled, scrutinized, and stripped down to her underwear—Janet Leigh is bathed in the shower. Isn't there something lovely in the way the knife comes in, too? We are on dangerous ground here, playing with our darker urges. And it begins with *Nosferatu,* nine years before the Bela Lugosi *Dracula* and so much more disturbing.

Bram Stoker (1847–1912) was Irish. For nearly thirty years, he was manager to the great actor Henry Irving, and so he was working in the pit of melodrama when film offered itself as the fresh, flaming sensation. He wrote *Dracula* in 1897, and it remains a very readable book in which the count is "a tall old man, clean shaven save for a long white moustache, and clad in black from head to foot." Any reader of the novel learns quickly that its vampirism is a metaphor for the sexual act. That also reminds us that the movies arrived at a moment when the mass population had to digest sexual experience and work out whether they liked it or not.

Nosferatu, by F. W. Murnau, does not put aside the sexual drive, but it adds more. It was based on a screenplay, taken from Stoker, by Henrik Galeen, in which the count is named Orlok (Max Schreck) and he is tall, emaciated, bald, with pointed ears, long fixed arms, and large white hands. His face is made up in the style of a skull. He is, shall we say, very ill, but he is part of an overall design that is natural. Murnau loved nature and light, and while he knew that *Nosferatu* existed in a sinister world it is still one of real forests, mountains, sunlight, moonlight, and the sea. In other words, *Nosferatu* forsakes the "easy" expressionist manner of *Caligari.* It wants a more filmic reality.

Murnau was at the start of his career still, and he was ready to try anything—stop motion, projecting negative footage, and some special effects that look comic now. And Murnau was not content with Stoker's interpretation: He feels the diseased soul and the malign religion in the confrontation. Above all, he sees Orlok as an emanation of the natural world—he is a mist and a vapor in mountains where cloud formations are often strange. Time and again, he makes the threat poetic, as if he feared the melodrama. Stoker felt that sex could only be melodramatic. In *Nosferatu,* the wife gives herself to the plague to save her husband.

Is *Nosferatu* frightening still? Or are we watching a relic in a scholarly mood? In the phantom ship and the uncanny apparition of Orlok I think there is fear still, but Murnau has caught the deeper dread: that the count is spiritually lost (like Norman Bates). And doesn't Norman have Orlok's frozen smile?

Nostalghia (1983)

There's a moment early on in *Nostalghia* when the Russian who is journeying through Tuscany tells his Italian interpreter that he's tired of all these beautiful paintings she's having him see. It's a rebuke that, sooner or later, in this film the viewer may wish to level at Andrei Tarkovsky, the director of *Nostalghia*. Except that if you do succumb to that crass and vulgar instinct, then Tarkovsky will hit you with an image so fresh and haunting, it takes your breath away.

This was Tarkovsky's first film made after leaving the Soviet Union, and the title of the film—I assume—refers to a deep love of country, a kind of homesickness, that goes beyond the normal. The film was shot in Italy, and it involves a Russian poet (Oleg Yankovsky) who is following the path taken by a great composer. I have to admit that I have seen the film three times, and I believe this is what it is about. I am not sure—but over the years I have grown accustomed to films where I'm not always sure what they're about.

The poet has an Italian interpreter (Domiziana Giordano), a woman of exorbitant beauty, long amber ringlets of hair, see-through clothes, and at least one great breast that is ready and waiting to be bared to the Russian, with the cry, "Is this what you want?" I think the woman is disturbed and I sometimes wonder what she is doing in the film. They also meet another disturbed man (Erland Josephson), who thinks the world is coming to an end.

That is about it in terms of narrative, except that it rains a great deal so that some of the ruins they visit are in a state of near flood. This waterlogged condition can get to you and to the characters. There is one moment when the Russian is smoking. He pulls at his cigarette and the sodden, tobacco-filled tube separates from the filtered end left in his mouth. But I'm not sure if it's a joke, one of those stray accidents that Tarkovsky left in, or . . . significant.

It's a film of two hours that seems to resolve nothing. But there are images to die for, like the last one of a huge ruined Gothic cathedral with a log-cabin house lurking inside it. I think this is old Russia being seen in old Italy. I'm not sure, but I love it.

Am I being too patient or dense? I first saw *Nostalghia* at the Telluride Film Festival of 1983, when Tarkovsky and Richard Widmark were two of the people being honored. On one night, Tarkovsky read (in Russian) a diatribe against America. Widmark was one who heard it. The next night was Widmark's tribute and he begged indulgence by saying that, whatever the faults of the United States, it had a tradition of trying to make movies that an audience could understand. It was a fair point, made with politeness. And for me it is part of a dispute that hangs in the air over *Nostalghia*—like the rain. You should see it and make up your own mind.

Nothing Sacred (1937)

How long does it take to make a good movie? *Nothing Sacred* is only 75 minutes long (but an hour and a quarter can seem a very long time in the wrong company). Ben Hecht is alleged (by Ben Hecht) to have written most of the script in four days, traveling by train across the country—and I'd guess that the train was kinder to screenwriting than air travel has ever been. Still, Hecht was hired in April 1937. He had one disastrous first attempt, and then the real script was in by late May. The picture opened November 25 at Radio City Music Hall.

It was David Selznick's partner, Jock Whitney, who asked for a "cockeyed comedy," like *My Man Godfrey.* Selznick said only Ben Hecht could do it, and everyone agreed that Carole Lombard ought to be in it—this was made easier and tougher by the fact that she was a client of David's brother, Myron Selznick. In fact, after his first no-hoper script, Hecht was put on a story from *Cosmopolitan* magazine. It was about a woman from the hinterland who claimed she was dying of radium poisoning. Hecht fussed with the story and came up with this: Hazel Flagg is dying, in Warsaw, Vermont—of boredom. So she puts the blame on radium poisoning. A reporter at the *New York Morning Star* hears the news and persuades his editor that it'll boost circulation. So they bring Hazel to town, even after she has learned from her doctor that he made a faulty diagnosis. She and the reporter fall in love.

Give Hecht his due: Once he had the image, of Lombard keeping a straight face as big-city hype went crazy over her sad story, the picture fell into place. Whitney had wanted Technicolor, when truly black-and-white would suit it better. But what's wrong with Lombard in color (photographed by Howard Greene)? Fredric March plays the reporter, and Walter Connolly is very good value as his editor, a windbag who can change his story line on a dime, and justify it—a man named Oliver Stone. Oscar Levant wrote some nice music. Lyle Wheeler did the sets. Travis Banton and Walter Plunkett did the costumes. And the ending was concocted by Ring Lardner, Jr., and Budd Schulberg. So *Nothing Sacred* is like a quick nap snatched during the years-long laboring over *Gone With the Wind.* And we all know that *Gone With the Wind* was more important, yet *Nothing Sacred* is such a relief in its assumption that movies might just as well be quick, throwaway, cynical, and funny as monuments to something or other. I don't mean to say *Nothing Sacred* is perfect—it's not as searching or as magical as *Godfrey* or *Bringing Up Baby.* But it's a true reflection of the "cockeyed" wisdom—that the world was a ridiculous place and it would be a good thing if a few smart young people saw that and said so in a way that makes you laugh. If you want to get the best, bravest insouciance in Hollywood of the thirties, you're better off going to comedies like this than the sagas. So Jock Whitney was not just rich, handsome, and a charmer—he was right.

Notorious (1946)

There are crucial hints—in *Rebecca,* in *Suspicion,* and in *Shadow of a Doubt*—of one character being taken over by another, or of some dark, neurotic reservation dragging on what might be a positive relationship, that show Alfred Hitchcock's development in his first years in America. So a case can be made for *Notorious* as his first deeply personal and fully achieved picture. I do not include *Spellbound* (1945) in this process. Despite its reputation, *Spellbound* is a grotesque mess, half-baked in its view of psychoanalysis, and the worst example of producer David Selznick's interference with his director.

Notorious was done through RKO under the Selznick banner, but while the producer was hopelessly tied up with the problems of *Duel in the Sun.* So the many excesses of that epic Western, onscreen and off-, helped shape and liberate this dark love story.

As the war ends, a Professor Huberman goes to prison for espionage. His daughter, Alicia (Ingrid Bergman), is left at liberty. She is depressive, alcoholic, promiscuous. Then she meets Devlin (Cary Grant), a cold, watchful intelligence agent. He recruits her, they go to Rio. She falls for him; he, more slowly, for her. They meet Sebastian (Claude Rains), a colleague of her father's. Sebastian wants to marry Alicia. She wants Devlin to stop it. But he wants the marriage—for reasons of espionage. So the recently saved woman agrees to destroy herself again.

Devlin is now running Alicia as an agent in an effort to uncover Nazi plots still active in South America, and soon enough Sebastian finds out. So he starts to poison the woman he loves. Only then does Devlin make an attempt to rescue the woman he loves and has nearly allowed to be murdered.

The espionage is a front: uranium ore in wine bottles, a silly MacGuffin that chanced to be close to a real secret. But Ben Hecht's very good script uses the front as a way into the deeply sadomasochistic love relationship between Devlin and Alicia. In turn, this exploits the tendency in Bergman to be victimized and an unyielding dark drive in Grant that only Hitch and Hawks recognized.

So the plot suspense and the romantic uncertainty are hinged and oiled to perfection. For the first time, Hitch had found the two levels at which he wanted films to work. Ted Tetzlaff did the outstanding photography—there are great love scenes and a fine staircase climax. Edith Head did the clothes, and the art direction is by Albert D'Agostino. And Hitch's direction reaches a new swiftness: Nothing gets in the way—the complete vision has come into its own.

You can say that Bergman and Grant are exactly cast, but they give a great deal beyond that. One should also stress the delicacy of Claude Rains—this is a story of two men led to a need to damage the woman they love. And there are good, showy supporting performances from Louis Calhern, Leopoldine Konstantin, and Reinhold Schünzel.

La Notte (1960)

In which a couple visit a dying friend in the hospital in Milan, where a deranged, nymphomaniac young woman throws herself at the man, and the first sign of moral helplessness or lassitude appears in his half-hearted denial. He is tempted to experiment with the happening. On the couple's life together—he is a writer, she is the wife of a writer. On how she wanders in the city and sees unfamiliar sights, how men in a fight believe she is watching them with intent. On an absurd striptease they witness at a night-club where engineering and athletics have eclipsed intimacy. And then an all-night party where he becomes attracted to a lonely woman, a younger version of his own wife. And the dawn comes up after the party and the couple are together, caught in an attempt to make love.

Because they are married, and because they are Marcello Mastroianni and Jeanne Moreau—above all, because she is Moreau—*La Notte* is the gravest movement in Antonioni's trilogy, the one with *L'Avventura* and *L'Eclisse* as its wings. In *L'Avventura* one love relationship breaks up because the woman vanishes, and then another woman takes over and is led to the point of wishing to disappear. In *L'Eclisse,* two strangers and unlikely friends meet, have an affair, and then silently turn away, leaving their rendezvous unoccupied. These are attempts at love that fail.

But a marriage is rather more than an attempt. Giovanni and Lidia are embedded in life: not just their apartment and his work (for which she is the first reader), but their dying friend (Bernhard Wicki). They have no children, but they have a life, and when Lidia strolls in parts of Milan where, perhaps, she has never been before we are close to that open sensibility in modern art, the one that measures the world—like Mrs. Dalloway seeing and feeling London, like Anna Karina probing at the texture of reality for Godard. And Moreau is not just stronger than Mastroianni as a screen presence. He lets the light slip over him; she inhales it, sniffs its fragrance. We might believe that she would make a better writer than Giovanni. And she is more potent, more vulnerable than even Monica Vitti (the girl met at the party). Moreau is a root vegetable, Vitti a flower. And in these years Moreau could take over the films of powerful artists and men in her defiant glance.

As time goes by, *La Notte* is the central structure in the trilogy, and the most moving part. Yet it is also the part most weighed down by conventional ideas of guilt and responsibility. And it is in *L'Avventura* and *L'Eclisse* that the air lightens so much with the possibility of chance. Lovers may forget each other—married people never. And Moreau's abandoned face is one of the great images of twentieth-century disaster.

La Notte was written by Antonioni, Ennio Flaiano, and Tonino Guerra from a story by Antonioni. It was photographed by Gianni Di Venanzo, and I think the grays are among the greatest ever filmed. Piero Zuffi did the sets, and the music is by Giorgio Gaslini. The trilogy is unique and precious (albeit foreboding in most respects), but *La Notte* is the central passage, in which minutes pass like the stones of a hard road.

Le Notti di Cabiria (1957)

Fellini followed *La Strada* with *Il Bidone,* in which Broderick Crawford and Richard Basehart played swindlers who masquerade as priests. The film was such a disaster that Fellini had great difficulty raising the money for his next film. In the end, he needed twin producers, Carlo Ponti and Dino De Laurentiis, for this to work. And it was always as a vehicle for Giulietta Masina that Fellini began to research the lives of prostitutes in Rome. Once more, he was looking for anecdotage and incident rather than social understanding. He actually employed the young poet Pier Paolo Pasolini to sharpen the hookers' talk, but he used none of the Marxist interpretation that was available with Pasolini.

The central character was named, portentously, after the heroine from early Italian cinema, but everything else about the role was Masina—the lack of prettiness or coarseness, the squashed gamine spirit, the plucky resilience, the tart with a heart. With Piero Gherardi, Fellini gave the rather nocturnal movie a raffish look, but again the gesture toward realism was more atmospheric than political. Aldo Tonti did most of the photography, though Otello Martelli took over at the end. The music was once more in the hands of Nino Rota, and music was as important as ever in protecting this winsome concept from the brutal realities of her job. We should not forget that in time *Le Notti di Cabiria* would inspire a musical, the 1966 *Sweet Charity,* by Neil Simon, Cy Coleman, and Dorothy Fields. That show imitated the film in its view of Cabiria as endlessly brave, despite the relentless way in which every man declined to fall in love with her. May we, just for the sake of adult entertainment and grown-up attitudes, observe that *Belle de Jour* came to exist in much the same time period?

Masina won the Best Actress prize at Cannes for her work, and soon enough she would come to be an emblem of a kind of fortitude that we should all honor, if we can. For my shoddy part, I still find her a cloying actress, a presence that makes me uncomfortable and a terrible barrier to deeper involvement. The men in the film include Franco Fabrizi and François Périer, though it was by now quite hard for anyone to play scenes with Masina except by succumbing to her music. Still, the film won a second Best Foreign Picture Oscar for Fellini at a time when American cinema was hardly permitted to touch prostitution as a subject. Though I am reminded of Tina (Marlene Dietrich) in *Touch of Evil,* only a year or two in the future, so much more economical, more alluring, and so lethally down to earth in her deflation of the male ego.

As you will have gathered, the film was a hit and a restorer of Fellini's box-office appeal. Still, I doubt that anyone struggling to hold back the laughter in *Cabiria* could have foreseen the great lunge toward gravity and modishness that was about to occur. Something called *La Dolce Vita* was brewing in his eager mind. He would tell the world it was depraved and have them lining up for more!

Now, Voyager (1942)

When Warner Brothers bought the Olive Higgins Prouty novel *Now, Voyager*, they had it in mind for Norma Shearer, Irene Dunne, or Ginger Rogers. Such wishes only bewildered Bette Davis, who believed it was uniquely suited to her—the story of Charlotte Vale, a repressed, shy, private woman who is drawn out by a psychiatrist, Dr. Jaquith (Claude Rains), and who then falls wondrously in love with Jerry Durrance (Paul Henreid). This shift called for a real change in looks (the loss of spectacles, the growth of hair, and so on), and whereas Davis was always eager for such alterations in herself, the other actresses were far more cautious about losing looks. So Davis got the part, and she would say later that she was instrumental in getting Henreid (after the studio had shot a lousy test) and in improving a lot of the dialogue. She can sound arrogant, but melodrama needs confidence as much as any genre.

The novelist had proposed an interesting idea to Warners: as a lover of silent movies, she suggested that the flashbacks be done as silent scenes, with a voice-over narrative. Over the years in film, that has often proved effective, as well as cheap. The idea of a voice studying the past is strangely potent. But Warners stayed literal-minded: The past should sound and feel real. Casey Robinson did the screenplay and wrote everything "straight." But Ms. Prouty prevailed on one other matter. The studio had been uneasy over the title—what exactly did it mean? But the novelist said it implied a mixture of romantic quest and immediate action. This is no small point. The titles of romance pictures are often the most poetic, and they clearly speak to the viewer. The very scheme of *Now, Voyager* is to suggest to any awkward, recessive woman that she can come into flower—now!—flowering in the dark.

Irving Rapper was hired as director (he had been a dialogue director), and this was his breakthrough picture. Sol Polito did the photography, and it benefits from one of Max Steiner's great string scores. For Bette Davis, it was always a favorite picture, itself a sign of her own emotionalism. She made a big fuss about better material, but she was always very good in "women's" pictures. When she does the big line—about the moon and the stars—it's clear forever that "big" is all about the magnification factor of her eyes. Rains is excellent as the doctor, and he was by now a subtle foil to Davis. As for Henreid, Davis enjoyed his company and helped him a lot—but he was often uncertain about the kind of hero he was most suited to. Studios saw him as a Charles Boyer and tried to prettify him, but Henreid was more retiring or modest and he seems a touch hidden or unreliable.

The rest of the cast includes Gladys Cooper (as Charlotte's mother), Bonita Granville, John Loder, Ilka Chase, Lee Patrick, Mary Wickes, and Janis Wilson. *Now, Voyager* was a solid hit. Davis and Cooper were both nominated for Oscars, and Steiner won one for his score.

The Nutty Professor (1963)

Which Jerry Lewis frightens you the most—the spastic jerk, or the ringmaster you used to be able to see on the muscular dystrophy telethon? Lewis has himself told the story that his wife would not let their children see *The Nutty Professor* because of the frightening ease with which he had carried off his strange "Hyde" persona in the film—Buddy Love. And it's not that Lewis was unaware of this. He has said that he had the idea for this film ten years before he made it, but he was frightened by what he might discover in the process. In short, although *The Nutty Professor* seems like a comic spoof of the Robert Louis Stevenson classic, I'm not sure that this Jekyll and Hyde may not be the clearest tribute to the power of the myth. This is a comedy only in its pretext. It's also a tense exploration of character, and maybe the first time Jerry Lewis put his popularity at risk.

He plays Julius Kelp, a chemistry professor at Mathews College. He is Jerry in horn-rimmed spectacles and wild hair. He has buckteeth and a silly grin. He is helplessly vulnerable to the fact that he is secretly in love with one of his own students, Stella Purdy (played by Stella Stevens, who has moments that are Monroe-esque).

So Julius takes a swig of some chemical elixir—to lose his shaming self, to be "bigger than life" (it is the same theme). He turns into Buddy Love, a monster of arrogance, armor-plated "cool," a hideously sophisticated cocktail lounge singer and insulter, a womanizer. Some people have always felt that Love was a version of the Dean Martin persona, the handsome guy that may have intimidated Jerry in all the years of their partnership. I'm not so sure. Jerry knew Dean was generous, harmless, and sweet-natured. But did Jerry really think that of himself? I lean to the theory—first proposed by Danny Peary, I think—that Love is the demon inside Jerry Lewis: the all-night vampire of money and sentimentality in the telethon; the total manipulator of all he sees in his film directing. The cruel perfectionist—the man who needs always to be right.

You can work it out for yourself in this extraordinary film, and test the evidence that Lewis is a self-conscious artist torn between the one-reel knockabout farce and a sermonizing film. Yes, it's an awkward mix, and one Chaplin had pioneered. *The Nutty Professor* was written by Lewis and Bill Richmond, but Lewis directed and coproduced, and as is clear from any study of his work, he conceived and controlled every item. There are a lot of good sight jokes along the way, but in the end it is the conflict of personalities that is most alarming. It's like one of those desperate moments in the telethon where Jerry sings to a sick kid. We feel as helplessly trapped as the child. But for once, at least, you feel the torment in Lewis himself.

Odd Man Out (1947)

It's hard to overestimate the importance of *Odd Man Out* to British cinema. For here was a film about the IRA, set in Belfast and to a great extent filmed there—already, so many awkward realities had been surpassed. It is also a story of twelve hours, tragic and suspenseful, and in its use of Robert Krasker's very bold black-and-white night photography it surely made a contribution to film noir not far short of that of John Alton. Above all, in presenting James Mason and director Carol Reed, it proved that Britain had the talent to carry very big pictures. To this day, *Odd Man Out* looks like a determined attempt to say that Britain—or Europe—can handle any modern drama.

It began as a novel by F. L. Green, published in 1945 and boosted by its sales as a Penguin paperback. Carol Reed picked Green to do his own screenplay, but he spent several months with him hacking it into existence. And then, R. C. Sherriff had his turn smoothing it out. In justice to the novel, and the increasing fever the hero suffers from his wound, *Odd Man Out* begins with the perfect realism of a daylight robbery and proceeds through dream and hallucination toward religious expressionism as the leader of the gang, Johnny McQueen (James Mason), goes on the run, pursued by his friends and enemies alike. And much depends on the handsome exhaustion of Mason's beautiful face.

The film takes no side in the IRA politics, but it has great sympathy for the gang and its loved ones. At the same time, the police are solemn and somber but not malicious or wicked. The one drawback to the film that troubles is the religious air it holds, and the way in which Johnny may be redeemed by his suffering. In terms of what was to come, the neutrality with which Harry Lime is observed may owe something to Reed's ultimate failure at keeping McQueen free from conventional patterns of guilt and atonement. And so the fabulous shadows Krasker had made for the film cannot help but take on Catholic undertones. In *The Third Man*, in Vienna, they are mere irony.

Ralph Brinton did the art direction for studio interiors to match the cobbled streets of Belfast—and Shoreditch in east London was used for some night locations. William Alwyn wrote the music. Many of the actors came from the Abbey Theatre in Dublin: the gang is completed by Dan O'Herlihy, Robert Beatty, and Cyril Cusack; Denis O'Dea is very good as the head constable; Kathleen Ryan is Johnny's girl; and other people in the city include Fay Compton, Beryl Measor, F. J. McCormick as Shell, the betrayer, and Robert Newton, generally thought to be too hammy or too drunk as the painter. Newton sweeps the film into Grand Guignol, and he helps make us see Belfast as a Dickensian city instead of just a place where a man waits for midnight or death.

Odds Against Tomorrow (1959)

Odds Against Tomorrow was a coming together of unexpected forces: the director Robert Wise; the blacklisted writer Abraham Polonsky; and the Harbel Company, which was Harry Belafonte, at that time a popular success as a singer and because of his performance in *Carmen Jones*, so that he was able to provide significant funding for this adventurous film noir. The source material was a novel by William P. McGivern, and Polonsky did the script, which was credited to John O. Killens and Nelson Gidding. (Polonsky had not had a credit since *I Can Get It for You Wholesale* in 1951.)

It's a story set in the Hudson Valley, to the north of New York City, and it concerns an attempted bank robbery. The leader of the robbery is Johnny Ingram (Belafonte), very much a new kind of black—smart, tough, not humble, not ingratiating, but a talented musician who is hung up on gambling. Polonsky's intent was to show a rounded character not remarked on, self-pitying or vengeful because of the way he has been wronged. In fact, Earle Slater (Robert Ryan), a white racist, has many of the characteristics of the alienated black man. And then there is Burke (Ed Begley), a veteran ex-cop embittered against the system.

The film was beautifully shot by Joseph Brun. Anna Hill Johnstone did the unromantic costumes. Leo Kerz was the art director. Dede Allen edited, and the music came from John Lewis, leader of the Modern Jazz Quartet (with Milt Jackson playing for Belafonte's character). With this level of craft work, and the high quality of acting, *Odds Against Tomorrow* amounts to probably the best picture of race relations in an American film until that time. It did not labor under a Stanley Kramer–like message. It did not encourage stereotype casting. And the only real reference to its theme is the ultimate state of Ingram and Slater: burnt to the point of being unrecognizable.

Belafonte was not the greatest of actors (certainly not as a young man), and he was somewhat impeded by his high voice. But Ryan is outstanding, and there is a trio of very good female performances—by Shelley Winters, Gloria Grahame, and Kim Hamilton. There is also a very good performance from the young Richard Bright as a homosexual.

Wise's direction is rather muted—this is not nearly as forceful a picture as Polonsky's *Force of Evil*. And compromises are evident along the way. But here was a film of real courage, sold by United Artists. It did not do well, but today it looks like a movie while the far more celebrated *The Defiant Ones* seems like a labored lecture. Belafonte was deeply disappointed; he did not act in films for another ten years. Equally, he never found a way of bridging the happy image of calypso singer and the man who held so many adult political opinions.

Of Human Bondage (1934)

Of Human Bondage, W. Somerset Maugham's autobiographical novel, was published in 1915, and its span of early life included the way in which Philip Carey, a medical student, became obsessed with a Cockney waitress and remorseless user of others, Mildred Rogers. Philip is crippled (he has a club foot), and it's a matter of profound mystery as to why he is drawn to Mildred—unless it is because she is his worst possible enemy, the abrasive edge on which he can file away his male surface or veneer. She is one of the most hateful of "heroines," yet you feel a self-scourging pleasure in how she is written.

Pandro Berman wanted to make the film at RKO. He had a script, by Lester Cohen, with some dialogue work by Ann Coleman. Leslie Howard had agreed to take the part of Philip. But director-to-be John Cromwell could only think of Bette Davis for Mildred. However, her employer, Warner Brothers, believed it would be the worst thing possible for her, and a sure way of killing her following. So the actress campaigned. She went in and asked every day for six months, until they gave in out of fatigue.

The script concentrated on the Mildred story—and even Davis admitted that she couldn't really conceive how Howard or Philip thought he was in love with her. She determined to pull no punches. Davis hired an English cleaning woman so she could study the accent, and she fiercely ignored the English cliquishness on the set. (Howard was allegedly surprised that an English actress had not been cast.)

Davis asked Cromwell if she could do her own makeup in the scenes of Mildred's decline. "I made it very clear that Mildred was not going to die of a dread disease looking as if a deb had missed her noon nap. The last stages of consumption, poverty and neglect are not pretty and I intended to be convincing-looking. We pulled no punches and Mildred emerged as a reality—as immediate as a newsreel and as starkly real as a pestilence." That was part of it—the rest was Mildred's gloating cruelty, her deliberate needling of Philip's good little boy, and Bette's radiant ugliness.

The supporting cast included Frances Dee, Kay Johnson, Reginald Denny, Alan Hale, and Reginald Owen. Henry Gerrard did the photography. The art direction was by Carroll Clark and Van Nest Polglase, and Max Steiner did a shocked score.

It worked. The picture was not popular, but no one could deny Bette's bitchiness. Warners was as horrified as they said they would be. She was a write-in candidate for an Oscar, but Bette believed that Warners ordered its members to vote against her (Claudette Colbert won for *It Happened One Night*). Davis was simply confirmed in her estimate that the studio was craven (she won next year for the flimsy *Dangerous*). A clash was inevitable. Years later, Bette looks brave and poisonous, but the question remains as to whether *Of Human Bondage* is a writer's justification for misogyny. It was remade, in 1946, with Eleanor Parker and Paul Henreid, and in 1964, with Kim Novak and Laurence Harvey. And it has never worked.

Oliver Twist (1948)

There is competition—even a musical version, *Oliver!*, which won Best Picture in 1968—but at the movies there is only the David Lean version, which stands not just as a warning to all followers, but as a model for the kind of serialization of classic novels developed by the BBC and famous in America under the rubric of *Masterpiece Theatre* (originally with Alistair Cooke as its urbane host). You could argue that Lean's film prospers to the extent that *Oliver Twist* (1837–39) is one of Dickens's more superficial, or surface-strong novels. *Oliver Twist* is a mystery story with fierce ordeals which turns out very nicely. It paints a vivid, frightening picture of the London underworld, but its message is not much more than "watch out"—every foundling may be a nobleman. Arguably, *Oliver Twist* today, taken from scratch, would be much more intriguing if Oliver became the leader of the gang, the cool head that surpasses Fagin and Bill Sikes and brings a little Corleone rationalism to it all. And then proves to be of noble birth. But easily steps over into politics with all his alarming prowess. Watch out for foundlings, indeed.

Lean and his producer, Ronald Neame, had undoubtedly been influenced by the Cruikshank illustrations. Still, designer John Bryan and photographer Guy Green found a nearly operatic noir style that is a beautiful partner to Dickens's visual descriptions. There was a very good score by Arnold Bax, and a kind of squalid energy in the textures of walls, streets, and clothes (call it dirt) that left M-G-M costume films of the same kind looking very laundered. Even *David Copperfield* suffers in comparison. And the great tradition of English clothes and props in such films begins with *Oliver Twist*.

Granted his approach (and admitting that it was Dickens, too), John Howard Davies was a fine Oliver, and again it's worth noting that he had many attributes of the real child—shyness, awkwardness, numbness—compared with the excessive, voluble articulation of the generation that included Freddie Bartholomew and Dickie Moore. I adore those two, but they were a little like miniaturized grown-ups (the thing Graham Greene observed in Shirley Temple). John Howard Davies seemed like a frightened boy.

As for Fagin, there were a few mild complaints in 1948 that it might be overdone, and even a little unfriendly to Jewishness. I don't agree. Fagin on the page is over the top because he playacts all the time for an audience of children. Alec Guinness got close to the illustrations, and he believed he was playing an inky villain without compromise or reflection upon Jewishness. We can take it. Otherwise, we would have to conclude that Robert Newton's Bill Sikes is very unfair to Brutes (don't Brutes have a heart and a union?) because he is so frightening. In other words, this kind of correctness is anathema to Dickens.

And then Lean showed how well he understood the necessary detail in smaller parts: Francis L. Sullivan as Bumble; Kay Walsh (Lean's wife then) as Nancy; Anthony Newley as the Artful Dodger; Diana Dors as Charlotte; and so on. Not a dud in the crowd. Even Bill Sikes's dog is one you flinch from.

Los Olvidados (1950)

There is no doubt about *Los Olvidados* being a turning point in Luis Buñuel's career. In the late 1930s, and in the age of war, he had led a wandering life, trying to be useful or to stay employed, but never dreaming of the kind of world in which he could make his art without hindrance. His impact in the late 1920s had been moderate at best, and restricted to avant-garde circles. In America, he had had jobs with the Museum of Modern Art and Warner Brothers, but without finding roots, let alone the chance to do what he wanted. There must have been times when he wondered if he would make another film—or what the world called a real film.

After the war, Buñuel moved to Mexico and began to make feature films there: *Gran Casino* (1947) and *El Gran Calavera* (1949). *Los Olvidados* was his next film, and it was plainly directed at an international audience. Its voice-over narration begins, "Concealed behind the imposing structures of our great modern cities are pits of misery, hiding unwanted, hungry, dirty and uneducated children . . . a fertile breeding ground for future delinquents. Although modern society attempts to correct these evils, the success of its efforts is still very limited . . ."

Worthy and reliable sentiments such as prompted many films in the 1950s—and hardly left the essential problem much better. In other words, despite the dream passages in *Los Olvidados*, despite its sense of a universal cruelty, this is a social problem picture as made by an earnest left-wing sensibility. André Bazin went so far as to say that *Los Olvidados* had a humanity that Buñuel's earlier documentary, *Las Hurdes*, had lacked. I take a different view: *Los Olvidados* seems to me a conventional protest, as if made in the assurance that the world can be improved. Whereas the true surrealist impulse finds no reason to credit or think of improvement.

So *Los Olvidados* is a surreal imagination firmly tempered by the attitudes embedded in Italian neo-realism, and as delivered by the sumptuous photography of Gabriel Figueroa, a man far more drawn to the picturesque than was Buñuel. The result was clear and useful: The movie won the prize for directing and the critics' prize at Cannes in 1951. It played all over the world (sometimes as *The Young and the Damned*). It made money, and it assuredly promoted Buñuel in Mexico and began to build his art-house audience.

The film is still worth seeing for historical reasons, and for the uninhibited yearning shown in the young people. But the treatment of characters is so different from the approach that really distinguishes Buñuel. This is, in the best sense, an upsetting film. Coming away from it, you want to help. Whereas the great Buñuel is a gentle, amused guide to the absurd dance we have been making all our lives. The film features hunger—real hunger, which is not to be disparaged. But the hunger that grows in *The Discreet Charm of the Bourgeoisie* is entirely neurotic.

Once Upon a Time in the West (1968)

Perhaps it was a warning sign, but nobody was sure how long it had been going on. In the mid-1960s, three men began meeting to talk about the Western and what it meant to them: Sergio Leone, Bernardo Bertolucci, and Dario Argento. Leone had had the go-ahead from Paramount to make a new, more personal Western, nothing as fixed and familiar as the *Dollars* pictures that Leone had just made with Clint Eastwood, Lee Van Cleef, and Eli Wallach. Those films were pastiches, parody, satire—but this new one would be "real." The three men started spinning off "ideas" for Westerns, which meant really the things they recalled from their own beloved films. As Bertolucci put it, Leone "had understood that cinema was changing, and that there was a need for people who wouldn't tell you the same old stories in the same old ways: in our treatment we put visual images and sensations rather than a lot of dialogue."

This was several years after the drastic redefinition of genre as managed by Jean-Luc Godard. And by that standard, the several months of Westernizing by those three men was an unmitigated disaster, a terrible sign of self-indulgence among film buffs cuddling their memories instead of carrying the medium forward into a new age.

The script was written by Leone and Sergio Donati, and you can annotate its references to classic Westerns if you like. But don't let that "intellectual" framework delude you into seeing *Once Upon a Time* as a reappraisal of the West. Instead, it is a druggy attempt by these Italian boys to make their own Western. So it's a grotesque mishmash of Monument Valley and such epic settings, a weird mix of Hollywood stars and Italian support, dialogue done in mistranslated riddles, with every situation dragged out like slow-motion sweat, and all beneath cobwebs of the mock symphonic music of Ennio Morricone. It is beautiful as photographed by Tonino Delli Colli, but this is beauty on novocaine.

Once Upon a Time was a fairy story, made under the guise of a return to reality. And while Leone may have intended an homage, it crushed the Western and was so ludicrously deranged in terms of real history that it cut off any attempt to develop the Western as a means of pursuing American studies. It was a way of saying that film artists need not look at the world, at nature, at life—just the anthology of movie imagery. Alas, it was a work acclaimed by many, with buffs looking for the longest possible version of this distended story (160 minutes is the favorite).

The cast included Henry Fonda (his black villain was the closest the film came to wit), Charles Bronson (as empty as the film was long), Claudia Cardinale, Jason Robards, Gabriele Ferzetti, Woody Strode, Paola Stoppa, Keenan Wynn, Jack Elam, Lionel Stander, and many others. Leone actually shot a good deal in America, but he was impervious to wherever he might be. His mind was so full of preconceived wide-screen compositions that he was blind to anything new or real. He was traveling on the screen, and he reckoned tracking shots were the only significant form of transportation.

One-Eyed Jacks (1961)

Some time in the spring of 1957, Marlon Brando decided that he wanted to make a Western. The word went out and he was offered a script derived from a Charles Neider novel, *The Authentic Death of Hendry Jones,* written by Sam Peckinpah, with Frank Rosenberg attached as producer. Rosenberg brought it to Brando, who thought he liked it, and in 1958 Brando wondered if Stanley Kubrick would be interested in directing it. But Kubrick hated the script. So Peckinpah was fired and Calder Willingham came on board.

Those script sessions, with Kubrick usually present but increasingly disaffected (and more and more obsessed with *Lolita*), might make a great movie. The story line changed, and some felt that it had to take in any fresh scene or character Brando thought of. The money kept going out. The story eventually settled on the friendship of Rio and "Dad" Longworth. They do a bank robbery but only one of them can get away. Rio goes to prison. He emerges years later and hears that Longworth is sheriff of a small town to the north, with a family. Rio goes after him.

It was when Kubrick heard that Brando had hired Karl Malden to play "Dad" (he had wanted Spencer Tracy) that the young director looked for his exit—and the exit strategy was that really Marlon wanted and needed to direct this film himself. Marlon acted taken aback, yet friends felt sure this had been his plan. And so the dire exercise came to pass. A strange location was found on the Monterey peninsula for much of the action. An unknown, Pina Pellicer, was hired to play "Dad"'s daughter and Rio's beloved. Kubrick left his imprint in the supporting cast: Ben Johnson, Timothy Carey, Slim Pickens, and Elisha Cook, Jr. Katy Jurado was hired as "Dad"'s wife.

The movie has its admirers. But at 141 minutes, it seems to me overdrawn but very uncertain. There is a vengeance story in there. There is a father-son story, full of recrimination, and Brando was well aware of hating his own father. There is a pathetic love story—though the real story of Brando and Pellicer is grim, and ends in her suicide. In the end, it seems like an untidy wreck with several lean, short films struggling for survival.

Alas, it's easy to conclude that this condition reflects what happened. Brando's patience wore out as filming went on, and as he found the need to make up his mind (and hold to it) so he felt burdened. Long before the film was finished, he had walked away from his own project and left the editing to others. He would never direct again, and yet he had a mix of self-pity and evasiveness that could blame the failure on film itself and the other people who were supposed to help him. And so our great actor bumped up against his own fatal limits—of being unable to sustain his own interest or be responsible to a larger work and its company. Yes, there are lively scenes in the film, but Brando was always a man fit for the moments more than the hours or the years. Natural actors are not always professional artists.

One False Move (1992)

According to IMDb.com, *One False Move* had a U.S. domestic gross when it was released of just over $1.5 million. Now, for a movie that is not a great deal. Yet I find that nearly everyone "in the know" has heard of this film, and many recommend it. As they might, for it is one of the few original thrillers made in America in the last twenty years. How can these things be reconciled? A gross of that number suggests that, at the most, 400,000 people saw the picture. That is a tiny sum by the standards of the movies—though if I or anyone could count on selling 400,000 copies of my next book, I'd be very happy. In the same way, a million and a half is chump change in any business sense. But for the characters in *One False Move,* it is real money. I don't think this is meandering thought about one movie. It's a way of getting at something profound in our culture: the lack of proportion over numbers, and the dislocation it represents.

So Carl Franklin's *One False Move* begins in Los Angeles, in the drug scene, with terrible violence—so much that some viewers are put off and anyone is left fearing worse. Two thugs, Ray Malcolm (Billy Bob Thornton) and Pluto (Michael Beach), kill some other people in the drug war and then they leave town fast, with a girl, Fantasia (Cynda Williams). At which point, the picture changes tone and direction. The cops have a lead that the killers are headed way east, and the action will settle eventually in a small town in Arkansas where a man named Dixon (Bill Paxton) is the law.

Two Los Angeles detectives (Jim Metzler and Earl Billings) go out to the country to consult with him, and there's a delightful clash of cultures—Dixon is a big talker, a line shooter, who thinks he's got one hook in a big case. He's charmed by his visitors and they're amused by him—they've never seen such a young and enthusiastic attitude. The new situation seems ripe for comedy, but then the action takes another turn and the rural police story slips over into a tragedy.

It was written by Tom Epperson and Billy Bob Thornton, and gradually it reveals itself as a movie intent on believing in a few lost souls. It prefers the country life, but it has no great illusion about anyone being especially safe or secure there. Indeed, this is a twisting, turning story about the way the past can catch up with you. It's made very simply—it can't have cost more than a million dollars—and it's the sign of some great talents. Carl Franklin is a very good director, indeed; *Devil in a Blue Dress* and the remarkable *One True Thing* came later in his career. The script is a series of misdirection clues. Cynda Williams holds the screen with a lazy authority that makes it all the stranger that she's not been seen much since. And the whole film brings sleepy, back-road Arkansas to life until we feel it as the center of the world and this story. So never trust the numbers.

One Flew Over the Cuckoo's Nest (1975)

In that very brief window between the exposé of Richard Nixon and the Iranian hostage crisis, there were a few cultural events that spoke of bitter victory. One of them was the movie of *One Flew Over the Cuckoo's Nest*, which seemed to believe that everything that might be wrapped up in the loose coat named "Jack Nicholson" was admirable, anarchic, liberated, and hopeful, while all those practices living beneath the white shroud tunic of Nurse Ratched were dead, destructive, chilling, and antilife.

But times have passed, and thirty years later I suspect that there are earnest, well-informed voices in favor of judicious shock therapy and deep narcotic immersion, just as there are those who would be very wary of the kind of dramatic sexual liberation of the Billy Bibbit character (the passage where Ratched sees what he has enjoyed and then reconstructs a trauma in his mind that will make for his suicide is her greatest act of evil—or fascism). Just as I have heard of young audiences nowadays who charge that James Dean in *Rebel Without a Cause* is self-pitiful and a pain in the neck, so I can believe that there are young makers of today's brave new world who would disapprove of Randle P. McMurphy.

The Ken Kesey novel was published in 1962. Then there was a play from the novel, with Kirk Douglas as McMurphy—and then he was convinced that a film had to be made of it. For this was *Spartacus* set in the life-style revolution of the sixties and seventies. No one would take it on until Michael Douglas and Saul Zaentz got the picture mounted—and walked away with the Best Picture Oscar. Casting Milos Forman as director was a brilliant move, for it meant that Kesey's anti-authoritarian attitudes took on the antibureaucratic experiences of someone who had grown up behind the Iron Curtain.

Moreover, Forman had the great insight of seeing the whole thing as a conflict in acting styles. So McMurphy is like a rogue teacher at the Actors Studio while Ratched represents the school of orderly and respectful public speaking. The vitality and the philosophy of the picture are alike in Nicholson's delighted role of lord of the rebels over a cast of oddballs—William Redfield, Brad Dourif, Sydney Lassick, Christopher Lloyd, Danny DeVito, and Will Sampson (as Chief Bromden). The script is by Lawrence Hauben and Bo Goldman, and it amounts to a testament of sixties radicalism—but I don't think there would have been any point in making the picture without that faith.

So here is the most drab and depressing of institutions risking insurrection as the inmates claim rights over their own scattered lives. And this just a few years before—to save money—President Reagan restored many inmates in mental hospitals to the streets. In which case, the nuts might as well speak up for themselves. The full tragic impact may have been confined to when the film opened. But Haskell Wexler's camera catching the shy, emerging realism of these crushed boys is something to be seen still.

Additional Oscars went to Forman, Nicholson, the script, and Louise Fletcher as Nurse Ratched.

Only Angels Have Wings (1939)

Oh, take me back to Barranca, where the steaks are the best and the coins are double-headers, and where a pilot's wife looking like Rita Hayworth is going to . . . Well, don't ask what she's going to do except wash her hair, file her lines, and read a little Hemingway while her husband flies the mail over the mountains. (Don't forget that while you're flying the mail, the other males can be floating your wife.)

If only the Nazis in 1939 had really been doing their background research on American camaraderie—if they'd looked at pictures like *Only Angels Have Wings*, couldn't they see that the insouciant brotherhood of Allied flyboys was going to be insuperable? Or did they, with all their deadly German efficiency, study the same picture and conclude that enemy purpose and heroism were all predicated on the most outrageous sense of fantasy?

Barranca is somewhere on the shoulder of Ecuador, a raffish seaport where sometimes a passing showgirl will be put ashore. The Dutchman has a kind of half saloon, half general store, half post office where he keeps a few pilots to operate the mail franchise—like Cary Grant and Thomas Mitchell, and a few young daredevils, one of whom, Joe, will risk a landing if it means getting a steak dinner with the showgirl. And, as Todd McCarthy has pointed out, Howard Hawks reckoned that the whole thing had the spice of documentary, while anyone else in sight could see that it was a set of guy dreams.

Apparently Hawks had written a few stories about the flyboys of Barranca, and the inevitable Jules Furthman turned them into a screenplay that swings for 121 minutes with nearly every line, gimmick, or MacGuffin hooking into others so that the whole thing feels like one shaggy dog story. With . . .

Well, what has it not got? First of all, it's got real flying stuff done in Nevada and Utah, with Paul Mantz and Elmer Dyer flying, with a 360-degree tracking shot to show the difficulty and the success of a plateau landing. And then it has the flagrant, Sternbergian set-making on $1.99 for the Barranca airfield (with plastic trees) and the mountain lookout where condors drift by like punch lines looking for a joke (art direction by Lionel Banks).

Joseph Walker shot it: Dimitri Tiomkin did some music. Richard Barthelmess is magnificent as McPherson, the pilot who has to recover his nerve and his reputation, and Rita Hayworth is not so much a discovery as his wife, Judy, as a shaky sensation. In truth, Hawks has some problems with Jean Arthur as Bonnie Lee—she wasn't too happy at the improv stuff and the casual attitude to continuity and what the whole cool thing was about. You feel Hawks being drawn to Hayworth.

But in the end it's a film about the guys, and Cary Grant's Geoff Carter, in gaucho pants, leather jacket, and sombrero, is in no danger of losing his nerve. He's uproarious in every way, except how he talks, and that's where the film is not just ecstatic, precise, and real but modern, absurd, and exhilarating. Here we are in 1939 as a genius sees that the medium is flimflam, and all the better for that.

On the Waterfront (1954)

Who's afraid of *On the Waterfront*? Or try answering these questions: Did Sam Spiegel produce a heartfelt political statement, as opposed to a rigged game? Do we believe that Terry Malloy (Marlon Brando) has spent time in the boxing ring, or is he just punch-drunk from Actors Studio improvs? Are we expected to believe that Terry and the girl (Eva Marie Saint) are going to settle down after this is all over and have pigeons? Is it likely that the criminal boss, Johnny Friendly (Lee J. Cobb), is going to sacrifice his mastermind, Charley (Rod Steiger)? And why is Charley killed? Finally, when the bloodied Terry staggers into work on the docks, what is that proving when this should be a picture about the need to strike against the corrupt waterfront practices?

These are first objections to the most specious "masterpiece" in American film. But backstory first. Years earlier, Elia Kazan and his pal Arthur Miller had planned a waterfront movie. Arthur was working on a script called "The Hook." At Columbia, Harry Cohn wondered if maybe the "problem" on the waterfront could be Red influence instead of criminal exploitation. Miller grew weary, and then worse than weary when he realized that Kazan (in 1952) was going to name names to the House Committee on Un-American Activities.

Whereupon, with a tidiness hard to be surprised by, Budd Schulberg (another confidant to HUAC) said, Well, I've got a waterfront script, about this boxer who informs on his criminal associates (had he been a little influenced by Abraham Polonsky's *Force of Evil*?). So off we go. Later on, Marlon Brando was one of the few who said he hadn't realized that *On the Waterfront* was about informing, but if he had known . . . ! All of which only goes to show that actors sometimes highlight their own lines in yellow and never read the whole script.

Now as a boys' melodrama *On the Waterfront* is good stuff—beautifully shot by Boris Kaufman in Hoboken, and directed with that lip-smacking, self-identifying glee that could make Kazan believe directing was more important than thinking. The waterfront becomes a kind of club in that everyone acts the same way: over the top, but with loving detail. For my money, Steiger's Charley ought to be the center of the film—he's the only character who behaves at all naturally. Everyone else is auditioning for posterity. And they're in. The picture is too celebrated for these words of disquiet to threaten it. Kazan would make better films. Brando, alas, was overwhelmed by this triumph. As for watching Lee J. Cobb, it is like observing meat in the act of pickling—and it's enough to destroy an ordinary appetite. *On the Waterfront* was nominated for twelve Oscars, and won eight, including Best Picture, Best Director (Kazan), Writing (Schulberg), Best Actor (Brando), and Best Supporting Actress (Saint). Leonard Bernstein did not win for music, and—here's the best joke—the collective strenuousness of Cobb, Steiger, and Karl Malden was overlooked in favor of Edmond O'Brien in *The Barefoot Contessa*. I can hear O'Brien laughing—but that's the end of *The Wild Bunch*.

Open City (1945)

Sometimes well-meaning critics say things like "Rossellini simply filmed the event, exactly as it happened in front of his camera." But he was much better than that. Much more the visionary artist, even if, sometimes, he found himself reduced to proclaiming the basics of documentary. Here's an example: there is a superb sequence in *Open City*—though still a difficult one to endure—in which we gradually appreciate the function of three adjoining rooms or spaces: a lounge, the office of the Gestapo, and the bare room where their prisoners are tortured. I don't think, in practice, the Gestapo had to suffer such limited means. But what Rossellini has done in putting three sets in a row, and then by having sound link them up—the noise of beating and the screams—and then, finally, the tracking camera in which some characters see what is going on is the truth of great art and cinema. The alignment is far-fetched—and never forgotten. This is a great director—or a great talent prompted by the extreme peril of his world.

I put it that way because the Rossellini before *Open City* is not as startling and innovative as the one I am describing. He was nearly forty when he did *Open City* and he had been a director since the late 1930s, without making a great impact. But *Open City* (it is often called *Rome, Open City*) is an episodic narrative film made only a short time after the events it describes. It had a tiny economy with scraps of film found here and there. But it is essentially the story of resistance to the German occupation. There again, the Germans are drawn in terms of stark villainy, whereas the Italians are allowed to be much more complicated. But what is most striking in the film is the sense of immediacy. Inside Italy and beyond, audiences felt they were seeing life under an occupation such as they had only imagined. Scenes like the carrying away of prisoners and the shooting down of Anna Magnani as she runs after the truck were devoid of artifice. Yet they are actually set in a real artistic context: For instance, we learn soon that Magnani's gesture was fruitless—because the prisoners are freed by other means.

The style is simple, direct, and authentic. Those who made it believed they were telling the truth as much as those—even Ingrid Bergman—who saw it. Years later *The Battle of Algiers* had a similar impact, though again we realize now that Pontecorvo and Rossellini were both accomplished, skillful shapers of what they wanted to see.

The script was written by Rossellini, Federico Fellini, and Sergio Amidei. Ubaldo Arata photographed it. And the impact overseas, with the coinage "neo-realism," was extraordinary, no matter that realism usually proves a tricky label. The script was nominated for an Oscar, and Ingrid Bergman was struck in the depth of her soul so that she felt compelled to work with the Italian. Alas, Rossellini would prove a trickier fellow than the genius of her imagination—but it is often difficult to know an artist too well.

Open Range (2003)

If you ever find yourself searching for an example of the sublime and lunatic manner in which films are our fantasies, without an atom of shame or irony, think of Kevin Costner. He had done very little until the late 1980s, when a rare stardom descended upon his Gary Cooperish humility. Give him his due, he never said he could act; and he has often revealed his awkwardness with a line. But he was handsome in an ordinary American way and got this notion of making films in which big dreams came true: I'll make a baseball field in Iowa (*Field of Dreams*); I'll have Sean Young, naked in my lap (*No Way Out*); I'll be Elliot Ness (*The Untouchables*); I'll be the spirit of baseball again (*Bull Durham*); I'll be a soldier who loves the Indians (*Dances with Wolves*).

It's harmless stuff, though closer to religious idiocy in *Field of Dreams* (a tranquil version of *Invasion of the Body Snatchers,* as ghosts come back to improve upon failed lives). But then Costner felt his power and his oats and the films rattled in, to increasing mockery: I'll be the man who defends JFK; I'll have an affair with a black rock singer. You can fill in the titles. But then the reach expanded, with *Waterworld, The Postman,* and *For the Sake of the Game* (how can my girl leave me if I pitch a perfect game?), and look at me, standing beside JFK!

It is a strange progress, yet our amusement stays quiet and generous. For there is an undeflected sincerity in Kevin's eyes and a nutty taste for integrity in his parables. He knows he is doing the right thing. Lo and behold, suddenly he was—as actor, producer, and director. In 2003 (and with far less attention than the earlier films had received) he made an enchanting Western in which Kevin seems to have said to Robert Duvall, "Lookee here, old buddy, how about we're the salt of the earth in the 1880s up on the high prairies." And Duvall, another amiable monster of self-persuasion, says, I reckon we could do that.

And I reckon they do. They play a pair of old pals, Boss Spearman and Charley Waite, who have been together a spell driving their cattle across the open ranges, never settling, seldom having a roof over their own heads, but protected against weather, hostiles, and progress by the great canopy of dream. Theirs is simple: they are good fellows, trying to get the other man to say two words where one will do. They have a dance, much aided by Duvall—the older, but far nimbler. And they come to a place where the local rancher (Michael Gambon) just can't abide open rangers or their kind of underplaying. Did I say that Annette Bening is there to make a nice cup of tea and living with her brother (so that the pals both think he must be her husband)?

Yes, it is like a scene preserved under a glass dome. It is quaint, nostalgic, and as daft as can be. But here in 2003 is a real Western, a Gary Cooper picture and a quite lovable thing. You can feel the breeze, smell Bening's fresh-washed face, and marvel at the fond double act of cowpokes not quite poking each other but . . . think of it as Sean Young in your lap.

Orphans of the Storm (1922)

The Two Orphans was a melodramatic sensation on stage in 1874 (and for decades thereafter). It was a translation of *Les Deux Orphelines* by Adolphe-Philippe D'Ennery. A foundling, Louise, is left on the steps of the cathedral. In fact she is the child of the de Vaudrey family, but their noble daughter had married a commoner! The baby Louise is taken in by a poor man. But then a plague kills the man and blinds Louise. So her adopted sister, Henriette, pledges to take care of her. They go to Paris seeking a cure for Louise's blindness. But they are separated. Henriette is kidnapped by the Marquis de Praille, and then rescued by one of the de Vaudreys (Joseph Schildkraut). Meanwhile, Louise is seized by Mère Frochard (Lucille La Verne), a wicked woman who turns her into a street beggar. Henriette and de Vaudrey search for Louise—they hear her voice singing in the street! De Vaudrey's father has Henriette imprisoned.

It's time for the French Revolution!

D. W. Griffith later admitted that it might have been rash of him to extend the established play into the era of the revolution—but anyone can see the appeal of the Terror, the guillotine, and panic in the streets. Under the pen name of the Marquis de Tolignac, Griffith wrote the screenplay himself, in which he established little bits of backstory like Henriette having made friends earlier with a man named Danton (Monte Blue) who can save them all. Not that we are deprived of a life-and-death race-against-time rescue mission with that eager diagonal blade wanting to kiss Lillian Gish's neck.

Enormous sets were built, and a budget of $1 million was surpassed. There were thousands of extras all perfectly costumed. The photography was fought over by Billy Bitzer and Hendrik Sartov, who were by now fierce rivals, and that surely led to delays. But the picture is a wonder to look at, especially in the tinted prints that Griffith intended. And in the early twenties, American film was desperate for ever more exotic locales and settings for the same old melodramas: DeMille would rebuild ancient Egypt; M-G-M experimented with real Rome and Culver City Rome on *Ben-Hur*. So Griffith's dream of recreating the Paris of the 1780s was not crazy. And the emotional pull of *The Two Orphans* was plain—it was remounted as a Broadway play in 1926. In addition, this is the Gish sisters film in which Dorothy really excels. Her blind gamine has great opportunities for pathos. To which, of course, Lillian turns a very sympathetic ear.

What troubles the modern viewer is the disproportion between accumulated verisimilitude and humbug, and the attitude to the revolution. There is actually a "helpful" title as the revolution gets under way: "The French Revolution RIGHTLY overthrew a BAD government. But we in America should be careful lest we with a GOOD government mistake fanatics for leaders and exchange our decent law and order for Anarchy and Bolshevism."

Such emphatic clarity only underlines the dilemma of a nation mad for story but bereft of history or a way of measuring consequences. Griffith was never able to invest his history with rounded human beings who spoke and thought as real people do.

Orphée (1950)

All Jean Cocteau did was take the legend of Orpheus and set it down in a deliberately plain, prosaic France of the postwar years where the paranoia left from the Resistance experience was likely to linger. And when we remember that Cocteau's official debut in film was *Le Sang d'un Poète* (1930), a very determined, arty movie, then the naturalness of *Orphée* and its readiness to be a film noir is all the more striking and impressive. There could be a rather ostentatious, swishy magician in Cocteau, not so much a showoff as a show-on. But within the cloak-carrying eccentric there was a very hardworking craftsman, always open to the new, always ready to learn. I don't think it's going too far to say that the restrained magic of *Orphée*, its fascinatingly humdrum exquisite moments, are lessons learned from such things as *Les Dames du Bois de Boulogne* and *Les Enfants Terribles*, projects on which Cocteau was simply the writer, or assistant, to more comprehensive film artists.

So, there's something to *Orphée* of the postwar Paris—shabby clothes, boxy cars, dusty roads, and the rhetoric of existential tirades, along with that inner feeling for vengeful, reactionary forces that had been left by occupation. Ask what that experience was like on film, and Cocteau's *Orphée* may be enlisted as evidence. So Jean Marais is the poet, a statue with a floppy forelock attached, a man of stone and flesh at the same time, but a man who has been a lion recently and has a new authority because of it. François Périer is a rather clerical Heurtebise, Marie Déa is Eurydice, like a girl from one of Jacques Becker's romances. Edouard Dermithe is Cégeste. The men wear slacks and open-necked shirts. Only death is dressed up—she is María Casares, with that enigmatic smile learned in *Les Dames*. Death's agents are black-leather motorcyclists. The poetry may be coming in on a car radio. Throughout the picture, the mundane parts of life are aglow with extra meaning, like umbrellas radiant with lightning.

Nicolas Hayer did the photography. Jean D'Eaubonne did the design, from models made by Christian Bérard—the film is dedicated to Bérard, a Cocteau regular who died in 1949. The costumes are by Marcel Escoffier, and the music is by Georges Auric. The cast also includes Juliette Gréco, Pierre Bertin, Henri Crémieux, Roger Blin, and Jean-Pierre Melville. The voice—and why not? for he had a magisterial voice for so slight a man—is Cocteau's.

And so Jean Cocteau—writer, poet, man of the theater, designer, artist, entrepreneur, provocateur: call him what you will—also found time to be a man of the movies, not just a filmmaker and a source of films, but an eminence at film festivals, a patron to the young. Simply to outline Cocteau's role in French culture of the twentieth century is to see America beset by internal frontiers and no-go areas. That a Cocteau could flourish speaks to the ease and assurance of French film.

Ossessione (1942)

The story of how *Ossessione* came to be is as interesting as the picture itself. In the late thirties, Luchino Visconti, an aristocrat, had gone to France to assist Jean Renoir. When Renoir came to Italy in 1940, for *La Tosca,* it was again Visconti who helped out when Renoir left for America. But they had talked about the kind of film Visconti might make as a debut: not a fascist film, of course, and not a white telephone romance—but a new kind of realism. Renoir mentioned the James M. Cain novel *The Postman Always Rings Twice.* Visconti made a script of it with Mario Alicata, Antonio Pietrangeli, Gianni Puccini, and Giuseppe De Santis. To their surprise, the Fascist authorities agreed that it could be made. But no one had bothered to seek rights to the book.

It was set in the Po valley in conditions of poverty never alleviated or romanticized by the film. Yet this poverty was paid for in great part by Visconti's private money. A drifter stops at an inn run by a couple. He and the wife start an affair. They are about to leave, but the wife decides to stay and the man moves on. Then there is a reunion, and now murder is plotted. The new couple take over the inn, but the man thinks the woman has only used him for the money. He starts another affair. The wife is killed.

In many ways, this is the toughest adaptation of the Cain novel, and one that shows a very different Visconti from the later stylist. He was in love with reality; he was not apparently an admirer of people, but he carried the difficult project past Fascist interference. He had Aldo Tonti and Domenico Scala as his cameramen and the imagery is hot before it becomes overheated, with a bleak indifference toward the meanness of place and action. Clara Calamai was the wife—and very good and sexy; Massimo Girotti was the drifter—lean, virile, and nasty; Juan de Landa the husband.

The authorities were amazed. They had never seen an Italian film so brutal or sordid, yet so human. Still, it was hard for the Fascists to see how it offended technically—except that anything that new might be dangerous. So the censor banned the film, and, apparently, young critics put pressure on Mussolini's son to get it released. By then, however, Italy was in such chaos that there were different cuts of the film, and few places where it could be shown. After the war, the illegal use of the Cain novel was revealed and the picture did not play in America until 1975.

As for Visconti, he seems to have taken time to digest the whole experience. He did not make another film for five years, and that interim was filled with the movies that are called neo-realist. *Ossessione* is sometimes still presented as their source. But that's hardly true. *Ossessione* had no overtly political sensibility and little liking for people or society. It is a Renoir film, if you like, but made by a cold misanthrope. And it is still very powerful.

It was with *Othello* that Orson Welles pioneered the itinerant or much delayed kind of production that would loom large in his later years—though the aborted *It's All True,* in various parts of South America, was the first sign of this method. The approach can be romanticized: thus it is said that Welles slogged through many minor things as an actor from 1949 to 1952, saving money and stealing costumes from Hollywood films for *Othello.* No one can deny the quixotic courage to persist, or the readiness to improvise. Still, movies are predicated on the most economical package of time for good reason, and on the determination (called the script) of what is to be filmed. Welles's method is both a hostage to money and an open excuse for the changed mind. Thus a work in progress in film may be never finished, or fixed in the mind. It might be anything, a potential, that often prevents it from being a satisfactory something.

Othello opened at Cannes in 1952. It did not premiere in the United States until 1955. And it was only in 1992 that a "restored" version appeared, with rerecorded music and a clearer sound track. I'm not sure that the clarified versions are truer to intent than the earlier renderings. Indeed, the condition in some of these Welles films where nearly every voice sounds ill-recorded, but faintly like Orson, may be more expressive of the approach than anything else. This is not a coherent production of *Othello* so much as variations on the Shakespeare—or an ongoing conversation about the play in Welles's head (the film it resembles is Al Pacino's musings over *Richard III*), and the company it needs is the 1979 *Filming Othello,* where Welles sits at the editing table yarning about the original.

Always open to melodrama, Welles made one key shift in the play. He begins with Othello's funeral, observed by Iago (Micheál MacLiammóir) from a cage hoist up on the battlements. And so the meaning of this *Othello* is more or less the affection and loathing that ties the two men together and which is unavoidably homosexual in feeling. Of course, that same tension runs through Welles's work, and the confusions of the shooting are held in place by the Iago figure—the one character who seems in charge of what is happening.

No one can deny the beauty, the spectacle, the heat and flourish of this film, but those things were second nature to Welles. It uses settings in Morocco and Italy with great aplomb and cuts them together in defiance of "continuity errors." Yet the single-stage-set *Macbeth* is more concentrated and powerful a film. This one spills out in every direction, and surely we are eager to know about the chaos of its making. But we have only the illusion of recovered unity and purpose. The rest is like a holiday in the sun—the best thing to account for Orson's deep tan and deeper voice. Suzanne Cloutier's Desdemona is not adequate, but there is loyal support from Robert Coote, Hylton Edwards, Fay Compton, Nicholas Bruce, Doris Dowling, and Michael Laurence.

Our Daily Bread (1934)

There's something so revealing about the creative naïveté of King Vidor that he could take his own hope for granted: that M-G-M would make *Our Daily Bread* just as they had been enthusiastic for his *The Crowd*. Vidor wanted to take the young couple from the silent film, John and Mary, broke, out of work, and behind with the rent in their city. But then an uncle gives them a plot of rural land. They go there. They try to live. But John realizes that he is ignorant as a farmer and so he approaches another unemployed farmer and suggests a cooperative venture. Within days, it seems, his bit of land is a parking lot for no-hopers: there's a carpenter, a stonemason, an undertaker, and even a violinist. John takes them all—he's making a story as well as a farm.

Vidor wrote the script with his new wife, Elizabeth Hill, and took it to Irving Thalberg. Time passed, and then Irving admitted he didn't think it was quite right for the studio. The studio system was not exactly part of the New Deal; indeed, the studios were very afraid of unionism, let alone cooperatives. Still, Vidor seemed not to notice or appreciate his own film with its stress on an all-for-one community and its wary attitude to banks and their decision to withhold funding. He fancied that other studios would jump at the opportunity. Or did he? He described it that way in 1953, but was he so innocent of business politics and life in America that he thought a small communist epic might help break the credit squeeze at banks?

In the end, he had to go to his pal Chaplin at United Artists for a guaranteed release, and he ended up hocking his own property to raise about $150,000. Still, the picture was only 71 minutes, shot largely on a disused golf course close to Hollywood (even that city was suffering!) and culminating in the exhilarating sequence where the community bands together to bring the water down to the land. They dig a ditch. They divert the water, chivvying and guiding, with what amounts to a human chain. And finally, they are a tribe reveling in their water and their communal efforts. Vidor shot that footage with a metronome and a bass drumbeat (adding Alfred Newman's music later), so there's a surging, Soviet-like rhythmn in the montage.

To say that Vidor was not suspicious of how this material would be welcomed is to deprive him of the kind of political sense that surely lies within *The Crowd, Street Scene,* and *Our Daily Bread.* He was fascinated by how American dreamers sustained their hopes when there was very little left to put on the table. But far more than *Our Daily Bread, The Crowd* touches on the real despair that can come with failure. What strikes one now in *Our Daily Bread* is the fun and spirit of a very odd camping expedition and the innocence that believes that if things work, then people will fall in line.

Joseph Mankiewicz actually wrote the dialogue (not his wittiest), and Robert Planck did the sunny imagery. Tom Keene is John (very cheery) and Karen Morley is really lovely as Mary—somehow in the hard years she keeps her sweeping false eyelashes. John Qualen is very good as one of the gang. How it fits with Vidor's *The Fountainhead* is another matter.

Outcast of the Islands (1950)

There is a view of Carol Reed that this was his last interesting film; there is a less friendly take that says this was the first dud, or the first picture where Reed seemed to have forgotten to care. All of which raises fascinating questions about how one quality lasts in a career, or how easily other factors betray the quality. I think it's true that Reed had three great films in a row—*Odd Man Out, The Fallen Idol, The Third Man*—and I fear it's the case that nothing after *Outcast* is as good. (Though *The Key*, 1957, is the one possible exception to that.)

So what do we conclude? That Reed reached a peak that was short-lived? That he was stimulated by the postwar state of the world? That a friendship with Graham Greene was an encouragement? And that, later on, Reed found his way of making films was terribly hampered by his status and by the greater amounts of money? Nicholas Wapshott's biography tells an interesting story of *Outcast:* how Reed, on his own, shot background footage on a research trip, only to discover that the camera union forbade its use because he'd shot it on his own. That was bureaucracy killing impulse, and it may have been symptomatic of things that depressed Reed.

Outcast of the Islands was based on Joseph Conrad's novel, published in 1896 as a prequel to *Almayer's Folly*. This was an Alexander Korda project, though the novel could easily have been Greene's recommendation—it is that side of Conrad that seems close to Greene, about a man, Peter Willems (Trevor Howard), who becomes obsessed with a native girl and who then loses confidence, luck, and design in his life.

Reed went off to what was then Ceylon to research the film and find locations, and along the way he made his famous discovery of Kerima to be the girl Aissa. There was a good deal of filming around Ceylon, and then interiors were done in England on sets designed by Vincent Korda. William Fairchild wrote the screenplay. Ted Scaife and John Wilcox did the photography. Bert Bates was the editor. The music was by Brian Easdale.

The film did not do well, but Pauline Kael would call it "one of the most underrated and unattended of modern films." I share that opinion, and I like the way she identifies the life force in Willems despite his every mistake. The story is not heavy on action. It is a mood piece, and I think Reed was making a very successful adaptation to a new way of regarding film—as a way of showing character and atmosphere. That no one else responded to it may have added to his dismay. Yet I cannot altogether rule out the chance of some kind of curse attached to Conrad with film, or stemming from the ennui in the central character. The cast includes Ralph Richardson, Robert Morley, Wendy Hiller, George Coulouris, Wilfrid Hyde-White, and Frederick Valk.

The Outlaw (1946)

The Outlaw is not a good film, but it does exist and it does come at a time when American movies may have been at their peak and when a man quietly going mad reckoned to himself, Well, if he could afford it, why not do it? These days we tend to romanticize every kid who can steal, beg, or borrow enough credit card debt to get a first film made. So why disparage a man who was able to take years if he wished, shooting by night, not necessarily because he was busy in the day—though he was, producing aircraft to save the free world—but because he really lived by night and had the best chance of designing a brave new brassiere then. You see, *The Outlaw* isn't just Howard Hughes, or even Pat Garrett meets Doc Holliday and Billy the Kid. It's Jane Russell.

We know this much. It was always a Howard Hughes production, but Howard Hawks was to direct from a treatment by Hawks and Ben Hecht and a script by Jules Furthman. Furthermore, it was Hawks who supervised the casting process. He got Thomas Mitchell as Pat Garrett and Walter Huston as Doc Holliday (which makes Huston the only actor who played Holliday and Wyatt Earp). And he did many tests of young unknowns before he cast Jack Beutel as Billy the Kid and Jane Russell as the girl, Rio. There's no doubt that Hughes had at least a voice of approval in this, and his lanky figure was sometimes seen in the distance. But it was Hawks who chose everyone and who shot for two weeks with Lucien Ballard on the camera. He shot some smart scenes, especially with the Kid and Garrett—though I think it was always apparent that Beutel was too languid (despite stories that Hawks had thought of him for the Montgomery Clift role in *Red River*).

So Hawks went away. The Arizona locations (near Flagstaff) were abandoned, and shooting resumed in Los Angeles, with Hughes himself directing, and Gregg Toland now doing the photography. That took about six months and deteriorated into endless sessions in which Hughes tried to get Jane's breasts to be themselves while standing up erect. Of course, the lady was big-bosomed and without support she was helpless. So Howard's aeronautical engineering came into play as he schemed over a brassiere that would not show.

Stories got out about the sex show that might be coming (this was all in advance of *Duel in the Sun*—or "lust in the dust"). There was a "rape" scene, plus scenes of the two young leads in the hay. And Hughes began to advertise such dreams in posters that featured an abandoned and voluptuous Jane Russell. All the while, she says, her master never laid a hand on her. And you can believe that, for voyeurism has seldom seemed so forlorn and lugubrious. Actually, the eye of the movie is more forlorn with Beutel.

Briefly, in February 1943, *The Outlaw* was released—so 1943 could be its day. But it wasn't properly shown until 1946. Its running time, once 121 minutes, dropped to 103. It could be shorter still, but it has ten minutes or so that are insolent and compelling. As for Jane, she seems very young and uncertain, yet far too intimidated to start laughing.

The Outlaw and His Wife (1918)

The surviving prints of *The Outlaw and His Wife* are of poor quality, something exacerbated by the heavy tinting of most scenes—so the stark glory of the pure black-and-white image has to be imagined. Still, there are scenes of the vagrant characters shot against such immense natural backgrounds (found largely in Lapland) that the excitement and the pantheism are intoxicating. To be sure, there are fine landscape effects in American film of this time—the battles in *Birth of a Nation*—but nothing matches the way in which the seemingly infinite wilderness and desolation of the north adds to this story, and animates its way of looking at the characters. You don't need the tinting when the distance is so majestic.

It's a melodrama, still, taken from a play by Jóhann Sigurjónsson, an Icelandic writer. Ejvind (Victor Sjöström) is wanted for sheep stealing. Rather than fight the matter out in courts, he retreats to the wild country of the north, with his beloved Halla (Edith Erastoff), a landowner. Halla is a remarkable character—not really beautiful, but very strong in her determination, and in many ways the driving force in the film. Erastoff and Sjöström had recently married—she was his third wife. (There is even a scene near the end, in mounting madness, where he says she looks like a horse!)

In the north, they hunt and fish, they live in stone huts or caves. They have a beautiful blond child. Their retreat is said to last sixteen years before the elements weaken and destroy them. At one time, they have a companion, Arnes (John Ekman), and he falls in love with Halla, so that he nearly kills Ejvind in a desperate crisis. There is a moment then when the film cuts away for just a second or two to a shot of Halla (her breasts exposed) that is a quicker resort to inner life than anything in film at that stage. Arnes overcomes his temptation, but the viewer is left excited by the directness with which thought is waiting to be expressed without symbolism or moral coding.

It's that real energy from life that makes the film so potent—plus the way the wife sacrifices her child and the absolutely unflawed acceptance of death at the end. In an American version of this film—if it had been attempted up in the Rockies—the "misunderstanding" would have been settled. The couple would have been redeemed and rescued. They would all have lived happily ever after.

But Sjöström's picture understands that the severity of the drama can match the extremism of the landscape—indeed, it has to. For a summer, the crew went up to remote places and put them on film. I suspect they hardly guessed how much sheer passion and primitivism those landscapes supplied. If Sjöström had known, then the central melodrama could have been less forced. But the sense of madness overtaking people, without a chance of relief, is waiting on his American film, *The Wind*, ten years ahead.

Out of Africa (1985)

It's not just Africa we're "out of"—here is a movie out of its mind with excessive taste, safari dreams, and poshlust. It's also significantly out of touch with Africa, the world made by whites there, and the very tricky, complicated mind of Karen Blixen. This is where the Peterman catalogue takes over from art or literature, or the alleged verities of light and space in Africa. Though its setting is Africa in the years from 1913 to 1931, it is a sweet evidence of how difficult it had become in the America of 1985 to imagine any other part of the world without resorting to flagrant fantasy. This is the high silliness that could be nominated for eleven Oscars then and win seven, including one for Sydney Pollack as Best Director.

It purports to be the story of Karen Blixen (Meryl Streep), who goes to British East Africa to live with her husband, Baron Blixen (Klaus Maria Brandauer). She learns there what a casual adulterer he is. She acquires syphilis from him. She meets a great white hunter, Denys Finch Hatton (Robert Redford), and travels with him, even letting him wash her hair on the slopes of Kilimanjaro. And she returns to Denmark.

Of course, Karen Blixen was the real name of Isak Dinesen (1885–1962), a great writer and an immense fabulist who, in old age, looked like a Gothic crone rather more deeply affected by syphilis than Kilimanjaro shampoo. Judith Thurman's biography was one basis for the film, and it makes clear how far Dinesen differed from and intensified Meryl Streep's very appealing presentation of a Hemingway ideal—brave white woman, good writer, active in sleeping bag, loves Africa, and not too demanding of wandering men. Equally Finch Hatton was not every dream that Robert Redford has ever held of the blond, solitary mountain man he yearns to be known as, but a pinched, disagreeable, vain Tory hunter.

The film claims Thurman's book and Errol Trzebinski's *Silence Will Speak* as sources, as well as every relevant book by Dinesen—all bundled up in a collection of clichés by Kurt Luedtke. In fact, the film belonged most to Pollack's brave ignorance of reality, to the spectacular photography of David Watkin, the I-want-to-live-there production design of Stephen Grimes, and clothes by Milena Canonero that make safari seem eternally chic.

Streep is very good and clearly striving for something she has found in the research, but is being hidden in the film. Klaus Maria Brandauer is excellent as the baron, and there are good performances from Michael Kitchen (he should have been Finch Hatton), Malick Bowens, Joseph Thiaka, Michael Gough, Suzanna Hamilton, Rachel Kempson, Graham Crowden, Leslie Phillips, Shane Rimmer, and Donal McCann.

It cost $31 million and had U.S. rentals of $43.4 million, so it did well enough in the end, with Oscars as trophies—it won Best Picture, Best Director, screenplay, sound, Art Direction for Grimes, Cinematography for Watkin, and Best Score for John Barry. I find it hard to credit that there is not an "Out of Africa" song (by Streisand), but there is a little bit of Mozart instead.

Out of the Past (1947)

Everyone loves *Out of the Past*—I even liked it in the old days in England, where it was known as *Build My Gallows High*. Not that the fatalism of Jeff Bailey (Robert Mitchum) is headed for judgment or execution. One of the pronounced things about this ultramoody picture is its offering no faith in law or order. Jeff is hired by Whit Sterling (Kirk Douglas) to find Whit's mistress, Kathie Moffat (Jane Greer), who has gone away. Actually she shot Whit and went off with $40,000 of his money. In due course, Jeff will settle with Kathie, but only after he has been in love with her, and crazy about her in Mexico, where he found her.

Of course, that's not how the story is told. The film begins in Bridgeport, a small town on 395, the road that goes up the east side of the Sierra. Jeff is working there in a gas station: He has a girl he might marry (Virginia Huston) and he has a mute boy (Dickie Moore, aged eighteen) who is his friend. Then two thugs drive by—Whit's men—quite by chance, and Jeff has to go back into his past to settle old scores and meet his fate like the idiot he is.

There, I have admitted at least the edge of doubt into all the noirista admiration of *Out of the Past*. Yes, it is terrifically well shot by Jacques Tourneur, and sixty years later it may stand as a definition of postwar modernism in that I still don't think its economy or impersonal eloquence can be faulted—it is hard-boiled, but full of feeling. And I know the scholarship (by Jeff Schwager) that established that Frank Fenton did the brilliant shooting script after previous work by Daniel Mainwaring—and Mainwaring was the Geoffrey Homes who wrote the novel *Build My Gallows High*.

But let me ask you this: Granted the robust, witty daring we see in Jeff, do we really believe in him holed up in Bridgeport looking for a new life? Does that fit with the guy who can't help but make a fool of himself with Kathie Moffat at every turn? And here we come to the big question: Were there times—like here—when it was asking a great deal for us to buy Robert Mitchum as so supreme, so omniscient, so lone and secure, and such a chump, too? This is a modest discontent, for I will always like the film—if only for Nicholas Musuraca's exquisite black-and-white. He and Tourneur together were a marvel of storytelling craft. And it's not that I dislike the tortuous nature of the plotline, it's just that I think Jeff needs to be several degrees more vulnerable or mortal. Because I have a sneaking suspicion that he's playing to the loathing of women and the trust in taciturn machoism that together go so far, sometimes, to spoil noir setups. Never mind, there's always Acapulco and that time of the evening when Kathie comes walking out of the night into the glow of a café. It's the place next to the movie house. And it's a perfect dream of going on the lam.

Outskirts (1933)

At first, Boris Barnet's *Outskirts* seems like a rare and loving re-creation of provincial Russian life before the war and the revolution. We are in a small town in 1914 where people have time to watch the shadows shift on a sunny day. A man accosts a woman on a bench, makes off with her eventually, and throws a lurid wink at the camera. A bored horse talks. And Yelena Kuzmina throws her ravishing smiles at us—one of the great smiles in the history of the cinema, even if Kuzmina does little else. (Barnet's other discovery at this time was Anna Sten, who is far livelier in his films than she ever was for Samuel Goldwyn.)

The style is comic, observant, and mundane—as if to say that was what Russia was like then. There is a strike in the town and Cossacks put it down, but the whole thing is muddled and so much less portentous or violent than similar scenes in Eisenstein. The sound is early and experimental: Individual sound effects are played against great sweeps of music (by Sergei Vasilenko), but many other sounds are simply left out as too difficult yet or too boring. Still, sound changes the perspective and signals the great war with Germany that no one in this Russia understands.

All of a sudden the picture is convulsed—epic battle scenes, wastelands at the front that might have influenced Kubrick. German soldiers are captured and imprisoned, and there is so little food in their camp that they are released to forage. One young soldier meets Yelena and takes up work in the shoemaking shop before paranoia and violence destroy the attempt at fraternization.

The alteration in tone and mood is uncanny, and it is arrived at through Barnet's steady eye for human nature. It has been observed before that this film "just happens," and seems coaxed into being by its own progress. But that is a way of masking Barnet's extraordinary artistic ambition: to show war as being in defiance of every instinct in human observation and contact. If I say the feeling is French, that is a way of guessing that *Outskirts* must have affected Jean Renoir as he came to make *La Grande Illusion* only four years later.

But Boris Barnet (whose roots were English) is still a neglected figure in film history. He does not fit the old idea of a Soviet montage maker; for that reason alone, the newcomer is likely to be nonplussed by *Outskirts*. That in turn only leaves us wondering what the film's title means (it was also known as *Borderlands*). But *Outskirts* shows very little mark of official Soviet intrusion—it is the work of an uncommon artist as much affected by Chekhov as by Bolshevik ideas. The look is like Dovzhenko (the photography is by M. Kirillov and M. Spiridonov). The comedy is near slapstick. And then we are facing the end of the world. To be seen to be believed.

The Ox-Bow Incident (1943)

It is a fable, only 75 minutes long, and the kind of film that may still be played in American high schools in the hope of conveying pity and decency and teaching civics. In 1885, two cowboys (Henry Fonda and Harry Morgan) ride into Bridger's Wells in Nevada. They find a community that has captured three men on charges of rustling and murder: a young family man (Dana Andrews); an old man, feeble (Francis Ford, John's brother); and an arrogant Mexican (Anthony Quinn). A lynching is called for and the sheriff is away. We hear the debate and we encounter the range of opinion in the small town. The lynching occurs and then the sheriff arrives with the news that there was actually no crime. Fonda reads aloud the last letter Dana Andrews was allowed to write to his young wife. Is there anyone around who would rather print heroic legends?

It is a novel by Walter van Tilburg Clark, published in 1940. A producer brought it to William Wellman, who ended up buying the property and offering it to Darryl Zanuck. To Wellman's surprise, Zanuck accepted it (though Wellman had to make two other films on the deal, *Buffalo Bill* and *Thunder Birds*). Lamar Trotti did the screenplay, simplifying the novel a good deal and making it more urgent and emblematic. This in turn was enhanced by a shooting strategy that did nearly all the exteriors on echoing sets with nailed-down sagebrush and gloomy studio lighting (by Arthur Miller). So we have no doubt about why we are there: We are witnessing a drama and a demonstration. It is good for us, even if we don't exactly feel good.

It is earnest, theatrical, and didactic—yet it works. And there, in 1943, is a film that quietly dismantles all the bombast of team spirit and rapid response. And along the way (if only because of some interesting bits of casting) it sheds a baleful light on some other Western movie mythology: Jane Darwell is quite hateful as a laughing bigot; Francis Ford is pitiful; and Fonda, for once, is helpless and stricken. Frank Conroy is the bloodthirsty Southern major, and Harry Davenport is very good as a voice of reason. It also has William Eythe and Mary Beth Hughes.

It was made very cheaply, with a somber folk-music score by Cyril Mockridge, but it was nominated for Best Picture, and of its own accord it came to be regarded as the kind of picture that Hollywood allowed itself every now and then. For Fonda, it leads directly to *12 Angry Men*, and you may decide that it is just as rigged as that study of the jury system. But miscarriages of justice are not so rare in the United States as to make the movie seem quaint. It is still watched by hunched teenagers falling out of love with the human race, whereas *Buffalo Bill* and *Thunder Birds* are on the shelf. Zanuck was a great judge of what mattered.

Paisan (1946)

Paisan is the Rossellini picture that followed *Open City*, and if it is less striking or forceful, it is more complex and searching. The situations in *Open City* are harrowing but clear-cut. What makes *Paisan* more interesting is that so many of the problems arise from failure of understanding, and from the reliably muddied state of human affairs, especially in war, where fear and insecurity are going to make mistakes. Once again, it is a kind of dramatized documentary, a film that uses nonprofessionals and real settings, but which acts out a series of scripted vignettes on life in Italy as the war reaches its final stages.

In the first, a Sicilian girl meets an American soldier. They can't talk to each other, because of the language barrier. The GI is shot by German sniper fire. Other Americans arrive and believe the Sicilian girl killed him. In turn, she is killed.

In the second, a boy from Naples picks up a black GI and steals his shoes. The angry GI tracks the boy but finds he lives in caves outside the city in unimaginable poverty. He does nothing.

In the third, some American soldiers enter Rome. A whore picks up one of the soldiers and realizes they met six months earlier, before she had turned to prostitution. The girl tries to revive the past. But her soldier cannot recognize her any longer. Six months in war is an age.

In the fourth, an American nurse realizes she is tending a Resistance leader. But the Resistance itself is damaged because of the false rumor that the leader was killed.

In the fifth, in a monastery, Italians are shocked to find they are looking after three American chaplains—one a Protestant, one a Jew.

And in the last episode, the Germans who are still fighting in the Po region execute Italian partisans who have been helping the Americans.

As Leo Braudy put it, "this episodic film is fascinated by the failures of relations between people, their separations and their misunderstandings." After the stirring plea for solidarity in *Open City*, Rossellini feels bound to admit the destructive climate of confusion. No matter the hope or the courage or the wish, people cannot be sure they are simply fighting for the same thing. The realities of politics are beginning to obtrude—and we are reminded that war is the history of politics carried on by other means.

In its way, it is like the doubts in *A Diary for Timothy* (1945) coming after the unified determination of *Listen to Britain* in the work of Humphrey Jennings. Moreover, this is a hint of what is to come with Rossellini: the series of postwar ordeals or tests that face the character played by Ingrid Bergman. The script was by Rossellini, Federico Fellini, Sergio Amidei, and Marcello Pagliero. The photography is by Otello Martelli. Far less of a banner or a cry for unity, *Paisan* is a superb portrait of muddle as the essential human condition. But just as uncertain endings put off movie investors, so *Paisan* is the kind of documentary that has great difficulty getting institutional support. After all, institutions believe in being right and in lasting verdicts.

The Palm Beach Story (1942)

Tom and Gerry, they are called. Tom and Gerry Jeffers. They live on Park Avenue and are just about perfect. He is Joel McCrea and he is an inventor. She is Claudette Colbert and she is simply well-dressed. But they are short on the rent and then a rich Texan, the "Wienie King" (Robert Dudley), shows up to rent the apartment. But he likes Gerry—he gives her the rent, in fact, as well as money for new clothes. Tom finds this shocking. But, darling, she protests, being attractive is what I do. I thought you liked it.

In many ways, this is the picture closest to the blithe heart of Preston Sturges. He had been an inventor, and he believed in being inventive. He did admire women for their cinematic presence, their look, and their way with clothes. So, Gerry hops off to Palm Beach and on the train she meets John D. Hackensacker III (Rudy Vallee), who takes a shine to her and invites her yachting. Meanwhile, the Wienie King has also given Tom money to fly south. That is where he meets John D.'s sister Maude (Mary Astor), who thinks he's terrific.

Of course, the more she sees of John D., the more Gerry gets her old yen for Tom. The two Hackensackers are very long-suffering about it all, but as they are jilted they do wonder whether Tom and Gerry don't have available siblings. They do, and so the screwball's roll ends in a double marriage and the title comes up: "And They Lived Happily Ever After . . . Or Did They?"

This is a very funny film. The dialogue sparkles, and the total devotion to a life of appearance is rich in irony. Moreover, the train journey south is an opportunity for Sturges to introduce the Ale and Quail Club, the best-ever excuse for his team of supporting players. But the screwball needs oil all the time if we are to avoid the squeak of pain or real emotional hurt. When the Breen Office saw the script, they thought they heard a kind of rapturous surrender to infidelity and sex—and they feared that might offend an American public at war. So Sturges kept carnality at a distance. Still, the fragility of marriage is all too evident, just as the kind of personality Sturges adored is seen as being truly dangerous. After all, the unquenchable lust in people—the desire for more appearance—is answered only by a flagrant trick (the doubling up of McCrea and Colbert), as if to say only movie's fraud can keep the ending happy. You could still take *The Palm Beach Story* and make a bitter lamentation out of it and the way the people screw up (in the sexual and the mechanical sense).

Whereas in *The Lady Eve* we see two contradictory people who are attached by love, in *The Palm Beach Story* lovers who are like brother and sister seem highly fickle and uncertain. You can begin to get hints of how the dream of being Preston Sturges faded. Still, the four leads are delights, and the froth of eccentricity elsewhere helps keep us from seeing that the fun is close to madness: Robert Warwick, Arthur Stuart Hull, Torben Meyer, Franklin Pangborn, Snowflake, William Demarest, Jack Norton, Robert Greig, Roscoe Ates, Chester Conklin, Jimmy Conlin, and Vic Potel.

Pandora's Box (1929)

It is one of the turning points in cinema: February 1929, the opening of *Pandora's Box* in Berlin. Yet the film is still silent, no matter that sound is conquering all. In the next few months, Dietrich will do her Lola-Lola at the Blue Angel, groaning out that "Falling in Love Again" chant in her lazy way. And for a moment Dietrich will rule the world of femmes fatales. Deservedly so. But here, a few months earlier, is the real turning point, as Lulu (Louise Brooks) waits for the embrace of a sexual maniac, and Jack the Ripper, her guy, is entranced by the knife, shining in the German Limehouse light. Her hand goes still, and we feel sure we heard something—the stretch of silk as a blade pierced it, her last sigh, her first scream?

Today, *Pandora's Box* plays at silent-screen festivals, or at any event where people are eager for the best films ever made. It is not the last silent film, but it may be the first modern movie, the first time someone has said, Let's do the orgy, the whole thing, let's make it about the way sensuality destroys itself. And let them—the ones in the dark—watch. Because the point of the film is, Really, are you going to stay in the dark all your life, or will you come up here into the German Limehouse light?

Pandora's Box is a reworking of material in plays by Frank Wedekind—*Erdgeist* and *Die Büchse der Pandora*. The script is by Ladislaus Vajda. The director of photography is Günther Krampf. The art director is Andrei Andreiev. And the costumes are by Gottlieb Hesch—in that last scene, Pabst told Hesch to take Miss Brooks's favorite outfit, rip it and soil it with grease, and tell her to wear that. Her own clothes. The cast was top-rank German people, some of whom hardly spoke to Miss Brooks, the Kansas dancing girl, imported for the film, the girl who wasn't a star. Dietrich's grave perplexity hung over it all: "Why should Pabst choose her when he could have me?"

In truth, because Louise Brooks was rather more the real thing than an actress. No, I don't mean she was Lulu, though there are episodes in her life still to come where she is an outcast and a reject. But Dietrich long before *The Blue Angel* was cute with knowingness—she could hardly move without tossing you that complicit grin. And Brooks was knowledge still looking like innocence. She is the natural being, a knife herself, a blade called beauty and desirability, thrust into the soft bourgeois flesh. Everyone wants her and she wants only to utter that scream that says "sound." "Let me talk" plays on her extraordinary mouth. Let me tell you how much I know. That is why the men in the film want to consume her, to stop her mouth with kisses.

This is the box where so many films are kept. Start here. With Fritz Kortner as Schön, Franz Lederer as Alwa, Carl Goetz as Schigolch, Alice Roberts as Anna Geschwitz, Krafft-Raschig as Rodrigo Quast, and Gustav Diessl as Jack the Ripper.

Paper Moon (1973)

In gorgeous black and white (by Lázsló Kovács) that seems to come from Hungary as much as the Midwest, and with period costumes and décor by Polly Platt, *Paper Moon* is the best-looking of Peter Bogdanovich's three hits in a row from the early 1970s. Every house and parlor repays scrutiny; any cap may have dollars in it. And in this deft story about looking sharply, one has to work to get every ounce of pleasure. You can say it's a Fordian throwback, but Bogdanovich has a tougher, sadder view of human nature than Ford and Capra. Then there's the degree to which a very sharp child has to educate her slow-witted father.

It comes from a novel by Joe David Brown, *Addie Pray,* which was turned into a screenplay by Alvin Sargent. The latter admitted that he got too bored to read the ending of the novel, so almost inevitably he changed it. In the book, Addie goes to live with a grandmother. But the movie is cute enough to know that it has actually discovered a love between Addie and her father, Mose. So the two go off together. A sequel would not come amiss, but it is Hollywood's principle to leave the really interesting films open-ended.

The coup of the film would seem to be casting Ryan O'Neal as Mose and Tatum, his real daughter, as Addie. She was ten when she won the Supporting Actress Oscar, and she has done nothing else to remind one of this flawless performance. Was it being with her dad that did it? Was it that Bogdanovich at that time had an assured way with actors? Or is it so good a role that any adult could play it? Whatever answer you prefer, I think this is among the toughest views of children in the unduly sentimental range of the American film. The real movie star of the years in which *Paper Moon* was set was Shirley Temple, whose goodness was as true as her dimples. Whereas Addie is born old and wise—and thus this is a film that every ambitious child loves.

Another point of view is to say that Tatum O'Neal is far more than a supporting actress in *Paper Moon.* Her role dominates the film. She is its mind, its conscience, its humor and fears. So if Tatum had got Best Actress (that went to Glenda Jackson in *A Touch of Class*), then a further justice could have been done—giving the Supporting Actress Oscar to Madeline Kahn for her superb Trixie Delight. There is much else, including John Hillerman in two parts, Randy Quaid, P. J. Johnson, and Burton Gilliam.

Bogdanovich's next film was *Daisy Miller,* starring Cybill Shepherd, but the first film done without Polly Platt. I cannot place later Bogdanovich films in this book, and I cannot entirely fathom his decline. But I feel the need, again, to pay tribute to these three in a row, the work of a man who deserves and deserved to be known in the pantheon of American moviemakers.

The Parallax View (1974)

There's no way for an audience to inhabit *The Parallax View*—this alone would account for the film's failure, without any testing of whether such steady play upon paranoia is ever going to be fun for anyone. But the very thing that seems to have drawn Warren Beatty to the project serves to keep an audience from identifying with him. For it's as if Beatty had entered his own Parallax test to see just how far he could go in being unlikeable in playing the lead role in a big picture. Why he should do that is another question, larger than this essay can take on, but it is close to what makes that intelligent man tick.

The greatest men of our time have been going down—we know that feeling if we survived the sixties and the seventies—and reporter Joe Frady reckons there is a conspiracy, with a large corporation, Parallax, that hires and trains assassins for all purposes. He will get himself hired on. That promises a scoop, perhaps, but it also threatens a full examination of Frady's personality. For he is not exactly Woodward and Bernstein. He is a user of people, a liar, a problem, someone who has not made peace with life. Is that why Parallax thinks he might be their kind of guy?

No one ever did this kind of stealthy thriller better than Alan J. Pakula; and Pakula was a man acquainted with depression and searching analysis. He ticks off the levels of the plot like a doctor assessing symptoms, so Paula Prentiss and Hume Cronyn are erased as friends or helps to Frady, and he explores an increasing solitude that rather becomes Beatty's uneasiness.

There's always the question of where this kind of intrigue can go. In *Klute*, Donald Sutherland did offer something like rescue to Jane Fonda. And in *All the President's Men*, there was the available opening in which some could believe that Redford and Hoffman had saved the Constitution. But Joe Frady has no ties, and Pakula is disinclined to trust him with victory. Thus, there is a greater, much darker film waiting in the wings in which—while telling himself he is still on the job—Frady does become an assassin. And a good one. Beatty always had the chilly smile to get away with that sort of efficiency. And there is a provocateur in him: just look at the way he elects to be a girl when crowded by the belligerent redneck in the bar.

So *The Parallax View* isn't right, and its fateful climax is altogether too glib and tidy. But the scene on the aircraft is brilliant, and it shows Frady beginning to lose his mind. It's one of those films in which two odd minds (Beatty and Pakula), no matter that they were at war (for Beatty tended to oppose everyone in those days), were on to something. The goal within reach, I think, was that Beatty might have recognized his killer's face in a last shot. Just before he pulls a trigger.

Paris Nous Appartient (1961)

None of the first New Wave films took as long to make as Jacques Rivette's *Paris Nous Appartient*. In the late fifties and early sixties, it became a legend of penurious dedication and steadfast anxiety. For, despite the optimism of its title, this was a film about unease, paranoia, and not belonging. Truffaut (who became one of its producers along the way) spoke of it as "the most directed" of New Wave films. He might have added that it was the most intellectually thorough, the most pensive and pessimistic, the film most alarmed by the world.

Rivette had a loan from *Cahiers du Cinema*. The camera and the processing were on credit, and Rivette was given ends of film from other productions. Actors were hired as participants in the production—a way of saying they worked for nothing. And yet, the event that serves as the focus of the film's story is an amateur production of Shakespeare's *Pericles*, an undertaking done for its own sake and as a gesture of defiance to all the forces of materialism and mistrust that beset the city.

Gerard (Giani Esposito) is putting on *Pericles*, but he is devastated by the death of Juan, who was composing music for the play. Juan's death is a mystery—some say suicide, but there are hints of murder. Gerard starts seeing Terry (Françoise Prévost), Gerard's girlfriend and a rather sinister fatale figure. She is also close to Philip (Daniel Crohem), an American who has fled McCarthyism and who believes that there is a hostile conspiracy in the city, out to get him and to stifle life and liberty.

It's part of Rivette's great talent that he makes this threat feel immediate and modern, yet a relic of the cities dominated by Dr. Mabuse. One of the most resonant moments in the film is a private screening of Fritz Lang's *Metropolis* (Rivette had been a great admirer of Lang). Rivette's camera style is objective, quite distant and classical—he is in the Renoir line, though without Renoir's exuberance. But the editing is conspiratorial, always leading us to suspect that there is more to a situation than we grasped at first.

Paris Nous Appartient was written by Rivette and Jean Gruault, though it's clear that the script took on a life of its own over the years as the actors were encouraged to improvise. Charles Bitsch did the photography, and Philippe Arthuys wrote the music. Betty Schneider plays the young girl who is an inquirer after mystery and obscurity.

The film did not do well, though many good judges regarded it as the most rich and thoughtful of the first New Wave films. In *Breathless* and *Les 400 Coups* there had been an affection for Paris that deserved Rivette's title. But Rivette's film was far more political than anything Godard had done yet. It spoke to a mood that would be made manifest as the sixties went on and assassinations defined our peril.

Paris, Texas (1984)

The movies play with age in a way that tempts us, for it caters to one of our most absurd hopes, the one about staying young, and never dying, perhaps, yet glowing like the sunset with wisdom or something that has been acquired in the process. But *Paris, Texas*—haunting as it is—is torn apart by this problem. The film opened in 1984, when Harry Dean Stanton was at least fifty-eight. Nastassja Kinski then was twenty-four.

They are offered to us as Travis and Jane, a couple who have been married and who have a son, Hunter (Hunter Carson), who must be six. That would mean, almost certainly, that the child was conceived when Jane was seventeen. It's not that such things can't happen, nor that Travis might not have left the marriage four years ago and gone to live in the American western wilderness, so that Jane sent Hunter to live with Travis's brother Walt (Dean Stockwell) and his wife, Anne (Aurore Clément). And I can accept the possibility that Travis comes walking out of the wilderness, that he collapses, and that Walt is called up to rescue him. So that the broken family comes back into focus, and Travis must consider how he can save them all.

May I say that it would have been a different film if Travis had been played by the screenwriter, Sam Shepard, who was forty-one at the time, and handsome and commanding in a scarecrow kind of way. In other words, I can believe that the teenage Kinski could have fallen for him and driven him crazy. But I'm not sure that she would have noticed Harry Dean Stanton. Well, you may say, actors do as they are told, for actors are trying to execute the purpose of the writer and the director. And perhaps it is intended that Travis and Jane were "wrong" for each other from the start so that it is rather a union that Travis has dreamed.

There is a long sequence, set in a kind of brothel in Houston, where Travis seeks Jane out in the effort to persuade her to resume life with Hunter. Its circumstances are odd: The two characters cannot really see each other; they do not look at each other. It is unbearably emotional and extended, and it is wonderfully played by both actors. And it works: Jane is reunited with Hunter while Travis watches this from an unbridgeable distance. It is nearly as if he is dead.

Every frame of the film lets us know that its director, Wim Wenders, loves the West, as a real place and as a very theatrical setting. I daresay the same could be said for Sam Shepard. The music, by Ry Cooder, is about as perfect as such music could be, and Robby Müller's imagery is very moving. But it doesn't work, or cohere—even though it moves one, and I'm not sure that many films are as moving and as incoherent. It is shot through with a kind of attitudinizing male romanticism that one can easily see coming from Nicholas Ray, a man Wenders knew and loved and filmed at his death in *Lightning over Water*. And it is as uncomfortable as that film. I used to like it very much. I now see it as a "problem" film. And I wonder if I will live long enough to hate it.

Une Partie de Campagne (1936)

It is only forty minutes, and if by chance it was the first film you saw you might automatically conclude, Why should any picture ever be longer, or shorter? It is a Guy de Maupassant story, about a Parisian bourgeois family having its Sunday in the country. The young woman, engaged to a dead end, meets a man on holiday at the country inn. They have a brief sexual encounter. Was it love or just a moment's sunlight on an overcast day? So life goes on, ruined, or whatever. Who knows—perhaps it would all have been worse if the young woman had gone off with her adventurer.

Jean Renoir took his cast and crew to a place on the river, the Seine, near Marlotte. He hoped for sun, in the mood of the day-trippers, and there are flashes of warm light in the film, but most of the time it rained—and one doubts whether rain or wind ruffling the water have ever been filmed with such feeling. As if he foresaw delays and anxieties, Renoir elected to play the patron at the country inn, Père Poulain, and there he is pattering in and out of the action, doing his best to offer encouragement. You can see now how it is a trial run for *La Règle du Jeu*, an experiment in being behind and in front of the camera at the same time—in both cases, Renoir is the host at the uneasy party, doing his best to keep the event moving along.

All this happened in 1936 and was not released until 1946. How easy it must have been then for the film to pick up its coda: *"Des années ont passé avec des dimanches tristes comme des lundis . . ."*

But do not forget the astonishing company: Jacques Becker was an assistant director, Henri Cartier-Bresson was another; Claude Renoir was on the camera; Marguerite Renoir would be the editor. And then, watching and absorbing, there were Claude Heymann, Luchino Visconti, and Yves Allégret. Joseph Kosma would do the great music—can't you hear the waltz that drifts down the river from Sunday to Thursday?

Yes, of course, the picture is a kind of tribute to French Impressionist painting, despite the black and white. And yes, there is nothing like the sense of airy opportunity as Jacques Brunius pushes the shutters open and light floods into the inn along with a glimpse of Sylvia Bataille standing on the swing in the garden outside. There is no discovery in all of film history as profound as Renoir feeling out spatial relationship—and *feel* is the only verb to use there, for the optics and the intellect of it all are dependent on the quality of being touched or noticed.

There is the river, also, with boats making their way on the patient current. And there is the shocking close-up of Mlle. Bataille in sex, in love—as erotic as cinema has yet managed.

So, here it is, a "spoiled" film from 1936. But maybe in the sum total of everything a film is greater than its basis, more humane and tragic than de Maupassant.

Essential.

The Passenger (1975)

We are passive, we are passengers. We watch, we are voyeurs. We close our eyes, and let ourselves go with the passing adventure on the screen. David Locke is an American who works for British media as a reporter. He is a well-known figure. When he is reported dead in a seedy desert hotel in North Africa, there will be earnest obituaries on London television. His wife watches in pain.

We never learn much about that marriage, or David's London life. We never go "inside" him enough to know why it is that after a dispiriting day in the desert he goes back to the hotel and finds a chance acquaintance—a man named Robertson—dead from a heart attack. We do not know why Locke quietly sticks his own picture in Robertson's passport, picks up the dead man's diary, and sets out to make the enigmatic appointments he has made. It's a scene rather like the one in *Purple Noon,* where Alain Delon tries to become Maurice Ronet. But we know about that: it's Ripley wanting money, the girl, and glory. Locke just wants to sleepwalk.

You may not quite agree with my description of the "action." You may marvel that I call it "action." There are people who find this a very pretentious, implausible existential thriller. I think it is one of the greatest films ever made: *The Passenger,* by Michelangelo Antonioni, a thriller, a mystery, and a sweet, faintly sinister parable on being so loose or free to let the vehicle of narrative, or of film running through the projector, carry you away.

It's from a Mark Peploe story, with a screenplay by Peploe, Peter Wollen, and Antonioni. You could say it's an escapist fantasy in which a bored man goes to Barcelona, meets a lovely girl (Maria Schneider) who doesn't ask any questions—you could say it's a dream come true. Or you could say that it's a dark ironic shape in which a searcher, giving up his old way of looking, tries another way and finds it leads him directly into the perilous heart of the intrigue he was hoping to report. But now he is a participant, a part of the story. Maybe the girl is bait in the trap. Either way, it all ends up at the Hotel de la Gloria at the close of the day in one of the most beautiful and suspenseful shots ever filmed—one shot, an acting out of liberty or imprisonment, depending on your point of view.

It's Antonioni and Jack Nicholson, and when the film was a flop, for years Nicholson owned it and looked after it. The photography is by Luciano Tovoli. The cast also includes Jenny Runacre, Ian Hendry, and Steven Berkoff. For myself, I watch it once a year and find that it grows richer and more suggestive, so that—while I think I know it—tiny things of intonation, a glance, or a background action grow like the blooming of the new year. So I am still unsure after thirty years whether it is a tragedy or a comedy. Try to decide.

La Passion de Jeanne d'Arc (1928)

As the public threatens to become a mob with the burning of the Maid, Warwick orders up fresh weapons. There is a staggering shot—a track and a pan, but part of a wheeling circle—as chain and mace flutter out of the window in a castle by Le Corbusier. The set is abstract, the weapons are authentic; the camera movement is giddy and sickening. This could be one of the deepest evocations of violence in all cinema. And it is from Carl Theodor Dreyer's masterpiece on the trial of Joan of Arc.

Warwick looks like a kind of Mussolini figure, yet the clerics are from Dürer (Antonin Artaud and Michel Simon are two of them). There are at the same time great pains to be true to period—and a stirring, spartan modernism: and so we get shots of the medieval crowd, tumblers, contortionists, jugglers, but framed from drastic, low angles against a white sky so that they are cutouts and cutaways within the flow of imagery (Rudolph Maté did most of the photography). The film is based on two warring structures: the documents of the real trial, and the seething close-ups that justify the word *passion* in the title.

And it is a succession of flagrant, composed images: of upside-down soldiers scurrying forward like beetles; of the execution stake, scorched, black with the nail that bore the damning inscription; of Joan hunched over in the furnace; of tears like the worms in the unburied skull, slipping down gross faces; of crows in the sky like kisses at the end of a child's letter. On and on, without slowing or remorse—a demented certainty that only art can accommodate these terrible events.

Long after the film is "known" and "digested," long past the point of its being taken for granted as an obligatory thing, *La Passion* will shock you. And I suppose that some will make the argument that no film ever came closer to the truth of sainthood, God, and sublime acceptance—so is it religion at work? I don't feel that. I know that Dreyer was religious in his way, yet I feel the film comes out of a desperate agnostic spirit—filled with conviction over the cruelty of the world and the coarse stupidity of authority. Yet, late at night, on television—Turner Classic Movies believes in the film enough for us to believe in them—its harsh grandeur and breathtaking beauty need only a few moments for the spell to be back. It is one of the most inspiring of films, and its inspiration is more art than God.

Yes, of course, we must speak of Renée Falconetti's Joan in a commitment to film and character that is exemplary, ravishing, and tragic. She was a comedienne onstage, it is said. So be it. Decades later, it is her face that touches Anna Karina when she goes to the movies in *Vivre Sa Vie*. By then, not even Godard had the zeal or the shamelessness to do close-ups in quite that stark way. But the method still leads the medium on. We have not yet caught up with its modernism.

Pat Garrett & Billy the Kid (1973)

Begin at the beginning? How would you know you were there? So start at the end? Well, the end in this case has a habit of changing, and it comes so long after the first ending you can believe it's starting again. Except that these old friendships and their fights are never over. There is a walled garden in the Western that likes to have its petty arguments over the facts and the legends, and which one ought to lead in the dance. Don't let these desperate men get in that garden, for they'll shoot your flowers to shreds and they'll be merciless in making you see that with everyone such damned liars there are few facts left, but just the range of drink and paranoia and terror and glory in men's heads. Somehow these heroes have to find a way to forget the terrible tongue-lashing a wife can give them.

So once upon a time the film began with the last farewell of old friends, Garrett and the Kid, as one says he's getting a new job and the other says he sees no reason to move on because of that. Nowadays, it has a fraternal beginning some thirty years later with Garrett being assassinated—you can look it up; such things happened; the cattlemen's ring took its bounty in due course; and of course everybody who had ever known the Kid would be dead one day.

Meanwhile, this is one of the most complex American films—see it in any and every version you can get, but generally go for the longer versions and on no account accept anything that does not have the scene where Garrett, sweet from the barbershop, goes home and finds a wife who simply tears him to pieces. This is the sharpest scene in Peckinpah where a woman tells one of the men not just to go to hell, but to stay there, because he's there already.

It was always a film of episodes, as Garrett tracks the Kid, captures him, has him escape, and then goes after him again, headed toward the Pete Maxwell place on the bank of the river—and there Garrett will work it out at last and get the job done. It barely touches the surface to add that this story of pursuit is also one of the saddest of broken-buddy films, where one man has to put on a badge and a mustache while another writes *Ben-Hur* and another floats by on a river raft with a gun at the ready.

The film was butchered, of course, and it's hard now to see that Sam Peckinpah expected anything less. But steak is steak, and whether it's a jailhouse escape, a shoot-out at the river, or Lew Wallace offering the brandy, the film takes its moments with the rueful expertise of Billy tipping Harry Dean Stanton out of Rita Coolidge's bed.

Rudolph Wurlitzer did the script, and it comes out of deep research into Garrett and Bonney. John Coquillon shot the film. A basketball team edited it—give attention to Roger Spottiswoode and Garth Craven. Friends of the film (like Don Hyde) have looked after it. I watch it a couple of times a year, and derive as much strength and helplessness from it as I do watching the light go out at the end of the day.

Was there ever a better cast? Kris Kristofferson is as plump and cocky as a college quarterback who has five girls getting him sundaes. This is *the* James Coburn film. Bob Dylan is fancy, odd, and a treat—and his music may be the best a Western ever had. Jason Robards is a man you want to know. And then there's Richard Jaeckel, Katy Jurado and Slim Pickens in a great duet, Chill Wills, R. G. Armstrong as keep-the-change Bob Ollinger, Luke Askew, John Beck, Richard Bright, Matt Clark, Jack Dodson, Jack Elam as Alamosa Bill, Emilio Fernandez, Paul Fix, L. Q. Jones, Jorge Russek, Walter Kelley, and Rutanya Alda (as Ruthie Lee). There are even Peckinpah and his son, making coffins—a steady job.

Paths of Glory (1957)

As they made *The Killing,* Stanley Kubrick and his producer, James B. Harris, found a novel, *Paths of Glory,* by Humphrey Cobb, published in 1935, based on the actual execution of five French soldiers in 1915 for mutiny. Dore Schary would not pursue it at M-G-M, but Kubrick-Harris bought the rights for $10,000 and apparently assigned it to pulp novelist Jim Thompson for a first draft. It was Thompson—if you can believe this—who softened the real ending. He had the five soldiers pardoned, and the wicked general exposed. No one was more shocked by this than Kirk Douglas, when the project came within his orbit. So a new script was done, largely by Calder Willingham, which is close to the unrelenting film we know. So the piece that supposedly opened up Kubrick's misanthropy might have been a lot softer because of his urge to make a popular film.

As part of the insane pattern of trench warfare, two corrupt officers, Generals Broulard (Adolphe Menjou) and Mireau (George Macready), plan one more frontal assault by the French forces. This materializes as one of the great movie attack scenes ever done, with astonishing tracking shots craning over a landscape already shattered by prior disasters. The lighting cameraman was George Krause, but we know that Kubrick himself was hand-holding a camera during the attack, and it's probable that he is directly responsible for most of the ravishing photography.

The attack is a disaster, and the generals conclude that cowardice was the reason why. They decree that three men should be made examples in court-martials and immediate executions—no one doubts the verdicts. The three men chosen are Ralph Meeker, Joseph Turkel, and Timothy Carey, and the officer chosen to defend them was one of the leaders of the attack, Colonel Dax (Kirk Douglas).

We know that Kubrick was very much under the influence of Max Ophüls as he made this film (he had been considering remakes of some Ophüls material), and it's clear—in the trenches and in the chateau where the staff is quartered—he was imitating the immense, rapid tracking shots so favored by Ophüls. (It is also worth noting that Ophüls died during the film's shooting.)

The spectacular movements are matched by a relentless examination of the characters. Dax is a paragon, of course—for Douglas was the star accounting for a third of the budget. But the others, officers and victims alike, are seen like monsters in their cages: craven, dishonest, feeble—it is a panorama of weakness in which the old-fashioned flourish of Menjou and Macready fits perfectly with the unpredictable turmoil of Timothy Carey. Other cast members include Wayne Morris, Richard Anderson, and Emile Meyer (deliberately miscast as a priest—there is no comfort in this world).

Yet even Kubrick flinched. He could imitate Ophüls's shots, but he could not understand the feeling in the master's view of people. Still, he knew this was hardly box office, so he dreamed up the conclusion in which a German girl sings to a crowd of French soldiers. He chose Christiane Harlan—and in time he would marry her. It is an odd sign of sentiment creeping into an immaculately cold enterprise.

La Paura (1954)

La Paura, or *Fear* or *Angst*—think of it as misery—is the end of the Bergman-Rossellini attempt to present themselves as more than a great, noisy scandal. But the actor playing with Ingrid Bergman in the film, Mathias Wieman, said they were tearing each other apart, and the reviews said enough was enough. As for Bergman herself, she noted, "The world hated the Rossellini version of me, so nothing worked. And he was stuck with me. What did he want with an international star? Nothing. He didn't know what to write for me. And, of course, by this time we both knew it. It was something we did not talk about. But the silences between us grew longer . . ."

Rossellini gave up finally in writing original material for Ingrid. When he did, everyone decided that the tortured story was their mirror. So he found his agonized narratives elsewhere—this time in a novel, *Die Angst,* by Stefan Zweig, which was turned into a script by Sergio Amidei and Franz Treuburg.

Irene Wagner (Bergman) is unhappily married to a man who owns a drug company (Wieman). She has a lover, Erich (Kurt Kreuger), but he doesn't satisfy her either. Then a woman, Giovanna Schultze (Renate Mannhart), starts blackmailing her. Irene thinks Erich is feeding information to the blackmailer, but in truth it is coming from the husband. Irene is devastated. She goes to her husband's factory and is on the point of poisoning herself with some of its chemicals. But then she resolves to do better and to love her unhappy children.

Alas, the story is reminiscent of *Journey to Italy,* where the matter of being delayed by a religious procession is enough to make a change of heart in the unhappy couple—or in one of them. You can feel both parties willing themselves to try again when every piece of mounting evidence argues to the contrary. *Journey to Italy* is the one film in which the shift may work, but then only because of the accumulated lessons derived from the woman's survey of antiquities. There is never a piece of action to which a desperate actress could cling. These scripts are infernally intellectual and assertive—and all the while Rossellini refused every offer for Ingrid coming in from other Italian directors, like Fellini, Visconti, and De Sica.

Of course, the setup is as promising as *Stromboli:* the use of a drug company might have opened the marital story up to so many other interpretations. But there's also a stress on the need for confession here that seems like the Catholicism of the lapsed. Irene does grow as a character, and there are moments where her courage mingles with the emotional resolve of a great actress. But by now, how Bergman must have hungered for the facile storytelling of *Gaslight* and *Casablanca.* Real story is so restful when you're lost in therapeutic improvisation.

Soon after *La Paura,* Jean Renoir appeared, and he suggested *Elena et les Hommes.* Roberto will say no, she told him. I'll ask anyway, said Renoir, and this time Rossellini approved.

The Pawnbroker (1964)

"*The Pawnbroker* is a terrible movie yet I'm glad I saw it," wrote Pauline Kael. What does she mean by terrible? I think it goes to this conundrum: that the more earnestly you try to do a decent job with this fearsome subject matter, the more calculating or tasteless you may appear. Let's take an example. Sol Nazerman is a Jewish pawnbroker who works in Harlem. He lost his family in a concentration camp. Every anniversary of the loss is unbearable. A scene comes up where he tells the Geraldine Fitzgerald character what happened to his family. It is the crucial scene of the film, in that at last we understand the whole story.

With his production designer, the excellent Richard Sylbert, director Sidney Lumet searched for an apartment on the West Side of Manhattan that overlooked the New York Central railroad yards. And thus, to quote Lumet, "Throughout the scene you can see and hear freight cars being shunted from track to track. That kind of visual and auditory corroboration of a scene's context is invaluable."

Well, I wonder. I know what Lumet means and I can understand the logic of his process, looking for a corollary or an equivalent. So the trains are a reminder of the trains that took people to the camps. But the trains are also a constant abrasion—in the way that living in that apartment might get on your nerves. So isn't the pursuit of equivalence crass and dumb? Do we need the facts or the idea of concentration camps to be made "expressive"? Or does the "rightness" of the art direction become hideously trivial?

In the same way, Lumet and his editor, Ralph Rosenblum, experimented with three- or four-frame cutaways to show the intrusive memories of the camps that defy all our processes of suppression. It was a stirring effect—yet I wonder if it didn't just expose the vulgarity of film when confronting such material. It left *The Pawnbroker* seeming a very mannered, worked-out film, when maybe only naked simplicity can handle such things. Suppose the window referred to earlier shows just a wasteland, with a three-legged dog running around. Is *The Pawnbroker* less expressive or more?

I think this is the paradox Pauline Kael was getting at—and I know I count myself in the band of people at the movies who say, Please, if you're going to take me to a concentration camp don't do it too well. Because your skill is not quite the point. I am troubled throughout *The Pawnbroker*, though I do not doubt the sincerity of those who made it. The script by David Friedkin and Morton Fine is from a novel by Edward Lewis Wallant. Quincy Jones did a heartfelt score that I find excruciating. And Rod Steiger is Sol. For me, Steiger became a nearly unwatchable actor as he grew older, and I fear that *The Pawnbroker* was the decisive step on that journey. He was inventive, ingenious, and egotistical as an actor—and I suspect that in such a man, Primo Levi–like, the ego has been burned away.

Peeping Tom (1960)

In the late fifties, all over the world, a shudder passed through filmmaking, the passing tread of a ghost or a warning. It took away the old innocence, and stopped some filmmakers dead in their tracks. From others, it drew a confessional outburst that might be vindicating or self-incriminating. Around 1960 there is a cluster of revealing films which seem to know the game is up—the magic is over. And they admit it, uncertain whether to be proud or ashamed, exultant or horrified: *Rio Bravo, Vertigo, Touch of Evil, Some Like It Hot, L'Avventura, Hiroshima Mon Amour, Psycho, Through a Glass Darkly, The Exterminating Angel, Lola, Peeping Tom.* As I say, the moods are various (*Peeping Tom* and *Lola*), some films are ends and some beginnings. But some secret law of film's displacement of reality has been felt.

So Michael Powell makes *Peeping Tom,* and has every reason to be taken aback by its vitriolic reception, but none at all—unless he intuits that loss of magic—for giving up, for going away to Gloucestershire. After all, to a man like Powell, vitriol was syrup on his pancakes!

There is still not enough known about Powell in the late fifties. But let's offer these things: His great days (the wave upon wave of the late forties) were over. A drab surge of realism was coming to British film (it was exemplified in the Woodfall films) and it was the smack of documentary that Powell loathed. His partnership with Emeric Pressburger had ended, and it's clear how far Emeric guarded Micky against his worst arrogance. Without Pressburger, Powell was vulnerable. And the recent films had done poorly; they seemed out-of-date.

And so Powell makes an alliance with Leo Marks (a former cryptographer), and Marks pours out this story of a young man in film—a focus puller—obsessed with the relationship between film and fear. He likes to photograph women in the moment of their murder. It would be a color film (photography by Otto Heller), but it made London feel like the city where Peter Lorre's *M* is hunted, a place where every passageway is psychological and anxious.

Powell gulped down the script (and Marks offered it as a shooting script) and then added his own things: the legion of redheaded women; himself and his own son in the home-movie footage of Mark Lewis's tortured upbringing; and Carl Boehm (instead of Laurence Harvey) as Mark—surely Boehm could be Lorre's brother.

The result is a masterpiece full of dread, raw with the vulgarity Powell allowed himself even as he imitated the aesthete. It is cold, nasty, and alienated and it knows how far those things are akin to the reptile machinery of film itself. It is a film in which you cannot tell disgust from exhilaration, because it is gripped by the real sadism of a serial killer. It's no wonder critics were shocked. The film was so far ahead of the game. It was as if a hero had proved a torture master. And something in Powell (only fifty-five) felt compelled to admit not just to what he had seen, but to how far the stress on seeing—on being a camera—might be a moral disaster.

Penny Serenade (1941)

During this prolonged tearjerker, there is a birthday party where Applejack (Edgar Buchanan), the family friend, presents Irene Dunne with a box of handkerchiefs. "You can never have too many," he mutters shyly, or like someone who has read the whole script. Some movies are padded out with "laughter pauses"; this one gets to 118 minutes because of crying spells.

At first, everything seems promising. How could one resist the prospect of people as smart and eloquent as Irene Dunne and Cary Grant being married? But wait, Grant is a bit of a big shot here, yet with an air of unreliability beneath it all. You wonder if it's going to be one of his great performances. Well, they lose a child and decide to adopt—they squeak through the process, even if his income is uncertain. They want a little boy, but they settle for a girl named Trina.

All of this is in a screenplay by Morrie Ryskind, from a Martha Cheavens story, that uses the awkward framing device of Dunne listening to old records accumulated during a marriage but on the point of divorce—it's the only way the title works. They handle the baby. There is even a droll scene where as the adoptive parents pass the hot potato back and forth, so Applejack steps in and gives the baby a bath. The time comes when probationary adoption has to be approved and Grant has lost his income. The film never says why, and never explores his aversion to work or discipline. But he goes before the adoption official (Beulah Bondi) and a judge and works his way toward tears. Then, after her first Christmas play, the daughter suddenly dies—off camera—from an unexplained illness. The couple crack up, and they are on the point of splitting forever when Beulah Bondi calls again with news of a little boy just like the one they asked for in the first place.

It was a Columbia film, directed by George Stevens, and Cary Grant was actually nominated for an Oscar. It's an excruciating experience, not only because the intelligence of the central players is strangled in the parent trap—they never talk about anything else—but because the step progression is relentlessly determined to get the tears out of us. George Stevens is not that much in evidence, though the monotonous household interiors are filmed (by Joseph Walker) with as much variety as possible.

Made on the eve of war, *Penny Serenade* was a big success, presumably because of every fear of loss it touched on. Not its least problem is that the children are so obvious and uninteresting. So American? Thank God, in real life, they manage to be so much more varied than the ones found for Hollywood pictures. The infant at the adoption hearing, a two-year-old, is used shamelessly for reaction cutaways, and her somewhat older sister is a bore—is it a malady of boredom that sweeps her away? But children will lose interest if their parents talk about nothing but the children. Here's a PhD thesis: that hardly anyone in Hollywood had ever experienced a normal family life, and so hysterical dysfunction mounts.

People on Sunday (1929)

The conventional history of German cinema in the twenties and thirties still functions in a poisoned nutshell, it's from Caligari to Hitler, the story of expressionism, formalism, and vigorous design eventually crushing life and real light in the medium. It's halfway true and half-baked, and nothing gives the game away so quickly as *People on Sunday*—or *Menschen am Sonntag,* that delicious urban trifle, put together by as cocksure a group of kids as ever collaborated on a new sort of movie. So, on the one hand, *People on Sunday* is like a launching pad for so many young talents. On the other, it leads to a simple question: How was this made in Germany in 1929? And the how is no small matter: It's as if the eye of G. W. Pabst (the closest Germany came to a naturalist or a humanist) had been joined with that of the French New Wave. It's as if the iconic fatalism of Louise Brooks suddenly succumbed to the sun and shadow and the flirty spontaneity of Anna Karina.

That comparison is not remote: for this is, quite simply, one of those weekend pictures where guys photograph their girlfriends—almost as a way of getting them into bed. Forget and forgive the brooding cityscapes of *M* and *The Testament of Dr. Mabuse,* this is about girl watching and inviting pickups off to the park for a picnic, a beer, a swim, and who knows where it will lead? This is a film about boredom and the craze for tanned skin. There were boys and girls in Germany—not just driven archetypes who never saw the sun! Just as its title suggests, it's not about the archetypal humiliated doorman, or Lulu and Jack the Ripper, it's about "people" on Sunday, ordinary people. Indeed, it is one of the few films that shows how between 1919 and 1939 you could be German and ordinary.

I hope there is no need to stress so large a political message, quite apart from its artistic or cinematic meaning.

How did it happen? Well, the oldest of the gang, and very likely the one with the camera was Eugen Schüfftan. He was a very technical photographer and soon he would work for Duvivier and Carné, but in the German context I suspect it was Schüfftan who loved the real light that fell in summer, a quality that comes back in Leni Riefenstahl's *Olympiad* and even in some of the burnished views of Nuremberg in *Triumph of the Will.* Billy Wilder supposedly did the script from an outline by Curt Siodmak—and it's tart, saucy, sexy. The direction was shared by Robert Siodmak and Edgar G. Ulmer. And Fred Zinnemann helped load the cameras at first.

But the eye-opening seductive force has to do with Berlin, the real light, the feeling of summer stupor and the mutual sensuality of a cast with names nobody knew—Brigitte Borchert, Christl Ehlers, Annie Schreyer, Wolfgang von Waltershausen, and Erwin Splettstösser.

Pépé le Moko (1937)

It is one of the great ideas in film: A Parisian gangster, a jewel thief and a bank robber, has to take shelter from the increasing police scrutiny; so he hides in the Casbah in Algiers—the Arab part of town, a no-go area for the police; but then along comes a beautiful socialite, a Parisienne, who catches his eye—he is a romantic; and in time he gives up the Casbah to be with her—and he is taken.

It came from a novel by Henri La Barthe, and it was produced by the Hakim brothers—Robert, Raymond, and André. They were Egyptian, but *Pépé le Moko* was their launch, and it led to an extraordinary and diverse career as producers (it included *La Bête Humaine, The Southerner, Plein Soleil, L'Eclisse, Eva,* and many others). They got Julien Duvivier to direct the picture and Henri Jeanson to do dialogue for it. They also elected to shoot some location footage in Algeria, while making a superb Casbah set in a Paris studio—with production design by Jacques Krauss. The photography was by Marc Fossard and Jules Kruger, and the music was a clever mixture of French romantic and North African.

Still, in history it rates as a Jean Gabin film. Gabin was thirty-three, not far from beautiful, but tough-looking, too, and while he became known as an actor who worked with Carné and Renoir, he owed a lot at first to Julien Duvivier who had cast him in *Maria Chapdelaine, La Bandera,* and *La Belle Équipe*, before making him the gift of Pépé le Moko, Parisian and North African, famous yet anonymous, very realistic yet self-destructively in love with love and with Mireille Balin, a beautiful former fashion model who would also have a great success with Gabin in Jean Gremillon's *Gueule d'Amour* (1937). In two-shots, she was elegant and he was raffish, but there was an erotic charge in their friction that was unmistakable. It's a bit of a mystery why Mlle. Balin did not last—she may have been set back by the way American interests sought to kill every print of *Pépé le Moko* once its remake, *Algiers* (1938), was set up.

That was a Walter Wanger production, directed by John Cromwell, in some places on a shot-for-shot basis lifted from Duvivier. Charles Boyer now was Pépé (not nearly tough enough) and Hedy Lamarr was Gaby (let me say it: not as beautiful as Mireille Balin). The American version also starred Sigrid Gurie, Joseph Calleia, Alan Hale, Gene Lockhart, and Johnny Downs. The French film had included Line Noro, Lucas Gridoux (as the sleazy cop, Inspector Slimane), Gabriel Gabrio, Fernand Charpin, Marcel Dalio, and Gaston Modot.

Of course, that kind of imperial suppression of competing films was common, and nearly always stupid. In recent years, however, Duvivier's *Pépé le Moko*—shot and created with skills worthy of Michael Curtiz—has reappeared in very good prints, and now the odd vulnerability of Gabin is reestablished. He was a great star, and one of the world's most natural screen actors.

Performance (1970)

Performance is a mirror: You look in it, and it shows you a kind of self you fear or dream of. If you were alive in London in the 1960s, the experience is certainly touched by nostalgia, though it leaves you knowing that you never quite had it that bad or that good. If you're on the artistic side, then the story teaches you that you can be a hard man. But if you're from the underworld, then it gives you heart—you might be an artist, too. It's part of the chronic English addiction to noir. It's a fairy story, poised between the godheads of Aleister Crowley and Jorge Luis Borges. It has moments that belong to the history of the musical. It has passages worthy of an anthology of the most pretentious films ever made. It takes itself so seriously that it can be very funny. And it has useful hints on how several people can inhabit one bath.

Clearly, it's romantic in its notion that the outlaw and the artist are alike, or twin figures. That comes from Donald Cammell, a remarkable fringe figure in film history, never satisfied or resolved, a suicide finally, but an emblematic hero in the rushing progress of change in Britain in the sixties. He wrote the script—he was the source of the ideas in the film. Then Nicolas Roeg came on board as his codirector and as the film's cameraman, perhaps because Cammell needed technical help, but also as a way of helping Roeg into a directing career.

Cammell's script was enriched a good deal by the input of David Litvinoff, someone on the edges of the art world and the underworld. Sandy Lieberson was a key figure as the producer. When Warner Brothers hated it, Frank Mazzola helped edit the final version. Christopher Gibbs was a design consultant.

It's the story of Chas, a gangster on the run, and Turner, a rock singer in exile from the world. Cammell had wanted Marlon Brando and Mick Jagger in the parts. He ended up with James Fox and Jagger. They are both good enough to hold the film in place, though the most powerful figure onscreen is Anita Pallenberg as Pherber, the seductive impresario.

Performance has to be seen—it is very visual. But it is very heady, too—and that element requires patience. The film may not have worn well. Cammell made other films, but never the masterpiece he required. Roeg became a very interesting director, and then a terribly vague figure, deeply affected by Cammell-like urgings. The film is not anywhere near as good as the stories that surround it. But if you ever doubt the tempest of repressed sensuality and pretension in the English soul, then *Performance* is a film to grapple with. By now there is enough written about it to nearly bury the film. So hold on to moments, like Jagger singing "Memo from Turner." Also with Michèle Breton, Stanley Meadows, Johnny Shannon, and Allan Cuthbertson.

Persona (1965)

It could not be simpler. A great actress, Elisabeth Vogler (Liv Ullmann), was playing in the last performance of a production of *Electra*. In the second act, she stopped. She would not take a prompt or a cue. It lasted a minute. Then she went on again, as if nothing had happened. She laughed afterward—she said she had this terrible fit of laughter in her. She had supper as usual with her husband. But next morning she was speechless. "This state has now lasted for three months." Tests reveal nothing in the way of a health problem or a hysterical reaction. These are the notes given to Nurse Alma (Bibi Andersson) as she prepares to meet Elisabeth Vogler. This is the start of Ingmar Bergman's *Persona*.

The nurse is amiable, decent, professional—I daresay she takes some pride in having common sense, a practical nature, a basic belief in people being healed. I mean, a nurse has got to believe that, just as an actress has got to hope that there are people out there who will be reached by the messages she believes she is sending. Anyway, the nurse cannot stand the silence. So she begins to talk and the film settles into a rhythm that we know—from being at the movies: one person talks and the other listens—and the listener becomes more powerful, for the more the talking person talks, the more surely plea and desperation creep in. And Alma the sensible is a mess—why do you think nurses wear starched white clothes, with a watch clipped to their lapel, if they aren't in terror of disorder?

But Alma has become an actress, too. It may be that in her jumbled life she has never talked so much to anyone, never performed, and never had the chance to find that level of self-expression. And thus Alma comes to the discovery that actresses know, and which sometimes tempts them into silence: that they are being used by the listeners, that they have become fantasy creatures, imaginary figures, personalities to play with. It could not be simpler: It is black-and-white, a little over 80 minutes, a film that might have been made over a long holiday weekend for next to nothing. And it is about vampirism and the power of one personality over another; it is about acting and being; it is about performance and silence. And it is what we had for films once upon a time. It is beside the point to say that Ullmann and Andersson are good in the picture. Rather, they are an event of primary importance: No one should be allowed to act professionally without seeing *Persona*. Of course, in life one cannot impose those rules. All I know is that with students—not just of film, but of every subject—I have shown *Persona* and had the conversation that followed go on and on until natural darkness overtook us. It could not be more complicated, or less lucid. It is as if Elisabeth Vogler fell silent in *Electra* because of her own memory of the film. We are in performance: It is a religious condition.

Peter Ibbetson (1935)

Gogo and Mimsey are childhood sweethearts living in Paris. But when Gogo's mother dies, an uncle ships him off to London. He grows up to be Peter Ibbetson, an architect, but not a happy man, in the nineteenth century. In Paris, on a visit, he meets a girl, Agnes, and remembers Mimsey. A job sends him to Yorkshire to restore stables belonging to the Duke of Towers. He meets Mary, the Duchess of Towers, and feels he knows her. Why not? She is Mimsey from his past. When Peter tries to run away with Mary, the duke intervenes and is killed in an accident. Peter is given the blame and life imprisonment. His back is broken. But he can still find Mary in his mind.

Perhaps aided by the barrier of subtitles, and the luster of Charles Lang's photography, André Breton was the first surrealist to pounce on this Hollywood film, made at Paramount, as a tribute to *l'amour fou*.

It was taken from the novel by George du Maurier (Daphne's grandfather), published in 1891, and certainly based in dream experience. But in 1935, how consciously was that past held up as an aim? Constance Collier adapted the book, and the screenplay was worked on by Vincent Lawrence, Waldemar Young, John Meehan, and Edwin Justus Mayer. Director Henry Hathaway was young, a devotee of Westerns and horse-riding films, yet intrigued by fantasy. No, he is not exactly the person likely to draw the idyll of romantic dream to the surface—though such a figure, Josef von Sternberg, was more or less at Paramount at the same time. What would Sternberg have done with it? Or is it possible that only a straightforward approach had a chance of making the subject work?

As always, look at the picture: Look at the aura in Lang's imagery and the elaborate, antique sets—by Hans Dreier and Robert Usher—with many suggestions of separation. And then look at the starry stillness of Gary Cooper and the impassive, somnambulist beauty of Ann Harding waiting to be occupied. There really was something happening. You can watch *Peter Ibbetson* as just the rather strange story it claims to be. But once you see the window to dream, it is irresistible, and the starry presence of Cooper is an amazingly clear path to follow.

No, I don't think this really suggests that Hathaway or Gary Cooper was poised to do the works of Magritte or Max Ernst. But equally the Hollywood film, so bent on action and character, is a dream we behold. *Vertigo* looks like a thriller until you realize that the outward mystery is silly compared with the inner malice. In other words, *Peter Ibbetson* is a lesson in how to look. You will find a few people who can hardly live without the film, and who treasure it as the key that opens the locked door. John Halliday is the Duke of Towers, Ida Lupino is Agnes, Virginia Weidler is Mimsey, and Dickie Moore is Gogo. Take a lesson, for there is hardly a flat movie with Dickie Moore in it—or Cooper—or Lupino. (If it had been me, I'd have put Lupino in the Harding role.)

The Petrified Forest (1936)

Robert Sherwood's *The Petrified Forest* opened on Broadway in 1935 and was esteemed for its wisdom. The title referred to a desolate stretch of Arizona, between Gallup and Indian reservations. The action takes place there in a roadhouse where a rather self-conscious and plaintive prophet of doom in the world, Alan Squier (Leslie Howard), will oppose a brutal gangster, Duke Mantee, and his response to depression and poverty. It was talky, but the Western setting was novel and exciting, and the play caught a current mood of cozy foreboding. Onstage, Mantee had been played by Humphrey Bogart in what was his biggest success to that date. Wearing no makeup and keeping his beard stubble, Bogart reminded audiences of Dillinger, who had just escaped from prison.

Warner Brothers led the open bidding on the play rights, and they at first announced Leslie Howard and Edward G. Robinson in the movie. But Howard stood by a promise to Bogart: If Warners wanted Howard, then Bogart must repeat as Mantee. He got the deal with $750 a week for three weeks.

Henry Blanke was the producer in charge, and he hired Archie Mayo to direct, while getting a screenplay from Charles Kenyon and Delmer Daves that is faithful to the stage work. Bette Davis was cast in the female lead role, the waitress who dreams of being a painter. Sol Polito was doing the photography, and art director John Hughes built a huge version of the roadhouse—it feels large enough for all the airy talk about humanity and the end of the world.

For some reason, they imported great quantities of dust and grit from Arizona and this began blowing about in the air conditioning on the sound stage. Illness and damage to equipment resulted, and the picture was proving extra expensive because the languid Howard was invariably late to turn up and serenely unaware of being in charge.

The story ended with Howard dead in Bette's arms and Bogart escaped—and it had cost $500,000 already. Was this a con or art? The question was asked very seriously at Warners, and some wondered if the high-mindedness of the drama didn't require a title or two to say what it was really about! Today, it looks like a very stilted show, and one can think of movie gangsters or tough movie producers who would have killed Howard's Alan off early just to stop him talking.

This may account for why Bogart's Mantee got such good reviews—he was a relief with his trust in rough action and put-down lines from old fight films. Indeed, by the time it opened, Warners had decided to give Bogart third lead status. He was established, at last, as a villain.

The Petrified Forest also starred Genevieve Tobin, Dick Foran, Joseph Sawyer, Porter Hall, Charley Grapewin, Paul Harvey, and Eddie Acuff. Though it had been a prestige production, it was shut out in the Academy Award nominations.

Phantom Lady (1944)

Perhaps he was going mad—I mean Cornell Woolrich (1903–68), arguably the most distinctive figure in the history of American noir. Woolrich was writing so much that as he completed *Phantom Lady* as a novel it was already serialized in a pulp magazine as *Phantom Alibi*. He was persuaded to adopt a pen name: William Irish was the name that came up. And at much the same time, the deeply unhappy Woolrich decided to go back to the Hotel Marseilles (in New York) and live with his mother. *Phantom Lady* is a magnificent book, in which a man unhappily married and uneasily placed in an affair elects to spend a whole evening in the city with a strange woman he meets in a bar. A number of apparently vivid incidents occur in the course of the evening. But when the man gets back to his apartment, two impassive men are waiting—policemen. The body of his dead wife is in the bedroom. He is the number one suspect.

That first chapter has been titled "The 150th Day Before the Execution," and the novel unfolds as the man's attempt to prove his innocence and find the alibi woman. Once he is incarcerated, the quest is carried on by his secretary. The quality of the book rests in the surrealism of this quest and our whole growing suspicion that the man's account of her may have been deranged. In the artistic sense, the question as to where she is or whether she is should never be answered. In the book, Woolrich was driven to pages of dotty explanation, best left unread. He was within reach of a masterpiece.

The movie followed quickly, and the key figure in its development was Joan Harrison (Hitchcock's trusty and very skilled assistant). She was associate producer on it for Universal. She got Bernard Schoenfeld to do the script, and she found Robert Siodmak and freed him from rather trashy horror pictures for his true métier. In turn, Siodmak got Woody Bredell to do the photography—every bit as startling and groundbreaking as their work together on *The Killers*. This is black-and-white that crackles and shines like a cellophane raincoat. You know if the woman had a scent you could catch, it would be nitrate—deadly nightshade.

Of course, the movie has to resolve its ending, and so a pretty obvious villain may be discerned, lurking, with a polite smile. In other words, the film becomes conventional. But along the way it has quite extraordinary scenes—as witness everything involving the hophead drummer Cliff Milburn, played by Elisha Cook, Jr. He was dubbed supposedly by Buddy Rich, and the sexual transference between Cook and Ella Raines in those sequences is such that you guess the censor lived with his mother, too.

The movie is a noir delight, with Alan Curtis, Franchot Tone, Aurora, Thomas Gomez, Regis Toomey, and Joseph Crehan. But if the narrative obsession could have been slipped, if Woolrich's great dream could have been honored, then you would have one of the great puzzle pictures, a movie fit for "Rosebud," a labyrinth with emptiness at the center, a story in which we are never quite sure whether the storyteller is wicked or demented. But it could be tried again.

The Phantom of the Opera (1925)

It is said that *The Phantom of the Opera* cost Universal over $1 million—and the picture turned big profits. Yet it was Lon Chaney's last film at Universal, the studio where he had started. Thereafter, he followed Irving Thalberg, his friend and supporter (he thought), to Metro-Goldwyn-Mayer. Yet his first film at the new home, the fascinating *He Who Gets Slapped*, cost just $172,000, and it was clearly a triangle film, with John Gilbert and Norma Shearer as important as Chaney.

It's also significant that the pictures Chaney made at M-G-M were on a much smaller scale than those at Universal. *He Who Gets Slapped* is 85 minutes; *The Unholy Three* is 72, *West of Zanzibar* is 65, and *The Unknown* and *London After Midnight* were less than an hour. And, of course, *London After Midnight* is one of just four Chaney films that do not survive. No one means to dump all that blame on Thalberg, but the pattern surely reflects a different way of using the actor—and perhaps a basic disdain of horror.

So it's a real treat to look at *The Phantom of the Opera*, worth all of its 111 minutes, fabulously photographed by Charles Van Enger and with some of the most potent sets in silent film, designed by E. E. Sheeley, Sidney Ullman, and Ben Carré.

The story is the one that will not go away: the novel by Gaston Leroux, first published in 1910. Erik (Chaney) is a deformed musician who lives in the cellars and sewers beneath the Paris Opera House. He loves Christine (Mary Philbin), a singer with the company, and he wants her to get lead parts. He kidnaps her and takes her to his subterranean realm. She rips off his mask and sees his hideous features. She is released, but she tells others about Erik, and in an immense finale she returns to the depths, defeats his plans, is reunited with her true love, and sees Erik thrown in the Seine.

Rupert Julian was charged with the direction, but he was apparently so difficult that a good deal was handled by Edward Sedgwick and Chaney himself. But this is authentic myth material, not far from "Beauty and the Beast," and soundly based in the concept of the underground world. The great Ben Carré (who had worked at the Paris Opera) did most of the designing for this, and someone knew how to frame and photograph the beautiful scenes of the Phantom taking his stunned beloved by tunnel and canal, deeper toward . . .

The face that Chaney reveals is not hideous by modern standards: Indeed, a face so alarming almost relies upon not being seen. But the key scene of the unmasking is superbly done, and the instinctive awareness of the unspeakable withheld but then delivered is profound and stirring. I'm not sure if any male actor in silent film digs deeper into our being now than Chaney at such moments. Thalberg may have flinched from horror (or thought it a touch vulgar)—but Chaney is the lode.

The Philadelphia Story (1940)

As I write this book, I begin to realize how many of George Cukor's films have to be included. Some are landmarks—you have to have *A Star Is Born, Gaslight,* and *Born Yesterday.* Some are fascinating failures—*Bhowani Junction.* Some become models—*David Copperfield.* And now I'm at *The Philadelphia Story,* which is only one of the essential American comedies.

And what a lovely thing the story of the *Story* is: how Katharine Hepburn was given the label "box-office poison" and thought to get rid of it; how her amiable would-be lover and producer Howard Hughes helped pay for it; how she got Philip Barry to write the play; how it opened in March 1939 and ran 417 performances with herself, Joseph Cotten as C. K. Dexter Haven, Van Heflin as Mike Conner, and Shirley Booth as Elizabeth Imbrie. And how it was the story of a stuck-up heroine, too perfect and chilly to feel enough, who is brought back to life and her very suitable first marriage on the doorstep of a second. The point is not stressed, but this scheme is Jane Austen–like in its focus on getting a paragon to behave naturally.

The movie started out as very much something Hepburn negotiated with Louis B. Mayer; she was one of the few stars who really got on with him. She had part ownership in the play and had asked for Gable and Tracy as costars. Mayer reflected and saw fit to teach her who was boss. You can do it, he said, but with Cary Grant and Jimmy Stewart—you see how brutal some moguls could be. Don't forget that Joseph L. Mankiewicz was the official producer on the venture, or that Donald Ogden Stewart was hired to do the screenplay.

At Metro, it was all too easy for the production values to reflect Barry's deep-seated belief that the rich are wonderful people. And this is one of those movies, screwball or verging on it, where wealth and style, wealth and manners, wealth and good clothes really do go together and give a lift to life. Joseph Ruttenberg's photography is like a high-key salon. Adrian did the clothes. For the first time in its young life, America began to seem like a cool place.

Hepburn shared in all this beauty. She found a modern look, with softer, longer hair that was becoming, and she held to it for several years. And she does fall for Mike—you feel the giddy rapture. Yes, it's odd that Stewart got the Best Actor Oscar instead of Cary Grant—not that Stewart is ever at fault. And yes, we need to note Ruth Hussey as Liz Imbrie, and all the rest of the cast. But Cukor knew just what he was doing, and he made a love story in which we are not sure until the very end which guy Tracy Lord is going to go with. Thus the knockout finale and one of the best last shots in pictures. You won't believe me—look it up—but *Rebecca* won the Best Picture Oscar that year. Not that *Rebecca* isn't pretty good, and so on.

The Piano (1993)

The Piano is one of those films that leaves one marveling at America's failure to imagine the inner life of its own earliest peoples. Of course, we have had our Western, and we are grateful for it, but the Western externalizes every issue. Whereas any traveler in the real West of today knows that it is a place of the spirit, where immense desolation looms over the human figure. We know the old cliché of the Western's "lone rider," but so few of them seem to have felt solitude.

Jane Campion wrote *The Piano* on her own—whereas she had often written in collaboration before—and it seems to me that she never sought to root this parable in studious research on early life in New Zealand. So things happen as they do in a story. Ada (Holly Hunter) is Scottish. She has a daughter, Flora (Anna Paquin), but we know very little about her early life—we do not know why she does not speak, any more than we understand why her piano means so much to her.

The two women and the piano are on a ship to New Zealand, for Ada has engaged (by post) to marry a settler named Stewart (Sam Neill). Stewart does not appreciate or like the piano. He leaves it on the beach, where it is rescued by Baines (Harvey Keitel), another settler. Baines buys the piano for land Stewart wants, and Ada agrees to teach him to play. Their bargain is blunt: For every note on the instrument, she is to give herself in sex to Baines. This transpires. Ada remains silent, but the feeling is very passionate. Then one day, out of neglect or whim, Flora gives them away to Stewart. In his rage he slices a tip off one of Ada's fingers. But Stewart is so horrified that he gives his wife to Baines. On another voyage she lets the piano go overboard and nearly drowns herself. Then she is better again. She speaks and plays with her silver-tipped finger.

There were some critics who said it was a smokescreen of the exotic and the erotic meaning very little. I think it is a fascinating story of pride and need, solitude and alliance, on which the stark beauty of New Zealand locations offsets the perilous state of these pilgrims. And, as with the best of Campion's other work (I think of *In the Cut*), it is more usefully seen as surreal than as naturalistic.

Stewart Dryburgh's photography is outstanding—wintry, cold but gorgeous. The lack of sunlight says a lot about Ada's lack of speech. Michael Nyman did a wonderful score. The acting is uncanny: Holly Hunter had never seemed to have such size or severity before. Keitel managed a very difficult part and the idea of a man inclined to sink into savagery. Sam Neill was as good as he always is in a supporting part. And Anna Paquin managed to make most prior child actors seem trained, coy, and phony. Hunter and Paquin won Oscars, as did Campion for her script. I have to say that she has not been as good or as piercing since. But *The Piano* is warning enough that she had wild and dangerous things in her, as well as a serious resolve to see the female side of our music.

The Piano Teacher (2001)

On the box that holds the DVD of *The Piano Teacher* (by Kino), it says that the film tells the story of "a middle-aged classical piano instructor who is trapped between her rigid passion for music and her suffocating home life." Well, you have to start somewhere. In Elfriede Jelinek's novel, this woman, Erika Kohut, is in her late thirties, and her mother is said to be old enough to be her grandmother. Late thirties, I think, is not quite middle-aged. And when the film opened, the actress playing Erika, Isabelle Huppert, was forty-six. The actress playing her mother, Annie Girardot, was seventy.

So something has shifted. The mother feels "right" in age. Erika is older than the novel intended—but Erika now is Isabelle Huppert, and that surely alters our response to the film. You see, Erika—a stranger when we open the novel, and for an instant as Michael Haneke's film begins—is not simply a woman of unusual strictness or severity who teaches piano to very good students in Vienna. No, she is a woman who attends pornography salons; who, before dinner one night, steps into her bath and, with a razor blade, cuts at her private parts; and who will demand of one young student, Walter (Benoît Magimel), that if he wants her he must engage in precise sadomasochistic sexual rites, binding her and beating her. It is a long letter she gives him in which she has written out the instructions—rather as if she might be giving him notes on a performance of Schubert.

It is Isabelle Huppert doing and asking these things, and you do not have to step very far back from the enthralling but alarming film to realize that, but for her, there would be no film. *The Piano Teacher* was not prohibitively expensive, perhaps. Still, it only proceeded to win prizes at Cannes and a place on art-house screens because Mlle. Huppert agreed to do it. Most reviews therefore observed her courage, her artistic daring—all fair enough—but things that get in the way of Erika Kohut's desperation and her . . . need (if that is the word).

Michael Haneke's *The Piano Teacher* is a riveting film; I think it's one of the few radical works of the last few years. And you can argue that it is about the conflict between a fevered sexual imagination and Erika's actual frigidity. But it is also, whether it likes it or not, a film in which celebrity, and unquestioned acting, have brought perilous material before us.

And one thing I want to stress, which may seem minor, is as follows. In the Kino account of it, they claim Erika has a passion for music. That is not stated in the book—and the book, by the way, is better than the film (Elfriede Jelinek is a Nobel Prize winner). Erika is offered as a great, unsentimental, uncompromising teacher. That she may be. But she is indifferent to the music in her being, and so is the character in the film. And here is my point: No one who had come close to Schubert's music (to pick just one composer) could lead the savagely compartmentalized life that Erika suffers. Therefore, she is a music teacher as a front. Therefore, she is very ill . . . And I am not quite sure that great acting and great reputation should be given to anything as unique (i.e., as rare in humanity) as such illness. But to begin to argue this matter, you have to see it.

Pickpocket (1959)

Dare one suppose that as Robert Bresson came to make *Pickpocket* something like an old-fashioned fantasy excitement overtook him—like Howard Hawks with a flying film, or Martin Scorsese in any scene where Joe Pesci is about to launch an unbridled attack on the least deserving person in sight? I do not mean to be facetious. I revere Bresson. But I find it delicious that the man who had applied himself so austerely to the occupations of country priest and would-be escapee in two previous films seems so thrilled by the recurrent actions of *Pickpocket.* Perhaps it is inevitable: Granted the occupation in question, and Bresson's nearly neurotic concentration on hands slipping in and out, how could this film not sometimes seem like on-the-job training, if not an encouragement like that in *Shane* where Alan Ladd teaches Brandon De Wilde how to use a six-gun?

Suffice it to say that Bresson, the model of thoroughness, went from day one and a first idea to opening the picture (75 minutes) in ten months. I can hear Richard Widmark giggling about the guy being a natural dip, and I note (en passant) that the cinema's two best pictures on this nefarious art end up side-by-side in this book. Yes, there is also *Harry in My Pocket,* which could have had an educational grant behind it, but no Bressonian intensity.

I would go a little further. Is there not some extra bond or attraction between the camera and the chosen actor (or presenter) in *Pickpocket*—Martin LaSalle? So much of what Bresson did in casting and directing was to get in the way of our identification with a character. On the other hand, so much also took that furtiveness for granted, and treated it as a forgivable sin. And I think the camera (at least) is in love with LaSalle. Thus, it moves through the film, at his hunched shoulder, with an uncommon urgency or curiosity, eager to assist him yet also preying on and for his being apprehended, or caught red-handed. This is the moment at least to ask the question, Am I crazy, or was Bresson gay? And if he was, can't we say so at last without the pantheon going into destruct mode? All I am getting at is the hand-in-glove complicity between the pickpocket and the presence of the filmmaking process.

I do understand that the religious allegory requires that he be captured and brought to grace in recognizing the girl who loves him (or his soul). And I am very happy with that treatment, rather than a film that shows our pickpocket getting sleek and cocksure in the job. But I watch films closely, and I love *Pickpocket* without being driven to exploring handbags on the subway or the texts of the Roman Catholic Church. I think there's a little bit of Montgomery Cliftism going on here. What I'm trying to say is that cinema has a unique kind of suspense whenever high church gets into the very low. And this is a heaven of a movie.

Pickup on South Street (1953)

What do the humorless slogans of the Cold War mean to the daily grind of a small-time pickpocket? Nothing! And so the dreads and pressures of a bogus era break upon the rocks of Richard Widmark's crooked grin and fatalistic personality—and the lesson is clear that Samuel Fuller was at his best whenever he had a hero or protagonist nobody would think of taking home to mother. This is authentic pulp cinema—and the pulp is the sediment that might come off the East River and be served up in the smart rat city as caviar; it is the open wound in Candy's face that, since he put it there, Skip McCoy considers he has every reason and right to explore. And it is the contents of Skip's mind—greedy, needy, mean and small, but a citizen of pulp, one who knows his rights and loves to snarl them in the face of the cops.

The opening is exemplary: the bored, slut face of Candy (Jean Peters) swaying on a sweaty subway; the insolence of Skip as he looks her dead cold in the eye, while the fish of his hand is in her bag. It could just as easily be up her private passage. And she would likely be as impressed. There's a wonderful sardonic humor to this hysterical toughness, but an unflinching certainty that that is all these lives are about. Widmark was an odd bird: an actor whose own nature fell aside as he itched to snarl, giggle, and push old ladies and their wheelchairs downstairs. Fuller was nearly alone in later years in knowing just how nasty the decent man yearned to be, and he may have had a great understanding of the masked malice.

But Fuller was just as daring and relentless in knowing that an American movie—one made for Darryl Zanuck, even—could make this Skip more and more loathsome, without ever losing us. Because whatever demon lurked in Widmark, we have it, too. We long to be dangerous, unwholesome, and laughing as the world closes in.

What Fuller supplies is the cheap talk, the scummy urban compositions in which the cockroach makes his sidelong movements, and the amazing battery of moving camera shots—cranes, trackings, and those moments where the camera just muscles in like pressure—that embody Skip's aggressive, taking attitude to the world. And, as we have been told so often, expect the cockroaches to survive if the Big One ever comes because they know their priorities and they are mercifully free from sentimental allegiance.

If you want more proof of that, just look at the two women in the film: Candy and Thelma Ritter's Moe, one of the sublime, exhausted hangers-on in film noir, or crime movies or whatever you want to call that genre. Her weary indifference to her own interest still bumps up against the foolish moment of her death. She is an outcast, a scrap of a thing, a nothing, yet she feels herself as grand as Falstaff, and just as subject to pain. She does not want to die, but she's tired. It is the film's glimpse of pathos and of a life worth living.

William Inge's *Picnic* came to Broadway in 1953, and it ran 477 performances, with Ralph Meeker as Hal, the ex-athlete vagrant who comes back to his small Kansas town in time for the Labor Day picnic, and to shake up so many settled lives. Joshua Logan directed the play, and just two years later there was the movie, at Columbia, with Logan directing Daniel Taradash's script.

Logan deserves great credit. Inge's play had been called *Front Porch* at first, and it never had the extended Labor Day sequences that are the luxuriant heart of the movie. But Logan got Harry Cohn to let the production go to Kansas. That brought in a real grain silo, and it allowed the film to find a meadow and an enchanted river where the flaming day changes (so reluctantly) and we get one of the best twilight scenes in American film.

Give credit also to William Holden, who artfully bends himself into the shape of Hal, without strain or pretension. Holden was a hip, urban type by nature. You suppose that he could handle himself, without being an athlete. But this Hal is beginning to be muscle-bound, to suffer from sports injuries, but when Holden takes off his shirt at one point you can feel every female character waver.

Yet Holden makes Hal decent, kind, sad, so that he wants to be important to everyone he finds in Kansas. He really wants to teach bookworm Susan Strasberg to dance. And he never notices her lush older sister, Madge, coming up behind, like a pink moth in the night.

And then it is, on the dock, with the river dark and burnished, that the music shifts from the local band to a studio orchestra playing "Moonglow" (the theme from *Picnic*, as it was called). Madge picks up Hal's beat and sidles onto the dance floor. The begging romance of the film's old-fashioned story is out in the open, and a kind of pure movie glamour lasts for as long as the music.

Kim Novak is Madge (it was Janice Rule on stage, and apparently she was grand). Novak is close to amateurish. When she tries to say "gentlemen," you wonder why she's being employed. But then she says "Hiya" to Hal, and you're watching a Kansas Juno. Her entry into the dance is shy, to say the least, but that suits her character. The movie is a very sweet dream about Hals and Madges finding each other and rescue in the Midwest. (Inge wrote that "happy" ending against his own better judgment.) It's not too far from shameful rot.

But don't let *Picnic* ever fade. There are CinemaScope compositions on the riverbank—one with Madge in a swing and poised goings on in the far distance—as great as Renoir. And the dance scene never loses its charm, even if it leaves you feeling pretty sheepish about settling for charm. Never mind—without charm, the movies would not have lasted. It is the key to the door called dream.

Picnic at Hanging Rock (1975)

St. Valentine's Day, 1900, in the Australian state of Victoria—a glorious summer's day. A party of adolescent schoolgirls will go from Appleyard College to Hanging Rock for a picnic. Hanging Rock is a volcanic eruption, perhaps millions of years old, a sign of the geological age of Australia and of a silent history in which it might have been many things. Is the rock beautiful or violent? Phallic or elemental? The girls in Victorian costume and corsets celebrate the heat and the festival by climbing up the rock. But at the end of the day, three of them and one teacher are missing. In the succeeding days, one girl is found alive. Another girl, who did not go on the picnic, is found dead, and the owner of the school, Mrs. Appleyard (Rachel Roberts), kills herself because her school cannot survive the scandal.

Joan Lindsay's book of the same name was published in 1967, and was written and presented with every air of reportage. Everyone took it for granted that such an incident had occurred, until detailed research failed to find any substantiation. The very school had not existed. There was no record anywhere of the deaths. People were not dismayed at this; they saw it as a fable on the relationship between Australian civilization (a pretty ribbon tied around the outside of the country) and the constant need to explain its age and emptiness, whether in terms of human ties to nature, or to some more mysterious or religious forces. It became clear that the book really was a novel, and the natural growth of a country consumed by the imagination and its sleeping hinterland. So you can say that *Picnic at Hanging Rock* is the festival of teenage girls on St. Valentine's Day becoming brides to nature. Or whatever you like to see in it.

Peter Weir's film, and its screenplay by Cliff Green, do not allude to the "fraud" of the novel—if that is the right word. And it's easy to see the anticlimax that comes with the knowledge—for in truth, this is the kind of case that almost demands a sort of Sherlock Holmes figure if the full clash of reason and the occult is to be made clear. The novel has such a figure in the young man Michael Fitzhubert (Dominic Guard), the last to see the vanished girls, and someone who falls helplessly in love with one of them.

The photography, by Russell Boyd, lends itself to the romantic-erotic aspects: the respectable Victorian nymphs in the wilderness; the blaze of the sun and the enigma of nature. So the sinister aspects of "disappearance" are as pantheistic as they are suggestive of crime. But removing people in a film is a tricky business—think of *L'Avventura*—in which an easy get-out is some kind of murder mystery. Weir does not take that route, and I think it's clear in the overall pattern of his work that he is susceptible to mysteriousness, without necessarily pressing the "ominous" pedal. So *Picnic* remains a curiosity, trapped by its own cunning perhaps, yet an admission of—even a volunteering for—the kind of spiritual subtexts to the epic riddle of Australia. *A Cry in the Dark*—really based on fact—is just one example of the obsessive wondering. So is *Walkabout*. And in turn that makes it intriguing as to why the American movie has so rarely felt those tremors of intent in the wild and empty places.

The Picture of Dorian Gray (1945)

Oscar Wilde's novel, published in 1891, is known yet not often read: In London, a beautiful young man, Dorian Gray, has his portrait painted by Basil Hallward (a real painter and an ancestor of Gloria Grahame, whose birth name was Hallward). Gray turns to what the blurbs call a life of vice—though it is somewhat vague in the book itself—and as he grows older, so Gray retains his "perfect" looks while the portrait (a living thing) seethes with the manifestations of his depravity and corruption. To put it mildly, it's a very moral tale, prim and censorious compared with the glorious liberty of Wilde's wit. Nevertheless, the novel counts as a classic, and I'm sure it had attracted filmmakers over the years, even if many of them must have shied away at the realization that you could hardly show the portrait without it being a letdown.

Albert Lewin (1894–1968) was not to be deterred. He was a graduate of New York University and Harvard. From being a drama and film critic for the *Jewish Tribune,* he moved into the industry and became a chief assistant to Irving Thalberg at M-G-M. He produced a number of important films (including *Mutiny on the Bounty* and *The Good Earth*) and then rose to become a director, starting with *The Moon and Sixpence,* in 1942. He then declared that he wanted to make *The Picture of Dorian Gray.* Louis B. Mayer wondered if he could stand such a thing, but Lewin assured the boss that he had the funds to do it independently if necessary. Whereupon, Mayer said do it at the studio.

Lewin seems to have believed that his greatest asset was the young actor Hurd Hatfield for the title part. (Apparently Garbo was also eager to give it a try.) Hatfield was a stunning looker and a competent actor, and he has a waxen look that serves him well. But it's difficult to make Gray interesting. What's far more impressive in the picture is its look, and its design. Gordon Wiles did a number of drawings that were incorporated as very elegant sets—the whole thing smacks of *The World of Interiors,* or a house where Lewin might like to live. Cedric Gibbons and Hans Peters helped bring this to life, and Harry Stradling's black-and-white photography is very impressive (he won an Oscar for it).

But early on you get the feeling that Lewin is filming the art, the statuary and the marble floors, instead of the people. The cast is good, but the film suffers from the discretion of the book and the great difficulty in filming debauchery head-on (as opposed to obliquely). Angela Lansbury is outstanding as a singer who is killed, and the rest features George Sanders, Donna Reed, Peter Lawford, Lowell Gilmore, Miles Mander, and Moyna MacGill.

And, yes, we do see the portrait, in a splash of color. It was painted specially for the movie by Ivan Albright, and it's not the worst job at invoking corruption, decline, and so forth. But the power of that picture depends on the horrified faces of those seeing it. There are far uglier things than Albright's painting in so many polite salons now. What frightens most of us is the mirror.

Pierrot le Fou (1965)

Like lovers on a beach at dusk, a giddy romance and a political gangster story are entwined, neither one trusting the other. And from the moment of reunion, as the babysitter arrives at the Griffons' apartment, so there is a lingering glance between the two of them, elasticized by the wide screen, full of longing and affection, but with hardly a glimmer of trust. You look at me with words, and I look at you with feelings, Marianne tells Ferdinand—and that struggle is not just a weather system for the couple, it's the storm in Godard's own head between being a writer or a filmmaker. For, if Samuel Fuller—the marooned director at the grisly cocktail party—is right, and cinema is about emotion, then the question hangs in the air: Is Jean-Luc Godard its ideal practitioner? After all, his protagonist can't read to his young daughter without expecting her to grasp the world of Velázquez and its relevance to *Pierrot le Fou.* (God damn it, call me Ferdinand, he bites back—as in Céline.)

So it's Louis-Ferdinand Céline versus Marianne Renoir, sense and sensibility, instinct and intellect, but which is which? Is she really less thoughtful than he is, or does he truly bow to her in terms of sensory immediacy? It hardly matters once we start getting those desperate, smoldering glances from Anna Karina, right into the lens, warning of infidelity and time. For this is the film that marked the end of the marriage between Godard and Karina, and sooner or later that would signify Godard's withdrawal from the attempt to make a new kind of B movie. Who could blame him? He'd done about a dozen of them in one of the great bursts of radical work the cinema has seen. And he had lifted Anna Karina from pinups to the pantheon.

Pierrot is based on the pulp novel *Obsession,* by Lionel White. Godard fashioned a story line as the company traveled south through France. But there was never anything as tidy as a script. So we get what they found: street theater; car theft; arbitrary slaughter on the roads; rivers and forests and the feeling of warmth and sun tan; the summer gaze of the South with the death's head using it as a mask. And the battle between pleasure and the visual goes on against commentary interruption and words—just words written on paper, wordplay, the attempt to order momentary experience. The unifying forces in the rhapsodic untidiness are Raoul Coutard's photography (feeding on red), Antoine Duhamel's funeral music and the wistful songs, the wild medley of supporting players (Germanic thugs, a dwarf, the Princess Aicha Abadir, Jean Seberg in a movie house, Raymond Devos on a pier telling an eternal story).

Plus the extraordinary presence of Belmondo and Karina. Of course, this is Karina's great test in a part that is half Lolita and half Phyllis Dietrichson. She is magnificent, pained, sensual, impulsive; she is the moment, the seconds. While he is the museum, the bookstore, the manuscript, the corrective, reflective process. And still a man brought back from living death so that he can die properly, And the way to death for him is a simple equation: *l'amour = la mort.* The last great romantic movie. The end of Godard's youth.

A Place in the Sun (1951)

Theodore Dreiser's *An American Tragedy* (1925) had been filmed before, by Sternberg in 1931, with Sylvia Sidney as the female lead, playing Roberta Alden, the girl Clyde Griffiths meets in the shirt-collar factory. But it's distinctive of George Stevens's remake that now the rich girl Angela (Elizabeth Taylor) has become central in her rapturous agony with George Eastman (Montgomery Clift). The Clift-Taylor bond is often cited as an example of screen chemistry. And that leaves the factory girl (Shelley Winters) as not just plain, whining, and awkward but as someone the entire audience wants to see murdered—so great is the gravitational pull of the "perfect" romance between George and Angela.

To say that this is a discredit to Dreiser and unfair to life is not going far enough. *A Place in the Sun* cheats. On the other hand, it is an overwhelming romance, and one of those films that lets us share the madness of unfettered desire. This result would not be as interesting if the film were not meticulously made. But one can feel Stevens's own pain over his hero's quandary and the telephoto close-ups that he employed for the lovers' big scenes—the kisses so close and so far—are inspired and very moving.

The screenplay was the work of Harry Brown and Michael Wilson, though Ivan Moffat had an important role as an assistant. And it's plain from the script that the social ironies in Dreiser are being abandoned for a straightforward story of American humility making it all the way to the top. At the outset, George hitchhiking (in a leather jacket) sees a highway poster of a girl who resembles Angela and who is advertising "Eastman" clothes (and happiness in wealth). He is the poor sheep of the family, with a religious mother (Anne Revere), but he is Montgomery Clift, arguably the angel of black-and-white cinema in 1951. And when we meet the rich people—the Eastmans *chez lui*—they are decent, urbane, good-natured—very far from the rich as Dreiser knew them. Angela looks like Elizabeth Taylor's eighteen years, but she is a paragon, and she eclipses any sad memories of Shelley Winters.

And so the death occurs (though the film lets us think of it as an accident, despite George's deep desire for it). The scenes in the woods near Tahoe are very atmospheric, and the gloom that gathers lasts through the trial to the death cell. William Mellor's photography is outstanding, and the Franz Waxman score is one of the most potent Hollywood ever made.

So a great novel has been gelded, and a "murder" is set aside by our own longings. And it works. What remains is one of the most intriguing examples of Hollywood offering desire in place of realism, common sense, or morality. Stevens, the score, and the script won Oscars, and shelley winters was nominated, but the film hinges still on the exquisite distress of the impossible glance between Clift and Taylor—one of the great Hollywood romances just because it was ruined.

Planet of the Apes (1968)

It was in the air. Anthropologist Desmond Morris had a popular best seller with *The Naked Ape* in 1967. In Stanley Kubrick's portentous *2001*, the world begins with apes tossing their bone in the air and deciding what to do with it. The first entirely synthetic pop group was achieved in the laboratories in the sixties: the Monkees. And Arthur P. Jacobs, a producer, had the idea for *Planet of the Apes* at Fox. There was a novel, by Pierre Boulle (the author of *The Bridge on the River Kwai*), and it was itself a little best-sellery in the notion that a hair's breadth separated us from the apes (try taking your ape to *Bringing Up Baby*—they don't get it). The screenplay of the first film was given over to Michael Wilson and Rod Serling. Serling, of course, was the man behind *Twilight Zone*, on television, and a talented, witty writer. Alas, that sprightliness seldom found its way into *Planet of the Apes*.

But the idea was that a band of American astronauts under the dogged command of Charlton Heston crash on an unknown planet. They don't know where they are or what time it is. But the realization dawns that this is Earth still in an age when the apes are in charge. Thus, the men have to avoid the condition of slavery that is regarded as their proper status. This allowed for a fair amount of sardonic commentary on the supposed differences between the two, most of which was delivered by running characters played by Kim Hunter and Roddy McDowall—the Diana Trilling and Gore Vidal of the ape world. As you may imagine, the ape kingdom was run by far worse brutes and tyrants, riding on horseback and given to very nasty ape jokes.

Franklin Schaffner directed the pilot (as it were). And I can only say that it's a style that monkeys wouldn't sit through. I have no leg to stand on, because the first film had rentals of $15 million, thus encouraging sequels like *Beneath the Planet of the Apes* (1970) and *Escape from the Planet of the Apes* (1971), in which the direction was reassigned and Heston gracefully withdrew. As it was, Chuck had looked pretty good in animal skins, and he had had a thing going with Linda Harrison, who was rather more in her own skin.

The points made about the irony in the reversal of roles soon palled, and when Tim Burton tried to revive the franchise in 2001, there seemed nothing left but cruelty and the ape suits. But we all love monkeys, and Kong—whether a trembling doll or a man in a suit—can be very winning. Still, for myself I think I prefer real gorillas and Sigourney Weaver picking edible bugs out of each other's hair in *Gorillas in the Mist*, or Charlotte Rampling eyeing her monkey in Nagisa Oshima's neglected *Max, Mon Amour*. Best of all, I like the moment when the ape head comes off in *Blonde Venus* and you can see that it's Dietrich. As for the preposterous idea of the apes running the world—let them make sense of the movies first!

Platinum Blonde (1931)

Until late in the day, Columbia was confused over what to call this film. One title was *The Gilded Cage*—as if to describe the fate of the young reporter who marries into a high society family and then feels trapped. But others favored *Gallagher*, the name of the woman reporter who loves the man and then waits to see if he will give up his social prize. Late in the day, the studio harked back to *The Blonde Lady* (referring to the society girl—the other point of the triangle) but went one better. Taking advantage of Jean Harlow's unique hair, they called the film *Platinum Blonde* and even launched a contest to see if anyone in the audience could copy the exact hue of Harlow's hair. No one could.

Yet, truly "Jean Harlow in *Platinum Blonde*" is not as exact or acute as "Robert Williams in *The Gilded Cage*." Stew Smith (Williams) is sent by his paper to the Schuyler mansion because the son of the house is having a romance with a showgirl. There are incriminating letters involved. Stew gets hold of them and instead of asking for money he simply gives them back to Anne Schuyler (Harlow). That sets off a romance. A marriage ensues. But Stew isn't "right" in the Schuyler house, and in the end he learns that and he goes off with Gallagher (Loretta Young), his more than loyal chum.

Now, extract the real story from the title and you have: Young man becomes infatuated by class. He marries into it and learns his mistake. He opts for the real class of his natural partner. Add to that the fact that Robert Williams died of peritonitis just a few days after the film opened. He was thirty-two, with a striking resemblance to Scott Fitzgerald—lazy, sexy, a great talker, a wit. How good was he? Well, good enough to make us realize quite forcefully that this film is mistitled and that the rapport between Williams and Loretta Young is the most interesting thing on view.

So, it's an odd dislocation, and no kindness to Harlow, although Frank Capra throws in a couple of great shots where you get Jean's breasts on a plate. One can't tell about Williams, but there's enough there to leave one wondering and wistful. Young is better than she ever was (and there's a shot of her bare back to die for) when she added moral underlining to her work. But the idea of class (or privilege) being something a smart young man might be seduced by is so much more intriguing than two-thirds of the ideas in American comedies. And this film does lead its hero toward a quite necessary divorce—in turn, that's a way of defining vitality and freedom as something the rich don't have.

So, almost incidentally, it's one of Frank Capra's most appealing pictures—written by Dorothy Howell and Jo Swerling, with dialogue by Robert Riskin from an idea by Harry E. Chandlee and Douglas Churchill. More still, for 1931 this is very agile and alert and a film that shifts its own basis as it proceeds. What seems like a comedy is really a love story. And there's a lesson: Hide your true genre in the lineaments of another.

Platoon (1986)

Platoon is clearly the high point of the fierce, self-lacerating arc known as Oliver Stone. And it says something very intriguing, something occasionally remarked upon by nations that have had to fight the U.S., which is that, despite every strenuous argument of justification for each and every war, there is something in some Americans that just loves war, and which often loses sight of foreign enemies because it is really waging a contest within, a battle between purity and its opposite. One element of this America is its inescapable habit of fighting other Americans. *Platoon* illustrates this thesis perfectly. For here is a movie that bothers to say very little about the reasons for the Vietnam War, but sees it in the lurid light of the partisanship within America. Thus, it's the battle between two sergeants, Barnes (Tom Berenger) and Elias (Willem Dafoe)—between compromise and the denial thereof. It's another version of the struggle between Robert Ryan and Aldo Ray in Anthony Mann's seminal picture, *Men in War* (1957).

Yes, it's true, Oliver Stone was in Vietnam, and he has not been shy about the way the experience shaped him. Moreover, I think it can be said that the sense of the jungle, the unexpected terror of combat, and the sheer urge to survive are brilliantly rendered in *Platoon*. The feeling we have of being there in that jungle with these guys is overwhelming, and the film offers no relief or rest. That is where its power lies, just as its meaning is in Barnes vs. Elias—the conflict between an austere, cruel, warped martinet and a loose, hip, druggy freedom fighter. Of course, the hero-worshipper in Stone makes both men extraordinary fighters: The gentle Elias has magical instincts and exceptional courage. And Barnes is the kind of sergeant fearful troops cling to. But Stone's own allegiances are too clear and too obvious. He wants Elias because Elias doesn't believe in being in Vietnam.

The film and its power struggle are weighed through the eyes of a newcomer (Charlie Sheen), and virtually every minute is electric. Of course, the opposite is true in real war: boredom is the constant climate—and boredom is never going to be Oliver Stone's subject. His platoon is under intense pressure, and it follows that a kind of hysteria dominates the film. This is unquestionably powerful, but it makes it hard for complex ideas to breathe and work upon us. So *Platoon,* I think, has dated and simplified where other Vietnam War studies seem more challenging.

But Stone would have said he wanted to convey the feeling—and at that he succeeds. The photography, by Robert Richardson, was groundbreaking in its natural power of hallucination. The rigorous editing, by Claire Simpson, won an Oscar. And the platoon members are a terrific team of young actors. Apart from the leads, there are Forest Whitaker, Francesco Quinn, John C. McGinley, Richard Edson, Kevin Dillon, Reggie Johnson, and Keith David.

It won the Best Picture Oscar as well as Best Director for Stone.

The Player (1992)

Even if you accept the view that *3 Women* is a major Robert Altman film (and not everyone does), still there had been years of wandering or uncertainty after 1977. Fifteen of them, filled with theatrical adaptations, a few real films, but nothing that seemed to grip Altman himself. I suspect he felt this, because *The Player* opens with maybe the second-most-famous opening shot in American film—an immense, intricate tracking shot. Number one is Orson Welles's *Touch of Evil,* and that film marked a return of one of Hollywood's mavericks. It suggests that, from the outset, Altman knew *The Player* was his material and his comeback.

But all of that depends rather on whether the Hollywood depicted in this sardonic film is a place anyone would want to get back to. As written by Michael Tolkin, and adapted from his novel, *The Player* is a shrewd, general satire—shrewd because it picks on no real villains or no one really responsible. And if no one is hurt or offended, then the satirist can hope to stay in work. Nevertheless, and granted that it was made on the eve of the real dominance of computer and cell phone (so that it now has a technological charm), this is a very good, tart portrait of Hollywood attitudes to others and the self. Indirectly, therefore, it is a lucid explanation as to why the films coming out of the system are so compromised, and negligible.

In the end, despite its wit and smarts, *The Player* is similarly neutralized. But nothing takes away from a much younger man's deftness with the camera (and the microphones) and his uncanny ability to get at the nuances of social interaction. The thriller structure is neither thrilling nor especially interesting: it's a kind of MacGuffin, the string that holds the bait—the money, the success. What the film gets brilliantly are the power shifts, the paranoid intimations, the total insecurity. And Altman's Steadicam coverage and long takes are very good at catching that vulnerability. So, in matters of pure style and the use of space and barriers, windows, and vantages, the film is far more interesting than its set "story." As so often in Altman—and this is key—you feel that he doesn't quite care what happens to people. There really is a misanthrope in there. *Short Cuts* is the film *The Player* is preparing for—and a tryout with its soft, treacherous light.

Still, it's an entertainment for anyone interested in L.A., the movies, or Altman, and you'll never get bored with actors like these to study: Tim Robbins (always equivocal as Griffin Mill), Greta Scacchi (wasted), Fred Ward, Whoopi Goldberg (not very good), Peter Gallagher, Brion James, Cynthia Stevenson, Vincent D'Onofrio, Dean Stockwell, Richard E. Grant, Dina Merrill, Sydney Pollack, and many others, some of whom are what are known as cameos.

Playtime (1967)

Films cannot help but be of their time, and Jacques Tati's *Playtime* had the misfortune of being reviewed in most places in 1968, a year in which it was hard for anyone of a radical temperament not to be uplifted by the possibilities of change and by the energy of young anger remaking the world. And, of course, anger is one of those emotions expressly missing from *Playtime*. Yet, over the years, its reputation has grown, and so I recall with great pleasure the 2006 festival at Telluride when *Playtime* in 70 mm was reaffirmed as a masterpiece—and by no one less than Jean-Pierre Gorin, perhaps the epitome of "1968."

As he introduced the film, Gorin made a distinction between comedians of pathos (Chaplin) and those of space (Keaton), and said that perhaps Tati was both. But it is a great mistake, I think, to see *Playtime* being in any way affected by that path of social criticism that deplores modern times. The world in *Playtime* may be silly, vain, pretentious—it may involve us all making idiots of ourselves—but there is no blame, no axe to grind. Rather, the fatuous world it describes in such omnivorous, loving detail is a source of joy.

But this kind of talk is idle if one does not stress that *Playtime* is a movie. It is a film that stays steady and affirmative in its faith in the long shot and the crowded frame. The camera is backed away, at an amazing (and amazed) distance, from which it can contain what seems to be an entire city. It comes as a shock to hear that Tati actually built this city, or the various aspects of it that intrigued him: the airport, the office, the restaurant, the shop. We feel we are seeing Paris, or any metropolis. That is a tribute to extraordinary precision in the art direction, but it is also a proof of the tranquil, amiable gaze that Tati maintains. There is nothing like the inclination to see ugliness, or unkindness, that actually builds pathos in Chaplin. Rather, Tati is charmed by the existence of things in space—and that is the beauty in Keaton.

The "action" of the film consists of the passage of a band of American tourists. These are the chief source of plot or dialogue, although their words are remote, isolated from synchronization, and so dubbed in as to seem dreamlike. Yet they are often funny and sharp enough—and they were done for the film by the columnist Art Buchwald, whose delicious squat figure appears on-screen toward the close of the movie.

The restaurant scene is the set piece of humor, simple duration, and human silliness, but as it builds—and as the viewer is looking this way and that so as not to miss something—so the sense of beholding the turmoil of life is irresistible. And the result is unique. Yes, this society is accident-prone and deserves to collapse or destroy itself, but its energy, its persistence, is beautiful and inspiring. It's like watching cells grow and divide. What alarmed 1968, I suspect, was the authentic optimism of the film, its exhilaration, and the gentle growing fondness between, say, the dark girl in green and Tati himself, who wanders in and out of his own world, auteur and bystander. Truly, a great film, the secret to the crowded frame.

Plein Soleil (1959)

It is often called *Purple Noon* in English-speaking movie houses, and it is an adaptation of Patricia Highsmith's *The Talented Mr. Ripley*—the novel that was remade forty years later by Anthony Minghella under the name elected by Ms. Highsmith. So it's worth pointing out that the René Clément film is the more faithful to the novel, and it is the one that has Alain Delon as Tom Ripley.

Clément is not much known today, despite his admirable resistance picture, *La Bataille du Rail* (1946), and the enchanting *Knave of Hearts* (1954), which has Gerard Philipe in London with some delectable women. And *Plein Soleil* is a very good psychological thriller that feasts on the contrast between the heat of the Riviera and the chill in Tom Ripley's calculating blood. As shot by Henri Decaë, it is a picture where sooner or later blood is going to have to take its place in the palette of sun-drenched primary colors. But what is most impressive about the film is the way the mere look of Delon is allied to the stealthy, voyeuristic way in which we are made to watch his conspiracy against friends, order, and life. To be brief, we become accomplices to Mr. Ripley—that is his talent, and that is the amoral journey that always interested Ms. Highsmith.

But so much more could be said about "the mere look of Alain Delon." I don't think there's any point in being strenuous or determined about trying to make a case for Delon the actor. He is probably too vain, too spiritually reticent, to be seen making any effort himself. But he is, sometimes, a presence of nearly infinite complexity or mystery. This happens in Jean-Pierre Melville's *Le Samourai* and even *Rocco and His Brothers*. It is a possibility that nearly always offers. But there is no film that watches so steadily or with such patience that gradually we begin to learn how to feel the corruption, and more, beneath the sheer beauty of his angel of death.

And the great skill in *Plein Soleil* is that we are so caught up in watching through Delon's eyes that the moral torpor, the narcissistic fatalism, really creeps up on us. As a result, this is one of those rare films in which beauty itself begins to sicken or depress us. And I daresay M. Delon had no idea of what was going on.

Of course, the Minghella film is richer by far, and it spreads its intimations of homosexuality as a response to Tom's "loneliness" as thick as jam. I put loneliness in quotes like that because for Highsmith that isolation is exhilarating and supreme. She takes it for granted; Minghella regrets it. That only demonstrates that Minghella is a more decent human being yet a more compromised artist.

His film has Jude Law—though it is perverse to cast him as Dickie Greenleaf instead of Ripley. *The Talented Mr. Ripley* is not Highsmith but it is a very good film with maybe half an hour of greatness. But Delon's cold gaze is still the razor that could slice Law and Matt Damon as thin, translucent, and fleshy as slices of prosciutto.

Plenty (1985)

In the late eighties, David Hare was much involved in film. He directed *Wetherby* (1985), *Paris by Night,* and *Strapless.* His play, *Plenty,* was brought to the screen by Fred Schepisi, and he adapted the novel, *Damage,* for Louis Malle. He remains an intriguing figure in the movie world (he also adapted *The Hours*) but he has not directed in a while and he has plunged back into a period of intense theater work, where he sometimes directs his own plays. Even that intermittent involvement establishes him as one of the more interesting English directors of the last twenty years. *Wetherby* remains a wonderful film, and *Plenty* is unforgettable.

When the play text was published, Hare added "A Note on Performance," which says, "To those of you who perform the play abroad, I can only say that its Englishness is of the essence." And yet, I don't feel that this film suffers from having an Australian director or an American lead actress. Hare adds in that "Note" that the English have a special way of being cruel, but quietly, to each other. And it is key to how his people fight each other very often, but there's no evidence to suggest that other peoples don't understand the hushed spite. Or aren't good at it.

Plenty was a play written in twelve scenes, first done in London in 1978 with Kate Nelligan as Susan Traherne. It covers the years from 1942 to 1962. Susan (Meryl Streep) is seen first as a resistance agent in German-occupied France. She is a little like the Virginia McKenna figure in *Carve Her Name with Pride,* except that she survives, albeit with shattered nerves. She is moderately famous because of this early life. She does talks on the radio. But her life is going nowhere, and this clashes violently in her spirit with the feeling during the war that there would be great days afterward. So she feels cheated by the peace. Betrayed by modernity, her nerve shot, she may also be bipolar—as written and played, Susan has a leaping unpredictability that is alarming. She is miserably married to a slow-moving diplomat named Brock (Charles Dance), and when she starts to make scenes she is an albatross around his career.

Susan is a rich part, and Streep is as extraordinary in the film as she is unappealing. Yet she's beautiful, talented, smart—she is a warrior who worries at her own guts. There's not a lot of story, and on film it's clearer how far some episodes repeat others. Instead, this is a portrait of a person who is likely to end her days locked up. Hare wanted the play to be enigmatic, yet perhaps the film adaptation needed a little more clinical diagnosis. If Susan's fierceness comes from having known terror, and being ruined by it, that could be more fully explained. Especially since Hare did the screenplay himself. But the very English thing about Hare is how his people make a fortress out of their problems.

The supporting cast is outstanding: Tracey Ullman, Sting, John Gielgud, Ian McKellen, Sam Neill, Burt Kwouk.

Point Blank (1967)

Some kind of criminal job has been done, and the three robbers meet in the abandoned Alcatraz prison, in San Francisco Bay, to share the loot. There's Mal Reese (John Vernon), Walker (Lee Marvin), and Walker's wife (Sharon Acker). But Reese turns on Walker, shoots him, leaves him for dead in a cell, and goes off with the wife.

Reese is not likely to have made a mistake. But we see Walker, wounded, falling into the famously cold and unfriendly waters off Alcatraz. And then night turns to day and we are on a tourist boat, looking at Alcatraz. Walker is gazing at the water, lost in thought. But someone else on the boat talks to him—it's Yost (Keenan Wynn), and he gives Walker the first leads in how to go after Reese and the $93,000 (his share in the job).

This is the opening of *Point Blank*, taken from a Richard Stark novel, *The Hunter*—Richard Stark being Donald Westlake. The script was by Alex Jacobs, and John Boorman was hired to direct, an Englishman—what did he know of Alcatraz and film noir? Enough, for this is not just a cool, violent pursuit film, it is a wistful dream and one of the great reflections on how movies are fantasies that we are reaching out for all the time—it's singin' in the rain again, the white lie that erases night.

With all the force of an implacable sleepwalker, Walker goes after his precise sum of money. Piece by piece, he takes out the levels of the Mob organization on the West Coast—is that what Yost wanted? The action goes from San Francisco to Los Angeles and back again. Walker finds his wife, and she kills herself. He finds his wife's sister, Chris (Angie Dickinson), and she agrees to help him. The steps involve a used-car lot, the rivers that run through L.A., a nice out-of-town house in the Hollywood hills, and back to San Francisco again, to Fort Point, for the payoff.

Walker is as in-our-face as Lee Marvin and as naturally brutal. But does he listen to what is said? Does he change his mind? Or is he dreaming? Is he actually dead or dying back in the cell on Alcatraz, constructing an immense journey in the name of revenge? Is his success real, or is it a modern myth?

The photography (Philip Lathrop) of California is harsh and schematic. The color schemes are bold, brilliant warning—Angie's orange dress in her great seduction scene is like flame. The supporting players include Carroll O'Connor, Michael Strong, Lloyd Bochner, and James Sikking. Boorman had a rare bond with Marvin, and no one ever used him better. Always frightening, even in repose, the actor had a power to suggest profound underground rivers of thought. Angie Dickinson is perfect as the brave woman in these dangerous spots. John Vernon is odious, and Sharon Acker is pathetic. Time and again, pulp films fail when they strive for ambition or poetry—and this has a form affected by Alain Resnais as much as Jim Thompson. But this is a masterpiece, endlessly intriguing—make what you will of it.

Poltergeist (1982)

The Freeling family lives in a suburban subdivision—it is the kind of place that covers the hills of southern California, now, like lichen. There are a mother and a father and three children. The father is a real estate broker; he works on subdivisions like the one where he lives. His younger daughter, Carol Anne (Heather O'Rourke), watches a lot of television and is fascinated by the white static that follows programs. When her budgerigar dies, her mother, Diane (JoBeth Williams), helps her bury it in the backyard. Carol Anne begins to hear voices in the TV set. The weather worsens, and in a great storm Carol Anne's brother, Robbie (Oliver Robins), is sucked into the set. The father, Steve (Craig T. Nelson), rescues him, but in the turmoil Carol Anne is sucked away and lost.

The Freelings learn that their house (and much of the subdivision) was built on an old burial ground (presumably Native American). They hire mediums and parapsychologists to advise on how to recover Carol Anne. In the crisis, her mother enters the TV set and retrieves the child. But scarcely has that ordeal ended than the ground erupts as the spirits of the dead come to claim the house. Finally, the Freeling house explodes—but the family has escaped to a motel.

In an examination paper on American film, one might present that synopsis and then ask students to explain why they'd assign it to this or that director. To be sporting, I think you'd have to allow the students a few changes in the story outline. So there might be an inspired Preston Sturges picture if we cut the graveyard eruption and simply suggested that the Freelings' cable package has this unusual extra—that members of the family can go off on short vacations to certain programs. A smart answer might see that this world and its family are not far from the archetypes offered in Steven Spielberg's *E.T.* But Spielberg in those days wasn't really associated with irrational horror—apart from *Duel*. So where did the savage conclusion come from?

In fact, we do have an answer: *Poltergeist* is credited to Tobe Hooper, the maker of *Texas Chainsaw Massacre*. It is "a Steven Spielberg Production"—the producers are Spielberg and his associate, Frank Marshall. Spielberg is credited with the story, and the script is attributed to Spielberg, Michael Grais, and Mark Victor. More significant, there were rumors from the set that Spielberg had been present a lot and that Hooper might even have been fired. Spielberg issued a statement congratulating Hooper on their unique creative relationship.

All that needs to be said is that *Poltergeist* is one of the most pregnant domestic horror films in which the family are beset with nightmarish specters—like a gaunt tree, dead, but able to grow into the house. Why not? If Spielberg and Hooper took turns, shot by shot, it's not likely to be dull. But the real coup here, and well worth fuller development, is the TV as the threshold for the other world. Matthew Leonetti shot it. Michael Kahn edited. Jerry Goldsmith did the music, and there are a lot of special effects credits. Also with Beatrice Straight, Dominique Dunne, and Zelda Rubinstein.

Portrait of Jennie (1949)

Here is one of the most intriguing "problem" films ever made in America. First, how does an 86-minute movie, almost all of it black-and-white, with a small cast, in 1949, cost $4 million? How does it make back only a quarter of that amount? And how does it contrive to work itself into frenzies of a strange half-erotic, half-faerie ecstasy over the eternally placid Jennifer Jones? After all, in 1949, this project—about a hard-luck painter who meets a strange girl in Central Park, a girl who seems out of her own time, and who finds himself in his desire to paint her—might have cast Moira Shearer, Jean Simmons, Pier Angeli, or even Grace Kelly (she was twenty-one on Broadway in 1949). All I mean to suggest by that brief casting list is that Jennie could have been ravishing, very sexy and very touching, a photographer's delight.

Of course, all the questions in the opening paragraph are tidied up with one answer: David O. Selznick. There he was in the late forties, the two-time winner of the Best Picture Oscar; a divorced man and the helpless guide to his discovery, Miss Jones; the titan in a business that was running out of audience and funds; the gambler whose many losses now drove him to even wilder plays than he had indulged before. Jennifer Jones in *Duel in the Sun* had raked in money and he had thrown it away in simultaneous gestures. The film had also proved the limits of Miss Jones and exposed Selznick to ridicule and the ordeal of trying to take over from a fired director.

Jennie came from a Robert Nathan novel, and Leonardo Bercovici, Peter Berneis, and Paul Osborn all worked on the script. But so did Selznick. William Dieterle directed, and no one can deny that there are some very beautiful, if not spooky, sequences in the picture, with Joseph August haunted by twilight in Central Park and Jennie as an apparition in period clothes. But it's at times like that, when the film gathers a true atmosphere, that its premise is most shaky. Do we believe in the occult? Does the look on Jennie's face drag us into the whirlpool in the way, presumably, Miss Jones had that effect on Selznick? Is it possible that the love story would be more thrilling if there was a little more use of suspense, or horror? As it is, there are frightening moments, at which the power of this dreamed woman seems ready to surpass the coziness (all thoroughly boring) of Joseph Cotten, Ethel Barrymore, David Wayne, and Lillian Gish.

And here we come to the fascinating point about the film. One cool observer of the whole fiasco was Alfred Hitchcock, at the end of his rope with Selznick and nearly free of the contract with him. My reason for saying that is the hunch that the man who would make *Vertigo* learned a lot from *Portrait of Jennie:* the erotic allure, the morbid sexual fantasy, the being in and out of life, the green light even (the original Jennie ended in a wash of green), and above all, the intuition that this love story would work best if allowed to strike dread.

The Postman Always Rings Twice (1946)

"Rip me, Frank! Rip me!" says Cora to Frank on the hillside at night after they've killed the husband and he has to smack her around so that she looks as if she just survived a car crash, but she has the idea that while he's hitting her he could really do her some good. Of course, they couldn't film that in 1946—but the great thing about then was that they didn't need to. You could just have the faces shining in the dark, and in every cinema in the land some guy would be telling his girl, or just reciting it under his breath: "Rip me, Frank!" You maybe didn't want the job of cleaning up afterward, but make no mistake about it, the underprivileged classes were getting sex for pleasure as a new habit, and without the movies it might not have happened.

The James M. Cain novel was published in 1934. It was done on the stage, and it was stolen in Italy for Visconti's *Ossessione,* but still that's how long it was before M-G-M took the plunge on a cunning script by Niven Busch (with Harry Ruskin doing just enough to share credit). It's the old story of that California roadside diner run by a Greek and his young wife and then one day this good-for-nothing, Frank Chambers, comes by. And sooner or later it's just Frank and Cora running the diner, except that they've got these clever lawyers in their life and nothing else is ever the same again. But the original was the perfect highway novel for the thirties, and every time anyone has tried it it works.

Tay Garnett was the assigned director, and he's exactly right. What wasn't exactly right was the Greek husband. The studio suddenly got scared of offending Greeks so they cast Cecil Kellaway, jolly, English, effete, all wrong. The role needed a stinking thug. So it was that much harder for John Garfield and Lana Turner to build up the heat, but they did it—and Turner all in her white sunsuit is probably Frank's idea of a madonna with a habit.

Everything else works, especially the stuff in court with the lawyers: Hume Cronyn is devious and hateful, and it's good to see Leon Ames with his benign smile wiped away. Audrey Totter is great as the other woman. It was remade in 1981, with a pile of credentials: Bob Rafelson directing, David Mamet writing, and Jack Nicholson and Jessica Lange as the lovers. That's a good film, too, though it strays a little in suggesting that the Cain might be a great novel. It's not. It's a great pulp novel. And the 1946 version feels that tension between the page and respectability. Nicholson and Lange go much further on the kitchen table—but in 1981 they made the journey, and in 1946 there is no question that its heady and dirty delight was being offered to us.

Pretty Woman (1990)

Not to get too solemn too quickly, but I think this may be one of the films that tells you most about Hollywood most nakedly. First of all, this is a story based on the toss of a coin that puts you in the Beverly Wilshire or in a shack off Hollywood Boulevard, a story in which one girl gets from one square to another without so much as shaking the dice—she does shake her hair. The next great myth to consider is that of the almightily rich, cold, suave, and distinguished man of business who can find a heart if he is first given the right kind of head by a girl young enough to be his daughter. Backup data: Julia Roberts was twenty-three at the moment of the film; Richard Gere was forty-one. Next myth: The process of prostitution is like washing your hands—this is of real utility in Hollywood because sooner or later in that business nearly everyone must consent to being screwed for money. Thus, two points: Though he may use whores, Mr. Gere still has an open heart and sweet feelings. He has not been compromised. If a princess comes along, he will fall in love. Second: Though for some time Julia Roberts's Vivien has been available for purchase on the street, she is still whole, virginal, and young. The film is called *Pretty Woman* as in Hemingway's classic line, "Wouldn't it be pretty to think so?"

Beyond that, the film is about three very compelling items in the American dream: sex, shopping, and transformation. Thus, Julia has sex with Gere—she strips down, she does it, she bathes with him, and in all this he is the pasha, serene, immaculate, tolerating his own pleasure. And then—as she is hired for the week at $3,000—she gets to go shopping on Rodeo Drive, a chance to despise the snobby element on that street while still having a fashion show. Just like Audrey Hepburn in *Funny Face*, Julia gets to wear the wardrobe—and some very handsome outfits. This culminates in the trip to San Francisco to visit the opera in a red sheath dress. And, of course, she remains herself while being a hit. She is accepted. She makes the grade and sows the seeds that Gere will have her educated next so that she is fit for marriage. (Alas, alas—the film we all want to see, *Vivien Goes to College*, has never been offered.)

Several hands worked on this script, and I suspect that the film only really materialized as Garry Marshall brought it to life. Gere is perfect—hardly there, without odor or disease. Hector Elizondo makes the film as the spirit of the hotel. Jason Alexander sucks up every bit of loathing. Laura San Giacomo has the hapless task of indicating what a real whore is like. And Julia Roberts is about as enchanting and magical and cloud-cuckoo-land as anyone has ever been in American film. She was Oscar-nominated. And in Hollywood's Golden Age she would have won by acclamation. But for 1990 the Oscar went to Kathy Bates in *Misery*. And—so I am told—millions of Americans all over the world dream every night of being that fierce defender of literature (who probably is still a virgin).

Prince of the City (1981)

Robert Daley's *Prince of the City* was a nonfiction book, published in 1975, about Detective Robert Leuci, a narcotics officer in the NYPD's Special Investigating Unit who becomes drawn into underground investigation and informing. At first the book was bought for the movies by David Rabe and Brian De Palma, and one can only be afraid of the theatrics they might have imposed on it. Another writer, Jay Presson Allen, saw the book—far more shrewdly—as a police procedural ideal for Sidney Lumet. Eventually, that's how it worked out, with Allen producing and writing a script after Lumet had done a treatment. They reckoned it would make a three-hour movie and it's close to that at 167 minutes, yet it had great understanding from studio boss John Calley.

Lumet's sense of reality and police behavior are at the root of the film, yet it does break through into that fascinating territory familiar from espionage films and the best modern police stories, of a hall of mirrors where no one is quite sure who can be trusted. Once upon a time, informers and audiences alike had a certain battered faith in turning up the truth, cleansing the system and reforming it. The great power of *Prince of the City* lies in the mounting awareness that no such hopes are justified, that the bureaucratic system is always likely to defend itself. It's the more striking in that *Prince of the City* was made before the great age of Internet and cell-phone hookups made ordinary human pursuit nearly impossible.

This may seem a dry subject, but it's clear already, I think, that the computer screen and the cell-phone closeup now dominate this kind of story—and inadvertently dramatize the isolation of the characters. We have somehow sold out our human rights in a deal whereby the toys—the machines—are meant to be solace enough in a world where we have less and less chance of uncovering the layers of corruption. So it's fair to say of even *Prince of the City* that in following a weak hero it was surely true to life, yet dispiriting, too. *Internal Affairs*, nearly a decade later, may be a more compelling film just because it clings to that cliché—a flamboyant villain (the Richard Gere role) as opposed to the new truth, that nearly everyone is shadowed by corruption.

Prince of the City is still very effective, beautifully shot by Andrzej Bartkowiak, with good production design by Tony Walton and costumes by Anna Hill Johnstone. Treat Williams played the lead role (and it's telling that he has never established himself as an iconic figure—he is an ordinary cop) and there is outstanding support from Jerry Orbach (who served more time in the NYPD than some cops), Richard Foronjy, Don Billett, Kenny Marino, Carmine Caridi, Tony Page, Norman Parker, Paul Roebling, Bob Balaban, James Tolkan, Steve Inwood, Lindsay Crouse, Lee Richardson, and many others.

Prince of the City is neither uplifting nor encouraging, and it helplessly suggests that citizens get used to the fix being in. At the same time, its insistence on reality as compared with the unfailing integrity of the leads in series like *Law and Order* is a last commitment to candor.

The Prisoner of Zenda (1937)

It's true that this adventure movie was conceived and carried out by David O. Selznick in the troubled time of the love affair between Mrs. Simpson and Edward VIII. Selznick, you see, was sufficiently Anglophile and enough of a monarchist to care about the threat to noblesse oblige—and he was still so good a showman as to see that *The Prisoner of Zenda* was a terrific trick for getting romantic audiences inside a court's inner circle and into the love affairs that can leave crowns and coronets at a tipsy angle. In other words, he took the nonsense seriously—and the history of movies attests to the virtue of that principle.

There was the novel by Anthony Hope (published in 1894), and done twice already as a silent film. This version is credited as follows: script by John Balderston from an adaptation by Wells Root of a play by Edward Rose; directed by John Cromwell. And no one wishes to allege that those gentlemen were not in attendance. But we know that Sidney Howard and George Cukor were asked for suggestions, and everyone dreaded Selznick's own brainwaves. If ever there was a picture put together by the system of taking classics and getting a movie at the other end, this is it. Yes, it worked out fine, but why? Is it the story? The look of the thing? The cast? Or is it just that in 1937 most people were happy to see this kind of story? One telling point: By the 1952 remake (often shot-for-shot identical), *Zenda* was clearly a kids' entertainment. But in 1937 it was a flick for adults, too.

In hindsight, the color of the 1952 version seems automatic and drab, whereas James Wong Howe's rich black and white in 1937 is far more atmospheric and romantic, and far better at getting the forests, lakes, and castles of Zenda (just past Pasadena). The direction is as swift and tidy as a movie that is itching to arrive at swordplay. And the pacing is without fault.

Still, it's the efficiency and glamour of the playing (or the casting) that really carries the picture. No, you can't tell Ronald Colman's Rudolf Rassendyll from his king—so at least you understand the dilemma of all the other noble idiots in the picture. In fact, Colman serves as a ball boy to some more favored players: Madeleine Carroll, who is so lovely as Flavia that it's easy to believe that Selznick's partner, Jock Whitney, fell for her; Mary Astor, who is allowed for once to be naughty as Antoinette; C. Aubrey Smith as Colonel Zapt; David Niven as Fritz; Raymond Massey as Michael—or Black Michael, as the cast has it, in case you've missed the hints in Massey's acting. I have left the best to last, because Douglas Fairbanks, Jr., was usually such a junior and so wet. But really his Rupert of Hentzau is delicious, and one of the most appealing villains in screen history. I suspect Rupert was grandfather to a man named Bond.

The Private Life of Sherlock Holmes (1970)

This is a famous tragedy, so where should we begin? Well, in the first instance, Billy Wilder's preferred cut was a 200-minute film, but the picture as eventually released was 125 minutes (and it frequently feels painfully slow). It cost $10 million, with enormous sets—one, an ocean liner, turned out so big, they couldn't film in the studio pool and had to go to sea! It earned $1 million. And Wilder himself consented to the massive cuts, including a couple of self-contained Holmes "cases." But what are self-contained cases doing in a film of this length?

Wilder had been thinking about Holmes since his days in Berlin. He felt drawn to the cool brain of the man, the misogyny, the boredom, the disbelief in all sentiment. As early as the 1950s, Wilder had had talks with Alan Jay Lerner, Frederick Loewe, and Moss Hart about a musical, with Rex Harrison as the detective. That passed, but then Wilder and I. A. L. Diamond started working on a script (it would be a ten-year venture) with dreams of Peter O'Toole and Peter Sellers in the two roles.

It's clear that Wilder planned something fresh on Holmes—a new but searching character study; an explanation of his problem with women, and his flirtation with homosexuality. Wilder had fought censorship through the forties and fifties, slipping his sex, nastiness, and double meanings in between tablets of stone. Then censorship gave up and said, virtually, Do what you like. A case can be made that such opponents of censorship as Hitchcock, Preminger, and Wilder were suddenly lost. They had specialized in being naughty—now they could be frank. And I suspect that Wilder was not ready to make an open film about gayness. The sexual material was left naked by the new fashions, but Wilder was not the man to be so open. So the heart of the film is muffled.

Then something strange happened: O'Toole dropped out and Wilder replaced him with Robert Stephens after a very brief meeting, without ever seeing Stephens on stage or screen. He simply told Stephens to be perfect and then nagged him endlessly about fine nuances until Stephens was lost. It is said the actor even attempted suicide in the crisis that developed. So I think it has to be admitted that the casting was wrong—Stephens is not right for what Wilder intends. Nor is Colin Blakely much help as Watson.

Alexandre Trauner did the sets and spared nothing, but the sets are inert, not fun, and not often explored by the action. Miklós Rózsa gave a treasured violin concerto—and it's not memorable. Christopher Challis did the color photography, but it's hard to recollect the imagery. Toward the very end, there are excellent scenes between Holmes and the woman (Genevieve Page—Wilder turned down Jeanne Moreau) that are good enough to show a way to reconstruct the film with Holmes truly uncertain over his own sexual nature. The long version plays sometimes. But it's no help: In so many ways, this great attempt was wrong. Also with Christopher Lee, Irene Handl, Clive Revill, Tamara Toumanova, Stanley Holloway.

The Producers (1968)

Everybody now has seen *The Producers* onstage, or they have their stories about how they just missed a ticket. Long ago, the daring of the show and its concept have collapsed under the weight of the money it has earned. And yet, as its success threatens to surmount so many records in show business, when *Springtime for Hitler* opens in the show within the show, some members of the "audience" walk out until it is perceived as a satire on Hitler. And all of this began nearly forty years ago—it says something odd about Mel Brooks, and us, that the story hasn't grown along the way. It just sits there, the supposed comic tribute to a Jewish way with show business and making money that has become money itself. How can or should Brooks keep the aghast tone of self-congratulation out of his voice?

The strength of the film, it seems to me, is still the rare charm in bringing Zero Mostel and Gene Wilder together as Max Bialystock and Leo Bloom. Thank God they don't have to do numbers together—but that's because they are so intent on the other numbers, the ones that could make a success out of a disaster. They will put on a flop show and take the money from investors. The worst play they can find is *Springtime for Hitler*, a happier reprise of that story, written by Franz Liebkind (Kenneth Mars). But when the first light of "satire" dawns on the audience, *Springtime* becomes a hit and the guys have to blow up the theater to stop it all. So they end in jail with plans for a new show, *Prisoners of Love*.

Mostel and Brooks shone with fondness for each other. It was as if they knew that they were being so scurrilous and inventively funny about Jewishness that their game together was a riposte to Nazism—instead of a deeply plausible response. It was as if they had elected to believe that show business was truly the Jewish religion. Non-Jews could see other things in Jewry, but the Jews themselves realized that show business and storytelling were the secret. And these two dainty, filthy guys together gave the first film a touching relationship that held together in the spasms of schtick that took over. For me, succeeding partnerships—especially Lane and Broderick—never came near this furtive pleasure. Never even seemed Jewish.

Like most things touched by Mel Brooks, it has all gone too far, and yet the first film—coming in those smugly disapproving sixties—was truly out-of-its-mind and in-our-face. It was a small outrage, but that was its métier. As a huge success, it suddenly raises so many other, larger worries—like would these two guys really do this? Or like raising the hope for a far more dangerous work, one in which a couple of schmucks run coach trips to Auschwitz and Dachau, with a sideline in selling Nazi memorabilia and souvenirs.

Providence (1977)

You could take a long time to tell the story of *Providence*, but you can tell it very quickly, too. Clive Langham (John Gielgud) is a famous writer, a novelist. He lives in a large house on an estate, and he is dying in some pain. He is writing a book, or trying to, and he is reliving the events of his life, yet trying not to. That double flex is the energy of the film, for his novel is peopled by versions of the figures in his life: his son, the lawyer, Claude (Dirk Bogarde); his illegitimate son, Kevin Woodford (David Warner); Claude's wife, Sonia (Ellen Burstyn); and his own wife, Molly, and his mistress, Helen (both figures filled by Elaine Stritch).

The script is by David Mercer (who is referred to with fond exasperation in the story). The astonishingly atmospheric camerawork is by Ricardo Aronovich. The art direction—in houses inhabited and houses that are like stage sets (and meant to be)—is by Jacques Saulnier. The costumes are by Claude Serre, John Bates, and Yves Saint-Laurent. The music is a deliciously old-fashioned score by Miklós Rózsa.

And the director is Alain Resnais, the maker of *Night and Fog* and *Hiroshima, Mon Amour* (which is to say, grave works that lead us to the brink of our modern abysses). But Resnais is also the director of *Last Year at Marienbad*, which is constructed on the idea of play or gamesmanship. And *Providence* is one of those rare masterpieces able to stand back from the process of creation—in this case the making of a novel—and see what a serious game it is.

There is no doubt in my mind that the very opening—in which a camera tracks through the large, deserted house, to find a man who drops something on the floor, is a reference to the opening of *Citizen Kane*. In turn, that is a way of saying that some of the wisest and greatest works in our art are reflections on the very process of making film.

The film is very funny, not just in terms of its incidents, but in the way a crazy rhyming holds reality and the novel together. There is a sublime surprise here that amounts to the most basic openness to what happens in life. And it's part of that that the performances are exquisite: the archetypal lecherous cantankerousness, the thirst for wit in Elaine Stritch; the elegance and the profundity of Ellen Burstyn; the intelligence and the gay loneliness of Dirk Bogarde—this is not just one of his best performances, but a confession from the man; and the divine mixture of the spirit and the smart, witty flesh in John Gielgud.

As for Resnais, let us just note the effortless and eloquent English here from a director who has no superior at his use of the French language. This is literature written for and, on the screen. The cast also includes Samson Fainsilber, Tanya Lopert, Cyril Luckham, Milo Sperber, Peter Arne, and Kathryn Leigh Scott.

The Prowler (1951)

Nothing could be tidier. A married woman (Evelyn Keyes) reports a prowler. Van Heflin is the cop who comes to investigate. They become attached. They kill her husband. It all ends in the desert, with the police pursuing Heflin up a manmade mountain of earth. The possibility lingers that Heflin himself was the prowler at the beginning.

This was Joe Losey's third film, after *The Boy with Green Hair* and *The Lawless*. He was asked to do it by a strange Austrian producer going under the name of S. P. Eagle. The budget was low, the schedule was nineteen days, but Eagle had acquired Arthur Miller to do the camerawork. With a veteran like that on hold, Losey elected to save time by going for long takes. The result is his first deeply personal and unmistakable film, a bleak parable on the restless urge in postwar America to get ahead.

There was a screenplay of sorts, but Losey was able to get Dalton Trumbo and Hugo Butler to do a substantial rewrite in which their terse nihilism would match the unsentimental (and makeup-deprived) performances of the two leads. Keyes and Heflin are brilliant, and a demonstration of how many small stars lived in the hope of getting this kind of B picture. The overall regard for the characters—as helpless figures driven past morality by ambition—may have helped foster the suspicion that Losey (and others) were Communist. It's far more the fusion of film noir with an adult intelligence. And that may be why *The Prowler* seldom rates in the self-pitying annals of film noirs we love to see over and over again. The violence and the human weakness are not neurotic here. Nor are they gloated over. They are the heartbeat of the nation.

Losey would survive. He moved on and did more great work. Robert Aldrich, his assistant director on *The Prowler*, had a few good years to come. But Heflin and Keyes are the real casualties, two very smart players who hardly knew that this very modest picture was probably going to be their greatest moment.

One other aspect needs treatment. As he came to make *The Prowler*, Losey had lunch with John Huston (an unofficial assistant to Eagle, or Sam Spiegel). Losey was genuinely asking for an education, and Huston said, "Remember, the screen is three-dimensional." What he meant, Losey gathered, was that the illusion of depth and space was vital. It was in that spirit that he used John Hubley unofficially as a design consultant—the actual sets were credited to Boris Leven. And so *The Prowler* is the first Losey film in which we feel a keynote of his vision: the interaction of place and character, and the way in which the camera can move through space with the human figures. Example: The brilliant shot of Heflin in his bare lodging, endlessly throwing paper basketballs at the lamp bowl. Physical obsession can be established in a great movie in five seconds (if you see the ceiling shot).

Psycho (1960)

In Phoenix, Arizona, Friday, December 11, at 2:43 p.m., the world changes, as the camera slithers in through a window in a cheap hotel to discover a man and a woman, naked by 1960s standards, flagrantly in heat by the conventions of a Phoenix Friday when even if it is winter, it's stifling, headachy weather in which Marion Crane (Janet Leigh), not satisfied in the hotel room, will feel so little air in her life that rather than bank the $40,000 from a realty deal that her boss has handed her, she'll take to the road with it. And in her lack of satisfaction, she is not alone.

In the first forty minutes, we see Marion in her underwear three times, without having a proper chance to rip her flesh from her smile. Hold on, it is coming. After one of the great night drives in American film, with torment in the rearview mirror, Marion comes to a shabby motel bypassed by the new highway—in the fifties, America's rural character was erased by freeways. Yet something remained in the bypassed spots—rancor, regret, revenge, as mothers and sons huddled together in the same lamplight. And in a bathroom as bright as a furnace, the knife would go in. Oh no, explained pious Alfred, never quite in, not in our state of censorship. Never quite in—satisfaction is not my game.

The world changed? I think so. Here is a Hollywood film cut to ribbons by its own internal energy, long before it can end—cut up by a process of pastiche, camp mockery, and what did we ever think we were doing by using the word "horror"? So *Psycho* is the most shocking film made in America (no one allowed in after it had started) and yet a startling new comedy, where we have to laugh at our own outrage. The very warning offered in *Vertigo,* of our culpability at the movies, was screaming at us now like Bernard Herrmann's strangled chords.

In addition, at the cost of about $1 million, it took in around $20 million and it made fear, unimaginable violence, and the expectation of the upraised knife key dynamics in a new cinema. At the same time, it was brilliant and so full of understanding of the medium that it became harder to love the medium. And as for "psycho" itself, that word, the name, the film turned it loose on the culture like a mad dog, and it shifted the Freudian age of potential treatment into one of licensed glee.

In conjunction with that, Anthony Perkins was allowed to make Norman Bates the most gentle and sympathetic character in the film—that's where Hitchcock's humor was going. Janet Leigh became the Fay Wray of stardom—the iconic sacrificial victim. And the film was full of nasty, suspicious, grudging people—John Gavin, Vera Miles, Martin Balsam, John McIntire, John Anderson, Pat Hitchcock, Frank Albertson, Vaughn Taylor, Mort Mills, all the way to Simon Oakland, who manages to be the necessary explainer of it all as well as the bomb under any explainer's seat. Of course, Norman has the last look and the last word—as well as the greatest curse in American film—"Mother!"

Public Enemy (1931)

There's a sly coyness about *Public Enemy.* That's why it picks a forbidding and impersonal title when it really wants to offer us the gutter charms of James Cagney as gangster Tom Powers. It's as if the film is wondering: Can we get away with it? But don't forget that initially, Cagney and Edward Woods were cast in opposite roles: Woods would be Powers and Cagney would be Matt Doyle, killed along the way. But the more William Wellman looked at his two actors, the more clearly he saw Cagney's edge of punchy humor and lethal seductiveness. He's the guy they want to see, Wellman decided. And if Cagney asked what this meant, he was told, Just be yourself, Jimmy; be wicked, outrageous, cocky, funny, a pile of trouble. If there was any doubt in milking this dangerous energy, the film could remind itself that Cagney's role would wind up dead.

Better than dead. Starting in 1909, Tom and Matt are childhood friends on the make in the city—naughty kids, but you've got to love them. Fifty years later it was the same thing with Al Pacino and Steven Bauer in that first part of *Scarface,* joshing each other, flirting with girls, strutting their stuff and taking on vicious opponents—what was not to love? And when the point comes that Pacino and Cagney have gone too far, let them go a little further, because they've agreed to die. So in *Public Enemy,* Matt is killed and Tom is shot to pieces. His family lines up at Matt's hospital bed—the mother, the good brother, and Matt's sister. They are reconciled. But then, before you can blink, the word comes that the scum have got Tom. There's a knock at the door, and there he is, a corpse rolled up like a mummy, pitching forward into the camera. You can hear the connoisseurs sighing at this spiffy death.

Public Enemy was written by Harvey Thew from a story, "Beer and Blood," by John Bright and Kubec Glasmon. Darryl Zanuck was the producer, keeping an eye on the script and giving Wellman the confidence to go with Cagney—make it a gangster picture. That's how the grapefruit business works. One morning, seeing a cut fruit on the breakfast table, Powers rams it in the face of Mae Clarke (one of his girls). It's shocking. It's talked about. You wouldn't want it to happen to you, but there's panache in doing it to a sour-faced broad. The gangster can do and say things that are over the top. If the film's a hit, you'll find kids on the street repeating the trick in a few weeks.

So you can pump out the stories that Cagney was a gentle soul, really. You can put your hand on your heart and say we never had a gangster we didn't bury—until Michael Corleone. But the public can read your wink and they know the public enemy is a treat, a hell of a guy. *Public Enemy* is as terse as good journalism, with good side bits by Jean Harlow, Joan Blondell, Donald Cook, Leslie Fenton, and Frankie Darro. There had never been anything as cheerful and dangerous before.

Pulp Fiction (1994)

Rest assured: The jazzy, cool assurance and the bravura exhilaration of *Pulp Fiction* still work as it lies coiled, like a sleepy mamba or a Möbius strip, on a child's daydream version of underworld Los Angeles. And it's not just the famous and much repeated comic verve of the chatter (the "royale" stuff, or Mr. Winston Wolfe's wicked cleanup patter), but the lovely, elegant way in which the story is always our snake, wondering when to eat its own tail.

It is a terrific screenplay—by which I don't mean to assert that the shapes were always there in the script, or that they arose, like champagne bubbles, in the editing. But the ways in which the John Travolta character is alive yet not, and the final QED of the people in the diner, are exquisitely worked out and something of profound aesthetic pleasure. It is both a marvel and a disgrace that there wasn't enough in Quentin Tarantino's makeup or our culture's imperatives to say, There, see that, study that, do more of that. Whereas, more or less, he has chosen to follow up individual stories when his enormous naïveté and innocence were so protected by his urge to make a crazy quilt film, and by the way it never threatened his unawareness of nearly everything except sweet movie impact.

Still, it is mysterious to see how easily he had risen above the blood-soaked violence and the gloating cruelty of *Reservoir Dogs*. There are things of huge potential grotesquerie in *Pulp Fiction*—the mess in the back of the car, adrenaline straight to the heart, and the little shop of perverts—but the energy and comic curiosity of the picture drive straight through those worries as if they were paper walls. Somehow or other Tarantino knew he had a story that worked, and a band of actors who could do it all in his sleep—no, they are awake, but Quentin is dreaming, and the playing is perfectly in key with his trance.

So it's magic when a puffy Travolta gets up to dance, and Uma Thurman for once in her life was revealed as a collection of foxy, Egyptian moves. I don't think Bruce Willis was ever better, just as Harvey Keitel will never be so likeable, useful, and practical. Tim Roth and Amanda Plummer are enshrined in their diner with their loving rant, and while staring into the camera Christopher Walken seems to have faced and accepted the proposition that yes, he really is a very strange guy, the more so when he tries to be salt of the earth.

So nothing is really off or wrong, and Tarantino whips 154 minutes by in a cool hurry. It's sheer movie, and no wonder the American business (let alone the art) reeled with the thought that it had tossed off a work of natural genius. But then you have to face the failure to ditto, or to make any real advance (despite *Jackie Brown* being worthwhile and interesting). More and more, it becomes apparent that only the snake and the shape knew what they were doing. As for Quentin, he was in a trance.

The Puppetmaster (1993)

Hou Hsiao-hsien was born in mainland China in 1947, but in a year he was taken by his family to Taiwan. He is one of the great masters of film alive and working now, and it's fascinating and appropriate that *The Puppetmaster* is an account of the career of Li Tien-lu, one of Taiwan's most famous puppeteers and a man who was born in 1909, only a few years after Japan had begun an occupation of the island that lasted until its military defeat in 1945.

So, the years of Li Tien-lu's early life might easily be presented as an era of hardship and deprivation under a cruel occupying force. Children and old people alike die of untended illness and even starvation. Japanese officials visit the family home one day and insist that the old Chinese pigtails must be cut off as a sign of subservience. In return, the Chinese are given tickets to the Japanese opera. It is the bargain of tyranny, of course, but Li Tien-lu is fascinated by the opera, and Hou Hsiao-hsien allows us several minutes of an uninterrupted long shot to observe and absorb the show. It is felt as nourishment.

But to speak of Hou's long shots is to get to the heart of this film. Just as the commentary of the master puppeteer is phlegmatic and resigned to fate, so Hou's camera prefers withdrawn, static setups in which a good deal of action flows back and forth across the frame, without the film resorting to cuts or close-ups to point up the details. In a way, the overall has taken over from the detail. It is the refusal to take sides that is so distinctive. Yet, here's an interesting extra. The style I have just described could fit the Japanese director Ozu, and there are resemblances. But the very opening shot of *The Puppetmaster*—fixed and remote—is teeming with family life, with people moving back and forth, freely and boldly, from instinct and liberty. It actually feels more like a modern Western family than those Ozu films where something in the air—some caution, some chill of respect—has frozen people into a position. I have talked elsewhere about a growing sense of restriction in Ozu—and I can only say that it emerges more clearly when set beside the work of Hou Hsiao-hsien.

The Puppetmaster uses on-camera interviews with, and voiceover narrative from, Li Tien-lu, but he's far from a sentimental old-timer catering to an audience. He's dry, withered, very professional, and startlingly given to fate and accepting its considerable inroads. Gradually, too, we wonder at his reliability. There's a superb scene of wartime activity set on a dank, misty hilltop, with soldiers quarreling over hygiene, all done in one long shot that is remarkable in its refusal to depict the Japanese in cliché terms. There is also a great deal of puppet theater, including a play about a raid behind American lines. It is this steady sense of story or play commenting on life that makes the film so complex and challenging. We learn a great deal about Taiwan, not least the existence there of an ironic sense of theater.

Pursued (1947)

Every now and then in film history, someone offers a classic summation of the movies. So one afternoon in the summer of 1983, there I was in his study with Niven Busch (author of *Duel in the Sun*), overlooking the Golden Gate Bridge. He was screenwriter and producer on *Pursued,* and this is what he said: "It has kind of Greek overtones—incest feeling, and all that—which the West was like. Greece in the ancient days must have been very much like the West. Passions were powerful and arms were at hand." It sounds like some Hollywood producer, snarling as he tries to hold on to his cigar. But Niven Busch, my dear friend, was an educated man. He had been to Princeton and written for *The New Yorker*—not that he ever let such things get in his way.

Still, he'd read enough of the Greeks to see that the Western was déjà vu, and he had enough innate knowledge of psychology to see that within the myths of the Western there were Freudian truths. So *Pursued* is the story of a man intent on finding the killers of his father. And in a West where families might be split up, you just have to take care to remember which was your father and which the killers. In other words, pause before you fire—you may be shooting yourself. Jeb (Robert Mitchum) has fragmented memories: a woman (Judith Anderson), a pair of spurred boots, and flashing lights.

The very clever script (influenced by Robert Louis Stevenson's *The Master of Ballantrae*) is told in flashback: Jeb and Thorley (Teresa Wright—Mrs. Niven Busch) are in the ruins of his childhood house waiting for Grant, Thorley's father and a crooked lawyer, a man with one arm (Dean Jagger). The truth as it spills out involves sex and incest and the way so many families could hardly draw their own family tree.

It is a wonderful story, set against Monument Valley, photographed by James Wong Howe, and directed by Raoul Walsh. In time, critics came to see it as a Walsh film, but it's hard to find anything else as intricate or potent in Walsh's work. Truly, I think this is a Busch film, in which even the casting of Teresa Wright had special overtones. The lead part went to Mitchum only after several other actors had turned it down, and the film was close to Mitchum's heart just because it had required him to act. Howe made it a Western noir, and it seems magical now that the Western apparatus lends itself so easily to a story of the inner life. Max Steiner's score is a further underlining of the lineaments of dread.

The use of Monument Valley is intriguing. That is Ford's territory, of course, but Ford uses it as spectacle whereas Busch and Walsh turn it into a psychic setting for characters who have offended the gods. Pursuit, tracking, searching have their outward meanings. But put an American in the wilderness and he is so astounded that he decides space is a projection of his mind.

Pygmalion (1938)

George Bernard Shaw knew enough about the twentieth century and the reputation of authors to understand that he had to be a hit in the movies—it was the only way the world might be saved for common sense and literacy. But over the years, the few screen adaptations of his work had failed dismally. Moreover, Shaw had given early warning of his ambitions. On meeting Samuel Goldwyn, and talking to him about a project, Shaw said, "The trouble is, Mr. Goldwyn, you are interested in art, whereas I am interested in money."

But in the mid-1930s, *Pygmalion* (a play that opened in 1913) was filmed in Germany and Holland. Why not in English? Shaw wanted to know. And the object of his question was Gabriel Pascal, a Transylvanian he had met one day on the beach. The world tended to suppose that Pascal was a brilliant entrepreneur who had wooed the playwright. It was the other way round: Shaw had got his hooks into Pascal, and soon enough he would draw blood.

You know the story. No one quite understands the odd "collaboration" on the script. Shaw got the screenplay credit (and he won the Oscar for it), but W. P. Lipscomb and Cecil Lewis helped on the screenplay, and there was extra dialogue work by Ian Dalrymple, Anatole de Grunwald, and Kay Walsh, the actress who would later marry David Lean. By some weird arrangement, Pascal agreed to let the directing credit be shared by Anthony Asquith and Leslie Howard—Asquith actually directed the film, but Howard gave some notes to the cast. And, of course, Howard played Professor Henry Higgins, a shrewd box-office ploy at the time, and a way of guiding the film toward romance, but not necessarily the best casting available. On the other hand, Wendy Hiller, twenty-six at the time, is arguably the best Eliza there has ever been—coarse and delicate, and both from the heart. Added to which, you have the rare Wilfrid Lawson as Doolittle, one of the outstanding "unknown" English actors in history. What this all means is the play—a smart comedy of manners and a subtle romance—is played as such. You may wonder where the songs have gone. But not for long. Shaw was in heaven: The film was a hit, and it was absolutely faithful to what he had written.

Harry Stradling was brought in from America for the photography. The young David Lean was the film's editor. And John Bryan did splendid art direction. The costumes were by Ladislaw Czettel, but gowns for the Ascot scene came from Worth and Schiaparelli. The supporting cast included Marie Lohr, Scott Sunderland, Jean Cadell, David Tree, Everley Gregg, and Cathleen Nesbitt.

The film's success launched a heady plan for a complete Shaw, but the next step was *Major Barbara* (a flop, despite having Wendy Hiller and Rex Harrison), and then *Caesar and Cleopatra* (with Claude Rains and Vivien Leigh) which proved one of the biggest money losers in British film.

Quai des Brumes (1938)

This is the one where Michèle Morgan plays the seventeen-year-old girl, wearing a cellophane raincoat (Coco Chanel did the costumes). Morgan was the right age, but she looks like a crazy angel who has seen enough darkness for a couple of lives. She's Nelly, the ingenue, the girl who wins Jean Gabin's deserter soldier the instant he sees her, the one who lures him off the boat for a last farewell when he's safe and on his way to Venezuela.

It came from a novel by Pierre Mac Orlan, published in 1927 and set in Montmartre. Marcel Carné and writer Jacques Prévert both loved the novel, but they felt it couldn't be done in its real setting. So they thought of Hamburg and had proposed it to Ufa as a German film. But then the word came down from Dr. Goebbels that the material had some unpleasant elements. So it was reassigned, to a Jewish producer (Gregor Rabinovitch), and they decided to relocate to Le Havre.

That's where Jean (Gabin) arrives, a truculent deserter with no backstory—the overall air of defeatism is so great it makes up for every vagueness. He's given a helping hand by Panama (Édouard Delmont), and he meets the sweet, melancholy painter, Michel Krauss (Robert Le Vigan). But he's also met Nelly, who is terrorized by her guardian, Zabel (Michel Simon), and the gangsters he knows.

Quai des Brumes is the first of the Carné-Prévert collaborations, and it has a lofty reputation for being down and dirty. Yet there's plenty wrong with it. Gabin is too quickly aggressive as the soldier, and he really needs some nasty backstory, enough to make Nelly's nostrils quiver. And then there's the unlikely but so convenient suicide of Krauss, opening up the story line but proving a tough act to follow even for Le Vigan.

But the real problem is that, with that great title and a mood of fate closing in, far too much of the film is bright-looking. The Le Havre exteriors are very good, especially Panama's shack on a spit of land, and Alexandre Trauner did great interiors back in the studio. But the lighting is downright wrong (for once), no matter that Eugen Schüfftan did the photography and the camera operators included Henri Alekan and Philippe Agostini.

Gabin is as moody as can be, and he's very effective slapping Pierre Brasseur around. But Michel Simon's villain is a bit of a disappointment, and Morgan seems far too knowing to be the innocent girl. Maurice Jaubert did the music. Pauline Kael was not impressed, and she thought the great reputation of the picture in the late thirties came from the sudden shot of despair on top of the gross overoptimism of so many American films. But that explanation doesn't work. There are American films of the same period, like *You Only Live Once*, that do the noir dismay a lot better. The cast also includes Raymond Aimos, René Génin, Jenny Burnay, and Marcel Perez. There's also a dog that refuses to give Gabin up.

Quai des Orfèvres (1947)

Quai des Orfèvres means "police headquarters" in Paris, and eventually this lush film becomes a whodunit that must be solved by a rather bad-tempered policeman (played by Louis Jouvet as a star turn). But what makes the film "lush" is the world in which the killing occurs—a cheap music hall, tiny bars, cramped apartments, dressing rooms, and the general clutter of backstage. And does Henri-Georges Clouzot love it! It's a movie of people with big egos squeezing together in narrow corridors and tight corners, and it has the most fabulous black-and-white photography (by Armand Thirard) so meticulously conveyed on the Criterion DVD that you know why "noir" was first recognized in France.

Maurice Martineau (Bernard Blier) is a failure in most respects. He's a little plump and he's losing his hair. He might have been a hot songwriter, but all he can claim now is that he is married to a star singer, Jenny Lamour (Suzy Delair), who has a sculpted body and a blackbird's voice. She's a treat, and Clouzot shoots her in patterned stockings, bombazines, underwear, every bit of saucy costume he can find. Jenny is relaxed and Maurice is not, so Jenny sees no reason not to have "lunch" with Brignon (Charles Dullin), a cadaverous lecher, because he might smooth her way to a movie part and some real money. On his side, Maurice knows just what Brignon is after as a percentage, and he threatens the predatory old man—in the hearing of others. Something that doesn't help when Brignon turns up hit over the head very dead. In his own apartment.

This comes from a pulp novel, *Legitime Defense*, by Stanislas-André Steeman, published in 1942. Author Luc Sante claims that Clouzot and Jean Ferry adapted the book from memory for the simple reason that they couldn't find a copy anywhere. The film has that freedom and—for Clouzot—a rare sense of fun and pleasure in the characters. Of course, in this sort of picture everyone needs to be capable of the killing—and so they are. Clouzot knows the atmosphere is what counts, and this is a film that reveals him as a genuine minor master of mise-en-scène. Thirard worked very closely with production designer Max Douy, and you can smell the sweat, the greasepaint, and the cheap perfume.

Jouvet is a little too proud, perhaps—the story needs a shabbier cop. But Blier is patently neurotic and living on the edge, with just the right wife to drive him crazy. But, of course, one thing that unites noir in all its contributing countries is the way in which men marry women they're going to want to murder. So it's a lightweight film and a tremendous entertainment. It doesn't have the real dread of *Une Si Jolie Petite Plage* (1949) or Clouzot's own *Diaboliques*, but it's hugely enjoyable. There are long passages where shot after shot improves on the last one—just like a perfect box of chocolates (with just one of the goodies containing poison).

Les 400 Coups (1959)

It made a difference, I realize, if you had been reading François Truffaut in *Arts* and *Cahiers du Cinéma,* for he was a terrific, terrier-like critic, a bit of Cagney and a bit of Bazin in him. Not that anyone outside Paris in 1959 could grasp the pathos in the way *Les 400 Coups* was the work of a wandering child dedicated to a kind of godfather—or that Bazin had not lived to see the finished film. I'm sure Bazin had faith in the kid, and knew him very well, yet I think Bazin would have been amazed. For the marvel of this movie is not just that Truffaut grew up in making it (he was twenty-seven when it opened), but that the toughie had become a lyric artist in the process. He had found Vigo waiting for him, and he had reclaimed that very brief life and its passion for film.

So expect to be moved. I do not mean that just because this is the story of an increasingly lost child in which an ordinary cinematic sentimentality comes into play. I mean, rather, that there is emotion locked in the grim, wolfish face of Jean-Pierre Léaud, and his flagrant naughtiness that gives you a hint of the young thug in Truffaut. I refer to the music by Jean Constantin, which I cannot hear without finding tears in my eyes. And I know that the trigger of that music comes also from the wondrous discovery that the kind of critic I had loved—and it was not comfortable exactly to admire Truffaut's writing in England then (it was not very *Sight and Soundy*)—had come home with a fabulous, simple film that did nothing less than pour movie into your lap.

This was also Paris in CinemaScope, with Henri Decaë handling it, and when the kids ran free in those gray streets and Constantin's poignant, halting melodies went with them, it was enough to say that the world itself was available for cineastes. Not that the potential misfortune and worse of ordinary delinquency is ever shirked by this casual piece of realism. This is a story of parental neglect and misunderstanding, of kids so unwanted that they can hardly voice their desperation for something to love.

Léaud has his chum (in a lovely performance from Patrick Auffay), but it is finally cinema that comes to his rescue. Hence the superb ending: The boy has escaped from reform school. He runs for a few minutes, or for a day. And he comes to that wan, foggy gray French sea—*la manche*—the sea he has never seen before. And then the tiring, handheld accompaniment to his run becomes the smooth, streamlined slide of the sloping beach. And Truffaut is so happy he shows the wheel marks of earlier tracking shots in the background—he loves cinema so, and is so proud to be a part of it. And so the boy paddles into the sea, and turns to face his camera and us, and the image freezes and begins to speckle. To be alive then and young.

The Queen (2006)

The dangers in choosing very recent films are made clear by picking *The Queen*. I like the film and its director (Stephen Frears) very much, and my only immediate cavil with the picture was that Frears had fallen rather in the way he imagines Cherie Blair warning her husband, Tony: "Are you going to be one of those socialists who fall in love with the royal family?" Of course, Blair could reasonably reply that he'd never realized he was a socialist. But you can't escape the fact that *The Queen* is probably the best bit of PR Elizabeth Windsor has had for years. And the republican in one laments the way in which the entertainment value of the film has ended up making HRH more endearing, more tolerable, more necessary.

I'm reminded that the very funny *A Question of Attribution* (written by Alan Bennett, directed by John Schlesinger, and with Prunella Scales as the Queen) had very much the same impact as far as the Queen's image counted. The great lesson of the entire Diana miniseries is that it was a television event far more than a period of history. And if the Windsors can think of nothing else to do, they'd better learn the lesson and hire some triumvirate of David Frost, Simon Cowell, and Oprah to handle themselves.

All of that said, *The Queen*'s imagining of the private life of the Windsors (as written by the very skilled Peter Morgan) is high entertainment and pretty good gossipy history. Just as with *The Deal*, a few years earlier (the story of Blair's finessing of Gordon Brown), Frears and Morgan worked very hard to put themselves in the position of guessing what was actually said behind closed doors. How? People leaked, just as they do in Hollywood. And the fusion of newsreel material (to show the reaction to Diana's death, the funeral, et cetera) is cunningly matched with the "at home" soap opera, where the Queen even talks to the animals sometimes.

Some say the venture depended on Helen Mirren's nerve and talent and her commitment to the part. Maybe. She is outstanding and was justly rewarded. But I think the rigor and the wit come from Morgan and Frears and from the overall audacity that the whole thing could be done in a relaxed way—it's a film made as if by Preston Sturges, not the hacks from London's tabloid press. Of course, it's also part 2 of the Blair story, and Michael Sheen's performance is even more uncanny than Mirren's. And some of the other performances—James Cromwell as Philip, say, or even Sylvia Syms as the queen mother—are not as accurate or as sure.

Finally, if the film ended up kinder than maybe Frears expected or intended, that is a measure of just how far it is in the Lubitsch tradition of regarding satirical subjects with tenderness. *The Queen* is not rebellious—it could even get Frears a knighthood, if HRH can summon up the poker-faced humor that Helen Mirren has given her.

Queen Kelly (1928)

We behold an enchanting valley in a rural setting, with brighter light falling magically on the grass and the dew so that we seem to feel every detail. It is Griffith Park, but it feels like a precious meadow somewhere in mittel-Europa, and this natural beauty is a setting for the meeting of two lines of people—the one of mounted cavalry with swords, breastplates, and helmets that bear the form of eagles; and the other a troop of convent girls in white frocks so bright they could be radioactive.

Make no mistake—the scene is hardly natural or plausible: Do the cavalry really exercise as if on the way to a coronation? And where do the convent girls think they are going? But the look of it all is hallowed, engraved, and very beautiful. There is only one respect in which I demur from Gloria Swanson's estimate of the footage: She says the photography made her look like sixteen. That day in Griffith Park, the great lady was thirty—and I would concede that she looks a winning thirty. However, what do I know? My limited knowledge of convent school girls is not just that most of them were turned loose before thirty, but on walks in the country they seldom went out Max Factorized, with false eyelashes or with underwear that collapsed at their ankles.

You see, Patricia Kelly (Swanson), a convent girl ready to be a mother superior for Luis Buñuel, does meet the Prince (Walter Byron) at the head of his column of cavalry, and yes, her prettiness does catch his eye. But somehow her panties are at her ankles. It is typical of director Erich von Stroheim that this is not explained—and it is typical of his provocation that he doesn't bother with that but moves directly to the embarrassment.

The Prince sees the problem and teases her so that the headstrong Catholic girl makes a ball of the panties and hurls them at him. He catches them and takes a quick sniff. When Ms. Swanson, a coproducer on the film, saw this scene, she could hardly believe it or the chance it had of getting past censors. Not long thereafter, with $600,000 spent and less than half the script shot, Swanson and her partner, Joseph Kennedy, called a halt on the picture.

I am talking about *Queen Kelly,* which survives in a version of about 90 minutes, overly full of the mittel-Europa stuff—though Seena Owen is terrific as the often-naked queen, whipping poor Patty Kelly, and with glimpses of the African scenes—where Patty inherits a bordello and accepts marriage to a drooling cripple, presented with full effect by Tully Marshall.

It would be foolish to make a great cause of *Queen Kelly.* It is trash, filmed sometimes with delirious detail and delight, and always threatening to get into the lewd and the lubricious—in heavy-handed ways that seem less sexy than helpless. Did Stroheim direct his downfall? It's a better explanation than "accident" or the notion that he was too deep into his art to notice. *Queen Kelly* is a great curiosity—to be seen, but not believed—and only a fraction of what *Greed* is in its butchered form.

The Queen of Spades (1949)

Alexander Pushkin's novella *The Queen of Spades* was published in 1834. It is one of the great works on gambling at cards and a very impressive portrait of nineteenth-century Russia, and it has a rather neglected film version, made in 1949 by Thorold Dickinson. Captain Herman Suvorin (Anton Walbrook) is a tsarist officer obsessed with cards. He hears a story that the old Countess Ranevskaya (Edith Evans) knows a secret way of winning. And so he insinuates himself with her companion, Lizoveta Ivanova (Yvonne Mitchell), in an attempt to learn the secret. Eventually, he is driven to threaten the old woman, and then to violence. But when he comes to play again, as supposed beneficiary of the secret, he discovers that he has not learned the whole answer.

Thorold Dickinson is a fascinating fringe figure in the British film industry. He made a few inventive feature films before the war, including a version of *Gaslight* (from Patrick Hamilton's play) in which Walbrook played the husband in a full-blooded melodramatic way. He then went into documentary before returning to fiction with *The Queen of Spades*. He ended up teaching film at the University of London.

Of course, in the late 1940s, British film had a very serious line in period films with lavish production design and costumes, and *The Queen of Spades* needs to be seen in that tradition. William Kellner was in charge of the imposing Russian sets, but a young Ken Adam was one of the draftsmen who assisted him. Oliver Messel did the rich costumes (you can hear them creak and sigh), and Otto Heller handled the black-and-white photography. The screenplay was done by Rodney Ackland, with some help from Arthur Boys; and the picture was produced by Jack Clayton (the suspense in his own *The Innocents* is plainly influenced by this film) and Anatole de Grunwald.

It may be a small touch, but this is one of the few films in which Anton Walbrook plays without a mustache. He looks a touch younger clean-shaven, and a great deal more vulnerable and less honest. Herman, in essence, is a hysterical type who believes as much in sinister atmosphere as he does in the fateful fall of the cards. The film is so constructed (like the novella) that there is probably no assured strategy at any card game. But Herman believes there may be, and while Herman is a panic-stricken officer on the edge of being broke, he is rich in superstition. But luck and magic are equally difficult to film: Each one feels like the other. And so Herman is especially prey to signs of the ghostliness in the old countess after he thinks he has disposed of her.

Edith Evans eats up her part (and rivals her own work in the later *The Whisperers*), and Yvonne Mitchell is plausibly Russian as the romantic lead. The rest of the cast includes Ronald Howard, Mary Jerrold, Anthony Dawson, Miles Malleson, Michael Medwin, Athene Seyler, and Ivor Barnard.

A Question of Attribution (1992)

This is not just the best thing John Schlesinger ever did. It is superior by so much that it leaves you wondering if anyone else turned up and directed it. Perhaps it's just that Alan Bennett's script is so gentle and yet cast-iron that the emerging film couldn't help but seem like his. But in that case, why isn't *An Englishman Abroad* (1983) less vulgar? That's the story of resident exile Guy Burgess (Alan Bates) reaching out for a little London gossip with actress Coral Browne as she comes to Moscow on a theatrical tour. That's a nice modest film for television, but just one sprig of thyme next to the full-scale daube of *A Question of Attribution.*

We are observing the life of Sir Anthony Blunt (James Fox), expert on seventeenth-century art, Keeper of the Queen's Pictures, an esteemed figure in the art world—and yet, the fourth man, which is to say a member of the espionage group (Burgess, Donald Maclean, Kim Philby, Blunt) that did so much to enliven British life in midcentury. He is already under examination from the Secret Service, and as our film begins he has a new interrogator—the blunt, dogged David Calder. This newcomer reflects the deft way Blunt has exhausted previous scrutiny with affable, empty small talk.

Blunt is also ill, so he is at the same time concerned to know the results of purely private X-rays and the X-ray photography of a picture (possibly Titian) in the Queen's collection. Is there another man in the painting? Covered up by another surface of paint? The three-card trick of painting-health-espionage is a little fusspot—but Alan Bennett is more likely to give you *Ten Little Spies* than *Detour.* Still, it's very intriguing and perfectly suited to Fox's camp overdone underplaying. Explanation? Fox in this film does decorative underplaying, a tradition in English acting observable also in Claude Rains, Laurence Olivier, and the sublime James Villiers.

The action reaches its height when on a visit to Buckingham Palace, Blunt encounters the Queen in the art gallery. She is played by Prunella Scales. Of course, these days, the Queen of England is Helen Mirren, and it's nearly treason to suggest anyone else. We know why: In the film *The Queen,* batting on a very treacherous wicket, Mirren invented a kind of limp-wristed but steel-nerved defense that made a heroine of the Queen. Scales, on the other hand, sees a very formal woman who knows how to apply the light lash of wit or even scorn.

The Queen-Blunt scenes are elegant confrontations in a comedy of manners, not episodes from a soap opera. And they leave us with the suspicion that the Queen knows exactly the degree of light and shadow in the keeper of her pictures. Moreover, the oblique way in which this movie comes on the question of attribution (or loyalty) cuts much deeper than we expect. It may be that Fox and Scales simply disdained any vulgarity in the playing. It could be that Bennett's script resists color. But there's no reason to deny Schlesinger credit here.

Que Viva Mexico (1931–32)

You can propose that Sergei Eisenstein's *Que Viva Mexico* is not a fictional film in any accepted sense of the term. But Eisenstein believed it was a collection of stories (more than a documentary). Above all, the story of its fortunes—tragic, comic, essentially cinematic—is irresistible and it helps furnish the definition of what the French have called *film maudit*—more or less, a film ruined or spoiled by something, usually "them." But remember: Every time the word *them* is employed, it's "us" using it.

In the spring of 1930, in Paris, Jesse Lasky of Paramount met Eisenstein and offered him and his associates, Tisse and Alexandrov, a modest contract if they would come to Hollywood ($900 a week to cover the three men). They arrived. They set up house, and they wrote scripts that struck Paramount as too expensive, impossible, or far too grim. (Others have disappointed Paramount for far larger sums.) The last of these was a version of Dreiser's *An American Tragedy*. So the trio were stranded when Paramount terminated the deal. It was then that Eisenstein thought of Mexico.

It's fairly clear that he had no wish to return to the USSR, and who can blame him? The painter Diego Rivera encouraged him to see Mexico and film it. They went to Chaplin for help (loaded with money) and he sent them to Upton Sinclair (well-off, but not loaded). It's a measure of Sinclair's curiosity and geniality that he and his wife advanced $25,000 for the trip, on a deal that would give the Russians 10 percent profit once costs were covered. So they set off.

The idea was for a four-month trip. It turned into fifteen months. Tisse went crazy for the faces, the pyramids, the decoration, and the light. Eisenstein loved the liberty (there was an element of homosexual holiday in it). They sent footage back to Sinclair for processing. He was more than impressed—but how did it all add up? It went on and on, with Eisenstein's concept enlarging as he learned more about Mexico. Then Stalin cabled Sinclair to say he didn't approve of Eisenstein. The footage was ravishing but unworkable. The money ran out. Eisenstein and his fellows went back to Russia (to harder times), and Sinclair kept the footage.

It was decades later before this material went back to Moscow. By then (1979) Alexandrov was the only one of the three left. He gave it the best shape he could, which is close to nil. He put a solemn commentary on it (read by Sergei Bondarchuk) and a dreadful musical score. It explains nothing about Mexico, but it is worth seeing for its intense, intermittent beauty and because of the atmospheric insinuations of how Eisenstein and the others were having the time of their life.

So, no, it's not a feature—but it cries out for one. And in a macabre way, changing names and numbers, the same story could be told of Orson Welles's *It's All True*, about ten years later and based in Rio. The best of the Welles footage is as lovely and as open-ended as the Tisse footage. It shows that Truth is a flimsy justification when you're dealing with film and money, and people are expecting a story. But the fascination of the great *films maudits* never dies. Is there even a secret urge in all great film artists to be *maudit*?

The Quiet Man (1952)

As John Ford's daughter, Barbara, surveyed the footage of *The Quiet Man,* she enthused in a letter to her father that it made Ireland look like "a fairy land." In time, Winton Hoch and Archie Stout shared an Oscar for making it look so enchanted and emerald, despite much adverse weather. And so far we're nowhere near the story itself.

Ford saw Ireland for the first time in 1921 (just after the birth of his son Patrick), and I think that to understand his conception of America it is important to see how he regarded Ireland. What follows from that is his helpless yielding to wishful thinking, and his celebration in *The Quiet Man* of a folksy, prettified Ireland. That twilight was finally set aside with the country's accession to the European Economic Community. *The Quiet Man* was a popular success in parts of the world accustomed to send money for guns to the IRA. It brought no comfort to those Irishmen who hoped to free their country from unreason, poverty, the tyranny of the Catholic Church, and the addled mixture of coziness, self-pity, boozy charm, and brutality known as "Irishness." *The Quiet Man* is the cheerful imprisonment of a real country in the confines of folklore and picture postcard. (It is the stifling of the voices of Joyce, Shaw, and Wilde, all of whom loathed the sentimentalization of Ireland.) Rather than see the real thing—the facts—Ford settled for the legend. He said as much about America, and it is time for this dangerous pipe dream to be exposed.

The film came from a *Saturday Evening Post* story of 1933, by Maurice Walsh, in which an Irish boxer goes home to Kerry, falls in love with a local girl, but finds himself at odds with the girl's brother over the dowry. There was a plan to do the film with Alex Korda just after the war, but that fell through. A few years later, for Argosy and Republic, it was revived. Richard Llewellyn did a first script, and then Frank Nugent turned it into a shooting script.

The boxer was made a bigger man; he became Sean Thornton, and John Wayne had the part. Rather more important to the lovelorn Ford was getting Maureen O'Hara into the role of Mary Kate Danaher. And for her brother, he cast Victor McLaglen, who had been a boxer—he fought Jack Johnson (no matter that McLaglen was thirty-four years older than O'Hara).

The concept of the film needs the three epic figures, with a gallery of "little" people gossiping about them. But whereas there is an authentic passion between Wayne and O'Hara (the actor thought the director was calling for love scenes to imagine himself with O'Hara), the prolonged fisticuffs with McLaglen is brutal and ponderous, as well as a travesty of how family really works in Ireland.

The gallery includes quite a bit of fun and sparkle with Barry Fitzgerald, Arthur Shields, Mildred Natwick, Ward Bond, Ken Curtis, Mae Marsh, Francis Ford, and—a standout—the young Jack MacGowran, not just really Irish but truly an actor.

It cost about $1.5 million and earned nearly $6 million. McLaglen got an Oscar nomination for Supporting Actor, and the film had a Best Picture nomination. Ford won his fourth Oscar as director.

Radio Days (1987)

Or suppose it all works through the ear? "It originated from an idea that I wanted to pick out a group of songs that were meaningful to me, and each one of those songs suggested a memory. Then the idea started to evolve: how important radio was to me when I was growing up and how important or glamorous it seemed to everyone."

Expect Woody Allen to tell a story and he gets tense with the fear that he will forget or fumble it. So he puts himself onscreen, as if that may help him keep control. But since he is so disastrous an actor, and so crippled by the demands of his ego, he spreads uncertainty in other actors. Pretending itself seizes up. But then sometimes Allen finds another way to go—he makes a picture that is an essay or a set of variations on a theme. And if he can persuade himself to get offscreen then something wonderful is in prospect. Like *Radio Days*, an event that all of a sudden makes it clear the guy was born to make movies, even if so much of the time he lets fear and pretension get in his own way.

So *Radio Days* takes a household living out by the shore—not simply autobiographical, but a way of organizing the memories: There's the kid, Joe (Seth Green), very natural, very relaxed and funny, and nobody's neurotic; there's Tess (Julie Kavner), the mother; Martin (Michael Tucker), the father; there's Aunt Bea (Dianne Wiest), dreaming of handsome guys; and Uncle Abe (Josh Mostel), feasting on fish. This is one of the most humble, robust, and lifelike families in American film, and without the matter ever being addressed in a narrative way (thank God), we get a sense of amazing warmth and solidarity, as well as a kind of chorus always ready to hum and dance to the songs on the radio.

It's a time of disaster hoaxes and real wars, with subs off Long Island looking like great fish, with local beauties dancing nude in their parlors like women waiting for Edward Hopper to paint them. It's the greater New York of seascapes and desolate streets that slope down to the water, as well as Radio City Music Hall and ratty nightclubs. And the film slips like wet fish on a marble slab—it's so alive. Carlo Di Palma shot it, and Santo Loquasto did the art direction, so the middle-class look is actually very richly provided.

Woody is the narrator—sad, wistful, excited, aroused—and he's perfect. He has a great enough radio voice that he isn't driven to sing. The songs keep coming like your favorite radio station, and you get a feeling of how movies and radio were once the bloodstream of a great nation. This is one of those quiet films that cuts America open to the eye, and leaves you longing for those old days (like *Ambersons*). It's a masterpiece, a one of a kind—with Mia Farrow as Sally, Danny Aiello, Jeff Daniels as Biff Baxter, Tony Roberts, Wallace Shawn, David Warrilow and Julie Kurnitz as Roger and Irene, and Diane Keaton singing "You'd Be So Nice to Come Home To." And like the sea, the fish, and sound itself, running through it all, the aching lament of "September Song," which can shift the mood in any direction you want.

Raging Bull (1980)

Between October 1942 and February 1951, Ray Robinson and Jake La Motta fought six times. Of those six fights, La Motta won only the second. Not that they were anything other than close fights, fought to the full limit of rounds, with Robinson winning on points in all except the last fight, a knockout. Robinson was the greatest boxer-fighter of his age. He was Sugar, an eloquent, smart black man who conducted himself like a prince. He was Ali in advance, as well as a sight to behold in the ring. So let's make a film about La Motta?

It really is the far-fetched decision, except that La Motta was white, Italian, and one of the neighborhood gang. He was known as the Bronx Bull, and he made a cult of stupid defiance. More than that, Marty Scorsese could identify with him as some kind of lonely hero who longs to be one of the boys. (But art *can* resist type: Nick Tosches wrote a great book about Sonny Liston.)

And so we trace the rise and fall of La Motta (Robert De Niro) through two marriages—first to an Italian girl (Theresa Saldana) and then to a white icon, the Lana Turner of the neighborhood swimming pool (Cathy Moriarty). Jake is sexy, but he knows he must apply ice water to his horn to keep it strong for the fights. So he pets with Moriarty and flirts with the boys. There is a very lively gay subtext here—hardly perceived by Scorsese—in which Jake is drawn into the ghastly macho circle of the fight crowd who secretly want to fuck each other.

Put that next to the immense, studied beauty of the film—the umbilical ring ropes in black and white but dripping red blood—and this is a very fancy film indeed. Nothing suggests anything but fear and loathing on Scorsese's part for the homosexual tendency, but there it is, in a film that plainly knows so little about boxing (and cares less) that it's happy to shoot it as somewhere between the bullfight and the ballet. It's pretentious and yearning, but reluctant to think its own feelings through. De Niro won the Oscar, not for insight so much as for the huge ordeal by which he made himself gross after looking like a brutal saint.

The result is fascinating, but truly confused. And it's the start of those films in which Scorsese can't close his eyes and ears to the foul patter of Italian guys, and it's the start of Joe Pesci (perhaps the great virus in Scorsese's work—the demon he cannot deny himself yet the force of destruction he fears to take on) taking the world over.

Paul Schrader and Mardik Martin wrote it, but not together—and their two voices may be at the heart of the turmoil. Michael Chapman did maybe the last great job in black and white—it's like Weegee in olive oil. Thelma Schoonmaker's editing is brilliant, even if it introduces a facility that helps Scorsese dodge his unsolved narrative. The great cast includes Nicholas Colasanto, Frank Vincent, and John Turturro. De Niro won his Oscar, and Pesci was nominated in support. *Raging Bull* has problems, but when *Ordinary People* beat it for Best Picture it was the moment for the Academy to retire into the night.

Raiders of the Lost Ark (1981)

At the time, everyone involved was making too much money to really explore first thoughts, let alone second, but in hindsight, *Raiders of the Lost Ark* looks like a very strange party game. Yes, it was the "natural" alliance of the two boy giants of the picture business, George Lucas and Steven Spielberg, and surely in their first great bounty they could be forgiven if they felt the urge to be kids again and to go back to the thrills of Saturday morning pictures. Don't you get it—*Raiders* and Indiana Jones are a fond throwback to a lost world? Well, yes, I think everyone got it after about three minutes. And it's not that *Raiders* wasn't fun. But did we need three of them?

The idea was hatched by George Lucas and Phil Kaufman, and I have heard rumors that Kaufman had expected to direct this first film—certainly there's a brotherhood of a kind between the leather-jacketed Indiana Jones (Harrison Ford) and the idealized version of Chuck Yeager (Sam Shepard) in Kaufman's far more interesting *The Right Stuff*. But the script was given to Lawrence Kasdan, and then Spielberg decided that he might as well direct, with Lucas serving as producer.

Indiana Jones is an archaeologist, and a rather humorless, deadpan jokester who has difficulties with women—let's face it, he has difficulties with just about everything. But he's determined to keep the Ark or the Holy Grail or the residuals of these pictures or whatever it is out of the hands of the Nazis and all other bad guys. The time is the 1930s, and you can easily think of *Gunga Din*, *Beau Geste*, and *Only Angels Have Wings*. Actually, you can easily see those films. And the "boys" might have realized that.

Experts on the series say that the original is the best, *Indiana Jones and the Temple of Doom* (1984) the least, and *Indiana Jones and the Last Crusade* (1989) a happy return. You can identify the series by its female stars—Karen Allen, Kate Capshaw, and Alison Doody (which amounts to an admission that they weren't very interested in women). But Spielberg directed all three, with humor here and there and secondhand panache everywhere. Harrison Ford became a grudging version of the most successful movie star of all time—though Sean Connery outshone him as a brusque Dad in number three.

It doesn't really matter, I suppose, except that along the way the photographing of adventure yielded to and helped discover computer-generated imagery in which everything was possible and nothing very interesting. Also, the pictures made amounts of money that altered the economy of Hollywood and made it seem orthodox to keep on making lightweight, silly, fun pictures. Here are the numbers.

Raiders (writing credits: Kasdan, Lucas, Kaufman)
budget: $20 million
worldwide gross: $384 million

Temple of Doom (writing credits: Lucas, Willard Huyck, and Gloria Katz)
budget: $28 million
worldwide gross: $333 million

Last Crusade (writing credits: Lucas, Kaufman, Menno Meyjes, Jeffrey Boam)
budget: $48 million
worldwide gross: $494 million

Rain Man (1988)

You can present *Rain Man* as exactly what Hollywood wanted from itself in the late eighties. It cost about $25 million, and it had a worldwide gross income of $354 million. More than that, it won Best Picture as well as several other Oscars. It is also a fond portrait of a man's world in which guys learn to blend sensitivity with success, gentleness with winning. Fifteen or so years after its great arrival, it looks curiously artificial and irrelevant. It's the kind of film that hopes to make contact with life through "stellar acting." But it's little more than a commercial for itself, stuffed with self-admiration and gloating coups. I don't think it goes too far to say that it's the smug movie of a culture charging down a dead-end street. It isn't simply that it's so removed from life. It's also the horrible comfort and cocksure bossiness it feels in that gulf.

Charlie Babbitt (and I think we are meant to hear the "everyman" reference in the name), played by Tom Cruise, is a smart, nasty, selfish hustler. He goes back to the Midwest for his father's funeral and gets a surprise (the last in the film). It turns out the father has left his considerable money to "another" brother: Raymond (Dustin Hoffman). This is Raymond as in Raymond from *The Manchurian Candidate,* but worse. Raymond is autistic, a kind of idiot savant. He is a simpleton with a tremendously rapid way of calculating numbers. And these brothers never knew about each other, but now they have to get along. They will try because Charlie feels very fraternal about Raymond's money. However, don't be surprised (or a believer) if Raymond gradually turns Charlie into a warm, loving human being—in short, a brother.

The story is by Barry Morrow, and the script was written by Morrow and Ron Bass. The film is directed by Barry Levinson, who in his time has done some really touching studies in male bonding. Cruise and Hoffman were powerhouses of different construction: Hoffman is a veteran car, cranky, quirky, eccentric; while Cruise is about the most streamlined and efficient wheels on the market. There is even a fatuous way in which you can read this as country and city or nineteenth-century and twentieth-century America. But it's best to confine yourself to Cruise's "I sit in awe at the feet of a master" act, along with Hoffman's "Why do you so admire me, my son?" I'm sure that Hoffman worked very hard at becoming autistic—it's just that it was a shorter journey than he ever reckoned. Cruise's acting, I think, is actually more thoughtful and very much quicker. But Hoffman wins on time of possession and hesitation after the catch. It all requires enormous patience and is a 90-minute film stretched to 133 minutes.

Valeria Golino is the girl. John Seale did the lustrous photography. Ida Random and Linda DeScenna did the art direction. Stu Linder edited the film and Hans Zimmer wrote the music. Other Oscars went to Levinson as director, to the script, and to Dustin Hoffman.

Raise the Red Lantern (1991)

Songlian is rebellious from the outset. When she is hired on to be the fourth wife, or concubine, of a rich man, she does not wait for the sedan-chair service that will pick her up. She packs her suitcase and walks, however far it is, in an attempt to show that she is her own fierce self, a young woman who has had enough of a university education to know that such practices as being married off in 1920 are archaic and absurd. Yet it happens to her, and the prison only draws in more tightly as the story unfolds. You can see this as one of the uncompromising social studies that began emerging from China—or you can see it as a Joan Crawford–like picture, with money from Hong Kong and Taiwan as well as China. After all, Songlian is also Gong Li, one of the great new actresses at the end of the twentieth century.

The house of Chen seems to exist in the provinces, yet we see no more of those exteriors than Songlian. There is an abiding master shot from a high angle, looking down on the courtyard that is the common space for the four houses of the four wives. The servants of the household are there to make their life easier—to massage their feet, to get their clothes, to arrange for a doctor to call—but they are guards, too, ensuring that the women do not escape. When Songlian arrives, she is the youngest and the freshest—the most sexual. Yet she is the least resigned or understanding. But she is smart enough to see that the four wives are in an eternal and futile competition to win the master's favor. So she plots to gain more power.

That is the delusion of the young. At first, she thinks she will be pregnant. She makes the claim, and Chen—hungry for an heir—comes to her regularly, with solicitude. Songlian thought that then, sooner or later, she would be pregnant. But an abused servant informs on her, and she is punished. The red lanterns that mark her house as a place of special privilege are taken down.

The film comes from a novel by Su Tong and a screenplay by Ni Zhen. Zhang Yimou is the director, and this was one of his breakthrough films—but notice that the Taiwan master Hou Hsiao-hsien was an executive producer, and Gong Li is in every sense a star. Her look—beautiful in Western eyes—and her acting (very fresh and forthright) are vital to the accessibility of this film. You'd also have to weigh the ravishing color photography of Zhao Fei and Yang Lun. Even untrained audiences notice that the new Chinese films had an expressive use of color that had nearly been given up in Western cinema.

It was Oscar-nominated for Best Foreign Language Film, and it played with great success on the international art-house circuit. But in its portrait of Songlian, it knew that old lesson Crawford had learned in the thirties and the forties—that the wronged woman should not expect mercy.

Rancho Notorious (1952)

In its first planning, *Rancho Notorious* was intended to marry Fritz Lang's fondness for Western iconography and his interest in gambling. Silvia Richards (with whom he was romantically involved, and who scripted *Secret Beyond the Door*) had done a treatment, "Chuck-a-Luck," featuring the kind of vertical roulette game of chance that figures in the story. But the treatment was shelved, and it was only when Daniel Taradash came on board as a new writer that it took off. It was Taradash who proposed a balladlike structure to the film, "The Legend of Chuck-a-Luck," written by Ken Darby.

Although Lang spent time researching exterior locations, this is the most set-bound of his Westerns—and the best. The two things are surely related. Whatever he might say about touring in the Southwest, Lang the artist preferred the control of studio shooting, and he never seemed dismayed by the "atmosphere" of cardboard rocks and painted vistas. So there were a few shots done at the Republic ranch, but most of it was filmed at the General Services studio, with Wiard Ihnen doing great work on the "mountain retreat" of Rancho Notorious, a kind of Berchtesgarden for wanted men, ruled by Altar Keane (Marlene Dietrich).

As photographed by Hal Mohr (in color) it looks very good—indeed, the cowboys have a slightly piratical air. The story is very simple: Vern Haskell (Arthur Kennedy) sets out to avenge the rape and murder of his sweetheart. The journey takes him to Rancho Notorious and is another study of vengeance as a warping force. Far less successful is his love affair with Altar and the romantic rivalry of Frenchy Fairmont (Mel Ferrer), a character somewhat mocked by his own name.

Indeed, Western enthusiasts only notice the artificiality of Rancho Notorious—but that is because Lang takes that for granted and makes this world a cockpit for moral energy that risks going mad. In that light, this film is very close to *The Big Heat,* even if the urban, black-and-white mood is kinder to the real subject. There are astonishing fights in this "Western," and they are like the fights that always thrilled Lang—less trials of strength than extreme geometric compositions (parallelograms of forces) in which humanity seems to be in the balance.

Arthur Kennedy is very good, and his Vern fits in easily with the Westerners he was playing at the same time for Anthony Mann and Edgar Ulmer. The supporting cast has a number of vivid cameos—William Frawley, Jack Elam, Dan Seymour, Frank Ferguson. Lang said that he and Dietrich were romantically involved during the film. Maybe, but it doesn't show. Dietrich here was fifty, and her makeup begins to look heavy. She lacks songs (apart from "Get Away, Young Man"), and she misses Sternberg. Without him, she was not the easiest person to put in a movie story. After *Rancho Notorious,* she did nothing until *Witness for the Prosecution.*

Rashomon (1950)

Even if you haven't seen *Rashomon,* you've likely heard of it. You vaguely know the way in which "Rashomon-like" applies to a story in which you get several points of view that amount to a total contradiction and a revelation of the lies we tell. I wonder how far Akira Kurosawa guessed at the time that the new art-house film circuits of Europe and America were bursting for this kind of agnosticism? Was his whole American career worked out as carefully as Addison DeWitt (same year) sculpted the rise of Eve Harrington in *All About Eve*? It won the Grand Prix at Venice and went on to the Academy Award for Best Foreign Picture. And it was the start of Kurosawa as an international figure.

It's not that Kurosawa didn't deserve some success. He's a terrific, vigorous, single-minded director. And in such varied things as *Seven Samurai* and *Ikiru* he's well worthwhile, even if you can predict those films in detail from about fifteen minutes in. He's also close to an amateur when it comes to taking us back to early Japan and having us feel the lawlessness and the threat to culture in those times. So *Rashomon* leaves us like smarty-pants who don't trust truth. But *Sansho the Bailiff* (just a few years later) leaves a feeling of fear and miracle in the world. To be brief, I don't mind *Rashomon* being celebrated—it's good clean fun, spectacular, and absorbing. But when its fans don't know Mizoguchi I get upset.

So, in *Rashomon,* three characters meet in the woods: a nobleman, his wife, and a bandit. And they are observed by a fourth, a woodcutter. At the end, the nobleman is dead and the woman appears to have been raped. But what really happens? As in most expert thrillers, the secret to that last question is that it doesn't matter—for grave issues of character, action, and society are not being called into being. A game is being played in which ninth-century Kyoto is an excuse for costume, swords, and a way of filming the woods that might occur more naturally to a Japanese artist. The fundamental issues of freedom and slavery in *Sansho,* or of hope and loyalty in *Ugetsu,* are never broached. Instead, it's a shorthand for getting from "You never knew" to the assumption of wisdom that actually eliminates all responsibility or consequence. Because you don't know what happened, nothing happened.

On the plus side, the film was quick and vivid, and in many ways (i.e., the fighting) it catered to Western curiosity. The rapid tracking movements were full of fun and energy—if empty of meaning. Toshiro Mifune introduced his bristling wild guys. Machiko Kyo played the woman as if determined to have no future claim of rape trusted. Masayuki Mori is the nobleman, and Takashi Shimura plays the woodcutter. Of course, the film is a drama. It's only later on that one reflects how far the *Rashomon* method is more interesting if applied to comedy, and in a situation where everyone is sure they are telling the truth.

Yes, there was a direct remake, *The Outrage* (1964), shifted to Mexico, with Paul Newman, Claire Bloom, Laurence Harvey, and Edward G. Robinson. It is a tranquilizer.

Raw Deal (1948)

This book has to include at least one of the luminous noirs made in the late forties by Anthony Mann and photographer John Alton. But can it find room for more than one? Mann had been Emil Anton Bundsmann (born near San Diego in 1906). The child of philosophy teachers, he tried acting first, and then joined the Selznick company to direct screen tests. He started directing low-budget films in 1942, and he became established, and respectable, around 1950 with the James Stewart Westerns. John Alton was five years older, born in Hungary. He roamed the world working as a cameraman, and studying the infant art, and he ended up in Hollywood in 1940. He did five films for Mann, all black-and-white—they are *T-Men, Raw Deal, Reign of Terror, Border Incident*, and *Devil's Doorway*. Alton also shot *He Walked by Night*, credited to Alfred L. Werker, but also worked on by Mann (and the most abstract of them all). From these beginnings, Alton went on to win an Oscar for the entirely different color photography on *An American in Paris*. That was for M-G-M, where Alton became a celebrated but conventional artistic cameraman.

It's hardly original to say that the two guys had a great time on their five films—the cinematic excitement jumps out at you from every shot, and surely these films had a huge impact on certain French critics (often reliant on the subtitles) in finding beauty at the lowest level of American moviemaking. Equally, the label "every shot like a painting" is a mixed blessing that often goes too near the dream of saving trash with artiness—that shining white lie and pathetic fallacy is painfully evident in *Reign of Terror*, the most spectacular of the films, largely because it is a re-creation of revolutionary France. Every shot is breathtaking, but lack of breathing is not helpful to feeling oneself taken up in the atmosphere of a movie. *Reign of Terror* is frantic, show-off time—nothing is natural about it, and it is a tough act to inhabit.

That's why I opt for *Raw Deal*, a brutal vengeance story in which Dennis O'Keefe escapes from prison resolved to nail the people who put him there. The savage compositions of light and shadow fit this hard-boiled and luridly unfair world. There are superb cameos in villainy, by Raymond Burr and John Ireland, while O'Keefe and Claire Trevor are perfectly suited to the bittersweet, sadomasochistic "romance." One can breathe while watching the film, and one can feel that the noir story is adjusted to the bravura styling. In *Reign of Terror*, there is a grotesque gap between Robert Cummings's sunny hero and Richard Basehart's Robespierre. Cummings is making an entertainment while Basehart suspects he may be in a work of art.

The most interesting question is what this partnership did in educating Mann. Surely his eye was assisted and provoked—yet Mann has one of the great cinematic eyes (arguably a lot more interesting than Alton's). So maybe it was Mann who helped Alton. Mann was working his way toward a kind of calm distancing from people that is emphatically at odds with Alton's graphic underlining of everything.

Rear Window (1954)

There are great films and great entertainments. Sometimes one film is both—take *Rear Window*. L. B. Jefferies (James Stewart) is in his Lower Manhattan apartment with a broken leg. There it is, in white plaster, as long and hard as a telephoto lens. He is a photographer and a sensationalist. He specializes in taking pictures of dangerous events. This time he got too close—thus the broken leg. So the wanderer and adventurer is a trapped spectator, seated in front of the lives in the courtyard where he lives, trapped by the offers of marriage from his perfect girlfriend, Lisa Fremont (Grace Kelly). He can only watch—remind you of anyone?

There are windows in the courtyard, windows and lives: the honeymoon couple; the composer; the lonely romantic woman; a young dancer; an elderly couple with a dog; and the Thorwalds—Lars and his wife. They argue a lot: the wife is bedridden; she nags Lars. He seems bitter. So many of the windows are playing love or marriage movies—as if Lisa had programmed them. Then one night when L.B. is only half awake, he thinks . . . did he see a part of a murder? Where is Mrs. Thorwald?

His masseuse, Stella (Thelma Ritter), tells him voyeurism is an unhealthy habit. His friend the cop, Doyle (Wendell Corey), tells him he's crazy. But Lisa begins to think they might both be right. They will play detectives together.

This comes from a novelette by Cornell Woolrich and a script by John Michael Hayes that is among the most perfect ever written. For as the intrigue grows, as the crazy notion picks up dark detail, and credibility, so our love story deepens. Lisa will go across the way to the Thorwalds' apartment while he is out and she'll look for the wedding ring. If Mrs. Thorwald took a vacation, as Doyle says, she'd hardly leave that behind. So over she goes, with Jefferies and us watching, and Oh, my God, here's Thorwald coming home. He gets her, but Jeff calls the police and they come just in time. Then cock-a-hoop Lisa is wiggling her hand at Jeff because she's wearing the wedding ring. And Lars Thorwald follows the line of her signal and looks straight at us.

Robert Burks did the photography. Hal Pereira led the art direction team. Edith Head did Lisa's great clothes. Franz Waxman wrote the music. The windows use players like Judith Evelyn, Ross Bagdasarian, Georgine Darcy, Irene Winston, and Lars Thorwald is Raymond Burr in white hair—he looks like . . . David O. Selznick, that bête noire in Hitchcock's life.

It's 112 minutes. It's funny, tart, tender, thoughtful, desperate, and as neat and tidy a moral parable about looking at things and getting involved as you're ever going to find. I suppose I've watched it forty times or so, and I'm still waiting for it to taste like less than a Meyer lemon fresh from the tree. But as time passes, the suspense falls away, and the bones of greater comedy emerge.

Rebecca (1940)

When Joan Fontaine came on the set of *Rebecca* (having overcome Vivien Leigh, Margaret Sullavan, Loretta Young, and Anne Baxter in the casting contest), she was taken aback that both Laurence Olivier and Alfred Hitchcock treated her with a coolness close to disdain. But why not? Fontaine was playing an interloper in a settled household, a real girl daring to challenge the power of a ghost, and she didn't have a name to call her own. Hitchcock knew a lot about intimidation, and Olivier was so crazy about Vivien then that he thought he would have preferred her on the set.

But that was by no means the biggest battle on *Rebecca.* Producer David O. Selznick had tempted Hitch to come to America, and then he offered him the Daphne Du Maurier novel that had been recommended to the Selznick organization by Kay Brown (the same way they had got *Gone With the Wind*). So Selznick the book man was certain the adaptation should be faithful. There was the start of trouble with Hitch, who had often made big departures on books he was filming—tossing in a girl in *The 39 Steps.*

So there was dispute on the script with Selznick bitter and bewildered at Hitch's casual departures. In the end, Selznick won that battle on a script that was credited to Robert E. Sherwood and Hitch's assistant, Joan Harrison. Moreover, in nearly every detail of that squabble, Selznick was right: he knew what a strange bird *Rebecca* was—a mixture of romance, mystery, obsession, and even horror. To this day, it is striking for the way it overlaps genres and allows hints of perversity—especially in the role of Mrs. Danvers.

But the real struggle came in the shooting and the amazed reaction to rushes. Selznick was used to ample coverage (if in doubt, shoot another angle), and he fancied himself as an editing-room master of ceremonies. Whereas Hitchcock liked to envisage every aspect of a sequence in his head, then shoot it, so that the pieces of film only needed assembly. He left no fun to the editing—and no power. Selznick roared in distress.

Forever afterward, Hitchcock complained at Selznick's interference—and nobody could deny that habit in the producer. But Hitch's way of shooting was not just very difficult to interfere with. It was immaculate, and it worked. *Rebecca* is often a suspense film, and Selznick had never managed that as well as Hitch could. So both sides could claim victory, if only because the movie won the Best Picture Oscar and was a box-office success. The battle between producer and director would be settled another day.

Who won? We won, for this is a very sophisticated entertainment, one of the best films Selznick would ever make, but deeper and tauter than anything Hitch had done so far. Fontaine is superb (this is her real Oscar performance). Olivier is very interesting and repressed. George Sanders is a treat. But over the years Judith Anderson becomes uncanny as Mrs. Danvers—she was defeated for Supporting Actress by Jane Darwell in *The Grapes of Wrath* (a travesty).

Rebel Without a Cause (1955)

This is a key moment in American film, poised on the brink of rock 'n' roll and the kingdom of the American teenager, yet bringing to a close the era of the brooding existential hero, the tradition that had gone from John Garfield to Brando and Clift, and which had suddenly risen up in the untidy life of Nicholas Ray as that ghost-in-waiting, James Dean. And for a moment, two nervous wrecks—the actor and the director—were looking in time's mirror and the result was a film that survives as emotional melodrama, as a portrait of high school and of the impossible remaking of family in America. There are moments of pretension, of stilted lines and unfulfilled striving. (Why not? It's about being a teenager.) On the other hand, it's as perfect an expression of the moment as a great song.

The possibility of the film had been around for several years. It might have been a Marlon Brando picture. But it came together at Warner Brothers, produced by David Weisbart and written by Stewart Stern, apparently from an idea by Ray, with some further work by Irving Shulman. Still, much of the mood was derived from study of actual Los Angeles gangs—albeit white, white, and white. Thus, it is also a history of a city that is no more. Jim Stark (Dean) comes to town, and finds himself confronted with the gang led by Buzz (Corey Allen), with Judy (Natalie Wood) as the princess, and Plato (Sal Mineo) as the only other outsider. The film never asks why Plato is beyond the group, but his parents are nowhere, he has a black nanny, and he wants to be looked after in the profoundest way. Of all the gang—and it includes Dennis Hopper, Frank Mazzola, and Nick Adams—only Judy is played by a teenager (so Ray had an affair with her as a salute, and as an attempt to feel the young pulse).

It was photographed by Ernest Haller (who had done *Gone With the Wind*), and yet the film has some of the greatest CinemaScope framing ever seen, as well as a camera spinning on its axis. Despite Warnercolor, the color scheme is electrifying and creative. And the music, by Leonard Rosenman, means as much as Steiner's score on *Gone With the Wind*. Its scenes are still the stages of teenage initiation. Its reformed family (Jim, Judy, and Plato) is heartrending, and maybe the planetarium in Griffith Park still stands because of this film's poetic grasp of being on the edge of deep space and nuclear apocalypse.

Yes, the film announced an appalling surrender to teenagerism that we still suffer from. Yes, Deanism is a cunning version of self-pity, as seductive as a snake's stillness. Yes, the point of view of the parental generation (Jim Backus, Ann Doran, William Hopper—all excellent) is travestied. But there are movies in which beauty or grace is so allied with timeliness, there is no stopping or forgetting it. This is the only film where Dean was a kid now—and he only needed to do it once. If you came of age around the same time as this film, then you are lost—and we understand. Growing up was over. But the dysfunctional family was a new institution. No one could swallow the happy bromide again.

The Reckless Moment (1949)

How quickly film noir improves on itself if put to an extra human challenge. So here is a story based on murder and blackmail. But it leaves a film that is unmistakably a love story as well as proof that, given the chance, criminal incident will bring out the character in people. It's a story about human family as a duty and taskmaster under which the individual may lose his or her own liveliness. Lucia Harper (Joan Bennett) is a wife and mother in this predicament. She has a daughter, Bea (Geraldine Brooks), and Bea has a lover that the mother doesn't approve of. One day, the lover's corpse turns up and Lucia assumes that Bea is the killer. So, on her own, she disposes of the body and lives with the hopeless dream that nothing more will happen.

Then a man appears, Martin Donnelly (James Mason), an enchanting, amiable man, not at all what you'd expect of a blackmailer. But that's what he is, goaded on by his much blunter partner, Nagel (Roy Roberts). They know what happened, and they begin to blackmail Lucia—for money, they will say nothing. Martin is the messenger in these nasty negotiations, yet he becomes the wife's friend. He sees how smothered or trapped she is by her family, yet he looks upon those ties with the fondness of an outcast who has never enjoyed them himself. He falls in love with Lucia. She has a husband, but she is stirred by this odd man, struggling in his own trap. What can Martin do to end the pressure on her? It's foreseeable, maybe, yet it comes as a surprise, too, and it raises the film to the level of tragedy.

It came from a novel, *The Blank Wall*, by Elisabeth Sanxay Holding. The adaptation was done by Mel Dinelli and Robert E. Kent, and the screenplay was the work of Henry Garson and Robert W. Soderberg. The producer was Walter Wanger, who was married to Joan Bennett. Wanger used two great European directors, Fritz Lang and Max Ophüls, to showcase his wife—and clearly this subtle investigation of mixed motives is Ophüls material. His handling of Mason is exemplary, and he was always a director who sympathized with the traps in which women found themselves. But this relationship is one of the most complex in his work, and it makes for a novel-like movie, full of nuance and detail.

Burnett Guffey did the photography, and Hans Salter contributed a good score. The cast also includes Henry O'Neill and Shepperd Strudwick.

The story was remade in 2001 as *The Deep End*, with Tilda Swinton as the wife. That film tended to be a vehicle for her and so it did not uncover the offbeat love affair that is so haunting in the Ophüls film. But the character of a director—let alone the greatness—is always going to be apparent in how he reads a story and in the space he finds between the lines.

Red Dust (1932)

It was Labor Day weekend, September 1932, when the servants came into the house on Easton Drive in Beverly Hills and found Paul Bern, naked, shot dead, with a note nearby apologizing to his wife, Jean Harlow. At the time, she was shooting *Red Dust* at M-G-M, with Clark Gable. It looked like being a smash hit. But when the death was reported, Louis B. Mayer concluded that Harlow would be in no state to complete the picture. So he talked to Tallulah Bankhead about taking over. Harlow rallied.

Red Dust had been a play, by Wilson Collison. It flopped, but the studio saw potential. It was a story set in the jungles of Indochina. Dennis Carson is a rugged rubber planter. He meets Vantine, a Saigon hooker escaping from the police. They get acquainted, but then a couple of highbrows arrive, Gary and Barbara Willis, an engineer and his wife. Barbara becomes infatuated with Dennis, but finally Dennis realizes that the Saigon hooker is more his type.

With Hunt Stromberg producing, John Lee Mahin wrote a script, and there was some doctoring by Donald Ogden Stewart. Dennis had been earmarked for John Gilbert, but Mayer overrode that and put Gable in instead. Jean Harlow was to be Vantine—she and Gable had had a few effective scenes together in *The Secret Six,* and *Red Dust* was meant to be a sexy collision for the two of them. Indochina was built on a set by Cedric Gibbons and Arnold Gillespie, with a lot of mud and heat and a general drenched look that made clear what assets the stars had. There was a good deal of suggestive stuff with liquid rubber, and a moment where Mary Astor had to watch a black slug squirt out of a tree. It was raunchy for its day, and there was a notorious bath-in-a-barrel scene where Harlow had done her bit for Clark and then stood up to allow the crew a good look at her breasts.

It was one of Hollywood's class stories, with plenty of automatic racism and an attitude to Indochina that boded no good if you cared to think ahead thirty years. Gable's attitude was live for today, and Gene Raymond and Mary Astor were the educated couple, with sex the great leveler. And, of course, there was a strange way in which the Bern-Harlow tragedy was just a cultured man and a raw doll, a famous sexpot and a guy who wasn't sure about his sex drive. Victor Fleming directed the film, and everyone agreed that Clark and Jean were made for each other.

Then came Paul Bern's death, hiatus, and then Jean came back to work, too eager to see her great chance disappear. Her hunch was right. The picture cost about $400,000 and it grossed three times that amount. Gable and Harlow would do four more pictures together, though she was dead before the last one—*Saratoga*—came out.

Twenty years later, it was remade as *Mogambo,* with Ava Gardner and Grace Kelly as the women, and Gable still living rough. John Ford directed.

Red-Headed Woman (1932)

When M-G-M signed Jean Harlow, they were a little nervous about owning up. On screen, in *Platinum Blonde,* for instance, she had been a lady. In life, she was Jean Harlow, so full of sex and mischief and available skin that it seemed stupid to ask anything else of her. But the studio did not wish to be seen as so brazenly lascivious, so low-down. So they tried to kid themselves that Harlow was more than what she was—and maybe that's one reason why Paul Bern ended up looking after her. Bern was the man to advise exotic foreigners, shy spectacles, and people generally less self-satisfied than Jean Harlow.

On the other hand, the studio had a property, *Red-Headed Woman,* from a novel by Katharine Brush, complete with a script by F. Scott Fitzgerald that pleased nobody—Fitzgerald had apparently tried to class it up. It was about a tramp who makes her way to the top by doing the very thing everyone could believe of Harlow. Jean didn't much like the material, but the studio got a new script from Anita Loos and they put Harlow in it. Loos (an authority on blondes and gentlemen who succumb) took one look at the newcomer and wrote a script made for her.

Harold Rosson photographed it. Jack Conway directed and took about thirty days. The material was not very much altered. Harlow's character takes on a long line of men—Chester Morris, Lewis Stone, Henry Stephenson, Charles Boyer, and Harvey Clark. She had Leila Hyams, Una Merkel, and May Robson in the picture with her—and Paul Bern was watching over the whole thing as producer. The studio did the works: They asked Harlow not to wear a bra; they did scenes where she had just a satin sheet over her; and she delighted in wearing a skintight dress.

The picture opened in June. It had cost about $400,000, and it made the same amount in profit. Paul Bern wanted to marry her, while the public simply wanted more of her. The movie was banned in Britain, but in Culver City everyone had a new take on Harlow. She became engaged to Bern and no one raised an eyebrow—not even Thalberg, who must have realized that his studio was taking on a "slut," as opposed to all its ladies. It was Mr. Mayer who believed the M-G-M stars should be genteel (except when they were in his office with him). But the popular trend was toward sex, and Harlow had a unique vulnerable cheerfulness about it.

That would mean fifteen films made for them by 1937, despite the Bern scandal—or because of it. It's clear that the studio "handled" that killing with great shrewdness and maximum showmanship. With a mother and a stepfather on the dangerous side, Harlow needed a lot more care. But it was her misfortune that she came on tough, raunchy, or at least unflappable.

Red River (1948)

Like Bonnard or Dickens, Howard Hawks loved to be alive. Look at that, he says, time and again, whether it be smoke from wagons burning in the distance, or the gathering of cattle and men before sun-up that a circular panning shot can embrace and memorialize, or whether it is Dunson's hand waving cattle out of his way as he strides through the great herd—ownership with horns—to confront the man who took it away from him. Everything looks like the ugliness of revenge taking its toll (and revenge is a huge force in American film), but it is absolutely characteristic of Hawks that he is optimist enough, and enough a lover of life, that he sets that harsh call aside. And it is only by the most mature standards—those of Renoir, say—that the ending of *Red River* is right, even if father and son may never be at ease again.

It was meant to be the big film in Hawks's career, and loving life meant taking care of it. It would be a great hit film where he and his wife, Slim, took the real profits from ownership. But it is a film that asks searching questions of ownership. Though the film was a huge hit, there were unending legal troubles over the cattle, et cetera, and then there was a divorce—because Hawks loved liveliness too much, and couldn't settle for maybe the best wife a great director ever had.

What else? This is the one on how Tom Dunson, with Groot and Matthew Garth in tow, as well as a cow and a bull, makes a place for himself in Texas and then, after the Civil War, has to drive the herd to a railhead—wherever. And on the way, Dunson's anxiety makes him a tyrant, and Garth's cool presence makes him available as the rebel always waiting to see that no one else tangled with the father. The cattle stuff was all shot in a valley in Arizona—you can trace the geography if you study the backgrounds. But you can do that only if you want to miss the brilliant eye-and-glance action among the men.

You see two Dunsons: the young man from Republic, and for the first time an aging wolf—mean and nasty. You get two women—one not quite strong enough to insist, one certain that that is her destiny. You get Montgomery Clift proving that he could be a cowpoke too—even if guys like Richard Farnsworth helped him ride, fight, and roll a cigarette.

It's black and white, shot by Russell Harlan. The script is Charles Schnee from Borden Chase. The music is Dimitri Tiomkin. Aged eight, taken by an aunt, I saw the film and said I would stay to see it through again—just to be in that valley and with that group longer. My aunt looked at me. It is a film about insisting. She said she'd go shopping and come back. Ah, for the days of continuous performance. My favorite picture—but that is smoke in the wind.

With Walter Brennan, Joanne Dru, Colleen Gray, John Ireland, Harry Carey, Harry Carey, Jr., Noah Beery, Jr., Hank Worden, Paul Fix, Chief Yowlachie, and more cattle than anyone ever had a reliable count on.

Reds (1981)

Reds was an immense enterprise, a labor of years and love, but a film for which Warren Beatty—one of the most adroit producers in the history of Hollywood—would do no publicity. It makes no sense, not in Reagan's America, to say that a biopic on America's most attractive Communist should have to speak for itself. After all, in so many respects it was a film pledged to history, which may be the ultimate residence of politics. It was a film about what had actually happened in a young America, about the justice, nobility, and "rightness" of so many smart Americans once being so left. And even if times had changed, the film could not help but refer to the modern relevance of what they had said and believed in the years of the First World War. Yet Beatty would not testify on behalf of this five-year work and his own dedication.

It is the story of John Reed, scripted by the English playwright Trevor Griffiths, yet plainly made under the imprimatur of its producer. Nothing in the film is there because people persuaded Warren Beatty out of his own thoughts. And one has to admit that, despite the apparatus of the witnesses—ancient, broken faces, beautifully filmed, eloquent, and some dead before the film came out—the story (of Reed and Louise Bryant) is tricked out in Hollywoodish ways, even introducing an immense journey across the snows to save a beloved that resembles *Doctor Zhivago* but which did not happen.

It is two films—and that may be proper in dealing with a revolutionary figure in a sedate society who then goes into the cockpit of action. The first part is very exciting, and it hangs on Diane Keaton's Louise—the best work she has ever done—and enough of a portrait of a dynamic feminist for us not to notice how little of Reed we are getting. And Reed is Beatty—earnest, heartfelt, but self-effacing—the figure that has increasingly dominated the sultry kingmaker (and princess-taker). The photography (by Vittorio Storaro) and the décor (by Richard Sylbert) are glorious—though they smack so much of gift catalogues that it counts against the film's alleged Communist ideology.

Part two—with adventure, Russia, political tangles, and Zinoviev (Jerzy Kosinski)—is a mess and Reed becomes a decreasingly important or impressive figure. But the film cannot bring itself to ask whether he is simply washed aside by the tide or whether he becomes disillusioned with his own cause. Indeed, at the end, Reed is a kind of beaten-down kid such as Ronald Reagan could have liked—and when Beatty screened the film for the president, Reagan said he had hoped for a happy ending. By now, Beatty remembers Ron and Nancy as friends. That is not a mistake Reed would have made. But Reed would not have made so pretty a film or kept so straight a face when he got the Best Director Oscar for it. (This film is not directed; it is assembled like a souvenir issue of *Vanity Fair*—on the Red Look.) Reed wanted to change the world. Beatty wanted to secure his place.

Also with Jack Nicholson (overrated as Eugene O'Neill), Paul Sorvino, Maureen Stapleton, Gene Hackman, Edward Herrmann, and many others.

The Red Shoes (1948)

In *A Matter of Life and Death* (1946), Michael Powell and Emeric Pressburger had been charged with improving Anglo-American relations. Two years later, flagrantly against the grain of rationing and austerity in Britain they made a beautiful, extravagant, art-for-art's-sake movie, *The Red Shoes,* with the forbidding figures of J. Arthur Rank and his managing director, John Davis, looking over their shoulders as the budget rose. The bosses thought the whole thing was fanciful and would do no business. But then the film opened in America, and something in that country rose up with the cry "Gotta dance." In time the film would make a lot of money. More than that, a classic was established, that inspired generations of dancers or balletomanes. Much more than that, it inspired people to be part of those beleaguered groups that did "art."

There is a moment in Monte Carlo when the several members of the company begin to prowl around the vague notion of a Red Shoes ballet (or a film). Then they start to move in unison: Shared hopes are a prelude to the achievement itself. Lermontov (Anton Walbrook) says, "The Ballet of the Red Shoes is from a story by Hans Christian Andersen. It is about a young girl who is devoured by an ambition to attend a dance in a pair of red shoes. She gets the shoes and goes to the Ball. For a time all goes well. And she is happy. But at the end of the evening she is tired and wants to go home. But the red shoes are not tired. The red shoes are never tired. They dance her out into the street, they dance her over the mountains and valleys, through fields and forests, through night and day. Time rushes by, love rushes by, life rushes by, but the red shoes dance on."

Whereupon, Julian Craster (Marius Goring) interrupts—he writes the music and he loves the dancer. "What happens in the end?"

"Oh!" says Lermontov. "In the end she dies."

Well, no, nobody on the film died because of the film, though Albert Bassermann died four years later. Many found a new life. But they are all dead now. Not just Powell and Pressburger, and J. Arthur Rank, but Walbrook, Marius Goring and Moira Shearer, Leonide Massine, Ludmilla Tcherina and Robert Helpmann. Hein Heckroth, who did the production design; Brian Easdale, who wrote the music; Sir Thomas Beecham, who conducted it. One person is left (March 2008): Jack Cardiff, who did the color photography.

The ballet within the film was a novelty, but it inspired *An American in Paris,* just as *The Red Shoes* has a pioneering place in that special history of movies that are not simply musicals but stories with music—a tradition that includes Powell, Minnelli, and Kelly as well as Demy and Baz Luhrmann. The atmosphere of collaboration has never been done better. But neither has any film been so clear about the polar loneliness of a genius like Lermontov. And, please remember, that Victoria Page does die, her red feet severed from the rest of her—the red matched by the blood. This is from Hans Christian Andersen, and it has never been for soft hearts,

But *The Red Shoes* is never tired.

The Remains of the Day (1993)

How do we assess the nationality of films these days? Or, if I think I detect an echo of call and countercall in the formal exchanges between butler and housekeeper at Darlington Hall, is that my urge to feel a kind of Japaneseness (in that this film comes from a novel by Kazuo Ishiguro), or is it the real thing, a culture that treasures the way it has invented rituals that contain emotionalism? In which case, is this not also deserving of a high place in that English tradition that regrets the inhibition on feeling, but thanks God for it, too? In short, *The Remains of the Day* deserves to be watched very closely.

The watching is repaid, as it usually is with Merchant-Ivory films—meticulous is as meticulous does. Moreover, in this case, the project has not just the usual team (with Ruth Prawer Jhabvala adapting the novel for the screen), but a pair of producers of the utmost distinction—Mike Nichols and John Calley (one of the few Hollywood executives to sustain a reputation for being smart, likeable, and loaded with taste).

The setting is an English country estate in the 1930s. James Fox is lord of the manor and manners, well-intentioned, apparently amiable, but dangerous. His house is apparently run by Stevens (Anthony Hopkins), the butler, a man whose own life has been subsumed in the need to make order in the household. Two things threaten his calm: the fact that his elderly father (Peter Vaughan) is too old for service, and must either be retired or put down; and a new housekeeper, Miss Kenton (Emma Thompson), every bit as expert as Stevens, but more wayward in that she knows she could have an emotional life of her own.

These servants sustain appearances in a household where Lord Darlington is trying to avoid the Second World War. To that end, he has "conferences" to discuss the world, attended by French, German, and American figures, as well as a plain version of Oswald Mosley. And when the housekeeper takes on two European girls—very clean—as maids, it is the tranquil Darlington who says, Sorry, but they have to go, they're Jewish.

So there is a pleasing, meticulous balance, between plot and subplot, from which one might conclude that servitude is servitude and should end. In the main plot, this will be spelled out in Stevens's eventual inability to admit that he loves Miss Kenton. The acting of these scenes is as good as acting gets. When Stevens hides the book he is reading, the scene is great. With only one fatal disqualification: that Hopkins is so profoundly intelligent an actor he cannot quite become as stupid as Stevens is in reality. Acting stupid is a rare test, for which a refined intelligence can be an ultimate handicap.

So there's a flaw, and it matches Merchant-Ivory's reverence for the polished décor that is armor to the world they disapprove of. So there's a terrible tension all through the film over whether outright rebellion might not simply seem vulgar and lower class. The servants have taken the sweet poison of the system. And the "perfection" of so many scenes is somehow clammy, precious, and embalmed. But it's a fascinating dilemma and as good as the Ivory-Merchant business ever got. With Christopher Reeve, Tim Pigott-Smith, Hugh Grant, Michael Lonsdale.

Repulsion (1965)

Marnie (from 1964) and *Repulsion* would make a fairly intense double bill on morbid female psychology, except that I think the Hitchcock film would now look so dated as to be effete. Whereas the Polanski film is still startling—it deserves to be shown in London, at the old Paris Pullman, in one of those heatwaves that always take London by surprise. It is at least in the class of *Psycho* for its creative confusion over the genres of horror, suspense, and love—yes, I think it's love, the need for which aches in Deneuve's eyes. This is the film, above all, that suggested how hard it was going to be to make a dull film with Catherine Deneuve. And it indicated that Roman Polanski knew a good deal more about the workings of the mind than Hitchcock. But Hitch was always hopeful that if he knew how cinema worked, that would cover shortcomings in the other area.

Take a girl in whom there is a violent clash between her look and her inner being: She looks like a sexual dream, but she has feelings of nightmare over the body. There is no need for explanation—no need for a rough sailor in the house, a convenient poker, and so on. Take the neurosis as fact. This girl is left alone in her sister's apartment in South Kensington. The heat builds. The food rots. And every other organism flowers.

The script was by Polanski and Gérard Brach, and the superb photography—using very wide angles to get the emotional warping—was by Gil Taylor. But Polanski gave special credit to Deneuve, her commitment and understanding, even if she was driven close to crazy at the end of it all. Of course, an actress knows very often when a film belongs to her, and *Repulsion* offers neither cure nor rebuke for Deneuve's mania. She takes over. She becomes the pulse that is making the world and the film—and the only shocking thing about this was that just a moment ago, Deneuve had been the same engine in Jacques Demy's *Umbrellas of Cherbourg*.

Another thing to be said for *Repulsion* is Polanski's rapid identification of a kind of English supporting actor not in the mainstream, but edgy and odd with some unresolved anger or violence. *Repulsion* is full of them: Ian Hendry, John Fraser, Patrick Wymark, Yvonne Furneaux, and, not least, James Villiers (an actor much admired by Joe Losey, too).

Repulsion apparently cost £95,000, which was a lot of money in a silly way, and ridiculously cheap in another. It made black-and-white seem normal. It had a score by K. T. Komeda, the Polish jazz musician. It got an X certificate in Britain (properly), but it cleaned up and it was the first clear evidence of a rare balance in Polanski: He had a vision to delight the surrealists—but he had box office in his blood, too. It was likely that England was just a stepping-stone for him.

Ride with the Devil (1999)

We know Ang Lee nowadays as a major director based in America if not quite American. He has moved from Taiwan to Jane Austen to Annie Proulx without losing his balance, or his interest in the ground. He had the extraordinary success of *Crouching Tiger, Hidden Dragon*, a brimming entertainment, a tender estimate of female heroes, and a very artful marriage of Western and Eastern traditions. It may seem like a natural Ang Lee picture for inclusion in this book. Still, I prefer the far less well known *Ride with the Devil*.

Derived from a novel, *Woe to Live On*, by Daniel Woodrell, *Ride with the Devil* is a history of the American Civil War as seen through the experience of the border states, Kansas and Missouri, and through the eyes of several characters who are more and less than simply American. What is uncanny about the picture is not just the casual handling of extreme violence—including the raid on Lawrence, Kansas, by Quantrill's Raiders, an event scarcely known in America generally—but the larger re-creation of period, both in terms of objects, artifacts, and clothes and in the way people speak. This is a period film where you suddenly appreciate how little adjustment there is in talk in such movies. But the script (by James Schamus), Lee's direction, and the playing by a fine cast leads us directly to a different kind of sensibility. As ages pass, so thought changes and language is the record it leaves. Read letters from the Civil War period—the ones in the Ken Burns documentary—and you are living with elevated education and a blunt specificity that make this sentimental age seem soft and foolish. Yet here is a Taiwanese director getting into that level of discourse.

Frederick Elmes did the photography—brilliant in all respects, but in love with the dappled countryside and the simple architecture. Mark Friedberg did the production design, and Marit Allen did the costumes—all first-class work. Mychael Danna wrote the music. It's common enough by now in the Lee-Schamus films (often produced by Ted Hope) to see a kind of integrated craftwork that is uncommon in most films—and not always noticed. *Ride with the Devil* was not widely praised, and not seen as a film way out of the ordinary. But now, just a few years later, it has a tough texture and a kind of human practicality that leaves a work like *Cold Mountain* looking inflated and remote.

Tobey Maguire has never delivered so complete and sturdy a performance, or one with less need to be liked. Jeffrey Wright is outstanding. The singer Jewel is very touching and natural in the female lead, and there is outstanding work from Skeet Ulrich, Simon Baker, Jonathan Rhys Meyers (very scary as a psychopath), James Caviezel, and Tom Wilkinson.

Now, I understand that I may be troubling some readers in preferring this to *Crouching Tiger, Hidden Dragon*. But this is the superior film, truer to life and a very problematic situation.

Rififi (1955)

Jules Dassin had been blacklisted after *Night and the City* (1950). He was hanging out in Italy and France when suddenly a producer told him to read Auguste Le Breton's novel *Du Rififi Chez les Hommes* over the weekend. It was all in crooks' slang and Dassin's French was not up to the task. So he got a friend to read it to him aloud. He still didn't like the book very much, but when he went in to the Monday meeting he heard himself say yes. It was a magical decision.

Sitting there in our dark, quietly engaged in our own surreptitious tasks—like unwrapping a stick of chewing gum without making noise, or kissing the person beside you without being arrested—we are natural accomplices in furtive enterprise. How else does anyone explain the rapt attention and emotional support that the audience will bring to a scene of sustained robbery? So long as the criminals stay short of nasty violence, we are ready to watch them robbing our bank, our jewelry store, our house even. *Rififi* is the classic case of such participation, with a nontalking sequence of close to thirty minutes as the guys pull the job. If you want other examples of the same concentration try *Thief, The Killing, Heat,* the *Mission Impossible* films, or *Criss Cross.* Of course, Hitchcock took the voyeurist attraction several stages further when the crime became murder. But, to this day, *Rififi* is a morale booster for small crooks everywhere.

Dassin and René Wheeler turned the novel into a script, and Dassin knew that he could stretch the achievement or the prowess of the bad boys because in the end he would chart their downfall. The highest trick, like that in *Vertigo,* is to let the killer get off scot-free.

Philippe Agostini did the photography. Georges Auric wrote the music. Roger Dwyre edited the picture, and the production design was by Auguste Capelier and Alexandre Trauner. The cast is tough but quirky (just the way we like our criminals): Jean Servais, Carl Möhner, Robert Manuel, Janine Darcey, Pierre Grasset, Robert Hossein, Marcel Lupovici, Dominique Maurin, Magali Noël, and Dassin himself (under the name Perlo Vita).

Now shift your point of view. You come home to find your home violated—the clever job becomes an outrage. Anthony Minghella's film *Breaking and Entering* is a measure of the sexual undertones when real robbery fills us with horror and a sense of invasion. The contrast leaves one dreaming of Buñuel doing a two-hour film in which a man enters a sleeping woman's bedroom and deprives her of everything. She wakes up and calls the police, of course, but the investigating officer cannot quite understand why she is so elated. In life, of course, the feeling is the opposite. All of which only helps indicate what a very strange and transforming place the movie house is.

Rififi was at Cannes, and Dassin won a prize—much to the consternation of American authorities who still harbored that old anti-Red grudge. But Dassin was buoyant—for it was at that same festival that he met a dazzling Greek actress, his future wife, Melina Mercouri.

The Right Stuff (1983)

Terms of Endearment, in which Jack Nicholson plays a retired astronaut, won the Oscar for Best Picture for 1983. Philip Kaufman's *The Right Stuff* was a nominee, but it was also a serious box-office disappointment and a film that seemed overshadowed by the concurrent real-life political uncertainty of John Glenn. Maybe the Ladd Company did a poor job distributing the film. Maybe there was a remaining feeling that agreed with the original screenwriter, William Goldman, and the writer of the best-selling book, Tom Wolfe, that Kaufman had erred in subjecting his heroic chumps to a more ironic treatment. But, in hindsight, I think it was all a sad reflection on the way the film business and the audience was retreating from being grown-up in the 1980s. *The Right Stuff*—tongue in cheek (how else can you say that title?)—is one of the great American movies, and its failure spelled our decline and our decades of dismay yet to come.

It's not that Kaufman ever doubted the heroism of Chuck Yeager or felt less than love for flight. Sam Shepard in a faded brown leather jacket looking for chewing gum is Gary Cooper, but a fond detachment from Cooper, too—and don't forget that the real Yeager (a demon of self-promotion still in 1983) is a grinning face in the background in the desert cantina scenes. As for the next generation, they are spam in a can, very human but the creation of PR spin, and whirling on their own daft axes. Above all, the humor brought to those Cold War years is so warm and tender—just look at the cartoon characters of LBJ and the German rocket experts. Just feel the larger, liberal air of merry silliness that kept the Cold War busy, the "space race" and every armaments contest. It's as if the wry voice of A. J. Liebling (a great journalist of the period) has been used to deflate the silly balloon of tension.

Then count the glories: the dazzling feeling of being in the air, buffeted by devils and clouds; the loving employment of the desert. Southwest (largely filmed around Edwards Air Force Base); and the chorus that is the press corps—feverish and frantic, and the best measure of the film's American awareness. The result is a mix of beauty and satire, comedy and pathos, character and reputation, that is endearing and challenging. It is hardly possible to watch *The Right Stuff* without growing into a critique of America—and there, I guess, you have a key reason for its failure.

It follows in such a panorama that many actors do fine work: Dennis Quaid is as bouncy as a new ball; Scott Glenn is a mockery of laconic toughness; Ed Harris is so much more appealing than the real Glenn; Shepard is just fine—and kindly untested as an actor; Barbara Hershey is a ripe peach; Jeff Goldblum, Levon Helm, Pamela Reed, Fred Ward, bring them all on, all the way down to Royal Dano's stark preacher. It's a delight still, and I'd guess that its current rentals on DVD are five times those of *Terms of Endearment*.

Rio Bravo (1959)

Long before the measured fade-in that introduces the languid self-delight of Dean Martin and the jailhouse singsong, *Rio Bravo* had shrugged off the tight harness of a regular Western. Yes, we are holed up in a little town on the edge of the desert, with an ornery prisoner and a perverse posse from hell waiting for a false move, but . . . Let's be candid, could this ordeal go on forever? This is not exactly the West, but Illyria, or paradise. Time is there for the Dude to make his slow recovery from booze, for Colorado to act cool, for Feathers to talk John T. Chance into the ground (is he so bad-tempered because he ended up with a name like "Chance"?), and so that Stumpy can grow old. As for the Burdettes, the villains, let's allow that they are a minor order of angels, snarling and shooting from time to time, but as solid as the wall in squash, ensuring that the ball bounces back.

So, it is 1959 and that dazzling moment when you can see Hollywood breaking up like old concrete, with beautiful new flowers creeping through the cracks. And this is Howard Hawks's last great film, which is not to disparage several nice small ones still to come. But just as *Vertigo,* say, is one man's testament on film, and not comforting, so *Rio Bravo* is an old-timer's reverie, and it is the proof of what we have seen all along: that it might be fun to do a movie.

Of course, Hawks's trick is to make it look easy, too. Is there a film from the fifties so free from strain, or one in which the drift of song is there all the time—I refer not just to the cutthroat song or Dimitri Tiomkin's dainty music, but the notion (a few years ahead of Demy) that really every line could be sung. And whereas it is easy enough to romanticize a final Western grouping like *The Wild Bunch* (and I really like *The Wild Bunch*), isn't this grouping more civilized, more sexy, more chatty, and more safely lodged in what I will call culture? This little town could be in Arden.

The screenplay is by Jules Furthman and Leigh Brackett. Russell Harlan took the pictures. It's 140 minutes, and I wonder if even at 14 hours Hawks would have succumbed to boredom. The routines are not all brand-new, though Feathers is without doubt the most Coltraneish voice in American film, going on and on and getting better all the time. What is it about? Is it about courage and character and conversation? Yes, but it's about rolling a cigarette, black tights, and waiting for a flowerpot to come through the window. It's about teasing Ward Bond rotten for *Wagon Train.* It's about blood drops in a glass of beer.

Ricky Nelson did well enough. Dean Martin altered the way the world thought of him. John Wayne watched over everyone like a football coach with rookies. And Angie Dickinson took her moment the way Bob Beamon jumped in Mexico City in 1968. With fond thanks to John Russell and Claude Akins as the Burdette brothers, to Pedro Gonzalez and Estelita Rodriguez (I think they're meant to be Mexicans), and to everyone else.

The River (1951)

So a Frenchman went to India to make an English film. It's an encouraging sign of how, after 1945, film nationalism started to leak. Films made by travelers became increasingly common, whether documentary or feature. But for Jean Renoir, the emergence of *The River* was also a way of healing the past. He had not made a picture since *The Woman on the Beach* (1947). He was not sure where he belonged, or how to proceed. Then he was approached by a former florist, Kenneth McEldowney, who had heard of Renoir's interest in Rumer Godden's novel *The River*. McEldowney bought the book (Renoir had an option already) and arranged $500,000 for the picture.

It is the story of an English family in India: the father (Esmond Knight); the mother (Nora Swinburne); two English girls, teenagers, Harriet (Patricia Walters) and Valerie (Adrienne Corri), and their Indian friend, Melanie (Radha Sri Ram). There is the little boy of the house, Bogey (Richard Foster), and Captain John (Thomas E. Breen), the American who lost a leg in the war. Brando was considered for Captain John (along with a dozen other actors), but the part went to the son of the censor (Joseph Breen), who had already lost his leg in the war.

Claude Renoir agreed to be the photographer and Eugene Lourie the designer—and of course, in India, the film had to be Renoir's introduction to Technicolor. It is a small family story, I suppose, and not without that English indifference to extraordinary foreign places where they are posted. It is also that rare thing, a story about adolescence, with three girls infatuated with the wounded captain, and making idiots of themselves. There's the point. If everyone has his or her reasons, we all know we can be wrong and make fools of ourselves.

There is drama on a hot afternoon—Bogey is taken by the great cobra he adores. And there is melodrama, with red hair and temperament flashing in the sun. But there is India, hardly noticing it all—the India of so much larger tragedies that individuals have a very small claim on our time. Renoir had always loved individuals, the specifics of the human case, but here there is an attitude—tranquil, half-sleepy, resigned—that knows their tempests come and go. And just as Rumer Godden supplies the English family mood to perfection, so Renoir recognizes how India alters everything.

This is the resumption of a great career and one of those postwar films that finds the larger world as its subject. It would be foolish to link it too closely to Indian religion or philosophy. Renoir was only a traveler and a visitor. But he had had his mind enlarged, and there is a way in which this river—the Ganges—is attached to the river in *Partie de Campagne* (1935), and the notion (spelled out in the book *Renoir My Father*, published in 1962) that we are just corks bobbing on the stream. Some say *The River* is picturesque, or for children, or a holiday excursion. Whereas it is the start of Renoir's last great burst of action.

Robin Hood (1922)

The Fairbanks unit was a gang of athletic boys who, first of all, had to keep Doug amused: the idea and practice of boys' adventures turning into immense movies really operates with Douglas Fairbanks. So it was Allan Dwan, apparently, who first had the idea of Doug playing Robin Hood. But Doug wasn't interested. He had Jack Dempsey as a visitor and everyone was watching the great boxer. Then Dwan had an idea: get some real archery equipment with targets on the lot and challenge Doug to hit a bull's-eye. It was a new game, and it worked. Within a couple of days, the star was hooked on playing Robin Hood. What's more, it turned into the most expensive film made in America to date.

Dwan and the writers read up on the subject as best they could, but they were candid in admitting that it hardly mattered whether Robin of Locksley had even existed. It was the story of a king, Richard the Lion-Hearted, who goes off on the Crusade. In his absence, that wicked brother Prince John and the Sheriff of Nottingham seize the country. Who shall defend the nation? Robin—that's who!

Dwan would direct. The script came from Lotta Woods and Doug himself. And a whole lot of building was entrusted to art directors Wilfred Buckland, Irvin J. Martin, and Edward M. Langley as well as the costumer Mitchell Leisen, hired in from DeMille. They built a castle in Santa Monica on the principle that guys in Europe had been halfhearted about it. With Bob Fairbanks, Dwan built immense sets with an interior hall that was 450 feet long—big enough for a football field. Doug was daunted when he saw them, but then Dwan taught him how the sets could be rigged as gymnasia, with handholds, slides, and chutes behind the tapestry wall covers so Doug could do his great chase sequences. And once Doug could move across these sets, the film became his. He had a pretty bizarre wig, and no one enjoyed wearing the armor. But put him in tights and he was Tarzan in the castle. And all the while, Leisen was designing the knights' tabards so they matched the illuminated manuscripts.

Arthur Edeson shot it, and Richard Rosson was the assistant director handling the crowd scenes. But the adventure stuff was done by Doug and Allan Dwan, and it was a matter of vaults, swinging sashes, balconies, staircases, and sudden appearances. Plus archery and sword fighting. Children today are blasé technocrats: They take color and sound for granted—they are used to fabulous scenery. But strap them to the sofa and the gnashing of protest and fury can still be silenced by Doug's exuberance.

Wallace Beery is King Richard, Enid Bennett is Lady Marian, Sam De Grasse is Prince John, Willard Louis is Friar Tuck, and Alan Hale is Little John. The estimate is that it cost \$1.5 million, and it earned \$2.5 million in America alone.

Robinson Crusoe (1952)

Sometimes known as *The Adventures of Robinson Crusoe,* this film was a major step in the world's rediscovery of Luis Buñuel—and his first film in color. In so many ways, it's a fitting subject for him: for the original novel, by Daniel Defoe, is an immense, conscientious, and self-congratulatory reestablishment of a bourgeois existence, after our hero has suffered the misfortune of a shipwreck. That's why Crusoe has it in him to be smug, ultramaterialist, and an unblinking visitor from capitalist Europe, utterly secure about his superiority. Inasmuch as Buñuel made a faithful adaptation of Defoe—not just in terms of action, but in living up to the familiar imagery of the novel—it is remarkable that this should end up so alarming a portrait of an increasingly lonely and incipiently crazy man.

The film was produced by Óscar Dancigers (Buñuel's regular producer in his early Mexican years). Buñuel did the screenplay with Philip Roll (a pen name for Hugo Butler). And the film was shot largely in a jungle area near Acapulco, by Alex Phillips, using Pathécolor. The look of the film is naturalistic, though there are arresting scenes of Crusoe "talking to" his own echo in the mountains, and of a trailing torch being quenched by the sea. There is also a moment when Friday becomes "naughty" and the film hints, comically, at a direction it might take. But Crusoe remains heroic, and there may have been a tension in Buñuel between honoring that box-office need and digging deeper into loneliness and hallucination. As it was, the picture cost $300,000, a huge sum for the Mexican industry, and one that required some money from the United States.

No one seems to have enjoyed the shoot very much. The jungle proved hot, with scorpions. Buñuel was observed to be drinking a lot. And he was not, at first, on easy terms with Dan O'Herlihy, his Crusoe. It seems that the producers had wanted Orson Welles, having seen him in *Macbeth.* And when that proved fruitless, their eye fell on Macduff in that film. O'Herlihy was always a good actor, but he spoke no Spanish and he did not swim. At first, he was taken aback by Buñuel's dogged insistence that he not act for effect.

Under the circumstances, O'Herlihy gives a solid performance (he got an Oscar nod—Brando won in *On the Waterfront*), and there is an amusing interplay between him and Jaime Fernández (Man Friday). Of course, a Buñuel film without women is an anomaly, if not a perversion. Crusoe is moved by a dress on a scarecrow blowing in the wind—and I think in hindsight that Buñuel's Crusoe cries out for some of the small indiscretions that Fernando Rey might have brought to the part. But it's clear how far Buñuel was still learning as he struggled to become a professional filmmaker as well as the source of outrage. The Mexican work is not consistent. It seldom has the poetry that would come in the sixties and the seventies. But it's as if Buñuel had only begun to ask himself practical questions in the fifties.

Rocco and His Brothers (1960)

We should remember the rush of films in 1960. It was the year when the French New Wave broke upon the shore. It was the time of *Psycho, The Apartment*, and *The Bellboy*. And in Italy, these films had their opening—*L'Avventura, La Dolce Vita,* and *Rocco and His Brothers*. Of those three, the last—by Luchino Visconti—is certainly the least known today. But have no doubt about it: In 1960, *Rocco* was a shattering experience. I recall its screening at the London Film Festival with audience members crying out at the concluding events of the melodrama. There was a terrible sense of wound and loss. The film worked.

When Visconti made *La Terra Trema,* he had had a scene of a few men leaving Sicily for the north. In the fifties, this became a heavy migration. So Visconti had the idea of picking up that story. But in the years that had passed, he had become so distant from the man who made *La Terra Trema.* In that documentary-like film, Visconti had used natives and amateurs. In *Rocco,* the title part—that of a boxer—was taken by Alain Delon, not just French, not just uncommonly beautiful and delicate for a boxer, but an actor who reckons he is playing something like the noble brother Alyosha in some Karamazovian scheme.

The operatic and the literary sensibility had surfaced in Visconti, and not too much was left of the communist or the realist. In his family grouping, there are two brothers—the saint and the beast, Simone (Renato Salvatori). Their antagonism turns on Nadia (Annie Girardot), the woman they both love. In the final passages of *Rocco,* Simone rapes Nadia, then beats up Rocco (who has been compelled to watch the rape). Then after Rocco has told Nadia that he cannot see her anymore—a sacrifice all the more portentous for being shot on the roof of Milan Cathedral—Simone murders Nadia, stabbing her repeatedly while she adopts a crucifixion-like posture. I didn't say it was good—just shattering.

Visconti wrote the picture with Suso Cecchi d'Amico and Pasquale Festa Campanile, and the ravishing black-and-white photography (like a very velvety noir) was entrusted to Giuseppe Rotunno. The music, ornate and romantic, was by Nino Rota. It's hard to exaggerate how far removed these characters were from Sicily—let's say that they were as glamorous, as dark, and as theatrical as the figures in *The Godfather.* And Visconti was surely aiming at a kind of international audience. In *La Terra Trema* he had used rare dialects. In *Rocco,* several of the cast were dubbed because they could not speak Italian. The central trio—all of whom are very powerful—were backed up by Katina Paxinou as the mother, Roger Hanin, Suzy Delair, Paolo Stoppa, and the young Claudia Cardinale.

I suspect that *Rocco* looks dated now, and I have to say that it marks a process of self-betrayal in Visconti that is the opposite of true development. From now on, he was an habitué of the studio, of art directors and designers, of starry casts and obsessively pessimistic and literary conclusions. But in 1960, there were people who felt that *Rocco* was the best Italian picture of the year.

Rocky (1976)

There is a fond school of thought that sees the economy, the daring, and the quality of American movies in the early 1970s (the term "silver age" has been used) being crushed by two very big events: the opening of *Jaws* and *Star Wars*. No matter that those two films came from apparently promising new directors, they ended up making life harder for new directors. But there is a third film in that dire pattern of influence, the most excruciating and the least explicable—we have come to *Rocky*.

Sylvester Stallone was twenty-nine in 1975, real name Michael, with eyes stolen from a very sad bloodhound. He had been acting a little and in three days he wrote a script about a hard-luck club fighter, Rocky Balboa, who goes up against the champion, Apollo Creed (Carl Weathers). Stallone was quite proud of the three days, but I think it suggests that he rested a lot. Well, it was taken up by Robert Chartoff and Irwin Winkler, producers, who reasoned that it was so simple, so stupid, and so made for Stallone's lovelorn look, why not risk a million on it?

They shot it fast in twenty-eight days, with John G. Avildsen directing. James Crabe did the photography. Bill Cassidy did the production design. Scott Conrad and Rick Halsey would edit it. Bill Conti wrote some music, and Sly's brother Frank wrote a song, "Take Me Back."

It was about this pretty boy palooka, his girlfriend Adrian (Talia Shire), his trainer (Burgess Meredith), and Burt Young as his brother. It was either Capraesque or it was raw corn—depending on your take. It was also comic-book blatant, full-frontal and inspirational. Everyone began to catch Stallone's fever for wishful thinking (Sly was shy until he started talking, and then he was over the top). And he seemed to be the one guy who believed in it all.

It's when the picture reaches the fight that you realize what a travesty it means to be. The fighting is not just implausible, it's not far from slapstick ballet, and all based on a way of fighting in which no one bothers with defense. (Stallone says that he got his idea from seeing Chuck Wepner fight Muhammad Ali.) It's shameless and brutal, and deeply sentimental in every way. But the public loved it and responded to the sudden stardom of this young writer-actor. There were even those who reckoned that a Wellesian "talent" had been unleashed upon us all.

It won the Oscar for Best Picture—against *Network*, *Taxi Driver*, and *All the President's Men*. Avildsen then won for directing (Ingmar Bergman was one of those he beat). Sly was nominated as actor and writer. Talia Shire, Burgess Meredith, and Burt Young were all nominated. The madness knew no end. Balboa became a patron saint of Philadelphia—allegedly a tough city on sports heroes. And, of course, the film grossed $225 million worldwide.

The series went to *Rocky V*, with Stallone himself directing parts 2, 3, and 4. (Then in 2006 came the pensioner Rocky.) There were also three Rambos, plus Rambo on Social Security, to say nothing of the film careers of Arnold Schwarzenegger, Steven Seagal, and sundry other superheroes with empty, puffed-up faces.

Roman Holiday (1953)

In 1953, the movies believed in princesses and the millions who would be captivated by the thought of a holiday in Rome. That's worth stressing because the movies have been a measure of how up-to-date we are or aren't, and of how we advertise such sweet messages to ourselves. In 2008, what equal idiocies are there prompting entire movies?

It's easy now to see how in 1953 (the year of the coronation of Queen Elizabeth II—a landmark in the spread of TV sets in Britain and Europe), Hollywood could envisage Audrey Hepburn as a princess (a Princess Margaret who had swallowed her politeness pills, was X degrees prettier, and spoke the Queen's clear English, not Margaret Windsor's drawl), instead of Grace Kelly. (Question: Would it have been to the benefit of the movies and/or Monaco if Prince Rainier had married Audrey and Grace had been free to do *Vertigo*, *Marnie*, and *Wait Until Dark*?)

Roman Holiday was directed by William Wyler, who had done a number of grown-up films with complicated women. It was written by John Dighton and Ian McLellan Hunter, though it would turn out that Hunter was fronting for Dalton Trumbo. And Gregory Peck as the American journalist who gives Audrey's princess a brief vacation from duty had done a lot by then—not just Lewt in *Duel in the Sun* and *Twelve O'Clock High*, but *David and Bathsheba* with Susan Hayward. There was every indicator at "go" in the public mind that, offscreen, Gregory Peck could make love in a movie.

But *Roman Holiday* was a fairy tale, simply because of the radiant presence of Audrey Hepburn, in her first starring role (after doing *Gigi* on Broadway), and so sublimely set apart from changing times, the idioms of talk and what a girl might do, that the film could have been silent. Audrey is the auteur of the film. It's not just that with any other actress the film alters—it's far more likely that it was made only because this creature called Audrey came along: unreasonably beautiful; completely likeable; entirely thin—and yet for the 1950s, not absurd, but palatable. Try to think of a comparable event in movie history and the closest I can come is Julia Roberts in *Pretty Woman*—made in a completely different degree of sexual candor, but with Julia's charm simply warding off any foul suggestions in the script, her costume, and what she does. She was perfect, and it's films like these that show how insane the public can be. Another example—far tougher to explain: Diana in her strange real life.

Who knows what Wyler thought? Or Trumbo? His story won an Oscar for Hunter. The picture was nominated as Best, Wyler was nominated, and so was Eddie Albert for Supporting Actor. And Audrey beat Deborah Kerr in *From Here to Eternity* for Best Actress. Seen today, *Roman Holiday* is hard to finish, because it has only its charm. There is no world, no masked meaning behind it. My one comment would be to juxtapose two photographs: Audrey in 1953, with Princess Margaret, not as pretty or charming, hopelessly human, and hoping against hope for a life.

La Ronde (1950)

In more recent times, *La Ronde* has been redone as *The Blue Room,* scripted by David Hare and directed by Sam Mendes, with Nicole Kidman starring. But this is the real thing, a movie version of the Arthur Schnitzler play *Der Reigen,* set in Vienna in 1900, adapted for the screen by Jacques Natanson and Max Ophüls, and directed by Ophüls. It's in black and white, photographed by Christian Matras. Jean d'Eaubonne did the sets. The music is from Oscar Straus.

In its day, *La Ronde* was perceived as the classically "naughty" French film. Another word was "sophisticated." And I suppose the views came from the antisentimental notion that amorousness, or seduction, or sex made its natural way through society, circulating as freely as money, or infection. So the idea had been used before of a coin or a banknote passing through many hands in one day. In *La Ronde,* what was being passed was the sexual urge—the hard-on, if you will, or even the same bodily fluid. I use that metaphor poetically, but today no inspector of infectious diseases could be quite so amused. *La Ronde* is a demonstration of dangerous practices. Yet in 1950, all people noticed was that sex could be enjoyed without love being declared.

Not that Ophüls is so lacking in tenderness, or that the renewal of romantic urgings had not always been a part of his philosophy. The figures in *La Ronde* are toys, or horses on a fairground carousel, if you prefer. And their presence as figures in a pattern or actors in a play are stressed by the key role of the *meneur de jeu,* the ringmaster or the director, embodied by Anton Walbrook: "Je suis l'incarnation de votre désir de tout connaître." Of course, he is a forerunner of the Peter Ustinov figure in *Lola Montès,* but he is also Ophüls himself stepping out of the dark. He is the director announcing, These people, these comedians, are mine. The first casting in the role was Louis Jouvet. And surely he would have been fine. What do we get with Walbrook? Something gentler and wiser, something Viennese and someone who might easily step off the carousel for a moment and be a king in the story.

So this is the perfect Ophüls film in a sense that leaves *Lola Montès*—damaged, abbreviated, maybe not ideally cast—as something more complex. Which do you prefer? It may be a matter of closeness to death. In *Lola Montès,* the show is nearly over. In *La Ronde,* it can run for years yet.

Apart from Walbrook, this is the cast: Simone Signoret (as the hooker); Serge Reggiani (as the soldier); Simone Simon (as the chambermaid); Jean Clarieux (as the brigadier); Daniel Gélin (as the young man); Robert Vattier (as the professor); Danielle Darrieux (as the married woman); Fernand Gravey (as her husband); Odette Joyeux (as the grisette); Jean-Louis Barrault (as the poet); Isa Miranda (as the actress—it was to have been Marlene Dietrich); and Gérard Philipe (as the count).

Room at the Top (1959)

What does a producer do in life? Often it is a matter of obtrusive mistakes or unobtrusive flights of genius. In the case of *Room at the Top*—which was a sensation in Britain when it opened such as would be hard to understand today—it was a matter of Peter Glenville and James and John Woolf offering the part of Alice Aisgill to Simone Signoret (and Glenville isn't even credited on the film, but he knew Signoret and helped it along). In John Braine's rather crude but best-selling novel, Alice Aisgill was as she sounds: Yorkshire through and through, albeit modern in her sexual thinking. So it was a risk as well as a coup to say, Forget the people who could play Alice as fortyish and Yorkshire (the part was apparently offered to Vivien Leigh): suppose she is French. And suppose she is Simone Signoret.

Of course, that's not the whole story. Braine's book had done well because it was a tough fable of social climbing and opportunism—of people who were deadly serious about getting to the top. So Joe Lampton betrays his mistress, Alice, in order to marry the boss's daughter (Heather Sears). He gets to the top, or Bradford's version of it, and he is reckoned to be doomed. That was the old-fashioned side of Braine's book. The new Britain coming, like the one Henry James had observed, was one where getting to the top did not necessarily carry any fatal moral consequence. But Joe (and Braine) were softies, really, and rather un-English—they couldn't stick the boot in without remorse.

Neil Paterson did the script, and Signoret for one believed that it was better than the novel (Mordecai Richler seems to have done some doctoring). Freddie Francis shot it, and Jack Clayton was the director. It was his feature debut and the start of a purple patch. They did location shooting in Bradford as well as studio stuff, and there are some rather old-fashioned supporting bits from Hermione Baddeley, Donald Wolfit, Donald Houston, Raymond Huntley, Allan Cuthbertson (as Alice's cad husband), and Ambrosine Phillpotts.

The strength of the project was Signoret, thirty-eight when the film was shot, but ravishing and very sexy for a British picture. Yet the core of the film was Laurence Harvey as Joe, and his casting was as clever, for Harvey was never quite likeable, and never too much in love with himself. That harshness works very well with Signoret's carnal abandon. You can see Joe longing to be as immersed in the love affair as she is. Signoret won the Oscar for Best Actress. Paterson won for the script. There were nods for Clayton, Harvey, and Best Picture.

The film made a lot of money and promoted everyone involved with it. There was talk of a British New Wave and certainly the North Country had an increasing voice in pictures being made. Signoret became an international star, but then her looks deserted her. Harvey was launched on his strange career, and Clayton was a fixture—until *The Great Gatsby*. But it takes a wise producer to know not to do as good a novel as that.

Rope (1948)

Rope was a play by Patrick Hamilton (his first, written when he was only twenty-five) produced in London in 1929 to great success. (Brian Aherne played one of the killers, and Ernest Milton was the detective-like Rupert Cadell.) It is the story of two young Englishmen who murder a friend (in their Mayfair flat) simply to prove that they can do it. It was assumed widely that Hamilton had been influenced by the Leopold-Loeb case in Chicago of 1924 (the basis for *Compulsion,* too). But he always denied that, and said he had thought of the idea in 1922. He also added that he was not especially interested in the Nietzschean ideas behind the murder: "I have gone all out to write a horror play and make your flesh creep." Thus, at the start of the play the murder is heard but not seen on a darkened stage.

Alfred Hitchcock was five years older than Patrick Hamilton, and it is certain that he saw the play in London—it is as easy to conclude that he would have been fascinated by its sense of murder as an exercise and by the gradual discovery of the crime by the Rupert Cadell character. The mystery is how no one sought to make a movie of it in the next two decades. Perhaps there really was an issue of dangerous taste involved.

Hitchcock was clearly drawn to *Rope* as a play: it is even said that he thought of doing it on stage: "I undertook *Rope* as a stunt . . . The stage drama was played out in the actual time of the story; the action is continuous from the moment the curtain goes up until it comes down again. I asked myself whether it was technically possible to film it in the same way. The only way to achieve that, I found, would be to handle the shooting in the same continuous action . . . And I got this crazy idea to do it in a single shot."

Not so much crazy as predetermined, academic, and laborious. Hamilton himself was hired as a first scenarist, and replaced with the young Arthur Laurents. Then Hume Cronyn did some dialogue revision. But Hamilton noted the difficulty of writing a script when the one-shot camera style (the ten-minute take, as it would be called) was a given.

There are eleven shots, and the result is . . . terrible. This is a ponderous picture founded on a dire theoretical mistake, the most disastrous proof of Hitch's urge to have a movie all in his head before he began. There may be some curiosity value in waiting for the "clever" invisible cuts. But only if you care to forget what is being said and done. That is possible because the creepiness of the Hamilton has been turned into a lecture—where James Stewart is badly miscast as Cadell.

It is said that Hitch wanted Cary Grant and Montgomery Clift as the killers, and one can see that being hilarious and unprecedented, a screwball comedy more than a gay subtext. Not surprisingly, the two actors backed off and so we are left with John Dall and Farley Granger, both of whom remind us of string, not rope.

Rosemary's Baby (1968)

When you consider that Roman Polanski went from *The Fearless Vampire Killers* to *Rosemary's Baby*, you get an idea of his nerve and his ability to handle whatever commercial situation came along. There's also little doubt left about his brilliance at that time, and his enthusiastic proclivity for nastiness. Some horror pictures date badly (*The Exorcist*, for one), but *Rosemary's Baby* is very disturbing still. In a way, the most alarming thing of all is Polanski's apologia. He read the Ira Levin novel, loved it, and thought great parts of it ready for film. But "being an agnostic . . . I no more believed in Satan as evil incarnate than I believed in a personal god; the whole idea conflicted with my rational view of the world. For credibility's sake, I decided that there would have to be a loophole: the possibility that Rosemary's supernatural experiences were figments of her imagination."

Now, if you as a viewer feel that "loophole," get through it fast. I always know I'm trapped with Satan in the film.

The rights to the novel had been bought by the horror movie veteran William Castle, and he had wanted to direct it himself. But Paramount and Robert Evans told him, No chance, and the project was offered to Polanski, who accepted fast and wrote the script himself. His plan was to film the New York apartment building, the Dakota, all in Los Angeles, and he has given great credit to Richard Sylbert (production designer) and Anthea Sylbert (costumes) for the suffocating look and feel of the film.

The lead parts presented problems, and Polanski had to be persuaded to see Mia Farrow in the role. But once she was cast, her anorexic, cropped-hair look became seminal. I think there's no question but that her physical, biological suffering is rendered throughout with extraordinary intensity. For the husband, Polanski thought of Redford and Beatty, but they were far too canny and image-protective to take on that forbidding role. So, finally, it went to John Cassavetes, which only suggests that the Devil is in casting when it suits him.

But Polanski was just as interested in the old-timers, the coven, that would surround Rosemary. Ruth Gordon was inspired casting, of course, but don't miss Sidney Blackmer, Maurice Evans, Ralph Bellamy, Elisha Cook, Jr., and Patsy Kelly.

At a cost of just under $2 million, the movie had rentals of $15 million, and it played a major part in the return of horror, with scenes where even a hardened viewer had trouble watching. It's easy to laugh at the idea—of health-food nuts who are really Satan's crew—but not during the film. It got very few Oscar nominations, but Ruth Gordon won for Best Supporting Actress and ensured her comeback. As for Polanski, he was established in his American reputation. But in the year after the picture came out, on Cielo Drive, in Los Angeles, his wife, Sharon Tate, was murdered when very close to full term in her pregnancy. It was an age when the Devil found every loophole.

'Round Midnight (1986)

Dexter Gordon died in 1990, uncommonly lucky among jazz musicians that someone had found the kindness, the ingenuity, and the money to make a proper celebration of him before that death. And if you are inclined, unhappily, to the suspicion that his generation is unlikely to be repeated in our musical history, then *'Round Midnight* is not just a grace note to Dexter but an eloquent memorial to a great art and its ruinous background. By which I mean the wretched life that black Americans lived to play as they liked.

It's not that anyone interested in the history of jazz can turn to Hollywood for help or illustration: In feature films, there is Nat King Cole as W. C. Handy; there are Louis and the boys on the bus out to Newport in *High Society*; and there are small wonders, like Marie Bryant singing for a moment in *They Live by Night*. There is Ellington at the road house in *Anatomy of a Murder*. There is Miles playing to Jeanne Moreau's face in *Lift to the Scaffold*. But the neglect is nearly complete, and it speaks to something horrible when you realize—naturally enough—that plenty of Hollywood people loved jazz. So the self-portrait in *'Round Midnight* is an item of treasure—and we owe it to a Frenchman, Bertrand Tavernier.

Tavernier had known François Paudras, the ordinary Parisian jazz fan who had done so much to help Bud Powell in his worst times—and Powell was very likely deranged as often as he was brilliant. Tavernier had also seen Gordon, whose European exile had been long because of his association with drink and drugs. Moreover, those things had left the handsome, tall man an unsteady wreck, as well as someone whose speech was hard to understand. Yet Tavernier had this idea that Dexter could act in a fiction movie, playing a version of himself, "Dale Turner."

Irwin Winkler offered to produce the picture, and I believe that one Clint Eastwood did a lot to persuade Warner Brothers to distribute the film in America. Then Tavernier and David Rayfiel wrote a script about Dale's friendship with a Frenchman, played by François Cluzet. The "story" is slight, but Dale wants to return to New York to see a daughter. It's enough, and it allows Gordon to improvise on the theme to startling richness. The nomination of Gordon for an Academy Award was a sentimental gesture, but not crazy or ridiculous. Gordon helps show us the profound links between modern jazz and the Actors Studio—which arrived in New York at much the same time. And if he is technically weak, that doesn't deny him sauce, wit, and a lovely creole mannerliness.

Beyond that, there are magnificent studio sessions, enormously enhanced by the art design of Alexandre Trauner. Some of the camerawork at these jam sessions is classic. The cast includes Sandra Reaves-Phillips, Lonette McKee, and Christine Pascal, and the musicians make a roll of honor: Herbie Hancock (who did get an Oscar for his score), Bobby Hutcherson, Billy Higgins, John McLaughlin, Pierre Michelot, Wayne Shorter, Ron Carter, Cedar Walton, Freddie Hubbard, Tony Williams.

The Round-up (1965)

We are on a sun-drenched plain of dust and blond grass; maneuvers are taking place. There are horses, a military band, and firing squads—it is all like toy soldiers in the long days. It is said to be the *puszta* of Hungary some time after 1848. The Austrian army, in cloaks, boots, and full uniform, have rounded up prisoners, some of whom may be remnants of the rebel army. There is a feeling of decades of antagonism between the administration in Vienna and the cowboy life on the *puszta*.

The career of Miklós Jancsó began only six years after the Budapest uprising. *The Round-up*, which caused a great stir at Cannes in 1965, was plainly both a historical study and a textbook demonstration on how prisoners might be interrogated, intimidated, and broken down. At the same time, it is a very formal film, made up of the regular outlines of compounds, stockades, and cells, surrounded by the infinite space and glare of the summer.

Written by Jancsó's regular colleague, Gyula Hernádi, and photographed by Tamás Somló, *The Round-up* advances like a theorem as the Austrians isolate possible troublemakers and then trick a couple of rebels into giving away the identity of the old revolutionary guard. This film is in black and white, and it was still only experimenting with long takes and very elaborate camera movements. By the time of *Red Psalm* (1971), which is astoundingly beautiful, Jancsó had brought the whole film down to twenty-odd shots, elaborate movements of people in different directions and a chorus of delectable young women in nothing but white skirts. *Red Psalm* won the Director's Prize at Cannes, but it was taken as a turning point in which this very individual director began to show signs of ostentatious formalism for form's own sake.

For his part, Jancsó claimed to be making films about freedom and power and their eternal conflict, but he did not seem to be much hindered or opposed by censorship. And there are great passages in *The Round-up* in which one feels the mathematics of liberty being steadily squeezed by geometry. It may be that only Hungarians, or people with a detailed knowledge of Hungarian history in the nineteenth century, can respond to these films. But long before the ending of the Iron Curtain, Jancsó felt he was making hymns to a strangled national liberty.

It is easily forgotten that Jancsó is still alive—and by many standards a master. Moreover, one can make the case for his influence—on Angelopoulos, on Béla Tarr, and even on Sergio Leone. No one had imagined the parade-ground elegance of his films until he made them, and just because Jancsó was so different from the films from, say, Poland or Czechoslovakia should not discredit him. Elegance is a Hungarian attribute—it was there in Alex Korda and Michael Curtiz. Meanwhile Jancsó's work is nearly as out of fashion as that of Eisenstein, and not much short of being that spectacular.

Ruggles of Red Gap (1935)

The Ruggles story goes back, and may well have its origins in more-or-less factual episodes from the picaresque history of the Wild West. Whatever, the notion of a servant (or a wife) won in a game of poker is rich in comic and menacing prospects—imagine Barrett won at a Mayfair card club in *The Servant*. Anyway, Henry Leon Wilson's story had been filmed twice as a silent, in 1918 and then in 1923, with James Cruze directing and Edward Everett Horton in the lead role.

Paramount decided on it as the last film in Charles Laughton's contract with them. Arthur Hornblow produced it; Leo McCarey directed; and the screenplay was officially by Walter DeLeon, Harlan Thomson, and Humphrey Pearson. However, it seems that Laughton's private writer, Arthur Macrae, was imported to doctor it to the star's liking.

The film has a great reputation still, but I'm bound to side with Laughton's biographer, Simon Callow, in saying that he gives an awkward, overdone, owlish impersonation of comedy without ever being funny. And Callow is surely right in his diagnosis: Laughton was not humble or self-effacing; he was nobody's servant. And there is the problem. Edward Everett Horton was a deferential actor, he understood in his true modesty the proper form in being a servant. Laughton was always more like a Barrett (from *Wimpole Street*), capable of digesting the entire household and becoming its mocking master.

Still, it's a nice idea, of Marmaduke Ruggles acquired in a bet by nouveau riche Westerners and then becoming a restaurateur (Laughton, we may recall, had been born into the hotel business, though in snobby Scarborough). The comedy of the film does exist, and it is to be found in the Flouds, Egbert and Effie (Charlie Ruggles and Mary Boland), the nervous-exuberant couple who are fearful of faux pas. The cast is also enriched by ZaSu Pitts, Maude Eburne, Roland Young, and Leila Hyams. McCarey directs the ensemble very well, and the Laughton-Pitts romance is as well observed as the Flouds' marriage. Yes, this is the film with the set piece where Ruggles confounds the Americans present with a quiet but perfect rendering of Lincoln's Gettysburg Address. Laughton does it well—but like a great actor. How interesting it would be to hear it coming from a true Jeeves. Of course, this was Laughton's heyday: He had just done *The Private Life of Henry VIII* and *The Barretts of Wimpole Street—Les Misérables, Mutiny on the Bounty,* and *Rembrandt* were ahead. He was unstoppable until *I, Claudius* came apart on the terrible gulf between him and Sternberg. But not too much of Laughton stands up well. The mystery is still there. Was he desperate not to emerge as gay, or was he locked in self-loathing? It seems that every picture was a hurdle in that race—a race never resolved. He passed from "greatness" to junk with surprising ease. In *Ruggles of Red Gap* he seems like the empty square. And Leo McCarey does not quite seem to notice.

The Rules of the Game (1939)

The shooting began on February 15, 1939, at the Chateau de la Ferte-Saint-Aubin in Sologne. So some time in that late winter, on the steps of the chateau, Marcel Dalio's Marquis would have stepped forward and explained that there had just been an accident. "And now, my dear friends . . . it is cold, you are running the risk of catching a chill and I suggest that you go inside." A few months later, on July 7, the film, *La Règle du Jeu*, opened in Paris. The war was weeks away and the film's portrait of a society that permitted such accidents, without daring to know their hideous consequences, was more than a jittery public could endure. But the time came, at Venice, in 1959, when a reconstituted version of the film opened. Where does it stand? It is the greatest film by the greatest director. Jean Renoir.

A house party has been arranged in a society where a virus called love has descended—everyone is in love with the wrong person. It is a condition of classic theater and farce, and we have many allusions to Mozart and Beaumarchais if we need instruction in misunderstanding—after all, isn't that the thing we do well and naturally? And once a dramatist recognizes that unstoppable proclivity in his figures, there's no need to approve or disapprove of them—they have their reasons and their energy. It is all a camera can do to keep up with them, to *see* them. So *La Règle du Jeu* is a film about hunting and pursuit in which almost certainly anyone will hit some wrong targets. Aim is not really a human facility so much as the helpless urge to fire.

There is also the tangle in lives (or plays) above stairs and below—once again, shown without judgment, but without any reliance on barriers that may keep people in or out. Class is only a way of organizing the others, so it is bound to occur, and certain to be overruled in a crisis. One valiant rule—one great seizing at hope—is directing: the idea that everything is under control. And there are occasions when this hurly-burly seems like a wild rugby match run by Octave (Renoir himself), our master of ceremonies and everyone's friend. But, alas, he becomes involved himself, and he is part of the tragedy.

From a script by Renoir, Carl Koch, Camille François, "and the cast." Jean Bachelet was director of photography. Eugène Lourié did the décor with Max Douy. Marguerite Houlet-Renoir did the editing. Dido Freire was script girl. Coco Chanel made the clothes, and Henri Cartier-Bresson was an assistant. More or less, it was the Renoir team, giving greatest rein to the deep focus, the camera movement, and the integrated shooting style that is forever the cinematic tradition and which Renoir had discovered in the thirties.

As for the actors, what can you say more than echo Renoir's realization that acting may be the best way to get through life. It ranges from elegant to slapstick, from insane to exuberant. In life, people go mad, and for actors, if they are working hard at the sane scenes, well, the madness is very difficult: Marcel Dalio, Nora Gregor, Roland Toutain, Mila Parély, Paulette Dubost, Gaston Modot, Julien Carette, Jean Renoir.

In the attempt to see an art in the movies, as well as entertainment, a culture as much as a business, I think that for some of us every attempt at judgment has come from this film's exhausted urging not to judge. But it is so hard not to be in love.

Rumble Fish (1983)

Seemingly at a low ebb after the failure of *One from the Heart* and the loss of his Los Angeles studio, but driven to make some money to save his family house in Napa, Francis Coppola went to Tulsa, Oklahoma, to make two films from the books about teenage life by S. E. Hinton—*The Outsiders* and *Rumble Fish*. The first was fairly conventional, but for its astonishing cast (a tribute to the casting acumen of Fred Roos): Matt Dillon, Ralph Macchio, C. Thomas Howell, Patrick Swayze, Rob Lowe, Emilio Estevez, and Tom Cruise. But by the time of the second picture, some deeper ambition stirred. So *Rumble Fish* is far from a routine job. It is a deeply poetic and personal essay on adolescence and a sure sign that Coppola is seldom the man you want to hire for a mainstream, moneymaking project.

It has a theme that is very close to Francis's often troubled relationship with his own brother, August Coppola. August was older, far more handsome as a kid, and seemingly more talented. People wondered how Francis could be anything other than daunted by August. This bond lies behind the fraternal relations in *The Godfather*, and now it leaped out again in the feelings of awe Rusty James (Matt Dillon) has for his older brother, the Motorcycle Boy (Mickey Rourke), who left home some time ago. It is when the Motorcycle Boy comes home that a crisis arises in Rusty James's life.

Whereas *The Outsiders* had been shot in realistic color, *Rumble Fish* was done in a very stylized, noirish black and white (handled by Stephen Burum) with just flashes of vivid color (for the tropical fish). It has dream sequences, fantasy scenes, and a very lyrical design sense, supplied by Dean Tavoularis. Stewart Copeland supplied a terrific rock score, and Barry Malkin was in charge of the editing. Coppola's two sons, Roman and Gian-Carlo, or Gio, worked as associate producers, and the cast includes a very young Sofia Coppola as Diane Lane's sister. The rest of the cast included Dennis Hopper (as the father to the two boys), Vincent Spano, Nicolas Cage (August's son), Christopher Penn, Larry Fishburne, William Smith, Michael Higgins, and Tom Waits.

I don't mean to overpraise *Rumble Fish*, but I think it is a haunting evocation of teenage years and maybe the most satisfying picture Coppola made after *Apocalypse Now*. I know that range includes *Tucker*, *The Godfather Part III*, and *Bram Stoker's Dracula*. But in fact only *Apocalypse Now Redux* seems to me in the same class as *Rumble Fish* and the great films of the early seventies. There's nothing too remarkable about that decline, or the loss of focus. There are many directors in America whose halcyon days have been quite short-lived. What happens in that loss of dedication, or the psychic need that powers it, is a fascinating question. There are no easy answers—and few striking comebacks. So Coppola has just four films to stand for his greatness. Of course, one would be enough.

Run of the Arrow (1956)

The charitable interpretation of John Ford's *The Searchers*—that it pays heed to the civil rights movement of the 1950s—should keep in mind that *Run of the Arrow* comes in the same year and surely recognizes an America raw with unhealed war wounds, racial hostilities, and that intransigent energy that makes Samuel Fuller so fascinating and alarming. Fifty years after the two "classics" were made, the Ford is a set piece with wondrous resonance here and there. But it is a fanciful view of what life was like in its America. Whereas *Run of the Arrow* is as fresh and scorched as a recent report carried through fire and ice, conceived and delivered in momentous anger. I'm not sure if there is another American movie that indicates so thoroughly the way the impact of an unresolved war has been branded on America.

O'Meara is one of the most unbridled, odious heroes in the Western. Give some credit to the rebellious Rod Steiger, granted free rein, but the entire conception is Fuller's—an Irish Confederate, a rebel who, having fired the last shot of the war (a hit), defies the peace and the weariness that may have overtaken General Lee. This is a man who will fight on, a spirit for whom the war was a convenience, even if it captured many of his innermost prejudices. O'Meara is an extraordinary picture of a type of Southerner who still drives America on to a fearsome date with destiny. And so *Run of the Arrow* and the journey of the film are kinds of wicked, drunken pilgrimage, mockeries of real spiritual inquiry, yet aching with O'Meara's cruel ego. That's why the desert is his proper destination (the film was shot near St. George, Utah), whereas the Monument Valley of *The Searchers* is simply an inane place for settlement.

This is a film of 86 minutes, with its own concessions to "Hollywood"—like Charles Bronson as Blue Buffalo, and Angie Dickinson reading the dialogue for Sarita Montiel's squaw. No matter, it is a properly violent fable in which that old word "savage" seems to fit our hero better than the "Indians" he finds in the wilderness. Ralph Meeker and Brian Keith are brilliantly articulate as cavalry officers with alternative answers (or failures to answer) the question of where America is going. And Steiger is a wild man such as few American films (or stars) could tolerate.

It is often said that Fuller films like a journalist reporting, but that point is not right. A journalist describes a scene. Fuller has had the daring and the historical acumen to imagine an action that may never have been. Never mind: As we watch, we seem to be seeing the uniquely dangerous Eden that America's melodrama required. It is taken for granted in this approach that the Indians are doomed. But there is the same bleak open-mindedness left for the larger enterprises—the West, America, civilization. For, in the end, this is a film about outcast fury—the energy that made America—and its longing for death.

The Sacrifice (1986)

We are on a flat shore by a lake or an inland sea (it is Gotland in the Baltic). The grass is that wintered green that has been hidden by snow. A man is trying to plant a tree by the shore, and he is talking to a child, his grandson. The camera stays fixed, at a remove, covering slightly, as a postman arrives, weaving figure eights on his bike as he talks to the man. It is the man's birthday: he is a writer, a critic, a philosopher, and a teacher (he was an actor once, but he found he could not speak onstage). We move inside the house; it is a lovely study in white, brown, and gray. People gather for the party—the man's English wife, a few friends. Gifts arrive—an old map of Europe. But then there is a roar in the air. Low-flying jets crush the scene. A pitcher of milk falls from a shelf. There is a terrible intimation of terminus. A great passage of film has been achieved.

This is the opening of Andrei Tarkovsky's last film, *The Sacrifice*. The light is Swedish, rendered by Sven Nykvist, and much of the mood and the place comes from Bergman, along with the brooding on the end of the world. The man is played by Erland Josephson. His wife is Susan Fleetwood. The grandson is played by Tarkovsky's young son, Andriosha. Tarkovsky himself dies in 1986.

As befits a film made in the last light of life, the beauty is not just heartfelt but perilous. There is a sense of time running out that comes even before the warnings of what is World War III. And the life on the shore is a semblance of that last rational but hedonistic version of life that must succumb to the poison in due course. But this is not simply a rational film in which the philosopher and everyone else faces extinction. It is a deeply religious story in which, perhaps, the worst can be avoided in the spirit of sacrifice. If the man can give up much of his great place and calm, then perhaps life will persist for the grandson.

In turn, *The Sacrifice* touches on the supernatural and the divine. There is a character who could be a saint or a witch. There will be nightmares—and the act of sacrifice. Some people get this terminology wrong. In truth, this film is one of those meetings with death and disaster that are so very hard to steer away from horror or the nearly hysterical hope for regeneration. The immense beauty of the first third of the film gives way, gradually, to increasingly contrived spectacle and the special mood of salvation. And by then, I fear, the authentic poetry of the opening has yielded to specious scenarios that remind us that Tarkovsky, too, was dying and that he found it very hard to bear. Why not—with his infant son playing in the grass?

What I am trying to say is that *The Sacrifice* is plainly the work of a master and for at least thirty minutes its poetry is impeccable. What follows fails . . . or it is less impressive. But that doesn't really matter. The attempt in *The Sacrifice* is what counts. And the mannerism that follows, the vanity even, are a forgivable despair. It is worth stressing that as he died, Tarkovsky estimated that the only cinema that would last would be that of the poets. Of course, he was laying down the law, for his son and every would-be poet.

Sadie Thompson (1928)

W. Somerset Maugham wrote "Rain" as a short story in 1921—it was published in the collection *The Trembling of a Leaf*—and the title speaks for the use of weather to enhance the story's sexual tensions as a whore meets a strict clergyman. In 1922, John Colton and Clemence Randolph had turned it into a Broadway play, *Rain,* that ran for 648 performances and starred Jeanne Eagels as Sadie Thompson with Robert Kelly as the Reverend Alfred Davidson.

This was a story in which Davidson first castigates Miss Thompson and then as he realizes how attracted he is to her he kills himself. The topic of sex and the critical view of a man of the church were both certain sources of trouble with the Hays Office. But Gloria Swanson was determined to do it. She and her backer, Joseph Kennedy (later U.S. ambassador to London), bought the rights to both the story and the play—later, she even asked Maugham to write a sequel (which he said he would do for $25,000). Then Joe Schenck and United Artists mounted a big protest because the story had been banned. It's the same old story with censorship, a fight for naughty love and hollow glory.

The whole thing came to pass. There had been a first thought of going to Samoa itself, but wiser and cheaper plans prevailed and Catalina Island was reckoned close enough to "Pago-Pago," with William Cameron Menzies doing the interiors at a studio in town. There were other obstacles. George Barnes was hired as photographer, but then Goldwyn pulled him off it and in turn Robert Kurrle and Oliver T. Marsh took over (with Charles Roshier working occasionally). Swanson's chief support in all this was her director, Raoul Walsh, and one day she determined that he was ideal to play Sergeant O'Hara—and she was right. Meanwhile, securing Lionel Barrymore for Davidson was key to the project.

The original version was 97 minutes, but some damage was suffered so that only a 91-minute version remains. Still, it shows a fine American production at the end of the silent era, well played and well directed, and a role very well suited to Swanson's self-confidence. The film did pass the Code—or rather the Code came in a distant second. There was never going to be any stopping the movies as a conveyor of the idea of sex. Of course, the reality is another matter. But *Sadie Thompson* speaks to the health and candor of Sadie's attitudes, and the film took in a million dollars.

A few years later, Joe Schenck persuaded Joan Crawford to do a remake, *Rain* (with Lewis Milestone directing and Walter Huston as Davidson). It was not a happy or relaxed experience, and Walter Catlett, a supporting actor, told Joan, "When Jeanne Eagels died, *Rain* died with her." By 1953, *Miss Sadie Thompson* (with Rita Hayworth and Jose Ferrer) only showed how the material had dated. Swanson struck while it was dangerous, and hers is the best version (even with the ending lost). Swanson was nominated for the first Best Actress Oscar, but lost to Janet Gaynor.

Safety Last! (1923)

Several years before *Metropolis*, there he is, modern man, clinging on for dear life to the hands on a great city clock. But not for Harold Lloyd the urban doom that pervades Fritz Lang's film: Harold is attached to the clock in no metaphorical sense. He's there for bare survival, as he tries to win promotion at the department store where he works and get his girl to marry him. Yes, you can say it was safer than it looked, but in fact Lloyd dragged his arm out of its socket doing the routine. And still to this day, there you are in downtown Los Angeles—when it was a very different place—and you can see all the life and bustle going on at ground level, while Harold flirts with his mission impossible.

Is it just me, or isn't there something of Tom Cruise in Harold Lloyd? The slight figure. The shock of dark hair. The inner numbness wiped away by the terrific friendly grin. And, more than anything, the innocent yet determined notion of getting ahead and being a success. It's typical of Lloyd that he has a girl (Mildred Davis) whose attitude to him is that she'll marry him, not when he discovers El Dorado or the Holy Grail, but when he gets ahead in the modern race. And so, he leaves Great Bend for the big city, narrowly avoiding carrying a black baby with him instead of his suitcase, and only just reclaiming the train after he's been picked up by a horse and carriage. Harold is always going somewhere, but he has a sublime talent for getting the wrong lift.

Lloyd had seen a steeplejack on the side of the Brockman Building in Los Angeles, and he conceived the whole picture out of that set piece. In his case, they'd climb the International Bank Building (with the aid of Bill Strother). Hal Roach himself filmed as they built sets attached to the skyscraper and had catching cradles out of camera view. The climax comes as Harold reaches the top, is knocked half-conscious by a whirling wind vane, and does a lovely staggery dance on the parapet ledge.

It was a Roach production for Pathé release, with Fred Newmeyer and Sam Taylor as directors, and Roach, Taylor, Tim Whelan, and Harold himself doing the story. Walter Lundin shot the film, and on a budget of $121,000 it earned $1.588 million. Thus, the immense fortune of Harold Lloyd and the absolutely honest emphasis on getting ahead. He was kind, good-hearted, and boyish, without a trace of cunning or intrigue to him. He stands for the days when the American audience liked nothing better than identifying with a good kid, a go-getter, and a fellow whose blue sky knew not a cloud of neurosis. People were scared for Lloyd in his stunts, but they trusted him to take care of himself. In the same way, we look at the youthful energy of the central character and the patient way the camera waits on him, and we know that the films are effectively directed by what Lloyd decides to do. And so a movie, a classic, came from the idea that a man climbing a building would draw a crowd.

Sait-On Jamais . . . (1957)

As the few people helping build the contents of this book exchanged lists, Bob Gottlieb wondered about Roger Vadim's *And God Created Woman,* if only because that famous if silly picture surely established Brigitte Bardot (who is historically interesting). But I guessed I would have a chance to talk about Bardot with *Le Mépris,* and I knew that the only Vadim film I cared about was variously known as *Sait-On Jamais,* or *When the Devil Drives,* or *No Sun in Venice.* Of course, the title it cries out for is simply *Death in Venice.*

It must be well over thirty years since I've seen *Sait-On Jamais,* and I have been unable to find a print of it now (which is unusual), so I have to admit I cannot remember too well what it is about. But that strikes me as a minor complaint. There must be some criminal enterprise involved, yet all I can really recall of "plot" is the rivalry over Françoise Arnoul between Christian Marquand and Robert Hossein. Is it possible that it's just a love story? That could explain how I recall in some detail a prolonged scene in which Hossein pursues Arnoul through a wintry Venice with just a crimson flower as his lure.

You see, Vadim is one of those filmmakers who could handle space. One of the things admired about *And God Created Woman* (in a rather camp way) was how he could arrange Bardot in a CinemaScope frame. But if you have ever loved Venice, or known it in winter, just consider what a CinemaScope frame can do with its alleys and steps, its sudden prospects and its claustrophobic tight corners. I don't believe it matters too much if this film is about very little, or next to nothing, because it is about space and movement in Venice, when the colors are gray, white, russet, and stone—the colors of a winter city.

That photography is handled by Armand Thirard, and I trust that it survives somewhere. Jean André did the production design, and Victoria Mercanton edited the film. Marquand is in his element as a rather lazy adventurer, Françoise Arnoul is very pretty, and I don't think she ever removes any clothing (I think I would have remembered). Robert Hossein is nasty and frightening, and O. E. Hasse was another villain.

I have left the best to last. There is a sound-track to the film, written by John Lewis and played by the Modern Jazz Quartet (Lewis, Milt Jackson, Percy Heath, Connie Kay). There are some who may charge that John Lewis writes genteel chamber jazz—that he is too cool to be the real thing. Perhaps. Still, this seems to me the best jazz score written for the movies, which isn't to say that it doesn't sometimes rival the bells and chimes of Venice. But I recall those spaces, the tracking shots, and the chasing swirls of Lewis and Jackson, piano and vibraphone. No, it's not a great movie, but it's a mystery why it's not better known.

Le Samourai (1967)

Is this authentic movie history, or the stuff of dreams? Is there a difference? It seems that Jean-Pierre Melville had wanted to do such a film as this for several years, and had had only Alain Delon in mind for the central part. And so, eventually, he cornered Delon and began to read him the script. After a few minutes, Delon stood up and stopped the director. "This is seven and a half minutes," he said, "without dialogue. I'll do it. What is it called?" Melville replied, "*Le Samourai,*" and Delon got up and led Melville to an inner room of the house that contained a leather couch, and the sword and lance of a samurai.

Well, this is a film about inner rooms of that kind, which leaves just this question hanging: Are the occupants of such private places really the grave heroes of our time, or are they solemn kids in love with disastrous fantasies? Or, to put it another way, is this the perfect, ritualistic tribute to the solitude of the hit man, or is it a superb piece of absurdist humor resting on the fact that no one—onscreen or in the audience—dares begin to smile, let alone laugh? It is as if the great beauty of Delon—though fatuous—dares us to observe his silky pretensions and stay in chilled respect, or to start to vibrate with buried laughter.

Jef Costello is a man in a raincoat and a fedora hat—they seem like soft, fabric materials, but they might be steel cast by Brancusi. There is no deviation or untidiness. He is a hit man in a world where nearly everyone could be hit. He carries out his assignments with a dreamy perfection. It is not just that he is brave, accurate, expert, and cool—but is he cool? And beautiful? So much so that our seeing him is like bearing witness to an angel's mission. (It could as easily be Buster Keaton as Delon.) Except that he is seen on a job by an apparent stranger—by a black woman singer at the club. And so, fatalistically, Jef moves toward his destiny, for somehow he cannot blame this innocent bystander or hit her. She is another angel.

Melville films all this as if it might be the only film he would ever make. Indeed, he makes it look like Bresson, and I think it is far more productive to see the links with *Pickpocket,* say, than with *This Gun for Hire,* the Frank Tuttle film from the Graham Greene novel. Henri Decaë shot it in subdued colors, and Delon seems to know that this is the film for which he will be remembered. He might even have concluded from this film that he could as well rest with tranquillity beneath the snow of rumors about his own underworld life. There is an implacable suggestiveness to the picture that leaves no room for argument.

It is a perfect film, until you realize that this same Melville once made *Le Silence de la Mer* and *Les Enfants Terribles*—and then its immense aplomb can shrivel up, just like the Wicked Witch of the West when a drop of water hits her.

In short, I love the film, but I am daunted by my feelings.

Samson and Delilah (1949)

If you recall, there is a moment in *Sunset Blvd.* when Norma Desmond gets out the car and has Max von Mayerling drive her over to Paramount, where she will talk to Cecil B. DeMille about her script. The assumption behind *Sunset Blvd.* is that Norma is crazy to think that a working professional, let alone the great DeMille, would countenance her garbage. This seems reasonable, but for one thing: At Paramount, at that moment, DeMille was making *Samson and Delilah*, which is beyond trash.

The screenplay required at least eight hands—Fredric M. Frank, Vladimir Jabotinsky, Harold Lamb, and Jessie L. Lasky, Jr. I'm sure Norma Desmond could have done it on her own—and who can rule out the chance that she actually wrote it in childish longhand? For this is the story of Samson, a very strong man among the Israelites and easily seen as a threat to the Philistines. So those wicked and malign occupiers set Delilah, their most beautiful babe, to seduce Samson. She thereby discovered that his strength lay in his hair, and while he was in a drugged sleep she cut it off. Then was Samson reduced and humiliated by the Philistines and brought into the Temple to be mocked. But Samson called out to God, got an extension of his old strength, and pulled down the Temple. Big finish. Samson and Delilah crushed in the ruins. Philistines defeated.

Dewey Wrigly was credited with "Holy Land Photography," but most of the picture was done at Paramount with George Barnes handling the Technicolor (very rich in the red-brown range), which got an Oscar nomination. Edith Head and a team of others (including Dorothy Jeakins) were nominated for costumes, though Hedy Lamarr had her own designer, Elois Jenssen. But the key Oscar went to the design quartet—Hans Dreier, Walter Tyler, Sam Comer, and Ray Moyer—who did the Temple in its destruction.

Still, I have to say, you could have Samson and Delilah naked on a simple sofa and the picture would still be a wow if you had Victor Mature and Hedy Lamarr. Mature's good nature was as ample as his muscles, and he plunges into the pathos here without shame or coyness. Indeed, Mature could have played King Kong. But Hedy Lamarr (aged thirty-six) was genius casting. Her career was in decline by then (maybe she was putting in too much time on her inventions—her brow does look furrowed). But she had a kind of gloomy sexuality that places the story in that intriguing ground where biblical overlaps with screwball—bibleball?

Nor is this the end of the fun. Let me just add that the leading Philistine aristocrats are George Sanders and Angela Lansbury, both of whom have the English background that so naturally inspires thoughts of vicious corruption. The cast also includes Henry Wilcoxon, Olive Deering, Fay Holden, Russ Tamblyn, George Reeves, Tom Tyler, and Mike Mazurki.

The picture had first rentals of $11.5 million, a Paramount record at the time.

San Francisco (1936)

Timed for the thirtieth anniversary of the 1906 earthquake and fire, *San Francisco* is a fine example of Metro-Goldwyn-Mayer's attitude to the world's problems: Surely star power, high-mindedness, prayer, and song will get us through. San Francisco is depicted as the expression of three personalities: Mary Blake (Jeanette MacDonald), a sweet girl with a sweeter voice, just as good with opera as she is with the "Battle Hymn of the Republic"; Father Tim Mullin (Spencer Tracy), a robust churchman, the model of piety standing in for civic enlightenment; and Blackie Norton (Clark Gable), saloon keeper, expert in a pretty corrupt world, but with his heart so firmly in the right place that he can be redeemed. When the act of God strikes San Francisco, it's Jesus and melody that carry the spirit of determination that will build the city back up again.

The script job was given to Anita Loos and Robert Hopkins (both San Franciscans originally), and they based the Gable role on Wilson Mizner, a man about town. It had been a Thalberg production, but when Irving died it was reassigned to Bernard Hyman, and he enlisted Woody Van Dyke to direct. It was a big picture that cost $1.3 million in the end. By far the most beautiful and cinematic part of the film is the exciting Slavko Vorkapich montage that depicts the earthquake—and there was a lot more in the way of special effects from James Basevi. But Jeanette MacDonald is Metro's idea of spectacle, singing opera and then coming in at the end with the terrific first four notes of "San-Fran-cis-co," the epitome of easy courage and studio politics.

There is a scene where Blackie knocks Father Tim off his feet, and the Breen Office said it had to go because it showed lack of respect for the Church. So Loos and Hopkins threw in another scene, in the gym, where we see that Father Tim is actually a far better boxer than Blackie—you see, he only let himself be knocked out! The key song was written by Bronislau Kaper and Walter Jurmann, and Gus Kahn added the lyrics. To this day, the organist at the Castro Theater plays it every night as a finale, and it stands as the San Francisco anthem.

Considering the real place of earthquake threats in California, it's a foolishly cheerful, detached film. Indeed, it views natural disaster the way studios regarded the war effort. But it got a Best Picture nomination, and it made a huge profit of $2.23 million. No other Metro picture of that era came close to it. Of course, in the thirties, natural disaster was a blip on the screen. In the current climate of Hollywood, no one would dare to make a film about Katrina—not just because they'd fear the likelihood of being attacked for a partisan job, but because no studio recognizes the responsibility. San Francisco may be ruined by a second "big one," a blow that takes the smile off the California face. But for 1936 this film sufficed as a rousing affirmative and a rehearsal for war. Did anyone look at the Vorkapich rhapsodies on collapse and imagine?

Sansho the Bailiff (1954)

Watching *Sansho the Bailiff,* and wondering why it has that title, I ask myself how far Jean Renoir and Kenji Mizoguchi knew each other. I cannot find references to understanding, but Mizoguchi was winning prizes at European festivals during Renoir's great surge in the 1950s. (*Sansho* won the Silver Lion at Venice, the third Mizoguchi in a row to take that prize.) Surely they felt some kinship. For the humanism in Mizoguchi and the Shakespearean sweep of time and society are akin to Renoir's vision of life's theater carrying on in India, in Montmartre, and in the theater. Their language was the same: the way camera movements expanded consequence; spatial connections that spoke to likeness; and the suffering. Let us be clear: There is more suffering in Mizoguchi. His work of the fifties is the great tragic moment of cinema. Yet *Ugetsu* finds a calm in story itself—and that was Renoir's compassion, too.

We are in eleventh-century Japan. The governor of Tairo province, Masauji (Masao Shimizu), has to go into exile. He has challenged the system of corruption and slavery. His wife, Tamaki (Kinuyo Tanaka), undertakes a journey to join him. But she and their two children are waylaid by bandits: The mother is sold into prostitution; the two children become the property of Sansho the cruel bailiff.

Ten years pass. The children are grown: They are Zushio (Yoshiaki Hanayagi) and Anju (Kyoko Kagawa). Zushio has declined. But Anju urges him to escape and find their parents. When he does escape, Anju stays behind and kills herself. Zushio hides in a temple, protected by Taro, the son of Sansho. He learns that his father is dead, but when he seeks justice he is made governor of Tairo, like his father. He ends slavery. He searches, and finally at the seashore he finds his mother, old, crippled, and blind.

As a story of family separation and search, *Sansho* comes without the odd, brief mercy that *Ugetsu* holds. But *Ugetsu* is a story of spirits. *Sansho* is a chronicle, nearly Lincolnian in its study of a man who might free slaves. Its method is discreet: long shots, camera movements, sudden glimpses into the abyss—like Anju walking slowly into a pool, setting off her own ripples. It comes from a novel by Ogai Mori. Kazuo Miyagawa did the photography. Near the end of his life, though only in his fifties, Mizoguchi was working very hard. He knew that he and his characters were on the same path.

Sansho is two hours long, and the ten-year gap is the clue to its Shakespearean ambition. But you are left in no doubt about old people waiting for the young to grow up, and then forgetting what they are waiting for. This is a perfect film, one in which we never notice execution or exactness. We are waiting for the ending, its bleakness, its happiness, its dread. You can take those few years around 1955 and still be amazed that such staggering films were made. And I cannot help but wonder whether in their travels, in their work, Renoir and Mizoguchi ever quite realized how they were looking for each other.

Saturday Night Fever (1977)

By the mid-1970s, the American movie musical hardly existed with any vitality or novelty. There had been great hits—like *West Side Story* and *The Sound of Music*—but it is an act of charity to call them movies. *Saturday Night Fever* came out of nowhere in 1977, and it was a new kind of musical, one that found a way to harness the new youth audience that liked to dance, and here was a story about a Brooklyn kid with few assets but a great urge to make it. He dances in the way earlier movie characters boxed, played the violin, or turned to a life of crime. In fascinating ways, Tony Manero combined all those urges—and the public went with him in a rush, John Travolta became a major star, and disco music (not our finest hour) was elevated.

To that extent it was a film with a story or a question—will Tony get out of Brooklyn?—to which songs, or a kind of Muzak, had been added in the form of the background music to his chosen way—disco dance contests. The film was produced by Robert Stigwood (who would then produce *Grease*). The screenplay was by Norman Wexler, based on a magazine story by Nik Cohn. And it was directed by John Badham. Yet I wonder whether any of those people had a claim for authorship to match either Travolta or the Bee Gees, the group that contributed the inspirational, sliding, gliding music that was disco.

The greatest interest in the film was the clash between that streamlined fantasizing in the music and the really gritty quality of the Brooklyn life. This isn't simply a story about two people who win the dance prize and fall in love. It's about the poverty of imagination and opportunity in Italian-American life, about families without much hope, about suicide and rape as some of the destinies these young people are headed for. Are those two things balanced? No, not quite. In the end, this is a picture that glimpsed the chance of cleaning up on the music—which is what happened. The real barriers to progress in places like Brooklyn remain. So few win a boxing title. So few win a dance cup.

But the impact on young imaginations was immense—just look at the spread of Tony's white suit (as designed for the film by Patrizia von Brandenstein). And then notice the heady bliss felt by Tony and his partner Stephanie (Karen Lynn Gorney) in the oddly plastic moves of disco dance. Disco may be the dance form of a diminished culture, but the dancing scenes here—to stuff like "How Deep Is Your Love," "More Than a Woman," and "Staying Alive"—is what made this a repeat experience for white kids. (The film does show a very white world, just as hip-hop was about to revolutionize music.)

As for Travolta, a TV high school kid was suddenly promoted to the big screen. He was a sweet, dumb, goofy boy, full of strut and acting instincts, but so palpably kind as to be like uncooked dough. He was twenty-three when the film came out, but he was as pulpy and unformed as sixteen. He still is.

Save the Tiger (1973)

John G. Avildsen is the director of one of the great rose-colored myths in Hollywood history—the humbug of a hopeless and used-up club fighter named Rocky Balboa fighting for the heavyweight championship of the world. (It was also the story of how a Hollywood unknown named Sylvester Stallone became one of the big men in town.) Four years before *Rocky*, this same John G. Avildsen had directed one of the most misanthropic of American films, *Save the Tiger*. Do we reconcile this contrast by taking it for granted that Avildsen had an alert proficiency that would do whatever he was offered? Or is there actually some common sense of the world, of its essential stupidity and indifference, in both the nightmare and the happiness dream?

There's no doubt that *Save the Tiger* was lifted way above its rut to a place where one wants to ask these questions because of Jack Lemmon's presence as the hero, Harry Stoner. Stoner has been a hero in the war and a real figure in his locality as a youth. But years have passed. He is unhappily married. He hates the dress company, Capri Casuals, that he runs with a friend. He is out of hope and energy and of that American delusion that the two together can still make everything turn out all right. It is his dreadful attempt at "everything" that makes him such a nonstop gloom merchant—and such a begging noise for an actor to mime to.

And let's not forget that Jack Lemmon got the Oscar as Harry Stoner (in a year when Brando, Nicholson, Pacino, and Redford were his rivals on split-screen night—your assignment tonight is a one-act play in which that quartet discusses the awards, the first line of which is Redford saying, "Of course, the thing about Jack is he always has done real").

Steve Shagan wrote this very actable piece, and it is pretentious enough to summon up a vague memory of Fellini at the end as Stoner, disconsolate to the *n*th degree after a night with a hooker, watches children playing ball—they are so innocent, he is so guilty. You sort of wish the kids would call the cops and accuse him of molesting them. How richly that would fit Stoner's horror of the world and its abuse of his tenderness. Lemmon rants, rails, laments, and assails. He goes unshaven. He stands there in the midst of it all, like a battered fighter offering up his reliable jaw—it is Rocky Balboa, at last, deserving to be champion griper. And surely we long for the script to hit him with more bad luck, low blows, and assaults on his faith in human nature.

This is the kind of terrible gravity that lifelong comics aspire to—it is Nobel stuff, with Jerry Lewis cooking up the dynamite. And it is a woeful glimpse of what plenty of Americans regard as art. Lemmon is unstoppable, untoppable, and yet so low you can't get beneath him either. It is so real and wearying you want to fall asleep, and it comes as a horrible shock after so many years of movies to find that the medium needed to read us this ill-tempered lecture about the awfulness of modern times.

Saving Private Ryan (1998)

The decision to open off Omaha Beach in one landing craft as dawn comes up on D-day is indicative of *Saving Private Ryan* in its great task—as a manual and philosophy of combat itself. We had had war movies since the beginning of film, but in those first twenty minutes Steven Spielberg established new standards for the din and chaos of combat, for the terrible, deafening blast and explosion of it all, for the natural terror and the decisive urge to stay attacking. And it is Spielberg's contention—and our hope—that that urge comes from ordinary moral decency. It's not that the Germans are badly treated in this movie, but *Saving Private Ryan* believes in the justness of its war.

The men under Captain Miller (Tom Hanks) make their objective; they secure the first beachhead in their section of German occupation. And then the wand of magic comes down on them. General Marshall (Harve Presnell—excellent) discovers that three out of four Ryan brothers have been lost already. The fourth, somewhere in Normandy, must be saved. It is an American sentimentality, if you like, the tremor of decency. Yet Miller's band of brothers may be lost in the saving attempt. Still, they will try, no matter that they grumble at the sudden illogicality of it all. Trained to survive, they are now to be educated in sacrifice. That's the theme of this remorseless study of combat—and I think it's fair to say of Spielberg and his America (of his filmmaking, too) that the grace note is the crown worn by democracy. Not that democracy ought to believe in kings.

The open-air stuff in Normandy (this is virtually the entire film) is staggering: Janusz Kaminski's photography is aware of passing grace notes as well as the great central thrust. The second set piece—the German attack on the bridge of Reimen—is actually more lucid and gripping than the first invasion: It's like an Anthony Mann attack. The use of the Upham character—educated, German-speaking, enlightened, afraid—is part of the overall stress on necessary force in combat. At the end, there is the attack and nothing else. In the heat of battle prisoners will be killed.

I would have had a few things different. When we learn who Miller is back home, it proves to be a classic Capra situation. I would have liked him to be a mess in real life, but a man who has found himself in war. And I would cut the finale, when Ryan the old man comes with his family to a cemetery to honor the grave of Miller and to wonder whether he deserved saving. We assume all these things—though it is nice to see Kathleen Byron as Ryan's wife.

Hanks is simple, ideal but infinite. Tom Sizemore has the blood of every screen sergeant. Among the men, look for Edward Burns, Matt Damon (as Ryan), Barry Pepper (as the sharpshooter), Adam Goldberg, Vin Diesel, Giovanni Ribisi, Jeremy Davies (as Upham), Ted Danson, and Paul Giamatti.

Sawdust and Tinsel (1953)

In choosing films for this book, the greatest directors present the most awkward problems. When I thought of Bergman first in relationship to 1,000 films, I thought of *Persona, Cries and Whispers, Wild Strawberries*, and *The Seventh Seal* as automatic choices, no matter that *The Seventh Seal* is by far the weakest of the four. But it was a landmark, and may still be the first Bergman picture the average person thinks about. Was that enough? I quickly thought of *Frenzy* (1944), because of the several things it introduced, not knowing how easily I (or readers) would see it again. In the later films, *Fanny and Alexander*? *The Shame*? *Autumn Sonata*? *Through a Glass Darkly*? You begin to wonder whether you can omit any films by the best directors. Which Bresson film is minor? And then I thought of the face of Harriet Andersson in *Sawdust and Tinsel*, and I looked at the film again. It's in. But something else will be out.

Bergman was born in Uppsala in 1918 and educated at Stockholm University. He moved straight into film and theater, a writer at first for movies and a would-be director onstage. *Frenzy*, in 1944, was his first scripting job, for the Alf Sjöberg film. He directed his own debut, *Crisis*, the next year. There is extraordinary development in his career, but that does not mean there are any stupid, juvenile, worthless films. By the time he made *Sawdust and Tinsel*, he was both a filmmaker and director of the Malmö City Theatre. Onstage, already, he had done *A Streetcar Named Desire* and *The Threepenny Opera*, and right after *Sawdust and Tinsel* he would do *Six Characters in Search of an Author*. By my count he had already had three wives and six children.

I spell it out like that to convey the small world he moved in and the almost academic intensity with which he scoured his own emotions. The third marriage had broken down because on location for *Summer with Monika* he had had an affair with Harriet Andersson—it is palpable in that authentically erotic film. He was living with Andersson but perhaps growing bored when he made *Sawdust and Tinsel*, which is a picture about the relationship between a circus master (Hasse Ekman) and his mistress (Harriet Andersson).

That *Sawdust and Tinsel* showed a deepening in Bergman's talent was almost entirely because of the nakedness with which he exploited his own relationship with Andersson. A little like *The Blue Angel*, it is a film about sadomasochism, humiliation, and betrayal, just as it reflects upon the endlessly renewable need of the director for a female muse and an obedient talent. It is the first film that defines the parameters—ugly but fascinating—of Bergman's relations with his actresses. This is not unique to Bergman, of course: *Sawdust and Tinsel* could easily be shown in a series and sequence that included *The Red Shoes, Lola Montès, La Strada*, the early work of Godard, and so much else.

In the totality of his career, *Sawdust and Tinsel* may reveal the nastiest side of Ingmar Bergman, but it is vital to the progress of a man willing, or even determined, to expose himself.

Scarface (1932)

The full title is *Scarface: The Shame of the Nation.* This refers to the add-on imposed on the Hughes company as it released its immensely enthusiastic endorsement of a certain Chicago gangster as "entertainer of the year." More or less, before enjoying the wanton strut, snarl, and tommy-gun fire of its gangsters, Hollywood had gone into a brief lamentation that social conditions should drive aimless young men to outlawry, and so on. Nobody was fooled. The nation was greedy for the rat-tat-tat of fire (with every detail and enhancement sound allowed) and the tumble of bodies that went with it. If only because of the presence of Jimmy Cagney in this new genre, it was not easy to split it from the musical or even a kind of antic, screwball comedy in which the kids' guns fired real bullets. (This dream goes on. I have just watched Al Pacino interviewed by James Lipton on *Inside the Actors Studio,* and when the turn came to discuss *Scarface* [1983], the audience gave a prolonged round of applause—hardly because of the moral uplift of that film but because it is one of the most enjoyable things even Pacino has ever done.)

Working for Howard Hughes, Howard Hawks approached Ben Hecht and suggested a ruling family in modern Chicago like the Borgias—the incestuous brother-sister relationship was there at the outset. Hecht told everyone that he wrote it very quickly, but research shows that other hands had a part, including W. R. Burnett, John Lee Mahin, Fred Pasley, Seton I. Miller, and Hawks himself. But what emerged is the portrait of a monstrous animal, closer maybe to King Kong than the regular tight-lipped Hawks hero. That role went to the sidekick, Guino Rinaldo (George Raft), unlucky enough to get involved with Tony's hot-blooded sister, Cesca (Ann Dvorak—also in bed with Hawks).

Nobody has suggested that this incest operated with any of Chicago's real mobsters, least of all Al Capone, but it clearly offers a way of reading the violence as coming from sexual dysfunction—that is even more pronounced in the remake, where cocaine has added to Montana's delusion.

That said, this is a sardonic, black-humored treatment of gangsters, full of gallows humor and X-marks-the-spot diagrams. There's no need to take sides, but who can resist the sport of this local war? Even without the later lectures that were tacked on to save face with law enforcement, this is a mocking treatment of law. United Artists said it was unforgivable. They wanted an ending with Camonte being hung. There were different cuts in different states.

There is a zest and intimacy in the playing that is shocking and gleeful. Paul Muni is brilliant in the title part, and his presence touches on all the ironies about being an American success. Dvorak is very sexy, Raft is taciturn, and then you've got Karen Morley, Osgood Perkins, C. Henry Gordon, Vince Barnett, Boris Karloff, Purnell Pratt, and Tully Marshall. Lee Garmes shot most of it and helped create the sultry twilight of lamps and wet streets. It cost $700,000 and earned about $1.2 million on its first run.

Scarface (1983)

Yes, crime and drug selling and the kind of violence that apply buzzing chain saws to human limbs are all very bad things, and if nations knew what shame was anymore they might feel ashamed. Do not repeat these practices at home, and do not even stoop to them on the road.

But still, by 1983, driven by two self-indulgent would-be hoodlums, Brian De Palma and Oliver Stone, there was no doubt that it could be a lot of fun to be Scarface. There is a moment near the end when Tony Montana, in his stupor from cocaine, feels that killing children may be going too far. And it's bogus, because everything rich and wondrous about Al Pacino's Tony is about going too far. If nothing else, as the terminal dullness of Reagan's America became intolerable and undeniable, someone made a film that was all about excess, delirium, and being out of control. There was a kind of nostalgia in it that longed wistfully for those great American days of murder, rape, and free enterprise.

And it is the absence of shame or moral reference in the story that is most exultant. To that end, it is a proper accompaniment that there is hardly any authority in evidence in *Scarface*. The one cop we ever meet—the terminally cynical Harris Yulin—is a complete sellout, horrified to realize in his last seconds that there's no dealing with Tony, that Tony is personally going to put a bullet in his stomach because that is known as the slowest and most excruciating way to die.

It is true that in the end Tony is alone and destroyed. He has killed his best buddy. He has seen his beloved sister die. And now his mansion is invaded by an enemy gang—we see the worms writhing in the cheese as the surveillance cameras pick up every detail of the Colombians' approaching menace. Tony will die in a hail of bullets and cocaine, and that's cool. But really the logic and the drive of the film should have him becoming mayor of Miami or governor of Florida, or . . . Why should there be any limit? Democracy can yield to this thug just as easily as Elvira, the wan Wasp princess he steals on the way up his ladder. And we have to wonder whether Michelle Pfeiffer ever guessed at the time, coming down in an aqua sheath dress and a glass elevator, did she know that nothing was ever going to get better? (Ferdinando Scarfiotti "helped" on the design.)

So the movie thrills to its own set pieces, which are everything from the way Pacino says "mon" and does his Cuban accent to the gradual vengeful process that will culminate in having F. Murray Abraham tossed out of a helicopter in flight. De Palma seems to know in this film that his "talent" was always training for the orgy, and this is the occasion where he relinquished all claim upon taste, refinement, or mercy. He gives the public what it wants and his method of direction is to tell Pacino to take ever greater risks. You can see the starch of Michael Corleone being purged from the actor's soul. He has been Montana ever since, brazen and excessive.

A masterpiece, and persuasive proof that so many movies lean toward trash.

The Scarlet Empress (1934)

A few years had passed since the moment when Josef von Sternberg delivered Marlene Dietrich to Paramount—and realized that just as he might possess her for a moment, though unreliably, she would haunt his dreams forever. But several things had emerged: Marlene had many love affairs, but stayed "loyal" to her husband, Rudy; Paramount had seen the shine fall from their new star—*Blonde Venus* and *Dishonored* had done poorly; she was urged to make films with other directors; and as the Depression extended, so Paramount fell on evil times.

All of which was perfect timing and positioning for *The Scarlet Empress,* the most extreme and by far the most expensive of her films with Sternberg. This time she would be the Princess Sophia of Prussia (played as a child by Marlene's own daughter, Maria), who becomes Catherine the Great, empress of all the Russias and—apparently—bedmate to most of her soldiers. The historical accuracy was regarded with disdain. This was the story of a sexual conqueror. And whereas once upon a time at Paramount, Marlene had had real men to challenge her—Gary Cooper and Cary Grant—now the men are just faceless, phallic uniforms, Sam Jaffe (the very image of a feeble, demented husband) and John Lodge, who was not really selected for acting ability. The empress is in a world of her own—and the film suffers because of it.

Everything went into the décor and the light and the recurring image of Marlene as a burning bloom in the center of so many hysterical arrangements. You can believe the statuary and the wall hangings were Russian if you like. It doesn't matter. This is the Russia of fever dreams. There is no attempt to measure the history or the politics of Catherine's rise to power. Her authority exists simply to make manifest the sexual glory of the woman who is in command of all this.

The Scarlet Empress is often hailed as the fullest demonstration of Sternberg's genius. In truth, I think it's out of control—and it is not a picture he talks about very much in his self-serving autobiography, *Fun in a Chinese Laundry.* The script (allegedly from Catherine's diaries) is by Manuel Komroff—and it showed how much Sternberg needed Jules Furthman (who did three of the previous four films). Hans Dreier did the sets, Travis Banton the costumes, and Bert Glennon photographed it. There were yards of classical music on the sound track. It was a disaster. Maybe people had had too much of this ogling of Marlene. Maybe Sternberg was being allowed to hang himself. But, in general, Hollywood in the thirties rather liked royal family stories. It admired and envied monarchy. When Edward VIII abdicated for Mrs. Simpson, there were people in Hollywood who were heartbroken. In short, the satire Sternberg intended cut against the ground of republican respect. He was doomed—but he would have said that that was his plan.

Scarlet Street (1945)

Wasn't there something going on between Fritz Lang and Joan Bennett? Hers was not the greatest of careers, but after Lang had used her as the whiny-voiced hooker in *Man Hunt*, he seems to have grown more and more interested. And *Scarlet Street* (derived from Jean Renoir's *La Chienne*—The Bitch), is the picture that digs into her casual, blowsy sexuality. Bennett was show business upper class—the daughter of Richard, she was the sister to haute snob Connie Bennett, and she was by now Mrs. Walter Wanger, but Lang delighted in revealing the slut in Joan Bennett. And nowhere is that clearer than in her "Lazy Legs" in *Scarlet Street*. There may have been a love affair, but it never stopped Lang from deriding Bennett's acting ability.

It was a wartime production of Diana Pictures, the company Wanger had set up with Bennett and Lang. But the project was one for which Ernst Lubitsch had bought the rights for Paramount. That it never got done there had to do with censorship objections. After all, in the old story Renoir had done, the Sunday painter killed his awful wife, let her pimp take the fall for it, and then wandered away into the world of Boudu. In America, no crime goes unrebuked (it is said), so what would become of the guy?

There was a brief association between Lang and Ludwig Bemelmans on the script before the author of *Madeleine* walked away with this riposte: "Am not overly fond of sitting in a rat trap and listening to the pronouncement of the pedantic professor that you are." So Dudley Nichols took care of the script with his customary ease. Milton Krasner did the photography, and the excellent sets—all silky clutter and garish mirrors—are by Alexander Golitzen. As for the paintings done by the Edward G. Robinson character, they were by John Decker.

Of course, in theme and central triangle, this was *The Woman in the Window* over again. But Chris Cross, the bank cashier and Sunday painter, is a tricky part: He must be homely but not absurd; he must have soul and desolation. Robinson was at his peak—remember, this is the moment of *Double Indemnity*, too. Suppose that insurance man, Barton Keyes, had a naggy wife at home, could Keyes become Cross? You feel that Robinson has all these characters in his mind, shuffling around each other. There was no star like him, and in his daring he opened up a range of parts usually given to supporting players.

Bennett is sexy, spiteful, unreliable—just the kind of girl that Lang the misogynist liked to dream of. She seems more relaxed than ever before. Whenever she went ladylike, she stiffened up. And, of course, Dan Duryea (in a series of clashing stripes), his forelock dripping off his lean head, his nasal voice arcing over that of Lazy Legs—he is a treat. The setting is said to be Greenwich Village, but it seems to be just a dark block away from *The Shop Around the Corner*.

Schindler's List (1993)

So many of the major enterprises of American film in the 1990s were trying to rediscover the place, or even the value, of big movies. Are they more than the spring that releases big money? And so in the same year, there was Steven Spielberg making *Jurassic Park*, because he knew he could, because he had the technology to keep the dinosaurs loping across the meadow, snapping at your heels, because film had reached that point of being able to re-create the distant past—as if it had been filmed yesterday. And at the very same time, he made *Schindler's List*, which in finding the Thomas Keneally novel had discovered a way of dealing with the concentration camps while keeping the movie big, and an uplifting event. Further, Spielberg must have realized—Oscars to Oskar—that he was at last in an impregnable position to have Hollywood give him proper respect. Their restraint toward his youth had lasted long enough. And just to show them, he'd make the two films at the same time, as if to prove that he was past being merely human.

It's hard not to see Spielberg's point about Hollywood's attitude to him. It is hard to resist his satisfaction that as that part of him covered by the past required some acknowledgment of his Jewishness, so the example of Oskar Schindler, manufacturer of enamelware—and the savior of over a thousand lives—was a decent way of telling the dire story with a positive attitude. Beyond that, with the help of Steven Zaillian's scrupulous and tender screenplay, *Schindler's List* is an uncanny version of the camps, the Krakow ghetto, the thing called the Holocaust, done with such steady application to all the crafts accessible to modern film, and with such an appalled sense of human nature that any kid coming to it fresh and suspicious might be sure the Holocaust happened.

But then, alas, some clerical fussiness flags that little girl's coat in red, so we will not miss it. That small touch exposed the uncrushable chutzpah of the most accomplished and "mature" filmmaker in America in 1992. With that one arty nudge Spielberg assigned his sense of his own past to the collected memories of all the films he had seen. All of a sudden, the drab Krakow vista became a set, with assistant directors urging the extras into line.

Schindler's List was a brimming example of Hollywood craft, and of maybe the most industrious and benevolent producer the system had ever known, but *Schindler's List* was also a disgrace to expressive power and our inescapable ties to the thing in our lives that used to be called "content." It was an organization of art and craft designed to re-create a terrible reality done nearly to perfection. But in that one small tarting up (not nearly enough to deter Oscars, of course), there lay exposed the comprehensive vulgarity of the venture.

Everyone was good, not just Liam Neeson, Ben Kingsley, Ralph Fiennes, and Embeth Davidtz, but all the children and the beautiful women who did not know whether the washrooms would give them water or gas.

The Searchers (1956)

Tell me the story again, Father—if you are my father. How Ethan Edwards comes back from the war late, with gold and his old Confederate coat. He comes back to the homestead of his brother, the wife and the children, in a place where no homesteading is really possible. Monument Valley looks like the beginning of time, or the end of it, but you can't farm there, and it is supposed to be Comanche territory. All of which shows how fast and loose John Ford would play with fact.

But the meaning or the purpose are elsewhere here, just as we feel Ethan has come back to see the brother's wife. Not a word is said, but there is a feeling of a love that passed there once, like a stream. Then Ethan is drawn away on a senseless posse mission and the Indian called Scar comes in the night, kills everyone, but is cruel enough to take Debbie, the youngest, until she can become Natalie Wood. And so the years and miles of searching begin as Ethan and Martin Pawley (Jeffrey Hunter), not a purebred anything, go after the scar and the wound and Martin realizes that he is there, just to be there, in case Ethan finds Debbie and makes certain of purity in the frontier way.

There are things in *The Searchers* that are cockeyed—notably the false eyelashes that Natalie Wood will wear as a Comanche bride. The subplot with Vera Miles and Ken Curtis becomes a bit more grinding every time you see the film. But then you are seeing the film again and again, because of its mystery. And every time, I find, I'm not quite sure how it's going to end, because I suspect Ford himself was in terrible doubt. But the simple confession in the ending of family and kin being reasserted is then magically defied when Ethan is not fit or ready to enter the house again. That last image of him in the breeze in the doorway, contemplating civilization and fury, and the door closing, is the greatest thing Ford ever does, and it is a tremendous moment in American film. But be careful deciding what it means.

Merian Cooper produced. Frank Nugent wrote the script. Winton Hoch did the beautiful photography. Max Steiner wrote the music—and the great, rolling theme. John Wayne's harshness, learned from *Red River*, came home. Jeffrey Hunter is fine, Natalie is adorable, and the rest of the cast is Vera Miles, Ward Bond, John Qualen, Olive Carey, Ken Curtis, Harry Carey, Jr., Hank Worden, and Henry Brandon as Scar. Someday in all this some new movie should tell Scar's story and of how Debbie loved him, and we should always recall that this comes from a story by Alan Le May and is the obverse of the story he wrote for Huston's *The Unforgiven*, where Audrey Hepburn is a Kiowa girl who has been taken by the whites.

Senso (1954)

The opening of *Senso* could hardly be more interesting. It is 1861, and we are at a performance of *Il Trovatore* at the Fenice opera house in Venice. We see the stage and then the packed house. In the upper gallery, leaflets and flowers are passed to the front for a demonstration against the occupation of Venice by the Austrian army—they are the officers in white sitting in the best seats. The excitement of two forms of theater, the Verdi and the political, is wonderfully done. And this is the old Fenice, so tragically burned in 1997 (and providing John Berendt for the occasion of his book *The City of Falling Angels*). There are moments when even feature film contributes to our historical record.

An emotional supporter of the demonstration is the Countess Livia Serpieri (Alida Valli). But in the aftermath, a close friend of hers and a leading activist (Massimo Girotti) goes so far as to challenge one Austrian officer—the insolently handsome Mahler—to a duel. In her efforts to have that dangerous silliness set aside, the countess attempts to meet Mahler (Farley Granger). He is in her box for the next delayed act of *Il Trovatore.* We see the singers in the background. "Can you see?" she asks. "Quite well," he answers, attending to the slope of her bosom. Some Austrians take culture where they can find it.

It is the start of a fatal love affair, in which the countess will be humiliated and Mahler will end up shot, all played out against superb battle scenes and a tense nocturnal moment when the countess's household, dogs included, is aroused as Mahler enters her bedroom, and Valli goes into such flights of desperation that she seems to grow older before our eyes. She died recently, and I wrote something to the effect that she seldom showed us a smile. As Anna, in *The Third Man*, there is not much to smile about, but there ought to be moments here in *Senso* when she loves Granger's wastrel. Perhaps, instead, she knows that he is unreliable—indeed, he is the one who smiles at the thought of her predicament. Just as he knows he is worth no one's love, so she falls to her ruin.

This mournful romance has not dated, and for many it is one of Luchino Visconti's cleanest and most satisfying films, in which the steady respect for décor is accompanied by a bleak lizard's stare for the human wrecks. Visconti had arranged to have Ingrid Bergman and Brando as the lovers. That seems like a huge loss. But Valli and Granger are more awkward and human; they are not icons of romance, but an unlovable beauty and a dishonest paragon. Their passion is never less than painful, and so a streak of realism looms up amid the lush visual treatment. The photography is by G. R. Aldo and Robert Krasker. Some of the music is Bruckner. An abbreviated, dubbed version, *The Wanton Countess,* had dialogue by Tennessee Williams and Paul Bowles! But the Italian script was by Visconti and Suso Cecchi d'Amico.

The Servant (1963)

Several years before the notorious house on Powis Square in *Performance*, Joseph Losey knew how to set an infernal mold in the structure and ambiance of a suitably upper-class residence. The house was by Richard MacDonald, of course, that hugely skilled designer so vital to Losey's rediscovery of himself and movie in England. I remember seeing the separate rooms all on one Shepperton sound stage, and realizing the way in which the webbing of camera movements could hold them in place. There, as the film was shot, you had a prescient feeling of a certain addled England stretched out in a morgue.

It was a trashy novel (by Robin Maugham), ostensibly uplifted by Harold Pinter's script. In fact, this was exactly the kind of trash—all rooted in intimidation, sadism, and shame—that Pinter understood. It was Losey, who was by then like a ferret pursuing the fat rabbit of English class, who knew what it could be. It was Losey who knew that Dirk Bogarde (that most secretive of English actors) could not fail to flower in the shit-beds of the hothouse. It was he who saw and nearly provoked a sexy affair between James Fox and Sarah Miles so that it would spill over on film, masking their limits as actors.

Yes, there is a decided lack of humor in the whole thing (or the decision to settle for Barrett's smarmy smile as comment). And there is finally a feeling of degradation and moral downfall for Fox's Tony that is way beyond his intellectual or spiritual capacities. (Invoking those things is the best joke in the film.) Still, this portrait of a helpless master and a cunning servant is icy, deliberate, and filled with loathing. And note that this vision came several years before that thing called the sixties really started to happen in Britain. So it's still relevant and useful to see *The Servant* as the climax to the unsettling films Losey made in the fifties in England.

But in all of those films, he faced problems of budget, script, and casting—to say nothing of his own uncertainty. The thing that strikes home in *The Servant* is the wintry assurance, the reptilian stealth of the takeover, and the final bleakness as England slips into the hands of its Barretts. Bogarde was a great strength during the filming: He helped the younger players, and I fancy that by his mere consent he gave courage to Losey. For Bogarde knew the swine he was becoming, and one part of his horrible smile is for all the aunts in England who would be mortified by it.

This is one of the great English films, and I don't think it could have been made in any other country without such surgical malice, or such American disinterest. Indeed, it leaves *Performance* looking not just imitative, but pretentious and romantic (Donald Cammell believed too much of his own guff). Losey knows that the Tonys will go on, dead inside, just as the Barretts would dream up their Blair. But those consequences are only there if you feel inclined to do the autopsy. First observe the death.

Se7en (1995)

In a city where it rains, a serial killer is on the loose. The police call him "John Doe" in advance of finding him, and the chief responsibility for that falls on Detective William Somerset (Morgan Freeman), who has seven days to go until his retirement, and a much younger cop, David Mills (Brad Pitt). Rookie and veteran, the two men make friction first, and then friends. Mills has Somerset home to dinner to meet his pregnant wife, Tracy (Gwyneth Paltrow). At dinner, their apartment shakes as the subway train goes past. Nowhere in this city is still, dry, or comfortable. But the dinner party is nearly sacramental in David Fincher's misanthropic film—it is a small haven of amity and understanding. It will not deter Somerset from retiring. But perhaps it restores his faith in the human race. More fool him.

No one I have ever met seeks to deny the aggressive talent in David Fincher, the director of *Se7en,* nor even the suggestion that he may be the closest rival to Michael Mann at putting eloquent imagery on a screen. But is that enough?

The city in *Se7en* is not named; it is "metropolis" again—which is fair enough and quite beautiful in the way Darius Khondji has made its shit-wash radiant. And the deliberate squalor that comprises gray slums and trashy luxury is equally well handled in the production design of Arthur Max and Gary Wissner's art direction. This is an odious place, and the hatefulness—we feel—has arisen naturally out of the malice, the disgust, and the unbridled evil in the world. (It comes from the computers, too.) Alas, the cops are no longer vigilantes or protectors. They are not people who can save the world. They are sacrificial victims—they are the idiots whose dogged pursuit pays tribute to the intelligence of the killer. More fool them. More brilliant him.

The killings in *Se7en* are modeled on the seven deadly sins, and they are hysterically brilliant in their presentation and the way in which the film offers them to the detectives and to us as puzzles to be solved. This bleak intellectual command—it's deadpan Meet John Doe—comes to reside in Kevin Spacey, in his revealing performance (Spacey, I think, was born to be hateful—grant him that, and he comes alive). And the killer wins: He assures his own death (always part of his plan), and he completes his mission, which includes striking horror in Somerset and Mills, and in us. More than the director knows, or gives himself a chance to notice, the film identifies with and embodies the cruel intellectual superiority of the killer. To that extent, *Se7en*—quite beautiful and piercing—is one of the most truly sadistic works the cinema has produced. Its very achievement is disgusting.

Spacey controls the film: After all, he knows the script (by Andrew Kevin Walker); he has designed the mise-en-scène. Freeman and Pitt are valiant, Paltrow is sweet and woeful. There are good supporting performances from R. Lee Ermey and Richard Roundtree.

Seven Brides for Seven Brothers (1954)

Who's to argue with the president at the time, Dwight D. Eisenhower, who said, "If you haven't seen it, you should"? Still, it seems to me that *Seven Brides for Seven Brothers*—deemed innovative, groundbreaking, and sensational in its day—has fallen out of fashion. It was a big hit in 1954, and it was actually nominated for Best Picture. Is it possible that the rise of feminism has taken away a lot of an innocent age's enthusiasm?

It was a Jack Cummings production, driven forward by Stanley Donen, who was working on his own and obviously had a lot to prove in delivering a musical (without any stage original) where the story was carried in song and dance. Indeed, the most daring thing about this film is the breakup of the old musical tradition in which illustrative numbers halt and summarize the small talk. Donen deserves high credit for a musical where the music hardly stopped. This wish to be new showed up in strained relationships with the first screenwriters, Frances Goodrich and Albert Hackett. They had worked from the Stephen Vincent Benet story "The Sobbin' Women." But Donen was unhappy. So they backed off and Dorothy Kingsley came on board. It was she who worked out that the female lead (Jane Powell) should be far more instrumental in the plot maneuvering.

So, here are these seven brothers out in the backwoods when one of them, Howard Keel, feels the need for a wife—whereupon his brothers all get the same itch. More or less, the model for the story is the *Rape of the Sabine Women,* though it's doubtful that that was noticed in the Eisenhower age. High spirits and animal energy overwhelm sexiness—that's what the dancing is all about.

The songs were written by Gene de Paul and Johnny Mercer, and they include "Bless Your Beautiful Hide," "When You're in Love," "Lonesome Polecat," and "It's Spring, Spring, Spring" (is it just three springs?). But it's the choreography of Michael Kidd that is the driving force (granted that Donen was himself a dancer and choreographer) filling the CinemaScope frame with dynamism, especially in the barn-raising ballet.

Keel and Jane Powell were not dominating actors or star personalities, but they did not need to be. This really is an ensemble musical, with Marc Platt, Jeff Richards, Matt Mattox, Russ Tamblyn, Tommy Rall, and Jacques d'Amboise among the men. The other brides are Virginia Gibson, Julie Newmeyer (later Julie Newmar), Nancy Kilgas, Ruta Kilmonis (Ruta Lee), Betty Carr, and Norma Doggett.

As so often, looking at this classic again only underlines the timidity of the business and the art in not moving further ahead with integrated musicals. The energy of *Seven Brides,* the exuberance, is still astonishing and exhilarating. And the chorus line of bursting talent tells its own story. Giving up on the musical, though, goes hand in hand with the decline of popular song and jazz. How did the music go out of America?

Seven Chances (1925)

If ever the comedian was born to reflect on the meeting place of—or the abyss between—"true love" and life's chronic tendency toward gambling, it was Buster Keaton. In *Seven Chances,* Buster is a man, Jimmy Shannon, with a "true love"—Mary Jones (Ruth Dwyer)—and he will end with her, which is nice if you believe in nice. But Buster plainly is a man inclined toward a belief in nothing but mathematics and absurdity. Thus, he does not laughingly reject his predicament—to be married by 7 p.m. on his twenty-seventh birthday—but he obediently falls in with it, like a number that has always been searching for the right equation. Look at his face—as beautiful but as inhuman as a butterfly—and you see that utter failure to identify sentiment, as opposed to identification. Buster is a Monopoly player who, told that his emblem is the boot, never thinks to ask, Is the boot me? He says, "I am the boot. The boot is like me. I like a boot. Give me a boot." And life obliges. Why seven?

Faced with his need (he has to be married by 7 p.m. to get his grandfather's money), Jimmy bungles his plea to Mary, not because he's shy, but because, again, he is not exactly human—he gets things wrong. And then he goes along with his pal's idea, to make a short list of the next seven possibilities. With Buster, you begin to wonder if it might not be easier for him to marry seven girls instead of one. Was the grandfather trying to say something in all the stress on 7? In other words, that horse-and-carriage act we all cherish, love and marriage, is getting the runaround.

So the film turns into a fantasia on number. Buster at the church is suddenly in an immensely crowded frame because the position of his consort, or 7-up, has been advertised. And then it's Buster being pursued by a horde of marriage-mad women. No wonder Buñuel adored this kind of thing—for we are as close to horror as we are to farce. Then we get an avalanche of rocks before the whole thing (not even 70 minutes) gets sorted out. And Buster ends up with Mary, except that she is clearly worried out of her mind by that blank look in his face. He has eyes like roulette wheels.

This is Keaton at M-G-M, with Joe Schenck producing and Clyde Bruckman serving as "writer." And in many ways, this is the purest of Keaton films in which a poor boot is going to be pursued by all the 7s. So many silent films now seem woefully out-of-date. But *Seven Chances* is ahead even of the other Keatons in that it takes for granted the coming of a society where transactions between men and women (or whatever) are akin to throwing dice. The jokes are hilarious, but we dare not laugh out loud for fear of waking Buster from his endless dream. From time to time, in this book, I have remarked on the gap between film and literature in the twenties. Yet Keaton was instructing Franz Kafka on the pitiless futility of taking sides in life.

Seven Samurai (1954)

In sixteenth-century Japan, an idyllic village, in a valley below steep mountains, discovers that bandits will attack as soon as the barley crop is ripe. They have suffered before—should they yield again, or fight back? A small committee is appointed to find samurai who will defend the village. This is a long film, drawn out by a master of suspense and control (over 200 minutes in its full version). We meet the seven samurai. We see them living in the village, doing their best to train the farmers and work out a strategy. And then there is battle, begun in sunlight and ending in pouring rain. Why seven?

The film is over fifty years old now, and it is impossible for anyone to see it today without thinking of the traditions it inspired: not just *The Magnificent Seven* and the Sergio Leone pictures; not just the immense field of martial-arts films based on the Western fascination with samurai armor and Japanese discipline; not just Melville's *Le Samourai*, or Frankenheimer's *Ronin*, but the laser-beam sword battles of the *Star Wars* series. (George Lucas was a huge admirer of Akira Kurosawa—and the eventual coproducer on *Ran*.)

Yet I urge you to do your best to regard this film with the eyes of 1954, and to see the astonishing vigor from Kurosawa that goes into every frame and meeting. I suspect that by the time he made *Seven Samurai*, he was well aware of and much in love with tropes from the American Western. But then consider the things that are uniquely his: the restless camera movements, the urge like that of a mettlesome horse, to be galloping and moving; the intense, burning close-ups and the way in which the cadet samurai can look at the weary master and say, "You are simply great!," and we feel the justice of it, but understand the sad smile on the master's face. There are the lovers on the forest floor, spread-eagled and surrounded by wildflowers. There is the terrible look on the face of the kidnapped wife as she realizes her husband is about to rescue her. There is the sudden use of slow motion (so that you wonder if you really saw it). And the sounds of running water, of bird cries, of the wind and of Toshiro Mifune's snorts of derision for everyone—himself included. These images and sounds are like moments in Shakespeare.

You can say that the film was a canny attempt to win Western audiences—and it undoubtedly achieved that. But over fifty years later, you can marvel at the rich black-and-white, the natural sounds, the drumbeats, the hooves on the ground and the music. It is a landmark in action films, but in its treatment of heroism, too. These samurai work and some of them die, for mere food. You wonder if they may seize the village, or be turned on by the villagers, for there is not too much trust between those parties. But the integrity of the contract prevails. There has always been a vein of cinema in which people do the right thing. And *Seven Samurai* comes as that notion was being treated with cynicism. But there is no denying or forgetting the faces of these men. They are the seven samurai, and they have found themselves. They do not need to say so, because we understand it.

7th Heaven (1927)

Austin Strong's play *7th Heaven* opened on Broadway in 1922, and it was a smash hit for nearly two years. It could be set anywhere, but in fact it's Paris—what it's palpably not is anywhere in the United States. Diane is a waif of the kind that depends on being unable to speak and not inclined to think. Her sister tries to force her into prostitution as a way of getting along. But she is saved by Chico, a sweet-smelling sewer worker, who takes her up to his seventh-floor heaven. They fall in love, but then war comes along—it has to be the First World War. Chico goes off to fight, and Diane takes a job in a munitions factory. She thinks Chico has been killed and starts seeing another man, Brissac. But then Chico comes back—blind. So he does not notice Brissac.

Onstage, the key parts had been played by Helen Menken and George Gaul. When Frank Borzage was given the assignment by Fox, he auditioned or tested a lot of players. He was looking for chemistry, and he emerged with Janet Gaynor and Charles Farrell. Benjamin Glazer did the screenplay, and he deleted the threat of prostitution at the start, just as he downplayed Brissac as a rival at the end. Moreover, he introduced a heavy religious element. For example, Diane and Chico stage their own marriage, and then finally a great deal too much is said about how good God has been to them.

The picture is a landmark in one sense: It inaugurated the Gaynor-Farrell partnership. It won an Oscar nomination for Best Picture, and Borzage actually took the Best Director prize. Gaynor also won Best Actress (though for three films—this, *Street Angel,* and *Sunrise*). Alas, it seems like a picture stranded on the far side of the sound barrier. Borzage is genuinely impressed by the love felt between separated people, but he lets the film work more at the level of sentimental separation than that of dream. In other words, Borzage is slow and cautious with his own effects. He does not seem to feel the wind of our desire lifting and carrying the characters.

Ernest Palmer photographed the picture, and Harry Oliver designed the overly pretty "7th Heaven" itself. It's also surprising to see how much screen time is given to events in the war during which Chico seems like an ordinary enough guy, capable of surviving. As it developed in the thirties, Borzage's style was to surround his lovers with a drab darkness and wait for the light to find them. His touch then could be extraordinary. But *7th Heaven* is too good to be true, and it has the effect of making the characters and the actors seem listless.

Of course, the characters need to talk, and I think that the gap between their poverty and their dreams should have been developed more. Gaynor is plainly the heir to Lillian Gish, but Gish had lost her treasury because of her sober decorum. So *7th Heaven* is meant to be a shrine, but increasingly it feels like a prison. Desire has been ensured at the end, but can there be sex? In the cinema, can a blind person have life?

The Seventh Seal (1956)

The Seventh Seal is one of the most important pictures in the history of international cinema. It gave a huge boost to intellectual dating, chess, and medieval studies, and it made Bergman a controversial yet austere figure all over the world. It was to see the earlier work of Ingmar Bergman that I joined the National Film Theatre in London in 1957—and while that quest was heartfelt and patient with long lines, it was also pretentious and social climbing, a way of insisting that the cinema was as serious as any of the arts. So Bergman laid the foundation for international art-house theaters in a way that Fellini, Antonioni, and the New Wave capitalized on. There was also the fact that, in its time, the medieval allegory and the game of chess with Death were a dramatization of the fate of a world that had bought into atmospheric nuclear testing and the bullying defiance of the Cold War. Anyone could see that there was a lot at stake, and *The Seventh Seal* referred to biblical apocalypse with the confidence of Elmer Gantry.

The time is the fourteenth century. A knight (Max von Sydow) has returned from the Crusades. Like so many noble people a decade after Hiroshima and the opening up of Auschwitz, the knight has lost his faith, though his squire (Gunnar Björnstrand) still prays out of habit. Death appears (Bengt Ekerot), tall, pale, in black robes. It is time for the knight to die, but he challenges Death to a game of chess to delay his end. Meanwhile a troupe of players are attempting to bring comfort and consolation to an oppressed people, threatened by the Black Death. It sounds like an epic, but it was 96 minutes and astonishingly modest by the standard of Hollywood budgets. The film played and played. The knight goes his only way, but the players (Nils Poppe and Bibi Andersson) live on.

Bergman was not quite forty when he made *The Seventh Seal,* and in hindsight there are ways in which his mastery then was as slick as it was austere. I don't believe the film endures as a masterpiece, but that has nothing to do with its astonishing impact at the time. Bergman had already become the dominant figure in a country where film and theater were interlocked, and he had his company of actors working happily in both mediums. Time has proved their quality and their eminence. In Gunnar Fischer, he had a great black-and-white cameraman—and, of course, Bergman had not yet tried color.

So, if you were there at the moment, I suspect you'd have a hard time seeing *The Seventh Seal* again. But if you're a good deal younger than the film, then its intellectual showmanship is very impressive. The really remarkable thing is how, in finding a great audience (with invitations to do what he liked), Bergman also discovered the prospect of doing much better work. But the ability to look at your own success and establish higher standards is a definition of art. And this is unmistakably art.

The Seventh Victim (1943)

The producer Val Lewton had had three B picture hits in a row at RKO—*Cat People, I Walked with a Zombie, The Leopard Man.* So the studio bosses called him in for congratulation, and told him that his next film would be an A release! Terrific, said Lewton, because, as a matter of fact, the next story was one especially close to his heart. What will that be? asked the bosses. *The Seventh Victim,* said Lewton. Great title, they agreed: who is going to direct it? Whereupon Lewton explained that Jacques Tourneur, director of the first three, was unavailable. Mark Robson, said Lewton—Robson had edited *Cat People,* but he had never directed before.

We can't have a novice director on an A picture! said the studio. Lewton could have made a change. But he was firm: He stood by Robson. So the studio said it would be another B picture—71 minutes for a cost of under $200,000. Perhaps it was for the best: No one ever knew what a Val Lewton A picture would look like.

The Seventh Victim is not so much a horror picture as a yearning for death—and once death has become desirable, fear hardly counts anymore. With a script by Charles O'Neal and DeWitt Bodeen, *The Seventh Victim* is the story of Mary Gibson (Kim Hunter). She is an orphan who comes to New York in search of a vanished sister, Jacqueline (Jean Brooks). Mary makes a team with her brother-in-law, Gregory Ward (Hugh Beaumont). It turns out that Jacqueline has joined a cult. The other members try to kill her. But Jacqueline will take her own life. Mary and Gregory are left together.

As I said, death in this fable is a desirable destination. Little by little, the nihilistic mood takes over the film—not in a macabre way, not as the spell exerted by witches or devils, but as a necessary conclusion to all the vain fuss of life. Every horror film ever made or planned should look at *The Seventh Victim* because of its extraordinary grasp of spiritual emptiness, the beckoning alternative to action and activity.

It was shot in twenty-one days in May 1943 with a team that Lewton had come to trust: Nicholas Musuraca as director of photography; art direction by Albert S. D'Agostino and Walter Keller; set decoration (very important in a film where objects are heavy with dread) by Darrell Silvera and Harley Miller; music by Roy Webb. Such teams were not uncommon in the great studio days: The factories employed the same workers. But Lewton's pictures have a common style, that of a mixed longing and apprehension, that we are not accustomed to seeing as the mark of a producer. In truth, there is very little internal evidence to say that Robson did direct this picture—or that Jacques Tourneur did not. The case for Lewton as auteur is very strong.

The acting is superb—above all Jean Brooks as Jacqueline, very beautiful, sultry, and doomed, yet fated not to have a great career. Kim Hunter is very good, and there are fine performances from Tom Conway, Isabel Jewell, Evelyn Brent, Erford Gage, and Ben Bard.

Sex, Lies, and Videotape (1989)

In hindsight, I daresay, the title *Sex, Lies, and Videotape* is like a generic definition of (or recipe for) American independent film—though you could go for further inclusive brevity still, and call it *Acting for Free,* which is a fairly accurate description of a great deal of what now passes for film or movie. Watch the person closely and try to decide whether he or she is more "into" life or acting. Do they wish to be assessed as pretenders or liars?

When writer-director Steven Soderbergh stepped up to receive the Cannes Palme d'Or in 1989, he is reported to have said, "Well, I guess it's all downhill from here." Wiser words than he ever guessed. Nearly twenty years later, we have had three *Ocean's Eleven* films to assess what the young name director can kill time with rather than pursue anything as slight, or as dangerous, as the original *Sex, Lies, and Videotape.*

Soderbergh may now regret the full-length diary of his first film that was published as a backup to its great success as a Miramax release. For here was a movie that nearly didn't get made, with the money coming in as bits and pieces, and the novice auteur having to do all he could to hold "creation" together under the multiple stresses of the occasion. And if you go back to the film itself, it's remarkable how piquant and astringent it still is—the story of a foursome, in love and in sex, bound together by suspicion and videotape recordings in which they either reveal themselves or discover how impossible that ambition is. What emerged, I suppose, was an odd air of triumph—the way in which a slight idea and uncertain plans could carry a movie project all the way to Cannes and considerable box-office success. What got buried, I fear, was a much more fascinating lesson on acting—that it was in a position to take over from all other types or versions of behavior. The clearest proof of this was the way in which James Spader (the eccentric engine of the film) was set on a career where his genuine novelty was flattened out in foolish eccentricities. To see the film again is to remember the feeling that Spader was about to become exceptional—whereas now he is just a cul-de-sac of oddity.

Walt Lloyd photographed the film. Cliff Martinez did the music. Soderbergh edited the film, and the other players were Peter Gallagher, Andie MacDowell, and Laura San Giacomo (with Ron Vawter excellent as the therapist).

It's too late for the sad jokes about what did happen to Soderbergh—except to say that he remains an observant, wry intelligence, which is a long way from being a creative artist. Soderbergh is that glum reality that now sits patiently behind the fuss of so many rather self-serving independent directors—he is and was a producer. And through thick or thin, the business history of the American film has been to defend and enrich and secure that slug of a fellow.

Sexy Beast (2000)

There have been several gangster films from Britain in the last fifteen years or so which speak to the perverse charm of some criminals being prosperous citizens. Too many of them have been miserable excuses for attitudinizing and violence. But there are some exceptions, notably the comedy of *Love, Honor and Obey* (by Dominic Anciano and Ray Burdis) and the phenomenon of *Sexy Beast,* where the violence and the comedy are literally inseparable. It's a little hard to tell from this novel film how promising director Jonathan Glazer is—and his second film, *Birth,* also flirted with prospects it couldn't always reach. Still, *Sexy Beast* may be the first film in an authentically surrealist career. It has to be seen because there is no other film like it.

"Gal" Dove (Ray Winstone) is a retired thief, and now a pillar of the Costa del Sol. He lives there in his villa with his wife, Deedee (Amanda Redman), and a couple of friends, Aitch (Cavan Kendall) and Jackie (Julianne White). He basks in the sun, his belly and his fat face at risk of burning. They lounge in the pool. They have the easy life.

But then the word comes that the Mob in London require one further job from Gal, and they are sending Don Logan (Ben Kingsley) to persuade him to toe the line. Don is a beast, a nutter, a force beyond restraint or predictability. People are afraid of Don, of his ranting talk, his foul mouth, and his unquestioned proclivity for nastiness. He is also an actor. Kingsley got awards and nominations for his Don Logan, including a Supporting Actor Oscar nomination. This flagrant air of performance is used to offset the exceptional danger in the man, and it has the uncommon effect of making Don as hilarious as he is frightening.

In time, Gal handles Don rather well, and life in the Costa del Sol resumes its even tone. This happens because Winstone's Gal is as clever as he seems lazy. He goes back to London and is involved in the mob scene there, a setup that includes such archetypal figures as James Fox and Ian McShane (both of whom bring considerable baggage to a film like this).

So *Sexy Beast* rests somewhere between a gangster film and a game in which the elements of gangsterism are pieces on the board. It was written by Louis Mellis and David Scinto (with uncredited help from Andrew Michael Jolley), and we know early on that it's a screenplay that relishes chat and verbal structures. Don's way of speaking is often insane, and sometimes wildly theatrical. But the interaction is very compelling. Ivan Bird did the photography, and he makes Spain seem like a daft never-never land. The production design is by Jan Houllevigue, and the music is by Roque Baños. There are dream sequences and nightmares, and there are some reasons for thinking that pretension risks going out of control. But *Sexy Beast,* and *Birth,* have ravishingly effective scenes and an overall air of mystery that is enchanting.

Shadow of a Doubt (1943)

Over the years, Alfred Hitchcock would often say that *Shadow of a Doubt* was his favorite picture. It's an intriguing pick, and I think it points toward areas of creative liberty that Hitch felt opened up on that picture, as well as the crucial cross-identification of the two Charlies which is so important to his evolution. Still, in larger retrospect, I think there are several better pictures than *Shadow*—and several reasons for seeing it as a transition from certain English modes or habits to the more extensive pessimism of his American work.

It was the second picture made on his Universal deal (following *Saboteur*), with Jack Skirball as an amiable producer who left Hitch alone to do his thing. And though the film comes from a story by Gordon McDonell, it's much closer to an original worked up for the screen by Thornton Wilder, Sally Benson, Hitch, and his wife, Alma. Hitch had wanted Wilder because of *Our Town* and his wish to be true to small-town life. Yet, I wonder if that artfully worked up background atmosphere doesn't get out of hand—indeed, doesn't even become a pressure that could explain murder. If only the young Charlie were more eager to get away from the stifling world.

You see, the thrust of the action is more that of a mathematical theorem than a story. Charlie Oakley (Joseph Cotten) is seemingly trapped in a harsh urban world (New York). He is a killer, too, increasingly pursued by police. So he thinks to make an escape, all the way across the continent, to Santa Rosa, in California. That's where his married sister (Patricia Collinge) lives with her daughter and Charlie's niece, "Charlie" Newton (Teresa Wright). But as the journey works out, the young, adoring Charlie will realize the older one's dark truth and will prompt his demise.

The bond between uncle and niece is fascinating, and it points to the subtle bonds between characters in later Hitchcock (Melanie and Lydia in *The Birds*, say). But it needs some help that might come if the niece had a little more danger or violence in her, just a touch more of the uncle. As it is, they are so different, the bonding seems imposed and threatened by the dense undergrowth of Santa Rosa life—Collinge, Henry Travers, Hume Cronyn—much of which has dated badly and become a heavy-handed commentary on law-abiding interest in the grisly aspect of murder.

So the film lurches in and out of its own smooth poison, and the repeated use of the "Merry Widow" dance device becomes intolerable. But Cotten and Wright act beautifully, and seem to feel more and more strands of DNA becoming tangled as the picture goes on. So the greatest interest is to see Hitch feeling his way into that tangle where good nature and a darker opposite become mutually dependent. He is getting toward the way in which "good" characters feel a stronger impulse toward "bad" than they ever reckoned on, and that is the real turning point in Hitchcock's cinema.

Shadows (1960)

When *Shadows* opened in London, at the National Film Theatre, in 1959, it was part of a season entitled "Beat, Square and Cool" that looked back to the experimental films of the 1950s, or even earlier. But the film had an end-credit boast, "The film you have just seen was an improvisation," that seemed to hark forward and that caught some of the mood of the Actors Studio, which seemed to be the core of the new American acting. It had given us Brando, Clift, and Dean, but still to come were Nicholson, Pacino, Beatty, and De Niro. In many ways, the actor John Cassavetes, who made *Shadows*, seemed to fall in line with those names. After years of failure in the early fifties, he had had a breakthrough in Martin Ritt's *Edge of the City* (1957), in which he had seemed torn between a rebel intransigence and the self-pity that was helping Method actors become stars.

But John Cassavetes was something else. *Shadows* had been improvised in only a few places. Cassavetes also claimed that it had been shot in six weeks. But we know now that the process was much more extended and conventional. *Shadows* was a project that Cassavetes introduced at his Drama Workshop in 1957. The situation: that of a light-skinned black family, some of whom sometimes passed for white. The roles were assigned and then improvisation was used to discover the right dialogue and structure—this is close to the method Mike Leigh would employ in England. Long before the shooting started, Robert Alan Aurthur (cowriter on *Edge of the City*) came in to help on the script. The movie started shooting in 1957 and went on over a period of two years. It was shot, on 16 mm, by Erich Kollmar; it was edited by Maurice McEndree and Cassavetes; and it acqured a musical score that featured Shafi Hadi and Charles Mingus. It is said to have cost $40,000.

More or less, it looked like the New Wave films coming out of Paris yet it had an American subject: interracial love relationships, with striking performances from Ben Carruthers, Lelia Goldoni, Hugh Hurd, and Anthony Ray (Nick's son). It was the awkwardness, I think, that led to thoughts of improvisation, but it was the faces of these actors—totally committed—that carried the energy of the film and seemed to characterize a fresh realism.

Considering the impact of the film, it's remarkable that none of the actors really "took" in a career sense. Because they seemed very good at first. So Cassavetes (and by implication his wife, Gena Rowlands) fell into a lifelong "bargain." They might do industry films occasionally, but they were pledged to their group and its ability to dig out important inner subjects in a form of acting that was far more group-related than given to new social or political ideas. Seen now, *Shadows* looks like an intriguing but isolated experiment. For years, Cassavetes regarded it as a new model. Today, it looks like a warning that actors are seldom smart enough to know what to say on their own.

Shakespeare in Love (1998)

If you were ever moved by the depiction of the Globe at the start of Olivier's *Henry V*, then *Shakespeare in Love* comes as a very belated sequel and one of those few modern films that takes possession of the audience. Quite simply, it is a clever idea, to go back to the life and times of Shakespeare, to trace the show business intrigues of Elizabethan theater, and to tell a fresh, vivid love story that surely helps anyone feel *Romeo and Juliet* on the pulse. More than that, the whole thing is done in great good humor, with a few knowing winks to the audience of 1998, as if to say, Well, of course, no one knows for sure what Will Shakespeare was like—but isn't this plausible?

The project had been in waiting a long time, and Marc Norman's place on the screenplay credits points to long research and probably many drafts. And Tom Stoppard? He comes in late in the day, with a touch of Will about him, and smartens up the whole enterprise so that the wit works on many levels and the whole thing suddenly coheres. The battle between theatrical companies (Burbage and Henslowe), the attempts by the chamberlain, Tilney, to keep women off the stage, the love affair between Will and Viola De Lesseps, and the bringing into being of *Romeo and Juliet*—all these things are beautifully integrated, with Elizabeth herself keeping a stern but fond eye on the proceedings. The result is funny, sexy, a serious tribute to the writing and to theater, and a film that ought to help any student grappling with Shakespeare.

John Madden directs, and I don't say he does more than keep the many balls in the air—but that is no small achievement. Richard Greatrex did the photography. The production design is by Martin Childs—using clever sets and real buildings. The music is by Stephen Warbeck, and the really glowing costumes are by Sandy Powell. Ingenuity fizzes like champagne, and I don't think it's going too far to remark on a true affinity between the raptures of storytelling skill in the film with the spirit of Shakespeare himself.

Joseph Fiennes is Shakespeare, and he's so dynamic you wonder what happened to his career afterward. Gwyneth Paltrow is lovely and eager as Viola De Lesseps, and she got her Oscar for it. Simon Callow blusters and cringes at the drop of a hat as Tilney. Colin Firth is a villainous Wessex. Ben Affleck is Ned Alleyn. Geoffrey Rush is Henslowe, and Martin Clunes is Burbage. Tom Wilkinson is superb as Fennyman, and still the cast includes Antony Sher, Jim Carter, Mark Williams, Imelda Staunton, and Rupert Everett (uncredited) as Marlowe.

The picture cost $25 million (a miracle, for it feels lavish) and the U.S. gross was over $100 million. Its seven Oscars included Best Picture and Script, to Ms. Paltrow (Best Actress) and to Ms. Dench (Best Supporting Actress) for her queen of the revels. A genuine delight—and where is the sequel as Viola is shipwrecked on an American shore?

American friends are shocked that I rate this so highly. Is it that the English long to love their Will?

Shame (1967)

We know that Ingmar Bergman had lived on an island off the Swedish coast for the last years of his life, and *Shame* is a work that helps explain this retreat. For all anyone knows, or ever knew—with blueberries, wild strawberries, fish in the sea, and a little wheat to make your bread—such an island may have been a survivalist ideal. *Shame* opens on just such a becalmed rural setting, the place where Jan (Max von Sydow) and Eva (Liv Ullmann) have gone to. But something is wrong, and gradually we become aware of some indistinct state of civil war, without prospects or better escapes. It is not a modern war, but one that might have been fought by Godard's *Les Carabiniers*. It is a kind of makeshift war into which every sophisticated dread—fallout, torture, the loss of standards—can be accommodated. I'm not sure if the "shame" talked about is the regret that sees such loss of standards, or guilt over the notion that anyone can or should escape such a dilemma.

Coming very soon after *Persona, Shame* has an air that seems to say: Intellectual discussions of identity are all very well, but the bleak stories of survival are all that are left. It shows also how thorough Bergman's own pessimism was, and how completely it could take away his humor; after all, the paradox of a silenced actress in *Persona* is comic, so long as no one laughs. And it's not that the fear of civil war and the breakdown of civic and civil standards has gone away—the wind called Katrina brought it home, even if we have grown accustomed to forgetting reports of famine and civil war in Third World countries where such things are common.

Beautifully shot by Sven Nykvist in somber black and white, *Shame* is *The Seventh Seal* acted out in modern times, without any benefit or allusion to the holy family that can survive. Jan and Eva were artists once, musicians, but they are childless and their indignity now is only underlined by that very impractical career. Time passes during the film, and life is degraded step by step. The last survivors end in a boat, uncertain whether to drink poisoned water or not.

There are times, and *Shame* is an example, when Bergman's despair began to threaten his stamina as an artist—or so I feel. I wonder whether true despair can be so fertile and articulate. Shouldn't it have the grace to shut up? And in this mood, Bergman becomes sometimes monotonous and foreboding. It's easy enough to imagine the end of the world, happening down the street, and to guess how badly neighbors (and we ourselves) may behave. But there may be humor, too, and kindness and a remembrance of better things. So it was a great encouragement to see Bergman rallying after the grim sixties. Not always in sunshine and frolic—*Cries and Whispers* is not cheerful. But it is robust and full of life. And in the decades since, Bergman emerged into a kind of shocked, half-broken kindness, a mood of optimism even.

Shampoo (1975)

Somehow or other, over the years, the newspapers have found the nerve or the gullibility to ask themselves the question "Is Warren Beatty running?"—as in, Is he running for elective office? Among many other things, *Shampoo* is the definitive answer to that question, and his way of suggesting that there are always going to be other people (individuals) that divert him from working for people (the mass). These days, the people beckoning him are his children and his wife, for Warren has changed. But no one could change enough to dissuade the voters from what was once a favorite American dream—that he was catnip.

In *Shampoo* (a title that could have a sexual connotation, I suppose), he plays George Roundy, one of the genius hairdressers in Los Angeles and a man who is thinking of opening his own salon—that is the extent of his political ambition. The ladies like him—and not just because of what he can do with their hair. And George surely likes the ladies. In the brief period in which we see him, he is "going with" Goldie Hawn, and he is very vulnerable to an old flame, Julie Christie, the mistress of Jack Warden, whose wife, Lee Grant, is also determined to have George's dryer on her hair. And then there is Lee's teenage daughter, Carrie Fisher, in her first film part.

Shampoo grew out of the friendship between Beatty and his house writer, Robert Towne. They shared the nomination for original screenplay, though it may be that Beatty believed that his being the living model for George deserved a share in the prize. Let's say Towne wrote the script, while Warren fixed it. It takes place on election day 1968 (the first Nixon victory), and it is not just a portrait of sexual promiscuity and of having one's life ruled by one's dryer, but a panorama of L.A. too. In the end, the Beatty character's chronic womanizing is left like a bull, bristling with banderillas, trapped in a corner—but still horny. Beatty is absolutely brilliant in the part, and it's hard to believe that he is not improvising some of the speeches—or confessing.

Shampoo was directed by Hal Ashby, and it is full of Ashby's constant good nature and his love of Los Angeles. Of course, this is the world before AIDS, which helps us see the picture now as a time capsule of the last great era of self-confidence, if not cockiness, in Hollywood. Seen today, it is startling just how free and easy pictures could be with sex then. If movies' real social purpose was to train us in sex, there must be the beginning of a suspicion that since 1975 we have been letting ourselves lose the habit.

Shampoo is very funny when it is most urgent, as with Julie Christie under the table and Warren trying to keep his aplomb. This may be as close as we have come to a modern screwball classic—we can only marvel that it doesn't stimulate imitation.

Shane (1953)

It's hard to realize now that anyone ever lacked for confidence in *Shane*. But the film was shot in Jackson Hole, Wyoming, in the summer of 1951, and it was ready for the screen long before its release in April 1953, when Paramount proudly announced, "There never was a film like *Shane*." Something was amiss somewhere in estimates of this nearly perfect arc of story in which the slender buckskin saint yet gunslinger rides out of one horizon, and then rides out the other, and somehow the warring state of the land he passed through has been settled. No one really thinks the West was like that—everyone wishes that it had been. *Shane* is a fairy-tale Western, as the critic Robert Warshow knew:

> Shane was hardly a man at all but something like the spirit of the West, beautiful in fringed buckskins. He emerges beautifully from the plains, breathing sweetness and a melancholy which is no longer simply the Westerner's natural response to experience but has taken on spirituality; and when he has accomplished his mission, meeting and destroying in the black figure of Jack Palance a Spirit of Evil just as metaphysical as his own embodiment of virtue. He fades away again into the more distant West, a man whose "day is over," leaving behind the wondering little boy who might have imagined the whole story.

Shane was a short novel by Jack Schaefer, published in 1949, and the film (scripted by A. B. Guthrie, Jr.) had the good sense to make a very faithful adaptation. The story is very simple: A man, a gunslinger once, stops awhile in a valley where the farmers and the ranchers are at odds. He settles matters and rides on. George Stevens, just off *A Place in the Sun*, was at the top of his game and had become a very good handler of landscape to back up human story. And maybe the first thing that strikes us about *Shane* is its photography (it won an Oscar for Loyal Griggs), which is as tender to deep space as it is to the cramped cabin where the Starretts live.

In many ways, Alan Ladd was not natural casting. Though he had a great, deep voice, he was famously short and slender. The film involves him in a tremendous barroom fight with Ben Johnson, and Johnson told wry stories about how he had to go easy with the lightweight to get beaten up properly. And Ladd in buckskins now is a little too close to gay iconography maybe. There must have been other thoughts along the way. Yet Ladd is astonishing: He seems to know that his rather humdrum life is being ennobled. He acquires grace.

Van Heflin and Jean Arthur—the Starretts—were always very good actors. Brandon De Wilde announced himself with Joey. And then there are supports—Elisha Cook, Jr., John Dierkes, Emile Meyer, Edgar Buchanan, and Walter Jack Palance, the greatest mean ornery arrogant gunfighter there ever was, or will be. There are stories—far rarer in practice than you might guess—that coming home from Wyoming, everyone knew they had made something special. So Paramount made them wait.

Shanghai Express (1932)

Facts are facts: This film was made at Paramount in the middle of industrial Los Angeles, and not just in a Paris loft apartment with a few gestures toward scenery and an absolute determination to make a small, private movie that was a mockery of Hollywood conventions and a tribute to absolute love—as if that were an archaic religion once claimed by the Persians. Yes, there is a shot of a locomotive leaving a depot, but it is so sublimely shot from above that it might be just a series of floats drawn beneath a camera. As for being in China, that expensive, time-consuming chore is regarded with perplexity—as if anyone with the least imagination ever "needed" to be anywhere else.

How did Josef von Sternberg get away with the masquerade? Well, because Marlene Dietrich was a phenomenon still, especially when treated with her lover's hopeless, sultry languor. Just like the film shot in the loft on strips of film that the girl has stolen during 5 p.m. love nests with a Big Producer, this is a man and his girl shooting scenes during their own romance, and trusting that the scenes may somehow extend the natural history of the sexual act. They surely do: Not enough attention has been paid to Sternberg's close-ups as orgasmic moments of the sort experienced with other people in the room so that you have to keep your quiet as intense as the dark. The exquisite shot of Dietrich in prayer (to save Clive Brook's life) is such a one—so poised, so composed, so still, so hushed, like a bomb on the edge of going off.

And don't rule out the possibility that Sternberg was tickled to see whether Paramount or the public would tumble to the fact that he was asking them both to see and take seriously films about his and Marlene's coming. The great trick of the films, of course, is to say they are about true love—thus, we are meant to suppose that Lily and Donald have waited desperately to meet again and now will be married (I want to see the film where Lily goes back to be lady of the house in Shropshire) instead of just sexes passing in the night, coming and going. To that extent, all of Sternberg is a withering satire on the alleged function and entertaining purpose of these things called movies.

But it was done at Paramount. Jules Furthman wrote a script. Lee Garmes did the photography. And you can see Anna May Wong, Warner Oland, Eugene Pallette, Lawrence Grant, Louise Closser Hale, Gustav von Seyffertitz, and Emile Chautard as other drugged guests at the party, sauntering in and out of the light in a world where the light and the dark are like being in bed or not. It is ridiculous and lovely, just like an orgy for people who know nothing lasts. Yet the film is seventy-six years old as I write and still a monument of erotic art. Moreover, it is one of the few great surrealist experiments ever paid for by a studio and people raised to the tough rules of the rag trade.

The Shawshank Redemption (1994)

Polls of the general public have discovered a very high opinion of *The Shawshank Redemption,* and I'm prepared to take that as a sign of the innate longing in most of us for feeling good and getting a bit of salvation. At the same time, I am not yet persuaded that Frank Darabont has enough muscle in his head to resist a weakness for adult fairy tales. Anyone with that malady should recall how severe the best fairy stories are, and how unforgiving the bent of children is. I still find *The Shawshank Redemption* a veiled testimony to the idea that being in prison is not so bad. Whereas I think in our world and time that being in prison is not just bad, not just an effective way of organizing and extending crime, but one of those things over which we should be most ashamed.

It comes from a novella by Stephen King broadly dedicated to the notion that good nature will come through in the end, yet this is a principle that seldom operates in Mr. King's customary horror works. Tim Robbins plays a man wrongly imprisoned on murder charges, a man whose natural decency will subtly alter the nature of prison life and ensure that he and his pal (Morgan Freeman) get their just deserts at the end of a very long (142 minutes) and rather slow film in which "parable" creeps in as realism beats a retreat.

There is another interpretation of prison: that it is the sweeping place for all the worst defects of poverty and inequality in society, and a way in which the better-off parts of that same society can overlook the disparities and any kind of guilt that may result from it. That would be called politics, and that is something the American movie is very fearful of getting into. It means that the question of chance sending one to prison (or making one a genius in Las Vegas) is very fertile as a way of getting at the hypocrisies of America. But Darabont's film spends so much time establishing the Gothic nature and look of the prison, and so little on its ambiguous moral light.

In the thirties, and even as late as *Birdman of Alcatraz* (1962), there was a notion in our films that dedication, hard work, and rehabilitation were possible. So it's interesting to note the widespread feeling now that prison is a form of gaming—you win or you lose, you're in or you're out. Surely this makes it far easier for the lucky to disregard any ideas of social consequence and responsibility. And so we have other prisons where the unnamed and the uncharged are also tortured.

It goes without saying that Tim Robbins is very good in the film, while Morgan Freeman is immaculate. But such things do not guarantee intelligence. Both actors, I think, are worldly enough to know the white lies being trafficked here. The cast also includes Bob Gunton, William Sadler, Clancy Brown, Gil Bellows, and James Whitmore.

The Sheltering Sky (1990)

Don't try telling the picture business, or the audience, that *The Sheltering Sky* was just another version of *The Sheik,* with a white woman (Debra Winger) swept off her feet, her camel, and her existential worldview by a glorious Arab, Belqassim (Eric Vu-An). The picture cost at least $25 million, and it grossed just over $2 million in the American market. That is doom, and I daresay the failure helped to hurry Winger into premature retirement just as it led the business to see that whatever John Malkovich had, it had little to do with charm and being a romantic lead.

Not that *The Sheltering Sky* can be a romance. It is the Paul Bowles novel of 1947, and there is the ancient Bowles sitting in a café, like a wise lizard, watching over his characters and offering a sparse, unsentimental narration. Kit and Port Moresby (Winger and Malkovich) come from America to North Africa with Tunner (Campbell Scott), who would like to get into bed with Kit. But Tunner is not quite attuned to the fatalism that attends the Moresbys. They are, in turn, a version of Paul and Jane Bowles, whose sexual agenda was not fixed but who had half a mind to disappear into the desert as a response to the thankless life exposed by the recent events in Europe.

I don't claim the film as a total success, let alone on a par with the novel, though I would say that Bernardo Bertolucci and Vittorio Storaro make the desert seem both enthralling and sinister. Nor is the adventure of Kit and Belqassim revealed as fully as it needs to be—but if you read the book, it would be a challenge. What does work is the affectless hostility of Malkovich and the girlish gloom of Winger—they really give very good performances, above all in touching the affection that has lost the habit of trusting itself. Then there is the exquisite extra of a raddled Jill Bennett and a toady Timothy Spall as the Lyles. Their role is small, but they are never off target.

With music by Ryuichi Sakamoto (as well as Lionel Hampton doing "Midnight Sun" over the credits), production design by Ferdinando Scarfiotti, and a clever script by Mark Peploe, *The Sheltering Sky* really does bring us to the lip of horror and a terrible Western dismay at the confrontation with emptiness and alienation. The novel is bleak and austere enough for the end of the world, and in a way that's its true subject. The film runs the risk of seeming like just a bad trip (though it might be really shocking with more hints of Kit going native, or feeling the gravitational pull of her escape from European culture). Of course, in the years since *The Sheltering Sky* was made, our experience has turned away from any exploratory relationships with Islam. And it's possible that Bertolucci was timid about that before he began. But I think the picture will emerge with more distinction as a portrait of two literate and brave Americans lost in the desert.

Sherlock Jr. (1924)

And so it was that Buster Keaton's fondness for mechanics turned to the projector itself. *Sherlock Jr.* is not much more than 40 minutes long, as if Keaton thought to himself, This joke can only go so far, don't let's grind it into the dust. Still, it was a proper Joseph M. Schenck production, like the others, and in the largeness of its surreal vision it is not just as important as the longer features: It is a breakthrough. It is as if a filmmaker had at last learned the point of the whole thing.

Buster plays a dreamy movie projectionist, an aspiring soul who sits beside his apparatus, beholding the wonders of the screen, and content for the moment to imagine himself there—as one of the famous screen characters, "Sherlock Jr.," ace detective. But then the time comes when Buster is drawn like a bubble to the surface. He goes up to the screen, studies it for a moment, as if it were a Magritte canvas entitled *This Is Not a Place*, and enters. He steps into the action, and the first joke is that the image in which he has found himself starts cutting violently so that he goes through the slapstick of readjustment. This is hilarious, and it does embody the ultimate world of Buster—where a machine can make a chump of him by ringing its very simple changes.

Buster then takes the part of the detective and manages not just to find a string of pearls but to shoot some devilish pool without having the "13" ball blow up in his face. But then he comes back to the real world and meets his sweet girl again—this time it's Kathryn McGuire—and when it comes to kissing her, why, he looks through the projection window (directly at us) and takes lessons in technique from the couple on the screen. All of a sudden, someone has observed, with humor, that the picture show is there as an enchanting if uncertain teaching tool for how we do the little things.

Keaton directed this himself, and in the scenes where he is in the screen—in straw hat and late-nineteenth-century costume—there are some classic images of him in the desert like the spirit of Americana. So often, in period setting and costumes, Keaton harked back in time, but without the heavy sentimentality of Griffith. He is a pioneer figure, a smart little man on the prairie and the range, not intimidated by the scale of it all, but deeply impressed. That is why he is gazing. And that is one reason why he is so alert to the new mechanics of the age. So *Sherlock Jr.* is not really a comedy—it's not one of Keaton's funniest—but it is a tender, wistful reflection on the new laws of physics, of being there and falling in the water when the shot changes. Indeed, Keaton sees it as a new species of wild beast—not one he thinks he can get along with. The only question is, Will he one day disappear into that screen world where the shocks are instant and pain-free?

She Wore a Yellow Ribbon (1949)

There's a memo that John Ford wrote to potential scenarist James Warner Bellah about *She Wore a Yellow Ribbon* that is deeply instructive on Ford the artist: "Jim, I think we can make a Remington canvas . . . broad shoulders . . . wide hats . . . narrow hips . . . yellow strips down the pants leg . . . war bonnets and eagle feathers trailing in the dust . . . the brassy sound of bugles in the morning . . . the long reaches of the prairie . . . the buttes and mesas in the distances and the buffalo . . ."

Is there a better demonstration of heroic impressionism, or of Ford's natural inclination to paint a fond picture of an idealized life—as opposed to telling the accurate history of what happened in the West? All I ask Fordians to notice here is how far the director's entire approach was imbued with the wishful thinking of legend making. The other thing to say is that Ford seems a lot more comfortable in *She Wore a Yellow Ribbon* than he did in *Fort Apache,* the first film in the cavalry trilogy and the one that addresses history the most.

"Custer is dead," *She Wore a Yellow Ribbon* begins, but only as a marker. It is clear that the cavalry is on its way to avenging that defeat, even if Ford makes nothing of the politics behind that need. But this is really a day in the life of the cavalry as measured through the person of Captain Nathan Brittles (John Wayne), who has mere days left in the service but time to make a small advance in the campaign against the Indians. Filmed in color, *Yellow Ribbon* is fond, uncritical, nostalgic, and drunk on the Army.

The younger people at the fort—the bustling good humor and daredevil riding skills of Ben Johnson, John Agar, and Harry Carey, Jr., and the prairie glamour of Joanne Dru (she wears the yellow ribbon) blend in with the veteran stock company that is Victor McLaglen, George O'Brien, Mildred Natwick, and Francis Ford. There's precious little story and Wayne is duly older, creaky, amiable, benign, a pussycat and a model for others. Ford had seen him in *Red River* and been impressed by his acting, but as yet he had not realized how far that ability depended on Wayne exposing an uglier side of himself.

In fact, the script was done by Frank Nugent and Laurence Stallings, and it is free from contentious issues. The photography by Winton Hoch is legendary—not just in what it renders, but in the famous thunderstorm sequence where Hoch got the forks of lightning tarting Monument Valley up a bit. Of course, Brittles is a widower—he talks to his wife's grave in the amber light. But she doesn't talk back, alas. It's possible that women ended up a little more bored and less self-satisfied than the Brittles of the regiment. But women don't really figure in the scope and texture of the Ford legend: They may be seized by a chief named Scar, but they aren't allowed a relationship with him.

The Shining (1980)

The Overlook Hotel was designed, as the credits attest, by Roy Walker and Les Tomkins, but it looks and feels as if Albert Speer and Leni Riefenstahl might have worked on the night shift. The air is crystal. Sound carries in the thin air. And shining lasts, sometimes for decades. There is a magnificent opening where the hotel manager (Barry Nelson) tells Jack Torrance (Jack Nicholson) how the place needs a caretaker in winter. It's a case of one bullshitter shitting another, and it's so cozy it gives you the creeps. And there you are listening to this guff about the magnificent, comprehensively appointed hotel which is useless, alas, in winter. Why? Because it snows! DID NO ONE EVER TELL THEM ABOUT SKIING?

Anyway, the hotel needs a caretaker, some sort of natural loner with a family that gets under his skin and a great novel to write in the quiet winter. But a guy who will appreciate throwing a ball against the pine-tree walls at the Overlook and imagining he's in the World Series. Let's face it, it needs Jack: In a way, the *2001* way, the Overlook is Jack's special obelisk. "You've always been the caretaker, sir," says Philip Stone's plaintive Grady (Stone in late Kubrick is a touchstone). After all, Jack can shamble down to the Gold Room ballroom, shut up for the winter. He can sit at its long bar, hide his eyes in hope, and there's Lloyd, the immaculate barman, only slightly resembling a cadaver, with, "What'll it be, Mr. Torrance?"

What indeed? The Overlook is Jack's palace of desire, his eternal movie house. It plays his slow horror pictures, the ones where all the loathing of his own family will find a home. And, truly, this is a movie about home—and being caught in someone else's.

Yes, it's a novel by Stephen King, and King got very indignant that Kubrick's film hadn't been scary enough. Oh, poor Mr. King—who even made a TV version to show what he meant, unaware that it would miss the deep-seated humor and hominess of Kubrick's version. This is surely Kubrick's great film, serenely unanchored in any fixed genre, effortlessly invented, inspired alike by the hollow brain of a house and the naughty little germ of a man, Jack. It would not work if Jack were not endearing, hammy, and so stupid—but over the years no actor has done stupid as well as Jack.

Shelley Duvall as wife is grating—but she's meant to be. Danny Lloyd is one of the great sinister children of modern film. And there are the supporting players, Barry Nelson and Philip Stone, for sure, but Scatman Crothers and the sublime Joe Turkel as Lloyd. This is not quite horror; it's more dread which seldom has climaxes but never goes away. The novelist Diane Johnson wrote the script. John Alcott did the lovely shiny photography, and the music comes from Bartók, Penderecki, Wendy Carlos, Rachel Elkind, and Gyorgy Ligeti. A masterpiece. How wonderful that this straining, chilly, pretentious, antihuman director should have stumbled into it.

Shoeshine (1946)

The harsh black and white of *Shoeshine's* photography takes us back to that ancient discovery of the medium—that while you may envy the lavish life of the wealthy, still the imagery of poverty is imprinted on the viewer's soul. There is no need in this film to spell out the intricacies of justice when vagrant kids are charged with stealing. The wolfish faces of the boys tell the whole story. *Shoeshine* is like Dickens simply reporting the life of the streets and the courts, daring us to look away or forget. *Bicycle Thieves* is a very moving picture, and *Paisan* and *Open City* reflect a growing historical intelligence. But *Shoeshine* trembles with a bare need to get its message home. Its children are not sentimentalized (and the boy in *Bicycle Thieves* is). They are tough, spunky, becoming increasingly broken down and demoralized by their life. There are scenes in Sergio Leone's *Once Upon a Time in America* (1984), pretty pastel scenes, of the kids who will become the gangsters, and their childhood is romanticized from start to finish. See *Shoeshine* and you cannot feel that. The children are the natural victims of war.

In this case, we follow two boys, Giuseppe and Pasquale, who are shoeshine artists—they see the world from the ground up, and they polish the shoes of Romans and American soldiers alike, hoping for a scrap of money. They are already edging into the black market, and they are the easiest of those criminals for the police to catch. So there are trials and sentences, and they are confined in a children's prison—there is no other word for it—where their criminal training intensifies. De Sica's film does not preach about such consequences, but there is no escaping them.

The story came from Cesare Zavattini, and he, Sergio Amidei, Adolfo Franci, and C. G. Viola were duly Oscar-nominated for Best Original Screenplay (they lost to Sidney Sheldon for *The Bachelor and the Bobby-Soxer*). What is so vital about *Shoeshine* is this decline in the boys and the way they hold to their great dream of having horses. They are already, in their way, part of the consumer society, but diverted and distracted by the pressures around them. Indeed, one boy will kill the other finally—the struggle for survival has become so intense.

The two boys are Rinaldo Smordoni and Franco Interlenghi, and I don't think their naturalness was surpassed in any of the neorealist films. Justifiably, they are famous for seeming drawn from the streets—yet Interlenghi had a career waiting for him: in *Teresa, I Vitelloni,* and *The Barefoot Contessa,* and even married to Antonella Lualdi (a boy could get his horse).

Today, the black and white of *Shoeshine* would be rejected by nearly every production. And so the anodyne color that has replaced it torments us with the thought that we have done away with poverty and the damage shown in *Shoeshine.* Nothing could be further from the truth. It is simply that we are too cool now, or too dishonest, to stomach "realism."

The Shop Around the Corner (1940)

Onscreen—never mind the other place—there was an enchanting chemistry between Jimmy Stewart and Margaret Sullavan. They had found the mirror in which each one could look adorable. He craned over her and she arched back to look up at him. Their two voices dropped to a hush as intimacy took their breath away. So of course it is inspired of Ernst Lubitsch and Samson Raphaelson to launch this film on the notion that they can't stand each other. It works deliciously. They rub each other up the wrong way, but we know that that kind of stroking is only prelude to a fonder friction. And their characters, Miss Klara Novak and Mr. Alfred Kralik, are quite safe, because in their dreams they still go to movies with Jimmy Stewart and Margaret Sullavan making like the trellis and the vine. And out of all this emerges something fit for Shakespeare or Mozart—that the head and the heart fall in love at different speeds. Which is not to say that reconciliation is certain. The one could easily crush the other. And when Klara looks into an empty mailbox and Sullavan's wounded eyes widen, we are so close to tragedy we have to hold on very tight.

The next matter of joy is the way Budapest is re-created on the Culver City lot, no matter that by 1940 I daresay a Lubitsch was taking or giving odds on whether the real city could survive a regime that took precedence over power plays at Matuschek's. The aplomb with which refugees and narrow escapees preside over a dream Second World War in Hollywood is not the least measure of character and courage in the American movie. And, almost inadvertently (that is the Lubitsch touch—of happening upon the given), the delicacy of amatory affairs is not the least part of the whole code and structure of freedom that the war was being fought over.

So this is a comedy in which earnestness or gravity endangers true love, and Lubitsch's other touch—the casting wand—is able to see that both Stewart and Sullavan had a humorlessness, a stiff-backed pride, that would bring them so close to the lip of disaster. It's not that Lubitsch really believes in true love, or in its ability to last much more than twenty minutes, but he does tremble a little at the thought that this lovely chemistry he finds himself with might be too high-minded to make a modest equation or a warm explosion.

We are taught how to regard Klara and Alfred by the fond, yet wry attitude for all the supporting players—Frank Morgan is humbug, fusspot, and a real ruin discovered at Christmas in a quite Dickensian performance; Joseph Schildkraut is the fascist in the shop—if the brownshirts do come calling he is their man—and Felix Bressart is the eternal wall off which so many jokes and reaction shots need to bounce.

Moral of it all: *The Shop Around the Corner* was nominated for nothing in 1940. Neither did Lubitsch ever win an Oscar. That's how good Hollywood was then: The gems were smuggled out with the costume jewelry.

Short Cuts (1993)

There were those who complained that too much of the material taken from Raymond Carver short stories wasn't exactly or faithfully Carver. And there were those who argued that this sweeping panorama (if white is all you can see) of life and death in Los Angeles was not very comfortable or inspiring. There's truth in both claims: but Robert Altman always tricked and exploited and hurt writers; and he is head-and-shoulders taller than so many directors in that he never attended to the bromide that he ought to try to like people more. He could respond that anyone who treats actors so well must have a soft spot for humankind.

Altman did the script himself, with Frank Barhydt, yet I think the real structuring of the film was probably established in the editing. That's where this extended ronde of L.A. stories really comes together; that's how the artless resemblance in so many lives begins to mean more. In that sense, *Short Cuts* was a very influential film—it surely stands behind both *Magnolia* and *Crash,* two of the most striking films about L.A. in the last ten years, and both of them were composed as circling overviews where propinquity and coincidence—chance and meaning—have to be assessed and reconciled by the viewer. However, the comparison with those two films does point up a bizarre thing about Altman's city—so palpably L.A. in most respects—which is its absence of black, Hispanic, or Asian characters.

That's what we don't have—along with the question of why. (Was it really overlooked?) Let's now concentrate on what we do have: There is the trio of boys who go fishing (Buck Henry, Fred Ward, Huey Lewis); there is the warmly lugubrious romantic pairing of Lily Tomlin and Tom Waits; there are the four friends, Chris Penn and Jennifer Jason Leigh and Robert Downey, Jr., and Lili Taylor, who will go to Griffith Park and feel the earthquake that ties the city together; there is the strange marriage of Penn and Leigh, with her doing phone sex like knitting while he gazes on like a crushed romantic—and his terrible response to this alienation; there is the family of Andie McDowell and Bruce Davison, their son, the weird traffic accident (such a slight passing—did it do damage?) and the grandfather, Jack Lemmon; there are Peter Gallagher and Frances McDormand; there are Lori Singer and Annie Ross—and how good it is to have Ross's songs on the sound track. And still I haven't come to Anne Archer and Tim Robbins, Julianne Moore and Matthew Modine, Lyle Lovett's baker or the sisterhood of Madeleine Stowe and Julianne Moore, and the ginger flourish of Moore's pubic hair.

This is a world riddled with loss and tragedy. It is a place without much hope or daydream, things allegedly made in L.A. It is a film not too far from despair. But there was Altman, nearly seventy, introducing a masterpiece that told the film world, Look at the city, film what you see and feel, in ways that could change the history of movies.

Show Boat (1936)

Show Boat was a novel first, written by Edna Ferber and published in 1926. Carl Laemmle bought the film rights for Universal but did nothing because a stage show came into being, a musical, the book and lyrics by Oscar Hammerstein and the music by Jerome Kern. The cast included Charles Winninger and Edna May Oliver, with Norma Terris as Magnolia, Helen Morgan as Julie, and Jules Bledsoe as Joe. The songs included "Ol' Man River" and "Can't Help Lovin' Dat Man." Opening in late 1927, the stage musical ran 575 performances. Laemmle then paid some more for the song rights, and in 1929 he released the first film of *Show Boat,* directed by Harry A. Pollard and starring Laura La Plante and Joseph Schildkraut, with featured appearances from Helen Morgan and Jules Bledsoe. It was a failure, chiefly because it was not an all-talking picture.

So Laemmle vowed to try again. He hired Zoe Akins to write a new script and he talked about Frank Borzage as the director. Few people liked the Akins script, so Oscar Hammerstein was engaged to do a new one. By then, at least $200,000 had been spent on the project. It was at that point that Laemmle startled most of show business by announcing James Whale (the master of horror) as director. Irene Dunne was set to play Magnolia—she had played the part in the road show. Charles Winninger beat out W. C. Fields for Cap'n Andy. Helen Westley stepped in to replace a weary Edna May Oliver. Allan Jones was borrowed from M-G-M. And in two key respects, Whale insisted: He wanted Helen Morgan, no matter that her alcoholism had worsened. She got it for $3,000 a week, but she was to forfeit the role with one failure to appear on time and she would have to pay for a replacement. In addition, hearing that it had always been Jerome Kern's wish, Whale insisted on Paul Robeson for Joe.

Shooting began late in 1935, using three-fifths of the Universal lot, but at the moment when Carl Laemmle was offering the studio for sale. John Mescall (another drunk) was doing photography, and Charles Hall was art director. It wrapped in March 1936, $400,000 over budget and with fifty-five hours of material. And all the while, the sale of Universal was up in the air.

It would have been no wonder if the pressure had crushed Whale—and he had his critics (Irene Dunne included). But the film is wonderful, and leaves no doubt about why the stage show prospered or why the work has become a classic. Robeson's "Ol' Man River," scripted by Akins as a set piece with camera movements, is transcendent—the grandeur of the treatment (a 270-degree pan shot) only inspires Robeson (the two men got on very well). But Helen Morgan's "Bill" tops it, and is as quiet and modest as "Ol' Man River" is large. It is our best assurance of Morgan's talent, a profound comment on mixed race, and one of the great, sad torch songs in the history of the musical.

M-G-M remade *Show Boat* in 1951 with Kathryn Grayson and Howard Keel, and with Ava Gardner mouthing "Bill" as Annette Warren did the singing. (Lena Horne was considered—and denied.)

Show People (1928)

There's a delightful moment in *Show People*, when Peggy Pepper (Marion Davies), a hot newcomer at Metro-Goldwyn-Mayer, gets to have a meal at the studio commissary. The place is packed with real stars and director King Vidor allows Peggy a lovely, sidelong stare at none other than Marion Davies herself. The look on Peggy's face—awed, wary, but skeptical—says it all. Peggy can handle this one.

It's a famous story, how William Randolph Hearst took a fancy to a girl in the Ziegfeld Follies, Marion Davies. He formed a company, Cosmopolitan, to make her pictures and, after a few years based at Paramount, the company moved over to M-G-M in 1924 because of the great friendship between Hearst and Louis B. Mayer. It is said that Hearst lost a good deal of money on Cosmopolitan, but in part at least that was because his lover's esteem for Marion preferred to see her in large dramatic roles, whereas anyone who knew her judged that comedy was her forte.

By the time of *Show People*, Marion was past thirty, though Hearst's fondness had not waned any more than his creative misinterpretation of her. Still, *Show People*—under the guise of being a satire on Hollywood—is the film above all that shows how mistaken Hearst was. It was the second film she made for King Vidor at Metro, following *The Patsy*, but it was still officially a Cosmopolitan production, the story of Peggy Pepper from Georgia who launches herself at Hollywood and becomes "Patricia Peppoire," a grand lady of the screen. It was written by Agnes Christine Johnson, Wanda Tuchock, and Laurence Stallings, but Vidor was intimately involved in that he had become a favored guest at San Simeon, the estate Hearst kept up the California coast, where Marion was first lady.

Without reverence or foolishness, *Show People* makes a lot of fun at Hollywood's expense—particularly at pretension and any tendency to forget one's roots. So it was Vidor's intention to have Patricia brought back to Peggy's common sense by William Haines throwing a custard pie in her face. This was to remind her of her humble origins in comedy. However, Mr. Hearst went very quiet whenever this pie was mentioned. He thought it unbecoming. He could not bear to see his Marion humiliated. And so he spoke to Mr. Mayer, Mayer spoke to Vidor, and all Patricia gets is a gentle soaking from a soda syphon.

It doesn't detract from the fun or the naughtiness of the film, and it leaves us in no doubt that Marion was a very good comic mime—she does Chaplin very well, no matter that she had probably been Chaplin's lover earlier. John Arnold did the photography. There was a synchronized score, but no dialogue, and the supporting cast includes William Haines, Dell Henderson, Paul Ralli, Tenen Holtz, Harry Gribbon, Polly Moran, and Albert Conti, as well as every Metro star they could round up (including King Vidor). But no one persuaded Mr. Hearst to take a bow.

The Sign of the Cross (1932)

"Bib-lit" is mercifully light on the ground these days, but in a world afflicted by bank closures and food lines, thoughts of sin and the sinning class could be stirred. No one had more history in this than Cecil B. DeMille, and as it turned out *The Sign of the Cross* is one of the more intriguing social commentaries of 1932, even if one is not quite sure whether it is a Marx Brothers film or not. No, it can't be—it moves too slowly.

There was a play, by Wilson Barrett, which seems to owe a few centavos to Henryk Sienkiwicz's *Quo Vadis?* in that it involves Christians, lions, and Nero. Waldemar Young and Sidney Buchman shrugged off whole libraries of "research" to come up with a script in which a noble Roman, actually named Marcus Superbus (Fredric March) falls for a coy handmaiden (Elissa Landi), and thereby rejects the sinuous offerings of the Empress Poppaea (Claudette Colbert), whose sexual energies are not exactly fulfilled by Nero (Charles Laughton).

This is the one where Colbert takes a bath in asses' milk. The man who handled that scene was DeMille's top designer and costumer, Mitchell Leisen. DeMille wanted an effect whereby Ms. Colbert's nipples might fleetingly appear, like bubbles, above the milk. So Leisen and the actress had a lot of fun measuring and pouring, while DeMille—apparently—was in the wings trying to get a glimpse. Colbert takes her bath like a good sport, and it's apparent that she's wearing nothing. But then, under the lights of Karl Struss, the bath began to demonstrate the fermentation process that makes cheese. The story is that Leisen and Colbert went out to dinner, and while they were out the milk hardened so that a visitor to the set thought it was marble, fell in, and was only just saved. You don't have to believe all this, but the surge in yogurt sales in Los Angeles plainly dates from this period.

What you cannot avoid believing—because it's there onscreen—is the unbridled way in which Laughton seems to say to Colbert, "Well, if you're the empress, I'm the queen!" In other words, he gives what is the most flagrant and fleshy portrait of an abandoned homosexual spirit seen in an American film until that time. DeMille was said to be unsure of what was happening. He tried to direct Laughton, but it was impossible. And at the end of it all, when DeMille asked Laughton whom he wanted to play next, Laughton answered, "You!"

Rome burns, Nero plays the harp. Christians are gnawed by lions—Leisen said they used prime rack of lamb to get the lions interested. (Otherwise, Leisen said, they were inclined to chat about the last film they'd made.) DeMille reissued the film in 1944, with fresh scenes and a prologue written by Dudley Nichols. Apparently he had had a vision that the Nazis were like Nero. It is a business terribly vulnerable to visionaries. But Nero and Poppaea are more than they seem: They are the first onscreen portrait of the Hollywood marriage where he's gay and she's viciously carnal because of it. And you can still see that today.

La Signora di Tutti (1934)

The Italian movie star Gaby Doriot (Isa Miranda) tries to kill herself. The process of the operation to save her is the threshold to flashbacks on her life. As a girl, she is taken out of school by her parents, because of a scandal, and sent to the country. She meets Leonardo (Memo Benassi), the son of a banker, Roberto (Federico Benfer), and a crippled mother. It is while Gaby is involved with the father that the mother (Tatiana Pawlova) falls down stairs and dies. The banker then takes up with Gaby in a long period of travels in Europe. His business suffers, and he is tried for fraud. It is while he is in prison that Gaby becomes a film star. Coming out of prison, the banker tries to see her new film, *La Signora di Tutti*, and is killed in a street accident. Leonardo returns and Gaby realizes he loves her—even though he has married Gaby's sister, Anna (Nelly Corradi). Gaby dies during the operation.

Max Ophüls was invited to make *La Signora di Tutti* in Italy by the publisher Angelo Rizzoli. The film came from a novel by Salvatore Gotta, and the script was written by Ophüls, Hans Wilhelm, and Curt Alexander. Italy was already a Fascist country, in which—we assume—the Italians could hardly do "good work," and yet here is a Jewish exile arriving and making a near masterpiece.

Anyone can see how easily the structure of *La Signora di Tutti* fits that of *Lola Montès*, more than twenty years later. This is a more personal story, and it is far more attentive to individual details as well as the Freudian interpretation of a woman loved by father and son—but don't forget how in one episode the teenage Lola makes off with her mother's lover. *Lola Montès* is far more aware of its archetypal parable and gloomier about show business. Indeed, the operation is a more conventional, Hollywoodesque way of telling its story—and so much less intriguing than the life as a circus act formula.

But Ophüls is already fully aware how "everyone's woman" belongs least of all to herself. Gaby does not just surrender her real name. She consents to being a dramatic element in the overbearing lives of others. And so, the resort to acting and films is a good metaphor for the kind of personal helplessness Gaby feels. She becomes other people when her own freedom of decision is taken away. And notice how, all through, her ability to fly creatively is weighed upon by the terrible accidents that make others earthbound.

All of that said, this is an Ophüls film in the movement of the camera (photography by Ubaldo Arata) and the beautiful uncertainty of the actress (Miranda). Haunted by mirrors and physical impasses, she is like a bird in a dead end, bright and adorable, but waiting to be crushed. The music is by Daniele Amfitheatrof, who would work for Ophüls again on *Letter from an Unknown Woman*.

Une Si Jolie Petite Plage (1949)

It is late at night, too late to be out. A wretched local bus lances through the dark and the rain. It carries a passenger who has come to stay at the only hotel open in winter. The walls of the place are stained with moisture and decay. He is beautiful in a harrowed way. He wears a soaking raincoat and he is too tired to eat. He has the doomed face of Gérard Philipe, who would be dead at thirty-seven. Everyone in the town tells him, Oh, wait until morning, or wait until summer, or wait until you're dead—it's such a pretty beach. Nonsense, the place is hell, and you are caught in one of the gloomiest of French noirs, beside which *Quai des Brumes* (1939) feels like a merry weekend in Knokke-le-Zout.

Philipe's character says he is a student, with a touch of consumption. But I think any moviegoer realizes that his problem is existential dread. There's a speechless old man in the hotel who seems to recognize the newcomer. And then a day later, a pursuer arrives (it's Jean Servais): He takes his meals in his room while Philipe eats in the bar—so Philipe is not even sure that he is being tracked. As a rule, in this town it rains—though sometimes it rains harder. And whenever it clears, we see the beach, a flat stretch of drab sand, a place where sickly ghosts might take their promenade.

Philipe's character is a mass of indicators: There's a gun in his luggage, but he sobs himself to sleep. He has a lifeless romance with the waitress (Madeleine Robinson). I'm not going to spoil what happens, except to say that Philipe plays an orphan, and the film carries a fulsome defense of orphans and those who take care of them—to stress that nothing like what happens in this film could occur in life. No comfort. You know it's going to end on the beach and it does, with a last shot that defies belief.

Yves Allégret directed, and if there's a load more atmosphere than substance, never mind—this is the kind of noir that leaves a lot of American films seeming like poseurs. Jacques Sigurd wrote the screenplay. Henri Alekan photographs it all with available light and a few stage lights—natural light in this place is nearly a contradiction in terms (it was apparently shot in Barneville-Carteret, in Manche, a place that might as well have closed down). Maurice Colasson did the grunge design, and Maurice Thiriet wrote the music.

The rest of the cast includes André Valmy, Christian Ferry, Jeanne Marken, Mona Dol, and Julien Carette (with a mustache). But it's Gérard Philipe's film, and the one thing it misses is his interior monologue—harsh, desperate, self-pitying, and riveting. Allégret tries to show the character objectively, but we need to hear the inner torment that is reduced to sobbing at night. His voice, glowing in the dark of his room like a cigarette, could be the chat of madness.

And every time Philipe walks on that beach, you feel the wind sanding at his fragile soul.

All of film, I suppose, is straining toward a love story: The spectator desires that landscape, that house, that woman. To be very blunt about it, the being in the dark is not entirely crepuscular or nocturnal; it yearns to be up there in the light of the screen. But there is no direct way up there. And so, time and again, the great love stories on film are the impossible ones, the ones where gazing is the measure of eros (that's the lesson we learn in the dark). It's like Buñuel's bourgeoisie looking at their receding dinner; it's like the faces of Trevor Howard and Celia Johnson in *Brief Encounter* (which by the standards of postcensorship cinema is no encounter at all); or it's like Jean-Pierre Melville's *Le Silence de la Mer,* a beautiful debut, a film with snow on the ground to signal not just war but the way love has been turned into espionage by politics.

It is based on the novel by Vercors, published in 1942. Apparently, Melville, in London, read the English translation, published by Cyril Connolly. A German officer, Werner von Ebrennac (Howard Vernon), is billeted in the country house of an old man and his niece (Jean-Marie Robain and Nicole Stéphane). They respond to this imposition with silence. So the German talks about his love of French culture and history. When he talks of "Beauty and the Beast," we suspect he loves the niece. We learn he has dropped his fiancée. And then after a leave he comes back and admits he has learned about the concentration camps and the real nature of the Reich. He volunteers for a posting to the eastern front. The niece says, "Adieu," her one word to him. The story is told by the uncle, and it turns into the pages of Vercors's underground novel.

The film was shot at Vercors's own house in Villiers-sur-Morin, in Seine-et-Marne, in the early winter of 1947–48. The photography was by Henri Decaë, and Decaë and Melville together edited the picture. There are still disputes as to whether Pierre Braunberger produced or just helped. Nor is it plain what it cost. Melville said 120,000 francs, with half of that going for the rights and the score, by Edgar Bischoff. It was not released until 1949, which suggests that the shooting was intermittent and fragmented. No matter, the intensity of the concept holds everything together, and the history of a Resistance situation merges with the universal capacity for desire and affection as contained in the mechanics of cinema.

That the German is "a good German," no matter that this film comes so soon after the war, owes something to the real officer, Ernst Junger, billeted in the house of Vercors. But it is also an immediate sign of Melville's realization that all manner of ambiguities live under uniform. As it is, Howard Vernon is the central actor in the film: He fills silence and nullity. But the silence endures. This film was one of the shared models for every director of the New Wave. Its methods, its light, its situations, and its grace are recurring gifts.

The Silence of the Lambs (1990)

Clarice Starling (Jodie Foster) is Southern, from white trash, an earnest girl who is hauling herself up from the dirt in the service of the FBI. She is not quite grown up. Her boss (Scott Glenn) recruits her to go to see the imprisoned Hannibal Lecter (Anthony Hopkins) in an attempt to gain insight or information on a serial killer, known as Buffalo Bill. The sequence that follows is a landmark in modern film. The prison is a nearly Victorian dungeon that still surrounds Lecter with ultramodern safety devices. Clarice must run the gauntlet to reach him—this gauntlet is sexual and moral. And when she reaches Lecter, he is cold, austere, reptilian, clerical (he is like a library compressed into human form—a computer). But he likes her. He smells her. He begins to slip into a paternal attitude to her. And she is like the pilgrim seduced by the dark magician. And if she succumbs—what chance have we?

While it is clear that Lecter is a monster, he begins to make the strange journey that was to be finalized in *Hannibal,* where he manages to serve up Gary Oldman's brain while becoming like an uncle, or even a lover, to Clarice. For in truth, he does help her discover Buffalo Bill, and then at the end he melts into the crowd, the larger world—not just escaped from detention, but bent on following his archenemy (Anthony Heald) and having him for dinner.

Taken from the novel by Thomas Harris, adapted by Ted Tally, and directed by Jonathan Demme, this is a crucial example of the moral nature of an art being sacrificed to the requirements of a cold-blooded entertainment business. For this is horror (and it is often very disturbing) shot through with arch comedy and a furtive but self-congratulatory love story. The film was a great success in every way, but it seems to have fallen on the genuine decency of Demme and left him numb or stricken. He has never been the same again, and now seems incapable of the humanity or the daring of *Melvin and Howard* or *Something Wild.* Equally, he has never again returned to the macabre gloating of this film, or to that mixing of genres that can find a love story between Lecter and Clarice. Yet the movies have only themselves to blame, for film has been falling in love with monsters for decades.

Thirty years after *Psycho,* the lock clicked home: The way in which that shocker had been entrusted to Norman Bates at the end was now fulfilled and celebrated by the insinuation of Lecter as almost the deepest presence and standard in the film. It's interesting to recall that Anthony Hopkins (who is not onscreen for that long—not really long enough for a lead performance) said that once he had the look and the manner it was easy to do the rest. For it hangs on fascination in itself. If evil looks us in the eye, without shame or coyness, we are hooked.

It won Best Picture, as well as Oscars for Tally, Hopkins, Foster, and Demme.

Silk Stockings (1956)

I'm fond of Lubitsch's *Ninotchka,* but put to some acid test I'm going to prefer Rouben Mamoulian's *Silk Stockings.* I'll try to explain, but first the history: *Ninotchka* was a hit film of 1939, and later on (in 1955) there was a Broadway musical adaptation written by George S. Kaufman, Leueen MacGrath, and Abe Burrows, with songs by Cole Porter. It starred Don Ameche and Hildegarde Knef. In the stage show, Ameche played a theatrical agent, and Knef's Ninotchka is a Soviet commissar sent to Paris to protect the work of a Russian composer.

The movie rights went to M-G-M, where it would be Arthur Freed's last production. Leonard Gershe and Leonard Spigelgass wrote the script, going back to *Ninotchka* wherever they could and turning the male role into a movie producer. Freed appointed Rouben Mamoulian to direct, largely because he was Russian and had worked with Garbo. And it was Mamoulian who coaxed Fred Astaire to take part. Initially Astaire had felt he was too old. But Mamoulian insisted they were doing a love story, where dance was the love. Eugene Loring was doing choreography, but Hermes Pan was brought in to work on the numbers involving Astaire. The female lead was Cyd Charisse, though her singing was dubbed by Carole Richards. Robert Bronner did the photography, in CinemaScope.

There are three big dances. In his hotel room, Fred talks to Ninotchka about love. She says in Russia it is "chemical reaction." Whereupon, he breaks into a six-minute version of "All of You," in which she wears a long, belted jersey dress and in which his seductive moves draw her into an irresistible delight. The impassivity of Charisse (her normal acting state) makes a fascinating contrast with the voluptuousness of her body, and it is a fact, I think, that the ideological meeting of liberty and discipline ends up in liberty's favor, but only in the most relaxed formalism of a pas de deux.

The second is a solo dance for Charisse in her hotel room, as she puts on the various pieces of capitalist lingerie she has secretly acquired. It is one of the most purely erotic dances in the American musical, and it is akin to an aria on sexuality.

Third is achievement, marriage, bliss: It's Fred taking Ninotchka onto an empty film set and then leading her into "Fated to Be Mated," a routine with some exhilarating camera movements and edits to dramatize the unison and the happiness of the two together.

Those three numbers are the spine of the film, and very supple. But there is more: Janis Paige as the cartoon version of a movie star; Astaire doing "The Ritz Roll and Rock," which he persuaded Cole Porter to write for him; and the three commissars Jules Munshin, Joseph Buloff, and Peter Lorre doing "Siberia," with Lorre hanging on to two chairs for support.

It was the end for Freed, for Fred and Cyd (their last musical), and for Cole Porter (his last show). All of which is a terrible letdown to this alleged celebration of America's capacity for thinking pink and beating the Reds.

Silkwood (1983)

Silkwood may be the first movie for which director Mike Nichols worked to make an accurate sense of place and social climate vital elements in a picture. So many of his earlier films give up those things to establish a witty air of "stage" where the drama is unfolding. Thus, *Who's Afraid of Virginia Woolf?* would probably work better on a more stylized set (as opposed to the attempt at a real house), and *The Graduate* makes a mess at anything more than a cartoon California. But in *Silkwood,* we feel we are out in the desolate places of Oklahoma, and in the unnoticed dark fields of the republic, where ordinary life goes on. To match that feeling of place, *Silkwood* is deliberately slow—as if to suggest the very gradual onset of horror in the minds of its characters.

Of course, it is based on real events, and when the film came out there was an unavoidable controversy over how accurate the script by Nora Ephron and Alice Arlen was—whether as journalism or as paranoia. That moment has passed and so now it's easier to see this movie as a study in the way certain modern corporations reckon to mislead their own employees. The horror comes in the sheer details of radiation poisoning, and the harsh methods applied to detect it or guard against it.

But the real strength of the film is the decision to let Karen Silkwood (Meryl Streep) be a wolflike maverick, sexy, insolent, and rebellious, but casual and lazy, who finds a stiffening of her own spine as she realizes how dangerous her everyday, boring work is. This is a striking piece of acting just because it cuts itself off from so many obvious sources of sentimentality. There, too, it shows a development in Nichols, who had tended to make films about caricatures, or people separated from their own motivation—think of Mrs. Robinson in *The Graduate.*

So the film works because of the subtle contrasts between the hippie untidiness of the place where Streep, Cher, and Kurt Russell live and the sterilized nuclear factory, and by the way these décors build into a profound philosophical antagonism. Cher was better than anyone expected, and Russell does nothing to get in the way. But then one has to note the very good supporting cast—Craig T. Nelson, Diana Scarwid, Fred Ward, David Strathairn, Tess Harper, Ron Silver, and so on.

Of course, it's a subject that we all prefer to forget—and clearly it owed its movie existence to the recent example of Three Mile Island. But its power comes not from the situation, but from the true portrait of a trio of rednecks suddenly having to think. Notably, it was not nominated for Best Picture—*Terms of Endearment* won, and Shirley MacLaine won for Best Actress over Streep. Cher's was the popular nomination, though she lost, too. These days, *Silkwood* is still a gripping picture whereas *Terms of Endearment* is a mystery.

Since You Went Away (1944)

With its four-word title and its span of meaning, *Since You Went Away* was David Selznick's most significant follow-up to *Gone With the Wind*, and it was also the producer's contribution to the war effort. It was characteristic of Selznick's favored view of life that he regarded war as a panorama of women left at home—as opposed to that of the men who went away. Of course, historically, even though they were not of the same year, the Selznick picture was eclipsed by Goldwyn's *The Best Years of Our Lives*, a film that did not neglect men or the begging scenes of reunion. Indeed, for a film as ambitious as this (172 minutes, despite wartime restrictions) and with the hope of making a total statement, it is striking how dark, depressive, and forgotten *Since You Went Away* now looks. Is it because of the presence of Stanley Cortez and his fondness for darkness, or is it Selznick's natural melancholy, that the film looks like a film noir in which the menace never quite materializes?

The film was taken from Margaret Buell Wilder's book about a family of women left behind, and it inspired Selznick to do the whole screenplay himself. Alas, that's where the enterprise breaks apart. For Selznick is fatally committed to likeable, ordinary people, and that in turn promotes so many long-drawn-out scenes of small talk. Nothing really happens—which may be true to the very domestic situation, but makes for lassitude in the film, especially when its few men are as nice and polite as Joseph Cotten and Robert Walker.

The look supplied by Cortez cries out for building neurosis and edginess in the women—not just sexual or romantic frustration, but a kind of alienation or loneliness in which the women are advancing on crack-up. The sociological truth of World War II is that it altered the position of women, their attitudes to work, love, family, and self. But those strains hardly figure in *Since You Went Away* because Selznick is far too devoted to the passivity and the self-sacrifice of women.

The intelligent view might have had that when the men came home, they would find their woman changed—not even the Goldwyn film really faces that. And, as I say, the undermining is there in the imagery and in a plot structure that needs one disaster after another in the third hour if survival is to count for enough. It needs Antonioni, perhaps, someone who can show an overall mood turning sour or hollow. As it is, the film is a proof that Selznick hardly understood the world or the audience after 1939. The central trio—Claudette Colbert, Jennifer Jones, and Shirley Temple—are a lot too good to be true, or compelling. It would surely have been in accord with the facts if some loyalties had lapsed and some loves been lost. But Selznick was not grown-up enough to grasp those changes—no matter that his life was rife with them at the very same time.

The Singing Detective (1986)

I realize that *The Singing Detective* was not exactly a feature film, but a six-part television serial that played on the BBC in November and December 1986. Still, it seems to me such an achievement, with so great an influence, that it would be absurd to bypass it. As it is, a good deal of British material in this book was made ostensibly for the small screen. But it would also be fanciful to do a book like this without including something from Dennis Potter—so why not go for his masterpiece?

Potter wrote it, yet it's fair to say that in the entire production that followed, he was regarded as the "author" of the piece—and not just because he and his hero had illnesses in common. This was regarded by the BBC as a "play," and Jon Amiel, the director, took it as his task to serve the writer. So it's the story of Philip Marlow (Michael Gambon) in bed, in hospital, with a dire skin disease that is disabling. One strand of the work is hospital life in which he is being treated (there are fates close to death, yet more torturing) by Nurse Mills (Joanne Whalley). Another strand is the kind of thriller that Marlow writes, which tracks the seduction of his wife, Nicola (Janet Suzman), by the nasty Mark Binney (Patrick Malahide). Yet a third strand is the childhood that Philip knew in the Forest of Dean, which will turn on another marital betrayal.

The production was led by Kenith Trodd and Rick McCallum and John Harris. Ken Westbury did the photography. Jim Clay was in charge of design. I don't know the economics, but I doubt very much that the six parts of *The Singing Detective* (300 minutes on air) cost more than a million pounds. In other words, this was factory filmmaking reliant on an agreed script, intense preparation, very good casting and acting, and an overall attitude that this kind of work—which provoked huge controversy over matters of taste—was "right" for the public.

That's where the producers' sense of the writer comes in. For there was no audience in Britain to say, Give us *The Singing Detective*, with the surreal excursions into musical, please. There was every warning that conservative views would be shocked by being offered so much sex. Yet surely Potter's vision—of childhood making and warping the man, and of illness as a social metaphor—was profound and valuable. Dennis Potter on television has mattered as much to Britain as Bacon and Freud on gallery walls: Britten, Courtney Pine, and the Beatles playing music: David Hare and Harold Pinter onstage, as well as novels by . . . Well, name your favorites.

The large cast was distinguished by Gambon's courage and vulnerability, and the other leads, but it was rich through and through: Lyndon Davies as Philip the boy, Bill Paterson, Jim Carter, Alison Steadman, David Ryall, Imelda Staunton, Gerard Horan, Leslie French, David Thewlis.

Singin' in the Rain (1952)

In the general agreement these days that *Singin' in the Rain* is the greatest of the M-G-M musicals, and perhaps the best American musical altogether, everyone quickly adds, ". . . because it's about something." It has a story and a subject: the turmoil in Hollywood that greeted the coming of sound and the way one star, Lina (Jean Hagen), an empress in silence, became a fishwife when miked and had to give way to youth, spunk, and gotta-try (Debbie Reynolds).

It has to be said that the scenes that trace attempts to record sound and picture at the same time are very funny—"I can't make love to a bush!" screams Hagen. In turn, that owes a lot to the script—by Betty Comden and Adolph Green—which is researched, funny, and in complete subservience to Gene Kelly's Don Lockwood, and Gene's certainty that nothing should ever stand in the way of his panzer smile. So, if the film is about something, it could be a little more about Lina's loss and a little less about Don's heartless exuberance.

But this was Kelly at his peak, and the codirecting title he shared with Stanley Donen was generally taken as a kindness to Donen. Kelly ran the numbers, and he had a way of seeing the numbers start before others were counting. That said, so much had been learned on *An American in Paris,* and now Kelly was in home territory, given material that was a celebration of a song-and-dance man, and which had the complete backing of Arthur Freed for the very good reason that the picture was going to use many of Freed's songs (done with Nacio Herb Brown).

Freed let himself be kidded in Millard Mitchell's broad version of the studio boss who still "can't quite visualize it" after a number has run. And the songs are bouncy, lively, and second-rate—but if this is the greatest musical, where is the great song? I love Donald O'Connor doing "Make 'em Laugh," even if it is stolen from Cole Porter's "Be a Clown," and "You Were Meant for Me" has a sweet glide to it. The Broadway ballet is a knockout, and it introduces Cyd Charisse in lime green and legs forever.

Of course, there is one great number. Kelly gave Roger Edens credit for the humming intro to "Singin'" itself. It got him moving and it indicated the wistful, elegiac keynote to the number. It is night. He is largely alone. There are climaxes to the number, but it's an inward, idyllic lyric—and with some quite lovely crane movements (Donen or Kelly? we'll never know), it becomes one of the most intricately worked-out routines—not just a novelty, but a mood piece, and a song that, finally, resembles the whole point of the movies. For millions, all over the world, all the movies were singin' in the rain—giving us a chance of mercy or delight when times were hard and the rain seemed toxic. That's why the number lifts the whole film, and how it eclipses Kelly's rather frantic ego.

La Sirène du Mississippi (1969)

I realized some time ago that I love this film beyond reason, and so I have had to learn not to make strenuous efforts of persuasion. Just state the facts, and let them sink in. Sooner or later, the people one might have thought to educate see the connection—that the film itself is about a love beyond reason. So they steer clear of me or give me a funny look—however you care to put it, they feel they have got my number. But numbers are infinite, aren't they?

So let me tell you the story again; I can tell it forever. Louis Mahé (Jean-Paul Belmondo) lives on the island of Réunion, a French possession in the southern Atlantic, a place off on its own, not sure whether it is lonely or eccentric. He is a tobacco farmer, well-to-do. He has a very good, large house, but he is single. So he has resorted to the correspondence columns in the newspapers to find himself a possible bride. He makes an epistolary contract with one, named Julie Roussel. And when her ship sails in, he goes down to the docks eager to meet her, her photograph in his hand and in his memory.

But he cannot find the woman in his photograph at the docks. Instead, there is a beautiful woman who says her name is Julie Roussel (Catherine Deneuve). She is a good deal more beautiful than the woman in the picture, whereupon he forgets the picture. The relationship is a little uneasy: the wedding ring purchased from a loop of string Mlle. Roussel had sent him does not fit. But she is Deneuve with auburn hair, bare-legged in the moist warmth of Réunion, extraordinarily beautiful. Is he an idiot, or just a fool? They marry. He feels they are in love. Snap—she is gone, with most of his money.

He hires a detective to track her down (Michel Bouquet). But then he goes to Europe to pursue her himself. And one day, by chance, he sees her on television. So he tracks her down in a shabby hotel room. She is contrite: Oh, my darling, she says, if only you knew. She has had an appalling life—she recounts her woes—and he is in love with her again. But the damned detective shows up, too stubborn to be let go. So Louis kills the man. They retreat into the country, to a cabin in the snows. He is ill. He guesses she is poisoning him. But he still loves her.

François Truffaut adapted this from the Cornell Woolrich novel *Waltz into Darkness*, and he has made it more gentle. In the Woolrich, the woman needs to kill Louis and he wants her hand to close his eyes. But Truffaut makes it a love story. At every deceit, Julie confesses and Louis is hers again. Their pursuits and reunions may repeat. Already, there is a longer version of the film. It could go on forever, this story. I wish it would.

The Sixth Sense (1999)

The power and the opportunity of the cinema to explore extrasensory stories may be one of its greatest challenges—and risks. It could even pioneer the opening up of that domain in real life. But the dangers are just as real, and the charm of *The Sixth Sense* is the adroitness with which it steers between horror and whimsy. I still admire the film, yet the career of writer-director N. Night Shyamalan ever since (one wreck after another) only underlines the rarity of this picture. It was sold as a kind of horror film, and it was a sleeper success (cost $55 million—earnings $293 million), but to call it that is to miss so much.

The setting is Philadelphia, Shyamalan's own city, photographed by Tak Fujimoto so as to seem pregnant with possibilities. Malcolm Crowe (Bruce Willis), a successful psychologist, is celebrating with his wife, Anna (Olivia Williams), when a crazed former patient (Donnie Wahlberg) breaks in. He shoots Malcolm and then kills himself. After the time a recovery would take, Malcolm is back at work and dealing with a new case, that of Cole Sear (Haley Joel Osment). Gradually, Cole will tell Malcolm that he "sees" dead people. And so the story proceeds, with Cole proving able to help several people he meets. In the end, in a gentle plot pivot that comes as a surprise to newcomers, he is able to help his own therapist.

Rather like James Cameron's first *Terminator, The Sixth Sense* is one of the few modern films that springs an authentic narrative surprise where ingenuity and plausibility are held in balance. For what happens here isn't just a shock trick: it's a tender realization of how mourning works and a state of mind finally that is not afraid of death, or daunted by it. The cinema has always had fantastic success in showing us the fact (the face, the person) and then stimulating us to feel sympathy or fear. After all, at the movies, we see dead people or strangers so unreachable they are, literally, on the other side. It was Shyamalan's grasp of that and his ability to relate his story to the workings of movie that seemed so promising.

In addition, of course, it is a film rooted in a generous sense of how the mind may work, or employ openness, that is very sympathetic or encouraging to the possibility of telepathy. Shyamalan uses two shots of people who are not really together that are beautiful, sad, and also faintly comic. It was a rare delicacy that promised so much. Yes, I know, the years since have been crushing and the wisdom in Shyamalan has turned adolescent and fake. Never mind: This film still speaks for itself. The director was blessed to have Osment, easily the most interesting child actor in an age rich in that breed. But the subtle performance of Bruce Willis is very much a matter of the director's vision and insistence. Add to that two wonderful pieces of work from Olivia Williams and Toni Collette (as Cole's mother).

The Small Back Room (1949)

This is a war film, and a film noir; it's even a story about a man struggling to overcome the twin handicaps of self-pity and booze. And such familiar genres are not common in Powell and Pressburger films, which had little taste for slices of ordinary life. Sammy Rice's life is not commonplace, but it's very real: He has to lie on the shifting pebbles of an English beach, trying to dismantle a bomb or a mine such as the Germans have not used before, and describing what he is doing over the radio-telephone in case he blows himself up.

Sammy limps. He has been wounded before, badly enough to have a tin foot. He despises the bureaucracy that endangers his work, and his fear of being under such pressure has driven him to drink and to the certainty that he is unlovable. Of course, there is a girl, but she has to ignore his gloom and his insults.

This comes from a Nigel Balchin novel, and Balchin helped the Archers with the screenplay—Michael Powell would compare his dialogue to that of Pinter, and in the dark and terse love scenes between David Farrar and Kathleen Byron there is a note of Hawks sometimes, of desperate fatalism. And of a need that voices itself as challenge. Sammy's problem with life is also beautifully mirrored in the form of a Corporal Taylor (Cyril Cusack), an expert with lethal fuses, but a man haunted by the infidelities of his wife. He has been reduced to a dire stammer, and Sammy's tin leg squeaks against the pebbles as he struggles to make sense of a bomb—Powell rejected the idea of a sandy shore and filmed at Chesil Beach. He wanted those pebbles in a film where sound is crucial and excruciating.

There are also nightmares where Sammy's small back room is nearly crowded out by a monstrous whiskey bottle—these scenes are very impressive, yet in truth they work against the realist tension of the rest of the film and the restraint in Farrar's performance. The bottle is one of those things where Powell goes too far and looks arty because of it.

The picture was made for Alexander Korda, with Christopher Challis doing the black-and-white photography, Hein Heckroth as the production designer, Brian Easdale writing the music (there's a jazz club sequence, too, with Ted Heath and Kenny Baker), and Reginald Mills as the editor. Farrar is one of those actors let go by the British film industry, and he is very powerful here, just as Kathleen Byron had clearly become a Powell muse. ("She was too straight to be an actress," Powell would write. "But she was a good one.") The film was a failure (were war films going out of style, or is it too dark and personal?). To that extent, it's a badly neglected film in the Powell-Pressburger collection, and it has fine supporting performances from Jack Hawkins, Leslie Banks, Michael Gough, Milton Rosmer, Emrys Jones, Michael Goodliffe, Renée Asherson, Anthony Bushell, Sidney James, and Robert Morley as "the Minister."

Smiles of a Summer Night (1955)

Does Ingmar Bergman get a royalty every time "Send In the Clowns" is sung? Well, why not? And if that sounds like a trivia question, let's be unashamed of using the Broadway musical to advertise one of those fascinating Bergman works from the fifties, before he was exactly "Ingmar Bergman" and when he was trying on various hats to see what worked and thought he might try to be romantic.

Smiles of a Summer Night is a complex dance in which, at the moment of midsummer, some allegedly sophisticated but actually rather numb characters gather for a country house weekend in which the games, official or otherwise, will play out most of the sexual variations they long for but which are beyond their accomplishment. So it's a potion against sadness, and thus one of Bergman's more therapeutic films, even if its tone is often sardonic and even cruel. It is beautifully photographed by Gunnar Fischer, and nowhere are Fischer's skills more refined than in the photography of Ulla Jacobsson—twenty-four here, exquisite, and arguably the loveliest of Bergman's women, if not the greatest actress (she would end up as a screaming wreck hustled out of *Zulu!*).

Still, enjoy her as you can in the magic of Swedish dusk, along with Eva Dahlbeck (great beauty and great actress), Margit Carlquist, Harriet Andersson, Gunnar Björnstrand, and Jarl Kulle. It is one of those films where Death does not appear, but his servants—neurosis and mortality—are everywhere. In other words, the festival of midsummer is more Viennese than Renoiresque. Never mind, Bergman with the idea of "pleasure" manages to be as shy and sinister as a cat with a big, fresh (but suspicious) fish.

The musical, *A Little Night Music*, came in 1973, lyrics and music by Stephen Sondheim and book by Hugh Wheeler. There's no doubt but that the young Sondheim responded to the tone of regret or dismay—and the summeriness of the musical is all in the halting pace of three-quarter time and a middle-aged ruefulness. But it's a great work compared with Woody Allen's foolish *A Midsummer Night's Sex Comedy*. The film of the musical (though directed by Hal Prince) is not very good—what am I saying? It's awful. And so "Send In the Clowns" is a song that acquires different meanings as the decades pass. Frank Sinatra clearly thought it meant him—but Judi Dench recovered it on the London stage.

All of which can serve as a gentle reminder to see the Bergman film again. In his last decades, under the polite rubric of "retirement"—despite majestic works like *Faithless* and *Sarabande*—it had been possible to believe that he was sleeping, or resting. Whereas the great body of his work builds and grows like a noble wine. Whenever people think of ten bests, they should cross their fingers and plow on regardless—"except for Ingmar Bergman." (He could so easily do all ten.) This is actually one of his best minor works. Elsewhere, I have suggested that as cinema began Sweden grasped it more surely than most countries. And now, past the end, who else can persuade you that the medium must be saved?

The Snake Pit (1948)

When you think about it, *The Snake Pit* is the title to a lurid adventure film—doesn't Indiana Jones have an immense ordeal in such a place? Yet, just as I was going to the movies seriously, or regularly (it was the same thing then), I was warned by fond relatives not to think about *The Snake Pit*—it was unpleasant, disturbing, beyond me, and (here was the final roadblock) it was about this unhappy woman. Somehow, I felt even then that there was an antagonism between the movies and unhappy women. So I caught up with the picture years later when it was easy to see how stilted it was in its treatment of madness (and its treatment of treatments), not to mention a thoroughgoing women's picture.

All of that is unfair. One has only to make the comparison with the dreadful nonsense of *Spellbound* (1945) to see that the postwar interest in madness and what to do with it could be earnest and grave. And I can see now that great credit goes to Anatole Litvak, who paid $75,000 of his own money to buy the rights to the novel by Mary Jane Ward and to sell the project to Darryl F. Zanuck. Moreover, the film was a great critical success and a surprising box-office performer. It grossed over $4 million, the same as *Johnny Belinda.* And those two films were nominated for Best Picture, along with *The Red Shoes, The Treasure of the Sierra Madre,* and *Hamlet* (the ultimate winner). You can see how much madness there was in 1948.

Litvak was nominated for the Best Director Oscar. Frank Partos and Millen Brand were nominated for Best Screenplay, Alfred Newman for his music, and, of course, Olivia de Havilland was nominated as Best Actress. Jane Wyman won for *Johnny Belinda,* but if de Havilland had won she would have had three in four years (with *To Each His Own* and *The Heiress*).

How does the film stand up? Well, it falls somewhere between the melodrama of its title and the kind of documentary-like work Fox was doing in those years. To see it now is to realize the enormous strides taken in fifty years in the general public understanding of mental disturbance. But it teaches us something else: about how far the various conditions of stress witnessed in war (to say nothing of the colossal dementia of the camps) had persuaded the public to pay attention to the inner life and how easily it could be unsettled. That is vital to film noir as well as all those movies that introduce this new character: the psychiatrist, the shrink.

And just because *The Snake Pit* is so much more sophisticated than *Spellbound,* and so truly horrified at the damage that can be done, you feel the pressure of public need and education. What remains fascinating and challenging, I think, is how far the fantasy-laden air of cinema was ever the right medium for that process. Are people sitting in the dark for their enlightenment ever going to find a way out? Does the medium eventually offer to treat the sick mind or glamorize it?

Snow White and the Seven Dwarfs (1937)

In Paris, in 1935, to receive an award, Walt Disney and his brother noted that one theater was playing a program of six Mickey Mouse shorts. Take it as a whole, said Walt, and that's a feature film. I suspect the idea of a full-length animated story film had been nagging at him much longer—there were examples in Europe. But it was the Paris revelation that started him off. Back home, he called an evening meeting of the company and said they were going to do *Snow White*. He reckoned it might be done for $250,000.

Thus began the most speculative period in the history of the Disney organization: Would a public sit still for a picture that turned out to be 83 minutes? There was a huge increase in the number of hired draftsmen. There was the creation of a multiplane camera that gave an added impression of depth. People worked six months on a minute of film. Above all, the Disney people had to work out the story components: a simple story that carried over an hour; attractive central characters, easily identified with; answer the question, Is it for adults or children?; find a way to get songs in, and to draw it so well that it felt like life. Disney was sure that if audiences noticed the artificiality they would never stay in their seats.

You can't blame Disney for coming up with such sweet, middlebrow answers for all those questions. He didn't realize that he was redefining the nature of movie entertainment and putting animation in a box from which it still has trouble claiming an adult audience. Disney was a pioneer, of course, but a conservative—it was like finding the Americas and calling them the USA.

Of course, it's not far-fetched to think of 1937 films still playing: It was a year that produced *The Awful Truth*, *Stage Door*, *The Prisoner of Zenda*, and *Easy Living*. Although *Snow White* cost close to $2 million (a million of which, Walt said, was research and development), it grossed $8 million worldwide, more than those four together. Of course, it had Technicolor—and I'm sure that that innovation was the key spur in Disney's thinking.

The next key was getting character right—and having seven unique dwarfs was vital. As for Snow White, the animators used a young dancer, Marge Belcher, as a physical model—she would become Marge Champion—and they gave her the voice of eighteen-year-old Adriana Caselotti. We know now that the voices of animation figures are very important in the process of identification.

The one question never settled—Is it for children or adults?—resulted in equivocation, and that may be the most important thing Disney ever didn't do. He said, Why not both? And what that ended up with—I think—was something deeply intuitive of the movies: adults who responded like kids.

The Academy was bewildered. No Best Picture nomination; a nomination for the score; no song nominated; but one Oscar and seven miniatures for the breakthrough.

Some Came Running (1959)

Nineteen fifty-eight was the year of *Gigi*. It won the Oscar for Best Picture. It was the one time that Vincente Minnelli won for Best Director. It got nine nominations and nine Oscars, and we are supposed to curl up like contented spaniels when we hear it. It makes me sick. I despise its prettified view of Paris. I find the Lerner and Loewe score grating. Leslie Caron has always been a mystery to me in films. And Maurice Chevalier delights himself more than he ever will me. The only thing I like in the film is Hermione Gingold, whose voice in "I Remember It Well" is the single thing in this fluff and organdy that might have passed the inspection of Colette. If you love Colette, *Gigi* is ghastly. If you don't love Colette, put this book aside.

Which is an introduction to my tribute to *Some Came Running*, where the same Minnelli was able to put aside "the musical" (his alleged forte) and explore the thing for which his talents were best suited: the psychological melodrama. In this case, it is a novel by James Jones, turned into a script by John Patrick and Arthur Sheekman. This is not a big story, despite the superb use of CinemaScope and décor to explore character and situation—this was an area latent in Minnelli, and so often frustrated by the garish codes of the musical. It's a story about small-town Midwest America (Indiana), of compromise, failure, and crushed hopes. In so many ways it's so much more useful or instructive a film than *Gigi*.

Frank Sinatra is a would-be writer come home from the Korean War, and this is one of his most heartfelt and modest performances—not least because he had the sense to trust the power of his supporting cast and resist any urge to intimidate them. So Sinatra is one in a group that includes Shirley MacLaine (never better or quieter), Dean Martin (in that emerging realization that he was an actor), Martha Hyer, and Arthur Kennedy, who never gave a performance that didn't deserve attention and master classes.

Vincente Minnelli was a great director, and I believe he was at his best when least distracted by those famous elements of design and decoration. Throughout his career, he pursued dramas, but few had such good material as this one, let alone the right cast. Some were painfully preachy, like *The Cobweb* and *Tea and Sympathy*. Others got overlooked simply because Minnelli was supposed to be a musicals man. But in maybe his best musical—*Meet Me in St. Louis*—he had also shown a respect for character and ordinary settings that flowers in *Some Came Running*.

So when people see Sinatra, Martin, and MacLaine together, they easily think "Rat Pack" and find this film disappointing. Try it again, and long after the sugar conceits of *Gigi* have dissolved, you will find that *Some Came Running* is about life. But Minnelli was a modest man, endlessly loyal to a studio that thought it knew what was best for him.

Some Like It Hot (1959)

First things first: There was a precedent—Billy Wilder remembered a silent German film, *Fanfares of Love*, in which two guy musicians had joined an all-girl band. I see no reason not to esteem the essential dirty mind of Wilder in guessing that this was going to be fruitful one day. After all, in the basic voyeuristic trick of the movies, guys in the dark watching girls in the light—the girls don't know the guys are there. They treat them like sisters.

Whereupon Wilder and I. A. L. Diamond got to work with the added hook that this would be a couple of guys fleeing from the St. Valentine's Day Massacre—they saw it! So the film becomes a sex comedy, while it is also an opportunity for parody of the gangster film. To Wilder, parody was next to character assassination. This was the man who had cast Erich von Stroheim as Gloria Swanson's director. So George Raft would play a version of himself. Edward G. Robinson's son would toss a coin under Raft's nose, and anything else anyone could think of would be crammed in, with the ultimate threat being that the gangsters convening in Florida (at the Coronado Hotel in San Diego, in fact) might recognize Joe and Jerry, thus demanding their masquerade as Josephine and Daphne.

I think it's clear that eyebrows were raised over the female impersonation and how to do it. Was it possible, in 1959, to get two name actors to be knockout dames? Remember, too, that Frank Sinatra was the first thought for Daphne. Jack Lemmon and Tony Curtis have made it clear over the years that doing the film was not a piece of cake. They were hours in makeup. They had to wear steel jock straps. They were teased unmercifully—not least by Wilder. And they had to wait and repeat everything until Marilyn got a decent take. Jack and Tony were by instinct quick studies. Once they had their take on the "girls," they knew what they were doing. And they cover a range: Josephine is pretty spiffy in a Kay Francis sort of way, but Daphne is out of English pantomime. In other words, you'd have to be as dumb as Marilyn to believe she's a girl. Anyway, it wasn't quite Sinatra's thing—and Frank under makeup is not a pretty thought. (Note: Wilder had had the dream long enough to think of Danny Kaye and Bob Hope—and they could have been hot.)

In great personal distress, Marilyn barely got away with it. Mitzi Gaynor was standing by—but with Mitzi Gaynor *Some Like It Hot* could have gone home. Marilyn is perfect because she doesn't get the masquerade—what that says about Wilder's esteem for her is not pretty either, but Billy Wilder was not a nice guy.

I suspect, literally, that no one knew the film was a gay breakthrough. If they had guessed, they would have taken fright. But here is another film from the late fifties that blows up every convention it can see and discloses miracles in the explosion. Everybody's perfect.

Something Wild (1986)

One of the functions of the movies has always been to take a representative figure from the middle of the middle class, the nerdy, safety-first brigade that makes up the huge majority of humanity, of us, and expose him to risk—great danger, or great delight. Thus the film says, Would you dare to do this—are you brave enough for something wild? It is an offer that turns upon the secret longing in the safe and the secure to be outlaws, to walk into the dark or the unknown, or to get to be with Melanie Griffith in her prime without a word of explanation or "sensible" preliminary getting-to-know-her first. In other words, will you jump in the deep end without knowing how deep it is, whether you can swim and whatever the actuarial odds on rescue? To be brief about it, film provides a chance to gamble with danger.

In so many cases, the gamble and its ordeal are heightened—they come as Horror, or a step beyond the abyss. But in *Something Wild*, the challenge is altogether human, humane, and deeply interesting. Jeff Daniels is our nerd—a nice guy named Charlie, decent but weak and fearful, conventional, yet a poet of action in his own shower. And then life becomes the shower. In the form of a "Lulu" (the name is emblematic and onomatopeic in cultural history), looking a little like Louise Brooks, and offering her Charlie not just "fun," but raptures that are exactly aligned with his repressed dreams. In other words, this Lulu is the phenomenon that Charlie has dreamed of but dreaded most of his life. And the film sinks in its big juicy hook for no better reason than that Melanie is intensely desirable and utterly direct—me, try me. What she offers is the obliteration of common sense—and in her clear urge to rape the camera, if necessary, she is an irresistible impulse.

But the real, inner cunning of this film—of the script by E. Max Frye, and Jonathan Demme's direction—is that as the runaway couple go into the hinterland (New Jersey and Pennsylvania), so Melanie slips back from Lulu to Audrey, sans wig, a more real, crushed woman with a very nasty menace in her life (in the form of Ray Liotta). And that's when Charlie has to learn what courage is really made of.

So, yes, there is a nice, cozy American moral (and morale) at the core of it all, and Charlie and Audrey will end up as the loves of their life, if that's what you want to believe. They will be happy together, and I'm not convinced that even the resources of Melanie can prevent a life so settled it may harden into rock, habit, and premature death. But Demme is plainly a kind man, not quite ready to grasp the surreal flame and risk being burned. Suppose Melanie remains wanton, depraved, the angel of death? Suppose Charlie's wild weekend restores him to a presettled family situation? Then *Something Wild* comes close to real horror—the idea that every mundane life in America could go mad.

As they say, it's a matter of taste. But even if you need to forgive the tidy ending here, there's no doubt about it: *Something Wild* is like an injection of some very powerful drug. You lose control, and inhabit the paradise of powerlessness. That's the movies. (And Margaret Colin is super.)

The Son of the Sheik (1926)

He was only thirty-one when he died. Filming *The Son of the Sheik* in the Yuma desert a few months earlier, he had complained of fatigue and a pain in his side. He was exhausted by his own success—he had made fourteen major films in the years since *The Four Horsemen of the Apocalypse* (1921). To this day, it is a matter of controversy how far he knew to look after himself, or let himself be pushed around by more powerful people. There were times when he looked older than his actual age. And even if he hadn't yet asked himself this question, the issue hovered—how was Valentino going to say lines like "I may not be the first victim, but by Allah I'll be the one you remember!" as he closed in on some patently Caucasian beauty posing as an Arab slave girl? If ever any great star faced the ridicule of being heard, it was Valentino, not John Gilbert—and not just because the voice might be high, sleepy, or too accented, but because the ethos of his lines and his screen character were so perilously archaic.

It was presumably because of that that Frances Marion had done a script for *The Son of the Sheik* that was clearly a parody of the original (made in 1921), even though it was adapted from a sequel novel by Edith Maude Hull. It was only when Paramount explained that Vilma Banky (a Rudy favorite) had been hired that a new script had to be written. This included the old sheik, Ahmed Ben Hassan, who had won Lady Diana five years earlier, and his son—in fact, Marion's first idea was for twin sons, but Valentino said he'd prefer to double up as father and son.

The studio got George Fitzmaurice to direct—for several years he was the man Valentino wanted. George Barnes did the photography. William Cameron Menzies was the art director and Hal Kern the editor. In the story, the father is a much older man, and Rudy apparently took delight in adding lines to his face and gray to his hair. But the son is our boy again, captured and tortured in one flagrantly masochistic sequence—he is strung up and whipped—and then the silent rapist in a classic scene that involves him and Yasmin (Banky) in a tent, with the ritual stripping of belt and knife and a lurid view of her eyes as he closes in. Fitzmaurice brings in the wind as a potent erotic force, and there is no denying the suggestiveness of the scene. But silence keeps it at a distance where there is no room for nuance or hint. There's no doubt it worked for female audiences, but the whole thing is on the brink of embarrassment. Four years later, eroticism had moved forward light-years to find the glances and the cryptic words of Dietrich and Cooper in *Morocco*.

But by the time *The Son of the Sheik* was in general release, the god was dead. On August 15, 1926, he was rushed to hospital with a ruptured appendix. On August 23 he died. A hundred thousand came to his lying in state at the funeral parlor. The new picture did extra good business, and it was easier at last to see that a curiosity had passed. He died in debt, but the income from the movies easily covered that up. And so it is that he is "known" still, if not always seen, the great lover and the secret pouf. He picked his moment.

Sophie's Choice (1982)

William Styron died this week (November 2006), and I suspect that many people were reminded of that long passage in the film of his *Sophie's Choice* in which Meryl Streep's white lace face presides over a dark background as she describes the occasion of her choice. How else would you film that moment? With Sophie in "real life," surrounded by mindless color and objects? Or as a voice-over? I ask these questions because I think something happened with the movie that was very far from the hopes of Styron, his careful director, Alan J. Pakula, or even the admirable Ms. Streep. The recollection of that moment at Auschwitz became a "scene," something enacted, something carefully considered, discussed, and played out—whereas, maybe, in life it could only be blurted out. I think what I am asking is whether a situation like the choice, in novel and movie, can be decently rendered in fiction without becoming an event, a great aria and a distancing of the reality in which our admiration of Ms. Streep (utterly deserved) confuses our response to Sophie Zawistowska.

I am not suggesting that things like the choice—and worse—did not occur. But I am not sure they can, or should be, made orderly, let alone beautiful—and the passage I have described is beautiful. There is a part of me—the Godardian part, perhaps—that would say simply have Ms. Streep pick up the text and read it in as flat a way as possible. The acting might be less—the reality might be more pointed.

It is something to think about in the course of a very moving picture, the story of a young writer, Stingo (Peter MacNicol), who meets a haunting couple, Sophie and Nathan Landau (Kevin Kline), lovers yet warring partners. Stingo comes to love them both, and as he does so the full story emerges—Sophie's trauma and Nathan's schizophrenic illness. Pakula wrote and directed this and produced it with Keith Barish, and it is an exemplary adaptation of a rather untidy novel. The Auschwitz scenes are extraordinary, yet they take us back to the problem discussed above that I think Nathan's illness may be the most frightening thing in the film. Why? Because it is more present, or more unsettled, I suppose. Film is less kind to the facts of the past. It likes to convert them into nostalgia but it tends to suggest that the facts do not matter because they are not now.

Some people say this is Pakula at his least effective—but it is foolish to ignore the extra ambition here. And just because Streep is "great" is no reason to blame her for being an actress. It could be said that Streep's intelligence already affords the chance for the unbearable to become manageable. Néstor Almendros shot the film wonderfully. George Jenkins did outstanding work on production design. And if it is seen rather seldom these days, it is not because anyone has forgotten what it is about or what it means. It stays in the culture, and it is that rarity: an American response to European experience.

Streep won the Oscar. That the film was not even nominated as Best Picture or for Best Director was not just monstrous, it was absurd. But I think too many people were too uneasy.

The Sopranos (1999–2007)

The first thing to be said is, Don't exaggerate your own fear of movies that run four hours, six, twelve, or twenty-four. After all, *The Sopranos* was eighty-six hours of film or story or screen time, drawn out over seven seasons and eight years, and at the end enough of us were watching and sliding off the sofa with screen-nearness-itis, desperate to see the ending first. And then, when blackness took over, there was a week nearly in which most talk was related to what that shutout had meant.

The next big point is here was a throwback: *The Sopranos* belongs to David Chase and HBO, but no one ever felt that it was "directed" except very tidily, thank you. There was a team of directors, and a team of writers: some were bigger names than others, but I really doubt that the greatest auteurists in the land could have identified uncredited episodes as coming from this person or that, Steve Buscemi or Tim van Patten. So the series honored the roots of television and factory filmmaking: it was the team that did it, and the team was the directors, the writers, and the cast of supporting actors. Week by week, integrity and eccentricity (consistency and originality) were as easily conveyed by the impulse of Tony Sirico or Edie Falco, or any of the others. Except that all those actors lived under a tyranny: Let me stay alive, Lord, from week to week and for the next season. And as befitted such a pressure, the skill and the cunning and the art of *The Sopranos* would be gripping from week to week.

The larger picture is another story. Some said *The Sopranos* was a great novel on TV—you should read those novels again. Frankly, I don't believe David Chase's assurance that it was all—just about—under control. If he thought that, he should have been fired. Eighty-six hours is a lot of story, but far too often the shapeliness of a great novel's design was gone. One day, I hope, we may get the inside story of the show, how Chase and HBO pondered the question of whether dramatic closure or syndication rights mattered most.

There was no closure in *The Sopranos*—though there had been in *The Godfather: Part II*, and that's why Coppola's six hours is a greater work of art. David Chase never quite made up his own mind about Tony Soprano's "I'm a good guy really," whereas Coppola knew the evil in Michael's heart. *The Godfather: Part III* is another, sadder story, not as bad as we thought at first, but too silly finally, and too nervous to grasp the only logical conclusion—Michael should go to Washington, not Rome, and we should see the resemblance of organized crime and our way of government.

But there's another problem: Great art, finally, concerns people of true nobility who nurse a flaw—the old models of tragedy are not just a myth. Story needs them. Long before the end, I fear, both Tony and James Gandolfini were bores—characters of an innately supporting nature who do not know or feel or aspire to enough to match their America. Michael Corleone is a great character in that we see his flaw grow from momentary impulse to obliterating disease. In the last analysis, *The Sopranos* occupied eighty-six hours; it did not turn them into great theater. *The Godfather* plays every year. *The Sopranos* in reruns will bore you.

The Sound of Music (1965)

For years, in the summertime, when newspapers had nothing to write about, they might cobble up stories about how many times a serial killer in Duluth had seen *The Sound of Music.* No, I'm kidding you, it was never a serial killer, though here and now I would like to propose a movie—it could be called *My Favorite Things*—in which some provincial woman has just two things in her life: seeing *The Sound of Music,* and killing off elderly patients in the nursing home where she works. I see it as a vehicle for Reese Witherspoon (the wonderful shocker from *Freeway,* but still capable of going blonde and pink when she's comforting the frail before she kills them). She is, of course, a mistress of trivia on the great show and film, and she has a way of singing "Climb Ev'ry Mountain" under her breath as she smothers her patients.

Yes, you're right: I am a very sick, vicious old man, but writing a thousand of these little recommendations can drive you crazy, especially when I come to a picture that I loathe but which—unquestionably—has to be in the book, if only because millions of the stupid and aggrieved will write in to the publisher, "Where was *The Sound of Music*?" if it is not. It is here.

I can believe that coach parties of out-of-towners kept *The Sound of Music* going for 1,443 performances after its Broadway opening in 1959—that, and its very pretty view of the Second World War as just a young nun, some sweet children, and the coming of the Nazis. It was Rodgers and Hammerstein, their last work together, with a book by Howard Lindsay and Russel Crouse derived from a work named *The Story of the Trapp Family Singers.* Some names fit.

Onstage, Mary Martin had played Maria at the age of forty-five—which rather shows how close the delight in musicals is to spiritual or irrational experience. The movie was the second collaboration of producer-director Robert Wise and screenwriter Ernest Lehman—they had killed *West Side Story* a few years earlier, which was a more serious crime than making *The Sound of Music,* because the latter had always been brain-dead.

There is that opening shot, with the camera hurtling in toward the outspread arms of Julie Andrews. But instead of a messy collision, her young plum voice breaks out in "The hills are alive." It goes on for 174 minutes, photography by Ted McCord, art direction by Boris Leven. Though dubbed (in "Edelweiss"), Christopher Plummer is caught between heavy boredom and the apparently serious urge to start kicking some of the children. He is having a terrible time, but somehow or other he must have signed a contract.

It won Best Picture, a second directing Oscar for Wise, and five Oscars altogether for ten nominations. In its initial rentals, it earned $72 million and took over the position of the most successful film of all time. *The Godfather* surpassed it in 1972—which reminds me of the proximity of this sort of rubbish and a murderous response.

Sparrows (1926)

Sparrows is still a picture that could frighten young children and anyone thinking of going to the South for a holiday. Deep in the swamps, old Grimes (Gustav von Seyffertitz) runs a baby farm—he takes in kidnapped children and then reckons to sell them off to fresh, unknowing parents. The setup is Dickensian, with Mama Molly (Mary Pickford) looking after seven children in a hovel surrounded by quicksand and crocodile swamps. And Molly is something to behold: In 1926, Mary was thirty-three, yet she looks less than five feet tall and in long shots you'd guess she was fifteen. In close-ups, she's older, but you wonder less about that than about how she has found not just a makeup salon in the swamp but a place where they can braid her pigtails every morning.

These inconsistencies don't matter. Written by C. Gardner Sullivan and directed by William Beaudine, this is a robust melodrama that leaves Griffith looking a little genteel. Mary looks great because she's the star and the heroine and because being so pretty is the sign that she hasn't given in yet—her glamour is hope, darn it. (That's why Warren Beatty is so cute in *Bonnie and Clyde*. He's good-looking because he's looking forward to things!) And Molly's dazzle would be more easily mocked or attacked if the film's situation weren't so authentically scary and nasty. Make no mistake, this view of the South is a breeding ground for all those Texas Chainsaw pictures and the films where pretty white girls get put in a Southern jail and—please don't ask!

In other words, give great credit to Beaudine, and to Mary the showwoman, for she was the driving force on these films, and she made sure they worked. Like hiring Charles Rosher, Karl Struss, and Hal Mohr to make the swamp look nasty and her look good. Moreover, when Mary and the little ones escape from the Grimes place and make a perilous journey through the swamp to civilization, you are left in no doubt at all that Charles Laughton saw *Sparrows* as he prepared *Night of the Hunter*.

And in 1926, this kind of stuff was believed. There were reports of such baby farms in the metropolitan press. There is even a scene with a ladder at a window where my wife and I burst out in unison with "Lindbergh!" As for Mary, she acts hard—a bit too hard maybe. She has a notion here of a country girl and she has an antic way of moving and dancing. Of course, she's endearing—and of course, she could still play a child in 1926 (like Pollyanna). But all you have to remember is that she was probably the richest woman in town already. Don't forget, too, that her father died when she was five so that Gladys Smith was left to help her mother raise a handful of children. The "sparrows" are the children, of course, and nothing is spared when it comes to their prettiness or their tears. But that was Mary's style—why spare a thing?

Spartacus (1960)

From the outset, *Spartacus* was a Kirk Douglas picture. At an early script reading, Laurence Olivier appeared in a three-piece suit, Peter Ustinov wore a summer suit. Charles Laughton came in a bathrobe. Whereupon Kirk appeared in sandals and a short leather skirt, brandishing a gladiator's sword. The British contingent started giggling, and Kirk knew what it was to be a revolting slave who still owned the picture.

There were other ironies in the name of freedom along the way. Owning the rights to Howard Fast's novel about the slave rebellion, Kirk heard that Anthony Quinn and Yul Brynner had a gladiator project under way, too. So Kirk pushed his budget so high that the other production got scared. They offered to amalgamate. Kirk demanded, and got, unconditional surrender. He also gave the screenplay assignment to Dalton Trumbo (with credit), thus helping to break the blacklist. Anthony Mann was the director (hired by Universal), and he did a couple of weeks (the gladiator school—with characteristic precision) before Kirk lost his temper at Mann's suggestions that Kirk was overacting. Instead, he hired in Stanley Kubrick, who was eager to satisfy his contractual commitment to Kirk after doing *Paths of Glory*. In addition, Kubrick, like Trumbo, came fairly cheap, and on a $12 million budget, Kirk was said to be looking for fat to trim.

Kubrick handled himself warily on the picture and never dared to encourage the suggestion that it was not Kirk's baby. But he could see the script was heavy and inert, and he began to give more of his time to the supporting cast (Woody Strode is very good, Tony Curtis is cute, and Olivier is like a snake). He dumped the unknown actress cast as Spartacus's wife and hired in Jean Simmons, who had refused it earlier and now went through the motions with tongue in cheek—sometimes she seems to smile at the camera as if hoping others are getting the joke.

Russell Metty did the camerawork and became increasingly bad-tempered with the boy genius director. A lot of it was filmed in America—the gladiator school is in Death Valley and the open-air pool is at San Simeon. But the battles were done in Spain—and they were expensive. Many crosses were required for the crucifixions. You can put a lot of this down to Kirk's monomania. But Hollywood, California, was never the culture that was going to do the story of a slave revolt and the loss of patrician privilege with relish. Neither the script nor the film comes to terms with this anomaly, or traces the real ambiguities of citizenship and slavery.

It is 184 minutes, and it had rentals of just over $14 million. Moreover, it came out in the season of John Wayne's *The Alamo,* and Kirk and the Duke were each determined they had made the best epic and launched devout Oscar campaigns in which much was made of the freedom of Texas and the freeing of the slaves. Neither film did well (though Peter Ustinov did win the Supporting Actor Oscar for his slave dealer). I suspect that a 45-minute documentary with Olivier, Laughton, and Ustinov telling stories of the film would still be a classic.

Spellbound (1945)

Spellbound is one of the most expensive vanity pictures ever made in America. The producer, David O. Selznick, was in a deep depression. There were disputes over why. He had killed his own desire by winning Best Picture twice in a row, with *Gone With the Wind* and *Rebecca*; he was in dire confusion over the state of his marriage and whether he really loved his discovery, "Jennifer Jones"; he was a manic-depressive waiting to hit a new low; he was dismayed that he could not help the "war effort." So he started seeing a practitioner, a woman named May Romm—who ends up with a credit, "psychiatric adviser," on *Spellbound*. In turn, she was rebuked by her professional associations for lending her name to such a fraudulent and witless treatment of psychiatry.

Of course, in the early and mid-1940s, stories with psychological content were hot in Hollywood, and in no small part that was due to the rise of psychiatry in the community—a development aided by the number of qualified people fleeing Austria and Germany. The real part that movement played in these films and in film noir is a fascinating subject.

Selznick jumped on the bandwagon but never bothered to ask how it functioned. So he got Ben Hecht (also a willing patient and a robust neurotic) to fashion a story from Francis Beeding's novel, *The House of Dr. Edwardes*. You won't believe it, but this is the story: Dr. Constance Petersen (Ingrid Bergman) works at a lunatic asylum. Dr. Murchison (Leo G. Carroll) is retiring as director. His replacement is Dr. Edwardes (Gregory Peck). No one notices anything untoward. Constance falls in love with him, and realizes he is a fake—he is, in fact, a mental patient himself. He thinks he killed Dr. Edwardes. We wonder, too. But Constance treats him according to the best therapy available—a lot of talk and some powerful kissing—and sets him straight. And us. The real villain was . . .

It says a lot for the skills of Hecht and Alfred Hitchcock, and for the beauty of Peck and Bergman together, that thousands of viewers did not start screaming and hold out their arms for a straitjacket (like the father in *The Conformist*). In fact, in 1945, the public seems to have swallowed the gibberish whole. It was nominated for six Oscars (including Best Picture)—it won for Miklós Rózsa's score (using the wail of a theremin).

Hitch had the good sense to break it down as a piece of nonsense with great scenes—and so it endures. The doors opening on other doors; the long tracking shot fixed on a razor in Peck's hands; the motif of lines on a white surface; and—notoriously—the Salvador Dalí dream sequence. Not all of that was allowed in the film (Hitch may have been jealous), and of course it is burdened by explanations. Hitch did dream sequences very well—he called them real life. And that is where *Spellbound* collapses. It has very little reality. Psychiatry survived, but May Romm never let her name be used on another film.

The Spirit of the Beehive (1973)

In a village called Hoyuelos, near Segovia, in 1940, two young girls, sisters, see James Whale's film, *Frankenstein*. They are Ana (Ana Torrent) and Isabel (Isabel Tellería), and people tell you in advance that *The Spirit of the Beehive* is extraordinary because of Ana Torrent, who was maybe six when the film was shot. And she is extraordinary, but only in the way of the whole film that allows an equal performance from Isabel Tellería as her older sister.

The country is flat near Hoyuelos, the buildings are sparse and simple. But the wind blows across the bleak fields. There is a well, and no child can know how deep its water goes. Their father keeps a beehive, and he writes out passages from Maeterlinck's *Life of the Bee*, as if trying to digest them or use them as a diving-off point into the black well water of a new book on bees. The family lives in a large but quite empty house where everything is like a magic breath on the embers of memory or metaphor. The bees struggle in their mysterious task. The mother, Teresa, writes letters that have no answer. Ana looks at photographs of her parents when they were young. Isabel tells Ana that the monster in *Frankenstein* is not dead. That sort of death is simply something they do in movies—the way one day Isabel pretends to be dead to frighten Ana. And Ana believes she will see the monster—though it will come as no surprise that when he appears he is gentle and sad. Ana has watched the scene in Whale's film where the monster and the little girl sit for a moment beside the lake.

Victor Erice films with a simplicity that matches the land near Hoyuelos, and yet after twenty minutes or so of this beautiful, grave film you know that every image is shot through with—let's call it "spirit." When the children set a small bonfire and jump through the flames, they are angels or demons. When Isabel is scratched by the cat, she puts blood on her lips like lipstick, like a femme fatale. When a deserting soldier hides in the barn, he is a harbinger of the monster appearing.

You could say that Erice has found a way of shooting—severe, yet without bottom—that is like the tremendous appetite of the two children for fantasy or storytelling. Yet one might discover in closer inquiry that this film, made at the end of Franco's life, and set in 1940, has many buried meanings about a country and its monstrousness. Enough for a burial ground.

You could argue, I suppose, that this is Spanish, a cultural attitude where these depths are more accessible if only because amid tyranny the people live on the brink of spirit, too. But you realize, too, how in America "spirit" has become a glib, empty word. We have to go as far as hideous horror to reach it, Erice has only to turn his head to see it. You could place Erice in Buñuel's line, though Erice seems content to be rural, mysterious, and childlike. Indeed, you feel he is drawn to Ana like a bee to the hive. But I think you could watch this film for years and have its possibilities grow larger all the time.

Splendor in the Grass (1961)

William Inge had his season of influence, and it lasted from *Come Back, Little Sheba* to *All Fall Down*, with *Picnic*, *Bus Stop*, and *Splendor in the Grass* included. His subject was the emotional and sexual repression in the American heartland. Nobody at this period complained of sexual repression in Warren Beatty, but his very handsome aggrieved look was important to Inge. They were friends. Beatty is the star of *All Fall Down* and *Splendor*, and his one stage performance was in Inge's play *A Loss of Roses*, which became the movie *The Stripper*.

Splendor in the Grass may be the most satisfying movie (as a whole) drawn from Inge, and I think that has to do with the authority and candor of Elia Kazan, and from the way actors could nearly scent the end of censorship in the air. There are "nude" shots of Natalie Wood in this film—they are not quite that, but we feel we have seen her naked—and in 1961 they were urgently required if only to say, Girls like her want sex and this is what it is going to look like. Kazan uses water in the film—and uses it brilliantly—as an old-fashioned metaphor for sex. But it can't help our craving: Let those two kids get at each other. Kazan and Inge met when Kazan directed Inge's play *The Dark at the Top of the Stairs*. In the course of that work, Inge told him the story in *Splendor*. Inge wrote it as a story. Kazan turned that into a script. And then Inge did some doctoring. Boris Kaufman did the photography (his first film in color). Richard Sylbert did magnificent work on production design—for this is a film about staid, deadening interiors and houses. Anna Hill Johnstone did the costumes: David Amram wrote the music.

It was Beatty's screen debut, and he is edgy, smouldering, and smart, but truly this was Natalie Wood's vehicle, and she is absorbing as the girl who goes mad from not having sex. She was nominated for an Oscar and lost to Sophia Loren in *Two Women*. She was never again as good, or as central to a movie. Of course, she and Beatty very soon were having a good deal of sex, and Wood was not a slow starter. But in many actors there is a superb yearning for sexual glory (or splendor) no matter how many times they have it. In all those senses, this was a very happy teaming and one that Kazan surely understood.

There are several very fine supporting performances, not least Barbara Loden as Beatty's sister—she would become Kazan's wife, so the director could score, too; Pat Hingle as his father; and a radiant but nervy Zohra Lampert as his wife. The cast also includes Gary Lockwood, Sandy Dennis, Lynn Loring, John McGovern (as the shrink), Phyllis Diller as Texas Guinan, and William Inge himself as the clergyman.

The Spy Who Came In from the Cold (1965)

Just a few years after the great splash of James Bond on the screen, here is an attempt to argue that international espionage is a grievous and hurtful business—one better served by the eternally wounded look of Richard Burton than by the cocksure smirk of Sean Connery. It's worth noting that John le Carré's novel—pessimistic in every way—was faithfully served by the screenplay of Paul Dehn and Guy Trosper. Yet Dehn had already been one of the screenwriters on *Goldfinger*.

It's a story of intrigue and intricate double cross, and of an attempt to discredit a Communist spy that goes wrong. When that burden is finally delivered it falls not just on Burton (one of the guiltiest of actors), but on Claire Bloom as his none-too-bright mistress. There is a set-piece scene of an investigative tribunal in Berlin (with Beatrix Lehmann as its head) in which the crushed anguish in Bloom and Burton (lovers in life) is very touching and in which the Le Carré message—of real lives being bandied about in espionage schemes—is fully delivered.

In many other cases, the cinema has not been able to resist a kind of humor in the espionage situation—of agile minds turning themselves inside out to do the double double cross first. Even in *The Russia House*, a touching love story, the scenes at the various intelligence headquarters are played in part for satire. But here, as in the later television adaptation of the George Smiley series, lives are broken and the girl is calmly shot in the rigged escape sequence.

Martin Ritt is not really the director one would have picked for this game of poker. Ritt liked to believe in trust and fellowship, and here the film really requires a level of mistrust that is closer to the gaze of Alan J. Pakula. So Ritt deserves high praise. He does not let the venture down, even if he might be accused of missing some of the English nuancing in the talk. A lot of help comes from the sunless black-and-white photography of Ossie Morris, culminating in a harsh Berlin wasteland where scathing searchlights make their tours of duty.

Burton and Bloom are very good as sacrificial victims, but the cast is richly endowed with supporting players: Oskar Werner is a Communist official whose arrogance is his undoing; Peter van Eyck uses his vulcanized baby face to excellent effect; and the shabby plausibility of British intelligence includes Michael Hordern, Bernard Lee, Robert Hardy, Rupert Davies, and an icy Cyril Cusack as Control. In the end, there's something clammy or narrowly depressive about this film, but still it seems an accurate portrait of the real compromises and nastiness in such work. It's a film that could encourage no one to enter that tricky service, and it offers a gallery of bleak cynics and broken people enough to make 007 curl up and die.

Burton was nominated for the Best Actor Oscar, but of course, the look of mortification on his face was specially sharpened by his experience of nomination and rejection.

Stagecoach (1939)

John Ford had not made a Western since 1926—the genre had fallen away as a source of A pictures in the 1930s. But it was restored to dignity by Ford's *Stagecoach*, which crams everyone and every last little thing in, epic adventure and social commentary, including public transport running across Monument Valley. In the real America, that has not come to pass yet, though tour buses come and go and the guides have to explain that the Apaches from *Stagecoach* are actually Navajo.

Someone drew Ford's attention to a magazine story, "Stage to Lordsburg," by Ernest Haycox (Lordsburg is in southern Arizona). No one is sure when Ford was reminded of Guy de Maupassant's story "Boule de Suif," in which a whore sleeps with a Prussian officer to ensure the safety of other travelers. But Ford had a notion of making the first Technicolor Western (working with Merian C. Cooper). Then there was a threat that Selznick might produce it. All of these things fell through, but Ford ended up with a Dudley Nichols script that he loved, and an arrangement to make it for Walter Wanger Productions.

They shot some of it in Monument Valley (being sold on the place by pictures sent from the Goulding family, who would build a lodge there), but the big Indian chase scenes were done on a dry lake bed in the Mojave (again, not a site for regular transport routes). That is where Yakima Canutt did his stunts, jumping from the coach to the line of horses; and then, as an Indian, falling from a lead horse and being dragged all the way under the coach on the ground. The chase scenes are very effective if a little stupid on the part of the Apache—they chase until they are shot, without another strategy.

The real function of the film for Ford was to present a cross-section of a hypocritical society that seems oblivious to the space, the wildness, and the new country. These are people secure in their greed and their bigotry. Thus, the Ringo Kid (John Wayne), the outlaw who seeks redemption, is not just the most natural American, but the one whose eye, skills, and character have become most attuned to the open spaces. He is a proper hero, and the film delights in the hope that he and Dallas, the hooker, may be "saved from the blessings of civilization."

Ford took some relish in saying it was a film about a coachload of rascals, but there's a clear, if not underlined, hierarchy of respect: he likes Ringo and Dallas (Claire Trevor); he admires the drunken Doc Boone (Thomas Mitchell); he feels nostalgia for the cavalry wife (Louise Platt), who happens to be very pregnant, and the Southern gent gambler (John Carradine). But the businessmen are despised—Donald Meek, Berton Churchill—while there's a knowing fondness for the pros, the sheriff (George Bancroft) and the driver (Andy Devine).

Ford needled Wayne from start to finish (the star was also the lowest-paid lead on the movie), but the picture changed the actor's status. *Stagecoach* did good business and it was nominated for Best Picture. Thomas Mitchell won an Oscar as Supporting Actor. Indeed, everyone is a supporting player, embalmed in a marinade of cliché.

Stage Door (1937)

As James Harvey puts it (his five pages on *Stage Door* in *Romantic Comedy in Hollywood* are bankable), the film "is like going to wisecrack heaven." It's one of those perfect American films where as little happens as possible but people (i.e., female people, here) simply exist and talk and give off a beguiling, dense air of gloomy pleasure. All the girls who live at the Footlights Club and who burn to get into theater complain about the place. Yet that's all they want to do. It's only when Terry Randall Sims (Katharine Hepburn) comes in sight and starts rhapsodizing over the dump that you realize how gauche she is. She's like a John Ford woman set down in a Howard Hawks dormitory.

It was a play by George S. Kaufman and Edna Ferber that opened in 1936, with Margaret Sullavan as Terry. Kaufman believed the movie was superior because it had less romantic action with men, and a stronger sense of the wisecracking sisterhood. Above all, the movie is the clash between Hepburn, in that airy loftiness the audience was beginning to hate, and Ginger Rogers, as the smartest tongue of the crowd and the stinging cold water on every dumb gesture toward altruism or high sentiment that Terry can muster. That Ginger had been in sight since at least *42nd Street*, but here she is one of the funniest women in American film, as edgy and sneering as Bogart—they might have been OK together. It's a useful reminder that that utterly meek, following girl in Fred Astaire's arms could give a lot better than she got.

The movie had quite a few changes for the good as it was written by Morrie Ryskind and Anthony Veiller (they got an Oscar nod), and then the whole thing was given to Gregory La Cava. Which is a way of saying that La Cava probably deserves to be numbered with the most proficient of American directors. The wiser and more wisecracking La Cava's material became, the better he was as a director. He did what little was needed to fuel the rivalry (aka dislike) between Hepburn and Rogers, and he was a master of sustained group compositions in which gossip, a piece of clothing, or the idea of a good dinner can bring female minds alive. Yes, of course, the talk is tip-top, but the ability to let talk fly by and seem like life is something that only a few could pull off.

And enough people understood the fabulous trick: *Stage Door* was nominated for Best Picture and La Cava got a nod for himself. So did Andrea Leeds, who plays probably the sappiest part in the outfit. Never mind, with Rogers and Hepburn doing Flynn and Rathbone while sitting down, this is pure entertainment and probably as fine a show of feminist glory as you'll find. Also with Adolphe Menjou, Gail Patrick (a La Cava favorite), Constance Collier, Lucille Ball (whatever happened to her?), Eve Arden (magnificent), Ann Miller, Ralph Forbes, Franklin Pangborn, and Jack Carson.

Stalker (1979)

In the late 1970s, though it was rusty, porous, and dilapidated in so many places, the Iron Curtain still stood, so it was possible to take Andrei Tarkovsky's *Stalker* as an immense, obscure meditation on strictures on freedom. Some said the film was so difficult to elucidate so that it would exhaust the patience of censors. But today, the Curtain is folded away for future use and one is left to recognize how far *Stalker*—despite its enormous metaphorical reach—simply reflects the appearance of decay, of chaos, of seepage, a universal malaise. Indeed, the rising moisture in Tarkovsky's work could even be the prospect of some flood set off by global warming. It is hardly the case that this situation, or its characters, are merely Russian, even if Tarkovsky the artist takes us back to the traditions of Dostoyevsky, and the great poets of Russian art, from Dovzhenko to Andrei Rublev.

His world is one of desolation, ruin, and breakdown. Nearly all structures are destroyed, abandoned, and repossessed. Thus, "home" has become a very unreliable concept. It is said that somewhere in the center of the world, a great meteor has landed and left a "Zone" which is guarded by police. Yet no one really knows why, or what the Zone holds.

The action of this very gradual, ruminative, 161-minute film is that of the Stalker (Aleksandr Kajdanovsky) taking two men, a Writer (Anatoli Solonitsin) and a Professor (Nikolai Grinko), toward the Zone. They argue and dispute over the right way there, over what may be there, and whether it is worth going. You can argue that the quest is as extensive and muddled as life itself, beset by the everyday doubts and neuroses of anyone who has ever sought to search for anything. As they reach the Room, or what may be the Room, the Professor says he has a bomb to destroy it. The Writer declines to enter the Room, as if afraid of what it will reveal about his inner desires. The Stalker wonders if anyone else can ever share his faith in the Room.

So what seemed in 1979 like a model of totalitarianism in decline may now be seen as liberty in tatters. Tarkovsky had reached a rare eminence at his death in 1986—he was only fifty-four and his intense spirituality, his immersion in beauty, and his tendency toward a lack of humor had raised him to a pinnacle of poetic or noncommercial cinema. It still remains to be seen where he will stand as film grows older. But he is a strange mixture of Eisenstein and Bergman (and very conscious of those twin traditions). His great films are as absorbing as any made—and I use that word advisedly—in that the feeling of all things moving slowly toward liquid is as powerful as it is creepy. It may be that the Room—if you ever get there—is an infinite, if dank, enclosure in which an uncertain number of strangers are watching the works of Andrei Tarkovsky. Equally, it may be that as malfunction of one kind or another covers the world, we may have a hard time distinguishing the Room, the Zone, and the local multiplex. For myself, I am in awe of the power—yet I have an itch to see Bob Hope playing the Stalker.

A Star Is Born (1937)

The legend is that *A Star Is Born* was made by a man, David O. Selznick, who so loved Hollywood, or who was so captivated by its romance, that just a few years after a movie full of warnings and unexpectedly dark views of lasting fame in pictures, he virtually reenacted its story by discovering a star of his own—he renamed Phyllis Isley Jennifer Jones, just as this movie takes Esther Blodgett and makes her Vicki Lester—and then slowly succumbed under the great burden of his "mistake." For every star turned on, another has to be turned off.

Of course, *A Star Is Born* was heavily indebted to Selznick's earlier *What Price Hollywood?*, where Constance Bennett was the discovery, and it was a collecting place for many rueful anecdotes about Hollywood history (its generosity and its cruelty).

The screenplay was credited to Dorothy Parker, Alan Campbell, and Robert Carson, from a story by Carson and William Wellman, but when Wellman got his Oscar for the story he admitted that really Selznick deserved his name on the prize. Furthermore, we know that such apprentices as Ring Lardner, Jr., and Budd Schulberg had a hand in it here and there. Howard Greene handled the Technicolor photography, and to this day footage from the movie is used as "documentary" material on Hollywood in its golden age. Lyle Wheeler did the art direction. Max Steiner wrote the music. And William Wellman brought energy and fatalism to the directing.

So Esther (Janet Gaynor), from the sticks, comes to town, longing to be in pictures. And she rescues a falling star, Norman Maine (Fredric March), from undue embarrassment when he is drunk. In turn, Maine takes her up, as discovery and then as love-mate. They marry, thus infuriating the studio publicist, Matt Libby (Lionel Stander), but as "Vicki" rises so Norman sinks deeper into alcohol. The benign studio boss, Oliver Niles (Adolphe Menjou—Oliver was the O. in Selznick's name), cannot save Norman. He walks off into the Pacific, like Captain Oates walking into the snow in 1912.

When the film was made, Gaynor was thirty-one and March forty—so he still seems in his prime, while she feels a bit too mature to be the ingenue. And Hollywood has not yet cast the film as its script requires: with a real newcomer. Gaynor is pretty, plucky, and very adept at the teary stuff, but really Maine is the great part and March has several very powerful scenes, not least those in the sanatorium where he seems to have seen his own future all too clearly. Stander is excellent as Libby, and this was one of the first times the key studio role of publicist had been properly identified. Menjou is smooth and not very believable. The cast also includes May Robson, Andy Devine, Edgar Kennedy, and Owen Moore. It was nominated for Best Picture and there were further Oscar nominations for Wellman, Gaynor, and March. Of course, "Vicki" wins an Oscar in the picture and announces herself as "Mrs. Norman Maine."

A Star Is Born (1954)

Long before the loving attempt at restoration made by Ron Haver, *A Star Is Born* was a curiously fragmented work—or something that didn't really fit its own title. This is not all bad, for there is a magical warmth between Judy Garland and James Mason in that he was a characteristic professional, happy to do anything to help her, while she will always be one of Hollywood's great self-inflicted crack-ups. So the effort to present "Vicki Lester" as an ingenue, as a star who might be born, is close to absurd. It's not just that Garland was thirty-two when the film was made. It's more that she looks overweight much of the time, puffy and rather used. This is patently someone at the end of a seventeen-year career that swallowed her childhood and exhausted many of us. It's not just what the public knew—it's what we see and feel. This is to say nothing of the imperfections of WarnerColor and the fact that cameraman Sam Leavitt was a strange choice for a film that needed glamour.

This labor of love was produced by Sid Luft, who was Garland's husband at the time—but this choice of material hardly gives one confidence in Luft's judgment. On the other hand, I wonder if the kindness of George Cukor and his steady encouragement of the insecure was ever better used. Cukor has a host of great performances to his credit, but in this case Garland and Mason are clinging to the wreck of a film, and Mason—I think—is enchanting (he lost the Oscar to Marlon Brando in *On the Waterfront,* which is not really a fair contest).

Even more problematic is the silly story, the reluctance to update it since the 1937 version or to admit the reality in Garland's presence. Moss Hart's screenplay is faithful to the original (a work of many hands, but credited to Dorothy Parker, Alan Campbell, and Robert Carson). This is a sappy view of Hollywood both in its view of lucky starlets and in its load of studio cruelty—all of which comes from Jack Carson's nasty publicist, Matt Libby, and none from studio boss, Oliver Niles (Charles Bickford). In 1954, four years after *Sunset Blvd.*, surely we deserved a studio setup where the publicist did what the boss ordered.

The film was 181 minutes as it opened and then it was cut to 154. The Haver restoration (using stills for lost scenes) is 170 minutes and a work of terrific scholarship and even greater love of the project—but still it's a mess. The "Born in a Trunk" number is garish and chaotic. On the other hand, the routine for "The Man That Got Away" (music and lyrics by Harold Arlen and Ira Gershwin) is among the finest musical numbers ever filmed. If it were all we had left of the whole venture, it would be enough. In the age of video we are at liberty to watch the scene over and over again, to exult in the smashing precision to Judy's emotionalism and to behold the ravished delight in Mason at getting to see such a thing.

The Stars Look Down (1939)

Those who regard John Ford's *How Green Was My Valley* (1941) so highly have probably never seen Carol Reed's *The Stars Look Down*. As a matter of fact, John Ford had seen Reed's film, and he apparently bought up a lot of its stock footage to use it in back projections and so forth. He should have tried to acquire much more.

Reviewing the film when it came out, Graham Greene thought it compared favorably with Pabst's *Kameradschaft,* and he felt that *The Stars Look Down* might be the best film Britain had made yet. It was taken from A. J. Cronin's novel, set in the Welsh mines where Cronin had been a medical inspector, published in 1935, which was an earnest plea for the nationalization of the mining industry (something accomplished only by the Labour government of 1945).

The rights for the film were bought by a new company, Grand National, with some money put up by holiday-camp pioneer Billy Butlin, and Carol Reed would be loaned out from Gainsborough. A budget of £100,000 was agreed on. The script for the film was done by J. B. Williams.

Michael Redgrave had been cast in the central role of Davey Fenwick, a man from a mining family who seeks education and a life above ground, but who returns from university to support his father's strike. Redgrave and a crew went off to Workington in Cumberland to film at a mine and in the miners' village. Redgrave went down into the pit and worked a drill, and designer Jim Carter took elaborate notes with a view to reconstructing the miners' village at Twickenham (the biggest set yet made for a British film). They also imported tons of coal and coal dust and a team of pit ponies. The photography was by Mutz Greenbaum and Henry Harris.

Margaret Lockwood was uncertain at first about playing Jenny, the girlfriend who decides to get herself a rich husband, but Carol Reed was close enough to the actress to persuade her to sign on. You can argue that the attempt at realism was partial, and it's true that Reed liked actors enough to want faces that stood out from the crowd. But that gap aside, his picture has nothing like the sentimentality of the Ford movie, and it is founded in a far tougher approach to the necessary development of mining. Also, the tragedy at the mine in *The Stars Look Down* is more natural, more right historically, and far less maudlin. The British were once a little ashamed of their cut-price social realism, and its documentary quality, but if you look at *The Stars Look Down* and *How Green Was My Valley,* it's often a matter of preferring overcast to the sunniest days the Welsh mountains ever knew.

The film was just finished as war broke out, and there was a feeling at first that it would be too depressing. But the wartime audience was ready to grow up, and the film was very well received. The rest of the cast includes Emlyn Williams, Edward Rigby, Cecil Parker, Nancy Price, Linden Travers, Allan Jeayes, and Milton Rosmer.

Star Wars (1977)

In 1979, when some innocence could still be excused, Michael Pye and Lynda Myles wrote, "*Star Wars* has been taken with ominous seriousness. It should not be. The single strongest impression it leaves is of another great American tradition that involves lights, bells, obstacles, menace, action, technology, and thrills. It is pinball on a cosmic scale." For me, it is also the line in the sand, the disastrous event, never mind its high, good, boyish intentions.

George Lucas had ample reason to be wary of Hollywood. *THX-1138* (still his most personal movie) had been a disaster. The success of *American Graffiti* had come despite gloomy predictions and stupidity from studio executives. Lucas was close to broke and determined to get his own back.

Lucas wrote a treatment for *Star Wars* in 1973. It was turned down by Universal and United Artists, but Fox bought it (for $10,000 down). A budget was agreed of $10 million ($3.9 million of which was to cover special effects). A sum of $750,000 covered the contributions of Lucas, his producer, Gary Kurtz, and all the leading players (though Sir Alec Guinness had 2.25 percent of the profits). In his best moments, Lucas reckoned the film could earn domestic rentals of up to $25 million. He had a trump card: In the negotiations with Fox, he had retained the major power of merchandising connected with the film, and the similar power over sequels. An empire was being formed in his mind, and this contract with Fox is among the seminal documents in film history.

The film was made, and it went one million dollars over budget. Fox was bemused by the picture, but by December 1980, it had a worldwide gross of $510 million. Half of that went to exhibitors. Fox took about $160 million. Lucas, Kurtz, and a few others shared $55 million. Guinness had $3.3 million. And the profits from the toys, the merchandising, the souvenirs, went largely to Lucas.

Of course, those numbers have built steadily in the twenty-five years since with video, television, DVD, boxed sets, and so on. And with a remorselessness that seemed to pain George as much as it did his followers, the original plan was enforced. It speaks weirdly to his narrative sense, perhaps, but the first film was really part 4 of a six-part series. And so the sequels came: *The Empire Strikes Back* (1980, Irvin Kershner), which introduced Yoda (the most appealing figure in the series), and *Return of the Jedi* (1983, Richard Marquand).

That trio had all done very well—*The Empire Strikes Back* had a world gross of $538 million and *Return of the Jedi* took $475 million. Nearly a decade passed. Lucas invested more in Industrial Light and Magic, the company he had set up for special effects work, and surely in time these special effects became less special than the staple diet of film. In that process, photography itself was eclipsed by digitally generated imagery.

The narrative, cinematic value of the three films so far was slight. Yoda was cute. Harrison Ford and Carrie Fisher had their moments, and it was like Saturday morning movies and pinball—but so is pinball like pinball. But then Lucas rallied himself and personally delivered the three films as promised: *The Phantom Menace* (1999), *Attack of the Clones* (2002), and *Revenge of the Sith* (2005).

The return of Lucas as director promised authorship, but audiences recoiled from the coldness of the later films and the waste of good actors. Even the fun was gone. The numbers were not the same: *Clones* cost $120 million and grossed $310 million; *Sith* cost $113 million and grossed $380 million. The films were desertlike in that time and space made a common nullity, a place where no light falls.

Stavisky (1974)

When *Stavisky* opened in Paris, there were attempts made by Stavisky's heirs to block the movie. The tribunal that examined the matter said there was no malice or damage in the film—rather, it was a "rehabilitation." I think that's the way any viewer ignorant of the case (which is to say, nearly everyone outside France) will view it. Stavisky is an adventurer, and he is Jean-Paul Belmondo, still attractive, raffish, but obsessed with ruin. As Alain Resnais put it, "What did interest us was the man's personality: on one hand, an enormous generosity, a theatricality, a strong life impulse; and on the other, an almost inexorable thrust toward death. I have always been interested in the functioning of the human brain. Especially when there seem to be two very contradictory impulses warring within the same mind, as in the case of Serge Alexandre."

Serge Stavisky (1886–1934) was a Russian, born in Slobodka, who came to France when he was thirteen. He turned into an impresario and a speculator and a con man, and in the end there was an immense scandal in France at his fall and at the sums of money that were lost. Finally, he shot himself. Or is it possible that others killed him? For the scandal had affected many powerful people. *Stavisky* did poor business in France, perhaps because so many were still owed money by his firms.

Jorge Semprún had been asked to write a screenplay before Resnais was considered as a director. But the two men had worked together before, and they fell into a fruitful collaboration in which Stavisky would be seen both through his own eyes and as he appeared to others. So he shifts in the film from romantic to drab, from adventurous to irresponsible. It's a strong story line (and Resnais and Semprún kept to the facts as best they could), but it is a story with an overall attempt to show a whole era ending. Indeed, grant a few years' license, and it's easy to imagine Stavisky as a guest at the house party in *La Règle du Jeu*, taking a fateful phone call, but carrying on regardless.

Of course, Resnais's *Stavisky* is very beautiful, and very aware of iconography. The rich color photography is by Sacha Vierny, the set design is by Jacques Saulnier, and the costumes are by Jacqueline Moreau and Yves Saint-Laurent (he dressed Arlette, Stavisky's wife). So, it's rather as if the gorgeous décor and clothes of *Marienbad* had been given a shot of adrenaline with this compelling story. The music, by Stephen Sondheim, came from Resnais's sense of the way, in *Follies*, Sondheim could move from champagne to acid so quickly. You wonder if Stavisky could sing sometimes, like Chevalier, tempting destiny.

Belmondo personifies the film: He dresses well, with a love of clothes; he acts in a broad, very manly way, seductive yet shy, too; and we can credit that lurking pressure, the death wish. Anny Duperey is ideally elegant as Arlette. Charles Boyer is very fine as Baron Raoul—Resnais longed to work with him—and the cast also includes François Périer, Michael Lonsdale, Claude Rich, and Gigi Ballista.

At the end of John Ford's *Steamboat Round the Bend*, we are waiting to see which of two Mississippi paddle steamers appears first. The audience is in no doubt, for the *Claremore Queen*—under the benign, chatty, slow-cracking Dr. John Pearly (Will Rogers)—has been able to take the lead by adding its supply of hooch whiskey to the boat's furnaces. And then, as if the *Queen* were Stepin Fetchit (Jonah, Pearly's second in command and first in comradeship) it pops, creaks, stretches its joints, and starts to spout fire from its curlicued funnel. It was Ford's idea that, in victory, the *Claremore Queen* should explode altogether. That comedy was denied by the new boss at Twentieth Century Fox (the amalgamation had just occurred) and so a modicum of narrative realism prevailed at the end.

But what we have here is a dream or a farce, a piece of knockabout theater that smells of the studio in Los Angeles, and in which the studio shots sit awkwardly beside pretty footage of boats on the river. In other words, this is no more the Mississippi in the 1890s than Ford's Monument Valley is a reliable part of the West. And the dream in *Steamboat* is like the one in Ford's *Judge Priest* (a more interesting film), the offering of a South where Pearly and Jonah might be chums, and where the unyielding strains of history, race, and madness (the South of Faulkner) are buried in a minstrel show where everything is going to be all right, and where the injustice and the hanging of Duke (John McGuire) will be averted by a magic Ford is too bored to spell out—at least in *Judge Priest* the reversal of bad law is given due attention.

The film hangs upon the double act of Rogers and Fetchit, and they are sweet and cordial together even if today it is difficult to expect a black audience to swallow the simpleton in Fetchit. Joseph McBride quotes V. S. Naipaul on how adored Fetchit was in Trinidad in the forties, and how Fetchit and Rogers together "was like a dream of a happier world." That's valuable, but it hardly catches the problem of Fetchit for modern American audiences.

So there are lovely ironies, like the way Pearly's waxwork figures can become switched for convenience—Grant becomes Lee and two biblical prophets are turned into Frank and Jesse James. Most of this benevolence comes from the persona of Rogers, and one can argue that he is one of Ford's most intriguing heroes—an improviser, a "natural," yet pickled in limelight, a wise man yet as much a social outcast as Ethan Edwards. It should be added that Rogers was killed in a plane crash in Alaska before this film was released. He was fifty-five and he might have made many more films for Ford. But for good or ill?

As you might imagine, the film includes a great deal of broad playing: Irvin S. Cobb as the rival skipper, Eugene Pallette as a sheriff, Francis Ford as a drunk, Berton Churchill as a bombastic religious voice, and Anne Shirley as the girl who loves Duke.

Stella (1955)

If only someone had had the sense to cast Melina Mercouri in *The Barefoot Contessa*—that stately bore of a film might have suddenly sparked. In 1955, Mercouri was twenty-two, harsh, gauche, nervous, sexual, and rough—she went barefoot, bare-shouldered, and bare brazen. She was dark blonde, and she sang a bit and danced hardly at all—her arm movements were silly and repetitive, and she needed someone like Astaire to teach her how to dip her chin into her shoulders. It may seem strange to stress this detail, but look at *Stella* and you'll agree: She had great shoulders.

Stella was her first film, in which she is a café singer who just collects men—until one of them takes her out. The style is flat-out melodrama, and there's more than a little tourist trade in the movie with the suggestion that this is what Athens and Greece were like. Subtlety wasn't her thing. She did presence, with eyebrows like the fins on great fifties cars and a feeling that her eyes were always about to catch fire.

Michael Cacoyannis directed *Stella*, and it uses Athens locations very well, just as it conveys the slender margin between money and its absence. Indeed, there's a tinge of neo-realism to the film even if economics have been subsumed by fatal passion. The men in her life are a feeble dandy, a soccer player, and a kid. They're too close in age (and looks, maybe), and it would be nice to see Stella turning some older sugar daddy inside out. She laughs too much, and her laugh sounds as if it was recorded inside a tin sound box. But she looks fabulous and incendiary. Did I mention the shoulders? She could be the first girl to give you a hot shoulder.

In *The Barefoot Contessa*, she might have been sexier, more vulnerable and more needy than Ava Gardner—and, truly, in Mercouri you can feel the desperation of a European girl about to be taken up by the big show. *Stella* played successfully at the Cannes festival, and that's where she met Jules Dassin, who became her husband and cocreator.

But Cacoyannis was obviously mad for her, and it's always the person who gets those girls first who gets the truth and suffers the most. The finale in the film—the fatal meeting with a jilted lover—is done in a deserted city square, like a Western shoot-out, and the mock gravity is exactly right. The death blow is sudden and Stella is fulfilled by it. For Greece, at the time, the film was an astonishing breakthrough, and it's overloaded with bouzouki music, as if the Greek film industry was pushing its main chance as hard as possible. In later years, the tendency in Mercouri to overact was uncontrollable and less appealing than she seemed to think. But *Stella* is the moment, and you can still feel the heat and the sweat in her nervous armpits. For ninety minutes, at least, she had it.

Stella Dallas (1937)

This was always a Samuel Goldwyn property. He had read the novel, by Olive Higgins Prouty, published in 1923, and he loved it. More, he fancied it was him, no matter that the central character, Stella Martin, marries above her class, to Stephen Dallas. They have a daughter, Laurel. Stephen leaves her and then wants a divorce. He wants to marry again, to a socialite, to his own class. So Stella marries a man she knows, Ed Munn, a man of no quality, and Laurel moves away gradually to enjoy the "better" life her father offers. But Laurel is pained by her vulgar mother. And Stella adds to that crassness, to make the break easier, or out of her own misery. Laurel marries a rich man. Stella is outside the house, in the rain, watching—as if it were a movie.

The story was a hit in 1925, when Frances Marion wrote scripts. Henry King ended up directing. Belle Bennett was cast as Stella, after more famous actresses had declined the part. Lois Moran played Laurel. King shot it too slow, and Goldwyn and his editor, Stuart Heisler, had to go through the whole thing recutting before it played. In that work, day after day, Goldwyn was reduced to tears. Stella was him—he knew how it felt!

Twelve years later, Goldwyn wanted to remake it. He was still moved by the material. He had had a divorce and a daughter who suffered from it. In addition, Goldwyn had been Gelbfisz; he was Polish, he was famously ugly—in every *Last Supper*, someone said, Judas Iscariot looks like Goldwyn; he was treasured and mocked for his linguistic solecisms. He was a figure of fun. And he was the classic nouveau riche who might hope to see a daughter marry "well" in American society. Stella Dallas was Goldwyn—it was his own vision of himself that accounts for one of the all-time classic women's pictures, a work that cannot be touched without belief—as witness the dreadful modern version with Bette Midler as Stella.

So Vidor made the great version. In his book, *A Tree Is a Tree,* he says little about it; perhaps he knew it could never be his film. But he had Rudolph Maté shooting it, the man who had photographed Falconetti in Carl Dreyer's *The Passion of Joan of Arc.* The music would be by Alfred Newman. Richard Day was the art director. Tim Holt was Laurel's beau; Alan Hale was Ed Munn (brilliant casting); John Boles, limp and effete, was Stephen Dallas; Anne Shirley was Laurel; and Barbara Stanwyck was Stella. Stanwyck does a great job, even if she was a player whose chief ideal, always, was to seem cool and superior. Like so many stars, she had known hard times and humiliation—it all spilled out.

The picture had rentals of $2 million and there were Oscar nominations for Stanwyck and Anne Shirley. Today, the 1937 *Stella Dallas* cannot escape charges of camp, but only because the issue of class is now exposed as the throbbing heart of the film, and as a burning issue in an allegedly egalitarian country. It spoke from Goldwyn's heart, to be sure, but it is also a record of every awkward journey the self-made American has to suffer if he wants to appear classy. It follows that nearly every "women's picture" is knocking at this door.

The Sting (1973)

What a mystery this phenomenon is over thirty years later. I suppose on the one hand *The Sting* was the "sequel" to *Butch Cassidy and the Sundance Kid*—as such, it won Best Picture, Best Director for George Roy Hill (he was competing with Bergman for *Cries and Whispers*, Bertolucci for *Last Tango in Paris*, Friedkin for *The Exorcist*, and Lucas for *American Graffiti*—he could have been grateful for finishing fifth); and the Oscar for Adapted Screenplay went to David S. Ward. Robert Redford was nominated as Best Actor. You might like to pause over that fact and think about it for a few days.

I should add that the picture also made a ton of money: its domestic rentals were around $80 million. Yet I wonder how many people look at it today, or recall it. And if you are caught with it, you will marvel at the strange, abstract world it inhabits—it's as if the Dick Tracy sets had been built years too early and this flimsy film had thought to take advantage of them.

The title tells you what the movie is, or does. A sting is a kind of confidence trick, one that offers a sham apparatus. And so Paul Newman and Robert Redford propose an immense double-layered fraud that will free gangster Doyle Lonnegan (Robert Shaw) of much of his money. Even more so than with some of those movies where David Mamet films an elaborate trick, this is mere conjuring in which we are lucky enough to be invested on the winning side. There are no characters, no context, no time or place, and not the least gesture toward any other meaning. It leaves one thinking that *Butch Cassidy and the Sundance Kid* might have been written by Saul Bellow.

Is it relevant that this film won so many hearts and minds and dollars in the year Watergate broke open? Does it at least help explain the courage of some films from the early seventies that there was this weird "mainstream" in being, too—a mindless entertainment enough to captivate or console troubled citizens (and yet ones who knew they could no longer trust anything or anyone)? As a rule, Best Picture winners, whatever the quality, do have a bearing on their moment. But *The Sting* is almost a celebration of being unconnected and uninvolved.

This doesn't mean it isn't clever and pretty, though George Roy Hill, in my opinion, was a little troubled by plasticity and beauty. The use of the Scott Joplin rags (adapted by Marvin Hamlisch) undoubtedly had something to do with its novelty. And there are some decent supporting players—with a cartoonish comic menace seething out of Shaw. As for Newman and Redford, this halcyon period of their careers looks very odd now. Was there meant to be a gay subtext in the film, or is it helplessly there—like mice on sound stages? I see no sign that Hill got it, and I suspect the actors would have been horrified at the suggestion. But film is a spectacle that begs to be explained—and if you're awake, what else are you meant to wonder about?

The Story of the Late Chrysanthemums (1939)

Just because it comes from 1939, *The Story of the Late Chrysanthemums* makes me think of Hollywood. Didn't America own that heady year? But imagine this Japanese story done there: It's not hard, it's a show business success story. An actor of uncertain ability hears the truth about himself only from a humble maidservant. And so he forsakes the grand company where he worked. He goes on the road and she follows him. And in the end it will work out—except that she is not merely "adorable"; she is plaintive, a touch grating, enough to foster the tyrant in him. And he has ugly scenes—full of unfair recrimination, self-pity, selfishness—the things any actor can do without rehearsal. In other words, the human ambiguities of Kenji Mizoguchi's film are staggering, just as the camera style is already more confident and more beautiful than that of Renoir. I am trying to catch your attention, just like an actor: I want you to see and inhabit the depths of *The Story of the Late Chrysanthemums.*

The story is set in the late 1890s, and it is drawn from the career of a celebrated Kabuki actor, Kikugoru, a man Mizoguchi knew personally. In the film, he is named Kikonusuke, and he is a student actor with a splendid company. But a young woman, Otoku, has such love for him that she tells him he is still limited as an actor. He believes her—and all this is accomplished on a nocturnal walk, a long following shot, where we see the arrogant man altered by such calm kindness, and its gamble. He goes off on his own, and in time Otoku joins him and becomes his wife. She cares for him. She handles the money, and she steadily advises him on his career; he ignores her often, but her instincts are right. She does not seem unduly prescient, but she understands theater just as she accepts her own subservient role in the drama. He becomes everything they ever wanted—and we see and feel the progress in a picture that has several extended scenes of theater at work—but she is exhausted. The sacrifice has been made.

Compared with the late, period films, this is Mizoguchi intent on modern life, and this is the film in which he perfected his extended sequence shots that are withdrawn from the action, in order to open up the full context of the story. And just as in late Renoir, there is a superb poignant irony that hovers over the riddle of where theater ends and life begins. It is so moving that in film history, directors pursuing the same style should almost unwittingly discover the same. Of course, it is the balance between film and life.

The script is by Yoshikata Yoda and Matsutaro Kawaguchi (and the dialogue is unusually sharp). The photography is by Minoru Miki and the design by Hiroshi Mizutani. Kikunosuke is played by Shotaro Hanayagi and Otoku by Kakuko Mori—actors this great director used only the once, as if he had emptied them, or filled them.

La Strada (1954)

If only because of his association with Roberto Rossellini, it was assumed early on that Federico Fellini was a realist. The success of *I Vitelloni* had done little to dispute that, even if the film displayed very little interest in improving the social condition it faced—the apathy of young men. But in his next film, *La Strada,* Fellini either lurched away toward disloyalty, or began to reveal his true colors. You have to take your choice. He created a modern fable in which the background—the road, poverty in Italy—was a given, a source of the picturesque, and beyond reproach—and he hired in American actors in an effort to secure an international audience.

Of course, that tendency was apparent in Italian cinema with Rossellini himself, and careful historians should take note that the great director fell upon Ingrid Bergman not just with love, et cetera, but in an earnest endeavor to get his films to play in America. Thus, the imaginative trajectories of the two parties in that great romance moved in opposite directions. It looked like a tragic love story at the time, but it had all the ferment of comedy.

La Strada means "The Road," and that is where this odd double act pursues the meaning of life—the strong man and the waif, Zampanò and Gelsomina, in the persons of Fellini's wife, Giulietta Masina (they had been married since 1943), and Anthony Quinn (who had just won his first Supporting Actor Oscar in *Viva Zapata!*). I have to admit that there are several other roads I would take to avoid spending time with two such shameless hams. Even at the time, in Italy, leftist critics complained that this stagy allegory had wiped away any prospect of social commentary. But that's not really the grave or ugly question: What is it that remains? What sort of meaning is there in the very coy dance of these two life forces?

There is a third party to the action—Richard Basehart as more of a trickster figure—and I find him the only interesting person around. Fellini kept his team intact: Otello Martelli doing the camerawork, and Nino Rota writing the music. You might guess this, but the idea of the film is that the brutal strong man dominates and bullies the sweet, good girl but never conquers her spirit. Some find the question more pressing as to why she doesn't murder him—or why we remain loyal to the dark and this lurid fairy story. It's my hunch that not many people could endure *La Strada* today without some numbing potion. But you have to hand it to Fellini—he won the Academy Award for the Best Foreign Film, and he sank his teeth deeper and deeper in the soft American market.

These fables became more popular as the fifties advanced—*The Seventh Seal* was still to come. But in Bergman's world no one has to be lovable, and keeping up a plucky grin despite your tears isn't called for. I mean this as intelligent critical comment, but I always wonder whether Anthony Quinn might not have directed the movie.

The Strange Affair of Uncle Harry (1945)

We are in a town called Corinth in New Hampshire. Harry Quincey is called "uncle" by half the town. In fact, he lives with his two sisters, Lettie and Hester, not one of them married. It's a grand house, stuffed with old-fashioned furniture, but the family fell with the Depression. So Harry works as a pattern designer at the mill, while Lettie exists as a strange invalid, "like Robinson Crusoe on her chaise longue." In truth, Lettie loves Harry and can't think of letting him go. But then one day, modernity walks into these archaic lives in the form of Deborah, a new person at the mill from the Boston office. She's up-to-date in clothes and look. She's chic and smart. She's Ella Raines. And she and Harry fall in love. This is not one hundred percent credible, but the thought of it stirs Harry—and Harry all this while is George Sanders. This is one of the very few films in which that interesting, sad man was called upon to be a real actor. And the result is what makes the film touching and unusual.

Lettie meanwhile is Geraldine Fitzgerald, an actress as wasted as George Sanders was in the history of Hollywood. She looks a little like Ella Raines (which is good), and she plainly nurses a desire for Harry that the script hasn't the nerve to spell out. Still, this is a very unusual portrait of real familial obsession, and for about an hour it's a compelling picture.

The script was by Stephen Longstreet, with an intervening adaptation by Keith Winter, from a stage play by Thomas Job. But the producer on the film is Joan Harrison, Hitchcock's former assistant, and the woman who had put director Robert Siodmak on *Phantom Lady*. Siodmak is not interested in suspense or violence here. This is not a noir. But it's a picture of stifled emotion, and the art direction, by John Goodman and Eugène Lourié, is very telling about dead lives muffled by "stuff."

Harry loses Deborah. Apparently she has gone off to marry another man after Lettie has effectively squashed Harry's urge to be married. This is what drives Harry to thoughts of murder, and some rather fussy business with poison and cups of cocoa. So it's Hester (Moyna MacGill) who dies, and Lettie who gets the blame. None of this feels exactly right, and the ending of the film is a farrago of censorship and creative nervousness dragging a picture away from its own promising material. There's a title at the end of the film begging patrons not to divulge the ending. Instead, we should be attacking Universal for ever taking it on. But the message is clear: There was a fascinating family story to be told here, one descending into madness. The film is only 80 minutes long, and it's easy to see a lot of ways an extra fifteen minutes could have helped.

It may be that the heartfelt anguish on Sanders's face is his response to the way his best chance (for many years at least) was going to be spoiled. But there are many American films that cry out for braver hands and audiences who seek the end of controls.

Strangers on a Train (1951)

It's worth recalling that at this point in his career Hitchcock had just made three uncertain films, and three relative flops in a row: *Rope*, *Under Capricorn*, and *Stage Fright*. The misguided ten-minute-take period was over, and he was looking to recover himself. As is so often the case with Hitch, he found what amounts to a human diagram—criss-cross (a movie title from 1949): You do my murder, and I'll do yours.

The idea came from Patricia Highsmith, and that dark lady once told me that this was the movie from her work that she most enjoyed. She didn't mention Farley Granger. Which goes to suggest what this film owes to the remarkable late insolence of Robert Walker, an actor who had been cripplingly ingratiating, archetypally nice and decent, and forlornly appealing. Suppose that there was some much darker, less normal fellow inside Walker, and suppose that he had been wounded by the loss of his wife, Jennifer Jones—then this is an inspired piece of casting. It's true that this Walker is a little older and heavier—there seems to have been an illness or a setback of unusual proportion. Nevertheless, he drives the entire movie and may have taken Hitch to new prospects.

Guy Haines (Granger) is a tennis champion, about to be engaged to the daughter of a senator (Ruth Roman), but still married to a cunning small-town slut (Laura Elliott—very sharp), one of the more murderable figures in film. Bruno (Walker) knows all this; indeed, he is like an author, his own author—and Hitchcock's masterful style always favors those who know the most in his films. So Bruno offers what is truly a pretty idea, and he cannot comprehend that Guy doesn't pick up on its wit and wisdom. That Guy doesn't act on it is the least Highsmith part of the film. That he is so halfhearted in his refusal is a concession to censorship.

But the long sequence in which Bruno does kill the wife is still like a superb gift to the audience—note the way Bruno lowers her strangled body into our laps and our desires as a reward. What follows—Guy's desperate attempt to be champ and prove his innocence—is not nearly as enticing or as involving as Bruno's scheme. We want more of Bruno. We want a Guy who does fall in with the plan. For Hitch has grasped in this movie how ready we are to lend our immoral support to murderousness.

So in a way it's only half a film, with a good deal of padding: Pat Hitchcock, the awful tennis match—not to mention Ruth Roman. But the splendor of Bruno, his deadly flowering, is reward enough for those compromises. And in discovering the charm of villainy Hitchcock is charting out the ambiguity that will mean so much to him in the 1950s. So think of it as Bruno, on a train and making his way to a provincial fairground as dusk falls. It ends, properly, with his demon driving a carousel mad, and with his hand opening to reveal one of Hitchcock's great burning objects.

A Streetcar Named Desire (1951)

The Tennessee Williams play opened in New York, in December 1947, and it had thirty minutes of applause on the way to 855 performances. But those facts don't really explain its power or influence, or its standing as maybe the great American play written in the age of movies. It was, from the outset, a directed play. The Williams text, and the play's dynamics, had been through the maw and the needs of director Elia Kazan. I do not mean that as criticism. Kazan was at his height as a director, and 1947 is also the year of the foundation of the Actors Studio in New York, the focus of his psychological realist intensity and his sheer command of a new generation of actors. But Kazan's impact was greater still. He needed to identify with the text personally, and thus the story of Blanche DuBois (which is how the play reads) and its parable of homosexual desire was repressed (it's the only word) by Kazan's grasp of the Stella-Stanley scenes. He brought them out—to that end, he had an affair with Kim Hunter (Stella) during the production, and he had a bond with Marlon Brando (Stanley) that made Stanley the focal point of the action. Anyone who was there that night in 1947 will tell you it seemed like a play about Stanley. Yet if you read the text he is clearly secondary.

The film was a long time coming, no matter that the play's producer, Irene Mayer Selznick, was a child of the movies. It was impeded by censorship and the first feeling that so much of the play was simply not negotiable on film. In that process, Lillian Hellman actually wrote a version of it with a happy ending! Then there was the fear that with so tough a venture, the role of Blanche required a star. Many people were considered. Olivia de Havilland could have done it but she felt that Blanche was too sordid. So Vivien Leigh was cast—her second great Southern belle—and Kazan had to cleanse her of all the ideas she had picked up from the London stage production, where Laurence Olivier had directed her and Bonar Colleano played Stanley without becoming a sensation.

The film is censored in a good many places, and it is without Jessica Tandy, the first Blanche onstage. But it remains our best record of that original production, for Kazan did the film with the rest of the Broadway cast. And in a style and décor taken from the play. The screen distances it, of course—above all in the sex and violence—but it's still a very powerful piece in which Leigh bravely challenges Brando and fights him off. On film, Brando looks a setup, whereas onstage he must have been a startling surprise.

Harry Stradling photographed it. Richard Day was the art director. Lucinda Ballard did the costumes. Alex North wrote the rather heavy music. Vivien Leigh got her second Oscar (though the role increased her mental instability), and Karl Malden and Kim Hunter won in supporting categories.

Street Scene (1931)

Today, a play like Elmer Rice's *Street Scene* might seem naïve or unlikely. Yet in many cases people do live on streets still, and with the chance of community that that involves. In the East, on hot summer nights, the windows are open and people still sit on the steps watching the kids play, counting the passage of neighbors. But some accursed privacy has taken over: it is like the feeling in *Rear Window* (1954) that no one realizes they are being watched. They count on the solitude of their unit, and it is not just television they are locked up with. We live now with our dreams and fears; we practice our bad habits. So the gesture toward connectedness in *Street Scene*—like that in, say, *Short Cuts* or *Magnolia*—looks portentous or marvelous. Of course, if, as it suggests, there is still a thing called society, available to be seen, then there may still be politics, too.

Street Scene opened in 1929 and ran through the year of the Crash. It is, in a way, a play about its set: a stretch of urban street and lower-middle-class tenement housing; the collection of lives and ethnic groups (a cross-section is arranged—though without anyone of color), brought into focus by a murder that is committed. An Irish American discovers that his wife is having an affair with the milkman, and kills them both.

Goldwyn bought the rights and asked King Vidor if he would direct. So Vidor went to see the play and he puzzled over it. Then he saw a fly on a man's face, and he watched the fly move. That's how he would film *Street Scene:* ". . . we would never repeat a camera set-up twice. If the setting couldn't change, the camera could. We would shoot down, up, across, from high, from low, from a boom, from a perambulator, and we would move back and include not only the sidewalk but the street as well."

It took a superb set by Richard Day and the camerawork of George Barnes. To which was added the score by Alfred Newman, written by the composer after he had attended the shooting and meant to be one more sound effect, linking up the lines of talk. For here is one of the great early sound films, where the buzz of life accounts for the immediacy of the shooting.

For Vidor, as for Rice, it is also an experiment in community and the adaptation to poverty, with the young characters going through so many stages of the desire to leave, to get away, to be even more American than this cross-section. And just as in *Magnolia*, the abiding ties of kinship and association—of resemblance—are the poetry of it all. Vidor was one of those directors who thought hard about America, without being self-consciously political, and this is a sequel in many ways to *The Crowd*, where the liveliness of sound is a source of optimism.

Terribly neglected now, it is a classic, with a great cast and excellent natural acting: Sylvia Sidney, William Collier, Jr., Max Montor, David Landau, Estelle Taylor, Russell Hopton, Louis Natheaux, Greta Granstedt, Beulah Bondi, T. H. Manning, Matt McHugh, Adele Watson, and John Qualen.

Strike (1925)

There are versions of *Strike* available now which, in an earnest effort to be helpful, pile on the music (from Shostakovich to Duke Ellington—both subtly wrong in period) and horses' hooves when the tsar's troops attack the striking workers and their families. Avoid all such contributions if you can, and turn the sound down. There are some people who will tell you that *Strike* (based on an incident from 1912) is part of the Soviet revolution's rewriting of Russian history, a testament in the annals of communist solidarity. Maybe. I think you can argue that the workers, the factory owners, the troops, and the spies are all so clichéd that you can hardly trust a thing. There are history books that furnish the anguish and the real evidence.

But if you watch the film silent, you cannot fail to respond to the dynamic of the visuals and the thought that someone behind them is a graphic genius, and that the medium bearing them—film—is white hot and dangerous. It hardly matters what happened in the strike: you could drive the world mad with anger with this kind of movie. No one interested in the interaction of film and politics (much less the history of filmic expression) should fail to see *Strike*. But brood on what it means.

Sergei Eisenstein was twenty-six in 1924. He had studied civil engineering, and he had pursued all forms of graphic art, from painting to cartoon. He had had a crucial experience designing sets for Meyerhold at the Proletkult Theater, and he then led a splinter group of the theater, developing dynamic theatrical performance. It was in search of rapidly changing compositions that he fell upon film, and found himself ordered to make *Strike*. It was meant as part of a series. But Eisenstein went off on a personal track—it was his career-long failing in Soviet circles, of course, but it was his genius.

And so, with actors from the Proletkult, with Vasili Rakhals doing décor, and with Eduard Tisse as his cameraman, Eisenstein made a six-part chronicle of the strike. Leave aside the matter of justification or circumstances. The narrative is utterly one-sided, but the visuals are intensely ambitious. Eisenstein used close-ups like arias and geometric compositions as if his eyes and mind were overflowing. The giddiness, the hysteria almost, is as potent as the forms—the swirl of hose-pipe water playing on the strikers; the cavalry invading the apartment buildings—everywhere you look. There is hardly a calm or a plain shot. Nearly anyone can see *Strike* and say, Great God! Composition can do anything.

And it can. The actors make the owners brutes and the workers saints. But the imagery makes us excited about both of them. You want to be a striker and you want to be a cavalryman. Above all, you just want to be a filmmaker. You can still feel the way young artists must have swarmed around Eisenstein. At a bird-brained level, the film says, "Poor strikers." But it says, "Sweet policemen," too! It suggests something that has little to do with Communism: that film can harness energy, any energy. It's what Leni Riefenstahl knew. So watch out. And encourage written history and the preservation of documents.

Stromboli (1949)

So Ingrid Bergman wrote a letter to Roberto Rossellini: "I saw your films *Open City* and *Paisan*, and enjoyed them very much. If you need a Swedish actress who speaks English very well, who has not forgotten her German, who is not very understandable in French, and who, in Italian knows only 'ti amo' I am ready to come and make a film with you." She wanted reality, truth, beauty, art—or so she thought. He went wild at the letter because he wanted a name actress, money, fame. He wrote back at length and told her about a Latvian woman he had met in a refugee camp: "In her clear eyes, one could read a mute intense despair. I put my hand through the barbed wires and she seized my arm, just like a ship-wrecked person would clutch at a floating board."

Be careful what you wish for. Not very long thereafter, Bergman was Karin, a Lithuanian refugee, who agrees to marry Antonio (Mario Vitale), a young fisherman from the island of Stromboli. The island proves a far greater ordeal than the camp. The living conditions are harsh. Her husband beats her for speaking to another man. She hates the massacre of the tunny fish. And then the volcano erupts. She spends a night alone on the slopes of the volcano and cries out to God.

In real life, Ingrid and her director were lovers already on the island, but she cried out in another kind of despair at "these realistic pictures." "To hell with them!" said Bergman. "These people don't even know what dialogue is, they don't know where to stand; they don't even care what they're doing. I can't bear to work another day with you."

It's easy to read what happened in terms of the films they made together (a series of ordeals), but there is a comic side to it. And, truth to tell, even on the real Stromboli Ingrid never quite looks like the most deprived Lithuanian. In fact, *Stromboli* was a coproduction of Rossellini's company and RKO, with an American screenwriter, Art Cohn, helping out with Sergio Amidei and other Italian writers.

Yes, they went on location, and yes, the ground shakes beneath the cameras often enough as the volcano plays its part. In many ways, this is the most immediate and dramatic of the films Ingrid and Roberto made together just because the island speaks for itself and because Ingrid is so much more than a peasant or an amateur. The ordeal is like a penalty, but the film really rises to a climax. We do feel that a god or some spirit has touched Karin. The photography is by Otello Martelli, and the music—somehow—is a combination of Renzo Rossellini and Constantin Bakaleinikoff (from RKO).

There are different versions (and lengths), largely because RKO sought to minimize the ordeal and the damage. They apparently put $600,000 into the production (and there's no doubt but that impressed Rossellini), but they took only a fraction home afterward.

The Stunt Man (1980)

It was inevitable perhaps, after a full ten years of the auteur theory in America, that someone was going to identify the begging subject of the monster director, the egomaniac who might easily kill people or destroy cultures to get the right shot on screen. And so, somewhere between *Apocalypse Now* and *Twilight Zone: The Movie* came Richard Rush's *The Stunt Man,* in which the director's power over reality had been glorified by the subculture of picture making. In this case the director was called Eli Cross, and the name evoked "Noah Cross" (John Huston's character in *Chinatown*), just as Peter O'Toole's insouciant swagger left one wondering about his own memories of David Lean in Arabia.

The story is told through the startled eyes of Cameron (Steve Railsback), a fugitive from justice and an unhappy Vietnam veteran who takes cover from pursuit by taking the job of stunt man in Cross's World War I movie. He is enthralled and horrified by Cross's act—somewhere between Von Stroheim, Von Karajan, and "Vonderful, darlink!" (in other words, the satire wanders and is often betrayed by its own camp aspirations).

O'Toole's performance, I fear, is mistakenly overdone. It's as if he had been made giddy, or encouraged in giddiness, by the script. Whereas to be accurate and damning, this director needs to be as gregarious as Welles, as humble as Capra, as funny as Preston Sturges, and as religious as Scorsese (even if the Church is just Him). In other words, a director is a wondrous bag of tricks who can lose track of his own deviousness because he means to be all things to all men (and women).

The script is by Lawrence B. Marcus, from a novel by Paul Brodeur, and it's very much of that age that preferred its directors to be amiable boys instead of dangerous men. What's fascinating is the presence of Richard Rush in charge of it all. Rush (b. 1930) was a leading independent director in the 1960s, associated with drugs and bikers—he did *Hell's Angels on Wheels, Psych-Out,* and *Freebie and the Bean,* and seemed to have been promoted with *The Stunt Man.* Moreover, that picture did well in the United States, and it earned Oscar nominations for script, direction, and O'Toole. It seemed like a threshold for a career, yet Rush has directed just once since then: *Color of Night,* a disastrous attempt to make Bruce Willis erotic.

The Stunt Man doesn't wear too well: It manages to seem both obvious and pretentious now, and one longs for O'Toole to moderate his performance. But the idea of a demented fantasy in which a film director begins to resemble God or the other guy is funny and promising and true to life. *The Stunt Man* seemed to believe it was going to be a Great American Film. It isn't, but that's no reason for Rush to retire.

It was photographed by Mario Tosi, and Dominic Frontiere did the score (which also includes Dusty Springfield singing "Bits and Pieces"). It involves Barbara Hershey (as the actress in the film), Sharon Farrell, John Garwood, Alex Rocco, and Allen Goorwitz.

Suddenly (1954)

Don't tell me: The list of films omitted so that Lewis Allen's *Suddenly* should make the thoughtful thousand is enough to make a pantheon or an introduction to film course. It doesn't matter. We have to have this 77-minute killer, written by Richard Sale, about an assassin who takes over an ordinary suburban home because it has a great view of the railway depot in this town called Suddenly. How it got that name is just one of the things that could be answered in a remake. One thing it shows is America's readiness for "Action!"

You see, the president is coming through town on a train—can you imagine presidents traveling by rail?—and the hit man has a high-powered rifle which he will set up in the suburban home. And crack. Actually, it's stretching a point to argue that this assassin needs a rifle and bullets to do the job. Because the killer is Frank Sinatra, from whom mere glances could kill—just ask the cocktail waitresses, croupiers, and floor managers of Las Vegas.

The year of release is 1954—in other words, Frank has likely just won his Oscar; he may be on the point of losing Ava Gardner; but his voice is back on Capitol on things called long-playing records. Frank the hoodlum has been redeemed—so let's knock off a president. And make no mistake about it, the actor who could make a woeful Maggio in *From Here to Eternity* had it in him to be as nasty, creepy, and vicious as anyone on the American screen. The arrogance and sarcasm are like his toupee and his thin lips: forces for breaking backs. The cruelty and the malice are the fantasy acting-out of the shriveled runt, and they suggest an amendment to Ava's famous remark—that if Frankie only weighed 110 pounds, then 100 of that was vengeance.

There's a very good supporting cast that includes Sterling Hayden, James Gleason, and Nancy Gates, and you have the feeling that if the film had allowed itself more time and budget then Frankie's character (named John Baron) had schemes of torture lined up for all of them.

Why did Sinatra do it? He was making his way back in respectable films and pleasing musicals—*From Here to Eternity, Young at Heart* (though that shows his dark, fatalistic side, too), *Not as a Stranger, The Tender Trap, Guys and Dolls*. Surely nothing but deep psychic need prompted it—a chance for the little man to smack the world in the face. In which case, it turned out badly. In less than ten years, there were many people wondering whether Lee Harvey Oswald had seen *Suddenly*, and been encouraged. And after the shooting of John Kennedy, Sinatra took steps to have the film withdrawn, just as he was reluctant to let *The Manchurian Candidate* play very widely.

Did Oswald take the hint? Was Oswald the striker? There's still so little we know that the pitiless self-hatred of Sinatra's face is all the more alarming. He is not just a killer; he's a disappointed prophet in a world longing for religious incident.

Sullivan's Travels (1942)

John S. Sullivan (Joel McCrea) is a director of successful comedies—he has done *Hey, Hey in the Hayloft*, *Ants in Your Pants of 1939*, and *So Long, Sarong*. But he's getting just a little tired of his own success and a certain disrespect that goes with it—like no Oscar nominations (*Sullivan's Travels* would receive zero nominations). He lusts for dignity (a pose always likely to spell doom in the world of Preston Sturges). He wants to suffer a little, to see real, tough life. He wants to make a picture called *O Brother, Where Art Thou?* And thus Sturges launches his great Hollywood satire—all the better in that Sturges himself was torn in just the way of Sully.

There are very funny scenes in which the director's entourage tries to discourage him from this headstrong gambling. Again, it's typical of Sturges that those in the entourage are not craven, greedy idiots. They are the wise, sad men that Sturges kept as his stock company. They understand Sully—their man—it's just that he's going too far. But even in 1942, if a director got an idea in his head he could persuade himself he was at heaven's gate. Still, these scenes—with Robert Warwick and Porter Hall as studio men, with William Demarest as Jonesy, Franklin Pangborn as Casalsis, and Eric Blore as his valet—are among the best Sturges ever did, with a level of wit that is close to Oscar Wilde.

Sully is a chump. He goes. On a first forlorn effort he meets a girl (Veronica Lake)—there's always a girl in the picture—before ending up back in Los Angeles. Then he really goes for broke, and this time he makes it—does he ever! A real bum steals his possessions—that bum is then killed so that the death of Sully is reported. And Sully ends up on a chain gang in the South. That ordeal is rather tactfully presented. Still, it's a kind of hell, until one Sunday the convicts are led to a black church where they are shown a movie—it's *Playful Pluto*, a Disney picture from 1934. When the wretched guys laugh at it, Sully gets the message: There is something to be said for silly movies that make you laugh. So he engineers his escape (Sturges knew that this part of the film was feeble), and he goes back home, collects the girl, and resumes life as an Oscar-less favorite.

It's not that Sully is "right." It's rather more that the dilemma of whether to be Nicholas Ray or Preston Sturges goes on. Never fear—the system will get you whichever you choose. Yes, the film is far less morbid than *Sunset Blvd.* (eight years later at the same studio, Paramount—and John Seitz shot them both), but its ideas are trickier to resolve.

McCrea (a Sturges choice) is sublime: handsome, a bit thick, but decent. Veronica Lake was a discovery and difficult. She wanted McCrea to go to bed with her, and her being pregnant compelled Edith Head to put her in baggy clothes. The romance is fatuous, yet very Hollywood. The true love exists between Sully and his entourage—a group given screen life for the first time.

Sunday, Bloody Sunday (1971)

The most interesting thing about John Schlesinger's *Sunday, Bloody Sunday* is that in the central triangle of relationships, not one of them feels right or plausible. At first, you reckon that's an obvious failing in the film. But then as the story goes along something else comes into view—not very movielike, you have to admit—that suggests, well, maybe none of the relationships in life are exactly right. Is it, perhaps, that only the fantasy bonds from fiction are entirely gripping? Is it the case that in real life we all muddle along and make do as best we can?

Now, that is not the way Penelope Gilliatt's screenplay was presented when the film opened. Instead, it was the story of Bob (Murray Head), a young designer, who is having relationships with two people—Alex (Glenda Jackson), a divorced consultant in business; and Daniel (Peter Finch), a doctor—and Finch at that moment was fifty-five. Yes, you're correct. Bob and Daniel are both male, which means we have a homosexual relationship in a British mainstream movie, one in which the two actors kissed. We all saw it happen, and carried on muttering to ourselves about Peter Finch never having seemed gay. But that's part of the other problem I talked about.

John Schlesinger was gay, and I suspect there was a naughty streak in him itching to get that onscreen. And the picture was duly hailed for its gender pioneering. But Gilliatt's script (and she was a film critic in her day) is something else: It's a portrait of a professional Britain, not quite where jobs really matter, but peopled by characters who have rather put feelings on the shelf. Being with someone is a saving grace—or, at least, it avoids the disgrace of solitude. But it doesn't really fool anyone. And living together is one of those weird misnomers. Cohabiting is colder and more accurate, maybe. But people don't really live together, anymore than they sleep "with" each other. They sleep side by side, like prisoners in a row.

Sunday, Bloody Sunday isn't a great film, but it's a lot better than Schlesinger's more "daring" films (like *Darling*, which gets worse with time). And just as I give a lot of credit to the script, so I think the supporting players really assemble the air of crowded, untidy loneliness that is most intriguing and disconcerting—certainly far more than the dilemma of the central trio: Peggy Ashcroft, Maurice Denham, Vivian Pickles, Frank Windsor, Thomas Baptiste, Tony Britton, Harold Goldblatt, Hannah Norbert, Richard Pearson, June Brown, Caroline Blakiston, Bessie Love, and Jon Finch. The picture was photographed by Billy Williams, and Ron Geesin's score also makes clever use of material from *Così fan Tutte.* Luciana Arrighi did production design and Jocelyn Rickards the costumes on a film where décor means much more than usual.

Glenda Jackson is ideally cast—even if that's a way of wondering how such a mysterious movie career ever got off the ground. Peter Finch is touching and interesting. Whereas I cannot even recall what Murray Head looked like.

A Sunday in the Country (1984)

It's intriguing, I think, that Bertrand Tavernier thought to make *A Sunday in the Country* when he was only forty-three. After all, there is so much pressure in the film business to behave younger than one's actual age. So many stories seem to depend on their happening to kids. The conspiracy grows steadily: that "Life" (the big thing) is more eagerly felt and perceived by young people—or at least the age that has enough purchasing power to be lusted after by advertisers. Film directors quite often collect young wives (youth being what it is, they have to take on that challenge on a serial basis), and so they also like to find stories about young people.

So it says a lot for Tavernier's own breadth of vision—his curiosity, perhaps—that his most striking film may be the wondering on the part of a forty-year-old about the life of an artist nearly twice his age. Monsieur Ladmiral (Louis Ducreux) lives in the country, though within reach of the Paris train. He has a good house and garden and a housekeeper, and since he is a painter—rather in the Renoir school—we gather that these attributes are his subjects, too. The film focuses on one Sunday afternoon, but the Pierre Bost novel from which it is derived is called *Monsieur Ladmiral Va Bientôt Mourir.* And although neither the man nor the movie is morbid, that sense of what is coming is there in the warm-colored air he enjoys.

It is 1912, a tragic summer of happiness in France or anywhere else in Europe. For we cannot help but know some of the ways in which the peace and the stable, apparently, contented society is going to come apart. A man may die reasonably happy—but only if he spares himself the wondering of all the ways in which his children may be destroyed. And that future pregnancy was available, I suspect, in Tavernier's sensibility even before such films as *Life and Nothing But* (in which Philippe Noiret is a clerical military officer trying to keep track of the dead from the First World War) and *Safe Conduct,* in which the French countryside is the setting for Resistance violence.

What I'm trying to say is that Tavernier brings the mood of a novelist and a painter to film, as well as the historical sense of a man who is concerned to trace what has happened to France. *A Sunday in the Country* seems at first like a piece of nostalgia: the old man, his son and grandchildren, and even Irène (Sabine Azéma), his favorite perhaps, who does not visit often enough. His pictures are studies of the domestic life, yet the same subject nags at him and worries him. He feels its defects just as he suspects he may not be a great painter—I mean the kind of painter called great in history books.

Tavernier wrote this script with Pierre Bost and his then wife, Colo Tavernier. Bruno de Keyzer shot it, and Tavernier had the good sense to take his music from Fauré (who died in 1924). And it stands as a film about the artist, trying hard to be happy, and to be old graciously, but disturbed by the certainty that history has its own will. It is a sign of courage in any artist to look at old age—you get it in Welles, in Rembrandt, and Dickens, among others—but it shapes everything.

Sunrise (1927)

For years now, there has been such justified enthusiasm for the place of *Sunrise* in history that we may have begun to overlook what a very strange film it is. So, on the one hand, it is marvelous to see the streams of German and American cinema flooding together, and that, I suspect, was the overpowering reason why at the first Academy Awards *Sunrise* got an Oscar as the "most unique and artistic production," no matter that Best Picture went to *Wings*. That "classy" Oscar has never been given again, though one can argue that the Academy is still beset by wanting both kinds of cake. But then, you have to say that the German-American tension is palpable in our confusion over where this story is happening. The titles talk of every place and no place. But the film has a very strong sense of City and Country, and I have to point out the oddity of a film where the country girl spends so much time in the city and the woman from the city mopes her life away in rural torture (until nearly the last shot).

So here are the man (George O'Brien) and his wife (Janet Gaynor) living in the country. But he is deeply tempted by the woman from the city (Margaret Livingston), and he is on the point of murdering his wife when his conscience strikes. So instead of losing her in the lake he takes the wife to the city, and they have a grand time—let me add that I think their fun far exceeds that of the audience. When Murnau decides to be happy and funny, an audience can quickly lose interest. Nevertheless, all thought of his murderous attitude has left by the time they come home. But then there is a storm on the lake and the wife is lost. Irony of ironies? The woman from the country can't be sure what is happening—until the husband sees her and tries to kill her (one subtext not much discussed is his violence and his clear urge to kill someone).

The story ("a song of two humans") seems to me hokey and very "silent pictures." I know, one is supposed not to care or notice—look instead at the ravishing sense of the city (way ahead of anything of that time) and the superb traveling train shot into the city. I love it. But once I'm looking I can't help but notice the endless girlishness of Janet Gaynor and the fake spirituality ladled over a dark story.

I think the film was a stepping-stone, and Murnau was dead before he could touch ground. The art direction—by Rochus Gliese, Gordon Wiles, Edgar G. Ulmer, and Alfred Metscher—is phenomenal, and from a far more sophisticated film. The lighting (Charles Rosher and Karl Struss) and the camera movement are glorious. There are entire sequences here that see the medium altering. But the song of the humans is much harder to take and it stays obstinately in place. It's the scenario that is the problem: by Carl Mayer from a novel by Hermann Sudermann. What *Sunrise* needs is a grasp of character as subtle as the mise-en-scène. That would not come for years yet, and you can argue that it came in France and Japan more than in America. But don't doubt the impact of *Sunrise* on Hollywood—these are the first modern camera movements, carrying us toward desire.

Sunset Blvd. (1950)

People often tell themselves that *Sunset Blvd.* (the actual title) is a film noir, so let's say up-front that it's also a romance in which two broken dreamers get their heart's desires—that's one big reason why it made a musical. How so? Well, Norma Desmond has her comeback, on her own terms, and even if Norma is a famous crazy, Gloria Swanson delivered the pathos of a woman who is only in her early fifties. That ponderous screenplay she has labored on falls aside with one ecstatic traveling shot as she moves like a snake longing to wrap itself around the charmer's flute. She is ready for her close-up and once more having an affair with a camera. She is last seen, advancing, insinuating herself upon *Confidential* magazine and the entire library of scandalous celebrity—it is high time for a sequel, *The Trial of Norma Desmond* (of course, she gets off).

That interpretation may be sardonic, but it's obvious, too. The vindication of Joe Gillis is a little more oblique, but it's so much more lasting and interesting. For here is a ruined screenwriter: He needs Nancy Olson to rub his twisted nose in the mess of his idealistic youth. So all he wants now is a job and a killing. He gets both. The man who can't dream up a viable story line becomes the best pitch he'll ever hear. He is the story, and it is Billy Wilder's sour valedictory to let the ghost of Gillis tell the story, facedown in the gelid swimming pool, exactly the Hollywood reward that Joe gets only in his dreams. And so this breathtaking portrait of Hollywood failure is wrapped up in rueful, ruined success.

Famously, Louis B. Mayer scolded Wilder for biting the hand that had fed him. But the Oscars shunned the picture, and it was not originally a great popular hit, even if it caused a stir. For 1950, it was an audacious satire, and so much tougher than *The Bad and the Beautiful*, where the system and the showbiz optimism are left intact. But in *Sunset Blvd.*, there is enough cruelty and madness for everyone. Joe Gillis is not to be saved from doom—he loses his car, but his soul went earlier. And Max von Mayerling represents the role of the bereft, humiliated onlooker (and the kindest person left in this world). The sore thumbs are Nancy Olson and Jack Webb, dismissed as perfunctory nice guys and effective nonstarters in the Hollywood jungle.

Just how close this all comes to queasiness is spelled out in the old reminder that Montgomery Clift could have been "our" Joe Gillis. Clift's fear made Holden a star, but it saved the project. The romantic in Clift could hardly have avoided the horror of real sex between Joe and Norma—and there we are into a psycho horror film waiting for Robert Aldrich or something close to nightmare. It is Wilder's virtue that he keeps the picture comic—and that's why it's less a wounded noir than the first vision of a world in which all feeling waits to be ridiculed. So it's a hint of *Some Like It Hot*, and a first sense of how "story" and its variants have smothered real life.

Sweeney Todd (2007)

It's all very well for the ghost of Benjamin Barker to return from imprisonment in the colonies with a flash of white in his dark hair and the light of vengeance to illumine his ruined life. Still, even the great fans of *Sweeney Todd* (and I am one of them) have to gulp when his need for revenge and his right to it turn into the wanton throat-cutting of innocents (and women and children are spared only because they have less need to shave). No one is innocent in this world? Is that what the play is saying? Why then does it have at least three characters—with lovely, plaintive songs to sing—who are innocent or unnoticed? In the show itself, that awkward transition is masked by a comic song, "A Little Priest," in which Todd and Mrs. Lovett play cooing word games over the menu description of their latest pies. It is a funny song, normally done with dainty, macabre malice on the stage, but it knows that it's pulling a fast one on us, too. And what if the doing of that song isn't quite as sinister-comic as a tango for lame lovers? What if the voices are sublime—and quicklime?

Johnny Depp sings like . . . well, like Jack Sparrow, I fear: offhand, casual, apologetic. These can be endearing qualities in life but they are not the building blocks of *Sweeney*, much less the stirring grandeur of "Me, a Star" that fills the "Ballad of Sweeney Todd." (And so that great opening—as full of tragedy as bravado—has been dropped from the film. It is not a good start.) Helena Bonham Carter is the youngest and sexiest Mrs. Lovett anyone has ever seen—she is like the slut from *Fight Club* gone into trade, though in this case it would seem to be the wrong trade. All the odder therefore that she and Sweeney never get it on—and never soar in their duets.

Alan Rickman, who acts well (of course he does) has a voice so feeble that the entire role of Judge Turpin suffers. And yet Jamie Campbell Bower can sing—and so "Johanna" escapes the butchery.

And what can director Tim Burton offer in place of the music? Blood, my dear, though granted the Gothic pewter look of Dariusz Wolski's London, it is not quite real blood but a kind of liquefied lipstick—red for danger. And there's a monotony with the throat-cutting that killed the film's box office and not just the beards of London. You want this *Sweeney Todd* to be good, and you feel that Sondheim has left his great work up for grabs. Some regarded it as close to a masterpiece, but I fear it's a wretched hash and a surfeit of arty pessimism in place of tragedy. There are actions that can be indicated onstage in a gesture that are indelible. Spaced out on film they become torture.

Sweet Smell of Success (1957)

Before going overboard on this picture, I have to admit that Marty Milner is a stiff as the "cool" guitar-playing boyfriend, and I can hardly think of a duller band for him to be playing with than the Chico Hamilton Quintet. This is 1957, and there was a lot of really dangerous jazz then in New York; some of it was all black, and could have offered a way of life fit to pump raw vitality into this very controlled and negative picture. But those problems are modest compared with Susan Harrison's sister and the idea we are supposed to accept, that J. J. Hunsecker is so hooked on her as to be deranged. It just doesn't work, any more than the possibility that Tony Montana goes insane at the thought of anyone having sex with his sister (in *Scarface*). Hunsecker and Montana (now there's a movie) are so much into control that the idea of sex holding their attention is fanciful.

So the alleged "plot" of *Sweet Smell of Success* is fatuous, and the second half of the film is actually a good deal less compelling than the first. It doesn't matter: The exposition of the movie, its uncovering of a real Manhattan, and the seething relationship between J.J. and Sidney Falco—that remains one of the great setups in American film.

Yet where did it all come from? The script is a combination of an Ernest Lehman novella and Clifford Odets supposedly sitting in a trailer as they were shooting typing up dialogue. The talk is brilliant, and there's no question but that the original impact of the picture was that of a comedy double act who were steadily cutting each other to pieces. And while I'm happy to give a lot of the credit for that to director Alexander Mackendrick (Boston-born, but raised in Scotland), I have to say that Mackendrick never again got close to that sort of talk. So maybe something unusual belongs to the toxic chemistry between Burt Lancaster (J.J.) and Tony Curtis (Sidney Falco)—in Tony especially; there's a feeling of him having seen the first night's rushes and knowing he was home at last. As for Burt, is this one of the few films that really ruffled his soft-voiced intimidation and dug into the disturbed personality?

James Wong Howe's nocturnal photography is Weegee-like and very New York—his command of the light is the first plain proof of poison in the air. The Elmer Bernstein music is fine, but very melodramatic. There are good supporting performances from Sam Levene, Barbara Nichols, and the odious Emile Meyer. There is an undoubted conviction about the mood and ethics of a particular place. But what makes the movie famous are those sublime shots of J.J. at his table, with glasses for armor, and Tony settling in beside him, glowing at the smart of every fresh insult. I'm not sure that American film had ever previously suggested that people could be so nasty—and have so much fun with it.

And it's the title—for the movie does stink of drains and deodorant. But not enough to mask the rats and the flop sweat.

Swing High, Swing Low (1937)

Sometimes a very simple thing, a line or an image, holds a film in the collective memory—so *Swing High, Swing Low* is the one where Carole Lombard reclines in the crook of Fred MacMurray's arm as he plays the trumpet. He's Skid and she's Maggie, and that will do it as a touchstone of romance, and its fragility.

It comes from a play, *Burlesque,* by George Manker Watters and Arthur Hopkins, which opened in 1927, with Barbara Stanwyck and Hal Skelly in the leads. In the play, Skid is a comedian and their marriage turns on his wandering eye until she goes to New York to reclaim him. (There was an earlier movie, *The Dance of Life*—very good—with Skelly and Nancy Carroll.) What's remarkable about the 1937 movie is that that happy ending is given up; indeed, it's fairly clear at the end that, though they are reunited onstage, Maggie divorced him long ago and Skid is a wreck, not far from death. Their song plays on, "I Feel a Call to Arms," but the old image is a farewell, not salvation.

For Paramount: Arthur Hornblow was producing with Mitchell Leisen directing. The script, by Virginia Van Upp and Oscar Hammerstein II, recasts the story so that the couple meet, literally, as a cruise ship goes through the Panama Canal. With opposite movement and extreme verticality separating them, she is a hairdresser on board and he is a sentry. But from the start there's a perilous insouciance about him that clearly needs guarding. A superb scene follows—one of the great café scenes—where Skid plays a very hot trumpet and she is so held by it she hardly notices a young Anthony Quinn trying to pick her up. Mitchell Leisen says they used the two best trumpet players in town to do the sound track, but he omits to say who they were. (Suggestions?)

The interior photography, by Ted Tetzlaff, is lush and moody, and the whole film feels very noir for a romance. The erotics are there not just in the famous pose, but in the ravished gaze Carole Lombard has for the trumpeter. Hans Dreier and Ernst Fegté did the sets, and Travis Banton did the chic, deco clothes. These people are not rich, but they live in moderne sets above their station. It's the visual equivalent of their musical talent in what is really a tragic love story.

Dorothy Lamour is the chorus girl Skid falls for—and why not? Charles Butterworth is Skid's pal, and Jean Dixon is a good wisecracker as Maggie's girlfriend. The strong cast also includes Harvey Stephens, Cecil Cunningham, Charlie Arnt, and Franklin Pangborn.

It's only a romance, but the modesty of scale and the willingness to take a tough ending are what make this picture survive, and seem fresh, when so many more pretentious ventures have turned to dust. You can see here what a charming heel MacMurray could be. As for Lombard, it's difficult to watch any of her great films without feeling regret. She's a girl anyone would die for. This was Paramount's biggest hit of 1937, and one of those bittersweet delicacies where love story and musical are dancing together.

Swing Time (1936)

Consider American industrial production in 1936: *Swing Time* is 35 mm celluloid, 103 minutes. It cost $886,000, at the RKO factory. It grossed $1.624 million in the domestic market and $994,000 in the foreign. Apparently that made for a profit of $830,000. It was the Astaire-Rogers model, and some noted the curiosity that it had no musical numbers for its first twenty-eight minutes. Astaire's character was known as John Garnett, or "Lucky"—he is a stage dancer, and something of a gambler. Rogers's name is Penny Carroll, and she is a dance teacher.

Note that this is 1936, the height of surrealism, and consider that the blithe gem of a man, Garnett, is also drawn to gambling—the irrational pursuit of desire. Now, the triviality of the alleged story falls into place, along with the deliberate and entirely provocative first twenty-eight minutes without music or dance. This is a period of torment, a threshold of ordeal, a trial, before music is willing to begin. After that, it is a movie in which the classic Astaire-Rogers format of attraction-rebuff-happiness is doubled or tripled up, so that even within dance numbers there is the same repetition of structure, a hoppity tic within the toe-tapping, a hesitation or duplication of the beat, otherwise known as syncopation. This film was called *Swing Time,* though many critics noted that it made very little use of the jazz motifs or habits of "swing" music itself.

Pandro S. Berman presided in the form of producer at RKO. George Stevens was the director—and it may be worth adding that, for all his qualities, "swinging" is about the last verdict one would pass on the dogged, careful Mr. Stevens, which only suggests that these films did not really require directing. The dance director was Hermes Pan, whose principal function was to execute the desires of Mr. Astaire. The songs were written by Jerome Kern and Dorothy Fields. Robert Russell Bennett contributed additional music, along with Hal Borne, Astaire's personal pianist. The script—characters say things that resemble dialogue and plot points—was by Howard Lindsay and Allan Scott. David Abel was director of photography. Vernon Walker did the special effects; there is duplication of figures in the "Bojangles in Harlem" number, probably the first time Astaire had used such a device. Van Nest Polglase did the lovely sets in which rooms have the lateral length, empty space, and polished surface fit for dance. The supporting cast includes Victor Moore, Betty Furness, Eric Blore, Helen Broderick, and Georges Metaxa.

The numbers are "Pick Yourself Up," in which he shows her that he doesn't actually need to be taught to dance; "The Way You Look Tonight"; the "Waltz in Swing Time"; "A Fine Romance"; the "Bojangles of Harlem" number in which he dances with everyone except her; and "Never Gonna Dance," in which he plays with the idea and woos her with the theory that he might not dance. As so often, therefore, dance is offered in these films as Astaire's province or domain, a place where he will exist with a woman in unison, while alluding to the possibility of withdrawing permission. So dance is like an ecstatic or religious state controlled by the man, or the mannikin. If you love Astaire's art on film, how long before you wonder about his gayness?

Arlene Croce felt that this was the height of the Astaire-Rogers films.

Sylvia Scarlett (1935)

George Cukor used to tell a story how, in the battered aftermath of *Sylvia Scarlett*, Katharine Hepburn had wondered whether or when he started to lose confidence in the material. There may be something in the suggestion. Cukor was earnest in his gay life, but he did not like to be too gay about it. He knew that there was only so far he could go. *Sylvia Scarlett* was attacked by every critic in town, and it found no audience. Only a few years later, Cukor got dropped from *Gone With the Wind*. I don't think that had to do with his gay reputation, but Cukor never could be sure about that. He and Hepburn were the last people to be taking this risk. Who knows? If it had been Hawks and Margaret Sullavan, or La Cava and Stanwyck, *Sylvia* might be a classic.

But Cukor and Hepburn had volunteered to do it, rather as if some daring urge wanted to see if they could get away with it. It comes from a novel by Compton Mackenzie, and the script was by Gladys Unger, Mortimer Offner, and John Collier—though Cukor claimed that Collier did the real work. Henry Scarlett (Edmund Gwenn) has just lost his wife and fears an audit of the lace-making company where he works in Marseilles—he has borrowed funds for his gambling. So he and his daughter, Sylvia, decide to escape to England; she cuts her hair and dresses as a boy, "Sylvester." Why? Well, to avoid being caught? Because she . . . feels like it? The bold stroke is not substantiated. She needs to be on the run.

On the boat, they meet Jimmy Monkley (Cary Grant), a con man, and then the film is off—swindling and traveling theatricals, worlds in which Sylvia's masquerade feels as legitimate as any in the Forest of Arden. Of course, it is going to have to be explained—and then it gets awkward and stilted again, notably with the character of Michael Fane (Brian Aherne), Sylvia's true love. There's another key character, Lily (Natalie Paley), who ends up with Jimmy. But I think the problem Hepburn and Cukor had was the sudden shock of self-incrimination through this hokey material (the novel is Edwardian).

Pandro Berman produced the picture, Joseph August shot it, and Van Nest Polglase did the art direction. Over the years, it has always had a cult following, as if gays felt a duty to defend it. I think the task is forlorn. The picture really doesn't work, and I suspect that a more fixed heterosexual actress would have had the confidence it needed, and the wit to find extra flirtatious possibility. In a remake—if anyone had the courage—you could play it straight, or you could open up the gay angles. Best of all, Sylvia should be unaware of how fond some girls are. So often in Hollywood, the most daring treatments of gender have occurred when leading parties had no idea what was going on—like Charlton Heston in *Ben-Hur*, or Marilyn in *Some Like It Hot*. The real humor rests in the whispered question, "Can't you see she's a girl?" and the answer, "No, but my eyes felt something!"

Tabu (1931)

It is a story that demands a movie in itself: how two men felt the same sort of gravitational pull toward the South Seas, not just for the sake of the light there, the chance of idyllic native life, or because of the steady flux of the sea, but because their other world had gone sour on them. This was 1929 and '30, with the Great Crash seeming to indicate that every other social assurance was vulnerable. Would there have to be another war? Could anything survive that?

One of the men was Robert Flaherty, born in Michigan in 1884, an explorer in northern Canada who made *Nanook of the North* in 1922, and on the strength of that unexpected hit had got money to make *Moana* and then *White Shadows of the South Seas*, a documentary and a feature, set in the South Seas. But he knew he had not filmed the real thing there yet. The other man was Friedrich Murnau, German, born in 1888, an assistant to Max Reinhardt, a flier in the war; he later made *Nosferatu, The Last Laugh,* and then went to Hollywood for *Sunrise.* And was then himself drawn to the South Seas. Murnau was homosexual, hardly free in that life, and he had seen enough of Berlin and Los Angeles to have the most mixed feelings about the modern city. Two men, both capable of genius, very different, but joined in friendship.

They are transfixed by what they find, which is a few islands still untouched, still places where native peoples fish and dance and procreate and simply exist in the light. We are talking about the friendly peoples that changed the sense of law, society, and happiness for some of the men on the *Bounty.* But then on other islands "civilization" has reached out and turned the native life into business, with the beautiful people left defeated by money, toys, syphilis, and tuberculosis. So Murnau and Flaherty saw what seemed to them the last of the natural world, and as truth tellers and storytellers they were locked in their desire to film it.

The result is *Tabu*, a simple and even silly story about a fisherman who falls in love with a girl who has been declared untouchable: forbidden love, the heartthrob of Murnau's work as an artist. The music is strange and lofty, the plot is daft, and Murnau was resisting sound for its own sake and because he hardly knew how to direct the Tahitians. But the dancing, the movement in light, the imagery—in the hands of Floyd Crosby (he won an Oscar)—is not just the acme of silent cinematography, it is one more example of Murnau's ability to reach the soul through appearances.

Not unexpectedly, the two directors were pulling in different directions: Flaherty had documentary principles he adhered to; Murnau was a poet. I think it's also plain that Murnau felt a love for the natives that Flaherty could not share. So they parted ways, not in anger, but Murnau bought Flaherty out and made what is a Murnau picture. Seeing the film in 1931, a young Lotte Eisner responded to one moment: "A sail unfurls like a sheet of shining silk, and suddenly the dark bodies of natives are seen among the rigging like ripe clusters on a grape vine."

That is great film commentary, and it is the kind of feeling that runs through the whole film. Murnau had made an ode to a paradise that was vanishing. A week before his great film opened, he was dead, killed in a car crash, with a handsome new chauffeur.

A Tale of Two Cities (1935)

If only David O. Selznick had been told to confine his movie adventures to the works of Charles Dickens. He had begun so admirably with *David Copperfield*, and here in the same year is a splendid *Tale of Two Cities*—easily the best on film—even if it can't help but flash its royalist sympathies at us. But Dickens yielded to the same escape in the grim face of the guillotine. The novel is not one of the longest, but at just two hours the picture is crammed with detail and rarely flags. Dolly Tree's costumes are especially good, and Cedric Gibbons did the excellent sets in a photographic style that is invariably nocturnal—Oliver T. Marsh was the cameraman.

By 1935, Selznick was giving a lot of his time to thoughts of going independent, and that may have helped W. P. Lipscomb and S. N. Behrman with their studious adaptation of the novel. Some say that Dickens wrote for a screen and a medium that had not been invented yet. And certainly he had a way of signaling key moments. But I think the secrets to any successful approach to the classics rest in art direction and screenplay first and foremost. And one of the tricks of *A Tale of Two Cities* is to handle the way Sydney Carton is in fact on the periphery of the main story without any awkwardness resulting.

In turn, great credit is due to Ronald Colman, who is wise enough to see that Carton is only a supporting player, and who turns in a magnificent study of a self-loathing alcoholic. It is possible that this performance was based on observations of David Selznick's brother, Myron, the agent—in which case, the film is all the more somber in its sense of a life that has been wasted. In hindsight, it's startling that Colman was not even nominated for the Oscar—instead, nods went to Paul Muni, Gary Cooper, Walter Huston, William Powell, and Spencer Tracy—and Muni won as Pasteur.

The other keynote to the classics is the group playing, and here we have so much to behold: Edna May Oliver outstanding as Miss Pross; Reginald Owen as Stryver; Basil Rathbone, deeply cruel as St. Evremonde; Blanche Yurka, fixed in malice as Madame De Farge; Henry B. Walthall as Dr. Manette; and even Elizabeth Allan as Lucie Manette. Jack Conway directed—and without any evident problems. The best tribute to him is that one can imagine this as a theatrical show organized by Dickens himself. Of course, that is the highest tribute one can find for literary adaptation. What it also amounts to is the realization that in his unique fusion of the melodramatic and the solemn in theme, Dickens had made the movies more likely. We know he loved theater and performance, and it is clear from his writing that he was thrilled by drastic transition—such as the cinema made possible. But, years ahead of the screen, he made us see stories.

The Tales of Hoffmann (1951)

In 1950, Michael Powell and Emeric Pressburger took up the suggestion of Sir Thomas Beecham to do something else in the manner of *The Red Shoes*. He suggested Offenbach's *The Tales of Hoffmann*, and Beecham turned up at their meeting and went through the whole score on the piano, humming along, indicating the action. When he was done, he looked up with a bright idea: What about using that girl from *The Red Shoes*—Norma Shearer?

Moira, I think, said Michael. And before long he and Pressburger were sitting down with Vincent and Alex Korda. Ah yes, said Vincent, "Hoffmann, the hero of his own tale . . . There is a prologue in a beer hall where Hoffmann tells his fellow students the story of his three loves. Then, there are three acts, each one with a different love, each one with a different girl. At the end of his stories he is drunk and when his first love comes to see him he has—what you say—passed out. And she goes off with another boy—his rival always."

Alex Korda looked up: "Three girls?" It's always the same, you can film the Bible or Wittgenstein if there are girls.

The very ambitious production went ahead on a modest budget, with the entire score prerecorded (Beecham conducting), and the action mimed to the music—it was the way Hollywood musicals were done. And it was the swansong of the Archers group. Powell and Pressburger made a script from Dennis Arundell's adaptation of the Offenbach. Frederick Ashton did the choreography. Hein Heckroth did the very simple sets, and Christopher Challis ran the Technicolor cameras.

It is a story of the artist and his muse, brilliant in art and wretched in life, and it was a summation of Michael Powell's very self-conscious quest to make love to his stars. In the prologue and epilogue, Robert Rounseville was Hoffmann, Moira Shearer was Stella, Robert Helpmann was Lindorf, Ashton was Kleinsack, and Pamela Brown took the non-dancing role of Nicklaus.

The three scenes that followed had Moira Shearer, Ludmilla Tchérina, and Anne Ayars as the three girls, with Robert Helpmann and Léonide Massine sharing the male roles. The singing was handled by a cast headed by Owen Brannigan, Monica Sinclair, Rene Soames, and Bruce Dargavel.

Hoffmann is true to its original, and full of good, melodramatic dancing. But it is most cinematic as a series of jokes or asides about eyes and watching. Ten years ahead of *Peeping Tom*, and under the veil of artistic respectability, Powell had delivered an essay on voyeurism, or the love that travels on sight lines, that was obsessive, yet guilty, too. The design was amazing, but ordinary viewers never swallowed the story line. It was a film for the Festival of Britain, whatever that odd fair or the uncertain Britain would make of it. As he made it, Powell had plans to go to Stravinsky to do part of *The Iliad*, or a version of *The Tempest*. It is a line of filmmaking that did not advance until *Moulin Rouge* (which has a strong story and compelling characters). But in the British cinema of, say, 2006, it seems a flight of fancy or wild hope that *The Tales of Hoffmann* was ever considered, let alone made.

Targets (1968)

In 1966, a student named Charles Whitman climbed the bell tower on the campus of the University of Texas at Austin. He had a selection of weapons with which he killed or wounded forty-six people. Two years later, Peter Bogdanovich (who was twenty-nine) and his wife, Polly Platt, seized upon an offer from Roger Corman. He gave them a few days of Boris Karloff, the chance to use footage from *The Terror* (1963), and . . . According to Bogdanovich, Corman calculated that with 20 minutes of Karloff, 20 from *The Terror*, and 40 of something new he could have a brand-new Karloff picture. It was up to Bogdanovich and Polly Platt to find the new stuff and knit it all together.

Bogdanovich thought of Charles Whitman, and he did a script (inspired and helped by Samuel Fuller) in which the killer would end up behind the screen at the premiere of a Karloff film—he was called Byron Orlok in this new film, a disillusioned veteran of horror, increasingly aware that maybe the violence of his own pictures was leaving an imprint in society.

Corman gave the go-ahead: He said if the picture was picked up properly for distribution they'd call it *Targets*—and if it ended up with American International, then it was *Blood and Candy*. It cost $100,000, and Paramount picked it up with an advance of $300,000. Alas, released in 1968, the film coincided horribly with real assassinations: As a serious picture it was death; as *Blood and Candy* it might have broken records.

And it is a quite fascinating little picture and a terrific debut. The Whitman character is played by Tim O'Kelly, and we see the end to his home life before he goes on the rampage: He shoots his wife and his mother and a delivery boy. There is no explanation to this, thank God. What works best of all is the arbitrariness of what "Bobby" does and his own inability to work out a reason or even a context. It is the elderly actor who is driven to be seer and teacher, and it turns out that this is a burden that suits the elderly English gentleman in Karloff very well. Indeed, coming just a year before Karloff's own death, *Targets* is a gentle valedictory to him and a legitimate apprehension that maybe screen violence goes somewhere, from the screen to us.

You could argue that it was a film critic's film, not just in its urge to ruminate over the social place of movie, but in its several fond quotations from Hawks and Hitchcock. But it is also a very cool, authoritative piece of work, admirably shot by Laszlo Kovacs, and really a triumph in bringing together its disparate parts. Bogdanovich himself plays the young director in Orlok's film—a kid called Sammy Michaels. There's a lovely moment when the two film buffs—aged star and novice—fall asleep, side by side in the same bed. And as one great career ended, so another began with enormous promise.

The Tarnished Angels (1957)

Fifty years later, how could anyone believe that Hollywood ever found the courage, the sense, or the madness to make a black-and-white CinemaScope picture of William Faulkner's novel *Pylon*? You can hold the opinion that the literary pretensions of the Faulkner (with a great deal of reference to T. S. Eliot) join forces uneasily with studio melodramatics in the late fifties. But this is, quite simply, the best attempt at Faulkner ever made by the movies. Maybe that competition is less than intense. But maybe a mix of ambition and courage held sway then. How did that "archaic" industry, in so much more conservative a time, have a greater creative daring than we can muster?

Of course, this is a Douglas Sirk movie, even if he needed to persuade producer Albert Zugsmith and his studio, Universal, to take on such a task. Yet it's clear that Sirk had to make compromises along the way, as with Dorothy Malone and her parachute jump, when her filmy skirt went the way of all such things in a high wind. "I didn't have him [Faulkner] work on the *Pylon* script, because I didn't want it. And he didn't want it either. Faulkner always maintained he never understood the movies. I had [George] Zuckerman working with me again [on the script], and I seem to remember that he was instrumental in selling it to Zugsmith: I think he interested Zugsmith in the Malone part, particularly the parachute jump. He (Zuckerman) understood that the story had to be completely un-Faulknerized, and it was."

One might write a book on that paragraph. Yes, the novel has been "focused" so that the flying Shumanns are a marriage coming apart, into which the New Orleans newspaper reporter is drawn as . . . a third party, or a healing influence? The Shumanns (Robert Stack and Dorothy Malone) do a daredevil flying act in the era, just after the First World War, when that was a significant American entertainment. Rock Hudson is the reporter—an intellectual drunk—who sees them as models in a gypsy society.

It sounds garish and pretentious at the same time, but Stack and Malone are clearly aware that they are playing extensions of their characters in *Written on the Wind*, just a year before. There they were brother and sister; here they are married with a child, but torn apart by the crushing lack of confidence that is the emotional area where Sirk really joins with Faulkner.

This is not a comfortable film (in the way *Written on the Wind* never hesitates over its own logic), but it is remarkable and beautiful. The flying is rather fake now, but the erotic image of Malone needs to be an isolated dream. Hudson is far better than anyone had a right to expect, and there are fine supporting performances from Jack Carson and Robert Middleton. But still, the project seems so unlikely that the film's grace and gloomy momentum have to be experienced to be believed. And nothing can explain the certainty we have that Sirk understood Faulkner.

Tarzan and His Mate (1934)

Edgar Rice Burroughs (1875–1950) came along just in time. His first Tarzan book, *Tarzan the Ape Man,* was published in 1914, and by the end of the war Elmo Lincoln had acted the part for a movie. It is the story of an English aristocratic child stranded in the African jungle and raised by the animals. Only once really—in *Greystoke* (1984, directed by Hugh Hudson, but chiefly researched and written by Robert Towne)—has the original story been reimagined. Far more often, the picture business has settled for the myth: of a superhero, flawless in his ethical being, who has it in him to solve those African problems the script can concoct. As a rule, these have very little to do with Africa now, and do not divert Tarzan from Jane and a small white family in the woods.

Tarzan was a fixture of silent cinema, and many different people played the part. But it was only in 1932 that M-G-M reckoned the hero had authentic appeal in big pictures. In 1931, Mayer and Thalberg chose Johnny Weissmuller for the part. He was a handsome brute who had won five gold medals swimming at the 1924 and 1928 Olympics. He would not have to act, but he could wear a loincloth, he could swim, and he was in terrific condition. No man in American movies had worn fewer clothes. Exactly the same could be said for his mate, Jane (Maureen O'Sullivan), in *Tarzan and His Mate,* not the first in the M-G-M series, but the best and by far the sexiest.

Howard Emmett Rogers and Leon Gordon wrote the script from a story by J. Kevin McGuinness that had never exactly occurred to Edgar Rice Burroughs—but his longevity had been paid for in the contract. Harry Holt (Neil Hamilton) and Martin Arlington (Paul Cavanagh) are heading a trip into the interior, looking for ivory and for Jane—Harry's girlfriend, who dropped him for Tarzan on a previous trip.

The film, like early M-G-M Tarzans, employed some African footage from *Trader Horn,* but the "true" jungle was now built in the studio—immense tree trunks, fronds, vines, and ferns and secluded lagoons where T and J might skinny-dip. The lush photography is by Charles Clarke and Clyde De Vinna. The clothes were to die for: leather loincloths and bras that must have relied upon stickem to get past the censor. There is a lot of flesh on view, with clothes slashed to the waist, and no one at the studio failed to see the potential or use the old principle that people who had gone native—even respectable people with oiled bodies and false eyelashes—had an excuse for losing their clothes. Cedric Gibbons directed, and it's surely valid that his wife—Dolores Del Rio—had pioneered the Jane role with nude swimming in Selznick's *Bird of Paradise* (1932).

Weissmuller held the part until 1947—too long. By then Tarzan was B picture material, with a lounge-lizard hunk, Lex Barker. But in the early thirties, this was adult fare. *Tarzan the Ape Man* was 99 minutes; this is 92. The original cost $660,000 (more than *Red Dust*), and it had profits of close to $1 million.

A Taste of Cherry (1997)

As *A Taste of Cherry* begins, it is all rhythm—and just because Abbas Kiarostami's film seems "plain" or "simple" should not exclude the chance of something very sophisticated in that rhythm or the patterning. So the film relies on gear changes and cuts that take us from a view of Badii (Homayoon Irshadi) driving his white Land Rover to shots from his point of view in the driver's seat. And this is an intriguing contrast between narrative drive (or command) and the passivity or the openness of the world.

Except that, as he heads out of Teheran, Badii's road becomes narrower and dustier. At one point, he drives off it and relies on the enthusiastic help of a bunch of workers to lift him back onto the "road." Badii is calm, purposeful, yet sad, I think. He also has an air of class and education not simply due to ownership of a Land Rover. In the city, his vehicle is surrounded by young men offering themselves as day laborers. But he turns them down. He is looking for someone a little different—more of a loner, is it, or someone deserving? For he is looking for someone who will bury him after he commits suicide.

He picks up a soldier and repeatedly asks for his help, but the soldier refuses. He is not articulate. He is not drawn to say that suicide is wrong. But he doesn't want to be a part of it, and in the end he runs away. But then Badii finds Bagheri (Abdolrahman Bagheri), who seems more agreeable. Yes, he will do the deed. But then, as they drive on, Bagheri becomes expansive about the beauties of life—he talks of the taste of mulberries as one of those pleasures no man should give up on.

Is there a contract? It's not quite clear. Badii drops Bagheri off at the National History Museum, where he works. But he talks of doing it that night. Then at night—as if he were an actor in a film—a car comes for Badii and drives him out into the hills and his grave site. But in the morning he is still waiting. Soldiers are carrying out an exercise. A film crew is at work. Badii—or the actor—waits.

A Taste of Cherry won the Palme d'Or at Cannes in 1997, and it was a high point in the surge of Iranian cinema. It is only 99 minutes long, and it is filmed in rough color (by Homayun Payvar). It is characteristic of Kiarostami in that it offers a story situation from which it then withdraws a few degrees, as if to suggest that a kind of documentary is being shot. And so the story yields to the openness of life as a whole.

There's no doubt about Kiarostami's eye or his fruitful sense of cinematic repetition; he is a man obsessed with a quality of mystery or uncertainty in life that has found an interesting model in filming. It's still not quite clear whether this is his sole intent—or a manner and an allusiveness to which he is driven by conditions in Iran. Whatever our eventual answer, Kiarostami is an important new figure, and at the least a minor master.

Taxi Driver (1976)

It tests credulity that Travis Bickle was in the Marines for more than a few minutes. Are we meant to suppose that he is lying, or that Paul Schrader and Martin Scorsese shared a horrendous view of that institution? The question is worth asking in that Scorsese generally longs to be one of the gang, among the goodfellas, in the web. It pains him that natural allies fall apart in *Casino*. The envelopment of family appeals to him. But Travis expects to be alone—indeed, he knows he is alone even if some dream woman from the streets (Iris or Betsy) yields to his ominousness for a moment. Taxi drivers are alone. They have passengers now and then, but nothing really detracts from the knowledge that they are driving alone to nowhere, circling.

So in a real sense, *Taxi Driver* begins as the gangishness of Scorsese and the question in his own haggard eyes as to whether he can stand the initiation of looking at the worst things (like the high-angle autopsy of slaughter)—he can!—and the solitariness or the isolation of Paul Schrader, who saw the vivid yellow cab as a premature coffin and a symbol of paranoia, a place where the rearview mirror takes us straight into the driver's bleak soul.

It is a great idea, or clash of ideas, and the two authors had the ferment of Robert De Niro to fill the gap. And here is the first American film in which the modern city, noirishness, and the religious impulse sit together as naturally as cards in the three-card trick. The streets gasp with smoke or steam, and in the dank air it turns into Bernard Herrmann's rueful saxophone—his last and maybe his greatest score.

It rises naturally to its appointed and electoral climax in which, as if he were running for demented office, Travis may save Iris to win the city—but saving Iris eliminates so many voters and introduces us to the frenzy of blood that Scorsese needed. That is disturbing enough, but then there is the coda, where the damaged hero is back, lonelier than ever, still driving, still searching out the heart of isolation.

Taxi Driver is a great film, in which there was a clear and willing glimpse of disorder as the heart of America. And I doubt that Schrader or Scorsese could have done it alone—so the lesson emerges that even in this symphony of isolation, the contacts in life are vital if mysterious. The gesture toward urban realism exists, but the film is hallucinatory, beautiful and scarring. It is emotional at every turn, and it is a Bressonian attempt to ask whether any soul can save this city—or must he turn into an avenging angel?

Extraordinary photography by Michael Chapman, with exact performances from Albert Brooks, Cybill Shepherd, Jodie Foster (so knowing as to be terrifying), Peter Boyle, Harvey Keitel, Leonard Harris, and Joe Spinell. I watch the film again and again, unsure where it will take me this time. Or whether it is a return journey.

The Temptress (1926)

When the meeting occurred of the Mayer family with Garbo and Mauritz Stiller, Irene Mayer only had eyes for Stiller. Garbo seemed just a shy girl, but Stiller "frightened the life out of me. He was an awesome physical sight—enormously tall, with a very craggy face; a head, hands and feet huge by comparison even with his height; his voice had the rumble of something from under a deep mountain." At that moment, 1925, Stiller might have been the most sophisticated filmmaker in the world. He was Louis B. Mayer's target, though when they all sat down for Stiller's latest, *The Atonement of Gosta Berling*, the boss knew he had to have Garbo, too. Or Garbo above all. By the time he got to America, Stiller was a tall, rather sinister-looking outcast. The word was out that he was gay—he didn't command Garbo.

He got his shot, or ten days at it: He was to direct Garbo in her second picture in America, *The Temptress*. She was to play Elena, a femme fatale, very physical, a woman who would be reduced to following the one man she loved when he disapproved of her. It was from a Vicente Blasco Ibáñez novel, with a lousy script by Dorothy Farnum. Antonio Moreno was the male lead, and Stiller went to war over his mustache. Moreno said, I cannot survive without it (he may have been right), and he won the studio battle. Stiller was laughed at on set because he confused "Action!" and "Cut!," and the picture was beginning to look very florid and dangerously sexy.

The opening passages of the film are far and away the most beautiful and seductive. The story wasn't really Stiller material, but you feel a great eye in that opening and a kind of lethal frankness in Garbo. Then Stiller was fired. Fred Niblo came onto the set. People waited to see if Garbo would quit. She did not—we don't know what pressures were applied. Thereafter *The Temptress* gets sillier and sillier. Garbo has moments: There's a banquet where her breasts look as if they're on the menu; she lets a baby win her heart; and she wears all her clothes with flamboyant disdain.

But there's a ponderous passage in Argentina, where Robledo (Moreno) goes to build a dam. It is said that the film used some footage from Hoover Dam, but it's hard to believe. There's a whip fight with Moreno and another man that is faintly nasty. Lionel Barrymore plays a melodramatic villain. The story drags on over the years and only comes to life at the end. Robledo and his fiancée come to Paris. He is a famous dam builder now. Garbo is there on the streets, looking the worse for wear. Moreno notices her, but she is too far gone. Instead, she sits at a café, thinks she sees Christ (tall, gaunt, not long for this world—it should have been Stiller), and gives him a ruby ring. Most distributors hated that ending so they got another in which Elena snaps to, realizes it's Robledo, and they're happy at last. Stiller died in 1928, back in Sweden. He was forty-five. At last count, just ten of his nearly fifty films survive. He was a great director, but he is now known as the laughingstock who came as Garbo's baggage.

The Ten Commandments (1923)

It's all very well to marvel that Cecil B. DeMille made *The Ten Commandments* in 1923—and he'd have gone to eleven or twelve, if God had had other ideas. But don't forget that he repeated the process in 1956 (and got a Best Picture nomination for it). Not that those who recall Charlton Heston's Moses in the second picture have any idea of the chutzpah of the first.

The original *Ten Commandments*—story by Jeanie Macpherson, DeMille's favorite writer—is 146 minutes long, and it is two stories: the biblical adventure, with the Israelites quitting Egypt; and a modern story—as if the dire example of *Intolerance* had hardly been digested. In the old story, Moses is Theodore Roberts, Rameses is Charles De Roche, Miriam is Estelle Taylor, and Pharaoh's wife is Julia Faye. This involved enormous statues of sphinxes, a Golden Calf fit to be Rudolf the Red-Nosed Reindeer, and the erection of a city in the dunes at Guadalupe (near Santa Maria) in California.

Bert Glennon and Peverell Marley handled the photography, though Ray Rennahan did the two-strip Technicolor sequence at Guadalupe. The art direction was by Paul Iribe, and the costumes were by Howard Greer and Clare West. On the matter of costumes, one has to add DeMille's high relief that the biblical stories took place in hot climes where women were not obliged to wear too many clothes. Indeed, Estelle Taylor as Miriam sometimes needs little more than her husband, Jack Dempsey, would have worn in the ring.

The modern story is more fully dressed and a lot more amusing. The sturdy, Bible-reading McTavish family takes in a waif. They are Mother (Edythe Chapman), John (Richard Dix), and weakling Dan (Rod La Rocque). She is Waif (Leatrice Joy)—and Dan quickly sneaks off with her, headed for the fleshpots. They meet ruthless adventuress Sally Lung (Nita Naldi), a brazen hussy who has escaped from a leper colony! Dan develops leprosy. He shoots Sally and escapes. Whereupon Waif is reunited with John, who reminds her of the Ten Commandments and what a really handy guide to clean living they are. They will marry and populate the world—leprosy-free.

It was a huge popular attraction, and we can only explain that by the exoticism, the flesh on view, and the cheerful willingness to sort through our sins in the cause of human redemption. The picture cost $1.8 million, largely because DeMille went crazy over making Guadalupe impressive. We don't really know whether it was profitable in its time—though we know what DeMille said. At the very least, he survived well enough to take the biblical story by its horns again, give it 220 minutes, all in Technicolor, and only spend $13.5 million on it. The worldwide gross was $80 million—but there was no modern story. Had DeMille given up on us, or did he think we were better behaved? Another question: As the history of the movies and the fate of the world drift in opposite directions, will anyone ever do *The Ten Commandments* again? Of course—Kieslowski's *The Dekalog* is the answer.

The Ten Commandments (1956)

Cecil B. DeMille's first *Commandments* was in 1923, when the film ran 146 minutes. In his 1956 remake, the length had swollen to 220 minutes. Yet the grand old man held firm—not for him *The Seven Commandments,* or any compromise. This was 1956—the year of *The Searchers, Bigger Than Life, Invasion of the Body Snatchers, The Wrong Man, Attack!, The Killing, Lust for Life,* and *The Girl Can't Help It.* And yet, the films nominated for Best Picture that year were *Around the World in 80 Days* (the winner), *Friendly Persuasion, Giant, The King and I,* and *The Ten Commandments.* In a book that often refers to the Academy Awards, there has to be a moment when we observe that the Academy didn't know what was going on in its world.

Or is that right? Of the five films nominated in 1956, only *Giant* and *The Ten Commandments* get in this book—*Giant* because it is still worth seeing for episodes, and *The Ten Commandments* because of its existence. *80 Days,* I suspect, is seen by no one. *Friendly Persuasion* (no matter its Quaker message) has been forgotten, and *The King and I* has dwindled into an image of Deborah Kerr and Yul Brynner dancing.

The Ten Commandments won an Oscar for its special effects—the parting of the Red Sea, the printing of the tablets—but those set pieces are naïve now. Further, the saga of the Egyptians and the Israelites has become a feeble excuse for a film glorifying the wanton breaking of so many religious laws. Was there ever a population that fell for the stupendous confidence trick of such biblical films? Yes, there was. In 1956 "everyone" went to see it. It was the hit of the year with domestic rentals of over $34 million.

Moreover, this country now seems more religious than it did then. Mel Gibson's *The Passion of the Christ* went from being a film no one could see to a triumph. Yes, for our time and concern with moral issues, we have Krzysztof Kieslowski's *The Dekalog.* But DeMille's picture still plays on television, still rents, and still seems to some people to have been made by God.

It wasn't. It had a script by Aeneas MacKenzie, Jesse Lasky, Jr., Jack Gariss, and Fredric Frank, based on three novels about Moses, two of them by clergymen. It was photographed by Loyal Griggs and J. Peverell Marley. DeMille himself read the narration. And the cast included not just Heston but Yul Brynner as Rameses, Anne Baxter, Edward G. Robinson, Yvonne De Carlo, Debra Paget, John Derek, Cedric Hardwicke, Nina Foch, Martha Scott, Judith Anderson, and Vincent Price. Follow the twenty-nine-page printout of cast and crew and you will find that Fraser Clarke Heston (Charlton's boy) was the infant Moses, Woody Strode was the King of Ethiopia, Henry Brandon (Scar from *The Searchers*) was the Commander of the Hosts, Herb Alpert was a drummer on Mount Sinai, Richard Farnsworth was a chariot driver, Jon Peters was a boy on a donkey crossing the Red Sea, and Robert Vaughn was a spear carrier. The music was by Elmer Bernstein. The art direction was by Albert Nozaki, Hal Pereira, and Walter Tyler. Edith Head was one of five people doing costumes; over sixty people did makeup and hair. Farciot Edouart did the process photography. We could go on.

The Terminator (1984)

The last part of *The Terminator*—as the story becomes clear—is one of the great narrative passages in modern effects cinema, and I don't want to spoil it for you if you haven't seen the film. So, whatever your instincts, even if a vote for Schwarzenegger might be your least likely action, try the film. It comes from the best period of a giddy talent, James Cameron, and it is far superior to *Titanic*.

A cyborg (Arnold) has been sent to the future, from 2029 as it turns out, to eliminate a young woman named Sarah Connor (Linda Hamilton) who lives in L.A. now. Why? Wait and see. She is a very tough young hoodlum—indeed, in this film and *Terminator 2* (1991) Linda Hamilton introduced one of the most gutsy heroines American film has ever seen. She was not beautiful, but she was tough, brave, and no one to mess with. James Cameron (who had been married to his writer on this film, Gale Anne Hurd, and the movie director Kathryn Bigelow), later had a child by Hamilton—which is a kind of poetic justice.

In fact, Sarah is helped by another visitor from the future, though an ordinary man, not an indestructible cyborg. This is Kyle Reese (Michael Biehn), and he becomes very attached to Sarah. So what? What could the future care about all this? Work it out, or look at the movie.

There was a good deal of joking at the time that Arnold Schwarzenegger was the only actor in sight who could play a cyborg without much makeup. In fact, his face looks puffy and his red-light eyes can be very nasty, but he's a fascinating toy man in part because he manifests so much of Arnold's natural charm. Just as he is a fearsome and very dangerous something for Sarah, it's clear that the boy in James Cameron (a substantial part of the mixture) is delighted with his plaything, and in seeing just how damaged he can be but still keep ticking and hating. So it's a fair fight, and just as in *Aliens* (the next year), what Cameron brings to the screen is nonstop combat where we feel for both parties.

The script is by Cameron and Gale Anne Hurd, with some dialogue by William Wisher. But it was revealed later that Cameron had taken some inspiration from a couple of Harlan Ellison scripts, "Soldier" and "Demon with a Glass Head." The photography is by Adam Greenberg, and this is basically still a photographed film. Brad Fiedel did the music. Mark Goldblatt edited it, and George Costello did the art direction. The cast includes Paul Winfield, Rick Rossovich, Lance Henriksen, and Bill Paxton, though the minor characters are chaff in the wind of the intense central struggle. It's startling today to find that the picture cost only $6.4 million—yet it grossed $383 million. (It's old money meets new.) That profit margin was a huge stimulant to modern sci-fi, but it would be crazy to confine *The Terminator* to that genre. It tells a great story. It features a woman who might guard the world. And it helped us see that artificial personality ruled—or might govern.

Terminator 2: Judgment Day (1991)

While forsaking much of the original film's haunting narrative quality, above all in the feeling of a kinship between now and the distant future, *T2* does smooth the way for a box-office sensation with the sequel. But it's hard to complain, for this is one of the most exhilarating, unhindered battle films of all time. When people deride pure action films, and the heavy reliance on special effects and the digitalization of the image—and all three are viruses ready to destroy the world made by Bresson and Ozu—you can legitimately invoke *T2* as one of those films that manage to be "his story" written in lightning, if not quite history. (I refer to what President Woodrow Wilson is supposed to have said about *Birth of a Nation.*)

The essential situation of the first film is reprised: Linda Hamilton is living in scruffy Los Angeles with a young son (the one message left from the first film). As we realize now, this son (Edward Furlong, and a guttersnipe) is a serious threat to some kind of cyborg empire yet to come. And now a new menace comes back from the future to eradicate him. This is a new character who appears as a pristine policeman (Robert Patrick). But pristine verging on some new construction. He is not the old-model cyborg from 1984's film. Rather, he is a force that can be "stopped" by bullets and so on for only a moment. Then, his liquid metal constituency (think of it as glowing mercury) simply reforms. Blown apart, sundered, and really roughed up: If a few drops of the metal remain, then he can rebuild himself—as he moves forward—and the film has staggeringly beautiful scenes where the mercury takes shape and the shape becomes the cop without him so much as breaking stride. Robert Patrick's icy presence in this film, coupled with the malignant reanimation of Hugo Weaving in *The Matrix*, are landmark moments in the dramatic characterization of cyborg or cloned forms.

But now the forces of good have done their best in sending back another cyborg to protect the kid. At which point, as I outline this sequel, you might begin to wonder, "Where's Arnold?" Well, don't worry—with Schwarzenegger's reelection as governor of California in 2006 (an event once regarded as highly unlikely), it begins to be clear that he has a way of looking after himself. So, imagine Arnold watching the first film and saying to himself, "Gee—if I was likeable?" So here he is back again as a vigilante cyborg, often astride a motorcycle, in a deadly tourney with Robert Patrick. Now he's a cyborg a kid could hug. He takes a beating in *T2*, and stuntmen are detectable at key moments. But the modest re-jig is enough to give the sequel its ignition and a great thrust of adrenaline.

T2 is longer than *T* (and longer versions still come as DVD director's cuts—James Cameron can hardly kill anything he loves). And that's the great truth behind Patrick's cyborg: Like the cat in *Tom and Jerry* he suffers death by a thousand deaths, and almost immediately goes back to that nice, oozy, shiny silver shit—the stuff of life. For us, his pleasure comes in being destroyed, so his life must always be renewable—he is a start-again death trip.

This film cost $102 million (sixteen times the original), and it grossed $519 million (less than 1.5 times the original).

La Terra Trema (1947)

In the late 1950s, Luchino Visconti's *La Terra Trema* was still regarded as a monumental and valiant realist experiment. More or less, with funding from the Italian Communist Party and his own wealth, the "red duke" had gone to an extreme of Sicily (the Aci-Trezza area) to make a vast three-part account of the harsh life there. He would study the sulfur miners, the peasants, and the fishermen. At the outset, Visconti had had thoughts of using the works of the Sicilian novelist Giovanni Verga as the bare fictional basis, with the real poor serving as players in the drama.

In fact, he found the conditions of Sicily so overwhelming, and the difficulties so great, that *La Terra Trema* only deals with the fishermen. Still, it is 160 minutes long, and a clear sign of the first symphonic plans. There's no doubt but that Visconti's dedication was heroic, but even his great admirer, Geoffrey Nowell-Smith, concedes that he was also in the dark:

> Visconti brought to the project a great amount of revolutionary fervour, and an even greater ignorance of actual conditions. The whole project can be fruitfully compared to Eisenstein's equally grandiose and even less successful *Que viva Mexico!* Like *Que viva Mexico!*, *La Terra Trema* suffered from being abstractly conceived and unrealisable from the outset. . . . The contradiction was too great between what he wanted and what was there for him to see. Like Eisenstein, Visconti arrived on the scene as an outsider with the idea of making a film that would be at the same time a document and a call to arms.

In that, we can see the first great clash between Visconti the realist and radical and the man who would become such a devotee of studio design and art direction. He dreamed of a kind of living opera in Sicily. But he still struggled to have the amateur actors speak lines, no matter that their dialect was confined to their own village. And so it is a film of epic imagery, stark black-and-white footage of the sea, the sky, rocks, and ships, done by G. R. Aldo with Gianni di Venanzo as his operator (these are great stylist cameramen in the making). This imagery lingers for inscrutable flat talk, when really the film could and should have been silent save for some great score. There is music (by Willy Ferrero), but it is nowhere near satisfying or arousing enough.

The idea of this crew—it included the young assistant directors Francesco Rosi and Franco Zeffirelli—on location for six months in Sicily, with Communist funds and a taste for Rome's delicacies, striving to get the fishing people to look like a chorus is both moving and comic, and it's a valuable lesson in how documentary filmmakers (at least) need to look a long time before they decide what it is they can see. So *La Terra Trema* has receded today—and the nine-hour superwork would probably have been the final blow to any hopes of reform in tourism. But in the making of that odd man Visconti, this was a crucial folly.

The Testament of Dr. Mabuse (1932)

Here is a turning-point film, if you like, but one that needs very careful attention. First, let's say that it announces the triumph of sound pictures—not just because of the eerie music (by Hans Erdmann) or the sound effects (the car horns at the fatal traffic light; the bomb ticking in the flooded room); nor even the very punchy police-style dialogue; but in the headlong rush of the film and the way in which a narrative on such electric rails forces us to hurry and attend. Sound film made audiences hang on for dear life—and you cling to this *Mabuse* for fear of being left behind, and because already the natural interplay of all sound and vision has become poetic—let's just call it "cinematic." So the very names "Lohmann" and "Mabuse" are words, or cries, that resonate musically throughout the film.

Then there is this lever in time—call it 1932—with Fritz Lang urged by theater owners to bring Mabuse back. So he and Thea von Harbou (still married) did the script. The photography was in the hands of Fritz Arno Wagner and Karl Vash. And the superb décor is by Karl Vollbrecht and Emil Hasler—this is a film that needs everything from overstuffed salons to elemental stripped chambers. But always, the idea of the cell prevails and haunts the movie. Time and again in Lang, everything blooms from the frame and its interior frames.

So Mabuse is back and now he seems to be the demented, ever-scribbling ghost in an asylum (Rudolf Klein-Rogge), allegedly looked after by Dr. Baum (Oscar Beregi). But the ghost has wormed his way into the mind and the white coat of the "doctor," and so the figure of learned healing masks the demon—again. Indeed, Mabuse is so strong in Baum that he can even die and still direct his empire of crime. But the chilling new insight is not just that this empire seeks booty, so much as the spread of terror and unease. It seeks to dispel confidence.

On the side of good there is the reformed prisoner, Tom Kent (Gustav Diessl); his girl, Lilli (Wera Liessem); and Lohmann, the chief of police (Otto Wernicke). Lohmann smokes all the time. He is Germanic, gloating and not the most gentle of souls. Lang's police chiefs wear ambiguity the way they wear leather. Still it is a fair fight and a quite terrific suspense picture, enough to feed Hitchcock for years and keep 007 busy in decades to come. This is a seminal film in noir, paranoia, and the criminal web motifs.

What happened then? Dr. Goebbels loved it: here, for a moment is a Goebbels we might talk to. He added that Adolf had always liked Lang's films, too—so wouldn't Lang like to head the new film office for the Nazis? The legend is that Lang split fast. Patrick McGilligan's well-researched biography shows that the truth was more complicated. But Lang did leave eventually and settle on the side of the right. Still, don't kid yourself—the exhilaration of *The Testament of Dr. Mabuse*, and the sheer excitement of a real sound thriller (streets ahead of *Scarface*, say), with casual surface violence and a far more disturbing inner kind, raises the troubling question: Isn't the film itself half in love with this wondrous, terrible Mabuse?

That Hamilton Woman (1941)

The story goes that after *Rembrandt* and *I, Claudius,* Alexander Korda rather lost interest in directing. *Rembrandt* had proved a flop, and *I, Claudius* (in the hands of Josef von Sternberg) went from one disaster to another. But the orthodox thinking is wrong and you can see Alex flourish again with the glorious and intoxicating *That Hamilton Woman,* made in Hollywood but pledged to the sanctity of English honor and courage.

Once war broke out, his good friend Churchill was just one of those people urging Alex to make a picture for "morale." As was his custom, he plunged into history and had considered Wellington and Waterloo before he hit on Nelson. The great coup in the production was that Larry Olivier and Vivien Leigh were not just available at the same time in America, but in need of cash after a forlorn theatrical tour of *Romeo and Juliet.* Some said the blush had gone off the rose of their affair. Never mind, Alex was every bit as ardent about Vivien as Larry had been, and if the girl needed a little loving he would provide it.

So Alex and his brother Vincent (his designer) set up home at the General Services Studio. A script was furnished by Walter Reisch and R. C. Sherriff that would take as many liberties as it liked over the love affair between Nelson and Emma Hamilton—chiefly it made her a raving beauty still, no matter that the girl had put on weight in reality. Vincent Korda designed a great library for the Hamilton house in Naples and then quickly changed it to a bedroom—that is the set that has a quite beautiful shot of Emma running to the picture windows to see her beloved off the shore.

As for the battle scenes, rowing boats were reequipped as miniature men-of-war with one paddler in each hull—and it all looks stunning, thanks to Vincent's skill and the photography by Rudolph Maté. A serious issue of research arose over which eye and arm Nelson had lost by the end of his career. An elderly actor was discovered who had played Nelson long ago on stage. Which arm, which eye? he was asked. Well, he said, we never knew, so we changed it from night to night.

Miklós Rózsa wrote the flamboyant music. Alan Mowbray played Sir William Hamilton. Gladys Cooper was Lady Nelson and Henry Wilcoxon was Captain Hardy. The entire thing was shot in six weeks, and paid for almost entirely out of the pockets of Korda himself and Merle Oberon. It proved an enormous success, and very important in the war effort. It was even an inducement to Leigh and Olivier to marry in reality, though there were onlookers who wondered if she loved him as much as he loved him. But it was the best film they ever did together, in which her intense beauty makes a perfect romantic partnership with his ravaged, white-haired gaze. Korda would direct again, but never with the same panache.

Mathieu is a man of the world—very little shocks him or shakes his debonair stride. Neither nuclear fallout nor feminism has withered his mustache. He is French, secure, wealthy, alone, and sometimes on a train from Seville to Paris he is compelled to throw a bucket of cold water over a young woman. Indeed, if life is going to be providential with young women, then let us hope there are ample buckets of fresh water to hand.

What led to this? The most natural thing in the world. Mathieu took on a Spanish maid, Conchita (Angela Molina)—dark, voluptuous, needy, but eager—things a man like Mathieu (a natural connoisseur) could hardly fail to notice. He pursues his own maid, but does not notice that she is only Angela Molina sometimes. At other times she is Carole Bouquet—dark, sexual, needy, but aloof—things a man like Mathieu (a sensitive soul) is bound to appreciate. But how can he pin down "Conchita" when the phantom keeps separating, and he doesn't even know which is which?

This is the last film of Luis Buñuel, and it is worth waiting for. In their different ways, Conchita 1 and 2 can drive Mathieu crazy—not that a man of the world is likely to run amok or lose control in a vulgar, showy way. Still, when he had thought at last he was about to have Conchita, it is vexing to find himself on one side of a barred gate having to watch two or three other men take her instead. And it's not that she seems amazed, outraged, or ill-matched by two or three. Indeed, the sounds he has to hear are rather satisfied, if not self-satisfied.

As he came to his last film, the story goes, working from the novel, *La Femme et le Pantin*, by Pierre Louÿs, with a script from Jean-Claude Carrière, Buñuel had expected to have Maria Schneider for the lead role—for Conchita. But she dropped out. Did she think it might be a dirty film? Whereupon Buñuel had the saving idea—the ultimate weapon in the empire of casting—to cast two actresses and let them alternate scenes. It is inspired. The comedy becomes more than twice as funny and the spectacle of a man of the world who cannot actually tell one Conchita from another is adorable. As for the ladies, they are a perfect match—like two naughty kittens, but naughty in contrary ways. And Mathieu—of course—is Fernando Rey—suave, unflappable, yet demented.

Serge Silberman produced. Edmond Richard did the photography. Art direction was by Pierre Guffroy. Editing by Helene Plemiannikov. Costumes by Sylvie de Segonzac. The film is altogether as stylish as something by Mitchell Leisen. Yet it remains a work from Luis Buñuel, the director of *L'Age d'Or.* And that film and this one know the same secret passion and frustration of the cinema—of wanting your Conchita but being on the wrong side of the bars. The rapport between Rey and Buñuel is immaculate, silent, and as touching as that between Hawks and Grant. And not so very different. Think of this as *His Girls Friday.*

Thelma & Louise (1991)

Everyone agrees that *Thelma & Louise* altered gender studies—but what about genre studies? For the sake of argument, consider it as a Western (it is set in that red-state area to the west of Four Corners). And consider that two comely cows take it into their heads that bulls (or horses) are having all the fun. So the ladies take to the road—the ampersand in the title is for their bronzed arms interlocked on the bench seat—and eventually do just about everything those self-conscious guys have been doing. Indeed, at the end of it all, when police roundup is certain, and when these cows are going to be branded and corralled or made into hamburger, they simply take off. Their car launches off one mesa into the bright blue light that once drew Ethan Edwards away from the homestead in *The Searchers*. Cows can be wild things, too, and they have their merciful freeze frame (just like Butch and Sundance).

This picture comes from a spunky script by Callie Khouri (it won the Oscar), smart enough to rework the genre while ticking off every set-piece scene. Geena Davis (at her most gorgeous) is wastefully married to a cheat and a bore, and Susan Sarandon (an older version of the model) whisks her away to liberty—and death. The turning point is an attempted rape of Geena (done all too well) when Susan comes to the rescue shooting. So off they go, pursued by a sour cop well played by Harvey Keitel. They get to feel the fresh air, shoot up a gas tanker, and eventually Geena gets her rocks off (the couple, we learn, have never had an orgasm in marriage) when she picks up a wild and slippery cowpoke, beautifully embodied by newcomer Brad Pitt.

If it's a film about sisterhood as a new element in our discourse, then I think the suicide is as regrettable as the discreet absence of sex between the girls. Never mind: director Ridley Scott made this a very entertaining and good-looking movie, catnip to the liberal blue states yet funny enough and provoking enough to arouse the red ones, too.

The gallery of scummy men that the story needs are made up by Michael Madsen, Christopher McDonald, and Stephen Tobolowsky, but plainly the film works because of the girls. Davis and Sarandon were both nominated for Oscars (they lost to Jodie Foster in *The Silence of the Lambs*). Sarandon does the acting, but it's Davis who exists and really changes in the course of the film. I daresay that *Thelma & Louise* did better than any other "feminist" film before or since, and one finds that the title pairing of names has passed into common discourse. Whether or not one can bump into them driving around Arizona is another matter—but the driving is good for other reasons, and fantasy keeps the road humming by. Why should we turn on fantasy just because women got hold of it? The film was not nominated as Best Picture, which feels a little mean and disapproving in hindsight. This was a real sleeper, making far more money than anyone had hoped for. And changing some minds.

Theorem (1968)

People remember *Theorem* as a Terence Stamp film, so be warned that he disappears halfway through. Worse still, by far, instead of having his very dry Cockney voice observing the strange world rather in the spirit of Alfie, he is dubbed. And when you dub some actors, there's not much left except blue eyes and tight pants. You do begin to see what a very unnerving life it might be to be an angel of sex.

Still, that is what our Terry let himself in for in Pier Paolo Pasolini's *Theorem*. We are at the splendid house of an Italian industrialist (Massimo Girotti). The house is classical outside and moderne inside. The man lives there with his wife (Silvana Mangano), his daughter (Anne Wiazemsky), a son (Andrés José Cruz), and the maid (Laura Betti). No one seems to know who Terry is or how long he's staying, but he moves in like some kind of old friend, and very soon he goes through the household in a sexual way as if it were zabaglione.

These seductions are all shot in a rather simple way, with chunks of Mozart mixed in with Ennio Morricone (not that you'd know it was him). The family all seem to feel that Terry's the tonic that has changed their life, but although it's 1968 there's more therapeutic solemnity than flat-out sex. You may even come to the conclusion that the household is peopled with listless zombies—and so why doesn't Terry do a lot more emotional damage? But he moves on, and they are all changed in ways that are probably significant if you lived in Pasolini's head: The daughter goes catatonic; the son becomes an action painter who pees on his own pictures; the wife picks up strange young men; the father goes naked in Milan's railway station. And the maid decides to be buried alive.

Pasolini has an austere reputation: He was a Marxist, a poet, a homosexual, and a murder victim—it's a tough act to follow or gaze upon in cold blood. He had his moments, like *The Gospel According to St. Matthew*, and there is a profuse, carnal vitality in films like *Arabian Nights*. But *Theorem* is a key work and a crushing example of art-house gravitas. It rises to sublime heights of impossibility when it tries to lure Silvana Mangano into passages of wanton desperation—yet her false eyelashes remain as stiff and hieratic as the wings on a kite.

I am not being facetious in wishing that the whole thing had a voice-over delivered by Terence Stamp, not necessarily in character (it would be a bold friend of the film who claimed there was a character there), but as our Terry just in from London and telling us tales about making a load of lasagne like this. Am I saying it is pasta? No, not exactly—but I know how Italian cuisine can do wonders even with tripe, and I do think that *Theorem* is worth remembering as a lesson to us all about how addled art-house cinema can become.

Thérèse Raquin (1953)

Early on in *Thérèse Raquin*, Raf Vallone sees Simone Signoret for the first time. He assumes straightaway that she must be the sister to the feeble man in the house. Then, with hushed apology, he realizes that the two are partners trapped in an awful marriage. The whole film is there in a few moments. Signoret—in her early thirties, blonde, with dark eyebrows, a little heavy, a little sullen—is like a bomb. There's an odd resemblance to Kim Novak, and Vallone's character knows he's seen this film before and it would be far wiser not to get involved in any sort of remake. But then there's the impacted sexuality in Signoret, her look, her stare, the bomb that he can ignite. He's lost.

Thérèse Raquin has suffered as a film according to the wisdom that Marcel Carné never did anything worthwhile after the war. Whereas this version of the Zola novel, made for the Hakim brothers, is well worth tracking down. Carné did the screenplay with Charles Spaak, and it's offered as the kind of hard-luck story you might find under so many of those shabby Parisian roofs. Signoret is married to a weakling. They live with the mother-in-law—a small classic of malice and suspicion from the actress Sylvie.

The sexual charge in the setup scenes is palpable and really deserves more exploration. Something in the adulterous and murderous couple should change after their crime—that's why James M. Cain's *The Postman Always Rings Twice* is better and nastier, because the man turns weaker while the woman grows more powerful. You can argue that Carné is at a loss once the husband has been thrown from the train—and in truth he rather gives the film to Paul Frankeur as the loathsome blackmailer who arrives on cue.

Never mind: This is a real picture until its midpoint just because of the carnal charge in Simone Signoret. Yet she had an odd career, and she was already in semiretirement so that she could the better look after her new husband, Yves Montand. Well, once he met Marilyn Monroe—only a few years after *Thérèse Raquin*—Montand showed how tough a care job he was. And Signoret never quite flowered. There's not a moment in this film when she really smiles or turns her radiant sexuality loose. Did she lack the acting confidence to go with it?

Roger Hubert did the excellent black-and-white photography. Paul Bertrand was in charge of production design—there are cramped spiral staircases, mirrors and doors for hiding behind. Maurice Thiriet wrote the music. Carné knew exactly what he was doing—the direction is as fatalistic as could be—but still he fumbles the tragic fate of the couple and the way in which their brief liberated passion might turn sour or toxic. But that shift required the natural, poetic understanding of fate such as Carné had had to command in films like *Quai des Brumes* and *Le Jour Se Lève*.

There Will Be Blood (2007)

The credits say that it comes from Upton Sinclair's 1927 novel *Oil!,* but only in the matter of reading and inspiration, I think. Of course, the next thing to be said is that inspiration may be a far more reliable impulse for filming a novel than the dogged stitchwork of "adaptation." If Paul Thomas Anderson derived nothing else from reading Sinclair's novel, he thought of that kind of place, of the juggernaut of oil beneath the barren soil, and the kind of man who could endure the place and command the force. Just like the last section of *Greed, There Will Be Blood* is a study in lethal human ambition and its searching for power in a landscape that speaks not just to the enigma of frontier but all the old moral questions that hovered over biblical desert.

So it's worth noting that the Anderson who had been in love with human groupings (as in *Boogie Nights* and *Magnolia*) suddenly turns his attention to a man who has never seen a group he did not despise—including his real audience, the consuming public. And whereas in *Magnolia,* say, much of the meaning of the film lay in the interfolding of so many brilliant but effacing performances, so in *There Will Be Blood* we are in constant, unblinking confrontation with a single man and his force—a prospector who shifts his attention from silver to oil, who nags at the earth like a vulture with a corpse, one of the blackest figures in American film history, and an opportunity and a challenge to Daniel Day-Lewis.

His character, Daniel Plainview, uses the world as if it were his mirror, and he sees no one and nothing but his own ferocity. In turn, that prepares him to anticipate and preempt treachery and falsehood in others. What drives this paranoia? It is the simple need to be an American success, a figure of power, an engine in the land. Some people surmised that Day-Lewis was "doing" the honeyed voice of John Huston a lot of the time in the film. That is intriguing and plausible, for this is the Southwest desert such as Huston's Noah Cross may have plundered it. But you might just as well "hear" the voices of Charles Foster Kane or George W. Bush—for those are the lighthouses between which this perilous voyage steers its course.

Not enough happens? Couldn't there be a stronger story conflict, like the preacher saving the man's deafened son? Maybe. But I have to say that this is the most haunting film I have seen as I close the writing of this book, and I take it not just as vindication of the career of a man like Paul Thomas Anderson (now clearly the leader of his generation), but a sign that will and luck coexist still in America to make a resonant film about everything. Just as with *Citizen Kane*—or *Greed* or *Magnolia* or *Chinatown*—this could have been called "American."

The photography by Robert Elswit is lucid and suffocating. Jack Fisk's minimal design is vital. And the film has the best score in many years, delivered by Jonny Greenwood. In the cast, Day-Lewis has worthy aid from Paul Dano, Kevin O'Connor, Ciarán Hinds, and Dillon Freasier.

They Drive by Night (1940)

If you like Warner Brothers pictures around 1940, you can argue the occasional virtue of having three very strong male producers looking over a project—not just Jack Warner, official boss, but Hal Wallis, head of production, and Mark Hellinger, a journalist hired in to deliver a certain number of "tough" pictures, movies from a man's world, as suited a studio that favored macho guys. Hellinger (1903–47) had worked on *The Roaring Twenties,* and *They Drive by Night* was one of his first personal projects.

He had a novel, *The Long Haul,* by A. I. Bezzerides, about brother truckers in California—it was a perfect setup for George Raft and Humphrey Bogart (with Raft as the number one banana). Jerry Wald and Richard Macaulay did the script, and Raoul Walsh was assigned to direct. It seemed like a standard Warners product, with Arthur Edeson on the camera, montages by Don Siegel, music by Adolph Deutsch. It started shooting and all went well, though Wallis was nagging Walsh to make sure the extra money they'd spent on some street market sets came across as "atmosphere."

There was one unexpected factor. Ann Sheridan plays a girlfriend in her usual way. But the trucking boss, Alan Hale, has a wife who takes a shine to Raft and ends up killing her husband, with Raft framed for it. If you looked at the script quickly, you could say it was a femme fatale on her way to being a snake. Raoul Walsh had wanted Catherine Emery in the part, but Hellinger guessed that it deserved someone better. He had seen Ida Lupino as the blind girl in *The Light That Failed,* and he persuaded Warner and Wallis to go for her.

And so a routine picture, with Walsh getting the rough life on the road, the truckers' camaraderie (it's very pro-labor), and the atmosphere, turns into a court scene where Ida Lupino goes mad on the stand—not by giving a big, outpouring performance. All she does is go quieter, more private, and more intense. It is a staggering piece of work, the arrival of a major actress, and it nearly throws the film off balance—for what Lupino implies is that the men in Warners pictures, and maybe the studio as a whole, should watch what is happening to women more closely.

So Warners put Lupino under contract, and were so ready to promote her that in her next picture—*High Sierra,* a breakthrough for Bogart—Lupino got top billing. But Lupino delivers a person in *They Drive by Night* enough to stop the film in its tracks. The man's world, perfectly rendered by Raoul Walsh, has yet to appreciate the implicit social criticism—that living with monotonous tough guys may drive women mad. By the time Lupino got to direct—in the 1950s—she had fixed on these "dames" and made them the center in stories about the difficult position of women. It was Bette Davis and Olivia de Havilland who broke the contract system—but Lupino did her bit to change pictures.

They Live by Night (1949)

Maybe the most extraordinary thing about *They Live by Night* is that the film was finished and ready but waiting on the shelves at RKO for the best part of two years before it got released. Of course, it's a classic now, and clearly one of the great American debuts. But if Nicholas Ray had any incentive to believe that an angel of doom attended him, here was the opportunity. Long before the end, doom was in his system, like rot. But he had his reasons.

Early in 1947, the producer John Houseman found Edward Anderson's novel *Your Red Wagon* and loved it. He passed it to his friend, Nick Ray, to do a treatment, and in time Dore Schary gave it the go-ahead. Charles Schnee was brought in to turn it into a screenplay, but Ray got the directing job, in part because his musicological research had built up a great feeling for the Southwest in the Depression. He and Houseman were old friends, and it's clear that Houseman foresaw something out of the ordinary (he had been involved in great debuts before).

But he had not guessed how Ray would flower. A famously uncertain man, often confused or wandering in talk, Ray became enthused by visual storytelling from the first day, when he determined to use a helicopter to do the opening shot. This was groundbreaking, dangerous, and hardly appreciated by set attitudes. But Paul Ivano helped, and in the end they got an arresting and urgent shot that set the pattern for realism lit up by emotional intimacy.

Though the film is a love story—that of two young people, Bowie and Keechie (warrior names), who never have a real chance at life—Ray got George Diskant to give it the new noir look. Albert D'Agostino was in charge of set direction, and Darrell Silvera did the sets. Ray treated the young leads, Farley Granger and Cathy O'Donnell, as emblems of romance and surrounded them with a battered cast that seemed rough from country life. This emotional atmosphere is very touching, and it marked the start of the Ray style—bold, but trembling with hurt feelings. He could make events, flat in the script, spring to life. And his casts became not just servants to the story, but parts of it.

The supporting cast is brilliant—Howard Da Silva, Jay C. Flippen, Helen Craig, Will Wright, Marie Bryant (the singer), Ian Wolfe, and so on—and there's hardly a scene in the picture that doesn't feel like a fresh egg, just cracked open. You can say the picture is gloomy and a little sentimental, and Granger especially looks too pretty for it these days. But the mixture of tenderness and violence, of Depression grimness and romanticism, was undreamed of then.

RKO was bewildered (as Howard Hughes took over). There was much argument over what to call the film; *Your Red Wagon* and *Thieves like Us* were possible titles. And it didn't get released until late 1949, when it suddenly got rave reviews—from Richard Winnington, Dilys Powell, and a young writer named Gavin Lambert. There was a remake in 1974, *Thieves Like Us*, by Robert Altman.

They Made Me a Fugitive (1947)

This is one of the best, but least known, noir films that came out of Britain in the years after the end of the war—and it is the one that has the most direct comments on the war. Morgan (Trevor Howard) was an air force pilot and a prisoner of the Germans—a good, brave man. But he gets lost in the flux of peace and finds himself caught up in the black-market operations led by Narcy (Griffith Jones). He is framed for the killing of a policeman and sent to Dartmoor. His life and his hopes seem to be over. His girlfriend easily switches her affections to Narcy.

The narrative setup is not just intriguing, but part of a real postwar mood in which war service and sacrifice seemed to have been passed over by those who had taken advantage of wartime shortages that sometimes became more acute in the peace. Narcy is a rare English villain in that he seems to come from evil itself. His name refers to Narcissus, of course, but you can't help hearing "Nazi" in it, too. The script was written by Noel Langley, and Alberto Cavalcanti was the director.

The thing about Cavalcanti was always his ability to present reality and his lurking urge to get inside—at something crazy or distorted. And so in *They Made Me a Fugitive*, the world seen by Morgan as he gets out of prison is filled with malign eccentricity. The photography (by Otto Heller, who would do *The Queen of Spades*) was real, but the mood was nightmarish—as witness a woman who tries to get Morgan to kill her husband, and then does the job herself. The lighting is noir without the clear, stylized manner of, say, films by John Alton or Woody Bredell. But America and California are sunny places. Noir in some English films has as much to do with the country's habitual fogs, and the smoke in Dickens comes from something more sinister than mere industry.

The story works out well enough but without any effort to whitewash the world where very little is reliable or trustworthy. Indeed, there's a true feeling here of the disquiet in the novels of Graham Greene or Patrick Hamilton—it reminds us that the villain's name is also "Nasty" and that nothing is going to be nice again.

Trevor Howard is vital to this concept and its ambiguity. He makes us believe in Morgan as a decent man gone wrong, as well as someone raised to be very tough and quick in a crisis. Britain had its lighter heroes—Stewart Granger, Dirk Bogarde, John Mills—but Howard is from a darker league, less hopeful, more rueful, that includes James Mason and Stanley Baker. But Howard was a fit rival for Spencer Tracy; he believed in his own ordinariness and knew that the world was nothing to be taken for granted. He is one of the most grown-up figures in British film, even if that experience helped drive him to drink. Sally Gray is unusually good as the woman who helps Morgan.

They Shoot Horses, Don't They? (1969)

There was a lot of talk at the time that this movie had betrayed Horace McCoy's stringent pulp novel of the thirties in which the collapsing America is displayed in about 150 pages and a marathon dance contest. There is a story about how the James Poe screenplay was subtly undermined or softened that is told in Richard Corliss's *Talking Pictures.* Poe was set to direct with a cast of unknowns. Then everything went "known" and expensive. But anyone seeking out the picture now will be amazed that so bleak and desperate a picture was attempted, let alone released. It comes as a further surprise to see that a young Sydney Pollack directed it, and the discovery leaves one wondering what he would make of it now in the long shadow of his diminution.

It's not just that Pollack handles the frantic rhythm of surging activity and haunted rest with such authority. It is rather more that he seems perfectly at ease with the metaphor of the dance contest as America's unique survival test. Nor is it that the particular stories are tidily fashioned to make up the larger quilt. There are also two performances—Gig Young as the MC and Jane Fonda as the leading figure—that are beyond dispute the darkest voice of the thirties and its despair. Gig Young died some ten years after the film—for which he won the Supporting Actor Oscar—but it's a marvel that someone didn't recognize this performance and lead him away to some place of rest or oblivion. As for Jane Fonda, for all the enthusiasm for the way she has survived as a "pretty" woman of her age, you have to see her unflinching nihilism in this film to know what was survived.

There are some weak spots: Michael Sarrazin is too sentimental—or there is a pathetic need in the film to make him likeable. The mercy killing is overdrawn. Indeed, we hardly need it as a motif: Living on in this film is a greater curse than death. Susannah York is very good in her mad scenes, but they are a touch too stagey for the speed of this narrative, and again York looks like a feeble attempt to make the film more palatable, or even sexy.

There are many other fine supporting performances—Bonnie Bedelia (so close to stardom in films, but never quite, and seeming to guess it here); Bruce Dern—another near star very shrewdly cast; Red Buttons, so much better than in *Sayonara,* where he did win a Supporting Actor Oscar. But all the good work amounts to a superb, fatalistic ensemble in which Young and Fonda are the tireless sources of infection or disbelief.

They Shoot Horses, Don't They? didn't do well, and it has not survived as well as others of its time—notably *Midnight Cowboy.* But this is more lucid, more painful, and more American. It is unquestioned proof of a knowledge (in 1969) of how far show business itself was a corrupting energy that had driven the dream mad.

They Were Expendable (1945)

John Ford was in the Navy and in the Pacific during the war. He had his own movie group under the OSS, and his pictures included *December 7th* and *The Battle of Midway. They Were Expendable* was a nonfiction book, by William White, published in 1942, an account of the PT–boat campaign after the Japanese seizure of the Philippines and the retreat by General MacArthur. M-G-M had purchased the film rights, and they wondered if Ford might be available to do a feature film based on it. But his availability depended on prior commitments to the Navy and to Fox, and a realization that, once you've begun to film such things for real, it's harder to story them up again. In 1944, Ford would write about feeling abashed that "a great warrior like me should be in mockie-land while the good people are fighting."

Yet it worked out. Secretary of the Navy James Forrestal put in a word and Darryl Zanuck at Fox turned a blind eye to Ford's opinion that he had been wounded. *They Were Expendable* began filming at Key Biscayne, in Florida, in February 1945, with a script by Frank Wead and others. Joseph August did the photography, and he worked wonders in giving the bright look of Florida a duskier Pacific sheen. It's a film to conjure with—especially in comparison with the more roughly shot war documentaries—in games of "authenticity." *They Were Expendable* is "mockie-land," yet it feels as if we are there.

It's an episodic film, based on a series of strategic withdrawals. It is made out of intense, idealistic respect for the men of the Navy—people Ford had known and seen die—and it's worth stressing that Ford was at his best in the cohesion brought on by defeat. For me, Ford misconstrued the military and resolved to see it as a central "family" (whereas society is *the* American family). But still he was at his most heartfelt in seeing this family proved by defeat. What is most interesting, and left unanswered, is how far the fictional strength of the men in *They Were Expendable* sat beside his real experience of breakdown and worse under combat. It was a just war, and courage is a natural human resource, but so is fear. And there is no doubt, finally, that Ford was dedicated to the ideal and myth of the military—whether the war was just or not.

Long, and leisurely (135 minutes), *They Were Expendable* is a quiet epic, with Robert Montgomery as the lead and John Wayne as his second. They make a good contrast: The starchy Montgomery had served, whereas the Duke's terrific credibility had escaped service. Donna Reed is brave and lovely as a nurse. And the cast is fine all the way down in a film mercifully free from comic interludes, drinking scenes, and heavy sentimentality: Jack Holt, Ward Bond, Louis Jean Heydt, Marshall Thompson, Leon Ames, Cameron Mitchell, Russell Simpson.

Note: The film did not open until December 1945. Thus, in hindsight, its account of an initial defeat becomes all the more triumphant. And it is a film that shows officers airlifted out while ordinary men are left behind. Real soldiers and sailors may have been more caustic on such matters. Ford had mixed feelings about it, in part because M-G-M cut it without him.

The Thief of Bagdad (1924)

The sharpest eye cast on Doug Fairbanks was that of Alistair Cooke—it was the golfer studying the acrobat. And Cooke, who was a very good observer of movies and the movie scene, saw the first signs of limit in *The Thief of Bagdad*, made when Doug was forty—a dangerous age, of course. The story was out that *Bagdad* had cost $2 million (a prodigious sum), and it was Cooke's opinion that for that kind of money the audience deserved and expected nothing but absolute effortlessness in the leaps, the huge swinging movements, and the landings. It's a shrewd point. At the circus, say, after someone has done a triple somersault or some such marvel, we can forgive a stumbled landing—somehow it speaks to the actual difficulty. But on film, we entertain a fuller sense of perfection—something spiritual, expressive of a deep inner health and vitality, enough to overcome the roguishness of Doug's role in *Bagdad*. And in this film, he has a few moments of being out of breath or unsteady on his feet. All of a sudden people looked for sweat and the beginnings of a belly—and in *The Thief of Bagdad*, he had costumes that did show that part of the anatomy.

The story goes that it was Doug's first hope to have Maxfield Parrish design the film. That fell through (though Parrish did do a fine poster), and costumer Mitchell Leisen recommended William Cameron Menzies (it would be his first movie). There were palaces and grottoes by the mile, 3,000 extras a day as well as a real flying carpet. You can see where the money went.

This is not a casual reference to production values; rather it is a crazed urge to make Doug's gymnasium overpoweringly real or atmospheric—when truly his art was as abstract as gymnastics. But the dressing-up got out of hand. The décor began to smother the wonder of it all. Every Olympiad, the world is set alight again by the poetry of bodies moving through space. It is part of the essential dance in films, and Doug, like his friend Chaplin, was a study in motion. The sadness is that he never saw how far the simplicity was the secret.

The script was the work of Doug himself (under the name Elton Thomas), Lotta Woods, James T. O'Donohoe, and a certain Achmed Abdullah. Arthur Edeson did the photography, and William Nolan was the editor. There was a special score written for the picture, and it did well. The only question is whether it managed to get its money back. The supporting cast included Snitz Edwards, Charles Belcher, Julanne Johnston, Sojin, and Anna May Wong.

One last point: This is one of the films in this book (written during the direst years of the Iraq War) where the title refers to the country that was just a few years old in 1924. So let it be said that Doug's good humor and sweeping ignorance make assumptions about Baghdad and its people that are outrageous and so total that no one could really assume there would be no retribution. It is still fair to speak of Doug's vitality and innocence. But time has passed, and we know that neither quality is safe out of the house.

The Thief of Bagdad (1940)

Release dates don't often mean a lot, but this glorious adventure fantasy was opened at Christmas 1940, and there's no better way to think of it than as a sack full of wonders and presents when the world had little to look forward to. It was the brainchild of Alexander Korda, and the meeting ground for all the talents he could pull together. The marvel is that its style is so consistent when it almost certainly had six directors: Alex and Zoltan Korda and the designer William Cameron Menzies, not to mention the three credited directors—Ludwig Berger, Tim Whelan, and Michael Powell.

It's the sublime confrontation of two very different figures: Jaffar (Conrad Veidt), the great wizard, dressed usually in black, and Abu (Sabu), a native boy. Veidt was a recent refugee from Germany, one of the most handsome of men, but an actor with mime in his soul—he had been Cesare the sleepwalker in *The Cabinet of Dr. Caligari*. As for Sabu, he was fifteen, a boy from India, who had already done *Elephant Boy* and *The Drum*. He was pretty, quick, and agile, but it was his mischief, his merriment, and his sweet nature that made him a star. With Veidt, he had a cheeky chemistry that has not aged—it still seems as fresh and moist as the film's Technicolor.

That exquisite look was owed to many skills: to art director Vincent Korda, who doggedly followed every order from Alex or Powell to make the colors more intense or the designs less historically plausible; to a design crew that included Menzies, Percy Day, Ferdinand Bellan, and Frederick Pusey; to Oliver Messel, who did the costumes—themselves an act of defiance against wartime austerity; and of course to Technicolor, including its resident adviser, Natalie Kalmus, and the two cinematographers, Osmond Borradaile and Georges Périnal.

The script was by Lajos Biró, with dialogue by Miles Malleson. André De Toth was a production assistant. Who did what? I don't think anyone cared or remembers now. Powell, we know, did a lot of stuff with the ship, including putting an eye on it and then tracking into the eye. You have to give credit finally to the producer, to Alexander Korda, one of the most inspired men in his awkward craft—full of generosity, wit, panache, and taste, and always with a spare Hungarian up his sleeve and the conviction that the look of the Arabian Nights could be cut together with shots from the southern Californian desert and the Cornish coast. It's very hard to look at Korda's small empire during the war years without being touched. And this was maybe the wildest thing they ever did. If you have children, show them this film—and stay with it if they totter away, drunk on color.

The cast also included June Duprez (yes, Korda had an eye for women), John Justin, Rex Ingram (as the djinni), Miles Malleson (as the sultan), Morton Selten, Mary Morris (such a rare actress), Bruce Winston, Hay Petrie, Allan Jeayes, and Adelaide Hall. Oscars went to Vincent Korda, to Georges Périnal, and to Lawrence Butler and Jack Whitney for special effects.

The Thin Man (1934)

Don't worry about a thing: we know you take Dashiell Hammett very seriously (we all do), and yes, the thin man in Hammett's novel is a murder victim who can fit into a very narrow space, whereas in the films the thin man is evidently William Powell, and he's thin because thin is cool and suave and because he doesn't eat anything. And if you really owe allegiance to literature, you can tell yourself that Nick and Nora Charles are an allusion to the "glamour" of Dash and Lily (Hammett and Lillian Hellman). But in the end, it doesn't matter because really they are William Powell and Myrna Loy. Hammett and Hellman were just lucky to be involved.

In fact, the screenwriters on the first film, Frances Goodrich and Albert Hackett (married, too), encouraged the notion that the Charles couple were based on them. They did a script in three weeks for producer Hunt Stromberg after M-G-M had bought the book for $14,000. Stromberg hired Woody Van Dyke to direct (the key move), and Van Dyke hit on Powell and Loy for the leads (he had just directed them in *Manhattan Melodrama*). The studio was happy with Powell, but Louis B. Mayer objected to Loy. He thought she was too much of a lady. But Van Dyke fought for her and Mayer said, OK, if she's available in three weeks for another picture. And that is why he and James Wong Howe shot *The Thin Man* in sixteen days (with two days for retakes).

We are talking about chemistry here, as well as alcohol, and the fact that Powell and Loy would do fourteen pictures together. Loy accounts for it as well as anyone: "I played differently with Bill. He was so naturally witty and outrageous that I stayed somewhat detached, always a little incredulous. From that very first scene, a curious thing passed between us, a feeling of rhythm, complete understanding, an instinct for how one could bring out the best in the other."

They were sophisticates. When Nora joins Nick in a bar, she asks the barman how many he's had. Seven, says the husband, and she orders seven for herself to catch up. It's one of the most uxorious gestures in American film, a sweet raspberry to the memory of Prohibition (ended just the year before) and a sign of something very important about this married couple. As Loy said, doing married is hard—it's usually what happens when the film ends. But these two like each other. They drink in harmony. And if that damn dog lets them, they cuddle. There it is, a rarity in the system: a married couple who are still doing it.

They also shared the same bored amusement with the "explanation" scenes—who did it, how and why. They guessed that the audience wasn't listening. They were just reclining in Powell'n'Loy (a smooth cocktail). Don't bother to distinguish the plots in all the sequels. Just thank Van Dyke. The original also included Maureen O'Sullivan, Nat Pendleton, Minna Gombell, Cesar Romero, Natalie Moorhead, Edward Ellis, and Porter Hall.

The Third Man (1949)

How easily the great works of film become anthologies of their own highlights. How seldom we actually watch a picture like *The Third Man* again from start to finish—because how are we to muster the proper surprise when we know it inside out? But there is a writhing tension deep down inside, between the calm evil perpetrated by Mr. Harry Lime (we do not see the children destroyed by dud penicillin, but we see the harrowed face of Trevor Howard watching them—and with Trevor Howard's face in those days it was hard to make a flat movie) and the eloquent, sardonic, charm-for-sale effulgence of Mr. Orson Welles. Even the cat knew to perch on his shiny shoes, and surely Carol Reed knew how to get that knowing glance as the awoken light from the window above falls on his chubby smile.

That prompts a fascinating question: How in this postwar Vienna, where the strudel is short, is Orson so ecstatically well-fed? Is a private supply sufficient explanation, or do we need to conjure up the feasts of self-love to explain it? So yes, maybe Cary Grant (a very silly Holly, perhaps) and the knife mouth of Noël Coward as Lime would have been more chilling—or more Greene-ish. But when you put Joseph Cotten and Welles together, just those few years after *Kane,* it was impossible for the picture not to be a continuation of the Leland-Kane debate.

I think Carol Reed took that extra in his stride, and knew he had to give Orson some side dish—so he let him do the Switzerland vs. the Renaissance dialogue on the Ferris wheel, reckoning to get "free of income tax, old man" into the bargain. The result is one of those piercing studies in a certain kind of soft English friendship, where one old chum has been taking the other for a ride for decades. And, come to think of it, it's a picture about modern evil—which, I'm sure, is what Reed and Greene and even Alex Korda had in mind. That's the very thing that worried the other producer (the second third man?), David O. Selznick, into thinking these boys might be buggers.

So they might, and so their fondness, their betrayals, and their executioner's kindness is at the heart of it all. Alida Valli's somber Anna walks out on the film at the end not because she's learned she can't trust men, but because she sees how much of a stooge she was, someone to touch up the zither strings with, someone to be the "love interest." Whereas, of course, *The Third Man* is only interested in the preoccupation of rats—how to survive, how to wien.

I meant to say "win," but mistyping came to my aid—for surely this film is very Vienna and would have to be included in the great season of Vienna and the Movies. I had my wife take my picture in Lime's doorway once. I backed in. The door opened and an old woman inside took it all in at a glance. "Ah, that Harry Lime!" she sneered. But she loved the memory.

The 39 Steps (1935)

In all the merry briskness of *The 39 Steps* there's hardly time to notice that our hero, Richard Hannay (Robert Donat), is about the best original of James Bond you'll ever find. Except that I prefer Hannay, because he's not quite the rapist with drop-dead one-liners that Bond would become. As played by Donat, he's got the right Scots tinge, a hair-line mustache, and a saucy twinkle when he gets handcuffed to Madeleine Carroll.

John Buchan published *The 39 Steps* in 1915 as a quick story of espionage on the run, with Hannay being pursued by goodies and baddies alike. Charles Bennett did the screenplay with a free spirit, and Bennett himself—very sporting and fond of poor puns—might have been the best Bond of them all. It was a Gaumont-British film, and it has the air of having been shot in half an hour. Not that Hitchcock misses a trick. At the end, as the dying Mr. Memory (Wylie Watson) is pouring out the secret formula he has learned, with a lot of *r* squared, the screen is filled with heads gathered around him, but there's still a chorus line of flapping legs as the girls fill the stage behind. There was always that surrealist in Hitch, waiting for an opening.

It would be folly to say this means anything more than innocent entertainment, but if Hitch had a killing to do, he knew how. Out of nowhere, Lucie Mannheim staggers into the room, pitches forward, and there's a dagger in her back. And she has fallen, so that the light hits the handle a treat. Most of the time, the film is nocturnal and very noir (photography by Bernard Knowles), with lovely little stone-bridge sets and clumps of heather (art direction by Oscar Werndorff) when they get up into the Highlands.

Godfrey Tearle makes a good heavy, and there are delicious cameos from John Laurie and Peggy Ashcroft as a crofter and his wife. (Donat notices her, too—for the 1930s, he had a very alert gaze, and it was clearly a tragedy when illness took off his edge.) Above all, he fits the sweet, nasty geometry of Hitchcock's traps and closing-ins, and he's insouciant, droll, and brave without being smug. As for Madeleine Carroll, this is one of those few films where you suddenly see that she was sexy. She doesn't have a lot to do except take her stockings off while handcuffed, but for 1935 that was inflaming. And her character, Pamela, was never even in the book. She and the handcuffs were supplied by Hitchcock.

Don't forget that Michael Balcon was the producer on this, with Ivor Montagu as his assistant. Alma Hitchcock and Ian Hay touched up the dialogue, but Bennett's script seems perfect. It was all done at Lime Grove Studios (later a stronghold of BBC TV) with the deft expertise required of episodic television. But it was a big hit, and it's still one of the best straight thrillers of the thirties.

The Thomas Crown Affair (1968)

Take one modern mastermind, a businessman turned by boredom toward thieving. Add a beautiful insurance investigator determined to capture him, but just as resolved to go to bed with him. It's fairly plain that *The Thomas Crown Affair* is a glorified fantasy festival—and it's a little less clear that Crown is another version of James Bond in that he is handsome, tailored, educated, class to his buffed fingertips—yet an outlaw at heart. And the woman is every Miss Perfect who wants to know what Bond keeps in his 00.

Coming off *In the Heat of the Night,* Norman Jewison was to produce and direct *The Thomas Crown Affair,* with a screenplay by Alan Trustman. He was taking his time contemplating which actor to cast as Crown when Steve McQueen started on a series of badgering calls. It's not for you, Steve, Jewison told him. You'd have to wear a tie. You've never been to college. McQueen grinned, and said less and less. He just went into his sardonic and superior act. Until Jewison saw that, yes, Steve McQueen could play Thomas Crown. It's that old principle in fantasy that goes back to Bulldog Drummond or Hawkeye: Make sure the gentleman can run through the forest or the bedroom barefoot.

Of course, putting *The Thomas Crown Affair* to any test of character risks solemnity. But you can see, in hindsight, how the larger hippie invasion of movies had left millions of people craving glamour, stylish clothes, and an Ivy League education (the asserted assets of Mr. Crown). And the story can turn sexy. For my money, Pierce Brosnan and Rene Russo in the remake are having sex while McQueen and Faye Dunaway are giving off signals. Still, they have their adherents. Norman Jewison meanwhile revealed himself as a mod by breaking up the frame in as many pretty shapes as he could think of. This was tiresome in 1968, and it's inane and incredible now. You realize that the Michel Legrand score, with "Windmills of My Mind," was doing a lot to hold the film in place; with lyrics by Alan and Marilyn Bergman, it won the Oscar for Best Song.

Alas, the one great asset of the rich in films of the thirties—their ability to say funny things—is missing here. But McQueen takes a supercilious pleasure in keeping his tie on, and Dunaway probably has a few wicked ideas about what she might do with it. They needed Buñuel. But it was asking too much of the system to realize that. Haskell Wexler did the photography, and he probably disapproved so much of the entire venture that he started doing things like waiting for the right light. As if the light mattered in a work so artificial. Also with Paul Burke, Jack Weston, Yaphet Kotto, Todd Martin, Sam Melville, and Addison Powell.

Thomas Graal's Best Film (1917)

Mauritz Stiller had an eye and a feeling for the great Scandinavian outdoors; thus, *Sir Arne's Treasure* (1919) is a revenge epic about Scottish mercenaries marooned on the Swedish shore because of the ice. It shudders with the cold and the prospect of slaughter, and it has many exciting moments. But put Stiller indoors, where frivolous but good-natured people can wear less clothing and show some awareness of a modern world, and that's when he comes to life. It's not just that he was so good a director—he was a natural director of smart comedies (and history teaches us that that is the hardest genre).

So *Thomas Graal's Best Film* is nothing less than an inside pictures story—not necessarily the first, but certainly the first in showing how far the need to conjure up film stories was changing the way people regarded the thing called life. So man-about-town Graal (Victor Sjöström) is a film scriptwriter and a ladies' man. But he can't think of a subject to do next! It's only when he hires a very lively Scots girl, Bessie (Karin Molander), as secretary that he sees how far her fantasies may give him material. Of course, the two of them fall in love, but it's part of Stiller's droll irony that they can never be quite sure whether they're in love with each other or the idea of the movie they are making.

The screenplay was written by Gustaf Molander (who would also write *Erotikon*), and it's clear that he was as much of a support to Stiller as Victor Sjöström. The actor-director (who would lead the way to Hollywood) was an earnest and humorless presence in his own films, and a grave figure in life, yet Stiller somehow freed a sense of comedy in him—or was it that the presence of the delightful and bubbly Karin Molander playing the Scots girl reminded Sjöström of fun? American movies were strong on girlish charm at this time (think of Mary Pickford), but Karin Molander was unsurpassed for naturalness, invention, and sheer charm. Everyone loved her, apparently, and several fellows ended up marrying her.

Thomas Graal's Best Film is photographed by Henrik Jaenzon, and naturally enough he plays a photographer in the film. The production design was by Axel Esbensen. The picture that survives is barely an hour long—and it was probably longer once. No matter, this is a cheeky film, full of insights into the ways of romance and romanticizing—and thus one of the first movies with a real comic understanding of the intricacies of picture making.

It proved such a commercial success in Sweden that Stiller decided to marry his two leading characters, and so in *Thomas Graal's Best Child* (1918) they collaborate on their biggest production yet—a child, but one that will be a credit to both of them. And we all know what a vexed thing collaboration can be in the picture business.

The Three Burials of Melquiades Estrada (2005)

Technically, this is a French and American picture, directed by Tommy Lee Jones and produced by Michael Fitzgerald, but largely financed from France by Luc Besson. Yet in most significant ways, it is a Mexican, or a Mexican-American, picture, written by Guillermo Arriaga, the author of *Amores Perros* and *21 Grams*, and the chronicle of a strange story of amity and loyalty worked out along the Mexican-American border. It is, legitimately, a Western, to the extent that it insists on an honest, humane look at some types of life now evident in the American West and along the border. From time to time, it summons up the iconography of Peckinpah and Huston, yet it is its own film, a rough but wry comedy in the end and a picture that takes for granted the shared, harsh times of most Mexicans and Americans.

Pete Perkins (Tommy Lee Jones) is a rancher in the town of Van Horn. He hires an illegal Mexican immigrant, Melquiades Estrada (Julio César Cedillo), and the two men become friends. Together, they date Rachel (Melissa Leo), a married waitress, and Lou Ann Norton (January Jones), the neglected wife of a border guard, Mike Norton (Barry Pepper)—the Nortons are from Cincinnati. Norton shoots and kills Estrada; it is an accident, but also the consequence of Mike's arrogance and his overreliance on his weapons and the echo of an early shot where a fox is mistaken for a coyote. So Perkins, who has learned the truth, kidnaps Norton and compels him to help carry Estrada back to Mexico for a proper burial.

The film becomes a lugubrious journey, with Estrada's body suffering badly in the heat and being subjected to some comic but grisly preservation techniques. The journey opens up the real nature of Mexico, as a place of amiable, decent people who muddle along as best they can in the blind shadow of American energy and purpose. In the end, the mood is probably closer to Faulkner than to any set movie examples. The penetrating survey of a real border and its ambiguities was offset by the serious neglect that the picture received on its American opening. The case remains that it is one of the best American films in recent years, and the fine elucidation of an intriguing actor as a considerable director.

As photographed by Chris Menges in ways that leave no doubt about the heat and the marginality of life, this is a picture that does what cinema has always been supposed to do: It sees through terrain to the heart of a treacherous social system. Tommy Lee Jones has been a brusque actor often, nearly brutal in his mercenary choices (the *Men in Black* films), but this movie is an uncovering of philosophy and tenderness and a beautiful proof of the independent spirit that may bring American movies back to life. Barry Pepper is outstanding as an unlikeable character. January Jones is excellent as a doll trying to be a woman. There are good supporting performances from Dwight Yoakam and Levon Helm (as a blind man who asks any passerby to kill him). Melissa Leo serves coffee and makes the world tick, but isn't going to get overly attached to any one man.

Three Comrades (1938)

We know much more than we might about *Three Comrades* because it was the picture on which F. Scott Fitzgerald was most heavily involved as a screenwriter (and the only one where he got a credit). This is the picture about which Fitzgerald implored producer Joseph L. Mankiewicz, "Can't a producer ever be wrong?" And this is the Fitzgerald who, a couple of years later, in the unfinished *The Last Tycoon*, would write an incisive portrait of how a studio like Metro-Goldwyn-Mayer worked. So it's useful to know—by way of Mankiewicz—that the chief objection to Fitzgerald's dialogue came not from the producer, but from Margaret Sullavan, who said, "These lines are unsayable!"

Three Comrades is from a novel by Erich Maria Remarque, published in 1937. The comrades are Germans who fought in the First World War and who try to make their way in the peace. Against a background of rising fascism, they meet Patricia Hollmann, a magical and inspiring young woman who is dying of consumption. One of the three, Erich, marries her. But in the end she dies by her own volition in the hope that Erich and Otto (the two left) may make their escape from Germany.

Mankiewicz was the appointed producer at Metro, and he had known Germany as a student in the late 1920s. Frank Borzage was the eventual director, and Edward Paramore was brought in as cowriter when Fitzgerald's script faced trouble. It also seems that David Hertz and Waldo Salt did some rewriting. There was a clash: Fitzgerald had been hired not just as a master of dialogue but as someone who knew the Europe of the Lost Generation firsthand. By instinct, Fitzgerald would have wanted German actors and a tough view of the changes in German society after 1933. But Metro was eager not to lose its German market (despite real knowledge of Nazi methods) and so it was very reluctant to offend Germany. Giving the project to Borzage—as opposed to, say, Fritz Lang—was a way of building the romance into a fit opponent of war. It made Sullavan more enchanting and more powerful. For Borzage excelled with stories where love could overcome depression, political unrest, or worse.

The wonder is that the picture ended up as good as it did. Joseph Ruttenberg did the photography, with montages by Slavko Vorkapich. The art direction was by Paul Groesse and Edwin Willis—though it's a stretch to say that we believe we're in Germany. We suspect we're at Metro, and we feel too many realities tugging at the flimsy structure. And though Margaret Sullavan is ethereal and breathless and everything anyone will ever tell you she was, the men are still Robert Taylor, Robert Young, and Franchot Tone. They feel like American guys—without that overcast that affected Europe in the 1930s. The cast also includes Guy Kibbee, Lionel Atwill, Monty Woolley, Henry Hull, George Zucco, and Charley Grapewin. It's not that Mankiewicz was wrong—rather, the project was at the wrong studio. (It should have been Warners?) You do not see *Three Comrades* and know that a terrible war is inevitable. You think the world is unfair to lovers.

The Threepenny Opera (1931)

Die Dreigroschenoper opened in Berlin in 1928, a musical play by Bertolt Brecht with music by Kurt Weill. In turn, it was a version of John Gay's *The Beggar's Opera* (1728), and Brecht retained the struggle between Peachum and Macheath, while bringing action forward from the eighteenth century to Soho in about 1840. And *The Threepenny Opera* is more or less world-famous because of the song "Mack the Knife," which has been through so many versions—no matter that few people have seen the work onstage, let alone the movie (which was in its day the subject of a fierce legal battle between Nero Films, the production company, and Brecht and Weill).

Brecht and Weill joined forces in the late 1920s and early 1930s on three shows—*Threepenny Opera, Happy End,* and *Mahagonny*—all of which were considered "epic theatre" thanks to the writing of Erwin Piscator. Epic was nonrealistic, an extension of cabaret, agitprop, and those things would be sharpened later by the way in which the works preceded Hitler and the Nazis. But something else needs to be said, and I think it applies to all three plays: that the texts and their drama is so much less than the power of Weill's music. Time and again, it is the sinister, seductive power of the songs—"Mack the Knife" and "Surabayya, Johnny" are outstanding examples—that holds the shows together. As for the writing, it treats hackneyed situations and clichéd characters. It rejects the poetry of spoken language and seems to disdain evident "big" speeches.

The film was set up by Nero and Tobis and Warner Brothers. It was an early and odd example of the international coproduction. The rights went for 40,000 marks and the budget was set at 800,000 marks. Seymour Nebenzal was the producer, G. W. Pabst was asked to direct, and immediately there was trouble.

Though the play had been a success onstage, Brecht and Weill felt that it was being softened for the movie. Nebenzal and Pabst were so much more impressed by naturalism and so much less given to the comic-book fragmentation of the theatrical production, with slogans and placards. The designer on the film was Andrei Andreiev (who had just done *Pandora's Box*), and it's certainly true that the film looks more like an attempt to produce London than the play's deliberate emphasis on staginess.

The authors must also have been alarmed that Nebenzal had hired in a trio of Hungarians to adapt the play: Léo Lania, Béla Balázs, and Ladislaus Vajda. So they sued. It was a famous case, and in the end Brecht lost and Weill won. The songs were to remain in their original positions in the show, but Brecht's worries were countered by his characteristic duplicity.

Fritz Arno Wagner did the photography, and it's clear that we are in a world where décor and costumes are meant to fill every inch of the screen. But some of the cast had been retained from the original show, and so the realistic intimacy of the look of the thing keeps breaking down in the abrupt theatricality of Rudolf Forster as Mackie Messer, Carola Neher as Polly Peachum, Valeska Gert as Mrs. Peachum, Reinhold Schünzel as Tiger Brown, Fritz Rasp as Peachum, and Lotte Lenya as Jenny.

3:10 to Yuma (1957)

The title refers to a train, and I wonder whether the very artful Elmore Leonard (the young man who wrote this story) wasn't having a little fun at the expense of *High Noon*. In that rather overdone classic, all hell will break loose when the twelve o'clock train hits town—and in this one the hellish dilemma is how a very nervous and reluctant deputy (Van Heflin) is going to get his prisoner (Glenn Ford) on another train with the gang watching and waiting for a mistake. All it proves is that movies and trains have usually liked each other.

Leonard was only in his early thirties, still hooked on the Western genre, though the lazy wit and the taste for talking in Glenn Ford's villain do show the way ahead for the writer. Indeed, this is one of the great talking Westerns. Heflin's character, Dan Evans, is a failure, a farmer who can't make it in Arizona, and who needs the danger money for getting Ben Wade (Ford) to jail (there was a famous one in Yuma—that's where they had Robert Ryan in *The Wild Bunch*). But Wade proves very sophisticated. He's like a devil tempting Evans with so many easy ways out—not least more money for doing the wrong thing. As such, this is one of the few pictures that ever dreamed of Ford as an articulate villain—and the experiment works so well it's a marvel more people didn't try him that way.

The screenplay is by Halsted Welles, and Delmer Daves is the director. To stress the emphasis on character and claustrophobia, the film is done in black and white and given a nice noir feel by Charles Lawton, Jr., who largely ignores the famous blasting light of Arizona. But the very skillful tension is in Daves's control, and it's so well done as to be spoiled by the booming song, written by George Duning and sung by Frankie Laine. Of course, in the spirit of *High Noon*, there had to be a song, but that kind of production extra takes away from the wind and the silence that are proper here.

Daves spends a lot of time getting the atmosphere of this barren part of the world, and weather plays an unusual part in the story. In a lot of this you can feel the natural inquisitiveness of Leonard, just imagining what it felt like in the legendary Wild West, waiting for the train and wondering if you were ever going to get a glass of cold water again. It does leave you thinking about what the Western lost when Leonard turned to modern Miami—and so on.

The real ambiguity builds, and it leaves us maybe a little more interested in the Ford character than the Heflin. But that's also a way of admitting how natural and real Heflin is, and how aroused Ford is by the lines he has. There's also a very well done scene in which Ford effectively seduces Felicia Farr. The rest of the cast includes Leora Dana, Henry Jones, and Richard Jaeckel.

Remade in 2007 with Russell Crowe as Glenn Ford and Christian Bale as Heflin. The remake had nothing of value from the original.

Three Women (1977)

The story got around that Robert Altman had reached a state of such confidence or euphoria that he reckoned he could make a film out of one of his own dreams. Of course, only a rather backward and very matter-of-fact sleep culture could be alarmed at that. Elsewhere in the world, people know that dream is a natural link to movie. But Altman made respectable noises to explain: "I didn't dream the story, but I'd had this succession of dreams all in one night in which I was making a film with Shelley Duvall and Sissy Spacek and it was called *Three Women* and I didn't know who the other woman was. It took place in the desert, and it was about personality-theft. And in my dream, I kept waking up and people would come into my bedroom—production managers—and I'd say, 'Go into the desert and find a saloon.' And when I did wake up, and realized that it was a dream, I was very disappointed, because I was really happy with what was happening."

So what emerged? It is a film in which Pinky Rose (Sissy Spacek) comes to work at a Desert Springs rehab center where elderly people take mineral baths. She is guided there by a Millie Lammoreaux (Shelley Duvall). I'd guess they are long-lost sisters to the two women in *Persona:* Pinky listens as Millie talks—and Millie is a singsong stream of clichéd consciousness, largely improvised by Duvall. They live together and they visit "Dodge City," a fake Western theme yard outside Desert Springs. It's run by a very macho cowboy, Edgar Hart (Robert Fortier). He has a wife, Willie (Janice Rule), speechless, but the painter of extraordinary murals—actually done by Bodhi Wind.

We feel a tension, a struggle for power—Pinky wants to become Millie. But there is a crisis: the pregnant Willie delivers a stillborn baby; Pinky sinks into a kind of coma; Millie asserts herself as the leader of the trio; Edgar is killed in an unexplained accident, and the three women settle as a trio.

If that is not enough basis for meaning for you, then *Three Women* is not your film. But if you are stirred at all by the film on the screen—with rainbow colors (by Charles Rosher) and the most fascinating interplay of tone, voice, and gesture among the women—then *Three Women* is a thing of beauty. I am in the latter camp, and I fear that the film's liberation from tidy plotting has still not been appreciated. But I think it frightened Altman, too, for he never really returned to its limpid, dazzling liberty, even if dream was there—like another drug—in his life.

Patricia Resnick worked on a script and was then dumped. Altman took credit for the script, which the actresses had done the most to work out—it was an Edgar-like gesture and hardly kind. Never mind: The film is extraordinary, and Duvall and Spacek were noticed. Spacek won Supporting Actress from the New York critics, Duvall shared Best Actress at Cannes. Diane Keaton won the Oscar as Best Actress in *Annie Hall.* The film is also notable for beautiful work from John Cromwell and Ruth Nelson (the one-time director and his wife) as an elderly couple. *Three Women* awaits rediscovery.

Throne of Blood (1957)

At the outset, we see a gloomy landscape lashed by rain and wind, and yet the sun is breaking through. It's a literal rendering of Shakespeare's fair and foul day in *Macbeth*, and it is a signal that the poetry of the play is more naturally delivered in language than as tricky weather systems. *Throne of Blood* is often described as one of Akira Kurosawa's great coups—a vivid retelling of Shakespeare's *Macbeth* that also incorporates elements of Noh theater. It's still worth seeing, and there are unquestioned high spots, but I'm not sure that this is even the best movie of *Macbeth*.

Washizu (Toshiro Mifune) is our main character, and you may be sure that he roars and snarls to perfection. He wears the clothes well. He seems like a warrior, and he is driven by some mixture of ambition and dread. As his wife, he has Asaji (Isuzu Yamada), playing in the Noh tradition with a makeup mask. She looks good, but actually fails to suggest the nagging, sexual force that urges her husband on. She is not a virus in his soul.

Further, Kurosawa has elected to do much of his story in interiors that are bare of décor, spacious and bright. All of a sudden, the viewer may feel nostalgic for the clammy castle walls and the pressing medieval darkness of the Orson Welles *Macbeth*. *Throne of Blood* is a different film, indoors and outdoors, and while it does a fairly spooky forest, still it settles for one male ghost instead of the witches (and it's the witches who help us understand Lady Macbeth). It's only in the climax, as the forest seems to move, that Kurosawa soars and finds a final thrust that is not Shakespeare, yet is very credible.

Who would have thought that Kurosawa would fall down on the atmosphere? But who can judge now exactly what he intended? In certain respects, his translation is very close to the play—in others it departs. But was he aiming at a Japanese audience, or an international one? The Welles version was done quickly and very cheaply, but it has unassailable virtues: Macbeth and his wife should be in terrible blood-pact concert; Macbeth is a man who can shift from quiet to full force; and there is the poetry.

With the Welles version, you feel Welles's terrible commitment to Macbeth's bloody ambition. You feel the urge to trample natural order and make an alliance with witchcraft. But those things are just gestures in *Throne of Blood*, a passing incident in a Japan beset by warlords. The language of Shakespeare is the difference because it takes us into an unrelieved confrontation with evil. By contrast, Toshiro Mifune is a big, noisy bully (his besetting liability as an actor). But Welles makes a noble man who has sold his soul. Yet in the history of film, *Throne of Blood* has the exotic advantage. It's different, and in the end it is a lot less than Shakespeare. Photographed by Asakazu Nakai, and also starring Minoru Chiaki, Akira Kubo, Takashi Shimura, Takamaru Sasaki, and Yoichi Tachikawa.

Tillie's Punctured Romance (1914)

In *My Autobiography*, Chaplin refers to *Tillie's Punctured Romance*, without naming it or giving any indication of its importance. For at just over 70 minutes, it was the first feature-length comedy. It was a success. It does not offer Chaplin as the Tramp character. And, yes, you've probably guessed it—it was a vehicle for someone else. So, in his book, it's enough for Chaplin to dismiss the unnamed venture as not having any special interest.

Marie Dressler (1869–1934) was Canadian, and she had been a veteran of the New York stage since 1892. She was a large woman who could quite easily be made to look like a man or be a figure of fun. She was also a very clever comedienne with a great following. *Tillie's Nightmare* was a stage play she had started doing in 1909: she played a flat-faced drudge who had dreams way above her station. And in *Tillie's Punctured Romance*—which was a Mack Sennett production—she was the poor, unsuspecting dunce (with a rich father, looking like half her age) who is deceived by the City Guy, a rather nervous fraud and womanizer, played by Mr. Chaplin.

The differences between the City Guy and the Tramp are not too many. The City Guy is better dressed, and he often wears a boater. Most distinctive of all, he has a quite different smile, one that shows too many teeth and ends up being quite unsettling. He is a gigolo and a cad, and Charlie must have known that he was gathering scant sympathy. Not the least element in his becoming the best known and most beloved person in the world was his desperate longing for love and attention. There are always actors who enjoy being nasty, and relatively minor in stature. But with Chaplin you feel the grievance and the damage it is doing to him. His access to sentiment is dependent on the thought that he is a fine, sad fellow. Yet he has a wicked streak of cruelty and cannot resist teasing the lumpish Tillie.

As for Dressler, it's clear that she is very accomplished, full of detail, and humor—but whereas Tillie, say, could attract sympathy onstage, she begins to let down the tremendous mass appeal of movies. She isn't sexy enough—and as if to point that up, the film gives the City Guy Mabel Normand as an accomplice and girlfriend. Even in poor prints, you can see Mabel chattering away in the silence, nudging Charlie like a naughty chum. They have chemistry—and in life it's easy to suppose they had a lot more. Indeed, Mabel looks like a sauce pot and a lot of fun. And she doesn't threaten Charlie in the way that Dressler does. Charlie knows he looks nasty next to the big lump, whereas Mabel flatters his spark and flair.

What does all this prove? That careers moved in fits and starts. Sennett obviously believed he could make Dressler a big star. It didn't happen, or not until sound, when she made a return (teaming with Polly Moran) and then became a real actress. As for Normand, she got involved in tragedy and scandal. She almost certainly did drugs. And she was dead in 1930 aged thirty-four. And then there's Chaplin.

Time Regained (1999)

Raoul Ruiz's Proust film, made as the century closed, is like a museum. There are many passages of the film where, for no apparent reason, there is a lapping movement on the screen—the camera goes this way and that, like waves making their attempt on the shore; or whole sections of a seated audience seem to shift sideways, and back again—not so much very important people as driftwood. It's possible, and required, I think, to relate these movements to the streaming or the fluidity that Ruiz puts beneath the credits, or the sea itself at Balbec that ends the film. But there's another comparison, just as useful: that we, along with Marcel Proust, are strolling through a museum that is the embodiment of Proust's novel and Ruiz's film.

This is not perverse, or far-fetched. Imagine yourself at a museum to see an exhibition (they call them shows these days) of the work of some painter, or movement, or some moment in the ages. Just as we are used to seeing Monet's Rouen Cathedral in different lights, so in such a show we see people at different ages. Turn a corner, and a woman may shift from novice to crone—only the eyes give the kinship away. There is even a moment in *Time Regained* where one character has two separate ages on his face—one side much older than another—and so as he turns in the turning commotion that is the engine of the film, he becomes his older self. *Time Regained* is not easygoing, no matter that it was a big-budget French-Italian-Portuguese production, with big stars. It is not easily followed if you don't have an outline of *À la Recherche du Temps Perdu* in your head, or on your lap. But it is maybe the most arresting film you will ever see about time's alteration, and our obsessive, childlike notion that it surely stands still while we move.

Of course, it says something of forbidding importance that a work finished in 1922, if only by the death of Proust himself, is so far beyond what film reaches now in matters of narrative organization, the ebb and flow of duration, the experience of time and memory. (What can it be that film does better?) And certainly Ruiz has confined himself to the last of the seven volumes, and then contrived to let many themes and situations from the book's past seep back into being.

His materials are the words of the book, a quite sumptuous photographic recreation in which we feel we are in a gallery on Tissot and Sargent in which the desires of the painted figures dictate our attention. I praise décor or production design a lot in this book, because the world created for films is neglected—here there is superb work by Bruno Beaugé and photographer Ricardo Aronovich. There is even a credit for "snow and rain." Marcello Mazzarella is Proust, Catherine Deneuve is Odette (at so many ages), Emmanuelle Béart is Gilberte, Vincent Perez is Morel, Pascal Greggory is Saint-Loup, Marie-France Pisier is Mme. Verdurin, Chiara Mastroianni is Albertine, John Malkovich is Charlus, and the rest includes Edith Scob, Arielle Dombasle, Dominique Labourier, Mathilde Seigner, and Patrice Chéreau as the voice of Proust.

A Time to Love and a Time to Die (1957)

"I have never believed in Germany at war," said Jean-Luc Godard, "so much as watching this American film made in time of peace." Of course, Douglas Sirk, the director, was also Detlef Sierck, born in Hamburg, and raised in German theater and film. The material is a novel by Erich Maria Remarque, actually titled *A Time to Live and a Time to Die,* and Remarque was present on the film, less as a writer than as the actor playing the professor. Said Sirk, "Some critics blamed me for not portraying the Hitler period more 'critically.' What was interesting to me was a landscape of ruins and the two lovers. But again, a strange kind of love story, a love conditioned. Two people are not allowed to have their love. The murderous breath of circumstances prevents them. They are hounded from ruin to ruin."

And just as in his romantic melodramas, Sirk constructs the passage of a mobile, inquiring camera passing through décor that is a deranged comment on the lives being observed, so this film is a somber but beautiful series of tracking shots through rubble and the shattered framework of buildings in which we see the ironic growth of a small, plain love. By Sirk's own standards, these are the humblest and quietest of lovers—they cannot avoid feeling that the time itself is at odds with love and how wistfully lucky they are as a result.

A young soldier, Ernst, comes home on leave from the Russian front—but "home" is a mockery now, a place very hard to find in the larger context of homelessness. He meets a girl, Elizabeth. They marry and have a brief idyll—it would make a lovely double bill with Minnelli's *The Clock*—before Ernst goes back to the eastern front, where he meets his death. There are Nazis in the film, but there is not much conventional laying on of guilt. The ruined city is a destroyed culture; that is the explanation for where we are. The lovers intuit that they have only moments to claim for themselves.

Sirk famously made films about people in love, yet threatened or undermined by the experience. The love is operatic sometimes. I suspect that these two are the quietest of Sirk's lovers. That owes a lot to the lack of starriness, glamour, or even great charm in John Gavin and Liselotte Pulver. It is not simply that they are restrained—they seem afflicted by their physical world. And to that extent it was vital in Sirk's strategy that the filming be done in Germany. In response, Germany turned a cold shoulder to the film. As Sirk put it, Germans were too deeply into self-pity to feel pathos for these characters.

No matter, it is a fine and touching film, with Russell Metty and Alexander Golitzen making the ruined world. There are good backup performances from Jock Mahoney, Keenan Wynn, and even the young Klaus Kinski as a Gestapo man.

Tinker, Tailor, Soldier, Spy (1980)

This is a movie, even if made for television, and one of those works that take us into serious duration. I know that some works by Rivette or Béla Tarr are of such length that a few people sigh and regret their lack of humor or economy. *Tinker, Tailor* is 290 minutes and it might be longer. If it were, it might be easier for people like me to understand what is happening, and why? I have seen it a couple of times over the years and I have the gist of it: It is a suspenseful and quite gripping playing out of an endless male ritual, the spy game. Let's say it's examining some hidden chalice so very closely, and talking about it in such rapt, cryptic ways that it never needs to be spelled out. It could be God, homosexuality, the rules of the club, a game of snooker, or a smell in the air.

It is adapted from a John le Carré novel by Arthur Hopcraft, and as far as I can see it has been done with tremendous fidelity and worship—and as if entranced by Le Carré's dogged, misogynist, and rather limited style. In theory, of course, the safety of the world is in balance in that the British Secret Service is supposedly sending George Smiley against the Soviet Karla. I don't think anyone really believes that tosh anymore—or sees it as less far-fetched than James Bond. Espionage is a sport—a very English communication system that works on denial, secrecy, and then astonishing coup. It means very little more than the average Harold Pinter play—and you can think of the dialogue as the raw material that Pinter turns into his own ping-pong. Self-parody is close at hand, and would be rampant but for the allegiance of that band of brothers, the English supporting actors, to which brotherhood, I daresay, Alec Guinness (Smiley) saw himself as patron saint, or chief D'Ascoyne.

Is it "cinematic"? Well, not really. It's not just that it's a series of talking heads so much as listening heads, all directed by John Irvin with the kind of concentration that solves crossword puzzles. Yet I could watch it day after day, and I actually see the brief bouts of "action"—Smiley entering a restaurant, or looking at the weather—as so much escapist flimflam. The key to enjoyment, I think, is the grave affinity between English actors putting on a brave yet tight-lipped show and spies, forever fondling small talk and adverbs as if they were tickling their privates. It is very English, very well done and cloud-cuckoo-land. Yet Guinness seems to have believed it as gospel of a sort, and his choir includes Joss Ackland, Michael Aldridge, Ian Bannen, Anthony Bate, Hywel Bennett, Bernard Hepton, Michael Jayston, Alexander Knox, Ian Richardson, Terence Rigby, George Sewell, John Standing, Patrick Stewart, Nigel Stock, and Thorley Walters. Bless them all. How and why the cast does not also include Cyril Cusack, James Villiers, or Robert Hardy I cannot explain. Siân Phillips is there as Anne Smiley—the Lucretia Borgia of the whole saga—and Beryl Reid is lovely as a neglected bit of crumpet.

Tirez sur le Pianiste (1960)

It was not that *Les 400 Coups* had been lacking. Still, there are first films with a joy or danger that is never regained (examples? Malick's *Badlands; Citizen Kane* even; Toback's *Fingers*). Then there was the undeniable fact that *400 Coups* was autobiographical—that engine might carry uncertain talent in its first thrust. And it was about a child. What would happen if François Truffaut yielded to adults? For all of those reasons, the suspense that attended *Tirez sur le Pianiste* was even greater than that which greeted the first film. Almost without drawing breath, here was something else as fresh as spit—or was it blood this time?

Moreover, in the story of the piano player who is a bit of a gangster (*Fingers,* anyone?), Truffaut had identified shyness as his central emotional subject. That would last all his career, yet it had bloomed in the person of a tremendous performer: the music-hall chanteur Charles Aznavour, who gave his sad face to the camera with the uncritical loyalty of a dog. More than that, Truffaut now explored the unhappy love affair—surely his forte onscreen—and the quite tragic loss of the Nicole Berger character, the first fatal woman in Truffaut's work, and the proof of women being magic just because of that instant in which they may be snuffed out.

Tirez sur le Pianiste was taken from the David Goodis novel *Down There,* in a script by Truffaut and Marcel Moussy, though I doubt many people would have recognized that. It employed Raoul Coutard as cameraman (in black and white and Dyaliscope again), and it reiterated the poignant beauty available to that format. Truffaut thought hard about image, and he went over to color as a habit quickly enough, but no friend to black and white can forget the emotions—harsh yet fragile—in his lurching camerawork and the gay, trigger-happy way his films could cut away or iris in and out on details. Truly, the screen was dynamic and he had a feeling for the image so total that he made Godard look orderly and calculated.

There are side quotes—the music box that plays music from Max Ophüls's *Lola Montès.* There is the tenderness of Georges Delerue's score and the jangling assertion of the café piano. But the speed with which asides and inserts could come and go, and the electric shift in mood from romantic to absurd, from lyrical to tragic—those things are still models for any filmmaker and a sign of how quickly film can work (this is a complicated movie of only 80 minutes). Marie Dubois is warm, Nicole Berger haunting, and the gangsters are so funny and yet so alarming. I find an extraordinary nostalgia in the mere sound of Delerue's music—and something just as compelling in the young man's amazed rapture at finding he could do anything with film. In a few years, it was clear that Godard was the more interesting artist, but the spearhead was Truffaut, and he was as sharp and challenging as any weapon.

First things first: In advance of the opening of *Titanic*, it was widely predicted as a disaster worthy of the great ship itself. Its budget had reached at least $200 million. In early distress because of that, the load and the copyright had been taken on by two companies, Fox and Paramount. At an early screening in Los Angeles, there was a good deal of gallows humor from those running the show that pink slips were not far away—and maybe worse. Whereupon, one or two critics came out of the 194-minute screening and said, Well, it's not that bad. And I still feel that way: It's not as awful as you think it's going to be. It went on to get domestic rentals of $324 million with worldwide earnings of as much as $900 million. And it's not that bad.

On the other hand, it is not a fraction as inventive as *The Terminator*, not nearly as exciting as *Aliens*, not as mysterious as *The Abyss*, and not as fascinating as all the stories that are told of the *Titanic* itself, that big story of 1912.

Does the James Cameron film look like 1912? Yes, I suppose so. The production design work (by Peter Lamont), all the art direction, and the costumes (by Deborah Scott) are coldly accurate, just as the model of the ship and the digitized animation of the sinking are relentlessly thorough. Does it feel like 1912? Not for a moment. Because the re-creation is all external. There is so little sense of period or class in the script and its understanding, and in 1912 most tales of horror from that sinking ship had to do with class differences. All Cameron has done is make a notional (but fanciful) bonding between an upper-class girl and a lower-class boy, while imposing all the malice of class on the Billy Zane character. In short, there is no sense of real history. (*Atonement* would do the same thing.)

But what Cameron has done is to devise a story arc that binds the past to the present and which gives us something to root for, no matter that we know how the story will end. So the girl, Rose (Kate Winslet), is alive still today in 1997 (and played gamely by Gloria Stuart), so that she can come to the aid of Bill Paxton as he attempts underwater recovery of the wreck. This is a good try, and the film gets away with it, though I'm bound to tell you that Ms. Stuart was two when the *Titanic* sank, and Cameron makes it clear in the nude-drawing sequence that Kate Winslet was better developed.

The "thrill" of the present looking at the past is feeble, I think, but it went a long way to giving the impression that the film was different. After that, it was painfully clear that a large audience existed that was uninterested in the history yet deeply impressed by the effects work of re-creation. And when the ship sinks, the spectacle is undeniable—just as the underwater sequences are clearly the ones that interested Cameron the most.

The acting doesn't really exist, yet it is said that Leonardo DiCaprio was made a sensation by the film. So be it. That did pass. The rest of the cast includes Kathy Bates (as Molly Brown), Frances Fisher, Bernard Hill, Jonathan Hyde, David Warner, Victor Garber, and Suzy Amis.

To Be or Not To Be (1942)

The point may be obvious. It may gloss over fine issues of taste. But in some total conflict, if one side is making *To Be or Not To Be* in the middle of a war and the other is not—you know which side to root for. No, there are no Nazi equivalents to this film, no film in which the Goethe Institute, let's say, sends a Schubert lieder singer on a tour of the United States and she tries to conduct an affair with a spokesman for the Bund. (You're tempted by the sound of it? But only because you've grown up in a culture addicted to irony, sarcasm, self-effacement, and that essential ingredient of American acting once identified by Kenneth Tynan—its Jewishness.)

It has to be said that Samson Raphaelson—Lubitsch's preferred writer—chose to be unavailable for this project, because he feared that it would end in charges of bad taste. So Melchior Lengyel shaped the idea and Edwin Justus Mayer wrote the script about a Polish acting company in Nazi-occupied Warsaw that has a hard time doing *Hamlet,* but which gets drawn into a masquerade against the Nazis that may help win the war. This is the company led by Maria and Joseph Tura (Carole Lombard and Jack Benny), when he is doing *Hamlet* and she has a Polish flier after her and she tells the boy to rendezvous in her dressing room just after her husband begins the speech "To be or not to be . . ."

What follows is nothing less than a farce in which the Nazis are the butt of the humor, but in which "So, they call me concentration camp Erhard, do they?" is relied upon to get repeated belly laughs. Some find it too much. I suggest that its brilliance lies in the concentration on actors at the heart of the story and the casting genius that saw how far the already wounded face of Jack Benny could consider no greater crime against humanity than walking out on his big speech. And then there is Carole Lombard, ravishing, sexy, happy, and glorious in her gowns. She was dead shortly after the film finished shooting, and it may be that that took away from audience numbers as much as any question of taste.

Alexander Korda was a coproducer on the venture and Vincent Korda did the sets. Those gowns are by Irene, and Rudolph Maté did the photography. The faultless cast also includes Robert Stack, Felix Bressart, Lionel Atwill, Stanley Ridges, Sig Ruman, and Charles Halton. Of course, it is an artifice, protected from the real horror of war. But it has moments when to see the Turas—vain, self-centered, essentially small-minded—is still to recognize how far cinema and egalitarianism can amount to models of ordinary decency. The American cinema has made few lastingly useful political statements, and it has often taken fright at the risk of trying. *To Be or Not To Be* is the sort of film that would have earned murder gangs if the other side had won. It is still brave, and it still bespeaks a wholesome insolence in many Americans toward tyranny and the way of life ready to rationalize the death of flirtation.

To Catch a Thief (1955)

It's clear in hindsight that *To Catch a Thief* was a holiday film—either because Hitchcock felt inclined to let the Riviera guide him, or because he saw the possibility of Grace Kelly exchanging one kind of stardom for another. There's no attempt to explore or dissect the Cary Grant character: He remains as upright and untouched as an Oregon pine—the sort of business his character, John Robie, claims to be in. Of course, one can see another angle in 1955: that several of these people, Robie included, were in the French Resistance, where there was a license to kill and steal (the cook, you recall, was a strangler). In all his films made in the 1950s, Hitch took his men apart. But Robie is never short of breath, let alone put under stress. He stands there and takes Grace Kelly's pale blue kiss, and he deflects her line, "Would you prefer a leg or a breast?" as if he were on probation.

All of which leaves the Riviera robbery plot like something from a previous age. Talking of which, let's admit that Cary Grant was several months older than Jessie Royce Landis, the mother of the Kelly girl. Now, I like Landis in the film, especially the way she laughs at Grant when he loses his roulette chip, and doubly so when she stubs out a cigarette in a fried egg. But there's an inescapable hint of the perverse in that scene where Cary and Jessie are flirting, but Grace is the real object of attention. Hitchcock in a nastier mood might at least have played with the possibility that Robie was drawn to mother *and* daughter.

For the rest, there is really just Grace Kelly to look at, and to grieve over. Who knows what satisfactions Monaco gave her? It's plain for anyone to see, I think, that she was both horny as hell and an amazing comedienne. The film is flimsy, but she sprawls through it like a wild, sexy girl home from finishing school and ready to seduce every man in the household, and any woman who gives her a second glance. Kelly did three films for Hitchcock, and this is the one in which she is most carefree, most nakedly available, and every bit as desirable as her own diamonds. I'm not sure if any actress since has been so celebrated for her glamour—and not much else.

Could more have been made of it all? You bet it could have. Suppose, for instance, that Kelly and Grant had joined forces as jewel thieves and cleaned up the Côte d'Azur. Yes, that's a fancy, but it's worth recalling that Hitch had Kelly in mind a few years later for the chronic thief in *Marnie.* Sooner or later, if she'd stayed in pictures, someone had to get at the duplicity beneath the blancmange in Kelly. She would have to be on the other side of the law, stealing to get her orgasms. As it is, here, she does all she can to give a signal of that. But, as I said, Hitchcock was on holiday.

In Little Hope, New Hampshire, and yet from the eternity of TV fame, too, Suzanne Stone turns to us—direct to camera—the freshest sundae, all pinks, creams, blondes, and custards, and goes into the lovely ad lib confession on what she did to her husband, when any idiot can see that why she did it was, quite simply, to be a sundae show on TV, to be not just the weather center in Little Hope, but the Whether Center in America (the question being whether Suzanne is just guilty or delicious—her show is called *Your Guilty Pleasures*, in which on reality TV you get to go through with the deepest, darkest longings you've ever had).

Well, no, the glorious *To Die For* doesn't quite reach that far. It stays in Little Hope with those grungy kids when its own great vaulting esprit indicates the chance that Suzanne could GO ALL THE WAY—she could be *Up Close & Personal*, she could be a Katie Couric, so wide-eyed and pretty that she can take in all of America in what amounts to the first TV blow job.

It's a brilliant try, taken from a dark, witty novel (based on a real case) by Joyce Maynard and very well scripted by Buck Henry, even if it falls short of some final manic, cartoon surge where one murder makes Suzanne a killer hit. It needs the zest of *Network*, that satirical energy, and the understanding that Suzanne Stone really is modern America—pretty, sweet, shallow, and a killer-diller.

It may be that Gus Van Sant was not quite the director for that kind of satire. He seems as interested in Joaquin Phoenix as he is in Nicole Kidman, and that's understandable at the New Hampshire level, because Phoenix is outstanding and very accurately observed. But Nicole—in claiming her own identity and naughty-flirty presence on our screen—was reaching for the stars, not just the George Segal figure, but the Robert Redford stiff from *Up Close & Personal* and a kind of Clintonian president who sees her and sighs, "Santa Monica!"

So the parents are cameo treasures, but the film lingers with them too long. And really Matt Dillon needs to be disposed of more quickly. Suzanne is the Bad Seed grown up, and Nicole is like a candy rocket willing to soar over the mediascape, shedding light and her panties wherever she goes. A masterpiece was in prospect—instead we have a very nice, tart, daring comedy and the sublime insight that so long as Suzanne is confiding in *us*, direct to camera, mouth to mouth, she can get away with anything.

So this was Nicole Kidman's real debut, yet look how far the business held back from putting her in more outrageous comedies, let alone pictures in which she rose like bubbles in champagne to the level of mass murder. Here is a unique sensibility, seductive and devouring, and all too often Ms. Kidman would be fobbed off with earnestness or cuteness. Terrific support from Illeana Douglas, Maria Tucci, Casey Affleck, Alison Folland, Dan Hedaya, and David Cronenberg.

To Have and Have Not (1944)

Published in 1937, *To Have and Have Not* is the closest Ernest Hemingway ever came to a political novel. Harry Morgan dies at the end with the gasping cry, "One man alone ain't got a chance." But in the Howard Hawks film, seven years later, a man alone—call him Harry Morgan—while he claims to be hard up, seems to be dressed by the J. Peterman catalogue; he has a boat and a sidekick named Eddie; he is insouciant about the war and taking any stance toward it; and he gets this odd girl, or "look," prepared to teach him to whistle. So *To Have and Have Not* is the Warner Brothers wartime movie in which Humphrey Bogart stays "above" the war.

There's more to it than that, but don't overlook the breathtaking charm of Hawks electing a story which has some nasty signs of Gestapo-tainted Vichy and still disdaining the war. So Harry Morgan is a relic from a sweeter past, hiring his boat out to ugly American fishermen, and getting along. At the hotel, the owner (Marcel Dalio) would like him to help some Resistance people—but resistance to what? Meanwhile, Harry has "her" on his hands, lolling in his doorway, and tossing insolent remarks at him along with boxes of matches and looks that might burn a man's toupee off him.

Hawks asked Jules Furthman to do a screenplay, and apparently let William Faulkner doodle a few scenes. It would all put Papa in his place. And then one day, Slim Hawks passed a fashion magazine over to Hawks, and there she was, Betty Perske, in a pretty hat, standing outside a Red Cross office, like a vampire. She was eighteen or so, and her voice was deep already. Hawks got Betty to wear "Slimmish" clothes. He took her voice lower. And he told Bogart that it would be a kind of love story if the girl kept topping him with insolent lines.

Bogart said that sounded fine, but he was overoccupied with his raucous wife, Mayo Methot, and Hawks had every reason to think that "Lauren Bacall" would be not just his contract property, but a new Slim, a bit slimmer and nineteen. Alas for lecherous dreams (and don't knock them as a major inspiration for good movies). Bacall had a soft heart—Howard always assumed that all the girls he discovered were as cool as he was. She fell in love with the actor, the drunk, and the toupee!

Meanwhile, it's a screwball classic posing as a war movie, with a little bit of musical as Hoagy Carmichael teaches Bacall to sing. Sid Hickox got the sultry Caribbean look. Charles Novi did the shabby sets. Max Steiner scored it, and Carmichael and Johnny Mercer did the songs. Effortless, serene, grown-up and childish at the same time. Is there a more "Hollywood" movie? Also with Dolores Moran, Sheldon Leonard, Walter Molnar, Walter Sande, and Dan Seymour. You kept the title? said Hemingway, perplexed. Sure, said Hawks—I had this girl and then I didn't have her. War is hell, Papa should murmur. But nothing's perfect.

To Kill a Mockingbird (1962)

These days you can't say "Boo!" to Boo Radley, and you'd better be careful about delivering a cross word on Harper Lee, Gregory Peck, or *To Kill a Mockingbird*. The novel and the film have passed easily into the pantheon of fictions that speak well and warmly of America, even if Atticus Finch does lose the crucial case, trying to defend Brock Peters against rape charges in a Southern town. I should add "wrongful" to those charges. This is not a Preminger-like film where we are left to make up our own minds.

The novel came out in 1960 and won a Pulitzer and was bought for the screen by that eminently sane and sensitive team, Robert Mulligan and Alan Pakula. In turn, they asked Horton Foote to do the screenplay, which retained the point of view of Scout, Atticus's young daughter, who is telling the story as a grown woman (her voice-over on the film is that of Kim Stanley). There's no doubt that, coming when it did, *To Kill a Mockingbird* was hugely welcome to and much glorified by liberal America. How far it hurried social improvement is another matter. Indeed, how extensive or real the social improvement is remains an embarrassing question. But there is a piety in the child's voice and a simple decency in Finch that have helped bestow the mantle of Lincoln on the character. Not that Gregory Peck was ever averse to that kind of ennoblement.

Peck does not seem entirely Southern—and I'm sure that was felt in the South above all. For this Atticus is not just enlightened; he is a little like a wise stranger. Of course, that is not to challenge or compete with the dignity, the sincerity, or the judiciousness that Peck brought to the role—all genuine, yet all labeled, too, whereas the character in the book, I think, was less solemnly conscious of the dangerous ground he was breaking.

The other great appeal of the film is owed to Mary Badham, who gives one of the finest performances by a child in American cinema. Robert Duvall made his debut as Boo Radley and is very good. The music was by Elmer Bernstein.

To Kill a Mockingbird was nominated for the Best Picture Oscar (it lost to *Lawrence of Arabia*). Mulligan was nominated for directing; Peck won his Oscar, overcoming Peter O'Toole, Burt Lancaster in *Birdman of Alcatraz*, Jack Lemmon in *Days of Wine and Roses*, and Marcello Mastroianni in *Divorce—Italian Style*. Mary Badham was nominated and lost to Patty Duke (age sixteen) in *The Miracle Worker*. Horton Foote won for his screenplay.

There's a rich movie tradition of the Southern trial: It includes *Judge Priest* and *Inherit the Wind* as well as movies like *Ghosts of Mississippi* or *Mississippi Burning* or *Intruder in the Dust*. All the movies whisper to us that, with human nature, it can't really be that bad. While the warmth of the South says, Yes, yes it is, because human nature has its habits. So if you're up in court in certain places, don't rely on the Finch Amendment.

Tokyo Story (1953)

Critics refer you to the Ozu style, but they are not generous in wondering what it means. So as I watch *Tokyo Story* again, I notice how often, after the "action" has ended, Yasujiro Ozu keeps the camera running on the space where it occurred. But are "action" and "space" the right words? The question is unnerving. Whether we rejoice in the cinema of "action" films, or simply remember the signal "action" that orders the camera to start rolling, we are pledged to believe in activity or incident. Yet, in candor, as you look at Ozu scenes, "activity" is not the best word. And that emptied or surrendered space after the "activity" may be meant as a direction to us—some guidance in how to look. After all, these cramped houses are empty sometimes: when the people who live there are "out"; when they have moved "off-camera"; or when they are dead.

These are not idle wonderings. Take the "story" that is *Tokyo Story*. An elderly couple who live in another city decide to visit their married children in Tokyo. It is a big journey. Everyone acts as if it is important. But, in reality, the family living in Tokyo hardly has room or time for the visitors. There is a problem of space in these houses, which leaves a question mark over the possession of inner space and how far the people can regard that as a right. So the parents are put up in a spa. And they go away from Tokyo disappointed. The mother falls ill on the way back. The relatives now hurry to get their last meeting with her. But they are too late. The mother dies. The widowed daughter-in-law—altogether the kindest person in the film—makes funeral arrangements. The father tells this daughter-in-law she should marry again—he is too impressed by loneliness to see another way. She doubts she will.

Some writers talk of Chekhov, and of the ordinary unkindness in families. The film itself admits to the implacability of life: It goes on, there are spaces left empty after people have gone, and there are ideals or "stories" of kinship and kindness that may be betrayed. Ozu's fondness for actors is immense, and his low-level, very still camera is gracious to acting: It lets it soak in; it permits time; and *Tokyo Story* is longer than Ozu usually allows himself. But I am not sure it is enough to say, simply, that Ozu sighs with regret and takes up a Chekhovian resignation. I am not sure it's enough to say this of Chekhov. For deep down—looking at people and their spaces—Ozu seems to know the profound outer loneliness in which people do not always play the role of son or father, or play it well. And there is no moral edge to his gaze. It is not that Ozu disapproves of his more abrupt characters any more than he sees *Tokyo Story* as a commentary on housing problems in the city and the nation. Though that point needs addressing, too, for Ozu seems to wonder always whether Japanese institutions are not prisons, too, confining human nature and taming it. Ozu is a master, but I think the message is more disturbing than just that of dismayed humanism.

Tol'able David (1921)

The silent cinema, it seems to me, was often by nature more interested in the nineteenth century, and America as a rural society, than it was in progress and urbanization. Of course, the cities meant larger audiences and bigger theaters. But still there were pictures so nostalgic for tamed space that they resemble the Western reestablished in glorious Eastern parks. That is where *Tol'able David* fits, and still works. Among other things, it is one of the most spectacular and heartfelt identifications with countryside ever managed onscreen. But it is the countryside as an expression of virtue and order. Don't forget that Hemingway's "Big Two-Hearted River" was written only a few years later. It bespeaks a modern sense of country, as a place of escape from civilization's plight.

This is the story of David Kinemon (as handsome, true, and thoughtful as Richard Barthelmess). In the first movement he harmonizes with his country life—his dog, his parents, his home and friends. All he misses is the chance to drive the U.S. mail. He is not man enough yet. But then Iscah Hatburn arrives with his two sons. They have escaped from prison and they terrorize the area. They kill David's dog and paralyze his brother. The Kinemons move, and David wonders if he has been a coward. One day, he gets to drive the mail, and as the Hatburns try to steal it so the chance for the great fight arises. He is a man.

This was a short story by Joseph Hergesheimer that Griffith planned to make with Barthelmess. But when the actor and director Henry King formed Inspiration Pictures together, Griffith traded them the story. The script was actually written by King and Edmund Goulding together, and King took great pleasure in researching locations in the Virginia countryside, in the area where he had been raised himself. Henry Cronjager opened the lens to that dappled light and delivered countless views of country life as a version of heaven.

I'm not sure I want to hear these people speak. Their initial comfort could be too stuffed to be endurable. And, really, the characters are so one-sided that they have little need for speech or thought. King's method is to find reveries and hold them rather too long. Barthelmess was probably the ideal actor for this. He had an interesting face, never without traces of doubt and anxiety (think of *Heroes for Sale* and *Only Angels Have Wings*). It was a face that was more interesting than many of his predicaments—and *Tol'able David* is tolerable in great part because of his modesty and his gradual emergence as a man of action.

The fight is grand, prolonged, and not one to bet on. But here in 1921 someone has suspected that great truth, that the movie fight is its trial at arms and its reason for suspense. It should be added that the setup in *Tol'able David* goes on: You can see it in *High Noon*, in *Straw Dogs* even, and in just about every film where revenge has rectitude (like King's *The Bravados,* even, where the fighting response is very confused).

The cast also includes Gladys Hulette, Walter P. Lewis, Ernest Torrence, Ralph Yearsley, Forrest Robinson, Edmund Gurney, and Marion Abbott.

Tom Jones (1963)

In his memoir, *The Long-Distance Runner,* Tony Richardson admits to feeling that *Tom Jones* was "incomplete and botched," despite its success, despite its winning the Oscar for Best Picture. The modesty is well-founded. The picture is a mess, sometimes called a romp, and a tribute as much as anything to the sudden new appetite for things English. Richardson talks in his memoir about how the film coincided with the first emergence of "swinging" London. I'm not sure that history would sustain that thought, but it is the case that *Tom Jones* caught the theatrical wave of the Royal Court and of Woodfall, the new film company that had made films of *Look Back in Anger, The Entertainer, Saturday Night and Sunday Morning, A Taste of Honey,* and *The Loneliness of the Long-Distance Runner.* It also harked back to the model of history with sex and indignity founded in *The Private Life of Henry VIII.*

It was Richardson who felt the urge to escape contemporary realism and who thought of Henry Fielding's *Tom Jones.* He asked John Osborne to do a screenplay from a treatment of the novel he made himself. No one was ever satisfied with Osborne's script (and he refused to do much rewriting). But with the sheer amount of story detail, costumes, and sets it was impossible to get the budget under £500,000. Columbia was to have backed it, but then David Picker arrived and United Artists took over.

Jocelyn Herbert was hired as designer, and after talks with Ossie Morris broke down, Richardson got Walter Lassally as his cameraman. They had locations all over the countryside—houses here, lanes there—and that sense of a rural society is the best thing about the picture. It's something Richardson summed up. He said it was an unhappy production (because of the script), "but there were many wonderful compensations—the English countryside in summer, heavy with the scents of grass seeds, dog roses and cow parsley, a green richness that seems to last longer than anywhere else. There were the great houses we used: one with a lake gorged with water lilies and yellow flags; another (Cranborne) majestic and elegant with a labyrinth of garden succeeding garden, glimmering with white and yellow roses."

The young Albert Finney tried to hold it together, but, as he knew, Tom is a passive part. Everyone else has more fun: Susannah York as Sophie, Hugh Griffith as Western, Edith Evans, Joan Greenwood, Diane Cilento, George Devine, Joyce Redman, Rachel Kempson, Wilfrid Lawson—and the narrator, Micheál MacLiammóir.

It made a fortune and won Best Picture. Richardson won for directing, Finney was nominated for acting—and three Supporting Actress nods went to Edith Evans, Diane Cilento, and Joyce Redman (they were beaten by Margaret Rutherford!). John Osborne got the Oscar for screenplay. *Lawrence of Arabia* had won Best Picture the year before and it was technically British. But *Tom Jones* was the breakthrough—the English were coming.

Toni (1934)

Based at Les Martigues, using the resources of the Marcel Pagnol Company, Jean Renoir intended *Toni* as a new commitment to realism. Everything was shot in real exteriors or in the kind of rough interiors where the action occurred. Inside and outside were as connected as they are in rural life. All sound was recorded live, on location, despite some imperfections. And the cast was an assembly of amateurs or of actors close in personal history to the parts they were playing. As for the story, it was picked up from a newspaper report, about an Italian immigrant worker in a tragic love affair.

"For the first time in my life," Renoir would write, "it seemed to me that I had written a script in which the elements completed one another, not so much through the plot as by a sort of natural equilibrium.

"*Toni* was to speed up my separation from the notion of the predominance of the individual. I could no longer be satisfied with a world which was nothing but the dwelling-place of personae having no link between them."

And thus, Renoir—the son of a portraitist—learned to set aside the close-up for the group shot (of course, his father was a master of complex social gatherings, too). In *Toni*, we can see Renoir feeling out physical context and the way personal relationships are defined by intervening space and the glance, or the regard. It looks a lot less dramatic, or melodramatic, than the films before the early 1930s—after all, the silent film often tried to bury itself inside anguished or ecstatic faces caught between massive plot forces. But now Renoir comes to see that intensity as a failure to honor the tangled contexts in which we live with others.

Toni has a new harshness in its photography (for the first time, Renoir had his nephew Claude Renoir doing the camerawork). But that is a response to the sunlight and the rocky terrain of the Midi. Despite that texture in the imagery, the compositions, the moving camera that exhausts so many passing compositions in one sweep, and the editing that is founded in the movement speak to a tenderness or kinship in peoples who must also respect the scheme that they are aliens to each other. The attitudes and the attention of actor Charles Blavette are exemplary in this process. (He is as influential as Dalio in *Rules of the Game*.)

Renoir noted that *Toni* was taken as a predecessor of Italian neo-realism, but he was suspicious of the bond—because he disliked the Italian habit of adding sound later, and because he noted the Italian custom of melodrama. In *Toni*, fateful instincts are played down by a kind of fatalism that knows everyone has his or her version of what happened. The purpose of the cinema, Renoir seems to say, or its opportunity, is to reconcile the brief outbursts of happiness or tragedy with the stoicism, or the duration, that sees all things happening and changing. That sensibility begins and ends in the style of the film, the way of seeing, and the human ability to imitate film itself by being burned but not destroyed.

Tootsie (1982)

I'm imagining how the headline, or something close to it, must have run: *Gandhi* beats *Tootsie*—and it gives ominous warning of Hollywood in the 1980s. I'd far rather see *Tootsie*, because it's a more interesting take on what wearing a robe can do to a man. But is it interesting, or dangerous, enough?

Tootsie is a show business story, one that is spurred on by a common problem: an actor who can't get work. Michael Dorsey is "difficult." That's why he isn't going to get a longed-for role in *The Iceman Cometh*. He has recently coached Sandy (Teri Garr) about being more assertive/butch as she tries for the part of hospital administrator in *Southwest General*, a successful TV soap opera. So, as a game and to show how un-difficult he can be, Michael dresses up as "Dorothy Michaels" and gets the part himself/herself. Once he's in, it was certainly possible for the many scriptwriters to have a lot of fun. But, please note, it's all a game and a demonstration of Dustin Hoffman's "versatility" that he can get away with it. Don't let's encourage any thought that Michael or Dustin are other than straight guys.

And so, on the one hand *Tootsie* is a bit of fun from the world of show business, no matter that that business has a higher incidence of homosexual behavior (in or out of the closet) than any other profession in America. In the same way, the audience for *Tootsie* was expected to discover anew how "brilliant" Dustin Hoffman was and is, without entertaining any doubts about him. A lot of actors—maybe the best equipped to play the part—would have ducked it.

The credits on *Tootsie* are story by Don McGuire and Larry Gelbart, screenplay by Gelbart and Murray Schisgal (enough to suggest that Gelbart really is a player). But stories were current about other writers—not least Elaine May—and the overall feeling that the people in charge (including director Sydney Pollack) had had a lot of trouble working out this story so that it remained good, "clean" fun. Once it gets going, that falls into place. For instance, Michael falls for Julie (Jessica Lange), an actress in the show, no matter that she wonders if Dorothy may be a little lesbian. And then Julie's father (Charles Durning) comes on to Dorothy, too.

When it was all over, the people in the film congratulated themselves for having made a class entertainment—the picture did very well, even if it missed out on most awards (Lange did win the Oscar for Supporting Actress). What's wrong with *Tootsie* is the idea that gender shock (or ruse) is just a game, as opposed to a constant subtext in show business (and life). Indeed, *Some Like It Hot*, more than twenty years earlier, is a great deal more suggestive of the way an unstable person may be swayed sexually—and so what, because nobody's perfect. *Tootsie* feels strained and tense, for all the fun, and Hollywood still turns the other cheek most of the time when gay questions arise. Also with Bill Murray, Dabney Coleman, Geena Davis, and Sydney Pollack (as an agent).

Top Hat (1935)

Everyone loved *Top Hat*—or so it seemed. It is the film from the Astaire-Rogers series that most people think of first, not because they really know it, but because the title embodies the affluence of the films as a whole and because there is that abiding image of Astaire dancing solo, in tails and top hat, flinging his cane down and catching it on the rebound. It was the most successful: On a budget of just over $600,000, it grossed $1.7 million at home and $1.4 million overseas. That meant a profit of $1.5 million.

On the other hand, there is a fascinating memo from Astaire to RKO producer Pandro Berman, responding to the script: Though it had been written for Astaire, he worries that he has no character and nothing to do but dance-dance-dance; he was a straight juvenile again, but "cocky and arrogant"; there's no real story; it's too close to *The Gay Divorcee*; I have too little comedy; I am "forever pawing the girl or she is rushing into my arms."

We all know the legend of Astaire the absorbed dancer, hardly knowing if his partner's feet were bleeding, and dedicating himself to the perfection of routines. So it's refreshing to see him unhappy over those questions that dog the theorist of the musicals—essentially, do musicals have to be "about" something? Moreover, although Astaire was entrusted with the dance routines in his films, and sometimes the songs came along because of his friendships with songwriters, he seems to have felt helpless in choosing and shaping material.

More or less, the Astaire-Rogers musicals have the personality of his stage shows, coupled with the odd myth that Fred was a high-society figure. Yes, his sister, Adele, was married into the British aristocracy and Fred was socially minded. But there were raw materials that pointed in other directions: he was Midwest, not rich and not handsome. Remember the early feeling at M-G-M that his charm was too slight to surpass big ears. Fred is odd-looking—and Ginger (she was all-American pretty) seems to know it. People still say he gave her class and she gave him sex. But since when has that been a regular American transaction? In the movies, sex was class—that's what made Gable a king. Whereas Fred was odd. I think he knew it and worried over it—which is not the same as knowing he was gay. He surely knew that that part of him would never get expressed. Yet knowledge seldom kills desire.

And so *Top Hat*—the one with "No Strings," "Isn't This a Lovely Day" (which is prompted by weather—something that feels like raw poverty in this world), "Top Hat," "Cheek to Cheek," and "The Piccolino," which is a Ginger song. They're all by Irving Berlin. Mark Sandrich directed. It is the classic (if not the best), and it's all about a mistaken-identity plot so much more ludicrous and less intriguing than the one that puts Fred in big pictures and says, Look, he's one of us. As Graham Greene said, he's about the nearest to a "human Mickey Mouse" we'll ever get.

Touch of Evil (1958)

Orson Welles had been away, in Europe, and the legend had spread that he had become lazy or inept after his early extravagance and monomania. He was brought back, apparently, because Charlton Heston, cast as the lead, observed that Welles (suggested for the villain) was a possible director, too. So Welles, enlarging his own size for the role of corrupt border-town sheriff Hank Quinlan, came back as the cleverest, most adroit director anyone had ever seen. *Touch of Evil* is made with sheer brilliance, from the single-take bomb-plant and explosion scene that went under the old credits to the pursuit and confession scene shot amid the trashy canals of Venice, California, standing in for the rancid Mexican-American border.

But more than that, granted that Welles had only a short time to rework the Paul Monash script, just look at the toughness of the Mexican-American attitudes—still years ahead of mainstream American film. Then reflect on the amazingly intricate camera movements in the motel sequence where evidence is "found," and consider the ambiguous examination of law and justice that goes with it. Think of the scary mood established at the other motel where Janet Leigh goes to "rest," and judge the audacity behind the performances of Dennis Weaver and Mercedes McCambridge.

The lurid photography, by Russell Metty, is as atmospheric as that in the Ambersons' house. The melodrama is played for full value, and yet it leaves room still for a mordant commentary on Welles himself—the incriminating "cane," the observations dropped like acid on candy-soft metal by the Marlene Dietrich character. It all makes for a fantastic mix—a tour de force filled with a terrible regret about expression itself that infects movie, life, and being. Here is a studio noir picture that stands up equally well as a private "diary" film.

As had happened before, Welles quit the editing and the film got itself into a studio version that has since been restored. The rebuilding of the sound track, by Walter Murch, is a more dubious achievement. Personally, I prefer the swagger of the old opening with the ticking and the Mancini score to the carefully compiled sounds of a real border town. This isn't an everyday place—it's pulp-town. It's a nightmare in a world that has vanquished all of Welles's old optimism. It's as if eloquence has lost the urge to talk any longer—and Quinlan's nihilism is not far from Welles's own dismay.

But try looking away for a second. The emotional impact is so much less than that of *Kane* or *Ambersons*, but what do we call this if it is not great film. Welles is hideous as Quinlan, and pathetic. Heston does a great job as the Mexican cop. And Janet Leigh is brave, sexy, and clever enough to conceal the plaster on her broken arm. Also with Joseph Calleia (wonderful), Akim Tamiroff, Valentin de Vargas, Mort Mills, Victor Milian, Joanna Moore, and Ray Collins.

Track of the Cat (1954)

This is one of those films that squeezes in because of its oddity, or perversity. After all, director William Wellman—a pillar of the Hollywood community—said he wished he had never made it. But the common sense and practical business-like acumen of Hollywood won't get you round the corner. "Being business-like" was certainly part of the Hollywood style, but it was so seldom observable in fact. The movie kingdom was a panorama of whims and irresistible impulses—look at the people they married, look at the films they made. *Track of the Cat* is strange, and the audience didn't get it. But when Joe Gillis tells the story, dead, from the swimming pool in *Sunset Blvd.*, the audience says, "Cool."

The crazy dream factor on *Track of the Cat* was Wellman's deep-seated urge to make a color film so that it looked like black-and-white. How do you do that? You make a Western in the winter in the snow country. He found a novel by the Reno author Walter Van Tilburg Clark (he had written *The Ox-Bow Incident*) about a family that is spooked by a black panther roaming in the woods. They shot exteriors up in the Sierra and interiors at Warners, and Wellman and his photographer, William Clothier, kept the secret to themselves. And no one remarked on it! Not even the labs where they could find so little color to print! Maybe the lab had sat down and reasoned that with Wellman directing it and Robert Mitchum starring it must be OK. Regular guys like that would never get themselves involved in anything so arty, would they?

Mitchum is in his nasty vein, and he's good, but maybe it needed a different actor—like Clifton Webb. I like the film a lot, especially its gloomy family mood, with a house full of Mitchum, Teresa Wright, Tab Hunter, Diana Lynn, and Beulah Bondi. As for the panther, you think you can see him anywhere.

Who even saw it? I saw it, and Wellman and Clothier saw it: "And when it was all over, we both cried. You know, you would have thought we were a couple of crying drunks—really, truly. It was so beautiful and so unusual. Warner saw it—the whole gang. They never noticed it. It went out. It was released. Nobody saw it. No one paid any attention to it. It was just a dream that went up like a bubble had burst. Really and truly. It just broke my heart. I said, 'For seven years I've been looking for a thing like this, Bill.' And Bill did a great job on it—got no mention as a photographer. Nothing. And it's absolutely beautiful."

And so it is. But the lesson is clear: Don't go arty for seven years and expect anyone to see it. You see, it's a closed club and everyone is being kind. If you were a rapist child-molester they wouldn't turn you in, either. So the only decent way for an American to see a film like this is by accident.

The Travelling Players (1975)

We know after half an hour, that, as non-native watchers, we are always going to be cut off from the roots of this extraordinary ritual become a film. Equally, we know that we are very far from the touristic world of *Zorba the Greek*. We sense that something innovative and beautiful is being done with the long take and the moving camera—it is said there are just eighty shots in a four-hour film, but who can keep count while being so physically caught up in these movements? Take the information on trust, and are we best advised to see these traveling shots as a version of Renoir, or Mizoguchi or Ophüls, or would we get more out of them if we knew more about the choral processions at the heart of Greek drama? For Theo Angelopoulos, the director, is not just an epic chronicler of Greece, he is someone who seems intent on finding a "musical" in Greek drama.

The Travelling Players, made when Angelopoulos was forty, was clearly the breakthrough film that marked his lavish and far-reaching style. In a nutshell, the film follows a traveling theatrical troupe in Greece in the years between 1939 and 1952 in its efforts to mount a production of a naïve play called *Golfo the Shepherdess*. These years are a time of war, first with Italy and then with Germany. That is followed by a fierce war of resistance, encouraged by Britain and America (not always with much understanding), to be followed by civil war because of the spread of Communist influence. In fact, the film begins in 1952, on the eve of the election of Papagos, and it then breaks into flashbacks that track the way the years of turmoil affected the company's plans. It is likely, in fact, that Angelopoulos used this very parochial format to avoid larger charges of breaking censorship, or commenting too directly on embattled issues.

A quick survey of Greece in those years will help any viewer, but then you are open to the beauty of the film itself, and the uncanny ways in which movement serves as a metaphor for history. There is not a director who moves so easily through space only for us to discover that a temporal journey has been made. But again, the traveling shot that fixes on a group is not just a record of a family troupe—it is an observation of a society in transit. The period can alter during the course of a single shot. So what we are seeing is pageantlike and theatrical (in the abiding sense of Greece being the founder of modern theater).

Of course, the panoramic effect cries out for a big screen, but Greek pictures of four hours are far more likely to be confined to the small screen these days. Still, Angelopoulos is a master, and this and several of the films to come are almost unbearably moving if you have caught the rhythm early enough. The color photography is in the hands of Giorgos Arvinitis, and the music here is by Loukianos Kilaidonis.

Treasure Island (1934)

The Robert Louis Stevenson novel, published in 1883, has been filmed so many times. There were, apparently, four silent versions, the most notable by Maurice Tourneur, with Lon Chaney as Long John Silver. It was inevitable, therefore, with sound that a new version—the most spectacular yet—be made in the great enthusiasm for literary adaptations. It was a book loved by Louis B. Mayer himself (the friendship of child and adult was always a theme that moved him). Hunt Stromberg took on the production, and John Howard Lawson and Leonard Praskins worked separately on an adaptation, before John Lee Mahin did the screenplay. Not that there was so much work to be done: Stevenson wrote with an uncanny sense of dramatization waiting at hand. His action sequences are carefully worked out. The reader can see the story.

The key step in the production was to cast Wallace Beery as Silver. This is good casting, respectful of the book, for Beery was close to fifty, commanding if homely, athletic and humorous. There's no evidence that others were thought of, but it's interesting to think of Tracy as Silver. As Jim Hawkins, the film cast the thirteen-year-old Jackie Cooper, who had already teamed with Beery in *The Champ* and *The Bowery*. But Cooper was tough and very American, and there's no doubt that the Englishness of the novel suffers in this version.

Victor Fleming directed, and, as so often, he judged nicely the balance of action and character that the work requires. One of the reasons why it is so hard to measure Fleming's own character is because, so often, he served his material closely. The photography was shared by Clyde DeVinna (the seascapes), Ray June, and Harold Rosson. Cedric Gibbons did the art direction, and Herbert Stothart wrote the score.

Lionel Barrymore plays Billy Bones, Otto Kruger is Dr. Livesey, Lewis Stone is Captain Smollett, and Nigel Bruce plays Squire Trelawney. Charles Sale is Ben Gunn, William V. Mong is blind Pew, and Douglass Dumbrille has the key role of Israel Hands (Jim's opponent in the best action scene).

There's nothing to fault here beyond the Americanness. Beery is droll and wicked—he is never quite the loner that seems waiting to be discovered in the novel. Tracy and, say, Freddie Bartholomew do, immediately, give promise of a different atmosphere, one in which we recognize Jim's need for a father figure.

The story does not rest. Byron Haskin directed a version for Disney in 1950, with Bobby Driscoll as Jim and Robert Newton as Silver. Newton commandeered the part and spawned a host of impersonations (notably by Tony Hancock), but Newton was drunk and Silver is not. Orson Welles was Silver in 1972, and really not very good. There is a TV version in 1990, with Charlton Heston as Silver and Christian Bale as Jim (it was directed by Fraser Heston). In truth, it is the best version of the novel. There is also a version by Raul Ruiz, postmodernist, ironic, playful, and a real treasure.

The Treasure of the Sierra Madre (1948)

John Huston had made efforts to secure the rights to *Treasure of the Sierra Madre* before he went off to the war. After all, the book had been published originally in 1927. But Warners had trouble locating its author, B. Traven, or verifying his identity. So the project dragged on and was revived after the war. Jack Warner was not happy: Huston wanted to do the whole thing in Mexico; some of the talk would be in Spanish; and there were no dames. In the end, it cost close to $3 million and it didn't do very well, probably because by then Bogart had a real romantic image and too many people were dismayed to see just how nasty and crazy his Fred Dobbs became. Still, when Jack Warner saw it, he reckoned it was one of the greatest pictures the studio had ever made.

Huston did the script, and Traven himself thought it was brilliant (he had only a few suggestions, which Huston followed). So they all went off to Mexico, with Ted McCord doing the black-and-white photography—I think it's a blessing that McCord delivered a rough look, whereas a Gabriel Figueroa might have lit the hell out of it (but there are too many camp sequences on painful sets where voices bounce off the wooden floor).

But the strength of the film is the unsentimental approach to the three treasure seekers, played by the director's father, Walter, Tim Holt, and Bogart. We have no illusions about any of them, even if Holt's Curtin comes dangerously close to being a regular fellow. But the old-timer was always crazy and the onset of Dobbs's paranoia is very well done. And it follows from that that, while the idea of "treasure" is sublime and all-powerful, Huston knows it for a trickster, too. It is the search that grips these men more than the finding. And the old man's mirth at the way the gold dust is scattered in the wind is an ancestor to the mad laughter that ends *The Wild Bunch*, and even the attitude to all the lost loot in Kubrick's *The Killing*. It's in Huston's nature, as much as the old-timer's, that treasure will give you a purpose in life—so long as you never get hold of it. Then you're done for. And this is actually very close to the notion within *The Man Who Would Be King*, that project that held Huston for decades.

And there are so many other things to enjoy: Bobby Blake as the Mexican kid at the start; John Huston himself in a white suit; Alfonso Bedoya, quite delicious as the bandit, though probably setting the general image of Mexico in American eyes back a hundred years. It was nominated for the Best Picture Oscar, and it got rave reviews despite the disappointing numbers—within a few years it was an accepted classic. Huston won as Best Director (beating Olivier for *Hamlet*). But what pleased him most was when his father got the Supporting Actor prize—just two years before his death.

The Tree of Wooden Clogs (1978)

Long before there were appealing stories of some movie-genic loner getting over a bad romance by buying a villa in (name the province of Italy where you intend to spend the rest of your days), the Italians themselves had worked out a simple kind of inducement, based loosely (or not) on the lives of the peasantry from another age. Ermanno Olmi was born in Bergamo in 1931, the child of peasants—and *The Tree of Wooden Clogs* is based upon the peasant life in a farmhouse community there at the very end of the nineteenth century. So, plainly, Olmi was delving into his own past in the age when Italy was struggling to be one nation, despite the unifying forces of the Church, the campagna, and the position of the peasantry.

It was a picture made for RAI (Italian television), and while it ran a full three hours, it could have been longer—or almost a daily account of life in the compound. In the long term, it declines to be angry or radical. Instead, it has a feeling that everything will work out for the best, that reflects Olmi's own allegiance to the Roman Catholic Church and which makes far too modest or polite an issue of ownership, authority, and disobedience.

Instead, a kind of sweetness prevails. Don Carlo, the rather absentminded landowner (he would prefer to play music all day), advises one of the peasants that a young son should be sent to school. But school requires shoes for the boy. And the father cuts down a tree on the estate to make wooden shoes. One day, the master sees the cuttings from the destroyed tree and wonders what happened. The father is fined and expelled from his home. No, Olmi does not believe that this is "right or wise," but neither is it the occasion of some radical dismay. It is assumed to be part of progress, and almost of a natural process as trees make way for shoes.

If you were a filmgoer at the time, you could have wondered how this version of history was meant to fit in with Bernardo Bertolucci's *1900*, made only two years, before, in which there was hideous violence and deep-seated antagonisms. The answer may simply be that Bertolucci was a Marxist and a city boy talking about country life. In turn, that is why the heroes and heroines from London or New York want to buy a hovel to improve in the right part of rural Italy—where the visitor has no real need to get caught up in local troubles.

Written and directed by Olmi, but also photographed and edited by him, *The Tree of Wooden Clogs* is a dramatized history inquiry—it's rather as if Ken Burns had made his Civil War out of lots of short stories instead of still photographs and contemporary letters. How you proceed says a lot for the cultural traditions in place, or the attitudes being gently imposed. The film was made with amateur actors, but that is a custom that seems inspired by the natural acting to be found in any Italian hill town.

The Trial (1962)

There were projects that Orson Welles nursed for decades, and carried with him through life changes, the death of some of his actors, and immense obstacles. But you get another side of his impetuous creativity when you realize that one day the Salkind brothers came to him with money for a modest film and a list of titles to choose from. Seizing upon the abandoned Gare d'Orsay in Paris for most of his sets, and going to Zagreb for the rest, Welles made a very complex film in just over two months, and had the film done and ready to show by December 1962. What's more impressive is that the view of Kafka is consistent throughout, faithful to the book and very compelling for young viewers who previously found Kafka "obscure." This is a film made with such control and panache. And it is pretty good Kafka as well as major Welles. Grant the popular image of Welles in the 1950s as a wandering wreck, and you have to admit that somehow he made three masterpieces in eight years: *Touch of Evil, The Trial,* and *Chimes at Midnight.*

Of course, Welles remains Orson. He introduces the story of Joseph K. with the story of the Man of Law—and he has this story delivered by the Advocate (a character played by Welles). In the book, this story comes in its place. In the film, it is clearly meant to be the explanation of the mystery that dogs Joseph K. and inasmuch as it is delivered by Welles personally it does suggest an omniscience that is not exactly Kafkaesque. On the other hand, it is a device of adaptation, especially if Welles had let another actor play the Advocate. As it is, the decision taken speaks volumes to his emotional need for positions of authority.

That said, the vision of Kafka's world is haunting and ingenious to a degree. This is one of the great paranoid films, because of the way space is stretched and insidious sound (whispers and creakings) seems to be creeping in through the cracks left, like a drug called radio. Edmond Richard did the photography. Jean Mandaroux was art director. Still, it's hard not to think that Welles's great experience at distorting space wasn't the key design element. It is as if the film was set in the Ambersons' house after it had suffered fifty years of rats and ghosts. As you tour the Gare d'Orsay in its modern manifestation as sophisticated art museum, it's a model of lateral thinking to remember what Welles saw could be done with its waiting neglect.

Anthony Perkins is Joseph, and it's a great, jittery performance, albeit one guided by the soft voice of Norman Bates throughout. In the scenes with ravenous women—Jeanne Moreau, Elsa Martinelli, Romy Schneider—one can feel how far it is also a homosexual horror story. The cast includes Akim Tamiroff, Arnoldo Foà, William Kearns, Jess Hahn, Suzanne Flon, Madeleine Robinson, Wolfgang Reichmann, Thomas Holtzmann, William Chappell, and Fernand Ledoux.

The Triplettes of Belleville (2003)

I'm not sure if I have ever seen an animated feature film in which there is less sense of piety or less burden about having undertaken animation altogether. In great films there is a visual momentum—often extreme, mannered, or expressionist—that still seems utterly necessary and demanding, so that it has burst out of the filmmaker like any other bodily fluid. Yet very often with animation there are intervening levels of self-explanation (often smug) that seem to say, "Well, I had this story, this idea, but then I thought I'd animate it. See how difficult it was? But see how I came through."

But Sylvain Chomet's exhilarating story about cycling and its mishaps has the speed and whir of a bicycle itself, spinning along so effortlessly that it's hard to think there was ever any premeditation or determination on story plus line equaling movie. Quite simply, Chomet sees things that way. Indeed, one of the keynotes of this film is the general agitation it shows about whether it can remember to do—or organize—everything it wants to do. It is so caught up with its own motion and commotion.

After all, it's an everyday story: Champion, a sad-faced orphan, wants to be a great cyclist. His grandmother Souza gets him a bike and trains him. He is in the Tour de France when wicked mafiosi kidnap him and two other cyclists. Why? Because they mean to employ their furious cycling energies in a form of popular theatre in Belleville (a mixture of New York and Montreal). Souza follows her boy to Belleville and there enlists the aid of an old vaudeville team—the Triplettes—in rescuing Champion.

The drawing is angular, often antique, except that Chomet is very versatile—in fact his is real drawing allied to the computer, and it is often a little like Toulouse Lautrec dating Betty Boop over an absinthe sorbet. There's a steady period feel to it all—and you can tell that Chomet likes fussy décor and clothes. Yet the attitudes of the story are spiced by a very modern anti-Americanism that is so refreshing after the hangdog self-satisfaction of so much American animation. And although there's a child, the energies and feelings are adult, smart, sarcastic, and superior. You have to hurry to keep up.

But it's the music and the songs (by Benoît Charest) that seem to bring sinister acceleration to the geared wheels turning—it's not too much to say that the film is like a giddy drug, a zest for turmoil, and an elegant resolve that seems to understand complex literary ideas. You could imagine Chomet doing an animated version of Proust—yet he has the old-fashioned trust in "wham!" that comes from an understanding of Tom and Jerry.

You can tell yourself that Pixar have captured a modern American attitude. But the sunniness behind those films seems to me essentially boring and complacent. It is as removed from Bush's age as Disney was from the thirties. *The Triplettes of Belleville* is about a kind of animated film that assumes the medium is ready for smart, devious, and rather wicked grown-ups. Down with childhood!

Tristana (1970)

At the end of his life, Luis Buñuel made three films in France: *The Discreet Charm of the Bourgeoisie, The Phantom of Liberty,* and *That Obscure Object of Desire.* They are films about frustration, using that word in the largest sense. Just before them, yet unfortunately lost in terms of our attention, is *Tristana,* another masterwork, and an icy study in the same tantalizing opportunity and deprivation. This is the more intriguing because it is a Spanish film, set in the Spain of Buñuel's own youth. It has another claim to fame: It is the one meeting of those two classic Buñuelian presences, Fernando Rey and Catherine Deneuve.

Toledo, 1929—filmed there, with the *there* looking like 1729 or 1529. Tristana (Deneuve) is an orphan, with long hair, brown-auburn-red. She goes to live with her guardian, Don Lope, a poor but noble man (Rey). She is innocent; he is not. He comes to desire her and she accepts the coming. They live as a couple. But Tristana feels trapped. Then a young artist, Horacio (Franco Nero), comes by. He and Tristana are a natural couple.

Tristana goes with Horacio to Madrid. Two years later, they return. She has a tumor on her leg. Don Lope is rich now and he lets the invalid woman live in his house. Her leg is cut off. She gets better. Lope asks Horacio to visit. Horacio asks Tristana to marry him. She refuses. The young man does not love her as Lope does. He is unquestioning. So Tristana marries Lope, but refuses to give herself to him. Lope is dying. Tristana is to call the doctor. But she does nothing except open up the windows and let cold air into his room.

Love was an immense ideal for Buñuel once, overpowering all things. But now those things have grown so wiry and cunning. In a perverse way Tristana goes from being the utterly obedient girl to the murderous victim of liberation (she is free but she is on crutches). The inscrutable Deneuve (very well wigged for the film) is doubly alluring on crutches—and there is a moment when she discloses the sight of her ruined but perfect body to a young boy (but not to us). Don Lope is also the man steadfast in love, no matter that he has been humiliated by youth. It is just that he is her jailer. And though she has come to have deep fondness for him, finally she does take the slender chance to be his killer. Great calm can end in the peak of revenge.

There are those who will say that life is not like this at all—that the film is a throwback to an archaic Spain. But if you fall victim to the dreamlike logic with which *Tristana* progresses, then you know you are seeing the ritual of a fable. And if you can see the profound simplicity in Buñuel for what it is, then you are watching the great filmmaker of his time just where Toledo 1929 becomes everywhere and always.

Trouble in Paradise (1932)

What was the Lubitsch touch? Here's one answer. Late in 1931 or early in 1932, the director King Vidor has a romance with the actress Miriam Hopkins. He takes her out to dinner and Ms. Hopkins comes with a script she's just been offered—by Lubitsch! They read it aloud together over dinner, their pleasure with the food regularly interrupted by the joys of the script and its encouragement to enacted romance. And there at the end of the typed pages is this handwritten comment: "King—Any little changes you would like I will be happy to make them. Ernst."

Happier, I daresay, to one-up a colleague than actually make changes. And who ever reckoned that *Trouble in Paradise* needed repairs? It came, supposedly, from a play, *The Honest Finder*, by Laszlo Aladar, but the screenwriter, Samson Raphaelson, declared the film was an entirely separate creation. It starts in Venice and moves to Paris, confident that in an age of depression the audience has a good-humored appetite for luxe and money, and the nerve that can win both. Make no mistake, *Trouble in Paradise* is disdainful of moral purpose and bromides about a better tomorrow. The political attitude is nihilist bar one thing—it is still stuck on sex and its great future. In the Lubitschian history of the 1930s, it was the Nazis' greatest mistake to lose humor.

Two thieves meet—Lily (Miriam Hopkins) and Gaston (Herbert Marshall). He is such a fabulous thief that Marshall's stiff leg seems like a hiding place for the loot. They are experts. Just sitting down to dinner they can pick each other's pockets in places where no tailor designed pockets. Indeed, his coup is to show her the garter he has somehow taken from her warm body. They pick upon a victim, Mariette (Kay Francis). But Lily is afraid that Gaston may fall for her for real. Perhaps she should act independently?

It's a film of talk, or innuendo, so theft is another idiom for sex. In which case, the moment when Francis simply takes off a heavy pearl necklace amounts to undressing. The drama of the film is a matter of which lady Gaston will settle with. And you could argue that this is a film that celebrates theft over loyalty. If in doubt, please play a double bill of *Trouble in Paradise* with Robert Bresson's *Les Dames du Bois de Boulogne*. *Trouble in Paradise* was so effortless in 1932 it rather slipped by. But it is now regarded, with justice, as one of the markers in American comedy—after all, isn't it crazy to prefer money to love? There is nothing better than the rising challenge to honesty between Gaston and Mariette:

GASTON: I know all your tricks.
MARIETTE: And you're going to fall for them.
GASTON: So you think you can get me?
MARIETTE: Any minute I want.
GASTON: You're conceited.
MARIETTE: But attractive.
GASTON: Now let me tell you.
MARIETTE: Shut up—kiss me! Wasting all this precious time with arguments.

It comes from a novel by John Gregory Dunne, with a screenplay written by Dunne and his wife, Joan Didion—so it's no wonder that everyone seems fond of the sad story. It's about the Spellacy brothers, Des and Tom, a priest and a cop, the one settled in the LAPD, the other rising steadily in the Catholic diocese of Los Angeles, the favored right-hand man of a cardinal played by Cyril Cusack at his most dreamy, fastidious, and vicious. And, straightaway, one realizes how seldom the screen takes being brothers seriously. These two know they're chalk and cheese, and they both fear and resent, yet are humbled by, the difference, and there's a kind of awful, gradual certainty whereby the cop is bound to ruin the priest's career, which the priest accepts inasmuch as he was not strong or inventive enough to destroy himself. Destruction being what he needed and what his precious career merited.

Robert De Niro is the priest and Robert Duvall the cop, and you can feel them flexing their ideas over the possibility that they might have swapped parts. Indeed, there is even a hint or an osmotic smear whereby they might, very gently and fondly, be "doing" each other—it's a great deal subtler and more beguiling than John Travolta and Nicolas Cage in *Face/Off*. But De Niro is very good indeed as the smooth careerist, doing the cardinal's dirty work, and watching the naughty world of real men pass by, like a whore he's giving a lift to.

I should have added that the drama is brought to a head by a barely disguised version of the Black Dahlia murders of 1947—when the parts of a pretty girl were found in a wasteland, cut up but organized artistically. This is the case that Duvall's detective takes up, and it is what connects so many people in what still seems a small Los Angeles. The period stuff is very warmly done, and Ulu Grosbard shows himself a tactful director of a good script. Incidentally, Rose Gregorio (Mrs. Grosbard) does a very nice job as a tough but caring madam.

As you might guess, the supporting cast is expert—Burgess Meredith is unforgettable as a stubborn little priest who gets kicked off to the desert because he won't play ball for Cusack; Kenneth McMillan is super as a fat, smart cop; Ed Flanders is as suave as silk, and Charles Durning—as the nastiest guy around—has a temper you can smell. There's a scene where Duvall goads him in public where you want to lip-read in case Duvall sneaked in some really nasty insult to Durning.

I heard Didion once say that this was her best experience with filmmaking (and I think she was speaking for Dunne, too). It's not a great film, but it's very well done and enjoyable, and it leaves you wondering why two writers as good as Didion and Dunne and knowing as much about the picture business didn't have a few more jobs as worthwhile. Yet most of their movies feel as if they were done for the health insurance.

The Truman Show (1998)

Nothing in the years since it appeared has taken away from the thought that *The Truman Show* was the mainstream phenomenon of the 1990s, the most original picture of a bland, if not stupefied, age, the movie in which the dread thing—the moment of real fear—occurred at high noon in a sun-swiped picture community, one that starts and ends with retirement. No other American film was clearer that the greatest threat to our existence was ourselves, and above all our decision to be cheerful, amiable, and pleasant. Thus, the great moment when we begin to realize that Truman Burbank (Jim Carrey) has had life itself—its risks, its decisions—taken away from him. But not taken by Communists, alien body-snatchers, or drugs. No, the weapon in the crime against life is that American staple, the long-running, lifelike show.

The screenplay was by Andrew Niccol, the direction by Peter Weir, but in many respects the daring of the venture consisted in its being a Jim Carrey picture in which comedy gave way to authentic nightmare, all the more alarming in that the sinister pedal was forsaken for the uplift. It was as if someone at last had realized that the most disconcerting or frightening thing about America was not the menace, not the black look of the humble zombie, but the bonhomie, the salesman oil, the "warmth" of citizenship. The blight of the nation's culture approaching the millennium was its betrayal of sincerity and sympathy. The archaic climate of film noir seemed ready to break up and be replaced by a film lumière, the kind of light that radiated commercials and which shone down upon the produce in our markets.

So the arc of *The Truman Show* is the gradual sense in our Lemuel Gulliver that he has been set up, that the busy ebb and flow of spontaneity in his cripplingly perfect community is nothing but mise-en-scène. Every soul is an extra; every incident is staged. *Truman* is a show that plays all the time on TV (banal but compulsive)—and please note that this film appeared a few years before the mocking glut of reality TV shows. After that, the haunting discovery is that a kind of godlike movie director (Ed Harris) is up there in his control room, hitting the switches, making the cuts, bringing the sidebars in and out with lethal tact. Thus, at a stroke, a film about film-making had asserted that it wasn't just the eroding money, the fools' glamour, or the celebrity of movie that was damaging, it was cinema's imitation of and supplanting of life.

In turn, this led to amazing images of an edge to the world—of the world beyond the dome of the show—that were as beautiful as the idea of Columbus so close to the edge he might fall off. So this is a great film—by far the best thing done by two awkward talents, Jim Carrey and Peter Weir. There is outstanding supporting work from Laura Linney, Noah Emmerich, Natascha McElhone, Holland Taylor, Paul Giamatti, and Harry Shearer.

12 Angry Men (1957)

At the outset of his movie career, you can almost hear Sidney Lumet saying to himself, Yes, I know this is far-fetched (that one sane voice sways the rest of a jury in 95 minutes), and I realize that that amounts to a whitewash of the jury system as a whole (so much more complacent than, say, *Anatomy of a Murder,* made two years later, where we are the jury, and can't quite decide). Still, within the limits of TV-into-movie, Reginald Rose had written a very deft script, with delineated characters. Lumet knew that he had an excellent cast, as well as Boris Kaufman ready to film it. So he tells himself, Don't fuck up. Don't get in the way.

If I say that I think that's what Lumet tried not to do on projects that range from *Long Day's Journey into Night* to *Q & A* or from *Network* to *Dog Day Afternoon,* it can sound mealy-mouthed. Not getting in the way is a high skill and a kind of modesty that is always looked upon kindly by writers and by those who have suspected that the auteur theory was a crock.

The original *12 Angry Men* still works very well. Indeed, the only thing that really mars it (apart from its excessive tidiness, and its willingness to settle for that) is Lee J. Cobb's overwrought performance and the assumption behind it that his character is a bigot. Somehow you feel that Otto Preminger would have made the man so much more charming, and then cast Henry Fonda in the part. Of course, that's already taking our analysis over the edge of simple enjoyment and into an appreciation of role-playing that Lumet never encourages.

Preminger knows that his courtroom is an arena where a great game is played; he takes it for granted, therefore, that he has actors playing actors. Whereas Lumet's reticence and self-effacement tell the actors they are playing real guys or types. And Cobb's being overcooked is very well demonstrated by the modulated ordinariness of people like Robert Webber, Martin Balsam, and Jack Warden. The less these jurors have to do, or stand up for, the more intriguing they are, and the more kindly Lumet looks upon them.

But where does that leave the Henry Fonda character? For me, then and now, he was always too much the teacher or the saint come down from heaven, or head office, to be among ordinary, sweaty men. Fonda is very relaxed, but it's hard for him not to be Lincolnesque or educational, and his white suit is an unnecessary clue, just as his classless eloquence is the giveaway to the kind of enlightenment he is meant to represent. He is not a common man, and anyone who has ever done jury service can guess that the attorneys would have rejected him early on. So his instrumentality shows like a halo. It's the fault of the play and the whole concept, for Fonda never gets angry. He just does his best to steer the result while keeping out of the way, and does it so well that Sidney Lumet never seems to notice that he suffers from the same crushing superiority.

Twelve O'Clock High (1949)

There are academic situations where Henry King's *Twelve O'Clock High* is employed in business schools or psychology classes for its lessons in man management and the maintenance of morale. That's fine, but I hope the business majors don't lose sight of the harsh beauty of a tense Gregory Peck, his hair and eyes as black as his leather jacket, or the rakish lines of the Air Force caps. For the iconography here goes way past acceptable managerial attitudes.

The framework of the film has Dean Jagger (he got a supporting Oscar), in civvies on a bike, coming back to the airfield in England where he was adjutant once. The tarmac is desolate, but then the roar of bomber engines comes in. There was a demoralized American unit there, enough to feel doomed or unlucky. Then Peck was the commander sent in to make sure they'd straighten up and fly right. He managed, but at the cost of his own crack-up. You see, bosses are not to become so fond of their men that they can't send them to their death.

So Peck drives himself crazy as he cuts out excuses, indiscipline, and friendship. Maybe that's like life, but I would advise keeping Joseph Heller's *Catch-22* in mind. *Twelve O'Clock High* is made from the point of view of obedience to authority and unquestioned acceptance of command. Yet there must have been a view that felt the war was insane, and gung-ho hysterical commanders exactly the leaders to avoid. *Catch-22* is a work of art, while this movie knows no reason to doubt the system.

Henry King was already an old-timer raised on the nobility of silent films and Richard Barthelmess as the Boy. Yet King and Peck were an interesting team, prepared to show the flaws in Peck's statue—*The Gunfighter* is somber and depressive; *David and Bathsheba* tries to be guilt-stricken; and *The Bravados* gives Peck a rare lease of wrath and disorder.

The air combat scenes (with some war footage and some very steady cockpit shots) suggest that man management can handle a dogfight—there's no room for panic, blind luck, or fuck-up, and little sense of the insanity of going up in a rattling steel box to lob bombs down Hitler's chimneys. Or was the target Dresden?

So this is a film that the Pentagon would have loved (and surely assisted), and it is guarded in history by Peck's ravaged sincerity and our larger feeling that that war was just (and fair?). Still, I hope military managers don't put too much reliance on its simple-minded homilies. And I must point out that Peck's crack-up is as brief and tidy as oversleeping. He sits still, oblivious and balefully intent, like a constipated Lincoln—and then, snap, he's all right again. So much for the real killer of combat stress. So, yes, this film needs the voice of Heller's Yossarian and at least the possibility that the command structure includes as much spite, folly, and madness as were permitted to show a few years later in *From Here to Eternity*.

Twentieth Century (1934)

Alas, we cannot rely on the movie archive to let us see how serious an actor John Barrymore was. But as to his command of comedy, there is no problem at all. *Twentieth Century* is one of the supreme screwball extravaganzas, confined to a moving train as if to demonstrate what *tour de force* means. It is also such a piercing dismissal (and celebration) of "acting" as fraud, self-service, and maneuvering for advantage that perhaps the first question—applied to Barrymore, or anyone else—is effectively out of order. Nothing is as hard or grave, or even as close to the grave, as comedy.

It all began as a play, *The Napoleon of Broadway,* by Charles B. Milholland. The director-producer Jed Harris looked at it and said it wasn't very good, so it should be passed on to Ben Hecht and Charles MacArthur. Milholland protested and said it was based on the impresario Morris Gest. Why not base it on me? said Jed Harris. Hecht and MacArthur duly turned it into *Twentieth Century,* which opened on Broadway in 1932, with Moffatt Johnston playing Oscar Jaffe and Eugenie Leontovich as Lily Garland.

The story? Jaffe is a theatrical producer in dire need of a success. He gets on the great train of the title hoping to sign up Lily, a big star, who is also traveling on the rails. He knew her first as the humble ingenue he discovered, Mildred Plotka. His star, his lover—doesn't she owe him one? She feels she owes him as many as there are pellets in a shotgun cartridge. There is a madman on the train (correction: it caters only to that breed), posing as a millionaire, and he gives a check for Jaffe's production of *The Passion Play*—Lily as Mary Magdalene.

Hawks worked on the play. Gregory Ratoff (who had played Jaffe in Los Angeles) urged him to make Lily as sharp and devious as Oscar. To convince Barrymore, Hawks had only to call the actor "the greatest ham on earth." For Lily, he went to his own second cousin, Carole Lombard. He told her that the movie would be total attack from the first scene. They should play it like a couple married and divorced many times—like Grant and Russell in *His Girl Friday,* "protected" by the legend of being eternal enemies. He broke through Lombard's reserve to the real woman—impetuous, foul-mouthed, and punch (or kick) first. It worked. It's hard to think that anyone had seen chemistry before *Twentieth Century.* We want this couple—as parents!

Joseph August shot it. Etienne Girardot repeated his stage success as the "millionaire." And for the rest, there are Walter Connolly, Roscoe Karns, Ralph Forbes, Charles Levison, Dale Fuller, Edgar Kennedy, Billie Seward, Snowflake, and so on. It may be a matter of taste as to whether you are more vulnerable to the comedy of mime or that of words and behavior—it seems to me inescapable, however, that *Twentieth Century* revels in the fraud of acting while so much silent film is laboring to believe in its artifice. Sophistication. Riot. Let the train go on forever. The comedy of confined actors is one of man's merciful triumphs.

Twenty Thousand Streets Under the Sky (2006)

The interaction of Patrick Hamilton (1904–62) and the movies becomes more fruitful as time goes by. He is not just the spirit of noir writing in Britain; he is a major novelist, who can stand comparison with Graham Greene, and with Harold Pinter—on whom he was a big influence. Hamilton plays—*Gaslight* and *Rope*—have their film interpretations, and *Hangover Square* is the origin of a famously lurid movie. But the enormous virtue of Simon Curtis's television filming of *Twenty Thousand Streets Under the Sky* was the tribute to Hamilton's writing and the rescue of one of the lesser-known books. In one stride it laid claim to being the best Hamilton on film, and the most instructive. Above all, in close-ups Curtis had found a style that addressed the wounding, terse conversation of Hamilton's books.

What Curtis and his screenwriter, Kevin Elyot, did was to make a three-part television series that exactly reflected Hamilton's plan: three short novels that worked together to make a portrait of life in a shabby public house on the Euston Road in the 1930s—the original novels, *The Midnight Bell, The Siege of Pleasure,* and *The Plains of Cement,* were published as a trilogy in 1935. The three central characters are a young barman (Bryan Dick), brash, likeable, romantic, and soaring in his ambitions; a pretty prostitute (Zoe Tapper), torn between the barman and the call of her trade, but hopelessly pushed into the position of betrayer; and another barmaid (Sally Hawkins), plain, quiet, watchful, and hopelessly in love with the barman.

The photography is very close to black and white, with a bruised coloring creeping in gradually as emotions rise higher—this is a fabulous recreation of the mood of the 1930s, and a photographic technique that has great potential. But the look of the film depends just as much on the openness and the disappointment in the faces and the outstanding level of movie acting by a little-known cast. I should add that the specially composed score, by John Lunn, was as potent and distinguished as some of the moodiest French movie music from the 1930s. In addition, Curtis used sets and real locations to build a stunning impression of London before the war.

It will be fascinating to see what a talent like Simon Curtis can or will do in feature films. But for the moment, here was one more testament to the natural place of television production in the history of British film. The material here is of the highest order, but the writer has always meant so much more in British television than in British film production. Of course, for Hamilton enthusiasts, a last great work remains to be filmed: *The Slaves of Solitude,* his masterpiece on boardinghouse life, published in 1947 (that key year in the history of noir)—if noir fans could only see that the mood and the movement is so much more extensive than a group of B pictures.

Two-Faced Woman (1941)

Two-Faced Woman opened just three weeks after Pearl Harbor, when no one felt compelled by so flimsy a romantic comedy—Garbo was to play Karin, a rather chilly ski instructress who becomes her own sexy twin sister to retrieve her husband, Larry Blake (Melvyn Douglas). But as war arrived, so the title seemed awkward. It carried intimations of espionage and dishonesty. Many other titles had been considered, everything from *Her Wicked Sister* to *Naughty Today and Nice Tomorrow.*

The film came from a Viennese play, *The Twin Sister,* by Ludwig Fulda, set in the fifteenth century! It was shifted to modern America by screenwriters S. N. Behrman, Salka Viertel, and George Oppenheimer, but without any sign of promise. Not that you have to blame other people. Garbo herself chose this script over *A Woman's Face,* the Donald Ogden Stewart reworking of the old Swedish picture about plastic surgery, the one that gave Joan Crawford a hit. Perhaps Garbo was afraid of that association with cosmetology.

She had a friendly team around her: George Cukor directed, Gottfried Reinhardt produced, Joseph Ruttenberg did the photography and Adrian the costumes, but the fact is that she was given an unkind haircut and some ugly clothes. (Adrian quit over the picture.) She doesn't look great—so you might look at the close-ups and start guessing how old she must be.

Was there studio sabotage at work? It doesn't seem so, so long as you discount the way several friendly forces allowed this disaster to happen. In addition, Garbo had to dance—the chica-choca, a kind of rumba, which she does with dance director Robert Alton, without grace or enthusiasm. Then throw in the fact that the picture is stolen away by two other women: Constance Bennett and Ruth Gordon. Then the Catholic Church picked on the movie: She was sleeping with another man, they said. It's her husband! answered Metro. He doesn't know it, said Cardinal Spellman. Thus the moral perils facing comedies of remarriage.

The reviews were bad and they stung Garbo. Another project came up, *The Girl from Leningrad* (she would have played a resistance heroine), but it passed over. So Garbo went to the studio and agreed that for $250,000 she would let them out of their contract with her. So began the list and the age of the films Garbo might have made. It's clear that she retained some dream of a comeback through most of the 1940s. In 1948, Walter Wanger tried to set up *La Duchesse de Langeais.* Max Ophüls was to direct. She had vaguely approved James Mason as costar, and she had done screen tests with William Daniels and James Wong Howe (they look better than *Two-Faced Woman*). Mason was to get $75,000—and Garbo $50,000. The budget was at $500,000. But it all collapsed: The money melted away, and Garbo was difficult. Ophüls went on to do *La Ronde.*

2 or 3 Things I Know About Her (1967)

Who or what is she? Jean-Luc Godard gives his answer over the credits, and it is the description of his future. Cinema is over. Social studies have begun. So "she" is *"la cruauté du neo-capitalisme"*; prostitution; *"la région parisienne"*; *"la salle de bains que n'ont pas 70% des Français"*; *"la terrible loi des grands ensembles"*; *"la physique de l'amour"*; life today; the war in Vietnam; the modern call girl; the death of modern beauty; *"la circulation des idées"*; *"la gestapo des structures."* And very soon, we see our central character, Juliette Jeanson (Marina Vlady), on a summer evening on the balcony of her apartment, on a high floor, above the city and in the air, saying, *"Oui, parler comme des citations de verité . . . C'est le père Brecht qui disait ça . . . Que les acteurs doivent citer."* That the actors ought to quote.

In fact, one can argue that Godard's transition from remade movies to the films of quotation lasted a few years, but *2 or 3 Things . . .* is the essential work, shot in a month of the summer of 1966, with an actress he had not worked with before, in Techniscope and color yet with an intimation of the endless videotape that might be required to watch the working out of solar systems where bubbles and liquid meet the air on tops of cups of coffee.

Already characters are slipping away to become archetypes, and already the charms of Paris are moving into the stricken conditions of Alphaville. The heroine represents Paris and vice versa—the symbiosis of fiction and sociology is a machine that has been turned on. Henceforward, Godard's films are to be theorems or tests of how a society can and cannot work. The film is shot by Raoul Coutard, and in its wide screen it has intense, liquid moments of urban beauty, but already a kind of recorded neutrality is setting in. What will there be to make its harsh record subtler, except the ways time may deform and fade the electronic record (old Xeroxes have become faint footprints)? Thus, the poetic justice we wait for is the machine's great sigh and the collective forgetting of electronic data. The moment when digitalization fades away and data lose their taste.

But here is the question: In the forty years since *2 or 3 Things . . .* have the collected works of Godard improved upon the anthology of the years 1959–67, or has he only demonstrated the fear, or the regret, or the lack of energy to make those films again? Of course, *l'école video-sociologie* is content. Its *annales* expand by geometric progression. But as she looks off at the air and as her hair moves through space and time, Marina Vlady cannot help but evoke nostalgia for those ghosts who were playing tennis in Paris in *Pierrot le Fou*, or Belmondo and Karina trying to start up a musical on the pine-tree shores of the Mediterranean.

Look back at the definitions of her, and the one that seems doubly ominous forty years later is *"le gestapo des structures."* One of those structures, I think, comes when actors quote instead of clinging to their wildness.

Between 1953 and 1964, Stanley Kubrick had made seven films. It was then that extended contemplation set in. It would be four years before he delivered *2001*. This was the era of man in space, from Yuri Gagarin to men walking on the moon. So it's not that people weren't interested in the topic, or wondering about whether there were other creatures in space.

Kubrick's first thought was a film about extraterrestrials. Then he saw *How the West Was Won* and imagined an equivalent for space, with documentary sections featuring learned heads talking about millions of miles. He was put in contact with Arthur C. Clarke, and the two agreed to collaborate on what became *2001*. Their starting point was a Clarke story called "The Sentinel," about a strange, manufactured pyramid discovered on the moon.

The film has four narrative sections. In the first, set millions of years ago, apes discover a black monolithic slab; the encounter sharpens their curiosity and their aggression. In 2001, a U.S. spaceship goes to the moon base Clavius to see the black monolith just found there; it emits a strange noise. Eighteen months later, the *Discovery One* is headed to Jupiter with two men, Dave and Frank, when their computer, the HAL 9000, seems to turn rogue; Frank dies, and Dave disconnects HAL. In the last part, Dave reaches the area of Jupiter, goes through an amazing light show, and comes to an antique bedchamber inhabited by himself, decades older; the monolith appears, again in orbit.

I have named characters, but Dave and Frank are no more personal than HAL—and they are not as interesting. HAL has a plot purpose. This is a film in which characters and story have succumbed to apparatus (mechanical) and vague speculation of a metaphysical kind. What it means is up to you, and it was noted at the time that the efficacy of the film seemed related to the smoking of grass in theaters as the light show passed by.

The film was shot at Shepperton Studios, with a novel use of large sets, space centrifuges, and special effects—though the effects were all of the old-fashioned, man-made kind. Despite having a computer as a character, the film was not computer-generated. The staggering photography was by Geoffrey Unsworth and John Alcott. The special effects supervisors were Wally Veevers (crucial to the film) and Douglas Trumbull. Alex North labored mightily on a forty-minute score, only to find at a preview that it had been dropped for Kubrick's original idea: bits and pieces of the classical repertoire, including "The Blue Danube" by Johann Strauss, "Thus Spoke Zarathustra" by Richard Strauss, and some pieces by György Ligeti. There are actors—Keir Dullea and Gary Lockwood and a few others—but they are merely photographed figures.

The film cost about $10 million and has earned at least twice that in U.S. rentals. The Academy regarded it as a technical exercise, though Kubrick was nominated as Best Director. I believe now, as I did in 1968, that *2001* was a lavish travesty and an elaborate defense of vacancy or the reluctance to use real imagination. Of course, space can still work on film—we have had *Alien*, *E.T.*, and others—but the lack of humanity is a dead end. So Kubrick was positioned now as a master, but too masterly for known material.

Ugetsu Monogatari (1953)

Some people believe in the supernatural; some believe in camera movements—they each shall be rewarded. Genjuro (Masayuki Mori) is a potter. He does good work, and he desires to be recognized and rewarded for it. He has an oafish assistant, Tobei (Sakae Ozawa), a man who dreams of being a samurai. It is a time of war and marauding bandits. The two men decide to take the pottery to town. They set off with wives and children. But the yearning of the two men tears apart the families. It permits separation, so that the two wives, Miyagi (Kinuyo Tanaka) and Ohama (Mitsuko Mito), are abandoned.

Tobei finds a dead samurai warrior. He takes his armor and weapons and so he becomes a samurai. Genjuro is approached by the beautiful Lady Wakasa (Machiko Kyo), who says she loves his work. He must go to live with her. He falls in love with Wakasa, who is a ghost. While he has an idyllic retreat with her, his wife and child are killed by bandits. Ohama is raped, and eventually her "samurai" husband meets her again as a shamed camp follower.

At last, Genjuro comes "home"—the man who had believed in ghosts and in camera movements in which a man might go from one state to another. His home seems deserted at first, but then as he moves to one side and the camera pans back again, it discovers a hearth, food cooking, his wife and child. Perfect for a night. But ghosts. Next day the real world begins again.

Ugetsu, which won the Silver Lion at Venice, comes from seventeenth-century stories and from de Maupassant. The script was by Yoshikata Yoda and Matsutaro Kawaguchi. In his excellent book on Kenji Mizoguchi, Mark Le Fanu reveals that Mizoguchi had wanted a harsher ending in which Genjuro returns and finds not even one night's relief or mercy. Daie, the studio, asked for something gentler and so the present ending was arrived at. I think Daie was correct. There is an irony and a brief tenderness in the way the man deluded once by a ghost now gets a respite because of another. That is a justification. What really "works," of course, is the single camera movement that transforms the cold and ruined house into a home for one night. The endings in Mizoguchi are magnificent: That in *Sansho the Bailiff* is unforgiving, helpless, and tragic—though it allows mother and son some time together. The ending to *Ugetsu* says to all of us—to the audience—to struggle on with the battle between dreams and life. For as long as there is film and hope, the struggle must be reencountered every day just as the potter or the artist begins again.

It follows from all of this that *Ugetsu* is a film of fateful camera movements—just study the terrible abruptness of the scene where Miyagi meets her end and the enchantment of the whole Wakasa passage. As for Genjuro—artist, dreamer, husband, lover—he is that essential cinematic hero, the one who will define his own comeuppance. He is a man who believed so strongly that he knew and understood things that he gave up on that other duty—"You must see."

Ulzana's Raid (1972)

Time passes. Word comes to a cavalry outpost that Ulzana has taken his Chiricahua Apaches off the reservation and started to raid homesteads in the area. This is not because Ulzana believes the old liberties can be regained, or history reversed. It is not that he feels special hatred for the whites he is killing. Rather, escape and raiding is his death wish, for he knows that this action will hasten and ensure his demise. Not that he has ever believed the latter was in doubt.

A cavalry patrol is sent out after him. Its leader is Lieutenant DeBuin (Bruce Davison); its aides are a veteran scout, McIntosh (Burt Lancaster), and a young Apache, Ke-Ni-Tay (Jorge Luke). The script was written by the novelist Alan Sharp, who clearly knew his film history enough to be well aware of *Apache* (1954), the earlier collaboration between Robert Aldrich and Burt Lancaster, in which a rogue chieftain, alone save for his resistant wife, took off into the wilderness.

It was said when *Ulzana's Raid* came out that it was a parable about naïve American soldiers going after a lethal native force fighting for survival (Vietnam?). That's surely there to be found, for DeBuin is close to an idiot in his ignorance of the enemy he must fight, and much of this film is a process of education in which McIntosh and Ke-Ni-Tay feel increasingly close to the man they are hunting. So it becomes a conflict of landscape and strategy, distance and surprise—a little bit like an Anthony Mann film—except that it resonates with Aldrich's love of doomed heroes. Yes, Ulzana is finished—and when his end comes he accepts it like a Roman—but McIntosh is on his last ride, too, and he has to teach DeBuin to carry on regardless.

Coming after a long decade of missteps—from *What Ever Happened to Baby Jane?* to *The Grissom Gang*—*Ulzana's Raid* was an astonishing chance to rediscover Aldrich and for him to reclaim his pungent economy, his natural violence, and his lack of sentiment. *Ulzana's Raid* is a classic, photographed by Joseph Biroc and with intriguingly sparse music by Frank De Vol. Above all, it is a movie that knows how cruel and demanding life could be on some of the American frontiers, not least the one where civilized ignorance confronted natural severity.

By 1972, Burt Lancaster was no longer the emerging industrial power he was at the time of *Apache*. But Burt had been as opposed as anyone to that film's decision to let its hero survive. So the deaths here may be seen as payment of an old debt. Let's say a word, too, for Joaquin Martinez as Ulzana—he hardly speaks; he is in no way humanized by the film's approach; he is a magnificent savage; and he is a figure in this film as grand as some of the rock formations and as hard to beat. Note, too, the presence of Richard Jaeckel, an Aldrich loyalist, as a sergeant who has seen everything in his time.

Umberto D. (1952)

Umberto D. is late in the history of neo-realism. Italy was hardly experiencing the worst of times any longer—and the thought may occur that Vittorio De Sica was at something of a loss about how to continue. But then he thought of the dog. To be precise, the story and the script came from Cesare Zavattini (and he got an Oscar nomination for it). Umberto Domenico Ferrari has worked thirty years in the Ministry of Public Works. He is retired now, and his landlady wants him out of the building where he has a room in Rome. Umberto has no relatives in the world. But he has a dog, a mongrel named Flike.

Umberto (played by Carlo Battisti) is silver-haired, but he doesn't smile much. Indeed, he's a touch severe or gruff, not endearing, and certainly not possessed of the charm for which De Sica was famous. I think that's the point. De Sica and Zavattini want us to feel the plight of an old man, without relatives or enough money to look after himself, and without enough movielike personality to win us over just like that. Let's say he's as stubborn and as alienated as many old people. Then there could be a grim but testing film about how he is forced to live on the streets. It's plain that he's conservative, not open-minded, yet he might have to learn to see vagrants as his fellows. That is a great subject, and it is still one that occurs in many cities.

But there's the dog. As he contemplates living on the streets, Umberto wonders what to do with Flike. He sees the city pound and the gas chamber. He tries to give the dog to a little girl, but her nurse complains that dogs are dirty and trouble. He tries to lose the dog, but clever old Flike finds him out. He contemplates suicide, and that does trouble the dog. But in the end, the two of them are reunited, and off they go, playing with a pinecone, down one of those long gray urban avenues that De Sica liked so much.

It's not that the film is less than touching, but it's Chaplinesque—long before the music wells up, you say to yourself that this is a Chaplin short drawn out to 90 minutes. Then the music comes (overdone by Alessandro Cicognini), and you remember how Chaplin can get on your nerves. The open-air sequences are very well filmed by G. R. Aldo, and as always De Sica has an eye for the city that is graceful. But the dog takes over the film—and surely (I hope) man has better emblems of his fate than his attitude to animals. Old men die on the streets, and I think it's telling that by 1952 De Sica couldn't face that subject. Or really address the reasons why old people may end up alone.

A year later, for Selznick, De Sica was directing *Terminal Station*—and not badly—but suddenly his material and his actors had gone Hollywood. And I fear he never quite recovered. But the place of neo-realism has not been filled, or its questions answered.

The Umbrellas of Cherbourg (1964)

Chance decisions play so great a part in the development of the arts. After all, how was it that the novel and the long-playing record avoided television's natural burden—that of having a little wedge of advertisements placed between two sixteen-page signatures, or in the gap already available between track 1 and track 2? As W. C. Fields noted, perhaps it was simply an oversight on the part of Charles Dickens—a busy man, after all—that he didn't employ a certain amount of juggling in every novel? How easily we could run on—why do people run forward rather than backward, and why isn't the talk in every movie sung?

So often, the realist's complaint about the musical is that awkward moment where the actors take a deep breath, the story goes on hold, and "it" breaks into song. What better cure for that hesitation, or the nausea that attends it, than having every line of dialogue sung? To which, the realist objects, Yes, but people don't sing all the time in life. Possibly, but neither do people go through life with music playing in their air—I am thinking of the musical "background" that we take for granted, and as our just deserts. How many times have I heard uneasy directors say of their rough cut, Just wait till we put a bit of music on it. In other words, the role of music is in no sense lifelike. Music is what life would have been like if Michel Legrand had been God.

Very well. *The Umbrellas of Cherbourg* is a small love story set in that town involving a very pretty girl from the umbrella shop and a sweet boy from the garage. They love. They part. They find others. They meet again. Life goes on. Except that Cherbourg (a pleasant but gray-brown town) has been turned into an enchanted place through a thing called décor, by the presence of Catherine Deneuve when she was so pretty, so adorable, she seemed dipped in liquid cocaine and you understood every fairy story better, and because of Legrand's score. Now, Legrand had already done two superb, conventional scores for Jacques Demy, in *Lola* and *Baie des Anges*, and ahead lay his song suite for Barbra Streisand in *Yentl*.

Legrand is not Mahler or Brian Wilson or Billy Strayhorn. But he may be the most natural music writer for the movies there ever was. What do I mean by that? I showed a group *Some Like It Hot* recently, and there is the tango sequence where Joe E. Brown and Jack Lemmon are having a night to remember. And as a finale, we cut to the tango orchestra and they are blindfolded. Someone asked me why. Well, I said, it's a joke, a tribute to that couple's abandon. But I thought harder and said that it's because they want to feel they're at the movies, in the dark. Legrand writes music where we need the dark to hide our trashy joy and our shameless tears. And for *Cherbourg*, with Demy doing the very agile lyrics, he simply opened up a new way for film to go. The team did it again in *Les Demoiselles de Rochefort* (which has ardent admirers). For me, I have to say that walking backward may be a once-in-a-lifetime way home. And as Dickens observed, a little juggling in *Copperfield* may be in order, but juggling in *The Old Curiosity Shop* is asking for trouble.

Under Capricorn (1949)

Under Capricorn is probably the least seen of the Alfred Hitchcock pictures made after 1939. In part, that's because Hitch tended to disown it in the long interview with François Truffaut, admitting that he was near enough infatuated with Ingrid Bergman and so eager to work with her that he paid too little attention to the script. But Hitch was also flustered by the major failure of an expensive venture. Indeed, the picture was reclaimed by the bank financing it, and that may explain why it has been hard to see. And recall that Hitch was once so dismayed by *Vertigo* that he kept it out of circulation.

Under Capricorn is not as good as *Vertigo*, but it is a lost treasure nonetheless. It came from a novel by Helen Simpson, for which Hitch hired James Bridie to do the script and then Hume Cronyn to do rewrites. He regretted both decisions, and he blamed Bridie above all for the weak ending. But it's easy to see why the idea appealed. In Australia in 1830, Sam Flusky (Joseph Cotten) is an uneasy member of the upper class. Uneasy because he has been a convict, sent down on a murder charge. But he is married to an English lady, Lady Henrietta Flusky (Ingrid Bergman), so that her status rubs off on him. Her cousin, Charles Adare (Michael Wilding), comes to visit from England, and he will fall in love with Henrietta, seeing Flusky as just a drunken Irish lout, an outlaw dragging the woman down. The truth is far stranger. Henrietta is an alcoholic. She committed the crime for which Sam took the blame. But she has a housekeeper now, Milly (Margaret Leighton), who is in love with Flusky and slowly poisoning her mistress.

The false reading of class, the love founded in terrible sacrifice, and the scheming housekeeper—these are all traits we know from Hitchcock. And at its best, *Under Capricorn* is filled with the same interest in sadomasochism that drives *Notorious*. This is still one of Bergman's great performances, and the long scene in which she confesses to her crime is a tour de force. In part, that's because Hitchcock was still under the spell of the ten-minute takes pioneered in *Rope*. But there the camera was burdened with the conceptual gimmick. Here, as if in the mood of Ophüls or Renoir, Hitchcock has actually seen the beauties in duration and moving through space. He isn't bound to ten-minute shots. But he is prepared to let the Technicolor camera (guided by Jack Cardiff) take immense, winding courses that are filled with emotional energy.

Sidney Bernstein produced the picture, and it was shot at Elstree, not in Australia. It's tempting to wonder how far that different air and sunlight might have affected it. Still, don't write this picture off. Apart from Bergman, Cotten is deeply troubled as Flusky, and it has a superb performance by Leighton as a Mrs. Danvers–like figure, and a strong British supporting cast that includes Jack Watling, Cecil Parker, and Denis O'Dea.

Underworld (1927)

"Underworld" or "innerworld"? In the hands of Josef von Sternberg, here we are in 1927 (that very provocative year) in which you can see what will be a standard "atmosphere" coming to life before your eyes—we call it "noir." And yet Sternberg's odd caprice is so alert to that thing made most precious in 1927—the unsaid—that this is about secret, psychic life as much as criminal undertakings. It was Andrew Sarris who first observed how *Underworld* was a Cocteau-like picture in which the manifestations of décor, clothes, and action were most eloquent as incendiary, subconscious matches bursting into flame. So here is a silent film itching to speak—yet a film in which people are like islands that might be sending code signals to each other. Above all, *Underworld* was influential in providing the confidence that the great figures of criminal existence could be beheld on their own without the obligatory confrontation with policemen.

So *Underworld* is a brooding power struggle between the brutish, yet nobly aspiring "Bull" Weed (George Bancroft), and the austere, stylish, and English mastermind figure, the thinking man, "Rolls Royce" (Clive Brook).

The original story was by Ben Hecht, and he got the first Original Story Oscar for it—a few years later, he would write *Scarface*, too. Hecht claimed to have strung together enough Chicago hoodlum incidents to make an eighteen-page outline. What made it tick, he said, was his catering to the public's delight in gangsters and their dames. Thereafter, the writer said, it was all he could do to stop Sternberg from ruining it with sentimental touches—like "Bull" coming out of a deflowered bank with the loot, and giving money to a beggar.

In truth, the two men worked better than that suggests, from a shooting script by Robert N. Lee. Sternberg encouraged a shameless integrity in his gangsters, a panache that was aimed at the public and which absorbs Bull's generosity with ease. Indeed, to be a gangster in this light is to be a star—it's something that seems to coincide with movie glory.

Bert Glennon did the photography and Hans Dreier did the sets—one of which will be shot to pieces in Bull's final standoff. But all that said, Evelyn Brent's "Feathers" McCoy, the gangsters' moll, is the film's most striking relic now. Brent made three films with Sternberg on the eve of his discovery of Dietrich. And in *Underworld* she apparently wore underclothes with feathers sewn into them. The scene of her coronation is one of the first great insane raptures in Sternberg's work—and hardly possible unless he felt something. But in his autobiography, she got short shrift:

> Perhaps she felt uncomfortable in the tickling garment, for at one time while I told her how to act, she threw a shoe at me. I had the shoe returned to her and asked her to leave the stage and walk back to her producer-husband. But he had seen some of the film, marveled at the transformation, and informed her that he was no idiot. So she divorced him, and continued with me to become a star. I liked her and after using her in three films I let her fly by herself, and she promptly plummeted to earth.

Underworld U.S.A. (1961)

When Samuel Fuller went to Columbia with the idea for this film, he did a grandstand version of his opening scene. The camera begins on the back of a woman. It cranes up to reveal a mass of women, scantily clad, arranged in the form of a map of the U.S.A. The woman turns to the camera and speaks. She is secretary-general of the union of prostitutes and her message is that the ladies of the night deserve some organization and some breaks for all they do to bring relaxation and consolation to the American public. Did he or did he not have the Columbia Statue of Liberty standing just offshore, naked?

It gives one a sudden picture of Fuller on a stepladder with a revolver in his hand, doing the entire picture like a Lars von Trier essay/comic book in which everything takes place in one huge interior set, as if it were a political convention.

Columbia suggested that this was pretty shocking and disgusting. OK, said Fuller, unabashed. There's this guy, Tolly. He's just a kid, and he sees his father rubbed out by the Mob. And he grows up and he sticks inside the Mob, but only because what he's really after is revenge. And he sets out to kill the guys who murdered his father. At this point, happy at last, the studio gave Fuller the go-ahead—what greater gift can you give a man than honorable revenge? You might have thought that the first comic-book idea was shelved, but it keeps coming up in the speeches Fuller gives the bosses—about how they have this notion of paying their taxes, donating to charity, and just lifting their regular criminal enterprises up to the level of regular business. *Underworld U.S.A.* is still sadistic and disruptive, because of its notion that, if it's organized, it's hardly crime.

The great bitter joke about the film is that Fuller chose upstanding Cliff Robertson as Tolly—the actor, married to an heiress, the guy who would play John Kennedy in *PT 109*, and the citizen who one day would start the end of David Begelman by telling the government about the fraudulently signed check. And the best thing of all is that Robertson makes a fine thug and lout, even if he lacks the distinctive whining voice of Richard Widmark in Fuller's *Pickup on South Street*.

Hal Mohr did the glossy black-and-white photography. Robert Peterson was in charge of the art direction. The cast includes Beatrice Kay, Larry Gates, Richard Rust—as a sleepy-faced hoodlum—and Dolores Dorn as the girlfriend, "Cuddles." She and Tolly have a couple of nice scenes where he paws at her bruised face to see how much it'll hurt. It's not quite as raw as *Pickup on South Street*, but it's seldom the case in a good Fuller film that the neurotic sexual urge in violence is neglected for more than five minutes. In truth, this is one of the last gangster films in which the gangsters are louts and people you wouldn't take home—from now on, they were on their way to being gents and fashion plates. So an air of nostalgia is there in Mohr's morgue photography.

Unfaithfully Yours (1948)

It seemed so promising. As Preston Sturges really set up on his own, away from Paramount, he was seized upon by Darryl Zanuck and Twentieth Century Fox. This left Sturges in the invidious position of being the third-highest-paid man in America (at $8,825 a week)—and third feels vulgar and competitive. The material Sturges found to entertain Zanuck was an old project, *The Symphony Story,* about an orchestral conductor. He is English and plainly based on Sir Thomas Beecham. He has a beautiful young wife, American, and he naturally develops some suspicions that she is being unfaithful to him. This melodrama was to be enacted through a single concert in which the music and the fantasies that went with it spelled out nothing less than him murdering his wife, to be followed by redemption and forgiveness.

This conductor, Sir Alfred De Carter, was meant first for James Mason—handsome, attractive, jealous, impulsive. Alas, Mason could not make the date, and so Sturges turned to Rex Harrison instead. It was a good match and the two men fell quickly into friendship, though Harrison in those days did not easily win audience sympathy. The wife's role was offered to Gene Tierney, and when she thought it too small it ended up with Linda Darnell, ecstatic to be working with Sturges. Other parts went to Barbara Lawrence, Rudy Vallee, Kurt Kreuger, Lionel Stander, Edgar Kennedy, Al Bridge, and Julius Tannen.

The three pieces of music were Rossini's overture to *Semiramide,* the reconciliation theme from Wagner's *Tannhäuser,* and Tchaikovsky's *Francesca da Rimini.* This was a lot of music and a lot of fantasy to go with it. Might there have been warning signs of a cultural overload, or even a lesson to be learned from *Monsieur Verdoux* that, whatever its secret urges, the public was uncertain about killing your wife and expecting a laugh from it?

It turned into a very big picture, one that cost as much as $2 million and left Sturges with a cut of 126 minutes. Zanuck intervened and about 20 minutes were dropped. There were even notions of titles to explain the music and the fantasy. Harrison was very good, but just as the film came to be released his mistress, Carole Landis, killed herself—a test even for Sturges's robust satire. The picture opened and did disastrous business. Later on, Sturges recalled seeing a play with his father as a boy. The father laughed helplessly throughout, and Sturges innocently congratulated them on having seen such good work. Nonsense, said the father, it's awful.

"It was years before I understood what he meant," wrote Sturges. "Then I forgot it and very stupidly made *Unfaithfully Yours.* The audiences laughed from the beginning to the end of the picture [they didn't]. And they went home with nothing. Because nothing had happened. He hadn't killed her; he hadn't killed himself. It just looked that way. The audience ate my seven-course special and went home hungry."

The Unforgiven (1960)

Seeing it years later on television, John Huston felt compelled to turn off *The Unforgiven* and to conclude it was the worst thing he had ever done. Well, some of us can supply a moderate list of Huston films far less worth seeing, and his own dismissal of it may speak to a rare disappointment, or a feeling of what might have been. At any event, it was a Ben Maddow script from an Alan Le May novel. It's not just that Maddow was a writer Huston liked (*The Asphalt Jungle*), but Le May (the brother of Strategic Air Command supremo Curtis Le May) was also the author of *The Searchers*. And that film and *The Unforgiven* are clearly related: In the Ford film, Natalie Wood has been kidnapped by and married into the Comanches; while in *The Unforgiven* Audrey Hepburn is a woman who has lived with Kiowa Indians before being "rescued" by a white family.

Huston complained that *The Unforgiven* was "bombastic" and that its racial tension or irony had been dispersed by the Hecht-Hill-Lancaster team that produced it. Yet that is not really so. Audrey Hepburn does a creditable job in her difficult role, and there are fine performances from Lillian Gish, Charles Bickford, John Saxon, and Joseph Wiseman. If there's a problem staring out of the film, I think it's Burt Lancaster, who may well have dragged the script toward making him a dull hero as well as a love interest for Hepburn. I suspect that Huston's dismay comes from that kind of battle.

Kate Buford's biography of Lancaster notes that it had originally been a Delbert Mann project, with a script by J. P. Miller. When that team was scrapped, Huston and Maddow came on board, but Buford suggests that Huston was more interested in the Mexican location than in the picture itself. The results onscreen (very well shot by Franz Planer) are too atmospheric to be written off. And the link to *The Searchers* (all in a time when American attitudes to race were altering by the moment) is too intriguing to abandon the picture. Suppose Hepburn and Lancaster were both miscast, or a sign of unhelpful directions in the material. Suppose that the leads might have been Robert Ryan (a more implacable man) and Susan Kohner (someone who could have been Kiowa). Suppose that romance horrifies the Ryan character and threatens him.

I'm guessing, and this may be too fanciful or generous. But the picture as we have it is full of hints of something very interesting and disturbing—and the thing that troubled Huston may have been the loss of that possibility. What makes the argument worthwhile, I think, is the whole vexed matter of the way the Western genre stopped short instead of taking on issues and topics from modern American life. That tragic error could still be remedied—the roots of modern America are all over the West still, and it's hardly as if the racial issue has been settled. I have a hunch that the full story of what happened on *The Unforgiven* could help the troubled movie endure.

Unforgiven (1992)

Very few American movie careers have been so carefully massaged as that of Clint Eastwood. And *Unforgiven* was the film that decisively ushered him into any establishment he cared to recognize. The man who had done *Rawhide,* the Leone trilogy, and the Dirty Harry films, as well as a steady supply of entertaining pictures that don't force their way into this book, came into gray eminence with *Unforgiven.* It won Oscars for Best Picture, for Best Director, and for Gene Hackman as Best Supporting Actor. And you could look at *Unforgiven* and hope that the famous male supremacist had welcomed old age, human limits, and mortality into his life. If you were a little more sentimental than Clint has ever been.

It was a script by David Peoples that Eastwood's company, Malpaso, had purchased in 1985 and done nothing with. Even when the movie went ahead, Eastwood never met Peoples or conferred with him. He just did the script, because Clint likes the minimum of fuss. It is the story of Will Munny (Eastwood), a widower of sixty who lives in a shack in the middle of a prairie with his two young children. Times are hard, Munny is broke, but he was a gunfighter once and so he yields to an offer from a band of whores in a faraway town to do a job. To this end, he leaves the children to fend for themselves in the middle of the prairie—there must be another film about what happened to them.

As he rides on his mission, he picks up two supporters: Ned Logan (Morgan Freeman) and the Schofield Kid (Jaimz Woolvett). The latter is a flash braggart; the former is old enough to be a somber Man Friday. When they get to the town where the whores have been wronged, it is under the control of Sheriff "Little Bill" Daggett (Hackman). We see him humiliate and thrash another gunslinger, English Bob (Richard Harris). And at first Will Munny gets the same treatment. Ned is whipped and killed by Little Bill. The Kid proves helpless. Only Munny can get revenge. But now he seems feeble with a gun, too old, too slow . . . Until by some magic, the elixir of lethal speed and the mantle of the angel of death return to him (and us). He vanquishes Little Bill.

Well, yes, in outline and three-quarters of the way this is a welcome visitation of adult moods and fears. Munny is shown to be a wreck of himself. There is stern talk about the stupidity of courage and the ordinary habit of cowardice. You think maybe Munny is a dead man, and those kids are orphans talking to the wolves. But then Clint cashes in: To respectability, he adds the luster of his very own killing machine, still firing on all cylinders. And the Academy fell for it.

It's a Malpaso picture, directed and produced by Clint, photographed by Jack Green, with décor by Henry Bumstead. Hackman and Freeman are terrific. Frances Fisher (Clint's squeeze at the time) is one of the whores. And he does look as if he'd been dragged backwards through a bush. But it's much less a change or a breakthrough than a shrewd hand-washing operation.

The Unknown (1927)

Tod Browning (1882–1962) is one of the most intriguing figures in early horror. Born in Louisville, Kentucky, he ran away from home to join the circus, and he was a contortionist and clown before being drawn to the movies. He acted for Griffith and became an assistant. At some point he seems to have recognized his own destiny was in creating suspense and grotesquerie.

The Unknown is part of his famous alliance with Lon Chaney at M-G-M. The setting is Spain, probably in the late nineteenth century. We see a circus in which Alonzo the Armless (Chaney) does a knife-throwing act. He throws with his toes (the way he smokes his cigarettes), and his first two knives take away his assistant's dress so that the next ones can outline her pretty figure. The girl is Joan Crawford, by the way, with a terrific suntan and huge shining eyes. She seems pretty and wholesome, but she has one hang-up that comes as a surprise in view of her candid gaze: She really can't stand those guys, like the strong man in the circus, who want to run their paws all over her.

Of course, Alonzo loves her from afar, and she does regard him as a perfect gentleman. The script is by Waldemar Young, from a story by Browning, but I have to say that the script is not nearly good enough. I know this is only 1927, and we are at M-G-M, where a film had to be fit to be shown to Mr. Mayer's teenage daughters. But still, the cult of Browning seems to me charitable in the extreme and blind to some frissons that a real Spaniard (call him Luis) might have picked up on in 1927.

The girl is attractive but frigid. Alonzo is a great lover but without the means of holding his love. So their "intercourse" is in the knives and—what else? Well, suppose that Alonzo has a habit of coming upon her while she is sleeping and smelling her fragrant body with sometimes a cold kiss placed on her warm thigh. Can you imagine the granite face of Chaney lost in that quiet rapture? Can you see the cutaway to Crawford's dreaming face—with just a flutter of her eyelashes? Here is a magnificent story of desire and frustration, with the knives coming closer at every performance. Perhaps before the end, at night, he even licks her wounds.

Alas, that is not *The Unknown*. For as soon as its situation is set up, Alonzo is revealed as a fake. He has a familiar (an ugly dwarfish man) who helps him take off the harness that binds his arms down. Alonzo has arms! It's just that on both hands he has a double thumb—all the more useful in his other trade of strangling. He is a killer hiding out. End of interest. The film is only slightly over 50 minutes, and it remains more of a curiosity than a developed work. But in the chemistry of Crawford and Chaney there was such potential, a truly perverse film that Mr. Mayer might not have noticed if his daughters were smart enough to keep their pleasure silent.

The Usual Suspects (1995)

When you round up the usual suspects, the gang's all here. In other words, start with the rudiments of one genre, and you may be establishing the mood of another. Or, film noir goes into screwball comedy. As the author of a novel, *Suspects* (1985), in which the characters are figures from film noir who enter into a new fiction, I am not the most objective observer of Bryan Singer's highly entertaining film. Yet I may be in an unusually favorable position for seeing how intense pursuit of film (and its very set codes, the genres) leads to the eventual collapse of those forms and the emergence of something new.

So some critics charged that *The Usual Suspects* was too clever for its own good, and far too much of an inside joke. But the film did quite well, thank you, which suggested that enough people were sufficiently conversant with genre rules to see them broken, while still taking pleasure in the playing of old tricks. *The Usual Suspects* works—and holds attention—as a mystery and a caper film, just as much as a metafiction on those themes.

Five guys are rounded up, five nice types: McManus (Stephen Baldwin), Keaton (Gabriel Byrne), Fenster (Benicio Del Toro), Hockney (Kevin Pollak), and Verbal Kint (Kevin Spacey). They are being interrogated, on suspicion or in anticipation, and yet we begin to feel that the gathering—the arrangement, the lineup—is just a casting call for another job yet to be done, one that involves that mythical Hungarian master criminal, spell it which way you like, Keyser Söze.

Note that everything is aboveboard: As photographed by Newton Thomas Sigel and designed by Howard Cummings, this looks like San Pedro and its waterfront. There is a ship at dock which may have loot. There will be a firefight there. There is a pretty girl in the offing (Suzy Amis). There is a mood of dread, a couple of pushy, cocksure cops (Chazz Palminteri and Dan Hedaya), and the unlikely pairing of a character named Kobayashi and an actor called Pete Postlethwaite.

Yet it's not really a story so much as a game, a kind of backgammon played on a long voyage, where if you play enough times you may get the thing to come out sweetly and rewardingly. There is a payoff (not disclosed here) and a happy sense of discovery, closely followed by a feeling of emptiness. For nothing really emerges in the finale except for the need to play the game again.

The script, by Christopher McQuarrie, won an Oscar, and it's very long on skill. But it doesn't really have the stamina or the vision to summon up much meaning. So Bryan Singer can only direct it for the sake of skill and intrigue—and in the end our concentration deserves more. So I think there's too much anticlimax for anyone's good—and the highly original method has not really gone much farther, though a crack here can become a hole elsewhere in *Being John Malkovich*.

Vampyr (1932)

So, how did Carl Dreyer move from *The Passion of Joan of Arc* to *Vampyr*? Prints of *Vampyr* have muttered German dialogue, a few faraway sound effects, and lengthy English subtitles in Gothic type. None of which really helps this novella-like tone-poem of a film. Further, coming in 1932, it has to be a film on which the participants had seen Murnau's *Nosferatu* and Lugosi's *Dracula*. In which case, it seems strange that Dreyer—a very sophisticated man—should want to believe so completely in the hokey business of vampires. Doesn't he see the inadvertent ways in which his film has drifted toward camp or even comic territory? Are we really expected to feel a spiritual equivalence between this and *The Passion of Joan of Arc*? In which case, I fear, *Vampyr* suffers a good deal. Any young audience seeing it today is likely to find it foolish and, worse than that, humorless.

All we know is that Dreyer got funding for this film from Baron Nicolas de Gunzberg, who also plays the lead, Allan Grey, under the name of Julian West. He looks a little like a lugubrious George Gershwin or one of those handsome young men in Buñuel's *L'Age d'Or*. He comes to a village in France that is afflicted by vampires. And thus, in just over 70 minutes, Dreyer spells out the details of the vampire technique and shows Grey's struggle to survive two sisters, and even to save one of them from the devilish bloodlust—the titles talk about the Devil a good deal.

Dreyer used as his basis *Camilla*, by Sheridan Le Fanu, but there is not really anything like narrative flow. Nor is the film frightening, until that passage where Grey is put in a coffin with a window in it. Instead, we find ourselves admiring a somewhat esoteric essay on vampiric urges. The history tells us that Rudolph Maté's camera equipment was faulty so that the film turned out fogged on some early scenes. Dreyer liked this effect and asked Maté to imitate it deliberately. This isn't the way to win a photographer's heart—but it accounts for the rare, misty gray look to the film.

There is some very striking imagery—a ferryman with a great scythe; a hand creeping up a banister; and even, occasionally, the faces of characters struck by horror. But there isn't suspense, or dread, or flow—and time and again we are left asking ourselves how far Dreyer really believed this stuff. Whereas, of course, the matter of belief is the rock on which *Joan of Arc* is made, and the substance that leaves one hardly noticing the silence of the film.

The screenplay is by Dreyer and Christen Jul and the art direction is by Herman Warm. The books say that it is a deeply atmospheric film. But I suspect that Dreyer needed to abandon all the obvious vampire apparatus to get at that. It's a picture that might have worked better if the word *vampyr* had never been used and if we had been left to deduce its presence from a disconcerting love story.

Vera Drake (2004)

How many Mike Leigh films can this book hold? He is a great figure, not just in the achievement, but in the seriousness of his approach. Leigh likes to gather actors in something like six months of rehearsal. They have outline characters, and they then build a life for their role in rehearsal. Through many improvisations, a tight written script is arrived at. Different methods work on different subjects and for different people. But I think Leigh's contribution to a theory of preparation is immense, and a most valuable link to theater.

But which Leigh films? I love several of the earlier pictures. Everyone admired *Secrets and Lies.* But in the end I must have *Vera Drake,* because it is so moving, so perfect a portrait of England in the 1950s, and so surprising in one aspect. Vera is a cleaning lady with a steady sideline: She helps girls who have got into trouble. She does this not as a feminist or a libertarian. She does it to be helpful. She doesn't even get paid. And—here is the surprise—in her tight-knit working-class family, she keeps it a secret from the others. I know, at first, that seems implausible, but I think it is part of the film's bleak truth to realize that in Britain then things were compartmentalized. Perhaps they still are.

Leigh was sixty when he made *Vera Drake,* and an established international figure, yet he had the greatest difficulty in funding a very low-budget film. This is worth stressing in that Leigh's commitment needs to be understood in a framework of very modest financial return. So *Vera Drake* had some British money, but some French money, too. And it found the money hard to get because even people who knew Leigh said, "The story of an uneducated back-street abortionist? It hardly sounds like a movie." When are such people trusted?

Now, of course, you know the film. You recall the respect and the prizes it won and you realize it did quite well. But I'm not sure if Leigh will ever be accepted, or able to relax. The film was shot in Super 16, by Dick Pope, in a most somber range of colors. It was shot, by Leigh, with a camera style that becomes more Ozu-like—and for the best reasons, because Ozu and Leigh are alike in locating a kind of unsentimental family focus in plain interiors, a place where family feeling exists—so long as you don't regard it as that American confection that obscures all other realities.

So the film is a grim lesson in the social services in the 1950s and on the nature of family life. There's so much small talk, and so little that is really said. This is a film in which Leigh gets the conspiracy of English lower-class life—to ignore every "it" they can think of—without condescension or cutesiness.

Imelda Staunton gives not a hint of performance as Vera, she simply is the benighted woman. And the film has a mass of fine supporting work from Phil Davis, Peter Wight (as the policeman), Alex Kelly, Daniel Mays, Adrian Scarborough, Heather Craney, Eddie Marsan, Ruth Sheen, Sally Hawkins, Lesley Manville, and Jim Broadbent (as the judge).

The Verdict (1982)

The Verdict is too simpleminded or self-righteous to be deeply interesting, no matter that it's very well made. After all, the Archdiocese of Boston (in the person of Edward Binns) behaves very badly and is ready to rely on a total cynicism in the judge (Milo O'Shea going too far, I think) and its saturnine legal mastermind (James Mason, exactly right—but who is surprised by that?). Wesley Addy's pinched, hangdog face was born to play the venal, lying doctor and Lindsay Crouse is heaven-sent as the honest admitting nurse who will come clean in the end. Of course, the awful judge excludes her testimony, but no jury is going to forget what they heard. And thus in the end, the jury, Ms. Crouse, and the legal team headed by the very shaky Paul Newman is 110 percent on the side of right.

I don't know the novel (by Barry Reed), so I can't judge whether the original has been smoothed out a little. But I'd trust David Mamet to deliver a rather bullying screenplay—heavy-handed, but monotonously righteous. Whereas what *The Verdict* really cries out for is a touch or two of Otto Preminger's skepticism about American legal process. In other words, we know Paul Newman has the case (if he can stay sober long enough to bring it home). We ache for the good guy he longs to be, and we are furious at the potential injustice of the wicked Church and its sanctimonious legal tools screwing this poor family out of any damages. When the jury comes in and asks if they can award over the limit, Jack Warden's gaze up to heaven is ours too—it's all too good to be true, and complacency actually takes away all the wan, wintry sensibility that there is in Andrzej Bartkowiak's superb lighting (the light for a graver film).

It has to be said that Sidney Lumet the craftsman can pay too much attention to crossing the *t*s and dotting the *i*s of a neat script and not enough to searching for something like doubt. And if you want to call a film *The Verdict,* don't you need more doubt or a less loaded case? But Lumet has always had a weakness for piling on.

Not that Paul Newman is less than magnificent—it was a travesty that he won his Oscar not for this but for *The Color of Money.* Still, the fascination in the film, I think, is there to behold, and see neglected—it's the Charlotte Rampling character, the betrayer, the one mess in the film. If only we knew more about her. If only we could see more of her ambiguity in the other characters. If only we were allowed a role as intelligent observers that meant we could not make up our minds as easily or tidily. As it is, you don't really see what—beyond sheer contrivance—has brought Newman's lawyer so low that he is the burnt-out case at the beginning. Justice needs a greater sense of doubt and frailty, and fewer people so automatically fit to be hissed or cheered.

Der Verlorene (1951)

In 1950, Peter Lorre was forty-six. Hungarian and Jewish (he was born Lászlo Loewenstein), he had been a well-known figure in German theater, though hard to cast. As such, he had been the murderer in Fritz Lang's *M,* a picture that made him and imprisoned him. He was forever afterward a killer or a monster, though one glimpse of his bulging eyes suggested a rare, if not warped, sensitivity. He was a "success" in Hollywood. He worked all the time—as villain, threat, coward—and he played the Japanese detective Mr. Moto in several films. He was world-famous, yet he was a wreck, a drug addict, a smiling refugee from his own legend. It was at that point that he returned to Germany—not to play Hamlet for the Berliner Ensemble (that was Brecht's offer), but to direct and star in *Der Verlorene* (*The Lost One*).

It would be a strange poetic justice if the adventure had turned out well, if Lorre had redeemed his haphazard career with a masterpiece and a success. In fact, *Der Verlorene* was a commercial mess, and it is not a great film. But it shows the large imagination of the man, as well as his desperate yearning. It is a remarkable, haunting picture, and one that deserves to be much better known.

It is the story of Dr. Karl Rothe, a man who worked in the Nazi camps but was appalled by the experiments there, and who in the years after the war becomes a homicidal maniac. There is some evidence to suggest that the story was based on a real figure, and Lorre sought out the novelist Benno Vigny in the attempt to make a script. Lorre wrote himself, but the thing never came clear. He drew in other writing associates: the director Helmut Käutner and Axel Eggebrecht. He got an old friend, Arnold Pressburger, to set the film up as a producer. He had every intention of doing it as a film noir—after all, Lorre had worked on several in America—and he engaged Václav Vích as director of photography. He cast the film with the utmost care. And it seems that there were moments when he believed it could all be a success. Who knows? Lorre was not well. He found postwar Germany depressing and uncongenial. And I think when there were script problems, he hoped "atmosphere" would bridge the gap. If only he had had Lang again to steady the ship.

But the attempt and its pathos are clear. The film is visceral and moody, and Lorre prowls through it like a ghost, looking older than he was, looking like death. The idea of murder as cruelty and vengeance is evident (really, it was a Lang film without the controlling geometry), and Rothe is the man in *M* in reverse, if you like: a humane victim driven to murder out of a feeling of retribution. Germany did not appreciate the film, and it got very little release anywhere else. But it remains a direct imprint of a very troubled soul. With Karl John, Helmuth Rudolph, Johanna Hofer, Renate Mannhardt, Eva-Ingeborg Scholz, Lotte Rausch, Gisela Trowe, Hansi Wendler, Kurt Meister, and Alexander Hunzinger.

Vertigo (1958)

A San Francisco cop, Scottie Ferguson (James Stewart), discovers his vertigo in a rooftop chase when another policeman dies trying to save him. He works at recovery, with his girlfriend, Midge (Barbara Bel Geddes), though she is painfully aware of his moderate feelings for her. Then an old school friend, Gavin Elster (Tom Helmore), calls him in. Can Scottie take a job? To follow Elster's wife, Madeleine (Kim Novak), who seems obsessed with an ancestor, Carlotta Valdes, who killed herself a hundred years earlier. Scottie follows Madeleine's strange day in the city, and she seems like a sleepwalker, a ghost or an actress playing a part.

But people watching actresses may fall in love with them. And when Madeleine jumps into the water at Fort Point, Scottie is compelled to save her. At last, they talk. They fall in love. He tries to rescue her from the curse of Carlotta. But at a nearby mission, she escapes him, climbs a tower as he suffers from vertigo, and hurls herself to her death. Scottie has a breakdown. And then one day as he tries to recover, he sees a woman on the streets of San Francisco—a redhead named Judy—who resembles Madeleine. He wonders if he can make her more like Madeleine.

In great mystery films, attempts to tell the story usually make mistakes. That has happened here. But I will go no further with this narrative in case there are readers who have not seen the film yet. For this is a film about watching, about making a film, and about directing an actress. It is also about being raised to a great height of suspense and risking a fall. For Hitchcock, therefore, it was very personal, and for us it raises questions about voyeurism and performance that may threaten our feeling for cinema as a whole.

It is also a film about extraordinary cruelty, for as the plot becomes clear—and several viewings are necessary for that—we appreciate Gavin's diabolical intrigue. (Whether Hitch grasped that is not so clear.) The darkness is buried in the glorious views of San Francisco, even more beautiful in 1957 than it may be now. And this is a film about desire and the black hole that can bury it—about light and dark, the ingredients of cinema.

So it is a masterpiece and an endless mystery—a love story, yet a hate story, too; an enchantment, yet an analysis of how stupid belief is. It failed when it came out. Perhaps it was too challenging. But we have learned how to watch it, and we have discovered the mortified figure Hitchcock often masked with his comedian persona. The performances are extraordinary. Stewart is truly frightening in that we face the limits in an otherwise reassuring presence. Kim Novak's attempt at her two roles is a touching achievement. But don't forget Bel Geddes, Tom Helmore, or Henry Jones. Bernard Herrmann's score is so extreme it is played in concert halls. Robert Burks shot the film, Hal Pereira and Henry Bumstead designed it. Edith Head did the clothes. It's a test case: If you are moved by this film, you are a creature of cinema. But if you are alarmed by its implausibility, its hysteria, its cruelty—well, there are novels. Alec Coppel and Samuel Taylor wrote the script from *D'Entre les Morts* by Pierre Boileau and Thomas Narcejac.

Une Vie (1958)

Just before the coming of the New Wave, Alexandre Astruc, the sometime novelist, critic, and essayist on film forms, made this beautiful, heartfelt adaptation of *Une Vie* that rapidly became lost in the new orthodoxy that nothing worthwhile was made as we waited for the wave on the shore. It was taken from the novel by Guy de Maupassant, published in 1883, and it would clearly be designed as tribute to the style of *Une Partie de Campagne,* even if Claude Renoir (the great director's nephew) had not been director of photography.

Astruc was the author of several key articles in the development of French film theory, including "La camera-stylo," written in 1948:

> . . . the cinema is quite simply becoming a means of expression, just as all the other arts have been before it, and in particular painting and the novel. After having been successively a fairground attraction, an amusement analogous to boulevard theater, or a means of preserving the images of an era, it is gradually becoming a language. By language, I mean a form in which and by which an artist can express his thoughts, however abstract they may be, or translate his obsessions exactly as he does in the contemporary essay or novel. That is why I would like to call this new age of cinema the age of *camera-stylo* (the camera as pen). This metaphor has a very precise sense. By it I mean the cinema will gradually break free from the tyranny of what is visual, from the image for its own sake, from the immediate and concrete demands of the narrative, to become a means of writing just as flexible and subtle as written language.

I wonder whether Astruc would now see the new dawn of 1948 as a happy moment—one with Welles, Mizoguchi, Ophüls, all at work, not to mention the coming of Antonioni, Nicholas Ray, and Alain Resnais, figures whose work must have delighted him. But today isn't it possible that the *"camera-digitale"* has been a horrible replacement for the pen and the camera, a machine that writes out reality as quick as a wipe, and just as synthetic? Moreover, it might be argued that the "tyranny" of the visual in filmmaking has set in with a vengeance.

So I would not be surprised if *Une Vie* continued to look like a very modern film, despite its nineteenth-century setting in rural Normandy. Jeanne Dandieu (Maria Schell) is of marriageable age. She meets and falls for the dark, rather sullen Julien de Lamare (Christian Marquand). He takes her without noticing her great romantic needs—she is an Emma Bovary in the passive voice. So in time Julien seduces her servant girl, Rosalia (Pascale Petit), and gets her pregnant. The child comes and Jeanne makes it her own. But the self-destructive Julien (there is a shot of him shaving that says how close he is to sardonic suicide) finds another lover, Gilberte (Antonella Lualdi). They are in a love-nest caravan together when an enraged husband (Ivan Desny) sends it over a cliff. *Une Vie* continues.

The rural colors, the camera movements, the subdued playing, the invariable sense of passionate detail and a set of great performances make it a classic—yet hardly seen or known today.

Violette Nozière (1978)

In 1933, a teenager, Violette Nozière, poisoned her parents and killed her father. They had lived in a wretched two-room apartment in Paris. Violette had been a wild girl, going out at night and coming back with syphilis. She said she had inherited it from her parents. She stole money from them, and had her eye on their savings. She was a dreamer, and it is not always clear what is fact in her life and what is fantasy. She has an imaginary father. She will say her nominal father raped her. She was arrested in August 1933 for the murder of her father. The mother denied the rape charges. In October 1934, she was condemned to death. But the case had provoked great public concern. The surrealists acclaimed Violette as a heroine in the battle against hypocritical bourgeois life. The death sentence was commuted and reduced to twelve years. She married the prison clerk's son. Just before her death, in 1963, her civil rights were restored.

This is one of the great unsolved crime pictures—and one of the best portraits of our attraction to figures like Violette. Director Claude Chabrol had said, "I fell in love with Violette long before I understood her." But do we ever understand anyone we are in love with? Thus, there is a fascinating tension between Chabrol's gaze (personifying those figures who may not even have existed—like the imagined father) and the bleak, impassive face of Isabelle Huppert as Violette, staring at herself in the mirror, waiting to see which face will blink or blush first. Mlle. Huppert was twenty-two at the time, and any viewer could see the struggle to disentangle a great new actress from a woman who might be a mercilessly selfish monster.

The film was scripted by Odile Barski, Hervé Bromberger, and Frédéric Grendel from a nonfiction account of the case by Jean-Marie Fitere. At every turn, that script is at pains to make the period authentic—and that is backed up in the look of the film (production design by Jacques Brizzio, set decoration by Robert Christides, and photography by Jean Rabier). The claustrophobia of the family apartment is odious, and Rabier said that he used lenses that existed in 1933—so it's arguable whether the color was well advised.

For most of his life, Chabrol has been intrigued by the myth of the femme fatale and the underlying reality of the woman who feels she is caught in a fatal trap. This is one of his greatest films, because it presents a conflict between Violette (the new actress) and her mother (played by Stéphane Audran, Chabrol's wife once and the enigmatic actress in many of his films). The viewer feels that antagonism, just as he or she cannot avoid the feeling that, whereas Audran was a good actress, Huppert is a phenomenon. Very little is explained. There is never a recess in the structure, where Violette confesses. The hard, lovely face of Huppert nurses the warning message: Try to decide.

With Jean Carmet as the father, Mario David as the prison director, Lisa Langlois as a friend, Jean-François Garreaud as Violette's boyfriend, and Bernadette Lafont.

I Vitelloni (1953)

Born in Rimini in 1920, and raised in that seaside town, Federico Fellini had made a name for himself as both actor and screenwriter before he began directing. His first few films—*Variety Lights* and *The White Sheik*—did not do well, but *I Vitelloni* was the picture that made his name. It is a striking companion to *8½* in that it shows Fellini discovering the lesson that, when in uncertainty, go back to yourself and what you know. And thus we get a hint of the ceaseless clash in Fellini—not always worked out comfortably—between the allegorical approach to life as a kind of traveling theater, and the simple stress on me, me. It remains a matter for history how far this indigestion will be appraised as the work of a master or a show-off. Now, spared the dazzling charisma of a Fellini alive, in person—Federico!—the jury is out.

In a lackluster Adriatic resort town we meet several young men, adolescents going on twenty-five, wasting away their days and lives, full equally of trite rebellion and inane hopes. (It comes as a welcome, tranquil corrective to American movies about such rebels in the 1950s determined to save the world by remaking it.) Fellini has little other concern or interest than whether any of these loafers can really get away and start a life. Meanwhile, they hang out and talk; they play practical jokes; they flirt with girls and prospects; but they are devoted to their own immaturity. In America, the film was called *The Young and the Passionate,* an early sign of America's flattery of its young. In Italian, it means "the big calves."

So the heroics, the melodrama, and fool's gold of young love are in short supply here. Fellini is generally despondent when he studies real people—until he can see them as kinds of archetypal actors. *I Vitelloni* is one of the good films about boredom and a view of life in which politics and education are by the way, and in which the passage from youth to whining old age seems very brief. The forlorn atmosphere is helped a lot by the photography of Otello Martelli and the score by Nino Rota.

Obviously, though, it's the guys that count, and Fellini's fond observation of types he has known and barely escaped being that really gives the film flavor and feeling. These actors are Franco Fabrizi, Alberto Sordi, Leopoldo Trieste, and Franco Interlenghi (who had been a child in De Sica's *Shoeshine*). This last character, Moraldo, is closest to Fellini—the director has said that he is the basis for Marcello in *La Dolce Vita. I Vitelloni* played widely throughout Europe and in America. Its comic-sad mood was just right for the time, in the way that *La Dolce Vita* caught the mounting metaphysical unease of the late 1950s. And surely Fellini learned the importance of keeping adjusted to that pulse.

Viva Zapata! (1952)

Elia Kazan had had thoughts of making a movie about Emiliano Zapata since 1943 and his first visit to Mexico. He was attracted to the real story, and he was in love with Mexicans, he said. But he also felt intrigued by the revolutionary who succeeds but is then confounded by real power. As he talked to John Steinbeck about doing a script, they both felt that the Zapata story traced their early romance with Communism and then the growing disillusion. Or was that just Kazan's retrospective tidiness and his ability to treat life as his mirror?

Steinbeck's script was confusing to Darryl Zanuck, but he pledged Fox to the venture—if Zapata had a white horse. At that time, Kazan took it for granted that he would film in Mexico itself, in Morelos province, where Zapata had been raised. But on a trip to Mexico, he met with Gabriel Figueroa, the cameraman, and a spokesman for the Mexican industry. Kazan was uneasy: He disliked the florid way Figueroa photographed things and his sentimentalization of the working class. But Figueroa was uneasy, too: Would Kazan's "gringo" Zapata (Marlon Brando) meet with government approval? So Figueroa disappeared with the script for a few days and came back with a government official and a lot of doubts. Kazan heard in all this the voice of those Communist Party officials he hated. But Figueroa was speaking for a country demoralized and in some ways warped by having its history fabricated by a powerful neighbor.

In the end, Kazan elected to shoot on the border, but from a base in Texas. With cameraman Joseph MacDonald, he achieved a wonderful, harsh look to it all—we believe we are in Mexico. But at the same time, Kazan felt this was his first "autobiographical" film—in other words, *he* was Zapata. At which point, we should add that this is the picture made just before Kazan decided to name names to the House Committee on Un-American Activities in 1952.

It's a very mixed result, far more "Mexican" than, say, *Viva Villa!* or most Hollywood pictures about that unlucky country. But how can these two countries understand each other living side by side but in such absurd inequality? As so often with Kazan, the hero is his own ego—and it's clear that the director was really more responsive to the details of Brando's performance than to Mexican history. Moreover, in casting Anthony Quinn as the brother, Kazan was stirring up the rivalry between two Stanley Kowalskis—Quinn had played the part in the touring company.

But the film is impressive: for Brando's intransigent, sulking simplicity, for Quinn's urban braggadocio, even for Jean Peters, who is surprisingly plausible as the wife to Emiliano, and for Joseph Wiseman as the loathsome commissar figure. Even the white horse works. And in the final scenes, with the epic death of Zapata and the stallion running free, Kazan comes close to his declared ideal—of the old Soviet way of filming. It's a high-bred venture through and through, as uneasy as Mexican-American relations are always likely to be. Brando was nominated, and Quinn won an Oscar for Best Supporting Actor.

Vivre Sa Vie (1962)

"Il faut se prêter aux autres et se donner à soi-même." It is the motto from Montaigne that precedes the twelve chapters of *Vivre Sa Vie,* and it means, "We must lend ourselves to others, and give ourselves to ourselves." And I think that still the most obvious meaning to that—and the one that signaled Jean-Luc Godard's first great film—was the extent to which the film had offered an entrance to Anna Karina and to her character, Nana. The hint had been there in *Le Petit Soldat,* but I don't think Godard felt then that he could ask Karina to carry a film. Equally, in *À Bout de Souffle,* Jean Seberg has a brazen stare, an armor, that may be her Premingerian training, her marriage, or her having a quarter of the budget to herself. In *Vivre Sa Vie,* Godard seems to relax, and he lets the woman conduct the film, or has it respond to her conduct. And just as he was helping her, or giving her kindness, so the spurt of benevolence surely refreshed his dry, bitter soul. He became, for the first time, attentive; he saw beauty.

And all of a sudden, his intense flirtation with the inner details of film style—with shots and cuts—becomes a far graver study of form. People with their backs to the camera; with their faces full on; in profile—like a drawing master, he goes through the opportunities. Nana writes a letter. Nana sees a movie. Nana dances to the music. There are set pieces of behavior, which though casual and mundane, become epics. Thus, her dance around the pool table is unquestionably one of the great scenes in the history of the musical.

There is also a documentary on the practice of prostitution, and obliquely, there is a speculation on how easily a girl trying to get into the movies—like the girl Godard himself had met, Anna—may come to imitate a prostitute. There is a darkness waiting, and we know now that in Godard's discriminating mind she would come to behave like a whore. But if acting is helpless, then surely sometimes direction must be responsible.

But still, there is the cleanliness of tragedy here, superbly photographed by Raoul Coutard again and the first really controlled score in a Godard film (by Michel Legrand, against his lyrical grain, and with a song, by Jean Ferrat and Pierre Frachet). Once more, Paris is the version of life that belongs to everyone, gray and abrasive, and sometimes looking positively ancient in this film.

The conversations are literary and philosophical, and no one would call them natural—and yet the film has a loving attention to passing moments and sheer noise that may be the closest Godard ever came to Renoir. As for Karina—whether looking at Falconetti or giving her impression of Louise Brooks—she is a sad beauty gazing at herself, at the camera and her stricken relationship with its owner. Yes, it is a film about a girl slipping into professional prostitution; but the same girl, in the same glances and moves, is passing into the heaven of filmmaking. It is a great film, and it is the only film of Godard's that does not seem to be locked up as just his.

The Wages of Fear (1953)

For a few years, in the early fifties, *The Wages of Fear* was the very model of a "foreign" film that could find an international audience. It was, in many respects, a film about the nihilism left by war—the four characters are all refugees from that war, on the run or stateless or just alienated, and driven to realize that none of the advertised codes (the right, the left, duty, for country, for mankind) function. They are on their own in a jungle, or in a rat-warren community, with only themselves and luck to rely on. This is one of the first modern films in which the Céline-like maxim is followed—you have to gamble with your life to give it value.

So the story outline begins, "In a wretched South American town, four men . . ." The country where this is happening goes unnamed, but Henri-Georges Clouzot never took his unit farther than the South of France (in the areas of Nîmes and Martigues). So the first achievement (thanks to art director René Renoux), was to convey the look and mood of a steaming jungle, high mountains, and crumbling towns through light and décor. One way to look at this film is as being in the school of *Only Angels Have Wings*—though Clouzot is far tougher on his guys than Howard Hawks ever managed to be.

The four men are Mario (Yves Montand), Jo (Charles Vanel), Luigi (Folco Lulli), and Bimba (Peter Van Eyck). Without prospects, they take an assignment: for $2000 each they will drive a truckload of nitroglycerine over the mountain to an oil field where the explosive is required to stop a burning well. "Nitro" was a new word and idea in 1953—a kind of magic—but its risk was that it could explode at just a bump in the road. And in this terrain, even in the South of France, the trick is to find the road in the bump.

It was all based on a novel by Georges Arnaud, and Clouzot did the screenplay with Jérôme Géronimi. But it was Clouzot's own cold-blooded attitude that treated the men as rats and which stressed the suspense in so sardonic a way. In some respects, this was like an old Hollywood film, but the view of the men was so reduced and de-romanticized—and only one of them will survive. Moreover, Clouzot saw a big film—156 minutes—with several sustained suspense set-pieces and a clear pattern of ordeal and relief.

The exciting camera-work was by Armand Thirard (in black and white), the editing was done by Madeleine Gug, E. Muse, and Henri Rust, and Georges Auric wrote a fine score. But it was Clouzot's triumph, a bold, nearly insolent adventure film that fit the troubled mood of postwar Europe and was full of tough performances—with Véra Clouzot as about the only woman in sight.

Not only did the picture do great business. It took the Grand Prix at Cannes (in a crowded year)—and Charles Vanel won the acting prize. Years later, William Friedkin tried a remake—*Sorcerer* (1977)—and the lesson was clearer still that Clouzot had had the instinct, the timing, and the luck to do it in 1953.

Wagon Master (1950)

A wagon master, or wagonmaster (both titles persist) was a man hired on by wagon trains starting out from the Midwest for Western liberties and new lives. He was not the leader of the traveling community, but he was captain of its ship, setting the course, maintaining the speed, and negotiating local difficulties. And so, by rights, he had probably made the trip before. If not, then he had to act sagaciously.

The story goes that while making *She Wore a Yellow Ribbon,* John Ford had got talking to some Mormon extras and admired their spirit and their story. So this wagon train is Mormon folk, led by Elder Wiggs (Ward Bond). They are kicked out of Crystal City by a reactionary sheriff happy to push all the dross, scum, outlaws, and outsiders into the capacious West. The wagon masters are two amiable cowboys: Sandy Owens (Harry Carey, Jr.) and Travis Blue (Ben Johnson—who had won Ford's faith as a rider first and then gradually as an actor).

It's the story of the journey the Mormons make to Utah in which the greatest danger is the Cleggs—a family of unwashed criminals who leech onto the wagon train. The Indians are friendly, and this is a prairie minus white outlaws. It has to be said that the journey is also without the inner, familial tensions that make a masterpiece out of *Red River.* Truth to tell, we don't really get characters in *Wagon Master* so much as landscapes with epic figures, safely set as good or evil (as if the Mormon vision were reliable). Ed Buscombe has written that the people are "less characters in a drama than figures in a pageant," and Lindsay Anderson regarded it as "one of the most purely lyrical films Ford has yet made."

That's sound commentary, but it leaves the film close to simpleminded, as something like a legend for Mormon children. The script was done by Frank Nugent and Ford's son Patrick, and Ford allowed that he liked it so much he actually shot a few pages of it! It is as easy to think that on location in Utah in November–December 1949, he let Bert Glennon exploit the sunny winter light and enjoyed himself in finding unusually splendid landscapes. It is a touch too picturesque, though there are awesome scenes of the wagons being hauled up a mountainside.

Along the way, they pick up traveling actors (Alan Mowbray and Joanne Dru), and Ford has a nice sense of actors joining in with all the other refugees. The Cleggs are Victorian nasty without being really threatening. Overall, the film glosses the extraordinary achievement of taking a wagon west, and it's regrettable that the Mormon characters are prim, almost clerical, instead of people who believed they were living a miracle. There are very few Hollywood films that touch on Mormonism or the religious fundamentalism that inspired many of these journeys. We need a film that has room for that God and for Donner-like sacrifices.

Walkabout (1971)

A father drives his two children—a girl of fourteen, and a boy of six—into the Australian desert. The kids think it is a fun outing, a picnic. Nothing ever explains the father's behavior—nothing, that is, except for the earlier splicing of radio small-chat with pieces of Stockhausen's "Hymnen" (the banal and immense meaning, and the offense that the one has caused the other). But he starts to fire at his children with a pistol. When that fails, he sets light to the vehicle and kills himself. There may be traces of grief and terror, but it may also be a measure of the father's sense of failure that his stranded kids simply begin to endure.

And so begins *Walkabout*, the first solo feature by Nicolas Roeg, and a film that could not have been more eagerly awaited after *Performance*. And surely the result is a tour de force, with Jenny Agutter and Lucien John (Roeg's own son) exposed to outback, desert, and jungle, to say nothing of the terror in being so abruptly separated from civilization. Roeg did his own photography and there is no question about the beauty of small figures in the large landscape. In time, the couple will meet and be saved by David Gumpilil, as an aboriginal youth on "walkabout," the ritual ordeal that will prove his manhood.

It is part of the baleful view of civilization, I fear, that the aborigine will be destroyed by the way in which the white girl disdains or ignores his courtship overtures. It is not that the girl is blamed for this, or condemned morally, though there is a glib flash-forward to her apparently happily married future (to a nice white) where she recalls the strange passion of the walkabout. I fear that it is Roeg's rather empty-headed conviction that the two English kids serve to destroy the aborigine's austere nobility. And therein begins the passionate limitation in Roeg's intellect, the first great drag upon his remarkable cinematic sensibility.

The script is by the apocalyptic playwright Edward Bond, and I suspect that Roeg meekly adopted his view of the wickedness or the antilife attitudes inherent in private school training. Whereas every urging in the glorious imagery encourages the girl to go native, to be a woman with her heroic rescuer. Another resolution—far more troubling—could have involved their brief bliss and then the way a rescuing white society tidied up the whole incident.

Early on there is a strange, arbitrary wall that appears—it yields access to the city as easily as the outback. I wish there was more of it, and more evident dream. For in fact, it is the literalness that is sometimes plodding and which in turn points to Donald Cammell as author of the great flights of fancy in *Performance*. Still, *Walkabout* is filled with the dread and wonder that a civilized society can feel in the wilderness, and there are passages still so poignant and primeval that one longs to see Roeg's version of the Bible (if Buñuel had done the script).

Wall Street (1987)

In *Platoon,* Oliver Stone had subjected Charlie Sheen to "adult" influences, and two ways to go in life. In *Wall Street,* the two sergeants are replaced by Gordon Gekko (Michael Douglas) as the master reptile of high finance and the sultry dream song, "Greed is good!" What does it say about Stone's casting instinct or his human judgment that he should have elected Charlie Sheen for his innocent, everyman figure, the weather vane of modern morality? What does it say of Mr. Stone but that he loves to have his cake and eat it, to wallow in the darker side of life and to be disapproving of that self-indulgence? He is our Cecil B. DeMille.

And yet *Wall Street* was one of the few American films to take on money and its making as subjects, and surely Stone was alert to the new rapacious mood of the eighties. It was uncannily shrewd to pick the streamlined self-love of Michael Douglas as the real silk suit in which Gekko would take a sin and turn it into a sermon. Thus, in Gekko's "greed is good" routine, you could feel a terrible moral indolence rising in the theater. It was exactly what weakness wanted to hear. It was the new interpretation that saw Budd Schulberg's *What Makes Sammy Run?* not as a condemnation of the movie world but as a textbook course on how to succeed in business without really sweating.

There's a wondrous greed in which Mr. Stone envisages the clothes, the décor, and the apparatus of success—it's there in the sleek hairstyle of Michael Douglas; in the cool modishness of Daryl Hannah; and in the absolute contempt felt for the kind of blue-collar decency represented by the Sheens, father and son. So Oliver Stone thinks he despises wealth, just as he is bathing in it. It's the moral schizophrenia in all his films, the how-I-love-the-thing-I-hate. In the end it is a tormented self-portrait that makes Stone unique in modern American film.

The "plot" is thumpingly commonplace, as is the notion that Douglas's character would take a second look at Charlie Sheen—the younger man's haircut is ample disqualification. But they get together, and the film then follows a test case that may bring Gekko down. Whereas a movie with any profound interest in money would know that the Gekko is a creature where if one perishes, a second and a third springs up in its place. The real complexity of high finance is the wall that makes it impenetrable—the real wall in *Wall Street,* whereby few prosecutors can see a way of dismantling it.

That's why finance is so tough a subject and why *Wall Street* is like an advertisement, more interested in sheen for its own sake than Charlie Sheen's aroused conscience. The meaning, you see, is that Oliver Stone cannot see a way of doing without money. Yes, he has a sermon against it, but one so witty, so sardonic, and so reptilianly winning—hence Michael Douglas and his Oscar—that we are sold.

Wanda (1970)

Wanda Goronski is first seen as a woman in white walking past piles of coal slurry to a court in Pennsylvania, where she will be officialy separated from her husband and children. She has no objection to the depiction of herself at the hearing as incompetent. She lets herself be discarded, and she starts to drift. She is picked up by an angry man named Dennis. He seems to be taking painkillers all the time—booze and pills—and his temper is short. They become companions, except that there is nothing like companionship. He gets her to be the driver on a bank robbery he plans.

Wanda was shot on 16 mm by Nick Proferes (he edited the film, too) as Barbara Loden wrote and directed it. When the film came out, Loden was close to forty and the second wife of Elia Kazan. In his memoir, *A Life*, Kazan said that she had had sexual cunning when young, and he cast her in his production of Arthur Miller's *After the Fall* and in his film *Splendor in the Grass*. She was noted for her promise and her sexy edge—but sexy edge is not an uncommon commodity, and it can wear out. Loden wanted to do her own work. She became more like a feminist. She got the idea for *Wanda* from a newspaper story, and Kazan says she asked him to direct it. He said it wasn't his kind of thing. He may have guessed she needed to do it on her own. Maybe he imagined she asked him.

You can say that *Wanda* has as little style or flourish as its character has hope—that it is neo-realism, or like Cassavetes. But I think it is tougher and more lucid than either. It is a remorselessly bleak portrait of a woman who is never going to get self-respect, let alone the credentials that might command respect. The film doesn't say why. We meet Wanda as a failure, as someone who has surrendered to her own incompetence. And she might be a victim, but only if she was more sentient or vulnerable.

In a way then it's natural that Dennis (Michael Higgins) becomes the center of the film, though it goes on long enough after his death for her passivity to be reasserted. It is a stark, unforgettable picture, full of pain and absurd humor—on the way to the bank, but lost, Wanda is stopped by a policeman. He tells her to present her license at the station. She asks him the way to the bank. The photography is rudimentary. There is no music. Loden has allowed herself to look as plain and hopeless as possible.

The picture won a prize at Venice. It played on the art-house circuit, and she and Proferes tried to set up another film but without any success. She developed breast cancer and she died in 1980. Kazan writes of her as a fierce woman and one of the few who never really yielded to him. It's a lack of compromise that shows in her film. The color on *Wanda* seems to be fading. I don't know how carefully the print is cared for. If ever there was a film with "lost" as its natural terminus, this is it. So guard it. Look at it. And remember her name.

War and Peace (1956)

No, of course, you can't film *War and Peace,* least of all with Audrey Hepburn's plaintive voice as Natasha. When Audrey is hurt, she sounds wounded. But when Tolstoy's heroine is hurt she begins to grow up. It's all very well for Natasha to be the kid swept off her feet by Prince Andrei. We want that to work. But when Andrei is Mel Ferrer, one can only conclude that Audrey's own private life was beyond our imagination. I'm not sure if any actress existed in 1955 who could have made a decent Natasha—or who could have done it in the English language, thus satisfying the first box-office requirement of a weird epic approach with Carlo Ponti and Dino de Laurentiis as coproducers.

That said, there is a great deal on the credit side, and nearly all of it has to do with King Vidor. To start with, Vidor was never afraid of anything, and if a movie director is intimidated he might as well go home. Second, the war, the retreat from Moscow, and the Russian guerrilla campaign under Kutuzov are brilliantly handled. Then there is the unexpected fact that Henry Fonda—awkward, shortsighted, far from a man of action—is actually a decent Pierre, and one who sharpens the need for a better script.

Under Carlo and Dino, six people were credited on the script—Bridget Boland, Robert Westerby, Vidor himself, Mario Camerini, Ennio de Concini, and Ivan Perillo. Almost certainly the numbers reflect division and defeat. How one longs to see a single strong writer doing the whole thing—Graham Greene, say—there is the voice that could make Pierre deeper and sadder. Yet Greene was also a movie person, quite capable of supplying Vidor with enough physical activity.

Added to which, the picture is very good-looking, with Jack Cardiff doing the first unit and Aldo Tonti on the battle scenes. The set design is by Piero Gherardi, who would later do such good production design for Fellini. And the music is by Nino Rota—though he quotes liberally from Tchaikovsky along the way.

In its full version it's 208 minutes, not just good-looking, but beautiful and crammed with outstanding supporting performances: Vittorio Gassman as Anatole (Audrey feels his charm, for sure); Anita Ekberg, surprisingly good as Helene; Oscar Homolka (never better, as Kutuzov); Herbert Lom a somber Napoleon; Wilfred Lawson as Bolkonsky, Barry Jones as Rostov, Helmut Dantine as Dolokhov; and John Mills quite haunting as Platon.

The film got just a single nomination—for Vidor's direction. And I would not deny him that much credit, for this *War and Peace* has a fluency and a power that no one had reason to expect. But the strength is in all the support and in the most challenging scenes—the huge movements of people. Audrey Hepburn was by then a major star as well as someone the public liked. But it is her presence that sets the film wrong. Imagine the young Jeanne Moreau instead—her English was good enough—and this could have been more than an unexpected pleasure.

Waterloo Bridge (1931)

In 1930, Robert Sherwood's play—about an American soldier in England in the First World War and a prostitute—did far better in London than New York. A movie version was fabricated in 1940, to capitalize on Vivien Leigh's new fame. By now she's a "ballet dancer" and he is Robert Taylor. Mervyn Le Roy directed and it was a straight love story. The 1931 version got lost in the rush—it seems that M-G-M bought it up and refused to let it be seen. And it has only recently come to light.

Universal got Tom Reed to do a treatment of the play, but director James Whale didn't like it at all—and having directed *Journey's End* in London and lived through the First World War, Whale was a very good test of the material. He was able to get a fresh writer, Benn W. Levy, and although the film is only 71 minutes, and opens up the cramped play rather too deliberately, it remains a very interesting pre-Code portrait of a hooker who has the chance of rising above her station.

Arthur Edeson does the photography. Charles D. Hall does the sets and makes a good contrast between Myra's place and the lush stately home to which her soldier boy belongs. Bette Davis appears as an ingenue, and there are good performances from Enid Bennett and Frederick Kerr as the soldier's parents. The soldier is Kent Douglass, who would later become Douglass Montgomery—and truth to tell he's not up to the level of his partner, Mae Clarke, the girl in whose face Cagney had planted a grapefruit in *Public Enemy*. This was after Rose Hobart had been cast. She was set in it for a while but then the studio declined to pick up her option and she went off in a huff.

Mae Clarke seemed like a star-in-the-making then, yet her long career (she only died in 1992) never made it as far as stardom. A few years after this she was plainly a supporting actress. Still, she's very appealing in *Waterloo Bridge*, and we feel the strain as well as the honesty in a girl who is truly a prostitute and who has to admit it finally. The attempts she makes to be ladylike are intriguing, and yet they never bury the sordid nuances. It's fascinating above all to see Bette Davis watching her. Davis was a beginner—Whale apparently did not like her very much. But she has terrific confidence in the film and you realize that Clarke is very insecure. That works for a while, but then it begins to betray the story.

Only a few years later, of course, Davis was Mildred in *Of Human Bondage*—an unrepressed performance—and I think there were things in that that she lifted from Clarke in *Waterloo Bridge*. It makes the juxtaposition of would-be stars so poignant, and it stresses the daring and the confidence that finally distinguish the great ones. *Waterloo Bridge* was cut in Britain, and the hooker was said to be a chorus girl. In America, it did better but not enough to lift Clarke out of her rut. How often she must have wondered about Myra as her dark mirror image.

Way Down East (1920)

Lottie Blair Parker's play *Way Down East* opened in New York in 1898 and passed into the popular repertory. It is said that the actress Phoebe Davies played the lead role over four thousand times. Anna Moore (Lillian Gish) is sent from her country village to see relatives in the city. There she encounters Lennox Sanderson (Lowell Sherman), a cad. He seduces her and pretends to marry her. Only when she declares her pregnancy does he reveal the fraud of the marriage. Anna's mother dies. The baby dies. Anna wanders around New England until strict squire Bartlett (Burr McIntosh) hires her as a servant. Well, she falls in love with the squire's son David (Richard Barthelmess). But Sanderson lives nearby and gossip carries the ugly story to the Bartlett house. Anna flees into winter and the snows and David eventually rescues her from the ice floes on a nearby river. Sanderson is exposed and ruined. Everything will be all right. Won't it?

I write as someone who, in the late 1970s, had the pleasure of welcoming Lillian Gish (a good deal sharper then than Anna was in 1920) to the community of Dartmouth College and taking her (with press accompaniment) to the banks of the White River (or was it the Connecticut?) there to marvel over the courage of those doing that scene nearly sixty years earlier. Still, I have to tell you that *Way Down East* is tough to take (the general version that survives is over two hours and the latest DVD is the 150-minute version). Griffith adapted the play, with Anthony Paul Kelly, and he had Billy Bitzer and Hendrik Sartov to photograph it for him.

There's no doubt that the melodrama is coherent, in the sense that the story can be followed. But if only it could not be predicted in every detail! If only the characters were more than their captions. I'm not sure if the period of the story is meant to be 1896 or as much as a hundred years earlier. Miss Gish may have splayed herself on ice floes (and white planks) for days at a time while the great finale was filmed, but she cannot make the story plausible or interesting. Whatever one's final opinion of Griffith the pioneer in films like *Birth of a Nation* and *Intolerance*, here he is in 1920 peddling material that never had a chance of being taken seriously. Nor is it really that good a vehicle for Gish. Anna does everything that her stupid society expects of her. She never demonstrates the least ability to be original or herself—to be a unique living person. So Gish goes through the repertory of expressions for the melodrama.

The one interest that is left, and which hangs over a lot of silent cinema, is that sentimental urge to trust country people while being wary of city folk. At a far higher creative level, that myth is still working in Murnau's *Sunrise*. But the fact remains: there was a weird bond between the new, technological medium and the old reactionary humbug that rural people were more sincere in their feelings. Silent cinema was dragged into the future kicking and screaming against progress—the very thing that it best demonstrated.

The Way We Were (1973)

It might be easier to know what "we" are expected to put up with from Hollywood junk if we knew exactly who "we" are meant to be. But in the film that endures, "we" is a concept borne on Marvin Hamlisch's soupy theme song, lyrics by Marilyn and Alan Bergman, that suggests "we" are all on the same ship of fools swept over time's Niagara by hurt feelings, Jew or Gentile, Red or suntanned, Streisand or Redford. So why make waves when we have "memories"—or residuals?

Let's try another tack: If Robert Redford had an ounce of the integrity or intelligence he likes to wear, he'd have taken gross offense at being asked to play Hubbell Gardner in this film. Why? Because the character in Arthur Laurents' novel, which Laurents adapted for the screen, is a sun-baked jerk, a natural athlete, sweet-looking, a charmer, flirting with the arts, and just about good enough to compose his own epitaph: "He was like the country he lived in. Everything came too easily to him." There it is, the all-time piercing of the southern California balloon, the crunch on charm.

Laurents tries to persuade himself and us that this empty paragon falls for Katie Morosky (Streisand), Jewish, radical, aggressive, Jewish. They meet at an Eastern university, and then some years later during the war an affair sets in. Hollywood beckons and we know that Hubbell is going to turn into a limp mix of Robert Redford and Sydney Pollack (our director), but he and Katie marry so that the romantic melodramatic tide can come in full and creamy. HUAC doesn't like Katie. Katie doesn't like Hubbell sleeping around and writing shitty pictures. So, despite being pregnant, she leaves him. This allows a few-years-later reunion, of course—by which time Hubbell is writing for television.

Now, clearly, by the inside standards of Hollywood in 1973, this was the kiss of death. But Hubbell still looks gorgeous and costarry and, really, something in this silly film needed to give him skin disease or make it clear that he is a cretin and just the kind of career story that helps explain why "we" are in the mess we're in. Hubbell Gardner has the ease and charm of a press secretary smoothing over a president's lies.

It turns out that Laurents was dropped from the film for a while. His dear friends Pollack and producer Ray Stark explained that "he" (Redford) was anti-Laurents—not because of the view of Hubbell, just because Hubbell's part was smaller or less chewy than Katie's. Later, Laurents came back, after several other writers had tried to steer the picture out of its mess. Now it looks and feels inevitable: the mismatched close-ups of Redford and Streisand are not regarded as satirical, and the Hamlisch music bridges all troubled waters. It's just that the picture is shitty—it's one that Hubbell must have written. And so the abiding fact of difference, and the possibility of politics, began to burn off in the light of the southern California sun. With Bradford Dillman, Lois Chiles, Patrick O'Neal, and Viveca Lindfors. Margaret Booth was the supervising editor at seventy-five—she could have cut it in her sleep, for this rhythm of evasion and lies was ancient and in her blood.

Went the Day Well? (1942)

In her BFI book on *Went the Day Well?*, Penelope Houston argues with characteristic shrewdness that the real threat the film plays with—of German invasion—had passed by the time it was made. Without a crushing victory in 1940 in the Battle of Britain, the German command were unable to launch a full invasion. There may have been other reasons—some weird superstition in Hitler, or even a residual sympathy for the country. (It was not that he didn't know there were Nazi sympathizers in Britain.) At any event, setting itself up in 1942, this Ealing film was confident enough to be more than a chiller—what if they had come with their Teutonic efficiency and fascist severity? It is also a reaffirmation of that typically Ealing sense of "little England" that could say to itself, "Well, of course, they wouldn't come, they may be nasty but they're not stupid." So the really telling contrast between *Went the Day Well?* and, say, Jean-Pierre Melville's *Army of Shadows* is just what would have happened in a Britain under occupation.

But don't forget that this very English film was made by the Brazilian Alberto Cavalcanti, a man whose contribution to British film cannot be underestimated. Ms. Houston also stresses that this film was prompted by a story by Graham Greene (though she believes Greene never saw the film). The story was "The Lieutenant Died Last." It describes a village called Potter, which was renamed for the film as Bramley End—and very pretty, too. The scripting was in the hands of John Dighton, Diana Morgan, and Angus MacPhail, with Michael Balcon as official producer. Cavalcanti had been working in British documentary, above all, but he had credentials that went back to silent and experimental days and he was well regarded by Balcon even if the two men sparred over Cavalcanti's dreams of surrealism. It was a good appointment, for Cavalcanti was likely to eliminate jolliness and parochialism. And as it turns out, *Went the Day Well?* is blunt about German sympathizers and the kind of violence required in a war like this. The film stops short of cruelty, and you can say it is ignorant of Nazi terror still, but you can't see it without the occasional shudder—this could have happened and been awful.

Wilkie Cooper did the photography (with Douglas Slocombe as an assistant). William Walton wrote the music. Sidney Cole was the editor, Tom Morahan the art director (with Michael Relph as his assistant). The excellent cast includes Leslie Banks, Valerie Taylor, Marie Lohr, Harry Fowler, Frank Lawton, Elizabeth Allan, Thora Hird, Muriel George, Patricia Hayes, Mervyn Johns, Basil Sydney, David Farrar, John Slater, and James Donald.

Of course, Britain had a real war, and Ealing dealt with it, from *The Foreman Went to France* and *The Next of Kin* to *The Cruel Sea* and *Dunkirk*. But to test the virtues of Cavalcanti's film, just look at the airy adventure of *The Eagle Has Landed* (1977), by John Sturges, no less, with its secret longing for the Germans to win in their ingenious raid—especially with Michael Caine as their officer.

Werckmeister Harmonies (2000)

The longer we look at a very plain image, the more susceptible it becomes to dreamscape, madness, or terror. Look long enough at some scruffy Hungarian town on days when the sun never pierces the overcast, and you can believe it is the end of the world that is awaited. Track closely with two men walking in silence and you can hardly tell whether they expect to see doom or glory. Did you ever, as a child, take one word and just keep repeating it over and over again until the repeated sound had lost all notion of meaning, but utterance was your song?

This is what happens, and though it is irrational, this thing that happens, we have the sense that it happens all the time (this is surely the miracle of film imprinting the whole medium—the explosive innovation that becomes as plain as habit). There is a young man (Lars Rudolph), with long wild hair and sunken eyes. Every night, at closing time in the pub, he conducts the strange dance of the solar system—it is a measure of his longing for knowledge. He has an uncle (Peter Fitz), an intellectual who speculates on the intervals between musical notes. But some dread hangs over the town where they live—and its harbinger is the arrival of a great truck that carries the stinking figure of a stuffed whale and the smaller marvel, the Prince.

The nephew looks at the whale and he doesn't know what to make of it. The feeling in the town becomes more ominous. Then Auntie Tünde (Hanna Schygulla—magnificent) asks the nephew to give the uncle a message, an offer—it is inscrutable but threatening. And violence breaks out in the town. The mob storms a hospital, beating inmates and mocking them. Tünde seems to be part of the military operation. Then calm returns but the nephew is a wreck, sitting on the side of his bed.

Where does this turn into meaning? As you watch it over and over again, possibly correcting errors I have introduced, it could be a metaphor for Balkan terror or for all of Hungary in 1956. You can propose that the film is an essentially Eastern European anticipation of trouble—made in the tradition of Miklós Jancsó, or Kafka. I don't know, and I suspect that the director Bela Tarr is far more interested in getting the universal application of this haunting parable.

In filmic terms, all is lucid and precise, even if the context is infinite in time and space. *Werckmeister Harmonies* demands steady attention, but then it becomes like a symphony of dread enough to make most horror pictures seem fussy. The script is by Tarr and László Krasznahorkai, and it comes from *The Melancholy of Resistance,* a book written by the latter. Tarr makes immense films with prolonged shots—as such he is a nephew to Ophüls and Tarkovsky. But in his insights, he has something of Lang. He can hardly see a doorway without knowing things can get worse. Unique, very hard to describe, the kind of work that merits the simple praise—"cinematic."

West Side Story (1961)

West Side Story is sometimes hailed as a movie landmark. It had rentals of $20 million on its first run. It got eleven nominations and ten Oscars. And, as much as anything, it began to overcome that earlier feeling of vulnerability in the American musical—that as story, literature, or content, it was so insubstantial. After all, this was *Romeo and Juliet* updated to 1950s New York. It was hip and cool. So be it. Millions will tell you they have had a good time at the movie, but I am here to say that the experience is a bit like sailing on a massive modern container ship whereas to see the stage show was like flying across the Indian Ocean on the *Cutty Sark*.

Onstage, it was the coming together of four big talents not always known for team spirit—Arthur Laurents wrote the book; Leonard Bernstein did the music; Stephen Sondheim was allowed to do the lyrics; and Jerome Robbins did the choreography. Of course there was a fifth man: Hal Prince, who was a codirector. It opened in September 1957, and it was a sensation—because of the artistic athleticism of the corps dancing as an expression of gang spirit (the Sharks and the Jets); and because of the elevation of the songs as something a good deal smarter and tougher than the abiding regime of Rodgers and Hammerstein offered. Above all, it was theater. Being there in the same space with those dancing gangs was the point of it. Their energy carried over the footlights. It was like a great prizefight. And, together, the anticipation in "America" and "Something's Coming" required the sixties.

Onstage, we had seen the city streets as sets, but in the movie there was a misguided attempt to use the real streets without softening Robbins's balletic dances. It did not mesh. Whether or not it could have done if Donen or Minnelli had been in charge, we'll never know. As it was, Robert Wise was coproducer and codirector (with Robbins). Wise has an honorable record in film, but not for energy, magic, or changing the rules. The partnership with Robbins was not fruitful. The movie broke down into gang scenes and love scenes. And then the real gloom set in, for three of the four leads could not, or did not, sing their songs. So the big close-ups Wise favored (as equaling love and sincerity) were made more unreal by listless dubbing.

Natalie Wood was Maria and she was beautiful, but she stank of film star instead of city girl. Richard Beymer was Tony and he was a lump. Rita Moreno was great in the dancing—"America"—but she did not sing either.

The result is 155 minutes of a pedestrian, epic musical. I just wonder what Minnelli could have done in 100 minutes on very stylized sets, with wild kids. The production design in the movie is by Boris Leven, and it's not bad, but the film never delivers the feeling of place. Ernest Lehman wrote the script—and if you think of going from *North by Northwest* to *West Side Story* in two years you have living demonstration of how deadly success can be.

Wetherby (1985)

Wetherby, in Yorkshire, is the site of a branch of the British Library—and one of the characters in the film actually works at the Library, telling an awkward, ardent young man that no, it's a reference library, you can't check the books out. It's in the way playwright-director David Hare works that the place therefore stands for two broad intellectual elements: the attempt to gather and organize life and experience; and the need to control and license it. It's the perfect corollary for a story about the difficulties in absorbing pain, loss, and tragedy into life. And it's a sign of the considerable potential in Britain—through theater and television—for complex ideas taking shape as movies.

It seems to be a settled world. There is a dinner party in the house of Jean Travers (Vanessa Redgrave), an old farmhouse. There is food and wine and talk: it is a kind of ideal of civilization. But one person is still and silent at the table—John Morgan (Tim McInnerny). He comes back the next day to talk to Jean. Without explanation or warning, he has a gun and blows his brains out. A policeman comes to investigate (Stuart Wilson) and he wonders why Morgan did it there, in the farmhouse, in front of Jean. He talks to Jean and she says, "Doesn't matter how well locked up you are, at times you're always going to have to let people in."

There it is, the heart of the matter—closure and entrance, self-sufficiency and conversation. The structure of Hare's film tells us that Morgan's shot has already broken the enclosure Jean has created—it has let her past bleed forward into her present life, and we know there was a love affair in those days that ended badly and which left Jean with the fear of someone coming in again. It may sound didactic, cut-and-dried, but Hare's talent is to root the larger implications in the small things or remarks of everyday life. And film's ability to juxtapose the now and the then enables him to treat Jean's life as almost an experiment in sensibility and sympathy.

Wetherby opened theatrically, but it's the kind of film that has sustained British television for decades—first with the BBC and ITV, then through Channel 4 and HBO: small subjects; very good writing; exact acting. Simon Relph served as producer, Stuart Harris did the photography, Jane Greenwood and Lindy Hemming did the costumes, and Hayden Griffin was the designer. The budget was plainly very small, and no one ever intended the picture as being for a mainstream audience. But then consider the quality of the cast: Vanessa Redgrave giving an astonishing performance in which emotionalism starts to break through the control; her own daughter, Joely Richardson, playing Jean as a young woman; with Judi Dench, Ian Holm, Suzanna Hamilton, Tom Wilkinson, Marjorie Yates, and many others. And this comes in a period when Hare seemed especially intrigued by film—enough to make *Wetherby, Paris by Night,* and *Strapless* all within the space of four years. They are all small stories, fabulously played, and situations that grow in recollection.

What Ever Happened to Baby Jane? (1962)

Joan Crawford had worked with Robert Aldrich in *Autumn Leaves* (1956), and she had asked him repeatedly for another picture. Then Aldrich heard about a novel, by Henry Farrell, about the Hudson sisters, movie stars from the old days but wrecks now and still living together. Aldrich heard that Bette Davis had read the book, too, and was interested. He found no studio ready to take it on, so he bought the rights himself and then worked out a deal with Kenneth Hyman at Seven Arts. Crawford would do it for $40,000 and 10 percent of the producer's profit; Davis agreed for $60,000 and 5 percent of the profits. Warners would release the film, and a paternal Jack Warner held a press conference with his two great stars from the past. They promised to behave.

Lukas Heller wrote the script, under Aldrich's guidance, and that's where the crucial tone was laid down. Even if the two actresses were grateful for a comeback opportunity and prepared to bury old differences, the picture would show them as warring gargoyles, sisters who had always been rivals. But what was special to this venture was the grisly black comedy of the approach and the closeness to real horror. It was not going to be a picture in which either sister won much audience sympathy. They were two grotesques, the opposite arrows in a classic sado-masochistic relationship. The picture would ask us to laugh at them. And to match the harsh tone, it would be shot in a rather hostile black and white. Bette especially was asked to wear exaggerated makeup—as if put on by a clumsy child—while Joan was a bedridden cripple, served rat for dinner. It's hard to miss, or forgive, the cruelty. On the other hand, Aldrich (without a hit of his own in several years) had been given a tough deal by Seven Arts—do the whole thing for under a million dollars.

It worked. Coming just a couple of years after *Psycho*, it moved black-comic horror into the mainstream and, even more than *Sunset Blvd.*, it treated old Hollywood as a deranged waxworks show. Crawford would make another five pictures and they were all exercises in horror. Davis had to take her share, too. Increasingly in life she let her makeup be influenced by that of Baby Jane Hudson.

The picture was a huge success: it covered its production cost in just eleven days of release. It's hard to take—it always was—though Davis especially is touching in the final beach scene. I think it shows a failure in Aldrich to handle extremes without exaggeration. But its influence commercially was enormous. Bette Davis was nominated for Best Actress. Had she won, it would have been her third success—a record. Joan was not nominated; neither was the picture nor Aldrich himself. (Anne Bancroft won in *The Miracle Worker.*) But Victor Buono got a supporting actor nod, and he caught the film's reckless catering to the gay regard for old Hollywood.

What Price Glory? (1926)

After *The Big Parade* (1925), everyone wanted a First World War picture that seemed fresh, and American. *What Price Glory?* was a play by Maxwell Anderson and Laurence Stallings that opened on Broadway in 1924 and ran for 433 performances. It centered on the amiable rivalry between Captain Flagg (Louis Wolheim) and Sergeant Quirt (William Boyd), and it employed a kind of language far closer to that spoken by soldiers than anything heard in a theater before.

Fox assigned the play to Raoul Walsh and he recast it with Victor McLaglen as Flagg and Edmund Lowe as Quirt. He also cast Dolores del Rio as the French girl, Charmaine, that they both fancy. Walsh hired in a hundred Marines and they did the battle scenes at night where Century City now stands. Apparently the police came to stop them several times and arrested a different assistant director every time. There were many complaints from neighbors about the bombardment, but in those days filmmakers did whatever they could get away with. Walsh reckoned that Fox had had to pay something like $70,000 in damages to be free of complaint.

In hindsight, the remarkable thing is that a play famous for its talk still held up as a silent film. The soldiers spoke in pretty rough ways during the filming and it became quite a craze for lip-reading audiences to write to the papers to report what was really being said in *What Price Glory?* But Walsh understood that the play depended on two guys artificially separated by being an officer and a sergeant. They were natural antagonists who lived by needling and teasing each other. And so the scheme (and entire genre) of wisecracking military buddies was born—whether or not it was something observable in war. Fighting men under stress in American films are licensed to be comics. Further, the repartee began to erase distinctions of ordinary soldier and officer—and so in *From Here to Eternity* there is very little respect for officers. It was something Walsh was ideally suited to—the rough friendship of different types in a war situation, the egalitarianism of the Army, and it's a topic he never really tired of.

Walsh's teaming of McLaglen and Lowe continued (with diminishing success) in *The Cockeyed World* (1929) and *Women of All Nations* (1931), where they continued playing Flagg and Quirt, and in *Under Pressure* (1935)—this after *What Price Glory?* had earned close to $2 million on a production cost of $350,000. But Walsh picked up the idea of a sparring twosome to great effect for *Me and My Gal, The Bowery,* and *They Drive by Night.*

John Ford had helped Walsh on the battle scenes for *What Price Glory?* And in 1952 Ford returned to the old chestnut, teaming Jimmy Cagney and Dan Dailey. Nobody could see why—and Walsh himself was by then planning *Battle Cry,* a celebration of the military group, featuring Aldo Ray as a very Walshian common grunt (a figure exploited further in *The Naked and the Dead* and in Anthony Mann's *Men in War*).

What Price Hollywood? (1932)

The regular way of thinking in Hollywood was that movies about the picture business seldom succeeded. But *What Price Hollywood?*, director George Cukor thought, was different for one clear reason—producer David O. Selznick had an unqualified love for the business, an idealism that could shrug off the normal pose of irony or cynicism. And so, Selznick used it more than once—for this, really, is the model for *A Star Is Born*, which came five years later.

It's an RKO film in which an alcoholic movie director, Max Carey (Lowell Sherman) helps a Brown Derby waitress, Mary Evans (Constance Bennett) become a movie star. And as she rises, so he sinks deeper. But this is less a love story than *A Star Is Born*. Indeed, Mary's romance is with an actor, Lonny Borden (Neil Hamilton), and that allows a more thorough portrait of Carey as a fallen master, a man who really understands the movies, but who has lost faith in them.

There is another major character, Julius Saxe (Gregory Ratoff), the producer, a man who tells his writers they should be able to tell their stories in fifty words or less—but who takes so much longer himself. Selznick and Ratoff were old friends, and Ratoff is older than his boss here, but there's a good deal of affectionate needling in the portrait of a rough-diamond producer.

The project began as a story by Adela Rogers St. Johns. Gene Fowler and Rowland Brown took it from there, and Jane Murfin and Ben Markson did the screenplay. Charles Rosher did the photography and there are some very lively montage sequences to suggest drunkenness and the whirl of hype in the movie business—not too far apart. A young Pandro Berman was the associate producer and Carroll Clark was the art director.

Connie Bennett is not the ideal waitress, maybe. In Hollywood, she was a very social figure and a leading clotheshorse. She makes no great effort to abandon those atmospheres, but she's amusing and she has a droll chemistry with Lowell Sherman, who carries the picture. Sherman (1885–1934) was a fascinating figure—as an actor he often played lecherous hounds (as witness *Way Down East*) and as a director he was a sophisticate, too (*She Done Him Wrong, Morning Glory*). He married three actresses, and he died—far too soon—of the same kind of excesses that affect his character in this film.

As for Cukor, he was just beginning, and a beneficiary of the friendship with Selznick—and that's the lesson, really: that Hollywood in those days was a small club in which friends stuck and worked together. Thus, just over the horizon, Cukor would meet Kate Hepburn and launch a lifelong friendship. In turn, that points to how valuable the protected gay community was in Hollywood, a center of wit and a steady, acerbic correction to the devout stress on happy, healthy love affairs between formulaic men and women. But as early as sound, Hollywood guessed attraction was a lot busier than that safe traffic.

What's Up, Doc? (1972)

What did Peter Bogdanovich do after the slow, moody exploration of landscape and relationships in *The Last Picture Show*? He made a screwball comedy that seemed unaware the genre had been dead for twenty-five years. It was as if Preston Sturges were taking a pee and would be back any minute. It only adds to the hallucinatory magic of this film that in the thirty-four years since it was made no one else has attempted a screwball comedy.

So where do we begin with the praise? Let's start at the script—by Bogdanovich and Buck Henry, Robert Benton, and David Newman—and its inner knowledge that in screwball it is necessary to like everyone and to see that madness exists in everyone, not just those spokesmen for gaiety who are acting crazy. Indeed, acting crazy may be the one chance at sanity anyone has. This is fabulously personified at that moment when Barbra Streisand awakens, discovers she is next to a piano, and starts, "You must remember this . . ." She knows she needs to sing, for sanity's sake, and without a cue or a pretext in the action.

The setting is San Francisco. Ryan O'Neal is a stupid musicologist who will be saved for fun (if he's lucky) by Barbra, who exists in the story like an unruly wind, or like Hepburn in *Bringing Up Baby* (the most obvious model for this film). But doing those routines with Grant and Hepburn was one thing. Let's remember that both Streisand and O'Neal had it in them to be insufferable—in which case their lightness of touch here is breathtaking. The momentum of look-alike bags, mistaken identity, and rapid double-take response mounts and ends in a chase that has elements of Keystone. The film was a huge success, and it made a lot of money. Only snobbery kept it out of the awards. Seen today, there is no mistaking the wit, the precision, the timing, the class.

True to form and training, Bogdanovich gives lavish attention to the smaller parts, especially the "idiots" required in screwball comedy. Madeline Kahn was making her debut as Ryan O'Neal's fiancée and she is perfect. Kenneth Mars is delicious as a fraudulent expert. And Austin Pendleton is quite lovely as the man who is hiring.

Polly Platt was production designer, and it's fair to suppose that she did a lot more. Bogdanovich has never said a word to deny her contribution to his early films. But here's the point: there is a skill and a precocious experience already in the making of *What's Up, Doc?* that hardly goes away. Yet in fact Bogdanovich has fallen on hard times and television work. He does not have people like Streisand ready to work with him today. And that is immensely to the misfortune of Ms. Streisand and the rest of us. I cannot put it any other way—this is a gem, the real thing, a riot. Oh, go see it!

When a Woman Ascends the Stairs (1960)

For much of his career, apparently, Mikio Naruse was placed in Japan as being another Ozu—yet not quite as good. However, I have tried in this book to probe Ozu a little just because I feel that his revered style contains or masks some rather bleak views of family life. So it's very useful to look at Naruse closely, and to say that perhaps he grants his female characters an extra degree of liberty and pain compared with Ozu. Relatively speaking, the best informed Western filmgoers know only a fraction of Japanese film, and not much more Japanese history.

To take just two examples of the difficulty this can lead to: Mizoguchi's *The Story of the Last Chrysanthemums* (1939), it seems to me, is more mature and complex in its views than any American films being made at that time. Does that mean that Japan, in 1939, was a more humane and developed society than the U.S.? Or, consider that Clint Eastwood's *Letters from Iwo Jima* (2006) has been a far more popular film in Japan than in America. That seems reasonable, because *Letters* pursues a Japanese point of view. But that is not the reason for the success. Rather, it is because sixty years later, the events of Iwo Jima were still largely unknown in Japan. How can that be?

In other words, most Westerners still need much more education in Japanese thought to grasp what many of their films are saying. And Naruse is a case in point in that for most of his career he pursued the social status of women. *When a Woman Ascends the Stairs* is about a working woman, Keiko (Hideko Takamine), who is manageress of a bar in the Ginza district. It is her job to keep the largely male customers happy while looking after the bar girls. The bar premises are above the place where Keiko lives—itself a striking arrangement in Western eyes, but perhaps normal in Japan. The movie is beautifully made, in an Ozu-like style that involves long takes and simple camera positioning—the material that allows us to see human interplay and to feel the impact of this life on Keiko. Moreover, Hideko Takamine—one of Naruse's favorite players—is superb.

So here is a fine piece of social realism and incipient feminism, from 1960, yet more lively in its action than most Ozu films. Indeed, as I suggested, Naruse can help us to feel the disciplinarian in Ozu, the formalist even. I do not mean to dispute the depth of feeling in Ozu, but I am still not sure how angered he is at accepting the situations he sees. He might have said that my difficulty came from a deluded rebelliousness or a Western sentimentality. Yet Naruse's film is closer to my mood. And Mizoguchi is another matter again in that he sees through every veil of form or face to recognize the human truth. And where do these films stand in the overall deployment of Japanese culture and attitudes? The question is so open that it compels one to see more Japanese films.

Whisky Galore! (1949)

It was in 1938 that Michael Balcon took over at Ealing Studios, and began one of the great careers as production chief—spurred and stimulated no doubt by the hardships of Britain at war and the relative dismay of the same country at peace. What better situation or demonstration of the latter could there be than the most fortunate, if unhappy, wreck (no lives lost) of a ship carrying fifty thousand cases of Scotch whisky off the shores of an island called Todday?

You will not find such a place on the maps, but you can locate Johnnie Walker, black and red label, in any reasonable liquor store. Imagine then the plight of serious drinkers in a time of peace when the word "plenty" was mocked by the scarcity of the real stuff. Moreover, you can see the risk—of the possible pollution and the damage to the fishing industry, to say nothing of the hazard if foolhardy swimmers went out there on their own to the rocks in an effort to make the place safe.

This came from a novel by Compton MacKenzie, based on a real wreck off Eriskay. It was apparently Charles Frend who proposed it as a topic—if not a crisis—at an Ealing board meeting, and Balcon jumped at it. The screenwriting job was given to Angus MacPhail (he had written *It Always Rains on Sunday* and was a developing alcoholic) and the directing job was given to Alexander Mackendrick. Technically, Mackendrick was born in the U.S., in Boston, because his parents were traveling. But that eccentricity was allayed by his being raised in Scotland and educated at the Glasgow School of Art. This was his first feature.

The unit was sent to the island of Barra to get the scenery and the atmosphere. Gerald Gibbs was the cameraman. Jim Morahan did art direction. There was music by Ernest Irving, and Joseph Sterling and Charles Crichton edited the picture. It proceeds sensibly with the old Scottish maxim that in a time of crisis free enterprise will prevail, and it shows how in a community like Scotland there may be no finer blender of conservative and socialist, man and woman, than whisky. It is part of an Ealing attempt to go to the corners of the British Isles and to show local independence. Mackendrick directs with a light hand, or with the generosity of a man who knows he has a natural hit here for the taking. So it proved. The film was a big success, especially in America, where it was called *Tight Little Island* and served to allay some of the reckless fears over mature drinking encouraged by films like *The Lost Weekend*.

Of course, Balcon was canny: not all the players were Scots—that could have called for subtitles. But there were enough natives scattered in there to satisfy purists: Basil Radford, Catherine Lacey, Bruce Seton, Joan Greenwood, Wylie Watson, Gabrielle Blunt, Gordon Jackson, Jean Cadell, James Robertson Justice, John Gregson, James Woodburn, and Duncan Macrae.

White Heat (1949)

By 1949, Bogart and Edward G. Robinson were set on very different courses away from their gangster past. So it says something profound about the demon in Jimmy Cagney that he wanted to get back to that outlaw, and that, when there, he was able to make him better than ever. The Cagney pictures of the 1930s were made very fast, and very conscious of their own factory. But *White Heat* is something else, even if it was seeing Cagney come back to vicious life that taught the others what this picture might be.

Virginia Kellogg wrote a couple of treatments on the story, which differs a great deal from the movie. It was only when Ivan Goff and Ben Roberts came onboard that it started to shape up. Cagney would visit them in their office and ask what they were after. "An evil man," they said, "but we want the audience to understand why." Jimmy lapped it up and it's worth saying that this was his first film where the nutsiness of his character was of interest.

Goff and Roberts did several drafts and the script came much closer to the movie—though Cagney improvised sitting in his mother's lap and kicking his girlfriend off the chair, two very memorable things in the picture. It seems to be set in 1949, though I think it feels at least ten years earlier. So Cody Jarrett is a man of about fifty with a mother, Ma Jarrett (Margaret Wycherly), who is plainly of far higher rank and greater intimacy than his nominal wife, Verna (Virginia Mayo). In an effort to break the gang, a government man, Vic Pardo (Edmond O'Brien), is put with Jarrett in prison, and in time he becomes a trusted confidant. But while Jarrett is doing his time, Ma dies—clearly because of the callousness of Verna and her stud, Big Ed (Steve Cochran).

Jarrett is tightly wound in all ways. When he hears of Ma's death—in prison, in the dining hall—his berserk dance of rage is breathtaking. And thereafter, you may decide, he is mad, though he remains sympathetic. Here is the trick of the picture. Cody is so much nobler than Verna and Ed. He is being betrayed by Vic. And who is his greatest pal? It is Ma who comforts him when his headaches come on and who advises him on how to intimidate the gang. And when Cody dies—in destructive splendor—she is the one he is talking to: "Made it, Ma! Top of the world."

Sid Hickox did the photography and Raoul Walsh was ready for every improv Cagney offered. Indeed, the direction is the primary level of Cody's support in the film—it's his privacy and his stage. Edward Carrere did the art direction and Max Steiner the music.

The supporting cast includes John Archer, Wally Cassell, Mickey Knox, Ian MacDonald, Fred Clark, Pat Collins, Paul Guilfoyle, Fred Coby, and Ford Rainey.

Who Framed Roger Rabbit (1988)

There were many people who regretted the breakdown in 1985 of the sequel to *Chinatown*. Robert Towne, writer of the original film, had been about to direct *The Two Jakes* when it collapsed. Well, it came back a few years later, as a broken thing. By then it mattered less than it might have because in a magical way, *Who Framed Roger Rabbit* had taken up the slack. We are talking about one of the most ingenious films—not just a profound and haunting fable on all the connects and disconnects between real people and the unreal on screen, but exactly the lament for Los Angeles in the new age of the automobile that Robert Towne had intended.

It comes from a novel, *Who Censored Roger Rabbit?*, by Gary K. Wolf. In turn this was made into a screenplay by Jeffrey Price and Peter S. Seaman. Robert Zemeckis would direct, but the venture had the backing of a team of producers that included Steven Spielberg, Frank Marshall, and Kathleen Kennedy. It had a nutshell idea: Eddie, a real, scruffy L.A. private eye (Bob Hoskins), is so down on his luck that he has to take toons for clients. What are "toons"? Well, toons are initially cartoon characters, people drawn, not made by God's wise and delightful processes. But that is much more than just the artifice that can keep them in the same frame—according to *Anchors Aweigh*. It is also an allegory for . . . well, whatever you want. But for Eddie (who has had trouble with toons before) there is an almost racial tinge to his hostility. And the toons are kinda wild. Let me just add that *Who Framed Roger Rabbit* falls close to the Rodney King incident and the episode called O.J. In other words, when I put this forward as an instructive American film, I am boosting not just the inspired fraternity of toons and people (essentially the work of animator Richard Williams) but the larger ideas behind it. And this is a film about cloning and race, as well as drawing style.

It is also a sexual delirium, thanks to the way Jessica Rabbit (Roger's wayward wife) is drawn, vocalized by Kathleen Turner (it's Matty from *Body Heat* on electric kool-aid), and sung by Amy Irving. And then you have the generally deranged and gob-smacked performance of Bob Hoskins, who can hardly move or breathe without having drawn arms around his neck. I often think that a little Hoskins goes a long way—but he is gorgeous here.

Joe McCoy and Alan Silvestri did the music. Dean Cundey photographed it. Arthur Schmidt did the editing. Roger Cain and Elliot Scott did the production design. And Joanna Johnston did the costumes.

The human cast also includes Joanna Cassidy, Christopher Lloyd (magnificent as Judge Doom), Charles Fleischer's voice doing Roger (and some others), Stubby Kaye, Alan Tilvern, Richard Le Parmentier, Joel Silver, and many voices by the incomparable Mel Blanc. It cost at least $70 million, but it grossed $154 million in the U.S. alone, and it is one of the last great works of wit and beauty, magic and terror, to come out of a Hollywood studio. They gave Best Picture that year to *Rain Man*.

Who's Afraid of Virginia Woolf? (1966)

Edward Albee's play opened in October 1962 and ran for 664 performances, with Uta Hagen, Arthur Hill, George Grizzard, and Melinda Dillon. Early reactions were that it was too foulmouthed and downbeat ever to make it to the screen, but Ernest Lehman persuaded Warner Brothers to put up the money for a film he would write and produce. Warners had to agree that no one under eighteen would ever see the film, and that helped formulate the modern ratings system.

In the play, George and Martha, the warring married couple, are in their early fifties. Elizabeth Taylor in 1966 was thirty-four. But Lehman reckoned that the part could be brought down a little while Taylor could let her looks go some. There was a meeting, and Taylor was tough, competitive, argumentative, a ballbuster. As they talked about it (and the talk meant her getting $1 million) they wondered about George. "What about him?" said Taylor, indicating Richard Burton on the other side of the room. Burton was only forty-one, though capable of looking older, or more tired. So casting's magic settled on the project, and all of a sudden the film became obvious.

Many directors were considered, but Lehman liked the chances of newcomer Mike Nichols, who had not made a film yet—though he had agreed to do *The Graduate.* Sandy Dennis was cast, and when Robert Redford absolutely refused the second male role it went to George Segal. Haskell Wexler was hired to do the photography, and Richard Sylbert created the production design. Later on, Sam O'Steen edited the picture. The casting had made it expensive, but this was at a moment when Burton and Taylor were still hot (as opposed to ridiculous), and it's plain that both of them were excited by the project and quite able to recognize its affinities with their own turbulent relationship.

Nichols let it play—what else was he to do with that text and that cast? There's no point in opening it up, though Lehman had decided that their child really had existed and killed himself. So it's a solid, talky picture, and a relic of those days when America still honored the theater as a place for intelligent, demanding plays. As a work, I fear it has dated badly, though it captures the drunken acrimony of faculty life all too well.

The picture had rentals of $14.5 million, a sign of gravity in the audience (as well as stamina), and of our modern taste for domestic diatribe. It was nominated all over the place and Taylor won her second Oscar. Burton did not win, but he never did. Other winners included Sandy Dennis, Wexler for photography that seems to me rather routine, Sylbert for the sets, the shabbiness, and the cigarette burns, and Irene Sharaff for the cardigans and other costumes.

What does it mean? Despite the aging down of the play, it really is about middle age and its seemingly endless trap. That is a discomfort that by today has been nearly exiled from American movies, so the sight and sound of these couples chatting away through their long night is reminiscent of things like long-playing records, canasta parties, and Norman Mailer.

The Wild Bunch (1969)

Made in the same year as *Butch Cassidy and the Sundance Kid*, Sam Peckinpah's *The Wild Bunch* manages to imitate its ending and demolish it. Butch and Sundance are badly shot up somewhere in Bolivia (their plan is: next stop Australia) with *federales* and soldiers surrounding their cramped courtyard. So, wisecracking to the end, they jump out into the light and space (the way they jumped off the cliff once) and only a freeze-frame saves them from annihilation. A freeze-frame! You can hear Peckinpah's sneer. He might slow down the fatal frames, but that is only so we can see every bullet bursting in flesh and blood. You can call that history's grim task, or self-destruction's last orgy. But nothing is spared.

In time, Deke Thornton (Robert Ryan) will come by to survey the corpses, and we remember his comment to the trash that make up his posse—"They're men, and I wish to God I was riding with them." The time is 1916 on the Mexican-American border, when automobiles and machine guns are making their appearance, when a bank robbery can get you no more than heavy casualties and several sacks of steel washers. Times are passing by, and the bunch are doomed men. They know it, and they have one nostalgia—to go with honor, if honor ever existed.

It had seemed possible ever since *Ride the High Country*, in 1962, that Peckinpah was going to make a great film if he could find the right scorched epic and keep nobility and despair in balance. Mindful of some Kurosawa films, Walon Green and Roy Sickner came up with it: the last days of a gang that lives on the border, robbing, whoring, riding, getting shot at and shot until someone takes them out. The bunch loses half its men in a first disastrous bank job, when Thornton and his trash are ambushing them. The survivors are Pike (William Holden), Dutch (Ernest Borgnine), the Gorch brothers, Tector and Lyle (Ben Johnson and Warren Oates), and Angel (Jaime Sanchez) the Mexican, their vulnerability and their way to honor when it is too late. And there is Sykes (Edmond O'Brien), the old-timer they leave behind, the man whose Hustonian laughter presides over the film.

But this is tougher and bloodier than John Huston, and it is a film in agonies over whether there is really honor in this bunch, or just a stupid, archaic code. They abuse women. They kid themselves. They'd rather get drunk than look at the great land. They are friends, yet they betray each other—Thornton was in the bunch once. And while he knows that his followers (Strother Martin, L. Q. Jones—hilarious but reptiles) are garbage, are they worse than the men following Pike?

The great desert light (by Lucien Ballard) is going out. Civilization is coming, and here is a pained cry of desire and lament from the America that never wanted any such thing. Peckinpah will always be restricted by his limitations, but when he was good you could taste the blood, the hooch, and the regret, and this and *Pat Garrett & Billy the Kid* are his great films.

The Wild Cat (1921)

It's a marvel (and a mistake) that in an age familiar with Marlene Dietrich and Louise Brooks, the world has rather lost track of Pola Negri. By all accounts, but chiefly her own, Negri was born Barbara Appolonia Chalupiec, in Poland—was one parent a fallen nobleman, the other a Gypsy violinist? Look at her, her eyes lemurlike in their kohl surrounds, and it's easy to believe all that and more. What's much nearer the point is that in coming to Berlin to join Max Reinhardt for the play *Sumurun* in 1917, she made herself available for the burgeoning career of Ernst Lubitsch. Apparently he found her something of a bore in person—or did he? Onscreen, he seems captivated by her. Perhaps he just went home and complained to his other ladies—"Another day with that awful Negri!"

The Wild Cat (sometimes *The Mountain Cat*) is their sixth and last film together, and it shows evident faith in her as a comedienne. In wild hair and leopard skins, Negri is the daughter of bandits who rule the snowy Alps and who capture a young lieutenant. It's true that Lubitsch and his photographer (Theodor Sparkuhl) did go on location to the snowy places, but don't look for too much realism in *The Wild Cat*. It is a satire upon military states, bandits, and femmes fatales, and it is glorious cover for every type of joke Lubitsch can float. It's worth remembering that this very playful picture was made in Berlin in the worst aftermath of the war. Yet it insists on ridicule from the moment when the young prince is leaving a town and a small army of children appear to cheer him on with "Daddy! Daddy!" There's not a hint of class commentary in the confrontation of bandit and aristocracy. Everyone's idiotic. The bandits live in a cave behind a curtain, and the aristos inhabit a kind of gingerbread palace. The décor is dreamlike, fussy, and cheapscape, and in the end the Alps seem as phony. In addition, Lubitsch invents masks for the screen itself. Nearly every image or sequence comes frilled or restricted by some apparatus. It's overdone, and a touch giddy, but it surely bespeaks Lubitsch's urge to satirize the whole show. But the visual is not as funny in the script (by Lubitsch and Hans Kräly) as the ironic dialogue would be ten years later. The reason is simple: we long to hear this mountain girl sounding like a wit and a sophisticate. Lubitsch was aching for sound and inclined to run visual riot in sets and costumes (by Ernst Stern and Emil Hasler). In any medium—like film or theater literature—where there are human figures, the comedy takes a more interesting turn if they can speak. Still, *The Wild Cat* would be reason enough for bringing Lubitsch to America. Negri came, too, in time, though not as part of the Lubitsch package despite the versatility that had also done Carmen, Ann Boleyn, and Madame Du Barry for him.

Wild Oranges (1924)

Wild oranges seem bitter at first, but then you get a taste for them. So says John Woolfolk (Frank Mayo), as he steps ashore on the wild Georgian coastline on a blue-tinted night. He has had a philosophical turn of mind ever since the day—a few years before—when he was out in a carriage with his young wife. A fluttering piece of paper spooked the horses. They were off. The carriage made a violent turn and the wife was thrown out as if propelled by a comic ejector seat. Dead as a doornail. Thus John's moodiness and his habit of sailing the seas with just his pipe and a pal, Paul Halvard (Ford Sterling).

The time is said to be not long after the Civil War, yet Joseph Hergesheimer's novel, *Wild Oranges*, was published in 1919 and has that air of disquiet that followed the Great War. At any event, the Georgia shore is a strange place. There is a wreck of a mansion visible beyond the wild orange groves and three people live there: Lichfield Stope (Nigel de Brulier), the gaunt, haunted figure of a veteran, a man afraid of everything; his daughter Millie (Virginia Valli), stricken with the same fear, yet somehow the beneficiary of a daily makeup artist; and Iscah Nicholas (Charles A. Post), a homicidal giant with a yen for Millie.

It is sort of sub-Faulkner—until you remember that in 1924 Faulkner was at the start of his career, and Faulkner's work is better and stranger than *Wild Oranges*, a Goldwyn film, directed by King Vidor, and plainly shot on location. And yet there is something as odd as the wild oranges themselves. There is a huge subtext, and we feel that it interests Vidor more than the heavy melodrama. John has sunk into depression or inertia. Yes, his ship sails on, but he is a passive creature. And Millie is afraid of everything—Ms. Valli rather overdoes this; she has a way of starting violently at every fluttering leaf that is fatiguing—for us. But the conventional romantic meeting of these two is actually made erotic by the sense of two lost souls who may cure themselves in becoming lovers. No, the subtext is not there; it's not delivered, as it might be in a novel. But you feel it, and—if you are of a mind—you may recall from the future a similar tendency in Howard and Dominique in *The Fountainhead*.

I don't mean to overpraise *Wild Oranges*, but its novelty is distinct and intriguing. It is not well played by Virginia Valli, though Mayo seems more aware of it. But something is happening in the American movie that seems ready to go beneath the routine level of melodrama.

Not that Vidor omits the blood and thunder (after all, he kept the rock drill in *The Fountainhead*). Before we are through there is a wild dog, a house burning down, and one of the greatest fistfights ever managed on the screen. It goes on and on in patient long shot—and it is clear that Mayo and Post had to carry a lot of it themselves. Mayo looks as if he has been through a couple of grinding millstones, and Post is an authentic monster.

Wild River (1960)

There are several films by Elia Kazan that are far better known—in part because of the sensational literary credentials, and because of high-powered central performances. There is no reason to nag at those films too much. They are what they are. Still, *Wild River* remains one of my favorites in his work, in large part because the subdued acting is perfectly in key with the historical subject and the unusually ambiguous approach. In so many Kazan films, there is little doubt about the characters we are meant to like and approve of—and the unrestrained acting is often a concession to their threatened righteousness. But *Wild River* begins and ends with an issue on which only fools take sides quickly.

The time is the 1930s. The place is Tennessee. The government has a plan to "improve" life for the people. Chuck Glover (Montgomery Clift) is a TVA agent who comes to spread the good news. It should be said at the outset that while Clift is a star and an intense romantic, this is Clift after his accident—not as beautiful, not as sure, but a muddler, a well-meaning mess, and a city guy out of his depth in this strange backcountry. It is the shabby ordinariness of Glover that is so important and instructive in how to watch the picture.

A dam will be built, so some small holdings must be cleared or sacrificed. This policy usually works well enough. But Glover confronts a matriarch, Ella Garth (Jo Van Fleet), who will not sell her land or quit it—no matter the benefits. She will have to be removed. Glover tries reason and blunt requirement; he even falls in love with Ella's granddaughter, Carol (Lee Remick). He finds himself hated by the local community, harassed, and beaten up. In the end, of course, the government "wins." Ella is taken away to a tidy new place she hates. We guess the change will kill her. But the dam will help Tennessee and Chuck will marry Carol and take her away.

Remember that in the 1930s Kazan made a short, *People of the Cumberland*—about another benign attempt to help poor people. *Wild River* came from two novels, *Mud on the Stars*, by William Bradford Huie, and *Dunbar's Cove* by Borden Deal. The screenplay was entrusted to Paul Osborn and his authentic regard for inarticulate people.

Time and again, the film works through restraint. This begins in Ellsworth Frederick's mournful, sodden landscape photography—in Scope and winter colors. It is there in Kenyon Hopkins's quiet music. And it is there in the strict objectivity of the script. Chuck is a decent guy, but he does damage. He may kill Ella and he troubles the society that finds him unfit for Carol. Nor does the film even suppose that Carol will be a glowing beneficiary. They make an awkward but touching couple—and just as Clift is prepared to let that show, Lee Remick is quite brilliant as someone of plainly lower intelligence than her own. What can you say about Jo Van Fleet—except that in life she was a whole five years older than Clift?

Wild Strawberries (1957)

In the "delivery" of Ingmar Bergman to the world, *Wild Strawberries* was the second shot, the clincher. *The Seventh Seal* had shared the Special Jury Prize at Cannes with Wajda's *Kanal*. The following year *Wild Strawberries* won the Golden Bear at Berlin, and it was a more accessible film, less dubious about man's future, but anchored to the presence of Victor Sjöström as the old professor, Isak Borg, whose journey to receive an honorary degree becomes a judgment of his whole life. Bergman over the years had often been tougher on his characters than his audiences liked. This tendency would reappear later and it was taken as part of his intimidating gloom and gravity. But Bergman revered Sjöström and came to love him. That showed, and it helped.

Borg is a professor of bacteriology at the Karolinska Institute in Stockholm, He lives alone, save for a housekeeper (Jullan Kindahl). He is seventy-eight, Sjöström's age when the project began. He is intending to fly to Lund for the honorary degree, but he has a dream—with handless clocks. A coffin falls from a hearse. A hand reaches out from within it to him. So he decides to go by road. The symbolism of this dream could be less oppressive. On the other hand, in opening up the casket of dream, the film is reaching into very fertile ground.

He travels in a 1937 Packard, driven by his daughter-in-law (Ingrid Thulin—in her Bergman debut). Along the way, in dream or reality, Borg will encounter the landmarks of his life—his son (Gunnar Björnstrand), his mother (Naima Wifstrand), his wife, now dead (Gunnel Broström). And they pick up a young hitchhiker, Sara (Bibi Andersson). The photography, by Gunnar Fischer, is unusually contrasty for Bergman—very black, very white—as if to convey an elderly impression of life.

Sjöström had been friend and example to Bergman. He was old, difficult, and not well (he died in 1960). As they made the film, Bergman had to abbreviate his hours and make sure Sjöström was done for the day with a whiskey by 4:30. He seemed distant—but Bergman saw that it was insecurity, the actor's fear. Then he saw Sjöström warm up in chatter with Thulin and Andersson. This is Bergman on the last scene:

> Isak Borg's great love of his youth takes him to a sunny hillside. Far away, he can see his parents beckoning to him. At five in the afternoon, the sunlight shone low over the grass and made the forest dark. Victor was angry and spiteful. He reminded me of my promise—on the dot of half-past four, home, his whisky. I appealed to him. Nothing helped. Victor stumped off. Quarter of an hour later, he was back. Aren't we going to take those damned scenes?
>
> . . . As he walked through the sunlit grass with Bibi in a long shot, he was grumbling and rejecting all friendly approaches. The close-up was rigged up and he went to one side and sat with his head sunk between his shoulders, dismissing scornfully the offer of a whisky on the spot. When everything was ready, he came staggering over, supported by a production assistant, exhausted by his bad temper. The camera ran and the clapper clacked. Suddenly his face opened, the features softening, and he became quiet and gentle, a moment of grace.

Winchester '73 (1950)

It's a dazzling idea that as a rifle, the Winchester '73 one-in-one-thousand (the one made best), changes hands, so the range and variety of the Western genre is defined, and all in 86 minutes in etchinglike black-and-white photography from William Daniels, so often a master of romantic lighting. There are other innovations: this was the first occasion on which Anthony Mann worked with Jimmy Stewart—there would be seven more films—and it was a landmark in that Universal, in hard times, worked out with Lew Wasserman a deal where Stewart got 50 percent of the profits, and likely made $1 million on this picture alone.

So there's a shooting contest in Dodge City, presided over by Wyatt Earp (Will Geer). There are brothers locked in hatred, Lin McAdam and Dutch Henry (Stewart and Stephen McNally). There's a saturnine Indian trader dressed in black (the admirable John McIntire), a raw soldier (Tony Curtis), a very broad-chested Indian chief, Young Bull (Rock Hudson), a coward and his girl (Charles Drake and Shelley Winters), Jay C. Flippen as an old-timer cavalry sergeant, Millard Mitchell as High Spade, Lin's lugubrious companion, and then, at the end, the wonderful drawl and leer of Dan Duryea's Waco Johnny.

Needless to say, this is a telescopic Western, in which Mann's eagle eye surveys great distances and the variation of terrain. You feel the space of the Western fable and you feel how close courage and resolve in the hero have come to harshness. Borden Chase, the writer, has said that Stewart did not seem ideal casting until people remembered the bomber missions he'd flown in the war. And truly this is a tougher, edgier Stewart, never too far from cracking up or turning cold. Mann was made into a more interesting dramatist by meeting Stewart.

Apart from that, one marvels at the speed of a story that circles so prettily without seeming contrived. The greater part of the action is out-of-doors, and the black and white adds to the sense of period. But this was a time when actors wore old leather and carried guns with aplomb. It's a delight to see the way Duryea moves, just as it is to contemplate Stewart's hat. The Indians are obediently savage and unfathomable, and the wild landscape is a place where only determination and shrewdness will triumph. Of course, there is also the gun—a beautiful object and a rare piece of engineering, and in 1950 still regarded without irony or shame as an instrument of progress and order.

There's no way America fifty-five years later could reinhabit those clothes and attitudes with confidence. That's one reason why the Western has gone. But Mann in the 1950s made a precious group of films, with a hero who was struggling between violence and decency, but a figure who expected to prove his virtue and purpose in a trial of arms. Stewart's experience in World War II made him a more challenging actor and it allowed *Winchester '73* to seem not just a genre film but a modern story—as up-to-date as its remarkable profits deal, another of the things that killed the honorable company of all the supporting players who put a hand and a fond glance on the esteemed rifle.

The Wind (1928)

The Wind is one of those silent pictures (made on the cusp) where much of the action is so dramatic, one is left only in suspense. And there are two endings (as if the production team was torn over what the picture was about). The tape I watched most recently has not just the happy ending that M-G-M called for but an elderly Lillian Gish appearing in an introduction—very pretty in color—lamenting the compromise they had to make. For Gish takes the line that Irving Thalberg entrusted her with the film. She was virtually its producer as well as its Letty.

Gish adds that she found the novel, by Dorothy Scarborough, sold it to Thalberg, and then wrote a four-page treatment that Frances Marion turned into a screenplay. Moreover, it was Gish who secured the directing job for Victor Seastrom (Sjöström as was).

We begin on the train going West. Letty is a lone traveler, coming all the way from Virginia—the destination is said to be Texas. Nothing is offered as an explanation of why she is making the journey, yet she is already anxious over the wind that batters the train windows and leaves dust everywhere. But a salesman, Wirt Roddy (Montagu Love) picks her up and warns her about the wind—the prospects of the wind are rather overdone, and when the train puts Letty off it is not in Texas but in the Mojave Desert. This is rather piling on. People and animals do live in much of Texas, where it can be unpleasantly hot and windy. They do not live or farm in the Mojave because life could not be sustained there. So the film cheats: when Letty meets Lige (Lars Hanson) there is a scene of them talking in the wind in which they both wear soft-brimmed hats that are going mad in the breeze. Fair enough: it shows the threat and the stress. But the other cowboys (like men in such places) wear the stiff-brimmed hats that Stetson made specially for that weather.

Letty is not happy in the West. She is not made welcome and she ends up marrying Lige, a rough, decent cowboy. Not that he touches her. It is around here in the film that you have to begin to ask yourself what the wind is symbolizing—and why did Letty go to live in the wind? Is it the sexual life she is afraid of? In which case, what should our attitude be? Lige reckons to save up the money and send her home—to Virginia (one of the few sane developments in the film). But Wirt Roddy comes back and has rape in mind. So Letty shoots him. It's a powerful moment, but Wirt's surprise is understandable. She has flirted with him earlier. What does she want?

Of course, people never get to say what they want. A few words would change this film. If that sounds sarcastic, don't let me take away from the bravura distress of Gish's performance. With airplane engines to whip up the wind, with Seastrom doing his sympathetic best, it's a near masterpiece. But in the West people go West out of courage, adventure, challenge, and hope—and Letty is without those things. In the happy ending she decides to make a go of it. In the unhappy close—which Gish believed was the right one—she totters out into the wind and the roaring furnace.

Wings (1927)

Flying in the First World War may have been our last order of knighthood. There was a code of chivalry and honor and every combatant was as moved by the fresh wonder of flight as by the thought of death. Or is it that the movies make it seem so? Was the real fighting in the air just a matter of desperate speed, blind luck, and survival? Or are we right to remember the moments, as in *Wings,* when the German ace Kellerman (Carl von Haartman) lets David Armstrong (Richard Arlen) get away when his guns jam? That Kellerman is ancestor to the mythic Ernst Kessler (Bo Brundin) in *The Great Waldo Pepper,* and even the crippled officer who runs a prison camp in *La Grande Illusion.* Perhaps it was all a pitiless mess in the air—but legend says it was *Wings.*

William Wellman's epic has not faded too much, even if it sometimes seems as if the First World War is being fought just to permit the rigmarole of fliers falling in and out of love with their girls and each other. So, on the one hand, it's the story of "buddies," Armstrong and Jack Powell (Buddy Rogers), in love with friendship, flying, and the same girl—Sylvia Lewis (Jobyna Ralston)—only because Jack can't see yet that Mary Preston (Clara Bow) is the one for him. And for us—Bow is authentic sweetheart material, captivated by the fun and silliness in romance. In comparison, Ms. Ralston never gets her wheels off the ground.

It was a mighty Paramount production, with weeks down in Texas waiting for the right combination of clouds in the sky. Wellman (a veteran of the Lafayette Escadrille) knew that you needed clouds to get perspective. Harry Perry was the head man in a team of a dozen photographers, most of them aloft during the brilliant dogfights.

The script is by Hope Loring and Louis Lighton and it has to give too much time (in 136 minutes) to the love stories. Never mind. The background story came from John Monk Saunders, who had been in the Army Air Corps and was a writer who specialized in fliers who had survived the war but with damage. It's from Saunders and Wellman, I suspect, that the film derives its real force—as a symphony to flight and fliers, and the laconic view of a brotherhood almost bent upon death. The war will be won, but *Wings* knows that the finest of men may die. It is the debut of the "Right Stuff," and nothing catches it better than the brief appearance of White (Gary Cooper), giving that curt salute so treasured by Hawks, among others, as he goes off on what must be his last mission—otherwise Gary Cooper would be starring.

It's the top-notch air film, better than *Hell's Angels* (and probably gentler on the staff). They say it cost $800,000—and it made that back several times over. So it had to win Best Picture-Production at the first Oscars, though Murnau's *Sunrise* also won a Best Picture award that year for "Artistic Production." Eighty years later, *Wings* is still a match for *Sunrise.*

Wings of Desire (1988)

In the cinema, we have several angels: there is Clarence in *It's a Wonderful Life,* a novice and apprentice, but able to put in a good word for life; in *A Matter of Life and Death,* angels run the whole afterlife business, with a starchiness learned in the British civil service; and there was Claude Rains in *Here Comes Mr. Jordan*—being as cool and urbane as possible about the big surprise. But that only teaches one to see that Rains's customary sangfroid was often verging on the angelic. After all, as the ultimate figure of law, order, and chance in *Casablanca,* you could say that Renault has his wings.

And here, I think, the idea of angels becomes very interesting indeed. Consider in how many films—especially those in which it has been moving, striving for flight, escape, or rescue—the camera is an angel. Think of the winged camera in Max Ophüls as being an angel that might want to catch Lola Montès in her perilous fall but can't intervene. That would be breaking an angels' rule. An angel watches, an angel sees, and we may presume that he or she prays. The rest is up to us.

That's the way in to *Wings of Desire,* a film written by Wim Wenders and Peter Handke, and then directed by Wenders, a film that imagines the plight of people who, just because they watch over us, have to see so much failure and tragedy. So much, that perhaps they become involved.

We are in Berlin—as it happens, not long before the wall that split that city came down. Two angels, Damiel (Bruno Ganz) and Cassiel (Otto Sander), are about their work. They are interesting "men," neutral, of course, objective, but given an extra glamour by the sepia tones that are their way of seeing. And when you look at Damiel, you see that Bruno Ganz could have been a contender, a god, even. So it is Damiel who desires more. He falls in love with a trapeze artist (Solveig Dommartin) and he thinks of coming to ground.

As photographed by Henri Alekan (he photographed *La Belle et la Bête* for Cocteau), this is a soulful examination of Berlin as a place aching for spiritual return. Wenders uses the architecture, the gargoyle figures, and even the stone angels (don't forget Peter Falk), as companions to these human figures, and he sees a modern city where religious faith has to take its chances with so many other hopes and fears. So it's a poignant metaphor, this idea that one or two noirish-looking onlookers are saintly, or waiting to plan our funeral.

I think the delicate idea falters a little. Truth to tell, it needs more comic energy than Wenders seems ready to give it. But this is a special, thoughtful movie, a perfect setting for Bruno Ganz—one of the great unidentified (or unclaimed) actors of our time—and probably Wenders's most interesting picture. Of course, it is also a very important step in the career of Peter Handke.

The Wings of the Dove (1997)

Did Henry James go to the movies, or with any sense of a narrative form coming into being just as he expired? He died in 1916, and it is far more likely that if he went to a show he would have gone to the theater, the arena in which he competed with a will but felt himself humbled and defeated. And yet, by a small stretch of history, one could imagine James living on long enough to see Murnau, Renoir, Antonioni—it's enough to make one wish for his collected film criticism.

All of which is a way of saying that at a certain moment when very young, I came to a fork in the path and followed movies rather than Henry James. I do not seek pity or forgiveness so much as the understanding that the choice remains hanging in the air. That is why I offer Iain Softley's *The Wings of the Dove* as the best example I know of James on film. No, the race is not crowded, though I can imagine other films having their backers—*The Heiress*, for instance, or Merchant-Ivory's *The Golden Bowl*.

The novel is set in 1902. Kate Croy loves an impoverished newspaper writer, Merton Densher. But he is too poor to be married. Kate makes a friend out of Milly Theale, American and an heiress but not well. Kate urges Merton to take an interest in her, and the mix of kindness and unkindness is utterly Jamesian. Milly falls in love with Merton, and though she learns of the plot against her she does leave money to him. When that check comes through, Kate poses this test: Merton must take the money or swear that he is not enthralled by Milly's memory. The love between Kate and Merton is over.

I tell the story because in James, so often, the arc or the circle of the story is the fatal enclosure. What distinguishes the Softley film first of all is a kind of confidence in the lethal tale that knows it can do without the immense written bedding in which these feeble lovers lie. The film is 101 minutes; the book is 500 pages. There can be no useful equation in which the one becomes the other. The only reason to begin is because Softley has been overpowered by the story and a need to tell it.

On that basis, this *Wings of the Dove* is an unbearable psychological thriller, set in London and Venice, so remorseless in its tracing of human intrigue and so sure of the survival of something finer that it reminds me of Bresson's *Les Dames du Bois de Boulogne*—there are similarities in the plot. Softley has done nothing else to match this (though he is an intriguing director). No one has seen or used the sinister air of disease in Venice so casually—the ghost of Luchino Visconti should have to see this film every day.

And then there is the central trio: Helena Bonham-Carter, Linus Roache, and Alison Elliott. Believe me.

The Winning of Barbara Worth (1926)

It was a novel first, *The Winning of Barbara Worth,* written by Harold Bell Wright in 1911, and depicting drastic floods on the Colorado River. It sold nearly 3 million copies—and is forgotten today. But the Colorado was an endless crisis and question mark. As the melting snow came down from the Rockies so the lower stretches of the river flooded. At the same time, all that hydroelectric potential was being lost. The Wright novel was so big, Sam Goldwyn had to pay $125,000 for the rights.

He was inspired equally by show business and patriotism and he was certainly prompted by the 1922 conference of western states that first agreed to build a dam on the Colorado. So Goldwyn got Frances Marion to turn the novel into a film, and he asked Henry King to direct. Barbara Worth (Vilma Banky) is the adopted child of desert ranchers. Willard Holmes (Ronald Colman), from East Coast money, comes West with a view to use the Colorado for irrigation. He also rivals local boy Abe Lee for Barbara's love.

The story hinges on where to build a town—high or low, thinking of floods. Worth goes high and calls the town "Barba." There are Wild West battles between the factions and in due course a great flood comes. But all is settled finally and Barbara and Willard will be married.

At King's insistence, the unit moved out to make a tent city—actually called "Barbara Worth" on maps of the time, near Gerlach in the Black Rock Desert (the site today of the Burning Man Festival). This ensured a great sense of veracity (with George Barnes doing the photography) mixed in with newsreel footage of actual floods. It's likely that Goldwyn was deliberately taking on *Greed* (which bore his name), but in this case the natural drama of place smothers the romantic story. And Ronald Colman looks decidedly out of place in the desert heat.

That's what led to the great discovery of the film. The role of Abe Lee was set for Harold Goodwin, but he was doing *The Honeymoon Express* for Lubitsch and that ran over. So the search was on for a natural cowboy. It unearthed Gary Cooper. At first King hired him as a rider. But when Goodwin failed to appear, Cooper was asked to do the scene when the exhausted Abe arrives with news. Goldwyn protested: it was a big scene and Cooper was a novice. But King stuck to his guns and even Goldwyn was amazed at the naturalism of "Coop." "He's the greatest actor I have ever seen in my life," raved the boss, a contract shaping in his mind.

In fact, that scene was so good it stole the picture and was dropped to save Colman's face! But the significance to history was clear: the Boulder Dam would be built (the Act funding it passed in 1928), and here in advance of sound, a hard-bitten economy of speech founded in inward belief was clear. Cooper was eclipsing Colman, and the "silence" that came to life in sound pictures could convey uncertainty, shyness, and doubt. The fatal gap between declaration and subtiles (so redolent of dishonesty) was gone forever.

The Wizard of Oz (1939)

Harold Arlen was thirty-three, and he had been engaged to do the songs for *The Wizard of Oz* with Yip Harburg as lyricist. It was a fourteen-week contract for $25,000. And Arlen was changing. In 1937, after years of debate and hesitation, he married Anya Taranda, a showgirl, not Jewish. He loved her enough to overcome that family obstacle. But he was stricken by it, and then Anya fell ill in the mind. But that was not quite yet. She was driving him down Sunset—he liked to be driven so he could close his eyes and let swoops and lines of song fill his head. At Schwab's, he asked Anya to stop the car. He got out, but he never made it inside. On the sidewalk, outside the drugstore, he wrote the basic line of "Over the Rainbow."

When they came to film that song, Judy Garland, their Dorothy, was sixteen. Her eager breasts were strapped down. She wore the braids and the gingham dress of a Kansas child. But no one could subtract from her woman's voice, or the way it grasped the grown-up wistfulness of Arlen's melody. Victor Fleming was directing the picture. But suddenly there was a crisis down the street at the Selznick lot. George Cukor, the director of *Gone With the Wind,* had been fired. The picture was on hiatus. Metro-Goldwyn-Mayer had a lot of money invested in it and so Victor Fleming was assigned to take over. But Fleming hadn't quite finished on *Oz* yet so he hurried and then Louis B. Mayer asked King Vidor if—as a great kindness to his old studio—he'd come in and finish.

So Vidor came in and looked at the barnyard set and he knew it would be in sepia like all the Kansas scenes. And roughly there had been a plan for Judy to sit on a bale of hay and sing the song—or mouth it to the playback. But Vidor heard the song and he felt the line in Arlen's music, the search almost, and so he added a twist—Judy would move across the set, and the camera, holding on her face, would move with her. And so they shot it.

The picture went to its first preview and studio people fidgeted during the song. "Why is she singing in a barnyard, of all places?" they asked. And Louis B. Mayer gave the order, "Lose the song." Arlen and Harburg were crazy with anger and grief. A few others—like Arthur Freed—thought it was a pretty song. The song is in the film. It won the Oscar for Best Song that year. And I think it is the moment where a very strange, confused movie puts its foot out on the ground and says "Home!" For the rest of her life, Garland could not get off a stage or a nightclub floor without singing the song. And no one should kid you that her life was better than wretched, yet maybe when she sang the song she was "home." And to this day, when that melody lifts, like eyes looking up at the sky, and you feel Judy or Dorothy becoming a woman, anyone who ever loved Hollywood is home.

You know the rest.

The Woman in the Window (1944)

Richard Wanley is played by Edward G. Robinson, so he's fifty-one in 1944, which makes him a touch elderly to have Bobby Blake as his young son—he says good-bye to his family at the rail station as they go off for the summer. And then he's on his own. He has a bachelors' dinner where old chum Raymond Massey teases him about his liberty. It's late at night (he had fallen asleep in his chair at the club) when he goes out on the empty street and stops to admire the portrait of a woman in a nearby art gallery. It's strictly photorealist, but she's lovely and then the woman herself floats into view on the glass of the window. And . . . well, one thing leads to another and soon Mr. Wanley has had to kill someone, in self-defense.

Cut forward maybe forty-five years and there I was in upstate New York, hoping to interview Joan Bennett—the woman in the window. And there she was in her living room sitting beneath the selfsame portrait. Alas, she hardly remembered what it was: her memory was gone and she would be dead in a few years. But don't take it for granted the dream of the movies won't come to you sometimes with a perfect present.

Nunnally Johnson wrote the script, and he was quite bitter in resisting Fritz Lang's feeling that this whole story should be a fantasy or a dream. Johnson was a smart man, a good writer, and a loyal, funny friend to many—in short, a good guy. Few people ever laid such charges at Lang's door. Still, trust the artist. Lang's method was always to stage every event as if he were quoting it from the scrapbook of dream images—what I mean by that is that the brilliant compositions always underline themselves; they are in italic, and thus a touch suspect, more haunting than reliable. And the dream structure places *The Woman in the Window* in that precious category of films that define cinema itself.

The suspense is tender, mocking, ironic, the violence is performed, and the outbursts of passion are like phrases of music, nearly. And so you imagine the "orchestra" of film technicians—fifty of them, maybe—laboring over the beauty of it all. The cameraman is Milton Krasner, the art director is Duncan Cramer, the clothes are by Muriel King. And somehow all those elements are like skins to the dream, layers of flesh or silk, the amazing texture that makes you feel you could reach out, touch and stroke, or pick up the crucial scissors yourself.

Fritz Lang's is not the easiest career to grasp or like. His genius is very formal, and he often deserves the charge of being formulaic and humorless. But *The Woman in the Window* is one of his signal films. Of course, its narrative setup is very like that of *Fatal Attraction*, and it's when you put those two films side by side that you see the difference between art and sensationalism, real eroticism and just having two movie stars who will pretend they are fucking. There's hardly anything that Lang didn't do long ago, in the days when fucking was just a matter of wondering.

A Woman of Paris (1923)

A Woman of Paris was the first picture Charlie Chaplin delivered under his arrangement to be part of United Artists. And it's an odd start—not a comedy, and a film in which Chaplin himself plays only a very small role. It wasn't what UA expected—least of all Mary Pickford. Yet it was Chaplin making a new start: a full-length film, aiming at romantic sophistication—and, deep down, it was a self-portrait (as if Chaplin could make any other kind of film). At first, no one was really satisfied. But the critics admired it and many filmmakers hailed it as a model for where films might be headed. It's in answering that question that *A Woman of Paris* remains most intriguing.

It's the story of Marie (Edna Purviance), a country girl who goes to live in Paris, and who is involved romantically with two men—Jean Millet (Carl Miller), a melancholy painter, who is guarded by his mother; and Pierre Revel (Adolphe Menjou), the "richest bachelor in Paris," an insouciant womanizer. Chaplin clearly saw the two men as aspects of himself—agonized artist and near libertine—and Menjou's performance is based on Chaplin himself. Moreover, in casting Edna Purviance, he was looking back on a long relationship that had ended with Chaplin marrying Mildred Harris, and hoping to free himself from Edna by launching her career.

So it's the story of sophisticated people, and one can feel Chaplin's instinct—that educated people relate to each other more quickly and with more irony. So, this is a film searching for a more rapid, internal level of storytelling. In many places, you can feel the cutting jumping ahead of the dialogue titles—as if half-glimpsing the idea that can be unspoken. But will the unsophisticated people be able to follow it? So it ends up tortured and striving, a film reaching for tacit understanding, but never quite getting it. For instance, Chaplin wanted to convey that, on and off, Pierre lives with Marie. He came up with Pierre keeping a stock of his perfumed handkerchiefs at Marie's house. Not bad, but one or two words of dialogue—a sigh, a grunt—could obviate the need for all the acting out. In other words, it is silence that is blocking the synapses and making the story so naïve—*A Woman of Paris* is a decade after *Dubliners*!

And it's not that Chaplin had the greatest eye for anything except comedy or pathos. He doesn't actually see sophistication. But he is trying hard, and the attempt is fascinating. It has great rewards: the ending—where a hay cart (Marie) passes a swish new car (Pierre), without either one noticing—is really ironic and without smug underlining.

Alas, the performances are tough to take: Edna Purviance was pretty, and she seems good-natured, but she isn't a beauty who draws us in. She has one great scene: reading of Pierre's engagement to another, but declining to notice. But that's all, and the film didn't ignite her career. Carl Miller is grave and charmless. Only Menjou really captures the spark of the picture.

Woman of the Year (1942)

There is hardly a movie that played so large a part in a star's career (and transformation) than *Woman of the Year.* Quite simply, it is crucial in the remarketing of Katharine Hepburn, a process willingly entered into by Metro-Goldwyn-Mayer but plainly driven by the star herself. And along the way, she met Spencer Tracy. It was the start of her immense popularity. But something was lost and you can see it go in the course of this adroit picture.

One day, the young writer, Ring Lardner Jr., visited a friend on the set of *Tom, Dick and Harry,* which was being directed by Garson Kanin. Kanin said he had an idea for Kate Hepburn, a picture to follow *The Philadelphia Story* that might be instrumental in killing off the box-office-poison legend attached to the actress. Kanin suggested that Lardner develop the idea with his brother, Michael Kanin—the idea of Hepburn as a Dorothy Thompson-like columnist, a smart modern woman.

They worked hard together on a script and made a novella out of it for easier reading. The novella was in the voice of the male sports writer who falls for the woman, and it was called *The Thing About Women.* Garson sent it to Kate, and she jumped at it. She took it to M-G-M, to Louis B. Mayer, and did the deal herself—$100,000 for her and $100,000 for the two writers. Joseph L. Mankiewicz was assigned as producer and it now seems certain that Hepburn herself asked for George Stevens as director—instead of her favorite, George Cukor. She wanted a more manly approach; she knew the project needed a director who would sympathize with the guy. She was lining up for her own subjugation.

She asked for Spencer Tracy to play the sports reporter—she had asked for him before on *The Philadelphia Story.* Tracy was committed to *The Yearling,* but when that was postponed he agreed to do *Woman of the Year.* They met on the steps of the Thalberg Building. She said, "Mr. Tracy, I think you're a little short for me," and Mankiewicz told her not to worry, the actor would cut her down to size. True story? Who knows? It smells of good writing, but who can resist that?

The next important thing was the way Hepburn looked in the picture—she looked beautiful and sexy, and that comes from Stevens, from cameraman Joseph Ruttenberg, from Adrian on clothes and Sidney Guilaroff on hair. She consented to this treatment—to glamour. She showed her legs as Tess Harding and she let Tracy beat her up in a figurative way. He took the shine off her.

More than that, Stevens changed the script in which Tess had been Sam Craig's superior all the way. Whether pushed by Hepburn or not, he made an ending (written by John Lee Mahin) in which Sam gets the better of her and she has to make breakfast for him as he waits in bed—just to show that some sexual revolution wasn't in the offing. The writers protested (they would get an Oscar), and they were allowed to doctor the new ending. But its thrust remained. Katharine Hepburn had been brought down, and eternity opened up before her.

A Woman Under the Influence (1974)

Married to the actress Gena Rowlands, John Cassavetes often asked her what she'd like to do. In the early seventies, she talked about a play that dealt with the new ideas about women—feminism. Cassavetes was not a card-carrying feminist (he disliked separate interest groups), but he wrote a play for Gena, and when she said that this play would be draining, demanding, exhausting, he wrote three plays. It was the process that led eventually to the script called *A Woman Under the Influence.*

Nick Longhetti (Peter Falk) is a sewer foreman—this film is one of the few efforts to deal with an authentic working-class experience. He would say he is a man's man, which means he is most comfortable with men. So he works late on an emergency job when he was supposed to be taking his wife Mabel (Rowlands) out. One of the crew asks him, "Did you call Mabel?" "How am I gonna call her?" he asks—he is incapable of explaining or apologizing. The other fellow says that Mabel "is a delicate, sensitive woman," whereupon Nick jumps on him, "Mabel is not crazy!"

There is the heart of the film. Mabel is being driven toward madness by a man who cannot deal in the terms of her "sensitivity." This is a marriage with noise but no communication, yet Cassavetes wants to believe it is a union of deeply kindred spirits, joined by affection and experience. What the film spells out—helplessly, because it is afraid to face this—is that the two people are unsuited to marriage and to the crowded emotional demands of family life.

Mabel goes away to a hospital, and then she comes back. To a welcome that is desperate, full of yearning, but unsuitable. Nick is probably more troubled or dysfunctional than Mabel. His work is an escape, like the friendship of guys—and it is very structured. In her home life, Mabel lives out a chaos that is destroying her. With more money, more resources of intellect, Mabel would try to discard the "influence" of Nick. But they both live a warm, close style of family life that is virtually confusion.

So this is not *A Doll's House* (from which the wife must walk away). Nor is it a story about a man needing to save himself. Rather, it's a study in wounding togetherness that would be better ended but that hangs in place because of the dogma of company. Cassavetes longs for people to be and stay together, when everything recommends separation. I think he feels the Longhettis are in love—but they're in prison. And to experience the film is like watching two beasts keep bumping into each other in a cramped space. It's touching but exhausting.

The film was shot slowly in family-like circumstances. There were several people doing camera: Mitchell Breit, Gary Graver, Caleb Deschanel, Fred Elmes, among others, and the camera is not unlike these characters, blind but striving to see. *A Woman Under the Influence* is the closest Cassavetes had to a breakthrough—it got nominations for direction and for Gena Rowlands and it probably earned close to $10 million on a $1 million budget.

The Women (1939)

There was a joke going the rounds in late 1938 that the M-G-M picture of *The Women* had been devised as a suitable and merciful dumping ground for ladies who had not been cast as Scarlett O'Hara. And several eventual stars had been very interested: Paulette Goddard (the favorite until Vivien Leigh showed up), Joan Crawford, Norma Shearer (in theory), and Joan Fontaine (more likely as Melanie—which went to her sister, Olivia de Havilland). But what really paid off in the joke was that by the time the cast was assembled, dressed, and ready to go, they had George Cukor as their director—just after his firing from *Gone With the Wind,* allegedly for giving too much time to the actresses.

It was a hit Broadway comedy from 1936, written by Clare Boothe—though George S. Kaufman helped get the show mounted. The idea comes from Nevada's 1931 law offering quickie divorces, the legislation that gave Reno its brief claim to fame. Norma Shearer wants a divorce because she found that her husband was having an affair with a shopgirl (Joan Crawford). Of course, she only learned this because the spiteful Rosalind Russell set it up that way. (The concept is full of the notion that women are best employed as their own enemies.)

Anita Loos and Jane Murfin did the script and they tried to stress bitchiness and catfights as much as possible. But compared with the original play, the language of the movie was toned down far too much. The dullest moments are whenever anyone turns "sincere"—a warning gong needs to be sounded. After that, the worst thing in the picture are the clothes (by Adrian) and the daft decision to interrupt the crackling action with a fashion show sequence, an attempt to get Metro involved with Technicolor and a subtle suggestion that they, the women, are lovely if they elect to shut up. Of course, divorce was relatively new in 1939, or risqué still. It's likely that the whole leverage has dated a lot in an age when people think they're behaving however they want.

Cukor doesn't overwork, but he likes his cast and lets them romp. Oliver T. Marsh and Joseph Ruttenberg did the high-key photography, and the picture contrives a fanciful and flattering view of Reno. (The real adventures of would-be divorcées, learning to ride and fly and gamble, must have been more interesting.)

Shearer is decent but out of her league. Goddard is as pretty and funny as she was in life. Russell steals the picture. But Crawford enjoys her nastiness to the hilt. The cast also includes Mary Boland, Lucile Watson, Phyllis Povah, Ruth Hussey, Virginia Weidler, Florence Nash, Margaret Dumont, Marjorie Main, and Hedda Hopper. Look as hard as you can—you won't find a man.

What's really missing is the clublike league of powerful women in Hollywood, the way it civilized the frontier town, and its gradual development into several demure lesbian relationships. After all, if movie fostered that dopey way of gazing at women, why shouldn't some dames fall for it, too?

Women on the Verge of a Nervous Breakdown (1988)

It's a great title, one that puts the era of screwball romance and post-Franco Spain in the same jostling madhouse with happy acknowledgments to all those films that have been bold or reckless enough to put "women" in the title, from Cukor's 1939 Road to Reno jaunt, *The Women,* to *And God Created Woman* to *Desperate Housewives.* Of course, Pedro Almodóvar is Spanish, surrealist, outrageous, sexually inflamed as a young terror, and still the kind of beloved enfant terrible who knows enough of the gay perspective to put women in their place—on a trembling screen where laughter always threatens the pathos.

Pepa (Carmen Maura) is forty-plus and still ravishing, a redhead who wears pink (with orange, green, and lemon accessories), and a woman who does lip-synching in the Spanish film industry—we see her working on scenes from *Johnny Guitar* (that uncertain guide to life). Well, her man dumps her (he leaves the message on a phone answering machine) and so the woman has 88 minutes of crisis, trying to chase the guy down while looking for someone else and remembering where the drugged gazpacho is. As always with Almodóvar, the film is a study of shoes, skirts, thighs, hairdos, lipstick—no one has ever surpassed this scruffy, half-deaf urchin's adoration of women, or so persuasively indicated that the secret equation of *l'amour fou* is homosexuals gazing at women. This is a Spain designed to make General Franco shudder in his grave—preferably to a mambo rhythm. It's like TV in that it's live, throwaway, and a weird mixture of junk and speed. But Almodóvar's secret credo is "not to be bored," and he knows that film is friendly to anyone who will try anything.

Is he Buñuel or Lubitsch? No. He can never quite bring himself to be the sucker for atmosphere that those two giants managed. Almodóvar is very productive, however, and there's no doubt but that he has altered the way Spain regards itself and the living tradition of screwball feeds on new jitters. It was nominated for the Best Foreign Picture Oscar and it won the European Film Award for Almodóvar and Maura. It's the anchor to his place in international art-house cinema. He works through florid coincidence and bizarre juxtaposition and he surely rivals Buñuel and the serene surrealist openness to the most unlikely things sitting together at the same table.

He worked for years with Maura, and helped us see what a volatile and versatile personality she is, but *Women* also uses Antonio Banderas and demonstrates Almodóvar's unprejudiced appetite for glorious babes and hunks. He is at the same time a man who understands the nightmare world of AIDS and the daft golden age of Sternberg and Jean Negulesco (*Woman's World* and *The Best of Everything,* ironic titles before that genre had been generally conceived of). But it is Almodóvar's special cozy homeliness that is at the root of his warmth and his sympathy for freakishness and all other disorders.

The World of Apu (1959)

In the third part of the Apu trilogy, following *Pather Panchali* (1955) and *Aparajito* (1956), Apu (Soumitra Chatterjee) is living in the city in great poverty. He wants to be a writer, but he needs to get a job. Then one day he goes to the country to see his friend Pulu. It happens that a marriage has been arranged during Apu's stay, but when the groom arrives it is painfully clear that he is insane. It does not matter the cause, if the marriage is canceled the bride will be disgraced and cursed. Apu, an educated man, protests this primitive attitude. But he changes no minds. And so he steps into the vacancy and marries the young bride (Sharmila Tagore).

They go back to the city to live and the bride puts on a brave face, no matter how distressed she is by their poverty. A son is born, but the mother dies during childbirth. Apu goes away, helpless, bitter. The baby is looked after by the grandfather. This is a movie rooted in Indian custom yet devoted to the example of De Sica and Italian neo-realism (a great influence on writer-director Satyajit Ray). By the time Apu returns from working in a coal mine, his son is alienated and intransigent. But the prospect of reunion and a new friend brings them together. So Apu walks into the future with his young son. The train he heard in the jungle as a child remains a vivid symbol. Once the train meant escape. Now the grandfather holds the boy's toy train in his hand as the boy begins to forget it.

Photographed very simply by Subrata Mitra, and with music by Ravi Shankar, the Apu trilogy shows Ray's preference for distancing drama—for instance, we do not see the young mother dying in agony. We have to read Apu's face to measure the loss. Still, this trilogy holds a deserved place in the history of humanist cinema, and if Ray never approached the level of, say, Mizoguchi or Ozu, still he helped introduce the idea of Indian film to the world—not Bollywood, but an Indian movie that could be identified and seen outside India.

Ray and Mitra were learning, along with their actors, and there were those—François Truffaut, for one—who declared they had no patience with such slow accounts of peasant life. Ray does seem slow early in his career, and in part that's because he rejects scenes of action in favor of long moments of sadness and reflection. That changed as he grew older, and as the dramatic instinct quickened so it became easier to see Ray's tender regard for all his characters. He was a shy man, and he honors shyness above many things in his films. But the films have not dated, and in general there was a move from the East—from Tarkovsky and Sokhurov, as well as Ozu and Ray—that we needed longer to look at some things for the necessary feelings to sink in. Indian cinema, meanwhile, is the most active on earth—in great part because the country has a population that still needs the communal movie experience we have lost.

Written on the Wind (1956)

This is perhaps the most respectable example of that dauntingly unrespectable tradition—the social melodrama, another quest for love and happiness that only proves the tormenting punishment held in reserve for Americans by insisting on their pursuit of happiness. And so we have the trembling image—half-satire, half-hysteria—of Dorothy Malone as a Texas oil heiress who has everything but understanding, cuddling a model oil derrick. Throw in a color scheme that is straight out of Freud, dazzling tracking shots that are the specialty of Douglas Sirk, and a theme song by Victor Young and Sammy Cahn in which the close harmony of the Four Aces hits us with "A faithless lover's kiss is written on the wind!" (I knew I put it somewhere!)

But just as that celebrated women's picture *Mildred Pierce* tells us so much about American society circa 1945, so *Written on the Wind* is an enticing key to the locked closets of Eisenhower's nation, musclebound on power but terribly shy of its own guilty secrets. Kyle and Mitch are boyhood friends, but just as Kyle is the heir to a vast oil fortune, so Mitch is the lower-class kid who has become the family's trusted operative. Mitch is adored by Kyle's sister, Marylee, but Mitch is so decent and noble a guy that he can see Marylee is Big Trouble and an alcoholic slut in the making because while she has derricks to hug there are none to go to bed with.

And then Kyle meets Lucy from the East and marries her and—wouldn't you know it—Mitch and Lucy fall quietly, discreetly, and impassively in love. Kyle begins to sweat. He can't make Lucy pregnant. He can't swing that heir. And he begins to suspect Mitch. Then Lucy does get pregnant. And Kyle turns nasty.

All of this is from a best-selling novel by Robert Wilder and a script by George Zuckerman. But it's the casting that is so fabulously intriguing. Dorothy Malone had always been a provocateuse, eager to lead, ever since the Acme bookstore in *The Big Sleep*. Robert Stack was a he-man with a glass jaw. Lauren Bacall revealed—in Sirk's gaze—her primness. And then there is Rock Hudson playing the stalwart. Yet surely Sirk, who made eight films with Hudson, knew his innermost yearnings. And thus the real secret text in the film is the unspeakable attraction between Stack and Hudson, and the relative emotional homelessness of the women.

Russell Metty's photography puts a seething tension in the décor and in the actors' gestures—there is an espionage-like mask always about to crack. There's no doubt that this power has survived, and it was made clearer by the films of Rainer Werner Fassbinder. Still, it's fair to say that the excitement of Sirk's great diagnoses of an unsound wealthy America came in the 1950s when the films were new. There's a way in which—polished as the films are—they feel like rehearsals moving ever closer to their own heart of darkness.

W.R.: Mysteries of the Organism (1971)

It has been an interesting discovery in doing this book that several films established as radical some decades ago, but not always seen in the passing years, take your breath away as you come back to them when checking on whether they deserve a place in the 1,000. So, as I planned lists toward this survey, I penciled in *W.R.* without too much thought. At the moment when I began teaching film, it was the rage. I then met Dusan Makavejev and became friendly with him—I believe we once talked about a kind of "Cinema Inferno," a film in which a child film buff in war-torn Yugoslavia hunts for the final reel to *The Wizard of Oz* (which he has never been able to see).

Well, things turned out rough in Dusan's country and his health has not always been of the best. So meetings became fewer—and he has not made enough films for someone of his extraordinary mind. And sometimes the films one has loved once are disappointments. Not this. *W.R.* is wicked, exuberant, funny, sexy; it is just one more film to suggest that the early seventies was a hell of a time, when all over the world it seemed there were brilliant minds finding quite new and startling ways to put films together and trap us in the middle of the experience.

Of course, 1971 was during the Cold War, which was harsh and cozy by turns, but which certainly allowed for more vigorous comedy than our current attitude toward Russia. *W.R.* means Wilhelm Reich, in one sense—the amiably dotty American theorist on sexual suppression and the creator of the orgone box. A good deal of the film traces his uneven life and shows various attempts at the enactment of his theories. In turn, this cuts against and into the story of Milena (Milena Dravic), an exemplary and liberated Yugoslavian girl who wants to assist and participate in the sexual liberation of a Soviet skating star.

In fact, Reich's kindred figure in the film is Josef Stalin, a massive if somewhat frozen sexual presence and a version of a political ice age in Makavejev's guerrilla thinking. It's clear he prefers Milena to Stalin, but it's equally apparent that the film realizes how very eccentric Reich is. The virtues of his thinking have not dispelled his comic isolation as an intellectual figure in the American hinterland. But Makavejev is and was a satirist who was reconciled to the likelihood of any deeply thoughtful person coming across as a madman (in the U.S. as much as in Russia).

At just 86 minutes, and photographed by Pega Popovic and Aleksandar Petkovic in a kind of instant color, *W.R.* is less a self-conscious film than a rabid examination of consciousness happy to try any method that comes to mind. Its origins lie in agitprop theater, and maybe in Serbian/Slav folklore as much as in the coded structures of television and advertising. There were thoughts and plans for Makavejev to make something—anything—in America, and it is plainly our loss that he was not made more welcome. He was never going to be a natural storyteller, but as a student of psychology, history, and ideology he is a fascinating commentator on fallacy and phallacy alike. But he is seventy-six now, and so it is up to books like this to insist on *W.R.: Mysteries of the Organism.*

The Wrong Man (1957)

"In 1952, I think," Hitchcock told François Truffaut, "a musician at New York's Stork Club went home at two o'clock in the morning. In front of his door he was met by two men who hauled him off to different places, like saloons, and asked various people there, 'Is this the man?' Anyway, he was arrested and charged with a hold-up. Though he was completely innocent, he had to stand trial, and eventually, as a result of all the trouble, his wife lost her mind and was put in an insane asylum."

Manny Balestrero is a stooped bass player, and we see the long fingers of Henry Fonda plucking at the strings as we hear the heartbeat of his music in this most mysterious of Hitchcock films. It's not that the master hadn't often teased us with stories of people of absolute innocence outraged by accusation. It's not that we ever forgot Hitch's story about how his father once had him locked up for an hour or so in the local police station. But the stories of outraged innocence are so often pitched on the edge of comic absurdity (*The 39 Steps, North by Northwest*) and I don't think there is a laugh in *The Wrong Man*. Indeed, you can hear in Hitchcock's own account of it how close this is to the expected horror of Kafka—one day, two men just took him away. It's not even that they had to say they were policemen. But don't we all deserve and expect, somehow, to be quietly apprehended—and never seen again?

So, it's immaterial that *The Wrong Man* is based on a real case when its entire atmosphere concerns an appointment foretold, or an arrest in the ordinary way of things. The mood goes through disbelief to anger to dread and all the time that blank air of normalcy beckons. Won't a time come when it seems proper? That's when we notice that the wife (Vera Miles) is not quite herself—and realize that Manny's ordeal has yet one more twist to take: that his wife will go crazy. And it's then that you feel how close this world has come to Bresson. For getting what you deserve—such a stalwart principle in American film—has gone out the window. And even if Manny is cleared, with that haunting moment when the right man walks forward and occupies the outline of the wrong man (like Hitch fitting his own silhouette on the TV show) still there is no mercy for the wife. Perhaps she will get better. But perhaps she can never recover from this glimpse of bad luck. How are you going to muster the nerve to go out tomorrow?

In the end, that's what *The Wrong Man* is about—the way in which nihilism or inertia can smother being and activity once bad luck is proved as a principle in the world. Of course, it is the film made before *Vertigo*, which only goes to sharpen the question, Do we earn all our bad luck? Or is there a fate that sometimes plays the game of getting us, too?

Wuthering Heights (1939)

Emily Brontë's great novel, published in 1847, has had a strange career in the movies: there is the Buñuel film, *Abismos de Pasión* (1950), sufficient to remind us that the novel was always a favorite of the surrealists and is a testament to forbidden or mad love; there is the Rivette film, *Hurlevent*, that touches on the novel; there have been two British versions, one with Timothy Dalton and Anna Calder-Marshall, the other with Ralph Fiennes and Juliette Binoche; there is even *Devotion*, a Warner Brothers biopic on the family, with Olivia de Havilland as Charlotte, Ida Lupino as Emily, and Arthur Kennedy as their brother, Branwell.

And there is the William Wyler picture, with Laurence Olivier and Merle Oberon, the famous one that got nominations for Best Picture, Best Director, for Olivier and for Geraldine Fitzgerald. The one where the Yorkshire moors north of Haworth are replaced with the rolling Conejo Hills of California. It was a Goldwyn production, and for once Wyler was unable to find or hold on to its saving reality. It is a terrible film (genteel and restrained) that seems to have no idea what the book is, how it works, or where its greatness lies.

The story of the film is bizarre. Ben Hecht and Charles MacArthur did a script on vacation and on spec. They got Walter Wanger interested in it, and Wanger had a mind to cast Charles Boyer and Sylvia Sidney. Then he quarreled with Sidney and sold the script to Goldwyn. All that mogul knew was it had to be directed by William Wyler. Wyler suggested Bette Davis. Goldwyn insisted on Merle Oberon, and then thought of Laurence Olivier. Searching in England, Wyler found Robert Newton and knew he was right for the part. It was a brilliant decision, for Heathcliff must be far from handsome—he must be rough, poor, and nearly ugly. Of course, Wyler thought of Vivien Leigh as he met Olivier, but he couldn't see her rising higher than Isabella. The proper casting? Newton and Wendy Hiller—but then Goldwyn would never have made it.

He tried to change the title, which he could not understand, but was told it was a classic and had to stay. So he worked away at everything else. Gregg Toland was hired to give it a shadow and candlelight look. The great out-of-doors was entirely wrong. Olivier was a matinee idol. And Merle Oberon was a travesty. Wyler grilled the actors. He went for take after take, as if he knew that the secret of the book was not coming across. But it is a book about houses as prisons as well as places of security. The outside—the open—is liberty itself, a world of spirits. And it is a ghost story. But its style should be rough, simple, and stark. Wyler made it a love story whereas it is a book about the hopelessness of love written by a young woman disposed to blow the china set called Jane Austen to smithereens. It is in no way a comfortable or classic novel. It is a book about ecstasy and loss.

The rich supporting cast includes David Niven, Flora Robson, Donald Crisp, Hugh Williams, Leo G. Carroll, Miles Mander, Cecil Kellaway, and Rex Downing.

Yankee Doodle Dandy (1942)

In 1939, George M. Cohan was sixty-one and ailing. He was also the supreme figure in the history of American musical theater—a songwriter, an actor, a singer and dancer, a playwright, and a producer. His heyday had been from about 1910 to 1930 and his great moment was America's involvement in the First World War and his 1917 song "Over There." In December 1939, he consulted with a play about his own life, *Yankee Doodle Boy,* written by the young Walter Kerr. It never made New York—the timing was off. But by 1941, the state of the war had changed. So Cohan tried to mount a movie about himself: he nearly got Goldwyn and Astaire to sign on, but Fred felt it was not quite him. Then a friend suggested Jimmy Cagney. Plainly, this was good casting, but Cagney was the more interested because he was being charged as a Communist. So Jimmy's brother, William, went to Warners. Cohan got $125,000 and 10 percent of the gross. Cagney got another 10 percent. A staggering contract.

The script job was given to Robert Buckner, with Cohan's request that his private life be omitted! Buckner absorbed a great deal of material from Cohan—but it was a tough grind, with very little humor. So the script was passed over to the Epstein brothers. They stressed the relationship between Cohan and his wife, Mary (Joan Leslie). They cut out a pack of Cohan cronies and they added comedy. But it was Buckner who had set up the framework of Cohan telling his story to Franklin Roosevelt—a role Cohan had played in *I'd Rather Be Right,* the 1937 Rodgers and Hart musical.

You can read the script and still wonder whether this was a viable project. But you have not yet encountered the glee with which Cagney took the part by the scruff of its own neck and shook it until it possessed him. I do not minimize the work of director Michael Curtiz—he was in charge of so many great entertainments, in such a range of moods, that he has to be honored. James Wong Howe shot it. But Cagney estimated that not many people really knew or recalled how Cohan had moved. So Cohan would be Cagney. John Boyle worked on the dance numbers, but Cagney was a trained hoofer and the toy soldier exuberance comes from him and it determines the way Cohan moves in the nonmusical scenes.

Thus it is that a mere name in theater history is one of the great moving images in film history—strutting, his ass pointed outward, his head jutting forward. It is punchy, elegant, dainty, and dangerous all at the same time. It was also a blessed choice, for which Cagney won the Oscar. For the rest, Joan Leslie is sweet, Walter Huston is very good as Cohan's father. The cast also includes Richard Whorf, Irene Manning, George Tobias, Rosemary DeCamp, Jeanne Cagney, Frances Langford, S. Z. Sakall, Walter Catlett, and Eddie Foy Jr.

Yankee Doodle Dandy premiered on May 29, 1942, at a gala that raised $4.75 million in war bonds. On November 5, Cohan himself died, a happy man.

The Year of Living Dangerously (1983)

Australia has its own view of the world, one that has no choice but to live in the Pacific. *The Year of Living Dangerously* is one of the few films that spring from that point of view, and asks us all what we know about Indonesia. More than twenty years after the film was made, do we know much more collectively? You can hope that the era of Sukarno has passed, and that is the crisis of Peter Weir's film, but now we know that Indonesia has a formidably large Islamic population, even if it is not "like" Arab countries. And we know that danger still lives there. How long is it before we see the equation between the danger and our ignorance? After all, elsewhere, we have lived to regret deposing one tyrant and his terrible order.

It's a story about an Australian journalist, Guy Hamilton (Mel Gibson), assigned to Jakarta in 1965. He is helped there by Billy Kwan, Chinese-Australian (Linda Hunt) and an endlessly mysterious figure. He also meets and has an affair with Jill Bryant (Sigourney Weaver), who is attached to the British embassy. But the situation deteriorates in Jakarta. Guy is badly hurt and he and Jill only just get away in time.

The story came from a novel by C. J. Koch, and Koch, Weir, and David Williamson all worked on a script that leaves a healthy place for the romance and is generally content to equate Indonesia's unfamiliarity with the mysteries of strange societies. But Billy is a remarkable character, torn in his own allegiances, very eager to be accepted, and almost the embodiment of complicated insights in his mixed racial identity and his considerable gender intrigue—it was clear that he was being played by a woman, even if sexual ambivalence was not a large part of the role.

But the other thing is that just as Peter Weir showed a terrific appetite for the erotic relationship that coexists with suspicion on both parts, so it's a film (a little like *The Third Man*) where we learn to trust no one and nothing. The feeling of menace or paranoia is very strong—and it comes in part from just one shot of "Sukarno" watching Guy. It's an actor, of course, and the film was shot in the Philippines, but there's a powerful sense of documentary implications.

The Billy character is himself fascinated with Javanese puppets and the role of puppet master, and sometimes this adds a bit too much "mysterioso" to nasty confrontations with crowds and police who do not speak our language. Of course, this was an Australian film financed by an American major (M-G-M/UA), and the sexiness of it all was played up along with the old notion that the East is a strange place. But Weir is too good to shuffle it all off like that, and in hindsight I'm inclined to guess that he might be just the filmmaker to get at a story that exposes the awkward gap in the way Europeans and Islamists think and feel. Also with Michael Murphy, Bill Kerr, and Noel Ferrier. Hunt won a Best Supporting Oscar (quickly—actor or actress?).

Yentl (1983)

Any venture including Barbra Streisand that asks for her not to be noticed or recognized—in other words, where attention is not being paid—is a stretch. It is not just that we may be skeptical about Barbra passing as a man, or a boy. It's the failure to register a superstar, or a very large ego, that is most far-fetched. And exactly that dislocation is evident in the film between the alleged hiddenness of her character and the vast, sweeping songs that seem eager to take on the sky and space itself—as well as the largest movie theater you can dream of. Isaac Bashevis Singer's Yentl—the girl who puts on men's clothes to get herself a male education—requires a concealed, shy yearning. And shy is not quite Barbra—as witness the nearly total way in which this picture was hers. In short, there are people who think *Yentl* is impossible.

But there it is—very well made, at certain points directed with flair and precision, and with one of the great scores in film history. I know, in the process it has become so large that it is a recipe for all kinds of feminism, and when Yentl sings "Papa, Can You Hear Me?," a beautiful, keening song, we were left in no doubt about the therapy rinse Barbra was giving to her own relationship with a father.

But Streisand also had the vision and the taste to know that Michel Legrand was the man to write this score. And then Legrand recognized the range of Streisand's unprecedented voice and delivered lines and musical moments that were a feast for her. The lyrics to these songs—by Alan and Marilyn Bergman—are a lot more uncertain. There's a feeling that this Yentl is going to end up in Las Vegas—and in truth an entire casino called "Barbra" would not be inconsistent with her talent.

Yes, the real charm of *The Umbrellas of Cherbourg* is that we never forget that Cherbourg is a small, provincial town without emotional underlining, and without the massive orchestration of this film. *Yentl* could have been done much smaller—by which I mean to say as quiet, Jewish songs sung a capella or to a single instrument. They become production numbers, and so Yentl needs to fly to get away from ordinary groundling feelings.

Never mind, the actual storytelling—with Mandy Patinkin, Nehemiah Persoff, and Amy Irving—is very well done. The songs are great and there is a way in which every uncertain Jewish beauty deserves a *Yentl* now and then the way inarticulate Italian gigolos want a *Rocky*. Both films are species of modern opera—in which case *Yentl* worked better because it has the score. So Barbra directed a film. The Academy turned their back on her (there was an Oscar to Legrand and the Bergmans), but stars of her size must adapt to that kind of ignorance in the world. And pass on, driven by song and forgiveness.

The "it" in American movie titles is often supposed to be sex, but Capra knew it was money. The film came from a hit play by Moss Hart and George S. Kaufman, that had opened on Broadway in 1936. It was a farce set in the Vanderhof household in New York City where everyone pursues his or her passion without much success until a granddaughter invites her fiance's rich parents to the house and there are several lessons about money, America, and how we're all poor when we're dead. It is a well-made play about eccentricity, a cozy reassurance about being poor, and a blithe hope that in troubled times Americans can stay "wacky." In short, it's screwball made under the shadow of a war that would wipe away most of those lazy attitudes. And as a reminder, the House Committee on Un-American Activities was formed in 1938, the year Capra's film of the play appeared, in which a charge is made that the Vanderhofs are "un-American."

Capra was in trouble after the financial failure of *Lost Horizon*—and anyone who could swallow that Utopianism in 1937 needed bed rest. He was about to plunge into a venture on Chopin and George Sand (with Charles Boyer and Marlene Dietrich), when the Hart-Kaufman play came into view, with a script by Robert Riskin. That recipe did the trick. *You Can't Take It with You* would win Best Picture. It did very nicely as a business venture, and it kept contact with the myth that Frank Capra had seriously radical ideas.

Joseph Walker shot it in fifty-six days with an all-star cast. The picture cost $1.64 million, and it would earn rentals of $2.13 million in its first year. Yet it has lasted less well than *Mr. Deeds* or *Mr. Smith,* precisely because it is enclosed, rather smug, and happy to be funny, while the two earlier films at least raise many problems and leave us with that queasy feeling that is still the most interesting thing about Capra. Deeds and Smith threaten many orthodoxies. The Vanderhofs are amiable nuts who rarely go out-of-doors. They are already confined.

Joseph McBride has raised the point that *You Can't Take It with You* was made as Capra was realizing that he was a millionaire and taking steps to guard his "it." So you can think of this as a picture where Capra got his confidence back, and in which he made a lightweight defense of eccentricity, and a first happy meeting with Jimmy Stewart. Graham Greene put his finger on it: "The director emerges as a rather muddled and sentimental idealist who feels—vaguely—that something is wrong with the social system." But don't ask what, and don't think too hard about solutions. The contrast with *La Règle du Jeu* is striking: two enclosed groups, both riddled with maverick tendencies. But for Capra "romance" was so simple a step, and for Renoir it is the disease that is making a plague.

Capra also won his third Best Director Oscar, a tribute to his unabating instinct for physical comedy and a crowded frame. The cast also included Jean Arthur (the most appealing person in view, sane and calm, but defending the nuts), Lionel Barrymore, Mischa Auer, Ann Miller, Spring Byington (nominated), Eddie Anderson, Donald Meek, Halliwell Hobbes, Harry Davenport, and Ward Bond.

Young Mr. Lincoln (1939)

The matter of legend and history hangs over the American cinema. Even those of us who believe that in certain key ways the medium once belonged to America (or was fashioned to express it), cannot dismiss the charge that those same movies have ruined a nation's sense of history. And when America becomes in so many respects not just the most powerful nation on earth but also the one that is most hungry to be admired, it has to be allowed that ruined history may be a prelude to an infinitely larger damage in the world. In other words, this issue would not be as important as it is if America had not insisted on being the world's star.

So consider Abraham Lincoln. What does he mean? More or less, people say that he was the greatest president the country has had. To be blunt, was that because he "won" the Civil War? Was it because he took the country into that war? Or was it because he quietly insisted on what that war was about—which is to say, a prolonged struggle between principle and practice which would not be solved in his lifetime? Was he a figure of more than human insight and understanding, or was he a man who could see beyond local interests and partisanship to recognize that the black Americans must be empowered, and all Americans remain citizens?

Why did John Ford think to make *Young Mr. Lincoln* in 1939? In all the immense commentary on the film that *Cahiers du Cinema* published, and in all the praise of Ford by American writers, this question goes unanswered. And the decision to make the film was personal. *Stagecoach* was by far Ford's "major" film of 1939: it was nominated for Best Picture and for director—*Young Mr. Lincoln* got neither nod and it did only modestly. There was no anniversary. But there was the sense of a coming crisis and the uncertainty as to whether Roosevelt should run again after his two terms in 1940. I think the urge to look at Lincoln came out of that questioning.

You can call that patriotic, or a sign of Ford's deep wish for some men to be like gods. Yet in the study of history, men are not gods, no matter how pious or benign they may seek to be. You cannot attempt good in the world without arousing those who charge you with harm. For every positive thing Lincoln did, you can point to the damage. The best explanation of how a man could look so weary, so sad, so accepting as he does in his last photographs is the nature of that burden. (The face of Lincoln is that of a man who has read the Faulkner novels not yet written.) Which is entirely human and historical. And in the same way there is no way of treating Lincoln except through the facts.

Yet *Young Mr. Lincoln* is a film about collective mood, about the national reference that has so many streets called Lincoln and which accepts the myth that this difficult, dangerous man (because he would not stop thinking) can be tidily put under glass and labeled "hero," or some such. The film—which imagines Lincoln's youth in Illinois in the most enchantingly casual, naturalistic, and matter-of-fact way—is religious. But Lincoln was not subject to religion.

So the film is a sublime dream, most artfully rendered, richly entertaining, with Henry Fonda in a kind of trance of worship, and Ford indulging every treasured feeling for a past he would have loved to inhabit. To the degree that Lincoln is a legend and film a dream, this is nearly perfect. But because Lincoln was real, actual, and made out of difficult thought, this film is a travesty and deeply antidemocratic. For it wants to believe that democracy does not rely on the steady application of human effort and compromise.

You Only Live Once (1937)

"ET" it says inside the hat—that's how Eddie Taylor (Henry Fonda) gets sent to prison as a third-time loser in *You Only Live Once*, which is Fritz Lang's most magnificent account of malign destiny snuffing out true love and a man's chance. Of course, the "ET" was somebody else.

It is said that the prospect of the story arose when Walter Wanger and Sylvia Sidney bumped into Theodore Dreiser, who had been writing an article about Bonnie and Clyde. What a subject, the novelist said, and what a part Bonnie Parker could be for Sylvia. Wanger was looking for a new project to release through United Artists and he got Gene Towne to come up with a treatment. In turn, Graham Baker wrote the screenplay. It was only then that Ms. Sidney, impressed by his direction on *Fury*, suggested that Fritz Lang might direct the picture.

Henry Fonda may have asked her later why she did that—for he found Lang boorish, humorless, and relentless and didn't like him, either. But Sylvia Sidney was getting an education. On *Sabotage*, in England, in 1936, she had been bewildered as to what Hitchcock was doing on the key sequences—everything was fragmented. Then she saw the result, and realized that she was great in the picture. Lang worked in much the same way—reaction shots in close-up to fit into the pattern.

Lang was a dictator, but the rewards are there on the screen. He composed everything in advance in detail, and made as much of an enemy of the cameraman Leon Shamroy as he did of Fonda. But then look at the emotional force in the compositions. Feel the growing sense of trap and enclosure, and see the way in which décor and lighting are being used to the same fateful ends. So many American crime films of this era made a pass at pointing to the social background or the man's violent nature as reasons for his criminal career. In *You Only Live Once*, it's as if the condition of being seen or photographed is enough to dramatize the desperate peril in every choice.

What is really remarkable is not just how fully Lang had adapted to American films and talk, as the way in which sound had been added to the visual as if it had always been there. Voices in the fog, gunfire, and the mood of music (Alfred Newman's) have been effortlessly incorporated. And Eddie becomes an Everyman, a nearly Bressonian character tossing a coin over God or life. Lang made such problems for himself and never really had a hit in America—but this is one of the most beautiful movies ever made.

In hindsight, it doesn't have much to do with Bonnie and Clyde. As Arthur Penn showed us, those sexy hoodlums just wanted to make a name for themselves and to hold on to their ampersand. They die happy—death is their coming. But Eddie and his girl Joan in Lang's world are models for the eternally underprivileged and unlucky. And Lang never lost his sympathy for those figures.

You, the Living (2007)

As I drew close to completing my selection of a thousand films for you, I yielded to the natural human hope for surprise. My deadline was December 2007—so I had a dream surprise lined up in my head: that on the brink of finality, I might encounter not just a very appealing film but a great director. And so, in August 2007, knowing my predicament, and taking a properly wicked pleasure in it, Tom Luddy asked me if I'd seen any Roy Andersson. No, I replied, though somehow I knew the name was double "s" from Sweden, and not a plumber's mate from Bethnal Green.

So a DVD appeared of *You, the Living*, which had played (to a prolonged ovation) at Cannes in 2007. I was staggered—not just by the exquisite medley of Célinean dismay, Chaplinesque optimism, amazing diagonal compositions, lugubrious color control—the film feels as if it's on heavy valium and needs more—but by the absolute clarity with which someone has said, "Look, look at me—or look at things a new way." I was immediately under the worst opposite pressure, for as I was delivering late entries my unique editor, Bob Gottlieb, was despairing at how many "greats" and "masterpieces" the book had already. So I must choose my words carefully—*You, the Living* is impossible to describe or forget. It helps open up a new and very becoming modern genre—I'd like to call it "film flat," in that it is founded in the absolutely calm, unexcitable view of the dreadfulness of life. "Film flat" is a noble tradition, easily accommodating Bela Tarr and Ozu, but open to so many others who elect to put a brave face, or a numb mind, on the worst of possible worlds.

Yet Andersson has not filmed Dachau, Darfur, or Dresden in its fire—no, I've heard Swedes say, "Oh, that's just Sweden," which sometimes volunteers for the status of utopia. And *You, the Living* is a variety of single-shot views or panoramas of the bored and boring dystopia.

If that sounds depressing, you have not encountered the extraordinary, ravishing humor of Andersson—thus a man going to the electric chair is told to think of something else. The clichés of stupidity ring through the film like the forlorn yet plucky brass-band instruments that he cherishes.

It will dawn on you that these random views of ordinariness are far from documentary: Andersson builds sets and keeps a tight body of players who take many parts. Then you begin to appreciate the courage and the beauty of this vision. Andersson knows how bad the world is, and he knows the fraud that distorts it for commercials (that is his main occupation). But this and the earlier *Songs from the Second Floor* (2000) are his conscience. And they are vital parts of the best of modern cinema. You must see it!

Z (1969)

Z was a political thriller attended by such controversy that it left you believing there was a real issue within the film. It is based on the murder of George Lambrakis, a Greek deputy, in 1963. The killing was the work of right-wingers, allegedly with the support of the police. It became a burning scandal and a self-sufficient incident in Greece—where "Z" can mean "he is alive still"—and by the time the film opened, all reference to the matter was banned in a Greece led by the colonels' junta. As a result, the film was made as a French production (shot largely in Algeria), though Mikis Theodorakis's score was apparently smuggled out of Greece, where he was living under house arrest. Almost as a concession to that courage and novelty, Z got a Best Picture nomination, and it has plenty of power even if it looks rather Warner Brothers from the 1940s next to *The Battle of Algiers*.

The movie was based on a novel derived from the real case by Vassili Vassilikos, and it was scripted by Jorge Semprún. At first, we see the Lambrakis figure (all names are changed and the country goes unnamed), played by Yves Montand, before he is killed. Then Jean-Louis Trintignant is the magistrate whose suspicions are enough to call it murder. Costa-Gavras directed in a very robust way, aided by some fine color photography by Raoul Coutard. The picture was made a good deal more impressive—and less likely to be ignored—by a starry supporting cast that included Irene Papas, Charles Denner, Georges Géret, Jacques Perrin, François Périer, Marcel Bozzuffi, Renato Salvatori, and Pierre Dux.

The tone is austere and I don't doubt the commitment of most of the filmmakers. But the trouble is that this kind of shadowy political intrigue had been common (and sometimes brilliant) in feature films for a long time. So it's very difficult for re-creations like Z to be better than, say, *Casablanca* or *The Third Man,* or to convey the authentic detail of a complex situation to a large audience. It is very difficult for the movies to do such cases as this and not leave the viewer uncertain about their veracity. The dead end of the whole process may be *JFK* and *Nixon,* overburdened with research, skill, and care in the acting but finally helpless confusions of history and legend. Television—drier, smaller, and quicker—has a far better record at bringing us the truth about these cases while we still feel angry.

One plain conclusion is that movie is not always a very helpful medium journalistically. Movies so easily yield to their own atmosphere and make the intrigue as dark as noir plotting. It's in that sense that *The Battle of Algiers* stays stirring and credible. Still, it's intriguing to see Trintignant's watchful face as the magistrate—and to compare it, next year, with his assassin in *The Conformist.* But no one had doubts over which was the better film, even if Z won the Oscar for Best Foreign Picture.

Zabriskie Point (1970)

Just as *Easy Rider* is a warning example of changing times in 1969, so is Michelangelo Antonioni's *Zabriskie Point*, where on the box-office strength of *Blow-Up* the utterly determined and unsharing artist was offered the U.S.A., a budget of $7 million, and Metro-Goldwyn-Mayer to make . . . just about whatever he wanted, or emerged with, from a strange period of rumination and improvisation. The result is something I love, no matter that it grossed about $800,000, and is altogether rather like Monica Vitti's faltering English trying to come to terms with the dry lucidity of Joan Didion.

The confusions and pretensions surely derived from the awe with which the studio regarded their Michelangelo, but it is evident in the array of screenwriters—Antonioni himself, Tonino Guerra (his regular), plus Fred Gardner, Sam Shepard, and Clare Peploe. Then you have to deal with the dumb Adam-and-Eve-like beauty of the raw leads—Mark Frechette and Daria Halprin—who simply could not act. And so the preparation became a weird mixture of consultations with Black Panthers and the creation of superb and insane Ozymandian houses in the desert, with sets by the very skilled Dean Tavoularis.

Two kids go on the lam from student politics and the very vague oppression of Americana and head for the desert. In fact, the vestiges of plot and narrative dialogue are so embarrassing that you train your sensibility to gaze past them at the distance, the shapes, and light. And that is where the film is. It would have been so much more coherent if Antonioni had been free of script or actors, and if he and cameraman Alfio Contini had just been let loose in the Southwest.

There is an orgy at Zabriskie Point itself, though orgy is a generous word for a director who closed his eyes in despair at the thought of sexual congress. Perhaps he did it to please his desperate studio who were just eager to get a bunch of kids out of their clothes and into the dust. Still, there are moments in that sequence in which the lovers begin to resemble the ashen ecstasies from Pompeii—I think of Rossellini's *Journey to Italy*, and the dogged resistance in American melodrama to what you might call novelistic cinema.

I would not include the film here—despite my attachment to Antonioni—but for the ending. With Pink Floyd's music, we see the repeated explosion of one of the desert mansions—and not just the blooming fire and smoke but also the prolonged, distended scattering of all the interior things in the house—clothes fluttering from closets, provisions bursting out of refrigerators, the pages of books riffling in the breeze (or in the water where these scenes were filmed). This rhapsody could stand alone—it should—as a magnificent short film, and a single denunciation of the collected television commercials of fifty years. In the montage of American movie, there have to be moments from this aria on disruption. Metro got their money's worth—even if their innocence remained intact.

Chronology

1895
L'Arroseur Arrossé
1903
The Great Train Robbery
1913
Fantômas
1914
Tillie's Punctured Romance
1915
The Birth of a Nation
1916
Intolerance
1917
Thomas Graal's Best Film
1918
The Outlaw and His Wife
1919
Broken Blossoms
J'Accuse
Male and Female
1920
The Cabinet of Dr. Caligari
Erotikon
Way Down East
1921
The Four Horsemen of the Apocalypse
Tol'able David
The Wild Cat
1922
Dr. Mabuse the Gambler
Foolish Wives
Nosferatu
Orphans of the Storm
Robin Hood
1923
The Covered Wagon
The Hunchback of Notre Dame
Safety Last!
The Ten Commandments
A Woman of Paris
1924
Greed
He Who Gets Slapped
The Iron Horse
The Last Laugh
The Navigator
Die Nibelungen
Sherlock Jr.
The Thief of Bagdad
Wild Oranges
1925
Battleship Potemkin
Ben-Hur
The Big Parade
The Gold Rush
The Joyless Street
Lady of the Night
Master of the House
The Merry Widow
The Phantom of the Opera
Seven Chances
Strike
1926
Faust
Flesh and the Devil
Mare Nostrum
The Son of the Sheik
Sparrows
The Temptress
What Price Glory?
The Winning of Barbara Worth
1927
The General
It
The Italian Straw Hat
London After Midnight
The Man with a Movie Camera
Metropolis
Napoleon
7th Heaven
Sunrise
Underworld
The Unknown
Wings
1928
Un Chien Andalou
The Crowd
Lonesome
La Passion de Jeanne d'Arc
Queen Kelly
Sadie Thompson
Show People
The Wind
1929
Applause
Blackmail
The Love Parade
Pandora's Box
People on Sunday
1930
L'Âge d'Or
All Quiet on the Western Front
Anna Christie
The Blue Angel
Earth
Hell's Angel's
Morocco
1931
The Champ
La Chienne
City Lights
City Streets
Dracula
Frankenstein
Kameradschaft
M
Le Million
Platinum Blonde
Public Enemy
Que Viva Mexico
Street Scene
Tabu
The Threepenny Opera
Waterloo Bridge
1932
Boudu Sauvé des Eaux
Dr. Jekyll and Mr. Hyde
Freaks
I Am a Fugitive from a Chain Gang
I Was Born But . . .
Liebelei
Love Me Tonight
The Music Box
Red Dust
Red-Headed Woman
Scarface
Shanghai Express
The Sign of the Cross
The Testament of Dr. Mabuse
Trouble in Paradise
Vampyr
What Price Hollywood?
1933
Baby Face
The Bitter Tea of General Yen
Dancing Lady
Dinner at Eight
Duck Soup
Exstase
42nd Street
The Gold Diggers of 1933
King Kong
Little Women
Outskirts
1934
L'Atalante
Imitation of Life
It Happened One Night
Judge Priest
The Merry Widow
Of Human Bondage
Our Daily Bread
The Scarlet Empress
La Signora di Tutti
Tarzan and His Mate
The Thin Man
Toni
Treasure Island
Twentieth Century
1935
Alice Adams
Bride of Frankenstein
David Copperfield
The Devil Is a Woman
The Informer
A Midsummer Night's Dream
Mutiny on the Bounty
A Night at the Opera
Peter Ibbetson
Ruggles of Red Gap
Steamboat Round the Bend
Sylvia Scarlett
A Tale of Two Cities
The 39 Steps
Top Hat
1936
Camille
Come and Get It
Le Crime de Monsieur Lange
Desire
Dodsworth
Fury
The Great Ziegfeld
Modern Times
Mr. Deeds Goes to Town
My Man Godfrey
Une Partie de Campagne
The Petrified Forest
San Francisco
Show Boat
Swing Time
1937
The Awful Truth
Black Legion
Un Carnet de Bal
Easy Living
The Good Earth
La Grande Illusion
History Is Made at Night
The Life of Emile Zola
Make Way for Tomorrow
Mannequin
Nothing Sacred
Pépé le Moko
The Prisoner of Zenda
Snow White and the Seven Dwarfs
Stage Door
A Star Is Born
Stella Dallas
Swing High, Swing Low
You Only Live Once
1938
The Adventures of Robin Hood
Alexander Nevsky
Angels with Dirty Faces
The Baker's Wife

Bringing Up Baby
Carefree
Holiday
Jezebel
The Lady Vanishes
La Marseillaise
Pygmalion
Quai des Brumes
Three Comrades
You Can't Take It with You

1939

Dark Victory
Destry Rides Again
Gone With the Wind
Gunga Din
Le Jour Se Lève
Love Affair
Midnight
Mr. Smith Goes to Washington
Ninotchka
Only Angels Have Wings
The Rules of the Game
Stagecoach
The Stars Look Down
The Story of the Late Chrysanthemums
The Wizard of Oz
The Women
Wuthering Heights
Young Mr. Lincoln

1940

The Bank Dick
Broadway Melody of 1940
Fantasia
The Grapes of Wrath
The Great Dictator
The Great McGinty
His Girl Friday
The Letter
The Mortal Storm
The Philadelphia Story
Rebecca
The Shop Around the Corner
They Drive by Night
The Thief of Bagdad

1941

Ball of Fire
Citizen Kane
High Sierra
Hold Back the Dawn
How Green Was My Valley
The Lady Eve
The Little Foxes
The Maltese Falcon
Man Hunt
Meet John Doe
Penny Serenade
That Hamilton Woman
Two-Faced Woman

1942

Bambi
Casablanca
Cat People
Gentleman Jim
The Hard Way
The Magnificent Ambersons
Now, Voyager
Ossessione
The Palm Beach Story
Sullivan's Travels
To Be or Not To Be
Went the Day Well?
Woman of the Year
Yankee Doodle Dandy

1943

Air Force
Cabin in the Sky
Day of Wrath
For Whom the Bell Tolls
Hail the Conquering Hero
Hangmen Also Die!
I Walked with a Zombie
The Life and Death of Colonel Blimp
Lumière d'Été
The More the Merrier
The Ox-Bow Incident
The Seventh Victim
Shadow of a Doubt

1944

An American Romance
Cover Girl
Double Indemnity
Frenzy
Gaslight
Going My Way
Henry V
Laura
Meet me in St. Louis
Ministry of Fear
The Miracle of Morgan's Creek
Mr. Skeffington
Phantom Lady
Since You Went Away
To Have and Have Not
The Woman in the Window

1945

Brief Encounter
The Clock
Les Dames du Bois de Boulogne
Detour
Les Enfants du Paradis
I Know Where I'm Going
Ivan the Terrible
Leave Her to Heaven
The Lost Weekend
Mildred Pierce
Open City
The Picture of Dorian Gray
Scarlet Street
Spellbound
The Strange Affair of Uncle Harry
They Were Expendable

1946

La Belle et la Bête
The Best Years of Our Lives
The Big Sleep
The Chase
Diary of a Chambermaid
Duel in the Sun
Gilda
Great Expectations
Humoresque
It's a Wonderful Life
The Killers
A Matter of Life and Death
My Darling Clementine
Notorious
The Outlaw
Paisan
The Postman Always Rings Twice
Shoeshine

1947

Body and Soul
Brighton Rock
The Cat Concerto
Crossfire
Daisy Kenyon
Le Diable au Corps
It Always Rains on Sunday
Kiss of Death
The Lost Moment
Monsieur Verdoux
Odd Man Out
Out of the Past
Pursued
Quai des Orfèvres
La Terra Trema
They Made Me a Fugitive

1948

Abbott and Costello Meet Frankenstein
Act of Violence
L'Amore
Bicycle Thieves
The Boy with Green Hair
Drunken Angel
The Fallen Idol
Force of Evil
Fort Apache
Germany Year Zero
Hamlet
Key Largo
The Lady from Shanghai
Letter from an Unknown Woman
Maclovia
The Naked City
Oliver Twist
Raw Deal
Red River
The Red Shoes
Rope
The Snake Pit
The Treasure of the Sierra Madre
Unfaithfully Yours

1949

Adam's Rib
All the King's Men
Caught
Colorado Territory
Criss Cross
The Fountainhead
The Heiress
I Was a Male War Bride
Kind Hearts and Coronets
Late Spring
Portrait of Jennie
The Queen of Spades
The Reckless Moment
Samson and Delilah
She Wore a Yellow Ribbon
Une Si Jolie Petite Plage
Le Silence de la Mer
The Small Back Room
Stromboli
They Live by Night
The Third Man
Twelve O'Clock High
Under Capricorn
Whisky Galore!
White Heat

1950

All About Eve
The Asphalt Jungle
Born Yesterday
D.O.A.
The Elusive Pimpernel
Les Enfants Terribles
Gone to Earth
Gun Crazy
In a Lonely Place
Miss Julie
Night and the City
No Man of Her Own
Los Olvidados
Orphée
Outcast of the Islands
Rashomon
La Ronde
Sunset Blvd.

Wagon Master
Winchester '73

1951

Ace in the Hole
The African Queen
An American in Paris
Diary of a Country Priest
M
A Place in the Sun
The Prowler
The River
Strangers on a Train
A Streetcar Named Desire
The Tales of Hoffmann
Der Verlorene

1952

Angel Face
The Bad and the Beautiful
Carrie
Casque d'Or
Europa '51
Forbidden Games
High Noon
Julius Caesar
The Lavender Hill Mob
The Life of Oharu
Limelight
Living
The Lusty Men
Monkey Business
Othello
The Quiet Man
Rancho Notorious
Robinson Crusoe
Singin' in the Rain
Umberto D.
Viva Zapata!

1953

The Band Wagon
The Big Heat
From Here to Eternity
Gentlemen Prefer Blondes
The Golden Coach
Journey to Italy
Madame de . . .
M. Hulot's Holiday
Pickup on South Street
Roman Holiday
Sawdust and Tinsel
Shane
Thérèse Raquin
Tokyo Story
Ugetsu Monogatari
I Vitelloni
The Wages of Fear

1954

Anatahan
Apache
Bad Day at Black Rock
The Barefoot Contessa
Beat the Devil
Carmen Jones
Dial M for Murder
The Glenn Miller Story
Johnny Guitar
Knave of Hearts
On the Waterfront
La Paura
Rear Window
Sansho the Bailiff
Senso
Seven Brides for Seven Brothers
Seven Samurai
A Star Is Born
La Strada
Suddenly
Track of the Cat

1955

Le Amiche
The Big Combo
Blackboard Jungle
Les Diaboliques
East of Eden
Empress Yang Kwei-fei
Floating Clouds
French Cancan
House of Bamboo
Kiss Me Deadly
Lola Montès
The Man from Laramie
The Man with the Golden Arm
Mr. Arkadin
The Night of the Hunter
Picnic
Rebel Without a Cause
Rififi
Smiles of a Summer Night
Stella
To Catch a Thief

1956

Attack!
Baby Doll
The Bad Seed
Bhowani Junction
Bigger Than Life
Bob le Flambeur
Bus Stop
Giant
The Girl Can't Help It
Invasion of the Body Snatchers
The Killing
Lust for Life
A Man Escaped
Moby Dick
Run of the Arrow
The Searchers
The Seventh Seal
Silk Stockings
The Ten Commandments
War and Peace
Written on the Wind

1957

Baby Face Nelson
Bitter Victory
The Bridge on the River Kwai
A Face in the Crowd
Forty Guns
Funny Face
The Incredible Shrinking Man
Jet Plot
Men in War
Le Notti di Cabiria
Paths of Glory
Sait-On Jamais . . .
Sweet Smell of Success
The Tarnished Angels
3:10 to Yuma
Throne of Blood
A Time to Love and a Time to Die
12 Angry Men
Wild Strawberries
The Wrong Man

1958

Ascenseur pour l'Echafaud
Ashes and Diamonds
Bonjour Tristesse
The Horse's Mouth
Man of the West
Touch of Evil
Vertigo
Une Vie

1959

Anatomy of a Murder
Ben-Hur
Fires on the Plain
Floating Weeds
Hiroshima, Mon Amour
Imitation of Life
North by Northwest
Odds Against Tomorrow
Pickpocket
Plein Soleil
Les 400 Coups
Rio Bravo
Room at the Top
Some Came Running
Some Like It Hot
The World of Apu

1960

The Apartment
L'Avventura
The Bellboy
Les Bonnes Femmes
Breathless
La Dolce Vita
Exodus
Eyes Without a Face
La Notte
Peeping Tom
Psycho
Rocco and His Brothers
Shadows
Spartacus
Tirez sur le Pianiste
The Unforgiven
When a Woman Ascends the Stairs
Wild River

1961

El Cid
The Hustler
The Innocents
Jules et Jim
Last Year at Marienbad
Lola
The Misfits
One-Eyed Jacks
Paris Nous Appartient
Splendor in the Grass
Underworld U.S.A.
West Side Story

1962

Advise and Consent
La Baie des Anges
Cape Fear
L'Eclisse
Eve
The Exterminating Angel
La Jetée
Lawrence of Arabia
Lolita
Long Day's Journey into Night
The Manchurian Candidate
The Man Who Shot Liberty Valance
The Miracle Worker
Mutiny on the Bounty
To Kill a Mockingbird
The Trial
Vivre Sa Vie
What Ever Happened to Baby Jane?

1963

The Birds
Cleopatra
Days of Wine and Roses
Le Doulos
8½
The Leopard

Le Mépris
Muriel
The Nutty Professor
The Servant
Tom Jones

1964

Bande à Part
Charulata
Dr. Strangelove
Gertrud
Goldfinger
Hamlet
A Hard Day's Night
I Am Cuba
The Killers
Kiss Me, Stupid
Lilith
Marnie
Mary Poppins
Mickey One
My Fair Lady
The Pawnbroker
The Umbrellas of Cherbourg

1965

Alphaville
The Cincinnati Kid
Doctor Zhivago
Fists in the Pocket
Loves of a Blonde
Major Dundee
Persona
Pierrot le Fou
Repulsion
The Round-up
The Sound of Music
The Spy Who Came In from the Cold

1966

Andrei Rublev
Au Hasard Balthazar
The Battle of Algiers
Blow-Up
The Chelsea Girls
Chimes at Midnight
Fahrenheit 451
The Good, the Bad, and the Ugly
La Guerre Est Finie
Who's Afraid of Virginia Woolf?

1967

Belle de Jour
Bonnie and Clyde
The Dirty Dozen
The Graduate
In the Heat of the Night
Mouchette
Playtime
Point Blank
Le Samourai
Shame
2 or 3 Things I Know About Her

1968

Bullitt
Faces
If . . .
The Immortal Story
Once Upon a Time in the West
Planet of the Apes
The Producers
Rosemary's Baby
Targets
Theorem
The Thomas Crown Affair
2001: A Space Odyssey

1969

L'Amour Fou
Army of Shadows
Bob & Carol & Ted & Alice
Butch Cassidy and the Sundance Kid
The Damned
Easy Rider
Midnight Cowboy
Monty Python's Flying Circus
La Sirène du Mississippi
They Shoot Horses, Don't They?
The Wild Bunch
Z

1970

Le Boucher
Claire's Knee
The Conformist
Five Easy Pieces
Little Big Man
M*A*S*H.
Performance
The Private Life of Sherlock Holmes
Tristana
Wanda
Zabriskie Point

1971

Blanche
The Ceremony
A Clockwork Orange
Death in Venice
Deep End
Les Deux Anglaises et le Continent
Dirty Harry
The French Connection
The Hospital
Klute
The Last Picture Show
McCabe & Mrs. Miller
Sunday, Bloody Sunday
Walkabout
W.R.: Mysteries of the Organism

1972

Aguirre, Wrath of God
The Bitter Tears of Petra von Kant
Cabaret
Cries and Whispers
Deliverance
The Discreet Charm of the Bourgeoisie
Fat City
Frenzy
The Godfather
The King of Marvin Gardens
Last Tango in Paris
Love in the Afternoon
The Mattei Affair
Ulzana's Raid
What's Up, Doc?

1973

American Graffiti
Badlands
Day for Night
Distant Thunder
Don't Look Now
The Exorcist
The Long Goodbye
Lucky Luciano
Mean Streets
The Mother and the Whore
Paper Moon
Pat Garrett & Billy the Kid
Save the Tiger
The Spirit of the Beehive
The Sting
The Way We Were

1974

Amarcord
Bring Me the Head of Alfredo Garcia
Céline and Julie Go Boating
Chinatown
The Conversation
The Enigma of Kaspar Hauser
F for Fake
The Godfather, Part II
The Parallax View
Stavisky
A Woman Under the Influence

1975

Barry Lyndon
Dog Day Afternoon
Hustle
Jaws
The Man Who Would Be King
Night Moves
One Flew Over the Cuckoo's Nest
The Passenger
Picnic at Hanging Rock
Shampoo
The Travelling Players

1976

All the President's Men
Carrie
Cria!
Illustrious Corpses
In the Realm of the Senses
Kings of the Road
Mikey and Nicky
The Missouri Breaks
Mr. Klein
Nashville
Network
Rocky
Taxi Driver

1977

Annie Hall
Close Encounters of the Third Kind
The Duellists
New York, New York
Providence
Saturday Night Fever
Star Wars
That Obscure Object of Desire
Three Women

1978

Autumn Sonata
Dawn of the Dead
Days of Heaven
The Deer Hunter
Fingers
Grease
Halloween
The Tree of Wooden Clogs
Violette Nozière

1979

Alien
All That Jazz
Apocalypse Now
The Black Stallion
Kramer vs. Kramer

Mad Max
The Marriage of Maria Braun
Stalker

1980

American Gigolo
Atlantic City
Bad Timing
Berlin Alexanderplatz
The Big Red One
Hitler, a Film from Germany
Loulou
Melvin and Howard
Raging Bull
The Shining
The Stunt Man
Tinker, Tailor, Soldier, Spy

1981

Chariots of Fire
Cutter and Bone
Heaven's Gate
Mephisto
Mommie Dearest
Prince of the City
Raiders of the Lost Ark
Reds
True Confessions

1982

Blade Runner
Diner
The Draughtsman's Contract
E.T.
Fanny and Alexander
Lola
Poltergeist
Sophie's Choice
Tootsie
The Verdict

1983

À Nos Amours
In the White City
The King of Comedy
Meantime
Nostalghia
The Right Stuff
Rumble Fish
Scarface
Silkwood
The Year of Living Dangerously
Yentl

1984

Amadeus
The Hit
Paris, Texas
A Sunday in the Country
The Terminator

1985

Brazil
Dance with a Stranger
Out of Africa
Plenty
Wetherby

1986

Aliens
Blue Velvet
Platoon
'Round Midnight
The Sacrifice
The Singing Detective
Something Wild

1987

The Dead
Empire of the Sun
Fatal Attraction
Hope and Glory
The Last Emperor
Radio Days
Wall Street

1988

Bull Durham
Cinema Paradiso
Dangerous Liaisons
The Firm
The Moderns
Rain Man
Who Framed Roger Rabbit
Wings of Desire
Women on the Verge of a Nervous Breakdown

1989

Close-Up
Crimes and Misdemeanors
Dead Calm
Do the Right Thing
The Fabulous Baker Boys
Sex, Lies, and Videotape

1990

GoodFellas
The Grifters
Life and Nothing But
Miller's Crossing
Pretty Woman
The Sheltering Sky
The Silence of the Lambs

1991

La Belle Noiseuse
Bugsy
The Double Life of Véronique
Into the Woods
JFK
Raise the Red Lantern
Terminator 2: Judgment Day
Thelma & Louise

1992

God Is My Witness
Hoffa
The Last of the Mohicans
The Long Day Closes
Malcolm X
One False Move
The Player
A Question of Attribution
Unforgiven

1993

Jurassic Park
The Piano
The Puppetmaster
The Remains of the Day
Schindler's List
Short Cuts

1994

Ed Wood
Forrest Gump
Pulp Fiction
The Shawshank Redemption

1995

Carrington
Casino
Fallen Angels
Heat
Leaving Las Vegas
Nixon
Se7en
To Die For
The Usual Suspects

1996

The English Patient
Fargo
Mary Reilly

1997

Boogie Nights
Happy Together
L.A. Confidential
Mother and Son
A Taste of Cherry
Titanic
The Wings of the Dove

1998

The Big Lebowski
Saving Private Ryan
Shakespeare in Love
The Truman Show

1999

American Beauty
Being John Malkovich
Election
Eyes Wide Shut
Magnolia
The Matrix
Ride with the Devil
The Sixth Sense
The Sopranos
Time Regained

2000

Sexy Beast
Werckmeister Harmonies

2001

Éloge de l'Amour
The Lord of the Rings
Moulin Rouge
Mulholland Dr.
The Piano Teacher

2002

Adaptation

2003

The Best of Youth
Dogville
Mystic River
Open Range
The Triplettes of Belleville

2004

The Intruder
Vera Drake

2005

Brokeback Mountain
A History of Violence
The Three Burials of Melquiades Estrada

2006

The Lives of Others
Longford
The Queen
Twenty Thousand Streets Under the Sky

2007

The Diving Bell and the Butterfly
4 Months, 3 Weeks, and 2 Days
Eastern Promises
No Country for Old Men
Sweeney Todd
There Will Be Blood
You, the Living

read more

DAVID THOMSON

GREAT STARS

BETTE DAVIS

Bette Davis was the commanding figure of the great era of Hollywood stardom, with a drive and energy that put her contemporaries in the shade. She played queens, jezebels and bitches, she could out-talk any male co-star, she warred with her studio, Warner Bros, worked like a demon, got through four husbands, was nominated for seven Oscars and – no matter what – never gave up fighting.

GARY COOPER

On screen he was the ultimate all-American hero: lean, laconic and masculine, a lone sheriff battling his enemies in *High Noon*, or a tough individualist in *The Fountainhead*. Off screen he bedded a host of leading ladies and carefully honed his image, making hundreds of movies and winning two Oscars in the process. David Thomson explores the career and the contradictions of 'Coop', the star who lived the dream in the golden age of Hollywood.

HUMPHREY BOGART

He became a legend as 'Bogie', the world-weary, wise-cracking outsider, but in reality Humphrey Bogart was plagued by demons. He was born upper-class yet made his name playing mavericks, drank with the rat pack and met four wives on set – including his great love, Lauren Bacall – yet always mistrusted stardom. Here Thomson reveals the man behind cinema's greatest icon.

INGRID BERGMAN

Adored by millions for her luminous beauty and elegance, at the height of her career Ingrid Bergman commanded a love that has hardly ever been matched, until her marriage fell apart and created an international scandal. David Thomson gives his own unique and original take on a woman who was constantly driven by her passions and by her need to act, even if it meant sacrificing everything.

Penguin History

PUBLIC ENEMIES
BRYAN BURROUGH

In the summer of 1933 an amazing group of chancers, misfits and psychopaths took to the roads of America. Fuelled by the Depression, fast cars and cheap guns, these freelance gangsters terrorized a vast swathe of banks and drugstores across the Midwest. Bonnie and Clyde, Dillinger, Machine Gun Kelly, Baby Face Nelson, the Barker gang, Pretty Boy Floyd and others went on a crime spree that turned them into legends in their own lifetimes.

As they tore across state lines, mocking the police and amassing fortunes, the gangsters had no idea that in Washington their nemesis was forming: J. Edgar Hoover's FBI. *Public Enemies* is the sensational story of the outlaws whose exploits became folklore, and the savage, myth-making response of those who hunted them down, leading to some of the bloodiest gunfights ever fought in America.

Bryan Burrough has delved into never-before-seen FBI files, read statements from the criminals and their gun molls, and heard eye-witness reports from the people who crouched behind teller cages as Dillinger robbed their neighbourhood bank, watched as Bonnie and Clyde shot innocent sheriffs and tossed baseballs with Baby Face Nelson. In a series of spectacular set-pieces he weaves together all the most infamous events both from the perpetrators' and from their pursuers' points of view, to make sense of the most ferocious crime wave in America's history. By turns engrossing, horrifying and exhilarating, *Public Enemies* is the true account of events that still seem incredible today.